**ATLA Bibliography Series
edited by Dr. Kenneth E. Rowe**

1. A Guide to the Study of The Holiness Movement, by Charles Edwin Jones. 1974
2. Thomas Merton: A Bibliography, by Marquita E. Breit. 1974

A Guide to the Study of
THE HOLINESS MOVEMENT

by
CHARLES EDWIN JONES

ATLA Bibliography Series, No. 1

The Scarecrow Press, Inc., Metuchen, N. J.
and
The American Theological Library Association
1974

ACKNOWLEDGMENTS

A host of people and libraries shared in the preparation of this Guide. Although too numerous to mention individually, I would like to thank literally dozens of association and church officials who made publications and information available to me. Particularly helpful were the Reverend O. Dale Emery of the Christian Holiness Association, the Reverend H. E. Schmul of the Interdenominational Holiness Convention, Mr. R. R. Hodges and the Reverend Marlow Salter of the Church of the Nazarene headquarters, and the Reverend Paul W. Thomas and the Reverend M. E. Dieter of the Wesleyan Church headquarters. Librarians associated with the following institutions were of immeasurable help: Brown University, Bethany Nazarene College, Olivet Nazarene College, Pasadena College, Nazarene Theological Seminary, Asbury College, Asbury Theological Seminary, Garrett Theological Seminary, Drew University, Houghton College, Messiah College, and Marion College. The long-support of my undergraduate and graduate teachers, Professors Fred Floyd and Merle Curti, of friends including Tom & Ruth Barton of Colorado College, Richard Gould, John Leax, James & Nancy Barcus of Houghton College, William McLoughlin, Marion Kesselring, Catharine Gravel, and Elizabeth Schumann of Brown University, Kenneth Scheffel of the University of Michigan, Martin Hamburg of Cornell University, Timothy Smith of the Johns Hopkins University, Kenneth Rowe of Drew University, and Robert Wedgeworth of the American Library Association. I am deeply indebted to Kenneth Scheffel and Ardele Hough for their criticism of the denominational write-ups and to Florence Lundy and my wife for considerable assistance in indexing. No small thanks is due my wife and son, Beverly and Karl, for their help and tolerance during an extended period of preparation.

Not all the works cited in the Guide could personally be examined, and despite care, errors have undoubtedly occurred; I would be grateful to be told of them.

Library of Congress Cataloging in Publication Data

Jones, Charles Edwin, 1932-
   A guide to the study of the holiness movement.

   (ATLA bibliography series, no. 1)
   1. Holiness churches--Bibliography. I. Title.
II. Series: American Theological Library Association.
ATLA bibliography series, no. 1.
Z7845.H6J65   016.2899   74-659
ISBN 0-8108-0703-3

Copyright 1974 by Charles Edwin Jones

Dedicated to
PROFESSOR FRED FLOYD
and
MRS. ELIZABETH ALEXANDER WILLIS HALL
who introduced me to the study of the
Holiness Movement and to bibliography

EDITOR'S FOREWORD

A significant development in the Christian world during the past several decades has been the rapid spread of what has come to be called the Charismatic Movement. Not only has the movement given new life to separate holiness or pentecostal churches, but also virtually every major denomination, including Roman Catholicism, now has its own charismatic wing.

One of the roots of this movement is the Holiness Movement in American Protestantism in the last century. Originating in Eastern cities by Methodist ministers and laymen in the 1850's, the Holiness Movement sought the power of the Spirit promised by Christ and evidenced in the early church. Soon the movement was sponsoring "holiness" camp meetings and revivals, issuing "holiness" books and periodicals, and forming regional "holiness" associations. The search for personal holiness, or Christian Perfection, thrived among the Methodists, and influenced other groups, especially Mennonites and Quakers. "Come-outism" in the 1880's led to an exodus of holiness movements from main-line Protestantism in the 1890's, thereby spawning a whole family of "holiness" denominations. Dr. Jones has assembled an invaluable guide to the literature of this complex movement, containing 7300 numbered entries covering 150 distinct "holiness" churches.

The American Theological Library Association Bibliography Series is designed to stimulate and encourage the preparation and publication of reliable bibliographies and guides to the literature of religious studies in all of its scope and variety. Each compiler is free to define his field, make his own selections, and work out internal organization as the unique demands of his subject indicate.

Charles Edwin Jones holds a Ph. D. degree from the University of Wisconsin in the field of American Religious Studies, specializing in the Holiness Movement in American Methodism. He has served in library and archival positions at Park College, Parkville, Missouri, and Nazarene Theological Seminary, Kansas City, Missouri, and is currently cataloger for history at Brown University Library, Providence, Rhode Island. We are pleased to publish his guide to the literature of the holiness movement as number one in our series.

Kenneth E. Rowe, Editor
Drew University Library
Madison, New Jersey

FOREWORD*

The current revival of interest in the idea of Christian holiness, and in the history of those small sects which in the twentieth century have promoted the idea, has many sources. Most obvious, of course, is the highly publicized growth of the neo-Pentecostal movement. Speaking in the "unknown tongue," both as a language of prayer and as a public sign of the experience of the baptism of the Holy Spirit, has become commonplace among earnest Christians meeting together for prayer on university campuses, in businessmen's breakfasts, or in "house churches." It has likewise captured the imaginations of pastors and lay people in many congregations of Lutherans, Roman Catholics, and Episcopalians in the United States.

Another factor in the perfectionist renewal has been the ethical reaction to the violence, the racism, and the corruption of our times, and to the despair which flows from these. Even William Sloane Coffin, Jr., chaplain at Yale College and representative of religious traditions far removed from that of the American holiness movement, declared occasionally in the late 1960's that the ethics of perfection had become the ethics of survival. The fascination with extra-rational experience which one finds in modern art and poetry as well as in the drug culture and the revival of the occult is matched by a rationalized and somewhat puritan commitment of increasing numbers of Christian groups to the search for a Christian discipline which eventuates in personal holiness.

Many laymen and clergymen, and most students of American

---
*by Timothy L. Smith, Professor of History, The Johns Hopkins University.

religious history, are aware that a long historical tradition lies behind these current developments. Some of them know a few of the basic general works which can provide an introduction to that tradition. Few, however, guess the immense complexity of the story, or realize how difficult it is accurately to reconstruct its details.

In this work of patient scholarship, Dr. Charles E. Jones has provided all who are interested with a guide to the inner life of the diverse sects, associations, and movements which trace their lineage back to the revival of the Wesleyan doctrine of Christian perfection which took place in the middle of the nineteenth century. A perusal simply of his table of contents will be an instructive beginning for all who are interested in the subject. The meticulous care with which he has assembled his brief summaries of the history of each of the religious bodies which are part of this tradition will excite the admiration of all who have worked in the history of popular social movements whose major and minor publications have largely escaped the attention of archivists and librarians. To be sure, some of the groups Dr. Jones describes are large, and their history sufficiently well recorded that his only task has been to exercise care and sound judgment. Most of them, however, have been small, and many only short-lived. To recover for students the names and brief histories of the latter, and to record the names of the periodicals, books and pamphlets from which their history can be reconstructed, is an immense achievement.

Readers familiar with the subject will recognize at once, of course, that the major portion of the modern "Pentecostal Movement" is not represented here. Dr. Jones includes only those bodies which have from the outset persisted in maintaining their ties to Wesleyan doctrine and discipline, adding to that doctrine only their conviction that speaking in the so called "unknown tongue" is the sign that a Christian has received the baptism of the Holy Spirit. Some will be surprised to find that the twentieth-century heirs of the nineteenth-century Wesleyan revival regard the

Pentecostal movement as separate from their own, though often indebted to it, and that leaders of the two movements have always been keenly conscious of their wide differences. Perhaps the publication of this volume will prompt the preparation of another which will give students a guide to the immense range of Pentecostal associations, denominations, and publications which have flourished among both white and black people in the United States and Canada, as well as among the several million Latin Americans whose conversion has come about under the influence of Pentecostal missionaries from those two countries.

Mr. Jones' training as an historian of the Wesleyan tradition, which began under the tutelage of Professor Merle Curti, who directed his Ph.D. dissertation at the University of Wisconsin, has included an assignment in two major American libraries and archival centers. He has made the best of that training in the preparation of this volume.

BRIEF TABLE OF CONTENTS

Editor's Foreword		v
Foreword		vii
Introduction		xvii
Abbreviations		xxii
Part I.	General Works	1
Part II.	Holiness Movement	7
1.	Christian Holiness Association	9
2.	Interdenominational Holiness Convention	466
Part III.	Keswick Movement	485
Part IV.	Holiness Pentecostal Movement	513
Part V.	Schools	537
Part VI.	Biography	567
Index		799

FULL TABLE OF CONTENTS

Acknowledgments	ii
Editor's Foreword, by Kenneth E. Rowe	v
Foreword, by Timothy L. Smith	vii
Introduction	xvii
Abbreviations	xxii
Part I. GENERAL WORKS	1
Part II. HOLINESS MOVEMENT	7
General	
1. Christian Holiness Association (1867-)	9
Association of Pentecostal Churches of America (1895-1907)	96
Baptists	
Alliance of the Reformed Baptist Church (1888-1966)	97
Free Baptist Church (-1962)	98
Brethren	
Brethren in Christ Church (1863-)	98
Pentecostal Brethern in Christ (18??-1924)	103
Calvary Holiness Church (1934-1955)	103
Christian Nation Church (1895-)	105
Christ's Sanctified Holy Church (1904-)	105
Church of Christ (Holiness) U.S.A. (1907-)	106
Church of God	
Church of God (Anderson, Indiana) (1880-)	108
Church of God (Apostolic) (1896-)	123
Church of God (Holiness) (1883-)	124
Church of God (Northern Indiana Eldership) (1876-18??)	129
Churches of God (Independent Holiness People) (1922-)	129
Churches of God, Holiness (1914-)	130
Churches of God in North America (General Eldership) (1830-)	131

xi

Church of the Gospel (1911-19??)	132
Church of the Nazarene (1895-1907)	132
Church of the Nazarene (1908-)	134
Churches of Christ in Christian Union (1909-)	203
Emmanuel Holiness Church (1916-)	205
Evangel Church (1933-1960)	207
Evangelical Church (1807-1946)	208
Evangelical Church of North America (1968-)	211
Evangelical Congregational Church (1922-)	211
Evangelical United Brethren Church (1946-1968)	212

Evangelistic Associations

Apostolic Christian Church (Nazarean) (1850-)	213
Apostolic Christian Church of America (1848-)	214
Bible Holiness Movement (1949-)	216
Central Evangelical Holiness Association (1890-1896)	216
Christian Congregation (1887-)	217
Church of Daniel's Band (1893-195?)	218
Emmanuel Association (1937-)	219
Evangelistic Tabernacle (1919-19??)	220
Faith Mission (1886-)	221
Fire Baptized Holiness Church (Wesleyan) (1895-)	222
General Holiness League (1891-189?)	223
Gospel Tabernacle Association (-1950)	223
Heavenly Recruit Church (1882-19??)	224
Hephzibah Faith Missionary Association (1892-1951)	224
Holiness Association of Texas (1899-1910)	227
Holiness Union (1904-190?)	228
Independent Holiness Movement (1907-)	228
Irish Evangelistic Band (1936-)	229
Kentucky Mountain Holiness Association (1925-)	229
Laymen's Holiness Association (1917-1922)	230
League of Prayer (1891-)	231
Lower Light Church (194?-1973)	234
Metropolitan Church Association (1894-)	235
Mexican Evangelistic Mission (1926-)	239
Missionary Bands of the World (1885-1958)	241
Northwest Texas Holiness Association (Aug.-Dec. 1899)	242
Peniel Missions (1886-)	243
Pentecostal Mission (1898-1915)	244
Pentecostal Rescue Mission (1897-1922)	247
People's Mission Church (1899-1925)	248
Pillar of Fire Church (1901-)	249
Primitive Holiness Mission (1889-190?)	256
Vanguard Mission (1881-1916)	256

Friends

Evangelical Friends Alliance (1965-)	258

California Yearly Meeting of Friends (1895-)	262
Central Yearly Meeting of Friends (1926-)	263
Kansas Yearly Meeting of Friends (1872-)	267
Evangelical Friends Church, Eastern Division (1813-)	268
Northwest Yearly Meeting of Friends Churches (1893-)	271
Rocky Mountain Yearly Meeting of the Friends Church (1957-)	274
God's Missionary Church (1935-)	274
Gospel Workers Church (1898-1958)	276
Holiness Christian Church (1882-)	277
Holiness Church (1880-189?)	278
Holiness Church (1880-1946)	279
Holiness Church, Donalsonville, Georgia (1902-1907)	281
Holiness Church of Christ (1905-1908)	281
Holiness Movement Church (1895-1959)	283
Immanueru Sogo Dendo Dan (Immanuel General Mission of Japan) (1945-)	286
Independent Holiness Church (1901-1905)	287
Independent Holiness Church of Christ (1888-1914)	288
International Holiness Mission (1907-1952)	288
Kodesh Church of Immanuel (1929-)	290
Methodists	
General	291
Apostolic Methodist Church (1932-)	303
Congregational Methodist Church (1852-)	303
Evangelical Methodist Church (1946-)	304
Free Methodist Church of North America (1860-)	306
Holiness Methodist Church (1900-)	325
Holiness Methodist Church (1911-1969)	325
Holiness Methodists (1913-19??)	326
Methodist Church (United States) (1939-1968)	327
Methodist Episcopal Church (1784-1939)	334
Methodist Episcopal Church, South (1845-1939)	361
Methodist Protestant Church (1830-)	367
People's Methodist Church (1938-1962)	368
Primitive Methodist Church, U.S.A. (1829-)	369
Reformed Methodist Church (1812-1952)	370
Wesleyan Methodist Church of America (1843-1968)	371
Missionary Church (1969-)	387
Missionary Societies	
Africa Evangelistic Band (1924-)	388
Africa Evangelistic Mission (1902-1962)	389
Bethany Fellowship (1945-)	390

Bethel Mission of China (1920-)	391
Bible Home and Foreign Missionary Society (1890-1924)	392
Evangelical Bible Mission (1939-)	393
Evangelistic Faith Missions (1905-)	394
Haiti Inland Mission (1949-)	395
Immanuel Mission (1890-1923)	396
India North-West Mission (1920-1955)	397
Japan Evangelistic Band (1903-)	397
Japan Rescue Mission (1922-1940/1)	404
Lebanon Missionary Bible College (1947-)	404
Oriental Missionary Society (1901-)	404
Union Bible Seminary (1911-)	408
Voice of China and Asia (1946-)	412
World Gospel Mission (1910-)	413
World-Wide Missionary Society (1921-1923)	415
World-Wide Missions (1950-)	416
World's Faith Missionary Association (188?-190?)	416
New Testament Church of Christ (1894-1905)	417
Nihon Horinesu Kyodan (Japan Holiness Church) (1917-)	418
Pentecostal Church of Scotland (1909-1915)	419
Pilgrim Church (1917-1922)	420
Pilgrim Holiness Church (1897-1968)	421
Salvation Army (1865-)	437
Sanctified Church of Christ (19??-)	447
Standard Church of America (1919-)	447
United Brethren	448
Church of the United Brethren in Christ (1800-1946)	448
Church of the United Brethren in Christ (Old Constitution) (1889-)	453
United Christian Church (1878-)	454
United Missionary Church (1853-1969)	455
Volunteers of America (1896-)	460
Wesleyan Church (1968-)	461
2. Interdenominational Holiness Convention (1947-)	466
Bible Missionary Church (1955-)	472
Church of the Bible Covenant (1967-)	474
Evangelical Wesleyan Church (1963-)	475
Evangelical Wesleyan Church of North America (1958-1963)	476
Evangelistic Associations	477
Midwest Holiness Association (1962-1963)	477

Voice of the Nazarene Association of Churches (195?-) ... 477
Independent Holiness Churches (1958-) ... 478
Methodists ... 479
  Allegheny Wesleyan Methodist Connection (Original Allegheny Conference) (1966-) ... 479
  Bible Methodist Connection of Churches (1966-) ... 480
Pilgrim Holiness Church of New York (1963-) ... 481
Pilgrim Holiness Church of the Midwest (1970-) ... 482
United Holiness Church of North America (1966-) ... 482
Wesleyan Holiness Association of Churches (1959-) ... 483

Part III. KESWICK MOVEMENT ... 485
Keswick Convention (1875-) ... 485
Christian and Missionary Alliance (1887-) ... 498
Evangelistic Associations ... 509
  Missionary Church Association (1898-1969) ... 509

Part IV. HOLINESS-PENTECOSTAL MOVEMENT ... 513
General ... 513
Baptists ... 518
  Holiness Baptists (1903-1914) ... 518
  Pentecostal Free-Will Baptist Church (190?-) ... 519
Church of God ... 519
  Church of God (General Assembly) (1886-) ... 519
  Church of God in Christ (1897-) ... 521
  (Original) Church of God (1886-) ... 523
Evangelistic Associations ... 523
  Apostolic Faith Mission (1907-) ... 523
  Apostolic Faith Movement (1900-) ... 525
Fire Baptized Holiness Church (1898-1911) ... 526
Pentecostal Holiness Church (1900-1911) ... 526
Pentecostal Holiness Church (1911-) ... 527
Tabernacle Pentecostal Church (1899-1915) ... 534
Triumph the Church and Kingdom of God in Christ (1902-) ... 534
United Holy Church of America (1886-) ... 535

Part V. SCHOOLS ... 537

Part VI. BIOGRAPHY ... 567

Index ... 799

INTRODUCTION

During the last decade the rise of Pentecostalism in the established churches has made talk of the baptism with the Holy Spirit respectable. In the preceding seventy-five years, however, Holiness proponents often faced rebuff as fanatics. While the popular press ignored the overwhelming Holiness majority, it focused attention on Holy Rollers and snake-handlers in remote Appalachian valleys as representative. Inaccurate and misleading, such characterizations cannot bear scrutiny. An examination of the so-called "Third Force" in American Christianity is long overdue.

With a present constituency of well over a million, the Holiness Movement represents the continuation of nineteenth-century Methodist evangelicalism in the twentieth century and, with its step-child the Pentecostal Movement, has perpetuated to a surprising extent the rural culture in which Victorian Protestantism thrived. A guide to the Holiness Movement should provide, therefore, materials for study of doctrine, worship, institutional development and personalities, as well as antecedent and related movements. Hopefully, this bibliography will serve to illustrate the history both of the Holiness Movement and the rural-urban transition in which it developed.

Though social overtones cannot be ignored, the foundation of the Holiness Movement is theological. Starting with John Wesley's contention that the road from sin to salvation is from willful rebellion against divine and human law to perfect love for God and man, Methodist holiness teachers in the mid-nineteenth century emphasized two crises in salvation: justification and entire sanctification. Simply stated, they taught that in the first experience man was freed from the sins he had committed; in the second, from the flaw in his moral nature which caused him to sin. As a natural kleptomaniac, he was forgiven for acts of theft in the first crisis and freed from the corrupt nature which compelled him to steal in the second. They called the crisis of conversion being saved, the crisis of healing of the sinful nature, entire sanctification or full salvation. Recognizing the necessity of spiritual growth before and after the crisis of entire sanctification, they maintained that as in human development, spiritual birth was necessarily a crisis. Feeling that the contrast between Jesus' disciples before and after Pentecost was explained by the sanctifying experience of that day, the Methodist holiness spokesmen of the National Holiness Movement, and their followers insisted that full salvation was accomplished in two crises and that purification of the corruption in human nature by the Holy Spirit must of necessity precede perfect love.

Responses to these emphases have provided the bases for several related, competing movements for which bibliographies are included. The predominantly Anglican Keswick Movement questioned the possibility of moral purity and suggested that suppression of evil tendencies might, after all, be all that was possible to mortal men. Emphasizing spiritual growth, Keswick spokesmen have preferred to talk of the Deeper Life instead of holiness.

Within Methodism opponents of crisis also preferred to talk of growth, sometimes even growth in holiness. Since the Methodist ritual required that ordination candidates avow their intent to be made perfect in this life, Wesleyan critics could hardly deny the foundation of the Holiness position. Instead, opponents centered attack on the second crisis and sinless perfection advocated by the holiness evangelists. In reply to champions of growth, holiness spokesmen charged Methodist critics with being followers of Nikolaus Ludwig Zinzendorf, the Moravian leader with whom John Wesley had disagreed over spiritual growth.

After the turn of the twentieth century, the claim by many holiness people that speaking in unknown tongues was evidence of the baptism with the Holy Spirit posed still another threat to the

Introduction   xix

National Holiness leaders. Often holding to conventional holiness beliefs concerning entire sanctification, the Pentecostalists separated the second crisis from the Holy Spirit baptism. Often they claimed the latter to be a distinct experience evidenced initially by tongues speaking, or glossolalia. The older holiness leaders utterly discountenanced the tongues phenomena. As a result only those Pentecostal groups which had espoused holiness before the 1906 Azusa Street revival (the birth of the present Pentecostal Movement) are included in the guide.

Though interdenominational by profession, the Holiness Movement was from its inception essentially Methodist. Principal leaders, both lay and clerical, were deeply committed to the Methodist Episcopal Church and regarded the revival of Christian perfection as a panacea for ecclesiastical reform. From the formation of the National Camp Meeting Association for the Promotion of Holiness in 1867 until the mid-1890's, established Methodist clergymen such as John S. Inskip and William McDonald kept most of the movement in the church. When growth of regionalism and the passing of the original leadership led to formation of independent churches after 1890, Methodist loyalists continued to dominate the National and state associations. And not until 1942 was the National Association led by a president affiliated with one of the distinctively holiness churches.

The rising power of the independent holiness churches in the holiness associations was in direct proportion to the decline of holiness influence within the Methodist Church. After World War II holiness denominationalism turned the formerly evangelistic National Association into a national council of holiness churches. Numerical growth and material prosperity pushed the churches steadily toward compromise. Relaxation of personal discipline was symbolized by fashionable dress and secular entertainment such as participation in athletics and the watching of television. As a result of conservative protest separatist movements troubled each of the larger holiness denominations and after 1955 a number of splinter groups appeared. Collectively these new groups supported the Interdenominational

Holiness Convention which, like the National Association seventy-five years before, regarded itself as the defender of primitive Wesleyanism.

The Guide is organized in six parts, three of them devoted to interdenominational movements (parts II, the HOLINESS MOVEMENT; III, the KESWICK MOVEMENT; and IV, the HOLINESS-PENTECOSTAL MOVEMENT). Part I is a short section on General Works--i.e., background works helpful to an understanding of the intellectual context in which the books in this Guide were written. Part V, SCHOOLS, includes an historical outline of names and locations of each institution with related bibliography. Part VI, BIOGRAPHY, is devoted to works on individuals.

Only those tongues-speaking churches which originated before 1907 as holiness groups are listed under Part IV, HOLINESS-PENTECOSTAL MOVEMENT. Under each movement materials are listed alphabetically by individual body grouped under such headings as denominational family (e.g., Baptists), evangelistic associations (groups which permit members to hold membership in other church bodies), and missionary societies (interdenominational missionary associations with foreign but no domestic work). Listings for individual associations or denominations include a historical sketch and subject bibliography.

For each association or denomination collective biographies will be listed under --BIOGRAPHY, in parts II through IV. Biography and related bibliography of individuals, however, is listed in Part VI. Each listing in Part VI is prefaced by a statement containing as much of the following information as possible: full name and dates, short biographical analytics, conventions attended or endorsed, denominational membership(s), occupation(s), birth and death dates and places. Bibliographies for Part VI, BIOGRAPHY, include works by and/or about the person listed. Sometimes included are works with no direct connection with the movement but of significance to an understanding of persons active in the movement (e.g., a pamphlet on skin cancer by a medical doctor active in the holiness movement).

Introduction

The arrangement of materials for associations and churches in parts II, III, and IV is as follows: entry under latest name of group with beginning and ending dates, a summary of name changes with inclusive dates, and an historical sketch of the group; this is followed in each case by the bibliography. The bibliography is divided into subject categories applied for the most part uniformly to all groups. Official publications are first and then general works; then the arrangement is alphabetical by specific subjects and, finally, alphabetical by geographical area. Publications of or about geographically based units of an association or church will be listed as official publications (e.g., CONFERENCES. NEW YORK.). Works by non-members published by the group to support its teaching are often separated by the subdivision -- --AUTHORITATIVE SOURCES. Issues crucial to Holiness discussion are grouped by issue as subdivisions of --DOCTRINAL AND CONTROVERSIAL WORKS. These subdivisions include -- --ESCHATOLOGY; -- --FAITH-HEALING; -- --GLOSSOLALIA; etc.

Works (in parts II, III, and IV) about particular hymns and gospel songs are listed under --HYMNS -- --HISTORY AND CRITICISM, while general treatments of church music are under --MUSIC. Works written in defense of the group are under --APOLOGETIC WORKS, but analytical works by members and non-members alike are under --CRITICAL WORKS. Works critical of other denominations are classed by denomination under --POLEMICAL WORKS, while those dealing with merger negotiations between denominations are under --RELATIONS WITH.... Collections of biographies or testimonies are under --BIOGRAPHY (individual biographies, as mentioned, are entered in Part VI).

References in the Index are to the serial number assigned to each paragraph and bibliographical entry. Additional subject approaches, not possible through the regular sequence of the Guide, are available through the Index. Inclusion of a group indicates a relationship at some point to the Holiness Movement. It does not imply, however, that Wesleyan perfection was stressed nor that commitment to Holiness teaching was emphasized by the group at all times or in all places.

ABBREVIATIONS

AEB	Africa Evangelistic Band
AFM	Apostolic Faith Movement
AG	Assemblies of God, General Council
AME	African Methodist Episcopal Church
APCA	Association of Pentecostal Churches of America
AssoRef	Associate Reformed Church
ATY	Akers. Tarry ye!
Bapt	Baptist Church
BHFMSNE	Bible Home and Foreign Missionary Society of New England
Bi. Chr	Bible Christians
BIC	Brethren in Christ Church
BM	Bethel Mission of China
BMiC	Bible Missionary Church
BMiU	Bible Missionary Union
BMW	Blews. Master workmen.
BPOH	Boyd and Harris. Projecting our heritage.
CA	Contemporary authors.
CBC	Church of the Bible Covenant
CC(H)	Church of Christ (Holiness) U.S.A.
CG(A)	Church of God (Anderson, Ind.)
CG(GA)	Church of God (General Assembly)
CG(H)	Church of God (Holiness)
CG(IHP)	Churches of God (Independent Holiness People)
CG(T)	Churches of God (Tomlinson)
CG(UHP)	Church of God (Unity Holiness People)
CGIC	Church of God in Christ
CHA	Christian Holiness Association

Abbreviations

CHC	Calvary Holiness Church
CHHMH	Companion to the hymnal; a handbook to the 1964 Methodist Hymnal.
Ch of Eng	Church of England
Ch of Ire	Church of Ireland
ChrAD	Christian Advent Church
CIOCC	Corbett. Influence of the country church.
CM	Christian Mission
CMA	Christian and Missionary Alliance
CN	Church of the Nazarene
COCICU	Churches of Christ in Christian Union
Cong	Congregational Church
COPN	Corbett. Our pioneer Nazarenes.
CU(NC)	Christian Union (North Carolina)
DC	Double cure; or, Echoes from National Camp-meetings.
DCSWM	DuBois. The chaplains see world missions.
DH	Door of Hope
Dis. Chr.	Disciples of Christ
DutchRef	Dutch Reformed
EA	Evangelical Association of North America
EAP	Earle. Abiding peace.
EBCM	Emmanuel Bible College and Missions
EC	Evangel Church
ECNA	Evangelical Church of North America
EFM	Evangelistic Faith Missions
EHC	Emmanuel Holiness Church
EmA	Emmanuel Association
EMC	Evangelical Methodist Church
Epis	Protestant Episcopal Church
ET	Evangelistic Tabernacles
ETWF	Eubanks. These went forth; biographical sketches of Pilgrim missionaries.
EUB	Evangelical United Brethren Church
EWC	Evangelical Wesleyan Church
FaM	Faith Mission

FBHC	Fire Baptized Holiness Church (Wesleyan)
FHOP	Pasadena, Calif. Bresee Avenue Church of the Nazarene. Fidelis Business and Professional Class honors our pioneers....
FM	Free Methodist Church of North America
Fr	Friends
FW Bapt.	Free Will Baptist Church
FYAB	Church of the Nazarene. Districts. Chicago Central. Fifty years ... and beyond.
GFIIH	Geiger. Further insights into holiness.
GFW	Garrison. Forty witnesses.
GHAI	Gish. Here Am I.
GIIH	Geiger. Insights into holiness.
GrOrth	Greek Orthodox Church
GTWATD	Geiger. The Word and the doctrine.
GWC	Gospel Workers Church
HA Tex	Holiness Association of Texas
HB	Holiness Baptists
H Bd	Holiness Bands
HC	Holiness Church
HCC	Holiness Christian Church
HC(T)	Holiness Church (Tennessee)
HFMA	Hephzibah Faith Missionary Association
HIM	Haiti Inland Mission
HM	Holiness miscellany
HMoC	Holiness Movement Church
HNTB	Hinshaw. Native torch bearers.
HU	Holiness Union
HWP	Hunter. Women preachers.
I	Independent
IAHC	International Apostolic Holiness Church
IAHU	International Apostolic Holiness Union
IAHUPL	International Apostolic Holiness Union and Prayer League
IGMJ	Immanueru Sogo Dendo Dan (Immanuel General Mission of Japan)

Abbreviations

IHC	International Holiness Church
IHM	International Holiness Mission
IHTA	Interdenominational Holiness Tabernacle Association
IndHC	Independent Holiness Churches
IntHC	Interdenominational Holiness Convention
JEB	Japan Evangelistic Band
JHC	Japan Holiness Church
KesC	Keswick Convention
KMHA	Kentucky Mountain Holiness Association
LDEFC	Lawson. Deeper experiences of famous Christians.
LDML	Lillenas. Down melody lane.
LHA	Laymen's Holiness Association
LIE	Leaders in education
LLITW	Lamson. Lights in the World; Free Methodist missions at work.
LMB	Leete. Methodist bishops.
LMGSS	Lillenas. Modern gospel song stories.
LOP	League of Prayer
Luth	Lutheran Church
M	Methodist Church
MAWACOSM	Metcalf. American writers and compilers of sacred music.
MB	Missionary Bands of the World
MBIC	Mennonite Brethren in Christ
MC	Missionary Church
MCA	Missionary Church Association
MCV	McClurkan. Chosen vessels.
ME	Methodist Episcopal Church
MEM	Mexican Evangelistic Mission
Menn.	Mennonite Church
ME, S	Methodist Episcopal Church, South
MetCA	Metropolitan Church Association
Meth(Can)	Methodist Church (Canada)
MethNC(Eng.)	Methodist New Connection (England)

MFATALW	Marston. From age to age a living witness.
MHP	McGraw. The holiness pulpit.
MHTWW	Miller. How they were won.
MHWMCOA	McLeister. History of the Wesleyan Methodist Church of America.
MLA	Montgomery. Living ambassadors.
MMAWODP	McLeister. Men and women of deep piety.
MOHMMH	McCutchan. Our hymnody; a manual of the Methodist Hymnal.
MOUS	Miller. Out under the stars.
MP	Methodist Protestant Church
MWWW in Ch. Hist.	Moyer. Who was who in church history.
Nat Cy of Am Biog	National cyclopedia of American biography.
NAW	Notable American women.
NHA	National Holiness Association
NHMS	National Holiness Missionary Society
NP	Nazarene pulpit.
NTCOC	New Testament Church of Christ
NVFML	Nee. Voices from many lands.
OMS	Oriental Missionary Society
PB	Pentecost Bands of the World
PC	Pilgrim Church
PCN	Pentecostal Church of the Nazarene
PCS	Pentecostal Church of Scotland
PeAC	Pentecostal Assemblies of Canada
PeFW Bapt.	Pentecostal Free-Will Baptist Church
PeHC	Pentecostal Holiness Church
PeM	Pentecostal Mission (London)
PenielM	Peniel Missions
Pent	Pentecostal
PeoMC	People's Mission Church
PFT	Pickett. Faith tonic.
PHC	Pilgrim Holiness Church
PL	Pentecostal League
PLOP	Pentecostal League of Prayer

Abbreviations

PlyBr	Plymouth Brethren
PM	Pentecostal messengers.
PM(N)	Pentecostal Mission (Nashville)
POF	Pillar of Fire Church
PPE	Palmer. Pioneer experiences.
PP in Am Meth.	Prominent personalities in American Methodism.
Pres	Presbyterian Church
PrimHM	Primitive Holiness Mission
PrimM	Primitive Methodist Church
PRM	Pentecostal Rescue Mission
PU	Pentecostal Union
RB	Reformed Baptist Church
RCath	Roman Catholic Church
REpis	Reformed Episcopal Church
RHOOF	Reynolds. Hymns of our faith; a handbook for the Baptist Hymnal.
RLOA	Religious leaders of America.
RMC	Reformed Methodist Church
ROG	The riches of grace; or, The blessing of perfect love.
RWBTB	Reza. Washed by the blood.
SA	Salvation Army
SBWTL	Sigsworth. The battle was the Lord's; a history of the Free Methodist Church in Canada.
SCA	Standard Church of America
SCC	Smith. Flames of living fire.
SCM	Simpson. Cyclopaedia of Methodism.
SCUH	Smith. Called unto holiness.
SEC	Synan. Emmanuel College: the first fifty years, 1919-1969.
SHBD	Smith. Heralds of a brighter day.
SWGHW	Storms. What God hath wrought.
TDOOP	Thomas and Thomas. The days of our pilgrimage.
TexHA	Holiness Association of Texas

UB	Church of the United Brethren in Christ
UM	United Methodist Church
UMC	United Missionary Church
Univ	Universalist Church
UPres	United Presbyterian Church
VanM	Vanguard Mission
VC	Voice of China
VCA	Voice of China in Asia
W	Wesleyan Church
WDCB	Wallace. Dictionary of Canadian biography.
WFMA	World's Faith Missionary Association
WHAC	Wesleyan Holiness Association of Churches
WHC	Wesleyan Holiness Church
WIWBA	Wingert. I was born again; a book of conversion stories.
WM	Wesleyan Methodist Church of America
WMAMH	Williams. Me and my house.
WMDCB	Wallace. Macmillan dictionary of Canadian biography.
WM(Eng)	Wesleyan Methodist Church (England)
WMK	Worcester. The master key; the story of the Hephzibah Faith Missionary Association.
WW	Who's who.
WWACUA	Who's who in American college and university administration.
WW among N. A. Authors	Who's who among North American authors.
WW in Am.	Who's who in America.
WW in Am. Ed.	Who's who in American education.
WW in Am. Meth.	Who's who in American Methodism.
WW in Meth.	Who's who in Methodism.
WW in the Clergy	Who's who in the clergy.
W-WM	World-Wide Missions
WWOTC	Willard. Woman of the century.
WWW in AM.	Who was who in America.

Part I

GENERAL WORKS

01 BURY, John Bagnell, 1861-1927.
The idea of progress; an inquiry into its origin and growth. Introduction by Charles A. Beard. New York, Macmillan, 1932. xl, 357 p.

02 ENCYCLOPAEDIA of religion and ethics, ed. by James Hastings, with the assistance of John A. Selbie and Louis H. Gray. New York, C. Scribner's Sons, 1908-1927. 13 v.
"Perfection (Christian)," by Frederic Platt: v. 9, p. 728-737.

03 EVANS, James Harrington
The spirit of holiness, by ... with an introd. preface by Octavius Winslow. New York, John S. Taylor, 1837. 252 p.

04 EVERETT, Walter Goodnow, 1860-1936.
Moral values; a study in the principles of conduct. New York, Holt, 1918. 439 p.
"Historical sketch of some perfectionist theories": p. 77-103.

05 FINNEY, Charles Grandison, 1792-1875.
Views of sanctification. Oberlin, Ohio, James Steele, 1840. 206 p.

06 FLEW, Robert Newton, 1886-
The idea of perfection in Christian theology. London, Oxford University Press, 1934. 422 p.

07 FOSS, Martin, 1889-
The idea of perfection in the western world. Princeton, N.J., Princeton University Press, 1946. 102 p.

08 HOUGHTON, Walter Edwards, 1904-
The Victorian frame of mind, 1830-1870. New Haven, Published for Wellesley College by Yale University Press, 1957. 467 p.

09 HUMPHRIES, Hugh Will
"Søren Kierkegaard's concept of sanctification." Unpublished Ph.D. dissertation, New York University, 1962. 249 ℓ.

10 JAMES, William, 1842-1910.
    The varieties of religious experience, a study in human nature; being the Gifford Lectures on Natural Religion delivered at Edinburgh in 1901-1902. New York, Modern Library, 1902. 526 p.

11 JAMES, William, 1842-1910.
    The will to believe, and other essays in popular philosophy. New York, Dover Publications, 1956. 322, 70 p.

12 JONES, Owen Roger, 1922-
    The concept of holiness. New York, Macmillan, 1961. 200 p.

13 KENDALL, Edith Lorna
    A living sacrifice; a study of reparation. London, SCM Press, 1960. 174 p.

14 LEEUW, Gerardus van der, 1890-1950.
    Sacred and profane beauty: the holy in art; preface by Mircea Eliade, tr. by David E. Green. New York, Holt, Rinehart and Winston, 1963. 357 p.
    Translation of Wegen en Grenzen.

15 LOSCHHORN, Albert
    Gerhard Tersteegens Auffassung von der Heiligung. Basel, Giessen, Brunnen-Verlag, 1969. 87 p.

16 PRIOR, Kenneth Francis William
    The way of holiness: the Christian doctrine of sanctification, by the Rev. Kenneth F. W. Prior. London, Inter-Varsity Fellowship, 1967. 128 p.

17 TAYLOR, William Stephens, 1905-
    "Perfectionism in psychology and in theology," Canadian Journal of Theology, V (July 1959), 170-179.

18 WARFIELD, Benjamin Breckinridge, 1851-1921.
    Perfectionism. New York, Oxford University Press, 1931-1932. 2 v.

19 WARFIELD, Benjamin Breckinridge, 1851-1921.
    Perfectionism; ed. by Samuel G. Craig. Philadelphia, Presbyterian and Reformed Publishing Co., 1958. 464 p.

20 WARNER, Sam Bass, Jr.
    Streetcar suburbs; the process of growth in Boston, 1870-1900. Cambridge, Mass., Harvard University Press and the

21 WHITE, Ernest, 1887-
    Christian life and the unconscious. New York, Harper, 1955. 190 p.

Part I. General Works 3

Massachusetts Institute of Technology Press, 1962. 208 p.

22 WILLARD, Willis Wardner, Jr.
"The evolution of the idea of holiness in the Old Testament."
Unpublished M. A. thesis, Drew University, 1934. iii, 98 ℓ.

23 WILSON, Byron R.
"An analysis of sect development, " American Sociological Review, XXIV (1959), 3-14.

24 WOLVERTON, Wallace Irving, 1905-
... The eighth-century prophets' idea of holiness. Chicago, 1937. 19 p.
Part of thesis (Ph. D.)--University of Chicago, 1934.
"Private edition, distribution by the University of Chicago Libraries, Chicago, Illinois. "

GENERAL WORKS--ANGLICAN AUTHORS

25 ASKWITH, Edward Harrison, 1864-
Christian conception of holiness. London and New York, Macmillan, 1900. 258 p.

26 LAW, William, 1686-1761.
A serious call to a devout and holy life, adapted to the state and condition of all orders of Christians. 6th ed. London, Printed for W. Innis and J. Richardson, 1753. vi, 499 p.
With this is bound the author's The absolute unlawfulness of the stage entertainment fully demonstrated, London, 1755.

27 LAW, William, 1686-1761.
A serious call to a devout and holy life; with an introd. by by J. V. Moldenhawer. Philadelphia, Westminster Press, 1948. xxv, 353 p.

28 LAW, William, 1686-1761.
A treatise upon Christian perfection. 1st American ed. Portsmouth, 1822.

29 MARSH, Edward Garrard, 1783-1862.
The Christian doctrine of sanctification considered in eight sermons, preached before the University of Oxford, at the Bampton Lecture, for the year MDCCCXLVIII. London, Seeleys, 1848. viii, 283 p.
Binder's title: Bampton lectures, 1848.

30 MARSHALL, Walter, 1628-1680.
The gospel-mystery of sanctification opened in sundry practical directions; suited especially to the case of those who labour under the guilt and power of indwelling-sin, to which is added, a sermon on justification. From the 12th European ed. New York, Southwick and Pelsue, 1811. 312 p.

31 NEILL, Stephen Charles, bp., 1900-
    Christian holiness. London, Lutterworth Press, 1960. 134 p.

32 TAYLOR, Jeremy, bp. of Down and Connor, 1613-1667.
    Holy living and dying: with prayers; containing the whole
    duty of a Christian and the parts of devotion fitted to all
    occasions and furnished for all necessities. London, G. Bell
    and Sons, 1883. 525 p.

33 TAYLOR, Jeremy, bp. of Down and Connor, 1613-1667.
    The rule and exercises of holy living; ed. and with an
    introd. by Thomas S. Kepler. Cleveland, World Publishing Co.,
    1956. 293 p.

GENERAL WORKS--CATHOLIC AUTHORS

34 BLANCHARD, Pierre
    Sainteté aujourd'hui. Paris, Desclée, De Brouwer, 1954.
    191 p. (Les Etudes carmélitaines)

35 CHAVCHAVADZE, Maria
    Man's concern with holiness, ed. by Maria Chavchavadze
    with contributions by Geoffrey Curtis [and others]. London,
    Hodder and Stoughton, 1969. 188 p.

36 CONFLICT and light; studies in psychological disturbance and
    readjustment, tr. by Pamela Carswell and Cecily Hastings.
    London, Sheed and Ward, 1952. 192 p.
    "Translated from Trouble et lumière ... published in French
    ... under the editorship of Père Bruno de Jesus-Marie."

37 FABER, Frederick William, 1814-1863.
    Growth in holiness; or, The progress of the spiritual life.
    4th ed. London, Thomas Richardson and Son, 1872. 528 p.

38 IMITATIO Christi. English.
    The imitation of Christ, ed. with an introd. by Thomas S.
    Kepler. Cleveland, World Publishing Co., 1952. 287 p.

39 IMITATIO Christi. English.
    The imitation of Christ, as written by Thomas à Kempis,
    translated by Richard Whitford, and decorated by Valenti
    Angelo. New York, Pocket Library, 1954. 305 p.

40 LAVELLE, Louis, 1883-1951.
    The meaning of holiness [as exemplified in four saints:
    St. Francis of Assisi, St. Teresa of Avila, St. John of the
    Cross, and St. Francis de Sales]. London, Burns & Oates,
    1954. xiv, 113 p.
    "This translation of Quatre saints was made by Dorothea
    O'Sullivan."

Part I. General Works 5

41 LOT, Myrrha (Borodine), 1882-1957.
La Déification de l'homme, selon la doctrine des Pères grecs; préf. par Jean Daniélou. Paris, Editions du Cerf, 1970. 290 p.

42 MEYER, James, 1883-
A primer of Christian perfection for everybody. Chicago, Franciscan Herald Press, 1946. viii, 184 p.

43 RODRIGUEZ, Alphonsus
The practice of Christian and religious perfection, written in Spanish...; tr. from the French copy of M. L'Abbe Regnier des Maris.... Dublin, Richard Coyne, 1846. 3 v.

44 TROUBLE et lumière. Burges, Desclee de Brouwer, 1949. 219 p.
Edited by Father Bruno de Jesus-Marie.

GENERAL WORKS--LUTHERAN AUTHORS

45 FEUCHT, Werner Christian Martin, 1929-1959.
Untersuchungen zum Heiligkeitgesetz. Berlin, Evengelische Verlagsantalt, 1964. 257 p.

46 GYLLENKROK, Axel, 1910-
Rechtfertigung und Heiligung in der frühen evengelischen Theologie Luthers. Uppsala, Lundequistska bokhandeln, 1952. x, 148 p.

47 HUBNER, Hans
Rechtfertigung und Heiligung in Luthers Römerbriefvorlesung; ein systematischer Entwurf. Witten, Luther-Verlag, 1965. 167 p.

48 HULME, William Edward, 1920-
The dynamics of sanctification. Minneapolis, Augsburg Publishing House, 1966. iv, 194 p.

49 JOEST, Wilfried, 1914-
Gesetz und freiheit; das problem des Tertius usus legis bei Luther und die neutestamentliche parainese. 2. aufl. Göttingen, Vandenhoeck & Ruprecht, 1956. 242 p.

50 KOBERLE, Adolf, 1898-
The quest for holiness; a Biblical, historical and systematic investigation, tr. from the 3d German ed. by John C. Mattes. New York, Harper, 1936. xi, 268 p.
Translation of Rechtfertigung and Heiligung.

51 KOBERLE, Adolf, 1898-
The quest for holiness; a Biblical, historical and systematic

investigation, tr. from the 3d German ed. by John C. Mattes.
Minneapolis, Augsburg Publishing House, 1938. x, 274 p.
Translation of Rechtfertigung und Heiligung.

52 PELIKAN, Jaroslav, 1923-
Fools for Christ; essays on the true, the good, and the
beautiful. Philadelphia, Muhlenberg Press, 1955. 172 p.

53 PELIKAN, Jaroslav, 1923-
Human culture and the holy; essays on the true, the good
and the beautiful. London, SCM Press, 1959. ix, 172 p.
American ed. entitled: Fools for Christ.

GENERAL WORKS--REFORMED AUTHORS

54 BARTH, Karl, 1886-1968.
Die Wirklichkeit des neuen Menschen. Zollikon-Zürich,
Evangelischer Verlag, 1950. 31 p.

55 BERKOUWER, Gerrit Cornelis, 1903-
Faith and sanctification; translated by John Vriend. Grand
Rapids, Mich., W.B. Eerdmans Publishing Co., 1952. 193 p.
(His Studies in dogmatics)

56 GOHLER, Alfred
Calvins lehre von der heiligung; dargestellt auf grund der
Institutio, exegetischer und homiletischer schriften. München,
C. Kaiser, 1934. 136 p.

57 HOEKEMA, Anthony A., 1913-
Karl Barth's doctrine of sanctification. Grand Rapids,
Mich., Calvin Theological Seminary, 1965. 23 p.

58 LANG, August, 1867-
Zwei Calvin-vorträge: Rechtfertigung und heiligung nach
Calvin; Calvin und der moderne gemeindegedanke. Gütersloh,
C. Bertelsmann, 1911. 64 p.

59 STALDER, Kurt
Das werk des geistes in der heiligung bei Paulus. Zürich,
EVZ-verlag, 1962. 523 p.
Thesis--Bern.

Part II

HOLINESS MOVEMENT

General

60 GAUSTAD, Edwin Scott, 1923-
Historical atlas of religion in America. New York, Harper & Row, 1962. 179 p.
"Holiness and Pentecostal bodies": p. 121-126.

61 GREER, George Dixon
"A psychological study of sanctification as a second work of divine grace." Unpublished Ph.D. dissertation, Drew University, 1936. 187 ℓ.

62 JOHNSON, Guy Benton, 1928-
"Do Holiness sects socialize in dominant values?," Social Forces, XXXIX (May 1961), 309-316.

63 JOHNSON, Guy Benton, 1928-
"A framework for the analysis of religious action, with special reference to holiness and non-holiness groups." Unpublished Ph.D. dissertation, Harvard University, 1954.

64 RAWLINGS, Elden Everette
"Other Wesleyan ecumenics," Christianity Today, XII (May 10, 1968), 35-36.

65 SHELDON, Joseph G.
"The Holiness Movement; a movement of social and religious protest." Unpublished M.A. thesis, University of Kansas City, 1961.

66 SNYDER, Howard Albert
"Unity and the holiness churches: a study of moves toward unity among selected American Protestant denominations affiliated with the National Holiness Association." Unpublished B.D. thesis, Asbury Theological Seminary, 1966. 415 ℓ.

67 WARBURTON, T. R.
"Holiness religion: an anomaly of sectarian typologies," Journal for the Scientific Study of Religion, VIII (1969).

68 WASHINGTON, Joseph R., 1930-
　　Black sects and cults.　Garden City, N.Y., Doubleday, 1972.
　xii, 176 p.
　　"Holiness and Pentecostal blacks: the permanent sects":
　p. 58-82.

Part II

Section 1

CHRISTIAN HOLINESS ASSOCIATION (1867-   )

[1867-1893 as National Camp Meeting Association for the Promotion of Holiness; 1893-1971 as National Association for the Promotion of Holiness, also as National Holiness Association]

Organized at Vineland, New Jersey, during the first distinctly holiness camp meeting its founders conducted, the association exists to promote entire sanctification as a crisis experience following justification. Known until 1893 as the National Camp Meeting Association for the Promotion of Holiness (from 1893-1971 the official title was the National Association for the Promotion of Holiness, usually shortened to the National Holiness Association), the organization was seen by its members as an instrument for reviving the Wesleyan doctrine of perfect love within American Methodism. Like the present Billy Graham Association, the National Camp Meeting Association was a group of evangelists. Unlike the Graham workers, however, the first National evangelists served as pastors during the winter months. The National Association owned no camp meeting grounds but conducted meetings upon invitation from local camp meeting committees. By 1874 the evangelists had not only made the association national by holding meetings in the South and West, but also international by extending their activities to India and Australia. Through books issued by the National Publishing Association for the Promotion of Holiness in Philadelphia and periodicals published in Philadelphia and Boston, the evangelists maintained contact with constituents between meetings. With leaders fiercely loyal to Methodism (until 1942 all National Association presidents serving as much as a year were ministers in the Methodist Episcopal Church), the National Association fought a losing battle. The passing of the original well-placed Methodist leaders and the growth of independent holiness churches forced a modification of the organization's activities. Although an ever-diminishing evangelistic and publication program continued until after World War II (the Christian Witness finally ceased publication in 1959), denominational membership largely replaced individual membership and interdenominational fellowship replaced revivalism as the group's chief function. Theological discussions and plans for cooperation among holiness churches have largely occupied the organization in recent years.

(General Works)

69 NATIONAL Association for the Promotion of Holiness.
Booklet, 1913-1914. n. p., 1913. 88 p.

70 NATIONAL Association for the Promotion of Holiness.
Booklet, 1924-1925. Syracuse, N. Y., Way of Holiness
Press, 1924. 99 p.

71 NATIONAL Association for the Promotion of Holiness.
The National Association for the Promotion of Holiness,
1932-1936. Chicago, Christian Witness Co., 193- . 59 p.

72 TINNEY, James S
"Distinguishing holiness: National Holiness Association
name change," Christianity Today, XV (May 7, 1971), 42.

--ANECDOTES, REMINISCENCES, SATIRE, ETC.

73 CARRADINE, Beverly, 1848-1931.
A bundle of arrows. Chicago and Boston, Christian Witness
Co., c1907. 258 p.

74 CARRADINE, Beverly, 1848-1931.
A church yard story. Chicago and Boston, Christian Witness
Co., 1904. 254 p.
Cover-title: Mississippi stories.

75 CARRADINE, Beverly, 1848-1931.
Living illustrations. Chicago and Boston, Christian Witness
Co., 1908. 290 p.

76 CARRADINE, Beverly, 1848-1931.
Mississippi stories.
See Carradine, Beverly, 1848-1931.
A church yard story.

77 CARRADINE, Beverly, 1848-1931.
Pastoral sketches. 2d ed. Louisville, Kentucky Methodist
Publishing Co., c1895.

78 CARRADINE, Beverly, 1848-1931.
Pastoral sketches. 5th ed. Chicago, Christian Witness Co.,
1896. 317 p.

79 CARRADINE, Beverly, 1848-1931.
Pen pictures. 3d ed. Chicago, Christian Witness Co.,
190- . 277 p.

80 CARRADINE, Beverly, 1848-1931.
People I have met. Chicago, Christian Witness Co., 1910.
265 p.

II. 1. Christian Holiness Association

81 CARRADINE, Beverly, 1848-1931.
    Remarkable occurrences. Chicago, Christian Witness Co.,
    1902. 270 p.

82 CARRADINE, Beverly, 1848-1931.
    Revival incidents. Chicago, Christian Witness Co., 1913.
    iv, 245 p.

83 CARRADINE, Beverly, 1848-1931.
    Yazoo stories. Chicago, Christian Witness Co., 1911.
    244 p.

84 HAYGOOD, Atticus Greene, bp., 1839-1896.
    The monk and the prince. Atlanta, Foote & Davies Co.,
    1895. 371 p.
    A fictionalized critique of the Holiness Movement in which shabby pious Savonarola (a Georgia Methodist Holiness preacher) confronts the world-wise Lorenzo de'Medici.

85 HELM, Kathryn
    The lure of Divine love; or, Experiences and their lessons, selected from a half century of practical Christian living, including many miracles of divine healing (A book of personal testimony written as letters to a friend). Cincinnati, Published for the author by God's Bible School and Revivalist, 1929. 607 p.

86 HOLINESS in doctrine and experience; a source book of quotable material; testimonies, experiences, definitions, illustrations, comp. anonymously by "A fellow servant of the master." Kansas City, Mo., Beacon Hill Press, 1951. 191 p.

87 ISAAC, Eben M.
    The extremely spiritual man; or, Holiness in action. Chicago, Christian Witness Co., 1907. 193 p.
    Fictionalized autobiography.

88 MOSELY, Harriett
    The power of grace; or, Memorials of Harriett Mosely [edited] by I.S. Leonard. London, R. S. Dickinson, 1888.
    150 p.

89 PAUL, John Haywood, 1877-1967.
    The Bethlehem wonder; [story of the eloquent Jew, a constructive fiction based upon true history written by a friend of the Hebrew people of our time]. Louisville, Herald Press,
    n.d. 44 p.

90 PAUL, John Haywood, 1877-1967.
    He witnessed the Bethlehem wonder. Louisville, Ky., Herald Press, 19- .

91 WHITTEMORE, Emma (Mott), 1850-1931.
    Frankie; or, The little conqueror.... New York, Door of Hope Repository, c1894. 67 p.

92 WINCHESTER, Charles Wesley, 1843-
    The victories of Wesley Castle. Chicago, Christian Witness Co., 1900. 211 p.

--APOLOGETIC WORKS

93 CHRISTIAN perfection, an address by the Southern holiness associations. Nashville, n. d.

94 EHLERS, W. C.
    Holiness and the opposition. Minneapolis, Northwestern Holiness Publishing Co., 1915.

95 HAYNES, Benjamin Franklin, 1851-1923.
    Facts, faith and fire; or, Chapters on the situation. Nashville, B. F. Haynes Publishing Co., 1900. 320 p.

96 JESSOP, Harry Edward, 1884-
    We the Holiness people; the things we believe and teach. Chicago, Chicago Evangelistic Institute, 1948. 110 p.
    "Endorsed and recommended by the National Association for the Promotion of Holiness."

97 JESSOP, Harry Edward, 1884-
    We the holiness people; endorsed and recommended by the National Association for the Promotion of Holiness. Chicago, Chicago Evangelistic Institute, 1948. 95 p.

98 KNAPP, Martin Wells, 1853-1901.
    Pentecostal aggressiveness; or, Why I conducted the meetings of the Chesapeake Holiness Union at Bowens, Maryland. Cincinnati, M. W. Knapp, 1899? 188 p.

99 PICKETT, Leander Lycurgus, 1859-1928.
    A plea for the present Holiness Movement. Louisville, Ky., Pickett Publishing Co.; Garland, Tex., Rev. M. A. Smith, 1896. 120 p.

--BIBLIOGRAPHY

100 DAYTON, Donald W.
    The American holiness movement: a bibliographic introduction. Wilmore, Ky., B. L. Fisher Library, Asbury Theological Seminary, 1971. 49 p.

101 JONES, Charles Edwin, 1932-

II. 1. Christian Holiness Association 13

Perfectionist persuasion; a social profile of the National Holiness Movement within American Methodism, 1867-1936. Ann Arbor, Mich., University Microfilms, 1968. 660 ℓ. Thesis (Ph. D.)--University of Wisconsin. Vita. Bibliography: ℓ. 520-660.

102 SMITH, Joseph Henry, 1855-1946.
Things behind and things before in the Holiness Movement. Chicago, Evangelistic Institute Press, 1916.

--BIOGRAPHY

103 ADAMS, John Quincy, 1825-1881, ed.
Experiences of the higher Christian life in the Baptist denomination; being the testimony of a number of ministers and private members of Baptist churches to the reality and blessedness of the experience of sanctification, through faith in the blood of Jesus Christ. New York, Sheldon & Co.,; Boston, Gould & Lincoln [etc., etc.], 1870. 287 p.

104 EARLE, Absalom Backas -1892.
Abiding peace. Boston, J. H. Earle, 1890, c1879. 126 p.

105 HOLINESS miscellany; essays [of] Dr. Adam Clarke and Richard Watson; experiences of Bishop Foster, Rev. Geo. Peck, D. D., Rev. Alfred Cookman, Rev. J. A. Wood, Rev. E. M. Levy, D. D. [and] D. Steele, D. D. Philadelphia, National Publishing Association for the Promotion of Holiness, 1882. 175 p.
John S. Inskip, comp.

106 HUNTER, Fannie (McDowell)
Women preachers; introd. by Dr. A. M. Hills. Dallas, Berachah Printing Co., 1905. 100 p.

107 McCLURKAN, James O., 1861-1914.
Chosen vessels; twenty-one biographical sketches of men and women, most of whom have been used of God in pioneering some great Pentecostal movement. Nashville, Pentecostal Mission Publishing Co., 1901. 199 p.

108 NEE, Gilbert Chibee
Voices from many lands; foreword by Henry Clay Morrison. Louisville, Pentecostal Publishing Co., 1936. 208 p.

109 [PALMER, Phoebe (Worrell)] 1807-1874.
Pioneer experiences; or, The gift of power received by faith, illustrated and confirmed by the testimony of eighty living ministers, of various denominations, by the author of "Way of holiness"; introd. by Rev. Bishop Janes. New York, W. C. Palmer, Jr., 1868. xii, 368 p.

110 PENTECOSTAL messengers: Seth C. Rees, B. Carradine, W. B. Godbey, A. M. Hills, S. A. Keen, E. H. Dashiell, Abbie C. Morrow, F. S. Heath, M. W. Knapp. Cincinnati, M. W. Knapp, 1898. 75 p. (Full Salvation Quarterly, vol. 5, no. 1)
Autobiographies except for sketch of Rev. Samuel Ashton Keen, by Rev. David C. Thomas.

111 PICKETT, Leander Lycurgus, 1859-1928, comp.
Faith tonic, 1 and 2 combined; being a series of articles by different writers, exemplifying God's dealings with those who trust Him. Louisville, Pentecostal Publishing Co., n. d. 102 p.

112 THE RICHES of grace; or, The blessing of perfect love, as experienced, enjoyed, and recorded by sixty-two living witnesses. Brooklyn, Henry J. Fox, 1854. 456 p.

113 SHAW, Solomon Benjamin, 1854-
The power of prayer; or, Touching incidents and remarkable answers to prayer; reprinted and enl. by Teunis Oldenburger. Grand Rapids, Mich., Calvin Press, 1945. 347 p.
Cover-title: Touching incidents; or, The power of prayer.
Previous editions published under title: Touching incidents and remarkable answers to prayer.

114 SHAW, Solomon Benjamin, 1854-
Children's edition of Touching incidents and remarkable answers to prayer. Grand Rapids, Mich., S. B. Shaw, 1895. 128 p.

115 SMITH, Bernie, 1920-   ed.
Contemporary conversions. Anderson, Ind., Warner Press, 1947. 131 p.

116 SMITH, Bernie, 1920-   ed.
Flames of living fire; testimonies to the experience of entire sanctification. Kansas City, Mo., Beacon Hill Press, 1950. 127 p.

117 WHITTEMORE, Emma (Mott), 1850-1931.
Mother Whittemore's records of modern miracles; foreword by her son and daughter and by Commander Evangeline Booth; tribute by Miss Sara Wray of the Eighth Avenue Mission, New York City, ed. by Rev. F. A. Robinson. Toronto, Missions of Biblical Education, 1931. 310 p.

118 WIMBERLY, Charles Franklin, 1866-1946.
Beacon lights of faith; introd. by Dr. M. E. Lazenby. New York, Revell, c1929. 191 p.

II. 1. Christian Holiness Association   15
                    --CAMP MEETINGS

119   NATIONAL Holiness Association.
      Camp meeting manual, prepared by the National Holiness
      Association Camp Meeting Seminar, Bishop Henry A. Ginder,
      director. Marion, Ind., 196- . 48 p.
      Mimeographed.

120   BLANCHARD, Charles Lorraine, 1902-
      "A study of the modern camp meeting." Unpublished
      Th. M. thesis, Louisville Presbyterian Theological Seminary,
      1962. 315 ℓ.

121   CARY, William Walter, 1887-
      "Sychar, an holiness camp meeting." Louisville, Ky.,
      Pentecostal Publishing Co., 1933. 64 p.

122   THE DOUBLE cure; or, Echoes from National camp-meetings.
      Boston and Chicago, Christian Witness Co., 1887. 442 p.
      Thirty-three sermons preached at various encampments
      of the National Camp Meeting Association for the Promotion
      of Holiness.

123   THE DOUBLE cure; or, Echoes from National camp-meetings.
      Boston, Christian Witness Co., 1894. 425 p.

124   GORHAM, B. Weed
      Camp meeting manual, a practical book for the camp
      ground; in two parts, with illustrative plates. Boston,
      H. V. Degen, 1854. 168 p.

125   HUGHES, George, 1828-1904.
      Days of power in the forest temple; a review of the
      wonderful work of God at fourteen National camp-meetings,
      from 1867 to 1872, with an introd. by Rev. Bishop Haven.
      Boston, J. Bent, 1873. iv, 453 p.

126   HUGHES, Howard Raymond
      "The history of Delanco Camp Meeting Association."
      Unpublished Th. M. thesis, Eastern Baptist Theological
      Seminary, 1961. v, 137 ℓ.

127   McLEAN, Alexander, 1826-1910, ed.
      Penuel; or, Face to face with God, ed. by Rev. A. Mc-
      Lean and J. W. Eaton. New York, W. C. Palmer, 1869.
      483 p.
      Origin of National camp meetings, descriptions of the
      Vineland, Manheim and Round Lake camps, with sermons
      preached at these camps.

128   POMEROY, B.
      Visions from modern mounts: namely Vineland, Manheim,

Round Lake, Hamilton, Oakington, Canton, with other selections. Albany, N.Y., Van Benthuysen Printing House, 1871.

129 WALLACE, Adam, 1825-1903, ed.
A modern Pentecost; embracing a record of the sixteenth National Camp-Meeting for the Promotion of Holiness, held at Landisville, Pa., July 23d to August 1st, 1873. Philadelphia, Methodist Home Journal Publishing House, 1873. 224 p.

130 WESCHE, Percival A.
"The revival of the camp-meeting by the holiness groups." Unpublished M.A. thesis, Divinity School, University of Chicago, 1945.

--CATECHISMS AND CREEDS

131 CUNDIFF, B. A.
A catechism on the second blessing. Louisville, Pentecostal Publishing Co., n.d. 22 p.

132 CURNICK, Edward T., 1850-1923.
A catechism on Christian perfection. Chicago, Christian Witness Co., 1885. 210 p.

133 FOWLER, Charles J., circa 1848-1919.
What we teach and what we do not teach. University Park, Iowa, Christian Witness Association, 194- .
Folder.

134 PAUL, John Haywood, 1877-1967.
Religion and reason; a systematic catechism of Christian doctrine: non-sectarian, topical light on several problems, and, The author's "Prize article" on sanctification. Louisville, Ky., Herald Press, n.d. 31 p.

--CHURCH WORK

135 [PALMER, Phoebe (Worrell), 1807-1874]
Promise of the Father; or, A neglected speciality of the last days, addressed to the clergy and laity of all Christian communities, by the author of The Way of Holiness.... Boston, Henry V. Degen, 1859. xvi, 421 p.

136 WRAY, Newton, 1854-
Fun and finance; a discussion of modern church novelties in connection with the subject of Christian giving, with an introd. by Rev. A.J. Gordon, D.D. Boston, McDonald, Gill & Co., 1890. 162 p.

II. 1. Christian Holiness Association   17

   --CLERGY

137   GODBEY, William B., 1833-1920.
         Holiness clergy bureau. Greensboro, N.C., Apostolic
      Messenger Publishing Co., n.d.

138   GODBEY, William B., 1833-1920.
         Woman preacher. Atlanta, Ga., Office of the Way of
      Life, 1891. 13 p.

139   GODBEY, William B., 1833-1920.
         Women preachers. Nashville, Tenn., n.d.

140   HUNTER, Fannie (McDowell)
         Women preachers; introd. by Dr. A.M. Hills. Dallas,
      Tex., Berachah Printing Co., 1905. 100 p.

   --CONDUCT OF LIFE

141   BOOTH, Catherine (Mumford), 1829-1890.
         Godliness; being reports of a series of addresses delivered at James's Hall, London, W., during 1881. Introduction by Daniel Steele. Philadelphia, National Publishing Association for the Promotion of Holiness, 1883. 158 p.

142   BOOTH, Catherine (Mumford), 1829-1890.
         Godliness; being reports of a series of addressed delivered at James's Hall, London, W., during 1881. Introduction by Daniel Steele. Boston, McDonald & Gill Co., 1893. 158 p.
         Reprint of 1883 ed.

143   CARRADINE, Beverly, 1848-1931.
         Golden sheaves. Boston, J. Gill, 1901. iv, 273 p.

144   CARRADINE, Beverly, 1848-1931.
         A great sermon. Are secret societies a blessing or a curse? An address by Rev. B. Carradine, D.D., pastor of the Centenary M. E. Church, St. Louis, before his congregation, January 4th, 1891. Chicago, Christian Witness Co., 1891. 19 p.

145   CARRADINE, Beverly, 1848-1931.
         Soul help. Boston and Chicago, Christian Witness Co., 1900. iv, 284 p.

146   CHURCH, John Robert, 1899-
         When saints disagree; and, How to be kept in perfect peace. Louisville, Herald Press, n.d. 59 p.

147 CORNELL, Clarence Ellsworth
    Sifted wheat; or, Helps to holy living; a special tonic for young people and a stimulus for those who are older. Chicago, Christian Witness Co., 1905. 276 p.
    Originally published in the Christian Standard, during 1902 and 1903.

148 THE DANCE: fifty statements concerning its morality, by a young woman, a great devotee of the dance before her conversion. Later she did all she could to warn young people of its evils. Chicago, Christian Witness Co., n. d. 15 p.

149 DODSWORTH, Jeremiah
    The better land; or, The Christian emigrant's guide to heaven. Columbia, S.C., L.L. Pickett, 18??. 312 p.

150 ELLYSON, Edgar Painter, 1869-1954.
    Holding out; written especially for young converts, also for new arrivals in the Canaan Land. Chicago, Christian Witness Co., 1894. 107 p.

151 ELLYSON, Edgar Painter, 1869-1954.
    Holding out; written especially for young converts, also for new arrivals in the land of Canaan. Cincinnati, M.W. Knapp, 1896. 107 p.

152 FITKIN, Abram Edward, 1878-1933.
    Tobacco, should a Christian ever indulge in it? Boston, Christian Witness Co., 1897. 22 p.

153 FREEMAN, Harry C.
    Holiness unto the Lord. San Francisco, F.F. Young Co., 1904. 136 p.
    Contents.--Only the baptism & its type.--The dance.--The theater.--The true route.--A glimpse of hell.--Redemption.--A glimpse of heaven.--Our mission.--Be filled.

154 GLASCOCK, James Luther, 1852-1942.
    Wholesome food for hungry people ... with an introd. by the Rev. M.G. Standley. Cincinnati, Revivalist Office, 1913. 165 p.

155 GOUTHEY, A. P.
    The tongue of fire. Louisville, Ky., Pentecostal Publishing Co., 1921. 29 p.

156 GRAVES, Albert Phelps, 1829-1911.
    From earth to heaven; as viewed in the sermons, Bible readings, and reform papers. 7th ed. Chicago, John Fairbanks, 1879. 341 p.

II. 1. Christian Holiness Association

157 GRAVES, Albert Phelps, 1829-1911.
Down grade; a book to save tempted young men. 4th ed. Chicago, J. Fairbanks, 1879. 180 p.

158 GRAVES, Albert Phelps, 1829-1911.
That railroad man. Philadelphia, Griffith and Rowland Press, 1904. xv, 206 p.

159 GRAVES, Albert Phelps, 1829-1911.
Twenty-five letters to a young lady. 4th ed. Chicago and New York, Fairbanks, Palmer & Co., 1883. 135 p.

160 HAMES, J. M.
How to keep sweet. Louisville, Pentecostal Publishing Co., n.d. 48 p.

161 HEATH, Frank Stowe
Soul laws in sexual, social, spiritual life.... 2d ed., rev. Cincinnati, M.W. Knapp, 1899. 125 p. (Pentecostal holiness library, vol. 2, no. 10)

162 HIGLEY, L. H., ed.
The brown god and his white imps; or, The evils of tobacco and cigarettes, prepared and ed. by L. H. Higley. 8th ed., rev. Butler, Ind., Higley Press, n.d. 126 p.

163 HUMPHREY, Jerry Miles, 1872-
Daily guide for the sanctified. Chicago, Christian Witness Co., 1917. 147 p.

164 HUMPHREY, Jerry Miles, 1872-
Spiritual lessons from every-day life. Lima, Ohio, True Gospel Grain Publishing Co., 1914. 210 p.

165 JACOBS, Simon P., 1847-1921.
Christ in ethics. New York, Broadway Publishing Co., 1912. 252 p.

166 KLETZING, Henry Frick, 1850-1910.
Stepping stones to success; or, Practical business and intelligent citizenship, by H. F. Kletzing and E. L. Kletzing. Naperville, Ill., Kletzing Bros., 1899. 379 p.

167 KLETZING, Henry Frick, 1850-1910.
Traits of character illustrated in Bible light, together with short sketches of marked and marred manhood and womanhood, by H. F. Kletzing and E. L. Kletzing.... Naperville, Ill., Kletzing Brothers, 1898. 371 p.

168 KNAPP, Martin Wells, 1853-1901.
Rescued!, or, The river of death, showing how people perish in it, and how they may be rescued. Rev. ed. Cin-

cinnati, Office of the Revivalist, 1898. 118 p.

169 McCONKEY, James Henry, 1858-1937.
The surrendered life; Bible studies and addresses on the yielded life. Pittsburgh, Silver Publishing Society, 1927. 123 p.

170 MAHAN, Asa, 1800-1889.
The true believer: his character, duty, and privileges. New York, Harper, 1847.

171 MILLER, Basil William, 1897-
Bible readings for Christian workers; rightly dividing the Word of Truth. Louisville, Pentecostal Publishing Co., 1930. 118 p.

172 PAUL, John Haywood, 1877-1967.
I choose to run; a handbook of the Christian life. Louisville, Ky., Herald Press, n.d. 47 p.

173 REES, Paul Stromberg, 1900-
Movies and the conscientious Christian. 2d ed. Grand Rapids, Mich., Zondervan, 1945. 23 p.

174 SELLE, Robert L., 1865-1929.
Which church would Jesus join? Louisville, Pentecostal Publishing Co., 1915. 148 p.

175 SHELHAMER, Elmer Ellsworth, 1869-1947.
Helps to holy living. Atlanta, E.E. Shelhamer, 1907. 128 p.

176 SHELHAMER, Julia (Arnold)
A message to men. Kansas City, Mo., Nazarene Publishing House; Atlanta, Repairer Publishing Co., 192?. 128 p.

177 SHELHAMER, Julia (Arnold)
A whisper to women; a companion book to A message to men. Kansas City, Mo., Nazarene Publishing House; Atlanta, Repairer Publishing Co., 1927? 127 p.

178 SMITH, Florence Ethel
Dancing as a modern amusement. Chicago, Christian Witness Co., n.d. 16 p.

179 TAYLOR, Bushrod Shedden, 1849-1935.
Pipe and quid; an essay on tobacco.... Des Moines, Iowa, Northwestern Holiness Publishing Co., 1891. 48 p.

180 VESS, Arthur L.
The loophole. Rev. and 3d ed. Oak Grove, La., Rev.

II. 1. Christian Holiness Association

Wilson Douglas; Pinellas Park, Fla., Revival Herald, 19?? 60 p.
On wedding rings.

181   WATSON, George Douglas, 1845-1924.
A pot of oil; or, The anointed life as applied to prayer, the mental faculties, the affections and Christian service. n. p., n. d.   129 p.

182   WATSON, George Douglas, 1845-1924.
A pot of oil; or, The anointed life as applied to prayer, the mental faculties, the affections and Christian service. Pittsburgh, G. Burgum, 1900.   156 p.

183   WATSON, George Douglas, 1845-1924.
Spiritual ships; an allegory of religious characters and experiences.   Wilkinsburg, Pa., Living Words Co., 1902. 156 p.

184   WATSON, George Douglas, 1845-1924.
Spiritual ships.   Cincinnati, Revivalist Office, n. d.

185   WATSON, George Douglas, 1845-1924.
Watson's Wise words for today; excerpts from "A pot of oil."   Cincinnati, Revivalist Press, n. d.   32 p.

186   WIGHT, J. B.
Tobacco, can it be defended?   8th ed., rev.   Butler, Ind., Higley-Huffman Press, n. d.   48 p.

187   WIMBERLY, Charles Franklin, 1866-1946.
The mastery of manhood; introd. by H. C. Morrison, D. D.   New York, Revell, c1924.   144 p.

188   WIMBERLY, Charles Franklin, 1866-1946.
The moving picture; a careful survey of a difficult problem.   Louisville, Pentecostal Publishing Co., c1917.   31 p.

189   ZEPP, Arthur Carroll, 1878-
Walking as he walked; or, Holiness in action, designed to show the practical side of sanctification in its outworking and application to daily life.   Chicago, Christian Witness Co., 1912.   134 p.

-- --AUTHORITATIVE SOURCES

190   FINNEY, Charles Grandison, 1792-1875.
Lectures to professing Christians, selected and abbreviated by E. E. Shelhamer.   3d ed.   Cincinnati, Revivalist Press, 1937.   119 p.
Reprint of 1928 ed.

191 WESLEY, John, 1703-1791.
Christian perfection as taught by John Wesley, by Josiah Henry Barr. Apollo, Pa., American Holiness Journal, 1946. 119 p.

--CONGRESSES

192 GENERAL Holiness Assembly. Chicago, 1885.
Proceedings of the General Holiness Assembly, held in the Park Avenue M. E. Church, Chicago, May 20-26, 1885. Grand Rapids, Mich., S.B. Shaw, 1885.

193 GENERAL Holiness Assembly. Chicago, 1901.
Echoes of the General Holiness Assembly, held in Chicago, May 3-13, 1901, ed. by S.B. Shaw.... Chicago, S.B. Shaw, 1901? 345 p.

194 LEONARD, Isabella S., ed.
Addresses on holiness, delivered at the Star Hall Convention, Manchester, November ... 1890. Edited by I.S.L. London, S.W. Partridge & Co., 1891. xii, 231 p.

195 LEONARD, Isabella S., ed.
Addresses on holiness. Second series. Delivered at the Star Hall Convention, Manchester, October ... 1891. Edited by I.S. Leonard. London, S.W. Partridge & Co., 1892? viii, 248 p.

196 PROCEEDINGS of Holiness conferences, held at Cincinnati, November 26th, 1877, and at New York, December 17th, 1877. Philadelphia, National Publishing Association for the Promotion of Holiness, 1878. 225 p.

197 WESTERN Union Holiness Convention. Jacksonville, Ill., 1880.
Proceedings of the Western Union Holiness Convention held at Jacksonville, Ill., Dec. 15th-19th, 1880. Bloomington, Ill., Western Holiness Association, L. Hawkins, agent, 1881. 83 p.

--CRITICAL WORKS

198 BEEBE, Theodore Eaton
Hatching chickens for the hawks. Long Beach, Calif., T.E. Beebe, 1920. 59 p.
"Poems in this book written by F.M. Lehman."

199 BRYANT, Thomas J., 1828-1893.
A protest and criticism on the Western Union Holiness Convention, reviewed by T. J. Bryant. Bloomington, Ill.,

II. 1. Christian Holiness Association   23

Printed by the Banner of Holiness, 1881. Cover-title, 32 p.

200   GODBEY, William B., 1833-1920.
      Satan's side-tracks for Holiness people. Nashville, Pentecostal Mission Publishing Co., 19??.

201   GOODELL, Charles LeRoy, 1854-1937.
      My ministry. New York, Fleming H. Revell Co., c1938. 185 p.
      Methodist clergyman critical of the Holiness Movement.

202   HUGHES, Edwin Holt, bp., 1866-1950.
      I was made a minister, an autobiography. New York, Abingdon, Cokesbury, 1943. vii, 328 p.
      Methodist bishop somewhat critical of the Holiness Movement.

203   IRONSIDE, Henry Allan, 1876-1951.
      Holiness, the false and the true. New York, Loizeaux Bros., 1953. 142 p.
      Reprint of 1912 ed.
      Includes spiritual autobiography and unfavorable critique of Holiness Movement.

204   WOODS, Leonard, 1774-1854.
      An examination of the doctrine of perfection, as held by Rev. Asa Mahan ... and others. New York, W.R. Peters; London, Wiley & Putnam, 1841. 140 p.

--DEVOTIONAL LITERATURE

205   BOUNDS, Edward McKendree, 1835-1913.
      Preacher and prayer. Chicago, The Christian Witness, n.d. 128 p.

206   DANFORD, Samuel Alexander, 1865-   comp.
      Holiness Bible readings. Chicago, Christian Witness Co., 1907. 74 p.

207   ELLYSON, Edgar Painter, 1869-1954.
      With Christ at prayer. Louisville, Pentecostal Herald print, 1908. 67 p.
      Chapel talks ... at Texas Holiness University, Peniel, Texas.

208   FOWLER, Charles J., circa 1848-1919.
      Thoughts on prayer, from sermon-talks. Chicago and Boston, Christian Witness Co., c1912. 112 p.

209 GODBEY, William B., 1833-1920.
Jesus only; a full salvation year book, by W.B. Godbey, Byron J. Rees, A.M. Hills, W.N. Hirst, E.H. Dashiell, J.M. Pike, C.W. Ruth, Abbie C. Morrow, C.E. Cornell, M.W. Knapp, B. Carradine, [and] Seth C. Rees. Cincinnati, God's Revivalist Office, n.d. 211 p.

210 HARNEY, William J.
Praying clear through; a book on a subject essential to all who would get into a state of grace, and grow therein; also for those who study to shew themselves approved unto God, workmen that need not to be ashamed. Cincinnati, God's Revivalist Press, 1915. 253 p.

211 HUMPHREY, Jerry Miles, 1872-
Dew drops from rifted clouds. Lima, Ohio, True Gospel Grain Publishing Co., 1917. 54 p.

212 HUMPHREY, Jerry Miles, 1872-
Fragments from the King's table. Lima, Ohio, True Gospel Grain Publishing Co., 1915. 213 p.

213 HUMPHREY, Jerry Miles, 1872-
Gleanings from Emmanuel land. Lima, Ohio, True Gospel Grain Publishing Co., 1911. 63 p.

214 HUMPHREY, Jerry Miles, 1872-
Impressive talks. Lima, Ohio, True Gospel Grain Publishing Co., 1918.

215 HUMPHREY, Jerry Miles, 1872-
Select fruits from the highlands of Beulah. Lima, Ohio, True Gospel Grain Publishing Co., 1913. 227 p.

216 MORROW, Abbie (Clemens)
Joy and rejoicing; Pentecostal Bible readings by Mrs. Abbie C. Morrow and Evangelist Chas. W. McCrossan. Cincinnati, M.W. Knapp, 1898. 93 p. (Pentecostal holiness library, v. 1, no. 12)

217 MORROW, Abbie (Clemens)
Prayers for public worship, private devotion, personal ministry. New York, M.E. Munson, 1902. 195 p.

218 RAVENHILL, Leonard
Revival praying. Zachary La., Fires of Revival Publishers, 1971, c1962. 176 p.

219 SMITH, Joseph Henry, 1855-1946.
Daily holiness text book. Cincinnati, God's Bible School and Revivalist, 1922.

II. 1. Christian Holiness Association   25

220   THOMPSON, John   -1899.
         Daily holiness text book, by John Thompson and E. I. D.
      Pepper.   Philadelphia, Christian Standard Co., 1896.   107 p.

221   WISEMAN, Peter, 1883-
         The Master's masterpiece on prayer; or, Lord, teach us
      to pray.   Louisville, Pentecostal Publishing Co., 1943. 32 p.

--DOCTRINAL AND CONTROVERSIAL WORKS

222   ACKERMAN, George Everett
         Old thoughts in new dress; or, Today's theology for laymen.   Louisville, Pentecostal Publishing Co., 1915. 154 p.

223   AKERS, Lewis Robeson, 1881-
         God's specific for sin.   n. p., n. d.   Unpaged.

224   ALLEN, Charles Bosne, 1857-
         Pardon-conversion, purity-sanctification.   Louisville, Pentecostal Publishing Co., 1911.

225   ALLIS, Mrs. Matilda
         Holiness briefs.   Fort Scott, Kan., Monitor Publishing House, 1889.

226   ALWOOD, J. K.
         Twenty-eight objections against the doctrine of double-birth perfection, commonly called the "second-work sanctification," together with a clear statement of the Bible doctrine concerning Christian perfection, also a chapter containing words of advice to young Christians.   Dayton, Ohio, Pub. for the author, 1880. 440 p.

227   ANDERSON, Tony Marshall, 1888-
         Truth for the times.   n. p., n. d.

228   AN APPEAL to Christian testimony on the doctrine and experience of Christian holiness, or entire sanctification.   London, E. Stock, 1870.   14 p.

229   ATWOOD, Anthony, 1801-1888.
         The abiding Comforter, a necessity to joyful piety and eminent usefulness.   Philadelphia, A. Wallace, 1874. 216 p.
         "Rev. J. T. Cran[e's] book, entitled, Holiness the Birthright of God's Children..., was the occasion of my writing this."--p. 6-7.

230   BABCOCK, C. H.
         Christ exalted.   Cincinnati, God's Revivalist, 1926.
      162 p.

231 BAIRD, Mr.
   Seed to the sower and bread to the eater. University Park, Iowa, Christian Witness Association, n. d. 16 p.

232 BAKER, Sheridan, 1824-1890.
   The hidden manna; being a view of Christian holiness taken from the standpoint of personal and general experience, with scriptural confirmations introduced with the author's experience. Boston, McDonald, Gill & Co., 1887. 278 p.

233 BAKER, Sheridan, 1824-1890.
   The new name; or, The soul's entire purification. Boston, McDonald, Gill & Co., 1890. 199 p.

234 BALDWIN, Harmon Allen, 1869-1936.
   Holiness and the human element. Louisville, Pentecostal Publishing Co., 1919. 123 p.

235 BOARDMAN, William Edwin, 1810-1886.
   He that overcometh; or, A conquering gospel. Boston, Henry Hoyt, 1869.

236 BOARDMAN, William Edwin, 1810-1886.
   The higher Christian life. Boston, Henry Hoyt, 1858. 330 p.

237 BOARDMAN, William Edwin, 1810-1886.
   In the power of the Spirit. Boston, Willard Tract Repository, 1875. 286 p.

238 BOOTH, Catherine (Mumford), 1829-1890.
   Popular Christianity; a series of lectures delivered in Princes Hall, Piccadilly. Boston, McDonald, Gill & Co., 1888. 203 p.

239 BOTTOME, Margaret (McDonald), 1827-1906.
   Death and life. Philadelphia, Christian Standard Co., 1897. 54 p.

240 BOWEN, George, 1816-1888.
   The amens of Christ; introd. by Daniel Steele. Boston, McDonald & Gill, 1886. 307 p.

241 BOWEN, George, 1816-1888.
   Love revealed: meditations on the parting words of Jesus with his disciples in chapters XIII, XIV, XV, XVI, XVII, of the Gospel by John. Philadelphia, Presbyterian Board of Publication, 1872. 392 p.

242 BOYNTON, Jeremy, 1824-1883.
   Sanctification practical: a book for the times; with an introd. and an appendix by Mrs. Palmer. New York, Foster and Palmer, Jr., 1867. 142 p.

II. 1. Christian Holiness Association

243 BRADY, J. W.
Grace magnified. Bloomington, Ill., Banner of Holiness Publishing Office, 1873.

244 BRASHER, John Lakin, 1868-1971.
The glorious church. University Park, Iowa, Christian Witness, 194?. 39 p.

245 BRASHER, John Lakin, 1868-1971.
The moods of the Spirit. Louisville, Ky., Herald Press, n.d. 27 p.

246 BROOKS, Delos Ferdinand, 1845-1935.
What is the carnal mind? Chicago, Christian Witness Co., 1905. 113 p.

247 BRYANT, Thomas J., 1828-1893.
A few out of many exclusive immersionist errors pointed out by T.J. Bryant. Camp Point, Ill., Journal Print, 188?. 51 p.

248 BRYANT, Thomas J., 1828-1893.
Plain things to holiness people; also popular errors concerning holiness teaching. Nevada, Iowa, Highway Press, 1887? 49 p.

249 BRYANT, Thomas J., 1828-1893.
Relay to Warner's Love without partiality, with an addendum. n.p., 1881? [19] p.
Cover title.

250 BRYANT, Thomas J., 1828-1893.
A survey of the field, and strictures thereon by J.P. Brooks, reviewed by T.J. Bryant. Bloomington, Ill., Printed by the Banner of Holiness, 1888? 25 p.
Cover title.

251 BURNS, Nelson   -1904.
Divine guidance; or, The Holy Guest; a discussion of the believer's privilege in Christ Jesus, the Holy Spirit as guide into all truth.... Brantford, Ont., Can., Book and Bible House, 1889. 288 p.

252 BUTLER, Charles William, 1873-1960.
A holiness manifesto. Louisville, Ky., Herald Press, n.d. 132 p.

253 BUTLER, Charles William, 1873-1960.
Salvation by faith; or, Faith versus the work and witness of the Spirit, by C.W. Butler; and, The fundamental of the fundamentals, by G.A. McLaughlin. Chicago, Christian Witness Co., n.d. 45 p.

254 CARRADINE, Beverly, 1848-1931.
The better way. 2d ed. Cincinnati, M. W. Knapp, 1896.
193 p.

255 CARRADINE, Beverly, 1848-1931.
Beulah land. Boston, Christian Witness Co., 1904.
276 p.

256 CARRADINE, Beverly, 1848-1931.
Bible characters. Chicago and Boston, Christian Witness Co., c1907.

257 CARRADINE, Beverly, 1848-1931.
A box of treasure. Chicago and Boston, Christian Witness Co., c1910. 336 p.

258 CARRADINE, Beverly, 1848-1931.
Gideon. Philadelphia, Pepper Publishing Co., 1902.
88 p.

259 CARRADINE, Beverly, 1848-1931.
Heart talks. Cincinnati, God's Revivalist Office, 1899.
278 p.

260 CARRADINE, Beverly, 1848-1931.
Holiness and its witnesses. Columbia, S. C., L. L. Pickett, n. d.

261 CARRADINE, Beverly, 1848-1931.
Jonah. Philadelphia, Pepper Publishing Co., c1902.

262 CARRADINE, Beverly, 1848-1931.
The old man. Louisville, Kentucky Methodist Publishing Co., 1896. 270 p.
On "whether or not there is a principle or nature of sin left in the soul after regeneration."

263 CARRADINE, Beverly, 1848-1931.
Sanctification. New Orleans, D. L. Mitchell, 189?.
124 p.

264 CARRADINE, Beverly, 1848-1931.
Sanctification; introduction by Rev. L. L. Pickett. Louisville, Pickett Publishing Co., 1890.

265 CARRADINE, Beverly, 1848-1931.
The sanctified life. Cincinnati, Office of the Revivalist, 1897. 286 p.

266 CARRADINE, Beverly, 1848-1931.
The second blessing in symbol, by B. Carradine. 2d ed., enl. Columbia, S. C., L. L. Pickett, 1894. 307 p.

II. 1. Christian Holiness Association   29

267   CHADWICK, Samuel, 1860-1932.
         Humanity and God. New York, F.H. Revell Co., n.d.
      xv, 356 p.

268   CHADWICK, Samuel, 1860-1932.
         Humanity and God. Rochester, Pa., H.E. Schmul, n.d.

269   CHADWICK, Samuel, 1860-1932.
         The way to Pentecost; with an introd. by Dr. Robert Lee
      Stuart. Berne, Ind., Light and Hope Publications, 1937.
      128 p.

270   CHAMBERS, Oswald, 1874-1917.
         Biblical psychology; a series of preliminary studies.
      Cincinnati, God's Revivalist Office, c1914. 273 p.

271   CHAMBERS, Oswald, 1874-1917.
         Studies in the Sermon on the Mount. Cincinnati, God's
      Revivalist Press, c1915. 122 p.

272   CHURCH, John Robert, 1899-
         A bird's eye view of God's plan. Louisville, Pentecostal
      Publishing Co., c1936. 63 p.

273   CHURCH, John Robert, 1899-
         Earthen vessels; or, The human element in holiness.
      Louisville, Pentecostal Publishing Co., 1942. 53 p.

274   CHURCH, John Robert, 1899-
         Earthen vessels; or, The human element in holiness;
      introd. by Dr. Paul S. Rees. Grand Rapids, Mich., Zondervan, 1942. 56 p.

275   CHURCH, John Robert, 1899-
         Earthen vessels; introd. by Dr. Paul S. Rees. Louisville, Pentecostal Publishing Co., 1942. 64 p.

276   CHURCH, John Robert, 1899-
         I am a skeptic. Louisville, Herald Press, n.d. 94 p.

277   CHURCH, John Robert, 1899-
         Is God responsible for our temptations? Louisville,
      Pentecostal Publishing Co., n.d. 59 p.

278   CHURCH, John Robert, 1899-
         A second grace, an adequate remedy for the sin. Louisville, Herald Press, 1942. 48 p.

279   CHURCH, John Robert, 1899-
         A second grace, an adequate remedy for sin. Grand
      Rapids, Mich., Zondervan, 1942. 45 p.

280 CHURCH, John Robert, 1899-
What does adoption mean to you?; and, God's plan for financing His church. Louisville, Deeper Life Press (Pentecostal Publishing Co.), n.d. 72 p.

281 CHURCH, John Robert, 1899-
Why baptize by sprinkling? Louisville, Herald Press, n.d. 82 p.

282 CHURCH, John Robert, 1899-
Why do the righteous suffer? Louisville, Pentecostal Publishing Co., c1936. 30 p.

283 CLARK, Dougan, 1828-1896.
From Elim to Carmel. Boston, Christian Witness Co., 1895.

284 CLARK, Dougan, 1828-1896.
The inner and outer life of holiness, ed. by Anna Louise Spann. Portland, Ore., Evangel Publishers, 1945.

285 CLARK, Dougan, 1828-1896.
The offices of the Holy Spirit, ed. by Anna Louise Spann. Portland, Ore., Evangel Publishers, 1945. 216 p.

286 CLARK, Dougan, 1828-1896.
The offices of the Holy Spirit. Philadelphia, National Publishing Association for the Promotion of Holiness, 1878. 288 p.

287 CLARK, Dougan, 1828-1896.
The theology of holiness. Boston, McDonald & Gill Co., 1893. 183 p.

288 COLLINS, J. H.
Sanctification: what it is, when it is, how it is. Louisville, Pentecostal Publishing Co., n.d. 63 p.

289 COLLINS, Mahlen Day, 1838-1904.
The common sense of Bible salvation. Philadelphia, Christian Standard Co., 1899. 69 p.

290 COOKMAN, Alfred, 1828-1871.
Familiar talks on the subject of the higher Christian life. University Park, Iowa, Christian Witness Association, 1947. 71 p.
New edition.

291 COOKMAN, Alfred, 1828-1871.
The higher Christian life. Boston, Christian Witness Co., 1900. 84 p.

II. 1. Christian Holiness Association 31

292 COUCHENOUR, H. M.
Sanctification; or, Deliverance from the inward foe.
Washington, Pa., L. P. Lehman and Staff, 1937.

293 COWARD, Samuel L. C.
Perfect love. Louisville, Ky., Pentecostal Publishing
Co., n. d. 26 p.

294 CULPEPPER, John B.
Sin. Louisville, Pentecostal Publishing Co., 1914.
91 p.

295 CUNDIFF, B. A.
Scriptural holiness. Louisville, Pentecostal Publishing
Co., 1928.

296 DANE, Charles Walter, 1875-1944.
Why, when and how of sanctification. Chicago, Christian
Witness Co., 1904. 92 p.
Cover-title: Sanctification: why, when, how.

297 DASHIELL, Edward Honeywood, 1873-1931.
The spirit of Jesus. Cincinnati, M. W. Knapp, 1898.
88 p. (Pentecostal holiness library, vol. 1, no. 5)

298 DAVIES, Edward, 1830-
The believer's hand-book; on holiness: showing how to
enter and how to dwell in the Canaan of perfect love. Reading, Mass., The author, 1877. 72 p.

299 DAVIES, Edward, 1830-
The contrast between infidelity and Christianity, as seen
in death-bed testimonies. Reading, Mass., The author,
1879. 95 p.

300 DAVIES, Edward, 1830-
The gift of the Holy Ghost; the believer's privilege.
Reading, Mass., E. Davies, 1877. 108 p.
Bound with his Select sermons on Christian experience;
and his The believer's hand-book.

301 DAVIES, Edward, 1830-
The law of holiness; an exposition of the Ten commandments, and also showing the relation of the Decalogue to the moral universe, and to the gospel. Reading, Mass., Published by the author at the Holiness Book Concern, 1880.
126 p.
With as bound: John Harris. Selections from Harris's
Mammon. Reading, Mass., 1880.

302 DAVIES, Edward, 1830-
The life of Rev. John Wesley, A. M., written from a

spiritual standpoint; introduction by Dr. Charles Cullis....
Reading, Mass., Holiness Book Concern; New York, Willard
Tract Repository; etc., etc., 1887. 261 p.

303 DAVIS, Henry Turner, circa 1833-
     Coals from the altar. Cincinnati, Office of God's Revivalist, 1902. 179 p.

304 DAVIS, Henry Turner, circa 1833-
     The shining way. Cincinnati, M.W. Knapp, 1900. 171 p.

305 DEMPSTER, Joseph S.
     Bread from heaven; introd. by E.I.D. Pepper. Philadelphia, Christian Standard Co., 1899. 287 p.

306 DOTY, Thomas K., 1833-1913.
     Lessons in holiness. Cleveland, The author, 1881. 224 p.

307 DOTY, Thomas K., 1833-1913.
     The two-fold gift of the Holy Ghost. Cleveland, Christian Harvester Office, 1890. 240 p.

308 DUNN, Lewis Romaine, 1822-1898.
     Relations of the Holy Spirit to the work of entire holiness. New York, W.C. Palmer, 1883.

309 EARLE, Absalom Backas   -1892.
     The higher Christian experience: questions answered....
     Boston, 1873. 13 p.

310 EARLE, Absalom Backas   -1892.
     The rest of faith. Boston, James H. Earle, 1873. 96 p.

311 ELLYSON, Edgar Painter, 1869-1954.
     God's man from Tishbi. Chapel talks on the life of Elijah, delivered at the Texas Holiness University, Peniel, Texas. Peniel, Tex., Pentecostal Advocate, 190?. 162 p.

312 ELLYSON, Edgar Painter, 1869-1954.
     Theological compend. Chicago, Christian Witness Co., 1908. 190 p.

313 ELLYSON, Edgar Painter, 1869-1954.
     Ye must; or, Some Bible imperatives. Marshalltown, Iowa, Christian Messenger Publishing Co., 1904. 167 p.

314 FERGERSON, E. A.
     Heart purity. Louisville, Pentecostal Herald Printers, n.d.

II. 1. Christian Holiness Association

315 FOWLER, Charles J., circa 1848-1919.
     Back to Pentecost. Philadelphia, Christian Standard Co., 1900. 144 p.

316 FOWLER, Charles J., circa 1848-1919.
     Chair-talks on perfection. Chicago, Christian Witness Co., 1918. 75 p.

317 FOWLER, Charles J., circa 1848-1919.
     Christian unity, its secret and success; with an introd. by Rev. Daniel Steele. Chicago, Christian Witness Co., 1907. 140 p.

318 GILL, Joshua
     Human heart: Bible reading. Boston, McDonald, Gill & Co., 1889.

319 GILL, Joshua, ed.
     Representation of the heart of man in its depraved state by nature, and the changes which it experiences under the influences of the Spirit of God operating upon it, to which are added directions for keeping the heart. Rev. and enl. Chicago, Christian Witness Co., 1893. 118 p.

320 GODBEY, William B., 1833-1920.
     Baptism: mode and design. Louisville, Pentecostal Publishing Co., c1883. 101 p.

321 GODBEY, William B., 1833-1920.
     Baptism: mode and design. Louisville, Kentucky Methodist Publishing Co., 1896, c1883. 74 p.

322 GODBEY, William B., 1833-1920.
     Baptism of the Holy Ghost. Greensboro, N.C., Apostolic Messenger Office, n.d.

323 GODBEY, William B., 1833-1920.
     Bible theology. Cincinnati, God's Revivalist Office, 1911. 418 p.

324 GODBEY, William B., 1833-1920.
     Commentary on the New Testament. Cincinnati, M.W. Knapp, 1896-1900. 7 v.

325 GODBEY, William B., 1833-1920.
     Current heresies. Cincinnati, God's Revivalist Office, 1908. 46 p.

326 GODBEY, William B., 1833-1920.
     Deeper things. Louisville, Pentecostal Publishing Co., n.d. 68 p.

327 GODBEY, William B., 1833-1920.
Demonology, by Rev. W.B. Godbey ... to which is added chapters on The devil and demons, by Evangelist L.L. Pickett; Demon possession in Russia, by Rev. F.B. Meyer; The devil, by Rev. Andrew Johnson; An angel visit, by Rev. J.M. Dustman. Louisville, Ky., Pickett Publishing Co., 1902. 68 p.

328 GODBEY, William B., 1833-1920.
Glorification. Cincinnati, Mrs. M.W. Knapp, 1902. 110 p.

329 GODBEY, William B., 1833-1920.
Holiness or hell? Louisville, Pentecostal Publishing Co., 1899, c1893. 151 p.

330 GODBEY, William B., 1833-1920.
Holiness or hell? Noblesville, Ind., J. Edwin Newby, Newby Book Room, 1972. 151 p.
Reprint of 1893 ed.

331 GODBEY, William B., 1833-1920.
The incarnation of the Holy Ghost. Louisville, Pentecostal Publishing Co., 19??.

332 GODBEY, William B., 1833-1920.
Life of Jesus and His apostles. Louisville, Pentecostal Publishing Co., 1904. 455 p.

333 GODBEY, William B., 1833-1920.
Outline on a debate on water baptism and the baptism with the Holy Ghost between Rev. W.B. Godbey ... and Rev. William Maupin, by Rev. Leroy McWherter.... Cincinnati, God's Revivalist Office, 1911. 32 p.

334 GODBEY, William B., 1833-1920.
Plan of salvation. n.p., n.d. 33 p.

335 GODBEY, William B., 1833-1920.
Sanctification. n.p., 1884. 112 p.

336 GODBEY, William B., 1833-1920.
Sanctification. Cincinnati, Elm St. Printing Co., c1884.

337 GODBEY, William B., 1833-1920.
Spiritual gifts and graces. Cincinnati, God's Revivalist Office, 1895. 83 p.

338 GODBEY, William B., 1833-1920.
Work of the Holy Spirit; introd. by Rev. L.L. Pickett. Louisville, Ky., Pickett Publishing Co., 1902. 75 p.

II. 1. Christian Holiness Association 35

339 GOUTHEY, A. P.
Things pertaining unto life. Louisville, Pentecostal Publishing Co., 1923. 29 p.

340 GREGORY, John
Sanctification, a gift for this life. Detroit, Truth Press Association, 1914.

341 HAMES, J. M.
Breaking the alabaster box. Louisville, Pentecostal Publishing Co., n.d.

342 HAMES, J. M.
Christ enthroned within. Louisville, Pentecostal Publishing Co., ndd. 53 p.

343 HAMES, J. M.
A cry for the supernatural. Louisville, Pentecostal Publishing Co., n.d. 46 p.

344 HAMES, J. M.
Fragrance from Beulah Land. Louisville, Pentecostal Publishing Co., n.d.

345 HAMES, J. M.
Fragrance, sweetness and power. Louisville, Pentecostal Publishing Co., n.d.

346 HAMES, J. M.
The fullness of Jesus. Louisville, Pentecostal Publishing Co., n.d.

347 HAMES, J. M.
God's wonders of tomorrow. Louisville, Pentecostal Publishing Co., n.d.

348 HAMES, J. M.
Golden graces. Louisville, Pentecostal Publishing Co., n.d.

349 HAMES, J. M.
Living in the heavenlies. Louisville, Pentecostal Publishing Co., n.d. 57 p.

350 HAMES, J. M.
Living in the heavenlies. Louisville, Pentecostal Publishing Co., 193?. 61 p.

351 HAMES, J. M.
Orthodox psychology; or, Vital Christianity. Chicago, Christian Witness Co., 1929. 166 p.

352 HAMES, J. M.
 The overcomer. Louisville, Pentecostal Publishing Co., n. d. 56 p.

353 HAMES, J. M.
 Select fruit from the Land of Beulah. Louisville, Pentecostal Publishing Co., n. d.

354 HAMES, J. M.
 The triumphant life. Louisville, Pentecostal Publishing Co., n. d.

355 HANEY, Milton Lorenzo, 1825-1922.
 The Inheritance Restored; or, Plain Truths on Bible Holiness. 4th ed., rev. and enl. Chicago, Christian Witness Co., 1897. 301 p.

356 HANEY, Milton Lorenzo, 1825-1922.
 Tares mixed with the wheat; a reprint of Unsaved church members, as published in The Christian Witness. Chicago, Christian Witness Co., 1910. 82 p.

357 HARDY, Chester Ernest, 1882-1972.
 Pentecost. Louisville, Ky., Pentecostal Publishing Co., 1929. 116 p.

358 HARRIS, John, 1802-1856.
 Selections from Harris's Mammon, by Rev. E. Davies. Reading, Mass., Pub. by the author at the Holiness Book Concern, 1880.

359 HARVEY, John W., 1854-
 The house of Abraham, illustrated; an allegory: Galatians 4:22-30. Sunset, Tex., C. A. McConnell, printer, 1900. 33 p.

360 HEGRE, Theodore A.
 The cross and sanctification, formerly published as Three aspects of the cross. Minneapolis, Bethany Fellowship, 1960. 276 p.

361 HEIRONIMUS, H. T.
 The theme of the ages; or, Handbook on holiness. Louisville, Pentecostal Publishing Co., 1924. 199 p.

362 HELM, Benjamin
 The abiding life (John XV). Louisville, Pentecostal Publishing Co., n. d. 106 p.

363 HICKS, Lawrence B.
 Holiness, the pride of God. Louisville, Pentecostal Publishing Co., n. d. 54 p.

II. 1. Christian Holiness Association

364 HILLS, Aaron Merritt, 1848-1935.
   The cleansing baptism. Manchester, Eng., Star Hall, 1910? 82 p.

365 HILLS, Aaron Merritt, 1848-1935.
   Dying to live. Cincinnati, God's Revivalist Office, 1905. 196 p.

366 HILLS, Aaron Merritt, 1848-1935.
   Holiness and power for the church and the ministry. Cincinnati, God's Revivalist Office, 1897. 382 p.
   Also issued under title: Holiness in the Book of Romans.

367 HILLS, Aaron Merritt, 1848-1935.
   Holiness and power for the church and the ministry. Manchester, Eng., Star Hall, 1913. 149 p.

368 HILLS, Aaron Merritt, 1848-1935.
   Holiness, not a modern fad. Manchester, Eng., Star Hall Publishing Co., n.d.

369 HILLS, Aaron Merritt, 1848-1935.
   Pentecost rejected; and the effect on the churches. Cincinnati, Office of God's Revivalist, 1902. 103 p.

370 HILLS, Aaron Merritt, 1848-1935.
   Pentecostal light. Manchester, Eng., Star Hall Publishing Co., n.d.

371 HILLS, Aaron Merritt, 1848-1935.
   Romans and sanctification. Manchester, Eng., Star Hall, 1910? 117 p.

372 HILLS, Aaron Merritt, 1848-1935.
   Satan's devices. Manchester, Eng., Star Hall Publishing Co., n.d.

373 HILLS, Aaron Merritt, 1848-1935.
   The secret of spiritual power. Manchester, Eng., Star Hall Publishing Co., n.d.

374 HORNER, Ralph Cecil, 1854-1921.
   Notes on Boland; or, Mr. Wesley and the second work of grace; introd. by J.V. McDowell. Boston, McDonald & Gill, 1893. 230 p.

375 HUFFMAN, Jasper Abraham, 1880-
   Golden treasures from the Greek New Testament for English readers. Butler, Ind., Higley Press, 1951. 160 p.

376 JACOBS, Simon P., 1847-1921.
   The real Christian. n.p., S.P. Jacobs, 1899. 338 p.

377 JESSOP, Harry Edward, 1884-
   The consecrating believer and the sanctifying God. Orlando, Fla., Holiness Book Ministry, n.d. 15 p.

378 JESSOP, Harry Edward, 1884-
   Foundations of doctrine in scripture and experience; a students' handbook on holiness. Chicago, Chicago Evangelistic Institute, 1938. 252 p.

379 JESSOP, Harry Edward, 1884-
   The heritage of holiness. Chicago, Chicago Evangelistic Institute, 1950. 94 p.

380 JESSOP, Harry Edward, 1884-
   Spiritual security; a meditation on the mutual responsibility of the Lord and the believing soul for eternal salvation. Intercession City, Fla., Central Florida Bible Institute; University Park, Iowa, Chicago Evangelistic Institute, 1953. 24 p.

381 JOHNSON, Zachary Taylor, 1897-
   The essentials of holiness. Louisville, Pentecostal Publishing Co., n.d. 168 p.

382 JOHNSON, Zachary Taylor, 1897-
   We believe; a study of the practical aspects of our Christian faith. Louisville, Pentecostal Publishing Co., n.d. 101 p.
   "A study in the fundamental doctrines of the Wesleyan faith as advocated in the charter of Asbury College."

383 JOHNSON, Zachary Taylor, 1897-
   What is holiness? Cincinnati, God's Bible School, 1936. 239 p.

384 JONES, W.
   The doctrine of entire sanctification scripturally and psychologically examined. Philadelphia, National Publishing Association for the Promotion of Holiness, 1890. xii, 255 p.

385 KEEN, Samuel Ashton, 1842-1895.
   Faith papers. Cincinnati, God's Revivalist, 1888. 144 p.

386 KEEN, Samuel Ashton, 1842-1895.
   Faith papers; a treatise on experimental aspects of faith. Louisville, Pentecostal Publishing Co., n.d. 41 p.

387 KEEN, Samuel Ashton, 1842-1895.
   Pentecostal papers; or, The gift of the Holy Ghost. Louisville, Pickett Publishing Co., c1895. 190 p.

II. 1. Christian Holiness Association

388 KEEN, Samuel Ashton, 1842-1895.
Pentecostal sanctification. Cincinnati, M.W. Knapp, Revivalist Office, 1897. 99 p.

389 KEEN, Samuel Ashton, 1842-1895.
Salvation papers. Cincinnati, Revivalist Office, 1896. 103 p.

390 KEITHLY, J. W.
The mission of the Holy Spirit. Dermott, Ark., J.W. Keithly, 1904.

391 KELLEY, Edward R.
The land of Canaan. Chicago, Christian Witness Co., 1922. 131 p.

392 KIMBER, John Shober
Following the star. Newport, R.I., Beulah Book Room, 1914. 79 p.

393 KIMBER, John Shober
Tabernacle talks. Los Angeles, Oriental Missionary Society, 1931. xv, 97 p.

394 KNAPP, Martin Wells, 1853-1901.
Christ crowned within. Cincinnati, God's Revivalist Office, 1886. 202 p.

395 KNAPP, Martin Wells, 1853-1901.
The double cure. Cincinnati, M.W. Knapp, Revivalist Office, 1895. 96 p.

396 KNAPP, Martin Wells, 1853-1901.
Holiness triumphant; or, Pearls from Patmos, being the secret of Revelation revealed. Cincinnati, God's Revivalist Office, 1900. 253 p.

397 KNAPP, Martin Wells, 1853-1901.
"Impressions." Cincinnati, M.W. Knapp, Revivalist Office, 1892. 145 p. (Pentecostal holiness library, vol. 1, no. 6)

398 KNAPP, Martin Wells, 1853-1901.
Lightning bolts from Pentecostal skies. Cincinnati, Office of the Revivalist, 1898. 307 p.

399 KNAPP, Martin Wells, 1853-1901.
Out of Egypt into Canaan; or, Lessons in spiritual geography. Boston, McDonald, Gill & Co.; Albion, Mich., Revivalist Pub. Co., 1889. 196 p.

400 LEVY, Edgar M., 1822-1906.
   The efficacy of the precious blood. Chicago, Chicago Evangelistic Institute Press, n.d. Unpaged (Spiritual Life Classics, no. 4)

401 McBRIDE, Joseph Benjamine, 1873-
   Christ in you the hope of glory. Cincinnati, God's Revivalist, n.d.

402 McBRIDE, Joseph Benjamine, 1873-
   In the citadel--on the throne. Louisville, Pentecostal Publishing Co., 1920. 207 p.

403 McCONKEY, James Henry, 1858-1937.
   The three-fold secret of the Holy Spirit. Harrisburg, Pa., F. Kelker, 1897. 116 p.

404 McCONKEY, James Henry, 1858-1937.
   The three-fold secret of the Holy Spirit. Harrisburg, Pa., F. Kelker, 1908. 123 p.

405 McDONALD, William, 1820-1901.
   Christian perfection. New York?, 1893. 16 p.
   Contents.--Christian perfection [as taught by John Wesley] by William McDonald.--An experience of more than fifty years ago, by A.M. Fowler.--The Pentecost, by A.M. Fowler.

405a McDONALD, William, 1820-1901.
   Modern faith healing, scripturally considered.... Boston, McDonald, Gill & Co., 1892. 112 p.

406 McDONALD, William, 1820-1901.
   The New Testament standard of piety; or, Our love made perfect. Rev. ed. Boston, McDonald & Gill, 1882. 287 p.

407 McDONALD, William, 1820-1901.
   Saved to the uttermost. Boston, McDonald & Gill, 1885. 76 p.

408 McDONALD, William, 1820-1901.
   Scriptural views of holiness. Philadelphia, National Publishing Association for the Promotion of Holiness, 1877. 320 p.

409 McKAIG, Robert Newton, 1842-
   The life and times of the Holy Spirit. Chicago, Christian Witness Co., 1908- .

410 McLAUGHLIN, George Asbury, 1851-1933.
   Inbred sin. Boston, McDonald and Gill, 1887. 99 p.

411 McLAUGHLIN, George Asbury, 1851-1933.
    A living sacrifice. Boston, Christian Witness Co., 1899. 74 p.

412 McLAUGHLIN, George Asbury, 1851-1933.
    Saved and kept; or, How to get saved and how to keep saved. Chicago, Christian Witness Co., 1903. 75 p.

413 McPHEETERS, Julian C., 1889-
    Religious trends of today. Louisville, Ky., Herald Press, 1938. 54 p.

414 MAHAN, Asa, 1800-1889.
    The baptism of the Holy Ghost. New York, Palmer & Hughes, 1870. 215 p.

415 MAHAN, Asa, 1800-1889.
    Christian perfection. New ed., with prefatory letter by the author, and an introd. by George Warner. London, F.E. Longley, 1874. 187 p.

416 MAHAN, Asa, 1800-1889.
    Doctrine of the will. New York, M.H. Newman; Oberlin, Ohio, R.E. Gillet, 1845. 218 p.

417 MAHAN, Asa, 1800-1889.
    Scripture doctrine of Christian perfection; with other kindred subjects, illustrated and confirmed in a series of discourses designed to throw light on the way of holiness. Boston, D.S. King, 1839. 237 p.

418 MAHAN, Asa, 1800-1889.
    Scripture doctrine of Christian perfection, with other kindred subjects illustrated and confirmed in a series of discourses designed to throw light on the way of holiness. 6th ed. Boston, D.S. King, 1841. 193 p.

419 MILLER, L. J.
    Lest we forget; or, What say the fathers? Louisville, Pentecostal Publishing Co., 1923. 62 p.

420 MOREHOUSE, Frank Eugene, 1854-1908.
    Bible readings on the double heart and kindred truths; introd. by O.E. Murray. Napoleon, Mich., F.E. Morehouse, 1898. 174 p.

421 MORRISON, Henry Clay, 1857-1942.
    Baptism with the Holy Ghost. Louisville, Ky., Herald Book Store, 1900. 39 p.

422 NELSON, Thomas Hiram, 1863-
    The contents of Calvary's cup; the vicarious atonement

and its purpose and fruit in character transformation. Portland, Ind., Tabernacle Press, 1937. 351 p.

423 NELSON, Thomas Hiram, 1863-
The Mosaic law in the light of modern science. Philadelphia, John C. Winston Co., 1926. 190 p.

424 NELSON, Thomas Hiram, 1863-
Nature's revelation of God and the Bible supplement.
New York, American Bible Society, 1940. 208 p.

425 OSBORN, Lucy Reed (Drake), 1844-
Light on soul winning. New York, Revell, 1911. 160 p.

426 PAGE, Isaac E., 1839-1926.
Fulness of grace: the believer's heritage, with an introd. by the Rev. W. E. Boardman. Philadelphia, National Association for the Promotion of Holiness; London, F. E. Longley, 1874. 160 p.

427 PALMER, Phoebe (Worrell), 1807-1874.
Faith and its effects; or, Fragments from my portfolio.
New York, Published for the author, 1854. 352 p.

428 PALMER, Phoebe (Worrell), 1807-1874.
Incidental illustrations of the economy of salvation, its doctrines and duties. Boston, H. V. Degen; Binghamton, N. Y., B. W. Gorham, 1855. 380 p.

429 PALMER, Phoebe (Worrell), 1807-1874.
A present to my Christian friend on entire devotion to God. New York, Published for the author, 1855. 192 p.

430 PALMER, Phoebe (Worrell), 1807-1874.
Present to my Christian friend; or, Entire devotion to God. New ed., rev. London, G. J. Stevenson, n. d. 130 p.

431 PALMER, Walter Clark, 1804-1883, ed.
Tracts on holiness. New York, W. C. Palmer, n. d.

432 PAPPAS, Paul John, 1898-
Conception of Christ in the Old Testament. n. p., n. d. 60 p.

433 PAUL, John Haywood, 1877-1967.
Scriptural holiness, the more excellent way; seven chapters and a sermon on the higher life. Louisville, Ky., Herald Press (Pentecostal Publishing Co.), n. d. 32 p.

434 PAUL, John Haywood, 1877-1967.
The way of power; a series of lectures delivered before the Japan Convention for Deepening of Spiritual Life at Karni-

zawa, stenographically reported. New York, Revell, 1918. 190 p.

435 PAUL, John Haywood, 1877-1967.
What is new theology? Wilmore, Ky., Department of Publications, Asbury College, 1921.

436 PAUL, John Haywood, 1877-1967.
When the Sun rose in the west; a story of the first Advent, with a Japanese setting. Louisville, Ky., Pentecostal Publishing Co., 1917. 38 p.

437 PEARSE, Mark Guy, 1842-1930.
Thoughts on holiness; introd. by Rev. W. McDonald. Boston, McDonald, Gill & Co., 1884. 219 p.

438 PECK, Jesse Truesdell, bp., 1811-1883.
The central idea of Christianity. Boston, Henry V. Degen, 1858. 389 p.

439 PECK, Jesse Truesdell, bp., 1811-1883.
The central idea of Christianity. Rev. ed., abridged. Louisville, Pentecostal Publishing Co., n.d. 48 p.

440 PHELPS, Alexander Alonzo, 1836-1904.
Purity and power; or, The twelve P's; a radical and scriptural treatment of the doctrine, experience and practice of Christian perfection. Boston, Advent Christian Publication Society, 1905. 600 p.

441 PICKETT, Leander Lycurgus, 1859-1928.
Holiness: the doctrine, the experience, the practice. Louisville, Ky., Pickett Publishing Co., n.d.

442 PICKETT, Leander Lycurgus, 1859-1928.
Leaves from the tree of life. Louisville, Ky., Pickett Publishing Co., 1899. 312 p.

443 PICKETT, Leander Lycurgus, 1859-1928.
St. Paul on holiness. Louisville, Pentecostal Publishing Co., n.d. 77 p.

444 RAVENHILL, Leonard
Tried and transfigured. Zachary, La., Fires of Revival Publishers, 1972, c1962. xiii, 144 p.

445 REID, Isaiah, 1836-1911.
Soul help papers; Tarshish ships and open doors. Des Moines, Published for the author by J.H. Welch Printing Co., 1904. 132 p.

446   RIDOUT, George Whitefield, 1870-1954.
       The beauty of holiness. Louisville, Ky., Pentecostal Publishing Co., n.d. 49 p.

447   RIDOUT, George Whitefield, 1870-1954.
       The deadly fallacy of fanaticism. Louisville, Ky., Pentecostal Publishing Co., n.d. 20 p.

448   RIDOUT, George Whitefield, 1870-1954.
       Dr. Fosdick answered; an exposé of Christian liberalism. Louisville, Pentecostal Publishing Co., 192?. 21 p.

449   THE RIGHT way; a symposium of teaching on the way of holiness. Foreword by Stanley Banks. London, Oliphants, 1964. 92 p.

450   ROBINSON, Reuben, 1860-1942.
       Honey in the rock. Cincinnati, Office of God's Revivalist, 1913. 288 p.

451   ROBINSON, Reuben, 1860-1942.
       Mountain peaks of the Bible. Peniel, Tex., Pentecostal Advocate, n.d. 164 p.

452   ROBINSON, Reuben, 1860-1942.
       Mountain peaks of the Bible. Louisville, Pentecostal Publishing Co., 1913. 164 p.

453   ROBINSON, Reuben, 1860-1942.
       A pitcher of cream. Louisville, Pentecostal Herald Print, 1906. 106 p.
       Sermons and excerpts on holiness.

454   ROBINSON, Reuben, 1860-1942.
       The story of Lazarus. Louisville, Pentecostal Publishing Co., 1909. 111 p.

455   RUTH, Christian Wismer, 1865-1941.
       Bible readings on the second blessing. Chicago, Christian Witness Co., 1905. 190 p.

456   RUTH, Christian Wismer, 1865-1941.
       Entire sanctification, a second blessing; together with life sketch, Bible readings and sermon outlines. Chicago and Boston, Christian Witness Co., 1903. 192 p.

457   RUTH, Christian Wismer, 1865-1941.
       The Pentecostal experience. Chicago and Boston, Christian Witness Co., 1909. 75 p.

458   RUTH, Christian Wismer, 1865-1941.
       Sanctification definitions, etc. Chicago, Christian Witness Co., n.d.

II. 1. Christian Holiness Association

459 RUTH, Christian Wismer, 1865-1941.
　　　The second crisis in Christian experience. Chicago, Christian Witness Co., 1913. 155 p.
　　　Date of publication corrected in manuscript from 1912 to 1913.

460 RUTH, Christian Wismer, 1865-1941.
　　　The second work of grace. Louisville, Pentecostal Publishing Co., 1920. 28 p.

461 SELLE, Robert L., 1865-1929.
　　　Food for the soul. Louisville, Ky., Pentecostal Publishing Co., 1915. 224 p.

462 SELLE, Robert L., 1865-1929.
　　　The holy nation. Cincinnati, M. W. Knapp, 1899. 67 p. (Pentecostal holiness library, vol. 2, no. 5)

463 SELLE, Robert L., 1865-1929.
　　　Sin: its origin, purpose, power, result, and cure. Louisville, Pentecostal Publishing Co., 1913. 60 p.

464 SELLE, Robert L., 1865-1929.
　　　Walking with Jesus. Louisville, Ky., Pentecostal Publishing Co., 1916. 158 p.

465 SHAW, Solomon Benjamin, 1854-
　　　God's financial plan; or, Temporal prosperity the result of faithful stewardship. Grand Rapids, Mich., S. B. Shaw, 1897. 267 p.

466 SHELHAMER, Elmer Ellsworth, 1869-1947.
　　　Popular and radical holiness contrasted. Atlanta, E. E. Shelhamer, 1906.

467 SHEPARD, William Edward, 1862-
　　　Holiness typology. San Francisco, W. E. Shepard, Publisher (Press of the Roberts Printing Co.), 1896. 197 p.

468 SHEPARD, William Edward, 1862-
　　　How to get sanctified. Cincinnati, God's Bible School and Revivalist, n. d.

469 SHEPARD, William Edward, 1862-
　　　Sin, the tell-tale; or, Be sure your sin will find you out. Cincinnati, God's Revivalist Press, 1917. 365 p.

470 SHEPARD, William Edward, 1862-
　　　Wrested scriptures made plain; or, Helps for holiness skeptics. Louisville, Pentecostal Publishing Co., 1900. 174 p.

471 SMITH, Joseph Henry, 1855-1946.
From glory to glory; or, Degrees in spiritual life. Philadelphia, Christian Standard Co., 1898. 178 p.

472 SMITH, Joseph Henry, 1855-1946.
Pauline perfection; being a series of expository messages upon various aspects of Christian perfection from the Pauline epistles, with an introd. by Evangelist Henry C. Morrison, president of Asbury College. Chicago, Christian Witness Co. 1913. xiv, 213 p.

473 SMITH, Joseph Henry, 1855-1946.
Proving our Father's will; Charity is perfect love; Divine union the goal of Christian perfection; and, Perfection not the end of progression. Chicago, Christian Witness Co., n.d. 33 p.

474 SMITH, Joseph Henry, 1855-1946.
Things of the Spirit. Souvenir ed. Chicago, Chicago Evangelistic Institute, 1940. 112 p.

475 STAUFFER, Joshua, 1891-1971.
"According to your faith." Berne, Ind., Light and Hope Publications, c1946. 165 p.

476 STAUFFER, Joshua, 1891-1971.
The divine conflict of the ages. Berne, Ind., Light & Hope Publications, c1959. 246 p.

477 STAUFFER, Joshua, 1891-1971.
When He is come; with introd. by Wm. M. Smith. Berne, Ind., Light and Hope Publications, c1948. 198 p.

478 STEARNS, Daniel Miner, 1844-1920.
The way to the kingdom. Harrisburg, Pa., F. Kelker, 1917. 121 p.

479 STEELE, Daniel, 1824-1914.
The gospel of the Comforter. Boston, Christian Witness Co., 1897. 371 p.

480 STEELE, Daniel, 1824-1914.
Half-hours with St. John's epistles. Chicago, Christian Witness Co., 1901. 261 p.

481 STEELE, Daniel, 1824-1914.
Half-hours with St. Paul, and other Bible readings. Boston, Christian Witness Co., 1904. 323 p.

482 STEELE, Daniel, 1824-1914.
Jesus exultant; or, Christ no pessimist, and other essays. Boston, Christian Witness Co., 1899. 334 p.

II. 1. Christian Holiness Association

483 STEELE, Daniel, 1824-1914.
????? Steele's answers ... ed. and arranged by E. L. Kletzing. Chicago, Christian Witness Co., 1912. 288 p.

484 SWEETEN, Howard W.
Must we sin? A treatise of the sin question from the standpoint of reason and revelation. Introduction by Rev. L. L. Pickett. Louisville, Pentecostal Publishing Co., 1919. 184 p.

485 TAYLOR, Bushrod Shedden, 1849-1935.
Full salvation. Des Moines, Iowa, Northwestern Holiness Publishing Co., 1886.

486 TAYLOR, Bushrod Shedden, 1849-1935.
The Gibeonites; a scriptural allegory.... Cincinnati, M. W. Knapp, 1896. 86 p.

487 TAYLOR, Bushrod Shedden, 1849-1935.
The Gibeonites; a scriptural allegory, in which graces, sins, and infirmities are compared with Israelites to be cultivated, Canaanites to be destroyed, Gibeonites to be repressed. Burlington, Ia. ?, 1924. 86 p.
Reprint of 1896 ed.

488 TAYLOR, James Morgan
Baptism of the Holy Ghost. Louisville, Pentecostal Publishing Co., n.d. 20 p.

489 TAYLOR, James Morgan
The carnal mind. Louisville, Pentecostal Publishing Co., 1909. 32 p.

490 TAYLOR, James Morgan
Knotty points; or, Truth explained. Knoxville, Tenn., James M. Taylor, n.d. 46 p.

491 TREFFRY, Richard, 1771-1842.
The true perfection which God requires, attainable on earth. Boston, McDonald and Gill, 1885.

492 UPHAM, Thomas Cogswell, 1799-1872.
Christ in the soul; or, Illustrations of some of the principles and experiences which characterize Christ's spiritual or inward coming and indwelling. New York, Warren, Broughton & Wyman, 1872. 173 p.
Poems.

493 UPHAM, Thomas Cogswell, 1799-1872.
The life of faith; in three parts; embracing some of the scriptural principles or doctrines of faith, the power or effects of faith in the regulation of man's inward nature, and

the relation of faith to the divine guidance. Boston, Waite, Peirce and Company, 1846. 480 p.

494 UPHAM, Thomas Cogswell, 1799-1872.
Principles of the interior or hidden life. Boston, Waite, Peirce & Co., 1846. 396 p.

495 UPHAM, Thomas Cogswell, 1799-1872.
Principles of the interior or hidden life; designed particularly for the consideration of those who are seeking assurance of faith and perfect love. 8th ed. New York, Harper & Brothers, 1848. 396 p.

496 UPHAM, Thomas Cogswell, 1799-1872.
A treatise on divine union, designed to point out some of the intimate relations between God and man in the higher forms of religious experience. Boston, Charles H. Peirce and Co., 1851. 435 p.

497 VANSANT, Nicholas, 1823-1902.
Entire holiness, is it a gradual or an instantaneous work? New York, W.C. Palmer, 1881.

498 WALKER, Edward Franklin, 1852-1918.
"Sanctify them"; a study of our Lord's prayer for his disciples. Philadelphia, Christian Standard Co., 1899. 160 p.

499 WATSON, George Douglas, 1845-1924.
Beauty for ashes; or, Heart wanderings: their cause and cure. Cincinnati, God's Revivalist Office, 1896. 38 p.

500 WATSON, George Douglas, 1845-1924.
The bridehood saints; treating of the saints who are the "selection from the selection," saints who are to make up the bride of Christ. Cincinnati, Office of God's Revivalist, 1913. 287 p.

501 WATSON, George Douglas, 1845-1924.
Coals of fire: being expositions of scripture on the doctrine, experience, and practice of Christian holiness. Boston, McDonald, Gill & Co., 1886. 151 p.

502 WATSON, George Douglas, 1845-1924.
Coals of fire; being expositions of scripture on the doctrine, experience, and practice of Christian holiness. Cincinnati, God's Bible School Book Room, n.d. 160 p.

503 WATSON, George Douglas, 1845-1924.
Fruits of Canaan. Cincinnati, Revivalist Office, n.d.

II. 1. Christian Holiness Association

504 WATSON, George Douglas, 1845-1924.
God's eagles; or, Complete testing of the saints. Cincinnati, God's Revivalist Office, 1927. 268 p.

505 WATSON, George Douglas, 1845-1924.
God's first words; studies in Genesis, historic, prophetic and experimental. New York, Revell, 1919. 228 p.

506 WATSON, George Douglas, 1845-1924.
The heavenly life; and, Types of the Hol Spirit. Cincinnati, God's Revivalist Press, n.d. 151, 85 p.

507 WATSON, George Douglas, 1845-1924.
The heavenly life ... to which is added: Preach the Lord's coming, by E.P. Marvin; Kadesh-barnea, by Rev. Evan H. Hopkins.... Louisville, Ky.; Greenville, Tex., Pickett Publishing Co., 1904. 151 p.

508 WATSON, George Douglas, 1845-1924.
A holiness manual. Newport, Ky., Printed for the author, 1882. 144 p.

509 WATSON, George Douglas, 1845-1924.
A holiness manual. Boston, Christian Witness Co., 1882. 144 p.

510 WATSON, George Douglas, 1845-1924.
A holiness manual. 2d ed., rev. by Isabella S. Leonard. London, Partridge & Co., 1891. 144 p.

511 WATSON, George Douglas, 1845-1924.
Love abounding, and other expositions on the spiritual life. Boston, McDonald, Gill & Co., 1891. 408 p.

512 WATSON, George Douglas, 1845-1924.
Love abounding, and other expositions on the spiritual life. Cincinnati, God's Revivalist Press, c1891. 408 p.

513 WATSON, George Douglas, 1845-1924.
Love and duty. Columbia, S.C., John M. Pike, n.d.

514 WATSON, George Douglas, 1845-1924.
Our own God. Cincinnati, Revivalist Office, 1904.

515 WATSON, George Douglas, 1845-1924.
Pure gold. Cincinnati, Revivalist Office, 1900. 156 p.

516 WATSON, George Douglas, 1845-1924.
The secret of spiritual power. Boston, Christian Witness Co., 1894. 160 p.

517 WATSON, George Douglas, 1845-1924.
Seven overcomeths, and other expositions from Revelation. Boston, McDonald, Gill & Co., 1889. 96 p.

518 WATSON, George Douglas, 1845-1924.
Soul food. Cincinnati, Revivalist Office, 1898. 143 p.

519 WATSON, George Douglas, 1845-1924.
Spiritual feasts. Cincinnati, Revivalist Office, 1904. 162 p.

520 WATSON, George Douglas, 1845-1924.
White robes; or, Garments of salvation. Chicago, Christian Witness Co., 1883. 160 p.

521 WATSON, George Douglas, 1845-1924.
White robes; or, Garments of salvation. London, Partridge & Co., 1891. 149 p.

522 WESLEYAN BIBLE commentary. [Editorial Board: Chairman and general editor: Charles W. Carter. New Testament editor: Ralph Earle. Old Testament editor: W. Ralph Thompson. Associate editor: Lee Haines] Grand Rapids, Mich., Eerdmans, 1964-1969; v. 1, 1967. 7 v.

523 WHEELER, Mary (Sparkes), 1835-1919.
Consecration and purity; or, The will of God concerning me. Ocean Grove, N.J., The author, 1913. 169 p.

524 WHITAKER, Charles B., 1855-
Entire sanctification, a second work of grace. Grand Rapids, Mich., Published by S.B. Shaw, Holiness Record Office, 1887. 167 p.

525 WHITE, Levi
The borderland of the supernatural. Rev. ed. Chicago, Christian Witness Co., 1905. 445 p.

526 WILLIAMS, Lewis Milton, 1862-
Jacob the heelgrasper; or, Some of God's pictures of the carnal mind. Oskaloosa, Iowa, L.M. Williams, 1907. 347 p.

527 WILLIAMS, Lewis Milton, 1862-
Walking before God; or, Saved through obedience. Cincinnati, Office of God's Revivalist, n.d. 316 p.

528 WILLIAMS, Lewis Milton, 1862-
The war of the ages. Chicago, Christian Witness Co., 1909. 339 p.

II. 1. Christian Holiness Association

529 WILLIAMS, Lewis Milton, 1862-
"Where art thou"; or, Spiritual earthquakes for saints and sinners. Cincinnati, God's Revivalist Office, 1905. 320 p.

530 WILSON, George Washington, 1853-1929.
Get right with God; or, There is another fact, and that is; with an introd. by Rev. James Leaton.... Jacksonville, Ill., Rev. G.W. Wilson, 1887. 240 p.

531 WIMBERLY, Charles Franklin, 1866-1946.
The cry in the night; a book of the times. 2d ed. Louisville, Pentecostal Publishing Co., 1913. 144 p.

532 WIMBERLY, Charles Franklin, 1866-1946.
Is the devil a myth? New York, Revell, c1913. 160 p.

533 WIMBERLY, Charles Franklin, 1866-1946.
Life's biggest ???; ten human mysteries. Louisville, Pentecostal Publishing Co., c1917. 36 p.

534 WIMBERLY, Charles Franklin, 1866-1946.
New clothes for the old man. Louisville, Pentecostal Publishing Co., n.d. 219 p.

535 WIMBERLY, Charles Franklin, 1866-1946.
Your heart and mine; a Bible text book on God's plan of salvation, for homes--schools and colleges, by Rev. C.F. Wimberly, D.D., and John C. Capehart. Seymour, Ind., J.C. Capehart, c1921. 124 p.

536 WISEMAN, Peter, 1883-
Biblical perfection; the theology of perfection as revealed in the Word of God, especially in the New Testament scriptures. Frome, Eng., Butler & Tanner Ltd., n.d.

537 WISEMAN, Peter, 1883-
The fact, faithfulness and fulness of God. Louisville, Pentecostal Publishing Co., n.d. 40 p.

538 WISEMAN, Peter, 1883-
The peerless book. Grand Rapids, Mich., Zondervan Publishing House, c1939. 108 p.

539 WISEMAN, Peter, 1883-
The peerless Christ. London, Edinburgh, Marshall, Morgan & Scott, 1937. 144 p.

540 WOOD, John Allen, 1828-
Mistakes respecting Christian holiness. Chicago, Christian Witness Co., 1905. 136 p.

541 WOOD, John Allen, 1828-
Perfect love; or, Plain things for those who need them; concerning the doctrine, experience, profession, and practice of Christian holiness. 22d ed. Philadelphia, Published for the author by Samuel D. Burlock; for sale by W.C. Palmer, Jr., New York, and the Office of the Methodist Home Journal, Philadelphia, c1861. 314 p.

542 WOOD, John Allen, 1828-
Perfect love; or, Plain things for those who need them, concerning the doctrine, experience, profession and practice of Christian holiness. Rev. and enl. ed. South Pasadena, Calif., 1891. 331 p.

543 WOOD, John Allen, 1828-
Purity and maturity. Boston, Christian Witness Co., 1899. 238 p.

544 WYNKOOP, Mildred (Bangs)
An existential interpretation of the doctrine of holiness; a message presented in chapel service, Western Evangelical Seminary, Portland, Oregon, November 3, 1955. Portland, Ore., Western Evangelical Seminary, 195?. 15 p.

545 ZEPP, Arthur Carroll, 1878-
Conscience alone not a safe guide. Chicago, Christian Witness Co., 1913. 150 p.

546 ZEPP, Arthur Carroll, 1878-
The crowing of the cock; or, The voice of conscience. Mountain Lake Park, Md., Modern Theses Publishing Co., 1926. 52 p.

547 ZEPP, Arthur Carroll, 1878-
Holiness in action. Chicago, Christian Witness Co., 1912. 134 p.

548 ZEPP, Arthur Carroll, 1878-
Progress after entire sanctification. Chicago, Christian Witness Co., 1909.

549 ZEPP, Arthur Carroll, 1878-
Walking as he walked. Chicago, Christian Witness Co., 1912.

-- --AUTHORITATIVE SOURCES

550 BENSON, Joseph, 1749-1821.
The life of the Rev. John W. de la Flechere: comp. from the narrative of the Rev. Mr. Wesley; rev. by Thomas O. Summers, D.D. Chicago, Christian Witness Co., 1925. 530 p.

II. 1. Christian Holiness Association

"Biographical notes of the Rev. Mr. Gilpin, from his own letters, and other authentic documents, many of which were never before published."

551 BENSON, Joseph, 1749-1821.
The life of the Rev. John W. de la Flechere: comp. from the narrative of the Rev. Mr. Wesley; the biographical notes of the Rev. Mr. Gilpin: from his own letters, and other authentic documents, many of which were never before published, rev. by Thomas O. Summers, D. D., University Park, Iowa, John Fletcher College, 1925. 530 p.

552 CLARKE, Adam, 1760?-1832.
Entire sanctification. Philadelphia, E. Jones, 1874. 36 p.

553 CLARKE, Adam, 1760?-1832.
Entire sanctification; being the twelfth chapter of his Christian Theology, with preview by John H. Paul. Louisville, Herald Press (Pentecostal Publishing Co.), n.d. 41 p.

554 FLETCHER, John William, 1729-1785.
Fletcher on perfection. Louisville, Pentecostal Publishing Co., n.d. 87 p.

555 GUYON, Jeanne Marie (Bouvier de La Motte), 1648-1717.
Autobiography of Madame Guyon.... Chicago, Christian Witness Co., 1917. 346 p.
Preface to 1917 ed. signed: E. L. K. [i.e. Elmer L. Kletzing]

556 GUYON, Jeanne Marie (Bouvier de La Motte), 1648-1717.
Letters of Madame Guyon: being selections of her religious thoughts and experiences, translated and re-arranged from her private correspondence; including her correspondence with Fénelon, abridged, by Mrs. P. L. Upham. New York, W. C. Palmer, Jr., 1870. 216 p.

557 GUYON, Jeanne Marie (Bouvier de La Motte), 1648-1717.
Sweet smelling myrrh; the autobiography of Madame Guyon, ed. by Abbie C. Morrow. Cincinnati, M. W. Knapp, 1898. 192 p.

558 HILLS, Aaron Merritt, 1848-1935.
Life of Charles G. Finney. Cincinnati, Office of God's Revivalist, 1902. 240 p.

559 MULLER, George, 1805-1898.
The work of faith through George Müller, ed. by Abbie C. Morrow.... Cincinnati, M. W. Knapp, 1899. 167 p.

560 ROGERS, Hester Ann, 1756-1794.
The experience of Hester Ann Rogers; also the funeral sermon. Chicago, Christian Witness Co., n.d. 105 p.

561 ROGERS, Hester Ann, 1756-1794.
Life and journal of Mrs. Hester Ann Rogers, condensed and combined by Rev. E. Davies. Reading, Mass., Holiness Book Concern, 1882.

562 TREFFRY, Richard, 1771-1842.
A treatise on Christian perfection. Boston, McDonald, Gill & Co., 1888. 215 p.

563 UPHAM, Thomas Cogswell, 1799-1872.
Life and religious opinions and experience of Madame La Mothe Guyon: together with some account of the personal history and religious opinions of Fenelon, archbishop of Cambray, by Thomas C. Upham. New York, Harper & Brothers, 1847. 2 v.

564 WESLEY, John, 1703-1791.
Christian perfection as taught by John Wesley, comp. by Rev. J.A. Wood. Boston, McDonald & Gill, 1885. 288 p.

565 WESLEY, John, 1703-1791.
Christian perfection, as taught by John Wesley. Compiled by Rev. J.A. Wood.... Introduction by Bishop W.F. Mallalieu.... Chicago and Boston, Christian Witness Co., c1921. 288 p.

-- --BIBLIOGRAPHY

566 NATIONAL Holiness Association.
A bibliography of the deeper life. Elkhart, Ind., Bethel Publishing Co., 1958. 7 p.

567 NAZARENE Theological Seminary.
Master bibliography of holiness works. Kansas City, Mo., Prepared by Nazarene Theological Seminary and published by Beacon Hill Press, 1965. 45 p.

-- --COLLECTIONS

568 BOYD, Myron F., bp., 1908-
Projecting our heritage; papers and messages delivered at the centennial convention of the National Holiness Association, Cleveland, Ohio, April 16-19, 1968, comp. by Myron F. Boyd and Merne A. Harris. Kansas City, Mo., Beacon Hill Press, 1969. 157 p.

569 GEIGER, Kenneth E., 1916- , comp.
Insights into holiness; discussions of holiness by fifteen

II. 1. Christian Holiness Association

leading scholars of the Wesleyan persuasion. Kansas City, Mo., Beacon Hill Press, 1963. 294 p.

Fifteen papers of the seminars on holiness doctrine, sponsored by the National Holiness Association, presented in the fall of 1961 on the campuses of various colleges and seminaries.

570 GEIGER, Kenneth E., 1916- , comp.
Further insights into holiness; nineteen leading Wesleyan scholars present various phases of holiness thinking. Kansas City, Mo., Beacon Hill Press, 1963. 349 p.

571 GEIGER, Kenneth E., 1916- , comp.
The word and the doctrine; studies in contemporary Wesleyan-Arminian theology. Kansas City, Mo., Beacon Hill Press, 1965. 429 p.

Presented at a Study Conference on the Distinctives of Wesleyan-Arminian Theology in Winona Lake, Indiana, Nov. 4-6, 1964, under the sponsorship of the National Holiness Association.

-- --ESCHATOLOGY

572 BORDERS, M. Edward
A better country. 3d ed. Chicago, Christian Witness Co., 1918. 102 p.

573 BORDERS, M. Edward
Coronation glories. Chicago, Christian Witness Co., 1915. 109 p.

574 CHASE, William R.
A catechism on the second coming of Christ. Chicago, Christian Witness Co., 19??. 37 p.

575 CHURCH, John Robert, 1899-
Did Jesus believe in eternal punishment? Louisville, Pentecostal Publishing Co., n.d. 57 p.

576 DASHIELL, Edward Honeywood, 1873-1931.
Heaven; or, The glory to be revealed. Federalsburg, Md., J.W. Stowell Printing Co., 1911. 319 p.

577 GOFF, Walter Roy, 1877-
The handbook of eschatology; or, A consistent Biblical view of the Lord's return, the resurrection of the dead and the judgment, with an introd. by Rev. Charles M. Stuart. Blairsville, Pa., Keystone Publishing House, 1917. 99 p.

578 GOFF, Walter Roy, 1877-
Jesus on His second coming; or, A consistent Biblical view of the Lord's return, the resurrection of the dead, and the judgment, with an introd. by Rev. Charles M. Stuart.

[New ed.] Blairsville, Pa., Keystone Publishing House, 1919. 135 p.
First published in 1917 under title: The handbook of eschatology.

579 HUMPHREY, Jerry Miles, 1872-   comp.
A soul's first day in heaven. Chicago, Christian Witness Co., 1917. 86 p.

580 HUMPHREY, Jerry Miles, 1872-   comp.
A soul's first day in heaven. Lima, Ohio, True Gospel Grain Publishing Co., 1917. 86 p.
"The greater amount of its contents has been selected from the writings of other authors."

581 JOHNSON, Andrew, 1875-
Postmillennialism and the higher critics, by the eminent evangelists and authors, Andrew Johnson ... and L.L. Pickett.... Chicago, Glad Tidings Publishing Co., 1923. 445 p.

582 McCONKEY, James Henry, 1858-1937.
The Book of Revelation; a series of outline studies in the Apocalypse. 2d ed. Pittsburgh, Silver Publishing Co., 1921.

583 McCONKEY, James Henry, 1858-1937.
The end of the age; a series of prophetic Bible studies upon the end of this present age. Pittsburgh, Silver Publishing Co., 1917. 129 p.

584 MORRISON, Henry Clay, 1857-1942.
Is the world growing better; or, Is the world growing worse? Louisville, Ky., Pentecostal Publishing Co., 1932. 176 p.

585 MORRISON, Henry Clay, 1857-1942.
The optimism of premillennialism. Louisville, Ky., Pentecostal Publishing Co., 1927. 147 p.

586 MORRISON, Henry Clay, 1857-1942.
The second coming of Christ. Louisville, Ky., Pentecostal Publishing Co., 1914. 120 p.

587 MORRISON, Henry Clay, 1857-1942.
The World War in prophecy; the downfall of the Kaiser and the end of the dispensation. Louisville, Ky., Pentecostal Publishing Co., 1917. 128 p.

588 NELSON, Thomas Hiram, 1863-
The gospel of cause and effect; or, The philosophy of rewards and punishments here and hereafter. Indianapolis, Grace Publishing Co., 1903. 258 p.

II. 1. Christian Holiness Movement

589   PAUL, John Haywood, 1877-1967.
    The climax of the Bible; a Question Bureau study of Revelation, with a sermon on The music of the River of Life and a Brief professional biography of the author. Louisville, Herald Press, n.d. 54 p.

590   PAUL, John Haywood, 1877-1967.
    The hereafter. Louisville, Ky., Pentecostal Publishing Co., 1910. 95 p.

591   PICKETT, Leander Lycurgus, 1859-1928.
    The Antichrist and some mistakes concerning him. Louisville, Ky., Pentecostal Publishing Co., 1928. 267 p.

592   PICKETT, Leander Lycurgus, 1859-1928.
    The renewed earth; or, The coming and reign of Jesus Christ. Louisville, Ky., Greenville, Tex., Pickett Publishing Co., 1903. 338 p.
    Introduction by Rev. John B. Culpepper.

593   PICKETT, Leander Lycurgus, 1859-1928.
    Who is the beast? Louisville, Ky., Pentecostal Publishing Co., 1919. 205 p.
    Rev. C.F. Wimberly, collaborator. cf. Introd.

594   PICKETT, Leander Lycurgus, 1859-1928.
    Why I am a premillennialist. Louisville, Ky., Pentecostal Publishing Co., 1927. 86 p.

595   SMITH, William Martin, 1872-
    Lessons in Daniel; an exposition of the Book of Daniel, the prophet. 4th ed., 1966. Noblesville, Ind., J. Edwin Newby, Newby Book Room, 1972. 192 p.

596   SMITH, William Martin, 1872-
    A primer of prophecy; with introd. by Rev. George E. Guille. Chicago, Bible Institute Colportage Association, c1914. 32 p.

597   STEARNS, Daniel Miner, 1844-1920.
    Studies in the Book of Revelation. Harrisburg, F. Kelker, 1921. 335 p.
    "These studies in the Revelation of Jesus Christ were given at Odd Fellows' Hall, Philadelphia, Pa., on Sunday afternoons, in January to May, 1896."

598   TAYLOR, Bushrod Shedden, 1849-1935.
    Death, hell and judgment. Cincinnati, M.W. Knapp, 1900. 67 p. (Full salvation quarterly, v. 6, no. 3)

599   TAYLOR, James Morgan
    The second coming of Christ and some reasons why I

think it is near, a sermon. Bismarck, N.D., The author, 1917. 80 p.
"Historical references": p. 80.

600 WATSON, George Douglas, 1845-1924.
Age to come. Cincinnati, Revivalist Office, n.d.

601 WATSON, George Douglas, 1845-1924.
Steps to the throne. Louisville, Pickett Publishing Co., 1898. 168 p.

602 WATSON, George Douglas, 1845-1924.
Steps to the throne. Cincinnati, God's Bible School Book Room, n.d. 168 p.

603 [WHEELER, Mary (Sparkes)], 1835-1919.
As it is in heaven, by one of the redeemed. Philadelphia, P.W. Ziegler Co., 1906. 408 p.

604 WILLIAMS, Leowin Bell, 1868-
The heavenly prospect; a synopsis of the future life, the resurrection of the dead, facts about the vastness of the universe, heaven, a place or a condition, recognition and conditions in the world to come. Louisville, Pentecostal Publishing Co., 1948. 117 p.

605 WILSON, George Washington, 1853-1929.
The sign of Thy coming; or, Premillennialism, unscriptural and unreasonable ... with an introd. by Rev. W.X. Ninde. Boston, Christian Witness Co., 1899. 366 p.

606 WIMBERLY, Charles Franklin, 1866-1946.
Behold the morning!; the imminent and premillennial coming of Jesus Christ. New York, Revell, c1916. 224 p.

607 WIMBERLY, Charles Franklin, 1866-1946.
The seven seals of the Apocalypse, unveiling past, present and future. New York, Revell, c1922. 175 p.

-- --FAITH-HEALING

608 CARTER, Russell Kelso, 1849-1926.
The atonement for sin and sickness; or, A full salvation for soul and body. Boston, New York, Willard Tract Repository, 1884. iv, 243 p.

609 CARTER, Russell Kelso, 1849-1926.
Divine healing; or, The atonement for sin and sickness. New ed., rewritten and enl. New York, J.B. Alden, 1888. 189 p.
Lettered on cover: A full salvation for soul and body.

II. 1. Christian Holiness Association

610 CARTER, Russell Kelso, 1849-1926.
"Divine healing; or, 'Faith cure', " Century Magazine, ns XI (Mar. 1887), 777-780.

611 CARTER, Russell Kelso, 1849-1926.
"Faith healing" reviewed after twenty years. Boston and Chicago, Christian Witness Co., 1897. 168 p.

612 CULLIS, Charles, 1833-1892.
Faith cures; or, Answers to prayer in the healing of the sick. Boston, Willard Tract Repository, 1879. 109 p.

613 CULLIS, Charles, 1833-1892.
More faith cures; or, Answers to prayer in the healing of the sick. Boston, Willard Tract Repository, 1881. 105 p.

614 CULLIS, Charles, 1833-1892.
Other faith cures; or, Answers to prayer in the healing of the sick. Boston, Willard Tract Repository, 1885. 160 p.

615 DAVIS, Henry Turner, circa 1833-
Modern miracles. Cincinnati, M.W. Knapp, 1901. 157 p.

616 GODBEY, William B., 1833-1920.
Divine healing. Greensboro, N.C., Apostolic Messenger Office, 1909. 42 p.

617 SHORT, John N., 1841-1922.
Divine healing; with a testimonial and introd. by Rev. N. Hammond Follin. Chicago, Christian Witness Co., n.d. 39 p.

618 SHULER, Robert Pierce, 1880-
"McPhersonism"; a study of healing cults and modern day "tongues" movements. Los Angeles, 1924? 63 p.

-- --GLOSSOLALIA

619 CHURCH, John Robert, 1899-
Which is right? One, two or three works of grace. Is speaking in tongues a sign of the baptism with the Spirit? Louisville, Pentecostal Publishing Co., n.d. 94 p.

620 PICKETT, Leander Lycurgus, 1859-1928.
God or the guessers; some scriptures on present day infidelity. Louisville, Pentecostal Publishing Co., 1926.

621 RIDOUT, George Whitefield, 1870-
The deadly fallacy of spurious tongues. Louisville, Ky., Pentecostal Publishing Co., n d. 16 p.

622 SHULER, Robert Pierce, 1880-
"McPhersonism"; a study of healing cults and modern day "tongues" movements. Los Angeles, 1924? 63 p.

623 ZEPP, Arthur Carroll, 1878-
The P's of Pentecost contrasted with the Corinthian manifestations. Chicago, Christian Witness Co., 1927. 32 p.

-- --PREDESTINATION

624 WIMBERLY, Charles Franklin, 1866-1946.
Falling from grace; 26 reasons why the possibility of apostasy is taught in the Word of God. Louisville, Pentecostal Publishing Co., c1917. 31 p.

-- --SPIRITUALISM

625 CARTER, Russell Kelso, 1849-1928.
The tree of knowledge; a startling scientific study of the original sin, and the sin of angels, with a history of spiritism in all ages. San Francisco, O.H. Elliott, 1894. 423 p.

--EDUCATION

626 HILLS, Aaron Merritt, 1848-1935.
Christian education and Anglo Israel, two addresses. Chicago, Christian Witness Co., 1906. 90 p.

627 SMITH, Joseph Henry, 1855-1946.
Educational limitation in the Holiness Movement. Cleveland, Ohio, Cleveland Bible Institute, 1922. Unpaged.

--EVANGELISTIC WORK

628 CORNELL, Clarence Ellsworth
Hints to fishermen; or, How to win souls. Chicago, Christian Witness Co., 1901. 110 p.

629 EARLE, Absalom Backas, -1892.
Winning souls. Boston, J.H. Earle, 1891. 501 p.

630 GLASCOCK, James Luther, 1852-1942.
Revivals of religion; before they occur, how to promote them, while they are in progress, and after they are over; with an introd. by Rev. H.C. Morrison. Louisville, Pentecostal Publishing Co., 1911. 109 p.

631 GODBEY, William B., 1833-1920.
Victory. Perryville, Ky., 1888; Published by J.H. Padgett, Ennis, Tex. Cover-title, 28 p.

I. 1. Christian Holiness Association

632 HARRIS, John William, 1870-
   God's plan; or, Redemption and salvation, a pocket reference book for Bible students of holiness; the plan of God for man's restoration to the holy state; a worker's manual for holiness workers. Indianapolis, Pub. for the author by Grace Publishing Co., 1904. 110 p.

633 HUMPHREY, Jerry Miles, 1872-
   The worker's secret of unction. Chicago, Christian Witness Co., 1921. 89 p.

634 JOHNSON, Zachary Taylor, 1897-
   We have an altar. Louisville, Ky., Herald Press, n.d. 40 p.

635 KNAPP, Martin Wells, 1853-1901.
   Revival kindlings. Cincinnati, God's Revivalist Office, 1890. 336 p.

636 PAPPAS, Paul John, 1898-
   Revivalism. n.p., n.d. 43 p.

637 PAUL, John Haywood, 1877-1967.
   Evangelism as a modern problem. New ed. Louisville, Ky., Herald Press, 1946. 62 p.

638 PAUL, John Haywood, 1877-1967.
   The next awakening; a group of essays on the principles of an expected world revival; or, Christ in a changing world. Louisville, Ky., Pentecostal Publishing Co., n.d. 32 p.

639 RIDOUT, George Whitefield, 1870-
   Revival blessings; or, Seasons of refreshing from the presence of the Lord. Louisville, Pentecostal Publishing Co., n.d. 128 p.

640 SELLE, Robert L., 1865-1929.
   Winning men to Christ. Louisville, Pentecostal Publishing Co., 1914. 112 p.

641 SHAW, Solomon Benjamin, 1854-
   The great revival in Wales, also an account of the great revival in Ireland in 1859. Chicago, S.B. Shaw, 1905. 191, [225]-285 p.
   "The great revival in Ireland" (p. [225]-285) reprinted from the author's Old Time Religion, retains the paging, chapter heading and running title of that book.

642 SHAW, Solomon Benjamin, 1854-
   ... Old time religion, including an account of the greatest revivals since Pentecostal days, and telling how to bring about an old time revival. Abridged ed. Chicago, S.B. Shaw, 1904. 285 p.

643 TAYLOR, Bushrod Shedden, 1849-1935.
Holy fire!, or, How, when, where and why to promote revivals of holiness. Saint Paul, Minn., Rich & Clymer, printers, 1887. 116 p.

644 WILKINS, Chester, 1918-
A handbook for personal soul-winning. Berne, Ind., Light & Hope Publications, c1950. 301 p.

645 WILKINS, Chester, 1918-
A handbook for personal soul-winning. 5th ed., rev. Kansas City, Mo., Beacon Hill Press, 1972, c1966. 320 p.

--HISTORY

646 AYARS, John E.
The holiness revival of the past century; commemorative of the National Holiness Camp Meeting Association, its work and the Philadelphia Friday meeting, with chronological notes from the writer's journal, supplementary. Philadelphia, J.E.A., 1913. 100 p.

647 CLARK, Elmer Talmage, 1886-1966.
The small sects in America. Rev. ed. New York, Abingdon Press, c1965. 256 p.
"Perfectionist or subjectivist sects": p. 51-84.

648 DIETER, Melvin Easterday, 1924-
"Revivalism and holiness." Unpublished Ph.D. dissertation, Temple University, 1972. 370 ℓ.

649 GADDIS, Merrill Elmer, 1891-
"Christian perfectionism in America." Unpublished Ph.D dissertation, University of Chicago, 1929.
Revised 1939.

650 JONES, Charles Edwin, 1932-
"Perfectionist persuasion: a social profile of the National Holiness Movement within American Methodism, 1867-1936." Unpublished Ph.D. dissertation, University of Wisconsin, 1968. 669 ℓ.

651 LUNSFORD, Robert Lloyd
"A historical background of the Holiness Movement." Unpublished M.A. in Theology thesis, Marion College, 1940.

652 ROSE, Delbert Roy, 1912-
A theology of Christian experience. Wilmore, Ky., Seminary Press, 1958. 234 p.
Mimeographed.
Includes account of the National Holiness Movement.

I. 1. Christian Holiness Association

353 ROSE, Delbert Roy, 1912-
A theology of Christian experience; interpreting the historic Wesleyan message. Minneapolis, Bethany Fellowship, 1965. 314 p.
Includes account of the National Holiness Movement.

354 SMITH, Timothy Lawrence, 1924-
"Popular Protestantism in mid-nineteenth century America." Unpublished Ph.D. dissertation, Harvard University, 1955.

355 SMITH, Timothy Lawrence, 1924-
Revivalism and social reform in mid-nineteenth-century America; chapters I-XI and XIV comprise the Frank S. and Elizabeth D. Brewer Prize Essay for 1955, the American Society of Church History. New York, Abingdon Press, 1957. 253 p.

356 TEED, Florence (Schleicher), 1901-1954.
"Papers, 1924-1954." 4 feet. In University of Michigan, Michigan Historical Collections.
Methodist minister and civic leader of Ann Arbor, Michigan; contain student papers, sermon materials, and sermons, including miscellanea relating to the Detroit Holiness Tabernacle, Chicago Evangelistic Institute, Asbury College, and holiness association activities and leaders, particularly Joseph H. Smith.

357 WILCOX, Leslie D.
Be ye holy; a study of the teaching of scripture relative to entire sanctification, with a sketch of the history and the literature of the Holiness Movement. Cincinnati, Revivalist Press, 1965. 395 p.

358 WILCOX, Leslie D.
Be ye holy; a study of the teaching of Scripture relative to entire sanctification with a sketch of the history and literature of the Holiness Movement. Rev. ed. Cincinnati, Revivalist Press, 1965. 407 p.

--HISTORY OF DOCTRINES

359 ARNETT, William Melvin, 1915-
"Current theological emphases in the American holiness tradition," Mennonite Quarterly Review, XXXV (Apr. 1961), 120-129.

360 CLARK, William A.
"Sanctification in Negro religion," Social Forces, XV (May 1937), 544-551.

661 COWARD, Samuel L. C.
Entire sanctification from 1739 to 1900. Louisville, Ky., Pentecostal Publishing Co., 1904. 371 p.

662 DIETER, Melvin Easterday, 1924-
"Revivalism and holiness." Unpublished Ph.D. dissertation, Temple University, 1972. 370 ℓ.

663 FORD, Jack, 1908-
What the holiness people believe; a mid-century review of holiness teaching. Birkenhead, Cheshire, Eng., Emmanuel Bible College and Missions, 1955. 70 p. (J.D. Drysdale memorial lecture)

664 LORD, J. C.
"Finney's sermons on sanctification, and Mahan on Christian perfection," Princeton Review, 2d ser., XIII (Apr. 1841), 231-250.

665 TRAINA, Robert Angelo, 1921-
"The atonement, history, and kerygma; a study in contemporary Protestant theology." Unpublished Ph.D. dissertation, Drew University, 1966.

666 WILSON, George Washington, 1853-1929.
"An exposition of recent teaching on holiness," Expository Times, V (1893-1894), 108-111.

--HYMNS

667 CARRADINE, Beverly, 1848-1931.
The best of all [ed. by] B. Carradine, C.J. Fowler, W.J. Kirkpatrick [and] H.L. Gilmour. Chicago, Christian Witness Co., 19??. Unpaged.
With music.

668 CARRADINE, Beverly, 1848-1931.
The best of all complete [ed. by] B. Carradine, C.J. Fowler [and] W.J. Kirkpatrick. Chicago, Christian Witness Co., 19??. 288 p.
With music.

669 CARTER, Russell Kelso, 1849-1926.
Songs of perfect love, ed. by Capt. R. Kelso Carter and John R. Sweney. Philadelphia, J.J. Hood, c1886. 128 p.

670 CULLIS, Charles, 1833-1892, comp.
Faith hymns.... New ed. Boston, Willard Tract Repository, 1870. 178 p.

II. 1. Christian Holiness Association

671 CULLIS, Charles, 1833-1892, comp.
Faith hymns.... New ed. Boston, Willard Tract Repository, 1882. 213 p.
Hymns preceding p. 122 without music.

672 CULLIS, Charles, 1833-1892.
Faith hymns.... New ed. Boston, Willard Tract Repository, 1887.

673 CULLIS, Charles, 1833-1892, comp.
Songs of victory. Boston, Willard Tract Repository, 1889. 159 p.

674 DAVIS, Grace (Weiser)
Favorite gospel songs; a hymn and tune book adapted to evangelistic meetings, prayer meetings, Sabbath schools.... Ed. by Grace Weiser Davis [and] Elisha A. Hoffman; Ira Orwig Hoffman, music ed. Jersey City, N.J., J.N. Davis, 1894. 173 p.

675 DAVIS, Grace (Weiser)
Favorite gospel songs; a hymn and tune book adapted to evangelistic meetings, prayer meetings, Sabbath schools, Epworth Leagues.... Ed. by Mrs. Grace Weiser Davis [and] Rev. Elisha A. Hoffman; Ira Orwig Hoffman, music ed. Chicago, Hope Publishing Co., 1901. 192 p.
On cover: New and enl. ed.

676 DAVIS, Grace (Weiser)
Gems of gospel songs. Baltimore, Sapp, 1884. Unpaged.

677 EARLE, Absalom Backas, -1892, comp.
Revival hymns. Boston, J.H. Earle, 1871. 63 p.

678 EARLE, Absalom Backas, -1892, comp.
Revival hymns. Rev. ed. Boston, J.H. Earle, 1874. 96 p.
Principally without music; some of the tunes indicated by title.

679 EARLE, Absalom Backas, -1892, comp.
Sought-out songs for Christian workers. Boston, J.H. Earle, 1899. [157] p.

680 [GILL, Joshua], ed.
Good news in song [for social and revival meetings. Evangelistic. Compiled by W.P. Ray, R.S. Robson and Joshua Gill. Rev. ed.] Boston, McDonald & Gill Co., 1891. 144 p.

681 GILL, Joshua
Good news in song, for social and revival meetings [by]

Joshua Gill [and] Geo. A. McLaughlin. Boston, Chicago, Christian Witness Co., 1891 [1886]. 255 p.
With music.

682 GILL, Joshua
Hymns of grace and glory, ed. by J. Gill, W. J. Kirkpatrick, and H. L. Gilmour. Cleveland, Mattill & Lamb, 1901. 224 p.

683 GILL, Joshua
Songs of redemption; [ed. by] Joshua Gill, Geo. A. McLaughlin, W. J. Kirkpatrick [and] Dr. H. L. Gilmour. Boston, Christian Witness Co., 1899. 256 p.
With music.

684 GILL, Joshua
The voice of triumph [by] Joshua Gill, Geo. A. McLaughlin, Jno. R. Sweney [and] W. J. Kirkpatrick. Chicago, Boston, Christian Witness Co., 1894. 255 p.
With music.

685 GILMOUR, Henry Lake, 1836-1920.
The silver trumpet: a collection of new and selected hymns; for use in public worship, revival services, prayer and social meetings, and Sunday schools, ed. by H. L. Gilmour and R. Kelso Carter. Philadelphia, J. J. Hood, c1889. 144 p.
With music.
Imperfect: p. 145 and ff. lacking.

686 GORHAM, B. Weed, comp.
Choral echoes from the church of God in all ages; a collection of hymns and tunes adapted to all occasions of social worship. Boston, H. V. Degen, 1864. 296 p.
Hymns with music: [43] p. at end.

687 GRAVES, Albert Phelps, 1829-1911, comp.
Jesus in song. n. p., n. d. 32 p.
Without music.

688 GRAVES, Albert Phelps, 1829-1911, comp.
Jesus in song-worship. Rev. ed. New York, Biglow & Main, c1882. Cover-title, 34 p.

689 HARRIS, John M.
Glorious gospel in song, number two, ed. by G. A. McLaughlin, C. J. Fowler, J. M. and M. J. Harris. Chicago, Christian Witness Co., 1912.

690 HARRIS, John M.
Songs of mounting up, no. 2, by J. M. Harris, R. E. McNeill [and] M. G. Standley. Cincinnati, God's Revivalist

II. 1. Christian Holiness Association

Office, c1915. [192] p.

691 HARRIS, Thoro, 1874-1955, ed.
Blessed hope hymnal. Editor: Thoro Harris. Associate editors: Orrin R. Jenks, Ross L. Fitch.... Chicago, Faith Publishing Co., 1910? Cover-title, [126] p.

692 HARRIS, Thoro, 1874-1955, ed.
Blessed hope hymnal. Revised and enlarged. For the Bible school, the mid-week meeting, young people's societies and all services of the sanctuary. Editor: Thoro Harris. Associate editor: C.B. Widmeyer. Chicago, T. Harris, 1911? Cover-title, [160] p.

693 HARRIS, Thoro, 1874-1955, ed.
Echoes of paradise; a choice collection of Christian hymns suitable for Sabbath schools and all other departments of religious work. Boston, C.H. Woodman, c1903. [262] p.

694 HARRIS, Thoro, 1874-1955, ed.
Eternal praise. Editor: Thoro Harris. Special contributors: Will O. Jones, S.L. Flowers. For the Bible school, the prayer circle, young people's societies and revivals.... Chicago, Windsor Music Co., 1913? Cover-title, [94] p.

695 HILLMAN, Joseph, 1833-1890.
The revivalist; a collection of choice revival hymns and tunes, original and selected, by Joseph Hillman, Rev. L. Hartsough, musical ed. Troy, N.Y., J. Hillman, publisher, 1869. 264 p.

696 HOPKINS, Mrs. E. B.
The gospel trumpet for the use of missionary societies and children's bands. Boston, McDonald, Gill & Co., 1890. 73 p.
76 hymns.
With music.

697 HUDSON, Ralph E., 1843-1901.
Salvation echoes, for Sabbath school, Gospel, prayer and praise meetings. Alliance, Ohio, 1882. 96 p.
Contains music.

698 INSKIP, John Swanel, 1816-1884, comp.
Songs of triumph, adapted to prayer meetings, camp meetings, and all other seasons of religious worship, selected and arranged by Rev. J.S. Inskip. Philadelphia, National Publishing Association for the Promotion of Holiness, 1882. 120 p.

699 JOHNSON, Ithiel Town, 1849-1931.
Hymns used by Rev. I.T. Johnson, evangelist. Provi-

dence, J.A. & R.A. Reid, 1880. Cover-title, 48 p.
Without music.

700 KIRKPATRICK, William James, 1838-1921, ed.
Pentecostal edition of Songs of praise and victory, by
Wm. J. Kirkpatrick and Dr. H.L. Gilmour, assisted by Rev.
Chas. A. Tushingham. Philadelphia, Pepper Publishing Co.,
1899. Unpaged.
Cover-title.

701 KIRKPATRICK, William James, 1838-1921.
Songs of praise and power, especially prepared for use
in prayer and evangelistic meetings, church services, Sunday
schools, missionary and all other religious gatherings [by]
Wm. J. Kirkpatrick, H.L. Gilmour, B. Carradine [and] C.J.
Fowler. Chicago, Christian Witness Co., 1909? 288 p.

702 KIRKPATRICK, William James, 1838-1921, ed.
Songs of praise and victory, by Wm. J. Kirkpatrick and
Dr. H.L. Gilmour assisted by Rev. Chas. A. Tushingham.
Philadelphia, Pepper Publishing Co., 1899. 76 p.
Cover-title.

703 KIRKPATRICK, William James, 1838-1921, ed.
Songs of the living way; ed. by Rev. E.L. Hyde, musical editors Wm. J. Kirkpatrick, Dr. H.L. Gilmour. Philadelphia, Pepper Publishing Co., 1900. 40 ℓ.
Cover-title.

704 KNAPP, Martin Wells, 1853-1901, ed.
Bible songs of salvation and victory, for God's people of
every land; suitable for revivals, the church, Sunday-schools
and the home. M.W. Knapp, ed.; R.E. McNeil [sic], musical ed. Cincinnati, M.W. Knapp, 1901. Unpaged.
With music.

705 KNAPP, Phoebe (Palmer), 1839-1908.
Notes of joy, for the Sabbath school, the social meeting
and the hour of prayer, by Mrs. Joseph F. Knapp. New
York, W.C. Palmer, Jr., 1869. 176 p.

706 McDONALD, William, 1820-1901.
Beulah songs; a choice collection of popular hymns and
music, new and old, especially adapted to camp meetings,
prayer and conference meetings, family worship and all
other assemblies where Jesus is praised, by Rev. W.
McDonald and Rev. L. Hartsough. Philadelphia, National
Publishing Association for the Promotion of Holiness, 1879.
96 p.

707 [McDONALD, William], 1820-1901.
Music for camp meetings, being a selection of the choic-

II. 1. Christian Holiness Association

est pieces published in the Advocate of Christian Holiness, and sung at the National and other camp meetings. Boston, J.P. Magee, 1872. Cover-title, 14 p.
With music.

708 McDONALD, William, 1820-1901, ed.
Songs of joy and gladness, ed. by W. McDonald, Joshua Gill, Jno. R. Sweney, and W.J. Kirkpatrick. Boston, McDonald, Gill & Co., 1885. 224 p.
With music.

709 McDONALD, William, 1820-1901.
Songs of joy and gladness, no. 2, [by] W. McDonald, Joshua Gill, Jno. R. Sweney, W.J. Kirkpatrick. Boston, McDonald, Gill & Co., 1890. 240 p.
With music.

710 McDONALD, William, 1820-1901.
The Sunday school vocalist; a collection of choice tunes and hymns for the use of Sunday schools. Boston, Henry V. Degen, 1858. 32 p.

711 McLAUGHLIN, George Asbury, 1851-1933, ed.
Glorious gospel in song, ed. by G.A. McLaughlin and J.M. & M.J. Harris. Chicago, Christian Witness Co., 191?. Cover-title, 160 p.
With music.

712 McLAUGHLIN, George Asbury, 1851-1933, ed.
Glorious gospel in song, number two; a book suitable for churches, sabbath schools, camp meetings, conventions, and all religious meetings. Especially adapted to revival work. Edited by G.A. McLaughlin, C.J. Fowler, J.M. and M.J. Harris. Chicago, Christian Witness Co., c1912. 192 p.
With music.

713 McLAUGHLIN, George Asbury, 1851-1933.
The golden trumpet, ed. by G.A. McLaughlin, J.M. Harris and W.J. Kirkpatrick. Chicago, Christian Witness Co., n.d.

714 McLAUGHLIN, George Asbury, 1851-1933.
Good news in song [ed. by] Joshua Gill [and] Geo. A. McLaughlin. Boston, Chicago, Christian Witness Co., 1891. Cover-title, 255 p.
Enlarged ed.

715 McLAUGHLIN, George Asbury, 1851-1933.
Songs of praise and salvation [by] G.A. McLaughlin, C.J. Fowler, W.J. Kirkpatrick [and] H.L. Gilmour. Chicago, Christian Witness Co., 1903? 126 p.
With music.

716 McLAUGHLIN, George Asbury, 1851-1933.
    Spiritual songs, ed. by G. A. McLaughlin and J. M. &
M. J. Harris. Chicago, Christian Witness Co., 19??. 2 v.
With music.

717 McNEILL, Robert E., ed.
    "Praise of His glory" songs, ed. by R. E. McNeill, J. F.
Knapp [and] M. G. Standley. Cincinnati, God's Bible School
and Revivalist, 1922. Unpaged.
With music.

718 PICKETT, Leander Lycurgus, 1859-1928.
    Cream of song, by Rev. L. L. Pickett, Evangelist O. B.
Culpepper and Wm. Edie Marks. Louisville, Ky., Pickett
Publishing Co., 1906. Unpaged.

719 PICKETT, Leander Lycurgus, 1859-1928.
    Gems; our motto: "Live to do good," by L. L. Pickett,
Geo. E. Kersey and O. B. Culpepper. Louisville, Ky.;
Greenville, Tex., Pickett Publishing Co., 1900. 214 p.
With music.

720 PICKETT, Leander Lycurgus, 1859-1928.
    Gems, no. 2; our motto: "Live to do good," by L. L.
Pickett and O. B. Culpepper. Louisville, Ky.; Greenville,
Tex., Pickett Publishing Co., 1904. 146 p.
With music.

721 PICKETT, Leander Lycurgus, 1859-1928.
    Tears and triumphs, comp. by L. L. Pickett, M. W.
Knapp and John R. Bryant. Cincinnati, Revivalist Publishing
House, 1894. 189 p.

722 PICKETT, Leander Lycurgus, 1859-1928.
    Tears and triumphs, no. 2; for Sunday schools, prayer
and praise meetings, young people's meetings and revivals,
by L. L. Pickett and M. W. Knapp. Cincinnati, Revivalist
Office, 1897. Unpaged.
With music.

723 PICKETT, Leander Lycurgus, 1859-1928.
    Tears and triumphs, no. 3, by Rev. L. L. Pickett, Rev.
E. A. Hoffman and Evangelist O. B. Culpepper. Louisville,
Ky.; Greenville, Tex., Pickett Publishing Co., 1902. Unpaged.
With music.

724 PICKETT, Leander Lycurgus, 1859-1928.
    Tears and triumphs, no. 4, ed. by L. L. Pickett, Edie
Marks [and] B. F. Butts. Louisville, Pentecostal Publishing
Co., 1910.

II. 1. Christian Holiness Association

725 PICKETT, Leander Lycurgus, 1859-1928.
Victorious songs. Louisville, Ky., Pentecostal Publishing Co., 1915. Unpaged.
With music.

726 POWER AND praise; a practical and resourceful collection of gospel songs, hymns and choruses for churches, Sunday schools, revivals and radio programs. Nashville, Tenn., John T. Benson Publishing Co., 1954. Unpaged.

727 ROWLEY, Charles E., comp.
Victory bells ... for revival services, prayer meetings, young people's societies & the Sunday school.... Toledo, Ohio, C. E. Rowley, 1900. Unpaged.

728 THE SONGS of the kingdom. Chicago, Christian Witness Co., c1916. Cover-title, 256 p.
With music.

729 STANDLEY, Meredith Goslin, 1879-
Songs of mounting up, ed. by Meredith G. Standley and Robert E. McNeill. Cincinnati, God's Revivalist Office, 1908? Unpaged.

730 STEVENS, G. S.
The American hymn and tune book; containing about 1000 hymns, adapted to nearly 300 of the most popular and useful tunes, ancient and modern, for use in public worship, prayer, conference and camp meetings, Sunday schools, seminaries, and the family or social circle, by G. S. Stevens, M. D. and Rev. W. McDonald. Boston, Henry V. Degen & Son, 1860. 383 p.
With music.

731 STEVENS, G. S.
The American hymn and tune book; containing nearly 1000 hymns, adapted to 280 popular and useful tunes, ancient and modern, for use in public worship, and the family or social circle, by G. S. and W. McDonald. Rev. ed. Boston, James P. Magee, 1863. 384 p.

732 SWENEY, John Robson, 1837-1899, ed.
Glad hallelujahs, replete with sacred songs [ed. by] Jno. R. Sweney and Wm. J. Kirkpatrick. Philadelphia, Thos. T. Tucker, c1887. 164 p.

733 SWENEY, John Robson, 1837-1899, ed.
The joyful sound; a collection of new hymns and music, with familiar selections. Editors: Jno. R. Sweney and Wm. J. Kirkpatrick.... Philadelphia, John J. Hood, c1889. 192 p.
With music.

734 SWENEY, John Robson, 1837-1899.
Melodious sonnets for sacred service, by John R. Sweney and Wm. J. Kirkpatrick. Philadelphia, John J. Hood, c1885. 128 p.
With music.

735 TAYLOR, Bushrod Shedden, 1849-1935.
"1000 old camp meeting songs," Life Line (Mooers, N.Y.) ser. no. 1 (1914).

736 TILLMAN, Charlie Davis, 1861-1943, ed.
The revival; suitable for all kinds of religious meetings. 15th thousand. Cincinnati, c1891. [144] p.
Hymns, with the music.
"For sale by J.W. Burke & Co., Macon, Ga.; Philips & Crew, Atlanta, Ga., and Charlie D. Tillman, Williston, S.C."

737 TILLMAN, Charlie Davis, 1861-1943, ed.
The revival, no. 3; songs for Sunday schools and special services. Atlanta, C.D. Tillman, 1899? [247] p.
With music.

738 TILLMAN, Charlie Davis, 1861-1943.
The revival, no. 4; suitable for all kinds of religious meetings. Atlanta, Charlie D. Tillman, 190?. Unpaged.
Cover-title.
With music (shaped notes)

739 TILLMAN, Charlie Davis, 1861-1943.
Revival 7; containing songs, both new and old possessing values yet untold. You'll find them on every page, familiar ones improved with age. Atlanta, Charlie Tillman Song Book Co., 192?. Unpaged.
With music (shaped notes)

740 TILLMAN, Charlie Davis, 1861-1943, ed.
Revival special, representing 5 song books. Atlanta, C.D. Tillman, 1905? [144] p.
With music.

741 TILLMAN, Charlie Davis, 1861-1943, comp.
Soul-saving songs. Atlanta, Banner Press, c1933.
Cover-title. [48] p.
Indexes on p. [2-3] of cover.

742 WILSON, George Washington, 1853-1929, comp.
The revival wave; a book of revival hymns and music, comp. by G.W. Wilson and B.H. Kennedy. Philadelphia, John J. Hood, c1887. 160 p.
With music.

II. 1. Christian Holiness Association

-- --HISTORY AND CRITICISM

743 LILLENAS, Haldor, 1885-1959.
Modern gospel song stories; introd. by Wm. M. Runyan. Kansas City, Mo., Lillenas Publishing Co., 1952. 157 p.

--MISSIONS

744 TAYLOR, James Milburn, 1873-
Interdenominational missionary work. Knoxville, Tenn., James M. Taylor, n.d.

745 TAYLOR, James Milburn, 1873-
An open door. Knoxville, Tenn., James M. Taylor, 1912.

746 TAYLOR, William, bp., 1821-1902.
Pauline methods of missionary work. Philadelphia, National Publishing Association for the Promotion of Holiness, 1879. 180 p.

--PASTORAL THEOLOGY

747 GODBEY, William B., 1833-1920.
God's gospel preacher: when, where, and how? Cincinnati, God's Revivalist Office, n.d. 32 p.

748 HOLLAND, William Webster, 1884-
The gospel of don'ts for parson and parish. n.p., 1945. Unpaged.

749 KNAPP, Martin Wells, 1853-1901.
Pentecostal preachers. Salem, Ohio, Convention Bookstore; Bicknell, Ind., Fellowship Promoter Press, 19??. 76 p.
Reprint of 189? ed.

750 McINTYRE, Robert, bp., 1851-1914.
Ordination address before the M.E. conference. University Park, Iowa, Christian Witness Co., n.d. 26 p.

751 REES, Seth Cook, 1854-1933.
The ideal Pentecostal church. Cincinnati, Revivalist Office, 1897. 134 p.

752 SHELHAMER, Elmer Ellsworth, 1860-1947, comp.
Heart searching talks to ministers, by various writers. Louisville, Pentecostal Publishing Co., 1914. 272 p.

753   SHELHAMER, Elmer Ellsworth, 1869-1947, comp.
        Heart talks to ministers and Christian workers. 3d ed.
      Cincinnati, God's Bible School, n.d.   160 p.

754   TAYLOR, William, bp., 1821-1902.
        The model preacher; comprised in a series of letters
      illustrating the best mode of preaching the gospel.   7th ed.
      Cincinnati, The author, 1860.   403 p.

755   WIMBERLY, Charles Franklin, 1866-1946.
        Messages for the times; introd. by Rev. H.C. Morrison,
      D.D. Louisville, Pentecostal Publishing Co., c1926.   205 p.

--PERIODICALS

756   ADVOCATE OF Holiness.   1- , 1886?- . Robinson, Tex.

757   ADVOCATE OF Holiness, and the Speedy Coming of the Lord!
        1, no. 1-8; Apr. 26, 1850-Apr. 16, 1851. Boston,
        Worcester, New Haven.
        Subtitle varies.

758   AFRICAN. ns no. 1-4, June-Sept. 1891. Vineland, N.J.,
        C.E. Welch.
        C.E. Welch, editor.
        Preceded by the African News, pub. in Vineland, N.J.,
      by T.B. Welch & Son from Jan. 1889 to Apr. 1891.
        Beginning with May 1891 the African News was also con-
      tinued by Ross Taylor under title, African News.   An illus-
      trated monthly journal of missionary progress.   In 1894 the
      title was changed to Illustrated Africa, and in July 1896 to
      Illustrated Christian World.

759   AFRICAN NEWS.... Information from and about Africa.
        Missionary news of Africa and other mission fields.
        1-3, no. 4, Jan. 1889-April 1891. Vineland, N.J.,
        T.B. Welch & Son.
        At head of title, v. 1-2: Bishop Taylor's Magazine.
        Editors: William Taylor, T.B. Welch.

760   AFRICAN NEWS. An illustrated monthly journal of mission-
        ary progress. Vineland, N.J., Chicago, etc., 3, no.
        5-6, no. 4, May 1891-Apr. 1894.
        Supersedes African News (Taylor and Welch)
        Superseded by Illustrated Africa, later Illustrated
        Christian World
        Editor: William Taylor

761   AMERICAN HOLINESS Journal.   1- , 1941- . Sandy Lake,
        Pa.; Apollo, Pa.

II. 1. Christian Holiness Association

762 AMERICAN OUTLOOK. 1- , 191?- . Nashville, Tenn.

763 ASBURY COLLEGIAN. 1- , 1915- . Wilmore, Ky.
Organ for students of Asbury College.

764 BANNER OF Hope. 1- , Feb. 22, 1883- . Bacup, Lancs., Eng.; Stockport, Ches., Eng. Feb. 22, 1883-1888 as Joyful News; ns 1-48, 1889-1892 as Joyful News, Banner of Hope.

765 BANNER OF Love. 1- , 1885?- . Washington, D.C.

766 BEULAH CHRISTIAN. 1- , 1907?-190?. Oklahoma City, Okla.

767 BEULAH LAND; a monthly devoted to evangelism and the spread of scriptural holiness. 1- , 1883- . Columbus, Ohio, Holiness Publishing Co.

768 BIBLE EVANGELIST. 1- , 188?- . Kansas City, Mo.

769 CHRISTIAN HARVESTER. 1- , 1873-1913. Canton, Ohio; Cleveland.

770 CHRISTIAN MESSENGER. 1- , 190?- . Marshalltown, Iowa.

771 CHRISTIAN STANDARD; a Holiness Journal for the Home.... 1-51, 1867-1914? Philadelphia, Pa.; Gainesville, Fla.; Upland, Ind.
1867-June 13, 1874 as Methodist Home Journal
Subtitle varies

772 CHRISTIAN STANDARD; an organ of Holiness work. 1-24, 1885-1886. London.

773 CHRISTIAN WITNESS and Advocate of Bible Holiness. 1-13, 1870-1881; ns 1-158, 1882-1959. Boston, Chicago, University Park, Iowa.
1870-1881 as Advocate of Christian Holiness;
1882 as Advocate of Bible Holiness

774 CHURCH VOICE and Banner of Holiness. 1- , Aug. 1, 1872-1890. Abingdon, Ill.; Bloomington, Ill.; Jacksonville, Ill.
Aug. 1, 1872-1883 as Banner of Holiness

775 CONSECRATED LIFE and Guide to Holiness. 1-47, July 1839-June 1865; ns 1-75, July 1865-Dec. 1901. Boston, New York, Philadelphia.
1-8, 1839-1842 as Guide to Christian Perfection;
9-47, ns 1-75, 1843-Sept. 1901 as Guide to Holiness

ns 1-33, July 1865-1880 also as os 47-76; occasional later volumes bear os numbering

776 CONTRIBUTOR. 1-21, no. 2, 1872-Feb. 1892. Boston.

777 CROWN OF Glory. 1- , 188?- . Indianapolis.

778 DIVINE LIFE. 1-27, 1878-1896. New York.

779 ERA OF Holiness. 1- , 191?-192?. Nashville, Tenn.

780 EVANGELICAL TIDINGS. 1- , 191?- . Owosso, Mich.

781 EXPOSITOR OF the Christ Life. 1- , 1881-19??. Toronto.

782 FIRE AND Hammer; advocate of Bible salvation and temperance by prohibition. 1-2, no. 10, Nov. 1883-Aug. 1885. North Topeka, Kan.

783 FLAME; a bi-monthly for the spread of full salvation. 1- , 1935- . Hillside, Southport, Lancs., Eng.; Grimsby, Lancs., Eng.

784 FOUNTAIN. 1- , 1948- . Freeport, Pa., Transylvania Bible School.
Supersedes Living Waters from David's Fountain

785 FULL GOSPEL and Rescue Journal. 1-4, no. 11, June 1905-1909. Chicago.

786 FULL SALVATION Quarterly. 1-6, 1895-1900. Cincinnati.

787 GOD'S REVIVALIST and Bible Advocate. 1- , 1888- . Albion, Mich.; Cincinnati.
1888-1900 as Revivalist

788 GOOD TIDINGS. no. 1-229, Dec. 2, 1880-Jan. 20, 1886. North Topeka, Kan.

789 GUIDE TO Holiness. 1- , 194?- . Los Angeles.

790 GUIDE TO Holiness (Wegweiser zur Heiligung). 1- , 1885-1910. Cincinnati.
Commonly known as German Guide to Holiness

791 GUIDE TO Perfect Love: an Evangelical Holiness Journal. 1- , 1921-1928? Philadelphia, Edgar J. Wrigley.

792 HAPPY PILGRIM. 1- , 188?- . Toledo, Ill.

793 HEART AND Life. 1-40, 1911-1954. Chicago, Ill., University Park, Iowa, Chicago Evangelistic Institute.

II. 1. Christian Holiness Association

794 HERALD, a Journal of Full Salvation and the Way of Faith. 1- , 1889- . Frankfort, Ky., Lexington, Ky., Louisville, Ky., Wilmore, Ky.
1889-1890 as Old Methodist; 1890-1891? as Kentucky Methodist; 1891?-1895 as Methodist; 1895-1897 as Methodist and the Way of Life; 1897-1932 as Pentecostal Herald; 1932-1942 as Pentecostal Herald and the Way of Faith

795 HERALD OF Gospel Freedom. 1-3, 1878-1880. Rome City, Ind., Indianapolis.
Merged with Pilgrim to form Gospel Trumpet

796 HIGHWAY. 1- , 1875-189?. Nevada, Iowa.
Also as Highway and Banner

797 HOLINESS CONSERVATOR. 1- , Oct. 1883-July 1887. Ada, Ohio.

798 HOLINESS EVANGEL. 1- , 1941-19??. Portland, Ore.

799 HOLINESS EVANGEL. 1- , 1948- . Birmingham, Eng., Holiness Missionary Fellowship.

800 HOLINESS EVANGELIST. 1- , 188?- . Oakland, Calif.

801 HOLINESS HERALD. 1- , 1932- . Seven Kings, Essex, Eng.

802 HOLINESS MISSIONARY Colporteur. 1- , 19??- . , Pa.

803 HOLINESS SENTINEL. 1- , 19??- . Freeport, L.I., N.Y., Long Island Holiness Camp Meeting.

804 HOLLOW ROCK Glad Tidings. 1- , 19??- . Kittanning, Pa., Hollow Rock Camp Meeting, Toronto, Ohio.

805 HOME HERALD, the New Voice of the Ram's Horn. 1-21, 1890-1910. Chicago.
1-17, 1890-1906 as Ram's Horn

806 ILLUSTRATED CHRISTIAN World. June 1894-May 1898. Vineland, N.J.; New York.
Supersedes African News
1894-June 1896 as Illustrated Africa
Merged into Christian Herald
Editors: William Taylor, Ross Taylor

807 INTERIOR ADVANCE. 1- , 189?- . Cumberland, Md.

808 INTERNATIONAL PURITY Journal. 1-30, 1887-1916. Morton Park, Ill.

1887-1900 and Apr.-Oct. 1910 as Christian Life (subtitle varies); 1901-Mar. 1910 as Purity Journal and the Christian Life

809 KINGDOM. 1-11, 1896-1906. Oakland, Calif.; San Francisco, Calif.
1-5, no. 2, 1896-1900 as Golden Gate Pentecost

810 KINGDOM TIDINGS. 1- , 1891?-19??. Germantown, Pa.

811 KING'S HIGHWAY; a journal of scriptural holiness. 1-29, no. 5, 1872-1901. London.

812 LAMP OF Life. 1- , 18??-19??. Toronto.
18??-Oct. 1901 as Interdenominational Holiness Berean

813 LAW AND Gospel. 1-5, no. 1, 1885-1890. Paris, Ill., Hutchinson, Kan., Springfield, Colo.

814 LIFE-BOAT; an illustrated monthly journal devoted to charitable, philanthropic, health and soul-winning work. 1- , 1898- . Hinsdale, Ill.

815 LIGHTHOUSE MESSENGER. 1- , 19??-1918. St. Louis, Mo., Lighthouse Mission.

816 LIVING WATERS from David's Fountain. 1-14, no. 1, 1936-1948. Freeport, Pa., Transylvania Bible School.
Superseded by Fountain

817 LIVING WORDS. 1- , 190?- . Wilkinsburg, Pa.

818 MICHIGAN HOLINESS Record. 1-7, Apr. 1883-May/June 1890, Michigan Holiness Association, Grand Rapids, Mich., Dutton, Mich., Saugatuck, Mich.
Apr.-May/June 1890 as Primitive Holiness Record

819 MIDNIGHT CRY. 1- , 1940- . Summerfield, Fla.; Tequesta, Fla.

820 NORTHERN INDEPENDENT. 1-7, 1856-1863. Auburn, N.Y.

821 OLD PATHS. 1- , 188?- . Savannah, Mo.

822 PACIFIC HERALD of Holiness. 1- , 188?- . San Francisco, Pacific Coast Holiness Association.

823 PAULINE ADVOCATE. 1- , 189?- . Upland, Ind.

824 PAULINE MISSION Chronicle. 1-8, 1893-1909. New York.

825 PENTECOST CENTURY. 1- , 1901-1906. Louisville.

II. 1. Christian Holiness Association

826 PENTECOSTAL CHRISTIAN. 1-4, Dec. 23, 1911-Dec. 1915. Providence, R.I.
Supersedes Beulah Christian

827 PENTECOSTAL ERA and National Advocate of Perfect Love. 1- , 1903-191?. Washington, D.C.

828 PENTECOSTAL EVANGELIST. 1- , -1904. Chicago.
Merged with Nazarene Messenger

829 PENUEL; an advocate of scriptural holiness. 1-9, 1876-1884. London.

830 PILGRIM. 1- , -1880. Indianapolis.
Merged with Herald of Gospel Freedom to form Gospel Trumpet

831 PREACHER; a herald of Christian liberty. 1- , 19??-19??. Pasadena, Calif.

832 PURE RELIGION. 1- , 188?- . Shellsburg, Iowa.

833 ROYAL PRIEST. 1- , 1887-189?. Kirksville, Mo.

834 SERMON QUARTERLY. 1- , Fall 1958- . Dallas, Evangel Press.

835 SHINING WAY; a Journal of Religious Reform. 1- , 188?- . David City, Neb.

836 SOUL WINNER. 1-14, no. 12, -Dec. 1915. Wilmore, Ky., Society of Soul Winners.

837 STANDARD OF Holiness. 1- , 1948-1957. Minneapolis, National Holiness Association.

838 TIMES OF Refreshing; or, Records of Christian Life and Christian Testimony. 1- , 1869-189?. Boston.

839 TRIUMPHS OF Faith. 1- , 1881-1913? Buffalo, N.Y., Oakland, Calif.

840 TRUE HOLINESS. 1- , 1898?-190?. McKinney, Tex.

841 VOICE OF the Family Altar. 1- , 194?- . Greensburg, Pa.

842 WAY OF Faith. 1-42, 1890-1931. Columbia, S.C., Oliver Gospel Mission.
Merged with Pentecostal Herald

843 WAY OF Holiness. 1- , 188?- . Chattanooga, Tenn.

844 WAY OF Holiness. 1-30, no. 5, Apr. 1909-Aug. 1928.
   Manchester, Eng., Star Hall.

845 WAY OF Life. 1- , 1882-1895. Atlanta, Ga.
   1882-188? as Tongue of Fire
   Merged with The Methodist to form The Methodist and
   The Way of Life

846 WESLEYAN THEOLOGICAL Journal. 1- , Spring 1966- .
   University Park, Iowa; Marion, Ind.

847 WESTERN RECORD. 1-4, no. 32, 1890-Sept. 19, 1893.
   Clay Center, Kan.; Kackley, Kan.
   1890-Aug. 15, 1892 as Pentecost Trumpet

848 WHISPERS OF Peace. 1- , 188?- . Brooklyn, N.Y.

849 WORDS OF Faith. 1-53, no. 6, 1874-Dec. 1927. Philadelphia.

850 ZION'S WATCHMAN. 1- , 1878-192?. Butler, Ind.

--POLEMICAL WORKS

851 SMITH, Hannah (Whitall), 1832-1911.
   Group movements of the past and experiments in guidance, by Ray Strachey, with an introd. by the Rt. Rev. H. Hensley Henson ... consisting of extracts from the papers of Hannah Whitall Smith, and a description of the times in which she lived and the curious religious sects which she investigated during the middle years of the nineteenth century. London, Faber & Faber, 1934. viii, 270 p.
   "First published in 1928 under the title: Religious fanaticism."

852 SMITH, Hannah (Whitall), 1832-1911.
   Religious fanaticism; extracts from the papers of Hannah Whitall Smith, ed. with an introd. by Ray Strachey consisting of an account of the author of these papers, and of the times in which she lived; together with a description of the curious religious sects and communities of America during the early and middle years of the nineteenth century. London, Faber & Gwyer, 1928. 276 p.
   Published also under title: Group movements of the past and experiments in guidance, 1934.

---CATHOLICISM

853 MORRISON, Henry Clay, 1857-1942.
Romanism and ruin. Louisville, Ky., Pentecostal Publishing Co., 1914. 213 p.

854 PICKETT, Leander Lycurgus, 1859-1928.
The danger signal; or, A shot at the foe. Louisville, Pickett Publishing Co., 1912, c1890. 313 p.
"Fourth edition."

855 PICKETT, Leander Lycurgus, 1859-1928.
Uncle Sam or the pope, which? Louisville, Ky., Pentecostal Publishing Co., 1916. 308 p.

---CHRISTIAN SCIENCE

856 BEERS, Forest William
Light and shadow; or, Christianity and the current religious "sciences." Rev. ed. Cincinnati, M.W. Knapp, 1899. 137 p. (Full salvation quarterly, vol. 5, no. 2)

857 BROOKS, Delos Ferdinand, 1845-1935.
Does St. John or Christian Science tell the truth? Chicago, Christian Witness Co., 1902. 83 p.

858 GODBEY, William B., 1833-1920.
Christian Science. Cincinnati, God's Revivalist Office, c1911. 29 p.

859 RIDOUT, George Whitefield, 1870-1954.
The deadly fallacy of Christian Science: its delusions considered, its claims examined, its false teachings investigated, its denials exposed. Louisville, Ky., Pentecostal Publishing Co., n.d. 22 p.

---JEHOVAH'S WITNESSES

860 GODBEY, William B., 1833-1920.
Russellism. Zarephath, N.J., Pillar of Fire, c1918. 38 p.

861 HUNT, Marion Palmer, 1860-
The exposure of millennial dawnism the preacher's imperative duty. Louisville, Pentecostal Publishing Co., 1934? 62 p.

862 RIDOUT, George Whitefield, 1870-1954.
The deadly fallacy of Russellism or Millennial Dawnism. Louisville, Pentecostal Publishing Co., n.d. 20 p.

-- --KESWICK MOVEMENT

863 HILLS, Aaron Merritt, 1848-1935.
Scriptural holiness and Keswick teaching compared.
Manchester, Eng., Star Hall, 1910?. 182 p.

-- --METHODISM

864 ATWOOD, Anthony, 1801-1888.
Causes of the marvelous success of Methodism in this country within the past century. Philadelphia, National Publishing Association for the Promotion of Holiness [pref. 1884]. 193 p.

865 RIDOUT, George Whitefield, 1870-1954.
The present crisis in Methodism and how to meet it; an address delivered at the Asbury College convention and commencement, Wilmore, Ky., May 26, 1921. Louisville, Pentecostal Publishing Co., 1921. 39 p.
"Addenda: Theological Schools": p. 27-39.

-- --MORMONISM

866 RIDOUT, George Whitefield, 1870-1954.
The deadly fallacy of Mormonism: its claims examined, its Bible uncovered, its duplicity exposed. Louisville, Ky., Pentecostal Publishing Co., n.d. 16 p.

-- --PENTECOSTAL MOVEMENT

867 HILLS, Aaron Merritt, 1848-1935.
The Tongues Movement. Manchester, Eng., Star Hall, 1910? 39 p.

-- --PLYMOUTH BRETHREN

868 STEELE, Daniel, 1824-1914.
A substitute for holiness; or, Anti-nomianism revived; or, The theology of the so-called Plymouth Brethren examined and refuted. 2d ed., with index and appendix by ... C. Munger. Boston, Chicago, Christian Witness Co., 1899. 370 p.

-- --PROTESTANTISM

869 WINCHESTER, Charles Wesley, 1843-
What Protestants believe. Chicago, Christian Witness Co., 1915. 240 p.

-- --SPIRITUALISM

870 MAHAN, Asa, 1800-1889.
Modern mysteries explained and exposed. Boston, J.P.

II. 1. Christian Holiness Association

Jewett and Co., 1855. xv, 466 p.

871 MAHAN, Asa, 1800-1889.
The phenomena of spiritualism scientifically explained and exposed. London, Hodder and Stoughton, 1875. 421 p.

872 RIDOUT, George Whitefield, 1870-1954.
The deadly fallacy of spiritualism: its denials of the truth, its perils exposed, its deceptions denounced. Louisville, Ky., Pentecostal Publishing Co., n.d. 13 p.

--POLITICAL AND SOCIAL CRITICISM

873 BOWES, Alpin Marshall, 1881-1930.
The time to strike; or, Our nation's curse.... Foreword by Rev. Charles B. Allen. Louisville, Pentecostal Publishing Co., 1908. 151 p.

874 FLOWERS, Sumpter Lee, 1881-1945.
The Black family: their character and influence. Kearney, Neb., Flowers Publishing Co., 1911. 59 p.
Story of Mr. Voter, his wife, Mrs. Law, and his three bad daughters, Miss Liquor Traffic, Miss Dance and Miss Prostitution.

875 HUNT, Marion Palmer, 1860-
Shall prohibition go? Louisville, Pentecostal Publishing Co., n.d. 21 p.

876 LEHMAN, Frederick Martin, 1868-
The white slave hell; or, With Christ at midnight in the slums of Chicago ... written and ed. by Rev. F.M. Lehman; slum data furnished by Rev. N.K. Clarkson.... Chicago, Boston, Christian Witness Co., 1910. 418 p.

877 MORRISON, Henry Clay, 1857-1942.
The battle of the ballots. Louisville, Pentecostal Publishing Co., n.d. 40 p.

878 PAUL, John Haywood, 1877-1967.
Main Street in Jericho; viewing social justice at its fountainhead. Butler, Ind., Higley Press, 1937.

879 PAUL, John Haywood, 1877-1967.
Main Street in Jericho; viewing social justice at its fountain head, with a friendly examination of "Christ's alternative to Communism," by E. Stanley Jones. Chicago, Christian Witness Co., 1937. 98 p.

880 PAUL, John Haywood, 1877-1967.
The Savior and the flag; the substance of two lectures

which the author has delivered on several occasions. Upland, Ind., Taylor University Press, 1928. 32 p.

881 PAUL, John Haywood, 1877-1967.
Silver keys to religious, social, civic and secondary perplexities. Louisville, Ky., Pentecostal Publishing Co., 1908. 284 p.

882 PECK, Jesse Truesdell, bp., 1811-1883.
The history of the great republic, considered from a Christian standpoint. New York, W.C. Palmer, Jr., 1871. viii, 710 p.

883 PICKETT, Leander Lycurgus, 1859-1928.
Al Smith and the presidency. 4th ed. Louisville, Pentecostal Publishing Co., n.d. 46 p.

884 PICKETT, Leander Lycurgus, 1859-1928.
The booze devil and how to kill him. Louisville, Pentecostal Publishing Co., 1914. 84 p.

885 PICKETT, Leander Lycurgus, 1859-1928.
The danger signal; or, A shot at the foe. Louisville, Pickett Publishing Co., 1912, c1890. 313 p.
"Fourth edition."

886 PICKETT, Leander Lycurgus, 1859-1928.
Songs and sayings for you; consisting of songs, facts and thrilling incidents, for use in temperance and prohibition campaigns in towns, counties, states and the national warfare against rum's murder mills, by Rev. L.L. Pickett. Louisville, Ky., Pentecostal Publishing Co.; Wilmore, Ky., L.L. Pickett, 1911. 56 p.
With music.

887 PICKETT, Leander Lycurgus, 1859-1928.
Uncle Sam or the Pope, which? Louisville, Pentecostal Publishing Co., 1916. 308 p.

888 REES, Paul Stromberg, 1900-
America: awake or perish. Grand Rapids, Mich., Zondervan, 1940.

889 REES, Seth Cook, 1854-1933.
Miracles in the slums; or, Thrilling stories of those rescued from the cesspools of iniquity, and touching incidents in the lives of the unfortunate. Chicago, Seth C. Rees, 1905. 301 p.

II. 1. Christian Holiness Association 85

--RELIGIOUS EDUCATION

890   HIGLEY'S SUNDAY School lesson commentary for 19??.
International improved uniform lessons.... Butler, Ind.,
The Higley Press, c19??. Annual.
"Founder: L. H. Higley."

891   TROKE, James Allan
What a Sunday school teacher should know about Palestine. Butler, Ind., Higley Press, 1942. 48 p.

--SERMONS

892   AYCOCK, Jarrette E., -1966.
The nightingale of the Psalms; an exposition of the 23rd Psalm, by Evangelist Jarrette E. Aycock. 2d ed. Louisville, Pentecostal Publishing Co., 1923. 32 p.

893   BOOTH, Catherine (Mumford), 1829-1890.
Aggressive Christianity; practical sermons. Introduction by Daniel Steele. Philadelphia, National Publishing Association for the Promotion of Holiness, 1883. 174 p.

894   BOOTH, Catherine (Mumford), 1829-1890.
Aggressive Christianity; practical sermons. With an introd. by Daniel Steele. Boston, McDonald & Gill, 1883. 174 p.

895   BOOTH, Catherine (Mumford), 1829-1890.
Aggressive Christianity; practical sermons. With an introd. by Daniel Steele. Boston, Christian Witness, c1883. 174 p.

896   BRASHER, John Lakin, 1868-1971.
Reckoning with the eternals, and other themes; introd. by President Joseph Owen. University Park, Iowa, John Fletcher College Press, 1927. 144 p.

897   CARRADINE, Beverly, 1848-1931.
Revival sermons. Chicago, Christian Witness Co., 1897. 340 p.

898   CARRADINE, Beverly, 1848-1931.
Revival sermons. St. Louis, W.B. Palmore, 1898. 340 p.

899   CHAPMAN, John A. M., 1829-1905.
The great command; a sermon. New York, W.C. Palmer, 1881. 18 p.

900 CHURCH, John Robert, 1899-
    The all-sufficiency of Christ. Louisville, Pentecostal Publishing Co., n.d. 35 p.

901 CHURCH, John Robert, 1899-
    Religion in the home. Louisville, Pentecostal Publishing Co., n.d. 62 p.

902 CHURCH, John Robert, 1899-
    Religion in the home. Wilmore, Ky., Seminary Press, 19??. 63 p.

903 CHURCH, John Robert, 1899-
    Why do the righteous suffer?; and, The all-sufficiency of Christ; radio talks delivered at Asbury College extension studio of WHAS, Wilmore, Kentucky. Louisville, Herald Press, 1936. 64 p.

904 CORNELL, Clarence Ellsworth
    Heaven or hell, which?; a message to the unsaved. Chicago, Christian Witness Co., n.d. 29 p.

905 CULLIS, Charles, 1833-1892.
    Tuesday afternoon talks. Boston, Willard Tract Repository, 1892. 197 p.

906 DAVIES, Edward, 1830-
    Select sermons on Christian experience. Reading, Mass. The author, 1877. 70 p.

907 EARLE, Absalom Backas, -1892.
    Growing, because abiding.... Boston, 1879. 13 p.

908 EARLE, Absalom Backas, -1892.
    The rest of faith; or, Soul rest. Chicago, Christian Witness Co., n.d. 27 p.

909 EARLE, Absalom Backas, -1892.
    Two sermons. Boston, J.H. Earle, 1884. 76 p.

910 ECKEL, Howard
    Preach the word; ten sermons. Cincinnati, God's Revivalist Office, 1904. 103 p.

911 [FERGERSON, E. A.]
    Gold from God's mint. Cincinnati, God's Revivalist Office, c1914. vii, 7-173 p.

912 [FERGERSON, E. A.]
    Streams from Lebanon. Chicago and Boston, Christian Witness Co., 1911. 272 p.
    Foreword signed: E.A. Fergerson.

II. 1. Christian Holiness Association

913 FLEMING, Bona
Bona Fleming: his testimony and red hot sermon preached at God's Bible School. n.p., 196?. 2 sides 33 rpm (19572). Introduction by Marshall Smart.

914 FLEMING, John   -1935.
Truth on fire, by John and Bona Fleming. Cincinnati, God's Bible School and Missionary Training Home, 1934. 256 p.

915 FOWLER, Charles J., circa 1848-1919.
Sermon: Judas Iscariot, his relation to Christ and Christian experience. Cincinnati, M.W. Knapp, 1896. 18 p.

916 FRAZEE, E. W.
The divine death on Calvary. Chicago, Christian Witness Co., n.d. 21 p.

917 GLASCOCK, James Luther, 1852-1942.
Some grapes from Eschol, a sermon on perfect love-- what it is, and how to obtain it ... also his experience, with introductions by Rev. E.I.D. Pepper and Rev. John Thompson. Cincinnati, M.W. Knapp, 1896. 53 p.

918 GODBEY, William B., 1833-1920.
Lost world. Greensboro, N.C., Apostolic Messenger Publishing Co., n.d. 31 p.

919 GODBEY, William B., 1833-1920.
The seven churches. Cincinnati, God's Revivalist, n.d. 40 p.

920 HAMES, J. M.
A feast of good things. Louisville, Pentecostal Publishing Co., 1929. 127 p.

921 HAMES, J. M.
The glory departed. Louisville, Pentecostal Publishing Co., n.d. 47 p.

922 HAMES, J. M.
The heavenly race. Louisville, Pentecostal Publishing Co., n.d. 43 p.

923 HILLS, Aaron Merritt, 1848-1935.
The whosoever Gospel. Cincinnati, M.W. Knapp, 1899. 91 p.

924 HUFF, William H.
The glory of his mission; preached in the General Convention for the Promotion of Holiness, Cadle Tabernacle, Indianapolis, Indiana, Sunday afternoon, September 16, 1923.

Louisville, Ky., Pentecostal Publishing Co., 1923. 32 p.

925 HUFF, William H.
Our three-fold nature. Louisville, Pentecostal Publishing Co., 1917. 22 p.

926 HUMPHREY, Jerry Miles, 1872-
50 ready-cut sermons. Chicago, Christian Witness Co., 1925. 243 p.

927 HUMPHREY, Jerry Miles, 1872-
Railroad sermons from railroad stories. Chicago, Messenger Publishing Co., 1917. 84 p.

928 HUMPHREY, Jerry Miles, 1872-
Sermons that never die. Chicago, Christian Witness Co., 1913. 174 p.

929 HUMPHREY, Jerry Miles, 1872-
X-ray sermons. Omaha, Neb., Anywhere Evangelistic Workers' Publishing House, 1924. 247 p.

930 HUNT, Marion Palmer, 1860-
A question of the ages: Is a lie ever justifiable? Louisville, Pentecostal Publishing Co., n.d. 19 p.

931 HUNT, Marion Palmer, 1860-
Old time revival sermons. Louisville, Herald Press, 194?. 128 p.

932 JONES, Samuel Porter, 1847-1906.
Lightning flashes and thunderbolts; a series of gospel sermons and talks by Rev. Sam P. Jones, the great Georgia evangelist, in Savannah, Ga., in 1901. Scenes and incidents of the meeting [by] George Stuart and others. Comp. by J.S. Shingler. Louisville, Pentecostal Publishing Co., 1912. 288 p.

933 JONES, Samuel Porter, 1847-1906.
Thunderbolts; comprising most earnest reasonings, delightful narratives, poetic and pathetic incidents, caustic and unmerciful flagellation of sin, together with irresistible appeals to the higher sensibilities of man to quit his meanness and do right. Introduction by Joseph S. Key. Nashville, Printed for Jones and Haynes, 1895. 584 p.
Edited by B. F. Haynes.

934 KELLEY, Edward R.
Messages from Isaiah. Chicago, Christian Witness Co., 1922. 128 p.

II. 1. Christian Holiness Association

935 MILLS, Abbie C., 1829-1917.
Quiet hallelujahs. Boston, McDonald & Gill, 1886. 255 p.

936 MILLS, F. J.
Broken fetters and other sermons. Louisville, Pentecostal Publishing Co., n. d. 152 p.

937 MORRISON, Henry Clay, bp., 1842-1921.
The simple gospel. Louisville, Pentecostal Publishing Co., 1919. 436 p.

938 MORRISON, Henry Clay, 1857-1942.
Will a man rob God? Louisville, Pentecostal Publishing Co., 19??. 16 p.

939 PAUL, John Haywood, 1877-1967.
Sermon on sin. Louisville, Ky., Pentecostal Publishing Co., 19??.

940 PEPPER, Eleuthera I. D., -1908.
Spices from the Lord's garden: Bible readings delivered by Rev. E. I. D. Pepper in the Philadelphia Friday Meeting, collected and arranged by Evangelist E. L. Hyde. West Conshohocken?, Pa., 1895. 82 p.

941 PETERS, Madison Clinton, 1859-1918.
Sanctified spice; or, Pungent seasonings from the pulpit. New York, Wilbur B. Ketcham, 1893. 216 p.

942 REES, Byron Johnson, 1877-1920.
Hulda A. Rees, the Pentecostal prophetess (Title suggested by Rev. E. I. D. Pepper); or, A sketch of her life and triumph, together with seventeen of her sermons. Philadelphia, Christian Standard Co., 1898. 152 p.

943 REES, Paul Stromberg, 1900-
If God be for us! Grand Rapids, Mich., Eerdmans, 1940.

944 RIDOUT, George Whitefield, 1870-
Amazing grace; messages on the grace of God as manifested in the soul's salvation and enrichment. New York, Revell, 1923. 146 p.

945 ROBINSON, Reuben, 1860-1942.
Bees in clover. Noblesville, Ind., J. Edwin Newby, 1972. 188 p.
Reprint of 1921 ed.

946 SHELHAMER, Elmer Ellsworth, 1869-1947.
Heart searching sermons and sayings. Atlanta, Repairer Publishing Co., 1917. 320 p.

947 SHELHAMER, Elmer Ellsworth, 1869-1947.
Plain preaching for practical people. Cincinnati, God's Bible School and Revivalist, 1929. 287 p.

948 SHELHAMER, Elmer Ellsworth, 1869-1947.
Searching sermons for saints & sinners. Cincinnati, Author or God's Bible School, n.d. 64 p.
"Two of these sermons have been taken from the large book, 'Pointed preaching for practical people'."

949 SMITH, William Martin, 1872-
The two-fold purpose of the baptism with the Holy Ghost. Westfield, Ind., Union Bible Seminary, 1950. 28 p.
Reprinted from The Gospel Minister.
"A sermon preached ... at a meeting of the Hamilton County, Indiana, Holiness Association.

950 STALKER, Charles Henry, 1876-
Holy Ghost messages. Leicester, Eng., J.W. Hemmings and Capey, n.d.

951 STANDLEY, Meredith Goslin, 1879-
The light that never fails. Cincinnati, God's Bible School and Missionary Training Home, 1934. 344 p.

952 STAUFFER, Joshua, 1891-1971.
Living under the weight of the cross. Owosso, Mich., Joshua Stauffer, 196?. 31 p.
"Sermon ... preached at God's Bible School Camp Meeting, Cincinnati, Ohio, June 12, 1960 ... revised for publication."

953 UPDEGRAFF, David Brainerd, 1830-1894.
Old corn; or, Sermons and addresses on the spiritual life. Boston, McDonald, Gill & Co., 1892. 383 p.

954 VENNARD, Iva (Durham), 1871-1945.
Upper room messages. Chicago, Chicago Evangelistic Institute Press, 1916. 128 p.

955 WALKER, W. B.
The cry in the night. Louisville, Pentecostal Publishing Co., n.d. 59 p.

956 WALKER, W. B.
The glory of the master, and other sermons. Louisville, Pentecostal Publishing Co., n.d. 47 p.

957 WALKER, W. B.
The gospel in the wind. Louisville, Herald Press, n.d. 32 p.

I. 1. Christian Holiness Association

958 WIMBERLY, Charles Franklin, 1866-1946.
The day of wrath and other sermons. Louisville, Pentecostal Publishing Co., c1940. 142 p.

-- --COLLECTIONS

959 AKERS, Lewis Robeson, 1881- , ed.
Tarry ye!; studies of Pentecost. Louisville, Pentecostal Publishing Co., c1930. 155 p.
With brief notices of the authors.

960 ENGSTROM, Theodore Wilhelm, 1916- , ed.
Victorious and fruitful living, and other sermons; a compilation of sermons written by leading teachers, preachers and evangelists in the Holiness Movement, C.W. Butler and others. Grand Rapids, Mich., Zondervan Publishing House, 1942. 116 p.

961 McGRAW, James, 1913- , comp.
The holiness pulpit. Kansas City, Mo., Beacon Hill Press, 1957. 128 p.

962 THE PENTECOSTAL pulpit; a series of select sermons on various topics by American preachers of the Holiness Movement. Louisville, Ky., Pentecostal Publishing Co., n.d. 176 p.

963 SIX PIONEER holiness sermons: Coals of fire, [by] Geo. D. Watson; Fire from heaven, [by] Seth C. Rees; The old man [by] B. Carradine; Out of Egypt [by] W.B. Godbey; Sanctification of the disciples [by] Bud Robinson; The way of holiness [by] John Thomas. Dallas, Evangel Press, n.d. 96 p.

964 TWENTIETH CENTURY holiness sermons, by twelve active ministers. Louisville, Pentecostal Publishing Co., n.d. 115 p.

-- --OUTLINES

965 CHANDLER, Ward B.
Chandler's choice series sermon outlines. Grand Rapids, Mich., Baker Book House, 1958. 161 p.

966 EIGHTY PIONEER holiness sermon outlines: the holiness fathers. Dallas, Evangel Press, n.d.

967 STAUFFER, Joshua, 1891-1971.
"Give ye them to eat"; or, Sermon outlines. Noblesville, Ind., Newby Book Room, 1972. 192 p.
Imprint on label.
Reprint of 1951 ed.

--WORK WITH YOUTH

968 DAVIS, Grace (Weiser)
Childhood conversions. Boston, Christian Witness Co., 1897. xx, 110 p.

969 HILLS, Aaron Merritt, 1848-1935.
Food for lambs; or, Leading children to Christ, a series of lessons illustrated by stories and incidents, for the use of parents and teachers in bringing children to Jesus, and preparing them for church membership. Cincinnati, M. W. Knapp, 1899. 202 p.

970 HUFFMAN, Jasper Abraham, 1880-
Young people and the Christ life. Chicago, Christian Witness Co., 1925. 123 p.

971 HUFFMAN, Jasper Abraham, 1880-
Youth and the Christ way. Cincinnati, God's Bible School and Missionary Training Home, 1934. 156 p.

972 PICKETT, Leander Lycurgus, 1859-1928.
Careful cullings for children. Louisville, Ky., Greenville, Tex., Pickett Publishing Co., 1903. 237 p.

973 SHELHAMER, Elmer Ellsworth, 1869-1947.
Heart talks to boys. 4th ed. Bridgetown, Barbados, B.W.I., The Student of Prophecy, n.d. 125 p.

974 SHELHAMER, Julia (Arnold)
Heart talks to girls. 4th ed. Bridgetown, Barbados, B.W.I., The Student of Prophecy, n.d. 126 p.

975 STANDLEY, Meredith Goslin, 1879-
Radio talks for the children. Cincinnati, God's Bible School and Missionary Training Home, 1934. 288 p.

--YEARBOOKS

976 CHRISTIAN HOLINESS almanac and yearbook, ed. by George Hughes. New York, Palmer and Hughes, 1884-1887. 4 v.

--AFRICA

977 DAVIES, Edward, 1830-
An illustrated handbook on Africa, giving an account of its people, its climate.... Reading, Mass., Holiness Book Concern, 1886. 91 p.

I. 1. Christian Holiness Association

--CARIBBEAN REGION

978 TAYLOR, James Milburn, 1873-
Campaigning for God in Caribbean waters. Knoxville, Tenn., James M. Taylor, 1912.

--IOWA

979 IOWA Holiness Association.
Yearbook and minutes, 1906. Oskaloosa, Iowa, Globe Presses, 1906.

--KANSAS

980 KANSAS State Holiness Association.
Fifty-fifth annual camp-meeting of the Kansas State Holiness Association, Beulah Park, Wichita, Kansas, 1944. Wichita, 1944.

--LATIN AMERICA

981 TAYLOR, James Milburn, 1873-
Baptized paganism in Latin America. Knoxville, Tenn., James M. Taylor, n.d.

982 TAYLOR, James Milburn, 1873-
The South American situation. Knoxville, Tenn., James M. Taylor, 1912.

--MARYLAND

983 WILLIAMS, Mrs. E. E.
Pentecostal services ... at Mountain Lake Park (Garrett Co., Maryland) ... 1896. Philadelphia, Published by Rev. John Thompson, 1896.

--MASSACHUSETTS

984 DAVIES, Edward, 1830-
Illustrated history of Douglas Camp Meeting; introd. by E.M. Levy. Boston, McDonald, Gill, 1890. 97 p.

--NEW YORK

985 HUGHES, George, 1828-1904.
Fragrant memories of the Tuesday Meeting and its fifty

years' work for Jesus; with an introd. by Rev. Bishop W. F. Mallalieu. New York, Palmer & Hughes, 1886. 154 p.

986 HUGHES, George, 1828-1904.
Fragrant memories of the Tuesday Meeting and the Guide to Holiness, and their fifty years' work for Jesus. Introd. to part I. by Rev. Bishop W. F. Mallalieu; and to part II. by Rev. Bishop William Taylor. New York, Palmer & Hughes, c1886. iv, 242 p.

987 WEISE, Arthur James, 1838-1910 or 11.
History of Round Lake, Saratoga County, N. Y. New York, Press of D. Taylor, 1887. 103 p.
Cover title: Round Lake.
Includes poems and hymns.

--NORTH DAKOTA

988 DANFORD, Samuel Alexander, 1865-
Spreading scriptural holiness; or, The North Dakota movement. Chicago, Christian Witness Co., 1913. 137 p.

--OHIO

989 KNAPP, Martin Wells, 1853-1901, ed.
Electric shocks from Pentecostal batteries; or, Food and fire from Salvation Park Campmeeting. Cincinnati, M. W. Knapp, Revivalist Office, 1899.

990 KNAPP, Martin Wells, 1853-1901, ed.
Electric shocks no. II from Pentecostal batteries; or, Pentecostal glories from Salvation Park Campmeeting, 1900. Cincinnati, M. W. Knapp, Revivalist Office, 1900.

991 KNAPP, Martin Wells, 1853-1901, ed.
Electric shocks no. III from Pentecostal batteries; or, Salvation Park Campmeeting, 1901. Cincinnati, M. W. Knapp, Revivalist Office, 1901.

992 KNAPP, Minnie C. (Ferle), 1868-1923.
Electric shocks no. IV from Pentecostal batteries. Cincinnati, Mrs. M. W. Knapp, Revivalist Office, 1902.

--OKLAHOMA

993 HOLINESS Association of Oklahoma.
Yearbook, 1906-1907. Oklahoma City, Okla., 1906.

II. 1. Christian Holiness Association

994 JONES, Charles Edwin, 1932-
"Background of the Church of the Nazarene in Oklahoma," B-PC Historian of the Bethany-Peniel College Historical Society, I (1953-1954), 18-31.

--PENNSYLVANIA

995 PENIEL Holiness Association.
Twenty-seventh annual encampment Peniel Holiness Association interdenominational camp meeting ... camp grounds, Conneautville, Pa. n.p., 1923. Unpaged.
Organized 1896; incorporated 1902.

--RHODE ISLAND

996 INTRODUCING PORTSMOUTH Camp Meeting, Est. 1891: 1971 season, Hedley Street, Portsmouth, R.I. For a vacation with an inspiration. Portsmouth, R.I., 1971. Folder.

997 REES, Byron Johnson, 1877-1920.
Hallelujahs from Portsmouth, no. 2; or, A report of the Portsmouth Camp Meeting. Springfield, Mass., Christian Unity Publishing Co., 1897.

998 SOUTH Providence Holiness Association.
A history of the revival of holiness in St. Paul's M.E. Church, Providence, R.I., 1880-1887; a statement of the circumstances which led to the formation of the South Providence Holiness Association and the People's Evangelical Church, published by order of the Association. Providence, E.L. Freeman & Son, 1887. 87 p.

999 WOODWARD, W. D.
Hallelujahs from Portsmouth; or, A report of the Portsmouth Camp Meeting. Springfield, Mass., Christian Unity Publishing Co., 1896.

--SOUTHWEST, OLD

1000 JERNIGAN, Charles Brougher, 1863-1930.
Pioneer days of the Holiness Movement in the Southwest. Kansas City, Mo., Pentecostal Nazarene Publishing House, 1919, 157 p.

--VERMONT

1001 DAVIES, Edward, 1930-
History of Silver Lake camp meeting, near Brandon,

Vermont. Reading, Mass., Holiness Book Concern, 1887? 20 p.

ASSOCIATION OF PENTECOSTAL CHURCHES OF AMERICA (1895-1907)

In December 1895 delegates of three independent congregations in Brooklyn, New York, met and formed the Association of Pentecostal Churches of America. Led by William Howard Hoople, son of a wealthy New York leather goods merchant who in the two years preceding had been instrumental in starting the member churches, the Brooklyn group was joined by the Central Evangelical Holiness Association of New England in November 1896. The Beulah Christian, published at Providence, Rhode Island, by Fred A. Hillery, one of the founders of the latter group, became the official organ. A Bible school, the Pentecostal Collegiate Institute, begun at Saratoga Springs, New York, in 1900, re-located in North Scituate, Rhode Island the next year. Foreign missionary work was started in India in 1898 and on Brava in the Cape Verde Islands in 1901. The work in North America grew rapidly, and by 1907, when the Association of Pentecostal Churches merged with the Los Angeles-based Church of the Nazarene, the group had spread as far west as Iowa, as far south as Washington, D.C., and as far east as Nova Scotia. At that time, it reported 45 congregations and 2407 members.

--HISTORY

1002   SMITH, Timothy Lawrence, 1924-
Called unto holiness; the story of the Nazarenes: the formative years. Kansas City, Mo., Nazarene Publishing House, 1962. 413 p.
Account of Association of Pentecostal Churches of America: p. 66-90.

--PERIODICALS

1003   BEULAH CHRISTIAN. 1- , May 1892-Dec. 9, 1911. Providence, R.I.
Supersedes Beulah Items, and Bible Christian
Superseded by Pentecostal Christian

II. 1. Christian Holiness Association

Baptists

ALLIANCE OF THE REFORMED BAPTIST CHURCH (1888-1966)

[Also as Reformed Baptist Alliance of Canada and Reformed Baptist Church]

In 1888 several Canadian Baptist ministers who had professed sanctification while attending the Old Orchard Beach, Maine, camp meeting, were disfellowshipped for preaching "entire and instantaneous sanctification." The following November about 75 people from New Brunswick, Nova Scotia and Maine met at Woodstock, New Brunswick, and re-formed a Baptist Church. At the end of its first year, the group reported 22 organized churches, twelve ordained clergy and 540 members. In 1894, it received a dominion charter. Methodist ideas of perfection had significant général effects on the Reformed Baptists, for, although they held to immersion as the right mode of baptism and adhered to Baptist ideas about the autonomy of the local church, they adopted the camp meeting as a means of evangelism and gradually developed a superintendency. Failing to organize churches outside the Maritime provinces and northern Maine, the group steadily lost members who migrated to New England, many of whom joined the Church of the Nazarene. In 1901 the group began publishing The King's Highway and sent its first missionaries to South Africa. Like other holiness churches, Reformed Baptists often engaged evangelists affiliated with the National Holiness Association. They also held membership in the Canadian Holiness Federation from its inception. In 1966, when it merged with the Wesleyan Methodist Church of America, the Alliance claimed 2,591 members in sixty churches and was supporting a Bible college in Nova Scotia and a missionary work with several hundred native members in South Africa.

1004   ALLIANCE OF the Reformed Baptist Church of Canada.
      Minutes. 1st-78th, 1888-1966. n.p.   -1966.
      Annual.

1005   REFORMED BAPTIST Church.
      Manual, 1958. n.p., 1958.   95 p.

--HISTORY

1006   ENCYCLOPEDIA CANADIANA. Ottawa, Canadiana Co.,
      1957-1958. 10 v.
      "Reformed Baptist Alliance of Canada" by Norman E.
      Trafton: v. 8, p. 432.

1007 MULLEN, Handley C.
"Some facts about the origin of the Reformed Baptist Church," The King's Highway, an Advocate of Scriptural Holiness, XXXVIII (July 15, 1957), 6; (Aug. 15, 1957), 6; (Aug. 31, 1957), 6, 8; and (Sept. 16, 1957), 3, 6.

--MISSIONS

1008 ENCYCLOPEDIA OF Modern Christian Missions; the Agencies. Burton L. Goddard, ed.... Camden, N.J., T. Nelson, 1967. xix, 743 p.
"Alliance of the Reformed Baptist Church, Department of Foreign Missions,": by A.D. Cann: p. 12-13.

--PERIODICALS

1009 KING'S HIGHWAY. 1-41, 1890-1967. St. John, N.B., Can.; Moncton, N.B., Can.

FREE BAPTIST CHURCH (-1962)

At the 1962 General Conference of the Pilgrim Holiness Church, the Secretary of Foreign Missions reported that a union with the Free Baptist Church, a small European group in South Africa, was in process. A long-established holiness work (Zion Church in central Johannesburg had often been used for general holiness gatherings), the Free Baptist Church merger promised to strengthen Pilgrim Holiness work among Europeans significantly, bringing the total white membership in South Africa to about five hundred.

1010 PILGRIM HOLINESS Church. General Conference.
Minutes of the Twenty-fourth General Conference of the Pilgrim Holiness Church, held at Winona Lake, Indiana, June 12-18, 1962. Indianapolis, Pilgrim Publishing House, 1962. 125 p.
Account of merger negotiations with the Free Baptist Church: p. 76.

Brethren

BRETHREN IN CHRIST CHURCH (1863-)

[Formerly as River Brethren]

An example of the impact of holiness revivalism on German Pietist groups, this group traces its American roots to eighteenth-

II. 1. Christian Holiness Association

century immigration to southeastern Pennsylvania. Originally part of the United Brethren in Christ movement, the group organized separately in 1863 but did not legally incorporate until 1904. In 1868 the second National Camp Meeting for the Promotion of Holiness was held at Manheim, in the heart of the Pennsylvania Dutch country, and from that time on the Brethren in Christ (also known as River Brethren because they lived near the Susquehanna River) were attracted in increasing numbers to Wesleyan perfectionism. After 1890 many of their Kansas members (including two uncles of Dwight Eisenhower) worked with the Hephzibah Faith Missionary Association. Tension between the Methodism latent in the holiness movement and the Brethren tradition has been perennial. Although it holds membership in the Christian Holiness Association whose current president is a Brethren in Christ minister, holiness sentiment within the church has passed its peak. The church sponsors Messiah College at Grantham, Pennsylvania, and Niagara Christian College at Fort Erie, Ontario, and carries on foreign missionary work in Nicaragua, Africa, India and Japan. The Evangelical Visitor is published at the headquarters in Nappanee, Indiana. In 1970 there were 10,203 members in 159 congregations.

1011 ALDERFER, Owen Hiram, 1923-
"The mind of the Brethren in Christ: a synthesis of revivalism and the church conceived as total community." Unpublished Ph.D. dissertation, Claremont Graduate School and University Center, 1964. 331 ℓ.

1012 BRETHREN in Christ Church.
Manual of doctrine and government of the Brethren in Christ Church, 1961. Nappanee, Ind., Evangel Press, 1961. 177 p.

1013 BRETHREN in Christ Church.
Manual of doctrine and government of the Brethren in Christ Church, 1961. Revision of 1968. Nappanee, Ind., Evangel Press, 1968. 180 p.

1014 BRETHREN in Christ Church. General Conference.
Minutes of the General Conference of the Brethren in Christ (River Brethren) of the U.S.A. and Canada.... n.p. v.
Title varies.

1015 SCHRAG, Martin Homer
"The Brethren in Christ attitude toward the 'world'; a historical study of the movement from separation to an increasing acceptance of American society." Unpublished Ph.D. dissertation, Temple University, 1967. 392 ℓ.

--DOCTRINAL AND CONTROVERSIAL WORKS

1016 BYERS, Charles B.
    Steps to victorious living. Elizabethtown, Pa., McBeth Press, 1952. 53 p.

1017 ZOOK, J. R.
    A guide for instructors to instruct penitance, doctrine of holiness and enpowerment and divine healing. Des Moines, Iowa, Kenyon Co., n.d. 12 p.

1018 ZOOK, J. R.
    Holiness and empowerment. Both defined: how to obtain them; how to retain them. n.p., n.d. 34 p.

--HISTORY

1019 BERT, Norman A.
    Adventure in discipleship. Nappanee, Ind., Evangel Press, 1968. 111 p.

1020 CLARK, Elmer Talmage, 1886-1966.
    The small sects in America. Rev. ed. New York, Abingdon Press, c1965. 256 p.
    Account of Brethren in Christ: p. 211-212.

1021 CLIMENHAGA, Asa W., 1889-
    History of the Brethren in Christ Church. Nappanee, Ind., E.V. Publishing House, 1942. 390 p.

1022 DODD, Gladys
    "The early career of Abraham L. Eisenhower, pioneer preacher," Kansas Historical Quarterly, XXIX (Autumn 1963), 233-249.
    In 1892 Abraham Lincoln Eisenhower, veterinarian of Hope and Abilene, Kansas, became an itinerant preacher. Turning his home in Abilene over to his brother, Dwight Eisenhower's father, Abraham Eisenhower toured Kansas in his Gospel wagon. In 1899 he and his wife started an orphanage in Oklahoma, a work which was ultimately turned over to the Brethren in Christ Church.

1023 DODD, Gladys
    "The religious background of the Eisenhower family." Unpublished B.D. thesis, Nazarene Theological Seminary, 1959. vi, iv, 436 ℓ.

1024 ESHELMAN, Wilmer J.
    The River Brethren denominations. Lancaster, Pa., 1948.
    Account of Brethren in Christ Church: p. 173-212.

II. 1. Christian Holiness Association

1025 MEAD, Frank Spencer, 1898-
Handbook of denominations in the United States. New 5th ed. Nashville, Abingdon Press, c1970. 265 p.
"Brethren in Christ (formerly known as River Brethren)": p. 59.

--HISTORY OF DOCTRINES

1026 ENGLE, Albert H.
"Complementary relationships between great truths of the Word of God." Unpublished M.A. thesis, Winona Lake School of Theology, 1953. 200 ℓ.

--HYMNS

1027 BRETHREN in Christ Church.
Spiritual songs & hymns; for use in all gospel services containing a large selection of standard church hymns, inspiring gospel songs and responsive readings. Nappanee, Ind., E.V. Publishing House, 1935. Unpaged.

--MISSIONS

1028 BRETHREN in Christ Church.
Hand book of missions of the Brethren in Christ Church....

1029 ENCYCLOPEDIA OF Modern Christian Missions; the Agencies. Burton L. Goddard, ed.... Camden, N.J., T. Nelson, 1967. xix, 743 p.
"Brethren in Christ World Missions," by Henry N. Hostetter and Mary C. Kreider: p. 96-97.

1030 EVANGELICAL VISITOR. 75th anniversary number. LXXV (Dec. 10, 1962).

--MUSIC

1031 SALTZMAN, Herbert Royce
"A historical study of the function of music among the Brethren in Christ." Unpublished D.M.A. dissertation, University of Southern California, 1964. 346 ℓ.

--PERIODICALS

1032 EVANGELICAL VISITOR. 1- , 1888- . Abilene, Kan.; Harrisburg, Pa.; Nappanee, Ind.

-- POLITICAL AND SOCIAL CRITICISM

1032a DAYTON, Donald W.
"A historical survey of attitudes toward war and peace within the American Holiness Movement," prepared by Donald W. Dayton and Lucille S. Dayton for the Seminar on Christian Holiness and the Issues of War and Peace, June 7-9, 1973, Winona Lake, Indiana, jointly sponsored by the Commission on Social Action of the Christian Holiness Association and the Peace and Social Concerns Commission of the Brethren in Christ Church. Unpublished paper, 1973. 25 p.
Mimeographed.

--STATISTICS

1033 U.S. BUREAU of the Census.
... Census of religious bodies, 1926; River Brethren: statistics, denominational history, doctrine, and organization; consolidated report.... Brethren in Christ, Old Order or Yorker brethren, United Zion's Children.... Washington, U.S. Government Printing Office, 1928. 15 p.

--WORK WITH YOUTH

1034 HEISEY, Ruth E.
"A survey of the congregations of the Brethren in Christ churches of the United States regarding the influence of religious education and church worship for the educable mentally retarded child." Unpublished M. Ed. thesis, Millersville State College, 1970. 105 ℓ.

--INDIA

1035 ENGLE, Anna R.
There is no difference; God works in Africa and India, by Anna R. Engle, John A. Climenhaga (Africa) [and] Leoda A. Buckwalter (India). Nappanee, Ind., E.V. Publishing House, 1950. xv, 386 p.

--RHODESIA

1036 DAVIDSON, Hannah Frances, 1860-
South and south central Africa; a record of fifteen years' missionary labors among primitive peoples, by H. Frances Davidson with photographs by the missionaries. Elgin, Ill., Printed for the author by Brethren Publishing House, 1915. 481 p.

II. 1. Christian Holiness Association   103

1037   ENGLE, Anna R.
         There is no difference; God works in Africa and India,
       by Anna R. Engle, John A. Climenhaga (Africa) [and] Leoda
       A. Buckwalter (India). Nappanee, Ind., E.V. Publishing
       House, 1950. xv, 386 p.

1038   KING, Paul S.
         Missions in Southern Rhodesia ... foreword by Vice-
       Admiral Sir Peveril William Pawlett.... Bulawayo, The
       Inyati Centenary Trust, 1959. 80 p.
         Contains chapter on the Brethren in Christ Church.

1039   SOWING AND reaping; the story of a work of God in Rho-
          desia, 1898-1948 ... issued as a memorial ... with the
          jubilee anniversary celebrations of the Brethren in Christ
          Church at Matopo Mission, July 6th, 1948. Bulawayo,
          Rhodesian Printing and Publishing Co., 1948. Unpaged.

PENTECOSTAL BRETHREN IN CHRIST (18??-1924)

   Descendants of River Brethren who settled in eastern Pennsylvania in the eighteenth century, the Pentecostal Brethren in
Christ emerged in the late nineteenth century as a product of the
impact of the Methodist holiness movement on German Anabaptist
groups.   Located in southwestern Ohio, a handful of Pentecostal
Brethren congregations led by twelve ordained and one licensed
minister united with the Ohio District of the Pilgrim Holiness
Church in 1924.   In addition to their church properties, the group
brought a fully equipped camp meeting ground at Springfield, Ohio,
to the merger.

1040   PENTECOSTAL BRETHREN in Christ.
         Faith and rules of the Brethren in Christ, 1910. n.p.,
       1910.

1041   THOMAS, Paul Westphal, 1894-1972.
         "The days of our pilgrimage; a history of the Pilgrim
       Holiness Church," by Paul Westphal Thomas and Paul Wil-
       liam Lee Thomas. Unpublished paper, 1968. 1 v. (various
       pagings)
         In archives of The Wesleyan Church, Marion, Indiana.
         Account of the Pentecostal Brethren in Christ: ℓ. 122-
       123.

CALVARY HOLINESS CHURCH (1934-1955)

   Founded in 1934 by four young ministers who had separated
from the International Holiness Mission, the Calvary Holiness

Church in Britain was the outgrowth of itinerant revivalism, called "trekking," which Maynard James, Jack Ford, Leonard Ravenhill and Clifford Filer had pursued for several years within the parent group. Several new congregations of the International Holiness Mission which were organized to nurture converts of the trekkers became a source of administrative tension. Disapproval of tongues-speaking by Mission officials led to separation in 1934. The new movement proved extremely evangelistic. Governmental power was largely in the hands of the founders who sat as the Executive Council. The Flame, a paper started by Maynard James in 1935, became the official organ the next year. In 1937 the church sent its first missionaries to Colombia. The Beech Lawn Bible College, established at Uppermill in 1947, was moved to Stalybridge the next year. Following World War II financial difficulties beset the movement, leading the Executive Council into talks with officials of the Church of the Nazarene, and in June 1955, at Manchester, England, a merger was effected. Largely because of a pledge not to countenance speaking in tongues in public worship, a half dozen ministers refused to unite. At the time of the union the Calvary Holiness Church consisted of about 22 congregations and 600 members.

--DOCTRINAL AND CONTROVERSIAL WORKS

1042 JAMES, Maynard G., 1902-
Facing the issue. Burnley, Lancs., Eng., Pilgrim Publishing House, 1948.

--EVANGELISTIC WORK

1043 JAMES, Maynard G., 1902-
Evangelize. Burnley, Lancs., Eng., Pilgrim Publishing House, 1945.

--HISTORY

1044 FORD, Jack, 1908-
"The Church of the Nazarene in Britain, the International Holiness Mission and the Calvary Holiness Church, with reference to holiness movements in Christian history." Unpublished Ph.D. dissertation, University of London, 1967.

1045 FORD, Jack, 1908-
In the steps of John Wesley; the Church of the Nazarene in Britain. Kansas City, Mo., Printed by Nazarene Publishing House, 1968. 300 p.
Thesis (Ph.D.)--University of London, 1967.

II. 1. Christian Holiness Association

--MISSIONS

1046 ENCYCLOPEDIA OF Modern Christian Missions; the Agencies. Burton L. Goddard, ed.... Camden, N.J., T. Nelson, 1967. xix, 743 p.
"Calvary Holiness Church, Missionary Society": p. 105.

--PERIODICALS

1047 FLAME; a bi-monthly for the spread of full salvation. 1- , 1935- . Hillside, Southport, Lancs., Eng.; Grimsby, Lancs., Eng.

CHRISTIAN NATION CHURCH (1895-)

In 1892 eight young men who called themselves "equality Evangelists" began work in the vicinity of Mount Victory, Ohio. Although few converts were made, the workers and some others met at Marion, Ohio, in 1895 and drew up a plan of government. The group incorporated as a church the next year. Doctrinally the Christian Nation Church stresses justification, entire sanctification, divine healing and the second coming of Christ. It holds that evidence of the experience of entire sanctification is not the exercise of any one spiritual gift. Worldly amusements, fashionable attire, sabbath desecration, and divorce are forbidden, and marriage between members and non-believers is discouraged. Large families are approved as being divinely sanctioned. In 1970 the Christian Nation Church had 3300 members in sixteen congregations.

1048 CLARK, Elmer Talmage, 1886-1966.
The small sects in America. Rev. ed. New York, Abingdon Press, c1965. 256 p.
Account of the Christian Nation Church: p. 82-83.

1049 MEAD, Frank Spencer, 1898-
Handbook of denominations in the United States. New 5th ed. Nashville, Abingdon Press, c1970. 265 p.
"Christian Nation Church": p. 68.

CHRIST'S SANCTIFIED HOLY CHURCH (1904-)

[1904-19?? as Colored Church, South]

As a result of holiness preaching in the Colored Methodist Episcopal Church in Louisiana, Christ's Sanctified Holy Church was organized in 1904. First known as the Colored Church, South, the group emphasizes entire sanctification "as a distinct experience ... wrought instantaneously" subsequent to justification. Rules--including abstinence from tobacco and alcoholic beverages--are strictly enforced. Candidates of both sexes are ordained to the ministry. The small size of the church (600 members in 30 congregations in 1957) makes sponsorship of permanent educational and missionary institutions impossible, but an annual summer school for ministerial training was, at last report, conducted at the group's headquarters at Jennings, Louisiana. Racial barriers have prevented much contact with the larger predominantly white holiness denominations.

1050   CLARK, Elmer Talmage, 1886-1966.
        The small sects in America. Rev. ed. New York, Abingdon Press, c1965. 256 p.
        Account of Christ's Sanctified Holy Church, Colored: p. 130.

1051   MEAD, Frank Spencer, 1898-
        Handbook of denominations in the United States. New 5th ed. Nashville, Abingdon Press, c1970. 265 p.
        "Christ's Sanctified Holy Church": p. 69.

CHURCH OF CHRIST (HOLINESS) U.S.A. (1907-)

In 1894 C.P. Jones and C.H. Mason, black ministers who had been excluded from the Baptist Church in Arkansas because of their holiness beliefs, founded an interdenominational movement which organized in 1897 as the Church of God in Christ. Mason left this group in 1907 to join the Pentecostal movement, taking a majority of the members with him. Jones reorganized those who remained as the Church of Christ (Holiness), which established its headquarters at Jackson, Mississippi. There, Jones supported himself by composing and publishing gospel songs, a number of which have been widely used by black and white holiness groups. Although the group briefly considered uniting with the Church of the Nazarene, race has prevented close relations with predominantly white holiness churches. In 1956 the Church of Christ (Holiness) reported 9,018 members and 151 churches. A Bible college is located in Jackson and a publishing house in Chicago. Missionary work is sponsored in Mexico.

1052   CHURCH OF Christ (Holiness) U.S.A.
        Manual of the history, doctrine, government, and ritual

II. 1. Christian Holiness Association

of the Church of Christ (Holiness) U.S.A., 1926. True holiness. 1st ed. Norfolk, Va., Guide Publishing Co., 1928. 83 p.

"Published by orders of the National Convention of the Church of Christ (Holiness) U.S.A., held in Jackson, Miss., August 22-29, 1926."

--HISTORY

1053 CLARK, Elmer Talmage, 1886-1966.
The small sects in America. Rev. ed. New York, Abingdon Press, c1965. 256 p.
Account of the Church of Christ (Holiness) U.S.A.: p. 120.

1054 COBBINS, Otho Beale, bp., ed.
History of Church of Christ (Holiness) U.S.A., 1895-1965. Chicago, National Publishing Board, Church of Christ (Holiness) U.S.A., 1966. 446 p.
Includes hymns, in part in shaped-note notation.

1055 MEAD, Frank Spencer, 1898-
Handbook of denominations in the United States. New 5th ed. Nashville, Abingdon Press, c1970. 265 p.
"Church of Christ (Holiness) U.S.A.": p. 69.

--HYMNS

1056 JONES, Charles P.
His fulness: anthems, songs and hymns; being a collection of choice, lovely, lively and powerful anthems for the choir with a number of special songs for special occasions--solos, duets, quartettes and choruses with also a happy collection of gospel songs for Sunday school or any service. Jackson, Miss., Truth Publishing Co., c1913. 119, 10 p.
With music (shaped notes).

1057 JONES, Charles P., comp.
Jesus only, songs and hymns; a collection of new and popular songs, hymns and tunes, for praise and prayer meetings, Sunday schools, camp meetings, holiness assemblies, etc., etc. Jackson, Miss., Truth Publishing Co., 1901. 67ℓ.

--MISSIONS

1058 ENCYCLOPEDIA OF modern Christian missions; the agencies. Burton L. Goddard, ed.... Camden, N.J., T. Nelson, 1967. xix, 743 p.

"Church of Christ (Holiness) U.S.A., Foreign Mission Board of the": p. 167.

   --STATISTICS

1059 U.S. BUREAU of the Census.
   ...Census of religious bodies, 1926; Church of Christ (Holiness): statistics, denominational history, doctrine, and organization.... Washington, U.S. Government Printing Office, 1929. 8 p.

   Cnurch of God

CHURCH OF GOD (Anderson, Indiana) (1880-)

Like other bodies with this name, the Church of God with general offices at Anderson, Indiana claims not to be a denomination, but a movement for reformation of the Church generally. About 1880 Daniel S. Warner, a minister in the Churches of God (General Eldership), a German pietist group, was sanctified under the ministry of National Holiness Association workers. Feeling that sectarianism was antithetical to true Christianity, Warner soon broke with his denomination and later, with the holiness association movement, which required church membership as a prerequisite to association membership. Through the Gospel Trumpet and Warner's own free-lance evangelistic work, churches sprang up in numerous places taking the New Testament name, the Church of God. No membership roll was kept since God alone knew who had been converted. Membership in denominational churches was considered sinful, and in any community those who identified with the Gospel Trumpet people considered themselves the true Church of God. Publication offices of the Gospel Trumpet moved several times: from Indiana to Michigan, to West Virginia, and finally (after Warner's death) back to Indiana. At Anderson, where the Gospel Trumpet moved in 1906 and where a Bible training school was established in 1917, the General Ministerial Assembly, which met in connection with the annual camp meeting, came to exercise administrative oversight of the paper, school and missionary activities. The Anderson group claimed nearly 150,000 domestic members and over 50,000 missionary adherents in 1968. It practices the washing of saints' feet and baptism by immersion and observes the Lord's Supper. Sunday school enrollment exceeds church membership by nearly 100,000. Though fear of sectarianism has caused the group to stand apart from other holiness groups, in recent years the Church of God has cooperated with the Christian Holiness Association. Other holiness churches have been wary of the Anderson group's cooperation with the National Council of Churches and of the alleged liberal theological tendencies of Anderson College and Theological Seminary. Though strongly evange-

II. 1. Christian Holiness Association

listic, the Church of God denies that the Second Coming of Christ will in any way be connected with the Millennium.

1060 CLEAR, Valorous Bernard, 1915-
"The Church of God: a study in social adaptation."
Unpublished Ph.D. dissertation, University of Chicago, 1953. 380ℓ.

1061 FERM, Vergilius Ture Anselm, 1896- , ed.
The American church of the Protestant heritage. New York, Philosophical Library, 1953.
Includes discussion on the Church of God (Anderson, Indiana) by Charles Ewing Brown, p. 433-454.

--ANECDOTES, REMINISCENCES, SATIRE, ETC.

1062 BYERS, Andrew L., 1869- , comp.
Things that happened; a collection of interesting anecdotes, comp. as vol. I of the Boys and Girls' Fireside Series. Anderson, Ind., Gospel Trumpet Co., c1918. 95 p.
Reprinted from the Shining Light, a periodical for children. cf. Pref.

1063 BYERS, Andrew L., 1869- , comp.
Trips and adventures; accounts of interesting and varied experiences, comp. as vol. II of the Boys' and Girls' Fireside Series. Anderson, Ind., Gospel Trumpet Co., c1918. 95 p.
Reprinted from the Shining Light, a periodical for children. cf. Pref.

1064 BYRUM, Enoch Edwin, 1861-1942.
Startling incidents and experiences in the Christian life; narratives of the wonderful dealings of the Lord with those who put their trust in Him and of their deliverance in time of adversity, trial, and temptation. Anderson, Ind., Gospel Trumpet Co., 1915. 414 p.

1065 BYRUM, Isabel (Coston), 1870-1938.
The poorhouse waif and his divine teacher; a true story. Anderson, Ind., Kansas City, Mo., Gospel Trumpet Co., 1919. 223 p.

1066 MITCHELL, Elizabeth Ann (Oldacre), 1876-
Anchored to the Rock. Anderson, Ind., Printed for the author by Gospel Trumpet Co., 1950. 142 p.

--APOLOGETIC WORKS

1067 STERNER, R. Eugene
We reach our hands in fellowship; an introduction to the Church of God. Anderson, Ind., Warner Press, 1960. 64 p.

--BIOGRAPHY

1068 BYRUM, N. H.
Familiar names and faces; a collection of cuts from photographs of ministers, gospel workers, writers, and others, whose names are mostly familiar to the readers of the Gospel Trumpet ... also a history of the Gospel Trumpet publishing work, with cuts representing the same and other things of interest. Moundsville, W.Va., Gospel Trumpet Publishing Co., 1902. 288 p.

1069 SMITH, John W. V., 1914-
Heralds of a brighter day; biographical sketches of early leaders in the Church of God reformation movement. Anderson, Ind., Gospel Trumpet Co., 1955. 144 p.

--CHURCH WORK

1070 BYRUM, Russell Raymond, 1888-
Problems of the local church; a manual of the principles and practise of local churches. Anderson, Ind., Gospel Trumpet Co., 1927. 271 p.

--CONDUCT OF LIFE

1071 BYRUM, Isabel (Coston), 1870-1938.
The value of a praying mother. Anderson, Ind., Gospel Trumpet Co., 1911. 173 p.

1072 OLDHAM, William Dale, 1903-
Give me tomorrow. Anderson, Ind., Warner Press, c1964. v, 95 p.

1073 OLDHAM, William Dale, 1903-
Just across the street; how to be a growing Christian. Anderson, Ind., Warner Press, 1968. viii, 160 p.

1074 OLDHAM, William Dale, 1903-
Living close to God. Anderson, Ind., Warner Press, 1957. 176 p.

II. 1. Christian Holiness Association

1075 WARNER, Daniel Sidney, 1842-1895.
Marriage and divorce. Anderson, Ind., Gospel Trumpet Co., n.d. 30 p.

-- --AUTHORITATIVE SOURCES

1076 RILEY, John Eckel, 1909-
This holy estate; guidance in Christian homemaking. Anderson, Ind., Warner Press, 1957. 191 p.

--DEVOTIONAL LITERATURE

1077 BYERS, Andrew L., 1869- , comp.
Treasures of poetry; being an extensive collection from the best productions of poetry and song representing as wide range of authors and containing poems of the home circle, narratives, beauties of nature, poems of sentiment and reflection, of sorrow and bereavement, of childhood and youth, etc., etc., and a large department of poems relating to religion and the spiritual life, comp. and ed. by A. L. Byers and Eva R. Johnson. Anderson, Ind., Gospel Trumpet Co., c1913. 607 p.

1078 BYRUM, Enoch Edwin, 1861-1942.
The secret of prayer; how and why we pray. New York, Fleming H. Revell Co., 1912. 209 p.

1079 ORR, Charles Ebert, 1861-
Odors from golden vials. Anderson, Ind., Gospel Trumpet Co., 1912. 155 p.
On prayer.

--DOCTRINAL AND CONTROVERSIAL WORKS

1080 BARNARD, Allison F.
Plain paths to the land of promise; or, Sanctification made clear; a series of simple and concise statements of truth for those seeking true holiness. Anderson, Ind., Gospel Trumpet Co., 1933. 128 p.

1081 BERRY, Robert Lee, 1874-
Adventures in the land of Canaan. Anderson, Ind., Gospel Trumpet Co., 1924. 128 p.

1082 BLACKWELDER, Boyce W.
The gifts of the Spirit. Anderson, Ind., Warner Press, n.d. 32 p.

1083 BOYER, Harold W.
The apostolic church and the apostasy; messages on the

church in history. Anderson, Ind., Warner Press, 1960. 79 p.

1084 BROWN, Charles Ewing, 1883-
The meaning of salvation. Anderson, Ind., Gospel Trumpet Co., 1944. 202 p.

1085 BROWN, Charles Ewing, 1883-
The meaning of sanctification. Anderson, Ind., Warner Press, 1945. 232 p.

1086 BROWN, Charles Ewing, 1883-
A new approach to Christian unity. Anderson, Ind., Gospel Trumpet Co., 1931. 205 p.

1087 BROWN, Charles Ewing, 1883-
The ordinance we forget. Anderson, Inc., Gospel Trumpet Co., n.d. 29 p.

1088 BROWN, Charles Ewing, 1883-
We preach Christ; a handbook of Christian doctrine. Anderson, Ind., Gospel Trumpet Co., 1957. 159 p.

1089 BROWN, Charles Ewing, 1883-
When souls awaken; an interpretation of radical Christianity, with an introd. by Gene W. Newberry. Anderson, Ind., Gospel Trumpet Co., 1954. 127 p.

1090 BYRUM, Enoch Edwin, 1861-1942.
The man of Galilee. Anderson, Inc., Gospel Trumpet Co., 1907. 175 p.

1091 BYRUM, Enoch Edwin, 1861-1942.
Ordinances of the Bible; showing the ordinances that have been abolished and those still in vogue. Moundsville, W.Va., Gospel Trumpet Co., 1904. 117 p.

1092 BYRUM, Enoch Edwin, 1861-1942.
Peter the fisherman preacher. Anderson, Ind., Warner Press, 1931. 141 p.

1093 BYRUM, Enoch Edwin, 1861-1942.
The secret of salvation, how to get it and how to keep it; showing the way of salvation, giving the reader the key with which to unlock its great storehouse of peace and happiness. Grand Junction, Mich., Gospel Trumpet Publishing Co., 1896. 408 p.

1094 BYRUM, Enoch Edwin, 1861-1942.
The secret of salvation; how to get it, and how to keep it.... Anderson, Ind., Gospel Trumpet Co., c1896. 403 p.

II. 1. Christian Holiness Association

1095 BYRUM, Enoch Edwin, 1861-1942.
What shall I do to be saved?; words of advice, warning, and encouragement to the unsaved, pointing out the way of salvation, and the requirements necessary to obtain it. Moundsville, W. Va., Gospel Trumpet Co., 1903. 200 p.

1096 BYRUM, Enoch Edwin, 1861-1942.
What shall I do to be saved?; words of advice, warning, and encouragement to the unsaved, pointing out the way of salvation, and the requirements necessary to obtain it. Anderson, Ind., Gospel Trumpet Co., c1903. 200 p.

1097 BYRUM, Russell Raymond, 1888-
Christian theology; a systematic statement of Christian doctrine for the use of theological students. Anderson, Ind., Gospel Trumpet Co., 1925. 680 p.

1098 BYRUM, Russell Raymond, 1888-
Holy Spirit baptism and the second cleansing. Anderson, Ind., Gospel Trumpet Co., 1923. 107 p.

1099 BYRUM, Russell Raymond, 1888-
Shadows of good things; or, The Gospel in type. Anderson, Ind., Gospel Trumpet Co., 1923. 192 p.

1100 DANFORD, Samuel Alexander, 1865-
Double cure. Anderson, Ind., Gospel Trumpet Co., 1928.

1101 GOSPEL Trumpet Company.
Wiederklange aus der Höhe. Moundsville, W. Va., 1904. 40 p.

1102 HALL, Kenneth F., 1926-
What do you believe?; a discussion for young Christians on some of the principal New Testament doctrines as taught in the Church of God. Anderson, Ind., Gospel Trumpet Co., 1958. 63 p.

1103 NEWBERRY, Gene W.
Primer for young Christians. Anderson, Ind., Warner Press, 1955. 112 p.

1104 ORR, Charles Ebert, 1861-
The gospel day; or, The light of Christianity. Moundsville, W. Va., Gospel Trumpet Co., 1904. 510 p.

1105 ORR, Charles Ebert, 1861-
The hidden life; or, Walks with God. Anderson, Ind., Gospel Trumpet Co., 1908. 224 p.

1106 ORR, Charles Ebert, 1861-
Das verborgene leben; oder, Der wandel mit Gott. Anderson, Ind., Gospel Trumpet Co., 1910. 220 p.
"Vorvort" signed: E.E. Byrum.
Translation of The hidden life; or, Walks with God.

1107 RICE, Hillery C.
Tell me about the church; with a foreword by Warren C. Roark. Anderson, Ind., Gospel Trumpet Co., 1956. 112 p.

1108 RIGGLE, Herbert McClellan, 1872-
The Christian church, its rise and progress. Anderson, Ind., Gospel Trumpet Co., 1912. 488 p.

1109 RIGGLE, Herbert McClellan, 1872-
Man, his present and future. Moundsville, W.Va., Gospel Trumpet Co., 1904. 206 p.

1110 RIGGLE, Herbert McClellan, 1872-
The New Testament church; spiritual, practical. Anderson, Ind., Gospel Trumpet Co., 1937. 196 p.

1111 RIGGLE, Herbert McClellan, 1872-
The sabbath and the Lord's day. 6th ed., rev. Anderson, Ind., Gospel Trumpet Co., 1928. 263 p.

1112 RIGGLE, Herbert McClellan, 1872-
Two works of grace. Anderson, Ind., Gospel Trumpet Co., n.d.

1113 ROARK, Warren C., 1902- , comp.
The church, comp. by Warren C. Roark; contributors: R.L. Berry, Herman E. Beyer, Boyce Blackwelder [and others]. Anderson, Ind., Warner Press, 1946. 144 p.

1114 ROARK, Warren C., 1902-
The Holy Spirit. Anderson, Ind., Warner Press, 1947.

1115 SMITH, Frederick George, 1880-1947.
Evolution of Christianity; or, Origin, nature, and development of the religion of the Bible. Anderson, Ind., Gospel Trumpet Co., 1911. 356 p.

1116 SMITH, Frederick George, 1880-1947.
The last reformation. Anderson, Ind., Gospel Trumpet Co., 1919. 256 p.

1117 SMITH, Frederick George, 1880-1947.
Sanctification and the baptism of the Holy Spirit. Anderson, Ind., Gospel Trumpet Co., n.d.

II. 1. Christian Holiness Association

1118   SMITH, Frederick George, 1880-1947.
What the Bible teaches; a systematic presentation of the fundamental principles of truth contained in the Holy Scriptures. Anderson, Ind., Gospel Trumpet Co., 1914. 576 p.

1119   SMITH, Frederick George, 1880-1947.
What the Bible teaches; a systematic presentation of the fundamental principles of Bible truth. 15th ed. Anderson, Ind., Gospel Trumpet Co., 1945. 365 p.

1120   SMITH, John W. V., 1914-
Members of His body and of one another. n.p., n.d. 32 p.

1121   WARNER, Daniel Sidney, 1842-1895.
Bible proofs of the second work of grace, or, Entire sanctification as a distinct experience, subsequent to justification, established by the united testimony of several hundred texts, including a description of the great holiness crisis of the present age, by the prophets. Goshen, Ind., E. U. Mennonite Publishing Society, 1880. viii, 493 p.

1122   WARNER, Daniel Sidney, 1842-1895.
The Church of God; or, What is the church and what is not. Moundsville, W. Va., Gospel Trumpet Co., 1902? Cover-title, 32 p.

1123   WARNER, Daniel Sidney, 1842-1895.
The Church of God; or, What is the church and what is not. Anderson, Ind., Gospel Trumpet Co., n.d. 31 p.

1124   WARNER, Daniel Sidney, 1842-1895.
The cleansing of the sanctuary; or, The church of God in type and antitype, and in prophecy and revelation, by D. S. Warner and H. M. Riggle.... Moundsville, W. Va., Gospel Trumpet Co., 1903. 541 p.

1125   WARNER, Daniel Sidney, 1842-1895.
The cleansing of the sanctuary; or, The church of God in type and antitype, and in prophecy and revelation, by D. S. Warner ... and H. M. Riggle.... Guthrie, Okla., Faith Publishing House, 1967. 541 p.
Reprint of 1903 ed.

1126   WARNER, Daniel Sidney, 1842-1895.
The sabbath; or, Which day to keep. Grand Junction, Mich., Gospel Trumpet Publishing Co., 1894. 184 p.

1127   WARNER, Daniel Sidney, 1842-1895.
The sabbath; or, Which day to keep. Moundsville, W. Va., Gospel Trumpet Co., 1899.

1128 WARNER, Daniel Sidney, 1842-1895.
Salvation, present, perfect, now or never. Grand Junction, Mich., Gospel Trumpet Publishing Co., n.d. viii, 9-118 p.

1129 WARNER, Daniel Sidney, 1842-1895.
Salvation, present, perfect, now or never. Moundsville, W.Va., Gospel Trumpet, n.d. viii, 118 p.
Biographical sketch of author: p. [v]-viii.

1130 WARNER, Daniel Sidney, 1842-1895.
Salvation, present, perfect, now or never. Anderson, Ind.; Kansas City, Mo., Gospel Trumpet, n.d. 96 p.

1131 WARNER, Daniel Sidney, 1842-1895.
What is the soul?; or, 100 scriptures proving that man possesses a spiritual and immortal element called the soul, the spirit, and the inner man, which goes to God at the death of the body. Grand Junction, Mich., Gospel Trumpet Publishing Co., n.d. 68 p.

1132 WILLIAMS, Carl Carnelius, 1903-
Things most surely believed. Anderson, Ind., Gospel Trumpet Co., 1955. 144 p.

-- --AUTHORITATIVE SOURCES

1133 RUTH, Christian Wismer, 1865-1941.
Sanctification of the Hall family. Anderson, Ind., Gospel Trumpet Co., n.d.

-- --ESCHATOLOGY

1134 RIGGLE, Herbert McClellan, 1872-
Beyond the tomb; or, Man, his nature and destiny. Anderson, Ind., Gospel Trumpet Co., 1929. 287 p.

1135 RIGGLE, Herbert McClellan, 1872-
Christ's kingdom and reign. Anderson, Ind., Gospel Trumpet Co., 1918. 300 p.

1136 RIGGLE, Herbert McClellan, 1872-
Christ's second coming and what will follow. Anderson, Ind., Gospel Trumpet Co., 1918. 317 p.

1137 RIGGLE, Herbert McClellan, 1872-
Jesus is coming again. Anderson, Ind., Gospel Trumpet Co., 1943. 156 p.

1138 RIGGLE, Herbert McClellan, 1872-
The kingdom of God and the one thousand years' reign. Moundsville, W.Va., Gospel Trumpet Co., 1899. 262 p.

II. 1. Christian Holiness Association

1139 SMITH, Frederick George, 1880-1947.
The Revelation explained; an exposition, text by text, of the Apocalypse of St. John, showing the marvelous development of the prophecies from the time of their delivery on the Isle of Patmos, the establishment and growth of Christianity, rise of Mohammedanism in the Eastern Empire, of the papacy in the western division, of Protestantism, the civil history of the territory comprising the ancient Roman Empire until the end of time, together with the conflicts and triumphs of the redeemed until the Final Judgment, and their eternal reward and home in the "new heavens and new earth." Anderson, Ind., Gospel Trumpet Co., c1908. 459 p.

1140 SMITH, Frederick George, 1880-1947.
The Revelation explained; a commentary on the Apocalypse of St. John. 11th ed., thoroughly rev. by the author and printed from new type. Anderson, Ind., Gospel Trumpet Co., 1943. 322 p.

-- --FAITH HEALING

1141 BYERS, Andrew L., 1869- , ed.
Two hundred genuine instances of divine healing; the doctrine explained. Anderson, Ind., Gospel Trumpet Co., c1911. 511 p.

1142 BYRUM, Enoch Edwin, 1861-1942.
Divine healing of soul and body; also, How God heals the sick.... Grand Junction, Mich., Gospel Trumpet Publishing Co., 1892. 248 p.

1143 BYRUM, Enoch Edwin, 1861-1942.
Divine healing of soul and body; also, How God heals the sick, and the conditions upon which they are restored.... Anderson, Ind., Gospel Trumpet Co., c1892. 254 p.

1144 BYRUM, Enoch Edwin, 1861-1942.
The Great physician and His power to heal. Moundsville, W.Va., Gospel Trumpet Publishing Co., 1899. 112 p.

1145 BYRUM, Enoch Edwin, 1861-1942.
Miracles and healing; scriptural incidents and evidences of the miraculous manifestations of the power of God, and of the healing of sicknesses and diseases. Anderson, Ind., Gospel Trumpet Co., 1919. 302 p.

1146 ROARK, Warren C., 1902- , comp.
Divine healing, comp. by Warren C. Roark; contributors: E.H. Ahrendt, Vivian Ahrendt, J. Grant Anderson [and others]. Anderson, Ind., Warner Press, 1945. 126 p.

-- --GLOSSOLALIA

1147   BROWN, Charles Ewing, 1883-
The confusion of tongues. Anderson, Ind., Gospel Trumpet Co., 1949. 32 p.

1148   CHESNUT, Lawrence J.
True Bible tongues: their proper place and use in the church. Oklahoma City, Okla., c1948. 96 p.

1149   JONES, Kenneth E.
What about the gift of tongues? n.p., n.d. 32 p.

--EVANGELISTIC WORK

1150   BYRUM, Enoch Edwin, 1861-1942.
Behind the prison bars; a reminder of our duties toward those who have been so unfortunate as to be cast into prison. Moundsville, W.Va., Gospel Trumpet Publishing Co., 1901. 150 p.

1151   STRONG, Marie
The spirit and method of altar work. Anderson, Ind., Warner Press, n.d. 32 p.

--HISTORY

1152   BROWN, Charles Ewing, 1883-
When the trumpet sounded; a history of the Church of God Reformation Movement. Anderson, Ind., Warner Press, 1951. 402 p.

1153   BYERS, Andrew L., 1869-
Birth of a reformation; or, The life and labors of Daniel S. Warner. Anderson, Ind., Gospel Trumpet Co., 1921. 467 p.

1154   CLARK, Elmer Talmage, 1886-1966.
The small sects in America. Rev. ed. New York, Abingdon Press, c1965. 256 p.
Account of the Christian and Missionary Alliance: p. 76-77.

1155   FORREST, Aubrey Leland
"A study of the development of the basic doctrines and institutional patterns in the Church of God (Anderson, Indiana)." Unpublished Ph.D. dissertation, University of Southern California, 1948.

II. 1. Christian Holiness Association

1156 GAUSTAD, Edwin Scott, 1923-
Historical atlas of religion in America. New York, Harper & Row, 1962. xii, 179 p.
Account of Church of God (Anderson, Indiana): p. 124.

1157 GOSPEL Trumpet Company. Editorial Staff.
Brief sketch of the origin, growth, and distinctive doctrines of the Church of God Reformation Movement. Anderson, Ind., 1926. 46 p.

1158 GOSPEL Trumpet Company. Editorial Staff.
Brief sketch of the Church of God Reformation Movement. Anderson, Ind., 1951. 48 p.

1159 MEAD, Frank Spencer, 1898-
Handbook of denominations in the United States. New 5th ed. Nashville, Abingdon Press, c1970. 265 p.
"Church of God (Anderson, Indiana)": p. 74.

1160 SMITH, Frederick George, 1880-1947.
Brief sketch of the origin, growth and distinctive doctrine of the Church of God reformation movement. Anderson, Ind., Gospel Trumpet Co., 1926. 46 p.

1161 SMITH, John W. V., 1914-
Truth marches on; a brief study of the history of the Church of God Reformation Movement. Anderson, Ind., Gospel Trumpet Co., 1956. 112 p.

1162 WARNER, Daniel Sidney, 1842-1895.
"Papers, 1866-1885." 1 reel of microfilm. In Anderson College and Theological Seminary, School of Theology Library.
Diary, personal notes, budget, record of sermons preached, sermon outline book, a history of the Gospel Trumpet Co., and papers relating to Warner's business transactions on behalf of the Gospel Trumpet Co.

--HYMNS

1163 CHURCH of God (Anderson, Indiana).
Hymnal of the Church of God. Anderson, Ind., Warner Press, 1953. 510 p.

1164 BYERS, Andrew L., 1869-
Children's praise and worship, for the beginners, primary and junior grades of the Sunday school; comp. and ed. by A. L. Byers, with Bessie L. Byrum and Anna E. Koglin as advisors.... Adapted to Sunday-school work generally. Anderson, Ind., Warner Press, c1928. Unpaged.
With music.

1165 BYERS, Andrew L., 1869- , ed.
Hymns and spiritual songs for Christian worship and general church work, ed. by Andrew L. Byers and B. Elliott Warren.... Anderson, Ind., Gospel Trumpet Co., 192?. 544 p.
With music.

1166 SONGS OF Zion; a compilation of favorite hymns and songs intended for all kinds of religious service, selected under the supervision of Gospel Trumpet Company. Published in round and shaped notes..... Anderson, Ind., Gospel Trumpet Co., c1940. [220], 217-228 p.

1167 WARNER, Daniel Sidney, 1842-1895.
Anthems from the throne, by D.S. Warner and B.E. Warren. 2d ed. Grand Junction, Mich., Gospel Trumpet Publishing Co., 1888. 145 p.

1168 WARREN, Barney Elliott, 1867-1951.
Echoes from glory; for Sunday-school and for prayer, praise and gospel meetings, with primary instruction in music, by Barney E. Warren and Daniel S. Warner. Grand Junction, Mich., Gospel Trumpet Publishing Co., c1893. 220 p.
With music.

1169 WARREN, Barney Elliott, 1867-1951, ed.
Junior hymns; prepared for the Sunday school and for religious meetings of children and young people generally by B.E. Warren and A.L. Byers. Anderson, Ind., Gospel Trumpet Co., 1914. 160 p.
With music.

1170 WARREN, Barney Elliott, 1867-1951, ed.
Salvation echoes; a new collection of spiritual songs hymning the tidings of full salvation, suitable for evangelistic work and gospel services in general, ed. by B.E. Warren, A.L. Byers, C.E. Hunter, and D.O. Teasley. Moundsville, W.Va., Gospel Trumpet Publishing Co., c1900. 224 p.
With music.

--MISSIONS

1171 ENCYCLOPEDIA OF Modern Christian Missions; the Agencies. Burton L. Goddard, ed.... Camden, N.J., T. Nelson, 1967. xix, 743 p.
"Church of God, Missionary Board," by Lester A. Crose: p. 170-171; and "Church of God, National Women's Missionary Society," by Axchie A. Bolitho: p. 171.

II. 1. Christian Holiness Association

1172 NEAL, Hazel G.
Madam President: the story of Nora Siens Hunter, founder and first president of the National Woman's Missionary Society of the Church of God, by Hazel G. Neal and Axchie A. Bolitho. Anderson, Ind., Gospel Trumpet Co., 1951. 148 p.

--PERIODICALS

1173 CHURCH OF God Missions. 1- , 1951- . Anderson, Ind.

1174 EVANGELIUMS POSAUNE. 1- , 1895- . Grand Junction, Mich., Moundsville, W. Va., Anderson, Ind., York, Neb., Racine, Wis.
German language ed. of Gospel Trumpet

1175 GOSPEL TRUMPET for the Blind. 1- , 1913- . Anderson, Ind.

1176 VITAL CHRISTIANITY. 1- , 1880- . Rome City, Ind.; Indianapolis; Cardington, Ohio; Bucyrus, Ohio; Williamston, Mich.; Grand Junction, Mich.; Moundsville, W. Va.; Anderson, Ind.
1880-1963 as Gospel Trumpet; a Weekly Holiness Journal

1177 YOUTH. 1- , 1919- . Anderson, Ind.

--POLEMICAL WORKS

-- --CATHOLICISM

1178 RIGGLE, Herbert McClellan, 1872-
Roman Catholicism in the light of their own Scriptures and authorities. Anderson, Ind., Gospel Trumpet Co., 1917. 182 p.

-- --MORMONISM

1179 ORR, Charles Ebert, 1861-
A religious controversy. Anderson, Ind., Gospel Trumpet Co., n.d. 92 p.
Concerns the nature of the Christian church, Mormonism, and the Church of God.

--PUBLISHERS AND PUBLISHING

1180 BYERS, Andrew L., 1869-
The Gospel Trumpet publishing work, described and

illustrated. Anderson, Ind., Gospel Trumpet Co., 1907. 87 p.

1181 BYRUM, N. H.
Familiar names and faces; a collection of cuts from photographs of ministers, gospel workers, writers, and others, whose names are mostly familiar to the readers of the Gospel Trumpet ... also a history of the Gospel Trumpet publishing work, with cuts representing the same, and other things of interest. Moundsville, W. Va., Gospel Trumpet Publishing Co., 1902. 288 p.

--RELIGIOUS EDUCATION

1182 BYERS, Andrew L., 1869- , comp.
Bible stories and studies, with illustrations and more than three hundred questions and answers, comp. as vol. V of the Boys and Girls' Fireside Series. Anderson, Ind. Kansas City, Mo., Gospel Trumpet Co., c1920. 111 p.
Reprinted from the Shining Light, a periodical for children. cf. Pref.

1183 BYERS, Andrew L., 1869- , comp.
Birds and animals ... comp. as vol. VII of the Boys and Girls' Fireside Series. Anderson, Inc., Gospel Trumpet Co., c1921. 96 p.

1184 BYERS, Andrew L., 1869- , comp.
Countries and customs ... comp. as vol. IX of the Boys and Girls' Fireside Series. Anderson, Ind., Gospel Trumpet Co., c1921. 95 p.

1185 BYERS, Andrew L., 1869- , comp.
Plants and insects; illustrated and interspersed with poems; comp. as vol. VIII of the Boys and Girls' Fireside Series. Anderson, Ind., Gospel Trumpet Co., c1921. 96 p.

1186 BYERS, Andrew L., 1869- , comp.
Things in nature, interspersed with illustrations and poems, comp. as vol. VI of the Boys and Girls' Fireside Series. Anderson, Ind., Kansas City, Mo., Gospel Trumpet Co., c1920. 111 p.
Reprinted from the Shining Light, a periodical for children. cf. Pref.

--SERMONS

1187 CAMP-MEETING sermons; sermons preached at the general annual camp-meeting of the Church of God, held at

II. 1. Christian Holiness Association

Anderson, Indiana, June 6-15, 1913.... Anderson, Ind., Gospel Trumpet Co., 1913. 494 p.

1188 MORRISON, John Arch, 1893-1965.
Triumphant living; with an introd. by Gene W. Newberry. Anderson, Ind., Warner Press, 1953. 128 p.

1189 OLDHAM, William Dale, 1903-
The enduring Word; a book of doctrinal sermons. Anderson, Ind., Gospel Trumpet Co., 1952. 127 p.

1190 OLDHAM, William Dale, 1903-
Messages of Christian brotherhood. Anderson, Ind., Warner Press, 1951. 128 p.

--STATISTICS

1191 U.S. BUREAU of the Census.
...Census of religious bodies, 1926; Church of God (headquarters, Anderson, Ind.): statistic, history, doctrine and organization.... Washington, U.S. Government Printing Office, 1928. 11 p.

--WORK WITH YOUTH

1192 BYRUM, Isabel (Coston), 1870-1938.
The pilot's voice; words of warning to the youth and enlightenment for parents. Anderson, Ind., Gospel Trumpet Co., 1916. 224 p.

--YEARBOOKS

1193 CHURCH OF God (Anderson, Indiana).
Yearbook of the Church of God. Anderson, Ind., Published by Executive Council of the Church of God, 1917- . v. Annual.

--CANADA

1194 ENCYCLOPEDIA CANADIANA. Ottawa, Canadiana Co., 1957-1958. 10 v.
"Church of God," by V.A. Lindgren: v. 2, p. 385.

CHURCH OF GOD (Apostolic) (1896-   )

[1896-1919 as Christian Faith Band Church]

A product of the Holiness Movement, the Church of God (Apostolic) was organized by Elder Thomas J. Cox at Danville, Kentucky in 1896. Until 1919, when it incorporated under the present name, the group was known as the Christian Faith Band Church. In addition to observance of baptism and the Lord's Supper, this group practices foot washing. At present there are about 600 members in 22 congregations. The Church of God (Apostolic) has little interchange with other holiness churches.

1195   CLARK, Elmer Talmage, 1886-1966.
       The small sects in America. Rev. ed. New York, Abingdon Press, c1965. 256 p.
       Account of the Church of God (Apostolic): p. 81.

1196   MEAD, Frank Spencer, 1898-
       Handbook of denominations in the United States. New 5th ed. Nashville, Abingdon Press, c1970. 265 p.
       "Church of God (Apostolic)": p. 73.

CHURCH OF GOD (Holiness) (1883-   )

[1897-1922 separated into Church of God (Independent Holiness people), and Church of God (Unity Holiness people)]

Originating in the Southwestern Holiness Association, which formed in 1879 at the National Holiness Association camp meeting at Bismark Grove (near Lawrence), Kansas, this group was one of the first to separate from Methodism because of holiness. Attempting to actualize the New Testament ecclesia, the first Church of God congregation was "set in order" and a class of eight ministers ordained at Centralia, Missouri, in 1883. Taking over the Association-sponsored paper and Bible school, the Church of God spread throughout rural areas of north central and western Missouri and eastern Kansas. Congregational in government, the group split in 1897 over whether congregations or ministers should be represented in the annual General Convention. Those favoring congregational sovereignty established headquarters at Ft. Scott, Kansas; those supporting elder supremacy, at College Mound, Macon County, Missouri. Re-united in 1922, the group regularly lost members to the Church of the Nazarene and other groups. Though churches have been established as far east as West Virginia and as far west as California and Oregon, most of the hundred-odd congregations are located in Kansas and Missouri. After the collapse in 1938 of a short-lived merger with Missionary Bands of the World, several former Missionary Bands leaders remained and occupied key positions in the Church of God.

In 1945 the publishing plant was moved to Overland Park, Kansas, a suburb of Kansas City, where a Bible college and an annual camp meeting had been established a few years earlier.

II. 1. Christian Holiness Association

Other schools are located at Gravette, Arkansas; Ava and Kirksville, Missouri; Ft. Scott, Kansas; Culloden, West Virginia; and Lamar and Littleton, Colorado. Missionary work is conducted in Jamaica, Cayman Brac, and the Virgin Islands, in Bolivia, on the Mexican border and among West Indian immigrants in England. Statistics are not kept but membership in the United States is probably less than 3000. The official organ, <u>The Church Herald and Holiness Banner</u>, is now in its ninety-third year of publication.

1197 CHURCH OF God (Holiness).
A handbook of faith and practice. Overland Park, Kan., Herald and Banner Press, 196?. 24 p.

1198 CHURCH OF God (Holiness).
A handbook of faith and practice. Overland Park, Kan., Herald and Banner Press, 1972. 24 p.
Reprint of 196? ed.

--CHARITIES

1199 THE HISTORY of the Church of God orphanage located at College Mound, Missouri. College Mound, Mo., 1911?

--DIRECTORIES

1200 CHURCH OF God (Holiness).
Roster of accredited ministers and church directory, 19??- . College Mound, Mo.; Ft. Scott, Kan.; Overland Park, Kan., 19??- . v. Annual.
Title varies.

--DOCTRINAL AND CONTROVERSIAL WORKS

1201 CHURCH OF God (Holiness). Unification Commission.
The New Testament Church, ed. by Dale M. Yocum, secretary. Overland Park, Kan., 1962. 64 p.

1202 BROOKS, John P.
The divine church; a treatise on the origin, constitution, order, and ordinances of the church, being a vindication of the New Testament ecclesia, and an exposure of the antiscriptural character of the modern church of sect. Columbia, Mo., Herald Publishing House, 1891. 283 p.

1203 BROOKS, John P.
The Divine Church; a treatise on the origin, constitution, order, and ordinances of the church, being a vindication of the New Testament ecclesia, and an exposure of the

anti-scriptural character of the modern church of sect. El Dorado Springs, Mo., Witt Printing Co., 1960. 283 p.
Reprint of 1891 ed.

1204 DINIUS, Will L.
Ekklesia. Fort Scott, Kan., Publishing Headquarters of the Church Advocate and Holiness Banner, 1907.

1205 KRING, James Arthur, 1873-
Trumpet blasts to the unsaved. College Mound, Mo., Herald Print, 1907. 91 p.

1206 SMELSER, Fred L.
Outline study of All about the Bible, by Sidney Collett. Gravette, Ark., Holiness Bible School, 194?. 54 p.

1207 SMELSER, Fred L.
A study on doctrines of Christianity; outline of Binney's Theological compend.... Gravette, Ark., Holiness Bible School, 194?. 73 p.

1208 SMELSER, Fred L.
A study on New Testament history, by Elder S. L. [i.e. F. L.] Smelser. Gravette, Ark., Holiness Bible School, 194?. 53 p.

1209 SMELSER, Fred L.
A study on Old Testament history. Gravette, Ark., Holiness Bible School, 194?. 2 v.

1210 SNEED, J. A., -1944.
One Church of God. College Mound, Mo., Church Herald Press, n.d.

1211 WATKINS, Aura Clay, 1885-1945.
Entire sanctification (the obtaining and retaining). Kansas City, Mo., 1915. 32 p.

1212 YOCUM, Dale Morris
Conformed to Christ. Cincinnati, Printed by Revivalist Press, 1962. 215 p.

-- --GLOSSOLALIA

1213 SMITH, George H.
The unknown tongue. 2d ed. Fort Scott, Kan., Church Herald and Holiness Banner, 1928. 62 p.

--EVANGELISTIC WORK

1214 WATKINS, Aura Clay, 1885-1945.
Pacific coast evangelistic tour; or, The opening of new

fields for holiness. Louisville, Pentecostal Publishing Co., 1914. 118 p.

--HISTORY

1215 COWEN, Clarence Eugene, 1904-
A history of the Church of God (Holiness). Ann Arbor, Mich., University Microfilms, 1949.
(University Microfilms, Ann Arbor, Mich., Publication no. 1365)

1216 COWEN, Clarence Eugene, 1904-
A history of the Church of God (Holiness). Overland Park, Kan., Herald and Banner Press, 1949. 233 p.

1217 JONES, Charles Edwin, 1932-
"Perfectionist persuasion: a social profile of the National Holiness Movement within American Methodism, 1867-1936." Unpublished Ph.D. dissertation, University of Wisconsin, 1968. 669ℓ.
Includes account of Church of God origins.

1218 KIERGAN, Arthur M., 1848-1933.
Historical sketches of the revival of true holiness and local church polity from 1865-1916. Fort Scott, Kan., Board of Publication of the Church Advocate and Good Way, 1972. Cover-title, 87 p.
Double columns.
Published at the decision of the convention of 1971 of the churches of God (commonly known as the Independent Holiness People).
Autobiographical.

--HYMNS

1219 GOOD WAY hymns and songs. Chillicothe, Mo., Good Way Publishing House, 189?. 202 p.

--MISSIONS

1220 DALE, Edith M.
The answer is a miracle; a drama which can be adapted for Christmas or missionary programs.... Overland Park, Kan., Herald & Banner Press, c1972. 16 p.

1221 ENCYCLOPEDIA OF Modern Christian Missions; the Agencies. Burton L. Goddard, ed.... Camden, N.J., T. Nelson, 1967. xix, 743 p.
"Church of God (Holiness), Department of Missions": p. 173.

--PASTORAL THEOLOGY

-- --AUTHORITATIVE SOURCES

1222 HOGUE, Wilson Thomas, bp., 1852-1920.
A hand-book of homiletics and pastoral theology. Overland Park, Kan., Herald and Banner Press, 1966. 454 p.
Reprint of 1914 ed.

--PERIODICALS

1223 CHURCH HERALD. 1- , 1901-1922. College Mound, Mo., Kansas City, Mo.
Superseded by Church Herald and Holiness Banner

1224 CHURCH HERALD and Holiness Banner. 1- , 1878- .
Savannah, Mo., St. Joseph, Mo., College Mound, Mo., Chillicothe, Mo., Fort Scott, Kan., Overland Park, Kar
1878-1896 as Good Way; 1896-1922 as Church Advocate and Holiness Banner

1225 CHURCH WITNESS. 1, May 11-June 22, 1900. Ft. Scott, Kan.
Merged with Church Herald

1226 GOOD WAY. 1- , 1897-1900. College Mound, Mo., The Good Way Association.

1227 JAMAICA CHURCH Herald. 1- , 1971- . Kingston, Jamaica, W.I.

--BOLIVIA

1228 FIRESTONE, Elvira R. (Englund)
Wonderful works of God. n.p., 195?. 126 p.
Autobiographical.

--MISSOURI

1229 GENERAL HISTORY of Macon County, Missouri. Chicago, Henry Taylor and Co., 1910. 945 p.
Edgar White, comp.
Account of Church of God (Independent Holiness people): p. 167-169.

1230 JONES, Charles Edwin, 1932-
"Disinherited or rural?; a historical case study in urban Holiness religion," Missouri Historical Review, LXVI (Apr. 1972), 395-412.

II. 1. Christian Holiness Association

CHURCH OF GOD (Northern Indiana Eldership) (1876-18??)

Separating from the Churches of God in North America (General Eldership) in 1876 over the latter's tolerance of secret societies, the Northern Indiana Eldership was deeply influenced by the National Holiness Movement. D.S. Warner, founder of the Church of God (Anderson, Indiana), served as editor of the quasi-official publication of the group. People formerly affiliated with Northern Indiana Eldership churches comprised the nucleus of the first congregation of Warner's group, which formed at Beaver Dam, Indiana in 1881. The Warner separation appears to have spelled the death warrant of the Northern Indiana Eldership which seems soon to have dispersed.

1231 SMITH, John W. V., 1914-
Truth marches on; a brief study of the history of the Church of God Reformation Movement. Anderson, Ind., Gospel Trumpet Co., 1956. 112 p.
Account of the Northern Indiana Eldership of the Church of God: p. 11-13.

CHURCHES OF GOD (Independent Holiness People) (1922-   )

A minority of the congregational sovereignty faction of the Church of God (Holiness) which did not re-unite in 1922, Churches of God (Independent Holiness People) has its headquarters in Ft. Scott, Kansas. There, for a number of years, it has issued The Church Advocate and Good Way. In 1972 fifteen churches were represented in the annual Convention. The constituency is scattered from Illinois to California. Little aggressive home missionary work has been conducted for many years, and the group, which never consisted of more than a few hundred people, appears to be dying. Support, however, is given to missionary work in Japan and Mexico and among American Indians in South Dakota and Wyoming. Unusual among holiness people, the Convention has every year since 1948 passed resolutions condemning Christian participation in war.

--DOCTRINAL AND CONTROVERSIAL WORKS

1232 JOHNSTON, Pearl Rose, 1856-
God and man; the law of God; the Christian sabbath; what is man?; the density of man. Fort Scott, Kan., The author, 1916. 160 p.

--HISTORY

1233 KIERGAN, Arthur M., 1848-1933.
Historical sketches of the revival of true holiness and

local church polity from 1865-1916. Fort Scott, Kan., Board of Publication of the Church Advocate and Good Way, 1972. Cover-title, 87 p.
Double columns.
Published at the decision of the convention of 1971 of the Churches of God (commonly known as the Independent Holiness People).
Autobiographical.

--PERIODICALS

1234 CHURCH ADVOCATE and Good Way. ns 1- , May 13, 1926- . Ft. Scott, Kan.
May 13, 1926 incorrectly numbered v. 2, no. 38

1235 MISSIONARY CHALLENGER. 1- , 1962- . St. Louis, Mo.

--JAPAN

1236 ENCYCLOPEDIA OF Modern Christian Missions; the Agencies. Camden, N.J., T. Nelson, 1967. xix, 743 p.
"Church of God at Baden," by L.W. Conway: p. 173-174.

1237 LABERTEW, Dorothy
The missionary barrel. Overland Park, Kan., Publishe for the Church of God at Baden by Herald and Banner Press 1972. 79 p.

CHURCHES OF GOD, HOLINESS (1914-)

Consisting in 1970 of 25,600 members in 32 congregations, the Churches of God, Holiness, is the outgrowth of the work of K.H. Burruss, a black evangelist. Beginning in Atlanta, Georgia, in 1914 and in Norfolk, Virginia, in 1916, the group spread rapidly. By 1922 when it incorporated as the National Convention of the Churches of God, Holiness, it had 22 churches in eleven states the West Indies and the Canal Zone. Stressing entire sanctification and divine healing (belief in the latter is a condition of membership), this black group has little contact with the large, predominantly white Holiness denominations. All pastors are appointe by one bishop elected by the national delegated convention.

1238 CLARK, Elmer Talmage, 1886-1966.
The small sects in America. Rev. ed. New York, Abingdon Press, c1965. 256 p.
Account of the Churches of God, Holiness: p. 120.

II. 1. Christian Holiness Association

1239   MEAD, Frank Spencer, 1898-
        Handbook of denominations in the United States. New
        5th ed. Nashville, Abingdon Press, c1970. 265 p.
        "Churches of God, Holiness": p. 87-88.

--STATISTICS

1240   U.S. BUREAU of the Census.
        ...Census of religious bodies, 1926; Churches of God,
        Holiness: statistics, denominational history, doctrine, and
        organization.... Washington, U.S. Government Printing
        Office, 1929. 8 p.

CHURCHES OF GOD IN NORTH AMERICA (General Eldership) (1830-   )

[1830-1845 as Church of God; 1845-1903 as Church of God in North America (General Eldership)]

An outgrowth of the evangelistic activities of John Winebrenner (1797-1860), the first congregation of the Churches of God in North America was organized at Harrisburg, Pennsylvania, in 1826. The eldership, consisting of seven preachers, was formed in 1830. Often called the Winebrennerian Church of God, this old German-American group espoused Wesleyan ideas of holiness in the late nineteenth century but has practically lost this emphasis in the twentieth. The group's chief contribution to the Holiness Movement was Daniel Sidney Warner (1842-1895), founder of the Church of God (Anderson, Indiana). The General Eldership sponsors a college and a theological seminary at Findlay, Ohio. Denominational headquarters is in Harrisburg. In 1970 the church claimed 356 churches and 35,905 members.

--HISTORY

1241   CLARK, Elmer Talmage, 1886-1966.
        The small sects in America. Rev. ed. New York,
        Abingdon Press, c1965. 256 p.
        Account of the Churches of God in North America
        (General Eldership): p. 81-82.

1242   GAUSTAD, Edwin Scott, 1923-
        Historical atlas of religion in America. New York,
        Harper & Row, 1962. xii, 179 p.
        Account of Churches of God in North America (General
        Eldership): p. 123-124.

1243   MEAD, Frank Spencer, 1898-
        Handbook of denominations in the United States. New

5th ed. Nashville, Abingdon Press, c1970. 265 p.
"Churches of God in North America (General Eldership)": p. 88-89.

--MISSIONS

1244 ENCYCLOPEDIA OF modern Christian missions; the agencies Burton L. Goddard, ed.... Camden, N.J., T. Nelson, 1967. xix, 743 p.
"Churches of God in North America, Board of Missions, Inc.": p. 186-187.

CHURCH OF THE GOSPEL (1911-19??)

[1911-1930 as Church of God]

Organized as the Church of God at Pittsfield, Massachusetts, in 1911, this group stressed entire sanctification as a second work of grace, the imminent second coming of Christ, and baptism by immersion. In 1930 the name was changed to the Church of the Gospel to avoid confusion with other groups bearing the title Church of God. With a handful of churches and less than a hundred members in 1949, the group was actively engaged in publishing and distributing "Narrow Way Tracts." No recent information or statistics are available.

1245 CLARK, Elmer Talmage, 1886-1966.
The small sects in America. Rev. ed. New York, Abingdon Press, c1965. 256 p.
Account of the Church of the Gospel: p. 82.

CHURCH OF THE NAZARENE (1895-1907)

The outgrowth of a tabernacle church organized in downtown Los Angeles in 1895, the Church of the Nazarene had spread into the Northwest and as far east as Chicago by 1907. Founded by Phineas F. Bresee and Joseph P. Widney, formerly prominent members of the Southern California Conference of the Methodist Episcopal Church, the church originally proposed to evangelize the urban poor. Widney, who had served as president of the University of Southern California, returned to the Methodist fold after a few years, leaving Bresee the sole leader. Acting much as a bishop, Bresee vigorously promoted the work. The Nazarene Messenger, a paper begun by the Los Angeles First Church, became

II. 1. Christian Holiness Association

the official publication. A Bible college was started in Los Angeles in 1902, and sponsorship of foreign missionary work in India undertaken in 1907. That year the denomination united with the Association of Pentecostal Churches of America under the title Pentecostal Church of the Nazarene. At the Chicago assembly in which the merger was ratified, the Church of the Nazarene reported 48 congregations and 3827 members, 1400 of which were affiliated with the mother church in Los Angeles.

1246 CHURCH OF the Nazarene (1895-1907). Assembly.
Proceedings of the ... annual assembly. 1st-11th; -1906. Los Angeles. Annual.

--DOCTRINAL AND CONTROVERSIAL WORKS

1247 WIDNEY, Joseph Pomeroy, 1841-1938.
The way of life; Holiness unto the Lord; the indwelling Spirit. Los Angeles, Commercial Printing House, 1900. 152 p.

--HISTORY

1248 GIRVIN, Ernest Alexander, 1857-
Phineas F. Bresee: a prince in Israel, a biography. Kansas City, Mo., Pentecostal Nazarene Publishing House, 1916. 463 p.

1249 REDFORD, Maury English
The rise of the Church of the Nazarene. Kansas City, Mo., Nazarene Publishing House, 1948. 208 p.
Account of the origin and growth of the Church of the Nazarene, 1895-1907: p. 46-81.

1250 SMITH, Timothy Lawrence, 1924-
Called unto holiness; the story of the Nazarenes: the formative years. Kansas City, Mo., Nazarene Publishing House, 1962. 413 p.
Account of the origin and growth of the Church of the Nazarene, 1895-1907: p. 91-150.

--HYMNS

1251 HARRIS, John M., ed.
Waves of glory; editors: J. M. Harris and W. J. Kirkpatrick. Los Angeles, Nazarene Publishing Co., 1905. 270 p.

--PERIODICALS

1252 NAZARENE MESSENGER. 1-14, 1896-1911. Los Angeles, Calif.
1896-1900 as Nazarene

--SERMONS

1253 BRESEE, Phineas Franklin, 1838-1915.
The certainties of faith; ten sermons by the founder of the Church of the Nazarene, with an introd. and notes on the author's life by Timothy L. Smith, Ph.D. Kansas City, Mo., Nazarene Publishing House, 1958. 95 p.

--INDIA

1254 THE STORY of Mrs. Sukhoda Benargees and Hope School, Calcutta, India. Los Angeles, Calif., Nazarene Publishing Co., 1906.

CHURCH OF THE NAZARENE (1908-   )

[1908-1919 as Pentecostal Church of the Nazarene]

The largest and most comprehensive of the Holiness denominations geographically, the Church of the Nazarene traces its origin to the union of the Holiness Church of Christ and the Pentecostal Church of the Nazarene at Pilot Point, Texas, in 1908. The latter group had been formed a year earlier at Chicago by the merger of the Church of the Nazarene centered in California and the Association of Pentecostal Churches of America concentrated in New York and the New England states. All had been deeply influenced by the National Holiness Movement and had large contingents of former Methodists. All had been in existence for less than fifteen years in 1908. At the outset the new group claimed 10,414 members in 228 congregations. Ardently defending entire sanctification as a definite second work of grace, this group has tolerated a variety of opinions relating to modes of baptism, the Millennium, and faith healing, but denies any connection between speaking in unknown tongues and the Baptism with the Holy Spirit. To dissociate itself from such an identity, in 1919 the Church of the Nazarene dropped Pentecostal from its name.

Aggressive evangelism, prudent administration, and accessions by merger with, and defections from, smaller Holiness groups, have swelled the membership to forty times its original size. Church government combines features from congregationalism

II. 1. Christian Holiness Association

and episcopacy, but has steadily moved toward centralization, particularly since 1923 when control of general church administration was vested in a single board. Since 1912, the denomination has had its headquarters in Kansas City, Missouri, where a large publishing plant is maintained and the official organ, the Herald of Holiness, is issued. In 1945 a graduate theological seminary was established there. The church sponsors liberal arts colleges at Wollaston, Massachusetts; Nashville, Tennessee; Mount Vernon, Ohio; Kankakee, Illinois; Olathe, Kansas; Bethany, Oklahoma; Nampa, Idaho; San Diego, California; and Winnipeg, Manitoba; and Bible colleges in Colorado, England, Germany, South Africa, and Australia. Mergers and missionary activity have extended the work of this group to all parts of North America and to every other continent. Augmented by additions from the Pentecostal Mission of Tennessee and the Pentecostal Church of Scotland in 1915, the Laymen's Holiness Association of the Dakotas and Minnesota in 1922, the International Holiness Mission and the Calvary Holiness Church of Great Britain in 1952 and 1955 respectively, and the Gospel Workers Church of Canada in 1958, the group has been highly self-conscious if not sectarian. By 1930, the "Nazarene" title had supplanted "Holiness" in church-sponsored college names. While cooperating with other Holiness groups informally, the Church of the Nazarene did not seek institutional membership in the National Holiness Association until 1968.

1255 CHURCH OF the Nazarene.
  Manual: history, constitution, government, ritual, 1907- . Los Angeles, Pilot Point, Tex., Kansas City, Mo. v.
  Quadrennial: 1911-1923, 1928-
  Subtitle varies.

1256 CHURCH OF the Nazarene. Board of General Superintendents.
  Quadrennial address. n.p., 1940. 24 p.

1257 CHURCH OF the Nazarene. General Assembly.
  Journal. 1st- , 1907- . Los Angeles, Kansas City, Mo. v.
  Quadrennial: 1911-1923, 1928-
  1907-1919 as Proceedings.

1258 MUELDER, Walter Goerge, 1907-
  "From sect to church; rural Pentecostal sects and the Church of the Nazarene," Christendom, X, no. 4 (1945), 450-462.

1259 PERKINS, Floyd J.
  "The Church of the Nazarene and its historical evangelical heritage." Unpublished M.A. thesis, University of Kansas City, 1952. 154ℓ .

1260 POWERS, Hardy Carroll, 1900-1972.
Manual: Church of the Nazarene, 1908-1958; comparisons and comments. Kansas City, Mo., Nazarene Publishing House, 1958. 80 p.

1261 RAWLINGS, Elden Everette
"Church of the Nazarene assembly," Christianity Today, XII (July 19, 1968), 50-51.

1262 REED, Harold William, 1909-
"The growth of a contemporary sect-type institution as reflected in the development of the Church of the Nazarene." Unpublished Th. D. dissertation, Graduate School of Religion, University of Southern California, 1943.

--DISTRICTS. CANADA CENTRAL.

1263 CHURCH OF the Nazarene. Districts. Canada Central.
Who knoweth whether thou art come to the kingdom for such a time as this? Twenty-fifth anniversary, Canada Central District, Church of the Nazarene, 1936-1961. Toronto, Ont., 1961. Unpaged.

--DISTRICTS. CHICAGO CENTRAL.

1264 MOORE, Mark Reynolds, 1916-
Fifty ... and beyond; a history of the Chicago Central District, Church of the Nazarene. Kankakee, Ill., 1954. 149 p.

--DISTRICTS. LOUISIANA.

1265 CARRUTH, Wallace E.
A history of the Louisiana District, Church of the Nazarene. Bossier City, La., Touchstone's, 1955. 124 p.

--DISTRICTS. MICHIGAN.

1266 U.S. WORK Projects Administration.
Inventory of the church archives of Michigan: Church of the Nazarene, Michigan District Assembly, prepared by the Michigan Historical Records Survey Project, Division of Community Service Programs, Work Projects Administration. Detroit, Michigan Historical Records Survey Projects, 1942. 50 p.

II. 1. Christian Holiness Association

--DISTRICTS. NEW ENGLAND.

1267 WASHBURN, Florence M.
Looking back over fifty years: New England District, Church of the Nazarene. n.p., 1957. 12 p.

--DISTRICTS. NORTHWEST.

1268 ZACHARY, E. E., comp.
Fiftieth anniversary book, comp. in commemoration of fifty years of progress, 1904-1954. Spokane?, Wash., Northwest District, Church of the Nazarene, 1954. Unpaged.

--DISTRICTS. WASHINGTON-PHILADELPHIA.

1269 BOWER, Reuben Edward, 1974- , ed.
Bird's-eye view of the Washington-Philadelphia District. Philadelphia, 1917.

1270 TAYLOR, Milton H., ed.
Pictorial review of the Washington-Philadelphia District. n.p., 1950.

--DISTRICTS. WISCONSIN.

1271 U.S. WORK Projects Administration.
Inventory of church archives of Wisconsin: Church of the Nazarene, prepared by the Wisconsin Historical Records Survey, Division of Community Service Programs, Work Projects Administration, sponsored by University of Wisconsin and State Historical Society of Wisconsin. Madison, Wisconsin Historical Records Survey, 1941. 58 p.

--ADDRESSES, ESSAYS, LECTURES

1272 CHAPMAN, James Blaine, 1884-1947.
Let the winds blow; selected writings comp. by Samuel Young. Kansas City, Mo., Beacon Hill Press, 1957. 102 p.

--ANECDOTES, REMINISCENCES, SATIRE, ETC.

1273 JONES, Lum
The new pastor. Kansas City, Mo., Nazarene Publishing House, 1926. 96 p.

1274 LEHMAN, Frederick Martin, 1868-
The man in black. Kansas City, Mo., Publishing

House of the Pentecostal Church of the Nazarene, 1913. 192 p.
Autobiographical allegory on the carnal mind.

1275 MARTIN, Paul La Rush, 1915-
Life in a Nazarene parsonage. Kansas City, Mo., Nazarene Publishing House, 195?.

1276 SMITH, Hannah (Brown)
"For heaven's sake," Atlantic, CLXXXI (June 1948), 71-74.

1277 SMITH, Hannah (Brown)
For heaven's sake. Boston, Little, Brown, 1949. 266 p.
An autobiographical novel of a girlhood spent in a Nazarene parsonage.

1278 STRANG, Clifford Benjamin, 1895-
Meeting life situations. Kansas City, Mo., Beacon Hill Press, 1945. 125 p.

1279 STRANG, Clifford Benjamin, 1895-
Over the doorstep. Kansas City, Mo., Beacon Hill Press, 1947. 93 p.

--APOLOGETIC WORKS

1280 CHURCH OF the Nazarene.
Church of the Nazarene: doors of opportunity. Kansas City, Mo., Nazarene Publishing House, 1933. Cover-title, 32 p.

1281 CHURCH OF the Nazarene.
The Church of the Nazarene. Kansas City, Mo., Nazarene Publishing House, 1946. 40 p.

1282 CHURCH OF the Nazarene.
The Church of the Nazarene.... Kansas City, Mo., 1947. 48 p.
Cover title: Church of the Nazarene: a bit of history, a brief statement of doctrine, some interesting statistics.

1283 CHURCH OF the Nazarene.
The Church of the Nazarene.... Kansas City, Mo., 1963. 12 p.
Cover-title: Church of the Nazarene: history, doctrine information.

1284 CHURCH OF the Nazarene.
Presenting your nearby Church of the Nazarene. Kan-

II. 1. Christian Holiness Association 139

sas City, Mo., Nazarene Publishing House, 1971. Folder.

1285 BEEBE, Theodore Eaton
Hatching chickens for the hawks. Long Beach, Calif., T.E. Beebe, 1920. 59 p.
"Poems in this book written by F.M. Lehman."

1286 FISHER, Charles William, 1916-
Why I am a Nazarene and not--a Mormon, a Roman Catholic, a Jehovah's Witness, a Christian Scientist, a Seventh-Day Adventist. Kansas City, Mo., Nazarene Publishing House, 1958. 144 p.

1287 HAMLIN, Howard H.
Let's look at our church. Kansas City, Mo., Nazarene Publishing House, 1969. 143 p.
"Second revised edition."

1288 PARROTT, Leslie, 1922-
Introducing--the Nazarenes. Kansas City, Mo., Nazarene Publishing House, 1969. 48 p.

1289 PRICE, Ross Eugene, 1907-
Nazarene manifesto; [the unique significance of the Church of the Nazarene in today's world]. Kansas City, Mo., Beacon Hill Press, 1968. 55 p.

1290 A QUADRENNIUM of progress, 1952-56, Nazarene Pastor, IX (June-July 1956).

1291 REED, Harold William, 1909-
You and your church. Kansas City, Mo., Beacon Hill Press, 1953. 96 p.

1292 SPRUCE, Fletcher Clarke
Now here is your church. Kansas City, Mo., Beacon Hill Press, 1971. 40 p.
Reprint of 1959 ed.

1293 YOUNG, Samuel, 1901-
The people called Nazarenes. Kansas City, Mo., Beacon Hill Press, 196?. Folder.

--BIOGRAPHY

1294 CORBETT, C. T.
Influence of the country church. Garden City, Kan., Elliott Printers, 1959. 28 p.

1295 CORBETT, C. T.
   Our pioneer Nazarenes. Kansas City, Mo., Nazarene Publishing House, 1958. 120 p.

1296 DuBOIS, Lauriston J., ed.
   The chaplains see world missions. Kansas City, Mo., Nazarene Publishing House, 1946. 157 p.
   "An authorized publication of the Missionary Study Committee, Church of the Nazarene."

1297 GISH, Carol (Spell)
   Here am I [the story of young people God called to the foreign mission field]. Kansas City, Mo., Nazarene Publishing House, 1960. 87 p.

1298 HINSHAW, Amy N.
   Native torch bearers. Kansas City, Mo., Nazarene Publishing House, 1934. 207 p.
   Woman's Missionary Society study book for 1934-1935.

1299 MILLER, Basil William, 1897-
   Out under the stars; life sketches of early Nazarene leaders. Kansas City, Mo., Nazarene Publishing House, 1941. 91 p.

1300 PASADENA, CALIF. Bresee Avenue Church of the Nazarene
   Fidelis Business and Professional Class honors our pioneers for faithful service to God and country. Pasadena, Calif., 1964. Unpaged.

--CATECHISMS AND CREEDS

1301 CHAPMAN, James Blaine, 1884-1947.
   Nazarene primer. Kansas City, Mo., Nazarene Publishing House, 1949. 64 p.

--CHARITIES

1302 JERNIGAN, Charles Brougher, 1863-1930.
   The Nazarene Home, a historic sketch. Bethany Station, Oklahoma City, Okla., 1912.

--CHURCH EXTENSION

1303 CHURCH OF the Nazarene. Department of Home Missions and Evangelism.
   Enlarge thy borders; the story of home missions in the Church of the Nazarene. Kansas City, Mo., Nazarene Publishing House, 1952. 124 p.

II. 1. Christian Holiness Association

1304 DAVIS, Leo C.
Today's pioneers; home mission miracles in southwest Indiana, with an introd. by Dr. Ralph Earle. Kansas City, Mo., Beacon Hill Press, 1954. 45 p.

--CHURCH WORK

1305 CHURCH OF the Nazarene. Commission on Christian Service Training.
The Christian Service Training Course; general bulletin, 1945. Kansas City, Mo., 1945. 47 p.

1306 LEWIS, Voyle H.
Christian worker's guide. Kansas City, Mo., Beacon Hill Press, 195?. 36 p.

1307 MILLER, Basil William, 1897-
Bible readings for personal workers. Kansas City, Mo., Nazarene Publishing House, 1941. 94 p.

1308 MOORE, Mark Reynolds, 1916-
The ministry of ushering. Kansas City, Mo., Beacon Hill Press, 1957. 76 p.

1309 PARROTT, Leslie, 1922-
Building today's church; how pastors and laymen work together. Kansas City, Mo., Beacon Hill Press, 1971. 228 p.

1310 PARROTT, Leslie, 1922-
How to usher, by Leslie [and Lora Lee] Parrott. Grand Rapids, Mich., Zondervan Publishing House, 1954. 61 p.

1311 PARROTT, Leslie, 1922-
The usher's manual; a spiritual and practical guidebook. Grand Rapids, Mich., Zondervan Publishing House, 1970. 64 p.

--CLERGY

1312 CHURCH OF the Nazarene. Department of Education.
Questions on the course of study for local preachers, licensed ministers, licensed deaconesses, song evangelists, ministers of music, and directors of Christian education, prepared by the Department of Education of the Church of the Nazarene. 1964 ed. Kansas City, Mo., Nazarene Publishing House, 1964. 181 p.

1313 BLANEY, Harvey Judson Smith, 1905-
"The attitudes of Nazarene ministers toward their profession." Unpublished Th.D. dissertation, Boston University, 1960. xii, 194ℓ.

1314 CHAMBERS, Joseph Leon
"Task identification and analysis for administration in the Church of the Nazarene." Unpublished Ed.D. dissertation, University of Southern Mississippi, 1966. 186ℓ.

1315 McGRAW, James, 1913-
"A comparison of MMPI scores and other variables with subsequent ratings of Nazarene ministers by their district superintendents." Unpublished Ph.D. dissertation, University of Kansas, 1969. 187ℓ.

-- --DIRECTORIES

1316 CHURCH OF the Nazarene. Department of Evangelism.
Directory of evangelists, Church of the Nazarene, prepared by Department of Evangelism. Kansas City, Mo., Nazarene Publishing House, 195?. 72 p.

-- --WIVES

1317 LEWIS, Esther (Lambert)
We also build; the role of the minister's wife. Kansas City, Mo., Beacon Hill Press, 1969. 111 p.

1318 PARROTT, Lora Lee (Montgomery), 1923-
How to be a preacher's wife and like it; introd. by Mrs. Billy Graham. Grand Rapids, Mich., Zondervan Publishing House, 1956. 99 p.

1319 WILLIAMSON, Audrey (Johnston)
Far above rubies; meditations for the minister's wife. Kansas City, Mo., Beacon Hill Press, 1961. 128 p.

--CONDUCT OF LIFE

1320 AIKEN, Irene
Mom's musings; random thoughts on home problems. Kansas City, Mo., Beacon Hill Press, c1972. 54 p.

1321 ANDERSON, Tony Marshall, 1888-
After holiness, what? Kansas City, Mo., Nazarene Publishing House, 1929. 128 p.
Also issued under title: After sanctification.

1322 AYCOCK, Dell (Davis), -1967.
Listen girls. Kansas City, Mo., Nazarene Publishing House, 1928. 50 p.

II. 1. Christian Holiness Association

1323 AYCOCK, Jarrette E., -1966.
Tithing--your questions answered. Kansas City, Mo., Nazarene Publishing House, 1955. 22 p.

1324 BENNETT, Willis G.
Conflicts of the intercessor. Kansas City, Mo., Nazarene Publishing House, 1929. 78 p.

1325 BENNETT, Willis G.
The hornet. 2d ed. Nashville, Bennett, 1940. 42 p.

1326 BROWN, Warren Shelburne, 1918-
Let's look at our rules; a study of our general rules. Kansas City, Mo., Beacon Hill Press, 1956. 31 p.

1327 CHANDLER, Ward B.
Family religion. Amarillo, Tex., Chandler's Publications, 1954. Unpaged.

1328 CHAPMAN, James Blaine, 1884-1947.
Ask Doctor Chapman. Kansas City, Mo., Beacon Hill Press, 1943. 192 p.

1329 CHAPMAN, James Blaine, 1884-1947.
A Christian, what it means to be one. 4th ed. Kansas City, Mo., Beacon Hill Press, 1941. 29 p.

1330 CHAPMAN, James Blaine, 1884-1947.
Your life, make the most of it. Kansas City, Mo., Beacon Hill Press, 1943. 32 p.

1331 CHISM, Fairy Steele, 1899-1971.
Tips to Christians. Kansas City, Mo., Beacon Hill Press, 1966. 48 p.

1332 CORLETT, David Shelby, 1894-
ABC's of stewardship. Kansas City, Mo., Nazarene Publishing House, 19??.

1333 CORLETT, David Shelby, 1894-
The Christian sabbath. Kansas City, Mo., Nazarene Publishing House, 1939. 32 p.

1334 DeLONG, Russell Victor, 1901-
The game of life; specifications for character engineering, by Russell V. DeLong and Mendell Taylor. Grand Rapids, Mich., Eerdmans, 1954. 89 p.

1335 DeLONG, Russell Victor, 1901-
Illnesses of the modern soul. Kansas City, Mo., Beacon Hill Press, 1965. 111 p.

1336 DIRKSE, Neal C.
        Now that you're sanctified. Kansas City, Mo., Beacon Hill Press, 1959. 40 p.

1337 DuBOIS, Lauriston J.
        Guidelines for conduct; an introduction to the General Rules of the Church of the Nazarene. Kansas City, Mo., Beacon Hill Press, 1965. 87 p.

1338 DuBOIS, Lauriston J.
        Life's intimate friendships. Kansas City, Mo., Beacon Hill Press, 1949. 95 p.

1339 DuBOIS, Lauriston J.
        Reverance in the Christian life. Kansas City, Mo., Beacon Hill Press, 1959. 72 p.

1340 DuBOIS, Lauriston J.
        Youth and recreation. Kansas City, Mo., Beacon Hill Press, 1948. 96 p.

1341 DUNNING, H. Ray
        "Nazarene ethics as seen in a theological, historical and sociological context." Unpublished Ph.D. dissertation, Vanderbilt University, 1969. 229ℓ.

1342 FISHER, Charles William, 1916-
        Don't park here! New York, Abingdon Press, 1962. 158 p.

1343 FLOWERS, Sumpter Lee, 1881-
        The serpent's fang. Kansas City, Mo., Nazarene Publishing House, n.d. 47 p.
        On evil speaking.

1344 GARSEE, Jarrell Willis, 1930-
        "Some developmental correlates of individually perceived generation differences in value role-taking." Unpublished Ph.D. dissertation, Ohio State University, 1972.

1345 GISH, Carol (Spell)
        Tips for teen-agers; your manners are showing. Cartoons by Ernest Lemieux. Kansas City, Mo., Beacon Hill Press, 1956. 80 p.

1346 GOODWIN, John Wesley, 1869-1945.
        Tithing, the touchstone of stewardship. Kansas City, Mo., Nazarene Publishing House, 19??. 48 p.

1347 GOODWIN, Paul John, 1896-
        Radio and the Spirit-filled life. Kansas City, Nazarene Publishing House, n.d.

II. 1. Christian Holiness Association

1348 HAMLIN, Howard H.
 From here to maturity. Kansas City, Mo., Beacon Hill Press, 195?. 94 p.

1349 HARDING, Ulla Earl, 1883-1958.
 An innocent vice? Pasadena, Calif., The author, n.d. 102 p.
 On smoking.

1350 HARPER, Albert Foster, 1907-
 Christian simplicity; an honest look at the dress question.... Kansas City, Mo., Beacon Hill Press, 1962. 15 p.

1351 HENSON, Jacob Cornelius, 1875-
 Faithful in stewardship. Kansas City, Mo., Beacon Hill Press, 1954. 27 p.

1352 HERRELL, Noah Benjamin, 1877-1953.
 Christ at the controls of life. Kansas City, Mo., Nazarene Publishing House, 1942.

1353 HESLOP, William Greene, 1886-
 The secret of a happy wedded life; thoughts, truths, anecdotes, verse and helps for everyone's inspiration. Grand Rapids, Mich., Zondervan Publishing House, 1941. 117 p.

1354 LEE, Earl G.
 The cycle of victorious living; Psalms 37: commit, trust, delight, rest. Kansas City, Mo., Beacon Hill Press, 1971. 55 p.

1355 LONDON, Holland Bryan, 1908-
 Pentecostal possibilities in youth. Kansas City, Mo., Nazarene Publishing House, 1939. 26 p.

1356 LONDON, Holland Bryan, 1908-
 This movie menace. n.p., 194?. 19 p.
 "Address ... delivered at Northwest Nazarene College."

1357 LOWN, A. J.
 Your purse and you. Kansas City, Mo., Nazarene Publishing House, 1960.

1358 LUDWIG, Minnie E. (Brink), 1877-1958.
 Living for Jesus. Kansas City, Mo., Pentecostal Nazarene Publishing House, 1916. 111 p.

1359 LUDWIG, Theodore, 1871-1957.
 The life of victory; or, Saved, sanctified and kept. Kansas City, Mo., Nazarene Publishing House, 1929. 93 p.

1360 LUNN, Mervel
   Treasures in heaven; the abundant life of stewardship.
Kansas City, Mo., Nazarene Publishing House, 1963.   93 p.

1361 McCLAIN, Carl Sheldon, 1899-
   Morals and the movies.   Kansas City, Mo., Beacon
Hill Press, 1970.   30 p.

1362 McCULLOUGH, Melvin
   The inevitable encounter; how teens can triumph over
temptation.   Kansas City, Mo., Beacon Hill Press, 1972.
80 p.

1363 MILLER, Basil William, 1897-
   The gold under the grass.   Nashville, Cokesbury Press,
1930.   230 p.

1364 MUNRO, Bertha, 1887-
   Not somehow, but triumphantly; talks to young people.
Kansas City, Mo., Beacon Hill Press, 1950.   119 p.

1365 PARROTT, Leslie, 1922-
   The art of happy Christian living; the principles and
practices of Christian living.   Grand Rapids, Mich., Zondervan Publishing House, 1955.   120 p.

1366 PARROTT, Leslie, 1922-
   Easy to live with.   Kansas City, Mo., Beacon Hill
Press, 1970.

1367 PURKISER, Westlake Taylor, 1910-
   Give me an answer; significant questions selected from
"The Answer Corner" of the Herald of Holiness.   Kansas
City, Mo., Beacon Hill Press, 1968.   120 p.

1368 PURKISER, Westlake Taylor, 1910-
   When you get to the end of yourself.   Kansas City, Mo.,
Beacon Hill Press, 1970.   70 p.

1369 REED, Louis Archibald, 1892-1952.
   Holiness and the Christian life.   Kansas City, Mo.,
Beacon Hill Press, 1947.   31 p.
   Prepared and distributed under the direction of the
General Stewardship Committee of the Church of the Nazarene.

1370 RILEY, John Eckel, 1909-
   This holy estate; guidance in Christian homemaking.
Kansas City, Mo., Beacon Hill Press, 1957.   191 p.

1371 RUTH, Christian Wismer, 1865-1941.
   Temptations peculiar to the sanctified.   Kansas City,

II. 1. Christian Holiness Association

Mo., Nazarene Publishing House, 1928. 51 p.

1372 SEAMANDS, John T.
On tiptoe with love; "where the Holy Spirit is, there is love." Kansas City, Mo., Beacon Hill Press, c1971. 107 p.

1373 SHAVER, Charles
You can quit smoking. Kansas City, Mo., Beacon Hill Press, 1969. 28 p.

1374 SHEPARD, William Edward, 1862-
Problems of the sanctified. Kansas City, Mo., Nazarene Publishing House, n.d.

1375 SPRUCE, Fletcher Clarke
You can be a joyful tither. Kansas City, Mo., Beacon Hill Press, 1966. 94 p.

1376 STOCKTON, John
Investments here and hereafter. Kansas City, Mo., Nazarene Publishing House, 1964. 84 p.

1377 TAYLOR, Richard Shelley, 1912-
The disciplined life. Kansas City, Mo., Beacon Hill Press, 1962. 102 p.

1378 TAYLOR, Richard Shelley, 1912-
Joy for dark days. Kansas City, Mo., Beacon Hill Press, 1964. 35 p.

1378a TAYLOR, Richard Shelley, 1912-
A return to Christian culture; Christian ideals in a sagging society. Kansas City, Mo., Beacon Hill Press, 1973. 94 p.
Based on the Ripper-Rothwell Lectures delivered at Bethany Nazarene College in February 1972.

1379 WELLMAN, Wendell
What's with entertainment? Kansas City, Mo., Beacon Hill Press, 1969. 24 p.

1380 WILLIAMS, J. E.
You're human too! Garden City, Kan., Commercial Department, Garden City Telegram, n.d. 27 p.

1381 WILLIAMS, Roy Tilman, 1883-1946.
Attitudes and relationships. Kansas City, Mo., Nazarene Publishing House, n.d. 95 p.

1382 WILLIAMS, Roy Tilman, 1883-1946.
Life's supreme choices. Kansas City, Mo., Beacon Hill Press, 1947. 79 p.

1383 WILLIAMS, Roy Tilman, 1883-1946.
Relationships in life. Kansas City, Mo., Nazarene Publishing House, 1948.
First issued under title: Attitudes and relationships.

----AUTHORITATIVE SOURCES

1384 DEAL, William Sanford, 1910-
Maturing gracefully. Kansas City, Mo., Beacon Hill Press, 1972. 88 p.

1385 SHELHAMER, Elmer Ellsworth, 1869-1947.
Helps to holy living. 4th ed. Kansas City, Mo., Nazarene Publishing House, n.d. 96 p.

1386 STEELE, Daniel, 1824-1914.
Hints for holy living; from the Milestone Papers. Kansas City, Mo., Beacon Hill Press, 1959. 80 p.

--CRITICAL WORKS

1387 BENNER, Hugh Clifford, 1899-
Rendevous with abundance. Kansas City, Mo., Beacon Hill Press, 1958. 126 p.

1388 FISHER, Charles William, 1916-
Our heritage and our hope; a tribute to the past, a promise to the future. Kansas City, Mo., Beacon Hill Press, 1958. 24 p.

1389 FLOYD, Fred, 1900-
"The Church of the Nazarene: its doctrines and responsibility." Unpublished B.D. thesis, Vanderbilt University, 1932. 119ℓ.

1390 MATTHEWS, John
The rise and fall of the Church of the Nazarene. n.p., 1920.

1391 PARR, F. O.
Perfect love and race hatred. Bourbonnais, Ill., The author, 1964. 111 p.
Mimeographed.

1392 PITTS, Joseph S.
Voices from the Philippines. Wilmore, Ky., 1958. 26 p.

1393 REHFELDT, Remiss, 1915-
Survival at stake. n.p., 195?.

II. 1. Christian Holiness Association

--DEVOTIONAL LITERATURE

1394   CHAPMAN, James Blaine, 1884-1947.
A day in the Lord's court. Kansas City, Mo., Beacon Hill Press, 1948. 144 p.

1395   CHAPMAN, James Blaine, 1884-1947.
Religion and everyday life. Kansas City, Mo., Beacon Hill Press, 1945. 141 p.

1396   CHAPMAN, James Blaine, 1884-1947.
Singing in the shadows. Kansas City, Mo., Beacon Hill Press, 1943. 183 p.

1397   CORNELL, Clarence Ellsworth
Words of cheer for each day in the year. Kansas City, Mo., Nazarene Publishing House, 1925. 199 p.

1398   CULBERTSON, Paul Thomas
More like the Master. Kansas City, Mo., Beacon Hill Press, 1966.

1399   GOODWIN, John Wesley, 1869-1945.
The secret place of prayer. Kansas City, Mo., Nazarene Publishing House, 1928. 191 p.

1400   HARPER, Albert Foster, 1907-
Holiness and high country. Kansas City, Mo., Beacon Hill Press, 1964. 380 p.

1401   KINNE, Clarence James, 1869-1932.
Prayer. Kansas City, Mo., Publishing House of the Pentecostal Church of the Nazarene, 1913. 85 p.

1402   KINNE, Clarence James, 1869-1932.
Prayer, the secret of power. Kansas City, Mo., Nazarene Publishing House, 1958. 72 p.
First published in 1913 under title: Prayer.

1403   MARTIN, Paul La Rush, 1915-
Good morning, Lord; devotions for youth. Kansas City, Mo., Beacon Hill Press, 1962. 64 p.

1404   MARTIN, Paul La Rush, 1915-
Have a good day; devotions for teens. Kansas City, Mo., Beacon Hill Press, 1971. 64 p.

1405   MUNRO, Bertha, 1887-
The pilgrim's roadmap; studies in Pilgrim's Progress. Kansas City, Mo., Beacon Hill Press, 1950. 79 p.

1406 MUNRO, Bertha, 1887-
Strength for today; companion volume to Truth for today. Kansas City, Mo., Beacon Hill Press, 1954. 384 p.

1407 MUNRO, Bertha, 1887-
Truth for today. Kansas City, Mo., Beacon Hill Press, 1946. 380 p.

1408 PARROTT, Lora Lee (Montgomery), 1923-
Devotional programs for women's groups. Grand Rapids, Mich., Zondervan Publishing House, 1952. 93 p.

1409 SEALS, B. V.
Beside the Shepherd's tent; brief, warm devotions, helps to the hungry in heart. Kansas City, Mo., Beacon Hill Press, 1956. 79 p.

1410 TAYLOR, Mendell, 1912-
Every day with Jesus; a day-by-day devotional book of the life, teachings, and interviews of Jesus. Grand Rapids, Mich., Eerdmans, 1961. 237 p.

1411 TAYLOR, Mendell, 1912-
Every day with the Psalms. Kansas City, Mo., Beacon Hill Press, c1972. 307 p.

1412 WILLIAMSON, Audrey (Johnston)
Overcome evil with good; meditations on Romans 12. Kansas City, Mo., Beacon Hill Press, 1967. 64 p.

1413 WILLINGHAM, Theodore Weber, 1893-
A basket of crumbs: thought-provoking meditations. Kansas City, Mo., Beacon Hill Press, 1972. 64 p.

1414 YOUNG, Samuel, 1901-
God makes a difference. Kansas City, Mo., Beacon Hill Press, 1954. 128 p.

--DIRECTORIES

1415 CHURCH OF the Nazarene. General Secretary.
Travel guide and church directory to Churches of the Nazarene in the United States and Canada...; an alphabetical list of Churches of the Nazarene by state and province. Kansas City, Mo., Nazarene Publishing House, 1968. 40 p.

1416 A DIRECTORY of the Nazarene churches in Australia, British Isles, Canada, Mexico, and the United States, including the location of some Holiness camp meetings with approximate dates, comp. and ed. by Kenneth E. Sullivan. Wollaston, Mass., E.N.C. Press, 1963.

II. 1. Christian Holiness Association   151

       92 p.

       --DOCTRINAL AND CONTROVERSIAL WORKS

1417   ALLEE, George Franklin, 1897-
       Complete consecration; the key to happy living. Kansas City, Mo., Beacon Hill Press, 1950. 32 p.

1418   ANDERSON, Tony Marshall, 1888- , ed.
       Our holy faith. Kansas City, Mo., Printed for Asbury College by Beacon Hill Press, 1966. 347 p.

1419   BEACON BIBLE commentary. Kansas City, Mo., Beacon Hill Press, 1964-1969; v. 1, 1969. 10 v.

1420   BELEW, Pascal Perry, 1894-
       The philosophy of providence. Butler, Ind., Higley Press, n.d.

1421   BENNETT, Willis G.
       Pentecost, its scope, power and perpetuation. Kansas City, Mo., Nazarene Publishing House, 1936. 158 p.

1422   BRESEE, Phineas Franklin, 1838-1915.
       Emmanuel. Kansas City, Mo., Nazarene Publishing House, 1927. 31 p.

1423   CAMPBELL, L. M.
       A cloud of witnesses; a series of Bible readings on the subject of holiness. Kansas City, Mo., Pentecostal Nazarene Publishing House, c1915. 125 p.

1424   CHALFANT, Morris
       A kindergarten primer on holiness. Danville, Ill., n.d. 63 p.

1425   CHAPMAN, James Blaine, 1884-1947.
       Christ and the Bible. Kansas City, Mo., Beacon Hill Press, 1940. 31 p.

1426   CHAPMAN, James Blaine, 1884-1947.
       Christ and the Bible. Kansas City, Mo., Beacon Hill Press, 1966. 23 p.
       "Revised printing."

1427   CHAPMAN, James Blaine, 1884-1947.
       Holiness, the heart of Christian experience. Kansas City, Mo., Beacon Hill Press, 1941. 79 p.

1428   CHAPMAN, James Blaine, 1884-1947.
       Holiness triumphant. Kansas City, Mo., Beacon Hill Press, 1946. 128 p.

1429 CHAPMAN, James Blaine, 1884-1947.
      The terminology of holiness. Kansas City, Mo., Beacon Hill Press, 1947. 112 p.

1430 CHAPMAN, James Blaine, 1884-1947.
      The touch of Jesus. Kansas City, Mo., Beacon Hill Press, 1945. 141 p.

1431 CORLETT, David Shelby, 1894-
      The ABC's of holiness. Kansas City, Mo., Nazarene Publishing House, n.d.

1432 CORLETT, David Shelby, 1894-
      The baptism with the Holy Spirit. Kansas City, Mo., Beacon Hill Press, n.d. 64 p.

1433 CORLETT, David Shelby, 1894-
      Holiness, the central purpose of redemption. Kansas City, Mo., Beacon Hill Press, n.d.

1434 CORLETT, David Shelby, 1894-
      Lord of all; a discussion of some important aspects of the Wesleyan doctrine of entire sanctification. Kansas City, Mo., Beacon Hill Press, 1962. 117 p.

1435 CORLETT, David Shelby, 1894-
      The meaning of holiness. Kansas City, Mo., Beacon Hill Press, 1944. 123 p.

1436 CORLETT, David Shelby, 1894-
      Symbols of Pentecost. Kansas City, Mo., Beacon Hill Press, 1939. 24 p.

1437 CORLETT, Lewis Thomas, 1896-
      Holiness in practical living. Kansas City, Mo., Beacon Hill Press, 1948. 80 p.

1438 CORLETT, Lewis Thomas, 1896-
      Holiness, the harmonizing experience. Kansas City, Mo., Beacon Hill Press, 1951. 94 p.

1439 EARLE, Ralph, 1907-
      Exploring the New Testament. Ralph Earle, editor, Harvey J.S. Blaney [and] Carl Hanson. Kansas City, Mo., Beacon Hill Press, c1955. 467 p.

1440 EARLE, Ralph, 1907-
      The Gospel according to Mark. Grand Rapids, Mich., Zondervan Publishing House, 1957. 192 p. (The Evangelical commentary on the Bible [2])

II. 1. Christian Holiness Association 153

1441 EARLE, Ralph, 1907-
Know your New Testament. Kansas City, Mo., Nazarene Publishing House, 1943. 221 p.
On cover; Christian service training course.

1442 EARLE, Ralph, 1907-
Meet the early church. Kansas City, Mo., Nazarene Publishing House, 1959. 95 p.

1443 EARLE, Ralph, 1907-
Meet the Major prophets. Kansas City, Mo., Beacon Hill Press, c1958. 128 p.

1444 EARLE, Ralph, 1907-
Meet the Minor Prophets. Kansas City, Mo., Beacon Hill Press, 1955. 109 p.

1445 EARLE, Ralph, 1907-
The quest of the Spirit. Norwood, Mass., Norwood Press, 1940. vi, 231 p.

1446 EARLE, Ralph, 1907-
The story of the New Testament. Kansas City, Mo., Beacon Hill Press, 1958. 128 p.
At head of title: Christian service training.
First published in 1941.
"Revised, 1956."

1447 ELLYSON, Edgar Painter, 1869-1954.
Bible holiness. Kansas City, Mo., Nazarene Publishing House, 1938. 141 p.

1448 ELLYSON, Edgar Painter, 1869-1954.
Bible holiness. Kansas City, Mo., Beacon Hill Press, 1952. 127 p.

1449 ELLYSON, Edgar Painter, 1869-1954.
Doctrinal studies. Kansas City, Mo., Nazarene Publishing House, 1936. 188 p.

1450 ELLYSON, Edgar Painter, 1869-1954.
Is man an animal? Kansas City, Mo., Nazarene Publishing House, 1926. 63 p.

1451 ELLYSON, Edgar Painter, 1869-1954.
Pentecost. Kansas City, Mo., Nazarene Publishing House, 1935. 32 p.

1452 ERDMANN, H. A.
The carnal mind and the cure for it. Kansas City, Mo., Beacon Hill Press, 1934. 64 p.

1453 FINCH, Oscar J., 1901-
Triumphant in temptation. Kansas City, Mo., Beacon Hill Press, 1945. 79 p.

1454 FISHER, William Edgar
Sound doctrine. Kansas City, Mo., Pentecostal Nazarene Publishing House, 1918. 175 p.

1455 GOODWIN, John Wesley, 1869-1945.
The gospel for our age. Kansas City, Mo., Nazarene Publishing House, n.d. 208 p.

1456 GOODWIN, John Wesley, 1869-1945.
Living signs and wonders. Kansas City, Mo., Nazarene Publishing House, 1920.

1457 GOULD, Joseph Glenn, 1896-
The precious blood of Christ. Kansas City, Mo., Beacon Hill Press, 1959. 110 p.

1458 GOULD, Joseph Glenn, 1896-
The Spirit's ministry. Kansas City, Mo., Nazarene Publishing House, 1941. 37 p.

1459 GOULD, Joseph Glenn, 1896-
The whole counsel of God. Kansas City, Mo., Beacon Hill Press, 1945. 133 p.

1460 GREATHOUSE, William M., 1929-
The fullness of the Spirit. Kansas City, Mo., Nazarene Publishing House, 1958. 104 p.

1461 GREATHOUSE, William M., 1929-
Who is the Holy Spirit? Kansas City, Mo., Nazarene Publishing House, 1972. 11 p.
Reprinted from the Herald of Holiness, May 10, 1972.

1462 GRIDER, Joseph Kenneth, 1921-
Repentance unto life; what it means to repent. Kansas City, Mo., Beacon Hill Press, 1965. 80 p.

1463 HAYNES, Benjamin Franklin, 1851-1923.
Beauty for ashes. Kansas City, Mo., Publishing House of the Pentecostal Church of the Nazarene, 1912. 72 p.

1464 HAYNES, Benjamin Franklin, 1851-1923.
The beauty of holiness. Kansas City, Mo., Pentecostal Nazarene Publishing House, 1912. 64 p.

1465 HILLS, Aaron Merritt, 1848-1935.
Eradication of carnality, why we teach it. Kansas City, Mo., Nazarene Publishing House, n.d. 46 p.

II. 1. Christian Holiness Association

1466 HILLS, Aaron Merritt, 1848-1935.
Fundamental Christian theology. Kansas City, Mo., Nazarene Publishing House, 1931. 2v.

1467 HILLS, Aaron Merritt, 1848-1935.
Standing grace; or, Romans and sanctification. Kansas City, Mo., Pentecostal Nazarene Publishing House, n.d. 104 p.

1468 HILLS, Aaron Merritt, 1848-1935.
The uttermost salvation. Kansas City, Mo., Nazarene Publishing House, 1927. 128 p.

1469 HOOKER, H. H.
Endless retribution. Kansas City, Mo., Nazarene Publishing House, 1939. 30 p.

1470 HOOKER, H. H.
God's financial plan for His church. 2d ed. Kansas City, Mo., Nazarene Publishing House, 1939. 32 p.

1471 JAMES, Maynard G., 1902-
I believe in the Holy Ghost. Nelson, Lancs., Eng., Coulton & Co., 1964.

1472 JAMES, Maynard G., 1902-
I believe in the Holy Ghost; foreword by Norman Grubb. Minneapolis, Bethany Fellowship, 1965. 167 p.

1473 JERNIGAN, Charles Brougher, 1863-1930.
Entire sanctification. Kansas City, Mo., Nazarene Publishing House, n.d. 32 p.

1474 JESSOP, Harry Edward, 1884-
Abram the Hebrew, the man who ventured out with God; high spots in a great life. Kansas City, Mo., Beacon Hill Press, 1958. 76 p.

1475 JESSOP, Harry Edward, 1884-
Studies in Christian essentials. Kansas City, Mo., Beacon Hill Press, 1945. 136 p.

1475a KNIGHT, John Allan
The holiness pilgrimage; reflections on the life of holiness. Kansas City, Mo., Beacon Hill Press, 1973. 111 p.
Presented originally as the Lienard Lectures on Holiness at Nazarene Theological Seminary, Kansas City, Missouri, in February 1971, and as the Gould Lectures on Holiness at Eastern Nazarene College, Quincy, Massachusetts, in April 1972.

1476 KRING, James Arthur, 1873-
   The conquest of Canaan. Kansas City, Mo., Printed for J.A. Kring by the Nazarene Publishing House, 1930. 263 p.

1477 LEHMAN, Frederick Martin, 1868-
   The man in black. Kansas City, Mo., Publishing House of the Pentecostal Church of the Nazarene, 1913. 192 p.
   Autobiographical allegory on the carnal mind.

1478 McCONNELL, Charles Allen, 1860-1955.
   The book's own story; four hundred stories of God's ancient people. Kansas City, Mo., Nazarene Publishing House, 1925- . v.

1479 McCUMBER, W. E.
   Holiness in the prayers of St. Paul. Kansas City, Mo., Beacon Hill Press, 1955. 121 p.

1480 McCUMBER, W. E.
   Our sanctifying God. Kansas City, Mo., Beacon Hill Press, 1956. 124 p.

1481 McGRAW, William David, Jr.
   Symbols of the Spirit. Kansas City, Mo., Beacon Hill Press, 1954. 30 p.

1482 MARTIN, Paul La Rush, 1915-
   The Holy Spirit today. Kansas City, Mo., Beacon Hill Press, 1970. 31 p.

1483 MARTIN, Paul La Rush, 1915-
   Sanctification: the big question for youth. Kansas City, Mo., Beacon Hill Press, 1970. 43 p.

1483a MARTIN, Sydney
   The gospel of power; the message of Paul for today's world. Kansas City, Mo., Beacon Hill Press, 1973. 86 p.
   Presented as the H. Orton Wiley Lectures at Pasadena College in May 1968.

1484 MATHIS, I. C., 1898-
   The beauty of holiness. Kansas City, Mo., Beacon Hill Press, 1939. 124 p.

1485 MATTHEWS, John
   The last eight days of the life of Jesus Christ. Kansas City, Mo., Nazarene Publishing House, 1924 180 p.

1486 MATTHEWS, John
   The love of God. Kansas City, Mo., Nazarene Publishing House, 1922. 154 p.

II. 1. Christian Holiness Association

1487 MAY, John W.
Even your sanctification. Kansas City, Mo., Beacon Hill Press, 1956. 47 p.

1488 METZ, Donald S., 1916-
Studies in Biblical holiness. Kansas City, Mo., Beacon Hill Press, 1971. 284 p.

1489 MILLER, Basil William, 1897-
"Cunningly devised fables": Modernism exposed and refuted, by Rev. Basil W. Miller, M.A., S.T.M., and Rev. U.E. Harding; with an introd. by Dr. James B. Chapman. n.p., 192?. 134 p.

1490 MILLER, Howard Vasser, 1894-1948.
His will for us. Kansas City, Mo., Beacon Hill Press, 1949. 80 p.

1491 MILLER, Howard Vasser, 1894-1948.
The path we take. Kansas City, Mo., Nazarene Publishing House, n.d. 23 p.

1492 MILLER, Howard Vasser, 1894-1948.
The sin problem. Kansas City, Mo., Nazarene Publishing House, n.d. 57 p.

1493 MILLER, Howard Vasser, 1894-1948.
When he is come. Kansas City, Mo., Nazarene Publishing House, 1941. 29 p.

1494 MITCHELL, T. Crichton
Mr. Wesley; an intimate sketch of John Wesley. Kansas City, Mo., Beacon Hill Press, 1957. 96 p.

1495 MORRISON, Joseph Grant, 1871-1939.
Achieving faith. Kansas City, Mo., Nazarene Publishing House, 1926. 166 p.

1496 MORRISON, Joseph Grant, 1871-1939.
The Christian sabbath. Kansas City, Mo., Nazarene Publishing House, 1939. 48 p.

1497 MORRISON, Joseph Grant, 1871-1939.
Our lost estate. Kansas City, Mo., Nazarene Publishing House, 1929. 187 p.

1498 NEELY, Benjamin Franklin, 1876-1967.
On to perfection. Kansas City, Mo., Beacon Hill Press, 1952. 124 p.

1499 PARROTT, Leslie, 1922-
What is sanctification? Kansas City, Mo., Beacon Hill Press, 1950. 48 p.

1500 PRICE, Ross Eugene, 1907-
You can be sanctified wholly. Kansas City, Mo., Beacon Hill Press, 1959. 24 p.

1501 PURKISER, Westlake Taylor, 1910-
Beliefs that matter most. Kansas City, Mo., Beacon Hill Press, c1959. 96 p.

1502 PURKISER, Westlake Taylor, 1910-
Conflicting concepts of holiness; some current issues in the doctrine of sanctification. Kansas City, Mo., Beacon Hill Press, 1953. 110 p.

1503 PURKISER, Westlake Taylor, 1910- , ed.
Exploring our Christian faith. Kansas City, Mo., Beacon Hill Press, 1960. 615 p.

1504 PURKISER, Westlake Taylor, 1910-
Exploring the Old Testament. W. T. Purkiser, editor [and others]. Kansas City, Mo., Beacon Hill Press, 1955. 448 p.

1505 PURKISER, Westlake Taylor, 1910-
Interpreting Christian holiness. Kansas City, Mo., Beacon Hill Press of Kansas City, 1971. 64 p.

1506 PURKISER, Westlake Taylor, 1910-
Sanctification and its synonyms; studies in the Biblical theology of holiness. Kansas City, Mo., Beacon Hill Press, 1961. 96 p.

1507 PURKISER, Westlake Taylor, 1910-
Security: the false and the true. Kansas City, Mo., Beacon Hill Press, 1956. 64 p.

1508 PURKISER, Westlake Taylor, 1910-
Security, the false and the true. Rev. ed. Kansas City, Mo., Beacon Hill Press, 1971, c1956. 60 p.

1509 RUTH, Christian Wismer, 1865-1941.
Entire sanctification. Kansas City, Mo., Beacon Hill Press, 1944. 111 p.

1510 SHARPE, George, 1865-1948.
The creed of Jesus, and other addresses on holiness. Glasgow, Scot., A. H. Burnett, 1924.

1511 SHEPARD, William Edward, 1862-
The palm tree blessing; a discourse on the various characteristics of the palm tree, illustrating the many features of the sanctified Christian life. Kansas City, Mo., Publishing House of the Pentecostal Church of the Nazarene

II. 1. Christian Holiness Association

1512 SHORT, John N., 1841-1922.
 The Bible Christian; or, Faith and its development. Kansas City, Mo., Pentecostal Church of the Nazarene, 1915. 159 p.

1513 SHUMAKE, C. E.
 Holiness in action. Kansas City, Mo., Beacon Hill Press, 1947. 36 p.

1514 SMITH, Arlis Milton, 1903-
 The twelve apostles. New York, Fleming H. Revell Co., c1940. 172 p.

1515 SWEETEN, Howard W.
 A more excellent way. Kansas City, Mo., Nazarene Publishing House, 1929. 191 p.

1516 SWEETEN, Howard W.
 Must we sin? A treatise of the sin question from the standpoint of reason and revelation. 4th ed., rev. and abridged. Kansas City, Mo., Nazarene Publishing House, n.d. 96 p.

1517 SWEETEN, Howard W.
 Sinning saints? Kansas City, Mo., Nazarene Publishing House, 1939. 160 p.

1518 TAYLOR, Richard Shelley, 1912-
 Life in the Spirit; Christian holiness in doctrine, experience, and life. Kansas City, Mo., Beacon Hill Press, 1966. 221 p.

1519 TAYLOR, Richard Shelley, 1912-
 Preaching holiness today. Kansas City, Mo., Beacon Hill Press, 1968. 216 p.

1520 TAYLOR, Richard Shelley, 1912-
 A right conception of sin; its importance to right thinking and right living. Kansas City, Mo., Nazarene Publishing House, 1939. 121 p.

1521 TAYLOR, Richard Shelley, 1912-
 Talks by the way. Portland, Ore., Better Book and Bible House, 1942. 88 p.

1522 WALKER, Edward Franklin, 1852-1918.
 Sanctify them; a study of our Lord's prayer for His disciples. Kansas City, Mo., Publishing House of the Pentecostal Church of the Nazarene, 191?. 95 p.
 Reprint of 1899 ed.

1523 WALKER, W. B.
The more excellent way. Kansas City, Mo., Beacon Hill Press, n.d. 61 p.

1524 WEATHERFORD, Fred Merle, 1888-
The Bible, the world's capsheaf. Kansas City, Mo., Nazarene Publishing House, 1931. 56 p.

1525 WEATHERFORD, Fred Merle, 1888-
Sanctification: the price of heaven. Kansas City, Mo., Pedestal Press, 1971. 176 p.

1526 WHITE, Stephen Solomon, 1890-1971.
Eradication: defined, explained, authenticated. Kansas City, Mo., Beacon Hill Press, 1954. 95 p.

1527 WHITE, Stephen Solomon, 1890-1971.
Essential Christian beliefs. Kansas City, Mo., Beacon Hill Press, 1940. 112 p.

1528 WHITE, Stephen Solomon, 1890-1971.
Five cardinal elements in the doctrine of entire sanctification. Kansas City, Mo., Beacon Hill Press, 1948. 91 p.

1529 WHITE, Stephen Solomon, 1890-1971.
Growth in grace according to Paul's prayer in the Philippian letter. Kansas City, Mo., Beacon Hill Press, 1947. 14 p.

1530 WILDE, Earle F.
Isms on trial; sermon by Earl F. Wilde, evangelist, Nazarene Church, Walla Walla, Wash., March 8, 1920. Kansas City, Mo., General Board of Foreign Missions, Church of the Nazarene, 192?. 27 p.

1531 WILEY, Henry Orton, 1877-1961.
Christian theology. Kansas City, Mo., Nazarene Publishing House, 1940-1943. 3 v.

1532 WILEY, Henry Orton, 1877-1961.
The Epistle to the Hebrews. Kansas City, Mo., Beacon Hill Press, 1959. 438 p.

1533 WILEY, Henry Orton, 1877-1961.
Introduction to Christian theology, by H. Orton Wiley and Paul T. Culbertson. Kansas City, Mo., Beacon Hill Press, 1959. 461 p.

1534 WILLIAMS, J. E.
Holiness and the human element. Salinas, Calif., Graphic Arts Printery, n.d.

II. 1. Christian Holiness Association

1535 WILLIAMS, Roy Tilman, 1883-1946.
The perfect man. Kansas City, Mo., Publishing House of the Pentecostal Church of the Nazarene, 1913. 143 p.

1536 WILLIAMS, Roy Tilman, 1883-1946.
Sanctification, the experience and the ethics. Kansas City, Mo., Nazarene Publishing House, 1928. 142 p.

1537 WILLIAMS, Roy Tilman, 1883-1946.
Temptation, a neglected theme. Kansas City, Mo., Nazarene Publishing House, 1920. 79 p.

1538 WILLIAMSON, Gideon Brooks, 1898-
Preaching scriptural holiness. Kansas City, Mo., Beacon Hill Press, 1953. 80 p.

1539 WINCHESTER, Olive May, 1880-1947.
Crisis experiences in the Greek New Testament; an investigation of the evidences for the definite, miraculous experiences of regeneration and sanctification as found in the Greek New Testament, especially in the figures emphasized and in the use of the aorist tense, ed. throughout, with final chapter and appendix by Ross E. Price. Kansas City, Mo., Beacon Hill Press, 1953. 110 p.

1540 WINCHESTER, Olive May, 1880-1947.
Moses and the prophets. Kansas City, Mo., Nazarene Publishing House, 1941. 128 p.

1541 WYNKOOP, Mildred (Bangs)
Foundations of Wesleyan-Arminian theology. Kansas City, Mo., Beacon Hill Press, 1967. 128 p.

1542 WYNKOOP, Mildred (Bangs)
A theology of love; the dynamic of Wesleyanism. Kansas City, Mo., Beacon Hill Press, 1972. 372 p.

1543 YOUNG, Samuel, 1901-
Faith in the midst of trial. Kansas City, Mo., Beacon Hill Press, 1955. 22 p.

-- --AUTHORITATIVE SOURCES

1544 BALDWIN, Harmon Allan, 1869-1936.
Holiness and the human element. 2d ed. Kansas City, Mo., Beacon Hill Press, 1952, c1919. 110 p.

1545 BROCKETT, Henry E.
Scriptural freedom from sin; a defense of the precious truth of entire sanctification by faith and an examination of the doctrine of "The Two Natures." Kansas City, Mo., Kingshighway Press, 1941. 188 p.

1546 BROCKETT, Henry E.
Scriptural freedom from sin; a defense of the truth of entire sanctification by faith and an examination of the doctrine of the "two natures." Kansas City, Mo., Beacon Hill Press, 1965. 188 p.
"First printing, 1941; fifth printing, 1965."

1547 CHADWICK, Samuel, 1860-1932.
The call to Christian perfection. United States ed. Kansas City, Mo., Beacon Hill Press, 1943. 110 p.

1548 CHADWICK, Samuel, 1860-1932.
The gospel of the cross. Kansas City, Mo., Beacon Hill Press, 1949. 95 p.

1549 COX, Leo George, 1912-
John Wesley's concept of perfection. Kansas City, Mo., Beacon Hill Press, 1964. 227 p.

1550 DeLONG, Russell Victor, 1901- , ed.
Evangelistic sermons by great evangelists; introd. by Bishop Arthur J. Moore. Grand Rapids, Mich., Zondervan Publishing House, 1956. 183 p.

1551 FLETCHER, John William, 1729-1785.
Checks to Antinomianism; abridged by Peter Wiseman. Kansas City, Mo., Beacon Hill Press, 1948. 333 p.

1552 FOSTER, Randolph Sinks, bp., 1820-1903.
Christian purity; abridged by John Paul, D.D. Kansas City, Mo., Beacon Hill Press, 1944. 108 p.

1553 LOWREY, Asbury, 1816-1898.
Possibilities of grace; abridged by John Paul, D.D. Kansas City, Mo., Beacon Hill Press, 194?. 121 p.

1554 McGRAW, James, 1913-
Great evangelical preachers of yesterday. New York, Abingdon Press, 1961. 159 p.

1555 PECK, Jesse Truesdell, bp., 1811-1883.
The central idea of Christianity; abridged by D. Shelby Corlett, D.D. Kansas City, Mo., Beacon Hill Press, 1951. 112 p.

1556 SIGSTON, James
William Bramwell and his experience of salvation. Kansas City, Mo., Publishing House of the Pentecostal Church of the Nazarene, n.d. 28 p.

1557 STEELE, Daniel, 1824-1914.
The gospel of the Comforter; an abridgment by Ross E.

Price, D.D. Kansas City, Mo., Beacon Hill Press, 1960. 160 p.

1558 STEELE, Daniel, 1824-1914.
The Holy Spirit and the church; selected materials from The Gospel of the Comforter, by Ross E. Price. Kansas City, Mo., Beacon Hill Press, 1961. 63 p.

1559 TURNER, George Allen, 1908-
The vision which transforms; is Christian perfection scriptural? Kansas City, Mo., Beacon Hill Press, 1964. 348 p.
"A thorough revision under ... new title of the author's thesis, first published in 1952 under title: The More Excellent Way; the ms. thesis (Harvard University) has title: A Comparative Study of Biblical and Wesleyan Ideas of Perfection."

1560 UPHAM, Thomas Cogswell, 1799-1872.
Principles of the interior or hidden life, designed particularly for the consideration of those who are seeking assurance of faith and perfect love; abridged by Olive M. Winchester, Th.D. Kansas City, Mo., Beacon Hill Press, n.d. 109 p.

1561 WESLEY, John, 1703-1791.
A plain account of Christian perfection. Kansas City, Mo., Beacon Hill Press, 1950. 62 p.

1562 WILKES, Alphaeus Nelson Paget, 1871-1934.
The dynamic of faith. Kansas City, Mo., Beacon Hill Press, 1943. 144 p.

1563 WILKES, Alphaeus Nelson Paget, 1871-1934.
The dynamic of redemption. Kansas City, Mo., Beacon Hill Press, 1946. 155 p.

1564 WILKES, Alphaeus Nelson Paget, 1871-1934.
So great salvation. Kansas City, Mo., Beacon Hill Press, n.d.

1565 WOOD, John Allen, 1828-
Perfect love; abridged by John Paul, D.D. Kansas City, Mo., Beacon Hill Press, n.d. 140 p.

1566 WOOD, John Allen, 1828-
Purity and maturity; abridged by John Paul, D.D. Kansas City, Mo., Beacon Hill Press, n.d. 96 p.

-- --BIBLIOGRAPHY

1567 NAZARENE THEOLOGICAL Seminary.
Master bibliography of holiness works. Kansas City,

Mo., Prepared by Nazarene Theological Seminary and published by Beacon Hill Press, 1965. 45 p.

-- --ESCHATOLOGY

1568 ALLEE, George Franklin, 1897-
I will come again; the doctrine of last things as related to Christ's promise of His return. Kansas City, Mo., Beacon Hill Press, 1968. 79 p.

1569 BEIRNES, George, -1942.
Pyramid symbolism and prophecy. W. Owen Sound, Ont., 19??. 51 p.

1570 CORBETT, C. T.
Ready for the rapture. Noblesville, Ind., Newby Book Room, 1971. 24 p.
First published in 1962.

1571 DAYHOFF, Irvin E.
The majestic hand in Bible prophecy. University Park, Iowa, 1968. 111 p.

1572 HESLOP, William Greene, 1886-
Heaven: our Father's home, God's city of gold. Grand Rapids, Mich., Printed for the Peniel Press by Nazarene Publishing House, 1937. 104 p.

1573 JAMES, Maynard G., 1902-
Daniel's forecast. Kansas City, Mo., Beacon Hill Press, 1964. 23 p.

1574 JERNIGAN, Charles Brougher, 1863-1930.
The World War in prophecy. Ponca City, Okla., Printed by Ponca City Democrat, 1918. 80 p.

1575 JESSOP, Harry Edward, 1884-
The final counterfeit: antichrist-superman-incarnate devil. Kansas City, Mo., Nazarene Publishing House, 1940. 61 p.

1576 MESSENGER, Frank Mortimer, 1852-
The coming superman. Kansas City, Mo., Nazarene Publishing House, 1928. 62 p.

1577 MESSENGER, Frank Mortimer, 1852-
The time of the end; or, Book of Revelation. Kansas City, Mo., Nazarene Publishing House, 1925. 192 p.

1578 MESSENGER, Frank Mortimer, 1852-
The World War; four horses of Revelation. Chicago, Messenger Publishing Co., 1918. 135 p.

II. 1. Christian Holiness Association

1579 TIDWELL, W. M.
The second coming of Christ. Kansas City, Mo., Beacon Hill Press, 1936. 64 p.

1580 WILLIAMS, J. E.
Wings of prophecy over the world. n.p., 1947. 48 p.

1581 WILLINGHAM, Theodore Weber, 1893-
The tornado in the sky, a prophetic study. Kansas City, Mo., Beacon Hill Press, 1958. 72 p.

-- --FAITH-HEALING

1582 DOOLEY, John Alexander, 1860-
Jesus Christ the great physician, by Evangelists Rev. John A. Dooley and Rev. Hannah M. Dooley. Minneapolis, Minn., 1928. 39 p.

1583 PURKISER, Westlake Taylor, 1910-
Spiritual gifts: healing and tongues; an analysis of the charismatic revival. Kansas City, Mo., Nazarene Publishing House, 1964. 23 p.

1584 SEARS, Lawrence Wayne, 1917-
The reality of Divine healing. Kansas City, Mo., Beacon Hill Press, 1955. 19 p.

-- --GLOSSOLALIA

1585 BLACK, Warren
"A Nazarene finds a new dimension," Full Gospel Business Men's Voice, XX (June 1972), 3-7, 26-28.

1586 CHALFANT, Morris
"Unknown tongues--tomfoolery or not?" Danville, Ill., n.d. 58 p.

1587 MATTHEWS, John
Speaking in tongues. n.p., 1925. 139 p.

1588 METZ, Donald S., 1916-
Speaking in tongues: an analysis. Kansas City, Mo., Nazarene Publishing House, 1964. 109 p.

1589 NEELY, Benjamin Franklin, 1876-1967.
The Bible versus the tongues theory. Rev. ed. Kansas City, Mo., Nazarene Publishing House, circa 1925. 79 p.

1590 PURKISER, Westlake Taylor, 1910-
Spiritual gifts: healing and tongues; an analysis of the Charismatic Revival. Kansas City, Mo., Nazarene Publishing House, 1964. 23 p.

-- --PREDESTINATION

1591 CORLETT, David Shelby, 1894-
   The meaning of Christian security. Kansas City, Mo., Nazarene Publishing House, 1939. 22 p.

1592 McKINLEY, O. Glenn,   -1970.
   Where two creeds meet; a Biblical evaluation of Calvinism and Arminianism. Kansas City, Mo., Beacon Hill Press, 1959. 123 p.

--EDUCATION

1593 ATWOOD, Alvin Ray, 1924-
   "A study of student personnel services available in colleges of the Church of the Nazarene in the United States with certain recommendations for improvement." Unpublished Ph.D. dissertation, East Texas State University, 1970. 265ℓ.

1594 CAMERON, James Reese, 1929-
   Eastern Nazarene College, the first fifty years, 1900-1950. Kansas City, Mo., Printed for Eastern Nazarene College by the Nazarene Publishing House, 1968. 420 p.

1595 DANSKIN, Donald Ralph, 1910-
   "Education for business in church-related liberal arts colleges." Unpublished Ed.D. dissertation, University of Oklahoma, 1955.

1596 GOULD, Joseph Glenn, 1896-
   The whole counsel of God. Kansas City, Mo., Beacon Hill Press, 1945. 133 p.
   "The function of a Holiness college (a supplementary chapter)," pp. 117-129.

1597 LUDWIG, Sylvester Theodore, 1903-1964.
   "The rise, development and present status of the educational institutions of the Church of the Nazarene in the United States." Unpublished M.A. thesis, University of Wichita, 1932.

1598 MEYERING, Chester
   "Values of Nazarene seniors in higher educational institutions." Unpublished Ed.D. dissertation, University of Denver, 1966. 196ℓ.

1599 MOORE, Ernest William
   "An historical study of higher education and the Church of the Nazarene, 1900-1965." Unpublished Ph.D. dissertation, University of Texas, 1965. 304ℓ.

II. 1. Christian Holiness Association

1600 PARROTT, Leslie, 1922-
"A study of student personnel services in six liberal arts church colleges." Unpublished Ph.D. dissertation, Michigan State University, 1958. 227ℓ.

1601 PERRY, Ralph Edward
"A study of the objectives in higher education of the six liberal arts colleges of the Church of the Nazarene." Unpublished Ph.D. dissertation, Bradley University, 1952. 290ℓ.

1602 PHILO, L. C., 1907-1972.
"The historical development and present status of the educational institutions of the Church of the Nazarene." Unpublished Ph.D. dissertation, University of Oklahoma, 1958. vii, 271ℓ.

1603 PURKISER, Westlake Taylor, 1910-
"Toward a definition of Christian education," Vital Speeches, XV (July 15, 1949), 602-605.

1604 ROBINSON, Kenneth Eugene, -1967.
"Educational development in the Church of the Nazarene." Unpublished B.D. thesis, Nazarene Theological Seminary, 1948.

1605 SHANNON, Ernest Boyd, 1911-1968.
"Personal services extended to students of selected church-related colleges in solving their problems." Unpublished Ed.D. dissertation, University of Oklahoma, 1955.

1606 STROPKO, Andrew John, 1945-
"Values of Nazarene college students on a public and a church sponsored campus." Unpublished M.A. thesis, University of Arizona, 1969. 70ℓ.

--EVANGELISTIC WORK

1607 CHURCH OF the Nazarene. Commission of the Mid-Century Crusade for Souls.
He that winneth souls; illustrations of personal evangelism in the Mid-Century Crusade for Souls, ed. by Alpin P. Bowes. Kansas City, Mo., Nazarene Publishing House, 1950. 125 p.

1608 CHURCH OF the Nazarene. Department of Evangelism.
The whole church evangelizing, comp. by the Department of Evangelism, Church of the Nazarene, John L. Knight, executive secretary. Kansas City, Mo., Nazarene Publishing House, 1970. 75 p.

1609 AYCOCK, Jarrette E., -1966.
Drawing the net; suggestions on how to give an invitation. Kansas City, Mo., Beacon Hill Press, 1953. 32 p.

1610 AYCOCK, Jarrette E., -1966.
Save some. Kansas City, Mo., Beacon Hill Press, 1953.

1611 AYCOCK, Jarrette E., --1966.
Win them. Kansas City, Mo., Beacon Hill Press, 1933.

1612 CHAPMAN, James Blaine, 1884-1947.
All out for souls; an address delivered to the District Superintendent's Conference at Kansas City, Missouri, January 9, 1946. Kansas City, Mo., Nazarene Publishing House, 1946. Unpaged.

1613 CORNELL, Clarence Ellsworth
Casting the net; or, Stringing the fish, with pertinent and practical suggestions on evangelistic methods and fruitfulness. Kansas City, Mo., Publishing House of the Pentecostal Church of the Nazarene, 1914. 96 p.

1614 DeLONG, Russell Victor, 1901- , ed. and comp.
All out for souls; a book of addresses delivered at the Conference on Evangelism held at the First Church of the Nazarene, Kansas City, Missouri, January 6, 7, 1947, under the sponsorship of the Nazarene Theological Seminary. Kansas City, Mo., Nazarene Publishing House, 1947. 144 p.

1615 DuBOIS, Lauriston J.
The pastor and visitation evangelism; manual prepared for use by pastors in conjunction with the manuals First steps in visitation evangelism and Soul winning through visitation evangelism. Rev. ed. Kansas City, Mo., Nazarene Publishing House, 1950. 118 p.

1616 ELLIS, J. William
We are witnesses, by J. William Ellis, in collaboration with Dr. Albert F. Harper, Executive Secretary, Department of Church Schools, Church of the Nazarene, Rev. W. A. Strong, pastor [and] Rev. Andrew Young, pastor. Kansas City, Mo., Beacon Hill Press, 1956. 121 p.

1617 FISHER, Charles William, 1916-
It's revival we need!: address delivered at the Conference on Evangelism at Kansas City, Missouri, January 12, 1966. Kansas City, Mo., Nazarene Publishing House, 1966. 72 p.

II. 1. Christian Holiness Association

1618   FISHER, Charles William, 1916-
       The time is now. Kansas City, Mo., Nazarene Publishing House, 1950. 79 p.

1619   FISHER, Charles William, 1916-
       Wake up and lift. Kansas City, Mo., Beacon Hill Press, 1955. 72 p.

1620   GILLILAND, Ponder W.
       Witnessing to win. Kansas City, Mo., Beacon Hill Press, 1958. 103 p.

1621   HARPER, Albert Foster, 1907-
       First steps in visitation evangelism, by Albert F. Harper in collaboration with Elmer H. Kauffman. Kansas City, Mo., Nazarene Publishing House, 1948. 103 p.

1622   JENKINS, Orville W.
       The church--winning Sunday nights. Kansas City, Mo., Nazarene Publishing House, 1961. 104 p.

1623   LAWLOR, Edward
       Wake up and witness; a message for the church. Kansas City, Mo., Nazarene Publishing House, 1963. 23 p.

1624   LEWIS, Voyle H.
       The church winning souls. Kansas City, Mo., Nazarene Publishing House, 1960. 92 p.

1625   LUDWIG, Minnie E. (Brink), 1877-1958.
       Living for Jesus. Kansas City, Mo., Pentecostal Nazarene Publishing House, 1916. 111 p.

1626   MEET MY saviour; a study of motivation and method in personal soul winning. Kansas City, Mo., Beacon Hill Press, 1966. 87 p.

1627   MONTGOMERY, James William, 1898-
       Personal evangelism. Kansas City, Mo., Nazarene Publishing House, n.d. 59 p.

1628   OKE, Norman R.
       We have an altar; a manual on altar work, by Norman R. Oke in collaboration with Dr. John L. Knight, Rev. Harold Volk, Dr. R.T. Williams. Kansas City, Mo., Nazarene Publishing House, 1964. 80 p.

1629   PERSHALL, Roscoe
       You can win them. Kansas City, Mo., Beacon Hill Press, 1966. 48 p.
       First published in 1960.

1630 POWERS, Hardy Carroll, 1900-1972.
Go ye next door; everyday evangelism through the Crusade for Souls Now, by the General Superintendents of the Church of the Nazarene.... Kansas City, Mo., Nazarene Publishing House, 1955. 48 p.

1631 PURKISER, Westlake Taylor, 1910-
The message of evangelism: the saving power of God. Kansas City, Mo., Beacon Hill Press, 1963. 112 p.

1632 STENBOCK, Evelyn
Soul-winning laymen; stories of contemporary lay witnesses. Kansas City, Mo., Beacon Hill Press, 1972. 80 p.

1633 TAYLOR, Mendell, 1912-
Exploring evangelism: history, methods, theology. Kansas City, Mo., Nazarene Publishing House, 1964. 647 p.

1634 WILKINS, Chester, 1918-
A handbook for personal soul-winning. 5th ed., rev. Kansas City, Mo., Beacon Hill Press, 1972, c1966. 320 p.

1635 WILLIAMSON, Gideon Brooks, 1898-
The labor of love; evangelism in the local church. Kansas City, Mo., Beacon Hill Press, 1953. 103 p.

--FINANCE

1636 MORRISON, Joseph Grant, 1871-1939.
The pastor and church finance. Kansas City, Mo., General Board of the Church of the Nazarene, n.d. 20 p.

1637 SPANGENBERG, Leonard, 1906-
Minding your church's business; a guide for pastors, church officials, and active laymen, with a foreword by Roger W. Babson. Kansas City, Mo., Beacon Hill Press, 1942. 142 p.

1638 WILLIAMS, Leewin Bell, 1868-
Financing the kingdom; a handbook of methods and suggestions for pastors, church officials, Sunday school teachers and officers of young people's societies on financing and promoting the kingdom of heaven. Grand Rapids, Mich., Wm. B. Eerdmans Publishing Co., 1939. 176 p.

--HISTORY

1639 BRESEE, Phineas Franklin, 1838-1915.
Sayings of our founder, comp. by Ward B. Chandler.

II. 1. Christian Holiness Association 171

Houston, Chandler and Roach Publications, 1948. 50 p.
First published in 1903; reproduced in 1948 and 1951.

1640 CHALFANT, Morris
Trade-marks of the holiness pioneers. Kansas City, Mo., Beacon Hill Press, 1962. 61 p.

1641 CHAPMAN, James Blaine, 1884-1947.
History of the Church of the Nazarene. Kansas City, Mo., Nazarene Publishing House, 1926. 160 p.

1642 CLARK, Elmer Talmage, 1886-1966.
The small sects in America. Rev. ed. New York, Abingdon Press, c1965. 256 p.
Account of the Church of the Nazarene: p. 74-76.

1643 GAUSTAD, Edwin Scott, 1923-
Historical atlas of religion in America. New York, Harper & Row, 1962. xii, 179 p.
Account of Church of the Nazarene: p. 125-126.

1644 MEAD, Frank Spencer, 1898-
Handbook of denominations in the United States. New 5th ed. Nashville, Abingdon Press, 1970. 265 p.
"Church of the Nazarene": p. 84-85.

1645 REDFORD, Maury English
The rise of the Church of the Nazarene. Kansas City, Mo., Nazarene Publishing House, 1948. 208 p.

1646 REDFORD, Maury English
The rise of the Church of the Nazarene. Kansas City, Mo., Nazarene Publishing House, 1961. 202 p.

1647 REDFORD, Maury English
The rise of the Church of the Nazarene. Rev. and abridged ed. Kansas City, Mo., Beacon Hill Press, 1965. 108 p.

1648 SCHAFF, Philip, 1819-1893.
New Schaff-Herzog encyclopedia of religious knowledge.... S.M. Jackson, editor-in-chief. New York, Funk, 1908-1912. 12 v.
"Pentecostal Church of the Nazarene," by H.K. Carroll: v. 8, p. 453.

1649 SMITH, Timothy Lawrence, 1924-
Called unto holiness; the story of the Nazarenes: the formative years. Kansas City, Mo., Nazarene Publishing House, 1962. 413 p.

1650 TWENTIETH CENTURY encyclopedia of religious knowledge; an extension of the New Schaff-Herzog Encyclopedia of Religous Knowledge. Editor-in-chief: Lefferts A. Loetscher. Grand Rapids, Mich., Baker Book House, 1955. 2 v. (xx, 1205 p.)
"Nazarene, Church of the," by Sylvester Theodore Ludwig: p. 789.

-- --SOURCES

1651 RAIRDON, Jack T.
"A descriptive guide to the resource materials of the International Headquarters, Church of the Nazarene, 1908-1948." Unpublished M.A. thesis, University of Oklahoma, 1950.

--HISTORY OF DOCTRINES

1652 DUNNING, H. Ray
"Nazarene ethics as seen in a theological, historical and sociological context." Unpublished Ph.D. dissertation, Vanderbilt University, 1969. 229ℓ.

1653 WINGET, Wilfred Lamont, 1930-
"The Holy Spirit and the holiness of the church: a study in the theology of the Church of the Nazarene." Unpublished Ph.D. dissertation, Vanderbilt University, 1966. 423ℓ.

--HOMILETICAL ILLUSTRATIONS

1654 ALLEE, George Franklin, 1897- , ed.
Evangelistic illustrations, for pulpit and platform. Chicago, Moody Press, 1961. 400 p.

1655 CHAPMAN, James Blaine, 1884-1947.
Chapman's Choice outlines and illustrations. Grand Rapids, Mich., Zondervan, 1947. 103 p.

1656 FUGE, Frederick Thomas, 1872-
Great illustrations. Grand Rapids, Mich., Zondervan Publishing House, 1944. 117 p.

1657 HESLOP, William Greene, 1886- , ed.
Five hundred and one sermon illustrations. Grand Rapids, Mich., Baker Book House, 1945. 140 p.

1658 HESLOP, William Greene, 1886-
Seed thoughts; outlines of sermons, sermon illustrations, points for preachers, seed for sowers, truth for teachers,

supplies for soul-winners. Grand Rapids, Mich., Zondervan Publishing House, 1943. 121 p.

1659 WILLIAMS, Leewin Bell, 1868-
Holiness illustrations. Washington, D.C., Williams & Son, 1940. 118 p.

--HYMNS

1660 CHURCH OF the Nazarene.
Glorious gospel hymns, for use in all services of the church; Haldor Lillenas, ed. and comp. Kansas City, Mo., Nazarene Publishing House, 1931. Unpaged.
With music.

1661 CHURCH OF the Nazarene.
Praise and worship hymnal. Kansas City, Mo., Lillenas Publishing Co., 1953? Unpaged.
With music.

1662 CHURCH OF the Nazarene.
Worship in song hymnal. Kansas City, Mo., Lillenas Publishing Co., 1972. Unpaged.
With music.

1663 CHURCH OF the Nazarene. Women's Foreign Missionary Society.
Quadrennial convention: June 13, 14, 15, 1940. n.p., 1940. 16 p.
Hymns, with music.

1664 [COVE, Mary Elizabeth]
Victory songs for juniors, with program material.... Wollaston, Mass., M.E. Cove, c1943. Cover-title, 32 p.
Most of the songs (in four parts, close score) by Mary Elizabeth Cove.

1665 KIRKPATRICK, William James, 1838-1921, ed.
Waves of glory, number two, ed. by W. J. Kirkpatrick, D.L. Wallace, C.J. Kinne. Kansas City, Mo., Lillenas Publishing Co., 1921. Unpaged.

1666 [LATHAM, Joy], comp.
Joyfully sing; a hymnal for juniors. Kansas City, Mo., Lillenas Publishing Co., c1968. Unpaged.

1667 LILLENAS, Haldor, 1885-1959, comp.
Evangelistic songs, for the church, Sunday school, campmeetings, revival services, young people's societies and other religious services. Kansas City, Mo., Lillenas Publishing Co., 1937. Unpaged.
With music.

1668 LILLENAS, Haldor, 1885-1959, ed.
Hymns of conquest, for use in all religious services.
Kansas City, Mo., Lillenas Publishing Co., 1940. Unpaged.

1669 LILLENAS, Haldor, 1885-1959.
Lillenas' Solos and duets, no. 2; for use by singing evangelists, gospel singers, choirs, glee clubs and other organizations of like nature. Kansas City, Mo., Lillenas Publishing Co., 1936. Unpaged.
With music.

1670 LILLENAS, Haldor, 1885-1959.
New songs of the old faith, number one; for the promotion of the full gospel of Christ and Christian zeal in all departments of the church, comp. by E.W. Petticord [and others]. Kansas City, Mo., Nazarene Publishing Co., 1925. Unpaged.

1671 LILLENAS, Haldor, 1885-1959, ed.
Songs of full salvation. Indianapolis, Lillenas Publishing Co., 192?. Unpaged.
With music.

1672 LILLENAS, Haldor, 1885-1959.
Songs of the sanctuary; comp. and ed. by Haldor Lillenas, assisted by J. Glenn Gould, A.E. Ramquist [and] P.H. Lunn. Kansas City, Mo., Nazarene Publishing House, 1945. [352] p.
With music.

1673 LILLENAS, Haldor, 1885-1959.
Songs of victorious faith, designed for use in all religious services. Kansas City, Mo., Nazarene Publishing House, 1935? Unpaged.

1674 LONDON, Holland Bryan, 1908-
Sunshine choruses; a collection of choruses and songs for use in Sunday schools, revivals, missions, young people's rallies, etc., comp. by Holland London and Haldor Lillenas. Enl. ed. Kansas City, Mo., Lillenas Publishing Co., 1934. Unpaged.

1675 REVIVAL MELODIES; special ed. for the world-wide revival. Kansas City, Mo., Nazarene Publishing House, 1921. Unpaged.

-- --HISTORY AND CRITICISM

1676 LILLENAS, Haldor, 1885-1959.
Modern gospel song stories; introd. by Wm. M. Runyan. Kansas City, Mo., Lillenas Publishing Co., 1952. 157 p.

II. 1. Christian Holiness Association 175

--MEMBERSHIP

1677 ARMSTRONG, Kenneth Shelby
"The Church of the Nazarene: a study of an institutionalized sect." Unpublished Th.D. dissertation, Iliff School of Theology, 1958.

1678 ARMSTRONG, Kenneth Shelby
Face to face with the Church of the Nazarene. Boulder, Colo., 1958. 87 p.
Based on dissertation, Iliff School of Theology.

1679 GARSEE, Jarrell Willis, 1930-
"Some developmental correlates of individually perceived generation differences in value role-taking." Unpublished Ph.D. dissertation, Ohio State University, 1972. 163ℓ.
Examines Nazarene college students' attitudes toward church standards in relation to those of older members.

1680 MEYERING, Chester
"Values of Nazarene seniors in higher educational institutions." Unpublished Ed.D. dissertation, University of Denver, 1966. 196ℓ.

1681 STROPKO, Andrew John, 1945-
"Values of Nazarene college students on a public and a church sponsored campus." Unpublished M.A. thesis, University of Arizona, 1969. 70ℓ.

--MISSIONS

1682 CHURCH OF the Nazarene. Department of Foreign Missions. Missionary policy. Kansas City, Mo., 1951. 48 p.

1683 BOWER, Reuben Edward, 1874-
The unreached Indian; a treatise on Indian life and Indian missions. Kansas City, Mo., General Board of Foreign Missions, Church of the Nazarene, 1920. 124 p.

1684 CHAPMAN, James Blaine, 1884-1947.
30,000 miles of missionary travel. Kansas City, Mo., Nazarene Publishing House, 193?. 167 p.

1685 COOK, Franklin
Discovery--Student Mission Corps. Kansas City, Mo., Nazarene Publishing House, 1969. 88 p.

1686 DeLONG, Russell Victor, 1901-
We can if we will; the challenge of world evangelism. Kansas City, Mo., Nazarene Publishing House, 1947. 285 p.

The 1947-1948 missionary study book authorized by the Commission on Foreign Missionary Study Literature.

1687 DuBOIS, Lauriston J., ed.
　　　　The chaplains see world missions. Kansas City, Mo., Nazarene Publishing House, 1946. 157 p.
　　　　"An authorized publication of the Missionary Study Committee, Church of the Nazarene."

1688 ENCYCLOPEDIA OF modern Christian missions; the agencies. Burton L. Goddard, ed.... Camden, N.J., T. Nelson, 1967. xix, 743 p.
　　　　"Church of the Nazarene, General Board, Department of World Missions," by Helen Temple: p. 180-183.

1689 FISHER, Charles William, 1916-
　　　　The time is now. Kansas City, Mo., Nazarene Publishing House, 1950. 79 p.

1690 FITKIN, Susan (Norris), 1870-1951.
　　　　Holiness and missions. Kansas City, Mo., Nazarene Publishing House, 1940. 93 p.
　　　　W.F.M.S. silver anniversary souvenir ed.

1691 GISH, Carol (Spell)
　　　　Here am I [the story of young people God called to the foreign mission field]. Kansas City, Mo., Nazarene Publishing House, 1960. 87 p.

1692 GOODNOW, Edith P., comp.
　　　　Distinctive days on mission fields. Kansas City, Mo., Nazarene Publishing House, 1943. 218 p.
　　　　The correlated missionary study book for 1943-1944.

1693 GOODNOW, Edith P., ed.
　　　　New missionary frontiers. Kansas City, Mo., Nazarene Publishing House, 194?. 112 p.
　　　　Missionary reading book authorized by the Missionary Study Committee, Church of the Nazarene.

1694 GOULD, Joseph Glenn, 1896-
　　　　Missionary pioneers and our debt to them. Kansas City, Mo., Nazarene Publishing House, 1935. 192 p.
　　　　Correlated mission study book for 1935-1936.

1695 HINSHAW, Amy N.
　　　　Native torch bearers. Kansas City, Mo., Nazarene Publishing House, 1934. 207 p.
　　　　Woman's Missionary Society study book for 1934-1935.

1696 JONES, Carl Warren, 1882-1963.
　　　　Look on the fields. Kansas City, Mo., Nazarene Publishing House, 1950. 92 p.

II. 1. Christian Holiness Association

1697 JONES, Carl Warren, 1882-1963.
Missions for millions. Kansas City, Mo., Published for the Department of Foreign Missions, Church of the Nazarene, by Nazarene Publishing House, 1948. 95 p.

1698 KINNE, Clarence James, 1869-1932.
The modern Samaritan; a presentation of the claims of medical missions. Kansas City, Mo., Pentecostal Nazarene Publishing House, 191?. 88 p.

1699 REHFELDT, Remiss, 1915-
So shall we reap. Kansas City, Mo., Nazarene Publishing House, 1958. 90 p.

1700 REYNOLDS, Hiram Farnham, 1854-1938.
World-wide missions. Kansas City, Mo., Publishing House of the Pentecostal Church of the Nazarene, 1915. 215 p.

1701 REZA, Honorato T.
Our task for today. Kansas City, Mo., Nazarene Publishing House, 1963. 136 p.
At head of title: Missionary study book, 1963-64.

1702 SPANGENBERG, Alice
The Master says, "Go." Kansas City, Mo., Beacon Hill Press, 1955. 144 p.

1703 TEMPLE, Helen Frances
I will build my church; stories about Christians who, under God, made lasting contributions to the cause of foreign missions. Kansas City, Mo., Beacon Hill Press, 1955. 96 p.

1704 VANDERPOOL, Daniel I., 1891-
In their steps. Kansas City, Mo., Nazarene Publishing House, 1956.

1705 VERNER, Clara
Our original citizens; the story of Nazarene work among the North American Indians. Kansas City, Mo., Nazarene Publishing House, 1971. 70 p.

1706 WILLIAMS, Roy Tilman, 1883-1946.
Glimpses abroad. Kansas City, Mo., Nazarene Publishing House, 1930. 250 p.
Account of foreign travel supervising missionary activity of the Church of the Nazarene.

-- --HISTORY

1707 CHURCH OF the Nazarene. General Board of Foreign Missions.

History of the foreign missionary work of the Church of the Nazarene. Kansas City, Mo., General Board of Foreign Missions, Church of the Nazarene, 1921. 59 p.

1708 SWIM, Roy Elliott, 1899-
A history of missions of the Church of the Nazarene; the correlated mission study book for 1936-1937. Kansas City, Mo., Nazarene Publishing House, 1936. 204 p.

1709 TAYLOR, Mendell, 1912-
Fifty years of Nazarene missions, by Mendell Taylor and Russell V. DeLong. Kansas City, Mo., Beacon Hill Press, 1952-1958. 3 v.

-- --SOCIETIES, ETC.

1710 CHURCH OF the Nazarene. Woman's Missionary Society.
Constitution and by-laws for local and district Woman's Missionary societies and Woman's General Missionary Council of the Church of the Nazarene, with recommendations and helps. Kansas City, Mo., Woman's General Missionary Council, 1932. 19 p.

1711 FITKIN, Susan (Norris), 1870-1951.
A brief history of the Woman's Missionary Society, Church of the Nazarene. Kansas City, Mo., Nazarene Publishing House, n.d.

--MUSIC

1712 BENNER, Hugh Clifford, 1899-
Singing disciples; toward better church music. Kansas City, Mo., Lillenas Publishing Co., 1959. 70 p.

--PASTORAL THEOLOGY

1713 AYCOCK, Jarrette E.,   -1966.
Add them to the church; a series of suggestions and methods for getting people to unite with the church. Kansas City, Mo., Beacon Hill Press, 1957. 52 p.

1714 CHAPMAN, James Blaine, 1884-1947.
The preaching ministry. Kansas City, Mo., Beacon Hill Press, 1947. 95 p.

1715 CHILTON, Claude L.
The Nazarene serviceman. Kansas City, Mo., Nazarene Publishing House, 1953. 64 p.

II. 1. Christian Holiness Association

1716 ELLYSON, Edgar Painter, 1869-1954.
 The pastor and his Sunday school responsibility. Kansas City, Mo., Nazarene Publishing House, 19??. 47 p.

1717 GIBSON, Charles Arthur, 1888-
 First things in the ministry. Berne, Ind., Economy Printing Concern, 1958. 100 p.

1718 GOULD, Joseph Glenn, 1896-
 Healing the hurt of man; a study of John Wesley's "cure of souls." Kansas City, Mo., Beacon Hill Press, 1971. 70 p.

1719 HILLS, Aaron Merritt, 1848-1935.
 Homiletics and pastoral theology. Kansas City, Mo., Nazarene Publishing House, 1929. 394 p.

1720 JONES, Lum
 The new pastor. Kansas City, Mo., Nazarene Publishing House, 1926. 96 p.

1721 PARROTT, Leslie, 1922-
 Building today's church; how pastors and laymen work together. Kansas City, Mo., Beacon Hill Press, 1971. 228 p.

1722 PAUL, Cecil Rowland, 1935-
 "The inclusion of pastoral counseling in the Church of the Nazarene; a comparison of Seward Hiltner and selected writers in the Church of the Nazarene." Unpublished Ph.D. dissertation, Boston University, 1968. viii, 220ℓ.

1723 WILLIAMS, Roy Tilman, 1883-1946.
 Pastor and people. Kansas City, Mo., Nazarene Publishing House, 1939. 75 p.

1724 WILLIAMSON, Gideon Brooks, 1898-
 Overseers of the flock; a discussion of pastoral practice. Kansas City, Mo., Beacon Hill Press, 1953. 250 p.

-- --AUTHORITATIVE SOURCES

1725 SHELHAMER, Elmer Ellsworth, 1860-1947.
 Heart talks with ministers. Kansas City, Mo., Nazarene Publishing House, n.d. 191 p.

-- --BIBLIOGRAPHY

1726 NAZARENE THEOLOGICAL Seminary.
 An annotated bibliography of books recommended for a pastor's library. Prepared by the faculty of Nazarene Theological Seminary. Edited and compiled by Robert E.

Crabtree. Kansas City, Mo., Nazarene Theological Seminary, 1964. 24 p. (The Seminary Tower, v. 19, spring 1964)

--PERIODICALS

1727 LA ANTORCHA Dominical. 1- , 1947?- . Kansas City, Mo.

1728 BIBLE SCHOOL Journal. 1- , 1910- . Los Angeles, Calif.; Kansas City, Mo.
1910-19?? as Bible School Teacher's Journal

1729 CHURCH SCHOOL Builder. 1- , Sept. 1946- . Kansas City, Mo.

1730 CONQUEST; a magazine for Christian youth. 1- , Oct. 1946- . Kansas City, Mo.

1731 HERALD OF Holiness. 1- , Apr. 17, 1912- . Kansas City, Mo.

1732 HERALDO DE Santidad. 1- , 1921-192?. Los Angeles.

1733 HERALDO DE Santidad. 1- , 1946- . Kansas City, Mo., Nazarene Publishing House.

1734 HIGHWAYS AND Hedges. 1- , 1909-191?. Bethany, Okla.

1735 HOLINESS HERALD. 1-4, 1913-1917; ns 1-32, 1922-1956. Glasgow, Scot.
1934-1952 as Way of Holiness; 1953-1956 as The Way; a Holiness Journal.

1736 HOLINESS HERALD. 1- , 1918?-19??. Bethany, Okla.

1737 JONES, Charles Edwin, 1932-
"An index of The Other Sheep, 1913-1918." Unpublished student paper, University of Michigan, 1955. xi, 186ℓ.

1738 NAZARENE PASTOR. 1-17, no. 1, Oct. 1947-Oct.-Nov. 1963. Kansas City, Mo.
Merged with Preacher's Magazine to form Nazarene Preacher.

1739 OTHER SHEEP. 1- , 1913- . Kansas City, Mo.

1740 PREACHER'S MAGAZINE. 1- , 1926- . Kansas City, Mo.
1964-June 1972 as Nazarene Preacher.

II. 1. Christian Holiness Association

1741 EL SENDERO de la Verdad. 1- , 1947- . Kansas City, Mo.

1742 SOUTH AFRICAN Nazarene. 1- , 1950- . Potchefstroom, Transval, S. Afr.
1950-1951 as Pastor's Bulletin.

1743 WUESTER, Alfreda (Huhnke)
"A system of subject access to the Herald of Holiness, official organ of the Church of the Nazarene. Unpublished M.A. thesis, University of Oklahoma, 1960.

--POLEMICAL WORKS

-- --CATHOLICISM

1744 FISHER, Charles William, 1916-
Why I am a Nazarene and not--a Mormon, a Roman Catholic, a Jehovah's Witness, a Christian Scientist, a Seventh-Day Adventist. Kansas City, Mo., Nazarene Publishing House, 1958. 144 p.

-- --CHRISTIAN SCIENCE

1745 FISHER, Charles William, 1916-
Why I am a Nazarene and not--a Mormon, a Roman Catholic, a Jehovah's Witness, a Christian Scientist, a Seventh-Day Adventist. Kansas City, Mo., Nazarene Publishing House, 1958. 144 p.

-- --JEHOVAH'S WITNESSES

1746 FISHER, Charles William, 1916-
Why I am a Nazarene and not--a Mormon, a Roman Catholic, a Jehovah's Witness, a Christian Scientist, a Seventh-Day Adventist. Kansas City, Mo., Nazarene Publishing House, 1958. 144 p.

-- --METHODISM

1747 BEEBE, Theodore Eaton
Hatching chickens for the hawks. Long Beach, Calif., T.E. Beebe, 1920. 59 p.
"Poems in this book written by F.M. Lehman."

1748 LEHMAN, Frederick Martin, 1868-
The man in black. Kansas City, Mo., Publishing House of the Pentecostal Church of the Nazarene, 1913. 192 p.
Autobiographical allegory on the carnal mind.

----MORMONISM

1749 FISHER, Charles William, 1916-
Why I am a Nazarene and not--a Mormon, a Roman Catholic, a Jehovah's Witness, a Christian Scientist, a Seventh-Day Adventist. Kansas City, Mo., Nazarene Publishing House, 1958. 144 p.

----SEVENTH-DAY ADVENTISM

1750 FISHER, Charles William, 1916-
Why I am a Nazarene and not--a Mormon, a Roman Catholic, a Jehovah's Witness, a Christian Scientist, a Seventh-Day Adventist. Kansas City, Mo., Nazarene Publishing House, 1958. 144 p.

--POLITICAL AND SOCIAL CRITICISM

1751 BANGS, Carl Oliver, 1922-
The communist encounter; [vital Christianity is the only adequate answer]. Kansas City, Mo., Beacon Hill Press, 1963. 94 p.

1752 CORLETT, David Shelby, 1894-
Prohibition at the crossroads. Kansas City, Mo., Nazarene Publishing House, 1932.

1753 TAYLOR, Mendell, 1912-
America at the crossroads. Kansas City, Mo., Nazarene Publishing House, 1966. 40 p.

1754 UPCHURCH, James T., 1870-
Behind the scarlet mask. Fort Worth, Tex., World Printers, 1924. 288 p.

1755 WILLIAMSON, Gideon Brooks, 1898-
"Meritocracy," Herald of Holiness, LII (July 22, 1964), 2.

--PUBLISHERS AND PUBLISHING

1756 HINSHAW, Amy N.
Your publishing house. Kansas City, Mo., Nazarene Publishing House, 1937.

1757 JORDAN, Oreus E.
"A history of the official publications of the Church of the Nazarene." Unpublished B.D. thesis, Nazarene Theological Seminary, 1949.

II. 1. Christian Holiness Association 183

1758 RAWLINGS, Elden Everette
"A history of the Nazarene Publishing House." Unpublished M.A. thesis, University of Oklahoma, 1960.

--RELIGIOUS EDUCATION

1759 BENSON, Erwin George, 1905-
Sunday-school handibook for pastors, Sunday-school superintendents, Sunday-school supervisors. Kansas City, Mo., Nazarene Publishing House, 19??. 64 p.

1760 ELLYSON, Edgar Painter, 1869-1954.
The Bible in Education. Kansas City, Mo., Publishing House of the Pentecostal Church of the Nazarene, 1913. 235 p.

1761 ELLYSON, Edgar Painter, 1869-1954.
The pastor and his Sunday school responsibility. Kansas City, Mo., Nazarene Publishing House, 19??. 47 p.

1762 ELLYSON, Edgar Painter, 1869-1954.
The principles of teaching, by E.P. Ellyson and H.O. Wiley. Kansas City, Mo., Department of Church Schools, Church of the Nazarene, 1931. 151 p. (Leadership Training Course)

1763 ELLYSON, Edgar Painter, 1869-1954.
...A study of the pupil, by E.P. Ellyson and H. Orton Wiley. 3d ed., rev. Kansas City, Mo., Nazarene Publishing House, 1930. 144 p. (Leadership training course)

1764 ELLYSON, Edgar Painter, 1869-1954.
A study of the teacher. 4th ed. Kansas City, Mo., Pub. for the Department of Church Schools, Church of the Nazarene, by the Nazarene Publishing House, c1929. 117 p.
At head of title: Leadership training course.

1765 ELLYSON, Edgar Painter, 1869-1954.
...A study of the teacher. 5th ed., rev. Kansas City, Mo., Nazarene Publishing House, 1939. 141 p. (Leadership training course)

1766 ELLYSON, Edgar Painter, 1869-1954.
The teaching agency of the church school. Kansas City, Mo., Department of Church Schools, Church of the Nazarene, c1929. 176 p.
At head of title: Leadership training course.

1767 ELLYSON, Edgar Painter, 1869-1954.
...The teaching agency of the church. 4th ed., rev. Kansas City, Mo., Nazarene Publishing House, c1934.

1768 ELLYSON, Edgar Painter, 1869-1954.
This is the will of God: Christian religious education. Kansas City, Mo., Nazarene Publishing House, 19??. 22 p.

1769 ELLYSON, Edgar Painter, 1869-1954.
The will of God: Christian religious education; anniversary address, tenth General Assembly, Church of the Nazarene, Department of Church Schools. Kansas City, Mo., 1940. Cover-title, 22 p.

1770 HARPER, Albert Foster, 1907-
The Nazarene Sunday school in the seventies; a blueprint for the teaching task of the church. Kansas City, Mo. Nazarene Publishing House, 1971. 256 p. (Christian service training course)
"Eighth revised edition."

1771 HARPER, Albert Foster, 1907-
The story of ourselves; a study in the growth of personality for teachers and parents. Kansas City, Mo., Nazarene Publishing House, 1944. 214 p.

1772 HARPER, Albert Foster, 1907-
The Sunday-school teacher. Kansas City, Mo., Beacon Hill Press, 1956. 115 p.

1773 HORN, Purl
Practical methods for building Sunday schools. 2d ed., rev. Pasadena, Calif., Purl Horn, 1953. 75 p.

1774 KELLY, M. Thomas
"An investigation into the status of the director of Christian education in the Church of the Nazarene." Unpublished M.A. thesis, University of Wyoming, 1952. 106ℓ.

1775 KNOTT, James Proctor, 1886-1963.
The vacation Bible school. Kansas City, Mo., Nazarene Publishing House, 1928. 48 p.

1776 McINTYRE, Ralph L.
Talking chemicals; simple object lessons with common chemicals. Kansas City, Mo., Beacon Hill Press, 1972. 52 p.

1777 METZ, Donald S., 1916-
"The development of religious education in the Church of the Nazarene." Unpublished D.R.E. dissertation, Southwestern Baptist Theological Seminary, 1956.

1778 MILLER, Basil William, 1897-
Putting the Sunday school across; addresses-in-print to Sunday School workers. 2d ed. Kansas City, Mo., Naza-

II. 1. Christian Holiness Association

rene Publishing House, n.d. 78 p.
Approved and recommended by the Department of Church Schools of the Church of the Nazarene.

1779 PENTECOSTAL LESSON commentary; helps on the International series Sunday school lessons.... Kansas City, Mo., Pentecostal Nazarene Publishing House, 1917- .
Editors: 1917- , E.F. Walker, B.F. Haynes.

1780 REED, Oscar Ferguson
"Some religious assumptions of the Church of the Nazarene and their impact upon religious education." Unpublished Ph.D. dissertation, University of Southern California, 1947.

1781 SAYES, James Ottis, 1922-
"The vocational religious education leader in the Church of the Nazarene." Unpublished D.R.E. dissertation, Southwestern Baptist Theological Seminary, 1956.

1782 WISE, Forest Franklyn, 1920-
"A study of the critical requirements of Sunday church school teachers of unmarried youth of certain Protestant denominations." Unpublished Ph.D. dissertation, University of Pittsburgh, 1958.

--SERMONS

1783 ANDERSON, Tony Marshall, 1888-
Searching the Scriptures. Kansas City, Mo., Beacon Hill Press, 1948. 140 p.

1784 AYCOCK, Dell (Davis), -1967.
More object sermons. Kansas City, Mo., Nazarene Publishing House, 1934. 70 p.

1785 AYCOCK, Dell (Davis), -1967.
Object sermons. Kansas City, Mo., Nazarene Publishing House, 1927. 86 p.

1786 AYCOCK, Jarrette E., -1966.
The crimson stream; a devotional sermon on the blood. Kansas City, Mo., Nazarene Publishing House, 1927. 32 p.

1787 AYCOCK, Jarrette E., -1966.
The grand old Book, a sermon on the Bible. Kansas City, Mo., Nazarene Publishing House, 1929. 40 p.

1788 AYCOCK, Jarrette E., -1966.
If Christ had not come, and other sermons. Grand Rapids, Mich., Zondervan Publishing House, 1944. 131 p.

1789 AYCOCK, Jarrette E.,   -1966.
"The prince of this world" (the devil) [John 14:30] by Evangelist Jarrette Aycock.... Kansas City, Mo., Nazarene Publishing House, 1941. 40 p.

1790 BELEW, Pascal Perry, 1894-
Seven golden candlesticks. Butler, Ind., Higley Press, 1956. 99 p.

1791 BRESEE, Phineas Franklin, 1838-1915.
The certainties of faith; ten sermons by the founder of the Church of the Nazarene, with an introd. and notes on the author's life by Timothy L. Smith, Ph.D. Kansas City, Mo., Nazarene Publishing House, 1958. 95 p.

1792 BRESEE, Phineas Franklin, 1838-1915.
Sermons from Matthew's Gospel. Kansas City, Mo., Nazarene Publishing House, n.d. 220 p.

1793 BRESEE, Phineas Franklin, 1838-1915.
Sermons on Isaiah. Kansas City, Mo., Nazarene Publishing House, 1926. 178 p.

1794 BRESEE, Phineas Franklin, 1838-1915.
Soul food for today, comp. by C.J. Kinne from the writings of P.F. Bresee. Kansas City, Mo., Nazarene Publishing House, 1929. Unpaged.

1795 BROWNING, Raymond, 1879-1953.
God's melting pot: Romans 8:28. Kansas City, Mo., Beacon Hill Press, 1951. 32 p.

1796 CHALFANT, Morris
Are you a crook? Elk City, Okla., Davis Printing Co. n.d. 36 p.

1797 CHAPMAN, James Blaine, 1884-1947.
Camp meeting sermons. Kansas City, Mo., Nazarene Publishing House, 1935. 92 p.

1798 CHAPMAN, James Blaine, 1884-1947.
Christian living in a modern world. 2d ed. Kansas City, Mo., Beacon Hill Press, 1942. 137 p.
First issued under title: Christian men in a modern world.

1799 CHAPMAN, James Blaine, 1884-1947.
Christian men in a modern world. Kansas City, Mo., Nazarene Publishing House, 1942. 137 p.

1800 CHAPMAN, James Blaine, 1884-1947.
The divine response. Kansas City, Mo., Beacon Hill Press, 1946. 137 p.

II. 1. Christian Holiness Association

1801 CHAPMAN, James Blaine, 1884-1947.
Some estimates of life. Kansas City, Mo., Nazarene Publishing House, n.d. 114 p.
Enlarged ed. of Ten little sermons.

1802 CHAPMAN, James Blaine, 1884-1947.
Truths that are vital. Kansas City, Mo., Nazarene Publishing House, n.d. 56 p.
"Special world-wide revival edition."

1803 CHAPMAN, James Blaine, 1884-1947.
With Chapman at camp meeting. Kansas City, Mo., Beacon Hill Press, 1961. 22 p.
"Second printing."

1804 DeLONG, Russell Victor, 1901-
Beyond tragedy--what?, and other sermons. Kansas City, Mo., Beacon Hill Press, 1956. 96 p.

1805 DeLONG, Russell Victor, 1901-
Clouds and rainbows, and other radio sermons. Kansas City, Mo., Beacon Hill Press, 1950. 112 p.

1806 DeLONG, Russell Victor, 1901-
Facts we hate to face, and other radio sermons. Kansas City, Mo., Beacon Hill Press, 1952. 108 p.

1807 DeLONG, Russell Victor, 1901-
The high cost of low living. Kansas City, Mo., Beacon Hill Press, 1949. 112 p.

1808 DeLONG, Russell Victor, 1901-
Mastering our midnights, and other sermons. Kansas City, Mo., Beacon Hill Press, 1953. 103 p.

1809 DeLONG, Russell Victor, 1901-
A temple or a tavern; thirty-four inspirational, informational, ethical, spiritual addresses. New York, Vantage Press, 1969. 176 p.

1810 DeLONG, Russell Victor, 1901-
There are no moral accidents. Kansas City, Mo., Nazarene Radio League, n.d. 94 p.

1811 DeLONG, Russell Victor, 1901-
The unique Galilean. Kansas City, Mo., Beacon Hill Press, 1957. 20 p.

1812 FISHER, Charles William, 1916-
Our goal is excellence; a compilation of radio messages. Kansas City, Mo., Beacon Hill Press, 1971. 112 p.

1813 GOODWIN, John Wesley, 1869-1945.
The living flame. Kansas City, Mo., Nazarene Publishing House, n.d. 176 p.

1814 GRAY, Joseph
The double cure and other holiness sermons. Kansas City, Mo., Beacon Hill Press, 1953. 142 p.

1815 HESLOP, William Greene, 1886-
The coming collapse and other sermons. Grand Rapids Mich., Peniel Press, 1937. 133 p.

1816 HICKS, Lawrence B.
"This is that"; the song of the sanctified. Kansas City, Mo., Beacon Hill Press, 1957. 37 p.

1817 HILL, Paul S.
The man in the garden. n.p., Published by the author, 1952.

1818 HUDSON, Oscar, 1874-
Gospel dynamite. Kansas City, Mo., Nazarene Publishing House, 1925. 202 p.

1819 KRING, James Arthur, 1873-
Vital gospel truths; sixteen sermons presenting the teaching of Scripture relative to sin and Christ's remedy for the universal malady. Kansas City, Mo., Beacon Hill Press, 1955. 123 p.

1820 LEIST, J. F., -1972.
The evangelist of Galilee. Kansas City, Mo., Nazarene Publishing House, n.d. 62 p.

1821 LEWIS, Voyle H.
No man can serve two masters. Kansas City, Mo., Nazarene Publishing House, 1964. 32 p.

1822 McCUMBER, W. E.
A good word, and other sermons. Kansas City, Mo., Beacon Hill Press, 1959. 77 p.

1823 MONTGOMERY, James William, 1898-
Christian certitudes, and other radio sermons. Kansas City, Mo., Nazarene Publishing House, n.d. 64 p.

1824 MONTGOMERY, James William, 1898-
The Christian way. Fort Wayne, Ind., n.d. Unpaged.

1825 MORRISON, Joseph Grant, 1871-1939.
Three loaves of bread; Faith for achievement; The mosquito scourge. Garden City, Kan., Telegram Publishing Co., 1956. 26 p.

II. 1. Christian Holiness Association

1826 THE NAZARENE pulpit; a collection of sermons from well known preachers. Kansas City, Mo., Nazarene Publishing House, 1925. 239 p.

1827 NEASE, Floyd William, 1893-1930.
Symphonies of praise; introd. by the Rev. Roy T. Williams. Kansas City, Mo., Nazarene Publishing House, 1931. 192 p.
Includes biographical sketch by Orval J. Nease.

1828 NEASE, Orval John, 1891-1950.
Heroes of temptation. Kansas City, Mo., Beacon Hill Press, 1950. 32 p.

1829 PRICE, Ross Eugene, 1907-
Faith in these times; sermons by Pasadena College ministers, commemorating fifty years of service by Pasadena College in the city of Pasadena, California, 1910 to 1960, ed. by Ross E. Price [and] Oscar F. Reed. Kansas City, Mo., Beacon Hill Press, 1961. 117 p.

1830 REED, Harold William, 1909-
Committed to Christ; messages to college youth. Grand Rapids, Mich., Baker Book House, 1960. 112 p.

1831 ROBINSON, Reuben, 1860-1942.
Bees in clover. Kansas City, Mo., Nazarene Publishing House, 1921. 188 p.

1832 ROBINSON, Reuben, 1860-1942.
Chickens come home to roost. Kansas City, Mo., Beacon Hill Press, 1958. 79 p.

1833 ROBINSON, Reuben, 1860-1942.
The moth-eaten garment. Kansas City, Mo., Beacon Hill Press, 1961. 39 p.

1834 ROBINSON, Reuben, 1860-1942.
My objections to a sinning religion. Kansas City, Mo., Beacon Hill Press, 1961. 31 p.
Selections from Bees in Clover.

1835 SMITH, Arlis Milton, 1903-
Seven sayings about the crucified. Kansas City, Mo., Beacon Hill Press, 1946. 124 p.

1836 SMITH, Bernie, 1920-
The thirteenth apostle. Kansas City, Mo., Beacon Hill Press, 1955. 95 p.

1837 SMITH, Bernie, 1920-
Triumph and tragedy in New Testament personalities. Kansas City, Mo., Beacon Hill Press, 1951. 69 p.

1838 SPARKS, Samuel F.
The better way. Louisville, Pentecostal Publishing Co. n. d. 45 p.

1839 SPRUCE, Fletcher Clarke
Fighting the stars, and other sermons. Kansas City, Mo., Beacon Hill Press, 1957. 90 p.

1840 THOMAS, James Melton, 1917
Great three-sixteens of the New Testament. Kansas City, Mo., Beacon Hill Press, 1955. 80 p.

1841 VANDERPOOL, Daniel I., 1891-
Living waters. Kansas City, Mo., Nazarene Publishing House, 1964. 123 p.

1842 WILEY, Henry Orton, 1877-1961.
God has the answer. Kansas City, Mo., Beacon Hill Press, 1956. 124 p.

1843 WILEY, Henry Orton, 1877-1961.
The harps of God, and other sermons; comp. and ed. by Ross E. Price. Kansas City, Mo., Beacon Hill Press, 1971. 86 p.

1844 WILEY, Henry Orton, 1877-1961.
The Pentecostal promise; and, "We all do fade as a leaf," anniversary message given on outstanding occasions. Kansas City, Beacon Hill Press, 1963. 24 p.

1845 WOODRUM, Lon Riley, 1901-
The security of surrender. Grand Rapids, Mich., Zondervan Publishing House, c1955. 29 p.

-- --COLLECTIONS

1846 THE NAZARENE pulpit; a collection of sermons from well known preachers. Kansas City, Mo., Nazarene Publishing House, 1925. 239 p.

-- --OUTLINES

1848 HESLOP, William Greene, 1886-
Sermon seeds from the Psalms. Butler, Ind., Higley Press, 1956. 144 p.

--STATISTICS

1847 CHAPMAN, James Blaine, 1884-1947.
Chapman's Choice outlines and illustrations. Grand Rapids, Mich., Zondervan, 1947. 103 p.

II. 1. Christian Holiness Association 191

1849 ARMSTRONG, Kenneth Shelby
"The Church of the Nazarene: a study of an institutionalized sect." Unpublished Th.D. dissertation, Iliff School of Theology, 1958.

1850 ARMSTRONG, Kenneth Shelby
Face to face with the Church of the Nazarene. Boulder, Colo., 1958. 87 p.
Based on dissertation, Iliff School of Theology.

1851 U.S. BUREAU of the Census.
...Census of religious bodies, 1926; Church of the Nazarene: history, doctrine, and organization.... Washington, U.S. Government Printing Office, 1928. 15 p.

--WORK WITH YOUTH

1852 COOK, Franklin
Discovery--Student Mission Corps. Kansas City, Mo., Nazarene Publishing House, 1969. 88 p.

1853 EDWARDS, Mildred (Speakes), 1904-
Opening doors of faith; guidance for the Christian home when children are one to five. Kansas City, Mo., Beacon Hill Press, 1953. 154 p.

1854 JONES, Elizabeth (Brown), 1907-
Together with God; guidance for the Christian home when children are six to eight. Kansas City, Mo., Beacon Hill Press, 1952. 158 p.

1855 LONDON, Allie S.
Is the lad going up with us? Kansas City, Mo., Beacon Hill Press, 1948. 24 p.

1856 LONDON, Allie S.
Youth for Christ. 2d ed. Kansas City, Mo., Nazarene Publishing House, 1941.

1857 PECK, Kathryn (Blackburn), 1904-
In favor with God and man; guidance for the Christian home when children are nine to eleven. Kansas City, Mo., Beacon Hill Press, 1952. 154 p.

1858 TAYLOR, Mendell, 1912-
Nazarene youth in conquest for Christ. Kansas City, Mo., Nazarene Publishing House, 1948. 159 p.

1859 WILLIAMSON, Audrey (Johnston)
Your teen-ager and you; guidance for the Christian home when young people are from twelve to eighteen. Kansas City, Mo., Beacon Hill Press, 1952. 96 p.

--YEARBOOKS

1860 CHURCH OF the Nazarene.
Yearbook, 1924; E.J. Fleming, ed. Kansas City, Mo., Nazarene Publishing House, 1924.

1861 CHURCH OF the Nazarene.
Yearbook, 1925; E.J. Fleming, ed. Kansas City, Mo., Nazarene Publishing House, 1925.

--AFRICA

1862 HYND, David, 1895-
Africa emerging. Kansas City, Mo., Nazarene Publishing House, 1959. 143 p.

--AFRICA, CENTRAL

1863 HALL, B. Maurice
I sought for a man; the story of Nazarene missions in Central Africa. Kansas City, Mo., Nazarene Publishing House, 1966. 72 p.

--AFRICA, SOUTH

1864 CHISM, Fairy Steele, 1899-1971.
"The Lord's doing"; Nazarene missionary achievements in South Africa ... by Fairy Chism, Ora V. Lovelace and C.S. Jenkins. Kansas City, Mo., Nazarene Publishing House, 1941. 235 p.
The correlated missionary study book for 1941-1942.

1865 ENCYCLOPEDIA OF modern Christian missions; the agencies. Burton L. Goddard, ed.... Camden, N.J., T. Nelson, 1967. xix, 743 p.
"The Church of the Nazarene in the Republic of South Africa," by Marjorie Wise: p. 184.

1866 ESSELSTYN, William C.
Nazarene missions in South Africa. Kansas City, Mo., Nazarene Publishing House, 1952. 153 p.
The 1952-53 missionary study book authorized by the Commission on Foreign Missionary Study Literature.

1867 HAYSE, George R.
The other side of the shield; [missionary work in the African locations]. Kansas City, Mo., Nazarene Publishing House, 1966. 96 p.

II. 1. Christian Holiness Association

--ALBERTA

1868 MANN, William Edward
Sect, cult, and church in Alberta. Toronto, University of Toronto Press, 1955. xiii, 166 p.
Includes description of the Church of the Nazarene.

--AUSTRALIA

1869 MINK, Nelson G.
Southern Cross salute; stories of men and women who are making history in the Church of the Nazarene in the South Pacific. Kansas City, Mo., Nazarene Publishing House, 1969. 72 p.

1870 TAYLOR, Richard Shelley, 1912-
Our Pacific outposts. Kansas City, Mo., Beacon Hill Press, 1956. 133 p.

--CALIFORNIA

1871 ECKEL, Howard
A plain statement of why the University Pentecostal Church of the Nazarene was disorganized. Pasadena, Calif., 1917.

--CANADA

1872 ENCYCLOPEDIA CANADIANA. Ottawa, Canadiana Co., 1957-1958. 10 v.
"Church of the Nazarene" by J. Fred Parker: v. 2, p. 385-386.

1873 PARKER, John Fred
From East to western sea; a brief history of the Church of the Nazarene in Canada. Kansas City, Mo., Nazarene Publishing House, 1971. 107 p.
A 50th anniversary project of Canadian Nazarene College.

1874 PARKER, John Fred
"The historical background of the Church of the Nazarene in western Canada." Unpublished B.D. thesis, Nazarene Theological Seminary, 1950. 145ℓ.

--CAPE VERDE ISLANDS

1875 GISH, Carol (Spell)
Mediterranean missions; a study of the missionary work of the Church of the Nazarene in Israel, Jordan, Syria,

Lebanon, Italy, and the Cape Verde Islands. Kansas City, Mo., Nazarene Publishing House, 1965. 158 p.
1965-66 missionary study book.

1876 MILLER, Basil William, 1897-
Miracle in Cape Verde. Kansas City, Mo., Beacon Hill Press, 1951.

1877 SPANGENBERG, Alice
Jerusalem and beyond; Christian missions in the Cape Verde Islands and the Middle East. Kansas City, Mo., Nazarene Publishing House, 1950. 160 p.

1878 TRACY, Olive Gertrude, 1908-
The nations and the isles; a study of missionary work of the Church of the Nazarene in the nations--Israel, Jordan Syria, Lebanon, Italy--and the isles--the Cape Verde Islands. Kansas City, Mo., Nazarene Publishing House, 1958. 251 p.

--CARIBBEAN REGION

1879 GISH, Carol (Spell)
The magic circle of the Caribbean. Kansas City, Mo., Nazarene Publishing House, 1953. 154 p.
The 1953-54 missionary study book authorized by the Commission on Foreign Missionary Study Literature.

1880 TEMPLE, Helen Frances
Other sheep I have; missionary stories from the Caribbean. Kansas City, Mo., Beacon Hill Press, 1953. 96 p.

--CHINA

1881 KINNE, Clarence James, 1869-1932.
Our field in China. Kansas City, Mo., Nazarene Publishing House, 1934. 62 p.

1882 OSBORN, Leon Clarence
The China story; the Church of the Nazarene in North China, South China, and Taiwan. Kansas City, Mo., Nazarene Publishing House, 1969. 80 p.

1883 RAMQUIST, Grace (Chapman), 1907-
No' respecter of persons. Kansas City, Mo., Nazarene Publishing House, 1962. 142 p.
Missionary study book, 1962-63.

1884 REED, Louis Archibald, 1892-1952.
The challenge of China, by L.A. Reed [and] H.A.

II. 1. Christian Holiness Association

Wiese. Kansas City, Mo., Nazarene Publishing House, 1937. 139 p.

--EAST (FAR EAST)

1885 EARLE, Ralph, 1907-
Fields afar: Nazarene missions in the Far East, India, and the South Pacific; missionary study book, 1969-70. Kansas City, Mo., Nazarene Publishing House, 1969. 127 p.

1886 FITKIN, Susan (Norris), 1870-1951.
Nazarene missions in the Orient, by Rev. S.N. Fitkin and Emma B. Word. Kansas City, Mo., Nazarene Publishing House, 193?. 112 p.

1887 TEMPLE, Helen Frances
These my brethren; missionary stories from the Far East. Kansas City, Mo., Nazarene Publishing House, 1962. 88 p.

--EUROPE

1888 JOHNSON, Jerry
Let's go Dutch; the Church of the Nazarene in Europe. Kansas City, Mo., Nazarene Publishing House, 1971. 64 p.

-GREAT BRITAIN

1889 FORD, Jack, 1908-
"The Church of the Nazarene in Britain, the International Holiness Mission and the Calvary Holiness Church, with reference to holiness movements in Christian history." Unpublished Ph.D. dissertation, University of London, 1967.

1890 FORD, Jack, 1908-
In the steps of John Wesley; the Church of the Nazarene in Britain. Kansas City, Mo., Printed by Nazarene Publishing House, 1968. 300 p.
Thesis (Ph.D.)--University of London, 1967.

1891 SHARPE, George, 1865-1948.
A short historical sketch of the Church of the Nazarene in the British Isles. n.p., 192?. 66 p.

--GUATEMALA

1892 BOWER, Reuben Edward, 1874-
Our friends in Guatemala. Kansas City, Mo., General

Board of the Church of the Nazarene, 1924. 61 p.

1893 HEAP, Gwladys
Pioneering in El Peten. Kansas City, Mo., Nazarene Publishing House, 1968. 79 p.

--HAITI

1894 CROW, Linda
Haiti, I love you, with photos by Walter and Linda Crow. Kansas City, Mo., Nazarene Publishing House, 1970. 71 p.

1895 ORJALA, Paul Richard, 1925-
Haiti diary; the intimate story of a modern young missionary couple's first two years in a foreign country, comp. from the letters of Paul Orjala and ed. by Kathleen Spell. Kansas City, Mo., Beacon Hill Press, 1953. 125 p.

1896 ORJALA, Paul Richard, 1925-
"Some implications of Haitian culture for leadership education in the Evangelical church in Haiti." Unpublished M.A. thesis, Hartford Seminary Foundation, 1956. 221ℓ.

--INDIA

1897 CHURCH OF the Nazarene. Missions and mission districts. India.
New India and the gospel, [by the] India Nazarene Mission Council. Kansas City, Mo., Nazarene Publishing House, 1954. 128 p.
"The 1954-55 missionary study book authorized by the Commission on Foreign Missionary Study Literature."

1898 BEALS, Prescott L.
India's open door. Kansas City, Mo., Nazarene Publishing House, 1940. 186 p.
The correlated missions study book for 1940-1941.

1899 EARLE, Ralph, 1907-
Fields afar: Nazarene missions in the Far East, India, and the South Pacific; missionary study book, 1969-70. Kansas City, Mo., Nazarene Publishing House, 1969. 127 p.

1900 RAMQUIST, Grace (Chapman), 1907-
No respecter of persons. Kansas City, Mo., Nazarene Publishing House, 1962. 142 p.
Missionary study book, 1962-63.

II. 1. Christian Holiness Association

1901 WILLIAMSON, Gideon Brooks, 1898-
"Yesu Masiki Jay" "Victory to Jesus the Messiah"; a first hand survey of Nazarene missionary progress in India, by Gideon B. and Audrey Williamson. Kansas City, Mo., Nazarene Publishing House, 1967. 111 p.

--ITALY

1902 GISH, Carol (Spell)
Mediterranean missions; a study of the missionary work of the Church of the Nazarene in Israel, Jordan, Syria, Lebanon, Italy, and the Cape Verde Islands. Kansas City, Mo., Nazarene Publishing House, 1965. 158 p.
1965-66 missionary study book.

1903 RAMQUIST, Grace (Chapman), 1907-
"And many believed," Acts 18:8; a study of Nazarene missions in Guatemala, Nicaragua, Peru, Argentina, Bolivia, and Italy. Kansas City, Mo., Nazarene Publishing House, 1951. 128 p.
The 1951-52 missionary study book authorized by the Commission on Foreign Missionary Study Literature.

1904 TRACY, Olive Gertrude, 1908-
The nations and the isles; a study of missionary work of the Church of the Nazarene in the nations--Israel, Jordan, Syria, Lebanon, Italy--and the isles--the Cape Verde Islands. Kansas City, Mo., Nazarene Publishing House, 1958. 251 p.

--JAPAN

1905 ECKEL, William A.
The pendulum swings. Kansas City, Mo., Beacon Hill Press, 1957. 144 p.
The 1957-58 missionary study book authorized by the Missionary Study Committee.

1906 ECKEL, William Dohn
Japan now! Kansas City, Mo., Nazarene Publishing House, 1949. 139 p.

1907 TEMPLE, Helen Frances
Many shall come. Kansas City, Mo., Beacon Hill Press, 1957. 92 p.

--KANSAS

1908 SEARS, Lawrence Wayne, 1917-
"A history of the origin and growth of the Church of

the Nazarene in Kansas." Unpublished M.S. thesis, Kansas State Teachers College, Pittsburg, 1949. 107ℓ.

--KOREA

1909 RAMQUIST, Grace (Chapman), 1907-
No respecter of persons. Kansas City, Mo., Nazarene Publishing House, 1962. 142 p.
Missionary study book, 1962-63.

--LATIN AMERICA

1910 LUNSFORD, Robert Lloyd
Tomorrow in Latin America, by R.L. and Esther Lunsford. Kansas City, Mo., Nazarene Publishing House, 1945. 204 p.
The 1945-1946 missionary study book authorized by the Commission on Foreign Missionary Study Literature.

1911 PRESCOTT, Lyle, 1913-1970.
Light in Latin America; missionary study book, 1961-62. Kansas City, Mo., Nazarene Publishing House, 1961. 192 p.

1912 RAMQUIST, Grace (Chapman), 1907-
"And many believed," Acts 18:8; a study of Nazarene missions in Guatemala, Nicaragua, Peru, Argentina, Bolivia, and Italy. Kansas City, Mo., Nazarene Publishing House, 1951. 128 p.
The 1951-52 missionary study book authorized by the Commission on Foreign Missionary Study Literature.

1913 REZA, Honorato T.
Prescription for permanence; the story of our schools for training ministers in Latin America. Kansas City, Mo., Nazarene Publishing House, 1968. 71 p.

1914 TEMPLE, Helen Frances
Called out of darkness; missionary stories from South America. Kansas City, Mo., Nazarene Publishing House, 1960. 87 p.

1915 TEMPLE, Helen Frances
More than conquerors; missionary stories from South America. Kansas City, Mo., Nazarene Publishing House, 1967. 79 p.

1916 TEMPLE, Helen Frances
Servants of the Most High; missionary stories from Mexico and Central America. Kansas City, Mo., Nazarene

Publishing House, 1968. 80 p.

1917 TEMPLE, Helen Frances
A sower went forth; missionary stories from below the Rio Grande. Kansas City, Mo., Beacon Hill Press, 1951. 80 p.

--MAINE

1918 SMITH, Keith Eugene, 1926-
"History of the Church of the Nazarene in Maine, 1893-1920 (the formative years)." Unpublished S. T. M. thesis, Boston University, School of Theology, 1964. v, 116ℓ.

--MEXICO

1919 REZA, Honorato T.
Washed by the blood; stories of native workers connected with the ministry of the Church of the Nazarene in the Mexican field. Kansas City, Mo., Beacon Hill Press, 1953. 80 p.

1920 VAUGHTERS, William C.
Men of miracle in Mexico. Kansas City, Mo., Nazarene Publishing House, 1966. 91 p.

--MISSOURI

1921 JONES, Charles Edwin, 1932-
"Disinherited or rural?; a historical case study in urban Holiness religion," Missouri Historical Review, LXVI (Apr. 1972), 395-412.

--NEAR EAST

1922 GISH, Carol (Spell)
Mediterranean missions; a study of the missionary work of the Church of the Nazarene in Israel, Jordan, Syria, Lebanon, Italy, and the Cape Verde Islands. Kansas City, Mo., Nazarene Publishing House, 1965. 158 p.
1965-66 missionary study book.

1923 SPANGENBERG, Alice
Jerusalem and beyond; Christian missions in the Cape Verde Islands and the Middle East. Kansas City, Mo., Nazarene Publishing House, 1950. 160 p.

1924 TRACY, Olive Gertrude, 1908-
 The nations and the isles; a study of missionary work of the Church of the Nazarene in the nations--Israel, Jordan, Syria, Lebanon, Italy--and the isles--the Cape Verde Islands. Kansas City, Mo., Nazarene Publishing House, 1958. 251 p.

--NEW GUINEA

1925 POWERS, Hardy Carroll, 1900-1972.
 And now New Guinea. Kansas City, Mo., Beacon Hill Press, 1955. 71 p.

--NICARAGUA

1926 GALLOWAY, C. Dean
 Nicaraguan nuggets. Kansas City, Mo., Nazarene Publishing House, 1968. 85 p.

--OCEANIA

1927 EARLE, Ralph, 1907-
 Fields afar: Nazarene missions in the Far East, India, and the South Pacific; missionary study book, 1969-70. Kansas City, Mo., Nazarene Publishing House, 1969. 127 p.

1928 MINK, Nelson G.
 Southern Cross salute; stories of men and women who are making history in the Church of the Nazarene in the South Pacific. Kansas City, Mo., Nazarene Publishing House, 1969. 72 p.

1929 RAMQUIST, Grace (Chapman), 1907-
 No respecter of persons. Kansas City, Mo., Nazarene Publishing House, 1962. 142 p.
 Missionary study book, 1962-63.

1930 TAYLOR, Richard Shelley, 1912-
 Our Pacific outposts. Kansas City, Mo., Beacon Hill Press, 1956. 133 p.

--OKINAWA

1931 BENNETT, Merril
 Okinawa lifeline. Kansas City, Mo., Nazarene Publishing House, 1964.

II. 1. Christian Holiness Association

1932 ENCYCLOPEDIA OF Modern Christian Missions; the Agencies. Burton L. Goddard, ed.... Camden, N.J., T. Nelson, 1967. xix, 743 p.
"Nihon Nazaren Kyodan (Church of the Nazarene)": p. 486.

--OKLAHOMA

1933 JERNIGAN, Charles Brougher, 1863-1930.
From the prairie schooner to a city flat. Brooklyn, The author, c1926. 140 p.

1934 JONES, Charles Edwin, 1932-
"Background of the Church of the Nazarene in Oklahoma," B-PC Historian of the Bethany-Peniel College Historical Society, I (1953-1954), 18-31.

1935 McCONNELL, Leona (Bellew)
"A history of the town and college of Bethany, Oklahoma." Unpublished M.A. thesis, University of Oklahoma, 1935.

1936 TAMBE, Narendra Govind, 1926-
"A comparison of selected administrative and organizational variables in the Jeevan Sadhana High School, Baroda, India, with that of the Bethany public school in Oklahoma." Unpublished Ph.D. dissertation, University of Oklahoma, 1965. v, 106ℓ.

--PERU

1937 CHURCH OF the Nazarene. Missions and mission districts. Peru.
Un estudio sobre los Aguarunas por el personal de la Iglesia del Nazareno en esa tribu. Monsefu, Imprenta nazarena, 1946. 59 p.
"Reconocimiento" signed R. S. W.

1938 DICKERMAN, Ethel (King)
The call of the Aguaruna; photos. by Clyde Golliher. Kansas City, Mo., Nazarene Publishing House, 1967. 80 p.

--PHILIPPINE ISLANDS

1939 COPELIN, Roy E.
Life in a Nazarene Bible college; the story of missionary education in the Philippines. Kansas City, Mo., Nazarene Publishing House, 1962. 87 p.

1940 PITTS, Joseph S.
Mission to the Philippines. Kansas City, Mo., Beacon Hill Press, 1956. 127 p.

1941 PITTS, Joseph S.
Voices from the Philippines. Wilmore, Ky., 1958. 26 p.

1942 RAMQUIST, Grace (Chapman), 1907-
No respecter of persons. Kansas City, Mo., Nazarene Publishing House, 1962. 142 p.
Missionary study book, 1962-63.

--RHODE ISLAND

1943 SCOPINO, Aldorigo Joseph, 1947-
"The Church of the Nazarene in Rhode Island, 1886-1972: a socio-historical approach." Unpublished M.A. thesis, Brown University, 1972. 73ℓ.

--SOUTHERN STATES

1944 REDFORD, Maury English
"History of the Church of the Nazarene in the South." Unpublished M.A. thesis, Vanderbilt University, 1935. 205ℓ.

--SOUTHWEST, OLD

1945 JERNIGAN, Charles Brougher, 1863-1930.
Pioneer days of the Holiness Movement in the Southwest. Kansas City, Mo., Pentecostal Nazarene Publishing House, 1919. 157 p.

1946 ROGERS, Dennis, 1858-
Holiness pioneering in the Southland. Hemet, Calif., 1944. 36 p.

--SWAZILAND

1947 CHAPMAN, Louise (Robinson)
Africa, O Africa; twenty years a missionary on the dark continent. Kansas City, Mo., Beacon Hill Press, 1945. 221 p.

1948 CHISM, Fairy Steele, 1899-1971.
The glow of the Veld fires, by Fairy Chism and Helen Irene Jester. Kansas City, Mo., Beacon Hill Press, 1949. 124 p.

II. 1. Christian Holiness Association

1949 ENCYCLOPEDIA OF modern Christian missions; the agencies. Burton L. Goddard, ed.... Camden, N.J., T. Nelson, 1967. xix, 743 p.
"The Swaziland Church of the Nazarene" by Marjorie Wise: p. 637.

--TENNESSEE

1950 GOMER, Thelma
"A mighty church moves on," Nazarene Weekly (Nashville), XLIII (May 6, 1973).
Historical sketch of the First Church of the Nazarene in Nashville, Tennessee, including an account of its relationship to the Pentecostal Mission.

1951 REDFORD, Maury English
"History of the Church of the Nazarene in Tennessee."
Unpublished B.D. thesis, School of Religion, Vanderbilt University, 1934. 148ℓ.

--TEXAS

1952 LYNCH, W. M., 1925-
"The rise of the Church of the Nazarene in Texas."
Unpublished M.A. thesis, Stephen F. Austin State College, 1956.

--TRINIDAD

1953 SAXON, Ruth O.
Flares in the night; the story of Nazarene missions in Trinidad and Tobago. Kansas City, Mo., Nazarene Publishing House, 1970. 86 p.

CHURCHES OF CHRIST IN CHRISTIAN UNION (1909-)

[1909-1952 as Churches of Christ in Christian Union of Ohio]

In February 1864 congregations which had withdrawn from the Methodist Episcopal, Baptist, Presbyterian, and United Brethren denominations over political preaching, met at Columbus, Ohio, and formed The Christian Union. Though holding to common evangelical teachings, this group opposed creeds as antithetical to Christian liberty. The impact of the Holiness Movement on Christian Union congregations in Ohio split the church, and in 1909 at Washington Court House, Ohio, the holiness faction organized the Churches of Christ in Christian Union of Ohio. After merger with the Reformed Methodist Church in 1952, "of Ohio" was dropped from the name. The denomination has since expanded into other states. From headquarters in Circleville, Ohio, where the church-sponsored Bible college also is located, the group issues The Advocate of Primitive Christian Union. In 1971, the Churches of Christ in Christian Union had over 250 congregations in a dozen states, and missionary work in Africa, the West Indies, Honduras, Bolivia, New Guinea and Korea as well as among American Indians in Arizona and Mexican Americans in Texas. United States membership stands at about 9000. The group holds membership in the Christian Holiness Association.

1954   CHURCHES OF Christ in Christian Union.
        Constitution and by-laws. Circleville, Ohio, Advocate Publishing House, 1955. 88 p.

1955   CHURCHES OF Christ in Christian Union.
        Constitution and bylaws. 1968 ed. Circleville, Ohio, Advocate Publishing House, 1968. 127 p.

1956   CHURCHES OF Christ in Christian Union. Annual Council. Ohio.
        Proceedings. 1st- , 1909- . Washington Court House, Ohio; Circleville, Ohio, 1909- .
        Annual.
        1950- includes Proceedings of the General Council.

--APOLOGETIC WORKS

1957   CHURCHES OF Christ in Christian Union.
        The Churches of Christ in Christian Union: history, organization, mission, what we teach. Circleville, Ohio, 1965.
        Folder
        "Third printing."

1958   CHURCHES OF Christ in Christian Union.
        Churches of Christ in Christian Union: history, organization, mission, what we teach. Circleville, Ohio, 1969.
        Folder
        "Fourth printing."

--CATECHISMS AND CREEDS

1959   HERMIZ, Thomas
        What we teach; a summary of the doctrines of the Churches of Christ in Christian Union. Rev. ed. Circleville, Ohio, Advocate Publishing House, 1965. 16 p.

II. 1. Christian Holiness Association

"1st printing, 1954; 2nd printing, 1965; 3rd printing, 1965."

--CONDUCT OF LIFE

1960 ANDERSON, Tony Marshall, 1888-
After sanctification; growth in the life of holiness.... Circleville, Ohio, Advocate Publishing House, 1970. 112 p.
"Fourth printing."
First ed. published in 1929 under title: After holiness, what?

--DEVOTIONAL LITERATURE

1961 ANDERSON, Tony Marshall, 1888-
Prayer availeth much. Circleville, Ohio, Advocate Publishing House, 196?. 93 p.

--MISSIONS

1962 ENCYCLOPEDIA OF modern Christian missions; the agencies. Burton L. Goddard, ed.... Camden, N.J., T. Nelson, 1967. xix, 743 p.
"Churches of Christ in Christian Union": p. 186.

--PERIODICALS

1963 ADVOCATE FOR Primitive Christian Union. 1- , 1906- .
Washington Court House, Ohio; Springfield, Ohio; Circleville, Ohio.
1906-19?? as Church of Christ Advocate.

1964 MISSIONARY TIDINGS. 1- , 1949- . Circleville, Ohio.

--YEARBOOKS

1965 CHURCHES OF Christ in Christian Union.
1971 yearbook of the Churches of Christ in Christian Union, 1909-1971. Circleville, Ohio, 1971. 1 v. (various pagings)

EMMANUEL HOLINESS CHURCH (1916-   )

[Also as Emmanuel Bible College and Missions]

Beginning with a single congregation at Birkenhead, Cheshire in 1916, the Emmanuel Holiness Church started a Bible school in 1921 and launched foreign missionary work three years later. Founded by J. D. Drysdale, a holiness evangelist, the group was oriented toward foreign missions from its inception. First called Emmanuel Missionary Training Home, the Emmanuel Bible College sent faith missionaries to Morocco in 1926, to the Formosa Territory (Argentina) in 1931, and to the Sahara in 1957. Expansion in Britain paralleled that in foreign lands and in 1947 the group organized as a denomination. Non-sectarian in outlook, the group readily cooperates with other denominations and participates in the annual interdenominational revival convention at Southport. The college issues Emmanuel quarterly. In 1973 a proposal for merger with the Free Methodist Church of North America failed ratification.

--DOCTRINAL AND CONTROVERSIAL WORKS

1966 DRYSDALE, John Douglas, 1880-1953.
Carnal nature, human nature, temptation, by J. D. D. 3rd ed. Birkenhead, Ches., Eng., 1938. 16 p.

1967 DRYSDALE, John Douglas, 1880-1953.
Holiness, by J. D. D. Birkenhead, Ches., Eng., 1938. 7 p.

1968 DRYSDALE, John Douglas, 1880-1953.
Holiness in the parables. London, Oliphants, 1952. 160 p.

1969 DRYSDALE, John Douglas, 1880-1953.
The new birth. 3d ed. n.p., 1938. 12 p.

--EVANGELISTIC WORK

1970 DRYSDALE, John Douglas, 1880-1953.
The price of revival. Birkenhead, Ches., Eng., Emmanuel, 1946. 185 p.
"Second edition."

--HISTORY

1971 DRYSDALE, John Douglas, 1880-1953.
Emmanuel: fourteen years after. Birkenhead, Ches., Eng., J. & L. Drysdale, 1931.

1972 DRYSDALE, John Douglas, 1880-1953.
Emmanuel: 25 years after. Birkenhead, Ches., Eng., J. D. & L. M. Drysdale, 1941.

II. 1. Christian Holiness Association 207

--MISSIONS

1973 ENCYCLOPEDIA OF modern Christian missions; the agencies. Burton L. Goddard, ed.... Camden. N.J., T. Nelson, 1967. xix, 743 p.
"Emmanuel Bible College and Missions," by Stanley Banks: p. 243-244.

--PERIODICALS

1974 EMMANUEL. 1- , 1927- . Birkenhead, Cheshire, Eng., Emmanuel Bible College.

1975 EMMANUEL NEWS Bulletin. 1- , 1963- . Birkenhead, Ches., Eng., Emmanuel Bible School and Missions. Reproduced from typewriting.

EVANGEL CHURCH (1933-1960)

[1933 as Holiness Evangelistic Association; 1933-1947 as Interdenominational Evangelistic Association; 1947-195? as Evangelistic Tabernacles]

The product of tension between a Fundamentalist holiness group and the liberal leaders of the California Yearly Meeting of Friends, this group was organized in 1933 after a committee of the Whittier Quarterly Meeting censured William Kirby, pastor of the Huntington Park Friends Meeting. Known successively as the Holiness Evangelistic Association, the Interdenominational Evangelistic Association, the Evangelistic Tabernacles, and the Evangel Church, the group at first identified closely with the non-denominational Training School for Christian Workers of Huntington Park, and supported the foreign missionary work of the National Holiness Missionary Society and the Oriental Missionary Society. It published a paper called The Evangelist at Huntington Park. When the Evangel Church merged with the Western Annual Conference of the Evangelical Methodist Church in June 1960, it had eight congregations, 35 ordained clergy, and about 400 members.

1976 EVANGEL CHURCH.
Manual, 1935-195?. Huntington Park, Calif., 1935-195?. 5 v. irregular.

--HISTORY

1977 BRACKETT, Charles H.
"The history of Azusa College and the Friends, 1900-

1965." Unpublished M.A. thesis, University of Southern California, 1967. iv, 152ℓ.

1978 COFFIN, T. Eugene
"History of California Yearly Meeting of Friends Churches, 1895-1955." Unpublished M.A. thesis, University of Southern California, 1956. vi, 93ℓ.
"Doctrinal difficulties": 48-57.

1979 PHILLIPS, Isaac N.
"A history of the Evangelistic Tabernacles." Unpublished M.A. thesis, Pacific Bible College, 1955. 74ℓ.

--PERIODICALS

1980 EVANGELIST. 1- , 1935?-1960?. Huntington Park, Calif.

EVANGELICAL CHURCH (1807-1946)

[1807-1922 as Evangelical Association of North America]

Founded by Jacob Albright (1759-1808), a Lutheran who had converted to Methodism, this German-American denomination was Methodist in theology and organization from its beginning. Known as the Evangelical Association until 1922, the group welcomed the revival of perfectionism and worked in cooperation with the National Holiness Movement. (The success of the second National Camp Meeting for the Promotion of Holiness held at Manheim, Pennsylvania, in 1868, was largely attributable to German support.) As coolness toward holiness teaching developed within the Methodist Episcopal Church, many of the dissatisfied joined the Evangelical Association. Former Methodist Episcopal ministers, who at the beginning of the century were instrumental in extending the Evangelical work into New England, soon found that their dispute with Methodism concerned church government as well as doctrinal teaching. As a result, most of the new congregations followed their pastors into the congregational Association of Pentecostal Churches of America. Though this incident cooled the fraternity of the Evangelical Association and the new holiness churches, Christian perfection remained an important emphasis until the merger of the denomination with the Church of the United Brethren in Christ, another German Methodist group, in 1946.

1981 EVANGELICAL ASSOCIATION of North America.
Doctrines and discipline of the Evangelical Association of North America. Cleveland, Publishing House of the Evangelical Association, 1893. 186 p.

II. 1. Christian Holiness Association 209

1982 BREYFOGEL, Sylvanus Charles, 1851-1934.
Landmarks of the Evangelical Association, containing all the official records of the annual and general conferences from the days of Jacob Albright to the year 1840; and the proceedings of the East Pennsylvania Conference together with important extracts from the transactions of the General Conference from 1840 to the present time.... Reading, Pa., Eagle Book Print, 1888. 436 p.
Cover-title: Evangelical landmarks.

--CONFERENCES. INDIANA.

1983 BAUMGARTNER, Samuel Henry, 1860-
Historical data and life sketches of the deceased ministers of the Indiana Conference of the Evangelical Association, 1835-1915. Compiled by S.H. Baumgartner.... Edited by E.W. Praetorius.... Cleveland, Publishing House of the Evangelical Association, 1915-1924. 2 v.
Title page of vol. 2 reads: Historical sketches of circuits, missions and stations of Indiana Conference of the Evangelical Association, 1835-1922. Also other important conference data. Edited by A.B. Heist and E.K. Roberts....

--CONFERENCES. KANSAS.

1984 PLATZ, M. C.
Fifty years in the Kansas Conference; a record of the origin and development of the work of the Evangelical Association. Cleveland, Evangelical Association, 1915. 363 p.

--DOCTRINAL AND CONTROVERSIAL WORKS

1985 BOWMAN, Hezekiah J., comp.
Voices on holiness from the Evangelical Association. Cleveland, Published for the author at the Publishing House of the Evangelical Association, 1882. 254 p.

1986 BOWMAN, Thomas, bp., 1836-1923.
The great salvation. Cleveland, Publishing House of the Evangelical Association, J.H. Lamb, Agent, 1909. 127 p.
First pub. in the Evangelical Messenger in 1906.

1987 PETTICORD, Emory W., 1880-
The Holy Spirit. Portland, Ore., Evangelism Publishing House, n.d. 19 p.

--HISTORY

1988 ALBRIGHT, Raymond Wolf, 1901-
A history of the Evangelical Church. Harrisburg, Pa., Evangelical Press, 1942. 501 p.

1989 CLARK, Elmer Talmage, 1886-1966.
The small sects in America. Rev. ed. New York, Abingdon Press, c1965. 256 p.
Account of the Evangelical Church: p. 68-69.

1990 SIMPSON, Matthew, bp., 1811-1884, ed.
Cyclopaedia of Methodism; embracing sketches of its rise, progress, and present condition, with biographical notices and numerous illustrations. Philadelphia, Everts & Stewart, 1878. 1027 p.
"Evangelical Association": p. 349.

1991 SPRENG, Samuel P.
History of the Evangelical Church. Cleveland, Ohio, Publishing House of the Evangelical Church, 1927.

--HISTORY OF DOCTRINES

1992 SCHWAB, Ralph Kendall
The history of the doctrine of Christian perfection in the Evangelical Association.... Menasha, Wis., George Banta Publishing Co., 1922. xiv, 153 p.
Thesis (Ph.D.)--University of Chicago, 1920.

--PERIODICALS

1993 EVANGELICAL MESSENGER. 1- , 1847-19??. Cleveland.

1994 EVANGELISCHE MAGAZIN für die Sonntags-schule und den Familienkreis. 1-24, no. 12, 1869/70-Dec. 1892. Cleveland.

1995 GUIDING STAR. 1- , 1878-1901? Farmersville, Pa.

1996 LIVING EPISTLE; an evangelical monthly devoted to the spread of Biblical knowledge, scriptural holiness and pure literature. 1- , 1866-190?. Cleveland.

--STATISTICS

1997 U.S. BUREAU of the Census.
...Census of religious bodies, 1926; Evangelical Church: statistics, denominational history, doctrine, and organiza-

EVANGELICAL CHURCH OF NORTH AMERICA (1968-   )

As a result of the merger of the Methodist Church and the Evangelical United Brethren Church in 1968, over 6000 members in 82 congregations of the Pacific Northwest, Montana, and Erie and Ohio Southeast conferences of the former Evangelical United Brethren Church left the denomination and formed the Evangelical Church of North America. Descended from the Evangelical Church which had merged with the Church of the United Brethren in Christ in 1946, the new group, like its ancestor, is deeply committed to holiness teaching. Joined in 1969 by the Holiness Methodist Church, the church established headquarters in Minneapolis. The Evangelical Church of North America holds membership in the Christian Holiness Association. Ministerial candidates normally attend the Western Evangelical Seminary in Portland. Editorial offices of the Evangelical Advocate, the official organ, are in Minneapolis.

1998   EVANGELICAL CHURCH of North America.
        Discipline of the Evangelical Church of North America, 1971. n.p., 1971. 253 p.

--PERIODICALS

1999   EVANGELICAL ADVOCATE. 1-   1969- .   Minneapolis, Minn.

EVANGELICAL CONGREGATIONAL CHURCH (1922-   )

This group represents the continuation of the East Pennsylvania Conference of the United Evangelical Church which refused to join in the 1922 reunion of that body with the Evangelical Association to form the Evangelical Church. Differences were governmental rather than doctrinal, and theologically the present Evangelical Congregational Church resembles the former Evangelical Church. Denominational headquarters and a school of theology are located at Myerstown, Pennsylvania. In 1970 there were about 175 churches and 30,000 members.

2000   CLARK, Elmer Talmage, 1886-1966.
        The small sects in America. Rev. ed. New York,

Abingdon Press, c1965. 256 p.
Account of the Evangelical Congregational Church: p. 70.

2001 MEAD, Frank Spencer, 1898-
Handbook of denominations in the United States. New 5th ed. Nashville, Abingdon Press, c1970. 265 p.
"Evangelical Congregational Church": p. 104.

--MISSIONS

2002 ENCYCLOPEDIA OF modern Christian missions; the agencies. Burton L. Goddard, ed.... Camden, N.J., T. Nelson, 1967. xix, 743 p.
"Evangelical Congregational Church, Board of Missions," by Thomas E. Paul: p. 254.

--STATISTICS

2003 U.S. BUREAU of the Census.
...Census of religious bodies, 1926; Evangelical Congregational Church: statistics, denominational history, doctrine and organization. Washington, U.S. Government Printing Office, 1928. 10 p.

EVANGELICAL UNITED BRETHREN CHURCH (1946-1968)

The result of the union of the Evangelical Church and the Church of the United Brethren in Christ at Johnstown, Pennsylvania, in 1946, the Evangelical United Brethren Church was, like its parents, a German Methodist church. Although the German language had fallen into disuse long before the merger, the ethnic heritage of the denomination remained. The ardent holiness element, particularly in the former Evangelical Church, saw the merger as a possible prelude to union with the Methodist Church, and warned of its intention to withdraw should the united body later join the Methodist Church. This fear was realized in 1968, when at Dallas, Texas, the 750,000-member Evangelical United Brethren Church joined the more than 10,000,000-member Methodist Church to form the United Methodist Church. Regarding the new body as the product of unholy compromise, more than eighty congregations in the Pacific Northwest, Montana, and the eastern Great Lakes areas withdrew and organized the Evangelical Church of North America.

2004 CLARK, Elmer Talmage, 1886-1966.
The small sects in America. Rev. ed. New York,

II. 1. Christian Holiness Association

Abingdon Press, c1965. 256 p.
Account of Evangelical United Brethren Church: p. 70.

2005 MEAD, Frank Spencer, 1898-
Handbook of denominations in the United States. 2d rev. ed. New York, Abingdon Press, c1961. 272 p.
"The Evangelical United Brethren Church": p. 101-103.

--CHURCH EXTENSION

2006 BLOEDE, Louis William
"Development of new congregations in the United States and Canada by the Evangelical United Brethren Church." Unpublished Th.D. dissertation, Boston University, 1960. 376ℓ.

--CONDUCT OF LIFE

2007 BEMESDERFER, James Orville
"Pietism and its influence upon the Evangelical United Brethren Church." Unpublished S.T.D. dissertation, Temple University, 1951. 227ℓ.

--MISSIONS

2008 ENCYCLOPEDIA OF modern Christian missions; the agencies. Burton L. Goddard, ed.... Camden, N.J., T. Nelson, 1967. xix, 743 p.
"The Evangelical United Brethren Church, the Board of Missions": p. 266; and "The Evangelical United Brethren Church, the Board of Missions, Division of Women's Service": p. 266.

Evangelistic Associations

APOSTOLIC CHRISTIAN CHURCH (Nazarean) (1850-   )

Distinguished by its emphasis on entire sanctification, this group is the result of work among Swiss and German immigrants begun by S.H. Froehlich about 1850. Although concentrated in Illinois and Ohio, small congregations are scattered from New England to the West Coast and in Canada. The Apostolic Christians are pacifists. Missionaries are at work in Brazil, Argentina, Australia and New Guinea. In 1970 the group claimed 51 congregations and 2347 members.

2009   CLARK, Elmer Talmage, 1886-1966.
         The small sects in America. Rev. ed. New York,
       Abingdon Press, c1965. 256 p.
         Account of Apostolic Christian Church (Nazarean):
       p. 70.

2010   MEAD, Frank Spencer, 1898-
         Handbook of denominations in the United States. New
       5th ed. Nashville, Abingdon Press, c1970. 265 p.
         "Apostolic Christian Church (Nazarean)": p. 25-26.

2011   TWENTIETH CENTURY encyclopedia of religious knowledge;
         an extension of the New Schaff-Herzog Encyclopedia of
         Religious Knowledge. Editor-in-chief: Lefferts A.
         Loetscher. Grand Rapids, Mich., Baker Book House,
         1955. 2 v. (xx, 1205 p.)
         "Apostolic Christian Church (Nazarean)," by Jacob
       Meyer: p. 55.

APOSTOLIC CHRISTIAN CHURCH OF AMERICA (1947-   )

[1848-1860 as Evangelical Bible Society; 1860-1906 as Apostolic
Christian Church]

     Like the other Apostolic Christian group, this denomination
is the result of evangelistic work among German-speaking Swiss
immigrants. Begun about 1847 by Benedict Weyeneth, the pacifist
group stresses entire sanctification. It feels that the sole mission
of the church is saving souls. The clergy, which receive no remuneration from the church, depend on the inspiration of the Holy
Spirit for sermon content. At present there are more than 10,000
members in 65 congregations, centered apparently in Illinois.

2012   BAUTZ, Friedrich Wilhelm
         Die Neuapostolische Kirche. Gladbeck, Schriftenmissions-Verlag, 1968. 32 p. (His Worte der Aufklärung und
       Abwehr)

2013   CLARK, Elmer Talmage, 1886-1966.
         The small sects in America. Rev. ed. New York,
       Abingdon Press, c1965. 256 p.
         Account of the Apostolic Christian Church of America
       p. 70.

2014   MEAD, Frank Spencer, 1898-
         Handbook of denominations in the United States. New
       5th ed. Nashville, Abingdon Press, c1970. 265 p.
         "Apostolic Christian Church of America": p. 26.

II. 1. Christian Holiness Association

2015 SCHAFF, Philip, 1819-1893.
New Schaff-Herzog encyclopedia of religious knowledge....
S. M. Jackson, editor-in-chief. New York, Funk, 1908-1912. 12 v.
"Apostolic Christian Church." by E. M. Bliss: v. 7, p. 389.

--HYMNS

2016 APOSTOLIC CHRISTIAN Church.
The Apostolic Christian hymnal; a collection of translations of hymns appearing in the "Zions Harfe" and other songs suitable for use in the services of the Apostolic Christian churches, Sunday schools and homes. Peoria, Ill., Apostolic Christian Publishing Co., 1921. 272 p.
Words with music for 4 voices.

2017 APOSTOLIC CHRISTIAN Church.
The Apostolic Christian hymnal; a compilation of hymns for the believers in Christ, containing the entire "Zion harfe" and "Heft" in English. For the greater part of the past century these hymns, first used in the German language, have been translated and sung to the same tunes in the following languages: Serbian, Roumanian, Hungarian, Slovakian. Chicago, Apostolic Christian Publishing Co., 1940. 525 p.
With music.

2018 APOSTOLIC CHRISTIAN Church.
Songs of praise and worship. Cleveland, Printed for the Apostolic Christian Church by the Evangelical Press, c1931. 101 p.

2019 APOSTOLIC CHRISTIAN Church.
Uj Sion hárfa; szent énekek és isteni dicséretek gyüjtémenye, a Krisztusban hivö gyülekezetek számára. 1953 kiad. Toldalékkal es enekiskolával. The Apostolic Christian hymnal; a collection of hymns compiled for believers in Christ, containing the entire Zion Harfe and Heft. For the greater part of the past century these hymns, first used in the German language, have been translated and sung to the same tunes in the following languages: Serbian, Roumanian, Hungarian, Slovak. Akron, 1953. xx, 160 p.
Principally with music.

--MISSIONS

2020 ENCYCLOPEDIA OF modern Christian missions; the agencies. Burton L. Goddard, ed.... Camden, N.J., T. Nelson, 1967. xix, 743 p.
"Apostolic Christian Church of America": p. 37.

BIBLE HOLINESS MOVEMENT (1949-   )

[1949-1972 as Bible Holiness Mission]

Organized at Vancouver, British Columbia, in 1949, this evangelistic association combines traditional Methodist theology and discipline with belief in the Baptism of the Holy Ghost and fire as an experience subsequent to entire sanctification. Members are not required to sever relationships with other groups, but to accept the discipline of the Movement as a means to vital Christian service. Work is carried on without direct financial solicitation. Plain dress and nonresistance are enjoined, and membership in secret societies including the John Birch Society and labor unions is forbidden. Foreign mission work was begun in West Africa in 1952 and in the Philippines in 1963. Led by Wesley H. Wakefield, the group, which until 1972 was known as the Bible Holiness Mission, is akin to the Independent Holiness Churches of Ontario and Saskatchewan. Truth on Fire, the official organ, is issued from Vancouver "bi-monthly or as often as the Lord permits."

2021   BIBLE HOLINESS Mission.
          Manual. n.p., 195?. 48 p.

--DOCTRINAL AND CONTROVERSIAL WORKS

2022   WAKEFIELD, Wesley H.
          Bible doctrine: what the Word of God teaches. Vancouver, B.C., Can., Bible Holiness Mission, 1951. 119 p.

--PERIODICALS

2023   TRUTH ON FIRE. 1- , 1964- . Vancouver, B.C., Can.

CENTRAL EVANGELICAL HOLINESS ASSOCIATION (1890-1896)

This association of independent holiness congregations, formed on March 13-14, 1890, at Rock, Massachusetts, was among the first efforts at collective action by holiness independents. Initially the Association consisted of the People's Evangelical Church of Providence, Rhode Island (organized in 1887 and the oldest remaining congregation in the Church of the Nazarene), the Mission Church of Lynn, Massachusetts, the Independent Congregational Church of Rock, Massachusetts, and a few other congregations in southeastern New England. During the first year these were joined by the Mission Church of Malden, Massachusetts, the Emmanuel Mission Church of North Attleboro, Massachusetts, and the Bethany Mission Church of Keene, New Hampshire. A loose, voluntary federation, the Central Evangelical Holiness Association

II. 1. Christian Holiness Association 217

was far from being a denomination, but it represented the first step in that direction. In November 1896, consultation between representatives of the Central Association and the Association of Pentecostal Churches of America, which consisted of three congregations in Brooklyn, New York, resulted in the union of the two groups under the name of the latter.

--HISTORY

2024 REDFORD, Maury English
  The rise of the Church of the Nazarene. Kansas City, Mo., Nazarene Publishing House, 1948. 208 p.
  "Central Evangelical Holiness Association": p. 82-97.

2025 SMITH, Timothy Lawrence, 1924-
  Called unto holiness; the story of the Nazarenes: the formative years. Kansas City, Mo., Nazarene Publishing House, 1962. 413 p.
  Account of Central Evangelical Holiness Association: p. 58-64.

--PERIODICALS

2026 BEULAH ITEMS. 1-5, no. 4, Sept. 1888-Apr. 1892.
  Providence, R.I.
  Superseded by Beulah Christian

2027 BEULAH CHRISTIAN. 1- , May 1892-Dec. 9, 1911.
  Providence, R.I.
  Supersedes Beulah Items, and Bible Christian
  Superseded by Pentecostal Christian

2028 BIBLE CHRISTIAN. 1- , -1892. Exeter, N.H.
  Merged with Beulah Items to become Beulah Christian.

CHRISTIAN CONGREGATION (1887-)

Like the Churches of God, the Christian Congregation originated in protest against sectarianism. Proposing to reinstate New Testament order and simplicity, this group was organized at Kokomo, Indiana, in 1887. The predominance of former Methodists among the early members appears to be the source of Wesleyan perfectionism in an organization which in other ways strongly resembles the Disciples of Christ. Strongly congregational, Christian Congregation affiliates are concentrated in states where the Disciples also are strong: Kentucky, Indiana, Ohio, Pennsylvania, Virginia, the Carolinas, and Texas. In 1970 there were 251 congregations and 44,914 members. Ironically the anti-sectarian teachings of the group have prevented fraternity with other churches. Perfectionism appears steadily to have decreased during the twentieth century.

2029 SCHAFF, Philip, 1819-1893.
    New Schaff-Herzog encyclopedia of religious knowledge.... S. M. Jackson, editor-in-chief. New York, Funk, 1908-1912. 12 v.
    "Christian Congregation," by E. M. Bliss: v. 7, p. 390.

2030 TWENTIETH CENTURY encyclopedia of religious knowledge; an extension of the New Schaff-Herzog Encyclopedia of Religious Knowledge. Editor-in-chief: Lefferts A. Loetscher. Grand Rapids, Mich., Baker Book House, 1955. 2 v. (xx, 1205 p.)
    "Christian Congregation," by Osceola J. Read: p. 240.

CHURCH OF DANIEL'S BAND (1893-195?)

Numbering four churches and 200 members in 1951, the Church of Daniel's Band was clearly Wesleyan in belief and practice. Evangelistic and perfectionist, the group, which was incorporated at Traverse City, Michigan in 1893, seems to have originated in a Methodist class meeting. It stressed separation from the world. Sunday schools were often held in cooperation with other groups, and the group conducted a small missionary work in Canada. It seems to have disappeared because of death and attrition sometime after 1951.

2031 CLARK, Elmer Talmage, 1886-1966.
    The small sects in America. Rev. ed. New York, Abingdon Press, c1965. 256 p.
    Account of Church of Daniel's Band: p. 77.

2032 MEAD, Frank Spencer, 1898-
    Handbook of denominations in the United States. 2d rev. ed. New York, Abingdon Press, c1961. 272 p.
    "Church of Daniel's Band": p. 104.

2033 SCHAFF, Philip, 1819-1893.
    New Schaff-Herzog encyclopedia of religious knowledge.... S. M. Jackson, editor-in-chief. New York, Funk, 1908-1912. 12 v.
    "Church of Daniel's Band," by E. M. Bliss: v. 7, p. 391.

2034 TWENTIETH CENTURY encyclopedia of religious knowledge; an extension of the New Schaff-Herzog Encyclopedia of Religious Knowledge. Editor-in-chief: Lefferts A.

II. 1. Christian Holiness Association

Loetscher. Grand Rapids, Mich., Baker Book House, 1955. 2 v. (xx, 1205 p.)
"Daniel's Band, Church of," by Elmer T. Clark: p. 320.

--STATISTICS

2035 U.S. BUREAU of the Census.
...Census of religious bodies, 1926; Church of Daniel's Band: statistics, denominational history, doctrine, and organization.... Washington, U.S. Government Printing Office, 1928. 6 p.

EMMANUEL ASSOCIATION (1937-   )

[Also as Immanuel Missionary Church, and Emmanuel Missionary Church]

Founded in 1937 by Ralph G. Finch, former General Superintendent of Foreign Missions of the Pilgrim Holiness Church, the Emmanuel Association is among the most conservative of Holiness groups. An evangelistic association rather than a church (members are not required to sever connections with other groups), the Association is unalterably opposed to worldliness. Members eschew vain and immodest apparel and worldly amusements including radio, television and the theater; they avoid unscriptural alliances, including secret societies, "organizations both of capital and labor," and the military. The group which before the founder's death in 1949 was dominated by the Finch family, has since freed itself from their control. Headquarters are in Colorado Springs, where the People's Bible College is located and the Emmanuel Herald is published. Most of the fewer than five hundred members live in Colorado and Indiana. In 1969 the group reported thirty-eight ordained and licensed ministers and seven foreign missionaries. Foreign missionary work is carried on in Guatemala. Annual foreign missionary giving is in excess of $20,000.

2036 EMMANUEL ASSOCIATION.
Guidebook. Colorado Springs, Colo., 1937- .
Quadrennial.

--HISTORY

2037 CARROLL, John H., 1884-1961.
Forty-seven years with the gospel plow; or, The life story of John H. Carroll. Shoals, Ind., Old Paths Tract Society, 195?. 152 p.
"Working in the Immanuel Missionary Church": p. 111-115.

2038 THOMAS, Paul Westphal, 1894-1972.
"The days of our pilgrimage; a history of the Pilgrim Holiness Church," by Paul Westphal Thomas and Paul William Lee Thomas. Unpublished paper, 1968. 1 v. (various pagings)
In archives of The Wesleyan Church, Marion, Indiana. Account of "The Finch Dissention": ℓ. 165-168.

--MISSIONS

2039 ENCYCLOPEDIA OF modern Christian missions; the agencies. Burton L. Goddard, ed.... Camden, N.J., T. Nelson, 1967. xix, 743 p.
"Emmanuel Association, General Council": p. 243.

--PERIODICALS

2040 EMMANUEL HERALD. 1- , 1944- . Colorado Springs, Colo.

--SERMONS

2041 FINCH, Paul W.
Revival messages: timely, helpful, urgent. Belfast, Printed by Nelson & Knox, 1954. 51 p.

EVANGELISTIC TABERNACLE (1919-19??)

[1919-19?? as South Side Mission, Ypsilanti, Michigan]

This Ypsilanti, Michigan, group was organized by Aaron F. Baughy as the South Side Mission in 1919. Little of the subsequent history of the Evangelistic Tabernacle is known except that in 1955 union with a California group with the same name was contemplated. Merger was not realized, however. At that time the group had a manual of governmental procedures, an indication of formal organization.

2042 EVANGELISTIC TABERNACLE.
Manual. Ypsilanti, Mich., 195?.

2043 PHILLIPS, Isaac N.
"A history of the Evangelistic Tabernacles." Unpublished M.A. thesis, Pacific Bible College, 1955. 74ℓ.
Includes account of Evangelistic Tabernacle, Ypsilanti, Michigan.

II. 1. Christian Holiness Association   221

FAITH MISSION (1886-)

[Associate missions: Africa Evangelistic Band (1924-); Faith Mission in Canada (1927-); Mission Foi Evangile (1960-)]

     Founded by John George Govan in 1886, the original purpose of this non-denominational group was the evangelization of rural areas of Great Britain and Ireland. Today about a hundred workers, called "Pilgrims," are engaged in this work. In each community workers hold a preaching mission of several weeks duration, visiting homes during the day and holding evangelistic services at night. Workers, who are drawn from and remain members of existing denominations, undergo a two-year training course in a mission-related Bible college in Edinburgh before going into the evangelistic field. The spread of the Faith Mission work outside Britain led to development of associate missions: the Africa Evangelistic Band in South Africa (1924); the Faith Mission in Canada (1927); and the Mission Foi Evangile in France (1960). Because of the difficulty of superintendence outside Britain, associate missions, though fraternal in attitude, are autonomous in government. With other holiness groups Faith Mission participates in the annual Southport Convention.

--EVANGELISTIC WORK

2044   CAMPBELL, Duncan
        The price and power of revival. Fort Washington, Pa., Christian Literature Crusade, n.d. 69 p.
        "Foreword," by P.S. Bristow.

2045   GOVAN, John George, 1861-1927.
        Workers together; suggestions for the promotion of aggressive Christian work. Rothesay, Scot., Christian Literature Co., 1902. 20 p.

--HISTORY

2046   CAMPBELL, Duncan
        God's standard; challenging sermons. Fort Washington, Pa., Christian Literature Crusade, 1967, c1964. 79 p.
        "The Faith Mission, 1886-1964": p. 77-79.

2047   ENCYCLOPEDIA OF modern Christian missions; the agencies. Burton L. Goddard, ed.... Camden, N.J., T. Nelson, 1967. xix, 743 p.
        "Faith Mission," by John G. Eberstein: p. 279.

2048   GOVAN, John George, 1861-1927.
        In the train of His triumph...; reminiscences of the early days of the Faith Mission ... arr. by I.R. Govan....

Edinburgh, Belfast, Bright Words Office, 1932. 63 p.

2049 GOVAN STEWART, Isabel Rosie, 1900-
Spirit of revival; biography of J. B. Govan, founder of the Faith Mission. Edinburgh, Faith Mission; London, Edinburgh, Marshall, Morgan & Scott, 1938. 208 p.

--SERMONS

2050 CAMPBELL, Duncan
God's answer; revival sermons. Fort Washington, Pa., Christian Literature Crusade, 1967, c1960. 95 p.
"Foreword," by John G. Eberstein.

2051 CAMPBELL, Duncan
God's standard; challenging sermons. Fort Washington, Pa., Christian Literature Crusade, 1967, c1964. 79 p.

FIRE BAPTIZED HOLINESS CHURCH (Wesleyan) (1895-   )

[1890-1945 as Southeast Kansas Fire Baptized Holiness Association]

Originating in the "third blessing" movement of the 1880's and 1890's, this group consists of the minority within that movement which opposed tongues-speaking. The church teaches three works of grace: regeneration, entire sanctification, and baptism with the Holy Ghost and fire. Before 1945, when the present name was adopted, the group was known as the Southeast Kansas Fire Baptized Holiness Association. Numbering fewer than a thousand members and concentrated near the Kansas-Oklahoma and Missouri Kansas borders, the church reports meetings as far west as California and Oregon and supports missionary work in New Guinea. At its headquarters in Independence, Kansas, it operates an elementary and high school and publishes two papers: The Flaming Sword for adults and John Three Sixteen for youth.

--HISTORY

2052 MEAD, Frank Spencer, 1898-
Handbook of denominations in the United States. New 5th ed. Nashville, Abingdon Press, c1970. 265 p.
"Fire Baptized Holiness Church (Wesleyan)": p. 107.

--PERIODICALS

2053 FLAMING SWORD. 1- , 1935- . Independence, Kan.

II. 1. Christian Holiness Association 223

2054   JOHN THREE Sixteen. 1- , Apr. 1891- . Vinita, Ind.
       Ter.; Tabor, Iowa; Independence, Kan.

GENERAL HOLINESS LEAGUE (1891-189?)

   Providing a means of fellowship among holiness believers
both inside and outside denominational churches, the General Holiness League aimed at counteracting pressure in New England
and the Midwest for a distinctly holiness church. Backed by
William McDonald, president of the National Holiness Association,
and Joshua Gill and Martin Wells Knapp, the Boston-based organization was designed to stem the flow of holiness Methodist members
into the Central Evangelical Holiness Association and like organizations. Faced by censure for holding meetings outside denominational control (such a resolution was adopted by the New England
Conference of the Methodist Episcopal Church in April 1892), the
League failed to take root. Opposition, on the other hand,
strengthened the movement toward independency. Although the
League soon disappeared, the organization apparently provided the
model for the International Apostolic Holiness Union and Prayer
League, parent of the Pilgrim Holiness Church.

2055   SMITH, Timothy Lawrence, 1924-
              Called unto holiness; the story of the Nazarenes: the
       formative years. Kansas City, Mo., Nazarene Publishing
       House, 1962. 413 p.
              Account of General Holiness League: p. 59-60.

GOSPEL TABERNACLE ASSOCIATION (-1950)

[Also as Trinity Gospel Tabernacle Association]

   At the General Conference of the Pilgrim Holiness Church
held at Frankfort, Indiana, in 1950, the Trinity Gospel Tabernacle
Association of Evansville, Indiana, joined the Indiana District of
the denomination. Led by A. L. Luttrull, the group consisted of
several small self-governing congregations with a few hundred
members.

       --HISTORY

2056   THOMAS, Paul Westphal, 1894-1972.
              "The days of our pilgrimage; a history of the Pilgrim
       Holiness Church," by Paul Westphal Thomas and Paul Wil-
       liam Lee Thomas. Unpublished paper, 1968. 1 v. (vari-
       ous pagings)
              In archives of The Wesleyan Church, Marion, Indiana.
              Account of the Gospel Tabernacle Association: ℓ.309.

HEAVENLY RECRUIT CHURCH (1882-19??)

[1882-1885 as Heavenly Recruits; 1885-1894 as Heavenly Recruit Association]

Like the Holiness Christian Church, the Heavenly Recruit Church derived from mission work begun in 1882 by a handful of workers in Philadelphia. Organized as the Heavenly Recruit Association in 1885, the work expanded to include mission churches in other eastern Pennsylvania towns and in Indiana, Illinois and other midwestern states. During a crisis over centralized administration in 1894, the majority reorganized as the Holiness Christian Association. The Indiana churches, however, modified the older title to Heavenly Recruit Church. In 1906 this group reported 27 organized congregations with 938 members, and had eight church buildings and 15 halls for worship. Reconciliation with their Holiness Christian brethren may account for their disappearance from records after 1806. A sizeable portion of the 2167 members of the Indiana Conference of the Holiness Christian Church, which in 1919 merged with the International Apostolic Holiness Church, may have been affiliated with the Heavenly Recruit Church.

2057   SCHAFF, Philip, 1819-1893.
New Schaff-Herzog encyclopedia of religious knowledge.... S. M. Jackson, editor-in-chief. New York, Funk, 1908-1912. 12 v.
"Heavenly Recruit Church," by E. M. Bliss: v. 7, p. 392.

HEPHZIBAH FAITH MISSIONARY ASSOCIATION (1892-1951)

[1892-1900 as Hephzibah Faith Home Association]

A product of the impact of holiness revivalism on German pietist groups such as the Brethren in Christ, the Hephzibah Faith Home Association was organized at Glenwood, Iowa, in 1893. Supporters of an orphanage at Tabor, Iowa, called Faith Home, the group set out on a course of aggressive evangelistic and missionary activity. Although support of Faith Home continued, "missionary" was substituted for "home" in the title after November 1900. The headquarters, a Bible training school and an annual camp meeting were established at Tabor. Here also, the Association published Sent of God, superseded in 1914 by Good Tidings Sent of God. Hephzibah workers, including an uncle of President Eisenhower, ranged over the Great Plains area from the Dakotas to the Indian Territory, holding school house revivals and establishing small congregations.

Foreign missionary efforts were extensive. Association workers arrived in South Africa in 1895, in India in 1898, and in

II. 1. Christian Holiness Association

China in 1905. Later workers were sent to work independently or with other groups in Mexico, Peru, North Africa and Haiti. Eventually the foreign work was turned over to other missions: that in China to the Oriental Missionary Society, in India to the United Missionary Society, in South Africa to the Church of the Nazarene, and in Haiti to the Wesleyan Methodist Church.

In the United States, the group (which in 1946 claimed 20 congregations, 700 members, and about 100 ministers and workers) faced the problems of an aging leadership and declining support. As a result most of the churches, an Indian school at Hot Springs, South Dakota, and the Haiti mission united with the Wesleyan Methodist Church in 1948. Three years later the Bible school and camp meeting at Tabor were accepted by the Church of the Nazarene.

2058 HEPHZIBAH Faith Missionary Association.
Association handbook. Mitchell, S.D., Hephzibah Association, 1936.

2059 HEPHZIBAH Faith Missionary Association.
Missionary year book.... Tabor, Iowa, 19??-19??.

--APOLOGETIC WORKS

2060 HEPHZIBAH Faith Missionary Association.
The work of the Hephzibah Faith Missionary Association. Tabor, Iowa, 19??.

--HISTORY

2061 CLARK, Elmer Talmage, 1886-1966.
The small sects in America. Rev. ed. New York, Abingdon Press, c1965. 256 p.
Account of Hephzibah Faith Missionary Association: p. 78.

2062 DODD, Gladys
"The religious background of the Eisenhower family." Unpublished B.D. thesis, Nazarene Theological Seminary, 1959. vi, iv, 436ℓ.

2063 McLEISTER, Ira Ford, 1879-1963.
History of the Wesleyan Methodist Church of America. Rev. ed. /i.e., 3d ed./ by Roy Stephen Nicholson. Marion, Ind., Wesley Press, 1959. 558 p.
Account of Hephzibah Faith Missionary Association: p. 275, 329-331, 446-447.

2064 MEAD, Frank Spencer, 1898-
Handbook of denominations in the United States. 2d rev. ed. New York, Abingdon Press, 1961. 272 p.
"Hephzibah Faith Missionary Association": p. 104-105.

2065 SCHAFF, Philip, 1819-1893.
New Schaff-Herzog encyclopedia of religious knowledge.... S. M. Jackson, editor-in-chief. New York, Funk, 1908-1912. 12 v.
"Hephzibah Faith Missionary Association, " by E. M. Bliss: v. 7, p. 392.

2066 WORCESTER, Paul W.
The master key; the story of the Hephzibah Faith Missionary Association. Kansas City, Mo., Printed for the author by the Nazarene Publishing House, 1966. 63 p.

--MISSIONS

2067 ENCYCLOPEDIA OF modern Christian missions; the agencies. Burton L. Goddard, ed.... Camden, N.J., T. Nelson, 1967. xix, 743 p.
"Hephzibah Faith Missionary Association, " by Roy P. Adams: p. 315-316.

--PERIODICALS

2068 GOOD TIDINGS Sent of God. 1- , 1914-1948. Tabor, Iowa
Supersedes Sent of God.

2069 JOHN THREE Sixteen. 1- , Apr. 1891- . Vinita, Ind. Ter.; Tabor, Iowa.

2070 SENT OF God. 1-22, 1892-1913. Glenwood, Iowa; Tabor Iowa.
Superseded by Good Tidings Sent of God.

--STATISTICS

2071 U.S. BUREAU of the Census.
Census of religious bodies, 1926; Hephzibah Faith Missionary Association: statistics, denominational history, doctrine, and organization. Washington, U.S. Government Printing Office, 1928. 8 p.

--AFRICA, SOUTH

2072 McCORD, James Bennett
My patients were Zulus, by James B. McCord with

John Scott Douglas. New York, Rinehart, 1951. 308 p.
Congregationalist missionary doctor who found natives inculcated with belief in faith healing as taught by George Weavers, Hephzibah Faith Missionary Association missionary, before McCord arrived.

HOLINESS ASSOCIATION OF TEXAS (1899-1910)

Despite its name, this group--formed in November 1899 at Peniel, a new suburb of Greenville, Texas--exercised many of the prerogatives of a church. Absorbing the Northwest Texas Holiness Association formed earlier that year, the Holiness Association of Texas attracted members of the Methodist Episcopal Church, South, and the Cumberland Presbyterian Church who had been ostracized for their holiness testimony. It issued licenses to holiness preachers denied recognition by old-line denominations. Association work paralleled the development of Texas Holiness University, established the same year at Peniel. Its activities were publicized in the Texas Holiness Advocate, known after 1905 as the Pentecostal Advocate. Though composed of "loyalists" who were reluctant to declare independence from the older churches, the Association was sympathetic with the independent church movement represented by the Holiness Church of Christ. When that group united with the Pentecostal Church of the Nazarene in 1908, so many members united with the new denomination as to threaten the future of the Association. The Holiness Association of Texas held its last annual meeting at Peniel in November 1910.

--HISTORY

2073   JERNIGAN, Charles Brougher, 1863-1930.
Pioneer days of the Holiness Movement in the Southwest. Kansas City, Mo., Pentecostal Nazarene Publishing House, 1919. 157 p.
"Holiness Association of Texas": p. 97-108.

2074   SMITH, Timothy Lawrence, 1924-
Called unto holiness; the story of the Nazarenes: the formative years. Kansas City, Mo., Nazarene Publishing House, 1962. 413 p.
Account of Holiness Association of Texas: p. 161-166.

--PERIODICALS

2075   PENTECOSTAL ADVOCATE. 1- , 1899-1911. Greenville, Tex.
1899-1905 as Texas Holiness Advocate.

HOLINESS UNION (1904-190?)

Formed in 1904 under the leadership of Henry Clay Morrison, this association sought, through local societies called unions, to provide fellowship for holiness believers in the old-line denominations, not to organize a new church. Morrison, an evangelist of Louisville, Kentucky, who owned and edited the Pentecostal Herald, had narrowly missed being removed from the ministry of the Methodist Episcopal Church, South, in 1896 when the presiding elder for Dublin, Texas, where Morrison was holding evangelistic meetings, brought charges against him. Believing that the opposition was due to his holiness preaching, Morrison formed the Holiness Union as a hedge against pressure to leave existing denominations and form a new holiness church. A convention held in Memphis in 1904 drew a large delegation from the Southern states, and for a brief time the Holiness Union plan appeared to be workable. Acceptance of tongues-speaking by large numbers of Southern Holiness people after the Azusa Street revival in Los Angeles in 1906, hastened the movement toward independency. In fact of the new trend, the Holiness Union simply disappeared.

2076   HOLINESS UNION.
Yearbook of the Holiness Union; containing a full report of the Holiness Convention held at Memphis, Tenn., Oct. 11-14, 1904, comp. by H.W. Bromley, secretary. Louisville, Ky., Pentecostal Herald Print, 1904? 82 p.

INDEPENDENT HOLINESS MOVEMENT (1907-)

Almost no information is available concerning this British group. Allusions in holiness writings indicate that the Movement, which was formed in 1907, was still extant in 1955.

2077   FORD, Jack, 1908-
In the steps of John Wesley; the Church of the Nazarene in Britain. Kansas City, Mo., Printed by Nazarene Publishing House, 1968. 300 p.
Mention of the Independent Holiness Movement: p. 29.

2078   FORD, Jack, 1908-
What the holiness people believe; a mid-century review of holiness teaching. Birkenhead, Ches., Eng., Emmanuel Bible College and Missions, 195?. 70 p.
Mention of the Independent Holiness Movement: p. 14.

2079   G. W.
The work of the Holy Ghost in modern times. Leicester, Eng., J.W. Hemmings & Capey, 1919.
Mention of the Independent Holiness Movement: p. 21.

II. 1. Christian Holiness Association

IRISH EVANGELISTIC BAND (1936-   )

Patterned after the Faith Mission, the Irish Evangelistic Band was formed in 1936. Workers receive no salary. As implied by the name, the Band concentrates its efforts in Eire.

2080   FORD, Jack, 1908-
In the steps of John Wesley; the Church of the Nazarene in Britain. Kansas City, Mo., Printed by Nazarene Publishing House, 1968. 300 p.
Mention of the origin of the Irish Evangelistic Band: p. 30.

KENTUCKY MOUNTAIN HOLINESS ASSOCIATION (1925-   )

This association of mission congregations in eastern Kentucky is the result of the work of Lela G. McConnell. A native of Pennsylvania trained for the Methodist Episcopal ministry at Chicago Evangelistic Institute and Asbury College, Miss McConnell went to Breathitt County, Kentucky, with the intent of establishing a school for the religious training of mountain youth. Lawson, Kentucky, served as a site for the Mount Carmel High School, established in 1925, and the Kentucky Mountain Bible Institute, established in 1931. Faculty and students conducted Sunday schools and revival work in neighboring communities and several holiness congregations were established. Since the beginning an annual camp meeting and workers conference has been held at the school, and school and evangelistic activities have been closely related. In 1952 over half of the 125 people who were serving in the schools and the radio station at Lawson, and in the mission churches related to the Association, were graduates of the Association-sponsored schools. Miss McConnell's work has maintained close ties with the National Holiness Association.

--HISTORY

2081   McCONNELL, Lela Grace, 1884-
God answers prayer in the mountains of Kentucky. Jackson, Kentucky Mountain Holiness Association, 1968. 2 sides   33 rpm   (80450)

2082   McCONNELL, Lela Grace, 1884-
Faith victorious in the Kentucky mountains; the story of twenty-two years of Spirit-filled ministry. Winona Lake, Ind., Printed for the author by Light and Life Press, 1946. 237 p.
Autobiography.

2083   McCONNELL, Lela Grace, 1884-
        Hitherto and henceforth in the Kentucky mountains; a
        quarter of a century of adventures in faith--the year of
        jubilee. n.p., c1949. 221 p.

2084   McCONNELL, Lela Grace, 1884-
        The Pauline ministry in the Kentucky mountains; or, A
        brief account of the Kentucky Mt. Holiness Association.
        Berne, Ind., Printed by Economy Printing Concern, 1942.
        200 p.
        Autobiography.

2085   McCONNELL, Lela Grace, 1884-
        The power of prayer plus faith. n.p., 1952. 229 p.

2086   McCONNELL, Lela Grace, 1884-
        Rewarding faith plus works. n.p., c1962. 174 p.

LAYMEN'S HOLINESS ASSOCIATION (1917-1922)

   In July 1917, during the Jamestown, North Dakota, holiness
camp meeting, a group of Methodist lay people organized to protest the treatment accorded two holiness leaders: S. A.
Danford, successful pioneer presiding elder, and his right-hand
man, J. G. Morrison. Following the forced removal of Danford
and Morrison to Oregon and Florida respectively, the Association
tried to force the Methodist bishop to appoint Morrison presiding
elder. When Morrison was ousted from the Methodist ministry,
the Association made him its president and editor of its paper
(which bore various titles but was called the Holiness Layman
during its most influential period). Morrison and other full-time
evangelists pushed the Association program vigorously, organizing
local groups in the Dakotas and a half-dozen other states and
Canadian provinces. Cut off from official Methodist standing,
Morrison was powerless to act when his own workers became
enamored with the Pentecostalism then sweeping the country. In
1922, despairing of saving Methodism, he joined the Church of the
Nazarene in Minneapolis. Over 1000 individuals associated with
him followed him into that denomination, greatly augmenting its
strength in the northern Great Plains. In the new church, Morrison filled posts of increasing responsibility serving as general
superintendent during the last years of his life.

2087   LAYMEN'S Holiness Association.
        Constitution of the Laymen's Holiness Association of
        America. n.p., 1920.

II. 1. Christian Holiness Association

--HISTORY

2088   DANFORD, Samuel Alexander, 1865-
Report for sixth year for Bismarck District of North Dakota Conference, M.E. Church. Bismarck, N.D., 1915.

2089   DANFORD, Samuel Alexander, 1865-
Spreading scriptural holiness; or, The North Dakota movement. Chicago, Christian Witness Co., 1913. 137 p.

2090   METHODIST Church (United States). Conferences. North Dakota. Historical Society.
History of the Methodist Church in North Dakota and Dakota Territory, written by the members of the North Dakota Conference Historical Society. Nashville, Tenn., 1960. 256 p.

2091   SMITH, Timothy Lawrence, 1924-
Called unto holiness; the story of the Nazarenes: the formative years. Kansas City, Mo., Nazarene Publishing House, 1962. 413 p.
Account of Laymen's Holiness Association: p. 298-315.

--PERIODICALS

2092   HOLINESS MESSENGER. 1- , 1908-1925. Jamestown, N.D.
1908-191? as North Dakota Methodist; 1916-1917 as Little Methodist; 1917-June 1918 as Methodist; July 1919-192? as Holiness Layman.

LEAGUE OF PRAYER (1891-   )

[1890 to Feb. 1891 as Pentecostal Mission Prayer Union; Feb. 1891 to 19?? as Pentecostal League; 19??-19?? as Pentecostal League of Prayer]

In 1887 Richard Reeder Harris, an Anglican layman, purchased Speke Road Hall in South London, which Moody and Sankey used three years earlier for meetings and began holding Sunday night evangelistic services. Influenced by the preaching of two American holiness evangelists at Speke Hall, two years later Harris and his wife, Mary, claimed entire sanctification. No ordinary mission superintendent (he had been financial adviser to the Bolivian government and a barrister who in 1894 became a Queen's Counsellor), Harris immediately championed the non-denominational holiness movement. Late in 1890 the Harrises re-named the Speke Hall Mission the Pentecostal Mission and organized the Pentecostal Mission Prayer Union, re-titled in February 1891 the Pentecostal League. Members were enjoined to pray for each other, for the mission, and for the infilling of the Holy Spirit. The first year the League launched a periodical called Tongues of Fire. Determinedly non-sectarian (in 1907 David Thomas, one of the Pentecostal League workers, left and founded the International Holiness Mission so that independent churches might be organized), the Pentecostal League has maintained its non-denominational character. In the early part of the twentieth century its name was changed to Pentecostal League of Prayer, later shortened to League of Prayer. Members participate annually in the Southport Convention.

--CONDUCT OF LIFE

2093   HARRIS, Reader, 1847-1909.
           Men's sins; an address to men only. London, H.R. Allenson, 1899. 16 p.

2094   HARRIS, Reader, 1847-1909.
           Men's sins; an address to men only. New and rev. ed. London, H.R. Allenson, 1901. 16 p.

2095   HARRIS, Reader, 1847-1909.
           Spiritual life leaflet series, nos. 1-3. London, S.W. Partridge & Co., 1919.

--DEVOTIONAL LITERATURE

2096   HARRIS, Reader, 1847-1909.
           Prayer and faith: addresses. London, S.W. Partridge & Co., 1899. 96 p.

--DOCTRINAL AND CONTROVERSIAL WORKS

2097   HARPER, James Albert
           The real thing; life in the Spirit.... London, Oliphants, 1964. 92 p.

2098   HARRIS, Mary Griffin (Bristow)
           The Song of Songs; a glimpse into the heart of Christ. Westminster, P.L. Publishing Co., 1916. 47 p.

2099   HARRIS, Mary Griffin (Bristow)
           Spirit pictures of the Pentecostal blessing. London, S.W. Partridge & Co., 1900. 94 p.

2100   HARRIS, Reader, 1847-1909.
           The atonement. London, S.W. Partridge & Co., 1902. 90 p.

2101   HARRIS, Reader, 1847-1909.
           The beatitudes. London, S.W. Partridge & Co., 1912.

II. 1. Christian Holiness Association

60 p.
A series of addresses.

2102 HARRIS, Reader, 1847-1909.
The case against atheism. London, Horace Marshall & Son, 1898. 93 p.

2103 HARRIS, Reader, 1847-1909.
The gospel of the Comforter. London, S.W. Partridge & Co., 1906. 84 p.

2104 HARRIS, Reader, 1847-1909.
Is sin a necessity?; a resumé of the recent controversy. London, S.W. Partridge & Co., 1896. 94 p.

2105 HARRIS, Reader, 1847-1909.
The Lord's Prayer. London, S.W. Partridge & Co., 1907. 72 p.

2106 HARRIS, Reader, 1847-1909.
The lost tribes of Israel. London, S.W. Partridge & Co., 1907. 89 p.

2107 HARRIS, Reader, 1847-1909.
The lost tribes of Israel.... 6th ed. London, Covenant Publishing Co., 1928. 61 p.

2108 HARRIS, Reader, 1847-1909.
The manuscript of God...; a series of seven addresses on the Ten Commandments. London, Arthur H. Stockwell, 1909. 61 p.
Delivered in Exeter Hall.

2109 HARRIS, Reader, 1847-1909.
Pentecost in the churches, and other addresses. London, S.W. Partridge & Co., 1897. 95 p.

2110 HARRIS, Reader, 1847-1909.
Six steps to the throne. London, S.W. Partridge & Co., 1903. 75 p.

2111 HARRIS, Reader, 1847-1909.
When He is come; or, The personality and work of the Holy Spirit. London, Andrews Bros., 1897. 84 p.

2112 STORRS, William Townsend, Vicar of Sandown, I.O.W.
Christian perfection: what it is not, and what it is; notes on a booklet of the Pentecostal League. Sandown, I.O.W., Eng., I.W. Chronicle Printing Works, 1900. 19 p.
Notes on Christian Perfection, by Reader Harris.

--ESCHATOLOGY

2113 HARRIS, Mary Griffin (Bristow)
The Great War, the herald of the Lord's return. London, S.W. Partridge & Co., 1915. 39 p.

2114 HARRIS, Mary Griffin (Bristow)
The Great War, the herald of the Lord's return.... 2d and enl. ed. London, P.L. Publishing Co., 1916. 56 p.

2115 HARRIS, Mary Griffin (Bristow)
Talks on the Apocalyse; studies in the Book of Revelation. London, S.W. Partridge & Co., 1913. 226 p.

2116 HARRIS, Reader, 1847-1909.
Daniel the prophet. London, S.W. Partridge & Co., 1909. 82 p.

2117 HARRIS, Reader, 1847-1909.
Things to come; signs of the times, ed. by Mary G. Harris. London, S.W. Partridge & Co., 1911. 52 p.

--HISTORY

2118 FORD, Jack, 1908-
In the steps of John Wesley; the Church of the Nazarene in Britain. Kansas City, Mo., Printed by Nazarene Publishing House, 1968. 300 p.
Thesis (Ph.D.)--University of London, 1967.
Account of the Pentecostal League: p. 90-97.

--PERIODICALS

2119 SPIRITUAL LIFE. 1- , Jan. 1891- . London.
1-25, no. 300, Jan. 1891-Dec. 1915 as Tongues of Fire; herald of the Pentecostal Mission.

LOWER LIGHT CHURCH (194?-1973)

[194?-1973 as Lower Light Mission or Lower Light Assoc.]

Formed in the 1940's as the Lower Light Mission, this congregation in Ann Arbor, Michigan, appears to have branched out into other communities in Michigan and Ohio. (The 1972 minutes of the Ohio Conference of the Bible Methodist Connection mention the possibility of a joint clergy meeting.) At most the group has a few hundred members in a handful of congregations. It is in fellowship with the new conservatives represented by the Inter-

II. 1. Christian Holiness Association

denominational Holiness Convention.

2120   BIBLE Methodist Connection of Churches. Conferences. Ohio.
     Minutes, July 12-15, 1972. n.p., 1972. 66 p.
     Mimeographed.
     Mention of the Lower Light Church: p. 37.

METROPOLITAN CHURCH ASSOCIATION (1894-)

[1894-1899 as Metropolitan Holiness Church]

     Long identified as the "Burning Bush" movement because of the name of its official publication, this group stemmed from a holiness revival in the Metropolitan Methodist Episcopal Church of Chicago in 1894. Until 1899 when the present name was adopted, the official title was Metropolitan Holiness Church. Strongly missionary and evangelistic in emphasis, the Metropolitan churches early placed great stress on emotional display in public worship and ascetic standards in personal behavior. Ironically the Association, which has adopted a communal form of organization, attracted several prosperous businessmen. (Frank M. Messenger, manufacturer of a nationally-distributed scripture-text calendar, was for a time affiliated with the Metropolitan Association). A training school for workers established in Chicago later moved to Waukesha, Wisconsin. Missionaries have been sent to South Africa, Swaziland, India and Mexico and evangelistic workers have gone to Great Britain. The India mission proved a success and today, churches there, which are headed by national pastors, have over 7000 members. Incorporated in Wisconsin in 1918, the United States group in 1958 reported 443 members in 15 congregations. The headquarters are now at Dundee, Illinois, near Chicago. The <u>Burning Bush</u> is presently issued from Lake Geneva, Wisconsin.

2121   METROPOLITAN Church Association.
     Discipline of the Metropolitan Church Association of Wisconsin, adopted Nov. 15, 1930. Waukesha, Wis., 1931. 64 p.

2122   METROPOLITAN Church Association.
     Discipline and rules for Christian conduct of the Metropolitan Church Association of Waukesha, Wisconsin. Waukesha, Wis., 1952. 20 p.
     Cover title: Discipline and Christian conduct.

        --ANECDOTES, REMINISCENCES, SATIRE, ETC.

2123   FARSON, Duke
     Raised a communist; life in a religious commune, illus.

by the author. Los Angeles, Farson Studio Publications, 1936. 142 p.
Fictionalized account of the author's boyhood.

--CONDUCT OF LIFE

2124 GRIFFITH, Glenn, 1894-
"Until death do us part." Dundee, Ill., Metropolitan Press, 1958. 32 p.

--DOCTRINAL AND CONTROVERSIAL WORKS

2125 METROPOLITAN Church Association.
Bible A-B-C book.... Waukesha, Wis., 1917. [46] p.

2126 METROPOLITAN Church Association.
Bible lessons; a treatise on evidences of religion, sin, repentance, consecration, and holiness, designed for Bible classes. Waukesha, Wis., Metropolitan Church Association, 1907. 189 p.

2127 METROPOLITAN Church Association
Favorite Bible stories.... Waukesha, Wis., Metropolitan Church Association, 1935. 47 p.

-- --AUTHORITATIVE SOURCES

2128 BOOTH, Catherine (Mumford), 1829-1890.
Repentance, saving faith, charity. Waukesha, Wis., Metropolitan Church Association, n.d. 42 p.

2129 CARVOSSO, William, 1750-1835.
Life of William Carvosso, sixty years a class leader. Waukesha, Wis., Metropolitan Church Association, n.d. 95 p.
Autobiography.

2130 EDWARDS, Jonathan, 1703-1758.
The perpetuity and change of the sabbath. Waukesha, Wis., Metropolitan Church Association, n.d. 45 p.

2131 EDWARDS, Jonathan, 1703-1758.
Sinners in the hands of an angry God. Waukesha, Wis. Metropolitan Church Association, n.d.

2132 EVANS, Christmas, 1766-1838.
The fall & recovery of man; also, A brief account of the author's views on religious manifestation of his time. Waukesha, Wis., Metropolitan Church Association, n.d. 28 p.

II. 1. Christian Holiness Association

2133 HENRY, George W., 1801-
History of the Jumpers; or, Shouting, genuine and spurious; a history of the outward demonstrations of the Spirit. Waukesha, Wis., Metropolitan Church Association. 1909. 379 p.

2134 HENRY, George W., 1801-
Shouting: genuine and spurious, in all ages of the church, from the birth of creation ... until the shout of the arch-angel, with numerous extracts from the Old and New Testament.... Chicago, Metropolitan Church Association, 1903. 305 p.

2135 PAYSON, Edward, 1783-1827.
The gospel invitation. Waukesha, Wis., Metropolitan Church Association, n.d. 28 p.

2136 PECK, Jesse Truesdell, bp., 1811-1883.
The great subject of holiness. Glasgow, Scot., Metropolitan Mission, n.d. 32 p.

2137 SIMPSON, Matthew, bp., 1811-1884.
The triumphant Christ. Waukesha, Wis., Metropolitan Church Association, n.d. 26 p.

2138 WESLEY, John, 1703-1791.
The scripture way of salvation. Waukesha, Wis., Metropolitan Church Association, n.d. 25 p.

--EVANGELISTIC WORK

2139 FINNEY, Charles Grandison, 1792-1875.
Revival fire; letters on revivals to all friends, and especially ministers, of our Lord Jesus Christ. Waukesha, Wis., Metropolitan Church Association, n.d. 96 p.

--HISTORY

2140 CLARK, Elmer Talmage, 1886-1966.
The small sects in America. Rev. ed. New York, Abingdon Press, c1965. 256 p.
Account of Metropolitan Church Association: p. 77-78.

2141 MEAD, Frank Spencer, 1898-
Handbook of denominations in the United States. New 5th ed. Nashville, Abingdon Press, c1970. 265 p.
"Metropolitan Church Association": p. 153.

2142 SCHAFF, Philip, 1819-1893.
New Schaff-Herzog encyclopedia of religious knowl-

edge.... S. M. Jackson, editor-in-chief. New York, Funk, 1908-1912. 12 v.
"Metropolitan Church Association," by E. M. Bliss: v. 7, p. 393.

2143 TWENTIETH century encyclopedia of religious knowledge; an extension of the New Schaff-Herzog Encyclopedia of Religious Knowledge. Editor-in-chief: Lefferts A. Loetscher. Grand Rapids, Mich., Baker Book House, 1955. 2 v. (xx, 1205 p.)
"Metropolitan Church Association," by Theodore G. Tappert: p. 735.

--HYMNS

2144 METROPOLITAN Church Association.
Burning bush songs, number one, selected by Music Committee of Metropolitan Church Association. Waukesha, Wis., Metropolitan Church Association, 1902. Unpaged.

2145 METROPOLITAN Church Association.
The joy-bells of Canaan; or, Burning bush songs, no. 2, selected by Duke M. Farson [and] Edwin L. Harvey. Waukesha, Wis., Metropolitan Church Association, 1905. 127 p.
With music.

2146 METROPOLITAN Church Association.
Message of victory; Burning Bush songs, no. 6, selected by Duke M. Farson, Edwin L. Harvey, Wm. T. Pettengill [and] Louis F. Mitchel. Waukesha, Wis., 1918. Unpaged.
Cover-title.

--MISSIONS

2147 METROPOLITAN Church Association.
Time for our annual missionary offering: Metropolitan Church Association, May 6-20, 1973. Lake Geneva, Wis., 1973. Folder.

2148 ENCYCLOPEDIA OF modern Christian missions; the agencies. Burton L. Goddard, ed.... Camden, N.J., T. Nelson, 1967. xix, 743 p.
"Metropolitan Church Association, General Assembly of the": p. 424.

II. 1. Christian Holiness Association   239

--PERIODICALS

2149 BURNING BUSH. 1- , 1902- . Chicago, Waukesha, Wis., Dundee, Ill., Lake Geneva, Wis.

--SERMONS

2150 HARVEY, Edwin Lawrence, 1865-
Sermons on Bible characters. Waukesha, Wis., Metropolitan Church Association, 1909. 242 p.

--SOCIAL CRITICISM

2151 MESSENGER, Frank Mortimer, 1852-
Catacombs of worldly success; or, History of Coarsellor Dell; a glimpse of the interior workings of a large industrial concern, showing its social and religious sides with relation to its business policies. Waukesha, Wis., Metropolitan Church Association, 1910. 235 p.

--STATISTICS

2152 U.S. BUREAU of the Census.
...Census of religious bodies, 1926; Metropolitan Church Association: statistics, denominational history, doctrine, and organization.... Washington, U.S. Government Printing Office, 1928. 9 p.

MEXICAN EVANGELISTIC MISSION (1926-   )

[1946 merged with Evangelical Methodist Church retaining former name; also 1954-1957 as Mexico District, Evangelical Methodist Church; 1957-present as Mexican Annual Conference, Evangelical Methodist Church]

Formed at Chihuahua in 1926 by Ezequiel B. Vargas, a former presiding elder in the Methodist Episcopal Church, South, the Mexican Evangelistic Mission is an indigenous group working in the states of Chihuahua, Durango, Coahuila, Nuevo Leon, Zacatecas and San Luis Potosi. In addition to village evangelism (there were 196 preaching points in 1964), 42 Mexican and eight United States workers conduct sizeable educational, relief and publication programs. With headquarters at Chihuahua, in 1964 the group claimed over 2000 baptized members and 43 organized congregations. In 1946 the Mission affiliated with the Evangelical Methodist Church. Designated as the Mexico District in 1954, the Mission became the first Mission Conference three years later. Independence was maintained by designating Vargas as general superintendent (Mexico), and the Mexican Evangelistic Mission continues to operate much as it did before joining the Evangelical Methodist Church.

2153 MEXICAN Evangelistic Mission.
    Disciplina: constitucion, doctrinas, gobierno y ritual. 42ava. Conferencia Anual, 1968. Chihuahua, Chih., Mex., Alffer Offset, 1968. 184 p.

2154 MEXICAN Evangelistic Mission.
    Mexico, land of contrasts and opportunity. Chihuahua, Chihuahua, Mex.; Eloy, Ariz., 1968? Folder.
    Also established as Mexican Annual Conference of the Evangelical Methodist Church in 1957.

2155 ENCYCLOPEDIA OF modern Christian missions; the agencies. Burton L. Goddard, ed.... Camden, N.J., T. Nelson, 1967. xix, 743 p.
    "Mexican Evangelistic Mission," by James H. Mumme: p. 424-425.

--HYMNS

2156 MEXICAN Evangelistic Mission.
    Himnario evangelistico. 6. ed. Chihuahua, Chih., Mex., 1956. 184 p.
    Without music.

--POLEMICAL WORKS

-- --CATHOLICISM

2157 UN SACERDOTE que predica solo a Cristo. Chihuahua, Chih., Mex., 19??. Cover-title, 17 p.
    Biography of Juan J. Arrien, converted Roman Catholic priest.

2158 VARGAS, Ezequiel B.,   -1965.
    Es Maria camino de salvacion? Réplica a los articulos del Sr. Presbitero Romano Emiliano Soria. 2. ed. Chihuahua, Chih., Mex., 1943. 64 p.

2159 VARGAS, Ezequiel B.,   -1965.
    Réplica al analisis del catecismo breve E. V. C. sobre el protestantismo. Chihuahua, Chih., Mex., Ebenezer, 19??. Cover-title, 63 p.

II. 1. Christian Holiness Association 241

-- --SEVENTH-DAY ADVENTISM

2160   VARGAS, Ezequiel B.,   -1965.
El adventismo del septimo dia. Parral, Chih., Mex.,
Imprenta Ebenezer, 19??. Cover-title, 35 p.

MISSIONARY BANDS OF THE WORLD (1885-1958)

[1885-1895 as Pentecost Bands; 1895-1925 as Pentecost Bands of the World]

In 1885 Vivian Dake, a Free Methodist pastor in Illinois, organized the young people of his congregation into a Pentecost Band, a society devoted to evangelistic and missionary activity. In an era when church-sponsored youth activities were almost non-existent, the Pentecost Band idea spread rapidly and Dake, a promoter of faith missions in this country as well as abroad, found himself head of a movement. Resistant to attempts at denominational control, the Pentecost Bands zealously pursued their evangelistic work independent of Free Methodist officials. After Dake's death in Africa in 1895, Thomas H. Nelson led the Pentecost Bands out of the church. Establishing headquarters in Indianapolis, the group operated on the "faith" principle: that God would supply material needs in answer to prayer without direct financial appeals or advance pledges. The Pentecost Bands tested candidates for foreign service by an apprenticeship in home missionary work conducted on the faith principle. Although a few small congregations were established in Michigan, Indiana and Illinois, emphasis was on foreign missions. Work was conducted at some time in Japan, India, Norway and Jamaica. In Indianapolis where the annual encampment (called in later years the Salem Park Camp Meeting) convened, the Herald of Light and Zion's Watchman was published. Threatened by tongues-speaking, in 1925 the group changed its name to Missionary Bands of the World. A union with the Church of God (Holiness), consummated in 1934, insured a larger base of support, but proved unsatisfactory to part of the Missionary Bands workers who secured independent status again in 1940. Aging personnel and declining support were perennial problems of the group, whose United States membership declined steadily. (In 1906 it reported 466 members; in 1936, only 222). In 1958, when it merged with the Wesleyan Methodist Church, the Missionary Bands was supporting twelve missionaries in India and Jamaica.

2161   PENTECOST Bands of the World.
Doctrines and discipline of the Pentecost Bands of the World.... Indianapolis, Publishing House of the Pentecost Bands, 1915. 72 p.

--HISTORY

2162 CLARK, Elmer Talmage, 1886-1966.
The small sects in America. Rev. ed. New York, Abingdon Press, c1965. 256 p.
Account of Missionary Bands of the World: p. 77.

2163 NELSON, Thomas Hiram, 1863-
Life and labors of Rev. Vivian A. Dake, organizer and leader of Pentecost Bands, embracing an account of his travels in America, Europe and Africa, with selections from his sketches, poems and songs. Chicago, Pub. for the author by T.B. Arnold, 1894. 508 p.

2164 PARSONS, Ida Dake
Kindling watch-fires; being a brief sketch of the life of Rev. Vivian A. Dake, together with a compilation of selections from his writings, sermons, and poems, to which is appended a few of his best songs with the music. Chicago, Pub. for the author by Free Methodist Publishing House, 1915. 209 p.

--PERIODICALS

2165 HERALD OF Light. 1- , 1894-193?. Indianapolis, Ind., Ft. Scott, Kan.
Title varies: Ram's Horn; Herald of Light and Zion's Watchman.

2166 PENTECOST HERALD. 1- , 190?- . Indianapolis, Pentecost Bands.

--STATISTICS

2167 U.S. BUREAU of the Census.
...Census of religious bodies; Missionary Bands of the World: statistics, denominational history, doctrine, and organization.... Washington, U.S. Government Printing Office, 1928. 8 p.

NORTHWEST TEXAS HOLINESS ASSOCIATION (Aug.-Dec. 1899)

Formed at Sunset, Texas, in August 1899, by John Stanfield, a Cumberland Presbyterian pastor who was suspended for espousing holiness, the Northwest Texas Holiness Association represented the first step toward independency by denominational loyalists in Texas. Its Form and Plan of Local Organization anticipated the transformation of local bands into independent churches. Supported by the Texas Holiness Banner, the Northwest Texas Association was soon

II. 1. Christian Holiness Association

absorbed into the Holiness Association of Texas.

2168   NORTHWEST Texas Holiness Association.
       Form and plan of local organization, adopted by the
       Association. Sunset, Tex., 1899.

2169   NORTHWEST Texas Holiness Association.
       Minutes of the Northwest Texas Holiness Association,
       held at the Holiness Camp Ground, Sunset, Texas, August
       9, 1899. Sunset, Tex., 1899.

--HISTORY

2170   JERNIGAN, Charles Brougher, 1863-1930.
       Pioneer days of the Holiness Movement in the Southwest. Kansas City, Mo., Pentecostal Nazarene Publishing House, 1919. 157 p.
       "Northwest Texas Holiness Association": p. 94-96.

--PERIODICALS

2171   TEXAS HOLINESS Banner. 1- , 1899-1900. Sunset, Tex.

PENIEL MISSIONS (1886-)

[Also as Peniel Missionary Society]

An outgrowth of the first rescue mission in Los Angeles, this faith group historically has made little distinction between domestic and foreign missionary work. Founded by T.P. and Manie Ferguson in 1886, by the turn of the century the group had established a number of branch missions on the West Coast and launched work in Alaska, Hawaii and Egypt. Fergusons supervised the Peniel work until their deaths. From the headquarters mission in Los Angeles they issued the Peniel Herald, recruited workers and raised support for other parts of the work. At their height the Peniel Missions in the United States never had as many as a thousand members; a government census in 1906 reported 703. P.F. Bresee and J.P. Widney, founders of the Church of the Nazarene in Los Angeles, served on the Peniel staff before starting the church in 1895. Mrs. Ferguson contributed "Blessed Quietness," a gospel song long popular in holiness circles. Haldor Lillenas, leading gospel song writer and music editor of the Church of the Nazarene, was converted in the Peniel Mission at Astoria, Oregon. In 1949 the Peniel work in Egypt and on the West Coast affiliated with the National Holiness Missionary Society. Under this arrangement rescue mission work in the United States continues under the old name. Headquarters are now at Sacramento, California.

--HISTORY

2172   CLARK, Elmer Talmage, 1886-1966.
        The small sects in America. Rev. ed. New York, Abingdon Press, c1965. 256 p.
        Account of Peniel Missions: p. 79-80.

2173   ENCYCLOPEDIA OF modern Christian Missions; the agencies. Burton L. Goddard, ed.... Camden, N.J., T. Nelson, 1967. xix, 743 p.
        "Peniel Missions, Inc.": p. 526.

2174   PICKETT, Leander Lycurgus, 1859-1928.
        Faith tonic, 1 and 2 combined; being a series of articles by different writers, exemplifying God's dealings with those who trust him. Louisville, Pentecostal Publishing Co., n.d. 102 p.
        Includes article entitled, "Peniel Missionary Work," by Manie Payne Ferguson: p. 3-35.

--HYMNS

2175   FERGUSON, Manie (Payne), 1850-
        Echoes from Beulah. Los Angeles, T.P. & M.P. Ferguson, 1913. 268 p.
        With music.

--PERIODICALS

2176   PENIEL HERALD. 1- , 1894- . Los Angeles; Sacramento, Calif.

--EGYPT

2177   TRACHSEL, Laura (Cammack), 1907-
        Kindled fires in Africa. Marion, Ind., World Gospel Mission, 1960. 123 p.
        "Kindled fires in Egypt": p. 107-121.

PENTECOSTAL MISSION (1898-1915)

[July 1898 to Nov. 1901 as Pentecostal Aliiance]

Inspired by the work of A.B. Simpson and the Christian and Missionary Alliance, the Pentecostal Alliance (known after 1901 as Pentecostal Mission) was organized in Nashville, Tennessee, in July 1898, by followers of J.O. McClurkan, a Cumberland Presbyterian evangelist. Though including a number of Presbyterians,

II. 1. Christian Holiness Association

this holiness evangelistic association was strongly Wesleyan from its inception. The work, which centered in McClurkan's tabernacle in Nashville, concentrated on mission work in Tennessee and other southeastern states and in foreign countries. A training school for workers was established in Nashville, where Zion's Outlook (later re-named Living Water) was published. Missionary zeal expressed itself in work in Cuba, Guatemala and India. Expansion repeatedly outstripped financial and organizational resources and the Mission, which by 1903 numbered 28 congregations (26 in Tennessee and one each in Atlanta, Georgia and Columbia, South Carolina), was forced to seek a larger base of support. As early as 1907 merger negotiations began with the Pentecostal Church of the Nazarene. In 1911, the Pentecostal Mission invited the Pentecostal Nazarenes to hold their General Assembly in Nashville. But it was not until 1915, a year after McClurkan's death, that the union was consummated.

--CONDUCT OF LIFE

2178 McCLURKAN, James O., 1861-1914.
Chosen vessels; twenty-one biographical sketches of men and women, most of whom have been used of God in pioneering some great Pentecostal movement. Nashville, Pentecostal Mission Publishing Co., 1901. 199 p.

2179 McCLURKAN, James O., 1861-1914.
How to keep sanctified. Nashville, Pentecostal Book and Tract Depository, 1900.

--DOCTRINAL AND CONTROVERSIAL WORKS

2180 GODBEY, William B., 1833-1920.
Satan's side-tracks for Holiness people. Nashville, Pentecostal Mission Publishing Co., 19??.

2181 HILLS, Aaron Merritt, 1848-1935.
Backsliders & worldly Christians. Nashville, Pentecostal Mission Publishing Co., 19??. 101 p.

2182 HILLS, Aaron Merritt, 1848-1935.
Secret of spiritual power. Nashville, Pentecostal Mission Publishing Co., 19??. 190 p.

2183 McCLURKAN, James O., 1861-1914.
Wholly sanctified; what it is and how it may be obtained. Nashville, Printed for the author, 1895. 114 p.

2184 McCLURKAN, James O., 1861-1914.
Wholly sanctified, what it is and how it may be obtained. Nashville, Tenn., Pentecostal Mission Publishing Co., n.d. 127 p.

-- --ESCHATOLOGY

2185   GODBEY, William B., 1833-1920.
Where are the dead? Nashville, Pentecostal Mission Publishing Co., n.d. 49 p.

--EVANGELISTIC WORK

2186   McCLURKAN, James O., 1861-1914.
Personal work. Nashville, Tenn., Pentecostal Mission Publishing Co., 1914. 187 p.

--HISTORY

2187   GOMER, Thelma
"A mighty church moves on," Nazarene Weekly (Nashville), XLIII (May 6, 1973).
Historical sketch of the First Church of the Nazarene in Nashville, Tennessee, including an account of its relationship to the Pentecostal Mission.

2188   HEATH, Merle (McClurkan)
A man sent of God; the life of J.O. McClurkan. Kansas City, Mo., Beacon Hill Press, 1947. 95 p.

2189   REDFORD, Maury English
The rise of the Church of the Nazarene. Kansas City, Mo., Nazarene Publishing House, 1948. 208 p.
"The Pentecostal Mission": p. 154-159.

2190   SMITH, Timothy Lawrence, 1924-
Called unto holiness; the story of the Nazarenes: the formative years. Kansas City, Mo., Nazarene Publishing House, 1962. 413 p.
"The Pentecostal Mission in Tennessee, 1898-1915": p. 180-204.

--HYMNS

2191   BENSON, John T., 1861-1930, comp.
Choice collections; a special selection of sacred songs, with brief sketches of the leading authors, comp. by Jno. T. Benson and M. Homer Cummings. Nashville, Pentecostal Mission Publishing Co., 1923? Unpaged
"Printed in both round and shaped notes."

--PERIODICALS

2192   LIVING WATER. 1- , May 30, 1891-1919. Nashville.

II. 1. Christian Holiness Association 247

1891-1896 as Tennessee Methodist; 1896-1902 as Zion's Outlook.

PENTECOSTAL RESCUE MISSION (1897-1922)

Organized in 1897 from a nucleus gathered in cottage and tent meetings the previous year, the Pentecostal Rescue Mission at first consisted of a single congregation at Binghamton, New York. Attracting most of its early workers from the Methodist Episcopal and Free Methodist churches, the Mission conducted week-night and Sunday services. It sponsored direct evangelistic work on the street and in saloons as well as among orphans and unwed mothers. On April 15, 1907, it began publishing News from Home, and from 1908 to 1911 operated the Pentecostal Mission Bible School in Binghamton. By 1920 membership stood at about 450 and the work had spread to other communities in south central New York, the Hudson Valley, Pennsylvania and New Jersey. Annual camp meetings were held in various locations and mission programs similar to the Binghamton one were carried on in several communities. In 1922, a year after Preston Kennedy, the long-time superintendent, left the group, the Pentecostal Rescue Mission merged with the International Holiness Church. At that time the group consisted of about sixteen congregations, operated an orphanage and two rescue homes, and supported missionary activity in Africa, South America and Alaska.

2193 PENTECOSTAL Rescue Mission.
   Doctrine and discipline, 1904.   Binghamton, N.Y., C.D. Pendell, Printer, 1904.

2194 PENTECOSTAL Rescue Mission.
   Discipline, 1910.   Binghamton, N.Y., Pentecostal Rescue Mission Press, 1910.

2195 PENTECOSTAL Rescue Mission.   Yearly Meeting.
   Minutes. 1-16, 19??-1921.   Binghamton, N.Y.; Easton, Md., 19??-1921.

--HISTORY

2196 THE PENTECOSTAL Rescue Mission: Pilgrim Holiness Church of New York; seventy-fifth anniversary diamond jubilee.   Binghamton, N.Y., 1972.   Unpaged.
   Added t.-p.: Celebrating the 75th anniversary of the Pentecostal Rescue Mission.   Motto: "Holiness unto the Lord."   A brief history.   Christ our way, truth, life: Pilgrim Holiness Church of New York, Inc.

2197 THOMAS, Paul Westphal, 1894-1972.
"The days of our pilgrimage; a history of the Pilgrim Holiness Church," by Paul Westphal Thomas and Paul William Lee Thomas. Unpublished paper, 1968. 1 v. (various pagings).
In archives of the Wesleyan Church, Marion, Indiana.
Account of the Pentecostal Rescue Mission of New York ℓ. 101-104.

--PERIODICALS

2198 NEWS FROM home. 1- , Apr. 15, 1907-19??. Binghamton, N.Y.

PEOPLE'S MISSION CHURCH (1899-1925)

Emanating from a rescue mission started in Colorado Springs in 1899, the People's Mission Church was largely the result of the evangelistic labors of William H. Lee. Nephew of Jason Lee, famous missionary to the Indians of the Northwest, Lee had been working with the Salvation Army in Kansas when in 1900 he went to Colorado Springs for a rest. While there he held a revival meeting in a mission started a year earlier after a tent meeting held by I.G. Martin, a well-known holiness evangelist. Lee's meeting was so successful that he was asked to become mission superintendent. Adopting as its motto "A work for the neglected, churchless, and Christless," the mission ministered to miners and drifters drawn to the nearby gold fields. Offering temporary housing and assistance in securing employment to its converts, the work incorporated in 1902 as The People's Mission Church and soon spread to other towns. Three years later the Western Holiness College and Bible Training School opened, and the group started issuing The Pentecostal Rescue Evangelist, a monthly. Through this paper and the annual Pike's Peak Holiness Camp Meeting, the church raised money for foreign missionary work. Seeking a wider base of support, in 1911 the People's Mission Church merged with the Pentecostal Church of the Nazarene, only to separate again after a few months due to administrative misunderstandings. Following Lee's death in 1919 the group, under the leadership of Paul W. Thomas, again sought a place within a larger denomination and in 1925 merged with the Pilgrim Holiness Church. People's Mission membership at the time was something less than 500.

2199 PEOPLE'S Mission Church.
Manual, 1921. Colorado Springs, Colo., General Headquarters, People's Mission Church, 1921.

II. 1. Christian Holiness Association

--HISTORY

2200 THOMAS, Paul Westphal, 1894-1972.
"The days of our pilgrimage; a history of the Pilgrim Holiness Church," by Paul Westphal Thomas and Paul William Lee Thomas. Unpublished paper, 1968. 1 v. (various pagings)
In archives of The Wesleyan Church, Marion, Indiana. Account of the People's Mission Church: ℓ. 123-128.

--PERIODICALS

2201 MISSION ADVANCE. 1- , 1920- . Colorado Springs, Colo.

2202 PENTECOSTAL RESCUE Evangelist. 1- , 1905-191?. Colorado Springs, Colo.

PILLAR OF FIRE CHURCH (1901-   )

[1901-1917 as Pentecostal Union; also as Pillar of Fire, and Church of the Pillar of Fire]

Known until 1917 as the Pentecostal Union, this group is largely the product of the labors of Alma Bridwell White. Until 1901 her husband, Kent White, served as a Methodist Episcopal pastor in Colorado. Then, his wife's free-lance evangelistic activities brought him into insoluable conflict with church authorities. Cooperating at first with the Metropolitan Church Association, the Kentucky-born couple started a rescue mission, a paper called Pillar of Fire and a Bible training school. Despite her husband's espousal of tongues-speaking and subsequent removal to England, Mrs. White carried on the work begun in Denver and developed a second center known as Zarephath near Bound Brook, New Jersey. Here a cluster of schools, a radio station and a second publishing plant were located. Having herself concecrated bishop, Alma White planted work in additional centers: Brooklyn, Newark, Philadelphia, Washington, Jacksonville, Cincinnati, Los Angeles, and London. In the 1920's Bishop White declared the Ku Klux Klan to be God's agent in maintaining social and racial distinctions; nevertheless, the Pillar of Fire established missionary work in the River Cess area of Liberia. Later Alma's sons, both of whom received master's degrees from Princeton, were made bishops and the group has remained under the direction of the White family. Highly sectarian, the Pillar of Fire is among the least fraternal of the Holiness churches. In recent years it has been reluctant to release statistics. In 1948, two years after Mrs. White's death, it reported 61 congregations and 5100 members. Present figures are undoubtedly much lower.

2203 PILLAR OF Fire Church.
Doctrines and discipline of the Pillar of Fire Church, 1918, written and comp. by Rev. Ray B. White, Zarephath, N.J., Pillar of Fire, 1918. 234 p.

2204 PILLAR OF Fire Church.
Discipline. Zarephath, N.J., Pillar of Fire, 1926.

2205 "FAITHFUL TREK to Zarephath Zion," Literary Digest, CXXII (Sept. 5, 1936), 30.

2206 "FUNDAMENTALIST Pillar," Time, XLVIII (July 8, 1946), 73-74.

--ANECDOTES, REMINISCENCES, SATIRE, ETC.

2207 WHITE, Alma (Bridwell), 1862-1946.
Modern miracles and answers to prayer. Zarephath, N.J., Pillar of Fire, 1939. 248 p.

--CATECHISMS AND CREEDS

2208 PILLAR OF Fire Church.
Catechism. Denver, Pillar of Fire, 1948. 208 p.

--CLERGY

2209 WHITE, Alma (Bridwell), 1862-1946.
Woman's chains; illustrated by Branford Clarke. Zarephath, N.J., Pillar of Fire, 1943. 184 p.

--CONDUCT OF LIFE

2210 WHITE, Arthur Kent, 1889-
Your home your college; or, "Throughly furnished." Zarephath, N.J., Pillar of Fire, 1922. 290 p.

--DOCTRINAL AND CONTROVERSIAL WORKS

2211 WHITE, Alma (Bridwell), 1862-1946.
The chosen people. Bound Brook, N.J., The Pentecostal Union, 1910. 313 p.

2212 WHITE, Alma (Bridwell), 1862-1946.
Everlasting life. Zarephath, N.J., Pillar of Fire, 1944. 341 p.

II. 1. Christian Holiness Association

2213 WHITE, Alma (Bridwell), 1862-1946.
The New Testament church. Denver, Pillar of Fire, 1907. 174 p.

2214 WHITE, Alma (Bridwell), 1862-1946.
The New Testament church. Bound Brook, N.J., Pentecostal Union, 1912- .

2215 WHITE, Alma (Bridwell), 1862-1946.
The New Testament church. Rev. ed. Zarephath, N.J., Pillar of Fire, 1929. 413 p.

2216 WHITE, Alma (Bridwell), 1862-1946.
Why I do not eat meat. Zarephath, N.J., Pentecostal Union, 1915. 213 p.

2217 WHITE, Arthur Kent, 1889-
A toppling idol--evolution [by] Arthur K. White ... [and] Ray B. White.... Zarephath, N.J., Pillar of Fire, 1933. 240 p.

-- --ESCHATOLOGY

2218 WHITE, Alma (Bridwell), 1862-1946.
The Ku Klux Klan in prophecy; illustrated by Rev. Branford Clarke. Zarephath, N.J., The Good Citizen, 1925. 144 p.

2219 WHITE, Alma (Bridwell), 1862-1946.
Restoration of Israel, the hope of the world. Zarephath, N.J., Pentecostal Union, 1917. 176 p.

-- --GLOSSOLALIA

2220 WHITE, Alma (Bridwell), 1862-1946.
Demons and tongues. Bound Brook, N.J., The Pentecostal Union, 1910. 86 p.

2221 WHITE, Alma (Bridwell), 1862-1946.
Demons and tongues. Zarephath, N.J., Pillar of Fire, 1919. 90 p.

2222 WHITE, Alma (Bridwell), 1862-1946.
Demons and tongues. Zarephath, N.J., Pillar of Fire, 1936. 128 p.

--EDUCATION

2223 LAWRENCE, Evan Jerry, 1918-
"Alma White College; a history of its relationship to the development of the Pillar of Fire." Unpublished Ed.D.

dissertation, Columbia University, 1966.

--EVANGELISTIC WORK

2224 PAIGE, Clara R., 1869-   , comp.
Alma White's evangelism; press reports, comp. by C.R. Paige [and] C. K. Ingler. Zarephath, N.J., Pillar of Fire, 1939-1940. 2 v.
"Drawings by Branford Clarke."

--HISTORY

2225 CLARK, Elmer Talmage, 1886-1966.
The small sects in America. Rev. ed. New York, Abingdon Press, c1965. 256 p.
Account of the Pillar of Fire: p. 78-79.

2226 MEAD, Frank Spencer, 1898-
Handbook of denominations in the United States. New 5th ed. Nashville, Abingdon Press, c1970. 265 p.
"Pillar of Fire": p. 165-166.

2227 WHITE, Alma (Bridwell), 1862-1946.
The story of my life and the Pillar of Fire. Zarephath, N.J., Pillar of Fire, 1935-1943. 5 v.
Autobiography.

2228 WHITE, Alma (Bridwell), 1862-1946.
Truth stranger than fiction. Zarephath, N.J., Pentecostal Union, 1913. 305 p.

2229 WHITE, Alma (Bridwell), 1862-1946.
Truth stranger than fiction. Rev. ed. Zarephath, N.J., Pillar of Fire, 1936. 256 p.

2230 WHITE, Arthur Kent, 1889-
Some White family history. Denver, Colo., Pillar of Fire, 1948. 432 p.

2231 WOLFRAM, Gertrude (Metlen), 1888-
The widow of Zarephath, a church in the making. Zarephath, N.J., Pillar of Fire, 1954. 244 p.

2232 TWENTIETH CENTURY encyclopedia of religious knowledge; an extension of the New Schaff-Herzog Encyclopedia of Religious Knowledge. Editor-in-chief: Lefferts A. Loetscher. Grand Rapids, Mich., Baker Book House, 1955. 2 v. (xx, 1205 p.)
"Pillar of Fire," by Elmer T. Clark: p. 880.

II. 1. Christian Holiness Association 253

--HYMNS

2233 PILLAR OF Fire Church.
Cross & crown hymnal, ed. by Bishop Alma White and Rev. Arthur K. White. Zarephath, N.J., Pillar of Fire, 1939. Unpaged.

2234 PILLAR OF Fire Church.
The harp of gold; or, Pillar of Fire praises, no. 2, ed. by Alma White [and] Arthur K. White. Zarephath, N.J., Pillar of Fire, 1925. Unpaged.
With music.

2235 PILLAR OF Fire Church.
The silver trumpet; hymnal of the church of the Pillar of Fire, ed. by Bishop Alma White.... Rev. Arthur K. White.... 3d ed. Zarephath, N.J., Pillar of Fire, 1929. Unpaged.
With music.

2236 WHITE, Alma (Bridwell), 1862-1946.
The bugle call; the hymns and songs of Alma White, with other favorite selections.... Zarephath, N.J., Pillar of Fire, 1943. [208] p.
With music.

2237 WHITE, Alma (Bridwell), 1862-1946.
Hymns and poems. Zarephath, N.J., Pillar of Fire, 1931. 224 p.

2238 WHITE, Alma (Bridwell), 1862-1946, ed.
Pillar of Fire praises, ed. by Mrs. Alma White, Arthur K. White [and] Mrs. Lillian O. Bridwell. Bound Brook, N.J., Pentecostal Union, 1909. Unpaged.

--MISSIONS

2239 ENCYCLOPEDIA OF modern Christian missions; the agencies. Burton L. Goddard, ed.... Camden, N.J., T. Nelson, 1967. xix, 743 p.
"Pillar of Fire," by Donald J. Wolfram: p. 535.

--PERIODICALS

2240 DRY LEGION; advocating social welfare, temperance education, national prohibition. 1- , Nov. 1934- . Denver.

2241 GOOD CITIZEN. 1-21, no. 6, 1913-1933. Zarephath, N.J. 4-16 also as no. 35-184.

2242   PILLAR OF Fire. 1- , Oct. 1910-19??. London.
        1-16, no. 2, Oct. 1910-Feb. 1926 as London Pillar of Fire.

2243   PILLAR OF Fire; devoted to the interests of the sanctified
        life. 1- , 1902- . Denver, Colo., Zarephath, N.J.
        1902-1907 as Rocky Mountain Pillar of Fire.

2244   PILLAR OF Fire Junior. 1- , 1906- . Zarephath, N.J.

2245   WOMAN'S CHAINS. 1- , 1924- . Denver, Colo.; Zarephath, N.J.

--POLEMICAL WORKS

-- --CATHOLICISM

2246   WHITE, Alma (Bridwell), 1862-1946.
        The truth in satire concerning infallible popes. Zarephath, N.J., Pillar of Fire, 1929.

-- --JEHOVAH'S WITNESSES

2247   GODBEY, William B., 1833-1920.
        Russellism. Zarephath, N.J., Pillar of Fire, 1918. 38 p.

--POLITICAL AND SOCIAL CRITICISM

2248   "PILLAR OF Fire Dry Legion acts out evils of liquor in
        Brooklyn church pulpit," Life, VIII (Jan. 29, 1940), 42-43.

2249   WHITE, Alma (Bridwell), 1862-1946.
        Guardians of liberty; illus. by Branford Clarke. Zarephath, N.J., Pillar of Fire, 1943- .

2250   WHITE, Alma (Bridwell), 1862-1947.
        Klansmen: guardians of liberty; illustrated by Rev.
        Branford Clarke. Zarephath, N.J., The Good Citizen, 1926. 160 p.

2251   WHITE, Alma (Bridwell), 1862-1947.
        The Ku Klux Klan in prophecy; illustrated by Rev.
        Branford Clarke. Zarephath, N.J., The Good Citizen, 1925. 144 p.

2252   WHITE, Alma (Bridwell), 1862-1946.
        The Titanic tragedy--God speaking to the nations.

II. 1. Christian Holiness Association

Bound Brook, N.J., Pentecostal Union, 1912. 213 p.

--SERMONS

2253   WHITE, Alma (Bridwell), 1862-1946.
Gospel truth. Zarephath, N.J., Pillar of Fire, 1945. 261 p.

2254   WHITE, Alma (Bridwell), 1862-1946.
Radio sermons and lectures. Denver, Pillar of Fire, 1936. 300 p.
"A collection of sermons given over the Pillar of Fire radio stations, viz. KPOF at Denver, Colorado, and WAWZ at Zarephath, New Jersey."--Foreword.

2255   WHITE, Alma (Bridwell), 1862-1946.
Short sermons. Zarephath, N.J., Pillar of Fire, 1932. 416 p.

2256   WHITE, Alma (Bridwell), 1862-1946.
The sword of the Spirit. Zarephath, N.J., Pillar of Fire, 1937. 375 p.

2257   WHITE, Arthur Kent, 1889-
The boys made good, and other sermons. Zarephath, N.J., Pillar of Fire, 1936. 352 p.

2258   WHITE, Ray Bridwell, 1892-1946.
The King's message, a volume of sermons. Denver, Colo., Pentecostal Union, 1916. 151 p.

--STATISTICS

2259   U.S. BUREAU of the Census.
...Census of religious bodies, 1926; Pillar of Fire: statistics, denominational history, doctrine and organization.... Washington, U.S. Government Printing Office, 1928. 10 p.

--WORK WITH YOUTH

2260   WHITE, Alma (Bridwell), 1862-1946.
Gems of life; short selections for children. Denver, Pillar of Fire Publishers, 1907. 110 p.

--YEARBOOKS

2261   PILLAR OF Fire Church.
Year book.... Zarephath, N.J.

PRIMITIVE HOLINESS MISSION (1889-190?)

[Also as Primitive Holiness Church]

This evangelistic association was organized in 1889 by S.B. Shaw, a Grand Rapids evangelist and publisher then serving as president of the Michigan Holiness Association. Like their leader (who had been affiliated successively with the Methodist Episcopal, Wesleyan Methodist and Free Methodist churches), members of the new group disliked formal organization. Consisting of a few poor rural charges in south central Michigan, the Primitive Holiness Mission was short-lived, disappearing without notice in a few years Shaw was suspicious of the wealth and worldly accommodation of some prominent National Holiness members, and sought through independency to demonstrate what a true holiness church would be like. He used the Michigan Holiness Association paper (re-named the Primitive Holiness Record) as a platform for radical reform. Group attitudes crystalized on such disparate issues as the right of women to preach; the wearing of jewelry, feathers and corsets as indicators of female vanity; the injustice of gate fees at camp meetings, and the un-Christian character of Masonry.

2262 SHAW, Solomon Benjamin, 1854-
" 'A new church'--not quite, " Michigan Holiness Record, VII (Sept.-Oct. 1889), 13.

2263 SMITH, Timothy Lawrence, 1924-
Called unto holiness; the story of the Nazarenes: th\ formative years. Kansas City, Mo., Nazarene Publishing House, 1962. 413 p.
Account of the background and formation of the Primitive Holiness Mission: p. 33-35.

--PERIODICALS

2264 PRIMITIVE HOLINESS Record. 1-7, Apr. 1883-May/June 1890. Grand Rapids, Mich., Dutton, Mich., Saugatuck, Mich.
Apr. 1883-Mar. 1890 as Michigan Holiness Record.

VANGUARD MISSION (1881-1916)

In 1881 Charles W. Sherman, a Methodist Episcopal minister, moved to St. Louis from Burnside, Illinois, and to promote holiness teaching began The Vanguard, a semi-monthly paper, and opened a downtown mission by the same name. Supporting himself by job-printing and evangelistic work, the Vanguard superintendent developed a large following not only in the city of St. Louis but throughout the Mississippi Valley as well. In 1890 Sherman, who

II. 1. Christian Holiness Association 257

was concerned with foreign as well as domestic missions helped sponsor the short African sojourn of R. L. Harris, future founder of the New Testament Church of Christ. The next year Sherman's daughter, Bessie, went to India as a faith missionary and in 1900, during a severe famine, Sherman visited her there. The visit resulted not only in appeals to Vanguard subscribers for contributions to relieve Indian suffering, but in establishment of an Indian work under Vanguard auspices. In 1904 Sherman supported the unsuccessful attempt of Henry Clay Morrison to confederate holiness Methodist loyalists into the Holiness Union. Thereafter, Vanguard support declined and in 1909 Bessie Sherman Ashton and her husband sought the support of the Wesleyan Methodist Church in the United States. The following year the Ashtons joined the Wesleyans and were appointed missionaries by the denominational board. In 1916, the India work became officially Wesleyan Methodist. The Vanguard apparently ceased publication at the end of 1914; presumably the mission in St. Louis also closed.

--PERIODICALS

2265 VANGUARD. 1-34, no. 19, 1881-Dec. 30, 1914. St. Louis.
27, no. 17-19 as 27, no. 15-17.

--INDIA

2266 ASHTON, Albert E.
Our work in the Orient, by Rev. Albert E. Ashton and Mrs. Bessie Sherman Ashton. Syracuse, N.Y., Wesleyan Methodist Publishing House, 191?. 32 p.

2267 BANKER, Floyd E.
From famine to fruitage; an account of fifty years of Wesleyan Methodism in western India, by Floyd and Hazel Banker. Marion, Ind., Wesley Press, 1960. 188 p.
Account of Vanguard Mission work in India: p. 1-70.

2268 ENCYCLOPEDIA OF modern Christian missions; the agencies. Burton L. Goddard, ed.... Camden, N.J., T. Nelson, 1967. xix, 743 p.
"Vanguard Mission": p. 681.

2269 McLEISTER, Ira Ford, 1879-1963.
History of the Wesleyan Methodist Church of America. Rev. ed. [i.e. 3d ed.] by Roy Stephen Nicholson. Marion, Ind., Wesley Press, 1959. 558 p.
Account of Vanguard Mission work in India: p. 148-149, 310-311.

Friends

EVANGELICAL FRIENDS ALLIANCE (1965- .)

[1947-1965 as Association of Evangelical Friends]

Coincident with the growth of holiness sentiment among American Methodists in the late nineteenth century was a movement toward evangelicalism among a significant minority of American Quakers. As a result of the work of Joseph John Gurney (1788-1847), an English Quaker who traveled extensively in the United States, many Friends adopted revivalistic methods. Associating the Inner Light with the Holy Spirit, the Gurneyites were receptive to Methodist holiness evangelism. Numerous local meetings and several yearly meetings, including the strong Ohio and Iowa ones, were deeply influenced. They replaced unprogrammed meetings with full-time pastors, and under David B. Updegraff, a holiness minister in Ohio, the ordinances of baptism and the Lord's Supper were observed. In 1887 when the first General Conference of yearly meetings gathered at Richmond, Indiana, with the Dublin and London yearly meetings and all North American yearly meeting except Philadelphia present, the Gurneyites secured a statement of principles which was saturated with Wesleyanism. The Richmond Declaration served as a basis for formation of the Five Years Meeting, a national body which by 1902 included all orthodox meetings except Ohio. But tensions over interpretation caused the eventual separation of most yearly meetings sympathetic to holiness--Oregon in 1926, Kansas in 1937--and formation of the Rocky Mountain Yearly Meeting (out of the Nebraska Yearly Meeting) in 1957. In 1947, these yearly meetings together with Ohio formed the Association of Evangelical Friends, re-organized in 1965 as the Evangelical Friends Alliance, representing over a fifth of all Quakers in the United States.

2270   ENCYCLOPEDIA OF modern Christian missions; the agencies. Burton L. Goddard, ed.... Camden, N.J., T. Nelson, 1967. xix, 743 p.
"Evangelical Friends Alliance."

--APOLOGETIC WORKS

2271   BARCLAY, Robert, 1648-1690.
A little apology (the gist of Barclay's), a condensation, or abstract, of the book, An Apology (1676 A.D.), by Robert Barclay [ed.] by Charles M. Kelly; the doctrines believed and taught by George Fox and Friends of the seventeenth century. Revised 1963. Newberg, Ore., Barclay Press, c1964. 81 p.

II. 1. Christian Holiness Association

2272 BARNETT, Paul W.
Why am I a Quaker? Emporia, Kan. ?, 1970. 118 p.

2273 FOX, George, 1624-1691.
Journal; ed. with an introd. and notes by Rufus M. Jones, with an essay on the influence of the Journal by Henry J. Cadbury. New York, Capricorn Books, 1963. 578 p.

2274 GURNEY, Joseph John, 1788-1847.
Observations on the distinguishing views and practices of the Society of Friends. New York, Friends Book and Tract Committee, 1888.

2275 MOTT, Edward, 1866-1954.
The Friends Church in the light of recent history. Portland, Ore., Loomis Printing Co., 1935.

2276 ROBERTS, Arthur Owen, 1923-
The people called Quakers. Newberg, Ore., Barclay Press, 1965. Cover-title, 18 p.
"Third edition."

2277 ROBERTS, Arthur Owen, 1923-
Through flaming sword; a spiritual biography of George Fox. Illustrations by Stanley Putnam. Portland, Ore., Barclay Press, 1959. 113 p.

--CONGRESSES

2278 ROBERTS, Arthur Owen, 1923- , ed.
Story of the Second American Conference of Evangelical Friends. Portland, Ore., Oregon Yearly Meeting Press, 1950.

--DOCTRINAL AND CONTROVERSIAL WORKS

2279 [ASH, Edward], 1797-1873.
Christian holiness: what it is and how to be attained. London, Book Society, 1873.

2280 CATTELL, Everett Lewis, 1905-
The spirit of holiness. Grand Rapids, Mich., Wm. B. Eerdmans Publishing Co., 1963. 103 p.

2281 CAVIT, Marshal
The will of my Father; messages on the relationship between holiness and missions. Newberg, Ore., Barclay Press, 1968. vi, 115 p.

2282   CLARK, Dougan, 1828-1896.
        The Holy Ghost dispensation. Chicago, Publishing Association of Friends, 1891. 169 p.

2283   DOUGLAS, Major
        George Fox, red-hot Quaker. Cincinnati, God's Bible School and Missionary Training Home, n.d. 105 p.

2284   MOTT, Edward, 1866-1954.
        The Christ of the eternities. Portland, Ore., Loomis Printing Co., 1936. 159 p.

2285   MOTT, Edward, 1866-1954.
        Christ preëminent. Portland, Ore., Oregon Yearly Publication Board, 1943. 174 p.

2286   PINKHAM, William Penn, 1841-1919.
        The defense of the faith. Cleveland, Soul-Winner Press, 190?.

2287   PINKHAM, William Penn, 1841-1919.
        The lamb of God; or, The scriptural philosophy of the atonement. Cleveland, Cleveland Bible Training School, 1895. 231 p.

2288   SMITH, Hannah (Whitall), 1832-1911.
        The Christian's secret of a happy life, by H.W.S.
        Chicago, Revell, 1883. 235 p.

2289   SMITH, Hannah (Whitall), 1832-1911.
        The Christian's secret of a happy life, by H.W.S.
        New ed., rev. and enl. Boston, Willard Tract Repository, 1885. 321 p.

2290   SMITH, Hannah (Whitall), 1832-1911.
        Every-day religion; or, The common-sense teaching of the Bible. New York, Revell, 1893. vii, 242 p.

2291   SMITH, Hannah (Whitall), 1832-1911.
        The God of all comfort, and the secret of His comforting, by Mrs. Pearsall Smith (H.W.S.). New York, Revell, 1906. 254 p.
        Published also under title: Living in the sunshine.

2292   SMITH, Hannah (Whitall), 1832-1911.
        Living in the sunshine, by H.W.S. New York, Revell, 1906. 254 p.
        Published also under title: The God of all comfort, and the secret of His comforting.

2293   WOODARD, Luke, 1832-
        What is truth? Auburn, N.Y., Press of Knapp, Peck & Thomson, 1901. vii, 167 p.

II. 1. Christian Holiness Association

--HISTORY

2294 SMITH, Hannah (Whitall), 1832-1911.
John M. Whitall; the story of his life, written for his grandchildren by his daughter, H.W.S.... Philadelphia, Printed for the family, 1879. 338 p.

2295 WILLIAMS, Walter Rollin, 1884-
The rich heritage of Quakerism. Grand Rapids, Mich., William B. Eerdmans Publishing Co., 1962. 279 p.

--HISTORY OF DOCTRINES

2296 MEKEEL, Arthur Jacob
Quakerism and a creed. Philadelphia, Friends Book Store, 1936. 171 p.
"An enlargement of a master's thesis ... Haverford College."

2297 ROBERTS, Arthur Owen, 1923-
"The concepts of perfection in the history of the Quaker Movement." Unpublished B.D. thesis. Nazarene Theological Seminary, 1951.

2298 ROBERTS, Arthur Owen, 1923-
"George Fox's concept of the church." Unpublished Ph.D. dissertation, Boston University, 1954. ii, 210ℓ.

--MISSIONS

2299 ENCYCLOPEDIA OF modern Christian missions; the agencies. Burton L. Goddard, ed.... Camden, N.J., T. Nelson, 1967. xix, 743 p.
"Evangelical Friends Alliance": p. 259.

--PERIODICALS

2300 CHRISTIAN WORKER. 1-24, no. 27, Feb. 15, 1871-July 5, 1894. New Vienna, Ohio; Chicago.
Subtitle varies
Merged with Friend's Review to form American Friend.

2301 CONCERN; the concern of Evangelical Friends for the fellowship of the gospel among all Friends. 1- , 1959- Portland, Ore.; Newberg, Ore.

2302 EVANGELICAL FRIEND. 1-10, 1905-1914. Cleveland.
Supersedes Soul-winner.

2303 EVANGELICAL FRIEND. 1- , 1967- . Newberg, Ore., Evangelical Friends Alliance.

2304 FRIENDS' EXPOSITOR. 1-6, Jan. 1887-Oct. 1892; index 1-6. Mount Pleasant, Ohio.

2305 MISSIONARY VOICE of Evangelical Friends. 1-13, Feb. 1955-1967. Portland, Ore.; Newberg, Ore., Joint Board of Missionary Publications of Ohio, Kansas, Oregon and Rocky Mountain Meetings of Friends Church.

2306 SOUL-WINNER. 1-4, no. 18, 1902-May 18, 1905. Cleveland.
Superseded by Evangelical Friend.

CALIFORNIA YEARLY MEETING OF FRIENDS (1895-)

From its establishment in 1895 to the mid-1930's the California Yearly Meeting was aggressively evangelistic. For over thirty years it supported the Huntington Park Bible School, a holiness school founded in 1899 primarily by Quakers. Holiness workers were instrumental in starting a number of Friends meetings and served in prominent positions in the state organization. A diverse group (in 1901 the California Yearly Meeting joined the more liberal Five Years Meeting), the Meeting lost some of its more ardent holiness members in 1933 when administrative bungling split the Huntington Park congregation and led to formation of the Holiness Evangelistic Association. Though numerous holiness members remained in the parent body, the schism largely neutralized their influence in the California Yearly Meeting.

--CATECHISMS AND CREEDS

2307 BALL, Charles S.
Remembering our heritage; studies in Friends beliefs. Whittier, Calif., California Yearly Meeting, 1964. 26 p.

--EDUCATION

2308 BRACKETT, Charles H.
"The history of Azusa College and the Friends, 1900-1965." Unpublished M.A. thesis, University of Southern California, 1967. iv, 152ℓ.

--HISTORY

2309 COFFIN, T. Eugene
"History of California Yearly Meeting of Friends

Churches." Unpublished M.A. thesis, University of Southern California, 1956.

2310 Le SHANA, David Charles, 1932-
"Friends in California; a study of the effect of nineteenth century revivalism upon western Quakerism." Unpublished Ph.D. dissertation, University of Southern California, 1967. 326ℓ.

2311 Le SHANA, David Charles, 1932-
Quakers in California; the effects of 19th century revivalism on western Quakerism, with a foreword by D. Elton Trueblood. Newberg, Ore., Barclay Press, 1969. ix, 186 p.

2312 PHILLIPS, Isaac N.
"A History of the Evangelistic Tabernacles." Unpublished M.A. thesis, Pacific Bible College, 1955. 74ℓ.

--MISSIONS

2313 ENCYCLOPEDIA OF modern Christian missions; the agencies. Burton L. Goddard, ed.... Camden, N.J., T. Nelson, 1967. xix, 743 p.
"California Yearly Meeting of Friends, Board of Missions," by R. Ernest Lamb: p. 105.

--PERIODICALS

2314 PACIFIC FRIEND. 1- , 1893- . Huntington Park, Calif., California Yearly Meeting of Friends.

CENTRAL YEARLY MEETING OF FRIENDS (1926-)

Formed in 1926 by several Friends meetings in eastern Indiana which had withdrawn from the Five Years Meeting because of its alleged liberalism, the Central Yearly Meeting has fraternity with the most conservative elements in the present-day Holiness Movement. With headquarters in Westfield, Indiana, where the related Union Bible Seminary and the editorial offices of the Friends Evangel are located, the group sponsors missionary work in Bolivia. In 1959 there were eleven congregations with 515 members in Indiana, Michigan and Arkansas.

2315 FRIENDS, SOCIETY of. Central Yearly Meeting.
Declaration of faith and discipline for Central Yearly Meeting of Friends. n.p., 1928.

2316 FRIENDS, SOCIETY of. Central Yearly Meeting.
Declaration of faith and discipline for Central Yearly
Meeting of Friends. n.p., 1940.

2317 FRIENDS, SOCIETY of. Central Yearly Meeting.
Declaration of faith and discipline for Central Yearly
Meeting of Friends. n.p., 1960. 74 p.

2318 FRIENDS, SOCIETY of. Central Yearly Meeting.
Minutes.... n.p., 1926- .

--CONDUCT OF LIFE

2319 STAUFFER, Joshua, 1891-1971.
Consideration of 7'C [i.e. 7 C's] in courtship: care, calling, character, conduct, compatibility, consideration, cheerfulness. Westfield, Ind., Union Bible Seminary, n.d. 31 p.

2320 STAUFFER, Joshua, 1891-1971.
Eternity in man, man in eternity. Westfield, Ind., Gospel Minister, n.d. 31 p.

--DOCTRINAL AND CONTROVERSIAL WORKS

2321 FRIENDS, SOCIETY of. Central Yearly Meeting.
Some distinctive views of Friends. Westfield, Ind., 1932. 31 p.

2322 FRIENDS, SOCIETY of. Central Yearly Meeting.
Some distinctive views of Friends. Westfield, Ind., Union Bible Seminary, 1957. 31 p.
"Second printing."

2323 NEWBY, J. Edwin, 1898-
Teachings of evangelical Friends, as gleaned from George Fox's Journal and Friends Disciplines; messages given at Central Yearly Meeting, 1952. n.p., 1952. 24 p.

2324 NEWBY, J. Edwin, 1898-
Two heaps of stones and what they mean. Indianapolis, n.d. 8 p.

2325 SMITH, Simeon O.
The Wednesday crucifixion of Christ. Westfield, Ind., Union Bible Seminary, 1965. 32 p.
Reprint of 1959 ed.

2326 SMITH, William Martin, 1872-
Bible doctrines. 2d ed., rev. Westfield, Ind., Union Bible Seminary, 1934. 223 p.

II. 1. Christian Holiness Association

2327 SMITH, William Martin, 1872-
By faith; an exposition and interpretation of the eleventh chapter of Hebrews. Westfield, Ind., Union Bible Seminary, c1959. 60 p.

2328 SMITH, William Martin, 1872-
Hannah's revival; a Bible study of Hannah and Samuel. Westfield, Ind., Union Bible Seminary, 1951. 35 p.
Reprint of 1911 ed.

2329 SMITH, William Martin, 1872-
Jonah the prophet: lessons from the experiences of a prophet of God; also, When pleasure is a sin. 2d ed. Westfield, Ind., Gospel Minister, n.d. 32 p.

2330 SMITH, William Martin, 1872-
Nicolaitanism, the thing that Jesus hates, and Laodiceanism, the thing that makes Jesus sick. Westfield, Ind., Union Bible Seminary, n.d. 24 p.

2331 STAUFFER, Joshua, 1891-1971.
The Psalms of the cross, the crook, and the crown. 2d ed. Westfield, Ind., Gospel Minister, n.d. 62 p.

2332 STAUFFER, Joshua, 1891-1971.
The witness of the Spirit. Westfield, Ind., Union Bible Seminary, n.d. 44 p.

2333 STAUFFER, Joshua, 1891-1971.
The wonders of seeds. Westfield, Ind., Gospel Minister, n.d. 111 p.

-- --ATHEISM

2334 SMITH, William Martin, 1872-
The infidel's grave and some strange incidents about it. Westfield, Ind., Gospel Minister, 19??. 40 p.
First published in the Gospel Minister in 1933.
Reprint with revisions of 1933 ed.
Impressions of Chester Bedell of North Benton, Mahoning County, Ohio.

-- --ESCHATOLOGY

2335 NEWBY, J. Edwin, 1898-
Chart messages on the history and prophecy of the Bible. Berne, Ind., Light and Hope Publications, 1951. 168 p.

2336 NEWBY, J. Edwin, 1898-
Chart messages on the history and prophecy of the Bible. 1970 ed. Noblesville, Ind., Newby Book Room,

1970. 168 p.
   Cover-title: Chart messages on Bible prophecy.

2337 SMITH, William Martin, 1872-
   Bible history of world government and a forecast of its future from Bible prophecy. 5th ed. Westfield, Ind., Union Bible Seminary, 1955. 208 p.

2338 SMITH, William Martin, 1872-
   Imminent signs of the times. Westfield, Ind., Union Bible Seminary, 1963. 38 p.
   Published serially in the Gospel Minister.

2339 SMITH, William Martin, 1872-
   Signs of the times. Westfield, Ind., Union Bible Seminary, 1956. 24 p.
   Address at Union Bible Seminary, May 13, 1956.

2340 SMITH, William Martin, 1872-
   Studies in Bible prophecy. Westfield, Ind., Union Bible Seminary, 196?. 103 p.
   Published serially in the Gospel Minister in 1960.

2341 SMITH, William Martin, 1872-
   The two desolations of Jerusalem; a comparative study of Matthew XXIV and Luke XXI. Westfield, Ind., Gospel Minister, 1947. 24 p.
   Reprint, with corrections, of 1922 ed.

--MISSIONS

2342 ENCYCLOPEDIA OF modern Christian missions; the agencies. Burton L. Goddard, ed.... Camden, N.J., T. Nelson, 1967. xix, 743 p.
   "Central Yearly Meeting of Friends Missionary Committee," by Lucille Williams: p. 124.

2343 ENYART, Mary H.
   "Dear Papa" (Biography). n.p., 197?. 42 p.
   Cover-title: "Dear Papa"; a biography of Paul C. Enyart.

--PERIODICALS

2344 FRIENDS EVANGEL. 1- , 1947- . Westfield, Ind.

II. 1. Christian Holiness Association

--POLEMICAL WORKS

-- --CATHOLICISM

2345 SMITH, William Martin, 1872-
What we need to know about Roman Catholicism; a review of some of its doctrines, practices, and purposes. Westfield, Ind., Union Bible Seminary, n.d. 30 p.

2346 TOOLE, I. N.
Eternal security in the light of the scriptures. Westfield, Ind., Union Bible Seminary, n.d. 23 p.

--SERMONS

2347 SMITH, William Martin, 1872-
Deliverance from hell; "How can ye escape the damnation of hell?" Matthew 23.33. 3d ed. Westfield, Ind., Gospel Minister, 1942. 16 p.
"A sermon ... on the Sunday of Central Yearly Meeting, August 30, 1936. Later it was rearranged and printed as an editorial in 'The Gospel Minister'."

2348 STAUFFER, Joshua, 1891-1971.
Romans 8:28; fourteen sermons. Westfield, Ind., Union Bible Seminary, 1967. 111 p.
First published in 1935.

2349 STAUFFER, Joshua, 1891-1971.
There was a man. Westfield, Ind., Union Bible Seminary, n.d. 48 p.

2350 STAUFFER, Joshua, 1891-1971.
The wonderful Christ. Westfield, Ind., Union Bible Seminary, n.d. 30 p.

KANSAS YEARLY MEETING OF FRIENDS (1872-)

From 1900 to 1937 the Kansas Yearly Meeting was affiliated with the Five Years Meeting. During these years and long after, the group was polarized around the Friends University of Wichita and the Friends Bible College of Haviland, Kansas, the former institution receiving the support of the majority. Reconciliation between the more liberal supporters of the Wichita institution and the holiness backers of the Haviland school, was made evident in 1957 when the Kansas Yearly Meeting joined in forming the Evangelical Friends Alliance. In 1961 the Kansas group claimed 8302 members.

2351 FRIENDS, SOCIETY of. Kansas Yearly Meeting.
Discipline of the Society of Friends of Kansas Yearly Meeting held at Lawrence in the year 1883, and reprinted by direction of the same in 1891.... Richmond, Ind., Nicholson Mfg. Co., 1892. viii, 128 p.

2352 FRIENDS, SOCIETY of. Kansas Yearly Meeting.
Discipline. Wichita, Kan., Day's Print Shop, 1943.

2353 FRIENDS, SOCIETY of. Kansas Yearly Meeting.
Discipline. Wichita, 1955.

2354 FRIENDS, SOCIETY of. Kansas Yearly Meeting.
Discipline. Wichita, 1966.

2355 FRIENDS, SOCIETY of. Kansas Yearly Meeting.
Minutes, 1872- . Lawrence, Kan., etc., 1872- .

--HISTORY

2356 JACKSON, Sheldon Glenn
A short history of the Kansas Yearly Meeting of Friend Wichita, Day's Print Shop, 1946. 95 p.

--MISSIONS

2357 ENCYCLOPEDIA OF modern Christian missions; the agencies. Burton L. Goddard, ed.... Camden, N.J., T. Nelson, 1967. xix, 743 p.
"Kansas Yearly Meeting of Friends, Board of Missions" p. 352-353.

EVANGELICAL FRIENDS CHURCH, EASTERN DIVISION (1813-)

[1813-194? as Ohio Yearly Meeting of Friends; 194?-1971 as Ohio Yearly Meeting of the Friends Church]

A Gurneyite group, the Ohio Yearly Meeting was probably more deeply influenced by Wesleyan perfectionism than any Friends meeting in the United States. It introduced pastors and programmed meetings, called its congregations churches and adopted a denominational order of government. Led into close fellowship with the National Holiness Movement by David B. Updegraff and Dougan Clark, the Ohio group made a significant contribution to the interdenominational movement through the Cleveland Bible Institute (now called Malone College), founded in 1892 by Walter and Emma Malone. Missionary work was established in China in 1890, in India in 1896, and in Formosa in 1953. As liberalism increased among Quakers in other states, the Ohio Friends welcomed into their

II. 1. Christian Holiness Association

fellowship local meetings from as far away as Ontario, Rhode Island, Virginia, North Carolina, and Iowa. In addition, they led in formation of the Evangelical Friends Alliance in 1956. Long known as the Ohio Yearly Meeting of the Friends Church, the group in 1971 changed its name to Evangelical Friends Church, Eastern Division, the explanatory phrase apparently an indirect invitation to other members of the Alliance to form a single denomination. The group holds membership in the Christian Holiness Association. In 1965 the Ohio Friends claimed 89 congregations and 7015 members in North America and 17 congregations and 987 members abroad.

2358 FRIENDS, SOCIETY of. Ohio Yearly Meeting of the Friends Church.
 Book of Discipline of Ohio Yearly Meeting of the Friends Church, revised August, 1961. Damascus, Ohio, 1961. 116 p.

2359 FRIENDS, SOCIETY of. Ohio Yearly Meeting of the Friends Church.
 Handbook for Friends. Rev. ed. Damascus, Ohio, 1963. 82 p.

2360 FRIENDS, SOCIETY of. Ohio Yearly Meeting of the Friends Church. Canton, Ohio, 1965.
 Minutes of the one hundred and fifty-third Ohio Yearly Meeting of the Friends Church, held at Canton, Ohio, 1965.... Salem, Ohio, Lyle Printing & Publishing Co., 1965. 192 p.

--HISTORY

2361 FRIENDS, SOCIETY of. Ohio Yearly Meeting of the Friends Church.
 Quaker sesqui-centennial, 1812-1962. Damascus, Ohio, 1962. 110 p.

--MISSIONS

2362 ENCYCLOPEDIA OF modern Christian missions; the agencies. Burton L. Goddard, ed.... Camden, N.J., T. Nelson, 1967. xix, 743 p.
 "Ohio Yearly Meeting, Friends Foreign Missionary Society of," by Walter R. Williams: p. 510-511.

2363 WILLIAMS, Walter Rollin, 1884-
 Me and my house, by Walter R. and Myrtle M. Williams; pen drawings by Anna Talbott McPherson. Grand Rapids, Mich., Wm. B. Eerdmans Publishing Co., 1957. 187 p.

--PERIODICALS

2364 EVANGELICAL FRIEND and Oriental News. 1- , Jan. 1929-1967. Butler, Ind., Damascus, Ohio.
1, no. 1 erroneously numbered 9, no. 4
Jan. 1929-July 1962 as Evangelical Friend.

2365 FRIENDS HERALD. 1-9, no. 3, Oct. 1921-Dec. 1928. Urbana, Ohio; Butler, Ind.

2366 FRIENDS ORIENTAL News. 1-51, 1911-1962. Damascus, Ohio.
Merged with Evangelical Friend to form Evangelical Friend and Oriental News.

--POLITICAL AND SOCIAL CRITICISM

2367 FRIENDS, SOCIETY of. Ohio Yearly Meeting.
An address to Christian citizens on the liquor traffic; issued by the meeting for sufferings of Ohio Yearly Meeting of Friends held near Barnesville, Ohio, 1894. 8 p.

2368 FRIENDS, SOCIETY of. Ohio Yearly Meeting.
An appeal for peace, issued by Ohio Yearly Meeting of the Religious Society of Friends held at Stillwater near Barnesville, Ohio, 1909. Stillwater?, 1909. [30] p.
With Mendenhall, A.H. Some social aspects of the Society of Friends in the 17th and 18th centuries. Salem, Ohio, 1914.

2369 FRIENDS, SOCIETY of. Ohio Yearly Meeting.
Capital punishment examined in light of Christianity.... Columbiana, 1896. 8 p.

--SERMONS

2370 BARNES, Horatio Nelson, 1806-1896.
Sanctification; a sermon delivered by N.H. Barnes [sic]. New Vienna, Ohio, Friends' Publishing House Press, 1875. Cover title, 8 p.

2371 LEWIS, David J., 1859-1899.
Word and work of David J. Lewis. Cincinnati, M.W. Knapp, Office of the Revivalist, 1900. 320 p.
Sermons of David J. Lewis: p. 82-320.

--AFRICA

2372 HOTCHKISS, William Ray, 1873-1948.
Sketches from the Dark Continent. Cleveland, Friends

Bible Institute and Training School, 1901. 160 p.

--CHINA

2373 WILLIAMS, Walter Rollin, 1884-
Ohio Friends in the land of Sinim; being a record of the missionary work in China under the direction of the Ohio Yearly Meeting of Friends Church. Mt. Gilead, Ohio, Friends Foreign Missionary Board of Ohio Yearly Meeting, 1925. 229 p.

2374 WILLIAMS, Walter Rollin, 1884-
These fifty years with Ohio Friends in China; an intimate story of missionary work in China, under the direction of Ohio Yearly Meeting of the Friends Church, 1890-1940. Damascus, Ohio, Friends Foreign Missionary Society of Ohio Yearly Meeting, 1940. 315 p.

--INDIA

2375 CATTELL, Catherine (DeVol), 1906-
Till break of day; pen sketches of life in Bundelkhand, Central India. Grand Rapids, Mich., Wm. B. Eerdmans Publishing Co., 1947. 213 p.

2376 COFFIN, Merrill M.
Friends in Bundelkhand, India; a brief 1896-1926, being a story in word and picture of thirty years service for Christ in India, under the auspices of the Foreign Missions Board of Ohio Yearly Meeting of the Friends Church in America. Mysore, Ind., Wesleyan Mission Press, 1926. 53 p.

NORTHWEST YEARLY MEETING OF FRIENDS CHURCHES (1893-)

[1893-193? as Oregon Yearly Meeting of Friends; 193?-1971 as Oregon Yearly Meeting of Friends Church; also, in Bolivia, as Iglesia Nacional Boliviana de Los Amigos]

Officially separated from the Iowa Yearly Meeting in 1893, the Oregon Yearly Meeting originally consisted of Friends meetings in the Willamette River valley, but as meetings were established in other parts of Oregon and in Idaho and Washington, they also were included. In 1902 the Oregon Friends joined the more liberal Five Years Meeting, but withdrew in 1926. Gurneyite and largely sympathetic toward the Holiness Movement, the Oregon group was never as uniformly committed to Wesleyanism as its Ohio counterpart. Ambivalence has in fact marked its reactions toward both the Quaker and the holiness traditions. The Oregon Yearly Meeting holds membership in the Evangelical Friends Alliance and works in cooperation with the Christian Holiness Association. It sponsors the George Fox College in Oregon and the Greenleaf Academy in Idaho and conducts foreign missionary work in Bolivia. In 1967 the group reported 6202 members in 50 congregations.

2377 FRIENDS, SOCIETY of. Oregon Yearly Meeting of Friends Church.
   Constitution and discipline of the Oregon Yearly Meeting of the Friends Church, adopted June 1945. Portland?, 1945.

2378 FRIENDS, SOCIETY of. Oregon Yearly Meeting of Friends Church.
   Constitution and discipline of Oregon Yearly Meeting of Friends Church, August 1970. Newberg, Ore., Barclay Press, 1970. 93 p.

--CATECHISMS AND CREEDS

2379 FRIENDS, SOCIETY of. Oregon Yearly Meeting of Friends Church. Board of Christian Education.
   Primary queries. n.p., n.d. Unpaged.

2380 [FRIENDS, SOCIETY of. Oregon Yearly Meeting of Friends Church].
   Quaker quiz; questions and answers concerning the Christian faith. Newberg, Ore., Barclay Press, n.d. 26 p.

2381 WILLCUTS, Jack L.
   A family of Friends; Friends Church membership course. Newberg, Ore., Barclay Press, 1960. 89 p.

--CHURCH EXTENSION

2382 ROSS, Milo C.
   Outreach, a handbook of church methods; being a manual of suggestions and ideas in church extension and home missions technique, prepared especially for use by the Friends Church. n.p., Board of Publication, Oregon Yearly Meeting of Friends Church, 1952. 142 p.

--DOCTRINAL AND CONTROVERSIAL WORKS

2383 BEALS, Charles Arthur, 1906-
   The essential baptism. Newberg, Ore., Board of Publication of Oregon Yearly Meeting of Friencs Church, n.d. 15 p.

II. 1. Christian Holiness Association

2384 MACY, Herman H.
What about the ordinances? Do outward man-administered rites have an important place in this the dispensation of the Holy Spirit? A consideration of what the New Testament reveals on the subject of baptism with water and the ordinance of communion. Newberg, Ore., Barclay Press, 1965. 40 p.
"Third edition."

2385 MILLS, Paul M.
The Bible and war. Newberg, Ore., Barclay Press, 1968. 24 p.
This new edition of The Bible and War is published in cooperation with the Board of Peace and Service of Oregon Yearly Meeting of Friends Church.

2386 SIMS, Edgar P.
Why baptizest thou? Newberg, Ore., Oregon Yearly Meeting of Friends Church, n.d.

--HISTORY

2387 FRIENDS, SOCIETY of. Oregon Yearly Meeting of Friends Church.
This is the story of Friends in the Northwest; Oregon Yearly Meeting of Friends Church, Newberg, Oregon. Newberg, Ore., Barclay Press, 196?. 29 p.

2388 BEEBE, Ralph K., 1932-
A garden of the Lord; a history of Oregon Yearly Meeting of Friends Church. Newberg, Ore., Barclay Press, 1968. vii, 288 p.
Chapter illustrations by Stan Putman.

2389 HAINES, Marie
Remembering 75 years of history; written in cooperation with the 75th Anniversary Committee, Oregon Yearly Meeting of Friends Church, August, 1967. Newberg, Ore., Barclay Press, 1967. 48 p.

--MISSIONS

2390 CAMMACK, Phyllis
Missionary moments; sixty diverse "moments" in the life of a South American missionary, with an introd. by Jack L. Willcuts [and] illustrations by the author, her sister, Mignon Pike, and nephew, Ted Pike. Newberg, Ore., Barclay Press, 1966. 134 p.

2391   ENCYCLOPEDIA OF modern Christian missions; the agencies. Burton L. Goddard, ed.... Camden, N.J., T. Nelson, 1967. xix, 743 p.
"Oregon Yearly Meeting of Friends Church, Board of Missions," by Jack L. Willcuts: p. 515.

--PERIODICALS

2392   FRUIT OF the Vine; Friends daily devotional readings. 1- , 1961- . Newberg, Ore.

2393   NORTHWEST FRIEND. 1- , 1918-1921, 1924-1967. Portland, Ore.; Newberg, Ore.
1918-1921, 1924-1942 as Friendly Endeavor.

ROCKY MOUNTAIN YEARLY MEETING OF THE FRIENDS CHURCH (1957-)

Set apart as a separate yearly meeting by the Nebraska Yearly Meeting in 1957, the Rocky Mountain Yearly Meeting consists of scattered Friends congregations in South Dakota, Nebraska, Kansas, Colorado and New Mexico. It holds membership in the Evangelical Friends Alliance and the Christian Holiness Association. In 1971 it reported 1588 members in 25 churches. The Rocky Mountain Yearly Meeting sponsors missionary work among the Navajo Indians in Arizona.

2394   FRIENDS, SOCIETY of. Rocky Mountain Yearly Meeting of the Friends Church.
Discipline of Rocky Mountain Yearly Meeting of the Friends Church. Pueblo, Colo., Riverside Printing Co., 1959. 94 p.
Printed by direction of Rocky Mountain Yearly Meeting.

2395   FRIENDS, SOCIETY of. Rocky Mountain Yearly Meeting of the Friends Church.
Supplement to the Discipline. n.p., 1964. 18 p.

2396   FRIENDS, SOCIETY of. Rocky Mountain Yearly Meeting of the Friends Church. Annual Assembly.
Minutes. 1st- , 1957- .
Annual.

GOD'S MISSIONARY CHURCH (1935-)

Formed in 1935 as the result of a dispute in the Pennsylvania-New Jersey District of the Pilgrim Holiness Church, the

II. 1. Christian Holiness Association

God's Missionary Church is even more conservative than its parent. (A recent annual conference opposed ownership of television sets, sex education, and standard gym suits and shower-taking in public schools.) Originating in east-central Pennsylvania (532 of the 595 members in 1971 still were affiliated with Pennsylvania churches) the group's traditional stricture against participation in war no doubt reflects the German Pietist background of many members. Headed by a general superintendent, the church issues <u>God's Missionary Standard</u>, a monthly periodical, and sponsors missionary work in Haiti and among Cuban refugees in Florida. Also of great importance to the group are the Penn View Bible Institute, Penns Creek, Pennsylvania, and three annual camp meetings. God's Missionary Church works in cooperation with the Interdenominational Holiness Convention.

2397 GOD'S MISSIONARY Church. Annual Conference.
 Conference minutes and journal. 1st- , 1936- . n.p., 19??.
 Annual.

2398 GOD'S MISSIONARY Church.
 Official handbook and discipline of God's Missionary Church, a non-profit, religious corporation, chartered under the laws of the State of Pennsylvania, A.D. 1935; revised by General Conference of 1970. Watsontown, Pa., Ellis Printing Co., 1971. 75 p.
 Cover title: Discipline of God's Missionary Church, 1971.

--PASTORAL THEOLOGY

-- --AUTHORITATIVE SOURCES

2399 BEDSOLE, Adolph
 The pastor in profile. Grand Rapids, Mich., Baker Book House, 1970. 163 p.
 Reprint of 1958 ed.

2400 HARMON, Nolan Bailey, bp., 1892-
 Ministerial ethics and etiquette. Rev. ed. New York, Abingdon Press, 1950. 215 p.

--PERIODICALS

2401 GOD'S MISSIONARY Standard. 1- , 1949- . Roaring Spring, Pa.

GOSPEL WORKERS CHURCH (1898-1958)

[1898-1918 as Holiness Workers Association]

At first known as the Holiness Workers, this group resulted from evangelistic efforts begun in March 1898 in the Georgian Bay area of Ontario by Frank D. Goff, a minister of the Holiness Movement Church. Most of Goff's converts joined existing denominations. In 1904 Goff and his supporters began publishing the Holiness Worker and in 1918 formally organized, published a discipline and obtained incorporation as the Gospel Workers Church. Democratic and Methodist in government and theology, the Gospel Workers established a camp meeting at Clarksburg, Ontario, and a small missionary work in Japan. In addition they supported foreign work of the Holiness Movement Church and the Oriental Missionary Society. Faced by a dearth of clergy and aging leadership, the churches looked to other groups, particularly the Free Methodists and the Nazarenes, for ministerial leadership. Many individuals joined other holiness bodies, and in September 1958 the remaining five churches and about 162 members under the Rev. Albert Mills, united with the Canada Central District of the Church of the Nazarene.

2402 GOSPEL WORKERS Church.
Discipline. n.p., 1918.

--DOCTRINAL AND CONTROVERSIAL WORKS

2403 GOFF, Frank D.
The promised enduement; or, The baptism with the Holy Ghost. Clarksburg, Ont., The author, 1921. 192 p.

--HISTORY

2404 ENCYCLOPEDIA CANADIANA. Ottawa, Canadiana Co., 1957-1958. 10 v.
"Gospel Workers Church" by A. Mills: v. 4, p. 394.

2405 PARKER, John Fred
From East to western sea; a brief history of the Church of the Nazarene in Canada. Kansas City, Mo., Nazarene Publishing House, 1971. 107 p.
Account of Gospel Workers Church: p. 66-67, 70-71.

--PERIODICALS

2406 GOSPEL WORKER. 1- , 1904-195?. Clarksburg, Ont., Can.

II. 1. Christian Holiness Association

1904-191? as Holiness Worker.

HOLINESS CHRISTIAN CHURCH (1882-   )

[1882-1894 as Heavenly Recruit Association; 1894-1897 as Holiness Christian Association; 1945-present as Holiness Christian Church of the United States of America]

     Originating in 1882 when three men and two women started holding street meetings in Philadelphia, the group, known at first as the Heavenly Recruits, had no intention of starting a church. In addition to street services, the workers conducted tent revivals and camp meetings in summer and held evangelistic meetings in rented halls during the winter months. To care for converts, the Heavenly Recruit Association felt compelled to provide pastoral care and, at a specially-called conference during a camp meeting at Linwood, Pennsylvania, in 1889, passed resolutions calling for a presiding elder and stationed pastors. Crises, such as the withdrawal of the Philadelphia church from the Association five years later, aroused sentiment in favor of stronger central administration and brought about the election of C.W. Ruth, a gifted young evangelist, as presiding élder. That year the name was changed to the Holiness Christian Association and, in 1897, to the Holiness Christian Church. Work in Indiana was organized into a separate conference, and home mission work begun further west. The editorial office of the Crown of Glory, a paper launched in 1892, soon moved to Indiana, as did the presiding elder. Contact with the western holiness precursors of the Church of the Nazarene fractured the group. Ruth himself joined the Pentecostal Church of the Nazarene and then, in 1908, led most of the Pennsylvania group (fifteen congregations) into the new denomination. In 1919 about fifty Holiness Christian churches in Indiana, Illinois, Missouri, Kansas and Oklahoma united with the International Apostolic Holiness Church to form the International Holiness Church. A remnant of the original group in eastern Pennsylvania slowly began to rebuild. In 1937 a new paper, the Holiness Christian Messenger, began publication and in 1945 the group undertook sponsorship of mission work in Jamaica. At the seventy-fifth annual conference in 1968, the Holiness Christian Church reported 47 congregations and more than 1500 members in the United States and Jamaica.

2407   HOLINESS CHRISTIAN Church.
       The doctrines of the Holiness Christian Church, by the General Conference, 1916, Elwood, Indiana, editor, John W. Clark. Elwood?, Ind., 1916. 132 p.

2408 HOLINESS CHRISTIAN Church.
The doctrines and discipline of the Holiness Christian Church of the United States of America (Incorporated). Latest revision, 1948. n.p., 1948. 69 p.

--HISTORY

2409 FIFTIETH ANNIVERSARY number, Holiness Christian Messenger, VI (Aug. 1943).

2410 HOLINESS CHRISTIAN Church of the United States of America.
Celebrating the 75th anniversary of the Holiness Christian Conference, 1894-1969; Christ our way-truth-life. Gibraltar, Pa., 1969. 47 p.

--HYMNS

2411 HEAVENLY RECRUIT praise hymns. Philadelphia, Hood, c1884. 80 p.

2412 HAAS, L. Frank, 1856-
Praise hymns used by the Heavenly Recruit Assoc. Philadelphia, J.J. Hood, c1891.

--PERIODICALS

2413 CHRISTIAN MESSENGER. 1- , 1937- . Gibraltar, Pa. 1937-195? as Holiness Christian Messenger.

2414 CROWN OF Glory. 1-15, 1892-1906. Chester, Pa.; Tipton, Ind.

2415 VOICE FROM Canaan. 1-6, 1906-1912? Carlinville, Ill.

HOLINESS CHURCH (1880-189?)

An early result of holiness evangelism in Great Britain, the Holiness Church, organized about 1880, was probably the earliest independent holiness body in that country. With thirteen congregations it began publishing the Holiness Advocate under the editorial direction of Mrs. S. Chambers in 1884. Cessation of this London publication during the next decade seems to indicate the demise of the group.

II. 1. Christian Holiness Association

--PERIODICALS

2416 HOLINESS ADVOCATE. 1-7, Jan. 1884-Dec. 1890. London.
Superseded by Pure in Heart.

2417 PURE IN Heart. 1-3, no. 10, Jan. 1891-Oct. 1893. London.
Supersedes Holiness Advocate.

HOLINESS CHURCH (1880-1946)

[1880-Aug. 1896 as Holiness Bands; and Southern California and Arizona Holiness Association]

The product of the Southern California and Arizona Holiness Association formed in 1880, this group has the distinction of being one of the first in the Holiness Movement to organize independent churches. Led by an evangelist named J.W. Swing, the Holiness Bands were composed largely of newcomers from the Middle West who kept close contact with home. Akin to the Church of God movement in Kansas and Missouri from which leaders such as B.A. and James F. Washburn had come, the group required candidates for membership to profess sanctification. From the beginning workers returned eastward in evangelistic effort. As early as 1886 Dennie Rogers and George Teel reached Collin County, Texas, winning converts who later would form part of the nucleus of the Church of the Nazarene in that area. Starting in 1885 the Bands issued The Pentecost from offices in Los Angeles. An annual camp meeting was held near Downey, California. In 1896 the churches adopted the Book of Doctrine, Rules and Regulations and incorporated as The Holiness Church. After 1906 the group lost many members to the Pentecostal Movement and progress was slow. In 1931, camp meeting grounds were secured near El Monte, California. The paper (renamed The Standard Bearer of Bible Holiness) located its editorial offices on the grounds and a Bible school known as the Holiness Evangelistic Institute was soon started there. In 1946, when the Holiness Church merged with the Pilgrim Holiness Church, it claimed about 400 members in 19 congregations. At that time Kentucky and Oregon had one congregation each; the rest were in California.

2418 HOLINESS CHURCH.
Book of doctrine, rules, and regulations. Los Angeles, 1896.

--DOCTRINAL AND CONTROVERSIAL WORKS

2419 TEEL, George M.
    The New Testament church. Los Angeles, Pentecost Printing House, c1901. 157 p.

2420 WASHBURN, B. A.
    Holiness links. Los Angeles, Pentecost Office, 1887. 216 p.

--HISTORY

2421 CLARK, Elmer Talmage, 1886-1966.
    The small sects in America. Rev. ed. New York, Abingdon Press, c1965. 256 p.
    Reprint of 1949 ed.
    Account of the Holiness Church: p. 114-115.

2422 CLARK, L. A., ed.
    Truths of interest; origin and distinctive teachings of the "Holiness Church." El Monte, Calif., Standard Bearer Publishing House, 1939.

2423 JERNIGAN, Charles Brougher, 1863-1930.
    Pioneer days of the Holiness Movement in the Southwest. Kansas City, Mo., Pentecostal Nazarene Publishing House, 1919. 157 p.
    "Holiness Church work in Texas": p. 91-93.

2424 ROGERS, Dennis, 1858-
    Holiness pioneering in the Southland. Hemet, Calif., 1944. 36 p.

2425 THOMAS, Paul Westphal, 1894-1972.
    "The days of our pilgrimage; a history of the Pilgrim Holiness Church," by Paul Westphal Thomas and Paul William Lee Thomas. Unpublished paper, 1968. 1 v. (various pagings)
    In archives of The Wesleyan Church, Marion, Indiana.
    Account of the Holiness Church of California: ℓ. 286-291.

2426 WASHBURN, Josephine F.
    History and reminiscences of Holiness Church work in southern California and Arizona. South Pasadena, Calif., Record Press, 1912? 463 p.

--PERIODICALS

2427 STANDARD BEARER of Bible Holiness. 1-2363, 1885-June

II. 1. Christian Holiness Association

19, 1946. Los Angeles; El Monte, Calif.
1885-1928 as Pentecost.

--STATISTICS

2428   U.S. BUREAU of the Census.
Census of religious bodies, 1926; Holiness Church: statistics, denominational history, doctrine, and organization. Washington, U.S. Government Printing Office, 1928. 9 p.

--PERU

2429   RUNDELL, Merton Russell, 1923-
"The mission of the Pilgrim Holiness Church in Peru." Unpublished M.A. thesis, Butler University, 1957.

HOLINESS CHURCH, DONALSONVILLE, GEORGIA (1902-1907)

An outgrowth of the work of the Georgia Holiness Association, this independent church was organized in 1902 largely through the influence of T.J. Shingler, a local merchant. Although a printed discipline was issued and a denomination envisioned, the movement seems never to have incorporated more than one congregation. The Donalsonville church joined the Holiness Church of Christ in 1907.

2430   HOLINESS CHURCH, Donalsonville, Georgia.
Discipline of the Holiness Church, headquarters, Donalsonville, Georgia. Louisville, Ky., Pentecostal Publishing Co., 190?.

--HISTORY

2431   JERNIGAN, Charles Brougher, 1863-1930.
Pioneer days of the Holiness Movement in the Southwest. Kansas City, Mo., Pentecostal Nazarene Publishing House, 1919. 157 p.
Account of Holiness Church, Donalsonville, Georgia: p. 27.

HOLINESS CHURCH OF CHRIST (1905-1908)

This group, formed by merger of the Independent Holiness

Church and the New Testament Church of Christ at Rising Star, Texas, in 1905, accelerated tendencies toward centralized administration begun in the parent groups before merger. Reaching from Tennessee and Mississippi to Texas and Oklahoma, the group established headquarters at Pilot Point, Texas, from which the Holiness Evangel, the official publication, was issued. A strong emphasis on missionary activity led to the establishment of a Bible training school and a home for unwed mothers in Pilot Point, and to the opening of rescue missions in downtown areas of larger towns. The church sent missionaries into Mexico, Japan, China, India and Africa. Holiness Church of Christ representatives, present at the union of the Association of Pentecostal Churches of America and the Church of the Nazarene at Chicago in 1907, persuaded their group to join also. As a result on October 13, 1908, during the second General Assembly of the Pentecostal Church of the Nazarene, held at Pilot Point, the two groups merged. At the time of the union the Holiness Church of Christ claimed 2307 members in 92 churches.

2432 HOLINESS CHURCH of Christ.
Manual, 1904-05; prepared by the Joint Committee on Union of the Independent Holiness Church and the New Testament Church of Christ, C.B. Jernigan, secretary. n.p., 1904.

2433 HOLINESS CHURCH of Christ.
Manual, 1905; adopted by the General Council at Pilot Point, Texas, November 7-12, 1905. Greenville, Tex., Holiness Advocate Publishing Co., 1905.

2434 HOLINESS CHURCH of Christ.
Manual. Pilot Point, Tex., Holiness Evangel, 1907.

2435 HOLINESS CHURCH of Christ. General Council.
Minutes of the General Council of the Holiness Church of Christ, Pilot Point, Texas, Nov. 7-12, 1905, Mrs. E.J Sheeks, secretary. Greenville, Tex., Holiness Advocate Publishing Co., 1905.

--DOCTRINAL AND CONTROVERSIAL WORKS

2436 CHAPMAN, James Blaine, 1884-1947.
Timely themes.... A book on holiness and kindred topics. Pilot Point, Tex., Evangel Publishing Co., 1907. 150 p.

--HISTORY

2437 JERNIGAN, Charles Brougher, 1863-1930.
Pioneer days of the Holiness Movement in the Southwest

Kansas City, Mo., Pentecostal Nazarene Publishing House, 1919. 157 p.
"Holiness Church of Christ": p. 122-124.

2438 SMITH, Timothy Lawrence, 1924-
Called unto holiness; the story of the Nazarenes: the formative years. Kansas City, Mo., Nazarene Publishing House, 1962. 413 p.
Account of Holiness Church of Christ: p. 171-179, 214-217.

--PERIODICALS

2439 HOLINESS EVANGEL. 1- , 1906-1909. Pilot Point, Tex.
1906 as Highways and Hedges.
Merged with Pentecostal Advocate.

2440 MISSIONARY EVANGEL. 1, 1906. Peniel, Tex.
Merged with Highways and Hedges to become Holiness Evangel.

--POLITICAL AND SOCIAL CRITICISM

2441 REST COTTAGE Association.
The white slaves of America. Pilot Point, Tex., 1907.

--YEARBOOKS

2442 HOLINESS CHURCH of Christ.
Yearbook, 1905; Mrs. E.J. Sheeks, recording secretary, ed. Greenville, Tex., Holiness Advocate Publishing Co., 1905.

HOLINESS MOVEMENT CHURCH (1895-1959)

[Also as Holiness Movement Church in Canada]

Founded at Ottawa, Ontario by Ralph G. Horner and his followers in 1895, the Holiness Movement Church merged with the Free Methodist Church in 1959. Horner, a charismatic leader who had worked as an effective but insubordinate evangelist in the Quebec Conference of the Methodist Church and with the Rochester Conference of the Wesleyan Methodist Connection, became bishop and ruled with an iron hand. Within five years the number of adherents reached 5653 and there were 118 places of worship and over 90 recognized clergy. Eventually the church spread to all provinces of Canada except the Maritimes, and to New York state and Belfast, Northern Ireland. A strong mission was early established among Coptic people in Egypt, and in 1904 missionaries were sent to China. Later work was also begun in the Sudan and in Brazil. From headquarters in Ottawa the group issued the Holiness Era, the Missionary Challenge, and the Young People's Guide. Bible training schools were maintained in Ottawa and Winnipeg. The Holiness Movement Church held membership in the Canadian Holiness Federation.

The Holiness Movement Church was clearly Methodist both in doctrine and organization. Pastors were appointed by the stationing committee of the Annual Conference, and leaders enjoyed long tenure. When, however, the aging Bishop Horner was asked to retire in 1919, he left the church and formed the Standard Church of America. Although the group survived another forty years and missionary work flourished (by 1959 there were over 5000 members in Egypt), only a few hundred Canadian members remained to unite with the Free Methodists.

2443 ...AN ACT to incorporate The Free Methodist Church in Canada. Ottawa, Queen's Printer and Controller of Stationery, 1959. Cover-title, 17 p.

2444 HOLINESS MOVEMENT Church.
The manual of the Holiness Movement Church: constitution, government, ritual (revised); published by authority of the General Conference held at Killarney, Manitoba, September 12-22, 1949. Ottawa, Ont., Can., Holiness Movement Book and Publishing House, 1949. 238 p.

--DOCTRINAL AND CONTROVERSIAL WORKS

2445 KETCHESON, W. G.
The pilgrim's pilot; a comprehensive treatise on religious subjects.... Deloraine, Man., Can., 1910. 539 p.

-- --AUTHORITATIVE SOURCES

2446 HENRY, George W., 1801-
Demonstrations of the Spirit called, Shouting, genuine and spurious; re-christened and re-printed by W. G. Burns. Ottawa, Ont., Can., Holiness Movement Publishing House, 1908. 317 p.

--HISTORY

2447 CLARK, Samuel Delbert, 1910-
Church and sect in Canada. Toronto, University of

II. 1. Christian Holiness Association

Toronto Press, 1948. xiii, 458 p.
Account of Holiness Movement Church: p. 368-378.

2448 HORNER, Ralph Cecil, 1854-1921.
Ralph C. Horner, evangelist; reminiscences from his own pen. Brockville, Ont., Can., Pub. for Mrs. A. E. Horner by Standard Publishing House, n.d. xxi, 215 p.

2449 MANN, William Edward
Sect, cult, and church in Alberta. Toronto, University of Toronto Press, 1955. xiii, 166 p.
Includes description of the Holiness Movement Church.

2450 POINTEN, Harold William
"The Holiness Movement Church in Canada." Unpublished B.D. thesis, Victoria University, 1950. 179ℓ.

2451 SIGSWORTH, John Wilkins
The battle was the Lord's; a history of the Free Methodist Church in Canada. Oshawa, Ont., Sage Publishers, 1960. 301 p.
Account of Holiness Movement Church: p. 238-241.

--MISSIONS

2452 HOLINESS MOVEMENT Church. Young People's Missionary Society.
A brief history of Holiness Movement missions [comp. by Nettie M. Hill and Norma A. Eves]. n.p., 1948. Cover-title, 40 p.

2453 ENCYCLOPEDIA OF modern Christian missions; the agencies. Burton L. Goddard, ed.... Camden, N.J., T. Nelson, 1967. xix, 743 p.
"Holiness Movement Church in Canada," by Nettie M. Hill: p. 318.

2454 EYRE, Marion
Supplement to Brief history of missions of the former Holiness Movement Church, which in 1959 merged with the Free Methodist Church, covering years 1949-1959. n.p., 1963. Cover-title, 12 p.

--PERIODICALS

2455 BUGLE OF Holiness. 1- , 1903- . Assiout, Egypt.

2456 CHILD'S TREASURE. 1- , 19??- . Ottawa, Ont., Can.

2457 HOLINESS ERA. 1- , 1892-195?. Ottawa, Ont., Can.

2458 MISSIONARY CHALLENGE. 1- , 1948-195?. Ottawa, Ont. Can.

2459 YOUNG PEOPLE'S Guide. 1- , 1898-195?. Ottawa, Ont., Can.

--POLEMICAL WORKS

-- --CATHOLICISM

2460 MORGAN, H. P.
By what authority? Ottawa, Ont., Can., Holiness Movement Publishing House, 1910. 59 p.

IMMANUERU SOGO DENDO DAN (Immanuel General Mission of Japan) (1945-   )

An indigenous Japanese denomination, this group was founded in 1945 by David Taugio Tsutada, who planned the organization while interned in a Japanese prison during World War II for preaching the second coming of Christ. Wesleyan in doctrine and episcopal in government, the Immanuel Church has grown from an original six members to more than 7000. Consisting of 100 congregations in 1967, the denomination maintains a Bible college, the John Wesley Press, a hospital and several kindergartens. It supports missionary activity in India, Jamaica, Taiwan and Laos. In 1952 it federated with the Japan mission of the Wesleyan Methodist Church of America to form the Immanueru Uesureyan Remmei (Immanuel Wesleyan Federation), so that it might utilize the services of missionaries without American control. Two years later, the World Gospel Mission in Japan also joined the Federation.

2461 JOHNSON, Harold
"Immanuel General Conference elects president, " Wesleyan Advocate, CXXIX (Dec. 13, 1971), 13.

--HISTORY

2462 ENCYCLOPEDIA OF modern Christian missions; the agencies. Burton L. Goddard, ed.... Camden, N.J., T. Nelson, 1967. xix, 743 p.
"Immanueru Sogo Dendo Dan (Immanuel General Mission of Japan), " by John M. Tsutada; and "Immanueru Uesureyan Remmei (Immanuel Wesleyan Federation), " by W. Conrad Cessna.

II. 1. Christian Holiness Association

2463 McLEISTER, Ira Ford, 1879-1963.
History of the Wesleyan Methodist Church of America.
Rev. [i.e. 3d] ed. by Roy Stephen Nicholson. Marion, Ind.,
Wesley Press, 1959. 558 p.
Account of the Immanuel Wesleyan Federation: p. 485-486, 505-506.

2464 TSUTADA, David Tsugio, -1971.
20 years retrospect of Immanuel General Mission in
Japan. Tokyo, Immanuel General Mission in Japan, 1965.
270 p.
Text mostly in Japanese with English captions.

INDEPENDENT HOLINESS CHURCH (1901-1905)

The Independent Holiness Church was organized at Van Alstyne, Texas, in 1901. Led by a talented young evangelist named C.B. Jernigan, the group extended its influence steadily by aggressive evangelism. After two years it numbered over twenty congregations. In 1905 it united with the New Testament Church of Christ to form the Holiness Church of Christ, which, in 1908, merged with the Pentecostal Church of the Nazarene to form what became the Church of the Nazarene.

2465 HOLINESS CHURCH of Christ.
Manual, 1904-05; prepared by the Joint Committee on
Union of the Independent Holiness Church and the New Testament Church of Christ, C.B. Jernigan, secretary. n.p.,
1904.

--HISTORY

2466 JERNIGAN, Charles Brougher, 1863-1930.
Pioneer days of the Holiness Movement in the Southwest.
Kansas City, Mo., Pentecostal Nazarene Publishing House,
1919. 157 p.
"Independent Holiness Church": p. 109-115.

2467 SMITH, Timothy Lawrence, 1924-
Called unto holiness; the story of the Nazarenes: the
formative years. Kansas City, Mo., Nazarene Publishing
House, 1962. 413 p.
Account of the Independent Holiness Church: p. 167-171.

INDEPENDENT HOLINESS CHURCH OF CHRIST (1888-1914)

[Also as Churches of Christ, and Holiness Church of Christ]

A loose federation of congregations, sometimes called Churches of Christ or Holiness Church of Christ, resulted from the evangelistic efforts of George Weavers (1840-1914), an English-born Baptist preacher who came into contact with holiness in the 1880's. Starting with the organization of Mount Zion Church in the country near Tabor, Iowa, the movement spread as its founder moved into southwestern Iowa, Nebraska, Missouri and Kansas. In 1892 a building in Glenwood, Iowa, formerly used as an opera house, was purchased as a church and headquarters building, and publication of Sent of God was begun. Weavers (in later years he dropped the final "s" from the name) was a founder of the Hephzibah Faith and a supporter of the World Missionary Association, and at times the activities of the three organizations were indistinguishable. The paper, begun as a project of the Churches of Christ, was taken over by the Hephzibah Association within a few years. Affiliated churches jointly sponsored camp meetings, and in 1909 the group purchased a permanent camp ground at Bellevue, Nebraska. At the 1914 camp, however, the group voted to move the meeting back to Tabor. With the death of George Weaver that year, the Independent Holiness Church of Christ movement began to disintegrate, most adherents being absorbed by the Hephzibah Faith Missionary Association.

--HISTORY

2468 WORCESTER, Paul W.
The master key; the story of the Hephzibah Faith Missionary Association. Kansas City, Mo., Printed for the author by the Nazarene Publishing House, 1966. 63 p.
Includes discussion on Independent Holiness Church of Christ.

--PERIODICALS

2469 SENT OF God. 1-22, 1892-1913. Glenwood, Iowa; Tabor, Iowa.
Superseded by Good Tidings Sent of God.

INTERNATIONAL HOLINESS MISSION (1907-1952)

[1907-1917 as Holiness Mission]

II. 1. Christian Holiness Association

This London-based group was organized in 1907 by David Thomas, a prosperous draper desirous of doing work outside denominational churches. Thomas, who had separated from the Pentecostal League to organize independent mission churches, established work at several locations around London. Soon others in England, Scotland and Wales followed his example. In 1908 the Holiness Mission Journal began publication in London and David B. Jones, the first foreign missionary, arrived in South Africa. Success in the African project caused the group to change its name from Holiness Mission to International Holiness Mission in 1917. Although aggressive evangelism continued to characterize the group after Thomas' death in 1930, sending missionaries and supporting the African work increasingly challenged the International Holiness Mission in Britain. The departure of four strong young ministers who founded the Calvary Holiness Church in 1934 further damaged the home base. Emphasis on foreign work required a substantial financial source which, in the early years, had been provided by a few prosperous businessmen within the membership. Their decease necessitated union with a larger body, and on October 29, 1952, at Leeds, England, the International Holiness Mission united with the Church of the Nazarene. At that time 28 congregations with about 1000 members in Britain were supporting 36 missionaries in South Africa: a foreign worker for each 28 members at home.

--HISTORY

2470 DAVID THOMAS, founder of the International Holiness Mission. London, International Holiness Mission, 1933.

2471 FORD, Jack, 1908-
"The Church of the Nazarene in Britain, the International Holiness Mission and the Calvary Holiness Church, with reference to holiness movements in Christian history." Unpublished Ph.D. dissertation, University of London, 1967.

2472 FORD, Jack, 1908-
In the steps of John Wesley; the Church of the Nazarene in Britain. Kansas City, Mo., Printed by Nazarene Publishing House, 1968. 300 p.
Thesis (Ph.D.)--University of London, 1967.

--PERIODICALS

2473 AFRICA'S SILENT Messenger. 1- , 19??- . London, International Holiness Mission.

2474 HOLINESS MISSION Journal. 1-47, 1908-1952. London.
Vols. 44-45 omitted in numbering.
Merged with The Way of Holiness to form The Way; a Holiness Journal.

2475 SOUTH AFRICA annual. 1- , 1920- . London.

--AFRICA, SOUTH

2476 BEDWELL, H. Kenneth
    Black gold; the story of the International Holiness Mission in South Africa, 1908-1936. Cape Town, S. Afr., Cape Times Ltd., 193??. vi, 103 p.

2477 BEDWELL, H. Kenneth
    Black gold, the story of the International Holiness Mission in South Africa, which united with the Church of the Nazarene, November 29, 1952, at Acornhoek, Transvaal, Union of South Africa. Rev. ed. Kansas City, Mo., Beacon Hill Press, 1953. 128 p.

2478 BEDWELL, H. Kenneth
    Tinsimu ta ku nkhensa, by H.K. Bedwell, D.J. Brown, and H.J. White. Cleveland, Trans., S. Afr., Central Mission Press, 1938. 64 p.

2479 BEDWELL, H. Kenneth
    Philip Lishali, a African firebrand. North Rand, Trans., S. Afr., International Holiness Mission, 1937. 20 p.

KODESH CHURCH OF IMMANUEL (1929-)

Founded at Philadelphia in 1929 by the Reverend Frank Russell Killingsworth and other dissidents from the African Methodist Episcopal Zion Church, the Kodesh Church of Immanuel teaches entire sanctification as a second work of grace but frowns on tongues speaking, foot washing and other practices as fanatical. The group endorses faith healing but not to the exclusion of doctors and medicine. With nine churches and 500 members in Pennsylvania, Virginia and the District of Columbia, the church recently opened a small missionary work in Liberia. Both foreign and domestic programs are supported solely by tithes and free-will offerings. Forbidding use of tobacco and alcoholic beverages, the Kodesh Church also condemns prideful dress, membership in secret societies, provocative dancing and attendance at inferior and obscene theatricals.

2480 CLARK, Elmer Talmage, 1886-1966.
    The small sects in America. Rev. ed. New York, Abingdon Press, c1965. 256 p.
    Account of Kodesh Church of Immanuel: p. 83.

II. 1. Christian Holiness Association

2481 MEAD, Frank Spencer, 1898-
　　　Handbook of denominations in the United States. New 5th ed. Nashville, Abingdon Press, c1970. 265 p.
　　　"Kodesh Church of Immanuel": p. 125.

2482 TWENTIETH CENTURY encyclopedia of religious knowledge; an extension of the New Schaff-Herzog Encyclopedia of Religious Knowledge. Editor-in-chief: Lefferts A. Loetscher. Grand Rapids, Mich., Baker Book House, 1955. 2 v. (xx, 1205 p.)
　　　"Kodesh Church of Immanuel," by Theodore G. Tappert: p. 630.

Methodists

(general)

2483 ANDERSON, William Ketcham, 1888-1947, ed.
　　　Methodism. Cincinnati, Methodist Publishing House, 1947. 317 p.

2484 BARNHART, Kenneth Edwin, 1893-
　　　"The evolution of the social consciousness in Methodism." Unpublished Ph.D. dissertation, University of Chicago, 1924. 145ℓ.

2485 BREWER, E. D. C.
　　　"Sect and church in Methodism," Social Forces, XXX (May 1952), 400-408.

2486 DAVENPORT, Frederick Morgan, 1866-
　　　Primitive traits in religious revivals; a study in mental and social evolution. New York, Macmillan, 1905. 323 p.

2487 DAVIES, Rupert Eric, 1909-
　　　Methodism. Harmondsworth, Middlesex, Eng., Penguin Books, 1963. 224 p.

2488 DIMOND, Sydney George, 1882-
　　　The psychology of the Methodist revival; an empirical & descriptive study. London, Oxford University Press, 1926. 296 p.

2489 HANDY, Robert Theodore, 1918-
　　　"The American religious depression, 1925-1935," Church History, XXIX (Mar. 1960), 3-16.

2490 KNOX, Ronald Arbuthnott, 1888-1957.
　　　Enthusiasm; a chapter in the history of religion, with

special reference to the XVII and XVIII centuries. New York, Oxford University Press, 1961. 622 p.

2491 LYLES, Albert M.
Methodism mocked; the satiric reaction to Methodism in the eighteenth century. London, Epworth Press, 1960. 191 p.

2492 NELSON, J. Robert
The Methodists. Glen Rock, N.J., Paulist Press (Paulist Fathers), 1966. 30 p.

2493 TO THE uttermost; commemorating the diamond jubilee of the Southport Methodist Holiness Convention, 1885-1945. London, Epworth Press, 1945. 79 p.

2494 WARNER, Wellman Joel, 1897-
The Wesleyan movement in the industrial revolution. London, Longmans, Green, 1930. 299 p.

2495 WHITNEY, Arthur P., 1912-
The basis of opposition to Methodism in England in the eighteenth century. New York, New York University, 1951. 77 p.
Thesis (Ph.D.)--New York University.

--ANECDOTES, REMINISCENCES, SATIRE, ETC.

2496 ASBURY, Herbert, 1891-
Up from Methodism. New York, Alfred A. Knopf, 1926. 174 p.

2497 SMITH, Charles Merrill
How to become a bishop without being religious. Garden City, N.Y., Doubleday, 1965. xii, 131 p.

2498 SMITH, Charles Merrill
When the saints go marching out; illustrated by Robert Osborn. Garden City, N.Y., Doubleday, 1969. xi, 225 p.

--APOLOGETIC WORKS

2499 CROOKS, George Richard, 1822-1897.
Why I am a Methodist? New York, Phillips & Hunt, 1887. 16 p.

2500 INSKIP, John Swanel, 1816-1884.
Methodism explained and defended. Cincinnati, H.S. & J. Applegate, 1851. 264 p.

II. 1. Christian Holiness Association

2501 KENNEDY, Gerald Hamilton, bp., 1907-
The Methodist way of life. Englewood Cliffs, N.J., Prentice-Hall, 1958. 216 p.

2502 TAYLOR, Jesse Paul, bp., 1895-
Goodly heritage. Winona Lake, Ind., Light and Life Press, 1960. 138 p.

--BIOGRAPHY

2503 TENNEY, Mary Alice, 1889-
"Early Methodist autobiography, 1739-1791; a study in the literature of the inner life." Unpublished Ph.D. dissertation, University of Wisconsin, 1939.

--CONDUCT OF LIFE

-- --AUTHORITATIVE SOURCES

2504 RUSSELL, Bernard Curry
"The theory and practice of Christian discipline according to John Wesley: its theological bases and its modern relevance." Unpublished Ph.D. dissertation, Drew University, 1951. 269ℓ.

--CRITICAL WORKS

2505 IMITATIO CHRISTI. English.
An extract of the Christian's pattern; or, A treatise of the Imitation of Christ. Written in Latin by Thomas à Kempis. Published by John Wesley, M.A. Bristol, Printed by W. Pine, 1770. vi, 7-306 p.

2506 BRYANT, Thomas J., 1828-1893.
A calm address to Methodist preachers and people everywhere in regard to questions growing out of the great holiness revival. n.p., n.d. 35 p.
Caption title.

2507 MORRISON, Henry Clay, 1857-1942.
American Methodist League; a brief statement of facts concerning the American Methodist League. Louisville, Ky., Pentecostal Publishing Co., 1915. 20 p.

2508 SANGSTER, William Edwin, 1900-1960.
Methodism can be born again. New York, Methodist Book Concern, 1938. 124 p.

--DEVOTIONAL LITERATURE

2509 CHADWICK, Samuel, 1860-1932.
The path of prayer. London, Hodder & Stoughton, 1931. 127 p.

2510 CHADWICK, Samuel, 1860-1932.
Through the year with Samuel Chadwick; devotional readings comp. by D.W. Lambert. London, Epworth Press, 1960. 67 p.

2511 GUYON, Jeanne Marie (Bouvier de La Motte), 1648-1717.
Poems; tr. from the French of Madame de La Mothe Guyon, by the late William Cowper ... to which are added, some original poems of Mr. Cowper, not inserted in his works. Newport-Pagnel, J. Wakefield; London, T. Williams, 1801. xii, 132 p.
Preface signed: William Hull.

--DOCTRINAL AND CONTROVERSIAL WORKS

2512 ARTHUR, William, 1819-1901.
The tongue of fire; or, The true power of Christianity, ed. by Thomas O. Summers. Cincinnati, Jennings & Graham, 1908. 376 p.

2513 ATKINSON, Joseph Baines
The beauty of holiness. New York, Philosophical Library, 1953. 160 p.

2514 BARKER, John Henry James
This is the will of God; a study in the doctrine of entire sanctification as a definite experience. London, Epworth Press, 1954. 110 p.

2515 BENNIS, Eliza, 1725-1802.
Christian correspondence; being a collection of letters, written by the late Rev. John Wesley, and several Methodist preachers, in connection with him, to the late Mrs. Eliza Bennis, with her answers, chiefly explaining and enforcing the doctrine of sanctification, now first published from the originals. Philadelphia, Printed by B. Graves, for T. Bennis, 1809. 349 p.

2516 CARMAN, Albert, bp., 1833-1917.
The guiding eye; or, The Holy Spirit's guidance of the believer. Toronto, Briggs, 1889. 221 p.

2517 CASSELS, Louis
Haircuts and holiness; discussion starters for religious encounter groups. Nashville, Abingdon Press, 1972. 128 p.

II. 1. Christian Holiness Association

2518 CHADWICK, Samuel, 1860-1932.
The call to Christian perfection. London, Epworth Press, 1936. 99 p.

2519 CHADWICK, Samuel, 1860-1932.
The gospel of the cross. London, Epworth Press, 1934. 110 p.

2520 CHADWICK, Samuel, 1860-1932.
Humanity and God. London, Hodder & Stoughton, 1904. xv, 356 p.

2521 CHADWICK, Samuel, 1860-1932.
The way to Pentecost. London, Hodder & Stoughton, 1932. 128 p.
Articles reprinted from Joyful News, ed. by J.I. Brice.

2522 COOK, Thomas, 1867-
New Testament holiness. London, Epworth Press, 1902. 158 p.

2523 ENTIRE SANCTIFICATION; or, Christian perfection, stated and defended by Rev. J. Wesley, Rev. A. Watmough, Rev. Dr. A. Clarke, Rev. R. Watson, Rev. R. Treffry. Baltimore, Armstrong & Berry, 1838. iv, 238 p.

2524 ENTIRE SANCTIFICATION attainable in this life. London, Charles H. Kelly, 1898. 281 p.

2525 EYRE, John
Full sanctification realized in the experience of Mrs. Elizabeth Jackson and letters to the Rev. John Wesley, to which are added others of equally eminent character. New York, Riker's Store, 1849. 235 p.

2526 HOBBS, James
Methodist standard holiness gems, with many additional articles, original and selected; including also Old and New Testament conspectus of holiness. New York, Palmer & Hughes, 1888. 220 p.

2526 HORNER, Ralph Cecil, 1854-1921.
Entire consecration; introd. by Rev. A. Carman. Toronto, W. Briggs, 1890. iv, 116 p.

2528 MEADLEY, Thomas Donald
Top level talks: the Christian summit meeting; studies in scriptural holiness or the doctrine of entire sanctification. London, Epworth Press, 1969. x, 241 p.

2529 POPE, William Burt, 1822-1903.
A compendium of Christian theology; being analytical outlines of a course of theological study.... London, 1875. 3 v.

2530 POPE, William Burt, 1822-1903.
A compendium of Christian theology; being analytical outlines of a course of theological study.... Second ed., rev. and enl. London, Wesleyan Conference Office, 1880. 3 v.

2531 SANGSTER, William Edwin, 1900-1960.
"The church's one privation," Religion in Life, XVIII (Winter 1949), 493-502.

2532 SANGSTER, William Edwin, 1900-1960.
The path to perfection; an examination and restatement of John Wesley's doctrine of Christian perfection. London, Epworth Press, 1943. 211 p.

2533 SCRIPTURAL HOLINESS; a series of papers by Rev. John Hartley, Rev. John Moore, Rev. J.D. Tetley, Rev. John Brash, Rev. I.E. Page, Rev. J.C. Greaves, Rev. B. Gregory, Rev. H.J. Staley, Rev. T. Brackenbury, Rev. Simpson Crump, Rev. W.G. Pascoe, Rev. J. Finnemore. London, A. Osborne, n.d. 192 p.

2534 STRACHAN, Alexander, 1793-1865.
The doctrine of entire sanctification explained and enforced in a dissertation on I Thess. 5:23-24. London, J. Mason, 1842. 92 p.

2535 STRACHAN, Alexander, 1793-1865.
The doctrine of entire sanctification explained and enforced. 2d ed. London, J. Mason, 1843. 128 p.

2536 WESLEY, John, 1703-1791.
Christian perfection as believed and taught by John Wesley, ed. and with an introd. by Thomas S. Kepler. Cleveland, World Publishing Co., 1954. 144 p.

2537 WESLEY, John, 1703-1791.
Explanatory notes upon the New Testament. London, Epworth Press, 1950. 1054 p.

2538 WESLEY, John, 1703-1791.
John Wesley [a representative collection of his writings] ed. by Albert C. Outler. New York, Oxford University Press, 1964. xvi, 516 p. (Library of Protestant thought)

2539 WESLEY, John, 1703-1791.
The message of the Wesleys; a reader of instruction

and devotion, comp. and with an introd. by Philip S. Watson. New York, Macmillan, 1964. 264 p.

2540 WESLEY, John, 1703-1791.
Selections from the Journal of John Wesley; ed. by Hugh Martin. London, SCM Press, 1955. 175 p.

2541 WESLEY, John, 1703-1791.
Works. Grand Rapids, Mich., Zondervan Publishing House, 1958. 14 v.
This ed. is a photo offset reprint of the authorized ed. published by the Wesleyan Conference Office, London, in 1872.

--HISTORY

2542 CLARK, Elmer Talmage, 1886-1966.
An album of Methodist history. New York, Abingdon-Cokesbury Press, 1952. 336 p.

2543 LUCCOCK, Halford Edward, 1885-
The story of Methodism, by Halford E. Luccock and Paul Hutchinson, with illus. by Harold Speakman. New York, Methodist Book Concern, 1926. 508 p.

2544 TREFFRY, Richard, 1771-1842.
Memoirs of the Rev. Joseph Benson. New York, Carlton & Phillips, 1853. 292 p.

--HISTORY OF DOCTRINES

2545 ANABAPTIST AND Wesleyan Tradition Seminar, Goshen College Biblical Seminary, Goshen, Ind., 1960.
The nature of the holy life; four papers. n.p., 1961. 46 p.
Held under auspices of the Institute of Mennonite Studies.
Reprint from the Mennonite Quarterly Review, vol. 35, April 1961.

2546 ANGELL, Edward D.
"The Methodist doctrine of personal experience as taught by John Wesley." Unpublished B.D. thesis, Evangelical Lutheran Theological Seminary, Capital University, 1947.

2547 BENNER, Forest T.
"The immediate antecedents of the Wesleyan doctrine of the witness of the Spirit." Unpublished Ph.D. dissertation, Temple University, 1966.

2548 CANNON, William Ragsdale, 1916-
The theology of John Wesley, with special reference to the doctrine of justification. New York, Abingdon Press, 1946. 284 p.

2549 CELL, George Croft, 1875-1937.
The rediscovery of John Wesley. New York, Holt, 1935. 420 p.

2550 CHILES, Robert Eugene, 1923-
"Methodist apostasy: from free grace to free will, " Religion in Life, XXVII (Summer 1958), 438-449.

2551 CHILES, Robert Eugene, 1923-
"Theological transition in American Methodism." Unpublished Ph. D. dissertation, Columbia University, 1964. 337ℓ.

2552 CHILES, Robert Eugene, 1923-
Theological transition in American Methodism: 1790-1935. New York, Abingdon Press, 1965. 238 p.

2553 COX, Leo George, 1912-
"John Wesley's concept of perfection." Unpublished Ph. D. dissertation, State University of Iowa, 1959. 395ℓ.

2554 COX, Leo George, 1912-
"John Wesley's concept of sin." Unpublished M. A. thesis, State University of Iowa, 1957. 193ℓ.

2555 CUBIE, David Livingstone, 1928-
"John Wesley's concept of perfect love: a motif analysis." Unpublished Ph. D. dissertation, Boston University, 1965. 341ℓ.

2556 EICKEN, Erich von
Rechtfertigung und heiligung bei Wesley, dargestellt unter vergleichung mit den anschauungen Luthers und des luthertums. n. p., 1934. 69 p.
Inaugural-Dissertation--Heidelberg.

2557 FUHRMAN, Eldon Ralph, 1918-
"The concept of grace in the theology of John Wesley." Unpublished Ph. D. dissertation, State University of Iowa, 1963. 505ℓ.

2558 HENSCHEN, Walter G.
Christian perfection before Wesley. El Monte, Calif., Deal Publications, n. d.

2559 JORDEN, E. E.
"The ideal of sanctity in Methodism and Tractarianism

with special reference to John Wesley and John Henry Newman." Unpublished Ph.D. dissertation, University of London, 1959.

2560 KNAPP, John Franklin
"The doctrine of holiness in the light of early theological and philosophical conceptions. Unpublished M.A. thesis, University of Cincinnati, 1924.

2561 KNIGHT, John Allan
"John William Fletcher and the early Methodist tradition." Unpublished Ph.D. dissertation, Vanderbilt University, 1966. 418ℓ.

2562 KOERBER, Charles J.
The theology of conversion according to John Wesley.... New York, 1967. 82 p.
At head of title: Pontificia Universitas Gregoriano.
Chapters III IV of a doctoral dissertation originally submitted to the Gregorian University at Rome in 1961.

2563 LERCH, David, 1903-
Heil and heiligung bei John Wesley, dargestellt unter besonderer berücksichtigung seiner Anmerkungen zum Neuen Testament. Zürich, Christliche vereinsbuchhandlung, 1941. ix, 180 p.
Inaugural-Dissertation--Zürich.

2564 LINDSTROM, Harald Gustaf Ake, 1905-
Wesley and sanctification; a study in the doctrine of salvation. Stockholm, Nya Bokförlags Aktiebolaget, 1946. xvi, 228 p.

2565 LINDSTROM, Harald Gustaf Ake, 1905-
Wesley and sanctification; a study in the doctrine of salvation. London, Epworth Press, 1950. 228 p.

2566 McINTOSH, Lawrence Dennis
"The nature and design of Christianity in John Wesley's early theology; a study of love and faith." Unpublished Ph.D. dissertation, Drew University, 1966. 266ℓ.

2567 MANIFOLD, Orrin Avery
"The development of John Wesley's doctrine of Christian perfection." Unpublished Ph.D. dissertation, Boston University, 1946. 203ℓ.

2568 MONK, Robert Clarence, 1930-
"John Wesley: his Puritan heritage; a study of the Christian life." Unpublished Ph.D. dissertation, Princeton University, 1963. vi, 382ℓ.

2569 MONK, Robert Clarence, 1930-
John Wesley: his Puritan heritage; a study of the Christian life. Princeton, N.J., Princeton University, c1963. vi, 382ℓ.
Thesis (Ph.D.)--Princeton University.
Abstracted in Dissertation Abstracts, v. 24 (1963), no. 6, p. 2592-2593.
Microfilm of typescript. Ann Arbor, Mich., University Microfilms, 1963. 1 reel. 35 mm.

2570 MONK, Robert Clarence, 1930-
John Wesley: his Puritan heritage; a study of the Christian life. Nashville, Abingdon Press, 1966. 286 p.
Based on thesis, Princeton University.

2571 MONK, Robert Clarence, 1930-
John Wesley: his Puritan heritage; a study of the Christian life. London, Epworth Press, 1966 [i.e. 1967]. 286 p.
Based on thesis, Princeton University.

2572 MUSSMAN, Robert Byron
"A study and evaluation of the primary nonscriptural influences of John Wesley's doctrine of Christian perfection." Unpublished Th.D. dissertation, Southern Baptist Theological Seminary, 1959. vii, 168ℓ.

2573 NYGREN, Ellis Herbert
"John Wesley's interpretation of Christian ordination." Unpublished Ph.D. dissertation, New York University, 1960. 276ℓ.

2574 SANGSTER, William Edwin, 1900-1960.
"Wesley and sanctification," London Quarterly and Holborn Review, CLXXI (July 1946), 214-221.

2575 SCOTT, Percy
John Wesleys lehre von der heiligung verglichen mit einem luterisch-pietistischen beispiel, mit einem geleitwort von prof. d. dr. Heinrich Frick, D.D. Berlin, A. Topelmann, 1939. 97 p. (Studien zur geschichte des nueren protestantismus, 17 bd.)
"Die arbeit ist von der Theologischen fakultät zu Marburg im S.S. 1937 als dissertation zur erlangung der würde eines lizentianten angenommen worden." p. [ix].

2576 SHIPLEY, David Clark, 1907-
"Methodist Arminianism in the theology of John Fletcher." Unpublished Ph.D. dissertation, Yale University, 1942.

II. 1. Christian Holiness Association

2577 STAPLES, Rob Lyndal
"John Wesley's doctrine of Christian perfection: a reinterpretation." Unpublished Th. D. dissertation, Pacific School of Religion, 1963.

2578 THOMAS, Wilhelm
Heiligung im Neuen Testament und bei John Wesley. Zurich, Christliche Vereinsbuchhandlung, 1965. 54 p. (Methodismus in Dokumenten, Heft 10).

2579 TURNER, George Allen, 1908-
"A comparative study of the Biblical and Wesleyan ideas of perfection, to determine the sources of Wesley's doctrine." Unpublished Ph. D. dissertation, Harvard University, 1946.

2580 WHEDON, D. A.
Entire sanctification: John Wesley's view. New York, Hunt and Eaton, n. d.

2581 WILLIAMS, Colin W.
John Wesley's theology today. New York, Abingdon Press, 1960. 252 p.

--HYMNS

2582 [WILLIAMS, J. A.], ed.
The wave of Sunday school song; a new collection of music for Sunday-schools, prayer-meeting, social and family circle. Toronto, Printed and published by S. Rose, at the Methodist Book Room, 1878. 216 p.

-- --HISTORY AND CRITICISM

2583 FLEW, Robert Newton, 1886-
The hymns of Charles Wesley; a study of their structure. London, Epworth Press, 1953. 79 p.

2584 LIGHTWOOD, James Thomas, 1856-
The music of the Methodist hymn-book; being the story of each tune with biographical notices of the composers. London, Epworth Press, 1935. xxiii, 549 p.

2585 RATTENBURY, John Ernest, 1870-
The evangelical doctrines of Charles Wesley's hymns. 3d ed. London, Epworth Press, 1954. 365 p.

2586 ROUTLEY, Erik, 1917-
The musical Wesleys. New York, Oxford University Press, 1968. xi, 272 p.

--PASTORAL THEOLOGY

2587 DYGOSKI, Louise Annie, 1911-
"The journals and letters of John Wesley on preaching."
Unpublished Ph.D. dissertation, University of Wisconsin,
1961. 374ℓ.

--PERIODICALS

2588 GUIDE TO Holiness and Class-leader's Magazine. 1-2, 1871-1872. London.

--SERMONS

2589 ADAMS, Joseph
The command of God, "Be ye holy"; a sermon preached in the Clarence St. Wesleyan Chapel, Newcastle-on-Tyne, on the 5th day of Nov., 1871. Bishop Auckland, Eng., Printed by M. Braithwaite, 1871. 8 p.

2590 BATT, John Herridge
The believers sanctification in Christ; an address delivered ... in the morning session of the convention held at Waterloo Road Chapel, Lambeth, May 5th, 1891. London, Bible Christian Bookroom, 1891. 16 p.

2591 BENSON, Joseph, 1749-1821.
Two sermons on sanctification. 2d ed. Birmingham, Eng., Printed by E. Jones, 1791. 72 p.
First published in 1782.

2592 FLETCHER, John William, 1729-1785.
An address to imperfect believers, who cordially embrace the doctrine of Gospel sanctification. Boston, Printed by True, Weston and Green, 1821. 48 p.

2593 FRENCH, Alfred J.
Life, light, and life: the principles of holiness; a discourse, delivered in Islington Chapel, Birmingham, July the 21st, 1879, in connection with the assembling of the Wesleyan-Methodist Conference and as the ninth lecture on the foundation of the late John Fernley. London, Wesleyan Conference Office, 1879. iv, 75 p.

2594 SANGSTER, William Edwin, 1900-1960.
Sangster of Westminster. London, Marshall, Morgan and Scott, 1960. 104 p.

2595 WESLEY, John, 1703-1791.
Sermons on several occasions; first series consisting

of forty-four discourses, published in four volumes, in the
years 1746, 1748, 1750 and 1760 (fourth edition, 1787); to
which reference is made in the trust-deeds of the Methodist
chapels, as constituting, with Mr. Wesley's Notes on the
New Testament, the standard doctrines of the Methodist
Connexion. London, Epworth Press, 1944. 596 p.

Methodists

(specific groups)

APOSTOLIC METHODIST CHURCH (1932-   )

Composed of followers of E.H. Crowson, formerly a minister in the Methodist Episcopal Church, South, the Apostolic Methodist Church was formed at Loughman, Florida, in 1932. Contending for Wesleyan fundamentals which it claimed no longer informed the teaching of the parent body, the new church adopted congregationalism and stressed second crisis sanctification and premillennialism. It enjoyed little growth, however, and as late as 1970 reported only three congregations and less than 100 members.

2596   CLARK, Elmer Talmage, 1886-1966.
The small sects in America. Rev. ed. New York,
Abingdon Press, c1965. 256 p.
Account of the Apostolic Methodist Church: p. 64-65.

2597   MEAD, Frank Spencer, 1898-
Handbook of denominations in the United States. New
5th ed. Nashville, Abingdon Press, c1970. 265 p.
"Apostolic Methodist Church": p. 148.

CONGREGATIONAL METHODIST CHURCH (1852-   )

Originating in 1852 in a separation from the Methodist
Episcopal Church, South, in protest of the itinerate system, the
Congregational Methodist Church is concentrated in the former
Confederate States. Headed by a president, the group continues
to champion the connectional approach to denominational administration, but cannot be considered congregational in that property
may not be alienated from the use of the denomination. The
church early incorporated entire sanctification in its doctrinal
standards and requires that ordained ministers profess the experience; lay officials must profess, or be seekers after perfect
love. The Congregational Methodist Church cooperates with the
Christian Holiness Association. In 1960 the group reported 223

churches and about 15,000 members. It sponsors Westminster College and Bible Institute, a junior college at Florence, Mississippi.

2598 CONGREGATIONAL METHODIST Church.
  Constitution and government. 1st- , ed.; 1852- .
  Baltimore; Eatonton, Ga.; Milner, Ga.; Anniston, Ala.; Decatur, Miss.; Dallas, 1852- . irregular.

--HISTORY

2599 FOWLER, Wilton R.
  A history of the Congregational Methodist Church. n.p., c1957. 109ℓ.

--MISSIONS

2600 ENCYCLOPEDIA OF modern Christian missions; the agencies. Burton L. Goddard, ed.... Camden, N.J., T. Nelson, 1967. xix, 743 p.
  "Congregational Methodist Church, General Mission Board," by Harold E. Pitts: p. 202.

--PERIODICALS

2601 CONGREGATIONAL METHODIST Messenger. 1- , 1913- . Dallas, Tex.; Florence, Miss.

EVANGELICAL METHODIST CHURCH (1946-)

[In Mexico also as Mexican Evangelistic Mission]

  On May 9, 1946, a group of Methodist ministers and laymen led by J.H. Hamblen of Abilene, Texas, met in Memphis, Tennessee, and decided to organize the Evangelical Methodist Church. Convinced that the main body of Methodists had become irretrievably modernist, the group held its first conference the following November in Kansas City, Missouri, and elected Hamblen (father of cowboy singer Stuart Hamblen) general superintendent. At this meeting the new church received the Mexican Evangelistic Mission, founded in 1926, into fellowship. In 1957 the Mexican mission was made the first Mission Conference and Ezequiel B. Vargas, its leader, designated as general superintendent (Mexico). Committed to traditional Methodist beliefs, the Evangelical Methodists adopted a modified congregational system of government. Augmented by mergers with the Evangel Church in 1960 and the People's Methodist Church in 1962, the group claimed 155

II. 1. Christian Holiness Association

congregations with 9788 members by 1971. Churches are concentrated in southern and southwestern states. Affiliation is maintained with John Wesley College, Greensboro, North Carolina; Vennard College, University Park, Iowa; Azusa Pacific College, Azusa, California; and the Western Evangelical Seminary, Portland, Oregon. The Evangelical Methodist Church is a member of the Christian Holiness Association.

2602 EVANGELICAL METHODIST Church.
Discipline. Chicago, Good News Press, 1949- .
Imprint varies.
Irregular quadrennial issue.

2603 EVANGELICAL METHODIST Church. Conferences.
Minutes.... 1946- .
Published 1946-1959 as Minutes of the annual and general conference; 1960-1963 there were separate volumes for each conference; 1964- combined the Eastern, Western and Mexican conferences.

--APOLOGETIC WORKS

2604 EVANGELICAL METHODIST Church.
The Evangelical Methodist Church presents a changeless faith in a changing world; a warm-hearted spiritual fellowship rooted in a rich Wesleyan tradition with a positive Christ-centered message. n.p., 196?? Folder.

2605 SHULER, Robert Pierce, 1880-
The Evangelical Methodist Church: what it is, and what it believes. Wichita, Kan., Evangelical Methodist Church, International Headquarters, 1952. 10 p.
Reprinted from the Methodist Challenge.

--HISTORY

2606 CLARK, Elmer Talmage, 1886-1966.
The small sects in America. Rev. ed. New York, Abingdon Press, c1965. 256 p.
Account of Evangelical Methodist Church: p. 65-66.

2607 MEAD, Frank Spencer, 1898-
Handbook of denominations in the United States. New 5th ed. Nashville, Abingdon Press, c1970. 265 p.
"Evangelical Methodist Church": p. 149.

--MISSIONS

2608 EVANGELICAL METHODIST Church. Board of World Missions.
Manual of operations of the Board of World Missions of the Evangelical Methodist Church (Includes Constitution and By-Laws). 1972 ed. n.p., 1972. 23ℓ.
Reproduced from type-written copy.

2609 ENCYCLOPEDIA OF modern Christian missions; the agencies. Burton L. Goddard, ed.... Camden, N.J., T. Nelson, 1967. xix, 743 p.
"Bible Methodist Missions," by W.W. Breckbill: p. 86-87; and "Mexican Evangelistic Mission," by James H. Mumme: p. 424-425.

--PERIODICALS

2610 VOICE OF Evangelical Methodism. 1- , 1953- . Wichita, Kan.

--RELIGIOUS EDUCATION

2611 EVANGELICAL METHODIST Church.
Christian education in the E.M.C. Cover-title, 30ℓ.

FREE METHODIST CHURCH OF NORTH AMERICA (1860-)

[1962-present also as Free Methodist World Fellowship]

In reaction to formalism and worldliness in the Genesee Conference of the Methodist Episcopal Church, the Reverend Benjamin Titus Roberts and others who had been "read out" of the church for their criticism of it, organized the Free Methodist Church at Pekin, New York, in 1860. (The Genesee Conference restored Roberts' ministerial credentials, posthumously, with apologies to his son, but a reunion was not effected.) Taking its stand for free grace, free pews, free men, freedom from oath-bound secret societies and lodges, and freedom in worship, the group was deeply committed to holiness from the start. Until 1943 the denomination forbade use of musical instruments in the church, a stricture symbolic of the asceticism and legalism that pervaded its membership in the formative years. Evangelistic fervor which led to separation of the Pentecost Bands in 1895, also characterized the parent body, which later sent foreign missionaries to China, Japan, India, the Philippines, Africa, Mexico, the West Indies and South America. Merger with the Holiness Movement Church of Canada in 1960 brought a large work in Egypt into the Free Methodist Church.

II. 1. Christian Holiness Association

After the death of Roberts in 1893, the group replaced "general superintendent" with "bishop" as the title of the chief denominational officer. Unlike other holiness churches, pastors are appointed rather than elected. Denominational headquarters had been established in Chicago in 1886 but were moved to Winona Lake, Indiana, in 1935. In 1964 the Free Methodist World Fellowship was established and general conferences formed in North America, Egypt and Japan. Legislation passed by any of the general conferences is reviewed by a constitutional council consisting of elected members from all three. Strongly committed to higher education, the church controls one junior and three senior colleges in the United States, supports another senior college in cooperation with other holiness churches, and maintains the John Wesley Foundation at the independent Asbury Theological Seminary in Wilmore, Kentucky, for ministerial training. The Free Methodist Church claims a world membership of 123,606. There are 68,656 members and 1147 churches in the United States and Canada. Merger talks are in progress with the Wesleyan Church. The Free Methodist Church holds membership in the Christian Holiness Association.

2612   FREE METHODIST Church of North America.
Doctrines and discipline, 1860- . Rochester; Chicago; Winona Lake, Ind., 1860- . v.
Quadrennial: 1862-1898, 1903-1955, 1960-1964, 1969- .

2613   FREE METHODIST Church of North America.
Yearbook of the Free Methodist Church around the world, 1906- . Chicago; Winona Lake, Ind., 1906- . v. annual.
1906- as Proceedings of the ... annual conferences....
Annual minutes.

2614   FREE METHODIST Church of North America. General Conference.
General conference daily. Greenville, Ill., S. K. J. Chesbro.

2615   FREE METHODIST World Fellowship. Winona Lake, Ind., 196?. Folder.

2616   HUFFMAN, J.
"Free Methodist vitality." Christianity Today, XIII (July 18, 1969), 13.

2617   LAMSON, Byron Samuel, 1901-
To catch the tide; [the World Fellowship story]. Winona Lake, Ind., General Missionary Board by Light and Life Press, c1963. 128 p.

--CONFERENCES. EAST ONTARIO

2618 FREE METHODIST Church of North America. Conferences. East Ontario.
 East Ontario Conference, 1895-1970; 75 years of progress in Canadian Free Methodism. n.p., 1970. Unpaged.
 Cover-title.

2619 FREE METHODIST Church of North America. Conferences. East Ontario.
 Focus on gains. n.p., 1966. cover-title, 11 p.

--CONFERENCES. KENTUCKY-TENNESSEE

2620 MAVIS, Marion
 A brief story of the Kentucky-Tennessee Conference, written for the 75th anniversary commemoration. Wilmore, Ky., 1970. 23 p.
 Cover-title: In the beginning; a history of the Free Methodist Church in Kentucky-Tennessee from its earliest beginnings until 1970.

--CONFERENCES. OKLAHOMA

2621 NELSON, Walter O.
 A history of the Oklahoma Annual Conference of the Free Methodist Church of North America. Siloam Springs, Ark., Silent Minister Booklet Press, 1949. 36 p.

--ANECDOTES, REMINISCENCES, SATIRE, ETC.

2622 HART, Edward Payson, bp., -1919.
 Reminiscences of early Free Methodism; with an introd. by Burton R. Jones. Chicago, Free Methodist Publishing House, 1913. xxi, 259 p.

2623 SIMS, Albert, 1851-
 Remarkable narratives; or, Records of powerful revivals, striking providences, wonderful religious experiences, tragic death-bed scenes, and other authentic incidents, to which is added some valuable hints for Christian workers. Kingston, Ont., The author, 1896. 352 p.

2624 SIMS, Albert, 1851-
 Remarkable narratives; or, Records of powerful revivals, striking providences, wonderful religious experiences, tragic death-bed scenes, and other authentic incidents, to which is added some valuable hints for Christian workers. Pittsburgh, Hague & Co., 1902. 352 p.

II. 1. Christian Holiness Association

--APOLOGETIC WORKS

2625 ROBERTS, Benjamin Titus, 1823-1893.
Why another sect; containing a review of articles by Bishop Simpson and others on the Free Methodist Church. Rochester, "The Earnest Christian" Publishing House, 1879. 321 p.

2626 TAYLOR, Jesse Paul, bp., 1895-
Goodly heritage. Winona Lake, Ind., Light and Life Press, 1960. 138 p.

--BIOGRAPHY

2627 BLEWS, Richard R.
Master workmen; biographies of the late bishops of the Free Methodist Church during her first century, 1860-1960. Centennial ed. Winona Lake, Ind., Light and Life Press, 1960. 303 p.

--CAMP MEETINGS

2628 TERRILL, Joseph Goodwin, -1895.
The St. Charles Camp Meeting. Chicago, T.B. Arnold, 1883.

2629 TREMAIN, Lloyd Carlos
"An evaluation of the organization and structure of the family camp program of the Pacific Northwest Conference of the Free Methodist Church." Unpublished M.Ed. thesis (project), Seattle Pacific College, 1968. iv, 57ℓ.

--CHURCH WORK

2630 MAVIS, Walter Curry, 1905-
Advancing the smaller local church. Winona Lake, Ind., Light and Life Press, 1957. 189 p.

--CLERGY

2631 COOK, Arnold Willis
"An analysis of the responsibilities and training of selected ministers in church business administration." Unpublished M.A. thesis, East Tennessee State University, 1970.

2631a ROBERTS, Benjamin Titus, 1823-1893.
Ordaining women. Rochester, N.Y., Earnest Christian Publishing House, 1891. 159 p.

--CONDUCT OF LIFE

2632 ALEXANDER, John Wesley, 1918-
    Thoughts from the sea. Winona Lake, Ind., Young People's Missionary Society, 1947. 159 p.
    Autobiographical.

2633 GHORMLEY, Newton Baxter, -1940.
    Our boys: for them and their parents. Neillsville, Wis., C. Robenstein, 1900. 133 p.

2634 HUMPHREY, Jerry Miles, 1872-
    Crumbs from heaven. Chicago, Light and Life Press, 1927. 144 p.

2635 LINCICOME, Forman, 1880-
    Three D's of the sanctified. Chicago, Free Methodist Publishing House, 1932. 63 p.

2636 MARSTON, Leslie Ray, bp., 1894-
    From chaos to character; a study in the stewardship of personality. Introduction by Bishop William Pearce; suggestions for study by Lois Wood-Woods. Greenville, Ill., Tower Press, Greenville College, 1935. 175 p.

2637 MARSTON, Leslie Ray, bp., 1894-
    From chaos to character; a study in the stewardship of personality. Study suggestions and worship guide by Lois Wood-Woods. Greenville, Ill., Tower Press, 1937. 192 p.
    "2nd edition."

2638 MARSTON, Leslie Ray, bp., 1894-
    From chaos to character; a study in the stewardship of personality. Study suggestions and worship guide by Lois Wood-Woods. Winona Lake, Ind., Light and Life Press, 1944. 192 p.
    "3d edition."

2639 TENNEY, Mary Alice, 1889-
    Blueprint for a Christian world; an analysis of the Wesleyan way. Winona Lake, Ind., Light and Life Press, 1953. 292 p.

2640 TENNEY, Mary Alice, 1889-
    Living in two worlds; how a Christian does it! Winona Lake, Ind., Light and Life Press, 1958. 118 p.

--CONVERTS

2641 HUMPHREY, Jerry Miles, 1872-
    The convert's homeward guide. Chicago, W.B. Rose, 1916. 126 p.

II. 1. Christian Holiness Association

--CRITICAL WORKS

2642   WEEKS, Sherwood, 1907-1968.
       The delusion of the holiness mystics and heresy in the holiness pulpits. Wauseon, Ohio, Gilson Press, 1955. Unpaged.
       Cover title: Mysticism, antinomianism and the positive gospel.

--DEVOTIONAL LITERATURE

2643   BALDWIN, Harmon Allen, 1869-1936.
       The fisherman of Galilee; a devotional study of the Apostle Peter. New York, Fleming H. Revell Co., 1923. 160 p.

--DOCTRINAL AND CONTROVERSIAL WORKS

2644   BALDWIN, Harmon Allen, 1869-1936.
       The carnal mind; a doctrinal and experimental view of the subject. Chicago, Free Methodist Publishing House, 1926. 183 p.

2645   BALDWIN, Harmon Allen, 1869-1936.
       Holiness and the human element. Louisville, Pentecostal Publishing Co., c1919. 123 p.

2646   BALDWIN, Harmon Allen, 1869-1936.
       Holiness and the human element. 2d ed. Kansas City, Mo., Nazarene Publishing House, 1952, c1919. 110 p.

2647   BALDWIN, Harmon Allen, 1869-1936.
       The indwelling Christ; with an introd. by Bishop Burton R. Jones. Vandergrift Heights, Pa., The author, c1912. 282 p.

2648   BALDWIN, Harmon Allen, 1869-1936.
       Lessons for seekers of holiness; containing numerous quotations from Wesley, Fletcher, and other standard authors, and designed to aid such as are groaning after purity of heart in entering upon the experience; introd. by Rev. John S. M'Geary. Chicago, S.K.J. Chesbro, 1907. 180 p.

2649   BALDWIN, Harmon Allen, 1869-1936.
       Objections to entire sanctification considered. Pittsburgh, For the author, 1911. 63 p.

2650   HAWKINS, Richard Watson, -1892.
       Redemption; or, The living way. Olean, N.Y., Herald Publishing Co., 1888. 497 p.

2651 HOGUE, Wilson Thomas, bp., 1852-1920.
 The believer's personal experience of Christ in the processes of salvation. Chicago, W.B. Rose, 1915. 58 p.

2652 HOGUE, Wilson Thomas, bp., 1852-1920.
 The Holy Spirit, a study. Chicago, W.B. Rose, 1916. 408 p.

2653 HOGUE, Wilson Thomas, bp., 1852-1920.
 A symposium of scriptural holiness. Chicago, Free Methodist Publishing House, 1896. 150 p.

2654 JOY, Donald Marvin, 1928-
 The Holy Spirit and you. New York, Abingdon Press, 1965. 160 p.

2655 JOY, Donald Marvin, 1928-
 The Holy Spirit and you. Winona Lake, Ind., Light and Life Press, 1965. 187 p.

2656 LINCICOME, Forman, 1880-
 The soul. Winona Lake, Ind., Light and Life Press, 1940. 64 p.

2657 LINCICOME, Forman, 1880-
 What is your life? Chicago, Light and Life Press, 1933. 64 p.

2658 MAVIS, Walter Curry, 1905-
 Beyond conformity. Winona Lake, Ind., Light and Life Press, 1958. 160 p.

2659 MAVIS, Walter Curry, 1905-
 Personal renewal through conversion. Kansas City, Mo., Beacon Hill Press, 1969.

2660 MAVIS, Walter Curry, 1905-
 The psychology of Christian experience. Grand Rapids, Mich., Zondervan Publishing House, 1963. 155 p.

2661 MINISTERS' CONFERENCE of Greenville College, Greenville, Ill., 12th, 1939.
 The Wesleyan message: its scriptures and historical bases; addresses delivered at the 12th annual ministers' conference, April 10-14, 1939. Winona Lake, Ind., Light and Life Press, 1940. 220 p.
 Foreword signed: George E. Kline, president of the Greenville Minister's Conference.

2662 MINISTERS' CONFERENCE of Greenville College, Greenville, Ill., 13th-14th, 1940-1941.
 The Wesleyan message bearing fruit; addresses de-

II. 1. Christian Holiness Association

livered at the 13th and 14th sessions of the Ministers' Conference of Greenville College, April, 1940-1941. Winona Lake, Ind., Light and Life Press, 1942. 176 p.
Foreword signed: George E. Kline, president.

2663 ROBERTS, Benjamin Titus, 1823-1893.
Holiness teachings, comp. from the editorial writings of the late Rev. Benjamin T. Roberts, A.M., by Benson Roberts, A.M. North Chili, N.Y., "Earnest Christian" Publishing House, 1893. 256 p.

2664 ROBERTS, Benjamin Titus, 1823-1893.
Living truths; ed. by E.D. Riggs. Winona Lake, Ind., Light and Life Press, 1960. Unpaged.

2665 ROBERTS, Benjamin Titus, 1823-1893.
Pungent truths; being extracts from the writings of the Rev. Benjamin Titus Roberts ... comp. and ed. by William B. Rose. Chicago, Free Methodist Publishing House, 1912. 379 p.

2666 SELLEW, Walter Ashbel, bp., 1844-1929.
Obligations of civilization to Christianity; or, The influence of Christianity upon civilization. Chicago, Light and Life Press, 1928. 58 p.

2667 SHELHAMER, Elmer Ellsworth, 1869-1947.
Bible holiness, how obtained, how retained. Chicago, Free Methodist Publishing House, n.d.

2668 SIMS, Albert, 1851-
Helps to Bible study with practical notes on the books of Scripture. Designed for ministers, local preachers, S.S. teachers, and all Christian workers. Uxbridge, Ont., 1886. iv, 196 p.

2669 SIMS, Albert, 1851-
Valuable bank notes; or, God's immutable promises, searched, tested and found true. Toronto, Ont., A. Sims, 1902. 85 p.

2670 TAYLOR, Jesse Paul, bp., 1895-
Holiness, the finished foundation. Winona Lake, Ind., Light and Life Press, 1963. 216 p.

2671 TENNEY, Mary Alice, 1889-
The Wesleyan message. Winona Lake, Ind., Light and Life Press, 1953.

2672 TURNER, George Allen, 1908-
The more excellent way: the scriptural basis of the Wesleyan message. Winona Lake, Ind., Light and Life

Press, 1952. 292 p.
Thesis (Ph. D.)--Harvard University, 1946.

2673 TURNER, George Allen, 1908-
The vision which transforms; is Christian perfection scriptural? Kansas City, Mo., Beacon Hill Press, 1964. 348 p.
"A thorough revision under ... new title of the author's thesis, first published in 1952 under title: The More Excellent Way; the ms. thesis (Harvard University) has title: A Comparative Study of Biblical and Wesleyan Ideas of Perfection."

2674 WARNER, David Snethen, bp., 1857-1927.
The anointing of the Holy Spirit. Chicago, Light and Life Press, 1925.

2675 WARNER, David Snethen, bp., 1857-1927.
The book we study; a brief tribute to the Holy Scriptures. Chicago, W.B. Rose, 1921. 76 p.

-- --AUTHORITATIVE SOURCES

2676 BARKER, John Henry James
This is the will of God; a study in the doctrine of entire sanctification as a definite experience. Winona Lake, Ind., Light and Life Press, 1956. 110 p.

2677 WOOD, John Allen, 1828-
Perfect love; or, Plain things for those who need them, concerning the doctrine, experience, profession and practic of Christian holiness. Rev. and enl. ed. Chicago, W.B. Rose, 1909. 331 p.

-- --ESCHATOLOGY

2678 BALDWIN, Harmon Allen, 1869-1936.
The coming judgment, general and at the end of time. Chicago, Free Methodist Publishing House, 1927. 184 p.

2679 SILVER, Jesse Forest
The Lord's return, seen in history and in Scripture as pre-millennial and imminent; with an introd. by Bishop Wilson T. Hogue.... New York, Revell, 1914. 311 p.

2680 SIMS, Albert, 1851-
Behold the Bridegroom cometh; or, Some remarkable and incontrovertible signs which herald the near approach of the Son of Man.... Kingston, Ont., Published by the auth 1900. 140 p.

2681 SIMS, Albert, 1851-
Deepening shadows and coming glories. Toronto, A. Sims, 1905. 256 p.

--EDUCATION

2682 FREE METHODIST Church of North America. Commission on Christian Education.
The study of Free Methodist higher education, sponsored by the Commission on Christian Education and the Association of Free Methodist Colleges; directed by David L. McKenna. n.p., 1962. 84, 61 p.
Appendix separately paged.

2683 NELSON, Marven O.
"The administration of guidance in colleges related to the Wesleyan and Free Methodist churches." Unpublished Ed.D. dissertation, University of Buffalo, 1952. 123ℓ.

2684 SCHOENHALS, Lawrence Russell, 1912-
"Higher education in the Free Methodist Church in the United States: 1860-1954." Unpublished Ph.D. dissertation, University of Washington, 1955.

--EVANGELISTIC WORK

2685 FAIRBAIRN, Charles Victor, bp., 1890-
The secret of true revival (holiness must be preached), with an introd. by Rev. J.T. Logan.... Chicago, Published for the author by Free Methodist Publishing House, 1929. 104 p.

2686 HOGUE, Wilson Thomas, bp., 1852-1920.
Revivals and revival work. Buffalo, N.Y., Pub. for the author, 1890. 64 p.

2687 ROBERTS, Benjamin Titus, 1823-1893.
Fishers of men; or, Practical hints to those who would win souls. Rochester, N.Y., G.L. Roberts & Co., 1878. 272 p.

2688 ROBERTS, Benjamin Titus, 1823-1893.
Fishers of men; or, Practical hints to those who would win souls. Winona Lake, Ind., Light and Life Press, 1948. 272 p.
Reprint of 1878 ed.

--HISTORY

2689 BOWEN, Elias, 1791-1871.
History of the origin of the Free Methodist Church. Rochester, N.Y., B.T. Roberts, 1871. 350 p.
"Sketch of the life of the author, by Rev. B.T. Roberts": p. iii-viii.

2690 HART, Edward Payson, bp., -1919.
Reminiscences of early Free Methodism; with an introd. by Burton R. Jones. Chicago, Free Methodist Publishing House, 1913. xxi, 259 p.

2691 HOGUE, Wilson Thomas, bp., 1852-1920.
History of the Free Methodist Church of North America; introd. by Bishop Edward P. Hart. Chicago, Free Methodist Publishing House, 1915. 2 v.

2692 HOWLAND, Carl Leroy, 1881-
The story of our church; Free Methodism, some facts and reasons. Winona Lake, Ind., Free Methodist Publishing House, 1939. 156 p.

2693 MacGEARY, John Samuel, bp., 1853-1931.
The Free Methodist Church; a brief outline history of its origin and development. Chicago, W.B. Rose, 1908. 224 p.

2694 MARSTON, Leslie Ray, bp., 1894-
From age to age a living witness; a historical interpretation of Free Methodism's first century. Winona Lake, Ind., Light and Life Press, 1960. 608 p.

2694a REINHARD, James Arnold, 1932-
"Personal and sociological factors in the formation of the Free Methodist Church, 1852-1860." Unpublished Ph.D. dissertation, University of Iowa, 1971. iv, 254.

2695 ROBERTS, Benjamin Titus, 1823-1893.
Why another sect; containing a review of articles by Bishop Simpson and others on the Free Methodist Church. Rochester, "The Earnest Christian" Publishing House, 1879. 321 p.

2696 SIMPSON, Matthew, bp., 1811-1884, ed.
Cyclopaedia of Methodism; embracing sketches of its rise, progress, and present condition, with biographical notices and numerous illustrations. Philadelphia, Everts & Stewart, 1878. 1027 p.
"Free Methodists": p. 379-380.

II. 1. Christian Holiness Association

2697 TAYLOR, Jesse Paul, bp., 1895-
Goodly heritage. Winona Lake, Ind., Light and Life Press, 1960. 138 p.

--HYMNS

2698 FREE METHODIST Church of North America.
The hymn book of the Free Methodist Church.... Rochester, N.Y., B.T. Roberts, 1883. 582 p.
Without music.

2699 FREE METHODIST Church of North America.
Free Methodist hymnal, published by authority of the General Conference of the Free Methodist Church of North America. Chicago, Free Methodist Publishing House, 1910. 498 p.
With music.
Prepared by Hymnal Commission including the Rev. A. T. Jennings, representative of the Wesleyan Methodist Connection (or Church) of America.

2700 FREE METHODIST Church of North America.
Free Methodist hymnal, published by authority of the Free Methodist Church of North America.... Chicago, Free Methodist Publishing House, 1915. 497 p.
Without music.

2701 FREE METHODIST Church of North America.
Choice hymns, a collection of hymns from the Free Methodist hymnal, especially adapted for revival services; comp. by William Pearce, Rollin E. Cochrane, Claude A. Watson [and] B.H. Gaddis.... Winona Lake, Ind., Free Methodist Publishing House, 1942. 112 p.
With music.

2702 FREE METHODIST Church of North America.
Hymns of the living faith. Winona Lake, Ind., Light & Life Press, 1951. 1 v. (various pagings).
"The Commission preparing Hymns of the Living Faith represents ... both sponsoring communions, the Wesleyan Methodist Church of America and the Free Methodist Church of North America."

2703 [LATHAM, Joy], comp.
Joyfully sing; a hymnal for children. Kansas City, Mo., Lillenas Publishing Co., c1968. Unpaged.
With music.
Adopted as the official children's hymnal by the Hymnal Commission, 1968, The Free Methodist Church [and] The Wesleyan Church.

2704 OLMSTEAD, William Backus, 1862-1941.
Gospel truths in song; adapted especially to Sunday schools, social worship, camp meetings and revival services. Chicago, W.B. Rose, 1915. Unpaged.
With music.

2705 OLMSTEAD, William Backus, 1862-1941.
Light and life songs; adapted especially to Sunday schools, prayer meetings and other social services. Editors: William B. Olmstead, Thoro Harris; associate editor: William J. Kirkpatrick. Chicago, S.K.J. Chesbro, 1904. Unpaged.
With music.

2706 OLMSTEAD, William Backus, 1862-1941.
Light and life songs, number two; adapted especially to Sunday schools, social worship, camp meetings and revival services. William B. Olmstead, ed.; Thoro Harris, assistant ed. Chicago, W.B. Rose, 1914. 224 p.
With music.

2707 OLMSTEAD, William Backus, 1862-1941.
Light and life songs, no. 4, for the Sunday school, social worship, missionary and evangelistic work, comp. and ed. by William B. Olmstead and Mr. and Mrs. Newton W. Fink. Chicago, Light and Life Press, 1928. Unpaged.
With music.

2708 PHILLIPS, Philip, 1834-1895.
Metrical tune book, with hymns, by Philip Phillips and J.G. Terrill. Chicago, Pub. for J.G. Terrill by T.B. Arnold, 1890. 230 p.
With music.

2709 PHILLIPS, Philip, 1834-1895.
Metrical tune book, with hymns and supplement, revised and enlarged by Philip Phillips, J.G. Terrill and T.B. Arnold. Chicago, T.B. Arnold, 1896. [5]-288, [282] p.
With music.

-- --HISTORY AND CRITICISM

2710 HOGUE, Wilson Thomas, bp., 1852-1920.
Hymns that are immortal, with some account of their authorship, origin, history and influence. Chicago, S.K.J. Chesbro, agent, 1906. 326 p.

2711 TAYLOR, Jesse Paul, bp., 1895-
The music of Pentecost. Winona Lake, Ind., Light and Life Press, 1951. 123 p.

2712 WESLEY, Charles, 1707-1788.
Living hymns of Charles Wesley: the singing saint [by] Bishop Leslie R. Marston; hymns that are immortal [by] Bishop W. T. Hogue; hymn poems [by] the Reverend Charles Wesley. Winona Lake, Ind., Light and Life Press, 1957. 64 p.

--MISSIONS

2713 FREE METHODIST Church of North America. General Missionary Secretary.
Go ... make disciples; 1963 annual report of Free Methodist world missions. Winona Lake, Ind., 1963. 32 p.

2714 FREE METHODIST Church of North America. General Missionary Secretary.
Missions cavalcade; 1968 annual report of Free Methodist world missions. Winona Lake, Ind., 1968. 30 p.

2715 HOWLAND, Carl Leroy, 1881-
Manual of missions; with an introd. by Bishop Wilson T. Hogue. New York, Revell, 1913. 176 p.

2716 LAMSON, Byron Samuel, 1901-
Lights in the world; Free Methodist missions at work. Winona Lake, Ind., General Missionary Board, Free Methodist Church, 1951. 220 p.

2717 ROOT, Helen Isabel, 1873-1945.
A corn of wheat. Winona Lake, Ind., Light and Life Press, 1943.

2718 WINSLOW, Carolyn (Van Valin)
Tomorrow. Winona Lake, Ind., Young People's Missionary Society, 1945. 123 p.

-- --HISTORY

2719 BURRITT, Carrie Turrell
The story of fifty years. Winona Lake, Ind., Light and Life Press, 1935. 213 p.

2720 ENCYCLOPEDIA OF modern Christian missions; the agencies. Burton L. Goddard, ed.... Camden, N.J., T. Nelson, 1967. xix, 743 p.
"Free Methodist Church of North America, General Missionary Board," by Byron S. Lamson: p. 289-292; and "Free Methodist World Fellowship," by Harold H. Ryckman: p. 292.

2721 LAMSON, Byron Samuel, 1901-
Venture! The Frontiers of Free Methodism. Winona Lake, Ind., Light and Life Press, 1960. 287 p.

--PASTORAL THEOLOGY

2722 HOGUE, Wilson Thomas, bp., 1852-1920.
A hand-book of homiletics and pastoral theology. 2d ed. Chicago, Free Methodist Publishing House, 1914. vi, 9-454 p.

--PERIODICALS

2723 CANADIAN FREE Methodist Herald. 1- , 1922- . Moose Jaw, Sask., Trenton, Ont., Stirling, Ont.

2724 CHRISTIAN MINISTER. 1- , 1949-1958. Winona Lake, Ind.

2725 EARNEST CHRISTIAN and Golden Rule; devoted to the promotion of experimental and practical piety. 1-58, no. 6, 1860-Dec. 1889. Buffalo, Rochester.

2726 GOSPEL FLAME. 1- , Sept. 1885-18??. Aquilla, Tex.

2727 LIGHT AND Life. 1- , 1868- . Chicago; New York; Aurora, Ill.; Sycamore, Ill.; Winona Lake, Ind.
Jan. 1868-June 1970 as Free Methodist.

2728 MISSIONARY TIDINGS. 1- , 1897- . Chicago; Winona Lake, Ind., Woman's Missionary Society of the Free Methodist Church.

2729 NEWS AND Views. 1- , 1962- . Winona Lake, Ind., Free Methodist World Fellowship.

2730 REACHOUT. 1- , 1942- . Winona Lake, Ind., Light and Life Press.
19??-197? as Teen Time.

2731 REPAIRER. 1- , 1895-191?. Atlanta, Ga.

2732 SALVATION TELEPHONE. 1, Jan.-Apr. 1885. Aquilla, Tex.
Jan. 1885 as Salvation News.

2733 YOUTH IN Action. 1- , 1941- . Winona Lake, Ind.

II. 1. Christian Holiness Association

--POLEMICAL WORKS

-- --CATHOLICISM

2734 PEARSON, Benjamin Harold, 1893-
The monk who lived again; a tale of South America. Winona Lake, Ind., Light and Life Press, 1940. 185 p.

--RELATIONS

-- --WESLEYAN METHODIST CHURCH

2735 JOINT COMMISSION of the Free Methodist and Wesleyan Methodist Churches.
Proposed discipline for the United Wesleyan Methodist Church. n.p., 1955. 122 p.

--RELIGIOUS EDUCATION

2736 ARNOLD'S COMMENTARY on the International Sunday
school lessons, uniform series. Chicago, Winona Lake, Ind., Light and Life Press [etc.]. Annual.
Began publication in 1895?
Title varies: 18??-1918, Arnold's practical Sabbath school commentary on the International lessons; 1919-1935, Arnold's practical Sunday school lesson commentary on the International lessons, improved uniform series (varies); 1936-1957, Arnold's practical commentary on the International Sunday school lessons, uniform series (varies).

2737 JOY, Donald Marvin, 1928-
"The effects of the value-oriented instruction in the church and in the home." Unpublished dissertation, Indiana University, 1969. 150ℓ.

2738 JOY, Donald Marvin, 1928-
Meaningful learning in the church. Winona Lake, Ind., Light and Life Press, 1969. 168 p.

2739 OLMSTEAD, William Backus, 1862-1941.
Handbook for Sunday-school workers; introd. by Rev. J.T. Logan. Chicago, W.B. Rose, 1907. 206 p.

--SERMONS

2740 BAKER, Harold Edwin, 1896-
Sparks from the anvil of truth. East Liverpool, Ohio, 1944. 175 p.

2741 BOYD, Myron F., bp., 1908-
To tell the world; thirty radio messages by Myron F. Boyd, speaker and director, The Light and Life Hour. Winona Lake, Ind., Light and Life Hour, 1964. 196 p. Biographical sketch by C. Dorr Demaray.

2742 LINCICOME, Forman, 1880-
A lot in Sodom. Atlanta, Repairer Publishing Co., 1932. 32 p.

2743 WHITCOMB, A. L.
Emmanuel and stepping stones to union with God. Winona Lake, Ind., Light and Life Press, n.d. 93 p.

--SOCIAL AND POLITICAL CRITICISM

2744 WATSON, Charles Hoyt, 1888-
... The employer, the wage earner, and the law of love. Lawrence, University of Kansas, 1917. 31 p. (Hattie Elizabeth Lewis Memorial Essays in Applied Christianity. 1st prize, 1917)

2745 WATSON, Claude A., 1885-
Repeal has succeeded. Winona Lake, Ind., Light and Life Press, 1945. 131 p.

--WORK WITH YOUTH

2746 JOY, Donald Marvin, 1928-
"A survey and analysis of the experiences, attitudes, and problems of senior high youth of the Free Methodist Church." Unpublished M.A. thesis, Southern Methodist University, 1960. ix, 123ℓ.

2747 MARSTON, Leslie Ray, bp., 1894-
Youth speaks. Winona Lake, Ind., Light and Life Press, 1939. 206 p.

--AFRICA

2748 ANDERSON, August Magnus, 1878-
African jungle. Anderson, Ind., Gospel Trumpet Co., 1928. 192 p.

2749 ANDERSON, August Magnus, 1878-
Nkosi; story of an African chief's son. Anderson, Ind. Warner Press, 1938. 160 p.

II. 1. Christian Holiness Association 323

2750 ANDERSON, August Magnus, 1878-
Ukanya; life of an African girl. Anderson, Ind., Anderson, Ind., Warner Press, 1931. 118 p.

2751 BRODHEAD, Chloe Anna (Sanford), -1927.
Our Free Methodist missions in Africa, to April, 1907. Pittsburgh, Aldine Printing Co., 1908. 77 p.

2752 GHORMLEY, Newton Baxter, -1940.
Land of the heart of Livingstone. Chicago, Free Methodist Publishing House, 1920.

--ALBERTA

2753 MANN, William Edward
Sect, cult, and church in Alberta. Toronto, University of Toronto Press, 1955. xiii, 166 p.
Includes description of the Free Methodists.

--CANADA

2754 ...AN ACT to incorporate The Free Methodist Church in Canada. Ottawa, Queen's Printer and Controller of Stationery, 1959. Cover-title, 17 p.

2755 SIGSWORTH, John Wilkins
The battle was the Lord's; a history of the Free Methodist Church in Canada. Oshawa, Ont., Sage Publishers, 1960. 301 p.

--DOMINICAN REPUBLIC

2756 JOHNSON, Pearl (Vennard)
Our neighbors the Dominicans. Winona Lake, Ind., Woman's Missionary Society, Free Methodist Church, 1942. 142 p.

--FORMOSA

2757 FREE METHODIST Church of North America. Woman's Missionary Society.
Entering the open door in Formosa. Winona Lake, Ind., Light and Life Press, 1956. 96 p.

--ILLINOIS

2758 TERRILL, Joseph Goodwin, -1895.
The St. Charles Camp Meeting. Chicago, T.B. Arnold,

1883.

--INDIA

2759 WARD, Ernest F., -1938.
Echoes from Bharatkhand, by Ernest F. Ward, with additional chapters by Mrs. Phebe E. Ward; introd. by Rev. Walter A. Sellew. Chicago, Free Methodist Publishing House, 1908. 174 p.

--JAPAN

2760 FREE METHODIST Church of North America. Woman's Missionary Society.
The living faith in Japan. Winona Lake, Ind., Light and Life Press, 1957. 96 p.

2761 ENCYCLOPEDIA OF modern Christian missions; the agencies. Burton L. Goddard, ed.... Camden, N.J., T. Nelson, 1967. xix, 743 p.
"Nippon Jiyu Mesojisuto Kyodan (Japan Free Methodist Church)": p. 488.

2762 KLEIN, Mattias
By Nippon's lotus ponds; pen pictures of real Japan. New York, Revell, 1914. 228 p.

--PANAMA

2763 PEARSON, Benjamin Harold, 1893-
Off to Panama!; a true adventure story of the opening doors for Christian missions in Panama. Los Angeles, Free Tract Society, 1935. 126 p.

--PARAGUAY

2764 THOMPSON, William Ralph, 1910-
"Factors in the establishing of a Free Methodist training school in Paraguay." S.T.B. thesis, Biblical Seminary in New York, 1950.

--PHILIPPINE ISLANDS

2765 FREE METHODIST Church of North America. Woman's Missionary Society.
Lighting the Philippine frontier. Presented by Free Methodist missionaries in the Philippines; editors: Ruby

II. 1. Christian Holiness Association

Schlosser and Gertrude H. Groesbeck. Winona Lake, Ind., Light and Life Press, 1957. 96 p.

HOLINESS METHODIST CHURCH (1900-   )

[1900-19?? as Lumber River Mission Conference of the Holiness Methodist Church; 19??-present as Lumber River Conference of the Holiness Methodist Church; formerly also as Lumber River Mission]

Organized in 1900 as the Lumber River Mission Conference of the Holiness Methodist Church (later re-named the Lumber River Annual Conference), this North Carolina group started as a home missionary movement devoted to spreading scriptural holiness. Unrelated to the North Dakota movement by the same name, the churches meet annually in a conference presided over by a bishop. Pastoral tenure is not limited. In 1959 membership in the seven congregations stood at 360, about half of the total twenty-five years earlier. The Lumber River group has little contact with other holiness groups.

2766   CLARK, Elmer Talmage, 1886-1966.
       The small sects in America. Rev. ed. New York, Abingdon Press, c1965. 256 p.
       Account of Holiness Methodist Church: p. 64.

2767   MEAD, Frank Spencer, 1898-
       Handbook of denominations in the United States. New 5th ed. Nashville, Abingdon Press, c1970. 265 p.
       Account of Holiness Methodist Church (North Carolina): p. 150.

2768   SCHAFF, Philip, 1819-1893.
       New Schaff-Herzog encyclopedia of religious knowledge.... S. M. Jackson, editor-in-chief. New York, Funk, 1908-1912. 12 v.
       "Lumber River Mission," by E. M. Bliss: v. 7, p. 383.

HOLINESS METHODIST CHURCH (1911-1969)

[1911-1920 as Northwestern Holiness Association]

A product of the Northwestern Holiness Association, an auxiliary of the National Holiness Association formed in 1911, the Holiness Methodist Church provided a home for sanctified believers uncomfortable in the Methodist Episcopal Church. Organizing as a church in 1920, the group consisted of small holiness bands scattered from Minneapolis to the West Coast. Aggressively evangelistic in 1948, the Holiness Methodists began missionary activity in

Bolivia. At headquarters in Minneapolis the church published The Holiness Methodist Advocate and operated the Holiness Methodist School of Theology. In addition, the twenty congregations of the group sponsored annual camp meetings in Minnesota, North Dakota and Washington. When it merged with the Evangelical Church of North America in 1969, the Holiness Methodist Church claimed about a thousand members in the United States and about six hundred in Bolivia. It cooperated with programs of the National Holiness Association.

2769 HOLINESS METHODIST Church.
Discipline; ed. by Committee on Discipline, rev. at the General Council of 1956. Minneapolis, Holiness Methodist Publishing Board, 1956.

2770 MEAD, Frank Spencer, 1898-
Handbook of denominations in the United States. New 5th ed. Nashville, Abingdon Press, c1970. 265 p.
Account of Holiness Methodist Church (North Dakota): p. 150.

--PERIODICALS

2771 HOLINESS METHODIST Advocate. 1- , 19??-1969? Minneapolis, Minn.

--BOLIVIA

2772 ENCYCLOPEDIA OF modern Christian missions; the agencies. Burton L. Goddard, ed.... Camden, N.J., T. Nelson, 1967. xix, 743 p.
"The Holiness Methodist Church, the Bolivian Holiness Mission,": by Henry C. Kurtz: p. 318.

HOLINESS METHODISTS (1913-19??)

Originating in a defection from the Wesleyan Methodist Connection (or Church), the group was organized at Forest City, North Carolina, by the Rev. H.C. Sisk and four others in 1913. In 1949 the Holiness Methodists claimed six hundred members in four congregations. No recent data are available.

2773 CLARK, Elmer Talmage, 1886-1966.
The small sects in America. Rev. ed. New York, Abingdon Press, c1965. 256 p.
Account of the Holiness Methodists: p. 65.

II. 1. Christian Holiness Association

METHODIST CHURCH (United States) (1939-1968)

Formed by the 1939 reunion of the Methodist Episcopal Church, the Methodist Episcopal Church, South, and the Methodist Protestant Church, the new Methodist Church was a product of compromise concerning governmental structure. Enjoying a numerical increase during its 29 years of existence of more than four million, the united body acted against its holiness minority in almost every area of controversy. Traditional modes of theological discourse and evangelistic outreach were practically abandoned, and social activism replaced missionary fervor as a collective ideal. Higher educational requirements transformed the clergy, often forcing ministers with little schooling into less desirable pulpits and discouraging poorly educated youths from seeking ordination. Although pockets of holiness sympathy remained in western Pennsylvania, Michigan, Iowa, Kentucky and Georgia, the perfectionist element within the church steadily declined. Of the independent colleges such as John Fletcher, Taylor, Ohio Northern and Asbury, which had championed the cause of Methodist loyalism in the early twentieth century, only Asbury continued to do so at mid-century. While annual camp meetings serving largely Methodist constituencies continued at Red Rock, Minn., Eaton Rapids, Mich., Wilmore, Ky., and Indian Springs, Ga., the exodus of holiness members to distinctly holiness churches continued. To many, the 1968 union of the Methodist Church and the Evangelical United Brethren Church to form the United Methodist Church merely emphasized trends long present in the parent groups.

2774 CAMERON, Richard Morgan, 1898-
Methodism and society in historical perspective, ed. by the Board of Social and Economic Relations of the Methodist Church. New York, Abingdon Press, 1961. 349 p. (Methodism and Society, vol. 1)

2775 GARBER, Paul Neff, 1899-
The Methodists are one people. Nashville, Tenn., Cokesbury Press, 1939. 144 p.

2776 HARKNESS, Georgia Elma, 1891-
The Methodist Church in social thought and action. New York, Abingdon Press, 1964. 172 p.

2777 JONES, Charles Edwin, 1932-
"Perfectionist persuasion: a social profile of the National Holiness Movement within American Methodism, 1867-1936." Unpublished Ph.D. dissertation, University of Wisconsin, 1968. 669ℓ.

2778 MacKENZIE, Kenneth M.
The robe and the sword; the Methodist church and the rise of American imperialism. Washington, Public Affairs

Press, 1961. 128 p.

2779 MUELDER, Walter George, 1907-
Methodism and society in the twentieth century, ed. by the Board of Social and Economic Relations of the Methodist Church. New York, Abingdon Press, 1961. 446 p. (Methodism and society, vol. 2)

2780 SCHILLING, Sylvester Paul, 1904-
Methodism and society in theological perspective, ed. by the Board of Social and Economic Relations of the Methodist Church. New York, Abingdon Press, 1960. 318 p. (Methodism and society, vol. 3)

--CONFERENCES. NORTH DAKOTA

2781 METHODIST CHURCH (United States). Conferences. North Dakota. Historical Society.
History of the Methodist Church in North Dakota and Dakota Territory, written by members of the North Dakota Conference Historical Society. Nashville, Tenn., 1960. 256 p.

--CAMP MEETINGS

2782 BAUGH, Stanley T.
Camp grounds and camp meetings in the Little Rock Conference, the Methodist Church. Little Rock, Ark., Epworth Press, 1953? 48 p.

--DOCTRINAL AND CONTROVERSIAL WORKS

2783 JOY, Donald Marvin, 1928-
The Holy Spirit and you. New York, Abingdon Press, 1965. 160 p.

2784 REED, Marshall Russell, bp., 1891-
Achieving Christian perfection. Nashville, Methodist Evangelistic Materials, 1962. 63 p.

2785 SANGSTER, William Edwin, 1900-1960.
The path to perfection; an examination and restatement of John Wesley's doctrine of Christian perfection. New York, Abingdon-Cokesbury Press, 1943. 214 p.

2786 SANGSTER, William Edwin, 1900-1960.
The pure in heart; a study in Christian sanctity. Nashville, Abingdon Press, 1954. 254 p.

II. 1. Christian Holiness Association 329

2787 SPANN, John Richard, 1891- , ed.
Fruits of faith. New York, Abingdon-Cokesbury Press, 1950. 240 p.
Lectures of 18 scholars at the 30th Annual Conference on Ministerial Training, Evanston, Ill., rev. and adapted to book form.

2788 STARKEY, Lycurgus Monroe
The work of the Holy Spirit, a study in Wesleyan theology. New York, Abingdon Press, 1962. 176 p.

--EVANGELISTIC WORK

2789 COLEMAN, Robert Emerson, 1928-
Dry bones can live again; revival in the local church. Old Tappan, N.J., Fleming H. Revell Co., 1969. 127 p.

2790 COLEMAN, Robert Emerson, 1928-
The master plan of evangelism; introd. by Paul S. Rees. Old Tappan, N.J., Fleming H. Revell Co., 1963. 126 p.

--GOVERNMENT

2791 HARMON, Nolan Bailey, 1892-
The organization of the Methodist Church: historic development and present working structure. 2d rev. ed. Nashville, Tenn., Methodist Publishing House, 1962. 287 p.

--HISTORY

2792 FERGUSON, Charles Wright, 1901-
Organizing to beat the devil: Methodists and the making of America. Garden City, N.Y., Doubleday, 1971. x, 466 p.

2793 THE HISTORY of American Methodism. New York, Abingdon Press, 1964. 3 v.

2794 HUGHES, Edwin Holt, bp., 1866-1950.
I was made a minister, an autobiography. New York, Abingdon, Cokesbury, 1943. vii, 328 p.
Methodist bishop somewhat critical of the Holiness Movement.

2795 "METHODISTS IN 1899," Independent, LII (Jan. 4, 1900), 37-42.

2796 SWEET, William Warren, 1881-1959.
Men of zeal; the romance of American Methodist beginnings. New York, Abingdon Press, 1935. 208 p.

2797 SWEET, William Warren, 1881-1959.
Methodism in American history. Rev. of 1953. New York, Abingdon Press, 1961. 472 p.

2798 TUTTLE, Alexander Harrison, 1844-1932.
"Methodism fifty years ago and now," Methodist Review, XCIX (Sept. 1917), 673-688.
Concerned with changes east of the Alleghanies.

-- --SOURCES

2799 SWEET, William Warren, 1881-1959.
The Methodists, a collection of source materials. Chicago, University of Chicago, 1946. 800 p. (His Religion on the American frontier, 1783-1840, vol. 4)

--HISTORY OF DOCTRINES

2800 PETERS, John Leland
Christian perfection and American Methodism. New York, Abingdon Press, 1956. 252 p.

2801 PETERS, John Leland
"The development of the Wesleyan doctrine of Christian perfection in American Methodism in the nineteenth century.' Unpublished Ph.D. dissertation, Yale University, 1950.

2802 SCOTT, Leland H.
"Methodist theology in America in the nineteenth century." Unpublished Ph.D. dissertation, Yale University, 1955.

2803 SCOTT, Leland H.
"Methodist theology in America in the nineteenth century," Religion in Life, XXV (Winter 1955-1956), 87-98.

2804 SHIPLEY, David Clark, 1907-
"Development of theology in American Methodism in the nineteenth century," London Quarterly and Holborn Review, CLXXXIV (July 1959), 249-264.

2805 THOMPSON, Claude Holmes
"The witness of American Methodism to the historical doctrine of Christian perfection." Unpublished Ph.D. dissertation, Drew University, 1949.

II. 1. Christian Holiness Association   331

2806   WILSON, George Washington, 1853-1929.
            Methodist theology vs. Methodist theologians; a review
        of several Methodist writers ... with an introd. by Bishop
        W. F. Mallalieu.... Cincinnati, Jennings & Pye, 1904.
        356 p.

              --HYMNS

2807   COKESBURY WORSHIP hymnal. Baltimore, Methodist Pub-
            lishing House, 1938. Unpaged.
            With music.

2808   METHODIST CHURCH (United States).
            The Methodist hymnal; official hymnal of The Methodist
        Church. Baltimore, Methodist Publishing House, 1939.
        695 p.
            With music.

2809   METHODIST CHURCH (United States).
            The Methodist hymnal; official hymnal of the Methodist
        Church. Nashville, Methodist Publishing House, 1966.
        Unpaged.
            With music.

              -- --HISTORY AND CRITICISM

2810   GEALY, Fred Daniel
            Companion to the Hymnal; a handbook to the 1964 Me-
        thodist hymnal. [Texts: Fred D. Gealy. Tunes: Austin
        C. Lovelace. Biographies: Carlton R. Young. General
        editor: Emory Stevens Bucke]. Nashville, Abingdon Press,
        1970. 766 p.

2811   McCUTCHAN, Robert Guy, 1877-
            Our hymnody; a manual of The Methodist Hymnal, with
        an index of scriptural texts by Fitzgerald Sale Parker. 2d
        ed. New York, Abingdon Press, 1937. 619 p.

2812   WASHBURN, Charles Campbell, 1868-
            Hymn stories. Nashville, Publishing House Methodist
        Episcopal Church, South, Whitmore & Smith, agents, c1935.
        80 p.
            Stories of hymns selected from The Methodist Hymnal,
        official hymnal of the Methodist Episcopal Church, the Me-
        thodist Episcopal Church, South, and the Methodist Protes-
        tant Church.

2813   YOUNG, Carlton Raymond, 1926-
            An introduction to the new Methodist Hymnal; ed. by
        V. Earle Copes. Nashville, Graded Press, Methodist Pub-
        lishing House, 1966. 31 p.

--LITURGY AND RITUAL

2814 METHODIST CHURCH (United States). General Conference. Commission on Worship.
The book of worship for church and home, with orders for the administration of the sacraments and other rites and ceremonies according to the use of the Methodist Church. Nashville, Methodist Publishing House, 1944. 549 p.
Cover title: Report [of the] Commission on Rituals and Orders of Worship [to the] General Conference [of] the Methodist Church, 1944.

2815 METHODIST CHURCH (United States). General Conference. Commission on Worship.
The book of worship for church and home, with orders for the administration of the sacraments and other rites and ceremonies according to the use of the Methodist Church, for voluntary and optional use. Nashville, Methodist Publishing House, 1945. xii, 562 p.
Prepared by the commission under its earlier variant name: Commission on Ritual and Orders of Worship.

2816 METHODIST CHURCH (United States). General Conference. Commission on Worship.
The book of worship for church and home, with orders of worship, services for the administration of the sacraments, and aids to worship according to the usages of the Methodist Church. Nashville, Methodist Publishing House, 1964. xviii, 437 p.
"Report of the Commission on Worship to the General Conference of the Methodist Church, 1964."

2817 METHODIST CHURCH (United States). General Conference. Commission on Worship.
The book of worship for church and home, with orders of worship, services for the administration of the sacraments, and aids to worship according to the usages of the Methodist Church. Nashville, Methodist Publishing House, 1965. 423 p.
"Adopted by the General Conference of 1964."

2818 COMPANION TO The book of worship. Edited for the Commission on Worship of the United Methodist Church by William F. Dunkle, Jr., and Joseph D. Quillian, Jr. Nashville, Abingdon Press, 1970. 207 p.

--MISSIONS

-- --HISTORY

2819 ENCYCLOPEDIA OF modern Christian missions; the agencies. Burton L. Goddard, ed.... Camden, N.J., T.

II. 1. Christian Holiness Association 333

Nelson, 1967. xix, 743 p.
"The Methodist Church, Board of Missions of," by J. Tremayne Copplestone: p. 407-418.

2820 BARCLAY, Wade Crawford, 1874-
History of Methodist Missions. New York, Board of Missions and Church Extension of the Methodist Church, 1949-1957. 3 v.

--RELIGIOUS EDUCATION

2821 HIRSCH, Helen Kathryn (Hubbard)
"A survey of the use of theological terminology with reference to Jesus Christ in selected church school curricula for adults," by Helen Kathryn Hubbard. Unpublished D.Ed. dissertation, University of Pittsburgh, 1966. 234ℓ.

--STATISTICS

2822 U.S. BUREAU of the Census.
... Census of religious bodies, 1926; Methodist bodies: statistics, denominational history, doctrine, and organization; consolidated report.... Washington, U.S. Government Printing Office, 1929. 137 p.

--ARIZONA

2823 JERVEY, Edward Drewry, 1929-
The history of Methodism in Southern California and Arizona. Nashville, Printed by the Parthenon Press for the Historical Society of the Southern California-Arizona Conference, 1960. 247 p.
Thesis (Ph.D.)--Boston University, 1958.

--CALIFORNIA

2824 JERVEY, Edward Drewry, 1929-
The history of Methodism in Southern California and Arizona. Nashville, Printed by the Parthenon Press for the Historical Society of the Southern California-Arizona Conference, 1960. 247 p.
Thesis (Ph.D.)--Boston University, 1958.

--VIRGINIA

2825 SWEET, William Warren, 1881-1959.
Virginia Methodism, a history. Richmond, Va., Whittet & Shepperson, 1955. xviii, 427 p.

METHODIST EPISCOPAL CHURCH (1784-1939)

This church, which until 1845 was the main body of American Methodism and from 1845 to 1939 the main Methodist body in the Northern states, was led during most of the nineteenth century by bishops favorable to the perfectionism latent in Wesleyan theology. At mid-century holiness leaders such as Dr. and Mrs. Walter Palmer, George Hughes, J.S. Inskip and William McDonald, were held in high regard in the church and had intimate friends among the bishops. Bishops endorsed and spoke at holiness meetings and holiness men held leading urban pulpits. By the turn of the century the situation had changed. The itineracy (periodic pastoral rotation) made it possible for a bishop unfriendly to holiness promoters to assign them to undesirable churches. In addition the death of the old respected holiness leaders and increasing opposition from the younger denominational leaders caused an ever increasing number of young holiness ministers and people to join new perfectionist groups such as the Church of the Nazarene and the Pilgrim Holiness Church. Membership continued to climb, but at a much diminished rate (from three million in 1906 to a little over four million 20 years later, only to drop to three and a half million in 1936). Although the 1939 re-union of the Methodist Episcopal Church, the Methodist Episcopal Church, South, and the Methodist Protestant Church was heralded as a victory over sectionalism, the declining membership of all three denominations before the merger apparently prompted their willingness to consolidate.

2826 METHODIST EPISCOPAL Church.
Doctrines and discipline, 1785-1936. Philadelphia, New York, Cincinnati, 1785-1936. 46 v.
Quadrennial: 1808-1936.

--CONFERENCES. NORTH DAKOTA

2827 DANFORD, Samuel Alexander, 1865-
Report for sixth year for Bismarck District of North Dakota Conference, M.E. Church. Bismarck, N.D., 1915.

--ANECDOTES, REMINISCENCES, SATIRE, ETC.

2828 ASBURY, Francis, bp., 1745-1816.
Journal ... from August 7, 1771, to December 7, 1815. New York, N. Bangs and T. Mason, 1821. 3 v.

2829 ASBURY, Francis, bp., 1745-1816.
Journal and letters. Elmer T. Clark, editor-in-chief, J. Manning Potts [and] Jacob S. Payton. London, Epworth Press; Nashville, Abingdon Press, 1958. 3 v.

Contents.--1. The journal, 1771 to 1793.--2. The journal, 1794 to 1816.--3. The letters.

2830 FLOWERS, Sumpter Lee, 1881-1945.
 The circuit rider; or, Suffering for Christ's sake. Olivet-Georgetown, Ill., Flowers Publishing Co., 1912. 183 p.
 Fictionalized autobiography.

2831 PECK, George, 1797-1876.
 Sketches and incidents; or, A budget from the saddle-bags of a superannuated itinerant. New York, Pub. by G. Lane & P. P. Sandford, for the Methodist Episcopal Church, J. Collard, printer, 1844-1845. 2 v.
 On t.-p. of vol. II: George Peck, editor. Vol. 1 pub. anonymously. Also attributed to Abel Stevens. cf. Allibone, Archibald, and Drake.

2832 SMITH, William C., 1818-1891, comp.
 Sketch book; or, Miscellaneous anecdotes, illustrating a variety of topics proper to pulpit and platform. New York, Carlton & Porter, 1860. 352 p.

--APOLOGETIC WORKS

2833 WISE, Daniel, 1813-1898.
 Popular objections to Methodism considered and answered; or, The convert's counsellor respecting his church relations, with reasons why Methodist converts should join a Methodist church. Boston, J.P. Magee, 1856. 256 p.

--BIOGRAPHY

2834 SMITH, William C., 1818-1891.
 Pillars in the temple; or, Sketches of deceased laymen of the Methodist Episcopal Church, distinguished as examples of piety and usefulness. Chronologically arranged. With an introd. by C.C. North. New York, Carlton & Lanahan; San Francisco, E. Thomas, etc., etc., 1872. 366 p.

2835 SMITH, William C., 1818-1891.
 Pillars in the temple; or, Sketches of deceased laymen of the Methodist Episcopal Church, distinguished as examples of piety and usefulness. Chronologically arranged. With an introd. by C.C. North. New York, Nelson & Phillips, 1872. 366 p.

--CAMP MEETINGS

2836 CAMP MEETING review; containing the proceedings of a camp meeting, and a confutation of the arguments which are produced in favor of the same, also showing that they are not for the good of society, written by a visiter [sic] to one of the meetings, also poems on other subjects. n.p., 1824. 30 p.

2837 FOSTER, John Onesimus, 1833-1920.
"The first Des Plaines camp meeting, Des Plaines, Ill., August, 1860," Journal of the Illinois State Historical Society, XXIV (Jan. 1932).

2838 GRIMES, John Franklin
The romance of the American camp meeting; golden jubilee etchings of the Lancaster Assembly and camp meeting, 1872-1922, illustrative of the camp meeting as an American institution. Cincinnati, Printed for the Semi-centennial Commission by the Caxton Press, 1922. 196 p.

2839 JOHNSON, Charles Albert, 1916-
"The frontier camp meeting: Methodist harvest time, 1800-1840." Unpublished Ph.D. dissertation, Northwestern University, 1951.

2840 JOHNSON, Charles Albert, 1916-
The frontier camp meeting; religion's harvest time. Dallas, Southern Methodist University Press, 1955. ix, 325 p.
Based on thesis (Ph.D.)--Northwestern University, 1951.

2841 JORCHOW, Merrill E.
"Red Rock: frontier Methodist camp meeting," Minnesota History, XXXI (June 1950), 79-92.

2842 LAKE BLUFF Camp Meeting Association, Lake Bluff, Ill.
Articles of association and by-laws of the Lake Bluff Camp Meeting Association, Lake Bluff, Illinois, incorporated 1875; principal office: Chicago, Illinois. Chicago, J.A. Van Fleet, 1875? 10 p.

2843 MEAD, Amos P., 1829-1886.
Manna in the wilderness; or, The grove and its altar, offerings, and thrilling incidents, containing a history of the origin and rise of camp meetings, and a defense of this remarkable means of grace; also an account of the Wyoming Camp Meeting, together with sketches of sermons and preachers. With an introd. by Rev. J.B. Wakeley, of New York. 3d ed. Philadelphia, Perkinpine & Higgins, 1860. 417 p.

II. 1. Christian Holiness Association

2844 OCEAN GROVE Camp Meeting Association of the Methodist Episcopal Church.
Ocean Grove; its origin and progress, as shown in the annual reports presented by the president, to which are added other papers of interest, including list of lot-holders, charter, by-laws, &c., &c., comp. by Rev. E. H. Stokes. Ocean Grove, N.J., 1874. 88 p.

2845 OCEAN GROVE Camp Meeting Association of the Methodist Episcopal Church.
City by the sea; fifth annual report of the president [E. H. Stokes] of Ocean Grove Camp Meeting Assc'n. Ocean Grove, N.J., 1874. 24 p.

2846 OCEAN GROVE Camp Meeting Association of the Methodist Episcopal Church.
Summer by the sea; sixth annual report and the historical address of the president [E. H. Stokes] of Ocean Grove Camp Meeting Assc'n. Ocean Grove, N.J., 1875. 45 p.

2847 OCEAN GROVE Camp Meeting Association of the Methodist Episcopal Church.
Centennial by the sea; seventh annual report of the president [E. H. Stokes] of Ocean Grove Camp Meeting Assc'n. Ocean Grove, N.J., 1876. 40 p.

2848 OCEAN GROVE Camp Meeting Association of the Methodist Episcopal Church.
Service by the sea; ninth annual report of the president [E. H. Stokes] of the Ocean Grove Camp-Meeting Association of the Methodist Episcopal Church. Ocean Grove, N.J., 1878. 39 p.

2849 OCEAN GROVE Camp Meeting Association of the Methodist Episcopal Church.
Golden ascent by the sea; twenty-ninth annual report of the Ocean Grove Camp Meeting Association of the Methodist Episcopal Church [Bishop J. N. Fitzgerald, president]. Ocean Grove, N.J., 1898. 71 p.

2850 OCEAN GROVE Camp Meeting Association of the Methodist Episcopal Church.
Upon the sands at Ocean Grove; forty-ninth annual report of the Ocean Grove Camp Meeting Association of the Methodist Episcopal Church. Ocean Grove, N.J., 1918. Unpaged.

2851 OCEAN GROVE Times, Ocean Grove, N.J.
...History of Ocean Grove, compiled in the year of its seventy-fifth anniversary by the Ocean Grove Times, in co-operation with the Ocean Grove Camp Meeting Association. Ocean Grove, N.J., 1944. 110 p.

At head of title: Diamond jubilee, 1869-1944.

2852 [PORTER, James], 1808-1888.
An essay on camp-meetings, by the author of "The True Evangelist." New York, Lane & Scott, 1849. 86 p.

--CATECHISMS AND CREEDS

2853 NAST, William, 1807-1899.
The larger catechism. Rev. ed. Cincinnati, Jennings and Pye; New York, Eaton and Mains, 1892, c1869. 149 p.

--CHURCH WORK

2854 JANES, Edmund Storer, bp., 1807-1876.
Address to class-leaders. New York, 1862. 46 p.

2855 WARD, William Thurman, 1871-
Variety in the prayer meeting; a manual for leaders. Introduction by Bishop William O. Shepard. New York, Methodist Book Concern, 1915. 192 p.

--CONDUCT OF LIFE

2856 ATWOOD, Anthony, 1801-1888.
The young man's way to intelligence, respectability, honor and usefulness. Philadelphia, Crolius & Gladding, 1842. 190 p.

2857 ATWOOD, Anthony, 1801-1888.
The young man's way to intelligence, respectability, honor, and usefulness. Philadelphia, J.W. Moòre, 1850. 188 p.

2858 ATWOOD, Anthony, 1801-1888.
Youth's guide to intelligence, respectability, honor and usefulness. 3d ed. Philadelphia, Methodist Book Rooms, n.d. 188 p.

2859 DAVIS, Henry Turner, 1832-
Perfect happiness. Cincinnati, Curts & Jennings, 1899. 224 p.

2860 McCARTY, Joseph Hendrickson, 1830-1897.
The black horse and carryall; or, Outdoor sights and indoor thoughts. Cincinnati, Jennings & Pye; New York, Eaton & Mains, 1873. 314 p.

II. 1. Christian Holiness Association

2861 PECK, Jesse Truesdell, bp., 1811-1883.
The true woman; or, Life and happiness at home and abroad. New York, Carlton & Porter, 1857. 400 p.

2862 SCHUH, Charles Gottlob, 1856-
God's treasure-house unlocked; authentic accounts of providential assistance, and how it may be obtained by all, original and comp. by Charles G. Schuh. Cincinnati, Cranston & Stowe; New York, Phillips & Hunt, 1887. 480 p.

2863 SCHUH, Charles Gottlob, 1856- , comp.
Die macht des gläubigen gebetes; eine sammlung von wohl-verbürgten gebt-erhörungen.... Nebst abhandlungen über die verschiedenen formen, bestandtheiele und geheimnisse des gläubigen gebets. Cincinnati, Gedrucht fur den autor von Walden & Stowe, 1883. 272 p.

2864 VINCENT, John Heyl, bp., 1832-1920.
Better not; a discussion of certain social customs. New York, Funk & Wagnalls Co., 1888. 86 p.

2865 WINCHESTER, Charles Wesley, 1843-
A temperance service for use in churches and Sunday schools. Rochester, N.Y., Whybrew & Ripley, 1882. 8 p.

2866 WISE, Daniel, 1813-1898.
Bridal greetings. New York, Hunt & Eaton; Cincinnati, Cranston & Curts, 1894. 144 p.

2867 WISE, Daniel, 1813-1898.
The path of life; or, Sketches of the way to glory and immortality, a help for young Christians. New York, Carlton & Porter, 186?. 246 p.

2868 WISE, Daniel, 1813-1898.
A saintly and successful worker; or, Sixty years a class-leader: a biographical study, including incidental discussions of the theory and experience of perfect love, of the class and class-meeting, and of the art of winning souls, suggested by the experiences and labors of William Carvosso. Cincinnati, Hitchcock & Walden; New York, Phillips & Hunt, 1879. 276 p.

-- --AUTHORITATIVE SOURCES

2869 IMITATIO CHRISTI. English.
An extract of the Christian's pattern; or, A treatise on the imitation of Christ, written in Latin by Thomas à Kempis. By Rev. John Wesley, A.M. New York, Carlton & Porter, 1857. 196 p.

2870   LAW, William, 1686-1761.
       An extract from Mr. Law's Serious call to a holy life, by the Rev. John Wesley, A.M. Philadelphia, Printed by Solomon W. Conrad, 1803. 216 p.

   --CRITICAL WORKS

2871   BEEBE, Theodore Eaton
       Hatching chickens for the hawks. Long Beach, Calif., T.E. Beebe, 1920. 59 p.
       "Poems in this book written by F.M. Lehman."

2872   CROOKS, George Richard, 1822-1897, ed.
       The present state of the Methodist Episcopal Church; a symposium. Syracuse, Hunt & Eaton, 1891. 96 p.

2873   HANEY, Milton Lorenzo, 1825-1922.
       Tares mixed with the wheat; a reprint of Unsaved church members, as published in The Christian Witness. Chicago, Christian Witness Co., 1910. 82 p.

2874   HUGHES, George, 1828-1904.
       Evenings with Grandfather Braddock, a veteran itinerant; showing his labors, joys, and triumphs in the Methodist itinerancy. Being an antidote to "My Grandfather Braddock." Advocating true reform, and unmasking pretended reformers in the Methodist Episcopal Church. By Rev. Frank F. Fairfield [pseud.] With an introduction, by Rev. Theophilus T. Trueman. Also a preface by Rev. Henry H. Hopeful.... Philadelphia, Published for the author, by Perkinpine & Higgins, 1859. 147 p.

2875   KULP, George B., 1845-1939.
       Battlefield of the church. Cincinnati, God's Bible School, n.d.

2876   LEE, Luther, 1800-1889.
       The debates of the General Conference of the Methodist Episcopal Church ... [and] a review of the proceedings, by Rev. Luther Lee and Rev. E. Smith. New York, 1845.

2877   MUNHALL, Leander Whitcomb, 1843-1934.
       Breakers! Methodism adrift. New York, Charles C. Cook, 1913. 215 p.

   --DEVOTIONAL LITERATURE

2878   CHADWICK, Samuel, 1860-1932.
       The path of prayer. New York, Abingdon Press, 1931. 133 p.

II. 1. Christian Holiness Association

--DOCTRINAL AND CONTROVERSIAL WORKS

2879 ACKERMAN, George Everett
Love illumined; with an introd. by Geo. T. Newcomb. Cincinnati, Curts & Jennings, 1900. 124 p.
"A few thoughts concerning Holiness, Sanctification, Perfect Love, Perfection, Purity."--p. 14.

2880 ATWOOD, Anthony, 1801-1888.
An exposure of Rev. Mr. Major's mistakes and a reply to his apology for wicked ministers in the Episcopal succession. Harrisburg, Pa., Printed by I.G. M'Kinley, 1844. 35 p.

2881 ATWOOD, Anthony, 1801-1888.
Manual on Christian baptism; or, The nature, subjects, and mode of this divine ordinance pointed out and defended. Philadelphia, Griggs & Co., 1840. 226 p.

2882 ATWOOD, Anthony, 1801-1888.
Methodism defended and prelatical succession refuted, being a reply to Tracts for the People, no. 4. Harrisburg, Pa., Printed by I.G. M'Kinley, 1843. 30 p.

2883 BALL, Ephraim, 1812-1872.
Review of a sermon on growth in grace in opposition to the Wesleyan doctrine of entire sanctification preached by A.J. Endsley, Jan. 22d, 1871 and subsequently published, by request, in the Pittsburgh Christian Advocate, by E. Ball. Canton, Ohio, Hartzell & Saxton, printers, 1871. 32 p.

2884 BANGS, Nathan, 1778-1862.
Letters on the necessity, nature, and fruits of sanctification. New York, Phillips & Hunt, 1881. 314 p.

2885 BEET, Joseph Agar, 1840-1924.
Holiness, as understood by the writers of the Bible; a Bible study. 2d ed. New York, Phillips & Hunt, 1889. 70 p.

2886 BINNEY, Amos, 1802-1878.
Binney's Theological compend, improved; containing a synopsis of the evidences, doctrines, morals, and institutions of Christianity, designed for Bible classes, theological students and young preachers, by Amos Binney and Daniel Steele. New York, Abingdon-Cokesbury Press, 1902. 195 p.

2887 BUTLER, William, 1818-1899.
The doctrine of holiness as taught in the Word of God. New York, Tract Society, n.d. 44 p.

2888   CRANE, Jonathan Townley, 1819-1880.
        Holiness, the birthright of all God's children. New York, Nelson & Phillips, 1874. 144 p.

2889   DUNN, Lewis Romaine, 1822-1898.
        Holiness to the Lord. New York, Nelson and Phillips, 1874. 219 p.

2890   DUNN, Lewis Romaine, 1822-1898.
        The Holy Spirit. New York, Bible House (W.C. Palmer), 1883.

2891   DUNN, Lewis Romaine, 1822-1898.
        A manual of holiness and review of Dr. James B. Mudge. Cincinnati, Cranston & Curts, 1895. 152 p.

2892   FLETCHER, John William, 1729-1785.
        Christian perfection: being an extract from the Rev. John Fletcher's treatise on that subject, to which is added a letter by Thomas Rutherford. New York, Published by T. Mason and G. Lane for the Methodist Episcopal Church, 1837. 141 p.
        Abridged from the author's Last Check to Antinomianism, by T. Rutherford.

2893   FLETCHER, John William, 1729-1785.
        Christian perfection: being an extract from the Rev. John Fletcher's treatise on that subject, to which is added a letter by Thomas Rutherford. New York, Published by Lane and Tippett for the Methodist Episcopal Church, 1847. 141 p.
        Abridged from the author's Last Check to Antinomianism, by T. Rutherford.

2894   FLETCHER, John William, 1729-1785.
        Christian perfection: being an extract from the Rev. John Fletcher's treatise on that subject, to which is added a letter by Thomas Rutherford. New York, Carlton and Porter, 185?. 141 p.
        Abridged from the author's Last Check to Antinomianism by T. Rutherford.

2895   FOSTER, Randolph Sinks, bp., 1820-1903.
        Christian purity; or, The heritage of faith; revised, enlarged, and adapted to later phases of the subject, with an introd. by Bishop Janes. New York, Nelson & Phillips, 1869. 364 p.

2896   FOSTER, Randolph Sinks, bp., 1820-1903.
        Nature and blessedness of Christian purity; with an introd. by Edmund S. Janes. New York, Harper, 1851. 226 p.

II. 1. Christian Holiness Association

2897 GORHAM, B. Weed
God's method with man; or, Sacred scenes along the path to heaven. Cincinnati, Hitchcock and Walden, for the author, 1879. 281 p.

2898 HUNTINGTON, DeWitt Clinton, 1830-1912.
Sin and holiness; or, What it is to be holy. Cincinnati, Curts & Jennings, 1898. 288 p.

2899 HUNTINGTON, DeWitt Clinton, 1830-1912.
What is it to be holy?; or, The theory of entire sanctification; an essay read before the Ministerial and Laymen's Association of Rochester District--East Genesee Conference. Rochester, Benton & Andrews, book and job printers, 1869. 71 p.

2900 KEEN, Samuel Ashton, 1842-1895.
Pentecostal papers; or, The gift of the Holy Ghost. Cincinnati, Cranston & Curts, 1895. 190 p.

2901 LOWREY, Asbury, 1816-1898.
"Dr. Mudge and his book," Methodist Review, LXXVII (1895), 954-959.

2902 LOWREY, Asbury, 1816-1898.
Possibilities of grace. New York, Phillips & Hunt, 1884. 472 p.

2903 LUMMUS, Aaron
Essays on holiness, in which prevailing mistakes about it, and the general want of it, are noticed. The doctrine is stated, proved, and defended, the experience and practice of it illustrated, and the subject practically applied and enforced. Boston, Conference Press, 1926. 229 p.

2904 McDONALD, William, 1820-1901.
The people's Wesley; with an introd. by Bishop W. F. Mallalieu. New York, Eaton & Mains, 1899. 62 p.
Revised and enlarged ed. published under title: The young people's Wesley.

2905 McDOUGLE, Leonidas I.
Salvation; or, The conditions of regeneration and sanctification, with an epitome of the churches' creed and the Christians chart of life. n.p., 1906. 47 p.
Reprinted from the Peninsula Methodist.

2906 MALLALIEU, Willard Francis, bp., 1828-1911.
The fullness of the blessing of the gospel of Christ. Cincinnati, Jennings and Graham; New York, Eaton and Mains, 1903. 168 p.

2907 MATTISON, Hiram, 1811-1868.
An answer to Dr. Perry's Reply to the Calm review, by H. Mattison.... New York, 1856. ix, 96 p.

2908 MERRITT, Timothy, 1775-1845, comp.
The Christian's manual; a treatise on Christian perfection, with directions for obtaining that state, comp. principally from the works of the Rev. John Wesley. New York, N. Bangs and J. Emory for the Methodist Episcopal Church, 1825. 160 p.

2909 MILEY, John, 1813-1895.
Systematic theology.... New York, Hunt & Eaton; Cincinnati, Cranston & Stowe, 1892-1894. 2 v.
Vol. II has imprint: New York, Hunt & Eaton; Cincinnati, Cranston & Curts.

2910 MUDGE, James, 1844-1918.
Growth in holiness toward perfection; or, Progressive sanctification. New York, Hunt & Eaton, 1895. 316 p.

2911 MUDGE, James, 1844-1918.
The life ecstatic. New York, American Tract Society, 1906. 223 p.

2912 MUDGE, James, 1844-1918.
The life of love. Cincinnati, Jennings & Pye; New York, Eaton & Mains, 1902. 140 p.

2913 MUDGE, James, 1844-1918.
The perfect life in experience and doctrine; a restatement, with an introd. by Rev. William F. Warren.... Cincinnati, Jennings and Graham; New York, Eaton and Mains, 1911. 311 p.

2914 MUDGE, James, 1844-1918.
The saintly calling. Cincinnati, Jennings and Graham; New York, Eaton and Mains, 1905. 260 p.

2915 MUNHALL, Leander Whitcomb, 1843-1934.
The highest critics vs. the higher critics. 3d ed., rev. and enl. New York, Eaton & Mains; Cincinnati, Curts & Jennings, 1896. 249 p.

2916 PEARSE, Mark Guy, 1842-1930.
The Christianity of Jesus, is it ours? Cincinnati, Jennings and Pye, n.d. 192 p.

2917 PEARSE, Mark Guy, 1842-1930.
The Christian's secret of holiness. Boston, Ira Bradley and Co., 1886. 272 p.

II. 1. Christian Holiness Association

2918 PEARSE, Mark Guy, 1842-1930.
Some aspects of the blessed life. London, T. Woolmer, n. d.

2919 PECK, George, 1797-1876.
The scripture doctrine of Christian perfection stated and defended, with a critical and historical examination of the controversy both ancient and modern; also practical illustrations and advices, in a series of lectures. New York, G. Lane & P. P. Sandford, 1842. 474 p.

2920 PECK, George, 1797-1876.
The Scripture doctrine of Christian perfection stated and defended, with practical illustrations and advices in a series of lectures, abridged from the author's larger work. New York, Lane and Tippett, 1845. 332 p.

2921 PECK, Jesse Truesdell, bp., 1811-1883.
The central idea of Christianity. New York, Carlton and Porter, 1857. 389 p.

2922 PECK, Jesse Truesdell, bp., 1811-1883.
The central idea of Christianity. Rev. ed. New York, Nelson & Phillips, 1876. 396 p.

2923 PECK, Jesse Truesdell, bp., 1811-1883.
"Holiness," Methodist Quarterly, XI (Oct. 1851), 505-529.

2924 PECK, Jesse Truesdell, bp., 1811-1883.
"Philosophy of Christian perfection," Methodist Quarterly Review, XXX (1848), 293-323.

2925 PERFECT LOVE; or, The speeches of Rev. E. L. Janes, Rev. H. Mattison, D.D., Rev. D. Curry, D.D., Rev. J. M. Buckley, and Rev. S. D. Brown in the New York preachers meeting, in March and April, 1867, upon the subject of sanctification; also Bishop Janes' sermon on sin and salvation at the Newark Conference Camp-Meeting, Morristown, Aug. 18, 1867. New York, N. Tibbals & Co., 1868. 129 p.

2926 PERRY, James H., 1811-1863.
Reply to Professor Mattison's "Calm review of Dr. Perry's late article in the Christian Advocate and Journal." New York, 1856. 55 p.

2927 SCOTT, Jane A., d. 1866.
Letters on Christian holiness; with an introd. by Rev. Enoch Stubbs.... 2d ed. Philadelphia, M. E. Book Rooms, 1879. xix, 161 p.

2928   SPICER, Tobias, 1788-1862.
        Spirit life, and its relations. Albany, N.Y., Munsell & Rowland, 1859. 216 p.

2929   STEELE, Daniel, 1824-1914.
        A defense of Christian perfection; or, A criticism of Dr. James Mudge's Growth in holiness toward perfection. New York, Hunt & Eaton, 1896. 136 p.

2930   STEELE, Daniel, 1824-1914.
        Love enthroned; essays on evangelical perfection. New York, Nelson & Phillips, 1875. 416 p.

2931   STEELE, Daniel, 1824-1914.
        Mile-stone papers: doctrinal, ethical, and experimental on Christian progress. New York, Phillips & Hunt, 1878. 287 p.

2932   TAYLOR, William, bp., 1821-1902.
        Infancy and manhood of Christian life. New York, Phillips & Hunt; Cincinnati, Walden & Stowe, 1880. 160 p.

2933   TAYLOR, William, bp., 1821-1902.
        Letters to a Quaker friend on baptism. New York, Phillips & Hunt; Cincinnati, Walden & Stowe, 1880. 163 p

2934   TAYLOR, William, bp., 1821-1902.
        Reconciliation; or, How to be saved.... New York, Phillips & Hunt; Cincinnati, Walden & Stowe, 1867. 208 p

2935   THOBURN, James Mills, bp., 1836-1922.
        The church of Pentecost. Cincinnati, Jennings and Pye 1901. 392 p.

2936   TUTTLE, Alexander Harrison, 1844-1932.
        Egypt to Canaan; or, Lectures on the spiritual meaning of the Exodus. New York, Eaton & Mains; Cincinnati, Jennings & Graham, 1912. 286 p.

2937   WALLACE, John H.
        An antidote to backsliding. New York, Carlton & Phillips, Tract Society of the Methodist Episcopal Church, 1855. 187 p.

2938   WATSON, Richard, 1781-1833.
        Theological institutes; or, A view of the evidences, doctrines, morals and institutions of Christianity. New York, Pub. by W. Waugh and T. Mason, for the Methodist Episcopal Church, 1834. 2 v.
        First edition published in 6 parts, 1823-1829.

II. 1. Christian Holiness Association

-- --AUTHORITATIVE SOURCES

2939 EDWARDS, Jonathan, 1703-1758.
The work of the Holy Spirit in the human heart; being two tracts on that subject, abridged by Rev. John Wesley, A.M. New York, Carlton & Phillips, 1853. 202 p.

-- --ESCHATOLOGY

2940 McDONALD, William, 1820-1901.
The annihilation of the wicked, scripturally considered. New York, Nelson & Phillips, 1872. 99 p.

-- --PREDESTINATION

2941 TAYLOR, William, bp., 1821-1902.
The election of grace. London, Hodder and Stoughton; New York, Nelson and Phillips, 1875. 247 p.

-- --SPIRITUALISM

2942 McDONALD, William, 1820-1901.
Spiritualism identical with ancient sorcery, New Testament demonology, and modern witchcraft, with the testimony of God and man against it. New York, Carlton & Porter, 1866. 212 p.

--EDUCATION

2943 PECK, Jesse Truesdell, bp., 1811-1883.
God in education; a discourse to the graduating class of Dickinson College, July 1852. Washington, Printed by R.A. Waters, 1852. 36 p.

2944 SWEET, William Warren, 1881-1959.
Indiana Asbury-DePauw University, 1837-1937; a hundred years of higher education in the Middle West. New York, Abingdon Press, 1937. 298 p.
"Omits reference to [Washington] DePauw's participation in the holiness revival."--Smith. Called unto holiness. 1962.

--EVANGELISTIC WORK

2945 BRUSHINGHAM, John Patrick, 1855-1927.
Catching men: studies in vital evangelism; introd. by Bishop Luther B. Wilson, foreword by Evan Roberts ... and contributions by other eminent specialists in evangelistic work. Cincinnati, Jennings & Graham; New York, Eaton & Mains, 1906. 222 p.

2946 BRUSHINGHAM, John Patrick, 1855-1927.
Spiritual electrology. Cincinnati, Jennings and Graham; New York, Eaton and Mains, 1912. 54 p.

2947 MALLALIEU, Willard Francis, bp., 1828-1911.
The why and how of revivals. New York, Eaton & Mains, 1901. 160 p.

2948 PECK, Jonas Oramel, 1836-
The revival and the pastor; introd. by J.M. Buckley, D.D. New York, Eaton & Mains; Cincinnati, Jennings & Pye, 1894. 279 p.

2949 TRUE METHOD of promoting perfect love; from debates in the New York preachers' meeting of the Methodist-Episcopal Church, on the question, What are the best methods of promoting the experience of perfect love? 3d ed. New York, Foster & Palmer, Jr., 1867. 136 p.

2950 TYSON, William Ainsworth, 1891-
The revival. Nashville, Tenn., Cokesbury Press, 1925. 287 p.

2951 WISE, Daniel, 1813-1898.
Revival miscellanies, by Daniel Wise and Allen W. Ralph. Boston, J. Magee, Agent, 1852. 442 p.

--HISTORY

2952 BRISTOL, Frank Milton, bp., 1851-1932.
The life of Chaplain McCabe, bishop of the Methodist Episcopal Church. New York, Revell, 1908. 416 p.
Chaplain of the 122d Ohio regiment, a prisoner in Libby, and later active in the work of the U.S. Christian Commission.

2953 DOUGLASS, Paul Franklin, 1904-
The story of German Methodism; biography of an immigrant soul, with an introd. by Bishop John L. Nuelsen. New York, Methodist Book Concern, 1939. 297, 64 p.

2954 ELLIOTT, Charles, 1792-1869.
The life of the Rev. Robert R. Roberts, one of the bishops of the Methodist Episcopal Church. New York, G. Lane & C.B. Tippett, for the Methodist Episcopal Church, 1844. 407 p.

2955 GOODELL, Charles LeRoy, 1854-1937.
My ministry. New York, Fleming H. Revell Co., c1938. 185 p.

II. 1. Christian Holiness Association

Methodist clergyman critical of the Holiness Movement.

2956 INSKIP, John Swanel, 1816-1884.
The experience and labors of the Rev. George D. Summers of the Methodist E. Church, a man who was born blind. Baltimore, Armstrong & Berry, 1838. 156 p.

2957 LEE, Jesse, 1758-1816.
A short history of the Methodists in the United States of America, beginning in 1766, and continued till 1809, to which is prefixed, A brief account of their rise in England in the year 1729, &c. Baltimore, Printed by Magill and Clime, Book-sellers, 1810. [Nashville, Tenn., Cokesbury Press, n.d.]. xii, 402 p.
Reprint of 1810 ed.

2958 THE M. E. churches, North and South. St. Louis, Southwestern Book and Publishing Co., 1872. 90 p.

2959 MATLACK, Lucius Columbus, 1816-1883.
The antislavery struggle and triumph in the Methodist Episcopal Church; with an introd. by Rev. D. D. Whedon. New York, Phillips & Hunt; Cincinnati, Walden & Stowe, 1881. 379 p.

2960 MATLACK, Lucius Columbus, 1816-1883.
The antislavery struggle and triumph in the Methodist Episcopal Church; introd. by D. D. Whedon. New York, Negro Universities Press, 1969. 379 p.
Reprint of 1881 ed.

2961 MATLACK, Lucius Columbus, 1816-1883.
"The disruption of Methodism," Methodist Quarterly Review, LVIII (April 1876), 292-308.

2962 MATLACK, Lucius Columbus, 1816-1883.
The history of American slavery and Methodism from 1780 to 1849; and, History of the Wesleyan Methodist Connection of America; in two parts, with an appendix. New York, 1849. 2 v. in 1 (368, 16 p.)

2963 MAY, James William, 1912-
"From revival movement to denomination: a re-examination of the beginnings of American Methodism." Unpublished Ph.D. dissertation, Columbia University, 1962. 378ℓ.

2964 SIMPSON, Matthew, bp., 1811-1884, ed.
Cyclopaedia of Methodism; embracing sketches of its rise, progress, and present condition, with biographical notices and numerous illustrations. Philadelphia, Everts & Stewart, 1878. 1027 p.

"Methodist Episcopal Church, The" p. 593-597.

2965 SPICER, Tobias, 1788-
Autobiography; containing incidents and observations, also some account of his visit to England. New York, Lane & Scott, 1852. 312 p.

2966 STEVENS, Abel, 1815-1897.
A compendious history of American Methodism; abridged from the author's History of the Methodist Episcopal Church. New York, Eaton & Mains; Cincinnati, Jennings & Graham, 1868. 608 p.

--HYMNS

2967 METHODIST EPISCOPAL Church.
A selection of hymns ... designed as a supplement to the Methodist pocket hymnbook. New York, J. Wilson, 1808.
Compiled by Francis Asbury.

2968 THE CAMP-MEETING hymn book: containing the most approved hymns and spiritual songs used by the Methodist connexion in the United States. 5th ed. Ithaca, N.Y., Mack and Andrus, 1835. 128 p.
Without music.

2969 CAMP-MEETING hymns and choruses. n.p., n.d. Unpaged
Without music.

2970 GILLMORE, Calvin, comp.
The camp-meeting hymn book, selected from various authors, for the use of those who worship God in the spirit. Geneva, N.Y., Printed for the compiler, by J. Bogert, 1830. 144 p.
Without music.

2971 GORHAM, B. Weed, comp.
Choral echoes from the church of God in all ages; a collection of hymns and tunes adapted to all occasions of social worship. Boston, H.V. Degen, 1864. 296 p.
Hymns with music: [43] p. at end.

2972 HENRY, George W., 1801- , comp.
The golden harp; or, Camp-meeting hymns, old and new, set to music. New York, 1853. 159 p.
With, as issued, his The golden harp; a supplement to the first edition of camp-meeting hymns. Oneida, N.Y., 1857; and, his Trials and triumphs in the life of G.W. Henry (familiarly known as blind Henry); or, Travels in Egypt, Twilight and Beulah. n.p., n.d.
Music: p. 99-152.

II. 1. Christian Holiness Association

2973 HULL, Asa
Camp meeting melodist; a collection of hymns and tunes suitable for all occasions of social worship. Boston, Asa Hull, agent, 1862. 32 p.
With music.

2974 KNAPP, Phoebe (Palmer), 1839-1908.
Bible-school songs for the use of Sunday-schools, prepared by Mrs. J. F. Knapp ... and J. H. Vincent. New York, Nelson & Phillips; Cincinnati, Hitchcock & Walden, 1878. 64 p.

2975 McDONALD, William, 1820-1901.
The Wesleyan minstrel; a collection of hymns and tunes for the use of Sunday schools and social worship. 3d ed. New York, Carlton & Phillips, 1852. 161 p.
With music.

2976 McDONALD, William, 1820-1901.
The Wesleyan sacred harp; a collection of choice tunes and hymns for prayer class, and camp meetings, choirs, and congregational singing, by Rev. W. McDonald and S. Hubbard. Boston, John P. Jewett & Co.; Cleveland, H. P. B. Jewett; New York, Sheldon, Blakeman & Co., 1858. 288 p.

2977 THE NEW camp-meeting lyre; or, A collection of hymns and spiritual songs, suitable to be sung at camp-meetings, during revivals of religion, and on other occasions. A new ed., improved and enl. by the addition of nearly one hundred hymns, many of which have never before been published. Philadelphia, J. Gladding, 1857. 256 p.
Caption and running title: The camp meeting lyre.
Without music.

2978 SCOTT, Orange, 1800-1847, comp.
The new and improved camp meeting hymn book: being a choice selection of hymns from the most approved authors, designed to aid in the public and private devotions of Christians. Published by the compiler. Brookfield, Mass., E. and G. Merriam, printers. 1830. 192 p.
Without music.

2979 SCOTT, Orange, 1800-1847.
The new and improved camp meeting hymn book: being a choice selection of hymns from the most approved authors, designed to aid in the public and private devotion of Christians. 2d ed. Published by the compiler. Brookfield, Mass., E. and G. Merriam, printers, 1831. 192 p.
Without music.

2980 SCOTT, Orange, 1800-1847, comp.
The new and improved camp meeting hymn book; being a choice selection of hymns from the most approved authors, designed to aid in the public and private devotion of Christians. 4th ed. Springfield, Mass., G. & C. Merriam 1833. 224 p.
Without music.

2981 SWENEY, John Robson, 1837-1899.
Anthems and voluntaries for the church choir, by John R. Sweney and Wm. J. Kirkpatrick.... Philadelphia, John J. Hood, c1881. 192 p.
Music with words.

2982 SWENEY, John Robson, 1837-1899, ed.
Bright melodies for the Sunday school and young people' societies, embracing praise hymns, work songs, invitation songs, primary songs, etc., etc. Editors: Jno. R. Sweney and J. Howard Entwisle. Philadelphia, Chicago, John J. Hood, c1899. 224 p.
With music.

2983 SWENEY, John Robson, 1837-1899, ed.
The garner; songs and hymns for Sunday-schools, prayer meetings, temperance, and gospel meetings, together with elementary instruction and exercises, for music classes Philadelphia, John J. Hood, c1878. 120 p.
Pieces with music unnumbered; 36 "familiar" hymns without music.

2984 SWENEY, John Robson, 1837-1899, ed.
Gems of praise; choice selection of sacred melodies. Philadelphia, Methodist Episcopal Book-room, J.B. McCullough, Agent, c1876. 176 p.

2985 SWENEY, John Robson, 1837-1899, comp.
Goodly pearls for the Sunday-school; a choice collection of new songs, duets, choruses, anthems, &c., suitable for anniversaries, and all the ordinary occasions of the Sunday-school; together with a selection of hymns for prayer and praise meetings, by John R. Sweney ... and John J. Hood. Philadelphia, J.J. Hood, c1875. 160 p.
With music.

2986 SWENEY, John Robson, 1837-1899, ed.
Melodies of salvation; a collection of psalms, hymns and spiritual songs. Editors: John R. Sweney, Hugh E. Smith, Frank E. Robinson. New York, Eaton & Mains; Philadelphia, J.J. Hood, c1900. [224] p.

2987 SWENEY, John Robson, 1837-1899, ed.
On joyful wing; a book of praise and song, [ed. by]

II. 1. Christian Holiness Association

> John H. Sweney and Wm. J. Kirkpatrick.... Philadelphia, John J. Hood, c1886. 352 p.
> 388 hymns (1-182, On joyful wing; 183-316, Melodious sonnets for sacred service; 317-388, precious hymns selected by Thomas Harrison).

2988 SWENEY, John Robson, 1837-1899.
> ...Organ score anthem book, by John R. Sweney and Wm. J. Kirkpatrick. Philadelphia, J.J. Hood, c1894. 160 p.
> At head of title: No. 2.

2989 SWENEY, John Robson, 1837-1899, ed.
> Our sabbath home praise book. Editors: Jno. R. Sweney and Wm. J. Kirkpatrick. Philadelphia, J.J. Hood, c1884. 192 p.
> With music.

2990 SWENEY, John Robson, 1837-1899, ed.
> Praise in song; a collection of hymns and sacred melodies, adapted for use by Sunday schools, Endeavor societies, Epworth leagues, evangelists, pastors, choristers, etc. Editors: Jno. R. Sweney, Philadelphia, John J. Hood, c1893. 224 p.
> With music.

2991 SWENEY, John Robson, 1837-1899, ed.
> Radiant songs: for use in meetings for Christian worship or work. Editors: Jno. H. Sweney, Wm. J. Kirkpatrick, and H. L. Gilmour. Philadelphia, John J. Hood, c1891. 192, i.e. 191 p.
> With music.

2992 SWENEY, John Robson, 1837-1899, ed.
> The royal fountain; new songs and familiar hymns for use in gospel, temperance and prayer meetings. Philadelphia, John J. Hood, c1877. Cover-title, 25 p.

2993 SWENEY, John Robson, 1837-1899, ed.
> Showers of blessing: a collection of hymns new and old. Editors: Jno. R. Sweney and Wm. J. Kirkpatrick.... Philadelphia, John J. Hood, c1888. 192 p.
> With music.

2994 SWENEY, John Robson, 1837-1899, ed.
> Songs of love and praise; for use in meetings for Christian worship or work. Editors: John R. Sweney, Wm. J. Kirkpatrick and H. L. Gilmour.... Philadelphia, John J. Hood, c1894. 224 p.
> With music.

2995 SWENEY, John Robson, 1837-1899, ed.
Songs of love and praise, no. 2. For use in meetings for Christian worship or work. Editors: John R. Sweney, Wm. J. Kirkpatrick and H. L. Gilmour.... Philadelphia, John J. Hood, c1895. 223 p.
With music.

2996 SWENEY, John Robson, 1837-1899, ed.
Songs of love and praise, no. 3. For use in meetings for Christian worship or work. Editors: John R. Sweney, Wm. J. Kirkpatrick and H. L. Gilmour.... Philadelphia, John J. Hood, c1898. 223 p.
237 hymns.
With music.

2997 SWENEY, John Robson, 1837-1899.
Songs of love and praise, no. 4. For use in meetings for Christian worship or work. Editors: John R. Sweney, H. L. Gilmour, J. H. Entwisle. Philadelphia, John J. Hood, c1897. 222 p.
234 hymns.
With music.

2998 SWENEY, John Robson, 1837-1899, ed.
Songs of love and praise, no. 5. For use in meetings for Christian worship or work. Editors: John R. Sweney, J. Howard Entwisle and the late Frank M. Davis. Philadelphia, John J. Hood, c1898. 223 p.
246 hymns.
With music.

2999 SWENEY, John Robson, 1837-1899, ed.
Songs of redeeming love.... Edited by Jno R. Sweney, C. C. McCabe, T. C. O'Kane, W. J. Kirkpatrick. Cincinnati, Cranston & Stowe, c1882. 160 p.
182 hymns.
With music.
Hymns no. 131-182 have separate half-title page reading: 52 hymns of the heart selected by C.C. McCabe.

3000 SWENEY, John Robson, 1837-1899, ed.
Songs of redeeming love, no. 2, edited by Jno. R. Sweney, C. C. McCabe, T. C. O'Kane, W. J. Kirkpatrick. Cincinnati, Chicago, Cranston & Stowe; Philadelphia, John J. Hood, c1887. ii, 3-160 p.
168 hymns.
With music.

3001 SWENEY, John Robson, 1837-1899, ed.
Sunlit songs: for use in meetings for Christian worship or work. Editors: Jno. R. Sweney, Wm. J. Kirkpatrick, and H. L. Gilmour.... Philadelphia, John J. Hood,

II. 1. Christian Holiness Association

c1890. 192 p.
With music.

3002 SWENEY, John Robson, 1837-1899, ed.
Winning songs: for use in meetings for Christian worship and work. Editors: Jno. R. Sweney, Wm. J. Kirkpatrick, and H. L. Gilmour.... Philadelphia, John J. Hood, c1892. 193 p.
With music.

-- --HISTORY AND CRITICISM

3003 METHODIST EPISCOPAL Church.
Hymn studies; an illustrated and annotated edition of the Hymnal of the Methodist Episcopal Church by Charles S. Nutter. New York, Phillips & Hunt, 1884. 475 p.
Without music.

3004 TILLETT, Wilbur Fisk, 1854-1936.
The hymns and hymn writers of the church; an annotated ed. of the Methodist Hymnal, by Wilbur F. Tillett and Charles S. Nutter. Nashville, Smith & Lamar; New York, Eaton & Mains, 1911. xvi, 567 p.
Without music.

--MEMBERSHIP

3005 COLEMAN, Robert Emerson, 1928-
"Factors in the expansion of the Methodist Episcopal Church from 1784 to 1812." Unpublished Ph.D. dissertation, State University of Iowa, 1954.

--MISSIONS

3006 BUTLER, William, 1818-1899.
Thy kingdom come; an anniversary discourse delivered before the Missionary Society of the Methodist General Biblical Institute, at Concord, N.H., Nov. 4, 1852. Boston, Rand, 1853. 52 p.

--MUSIC

-- --THEMES

3007 IVES, Charles Edward, 1874-1954.
[Symphony, no. 3].
Symphony no. 3: The camp meeting (1901-1912) New York, Associated Music Publishers, 1964.
Miniature score (33 p.)
Duration: about 17 min.

--PASTORAL THEOLOGY

3008 JANES, Edmund Storer, bp., 1807-1876.
The Christian ministry; a sermon preached before the New York preachers' meeting, Monday, February 8, 1876. New York, 1876. 29 p.

3009 McINTYRE, Robert, bp., 1851-1914.
Ordination address before the M.E. conference. University Park, Iowa, Christian Witness Association, n.d. 26 p.

3010 SMITH, William C., 1818-1891.
Tobacco in the ministry. New York, Printed by Phillips & Hunt, 1883. Cover-title, 32 p.

--PERIODICALS

3011 BEAUTY OF Holiness. 1-15, Jan. 1853-1864. Xenia, Ohio; Columbus, Ohio; New York.
Published by the Ohio and Pittsburgh conferences of the Methodist Episcopal Church, 1853-1858.
Merged into Guide to Holiness.

3012 DER CHRISTLICHE Apologete. 1-103, 1839-1941. Cincinnati.
Organ of the Central German Conference of the Methodist Episcopal Church, 1863-1923.

3013 INDIAN WITNESS. 1- , 1871- . Calcutta, Lucknow, Methodist Episcopal Church in Southern Asia.

3014 INLAND CHRISTIAN Advocate. 1- , 1886-18??. Des Moines, Iowa.

3015 LAMP OF Life. 1- , 1881-Nov. 1892. Bay City, Mich., Albion, Mich., Detroit, Mich.
Nov. 11, 1890-Nov. 1, 1892 as American Methodist.
Merged into Michigan Christian Advocate.

3016 METHODIST MONTHLY. 1-2, no. 4, May 1871-Apr. 1872. Indianapolis.

3017 ZION'S HERALD. 1-6, Jan. 9, 1823-1828; [ns] 1-38, 1829-1867; 45- , 1868- . Boston.
[ns] 1-4 as New England Christian Herald;
[ns] 13-38, 1842-1867 as Zion's Herald and Wesleyan Journal.

II. 1. Christian Holiness Association 357

--POLITICAL AND SOCIAL CRITICISM

3018   FOSS, Cyrus David, bp., 1834-1910.
"Politics and the pulpit," North American Review, CLV (1892), 538-547.

3019   HAMLINE, Leonidas Lent, bp., 1797-1865.
An address delivered in Zanesville, Ohio, at the request of a committee of the Zanesville and Putnam Colonization Society, on the 5th July, 1830. Zanesville, Printed by Peters & Pelham, 1830. 15 p.

3020   PECK, Jesse Truesdell, bp., 1811-1883.
The history of the great republic, considered from a Christian stand-point. New York, Broughton and Wyman, 1868. 710 p.

3021   SHELDON, Henry Olcott, 1799-1882.
The labor question; address delivered at the court house in Macon, Missouri, March 21st, 1870. n.p., 1870.

--SERMONS

3022   BAKER, Sheridan, 1824-1890.
Living waters; being Bible expositions and addresses given at different camp-meetings and to ministers and Christian workers on various other occasions, introduced with the author's experience in spreading holiness. 3d ed., corrected and enl. New York, Phillips & Hunt; Cincinnati, Cranston & Stowe, 1888. 314 p.

3023   DUNN, Lewis Romaine, 1822-1898.
Sermons on the higher life; with an introd. by Bishop Simpson. Cincinnati, Walden and Stowe, 1882. 385 p.

3024   EASTMAN, C.S., ed.
The Methodist Episcopal pulpit; a volume of sermons by ministers of the Michigan Conference of the M. E. Church in Michigan, with an introd. by the Rev. Joseph F. Berry. Monroe, Mich., Sermon Printing House, 1898.
"The damnation army, its victims and sponsors," by George B. Kulp: p. 242-255.

3025   FOSS, Cyrus David, bp., 1834-1910.
The faith once for all, a sermon, delivered at the dedication of Memorial Hall, Garrett Biblical Institute. Evanston, Ill., 1887. 20 p.

3026   FOSS, Cyrus David, bp., 1834-1910.
Religious certainties; sermons on special occasions [extemporaneously preached and stenographically reported].

Cincinnati, Jennings and Graham, 1905. 212 p.

3027 FOSS, Cyrus David, bp., 1834-1910.
Sermon "Our crisis" ... before the Pennsylvania state convention of the Methodist Episcopal Church.... Harrisburg, Pa., October 22-25, 1900. Harrisburg, Pa., 1900. 14 p.

3028 FOSS, Cyrus David, bp., 1834-1910.
Temperance and the pulpit, a sermon. New York, National Temperance Society and Publication House, 1871. 24 p.

3029 HUNTINGTON, DeWitt Clinton, 1830-1912.
Half century messages to pastors and people. Cincinnati, Jennings and Graham; New York, Eaton and Mains, c1905. 213 p.

3030 HUNTINGTON, DeWitt Clinton, 1830-1912.
Is the Lord among us? Cincinnati, Jennings and Pye, 1904. 163 p.

3031 TUTTLE, Alexander Harrison, 1844-1932.
The living word. Cincinnati, Jennings & Pye; New York, Eaton & Mains, 1904. 150 p.

3032 WINCHESTER, Charles Wesley, 1843-
The gospel of foreign travel. Rochester, N.Y., Press of Democrat and Chronicle, 1891. 236 p.
A course of Sunday evening sermons delivered in Medina (N.Y.) M.E. Church from Nov. 9, 1890 to April 19, 1891.

--AFRICA, SOUTH

3033 METHODIST EPISCOPAL Church. Missions and mission conferences. South Central Africa. Angola District.
"Records, 1885-1897, including minutes of regular and special meetings of the district, presiding elder's reports, and records of births, deaths, baptisms, marriages, ordinations, etc." In Library, Pacific School of Religion. 1 v.

3034 TAYLOR, William, bp., 1821-1902.
Christian adventures in South Africa. New York, Nelson & Phillips, 1875. xiv, xv, 557 p.
Introduction by William B. Boyce.

3035 TAYLOR, William, bp., 1821-1902.
The flaming torch in darkest Africa; with an introd. by Henry M. Stanley. New York, Eaton & Mains, 1898. 675 p.

II. 1. Christian Holiness Association

--INDIA

3036 PICKETT, Jarrell Waskom, bp., 1890-
Christian mass movements in India, a study with recommendations; foreword by John R. Mott.... New York, Abingdon Press, 1933. 382 p.

3037 THOBURN, James Mills, bp., 1836-1922.
The Christian conquest of India, by Bishop James M. Thoburn, forty-six years a missionary in India. New York, Young People's Missionary Movement, 1906. 10, 291 p.

3038 THOBURN, James Mills, bp., 1836-1922.
India and Malaysia. Cincinnati, Cranston & Curts; New York, Hunt & Eaton, 1892. 562 p.

--INDIANA

3039 SMITH, William C., 1809-1886.
Indiana miscellany: consisting of sketches of Indian life, the early settlement, customs, and hardships of the people, and the introduction of the gospel and of schools, together with biographical notices of the pioneer Methodist preachers of the state. Cincinnati, Published by Poe & Hitchcock for the author, 1867. 304 p.

3040 SWEET, William Warren, 1881-1959.
Circuit-rider days in Indiana. Indianapolis, W. K. Stewart Co., 1916. 344 p.

--KANSAS

3041 SWEET, William Henry, 1843-1919.
A history of Methodism in northwest Kansas. Salina, Kan., Kansas Wesleyan University, 1920. 546 p.

--KENTUCKY

3042 ARNOLD, William Erastus, 1862-
A history of Methodism in Kentucky. Louisville, Herald Press, 1935-1936. 2 v.
No more published.
Contents.--1. From 1783 to 1820.--2. From 1820 to 1846.
Comprehensive index to vol. 1, comp. by Mrs. Wade Hampton Whitley. Lexington, Ky., 1960.
14 p. (University of Kentucky Libraries. Occasional contribution no. 110)

--MALAYSIA

3043 THOBURN, James Mills, bp., 1836-1922.
India and Malaysia. Cincinnati, Cranston & Curts; New York, Hunt and Eaton, 1892. 562 p.

--MEXICO

3044 BUTLER, William, 1818-1899.
Mexico in transition from the power of political Romanism to civil and religious liberty. New York, Hunt & Eaton, 1892. xvi, 325 p.

--MICHIGAN

3045 MACMILLAN, Margaret (Burnham)
The Methodist Episcopal Church in Michigan during the Civil War. Lansing, Michigan Civil War Centennial Observance Commission, 1965. 75 p.

3046 PRESCOTT, William Ray
The fathers still speak; a history of Michigan Methodism. Lansing, Michigan Printing Service, 1941. 144 p.

--NEBRASKA

3047 DAVIS, Henry Turner, 1832-
Solitary places made glad; being observations and experiences for thirty-two years in Nebraska, with sketches and incidents touching the discovery, early settlement, and development of the state. Cincinnati, Printed for the author by Cranston & Stowe, 1890. 422 p.

--NEW JERSEY

3048 ATWOOD, Anthony, 1801-1888.
History of Methodism, Cape Island, N.J. Cape Island, 1867. 60 p.

--RHODE ISLAND

3049 McDONALD, William, 1820-1901.
History of Methodism in Providence, Rhode Island, from its introduction in 1787 to 1867. Boston, Phipps & Pride, printers, 1868. 136 p.

II. 1. Christian Holiness Association

--SOUTHERN STATES

3050 MATLACK, Lucius Columbus, 1816-1883.
"The Methodist Episcopal Church in the Southern states."
Methodist Quarterly Review, LIV (January 1872), 103-126.

3051 MORROW, Ralph Ernest
Northern Methodism and Reconstruction. East Lansing, Michigan State University Press, 1956. 269 p.

--TEXAS

3052 PHELAN, Macum, 1874-
A history of early Methodism in Texas, 1817-1866.
Nashville, Tenn., Cokesbury Press, 1924. 510 p. (History of Methodism in Texas, vol. 1)

3053 PHELAN, Macum, 1874-
A history of the expansion of Methodism in Texas, 1867-1902; being a continuation of the History of early Methodism in Texas, by the same author. Dallas, Tex., Mathis, Van Nort & Co., 1937. 525 p. (History of Methodism in Texas, vol. 2)

METHODIST EPISCOPAL CHURCH, SOUTH (1845-1939)

Organized in 1845 to uphold Southern attitudes toward slavery, this denomination was in most other aspects identical to its Northern counterpart. While defense of slavery disappeared with the Civil War, defense of the section and the culture which had fostered it continued long afterward. The Methodist Episcopal Church, South, was a much more aristocratic group than the Methodist Episcopal Church. Its members had a great deal at stake in the political and economic settlement after the war, and viewed the post-war extension of the Northern church into the South and the participation of Northern churchmen in radical Reconstruction with alarm. That a substantial portion of the bishops of the Methodist Episcopal Church were favorable toward the Holiness Movement and that the leaders of the National Holiness Association were, almost to a man, members of the Northern church, did little to arouse support for the movement in the Methodist Episcopal Church, South. Although pockets of sympathy existed, the Holiness Movement suffered severely from opposition in the Southern church. By the turn of the century holiness pastors, roughly treated by Southern bishops and presiding elders, were in increasing numbers leaving the church. Like its Northern sister, the Methodist Episcopal Church, South, increased in membership until the 1920's, then declined. In 1926 a government report put the membership at 2,487,000; in 1936, at 2,061,000. The participation of the Methodist Episcopal Church, South, in the 1939 merger resulting in The Methodist

Church, undoubtedly did much to neutralize holiness sentiment among other participants in the union.

3054 METHODIST EPISCOPAL Church, South.
    Doctrines and discipline. Richmond, Nashville, 1846-1938. 23 v.
    Quadrennial, 1894-1938.

3055 JAMES, John T.
    Methodism in the Southland. n.p., 1902. 199 p.

--APOLOGETIC WORKS

3056 HUDSON, Hilary T.
    The Methodist armor; or, A popular exposition of the doctrines, peculiar usages, and ecclesiastical machinery of the Methodist Episcopal Church, South. Nashville, Tenn., Publishing House Methodist Episcopal Church, South, Smith & Lamar, Agents, 1921, c1882. 319 p.
    "Ninth revised edition."

--BIOGRAPHY

3057 WIMBERLY, Charles Franklin, 1866-1946.
    Modern apostles of faith. Nashville, Cokesbury Press, 1930. 172 p.

--CLERGY

3058 ARNOLD, William Erastus, 1862-
    The H.C. Morrison case: a statement of facts; an investigation of the law. Louisville, Kentucky Methodist Publishing Co., 1897. 34 p.

--CONDUCT OF LIFE

3059 CARRADINE, Beverly, 1848-1931.
    Secret societies: are they right or wrong? Are they a blessing or a curse? An address by Rev. B. Carradine, D.D., pastor of the Centenary M.E. Church, St. Louis, before his congregation, Jan. 4, 1891. Syracuse, N.Y., A. W. Hall, 1891. 19 p.

3060 DODSWORTH, Jeremiah.
    The better land; or, The Christian emigrant's guide to heaven. Nashville, Southern Methodist Publishing House, 1861.

II. 1. Christian Holiness Association

--CRITICAL WORKS

3061 HAYNES, Benjamin Franklin, 1851-1923.
Facts, faith and fire; or, Chapters on the situation. Nashville, B. F. Haynes Publishing Co., 1900. 320 p.

3062 HAYNES, Benjamin Franklin, 1851-1923.
Tempest-tossed on Methodist seas; or, A sketch of my life. Louisville, Pentecostal Publishing Co., 1921. 310 p.
Autobiography.

--DOCTRINAL AND CONTROVERSIAL WORKS

3063 BOLAND, J. M.
"The problem and its critics," Quarterly Review of the Methodist Episcopal Church, South, ns XIII (1892-93), 339-353.

3064 BOLAND, J. M.
The problem of Methodism; being a review of the residue theory of regeneration and the second change theory of sanctification; and the philosophy of Christian perfection. 3d ed. Nashville, Tenn., Publishing House of the M.E. Church, South, for the author, 1888. 331 p.

3065 BOLAND, J. M.
"A psychological view of sin and holiness," Quarterly Review of the Methodist Episcopal Church, South, ns XII (1892), 342-354.

3066 BROOKS, John Rives, 1836-
Scriptural sanctification, an attempted solution of the holiness problem. 3d ed. Nashville, Publishing House of the Methodist Episcopal Church, South, 1899. 413 p.

3067 BROOKS, John Rives, 1836-
Scriptural sanctification; an attempted solution of the holiness problem, with an introd. by Jno. J. Tigert. Nashville, Tenn., Publishing House of the M.E. Church, South, 1903. xv, 413 p.

3068 CARRADINE, Beverly, 1848-1931.
Sanctification; introd. by Rev. L.L. Pickett. Nashville, Tenn., Publishing House of the M.E. Church, South, Barbee & Smith, Agents, 1891. 227 p.

3069 COLLINS, J. H.
Fruits & flowers (on the doctrine, experience, and practice of Christian holiness). Nashville, Southern Methodist Publishing House, 1886. 248 p.

3070   COLLINS, J. H.
        Sanctification: what it is, wher it is, how it is. Nashville, Southern Methodist Publishing House, printed for the author, 1885. 80 p.

3071   GODBEY, William B., 1833-1920.
        Christian perfection. Nashville, Tenn., Southern Methodist Publishing House, for the author, 1886. 128 p.

3072   GRANBERY, John Cowper, bp., 1829-1907.
        "Dr. Mudge on growth in holiness," Quarterly Review of the M. E. Church, South, XLIII (1896), 198-210.

3073   LEFTWICH, W. M.
        "The law of sanctification," Quarterly Review of the M. E. Church, South, XIV (July 1893), 370-385.

3074   MORRISON, Henry Clay, 1857-1942.
        Open letters to the bishops, ministers and members of the Methodist Episcopal Church, South. Louisville, Pentecostal Publishing Co., n. d.

3075   PICKETT, Leander Lycurgus, 1859-1928.
        The book and its theme. Nashville, Publishing House of the M. E. Church, South, 1893. 290 p.

3076   PICKETT, Leander Lycurgus, 1859-1928.
        The Pickett-Smith debate on entire sanctification, a second blessing: affirmative, Evangelist L. L. Pickett of Wilmore, Ky.; negative, Rev. M. A. Smith of North Texas Conference, both of M. E. Church, South. Louisville, Ky., Pickett Publishing Co.; Garland, Tex., Rev. M. A. Smith, 1897. 352 p.

3077   PICKETT, Leander Lycurgus, 1859-1928.
        St. Paul on holiness; Epistle to the Hebrews. Nashville, Printed for the author, Publishing House of the M. E. Church, South, J. D. Barbee, agent, 1888. 20 p.

3078   PIERCE, Lovick, 1785-1879.
        A miscellaneous essay on entire sanctification; showing how it was lost from the church and how it may and must be regained. Macon, Ga., Anderson Printing Co., n. d. 69 p.

3079   RALSTON, Thomas Neely, 1806-1891.
        Elements of divinity; or, A course of lectures, comprising a clear and concise view of the system of theology as taught in the Holy Scriptures; with appropriate questions appended to each lecture. Louisville, Morton & Griswold, 1847. 463 p.

II. 1. Christian Holiness Association

3080 RALSTON, Thomas Neely, 1806-1891.
Elements of divinity; or, A course of lectures, comprising a clear and concise view of the system of theology as taught in the Holy Scriptures; with appropriate questions appended to each lecture. Cincinnati, Poe & Hitchcock, 1861. 463 p.

3081 RALSTON, Thomas Neely, 1806-1891.
Elements of divinity; or, A concise and comprehensive view of Bible theology; comprising the doctrines, evidences, morals, and institutions of Christianity; with appropriate questions appended to each chapter, ed. by T.O. Summers, D.D. Nashville, Tenn., A.H. Redford, 1871. 1023 p.

3082 RALSTON, Thomas Neely, 1806-1891.
Elements of divinity; or, A concise and comprehensive view of Bible theology; comprising the doctrines, evidences, morals and institutions of Christianity; with appropriate questions appended to each chapter, ed. by T.O. Summers, D.D. Rev., with introd. Nashville, Tenn., Cokesbury Press, 1924. 1023 p.

3083 RALSTON, Thomas Neely, 1806-1891.
"Holiness and sin--new theory noticed," Quarterly Review of the M.E. Church, South, III (July 1881), 441-451.

3084 ROSSER, Leonidas, 1815-1892.
A reply to The Problem of Methodism by J.M. Boland. Nashville, Publishing House of the Methodist Episcopal Church, South, 1889. 126 p.

3085 SMITH, Joseph Thomas, 1851-
Entire sanctification (heart purity) and regeneration, as defined by Mr. Wesley, one and the same. Marshall, Tex., 1895.

--HISTORY

3086 DUREN, William Larkin, 1905-
The trail of the circuit rider. New Orleans, Chalmers' Printing House, c1936. 425 p.

3087 FARISH, Hunter Dickinson, 1897-
The circuit rider dismounts; a social history of Southern Methodism, 1865-1900. Richmond, Va., Dietz Press, 1938. 400 p.
Thesis (Ph.D.)--Harvard University, 1936.

3088 THE M.E. churches, North and South. St. Louis, Southwestern Book and Publishing Co., 1872. 90 p.

3089 SIMPSON, Matthew, bp., 1811-1884, ed.
Cyclopaedia of Methodism; embracing sketches of its rise, progress, and present condition, with biographical notices and numerous illustrations. Philadelphia, Everts & Stewart, 1878. 1027 p.
"Methodist Episcopal Church, South": p. 599-601.

--HYMNS

-- --HISTORY AND CRITICISM

3090 TILLETT, Wilbur Fisk, 1854-1936.
The hymns and hymn writers of the church; an annotated ed. of the Methodist Hymnal, by Wilbur F. Tillett and Charles S. Nutter. Nashville, Smith & Lamar; New York, Eaton & Mains, 1911. xvi, 567 p.
Without music.

3091 TILLETT, Wilbur Fisk, 1854-1936.
The hymns and hymn writers of the church; an annotated edition of the Methodist Hymnal, by Wilbur F. Tillett and Charles S. Nutter. Nashville, Publishing House of the M.E. Church, South, 1924. 567 p.
Without music.

--PERIODICALS

3092 LIVING WATER. 1- , May 30, 1891-1919. Nashville.
1891-1896 as Tennessee Methodist; 1896-1902 as Zion's Outlook.

3093 METHODIST CHALLENGE. 1-29, no. 2, Mar. 1922-Aug. 1960. Los Angeles.
1922-1944? as Bob Shuler's Magazine.

--POLITICAL AND SOCIAL CRITICISM

3094 CARRADINE, Beverly, 1848-1931.
The Louisiana State Lottery Company examined and exposed. New Orleans, D.L. Mitchel, 1889. Cover-title, 59 p.

3095 CARRADINE, Beverly, 1848-1931.
The Louisiana State Lottery Co., examined and exposed, two addresses and additional thoughts [delivered Feb. 24th, 1899 and Feb. 16th, 1890].... New Orleans, F.D. van Valkenburgh, 1890. Cover-title, 42, 59 p.
First address bound in following second address.

II. 1. Christian Holiness Association

--SERMONS

3096 CARRADINE, Beverly, 1848-1931.
Revival sermons. St. Louis, St. Louis Christian Advocate Co., 1897. 340 p.

--GEORGIA

3097 MANN, Harold William
Atticus Greene Haygood, Methodist bishop, editor, and educator. Athens, University of Georgia Press, 1965. viii, 254 p.
Includes comment on Holiness Movement in Georgia.

3098 PIERCE, Alfred Mann, 1874-
A history of Methodism in Georgia, February 5, 1736-June 24, 1955. Atlanta, North Georgia Conference Historical Society, 1956. 345 p.

--TEXAS

3099 PHELAN, Macum, 1874-
A history of early Methodism in Texas, 1817-1866. Nashville, Cokesbury Press, 1924. 510 p. (History of Methodism in Texas, vol. 1)

3100 PHELAN, Macum, 1874-
A history of the expansion of Methodism in Texas, 1867-1902; being a continuation of the History of early Methodism in Texas, by the same author. Dallas, Mathis, Van Nort & Co., 1937. 525 p. (History of Methodism in Texas, vol. 2)

METHODIST PROTESTANT CHURCH (1830-)

The Methodist Protestant Church was the most consistently friendly to the Holiness Movement of the three groups which united in 1939 to form the Methodist Church. (With less than 150,000 members, it was also the smallest.) Originating in 1830 in a dispute over the power of Methodist Episcopal bishops to appoint pastors, the Methodist Protestants strongly favored de-centralized administration. Before the Civil War, this church contemplated union with the Wesleyan Methodist Connection, a group which later identified with the Holiness Movement. Committed to administration through annual conferences, the Methodist Protestant Church suffered from vulnerability to local fracture. In 1911 the Louisiana Conference sent official negotiators to the Pentecostal Nazarene General Assembly in Nashville. While a formal union failed to materialize, a sizeable contingent of prominent clergy and lay members from Louisiana and Mississippi joined the new denomination. Nearly thirty years later, as a concession to the holiness sentiments of Methodist Protestants, the founding conference of the Methodist Church incorporated the Methodist Protestant statement on sanctification in the new discipline.

Several groups within the Methodist Protestant Church refused to enter the 1939 union. A group within the Eastern Conference formed the Bible Protestant Church, another in Missouri formed what is now the Fundamental Methodist Church; still another, which established headquarters at Brookhaven, Mississippi, succeeded in keeping the original name. The present Methodist Protestant Church, which claims to continue the original work of the denomination, is fundamentalist in its orientation. Through the Associated Missions of the International Council of Christian Churches, it sponsors a small mission in Mexico and another in British Honduras. The Methodist Protestant Church works in co-operation with the Christian Holiness Association.

--HISTORY

3101 BASSETT, Ancel H., 1809-1886.
A concise history of the Methodist Protestant Church, from its origin: with biographical sketches of several leading ministers of the denomination, and also a sketch of the author's life, with an introd. by William Collier. 3d ed., rev. and enl. Pittsburgh, William McCracken, Jr., 1887.

3102 DAVIS, Lyman Edwyn, 1854-1930.
Democratic Methodism in America; a topical survey of the Methodist Protestant Church. New York, Revell, 1921. 267 p.

3103 SIMPSON, Matthew, bp., 1811-1884, ed.
Cyclopaedia of Methodism; embracing sketches of its rise, progress, and present condition, with biographical notices and numerous illustrations. Philadelphia, Everts & Stewart, 1878. 1027 p.
"Methodist Protestant Church, The": p. 602-607.

PEOPLE'S METHODIST CHURCH (1938-1962)

[193?-19?? as People's Christian Movement]

First known as the People's Christian Movement, this group was organized January 1, 1938, in protest against the impending merger of the three main Methodist bodies. The church was led by the Rev. Jim H. Green and centered in Greensboro, North Carolina, where the non-denominational People's Bible School and College, also founded by Green, was located. Theologically conserva-

tive and committed to holiness, People's churches sprang up in
North Carolina, Virginia and Maryland. When the church merged
with the Evangelical Methodist Church in the summer of 1962, it
consisted of thirty churches with about a thousand members.

3104 EVANGELICAL METHODIST Church.
      1970 Minutes: 17th General Conference, 11th Eastern
   Annual Conference, 11th Western Annual Conference; July
   14-18, 1970, St. Louis, Missouri. n.p., 1970. 170 p.
      Account of People's Methodist Church: p. 12.

3105 MEAD, Frank Spencer, 1898-
      Handbook of denominations in the United States. 2d
   rev. ed. New York, Abingdon Press, c1961. 272 p.
      "People's Methodist Church": p. 161.

PRIMITIVE METHODIST CHURCH, U.S.A. (1829-)

   Formed in 1812 by converts of camp meetings held in England by Lorenzo Dow, an iconoclastic American Methodist evangelist, the Primitive Methodist Church was brought to the United States by British immigrants in 1829. Wesleyan teachings on justification and sanctification are emphasized. Governed by annual conferences and a quadrennial general conference first held in 1889, Primitive Methodists eschew superintendency and place denominational affairs in the hands of an elected president, vice-president, secretary and treasurer. Congregations extend calls to pastors on the basis of a preferential ballot. Pastoral tenure is unrestricted. Since 1922 the group has sponsored missionary work among Indians in Guatemala, raising $8.61 per member for that purpose in a recent year. The Primitive Methodist Journal is issued monthly. In 1959 the denomination reported ninety churches and 14,613 members in the United States. The Primitive Methodist Church works in cooperation with the Christian Holiness Association.

                    --HISTORY

3106 ACORNLEY, John Holmes
      A history of the Primitive Methodist Church in the
   United States of America from its origin and landing of the
   first missionaries in 1829 to the present time. Fall River,
   Mass., N.W. Matthews, 1909. 404 p.
      "Compiled by approval of the book and publishing committee of the general conference."

3107 ACORNLEY, John Holmes
      What is Primitive Methodism? Its origin, progress,
   characteristics and doctrines. Pottsville, Pa., J.W.

Cheetham, printer, 1881. Cover-title, 28 p.
An account of Hugh Bourne, the evangelist.

3108 CLARK, Elmer Talmage, 1886-1966.
The small sects in America. Rev. ed. New York, Abingdon Press, c1965. 256 p.
Account of Primitive Methodist Church: p. 62-63.

3109 MEAD, Frank Spencer, 1898-
Handbook of denominations in the United States. New 5th ed. Nashville, Abingdon Press, c1970. 265 p.
"Primitive Methodist Church, U.S.A.": p. 151.

3110 SIMPSON, Matthew, bp., 1811-1884, ed.
Cyclopaedia of Methodism; embracing sketches of its rise, progress, and present condition, with biographical notices and numerous illustrations. Philadelphia, Everts & Stewart, 1878. 1027 p.
"Primitive Methodist Connection, The": p. 995-997.

--MISSIONS

3111 ENCYCLOPEDIA OF modern Christian missions; the agencies. Burton L. Goddard, ed.... Camden, N.J., T. Nelson, 1967. xix, 743 p.
"Primitive Methodist International Mission Board," by Thomas W. Jones: p. 550.

--PERIODICALS

3112 PRIMITIVE METHODIST Journal. 1- , 1892- . Fall River, Mass.; Grand Rapids, Mich.

REFORMED METHODIST CHURCH (1814-1952)

The Reformed Methodist Church formed at Readsboro, Vermont, in 1814 in protest against the power of Methodist Episcopal Church bishops. Late in the nineteenth century the group espoused holiness. By 1952, having dwindled to fewer than five hundred members in a dozen congregations, the Reformed Methodist Church merged with the Ohio-based Churches of Christ in Christian Union. To the union the Reformed Methodists brought an established camp meeting at Port Crane, New York, and a foreign missionary field in the Island of Dominica. Their New York and Pennsylvania churches became the Northeastern District of the merged group.

3113 CLARK, Elmer Talmage, 1886-1966.
The small sects in America. Rev. ed. New York, Abingdon Press, c1965. 256 p.

II. 1. Christian Holiness Association

Account of the Reformed Methodist Church: p. 62.

3114 MEAD, Frank Spencer, 1898-
Handbook of denominations in the United States. 2d rev. ed. New York, Abingdon Press, c1961. 272 p.
"Reformed Methodist Church": p. 161-162.

WESLEYAN METHODIST CHURCH OF AMERICA (1843-1968)

[1843-1891 as Wesleyan Methodist Connection of America; 1891-1947 as Wesleyan Methodist Connection (or Church) of America]

Organized at Utica, New York, in 1843 as a protest against slavery and episcopacy, this group committed itself to a modified congregationalism from its inception. For over a hundred years it characterized its structure as a connection rather than a denomination, and called its general and regional conference officials presidents rather than superintendents. At the beginning, growth was spectacular (from 6000 to 15,000 members the first year), but the post-Civil War return of nearly a hundred ministers and thousands of members to the Methodist Episcopal Church left the Wesleyan Methodist Connection in 1875 with no larger membership than it had in 1844. Concentrated in upstate New York, western Pennsylvania and Ohio, Michigan and Indiana, the group increasingly identified with the Holiness Movement as the nineteenth century progressed. In 1853 church headquarters and publishing offices were established at Syracuse, New York, where they were to remain for over a hundred years (after a disasterous fire in 1957, the denominational offices moved to Marion, Indiana). In 1889 the group sent its first missionaries to Sierra Leone. It expanded its own program and absorbed work begun by the Vanguard Mission, the Hephzibah Faith Missionary Association, the Missionary Bands of the World, and the Alliance of the Reformed Baptist Church of Canada. When it merged with the Pilgrim Holiness Church to form the Wesleyan Church in 1968, the Wesleyan Methodist Church was sponsoring work in Japan, Taiwan, India, Australia, South Africa, Sierra Leone, the West Indies, and Colombia, as well as among American Indians in New York state and South Dakota. Twice the Wesleyan Methodist Church had rejected merger overtures of the Free Methodist Church with which it held much in common, largely because it feared the episcopal government of the latter. At the time of the union with the Pilgrim Holiness Church, the Wesleyan Methodist Church had about 45,000 members in the United States and a high rate of giving per capita when compared with other denominations. The church supported colleges at Central, South Carolina, Houghton, New York, Marion, Indiana, and Miltonvale, Kansas, and held institutional membership in the National Holiness Association.

3115   WESLEYAN METHODIST Church of America.
       Discipline. Boston; New York; Syracuse, N.Y.; Marion, Ind., 1843-1966. 33 v.
       Quadrennial: 1844-1864, 1867-1963.
       1966 ed. consists of revisions of the 1963 Discipline.

3116   WESLEYAN METHODIST Church of America. General Conference.
       Minutes. 1st-32d, 1844-1966. n.p.   -1966.
       Quadrennial, 1844-1864, 1867-1963.

--CONFERENCES. ALLEGHENY

3117   WESLEYAN METHODIST Church of America. Conferences. Allegheny.
       A white paper, by the minority of the Allegheny Conference of the Wesleyan Methodist Church of America. n.p., 1966. 24 p.

3118   McLEISTER, Ira Ford, 1879-1963.
       The Allegheny Conference centennial (1843-1943); the history of one hundred years of conference activities, by Rev. I.F. McLeister and Rev. J.B. Markey. n.p., 194?. 59 p.

--CONFERENCES. CANADA

3119   WESLEYAN METHODIST Church of America. Conferences. Canada.
       Fifty years of service for Christ and the Canada Conference of the Wesleyan Methodist Church. Brockville, Ont., Can., 1947. 12 p.

--CONFERENCES. CHAMPLAIN

3120   WESLEYAN METHODIST Church of America. Conferences. Champlain.
       One hundred and twenty-five years for Christ, 1843-1968; history of the Camplain Conference of the Wesleyan Methodist Church of America, by the Conference Historical Committee. West Chazy, N.Y., 1968. 102 p.

3121   NORTHRUP, A. O.
       One hundred years for Christ, by A.O. Northrup, Sr., W.F. Lewis, and L.C. Mattoon. n.p., Champlain Conference, 1943.

II. 1. Christian Holiness Association

--CONFERENCES. IOWA

3122 WOLTER, Gerald A., ed.
The Iowa Conference centennial, 1853-1953. Topeka, Kan., 195?. 98 p.

--CONFERENCES. KANSAS

3123 CALDWELL, Wayne
"The history of the Kansas Conference of the Wesleyan Methodist Church." Unpublished Th.D. dissertation, Iliff School of Theology, 1969.

--CONFERENCES. LOCKPORT

3124 WESLEYAN METHODIST Church of America. Conferences. Lockport.
Lockport Conference centennial, 1861-1961. Houghton, N.Y., 196?. Unpaged.
Cover-title: Our heritage; Lockport Conference centennial, 1861-1961.

--CONFERENCES. MICHIGAN

3125 WESLEYAN METHODIST Church of America. Conferences. Michigan.
"Records, 1852-1942." 9 v. In University of Michigan, Michigan Historical Collections.
Minutes, financial records, membership statistics, biographies of ministers; constitution and minutes of the Association for Ministerial Improvement of the Michigan Conference (1871-1917); minutes of the Leoni Wesleyan Methodist Church (1857-1860); and membership rolls and minutes of the Alton Wesleyan Methodist Church (1891-1906).

3126 RENNELLS, Charles Stephen, 1873-1962.
History of the Michigan Conference, Wesleyan Methodist Church of America; introd. by Ira Ford McLeister. Grand Rapids, Mich., Zondervan Publishing House, 1940. 121 p.

3127 RENNELLS, Charles Stephen, 1873-1962.
"Papers, 1852-1958." 60 items and 2 v. In University of Michigan, Michigan Historical Collections.
Personal papers and miscellanea collected by Rennells on Wesleyan Methodist churches in Michigan; ms. of his History of the Michigan Conference, Wesleyan Methodist Church of America (1940); a history of the Rennells family; a photograph album; and sermon records.

--CONFERENCES. OKLAHOMA

3128 WESLEYAN METHODIST Church of America. Conferences. Oklahoma.
　　　Oklahoma Conference history, 1904-1908 [i.e. 1968]; Raymond A. Tolle, Historian; Joe C. Sawyer, Conference President. Enid, Okla., 1968. 26 p.
　　　With as issued: Sixty-fifth annual session of the Oklahoma District of The Wesleyan Church, held at First Wesleyan Church, Enid, Oklahoma, July 15-21, 1968; Joe C. Sawyer, District Superintendent; Larry R. Hughes, Secretary. Enid, Okla., 1968.

--CONFERENCES. ROCHESTER

3129 WESLEYAN METHODIST Church of America. Conferences. Rochester.
　　　One hundred years of service for Christ in the Wesleyan Methodist Church, 1844-1944. Elmira, N.Y., 1944. 47 p.
　　　Chairman of the Historical Committee: Stanley W. Wright.

--CONFERENCES. SOUTH CAROLINA

3130 HILSON, James Benjamin, 1908-
　　　History of the South Carolina Conference of the Wesleyan Methodist Church of America; fifty-five years of Wesleyan Methodism in South Carolina. Introd. by Rev. Oliver G. Wilson. Winona Lake, Ind., Light and Life Press, 1950. 308 p.

--CONFERENCES. WISCONSIN

3131 WESLEYAN METHODIST Church of America. Conferences. Wisconsin.
　　　Wisconsin Conference centennial, 1867-1967. Eau Claire, Wis., 1967? Unpaged.

--ANECDOTES, REMINISCENCES, SATIRE, ETC.

3132 GIRANDOLA, Anthony
　　　The most defiant priest; the story of the priest who married. New York, Crown Publishers, c1968. 288 p.
　　　Spiritual autobiography of a Roman Catholic priest who married a former Wesleyan Methodist.

II. 1. Christian Holiness Association

3133 SHERWOOD, Mrs.
 Juliana Oakley. New York, O. Scott, for the Wesleyan Methodist Connection of America, 1847. 78 p.

3134 THE SOLDIER'S funeral. New York, O. Scott, for the Wesleyan Methodist Connection of America, 1847. 32 p.

3135 TAYLOR, Isaac, 1759-1829.
 The mine ... from the London edition. New York, O. Scott, for the Wesleyan Methodist Connection of America, 1847. 108 p.

3136 TAYLOR, Isaac, 1759-1829.
 The ship ... from the London edition, revised by the editors. New York, O. Scott, for the Wesleyan Methodist Connection of America, 1846. 102 p.

3137 [TAYLOR, Jefferys], 1792-1853.
 The farm, a new account of rural toils and produce. New York, O. Scott, for the Wesleyan Methodist Connection of America, 1847. 77 p.

3138 TAYLOR, Jefferys, 1792-1853.
 The forest; or, Rambles in the woodland. New York, O. Scott, for the Wesleyan Methodist Connection of America, 1846. 108 p.

3139 THE VILLAGE, a collection of interesting narratives. New York, O. Scott for the Wesleyan Methodist Connection of America, 1847. 69 p.

--APOLOGETIC WORKS

3140 WESLEYAN METHODIST Church of America. Administrative Department.
 The Wesleyan Methodist Church of America; established 1843. Marion, Ind., Wesley Press, 1961. 50 p.
 Cover-title: The Wesleyan Methodist Church of America; interesting facts for interested friends.

3141 WESLEYAN METHODIST Church of America. Department of Church Extension.
 These are the Wesleyan Methodists. Marion, Ind., 196?. Folder.

3142 LEE, Luther, 1800-1889.
 Wesleyan manual: a defence of the organization of the Wesleyan Methodist Connection, with an introd. by Rev. Cyrus Prindle. Syracuse, N.Y., Samuel Lee, Publisher, 1862. 190, 62 p.

With, as issued, his A synopsis of parliamentary rules for the use of ecclesiastical bodies and popular assemblies and conventions. Syracuse, N.Y., Samuel Lee, Publisher, 1862.

3143 SCOTT, Orange, 1800-1847.
The grounds of secession from the M.E. Church. New York, Arno Press & The New York Times, 1969. 229 p.
Cover-title: The anti-slavery crusade in America.
Reprint of 1848 ed.

--CATECHISMS AND CREEDS

3144 WESLEYAN METHODIST Church of America.
First studies in catechism. Marion, Ind., Department of Sunday Schools, Wesleyan Methodist Church of America, n.d. 38 p.

3145 WESLEYAN METHODIST Church of America. Editorial Department.
A guide to church membership. Marion, Ind., Wesley Press, 1963. 32 p.

3146 NICHOLSON, Roy Stephen, 1903-
Studies in church doctrines. 2d ed. Marion, Ind., Wesley Press, 1958. 55 p.

--CHARITIES

3147 HARNESS, Mary M.
Hephzibah poetry. Syracuse, N.Y., Department of Home Missions of the Wesleyan Methodist Church, 195?. 8 p.

3148 SWAUGER, John Robert, 1900-1955.
The Hephzibah Orphanage. Syracuse, N.Y., Department of Home Missions of the Wesleyan Methodist Church of America, 1950. 16 p.

--CHURCH EXTENSION

3149 WESLEYAN METHODIST Church of America. Department of Church Extension.
A decade of progress [1948-1958] in Wesleyan Methodist Churches. Conference by conference record with area and general summaries. n.p., n.d. [37]ℓ.

3150 SWAUGER, John Robert, 1900-1955.
The Wesleyan witness to America. Syracuse, N.Y.,

Department of Home Missions of the Wesleyan Methodist Church of America, 1950. 45 p.

--CHURCH WORK

3151 CARRADINE, Beverly, 1848-1931.
Church entertainments: twenty objections. Syracuse, N.Y., A.W. Hall, 1891. 97 p.

--CLERGY.

3152 LEE, Luther, 1800-1889.
Woman's right to preach the gospel; a sermon, at the ordination of Rev. Miss Antoinette L. Brown, at South Butler, Wayne County, N.Y., Sept. 15, 1853. Syracuse, N.Y., The author, 1853. 22 p.

--CONDUCT OF LIFE

3153 CARRADINE, Beverly, 1848-1931.
The bottle. Syracuse, N.Y., A.W. Hall, 1896, c1893.

3154 FAILING, George Edgar, 1912-
What's right with tithing? Marion, Ind., Wesley Press, 196?. Folder.

3155 McINTYRE, Robert W., 1922-
The Ten Commandments for teen-agers. Grand Rapids, Mich., Baker Book House, 1965. 40 p.

3156 McMILLEN, Sim I., 1898-
Cancer by the carton! Introd. by Gil Dodds and Bill Wade. Westwood, N.J., Revell, 1964, c1963. 64 p.

3157 McMILLEN, Sim I., 1898-
None of these diseases. Westwood, N.J., F.H. Revell Co., 1963. 158 p.

3158 PAINE, Stephen William, 1908-
The Christian and the movies. Grand Rapids, Mich., Eerdmans, 1957. 79 p.

3159 VAN WORMER, Ivah B.
Keep thy garments. n.p., 196?. 11 p.
Mimeographed.

3160 WILCOX, Leslie D.
Beacons for youth. Central, S.C., 1953. 62 p.

-- --AUTHORITATIVE SOURCES

3161   CARRADINE, Beverly, 1848-1931.
Secret societies: are they right or wrong? Are they a blessing or a curse? An address by Rev. B. Carradine, D.D., pastor of the Centenary M.E. Church, St. Louis, before his congregation, Jan. 4, 1891. Syracuse, N.Y., A.W. Hall, 1891. Cover-title, 19 p.

--DOCTRINAL AND CONTROVERSIAL WORKS

3162   BLACK, Ernest Watson, 1890-1948.
God's financial plan. Marion, Ind., Wesley Press, 1962. Cover-title, 15 p.

3163   COX, Leo George, 1912-
"In earthen vessels; or, A treatise on holiness as it is related to the human nature." Unpublished M. Rel. thesis, Marion College, 1944. 74ℓ.

3164   COX, Leo George, 1912-
"In earthen vessles; or, A treatise on holiness as it is related to the human nature." Revised and enlarged. Unpublished B.D. thesis, Marion College, 1945. 178ℓ.

3165   COX, Leo George, 1912-
John Wesley's concept of perfection. Kansas City, Mo, Beacon Hill Press, 1964. 227 p.

3166   DeWEERD, James Arthur, 1916-1972.
The realities of Christian experience; with an introd. by F. Lincicome. Fairmount, Ind., Christian Publications Inc. (of Indiana), 1940. xi, 222 p.

3167   DOTY, Thomas K., 1833-1913.
The two-fold gift of the Holy Spirit. Chicago, T.B. Arnold, 1891. 240 p.

3168   HALL, Alvin Willard, 1852-
The resurrection of Christ, and what it stands for. Syracuse, N.Y., Wesleyan Methodist Publishing Association 1905. 51 p.

3169   HORNER, Ralph Cecil, 1854-1921.
Original and inbred sin. Ottawa, Ont., Can., R.L. Crain, 1896. 148 p.

3170   KINDSCHI, Paul L., 1917- , ed.
Entire sanctification. Marion, Ind., Wesley Press, 1964. 80 p.

II. 1. Christian Holiness Association

3171 LEE, Luther, 1800-1889.
Elements of theology; or, An exposition of the divine origin, doctrines, morals and institutions of Christianity. New York, Miller, Orton & Mulligan; Syracuse, N.Y., S. Lee, 1856. viii, 580 p.

3172 LEE, Luther, 1800-1889.
Elements of theology; or, An exposition of the divine origin, doctrines, morals and institutions of Christianity. 2d ed. Syracuse, N.Y., S. Lee, 1859. viii, 584 p.

3173 LEE, Luther, 1800-1889.
Elements of theology; or, An exposition of the divine origin, doctrines, morals and institutions of Christianity. 11th ed. Syracuse, N.Y., A.W. Hall, 1892. 584 p.

3174 LEE, Luther, 1800-1889.
Natural theology; or, The existence, attributes, and government of God, including the obligations and duties of men, demonstrated by arguments drawn from the phenomena of nature. Syracuse, N.Y., Wesleyan Methodist Publishing House, 1866. 188 p.

3175 LEE, Luther, 1800-1889.
Slavery examined in the light of the Bible. Syracuse, N.Y., Wesleyan Methodist Book Room, 1855. 185 p.

3176 LEE, Luther, 1800-1889.
Slavery examined in the light of the Bible. Syracuse, N.Y., Wesleyan Methodist Book Room, 1855; Detroit, Negro History Press, 1969. 185 p.

3177 MATLACK, Lucius Columbus, 1816-1883.
A true church: its simplicity of character, dignity of position, relation to truth. New York, Book Room Office, 1848. 24 p.

3178 MEEK, J. H.
Entire sanctification. Syracuse, N.Y., Wesleyan Methodist Publishing Association, n.d. 45 p.

3179 NICHOLSON, Roy Stephen, 1903-
The Arminian emphases. Owosso, Mich., Owosso College, 196?. 167 p. (M.L. Goodman lecture series)

-- --AUTHORITATIVE SOURCES

3180 CARRADINE, Beverly, 1848-1931.
Beulah land. Syracuse, N.Y., Wesleyan Methodist Publishing Association, 1904. 276 p.

3181   CARRADINE, Beverly, 1848-1931.
        Sanctification; introduction by Rev. L.L. Pickett. Syracuse, N.Y., A.W. Hall, 1897. 222 p.

3182   CLARKE, Adam, 1760?-1832.
        Entire sanctification. Syracuse, N.Y., Wesleyan Methodist Publishing House, n.d. 22 p.
          Cover-title.

-- --PREDESTINATION

3183   BUCK, E. Parker
        The true Bible teaching versus the eternal security theory. n.p., 1962. 15 p.

3184   McKINLEY, O. Glenn, -1970.
        Where two creeds meet; a Biblical evaluation of Calvinism and Arminianism. Kansas City, Mo., Beacon Hill Press, 1959. 123 p.

--EDUCATION

3185   NELSON, Marven O.
        "The administration of guidance in colleges related to the Wesleyan and Free Methodist churches." Unpublished Ed.D. dissertation, University of Buffalo, 1952. 123ℓ.

3186   SMITH, Willard Garfield, 1911-
        "The history of church-controlled colleges in the Wesleyan Methodist Church." Unpublished Ph.D. dissertation, New York University, 1951.

3187   TAYLOR, Charles Winthrop
        "The history of the (higher) educational movement of the Wesleyan Methodist Church of America." Unpublished Ph.D. dissertation, Indiana University, 1959.

--EVANGELISTIC WORK

3188   LEE, Luther, 1800-1889.
        The revival manual. New York, Wesleyan Methodist Book Room, 1850. 108 p.

--HISTORY

3189   CLARK, Elmer Talmage, 1886-1966.
        The small sects in America. Rev. ed. New York, Abingdon Press, c1965. 256 p.
          Account of Wesleyan Methodist Church: p. 63.

II. 1. Christian Holiness Association

3190   JENNINGS, Arthur T., 1858-1914.
       History of American Wesleyan Methodism. Syracuse, N.Y., Wesleyan Methodist Publishing Association, 1902. 193 p.

3191   McLEISTER, Ira Ford, 1879-1963.
       History of the Wesleyan Methodist Church of America. Syracuse, N.Y., Wesleyan Methodist Publishing Association, 1934. 347 p.

3192   McLEISTER, Ira Ford, 1879-1963.
       History of the Wesleyan Methodist Church of America. Rev. ed. [i.e. 3d ed.] by Roy Stephen Nicholson. Marion, Ind., Wesley Press, 1959. 558 p.

3193   MARTIN, Joel
       The Wesleyan manual; or, History of Wesleyan Methodism. Syracuse, N.Y., Wesleyan Methodist Publishing House, 1889. 205 p.

3194   MATLACK, Lucius Columbus, 1816-1883.
       The antislavery struggle and triumph in the Methodist Episcopal Church; with an introd. by Rev. D.D. Whedon. New York, Phillips & Hunt; Cincinnati, Walden & Stowe, 1881. 379 p.

3195   MATLACK, Lucius Columbus, 1816-1883.
       The antislavery struggle and triumph in the Methodist Episcopal Church; introd. by D.D. Whedon. New York, Negro Universities Press, 1969. 379 p.
       Reprint of 1881 ed.

3196   MATLACK, Lucius Columbus, 1816-1883.
       The history of American slavery and Methodism from 1780 to 1849; and, History of the Wesleyan Methodist Connection of America; in two parts, with an appendix. New York, 1849. 2 v. in 1.

3197   MATLACK, Lucius Columbus, 1816-1883.
       The life of Rev. Orange Scott, comp. from his personal narrative, correspondence, and other authentic sources of information. New York, C. Prindle and L.C. Matlack at the Wesleyan Methodist Book Room, 1847-1848. 2 pts. in 1 v. (307 p.)

3198   MATLACK, Lucius Columbus, 1816-1883.
       Secession: a personal narrative of proscription for being an abolitionist. Syracuse, N.Y., 1856. 65 p.

3199   MEAD, Frank Spencer, 1898-
       Handbook of denominations in the United States. 2d rev. ed. New York, Abingdon Press, 1961. 272 p.

"Wesleyan Methodist Church of America": p. 163.

3200 SIMPSON, Matthew, bp., 1811-1884, ed.
Cyclopaedia of Methodism; embracing sketches of its rise, progress, and present condition, with biographical notices and numerous illustrations. Philadelphia, Everts & Stewart, 1878. 1027 p.
"Wesleyan Methodist Connection": p. 922-924.

--HISTORY OF DOCTRINES

3201 MEREDITH, Clyde W., 1901-
"Wesleyan theology of personal experience." Unpublished Th.M. thesis, Butler University, 1944.

--HYMNS

3202 WESLEYAN METHODIST Connection of America.
A collection of hymns for the use of the Wesleyan Methodist Connection of America. Boston, Published by O. Scott for the Wesleyan Methodist Connection, 1843. 510 p.

3203 WESLEYAN METHODIST Connection of America.
A collection of hymns, for the use of the Wesleyan Methodist Connection of America, comp. by Rev. Cyrus Prindle.... New ed. Syracuse, N.Y., Published by Lucius C. Matlack, for the Wesleyan Methodist Connection, 1855. 493 p.
Compiled by order of the General Conference of 1844.

3204 WESLEYAN METHODIST Connection (or Church) of America.
Sacred hymns and tunes, designed to be used by the Wesleyan Methodist Connection (or Church) of America. Syracuse, N.Y., A.W. Hall, agent, 1900. 169 p.

3205 WESLEYAN METHODIST Connection (or Church) of America.
The Wesleyan Methodist Hymnal, designed for use in the Wesleyan Methodist Connection (or Church) of America. Syracuse, N.Y., Wesleyan Methodist Publishing Association, 1910. 498 p.
Prepared by Hymnal Commission of the Free Methodist Church of North America, including the Rev. A.T. Jennings, representative of the Wesleyan Methodist Connection (or Church) of America.

3206 WESLEYAN METHODIST Church of America.
Hymns of the living faith; official hymnal of the Wesleyan Methodist Church of America. Syracuse, N.Y., Wesleyan Methodist Publishing Association, 1951. Unpaged.
"The Commission preparing Hymns of the Living Faith

represents ... both sponsoring communions, the Wesleyan Methodist Church of America and the Free Methodist Church of North America."

3207 BREWSTER, William H.
A collection of hymns for the use of the Wesleyan Methodist Connection of America. Syracuse, N.Y., Pub. by A. Crooks for the Wesleyan Methodist Connection, 1868, c1863. 648 p.

3208 PRINDLE, Cyrus, 1800-1885.
A collection of hymns for the use of the Wesleyan Methodist Connection of America. New ed. New York, O. Scott, 1846. 493 p.

--MISSIONS

3209 ENCYCLOPEDIA OF modern Christian missions; the agencies. Burton L. Goddard, ed.... Camden, N.J., T. Nelson, 1967. xix, 743 p.
"The Wesleyan Methodist Church of America, Department of World Missions," by Robert N. Lytle: p. 686-688.

3210 HENLEY, John H.
Mission work among the Mexicans. Syracuse, N.Y., Department of Home Missions of the Wesleyan Methodist Church of America, 1950. 11 p.

3211 WESLEYAN METHODISM among the Indians: Onondaga Indian Mission, by Hugh Newcomb; Brainerd Training School, by J.R. Swauger. Syracuse, N.Y., Department of Home Missions of the Wesleyan Methodist Church of America, 1950. 37 p.

--PERIODICALS

3212 BIBLE STANDARD; a monthly messenger devoted to practical Christianity. 1- , 1870-1892. Wheaton, Ill.; Syracuse, N.Y.
Merged with Wesleyan Methodist.

3213 WAY OF Holiness. 1- , 1864-19??. Syracuse, N.Y.

3214 WESLEYAN HERALD. 1- , 189?- . -----, Ohio.

3215 WESLEYAN METHODIST. 1-126, no. 14, 1842-July 3, 1968. Boston; New York; Syracuse, N.Y.; Marion, Ind.
1842-1850 as True Wesleyan; 1850-1883 as American Wesleyan.

Merged with Pilgrim Holiness Advocate to form Wesleyan Advocate.

3216 WESLEYAN MISSIONARY. 1-49, 1919-July/Aug. 1968.
Syracuse, N.Y.; Marion, Ind.
Merged with World Missions Bulletin to form Wesleyan World.

3217 WESLEYAN YOUTH. 1-33, no. 9, 1936-Sept. 1968. Syracuse, N.Y.; Marion, Ind.
1-8, 1936-1943 as Wesleyan Young People's Journal.
Merged with Pilgrim Youth News to form Win.

--POLEMICAL WORKS

-- --UNITARIANISM

3218 LEE, Luther, 1800-1889.
Discussion of the doctrine of the Trinity, between Luther Lee, Wesleyan minister, and Samuel J. May, Unitarian minister [commenced February 28th, 1854--contained eleven evenings] reported by Lucius C. Matlack. Syracuse, N.Y., Wesleyan Book Room, 1854. 160 p.

--POLITICAL AND SOCIAL CRITICISM

3219 LEE, Luther, 1800-1889.
The debates of the General Conference of the Methodist Episcopal Church ... [and] a review of the proceedings, by Rev. Luther Lee and Rev. E. Smith. New York, 1845.

--RELATIONS

-- --FREE METHODIST CHURCH

3220 JOINT COMMISSION of the Free Methodist and Wesleyan Methodist Churches.
Proposed discipline for the United Wesleyan Methodist Church. n.p., 1955. 122 p.

-- --PILGRIM HOLINESS CHURCH

3221 JOINT STUDY Conference on Church Growth, held at Marion, Indiana, on June 17-21, 1968; world missions of the Pilgrim Holiness and Wesleyan Methodist churches. n.p., 1968. 1 v. (various pagings)

3222 WILKINS, Chester, 1918-
"A review of the recently proposed union of the Wesley-

II. 1. Christian Holiness Association

an Methodist Church and the Pilgrim Holiness Church."
Unpublished M.A. thesis, Butler University, 1960. 80¢.

--SERMONS

3223 BLACK, Ernest Watson, 1890-1948.
Living messages from the Canaan journey. Kannapolis?, N.C., 1948. 230 p.

3224 CARTER, Charles Webb, 1905-
Road to revival. Butler, Ind., Higley Press, 1959. 152 p.

--ARKANSAS

3225 NOFSINGER, George F.
Wesleyan Methodism in the Arkansas Ozarks. Syracuse, N.Y., Department of Home Missions of the Wesleyan Methodist Church of America, 1950. 16 p.

--AUSTRALIA

3226 SWAUGER, John Robert, 1900-1955.
The Wesleyan Methodist Church in Australia. Syracuse, N.Y., Department of Home Missions of the Wesleyan Methodist Church of America, 1950. 29 p.

--INDIA

3227 ASHTON, Albert E.
Our work in the Orient, by Rev. Albert E. Ashton and Mrs. Bessie Sherman Ashton. Syracuse, N.Y., Wesleyan Methodist Publishing House, 191?. 32 p.

3228 BANKER, Floyd E.
From famine to fruitage; an account of fifty years of Wesleyan Methodism in western India, by Floyd and Hazel Banker. Marion, Ind., Wesley Press, 1960. 188 p.

3229 LIDDICK, Ruth (Sension)
Fifty years in India, 1910-1960. Marion, Ind., Department of World Missions, Wesleyan Methodist Church of America, 1960. Unpaged.

--KENTUCKY

3230 BLANCHARD, Charles Lorraine, 1902-
The Wesleyan work in the Kentucky mountains. Syra-

cuse, N.Y., Department of Home Missions of the Wesleyan Methodist Church of America, 1950. 26 p.

--NORTH CAROLINA

3231 POPE, Liston
Millhands & preachers; a study of Gastonia. New Haven, Yale University Press, 1942. 369 p.
Account of Wesleyan Methodist Church: p. 96-103, 127-128, 138.

--SIERRA LEONE

3232 BIRCH, Zola Dee (Kinnison), 1892-1950.
Sierra Leone facts-figures-faith. Syracuse, N.Y., Wesleyan Methodist Publishing House, 1939? 80 p.

3233 CARTER, Charles Webb, 1905-
A half century of American Wesleyan missions in West Africa. Syracuse, N.Y., Wesleyan Methodist Publishing Association, 1940.

3234 CARTER, Charles Webb, 1905-
Transformed Africans: on the conversion of an African village. Syracuse, N.Y., Department of Home Missions of the Wesleyan Methodist Church, 1938. 16 p.

3235 CLARKE, George H., -1929.
American Wesleyan Methodist missions of Sierra Leone, W. Africa, by George H. Clarke and Mary Lane Clarke. Syracuse, N.Y., Wesleyan Methodist Publishing Association, n.d. 256 p.

--SOUTH CAROLINA

3236 GAINES, Ina
Wesleyan Methodism in the Blue Ridge Mountains. Syracuse, N.Y., Department of Home Missions of the Wesleyan Methodist Church of America, 1950. 19 p.

--SOUTHERN STATES

3237 NICHOLSON, Roy Stephen, 1903-
Wesleyan Methodism in the South; being the story of eighty-six years of reform and religious activities in the South as conducted by the American Wesleyans, with an introd. by the Rev. J.S. Willett. Syracuse, N.Y., Wesleyan Methodist Publishing Association, 1933. 294 p.

II. 1. Christian Holiness Association

MISSIONARY CHURCH (1969-   )

Formed by merger of the Missionary Church Association and the United Missionary Church in 1969, the Missionary Church claimed 354 congregations and 21,250 members in the United States and Canada at its inception. Both parent groups had Mennonite founders and were strongly evangelistic. The united group has nearly 200 missionaries at work in nineteen countries. In addition to two Bible colleges in Canada, the Missionary Church sponsors Bethel College and Fort Wayne Bible College in Indiana. Per capita giving in a recent year was $275. Membership is concentrated in the Midwest, and denominational headquarters is in Fort Wayne, Indian. The Missionary Church works in cooperation with the Christian Holiness Association.

3238 CONSTITUTION PROPOSED as basis for union of the Missionary Church Association and the United Missionary Church. n.p., 196?. 31, 3 p.

3239 MISSIONARY CHURCH.
Constitution of the Missionary Church. Fort Wayne, Ind., 1969. 49 p.
Added t.-p.: Constitution and manual.

3240 MISSIONARY CHURCH. Merging General Conference.
Minutes, March 12-16, 1969, Detroit, Michigan. n.p., 1969. 38 p.
Mimeographed.

3241 MISSIONARY CHURCH. General Conference.
Minutes. 1st- , 1971- . n.p., 1971- .
Biennial.
Mimeographed.

--APOLOGETIC WORKS

3242 MISSIONARY CHURCH.
The Missionary Church in today's world. Fort Wayne, Ind., 197?. Folder.

--DOCTRINAL AND CONTROVERSIAL WORKS

3243 MISSIONARY CHURCH. General Board.
The assurance of the believer. Fort Wayne, Ind., 197?. Folder.
"Revised and adopted by the General Board of the Missionary Church."

----GLOSSOLALIA

3244 MISSIONARY CHURCH.
　　　　The gift of tongues; the official position of the Missionary Church. Fort Wayne, Ind., 197?. 5 p.
　　　　Reproduced from type-written copy.

--HISTORY

3245 MEAD, Frank Spencer, 1898-
　　　　Handbook of denominations in the United States. New 5th ed. Nashville, Abingdon Press, 1970. 265 p.
　　　　"Missionary Church": p. 153-154.

--MISSIONS

3246 MISSIONARY CHURCH.
　　　　Windows. Fort Wayne, Ind., 197?. Folder.

-PERIODICALS

3247 EMPHASIS ON Faith and Living. 1- , Mar. 1969- .
　　　　Fort Wayne, Ind.
　　　　Supersedes Emphasis, Gospel Banner, and Missionary Banner.

3248 REPORT; a bulletin highlighting the world outreach of the Missionary Church.... 1- , 1971- . Fort Wayne, Ind.

Missionary Societies

AFRICA EVANGELISTIC BAND (1924-)

　　　　An interdenominational faith mission, the Africa Evangelistic Band was founded in 1924 by three North Irish sisters, the Misses May, Emma and Helena Garratt. Formerly associated with the holiness-oriented Faith Mission of Ireland and Scotland, the women felt divinely led to pursue unsponsored missionary work in South Africa. As in the Faith Mission, workers are called Pilgrims. Band representatives work among all social classes, concentrating on remote areas, and cooperating with established local churches. Although the Band sponsors primary, secondary and Bible schools and does medical work, emphasis is on direct evangelism.

　　　　From the Union of South Africa work spread to Southwest Africa, Rhodesia and the Belgian Congo where twenty-five European

II. 1. Christian Holiness Association 389

missionaries were at work in the early 1960's. Training schools for native and European workers and bookstores for literature distribution are operated in key cities. Headquartered in Cape Town, the Africa Evangelistic Band issues The Pilgrim and Bethel News monthly.

--HISTORY

3249 CLOTHIER, M. James
　　　　The arrow of deliverance; the story of what God has wrought in and through the work of the A.E.B. during the past 25 years. Cape Town, S. Afr., Africa Evangelistic Band, 1949. 47 p.

3250 ENCYCLOPEDIA OF modern Christian missions; the agencies. Burton L. Goddard, ed.... Camden, N.J., T. Nelson, 1967. xix, 743 p.
　　　　"Africa Evangelistic Band," by H.G. Semark: p. 4-5.

--CONGO

3251 AFRICA EVANGELISTIC Band.
　　　　The first ten years in the Congo. n.p., 1947? 40 p.

--PERIODICALS

3252 BETHEL NEWS. 1- , 1959- . Kenilworth, Cape, S. Afr., Bethel Bible School, Kimberley.

3253 PILGRIM/PELGRIM. 1- , 1936?- . Kenilworth, Cape, S. Afr.; Mowbray, Cape, S. Afr.

AFRICA EVANGELISTIC MISSION (1902-1962)

This faith mission, which merged with the Pilgrim Holiness Church in 1962, resulted from the efforts of American missionaries: the Reverend and Mrs. Isaac O. Lehman and their son and daughter-in-law, the Reverend and Mrs. O.I. Lehman. Married in Africa, the elder Lehmans began evangelizing in the newly-opened gold fields around Johannesburg in 1902. Working among the more than 350,000 men there, the Lehmans encouraged converts to evangelize when they returned to their homes. As a result, the work spread from the Rand into eastern Transvaal and Portuguese East Africa. At the time of the merger, the Africa Evangelistic Mission was evangelizing on fifty of the 159 mine compounds on the Rand and 84 stations in Portuguese East Africa, with a total membership of 2185.

3254 ENCYCLOPEDIA OF modern Christian missions; the agencies. Burton L. Goddard, ed.... Camden, N.J., T. Nelson, 1967. xix, 743 p.
"Africa Evangelistic Mission": p. 5.

--HISTORY

3255 PILGRIM HOLINESS Church. General Conference.
Minutes of the Twenty-fourth General Conference of the Pilgrim Holiness Church, held at Winona Lake, Indiana, June 12-18, 1962. Indianapolis, Pilgrim Publishing House, 1962. 125 p.
Account of merger with Africa Evangelistic Mission: p. 75.

3256 THOMAS, Paul Westphal, 1894-1972.
"The days of our pilgrimage; a history of the Pilgrim Holiness Church," by Paul Westphal Thomas and Paul William Lee Thomas. Unpublished paper, 1968. 1 v. (various pagings)
In archives of The Wesleyan Church, Marion, Indiana.
"The Africa Evangelistic Mission": ℓ. 349-351.

BETHANY FELLOWSHIP (1945-)

[Also as Bethany Fellowship Missionary Training Center]

Formed in 1945 to promote evangelism by publication and worker training programs, this Minneapolis-based group takes a position on sanctification midway between the Holiness and Keswick movements. Subscribing to the doctrinal statement of the National Association of Evangelicals, the Fellowship sponsors the Bethany Fellowship Bible and Missionary Training Institute, issues numerous books and a periodical called The Message of the Cross, and since 1963 has conducted missionary work in Brazil. In addition to more than two dozen adult workers in Brazil, it supports more than sixty missionaries serving under other mission boards in over twenty countries. A warm relationship is maintained with Wesleyan holiness groups, a fact evidenced by the number of holiness authors published under the Bethany Fellowship imprint.

--DOCTRINAL AND CONTROVERSIAL WORKS

3257 HEGRE, Theodore A.
The cross and sanctification, formerly published as Three aspects of the cross. Minneapolis, Bethany Fellowship, 1960. 276 p.

II. 1. Christian Holiness Association

3258 HEGRE, Theodore A.
Three aspects of the cross. Minneapolis, Bethany Fellowship Press, 1960. 276 p.

3259 HEGRE, Theodore A.
The will of God--your sanctification. Minneapolis, Bethany Fellowship, 1961.

3260 JAMES, Maynard G., 1902-
I believe in the Holy Ghost. Foreword by Norman Grubb. Minneapolis, Bethany Fellowship, c1965. 167 p.

3261 STEELE, Daniel, 1824-1914.
Mile-stone papers: doctrinal, ethical, and experimental on Christian progress. Minneapolis, Bethany Fellowship, 196?. xii, 256 p.
Reprint of 1878 ed.

--EVANGELISTIC WORK

3262 RAVENHILL, Leonard
Why revival tarries; with a foreword by A.W. Tozer. Minneapolis, Bethany Fellowship, 1970, c1959. 175 p.
"Fourteenth printing."

--MISSIONS

3263 ENCYCLOPEDIA OF modern Christian missions; the agencies. Burton L. Goddard, ed.... Camden, N.J., T. Nelson, 1967. xix, 743 p.
"Bethany Fellowship, Inc.": p. 78.

--PERIODICALS

3264 MESSAGE OF the Cross. 1- , 1948- . Minneapolis, Minn.

BETHEL MISSION OF CHINA (1920-   )

The outgrowth of the work of Mary Stone (Shih Maiyü), a Chinese doctor educated at the University of Michigan and Johns Hopkins University, and Jennie V. Hughes, an independent missionary from California, the Bethel Mission is one of a very few missionary societies controlled and staffed largely by nationals. Founded in 1920, the original mission in Shanghai included an orphanage, a hospital, a nursing school, and elementary, secondary, and Bible schools for both sexes. When forced from the mainland by the Communists, four branch missions were operating in Shanghai and one in Hong Kong. The largest in China, the nursing school trained over 25,000 nurses. Educational and religious work among Chinese refugees spread from Hong Kong to Formosa and Indonesia. Bethel Mission directs nearly a hundred workers, from the Pasadena, California, headquarters established before Dr. Stone's death in 1954. Seeking support from other holiness groups (Dr. Stone and Miss Hughes were listed briefly as missionaries of the Pilgrim Holiness Church in the early 1920's), the Bethel Mission of China operates without denominational sponsorship. An illustrated newsletter is issued quarterly.

--BIOGRAPHY

3265 HU, Betty M.
Precious jewels. Pasadena, Calif., Bethel Mission of China, 1952. 142 p.

3266 SHANGHAI. BETHEL Mission.
Bethel heart throb surprises. Shanghai, 1932.

--HISTORY

3267 ENCYCLOPEDIA OF modern Christian missions; the agencies. Burton L. Goddard, ed.... Camden, N.J., T. Nelson, 1967. xix, 743 p.
"Bethel Mission of China, Inc.": p. 79-80.

3268 LAN, Alice Y.
We flee from Hong Kong, by Alice Y. Lan and Betty M. Hu. Rev. and enlarged ed. Pasadena, Calif., Bethel Mission of China, 1958. 150 p.

--PERIODICALS

3269 BETHEL MISSION of China.
Newsletter. 1- , 19??- . Pasadena, Calif.

BIBLE HOME AND FOREIGN MISSIONARY SOCIETY (1890-1924)

Launched by holiness people in Attleboro, Massachusetts, in 1890, the Bible Home and Foreign Missionary Society sponsored work on St. Thomas and St. Croix in the American Virgin Islands and on St. Kitts and Monserrat in the British West Indies. This faith mission depended on the support of holiness people in southeastern New England, particularly the constituency of the Portsmouth, Rhode Island, camp meeting. Over the years, the supporting group diminished. Additional backing became imperative, and in 1924 the Society united with the Pilgrim Holiness Church. At

II. 1. Christian Holiness Association

that time the group had four missionaries in the field.

3270 BIBLE HOME and Foreign Missionary Society.
By-laws, declaration of principles and articles of faith. n. p., n. d.

--HISTORY

3271 THOMAS, Paul Westphal, 1894-1972.
"The days of our pilgrimage; a history of the Pilgrim Holiness Church," by Paul Westphal Thomas and Paul William Lee Thomas. Unpublished paper, 1968. 1 v. (various pagings)
In archives of The Wesleyan Church, Marion, Indiana.
Account of the Bible Home and Foreign Missionary Society: ℓ. 120-121.

EVANGELICAL BIBLE MISSION (1939-   )

[1939-19?? as West Indies Bible Mission; 19??-19?? as East and West Indies Bible Mission]

This faith mission, organized in 1939 to back the work of G. T. Bustin, receives support at present from some of the smaller and more conservative holiness groups. While conducting tent meetings in Nebraska, Evangelist Bustin felt called to work in the West Indies. During the first nine years, he concentrated on the Bahamas and Haiti. In addition to direct evangelism, Bustin started a Bible training school and radio station in Haiti. Then in 1948, he embarked to a new field--Australia. There he came to feel that he should evangelize in the Central and Western Highlands of New Guinea, and with an Australian companion set out again. Although Bustin himself was in New Guinea only six months, the work that he and his companion began flourished. Within fifteen years, his followers established thirty mission stations, medical clinics serving over 20,000 patients per year, and Bible and English schools enrolling more than 200 students annually. In order to concentrate on New Guinea, Bustin relinquished the West Indian work to another group.

Before adopting the present name, Bustin's group operated as the West Indies Bible Mission and the East and West Indies Bible Mission. The Evangelical Bible Mission issues the Mission Messenger monthly from its headquarters in Summerfield, Florida.

3272 ENCYCLOPEDIA OF modern Christian missions; the agencies. Burton L. Goddard, ed.... Camden, N.J., T. Nelson, 1967. xix, 743 p.

"Evangelical Bible Mission, Inc.," by Charles M. Bustin: p. 253-254.

EVANGELISTIC FAITH MISSIONS (1905-   )

[Also as Faith Missions]

In 1905 Lewis Glenn, an Indiana school teacher inspired by Vivian Dake and the Pentecost Bands, set out as a faith missionary to Egypt. Gradually other American workers joined him, and in 1912 he began to publish a paper to marshal support, thereby laying the foundation for the Evangelistic Faith Missions. When the founder died in 1941, his son Victor assumed leadership. Since World War II expansion has marked the society's activities. In 1950 the group opened a mission in Eritrea; in 1960 it absorbed a small mission group in Guatemala; and in 1964 its workers entered El Salvador. Emphasis in all fields is on direct evangelism by national workers. Bible training schools and literature distribution programs are central to the group's program. From headquarters in Bedford, Indiana, the society issues over 40,000 copies of the Missionary Herald per month. Several groups affiliated with the Interdenominational Holiness Convention support the Evangelistic Faith Missions.

--BIOGRAPHY

3273   GLENN, Victor
       The price and product of missions. Bedford, Ind., Missionary-Evangelistic Ministries of the Evangelical Faith Missions, 1972. 40 p.
       Autobiographical.

--CONDUCT OF LIFE

3274   GLENN, Victor
       The victorious Christian, number one. Bedford, Ind., Evangelistic Faith Missions, n.d. Cover-title, 12 p.
       "This book was produced by Missionary Evangelistic Ministries of the Evangelistic Faith Missions."

3275   GLENN, Victor
       Victory over fear, number one. Bedford, Ind., Evangelistic Faith Missions, n. d. Cover-title, 12 p.
       "This book was produced by Missionary-Evangelistic Ministries of the Evangelistic Faith Missions."

3276   GLENN, Victor
       Victory over fear, number two. Bedford, Ind., Evangelistic Faith Missions, n.d. Cover-title, 12 p.

II. 1. Christian Holiness Association

"This book was produced by Missionary-Evangelistic Ministries of the Evangelical Faith Missions."

--HISTORY

3277 EVANGELISTIC FAITH Missions.
Losing to win: Victor Glenn, God's man in times like these. Bedford, Ind., 196?. 32 p.

3278 ENCYCLOPEDIA OF modern Christian missions; the agencies. Burton L. Goddard, ed.... Camden, N.J., T. Nelson, 1967. xix, 743 p.
"Evangelistic Faith Missions, Inc.," by Victor Glenn: p. 277.

3279 GLENN, Victor
Crossing continents with Christ; the amazing story of the miracle ministry of faith missions. Bedford, Ind., Evangelistic Faith Missions, 196?. 31 p.
"Sixth printing (revised)."

--PERIODICALS

3280 MISSIONARY HERALD. 1- , 1912- . Bedford, Ind.
19??-19?? as Missionary Holiness Herald and Vanguard; 19??-19?? as Missionary Holiness Herald.

--SERMONS

3280a GLENN, Victor
The victorious Christian. Bedford, Ind., Evangelistic Faith Missions, 197?. Cover-title, 12 p.
"This book was produced by Missionary Evangelistic Ministries of the Evangelistic Faith Missions."

HAITI INLAND MISSION (1949-)

[1964-present as Free Methodist Haiti Inland Mission; in Haiti, 1964-present, also as Croisades de la Grande Commission (Crusades of the Great Commission); 1964 merged with Free Methodist Church of North America]

Organized in 1949 to translate and print scripture portions into Creole, the Haiti Inland Mission merged with the Free Methodist Church in 1964. Now officially known in the United States as the Free Methodist Haiti Inland Mission, the work continues under the direction of Mildred E. Norbeck, the founder. An evangelistic program known as the Croisades de la Grande Commission is incorporated separately and has headquarters at Petionville, Haiti.

3281 HAITI INLAND Mission.
        Haiti Inland Mission: who, what, why. Intercession City?, Fla., 19??.

3282 NORBECK, Mildred E.
        The challenge of the hills. Intercession City?, Fla., 19??.

3283 NORBECK, Mildred E.
        The Haitian challenge and you. Intercession City, Fla., 1965.

--CONDUCT OF LIFE

3284 HOW TO repair broken fellowship (prescription for spiritual breakthrough). Sugar Grove, Pa., Great Commission Crusades, 19??. 15 p.

3285 WESLEY, John, 1703-1791.
        Prescription for spiritual breakthrough. (His sermon on "evil-speaking" abridged). Sugar Grove, Pa., Great Commission Crusades, 19??. 8 p.

--HISTORY

3286 HAITI INLAND Mission.
        Ten years in Haiti, 1949-1959: Haiti Inland Mission. Intercession City, Fla., 1960. Folder.

3287 ENCYCLOPEDIA OF modern Christian missions; the agencies. Burton L. Goddard, ed.... Camden, N.J., T. Nelson, 1967. xix, 743 p.
        "Haiti Inland Mission, Inc.," by Mildred E. Norbeck.

--PERIODICALS

3288 THE CALL from Haitian Hills. 1-16, 1949-1964. Intercession City, Fla.

3289 CHRISTIAN ACTION. 1- , 1965- . Intercession City, Fla., Great Commission Crusades.

IMMANUEL MISSION (1890-1923)

    In 1890, shortly after attending A.B. Simpson's missionary convention in New York, an English Wesleyan minister, named

II. 1. Christian Holiness Association 397

Samuel Bayley founded this independent holiness mission. It concentrated its efforts in Barbados and early utilized nationals in evangelistic work. In 1923, when the Mission (under the leadership of J.A. Humphrey, a West Indian) united with the Pilgrim Holiness Church, the group had ten stations. A year later, the Pilgrim Holiness Church absorbed the Bible Home and Foreign Missionary Society as well. The two additions greatly strengthened its missionary outreach in the Caribbean area.

--HISTORY

3290 IVES, R. Wingrove
A missionary's cry from Barbados; last chapter by Rev. R.G. Finch, General Missionary Superintendent of the Pilgrim Holiness Church. Kingswood, Ky., Missionary Office, 192?. 72 p.

3291 THOMAS, Paul Westphal, 1894-1972.
"The days of our pilgrimage; a history of the Pilgrim Holiness Church," by Paul Westphal Thomas and Paul William Lee Thomas. Unpublished paper, 1968. 1 v. (various pagings)
In archives of The Wesleyan Church, Marion, Indiana.
Account of the Immanuel Mission on Barbados: ℓ. 121-122.

INDIA NORTH-WEST MISSION (1920-1955)

[1920-1926 as Simla Hill States Mission]

A faith mission founded by British holiness people in 1920, the India North-West Mission merged with the Oriental Missionary Society in 1955. From 1920 to 1926 it was called the Simla Hill States Mission.

3292 ENCYCLOPEDIA OF modern Christian missions; the agencies. Burton L. Goddard, ed.... Camden, N.J., T. Nelson, 1967. xix, 743 p.
"India North-West Mission": p. 326.

JAPAN EVANGELISTIC BAND (1903-)

Organized in 1903 by Barclay F. Buxton (1860-1946) and A. Paget Wilkes (1871-1934), Anglicans who had served with the Church Missionary Society, the Japan Evangelistic Band is a nondenominational society intent on evangelizing through holiness conventions and training national workers. Both founders were prolific writers whose works have circulated widely in Japan, Britain and

America. (Two of Wilkes' works have long been required reading for ordination candidates in the Church of the Nazarene.) In 1905 the Band founded the Kansai Bible College, which had more than 300 graduates by the mid-1960's. Its encouragement of an indigenous church led to the establishment of the autonomous Nihon Iesu Kirisuto Kyodan (Japan Church of Jesus Christ) which has over 7000 members worshipping in fifty-nine churches located largely in southwestern Honshu and Shikoku. In addition, the Japan Evangelistic Band supports about twenty European and thirty Japanese workers who staff a large mission in Kobe, work with university students in Tokyo, and itinerate widely in rural areas distributing literature.

--BIOGRAPHY

3293   WILKES, Alphaeus Nelson Paget, 1871-1934.
        Moving pictures; or, Who's who? in the Japan Evangelistic Band. New and rev. ed. London, 1923. 31 p.

3294   WILKES, Alphaeus Nelson Paget, 1871-1934.
        Who's who? in the Japan Evangelistic Band. New and rev. ed. London?, 1926. 30 p.

--CONDUCT OF LIFE

3295   BUXTON, Barclay Fowell, 1860-1946.
        Following hard after God, a letter. London, Japan Evangelistic Band, 1947. 9 p.

3296   BUXTON, Barclay Fowell, 1860-1946.
        Life's possibilities: addresses. London, Japan Evangelistic Band, 1949. 75 p.
        Selected from The still small voice.

3297   CHAMBERS, Oswald, 1874-1917.
        The moral foundations of life; a series of talks on the ethical principles of the Christian life. London, Simpkin Marshall, 1936. 128 p.
        The chapters have appeared as articles in the B.T.C. Journal. cf. Foreword.

3298   SMITH, Allister
        "Made whole." London, Japan Evangelistic Band, 1956. 31 p.
        On personal Christianity.

3299   WILKES, Alphaeus Nelson Paget, 1871-1934.
        The dynamic of service. 4th ed. London, Japan Evangelistic Band, 1924. 310 p.

II. 1. Christian Holiness Association

3300 WILKES, Alphaeus Nelson Paget, 1871-1934.
The dynamic of service. 13th ed. London, Japan Evangelistic Band, 1955. 154 p.

--DEVOTIONAL LITERATURE

3301 CHAMBERS, Oswald, 1874-1917.
The discipline of prayer. 3d ed. London, Simpkin Marshall, 1936. 61 p.

3302 CHAMBERS, Oswald, 1874-1917.
The golden book of Oswald Chambers: my utmost for His Highest; selections for the year. New York, Dodd, Mead & Co., 1935. 375 p.
London ed. (Simpkin, Marshall & Co.) has title: My utmost for His Highest.

3303 CHAMBERS, Oswald, 1874-1917.
If ye shall ask.... New York, Dodd, Mead & Co., 1938. vii, 123 p.

3304 CHAMBERS, Oswald, 1874-1917.
My utmost for His Highest; selections for the year. London, Simpkin, Marshall & Co., 1927. 366 p.

3305 CHAMBERS, Oswald, 1874-1917.
The place of help; a book of devotional readings. London, Simpkin Marshall, 1935. xii, 240 p.

3306 CHAMBERS, Oswald, 1874-1917.
The place of help; a book of devotional readings. New York, Dodd, Mead & Co., 1936. viii, 286 p.

--DOCTRINAL AND CONTROVERSIAL WORKS

3307 BANKS, Stanley
The golden highway. London, Japan Evangelistic Band, n. d.

3308 BANKS, Stanley
Pathway to power. London, Japan Evangelistic Band, 1961. 44 p.

3309 BUXTON, Barclay Fowell, 1860-1946.
The baptism of the Holy Ghost: the essential preparation for all Christian work, a few words on Acts I & II. London, S.W. Partridge & Co., 1891. 39 p.

3310 BUXTON, Barclay Fowell, 1860-1946.
The Book of Jonah. London, Japan Evangelistic Band, 1930. 53 p.

3311 BUXTON, Barclay Fowell, 1860-1946.
　　　　The Book of Ruth: its message for Christians today.
　　London, Japan Evangelistic Band, 1929.　62 p.

3312 BUXTON, Barclay Fowell, 1860-1946.
　　　　Heavenly places; four Bible readings on holiness.
　　London, Japan Evangelistic Band, 1935.　40 p.

3313 BUXTON, Barclay Fowell, 1860-1946.
　　　　The royal anointing.　London, Japan Evangelistic Band,
　　1936.　22 p.

3314 CHAMBERS, Oswald, 1874-1917.
　　　　Baffled to fight better; talks on the book of Job.　4th
　　ed.　Oxford, Eng., Alden & Co.; London, Simpkin Marshall,
　　1931.　159 p.

3315 CHAMBERS, Oswald, 1874-1917.
　　　　Biblical psychology; a series of preliminary studies.
　　London, Simpkin Marshall, n.d.　viii, 269 p.

3316 CHAMBERS, Oswald, 1874-1917.
　　　　Biblical psychology.　London, S.W. Partridge & Co.,
　　1920.

3317 CHAMBERS, Oswald, 1874-1917.
　　　　Conformed to His image.　London, Marshall, Morgan &
　　Scott, 1950.　127 p.

3318 CHAMBERS, Oswald, 1874-1917.
　　　　He shall glorify me.　London, Simpkin Marshall, 1949.

3319 CHAMBERS, Oswald, 1874-1917.
　　　　If thou wilt be perfect.　London, Simpkin Marshall,
　　1939.　133 p.

3320 CHAMBERS, Oswald, 1874-1917.
　　　　The love of God.　London, Marshall, Morgan & Scott,
　　n.d.　183 p.

3321 CHAMBERS, Oswald, 1874-1917.
　　　　The making of a Christian.　London, Simpkin, Marshall,
　　1935.　37 p.

3322 CHAMBERS, Oswald, 1874-1917.
　　　　Our brilliant heritage.　Oxford, Eng., Alden Press,
　　1931.　47 p.

3323 CHAMBERS, Oswald, 1874-1917.
　　　　The philosophy of sin--and other studies in the problems
　　of man's moral life.　London, Simpkin Marshall, n.d.
　　82 p.

II. 1. Christian Holiness Association

3324 CHAMBERS, Oswald, 1874-1917.
The psychology of redemption. London, Simpkin Marshall, 1930. 147 p.
"Second edition."
"This book is compiled from verbatim notes taken of lectures given in 1915 to the students at the Bible Training College, Clapham, and in the following year to men of the Egyptian expeditionary force in the Y.M.C.A. hut, Zeitoun, Egypt."--Foreword.

3325 CHAMBERS, Oswald, 1874-1917.
Shade of His hand; talks on the Book of Ecclesiastes. Oxford, Eng., Alden Press, 1924. 153 p.

3326 CHAMBERS, Oswald, 1874-1917.
The shadow of an agony. London, Simpkin Marshall, 1933. 123 p.

3327 CHAMBERS, Oswald, 1874-1917.
So send I you; a series of missionary studies. London, Simpkin Marshall, 1930. 176 p.

3328 CHAMBERS, Oswald, 1874-1917.
Studies in the Sermon on the Mount. 5th ed. London, Simpkin Marshall, 1932. 111 p.
"First published 1911."

3329 WILKES, Alphaeus Nelson Paget, 1871-1934.
The Bible and modern thought. London, Japan Evangelistic Band, 1929. 41 p.

3330 WILKES, Alphaeus Nelson Paget, 1871-1934.
Christ's personal interviews.... London, Japan Evangelistic Band, 1935. 22 p.

3331 WILKES, Alphaeus Nelson Paget, 1871-1934.
Deliverance and joy. London, Japan Evangelistic Band, 1936. 15 p.

3332 WILKES, Alphaeus Nelson Paget, 1871-1934.
The dynamic of faith. Edinburgh, London, Oliphants, 1916. xii, 178 p.

3333 WILKES, Alphaeus Nelson Paget, 1871-1934.
The dynamic of faith.... 2d ed. Edinburgh, London, Oliphants, 1923. xi, 216 p.

3334 WILKES, Alphaeus Nelson Paget, 1871-1934.
The dynamic of faith. London, Edinburgh, Oliphants, 1956. 125 p.

3335 WILKES, Alphaeus Nelson Paget, 1871-1934.
The dynamic of life. London, Japan Evangelistic Band, 1931. xii, 305 p.

3336 WILKES, Alphaeus Nelson Paget, 1871-1934.
The dynamic of redemption; or, The blood of Jesus. London, Japan Evangelistic Band, 1924. x, 245 p.

3337 WILKES, Alphaeus Nelson Paget, 1871-1934.
Sanctification. 11th ed. London, Japan Evangelistic Band, 1947. 83 p.

3338 WILKES, Alphaeus Nelson Paget, 1871-1934.
A series of Bible readings [on the significance of the word "sanctification" in the New Testament] given at the J.E.B. annual conference.... London, Japan Evangelistic Band, 1923. 46 p.

3339 WILKES, Alphaeus Nelson Paget, 1871-1934.
So great salvation. London, Japan Evangelistic Band, 1928. 45 p.

-- --AUTHORITATIVE SOURCES

3340 BRENGLE, Samuel Logan, 1860-1936.
The guest of the soul. London, Marshall, Morgan and Scott, 1934. 127 p.

--HISTORY

3341 BUXTON, Barclay Godfrey
The reward of faith in the life of Barclay Fowell Buxton, 1860-1946. London, Lutterworth Press, 1949. 274 p.

3342 ENCYCLOPEDIA OF modern Christian missions; the agencies. Burton L. Goddard, ed.... Camden, N.J., T. Nelson, 1967. xix, 743 p.
"Japan Evangelistic Band," by Eric W. Gosden: p. 346.

3343 GOVAN STEWART, Isabel Rosie, 1900-
Dynamic: Paget Wilkes of Japan; foreword by B.G. Buxton. London, Edinburgh, Marshall, Morgan & Scott, 1957. 96 p.

3344 PATTISON, Mary Winifred Dunn
Ablaze for God; the life story of Paget Wilkes.... London, Japan Evangelistic Band, 1936. xii, 317 p.

3345 WILKES, Alphaeus Nelson Paget, 1871-1934.
Brimming over; or, Some incidents in the story of the J.E.B. London, Japan Evangelistic Band, 1923. 94 p.

3346 WILKES, Alphaeus Nelson Paget, 1871-1934.
His glorious power; or, The story of J.E.B. London, Japan Evangelistic Band, 1933. 182 p.

--PASTORAL THEOLOGY

3347 CHAMBERS, Oswald, 1874-1917.
Workmen of God; the cure of souls. New York, Dodd, Mead & Co., 1938. vii, 117 p.
"Books by Oswald Chambers": p. 117.

--PERIODICALS

3348 JAPAN EVANGELISTIC Band. 1- , Mar. 1906- . London.
1-20, no. 3 as Japan Evangelistic Band.
Quarterly Magazine; 21-52, no. 4, Jan./Feb. 1926-Oct./Dec. 1947 as Japan Evangelistic Band Magazine.

3349 JAPAN EVANGELISTIC Band.
News-letter for Prayer. 1- , 19??- . London.

3350 JAPAN EVANGELISTIC Band.
Witness series. 1- , 1948- . London.

3351 SUNRISE; newsletter for boys and girls. 1- , 1946- .
Colchester, Eng.

3352 SUNRISE; the junior quarterly magazine of the Japan Evangelistic Band. 1- , 19??- . Colchester, Eng.

--JAPAN

3353 GOSDEN, Eric William
Faith resurgent; God at work in modern Japan. London, Oliphants, 1967. 104 p.

3354 GOSDEN, Eric William
50 years on Theatre Street. London, Japan Evangelistic Band, 1968. 39 p.

3355 GOSDEN, Eric William
Take fire! James Cuthbertson of Japan; introd. by Paul S. Rees. London, Marshall, Morgan & Scott, 1960. 110 p.

3356 GOSDEN, Eric William
Upon this rock.... London, Edinburgh, Marshall, Morgan & Scott, 1957. 158 p.
On Sumi San, a Japanese nurse, and her conversion to Christianity.

3357 WILKES, Alphaeus Nelson Paget, 1871-1934.
Missionary joys in Japan; or, Leaves from my journal ... with an introd. by the Rev. Barclay F. Buxton. London, Morgan & Scott, 1913. xvi, 321 p.

JAPAN RESCUE MISSION (1922-1940/1)

Established about 1922 by George Dempsey, a British holiness worker who had visited Japan in 1918, the Japan Rescue Mission operated in the period between the world wars. The group disbanded in 1940 or 1941.

3358 FORD, Jack, 1908-
In the steps of John Wesley; the Church of the Nazarene in Britain. Kansas City, Mo., Printed by Nazarene Publishing House, 1968. 300 p.
Account of Japan Rescue Mission: p. 29, 34 (footnote 86).

LEBANON MISSIONARY BIBLE COLLEGE (1947-)

Graduates of this non-denominational holiness school at Berwick-on-Tweed, England, founded in 1947, currently serve under approximately thirty foreign mission boards.

3359 ENCYCLOPEDIA OF modern Christian missions; the agencies. Burton L. Goddard, ed.... Camden, N.J., T. Nelson, 1967. xix, 743 p.
"Lebanon Missionary Bible College": p. 363.

ORIENTAL MISSIONARY SOCIETY (1901-)

[1901-19?? as Cowman and Kilbourne Work; April 1973-present as OMS International; in Latin America as Inter-American Missionary Society]

In 1901 Charles E. Cowman and his wife, Lettie, went to Japan as faith missionaries. Joined a year later by Ernest A. Kilbourne, a telegrapher whom Cowman worked with in Chicago, the mission (known at first simply as the Cowman and Kilbourne Work) promoted its activities in a paper called Electric Messages. Aided by Juji Nakada, a Japanese native whom they had met in the United States, Cowman and Kilbourne stressed development of indigenous churches led by national pastors. Following establishment of a Bible school in Tokyo for the training of workers, between 1912 and 1918 they conducted a campaign of scripture distribution designed to place the Bible or a portion of it in every home in

II. 1. Christian Holiness Association

Japan. A nondenominational mission committed to holiness teaching, the Oriental Missionary Society maintained strong ties with the Holiness Movement in the United States and Great Britain, and secured a strong base of financial support. Prior to the advent of a strong, centralized denominational administration over the Pilgrim Holiness Church missionary program in the late 1920's, much support came from Pilgrim Holiness contributors since both the Cowmans and the Kilbournes were members of that group.

Following the Japanese precedent the society pursued a program similar in other fields: Korea (1907), China (1925), India (1940), Colombia (1943), Greece (1948), Brazil (1950), Formosa (1950), Ecuador (1952), Hong Kong (1954) and Haiti (1958). In 1957 it sent missionaries to the United Missionary Church in Nigeria. Known outside the Orient as the Inter-American Missionary Society, in 1967 it had 818 organized congregations with 1002 national workers and 141,000 baptized members. Long located at Los Angeles, headquarters moved to Greenwood, Indiana, in the 1960's. Early in 1973, to emphasize the world-wide scope of its work, the society's name was changed to OMS International and the name of the official organ to OMS Outreach. Since 1957 a men's auxiliary called Men for Missions International has promoted the activities of the Society. The Oriental Missionary Society works in cooperation with the Christian Holiness Association.

3360 ORIENTAL MISSIONARY Society.
Manual; rules and regulations governing the personnel and operations of the society in its overseas and domestic areas. Greenwood, Ind., 1967. 51ℓ.

--APOLOGETIC WORKS

3361 ORIENTAL MISSIONARY Society.
The time test; the faithful commitment to a unique mission. Greenwood, Ind., 196?. 35 p.

3362 PEARSON, Benjamin Harold, 1893-
Men + God = . Greenwood, Ind., Men for Missions International, 1967. 121 p.

--CONDUCT OF LIFE

3363 CRAMER, Raymond L., 1908-
The psychology of Jesus and mental health. Los Angeles, Cowman Publications, 1959. 262 p.

--DEVOTIONAL LITERATURE

3364 CARMICHAEL, Amy Wilson, 1867-1951.
If.... Los Angeles, Cowman Publications, n.d. Unpaged.

3365 COWMAN, Lettie (Burd), 1870-1960, comp.
Consolation. Los Angeles, Oriental Missionary Society, 1945. 369 p.
Tenth printing.

3366 COWMAN, Lettie (Burd), 1870-1960.
Handfuls of purpose. Los Angeles, Cowman Publications, 1955. 139 p.

3367 COWMAN, Lettie (Burd), 1870-1960, comp.
Manantiales en el desierto; traducción por Antonio Serrano. Los Angeles, La Sociedad misionera oriental, c1940. 336 p.

3368 COWMAN, Lettie (Burd), 1870-1960.
Mountain trailways for youth. Los Angeles, Oriental Missionary Society, 1947. 314 p.

3369 COWMAN, Lettie (Burd), 1870-1960, comp.
Springs in the valley. Los Angeles, Oriental Missionary Society, 1939. 371 p.

3370 COWMAN, Lettie (Burd), 1870-1960, comp.
Streams in the desert. Los Angeles, Oriental Missionary Society, 1925. 377 p.

3371 COWMAN, Lettie (Burd), 1870-1960, comp.
Streams in the desert. 11th ed. Los Angeles, Oriental Missionary Society, 1931-1966. 2 v.
Vol. 2 has imprint: Grand Rapids, Mich., Zondervan Publishing House.
On t.p. of v. 2: From the files and unpublished writings of Mrs. Charles E. Cowman.

3372 COWMAN, Lettie (Burd), 1870-1960, comp.
Traveling toward sunrise. Los Angeles, Cowman Publications, 1952. 254 p.
"Companion volume to Streams in the Desert."

--DOCTRINAL AND CONTROVERSIAL WORKS

3373 CRAMER, Raymond L., 1908-
The master key. Los Angeles, Cowman Publications, 1951. 138 p.

II. 1. Christian Holiness Association

3374 CRAMER, Raymond L., 1908-
The ministry of the Holy Spirit. Los Angeles, Cowman Publications, n. d.

3375 KIMBER, John Shober
Following the star. Los Angeles, Oriental Missionary Society, c1914. 120 p.

3376 KIMBER, John Shober
Tabernacle talks. Los Angeles, Oriental Missionary Society, 1931. xv, 97 p.

--HISTORY

3377 COWMAN, Lettie (Burd), 1870-1960.
Charles E. Cowman, missionary warrior; with portraits, illustrations and maps. Los Angeles, Oriental Missionary Society, c1939. 433 p.

3378 ENCYCLOPEDIA OF modern Christian missions; the agencies. Burton L. Goddard, ed.... Camden, N.J., T. Nelson, 1967. xix, 743 p.
"The Oriental Missionary Society," by Harry F. Woods: p. 516-517.

3379 ERNY, Edward
No guarantee but God; the story of the founders of the Oriental Missionary Society, by Edward and Esther Erny. Greenwood, Ind., Oriental Missionary Society, 1969. 116 p.

3380 PEARSON, Benjamin Harold, 1893-
The vision lives; a profile of Mrs. Charles E. Cowman. Los Angeles, Cowman Publications, 1961. 341 p.

3381 WOODS, Harry F.
"The story of a mission; or, Sixty years with God," Missionary Standard, LX (Jan. 1961), 3, 10, 11, 17.

--PERIODICALS

3382 ACTION. 1- , 1957- . Los Angeles; Greenwood, Ind., Men for Missions International, of the Oriental Missionary Society.

3383 OMS OUTREACH. 1- , 1901- . Tokyo; Los Angeles; Greenwood, Ind.
1901-1914 as Electric Messages; 1914-1944 as Oriental Missionary Standard; 1944-1949 as Oriental and Inter-American Missionary Standard; 1949-Mar. 1973 as Missionary Standard.

--POLEMICAL WORKS

-- --CATHOLICISM

3384 PEARSON, Benjamin Harold, 1893-
 The monk who lived again. Los Angeles, Cowman Publications, 1959, c1952. 178 p.
 "Fourteenth printing."

--CHINA

3385 LYALL, Leslie T.
 Come wind, come weather; the present experience of the church in China. Chicago, Moody Press, 1960. 95 p.
 "What of the night?"

--EAST (FAR EAST)

3386 BAKER, Richard Terrill, 1913-
 Darkness of the sun; the story of Christianity in the Japanese Empire. Nashville, Abingdon-Cokesbury Press, 1947. 254 p.
 "The resistance of piety": p. 133-144.

--JAPAN

3387 BURNETT family.
 "Papers, 1842-1919." 70 items. In University of North Carolina, Southern Historical Collection.
 Contain letters, 1911-1919, from members of the Oriental Missionary Society in Tokyo to Anna Burnett at Bynum, N.C.

3388 KILBOURNE, Ernest Albert, 1865-1928.
 The story of a mission in Japan. Tokyo, Cowman and Kilbourne, n.d.

UNION BIBLE SEMINARY (1911-)

Organized as a Bible training school in 1911, the Union Bible Seminary of Westfield, Indiana, sent its first missionaries to Bolivia in 1919. Although the school is largely supported by Friends of the Central Yearly Meeting, the Union Bible Seminary has (except 1933-1947) conducted its missionary work independently. In Bolivia there are 23 organized churches (the congregation in La Paz is the largest Protestant group in the city), a printing plant and a Bible training school. Seven American missionaries were working there in 1967. Both school and mission are promoted by The Gospel Minister, published monthly at Westfield.

--ANECDOTES, REMINISCENCES, SATIRE, ETC.

3389 "I ALONE survive"; the dramatic story of six show girls. Westfield, Ind., Union Bible Seminary, 19??. Folder.

--CHURCH WORK

3390 SMITH, William Martin, 1872-
The unfinished task. Westfield, Ind., Union Bible Seminary, 19??. Cover-title, 7 p.

--CONDUCT OF LIFE

3391 FINNEY, Charles Grandison, 1792-1875.
Finney on fashions; some principles stated by the eminent evangelist. Westfield, Ind., Gospel Minister, 19??. 15 p.

3392 HONEYWELL, E. I.
The Christian home. Westfield, Ind., Gospel Minister, 19??. Folder
"Reduced from an article ... in Missionary Holiness Herald and Vanguard."

3393 SMITH, Simeon O.
Mini-skirt, maxi-lust. Westfield, Ind., Union Bible Seminary, 197?. 8 p.

3394 STAUFFER, Joshua, 1891-1971.
Consideration of 7'C [i.e. 7 C's] in courtship: care, calling, character, conduct, compatibility, consideration, cheerfulness. Westfield, Ind., Union Bible Seminary, n.d. 31 p.

--DOCTRINAL AND CONTROVERSIAL WORKS

3395 A GREAT public meeting you will have to attend. Westfield, Ind., Union Bible Seminary, 19??. 2 p.

3396 SMITH, Simeon O.
The Wednesday crucifixion of Christ. Westfield, Ind., Union Bible Seminary, 1965. 32 p.
Reprint of 1959 ed.

3397 SMITH, William Martin, 1872-
Bible doctrines. 2d ed., rev. Westfield, Ind., Union

Bible Seminary, 1934. 223 p.

3398 SMITH, William Martin, 1872-
By faith; an exposition and interpretation of the eleventh chapter of Hebrews. Westfield, Ind., Union Bible Seminary c1959. 60 p.

3399 SMITH, William Martin, 1872-
Hannah's revival; a Bible study of Hannah and Samuel. Westfield, Ind., Union Bible Seminary, 1951. 35 p.
Reprint of 1911 ed.

3400 SMITH, William Martin, 1872-
Nicolaitanism, the thing that Jesus hates, and Laodiceanism, the thing that makes Jesus sick. Westfield, Ind., Union Bible Seminary, n.d. 24 p.

3401 SMITH, William Martin, 1872-
The precious blood of Christ. Westfield, Ind., Gospel Minister, 19??. Unpaged.

3402 SMITH, William Martin, 1872-
Studies in the genealogies. n.p., 19??. Cover-title, 16 p.

3403 STAUFFER, Joshua, 1891-1971.
There was a man. Westfield, Ind., Union Bible Seminary, n.d. 48 p.

3404 STAUFFER, Joshua, 1891-1971.
The witness of the Spirit. Westfield, Ind., Union Bible Seminary, n.d. 44 p.

3405 STAUFFER, Joshua, 1891-1971.
The wonderful Christ. Westfield, Ind., Union Bible Seminary, n.d. 30 p.

-- --ESCHATOLOGY

3406 SMITH, William Martin, 1872-
Bible history of world government and a forecast of its future from Bible prophecy. 5th ed. Westfield, Ind., Union Bible Seminary, 1955. 208 p.

3407 SMITH, William Martin, 1872-
Imminent signs of the times. Westfield, Ind., Union Bible Seminary, 1963. 38 p.
Published serially in the Gospel Minister.

3408 SMITH, William Martin, 1872-
Signs of the times. Westfield, Ind., Union Bible Seminary, 1956. 24 p.

II. 1. Christian Holiness Association

Address at Union Bible Seminary, May 13, 1956.

3409 SMITH, William Martin, 1872-
Studies in Bible prophecy. Westfield, Ind., Union Bible Seminary, 196?. 103 p.
Published serially in the Gospel Minister in 1960.

3410 SMITH, William Martin, 1872-
Why the church will not go through the tribulation and why the Antichrist has not come. Westfield, Ind., Gospel Minister, 19??. 14 p.

-- --PREDESTINATION

3411 TOOLE, I. N.
Eternal security in the light of the scriptures. Westfield, Ind., Gospel Minister, 19??. 23 p.

--MISSIONS

3412 ENCYCLOPEDIA OF modern Christian missions; the agencies. Burton L. Goddard, ed.... Camden, N.J., T. Nelson, 1967. xix, 743 p.
"Union Bible Seminary, Inc.": p. 647.

--PERIODICALS

3413 FRIENDS' MINISTER. 1-8, 1913-1920. Westfield, Ind.
Superseded by Gospel Minister.

3414 GOSPEL MINISTER. 1- , Jan. 6, 1921- . Westfield, Ind.
Supersedes Friends' Minister.

--POLEMICAL WORKS

-- --CATHOLICISM

3415 SMITH, William Martin, 1872-
What we need to know about Roman Catholicism; a review of some of its doctrines, practices, and purposes. Westfield, Ind., Union Bible Seminary, n.d. 30 p.

--SERMONS

3416 STAUFFER, Joshua, 1891-1971.
Romans 8:28; fourteen sermons. Westfield, Ind., Union Bible Seminary, 1967. 111 p.
First published in 1935.

VOICE OF CHINA AND ASIA (1946-)

[Also as Voice of China and Asia Missionary Society; 1946-19?? a Voice of China; in Hong Kong 1909-1951 as South China Peniel Holiness Missionary Society; in Hong Kong, Taiwan, Malaysia, Korea and the Philippine Islands, 1951-present as China Peniel Holiness Association]

Named for the "Voice of China" radio program started by Bob and Helen Hammond in 1946, the organization owes its origin to earlier missionary work by Mrs. Hammond's parents, Mr. and Mrs. A. K. Reiton. Going to Hong Kong in 1909, the Reitons established the South China Peniel Holiness Missionary Society. In 1939 their daughter and son-in-law joined them. Repatriated in 1942 after being imprisoned by the Japanese, both families returned to California for the duration of the war. The radio program, launched after the war to promote missionary activity in the Orient, identified the China work to Americans, and the Hammonds incorporated under that title. In Taiwan, Hong Kong, Malaysia, Korea and the Philippines, the work continued under the Peniel name, and in 1951 was incorporated as the China Peniel Missionary Society. From headquarters in Pasadena, California, the Hammonds promote and direct evangelism, churches, literature publication and distribution, orphanages, leprosaria, Bible and other schools, student centers, relief and hospital work. The society works in cooperation with the Christian Holiness Association. In the mid-1960's the Voice of China and Asia reported fifteen foreign missionaries in four fields.

3417 VOICE OF China and Asia Missionary Society. Stewardship Department.
Investments in stewardship; the sun never sets on God' missionaries.... Pasadena, Calif., 196?. Folder.

--HISTORY

3418 VOICE OF China and Asia Missionary Society.
Ministering for 60 years. Pasadena, Calif.; Vancouver B.C., Can., 1969. Folder.

3419 ENCYCLOPEDIA OF modern Christian missions; the agencies. Burton L. Goddard, ed.... Camden, N.J., T. Nelson, 1967. xix, 743 p.
"Voice of China and Asia, Inc.": p. 683-684; "China Peniel Missionary Society": p. 129-130.

3420 HAMMOND, Robert Bruce
Bondservants of the Lord; our experiences during the siege of Hong Kong, internment in Stanley Prison Concentration Camp, the establishment of Voice of China and Asia

II. 1. Christian Holiness Association

missionary work. Pasadena, Calif., Vancouver, B.C., Can., Voice of China and Asia (Missionary Society), 1963, c1943. 84 p.
Ninth ed.
First ed. published under title: Bondservants of the Japanese.

--PERIODICALS

3421 FLASHLIGHT. 1- , 1922- . Pasadena, Calif.
Also as Voice of China and Asia Flashlight.

--CHINA

3422 HAMMOND, Robert Bruce
Hate or love?: Red China; Hong Kong's troubled borders. Pasadena, Calif.; Vancouver, B.C., Can., Voice of China and Asia Missionary Society, 196?. 24 p.

--VIETNAM

3423 HAMMOND, Robert Bruce
After Vietnam what? Pasadena, Calif.; Vancouver, B.C., Can., Voice of China and Asia Missionary Society, 196?. 24 p.

WORLD GOSPEL MISSION (1910-)

[1910-1926 as Missionary Bureau of the National Association for the Promotion of Holiness; 1926-1954 (1926-1947 in foreign countries) as National Holiness Missionary Society]

Organized in 1910 as the Missionary Bureau of the National Association for the Promotion of Holiness, this mission was known from 1926 to 1947 in foreign countries, and from 1926 to 1954 in the United States, as the National Holiness Missionary Society. A non-denominational society, the group subscribes to Wesleyan-Arminian doctrine and attracts most of its support and missionaries from holiness churches. Since 1910 when it sent its first workers to China, the society has established and/or absorbed work in fifteen other fields: Kenya (1929), India (1937), Burundi (1938), Honduras (1943), Bolivia (1943), the United States-Mexico border area (1945), Egypt (1949), Mexico (1950), American Indians (1952), Japan (1952), Taiwan (1953), Lebanon (1955), Haiti (1965), Brazil (1966) and Indonesia (1969). In 1949 the Peniel Missions, with several rescue missions in California and a foreign work in Egypt, amalgamated with the society. More recently the Churches of Christ in Christian Union, the Evangelical Methodist Church, and the Congregational Methodist Church have chosen the World Gospel Mission as an official agency for sending foreign missionaries into the field. Operating on an annual budget averaging $1,100,000 in recent years, the Mission actively solicits prayer support. In a recent year it reported over 1500 prayer groups and "prayer affiliates." The Mission has issued the Call to Prayer since 1919. From 1926 to 1952 headquarters were in Chicago, since 1952 in Marion, Indiana. The World Gospel Mission continues to maintain close ties with the Christian Holiness Association.

--DOCTRINAL AND CONTROVERSIAL WORKS

3424 CAVIT, Marshal
　　　The will of my Father; messages on the relationship between holiness and missions. Newberg, Ore., Barclay Press, 1968. vi, 115 p.

--HISTORY

3425 CARY, William Walter, 1887-
　　　Story of the National Holiness Missionary Society. Chicago, National Holiness Missionary Society, 1940. 353 p.

3426 ENCYCLOPEDIA OF modern Christian missions; the agencies. Burton L. Goddard, ed.... Camden, N.J., T. Nelson, 1967. xix, 743 p.
　　　"World Gospel Mission," by George R. Warner: p. 699-700.

--PERIODICALS

3427 CALL TO Prayer. 1- , 1919- . Chicago; Marion, Ind.

3428 JUNIOR CALL. 1- , 19??- . Marion, Ind.

--AFRICA

3429 TRACHSEL, Laura (Cammack), 1907-
　　　Kindled fires in Africa. Marion, Ind., World Gospel Mission, 1960. 123 p.

--ASIA

3430 TRACHSEL, Laura (Cammack), 1907-
　　　Kindled fires in Asia. Marion, Ind., World Gospel Mission, 1960. 96 p.

II. 1. Christian Holiness Association

--CHINA

3431 TROXEL, Ellen (Armour), 1875-
Cecil Troxel, the man and the work; missionary to China with the National Holiness Missionary Society from its inception in 1910 until his promotion on June 9, 1944, by Mrs. Cecil Troxel and Mrs. John J. Trachsel. Chicago, National Holiness Missionary Society, 1948. 261 p.

3432 WATTS, Alice
Silver; the story of a Chinese girl whose life has been touched and set aflame by the Spirit of God, by Miss Alice Watts and Miss Bessie B. Cordell. Chicago, National Holiness Association Missionary Society, c1934.

--LATIN AMERICA

3433 TRACHSEL, Laura (Cammack), 1907-
Kindled fires in Latin America. Marion, Ind., World Gospel Mission, 1961. 144 p.

WORLD-WIDE MISSIONARY SOCIETY (1921-1923)

Dissatisfied with the administration of the foreign missionary program of the International Holiness Church, the Reverend H.J. Olsen organized the independent World-Wide Missionary Society on November 11, 1921. Operating from headquarters in Baltimore, Maryland, Olsen secured the support of numerous individuals in the parent denomination. In addition, the Society became the recognized missionary agency of the Pentecostal Rescue Mission, and the work expanded rapidly. When restored confidence in the management of the denominational program led to reunion in April 1923, the Society was supporting eighteen missionaries in Panama, Mexico, the West Indies, Africa and Alaska.

--HISTORY

3434 THOMAS, Paul Westphal, 1894-1972.
"The days of our pilgrimage; a history of the Pilgrim Holiness Church," by Paul Westphal Thomas and Paul William Lee Thomas. Unpublished paper, 1968. 1 v. (various pagings)
In archives of The Wesleyan Church, Marion, Indiana.
Account of the World-Wide Missionary Society: ℓ 109-111.

WORLD-WIDE MISSIONS (1950-)

An independent non-denominational mission, World-Wide Missions reflects the influence of Basil Miller, a minister, teacher and writer of the Church of the Nazarene. Miller founded the society in 1950 in response to readers of his missionary books, as a means of supporting indigenous foreign missions. Beginning with a subsidy for 35 churches in Nigeria, the work had by 1967 grown to include the support of more than a thousand foreign and national workers in over seventy nations. The society assists affiliated national churches which are governmentally independent. It issues a periodical, World-Wide Missions, from its headquarters in Pasadena, California.

3435 ENCYCLOPEDIA OF modern Christian missions; the agencies. Burton L. Goddard, ed.... Camden, N.J., T. Nelson, 1967. xix, 743 p.
"World-Wide Missions," by Basil Miller: p. 711.

3436 MILLER, Basil William, 1897-
Arms around the world: missions world wide. Pasadena, Calif., World-Wide Missions, 1971. 109 p. [Autobiography, vol. 4]

3437 MILLER, Basil William, 1897-
Dreams fulfilled: my mission career. Pasadena, Calif., World-Wide Missions, 1971. 109 p. [Autobiography, vol. 3]

--PERIODICALS

3438 WORLD-WIDE Missions. 1- , 1958- . Pasadena, Calif.

WORLD'S FAITH MISSIONARY ASSOCIATION (188?-190?)

[Also as World Missionary Association]

Founded at Shenandoah, Iowa, by R.R. Hanley, a medical doctor, this evangelistic fellowship was closely akin to and collaborated with the work of the Independent Holiness Church of Christ and the Hephzibah Faith Missionary Association. A congregation Hanley started in Shenandoah seems to have been affiliated with the Independent Holiness Church of Christ, and the World's Faith Missionary Association inspired formation of the Hephzibah Faith Missionary Association. The Association was designed to encourage evangelistic work and apparently consisted of Hanley's personal followers. Like the Independent Holiness Church of Christ, the World's Faith Missionary Association apparently folded with Hanley's death. J.B. Chapman, later to be general superintendent in

II. 1. Christian Holiness Association 417

the Church of the Nazarene, was at one time a member. Since Chapman was not converted until 1899, the World's Faith Missionary Society probably survived into the twentieth century.

3439 WORCESTER, Paul W.
    The master key; the story of the Hephzibah Faith Missionary Association. Kansas City, Mo., Printed for the author by the Nazarene Publishing House, 1966. 63 p.
    Includes discussion on World's Faith Missionary Association.

--PERIODICALS

3440 MISSIONARY WORLD. 1- , 1887-19??. Shenandoah, Iowa. 1887-190? as Fire-brand.

NEW TESTAMENT CHURCH OF CHRIST (1894-1905)

Organized July 9, 1894, at Milan, Tennessee, the New Testament Church of Christ was one of the first independent holiness groups in the South. The founder, Robert Lee Harris, a Texan who had served as an evangelist and faith missionary to Africa while affiliated with the Methodist Episcopal Church, South, died from tuberculosis a few months after organization, but work continued. Under his wife, Mary Lee, and several devoted followers strongly committed to congregational autonomy, the group spread to Arkansas and Texas. Unity was fostered by The Trumpet, a small paper issued from Milan, and, after 1899, by annual council meetings of representatives of the churches. But by 1902 the Texas group, which now had its own unofficial voice in The Evangelist published in Waco, had formed its own council. The trend toward denominational order continued apace, and conversations with representatives of the Holiness Baptists and the Independent Holiness Church led in 1905 to merger with the latter group under the name Holiness Church of Christ.

3441 NEW TESTAMENT Church of Christ.
    Government and doctrines of New Testament churches. Milan, Tenn.; Waco, Tex., 1894-1903. 4 v. triennial.

3442 NEW TESTAMENT Church of Christ.
    Minutes, council and guide book of the Churches of Christ, 1902; Mrs. Fannie S. Suddarth, secretary. Dallas, Penny Printing People, 1902.

3443 HOLINESS CHURCH of Christ.
Manual, 1904-05; prepared by the Joint Committee on Union of the Independent Holiness Church and the New Testament Church of Christ, C.B. Jernigan, secretary. n.p., 1904.

--CLERGY

3444 HUNTER, Fannie McDowell
Women preachers. Introduced by Dr. A.M. Hills. Dallas, Berachah Printing Co., 1905. 100 p.

--HISTORY

3445 JERNIGAN, Charles Brougher, 1863-1930.
Pioneer days of the Holiness Movement in the Southwest. Kansas City, Mo., Pentecostal Nazarene Publishing House, 1919. 157 p.
Account of the New Testament Church of Christ: p. 116-121.

3446 REDFORD, Maury English
The rise of the Church of the Nazarene. Kansas City, Mo., Nazarene Publishing House, 1948. 208 p.
"New Testament Church of Christ": p. 114-129.

3447 SMITH, Timothy Lawrence, 1924-
Called unto holiness; the story of the Nazarenes: the formative years. Kansas City, Mo., Nazarene Publishing House, 1962. 413 p.
Account of the New Testament Church of Christ: p. 153-159.

--PERIODICALS

3448 EVANGELIST. 1- , Dec. 1898-190?. Waco, Tex.

3449 TRUMPET. 1- , 1893-189?. Milan, Tenn.; Memphis, Tenn.

NIHON HORINESU KYODAN (Japan Holiness Church) (1917-   )

Established by the Oriental Missionary Society in 1917, the Nihon Horinesu Kyodan is an indigenous Japanese church. Originally composed of converts of Society missionaries who had arrived in Tokyo in 1901, the group, which was led from 1917 to

II. 1. Christian Holiness Association

1939 by Bishop Juji Nakada, is self-governing and self-supporting. Although in the 1930's the group claimed over 400 congregations and more than 12,000 members, World War II had disasterous effects. In 1925 the church sent a missionary to Brazil who six years later was instrumental in establishing the independent Brazil Evangelical Holiness Church. In 1955 evangelistic work was begun in Okinawa. Presently the group also sponsors work at Belem in northern Brazil.

3450   ENCYCLOPEDIA OF modern Christian missions; the agencies. Burton L. Goddard, ed.... Camden, N.J., T. Nelson, 1967. xix, 743 p.
"Nihon Horinesu Kyodan (Japan Holiness Church)": p. 484.

3451   ERNY, Edward
No guarantee but God; the story of the founders of the Oriental Missionary Society, by Edward and Esther Erny. Greenwood, Ind., Oriental Missionary Society, 1969. 116 p.
Includes account of Juji Nakada, first bishop of the Japan Holiness Church: p. 27-47.

PENTECOSTAL CHURCH OF SCOTLAND (1909-1915)

Formed in May 1909 by representatives of four holiness congregations, the Pentecostal Church of Scotland was the product of the influence of George Sharpe, founder of the Parkhead Pentecostal Church, Glasgow. A native Scotsman, Sharpe had from 1886 to 1901 been pastor in the Methodist Episcopal Church in upstate New York. While in America, he claimed entire sanctification under the ministry of L. Milton Williams, a Salvation Army officer. Returning home to accept a Congregational Church pastorate in 1901, his holiness preaching aroused opposition. While serving at Parkhead Church in Glasgow, in 1905, a crisis developed which resulted in separation of the pastor. Members sympathetic to him promptly organized a new church and called Sharpe as pastor. With the organization of the Pentecostal Church of Scotland three years later the Holiness Bible School was opened and a periodical called the Holiness Herald begun. The church early made contacts with other holiness groups in Britain and America. Star Hall, a well-known holiness mission in Manchester, was for a few years affiliated with Sharpe's group, and the founder himself held membership in the Pentecostal League of Prayer. Through L. Milton Williams and other American acquaintances Sharpe became interested in amalgamation with the Pentecostal Church of the Nazarene. Denominational officials from the United States visited; and Sharpe and his wife attended the 1915 General Assembly in Kansas City. In November that year the churches united.

--ANECDOTES, REMINISCENCES, SATIRE, ETC.

3452 SHARPE, George, 1865-1948.
This is my story. Glasgow, Messenger Publishing Co., 1948. 142 p.
Autobiography.

--HISTORY

3453 FORD, Jack, 1908-
In the steps of John Wesley; the Church of the Nazarene in Britain. Kansas City, Mo., Printed by Nazarene Publishing House, 1968. 300 p.
Account of the Pentecostal Church of Scotland: p. 35-63.

3454 REDFORD, Maury English
The rise of the Church of the Nazarene. Kansas City, Mo., Nazarene Publishing House, 1948. 208 p.
"The Pentecostal Church of Scotland": p. 159-164.

3455 SHARPE, George, 1865-1948.
A short historical sketch of the Church of the Nazarene in the British Isles. n.p., 192?. 66 p.

3456 SMITH, Timothy Lawrence, 1924-
Called unto holiness; the story of the Nazarenes: the formative years. Kansas City, Mo., Nazarene Publishing House, 1962. 413 p.
"The Pentecostal Church of Scotland": p. 237-242.

PILGRIM CHURCH (1917-1922)

[1917 as Pentecost-Pilgrim Church]

The Pilgrim Church originated in Pasadena, California, where in 1917 Seth C. Rees, former pastor of the University Pentecostal Church of the Nazarene, organized a tabernacle church primarily from the membership of his former congregation. Known at first as the Pentecost-Pilgrim Church, the group soon undertook sponsorship of a Bible training school in Pasadena and of missionary work in San Luis Potosi, Mexico. A few small congregations in other California towns and in Kansas sprang up as affiliates, and a paper known as The Pilgrim was published. Rees, in 1897, had been one of the founders of a midwestern group now called the International Holiness Church; and in 1922 he led the Pilgrim Church into union with that group as the Pilgrim Holiness Church. At the time of the merger the Pilgrim

Church claimed 457 members, 325 of whom were in Rees' congregation in Pasadena.

3457 PILGRIM CHURCH.
Handbook. Pasadena, Calif., 19??.

--HISTORY

3458 COLEMAN, John Paul
That our people may know. Pasadena, Calif., 1924.

3459 ECKEL, Howard
A plain statement of why the University Pentecostal Church of the Nazarene was disorganized. Pasadena, Calif., 1917.

3460 THOMAS, Paul Westphal, 1894-1972.
"The days of our pilgrimage; a history of the Pilgrim Holiness Church," by Paul Westphal Thomas and Paul William Lee Thomas. Unpublished paper, 1968. 1 v. (various pagings)
In archives of The Wesleyan Church, Marion, Indiana.
Account of the Pilgrim Church of California: ℓ. 104-108.

--PERIODICALS

3461 PILGRIM. 1-5, 1917-1922. Pasadena, Calif.

PILGRIM HOLINESS CHURCH (1897-1968)

[1897-1905 as International Apostolic Holiness Union and Prayer League; 1905-1913 as International Apostolic Holiness Union and Churches; 1913-1919 as International Apostolic Holiness Church; 1919-1922 as International Holiness Church]

The transformation of this group from an evangelistic association to a conventional denomination is registered in name changes during its first twenty-five years of existence. Originating with organization of the International Apostolic Holiness Union and Prayer League at Cincinnati in 1897, it became the International Apostolic Holiness Union and Churches in 1905, the International Apostolic Holiness Church in 1913, the International Holiness Church upon merger with the Holiness Christian Church in 1919, and the Pilgrim Holiness Church upon merger with the Pilgrim Church of California in 1922. Deeply committed to revivalism and to camp-meeting style worship, the group was led in its formative period by Martin Wells Knapp and George B. Kulp, former Methodists, and Seth Cook Rees, a former Quaker, all of whom had roots in the interdenominational National Holiness Movement. Absorbing a number of smaller bodies: the Pentecostal Rescue Mission of New York (1922), the Pentecostal Brethren in Christ of Ohio (1924), the People's Mission Church of Colorado (1925), and the Holiness Church of California (1946), the Pilgrim Holiness Church moved steadily toward denominational order. In 1930 a unified General Board of administration was created to exercise control between quadrennial delegated conferences, and denominational offices were moved from Cincinnati and Kingswood, Kentucky, to Indianapolis, and Pilgrim Holiness Advocate, established in 1922, re-located there.

With less than a dozen members at its beginning in 1897, the group counted 17,400 members in the United States in 1930, and 32,765 members when it merged with the Wesleyan Methodist Church of America in 1968. From 1901 when it sent its first missionary to Africa, the group was ardently mission-oriented. In 1930 foreign membership stood at 5044; in 1968, at 23,842 (roughly two foreign to three domestic members). Rating among the highest of American denominations in per capita giving, the Pilgrim Holiness Church in 1968 had 231 missionaries and 1061 national workers in more than twenty-five world areas. It sponsored one liberal arts and five Bible colleges in the United States and twelve Bible training schools abroad, with enrollments totaling 1244 students. The church held membership in the National Holiness Association.

3462   PILGRIM HOLINESS Church.
        The judiciary of the Pilgrim Holiness Church; an official supplement to the Manual of 1954. Indianapolis, General Board of the Pilgrim Holiness Church, 1954. 12 p.

3463   PILGRIM HOLINESS Church.
        Manual, 1897-1966. Cincinnati, Easton, Md., Indianapolis, 1897-1966.
        1897-190? as Constitution and by-laws.
        Irregular, 1897-190?; biennial, 1910-1916; triennial, 1919-1922; quadrennial, 1926-1966.
        1922 ed. includes directory of ministers.

3464   PILGRIM HOLINESS Church.
        Manual, 1946. Caribbean ed. Indianapolis, Pilgrim Publishing House, 1946.

3465   PILGRIM HOLINESS Church. International Conference.
        Minutes. 1st-26th, 1902-1968. Trappe, Md., Cincinnati, Indianapolis, Marion, Ind. -1968.
        Meeting called General Assembly, 1902-1938; General Conference, 1942-1962.

II. 1. Christian Holiness Association 423

Annual, 1902-1907; biennial, 1909-1915 and 1920-1926; quadrennial, 1930-1966.

--DISTRICTS. MICHIGAN

3466 U.S. WORK Projects Administration.
Inventory of the church archives of Michigan: Pilgrim Holiness Church, Michigan District; prepared by the Michigan Historical Records Survey Project, Division of Community Service Programs, Work Projects Administration. Detroit, Michigan Historical Records Survey Project, 1942. 27 p.

--DISTRICTS. NEW YORK

3467 THE PENTECOSTAL Rescue Mission: Pilgrim Holiness Church of New York; seventy-fifth anniversary diamond jubilee. Binghamton, N.Y., 1972. Unpaged.
Added t.-p.: Celebrating the 75th anniversary of the Pentecostal Rescue Mission. Motto: "Holiness unto the Lord." A brief history. Christ our way, truth, life: Pilgrim Holiness Church of New York, Inc.

--DISTRICTS. PENNSYLVANIA-NEW JERSEY

3468 RUTHERFORD, E. S., comp.
Pennsylvania-New Jersey District of the Pilgrim Holiness Church; a brief history of fifty years of service, 1913-1963, comp. by E.S. Rutherford, L.W. Chappell [and] Howard J. Frey. Allentown, Pa., 1963. Unpaged
Cover-title: Pennsylvania-New Jersey Pilgrims 50 years of ministry, 1913-1963.

--APOLOGETIC WORKS

3469 PILGRIM HOLINESS Church.
At work witnessing: Pilgrim Holiness Church; prepared by Pilgrim Information Agency. Indianapolis, 196?. Folder.

--BIOGRAPHY

3470 EUBANKS, Annie Laurie, 1926-
These went forth; biographical sketches of Pilgrim missionaries. Indianapolis, Foreign Missions Department, Pilgrim Holiness Church, 196?. Unpaged.

3471　GAYJIKIAN, Krikor, circa 1887-1972.
　　　　Twentieth century miracles. Cincinnati, 1943. Cover-title, 176 p.
　　　　Part 1 is the life story of Hosanna Gayjikian as told to E.S. Mueller.

--CATECHISMS AND CREEDS

3472　ROTHWELL, Mel-Thomas, 1905-
　　　　A catechism on the Christian religion; authorized by the General Board of the Pilgrim Holiness Church at its annual meeting, May 9-12, 1944, in Indianapolis, Indiana, Mel-Thomas and Helen F. Rothwell, authors and editors. Indianapolis, Ind., Pilgrim Publishing House, 1944. 100 p.

--CONDUCT OF LIFE

3473　DEAL, William Sanford, 1910-
　　　　The furnace of affliction; a treatise on the theme: How God through suffering develops Christian character. 5th ed. El Monte, Calif., Deal Publications, c1948. 80 p.

3474　DEAL, William Sanford, 1910-
　　　　A happy married life, and how to live it. Grand Rapids, Mich., Zondervan Publishing House, 1963. 117 p.

3475　DEAL, William Sanford, 1910-
　　　　Problems of the Spirit-filled life. Kansas City, Mo., Beacon Hill Press, 1961. 158 p.

3476　DEAL, William Sanford, 1910-
　　　　The victorious life; a guide book for victorious living. Grand Rapids, Mich., Eerdmans, 1954. 159 p.

3477　KULP, George B., 1845-1939.
　　　　Calloused knees; or, A man sent from God whose name was John. Cincinnati, God's Revivalist Press, c1909. 300 p.

3478　STAUFFER, Joshua, 1891-1971.
　　　　Spiritual guidance; a lesson how to determine God's will Owosso, Mich., Joshua Stauffer, n.d. 40 p.

--CONVERTS

3479　HAWKINS, Richard C.
　　　　Guidance for new converts. Indianapolis, Foreward Movement Committee, Pilgrim Holiness Church, n.d. Unpaged.

II. 1. Christian Holiness Association

3480 MILLER, L. L., -1957.
 The converts' class. Indianapolis, Ind., Pilgrim Publishing House, n.d.

--DEVOTIONAL LITERATURE

3481 DEAL, William Sanford, 1910-
 Daily Christian living. Grand Rapids, Mich., Baker Book House, 1962. Unpaged.

3482 STAUFFER, Joshua, 1891-1971.
 "Behold He prayeth." Kernersville, N.C., Herald Press, n.d. 181 p.

--DIRECTORIES

3483 PILGRIM HOLINESS Church.
 Directory, 1959. Indianapolis, Pilgrim Publishing House, 1959. Unpaged.

3484 PILGRIM HOLINESS Church.
 Directory, 1963. Indianapolis, Pilgrim Publishing House, 1963. Unpaged.

--DOCTRINAL AND CONTROVERSIAL WORKS

3485 BELTZ, Roy Allen, 1905-
 John Wesley, a great leader. Des Moines, Iowa, Boone Publishing Co., 1944. 47 p.
 Imprint covered by label: Chicago, Van Kampen Press.

3486 DEAL, William Sanford, 1910-
 What really happened at Pentecost? El Monte, Calif., Deal Publications, n.d.

3487 FLEXON, Richard G.
 Holiness and its relatives. 2d ed. Indianapolis, Pilgrim Publishing House, 1949. 55 p.

3488 FLEXON, Richard G.
 Rudiments of Romans. Indianapolis, Pilgrim Publishing House, 1952. 53 p.

3489 FLEXON, Richard G.
 Scriptural holiness. Indianapolis, Pilgrim Publishing House, n.d.

3490 JOPPIE, Alton S., 1906-
 The ministry of angels. Grand Rapids, Mich., Baker Book House, 1953. 97 p.

3491 MARSH, Elmer G.
The old man. Noblesville, Ind., Newby Books, 1972, c1931. 112 p.
Reprint of 1931 ed.

3492 MOURER, Charles Calvin, 1882-
Twelve [t]heological [t]ornadoes. Cincinnati, c1935. 271 p.
Title within lined border stating doctrines of the church.

3493 OLSEN, Henry John, 1879-1972.
Christ and Christian experience in the tabernacle; art work by Miss Edith J. Dawson. Indianapolis, Pilgrim Publishing House, n.d. 65 p.

3494 REES, Byron Johnson, 1877-1920.
The heart-cry of Jesus. Cincinnati, M.W. Knapp, c1899. 102 p. (Pentecostal Holiness Library, vol. 2, no. 1)

3495 REES, Seth Cook, 1854-1933.
The ideal Pentecostal church. Cincinnati, Revivalist Office, 1897. 134 p.

3496 STAUFFER, Joshua, 1891-1971.
A gospel picture. Owosso, Mich., n.d. 30 p.

3497 STAUFFER, Joshua, 1891-1971.
Joseph, a type of Jesus. Owosso, Mich., Joshua Stauffer, n.d. 40 p.

3498 STAUFFER, Joshua, 1891-1971.
Seven mighty miracles cluster around Calvary. Kernersville, N.C., n.d. 31 p.

3499 STAUFFER, Joshua, 1891-1971.
Ten aspects of faith. 3d ed. Owosso, Mich., n.d. 40 p.

-- --ESCHATOLOGY

3500 BEIRNES, William F.
Exposition of the Olivet discourse. Summerfield, Fla., Midnight Cry, 19??. 77 p.

3501 BEIRNES, William F.
God's prophetic calendar. Jupiter-Tequesta, Fla., Midnight Cry, 19??. 24 p.

3502 BEIRNES, William F.
Prophecies fulfilled and fulfilling. Summerfield, Fla., Midnight Cry, 19??. 38 p.

II. 1. Christian Holiness Association

3503 BEIRNES, William F.
Questions and answers on the Second Coming; a fascinating study of the Second Cpming of Christ, being a completely indexed compilation of questions submitted to the Midnight Cry magazine and answered by the editor. Summerfield, Fla., Midnight Cry, 19??. 40 p.

3504 BEIRNES, William F.
Resurrection glory, its mysteries unfolded. Summerfield, Fla., Midnight Cry, 19??. 63 p.

3505 BEIRNES, William F.
Revelation. Summerfield, Fla., Midnight Cry, 19??. 4 v.

3506 BEIRNES, William F.
Revelation. Jupiter-Tequesta, Fla., Midnight Cry, 19??. 284 p.
Printed by Voice of Faith, Seoul, Korea.

3507 BEIRNES, William F.
The sealed book revealed; a commentary on the Book of Daniel. Jupiter, Fla., Midnight Cry, 19??. 101 p.

3508 FLEXON, Richard G.
Thy kingdom come. Indianapolis, Printed by Pilgrim Publishing House, c1967. 104 p.

3509 PRATT, William H.
The home-coming of the Jews; up-to-date information regarding the Palestinian situation and disturbances in the Middle East, a study of these events and their relation to the present-day fulfillment of Bible prophecy. Revised ed. Terre Haute, Ind., Rev. William H. Pratt, n.d. 111 p.

3510 PRATT, William H.
Peace through the Prince of Peace. Terre Haute, Ind., William H. Pratt, n.d. 67 p.

3511 SMITH, William Martin, 1872-
The Bible history of world government and a forecast of its future from Bible prophecy. Greensboro, N.C., W.R. Cox, c1919. 244 p.

3512 SMITH, William Martin, 1872-
Bible history of world government and a forecast of its future from Bible prophecy. Greensboro, N.C., W.R. Cox, c1940. 196 p.
"Fourth edition, revised and enlarged."

--EDUCATION

3513 McCALLUM, Floyd Frederick, 1920-
"An investigation of the need for a liberal arts college for the Pilgrim Holiness Church." Unpublished Ed.D. dissertation, Michigan State University, 1955. 190ℓ.

--EVANGELISTIC WORK

3514 STAUFFER, Joshua, 1891-1971.
Mending our gospel nets. Owosso, Mich., Joshua Stauffer, n.d. 32 p.

3515 WILKINS, Chester, 1918-
A handbook for personal soul-winning. Berne, Ind., Light & Hope Publications, c1950. 301 p.

--HISTORY

3516 PILGRIM HOLINESS Church.
"The days of our pilgrimage; a brief historical sketch to the Pilgrim Holiness Church, revised to General Conference, 1962." Indianapolis, 1962. 7ℓ.
Mimeographed.

3517 PILGRIM HOLINESS Church.
"A historical sketch of the Pilgrim Holiness Church." Indianapolis, n.d. 2ℓ.
Mimeographed.

3518 CLARK, Elmer Talmage, 1886-1966.
The small sects in America. Rev. ed. New York, Abingdon Press, c1965. 256 p.
Account of Pilgrim Holiness Church: p. 76.

3519 1897-1947: JUBILEE issue, Pilgrim Holiness Advocate, XXVII (June 19, 1947).

3520 JONES, Charles Edwin, 1932-
"Perfectionist persuasion: a social profile of the National Holiness Movement within American Methodism, 1867-1936." Unpublished Ph.D. dissertation, University of Wisconsin, 1968. 669ℓ.
Includes account of Pilgrim Holiness Church origins.

3521 MEAD, Frank Spencer, 1898-
Handbook of denominations in the United States. 2d rev. ed. New York, Abingdon Press, 1961. 272 p.
"Pilgrim Holiness Church": p. 173-174.

II. 1. Christian Holiness Association

3522 SCHAFF, Philip, 1819-1893.
New Schaff-Herzog encyclopedia of religious knowledge.... S.M. Jackson, editor-in-chief. New York, Funk, 1908-1912. 12 v.
"International Apostolic Holiness Union," by E.M. Bliss: v. 7, p. 393.

3523 THOMAS, Paul Westphal, 1894-1972.
"The days of our pilgrimage; a history of the Pilgrim Holiness Church," by Paul Westphal Thomas and Paul William Lee Thomas. Unpublished paper, 1968. 1 v. (various pagings)
In archives of The Wesleyan Church, Marion, Indiana.

--HOMILETICAL ILLUSTRATIONS

3524 KULP, George B., 1845-1939.
Nuggets of gold, for the use of preachers, teachers, and all workers, gathered here and there, through over thirty years of active ministry; with an introd. by Rev. M.G. Standley. Cincinnati, God's Revivalist Office, 1906. 286 p.

--HYMNS

3525 PILGRIM HOLINESS Church.
Spiritual life hymnal; a treasury of 600 gospel songs, hymns and choruses, a varied collection that will meet the need of all services of the church, comp. by E.V. Halt. Indianapolis, Ind., Pilgrim Publishing House, 1948. 565 p.

3526 HALT, Eulice Vern, 1896- , comp.
Gospel ministry in song; a collection of songs carefully selected to meet the demand of all religious services. Indianapolis, Pilgrim Publishing House, 1940. 224 p.
With music.

3527 HALT, Eulice Vern, 1896- , comp.
Revive us again songs. Indianapolis, Ind., Pilgrim Publishing House, 1950. Unpaged.

3528 HALT, Eulice Vern, 1896- , comp.
Salvation songs; gospel songs, hymns and choruses for evangelism. Indianapolis, Ind., Pilgrim Publishing House, 1954. Unpaged.

3529 HALT, Eulice Vern, 1896- , comp.
The wondrous story in song. Indianapolis, Pilgrim Publishing House, 1945. Unpaged.
With music.

3530 MOURER, Charles Calvin, 1882-
The hobo, composed by C.C. Mourer, evangelist [and] trombone, guitar and saw-phone player. Cincinnati, c1925. Folder.
With music.

3531 MOURER, Charles Calvin, 1882-
Since I found that long lost gold mine in the sky, composed by Chas. C. Mourer. Indianapolis, Pilgrim Publishing House, c1939. Folder.
With music.

3532 MOURER, Charles Calvin, 1882-
This world means nothing to me, composed by C.C. Mourer, evangelist [and] trombone, guitar and sawphone player. Cincinnati, c1942. Folder.
With music.

3533 MOURER, Charles Calvin, 1882-
Thorns and roses, composed by C.C. Mourer, evangelist [and] trombone, guitar and saw-phone player. Cincinnati, c1936. Folder.
With music.

3534 MOURER, Charles Calvin, 1882-
When Jesus comes back, composed by C.C. Mourer, evangelist [and] trombone, guitar and sawphone player. Cincinnati, c1943. Folder.
With music.

--MEMBERSHIP

3535 STAUFFER, Joshua, 1891-1971.
What church members owe their pastor. Kernersville, N.C., n.d. 40 p.

--MISSIONS

3536 DEAL, William Sanford, 1910-
Thrilling experiences in missionary evangelism. Indianapolis, Ind., Pilgrim Publishing House, n.d.

3537 FLEXON, Mrs. Emma Laura
Among the other sheep. Indianapolis, Ind., Published by the author, n.d.

3538 MILLER, L. L., -1957.
Instead of the briar. Indianapolis, Ind., Foreign Missionary Office of the Pilgrim Holiness Church, n.d.

II. 1. Christian Holiness Association

3539 THOMAS, Paul Westphal, 1894-1972.
Regions beyond. Indianapolis, Ind., Foreign Missionary Office of the Pilgrim Holiness Church, 1935.

3540 WALTON, John Maxey
Unto the uttermost. Indianapolis, Ind., Foreign Missionary Office of the Pilgrim Holiness Church, n.d.

-- --HISTORY

3541 ENCYCLOPEDIA OF modern Christian missions; the agencies. Burton L. Goddard, ed.... Camden, N.J., T. Nelson, 1967. xix, 743 p.
"Pilgrim Holiness Church, Department of World Missions," by Charles Lewis: p. 533-535.

3542 EUBANKS, Annie Laurie, 1926-
These went forth; biographical sketches of Pilgrim missionaries. Indianapolis, Foreign Missions Department, Pilgrim Holiness Church, 196?. Unpaged.

3543 THOMAS, Paul William, 1921-
"An historical survey of Pilgrim world missions." Unpublished B.D. thesis, Asbury Theological Seminary, 1963.

3544 THOMAS, Paul William, 1921-
1967 historical sketches: Pilgrim world missions. Indianapolis, Pilgrim Holiness Church, Department of World Missions, 1967. Cover-title, 27ℓ.
Mimeographed.

--PERIODICALS

3545 AFRICA'S REVIVALIST. 1- , 19??- . -----, S. Afr.

3546 APOSTOLIC EVANGELIST. 1- , 1915-19??. Cambridge, Md.

3547 APOSTOLIC MESSENGER. 1- , 1901-1921. Greensboro, N.C.

3548 BETHEL HERALD. 1- , 1912-19??. Milton, Pa.; Allentown, Pa.
Merged with Apostolic Messenger.

3549 CHRISTIAN'S COMPANION. 1- , 1920?- . Bridgetown, Barbados, B.W.I.

3550 GOD'S MESSENGER. 1- , 19??- . Mooers, N.Y.

3551 GOD'S MESSENGER and Bible Advocate. 1- , 1905-19??
Easton, Md.

3552 INTERNATIONAL HOLINESS Church Paper. 1- , 1901-192?. Owosso, Mich.
1901-1919 as Apostolic Visitor.

3553 PILGRIM HOLINESS Advocate. 1-47, no. 13, 1921-June 29, 1968. Greensboro, N.C.; Kingswood, Ky.; Cincinnati; Indianapolis.
1921-Oct. 1922 as International Holiness Advocate.
Merged with Wesleyan Methodist to form Wesleyan Advocate.

3554 PILGRIM YOUTH News. 1-20, July 1948-1968. Indianapolis, Ind.
Merged with Wesleyan Youth to form Win.

3555 WORLD MISSIONS Bulletin. 1-30, no. 6, 1939-June 1968. Indianapolis, Ind.
1939-Feb. 1941 as Gift Box Missionary; Mar. 1941-June 1962 as Foreign Missions Bulletin.
Merged with Wesleyan Missionary to form Wesleyan World.

--POLEMICAL WORKS

-- --SEVENTH-DAY ADVENTISM

3556 WALTON, John Maxey
The sabbath question: Saturday or Sunday, which? 2d ed. Indianapolis, Pilgrim Publishing House, 1954. 39 p.
"First edition, 1943."

--POLITICAL AND SOCIAL CRITICISM

3557 REES, Seth Cook, 1854-1933.
Miracles in the slums; or, Thrilling stories of those rescued from the cesspools of iniquity, and touching incidents in the lives of the unfortunate. Chicago, Seth C. Rees, 1905. 301 p.

--RELATIONS

-- --WESLEYAN METHODIST CHURCH

3558 JOINT STUDY Conference on Church Growth, held at Marion, Indiana, on June 17-21, 1968; world missions of the Pilgrim Holiness and Wesleyan Methodist churches. n.p., 1968. 1 v. (various pagings)

II. 1. Christian Holiness Association

3559 WILKINS, Chester, 1918-
"A review of the recently proposed union of the Wesleyan Methodist Church and the Pilgrim Holiness Church."
Unpublished M.A. thesis, Butler University, 1960. 80¢.

--SERMONS

3560 ELLIOTT, Paul Frederick, 1869-1944.
The voice of God. Dayton, Ohio, Bethel Publishing Co., 1911. 141 p.

3561 HECKART, Robert H.
Behold the Lamb of God. Butler, Ind., Higley Press, 1959. 62 p.

3562 KULP, George B., 1845-1939.
The departed Lord; or, Words that burn. Cincinnati, God's Revivalist Press, 1921. 313 p.

3563 KULP, George B., 1845-1939.
Truths that transfigure: faith tonics; fifteen sermons for the saints published at request of laity and ministry. Cincinnati, God's Revivalist Press, 1927. 246 p.

3564 KULP, George B., 1845-1939.
A voice from eternity; or, Soul searching sermons. Cincinnati, God's Revivalist Office, 1909. 277 p.

3565 REES, Byron Johnson, 1877-1920.
Trumpet-calls (for the unsaved). Cincinnati, M.W. Knapp, 1899. 147 p.

3566 REES, Seth Cook, 1854-1933.
Fire from heaven. Cincinnati, God's Revivalist Office, 1899. 329 p.

3567 REES, Seth Cook, 1854-1933.
The holy war. Cincinnati, O., Revivalist Office, 1904. 246 p.

3568 REES, Seth Cook, 1854-1933.
The last prayer meeting. Independence, Mo., Gospel Tract Society, n.d. Folder.

3569 SLATER, Charles Livingstone, 1884-1950.
God's glorious challenge: a sermon. 2d ed. Indianapolis, 19??. 50 p.

3570 STAUFFER, Joshua, 1891-1971.
"All we like sheep." Owosso, Mich., Joshua Stauffer, n.d. 48 p.

-- --OUTLINES

3571 STAUFFER, Joshua, 1891-1971.
"Give them to eat"; or, Sermon outlines. Berne, Ind., Light and Hope Publications, c1951. 192 p.

--STATISTICS

3572 U.S. BUREAU of the Census.
...Census of religious bodies, 1926; Pilgrim Holiness Church: statistics, denominational history, doctrine and organization.... Washington, U.S. Government Printing Office, 1928. 11 p.

--WORK WITH YOUTH

3573 STAUFFER, Joshua, 1891-1971.
The ants are a people; little lessons for little people from little creatures. Owosso, Mich., Joshua Stauffer, 1955. 68 p.

--AFRICA

3574 EUBANKS, Annie Laurie, 1926- , comp.
Pilgrim missions in Africa, Indianapolis, Ind., Pilgrim Holiness Church, 1961.

--AFRICA, SOUTH

3575 BONNER, Norman Neal, 1917-
This is South Africa. Indianapolis, Ind., Foreign Missionary Office, Pilgrim Holiness Church, 1954.

3576 FUGE, Frederick Thomas, 1872-
The storm king; a collection of remarkable facts and illustrations. Greensboro, N.C., Apostolic Missionary Office, 1923. 213 p.

--ANTIGUA

3577 KING, Oscar Logan, 1887-1964.
Antigua. Kingswood, Ky., Missionary Office, n.d.

--BARBADOS

3578 HARTMAN, J.
What God hath wrought. Bridgetown, Barbados, B.W.I.

II. 1. Christian Holiness Association 435

Christian Mission Book Repository, 1904.

3579 IVES, R. Wingrove
A missionary's cry from Barbados; last chapter by Rev. R.G. Finch, General Missionary Superintendent of the Pilgrim Holiness Church. Kingswood, Ky., Missionary Office, 192?. 72 p.

--BRITISH GUIANA

3580 HILES, Lewis C.
South America, by Rev. and Mrs. L.C. Hiles. Kingswood, Ky., Missionary Office, n.d.

3581 WALTON, John Maxey
The Partamona trail. Indianapolis, Ind., Foreign Missionary Office of the Pilgrim Holiness Church, n.d.

--CARIBBEAN REGION

3582 EUBANKS, Annie Laurie, 1926-   , comp.
Pilgrim missions in the Caribbean area. Indianapolis, Ind., Pilgrim Holiness Church, n.d.

3583 FINCH, Ralph Goodrich, 1881-1950.
Full gospel work in the West Indies and South America, by Ralph G. Finch, J.M. Coone, and George Beirnes. Bridgetown, Barbados, B.W.I., R.G. Finch, n.d.

3584 PEISKER, Armor D.
Pilgrims in the northern Caribees. Indianapolis, Ind., Foreign Missionary Office, Pilgrim Holiness Church, 1953.

--CENTRAL AMERICA

3585 HIGGS, A. R.
Central America, by Rev. and Mrs. A.R. Higgs. Kingswood, Ky., Missionary Office, n.d.

--INDIA

3586 RASSMAN, A. E.
India, by Rev. A.E. Rassman and E.A. Meeks. Kingswood, Ky., Missionary Office, n.d.

3587 RASSMAN, A. E.
With Jesus in India's jungles. 2d ed. n.p., n.d.

3588   THOMAS, Paul Westphal, 1894-1972, comp.
       Pilgrims in India. Indianapolis, Ind., Pilgrim Holiness Church, n.d.

--JAMAICA

3589   FORD, Paul D.
       Jamaica. Kingswood, Ky., Missionary Office, n.d.

--MEXICO

3590   FLEXON, Richard G., ed.
       Mexico and the Pilgrim Holiness Church. Indianapolis, Ind., Foreign Missionary Office, Pilgrim Holiness Church, 1946.

3591   PEISKER, Armor D., ed.
       Mexico and the Pilgrim Holiness Church. Indianapolis, Ind., Foreign Missionary Office, Pilgrim Holiness Church, 1953.

3592   SOLTERO, Francisco H., 1892-
       Mexico, by Rev. and Mrs. F.H. Soltero. Kingswood, Ky., Missionary Office, 1927. 95 p.

3593   SOLTERO, Francisco H., 1892-
       Los Peregrinos in Mexico, by Rev. and Mrs. Francisco H. Soltero. Indianapolis, Ind., Foreign Missions Office, Pilgrim Holiness Church, 1958.

3594   SOLTERO, Nettie (Winans),   -1957.
       The romance of Pilgrim missions in Mexico, by Mrs. F.H. Soltero. Indianapolis, Ind., Pilgrim Holiness Church, n.d.

3595   THOMAS, Paul Westphal, 1894-1972.
       The Pilgrim Holiness Church in Mexico. Colorado Springs, Colo., Colorado Springs Bible Training School and Christian Academy, n.d.

3596   THOMAS, Paul Westphal, 1894-1972.
       25 years with Christ in Mexico; an account of the historic twenty-fifth annual conference of the Pilgrim Holiness Church across the Rio Grande. Indianapolis, Ind., Foreign Missionary Office of the Pilgrim Holiness Church, 1945.

--PERU

3597   RUNDELL, Merton Russell, 1923-
       "The mission of the Pilgrim Holiness Church in Peru."

II. 1. Christian Holiness Association

Unpublished M.A. thesis, Butler University, 1957.

--PHILIPPINE ISLANDS

3598 EUBANKS, Annie Laurie, 1926- , comp.
Pilgrim missions in the Philippines. Indianapolis, Ind., Pilgrim Holiness Church, 1960.

--RHODESIA

3599 SCHOOMBIE, G. A.
Rhodesian trek. Indianapolis, Ind., Foreign Missionary Office, Pilgrim Holiness Church, n.d.

3600 STRICKLAND, Romey E.
Over Livingstone's trail in Northern Rhodesia. Indianapolis, Ind., Foreign Missionary Office of the Pilgrim Holiness Church, 1948.

--TRINIDAD

3601 REES, O. W.
Trinidad. Kingswood, Ky., Missionary Office, n.d.

SALVATION ARMY (1865-)
[1865-1879 as Christian Mission]

Although known chiefly for its philanthropic work, the Salvation Army at its core is also a holiness church. Founded in 1865 in East London as the Christian Mission and led in its early years by William Booth, who until 1861 had been a minister in the Methodist New Connection, the group regarded sin as the source of social ills, and taught that the salvation of the individual was the first step toward social regeneration. Adopting the present name and military organization in 1879, the Salvation Army reached the United States the next year.

The "Articles of War," the Army's creedal statement, is Wesleyan and perfectionist. Its leaders, including General Booth, George S. Railton, and Commissioner Samuel Logan Brengle, have stressed entire sanctification, to the extent that even today the Sunday morning worship service at the Salvation Army citadel is called the Holiness Meeting. (The evangelistic service in the evening is called the Salvation Meeting.) While a large portion of the support personnel in social welfare activities of the Army are not members, those ultimately in charge are. Today 25,000 officers (evangelists) man more than 17,000 evangelical centers and 3000 social welfare institutions in 86 countries. In 1959 there were 253,061 soldiers (members) and 1259 centers in the United States. The Salvation Army holds membership in the Christian Holiness Association.

3602 HUXLEY, Thomas Henry, 1825-1895.
Evolution & ethics, and other essays. London; New York, Macmillan, 1901. xiii, 334 p.
Includes "The articles of war of the Salvation Army."

--ANECDOTES, REMINISCENCES, SATIRE, ETC.

3603 WAR CRY (periodical)
Holiness readings; a selection of papers on the doctrine, experience, and practice of holiness, reprinted from The War Cry. London, International Headquarters, Salvation Army, 1889. 194 p.
Reprint of 1883 ed.

--APOLOGETIC WORKS

3604 SALVATION ARMY.
All about the Salvation Army, incorporated October 24, 1884; amended charter, March 26, 1885. Brooklyn, N.Y., Salvation Army, 1885. 26 p.
Prose and poetry.
Hymns on front and back covers.
Without music.

3605 SALVATION ARMY.
What is the Salvation Army? An interpretation of its aims, methods and activities.... New York, 1924. 82 p.

3606 BOOTH, Catherine (Mumford), 1829-1890.
Mrs. Booth on recent criticisms of the Salvation Army; being an address delivered.... July 17, 1882. London, Salvation Army Stores, 188?. 32 p.

3607 BOOTH, Catherine (Mumford), 1829-1890.
The responsibility of Christians with respect to the Salvation Army. London, 190?. 8 p.

3608 BOOTH, Catherine (Mumford), 1829-1890.
The Salvation Army in relation to the church and state, and other addresses delivered at Cannon Street Hotel, city; with an appendix on the so-called "secret book." London, S.W. Partridge and Co., 1883. iv, 92 p.

3609 FRIEDERICHS, Hulda
The romance of the Salvation Army, with a preface by

General Booth.... London; New York, Cassell and Co., 1907.

--CHARITIES

3610 SALVATION ARMY.
Bridging the gulf, being a description of the prison work of the Salvation Army, coupled with the annual report for 1924-5. New York, 1925.

3611 BOOTH TUCKER, Frederick St. George de Lautour, 1853-
...The social relief work of the Salvation Army in the United States. Albany, N.Y., J.B. Lyon Co., printers, c1900. 37 p.
At head of title: Department of Social Economy for the United States Commission to the Paris Exposition of 1900.
"This monograph is contributed to the United States Social Economy Exhibit by the League for Social Service, New York."

3612 HAGGARD, Sir Henry Rider, 1856-1925.
The poor and the land; being a report on the Salvation Army colonies in the United States and at Hadleigh, England, with scheme of national land settlement and an introduction. London, Longmans, Green, 1905. xii, 157 p.

3613 SEARCH, Pamela
Happy warriors; the story of the social work of the Salvation Army. London, New York, Arco Publishers, 1956. 173 p.

3614 SMITH, Annie S.
The outsiders; being a sketch of the social work of the Salvation Army ... with an introd. by General Booth. 3d ed. London, The Salvation Army Printing Works, St. Albans, 1905-1906.

--CLERGY

3615 SALVATION ARMY.
The why and wherefore of the Salvation Army orders and regulations; intended especially for candidates for officership.... St. Albans, Eng., 1922.

3616 BOOTH, Catherine (Mumford), 1829-1890.
Female ministry; or, Woman's right to preach the gospel.... London, Morgan & Chase, 18??. 23 p.

--CONDUCT OF LIFE

3617 BOOTH, Catherine (Mumford), 1829-1890.
The highway of our God; selections from the Army mother's writings. London, Salvationist Publishing and Supplies, 195?. 114 p.

3618 BOOTH, Catherine (Mumford), 1829-1890.
Papers on practical religion. London, S.W. Partridge & Co., 1879. 151 p.

3619 BOOTH, William, 1829-1912.
Letters to Salvationists on religion for every day. London, New York, Melbourne, Salvation Army Book Department, 1902. 190 p.

3620 BOOTH, William, 1829-1912.
Salvation soldiery; a series of addresses on the requirements of Jesus Christ's service. 2d ed. London, International Headquarters, Salvation Army, 1890. 156 p.

--DEVOTIONAL LITERATURE

3621 ARNOLD, E. Irena
Poems of a Salvationist; with a foreword by Evangeline Booth. New York, Chicago, Fleming H. Revell Co., c1923 160 p.

3622 BOOTH, Catherine (Mumford), 1829-1890.
A few words on prevailing prayer. London, 18??.
8 p.

3623 BRENGLE, Samuel Logan, 1860-1936.
Wait on the Lord; selections from the writings of Commissioner Samuel L. Brengle, ed. by Brigadier John Waldron. Rev. ed. New York, Salvation Army Printing Dept. 1960. 32 p.
At head of title: The Salvation Army. William Booth, founder.

--DOCTRINAL AND CONTROVERSIAL WORKS

3624 SALVATION ARMY.
Handbook of doctrine. London, Salvation Army International Headquarters, 1969. x, 195 p.

3625 SALVATION ARMY.
Manual of Bible teaching, 1970. London, Salvation Army International Headquarters, 1969. vi, 266 p.
"Issued by authority of the General."

II. 1. Christian Holiness Association 441

3626 AGNEW, Milton Seccombe
More than conquerors. Chicago, Salvation Army, 1959.

3627 BOOTH, Bramwell, 1856-1929.
Handbook of Salvation Army doctrine, prepared under the ... supervision ... of the General. New York, 1923.

3628 BOOTH, Catherine (Mumford), 1829-1890.
Assurance of salvation ... an address.... London, Salvation Army Book Depot, 1880. 16 p.

3629 BOOTH, Catherine (Mumford), 1829-1890.
Holiness: being an address delivered in St. James Hall, Piccadilly, London. London, Salvation Army, 1881? 21 p.

3630 BOOTH, Catherine (Mumford), 1829-1890.
Life and death; reports of addresses delivered in London by Mrs. Booth of the Salvation Army. London, 1885.

3631 BOOTH, Catherine (Mumford), 1829-1890.
Papers on aggressive Christianity. London, S.W. Partridge & Co., 1881. 10 pts.

3632 BOOTH, Catherine (Mumford), 1829-1890.
Papers on godliness. London, S.W. Partridge & Co., 1882. 148 p.

3633 BOOTH, Catherine (Mumford), 1829-1890.
Popular Christianity; a series of lectures delivered in Princes Hall, Piccadilly. New York, M.B. Booth, 1887. 198 p.

3634 BOOTH, Catherine (Mumford), 1829-1890.
Popular Christianity; a series of lectures. 4th ed. New York, Salvation Army Publishing House, 1901. 127 p.

3635 BOOTH, William, 1829-1912.
Holy living; or, What the Salvation Army teaches about sanctification. 3d ed. London, Salvation Army Publishing Department, 1890. 31 p. (With his The doctrines of the Salvation Army)

3636 BOOTH, William, 1829-1912.
In heaven but not of heaven. New York, 1894. 24 p.

3637 BOOTH, William, 1829-1912.
A ladder to holiness; being seven steps to full salvation. Rev. ed. London, Salvationist Publishing & Supplies, 1951. 7 p.

3638   BOOTH, William, 1829-1912.
        Purity of heart; letters by General Booth to Salvationists and others. 2d ed. London, New York, Salvation Army Book-Room, 1902. 118 p.

3639   BRENGLE, Samuel Logan, 1860-1936.
        Heart talks on holiness. New York, Salvation Army Publishing House, 1900. 180 p.

3640   BRENGLE, Samuel Logan, 1860-1936.
        Helps to holiness (reprinted from the Red-Hot Library), with a preface by General Bramwell Booth. London, Salvationist Publishing and Supplies, 1896. 145 p.

3641   BRENGLE, Samuel Logan, 1860-1936.
        Helps to holiness. 8th ed. New York, Salvation Army Printing and Publishing House, 1914. xv, 194 p.

3642   BRENGLE, Samuel Logan, 1860-1936.
        Love-slaves. Atlanta, Ga., Supplies and Purchasing Departments, 1923. 132 p.

3643   BRENGLE, Samuel Logan, 1860-1936.
        The way of holiness. New York, Salvation Army Printing and Publishing House, 1920. 106 p.

3644   BRENGLE, Samuel Logan, 1860-1936.
        When the Holy Ghost is come. London, Salvationist Publishing and Supplies, 1909. 153 p.

3645   COUTTS, Frederick Lee
        The call to holiness. London, Salvationist Publishing and Supplies, 1957. 108 p.

3646   SMITH, Allister
        The ideal of perfection. London, Edinburgh, Oliphants 1963. 127 p.

--EVANGELISTIC WORK

3647   BRENGLE, Samuel Logan, 1860-1936.
        The soul-winner's secret. 3d ed. New York, Salvation Army Printing and Publishing House, 1911. 182 p.

3648   HEPBURN, Samuel
        Manual for holiness institutes and holiness clinics. Chicago, Salvation Army, n.d.

II. 1. Christian Holiness Association

--FINANCE

3649 BARTON, Bruce, 1886-1963.
Only one thousand dollars.... New York, 1922. Cover-title, 80 p.
Contains the Salvation Army statistics for the year ending September 30, 1921.

--HISTORY

3650 BEGBIE, Harold, 1871-
The life of General William Booth, the founder of the Salvation Army. New York, Macmillan, 1920. 2 v.

3651 BOOTH, Bramwell, 1856-1929.
Echoes and memories. London, Hodder and Stoughton, 1925. vii, 223 p.

3652 CHESHAM, Sallie
Born to battle; the Salvation Army in America. Chicago, Rand McNally, 1965. 286 p.

3653 COLLIER, Richard, 1924-
The general next to God; the story of William Booth and the Salvation Army. New York, Dutton, 1965. 320 p.

3654 MEAD, Frank Spencer, 1898-
Handbook of denominations in the United States. New 5th ed. Nashville, Abingdon Press, c1970. 265 p.
"Salvation Army": p. 196-198.

3655 NEAL, Harry Edward, 1906-
The Hallelujah Army. Philadelphia, Chilton Co., Book Division, 1961. xiii, 261 p.

3656 SANDALL, Robert
The history of the Salvation Army. Introduction by General Orsborn. London, T. Nelson, 1947-1955. 3 v.

3657 WISBEY, Herbert Andrew, 1919-
Soldiers without swords; a history of the Salvation Army in the United States. New York, Macmillan, 1955. 242 p.

--HYMNS

3658 SALVATION ARMY.
Musical pioneer; being a collection of songs and choruses composed by officers and soldiers of the Salvation Army. New York, 1890. 106 p.

3659   SALVATION ARMY.
         The Salvation Army songs and solos, as sung by the Happy Trio. Thos. E. Moore, General. Brooklyn, N.Y., 188?. Cover-title, 37 p.

3660   SALVATION ARMY.
         The Salvation songs, no. 3. Brooklyn, N.Y., T.E. Moore, c1887.

3661   SALVATION ARMY.
         Special songs for special meetings. New York, Salvation Army, 188?. Cover-title, 24 p.
         Without music.

3662   BOOTH, Ballington, 1859-1940, comp.
         Salvation songs, for the use of the Salvation Army.... New York, Salvation Army, 1889, c1890. 62 p.

3663   BOOTH, Evangeline Cory, 1865-1950.
         Songs of the evangel. New York, Salvation Army, c1927. 51 p.

3664   BOOTH, Herbert H.
         Songs of peace and war; original words and music by Commandant and Mrs. Herbert Booth.... London, Salvation Army Printing and Publishing Dept., 1890. 104 p.

3665   BOOTH, William, 1829-1912, comp.
         The Salvation soldier's song book. Philadelphia, Salvation Army, G.S. Railton, Commissioner, 1880. [262] p.

3666   BOOTH, William, 1829-1912, comp.
         The Salvation soldier's song book. Brooklyn, N.Y., Salvation Army, 1884. 67 p.
         Without music.
         Text on covers.

3667   BOOTH, William, 1829-1912, comp.
         Salvation Army songs. New York, Reliance Trading Co., 189?. viii, 260 p.

3668   BOOTH, William, 1829-1912, comp.
         Salvation Army songs. London, International Headquarters, Salvation Army, 1899. viii, 656 p.

3669   HOLINESS SONGS, especially adapted for holiness meetings and all-nights of prayer. New York, Salvation Army, 1891. 128 p.

II. 1. Christian Holiness Association

--MISSIONS

3670 ENCYCLOPEDIA OF modern Christian missions; the agencies. Burton L. Goddard, ed.... Camden, N.J., T. Nelson, 1967. xix, 743 p.
"Salvation Army," by John Grace: p. 567-569.

--MUSIC

3671 WIGGINS, Arch R.
Father of Salvation Army music: Richard Slater. London, Salvationist Publishing and Supplies, 1945. 80 p.

--PERIODICALS

3672 ALL THE World. 1- , 1952- . London.

3673 WAR CRY. 1- , 1880- . New York.

3674 WAR CRY. 1- , 1884- . Toronto.

--SERMONS

3675 BOOTH, Catherine (Mumford), 1829-1890.
Aggressive Christianity: the first of a series of sermons.... February 29, 1880. London, Salvation Army Book Depot, 188?. 16 p.

3676 BOOTH, Catherine (Mumford), 1829-1890.
The fruits of union with Christ. A sermon.... London, Salvation Army Book Depot, 1880. 15 p.

3677 BOOTH, Catherine (Mumford), 1829-1890.
Repentance ... a sermon.... London, S.W. Partridge & Co., 188?. 10 p.

3678 BOOTH, Catherine (Mumford), 1829-1890.
Saving faith, a sermon.... London, S.W. Partridge, 18??. 16 p.

3679 CAREY, Alfred Belmont
Holiness sermons. New York, Salvation Army Printing Department, 1926- .

--STATISTICS

3680 U.S. BUREAU of the Census.
... Census of religious bodies; Salvation Army: statis-

tics, history, doctrine and organization.... Washington, U.S. Government Printing Office, 1928. 14 p.

--WORK WITH YOUTH

3681 BOOTH, William, 1829-1912.
Training of children; or, How to make the children into saints and soldiers of Jesus Christ by the general of the Salvation Army. 2d ed. London, The Salvation Army, 1888. 263 p.

3682 BOOTH, William, 1829-1912.
Training of children; or, How to make the children into saints and soldiers of Jesus Christ. 3d ed. New York, Salvation Army Publishing House, 190?. 125 p.
"A few pages of current Army history": p. 123-125.

3683 BRENGLE, Samuel Logan, 1860-1936.
Can little children be really saved?; our task, which angels covet, a plea for the children. New York, Salvation Army Trade Department, n.d. 31 p.

--YEARBOOKS

3684 THE SALVATION Army year book, 19??-
London, Simpkin, Marshall, Hamilton, Kent & Co., 19??- .

--GERMANY

3685 GRUNER, Max
Revolutionares Christentum; 50 Jahre Geschichte der Hailsarmee in Deutschland. Berlin, Verlag der Heilsarmee 1952-1954. 2 v.

--GREAT BRITAIN

3686 BOOTH, Bramwell, 1856-1929.
...Work in darkest England in 1894. A review of the social operations of the Salvation Army with annual statement of accounts of the Darkest England Fund. With prefatory notes by the Ven. Archdeacon Farrar, D.D., and Henry Labouchere. London, 1894. 68, xv p.
"Note to third edition" dated 1895.

3687 BOOTH, William, 1829-1912.
In darkest England and the way out. London, International Headquarters of the Salvation Army, 1890. 285, xxxi p.

II. 1. Christian Holiness Association

3688 HAGGARD, Sir Henry Rider, 1856-1925.
Regeneration; being an account of the social work of the Salvation Army in Great Britain. London, Longmans, Green, 1910. 264 p.

--MICHIGAN

3689 HISTORICAL RECORDS Survey. Michigan.
Inventory of the church archives of Michigan. Salvation Army in Michigan. Prepared by the Michigan Historical Records Survey Project, Division of Community Service Programs, Work Projects Administration. Detroit, Michigan Historical Records Survey Project, 1942. 49ℓ.
Reproduced from type-written copy.

--NEW JERSEY

3690 HISTORICAL RECORDS Survey. New Jersey.
Inventory of the church archives of New Jersey. The Salvation Army. Jersey City. Prepared by the New Jersey Historical Records Survey Project, Division of Professional and Service Projects, Works Projects Administration. Sponsored by New Jersey State Planning Board and the National Archives. Newark, N.J., The Historical Records Survey, 1940. 34ℓ.
Reproduced from type-written copy.

SANCTIFIED CHURCH OF CHRIST (19??-)

This Black holiness group consists of a few small congregations centered at last report in Columbus, Georgia. In 1969 it was listed as cooperating with the National Holiness Association.

3691 NATIONAL HOLINESS Association.
Winter bulletin, 1969. Winona Lake, Ind., 1969.
Lists Sanctified Church of Christ as a cooperating denomination.

STANDARD CHURCH OF AMERICA (1919-)

Incorporated at Watertown, New York, in 1919 and in 1920 in Canada, this largely Canadian group was composed initially of followers of Ralph C. Horner dissatisfied with the treatment he had received in the Holiness Movement Church. Differing not at all in doctrine from the parent body, the Standard Church is Methodistic in administration and program. Organized into four annual conferences: Western, Kingston, New York and Egyptian, the group is very evangelistic. Pastors are stationed by the annual conferences for four-year terms. In the 1920's a Bible school, a printing establishment, and the church headquarters were located at Brockville, Ontario. From these offices the church issues the <u>Christian Standard</u>, the <u>Young People's Leader</u>, and the <u>Missionary Ambassador</u>, and directs foreign missionary work in China and Egypt. Statistics are not available, but total membership could not exceed a few thousand. The Standard Church is a member of the Canadian Holiness Federation.

3692   STANDARD CHURCH of America.
Manual and discipline of the Standard Church of America; authorized and published by the General Conference, 1956. Brockville, Ont., Can., Standard Publishing House, 1956. 192 p.

--HISTORY

3693   ENCYCLOPEDIA CANADIANA. Ottawa, Canadiana Co., 1957-1958. 10 v.
"Standard Church of America" by Irwin L. Brown: v. 9, p. 394.

3694   HORNER, Ralph Cecil, 1854-1921.
Ralph C. Horner, evangelist; reminiscences from his own pen. Brockville, Ont., Can., Pub. for Mrs. A. E. Horner by Standard Publishing House, n.d. xxi, 215 p.

--PERIODICALS

3695   CHRISTIAN STANDARD. 1- , 19??- . Brockville, Ont., Can.

3696   MISSIONARY AMBASSADOR. 1- , 19??- . Brockville, Ont., Can.

3697   YOUNG PEOPLE'S Leader. 1- , 19??- . Brockville, Ont., Can.

<u>United Brethren</u>

CHURCH OF THE UNITED BRETHREN IN CHRIST (1800-1946)

[Also as United Brethren in Christ]

II. 1. Christian Holiness Association

The product of the evangelistic work of Philip William Otterbein and Martin Boehm among German settlers in eastern Pennsylvania, Maryland, and Virginia, the Church of the United Brethren in Christ was organized in 1800 with Otterbein and Boehm as bishops. Methodist in theology and organization, the group readily accommodated to the Holiness Movement as it developed in the late nineteenth century. The denomination's German background and Wesleyan orientation contributed to fraternity with the Evangelical Church, and in 1946 the two groups merged to form the Evangelical United Brethren Church.

3698 UNITED BRETHREN in Christ.
Disciplines of the United Brethren in Christ. Part I. In English, 1814-1841. Part II. In German, 1814-1819, 1841. Translated and reprinted from the originals. Edited by Prof. A.W. Drury, D.D. Dayton, Ohio, United Brethren Publishing House, 1895. x, 232, 109 p.

3699 UNITED BRETHREN in Christ.
Minutes of the annual and general conferences of the Church of the United Brethren in Christ, 1800-1818. Translated and edited by A.W. Drury. Dayton, Ohio, United Brethren Historical Society, 1897. vii, 90 p.
Includes fraternal correspondence with Methodist Episcopal Church.

3700 UNITED BRETHREN in Christ. Board of Administration.
Partners in the conquering cause.... Dayton, Ohio, Board of Administration, United Brethren in Christ, c1924. 114 p.
Foreword signed: S.S. Hough, H.F. Shupe.

--CHARITIES

3701 UNITED BRETHREN Mutual Aid Society of Pennsylvania.
A compendium for the agents of the U.B. Mutual Aid Society of Pennsylvania, by I.L. Kephart.... Lebanon, Pa., Pub. by the Society, 1877. 131 p.

--DEVOTIONAL LITERATURE

3702 GUYON, Jeanne Marie (Bouvier de la Motte), 1648-1717.
Selections from the devotional writings of Madame de la Mathe-Guyon, comp. by D.D. Lowery. Dayton, Ohio, United Brethren Publishing House, 1904. 160 p.

--DOCTRINAL AND CONTROVERSIAL WORKS

3703 CASTLE, Nicholas, bp., 1837-1922.
A compendious dissertation of the value of the Bible and the insufficiency of reason in matters of religious faith and practice.... Elkhart, Ind., Printed by J.F. Funk & Brother, 1871. 24 p.

3704 CASTLE, Nicholas, bp., 1837-1922.
The exalted life.... Dayton, Ohio, Otterbein Press, 1913. 351 p.

3705 CASTLE, Nicholas, bp., 1837-1922.
The witness of the Spirit. Dayton, Ohio, United Brethren Publishing House, 1902. 84 p.

3706 DRURY, Augustus Waldo, 1851-1935.
Baptism, its place in the church visible. Dayton, Ohio, United Brethren Publishing House, 1902. ix, 11-90 p.

3707 DRURY, Augustus Waldo, 1851-1935.
Faith and knowledge; an address ... delivered September 7, 1892, at the opening of Union Biblical Seminary. Dayton, Ohio, United Brethren Publishing House, 1893. 23 p.

3708 DRURY, Augustus Waldo, 1851-1935.
Outlines of doctrinal theology, with preliminary chapters on theology in general and theological encyclopedia. Dayton, Ohio, Otterbein Press, 1914. 256 p.

3709 DRURY, Augustus Waldo, 1851-1935.
Outlines of doctrinal theology, with preliminary chapters on theology in general and theological encyclopedia. 2d ed. rev. and enlarged. Dayton, Ohio, Otterbein Press, 1926. 374 p.
Folded chart attached to back cover: Theological encyclopedia.

--HISTORY

3710 UNITED BRETHREN in Christ.
Origin, constitution, doctrine and discipline of the United Brethren in Christ. Circleville, Ohio, Printed at the Conference Office, 1837. 64 p.

3711 UNITED BRETHREN in Christ.
Origin, doctrine, constitution, and discipline of the United Brethren in Christ. Dayton, Ohio, United Brethren Publishing House, 1889. v, 7-170 p.

II. 1. Christian Holiness Association

3712 UNITED BRETHREN in Christ.
Origin, doctrine, constitution, and discipline of the United Brethren in Christ. Dayton, Ohio, United Brethren Publishing House, 1893. vi, 7-224 p.

3713 UNITED BRETHREN in Christ.
Ursprung, lehre, Constitution und Zuchtordnung der Vereinigten brüder in Christo. Harrisburg, Gedruckt bei Clyde und Williams, 1845. 104 p.

3714 CLARK, Elmer Talmage, 1886-1966.
The small sects in America. Rev. ed. New York, Abingdon Press, c1965. 256 p.
Account of the United Brethren in Christ: p. 68.

3715 DRURY, Augustus Waldo, 1851-1935.
History of the Church of the United Brethren in Christ. Dayton, Ohio, Otterbein Press, 1924. 821 p.

3716 DRURY, Augustus Waldo, 1851-1935.
History of the Church of the United Brethren in Christ. Rev., 1931. Dayton, Ohio, United Brethren Publishing House, 1924 [i.e. 1931]. 832 p.

3717 DRURY, Augustus Waldo, 1851-1935.
The life of Bishop J.J. Glossbrenner, D.D., of the United Brethren in Christ, with an appendix containing a number of his sermons and sketches. With an introd. by Rev. James W. Hott, D.D. Dayton, Ohio, Published for J. Dodds by United Brethren Publishing House, 1889. xv, 17-391 p.

3718 DRURY, Augustus Waldo, 1851-1935.
The life of Rev. Philip William Otterbein, founder of the Church of the United Brethren in Christ. With an introd. by Bishop J. Weaver, D.D. Dayton, Ohio, United Brethren Publishing House, 1884. xviii, 21-384 p.

3719 TWENTIETH CENTURY encyclopedia of religious knowledge; an extension of the New Schaff-Herzog Encyclopedia of Religious Knowledge. Editor-in-chief: Lefferts A. Loetscher. Grand Rapids, Mich., Baker Book House, 1955. 2 v. (xx, 1205 p.)
"United Brethren in Christ," by Raymond W. Albright: p. 1134.

--HYMNS

3720 UNITED BRETHREN in Christ.
Herzens opfer; eine sammlung geistreicher lieder, aus den mehrsten jetzt üblichen gesangbucher [sic] gesammlet;

zum öffentlichen und privat gebrauch fur liebhaber des göttlichen lebens.... Lancaster, Ohio, Gedruckt bey E. Schaffer, 1816. 352, [26] p.

--PERIODICALS

3721 HIGHWAY OF Holiness. 1-12, 1875-1887. Chambersburg, Pa.

3722 UNITED BRETHREN Review. 1-19, 1890-1908. Dayton, Ohio.
1-12, 1890-1901? as Quarterly Review of the United Brethren in Christ.

--PUBLISHERS AND PUBLISHING

3723 UNITED BRETHREN Publishing House.
Historical sketch of the United Brethren Publishing House, 1834-1894.... Dayton, Ohio, United Brethren Publishing House, 1894. 35 p.

--STATISTICS

3724 U.S. BUREAU of the Census.
...Census of religious bodies, 1926; United Brethren bodies: statistics, denominational history, doctrine, and organization; consolidated report ... Church of the United Brethren in Christ, Church of the United Brethren in Christ (Old Constitution), United Christian Church.... Washington, U.S. Government Printing Office, 1928. 22 p.

--YEARBOOKS

3725 UNITED BRETHREN in Christ.
Year-book. Dayton, Ohio, United Brethren Publishing House, -19??.

--CHINA

3726 UNITED BRETHREN in Christ. Foreign Missionary Society.
The call of China and the islands; report of the foreign deputation, 1911-1912, for every member of the United Brethren Church, by G.M. Mathews ... S.S. Hough ... foreword by Bishop W.M. Bell, D.D. Dayton, Ohio, Foreign Missionary Society, United Brethren in Christ, 1913? 122 p.

CHURCH OF THE UNITED BRETHREN IN CHRIST (OLD CONSTITUTION) (1889-)

[Also as United Brethren in Christ (Old Constitution)]

Dissenting from governmental changes adopted by the United Brethren in 1889, the Church of the United Brethren in Christ (Old Constitution) adheres doctrinally to the same standards as the main body. Both men and women may be ordained to the ministry, which consists of but one order, that of elder. Only clergy, however, are represented in the quadrennial general conference. Administrative supervision is exercised by presiding elders and bishops. The denomination sponsors a college and seminary at Huntington, Indiana, and foreign missionary work in Jamaica, Honduras and Sierra Leone. In 1970 there were 304 congregations and 22,568 members in the United States. The United Brethren work in harmony with other holiness churches.

3727 CLARK, Elmer Talmage, 1886-1966.
    The small sects in America. Rev. ed. New York, Abingdon Press, c1965. 256 p.
    Account of the United Brethren in Christ (Old Constitution): p. 69-70.

3728 MEAD, Frank Spencer, 1898-
    Handbook of denominations in the United States. New 5th ed. Nashville, Abingdon Press, c1970. 265 p.
    "Church of the United Brethren in Christ": p. 207.

--CATECHISMS AND CREEDS

3729 RASH, R. W., 1904-
    What the United Brethren believe; memory book, by R.W. Rash, J.L. Towne, and M.I. Burkholder, Huntington, Ind., Department of Christian Education, Church of the United Brethren in Christ, c1951. 55 p.

--MISSIONS

3730 ENCYCLOPEDIA OF modern Christian missions; the agencies. Burton L. Goddard, ed.... Camden, N.J., T. Nelson, 1967. xix, 743 p.
    "United Brethren in Christ, Church of the, Parent Board of Missions": p. 651; and "United Brethren in Christ, Church of the, The Woman's Missionary Association": p. 651-652.

--PERIODICALS

3731   UNITED BRETHREN. 1- , 19??- . Huntington, Ind.

--STATISTICS

3732   U.S. BUREAU of the Census.
...Census of religious bodies, 1926; United Brethren bodies: statistics, denominational history, doctrine, and organization; consolidated report ... Church of the United Brethren in Christ, Church of the United Brethren in Christ (Old Constitution), United Christian Church.... Washington, U.S. Government Printing Office, 1928. 22 p.

--SIERRA LEONE

3733   COX, Emmett D.
The Church of the United Brethren in Christ in Sierra Leone. South Pasadena, Calif., William Carey Library, 1970. xi, 171 p.

UNITED CHRISTIAN CHURCH (1878-   )

Between 1862 and 1870 a group in Pennsylvania led by the Rev. George W. Hoffman withdrew from the Church of the United Brethren in Christ because of convictions about infant baptism, military service, secret societies, and fashionable dress. Known as Hoffmanites the group was reluctant at first to organize, but in 1877 drew up a confession of faith. The present name was adopted at Campbelltown, Pennsylvania the next year. Evangelistic and doctrinally conservative, the United Christian Church believes in justification; entire sanctification; baptism (mode optional), the Lord's Supper and foot washing as ordinances; and strict observance of the sabbath. Through a cooperative arrangement with the Brethren in Christ Church, four missionaries are at work in Africa and Japan. In 1959 the church claimed 600 members in 12 congregations.

3734   CLARK, Elmer Talmage, 1886-1966.
The small sects in America. Rev. ed. New York, Abingdon Press, c1965. 256 p.
Account of the United Christian Church: p. 69.

3735   MEAD, Frank Spencer, 1898-
Handbook of denominations in the United States. New 5th ed. Nashville, Abingdon Press, c1970. 265 p.
"United Christian Church": p. 207.

II. 1. Christian Holiness Association　　　　　　　　　　　　455

　　　　　--MISSIONS

3736　ENCYCLOPEDIA OF modern Christian missions; the agencies. Burton L. Goddard, ed.... Camden, N.J., T. Nelson, 1967. xix, 743 p.
"United Christian Church, Mission Board": p. 652.

　　　　　--STATISTICS

3737　U.S. BUREAU of the Census.
...Census of religious bodies, 1926; United Brethren bodies: statistics, denominational history, doctrine, and organization; consolidated report ... Church of the United Brethren in Christ, Church of the United Brethren in Christ (Old Constitution), United Christian Church.... Washington, U.S. Government Printing Office, 1928. 22 p.

UNITED MISSIONARY CHURCH (1853-1969)

[In the United States 1853-1879 as Evangelical Mennonites; in Canada 1875-1879 as United Mennonites (formed by merger of Reformed Mennonites--founded 1874--and New Mennonites); 1879-1883 as Evangelical United Mennonites; 1883-1947 as Mennonite Brethren in Christ; missionary board 1921-1969 as United Missionary Society]

　　　　This group resulted from the mergers of a number of Mennonite revivalistic sects in America and Canada. In 1853, a group of Pennsylvania Mennonites who had adopted revivalist practices organized as Evangelical Mennonites. In 1874, Canadian Mennonites who had accepted Wesleyan teachings about sanctification from Evangelical Association itinerates formed the Reformed Mennonites. Joined in 1875 by a small group known as New Mennonites, the latter took the name of United Mennonites. In 1883, they united with a group seceding from the River Brethren under the title of Mennonite Brethren in Christ. Thoroughly imbued with Methodist ideas through contact with the Holiness Movement, the group retained Mennonite Brethren in Christ as its denominational title until 1947 when, during merger negotiations with the Missionary Church Association, the name United Missionary Church was adopted. As early as 1879, this group sponsored camp meetings, the first ones held among the Mennonites, and started publishing the Gospel Banner, a holiness paper. With other holiness people the Mennonite Brethren demanded abstinance from alcohol, tobacco, and other manifestations of worldliness, and taught eradication of inbred sin, divine healing for the body, and the imminent second return of Christ. As the United Missionary Society, it sponsored work in Brazil, Nigeria, the Middle East and India. In 1969 the United Missionary Church had one foreign missionary for every 100

North American members. With about 200 congregations and 10,000 members, it maintained two Bible colleges in Canada and Bethel College, a liberal arts school, in Mishawaka, Indiana. The denomination held membership in the National Holiness Association. In 1969, the United Missionary Church merged with the Missionary Church Association to form the Missionary Church.

3738 UNITED MISSIONARY Church.
Condensed doctrinal statement and membership application. Elkhart, Ind., Bethel Publishing Co., 1967. Folder.

3739 UNITED MISSIONARY Church.
Doctrines and discipline. Berlin, Ont.; Elkhart, Ind., 1880-1962. 14 v. irregular.
1956-1962 published under title: Constitution and manual.

3740 UNITED MISSIONARY Church. General Conference.
Proceedings. 1st-21st, 1885-1968. n.p. -1968.
Quadrennial 1888-1928, 1943-1959; triennial 1962-1968.

--BIOGRAPHY

3741 LAGEER, Ellis A., comp.
United Missionary Society presents Who's who. Elkhart, Ind., Bethel Publishing Co., 1960. Unpaged.

--CONDUCT OF LIFE

3742 HUFFMAN, Jasper Abraham, 1880-
Building the home Christian. Marion, Ind., Standard Press, 1935. 142 p.

--CRITICAL WORKS

3743 DEAN, William Ward, 1924-
The United Missionary Church: yesterday and today. n.p., 1956. Unpaged.

--DEVOTIONAL LITERATURE

3744 STORMS, Everek Richard
Bible reading and personal devotions in the United Missionary Church. Elkhart, Ind., Board of Evangelism of the United Missionary Church, 1960. Folder.

II. 1. Christian Holiness Association   457

--DOCTRINAL AND CONTROVERSIAL WORKS

3745   UNITED MISSIONARY Church. General Board.
           The assurance of the believer; a statement adopted by the General Board of the United Missionary Church. Elkhart, Ind., 196?. Folder.

3746   HUFFMAN, Jasper Abraham, 1880-
           Golden treasures from the Greek New Testament for English readers. Winona Lake, Ind., Standard Press, 1951. 160 p.

3747   HUFFMAN, Jasper Abraham, 1880-
           The Holy Spirit. Marion, Ind., Standard Press, 1938. 186 p.

3748   HUFFMAN, Jasper Abraham, 1880-
           Job, a world example; introd. by Evangelist Bud Robinson. New Carlisle, Ohio, Bethel Publishing Co., 1914. 94 p.

3749   HUFFMAN, Jasper Abraham, 1880-
           The meaning of Pentecost. Marion, Ind., Standard Press, 1940. 48 p.
           Reprint of 1926 ed.

3750   HUFFMAN, Jasper Abraham, 1880-
           The messianic hope in both Testaments; with an introd. by Charles R. Erdman. Marion, Ind., Standard Press, 1939. 285 p.

3751   HUFFMAN, Jasper Abraham, 1880-
           Old Testament messages of the Christ. Dayton, Ohio, Bethel Publishing Co., 1909. 181 p.

3752   HUFFMAN, Jasper Abraham, 1880-
           The progressive unfolding of the messianic hope; with an introd. by Prof. Charles R. Erdman. New York, Doran, 1924. 186 p.

3753   HUFFMAN, Jasper Abraham, 1880-
           Redemption completed; a treatise on the work of complete redemption, with an introd. by Rev. A.B. Yoder. Cincinnati, For the author by Western Methodist Book Concern, 1903. 196 p.

3754   HUFFMAN, Jasper Abraham, 1880-
           The stones cry out. Winona Lake, Ind., Standard Press, 1948. 108 p.
           Based on the author's Biblical confirmations from archaeology.

3755 HUFFMAN, Jasper Abraham, 1880-
Tithing. Winona Lake, Ind., Lambert Huffman, Publishers, 1967. 31 p.

3756 HUFFMAN, Jasper Abraham, 1880-
Voices from rocks and dust heaps of Bible lands. Marion, Ind., Standard Press, 1928. 132 p.

3757 TAYLOR, Donald M.
The Spirit-filled life; a doctrine and an experience in the United Missionary Church. Elkhart, Ind., United Missionary Church Headquarters, 1964. Folder.

--HISTORY

3758 CLARK, Elmer Talmage, 1886-1966.
The small sects in America. Rev. ed. New York, Abingdon Press, c1965. 256 p.
Account of Mennonite Brethren in Christ: p. 70-71.

3759 HUFFMAN, Jasper Abraham, 1880- , ed.
History of the Mennonite Brethren in Christ Church. New Carlisle, Ohio, Bethel Publishing Co., 1920. 283 p.

3760 MEAD, Frank Spencer, 1898-
Handbook of denominations in the United States. 2d rev. ed. New York, Abingdon Press, c1961. 272 p.
"United Missionary Church": p. 223-224.

3761 STORMS, Everek Richard
History of the United Missionary Church. Elkhart, Ind., Bethel Publishing Co., 1958. 309 p.

--MISSIONS

3762 UNITED MISSIONARY Church. United Missionary Society.
What is the United Missionary Society? Elkhart, Ind., 196?. Folder.

-- --HISTORY

3763 ENCYCLOPEDIA OF modern Christian missions; the agencies. Burton L. Goddard, ed.... Camden, N.J., T. Nelson, 1967. xix, 743 p.
"United Missionary Society," by Shirley J. Gall: p. 664-666.

3764 KAUFMAN, Edmund George, 1891-
The development of the missionary and philanthropic

II. 1. Christian Holiness Association

interest among the Mennonites of North America; with introd. by Archibald Gillies Baker.... Berne, Ind., Mennonite Book Concern, 1931. xix, 416 p.

3765 STORMS, Everek Richard
What God hath wrought; the story of the foreign missionary efforts of the United Missionary Church; with an introd. by Rev. R. P. Ditmer. Springfield, Ohio, United Missionary Society, 1948. 164 p.

--PERIODICALS

3766 GOSPEL BANNER. 1-91, July 1878-1969. Berlin, Ont.; Goshen, Ind.
Merged with Missionary Banner and Emphasis to form Emphasis on Faith and Living.

3767 MISSIONARY BANNER. 1-31, 1938-1969. New Carlisle, Ohio.
Merged with Gospel Banner and Emphasis to form Emphasis on Faith and Living.

--RELATIONS

-- --MISSIONARY CHURCH ASSOCIATION

3768 CONSTITUTION PROPOSED as basis for union of the Missionary Church Association and the United Missionary Church. n.p., 196?. 31, 3 p.

3769 HUFFMAN, Jasper Abraham, 1880-
The proposed merger: a frank statement. Winona Lake, Ind., 1955. 8 p.
Multilithed.

--SERMONS

3770 HUFFMAN, Jasper Abraham, 1880-
Upper Room messages. New Carlisle, Ohio, Bethel Publishing Co., 1915. 203 p.

--ALBERTA

3771 MANN, William Edward
Sect, cult, and church in Alberta. Toronto, University of Toronto Press, 1955. xiii, 166 p.
Includes description of the Mennonite Brethren in Christ.

--BRAZIL

3772 UNITED MISSIONARY Church. United Missionary Society.
The churches of Brazil. Elkhart, Ind., 196?. Folder.

--INDIA

3773 UNITED MISSIONARY Church. United Missionary Society.
The churches of India. Elkhart, Ind., 196?. Folder.

--NEAR EAST

3774 LAMBERT, Rose, 1878-
Hadjin and the Armenian massacres. New York,
Fleming H. Revell Co., c1911. 106 p.

3775 PYE, Ernest, 1881-
Prisoner of war, 31,163, Bedros M. Sharian. New
York, Fleming H. Revell Co., c1938. 202 p.

--NIGERIA

3776 SLOAT, L. Russell
Kwoshi, the Nigerian boy. Springfield, Ohio, United
Missionary Society, 1945. 32 p.

--ONTARIO

3777 BURKHOLDER, Lewis J., 1875-
A brief history of the Mennonites in Ontario, giving a
description of conditions in early Ontario, the coming of
the Mennonites into Canada, settlements, congregations,
conferences, other activities, and nearly 400 ordinations;
100 pictures of men and churches ... written and comp.
under the direction of the Mennonite Conference of Ontario.
Toronto, Livingstone Press, 1935. 358 p.

VOLUNTEERS OF AMERICA (1896-)

Founded in 1896 by Ballington and Maud Booth, son and
daughter-in-law of William Booth, the Volunteers of America is in
many ways like the Salvation Army from which it sprang. With
30,000 members in 1964, the Volunteers do religious and social
welfare work in over 600 centers in the United States. The present annual budget for this work exceeds $10 million. Unlike the

II. 1. Christian Holiness Association 461

parent body, their churches observe baptism and the Lord's Supper. An early emphasis on Wesleyan perfectionism has largely disappeared. The headquarters is located in New York City.

3778 MEAD, Frank Spencer, 1898-
 Handbook of denominations in the United States. New 5th ed. Nashville, Abingdon Press, c1970. 265 p.
 "Volunteers of America": p. 218-219.

--PERIODICALS

3779 VOLUNTEER GAZETTE. 1- , Apr. 11, 1896- . New York.
 Apr. 11, 1896-Sept. 10, 1898? as Volunteers' Gazette; Sept. 17, 1898-Nov. 18, 1899 as Christian Advance and Volunteers' Gazette; Nov. 25, 1899?-Nov. 1950 as Volunteers' Gazette.

--STATISTICS

3780 U.S. BUREAU of the Census.
 ...Census of religious bodies; The Volunteers of America: statistics, history, doctrine and organization.... Washington, U.S. Government Printing Office, 1928. 11 p.

WESLEYAN CHURCH (1968-)

Formed in June 1968 by the union of the Pilgrim Holiness Church and the Wesleyan Methodist Church of America, the Wesleyan Church represents a fusion of the two principal traditions in the American holiness movement: in the fervent evangelicalism derived from the revival and camp meeting and in the governmental practices and ideas about conduct inherited from Methodism. The group, which claims 80,000 United States and 40,000 foreign members, has its headquarters offices in Marion, Indiana. Numbering more than 2100 congregations in the United States and Canada, the group sponsors work in Australia, New Guinea, the Philippine Islands, Japan, Taiwan, India, South Africa, Rhodesia, Sierra Leone, Mexico, Honduras, the Caribbean, and South America. The denomination controls liberal arts institutions at Houghton, N.Y., Central, S.C., Marion, Ind., Bartlesville, Okla., and Miltonvale, Kan., and sponsors Bible colleges at Allentown, Pa., and Yarmouth, Nova Scotia. An officially recognized foundation for ministerial training has been established at the independent holiness Asbury Theological Seminary, Wilmore, Kentucky. The Wesleyan Advocate, official church organ, is published at Marion,

Indiana. The Wesleyan Church holds membership in the Christian Holiness Association. Exploration of the possibility of union with the Free Methodist Church of North America, with which the group has much in common, is underway.

3781 WESLEYAN CHURCH.
  The discipline of The Wesleyan Church; adopted by the Uniting General Conference of 1968, edited by the committee. Marion, Ind., Wesleyan Publishing House, 1968. 638 p.

3782 WESLEYAN CHURCH. General Conference.
  Minutes. 1st- , 1968- . Marion, Ind., Wesleyan Publishing House, 1968- .
  Quadrennial.

3783 ADAMS, J.
  "Holiness in Cincinnati; first national Wesleyan gathering," Christianity Today, XIV (Jan. 30, 1970), 37.

--CLERGY

3784 COOK, Arnold Willis
  "An analysis of the responsibilities and training of selected ministers in church business administration." Unpublished M.A. thesis, East Tennessee State University, 1970.

3785 THOMAS, Clifford William, 1916-
  "A descriptive study of ministerial education in the Wesleyan Church." Unpublished D. Ed. dissertation, Michigan State University, 1968. 151ℓ.

--CONDUCT OF LIFE

3786 DEAL, William Sanford, 1910-
  Maturing gracefully. Kansas City, Mo., Beacon Hill Press, 1972. 88 p.

--DIRECTORIES

3787 WESLEYAN CHURCH. General Department of Extension and Evangelism.
  Travel guide to Wesleyan Churches in the United States and Canada.... Marion, Ind., 1969. Folder.

3788 WESLEYAN CHURCH. General Department of Extension and Evangelism.
  Travel guide to Wesleyan Churches in the United States

and Canada.... Marion, Ind., 1973. Folder
Bound in Wesleyan Advocate, CXXXI (Apr. 2, 1973).

--DOCTRINAL AND CONTROVERSIAL WORKS

3789 DEAL, William Sanford, 1910-
Be filled with the Spirit. Kansas City, Mo., Beacon Hill Press, 1971. 45 p.

3790 FLEXON, Richard G.
Rudiments of Romans. Noblesville, Ind., J. Edwin Newby, Newby Book Room, 1972. 53 p.
Reprint of 1952 ed.

3791 FLEXON, Richard G.
Seven mysteries of the Bible. Noblesville, Ind., Newby Bookroom, 1969. 72 p.

-- --ESCHATOLOGY

3792 McMILLEN, Sim I., 1898-
Discern these times. Old Tappan, N.J., Fleming H. Revell Co., c1971. 192 p.
Foreword by Harold John Ockenga.

3793 McMILLEN, Sim I., 1898-
A study guide to Discern these times. Old Tappan, N.J., Fleming H. Revell Co., c1971. viii, 193-307 p.

3794 WARD, Cliff, 1909-
Christ's glory revealed. New York, Vantage Press, 1971. 367 p.

--EDUCATION

3795 BONNER, Norman Neal, 1917-
"An analysis of the attitudes of administrators and board members of church-related colleges." Unpublished Ed.D. dissertation, University of Tulsa, 1968. xi, 71ℓ.

3796 FERM, Lois (Roughan)
"Student characteristics and environments for learning in Wesleyan colleges." Unpublished Ph.D. dissertation, University of Minnesota, 1972. xiii, 256ℓ.

3797 THOMAS, Clifford William, 1916-
"A descriptive study of ministerial education in the Wesleyan Church." Unpublished D.Ed. dissertation, Michigan State University, 1968. 151ℓ.

3798 THOMAS, Walter Lee, 1938-
"The initial development of the differential value profile." Unpublished Ed.D. dissertation, University of Tulsa, 1969. xi, 196ℓ.

--EVANGELISTIC WORK

3799 WILKINS, Chester, 1918-
A handbook for personal soul-winning. 5th ed., rev. Kansas City, Mo., Beacon Hill Press, 1972, c1966. 320 p.

--HISTORY

3800 HUFFMAN, J. L.
"Wesleyan Church: Pilgrim Holiness and Wesleyan Methodist union," Christianity Today, XII (July 19, 1968), 52.

3801 MEAD, Frank Spencer, 1898-
Handbook of denominations in the United States. New 5th ed. Nashville, Abingdon Press, c1970. 265 p.
"Wesleyan Church": p. 219.

--HOMILETICAL ILLUSTRATIONS

3802 WILLIAMS, Ray L.
Lights from many windows. English, Ind., Rev. Ray L. Williams, 19??- .

--HYMNS

3803 [LATHAM, Joy], comp.
Joyfully sing; a hymnal for children. Kansas City, Mo., Lillenas Publishing Co., c1968. Unpaged.
With music.
Adopted as the official children's hymnal by the Hymnal Commission, 1968, The Free Methodist Church [and] The Wesleyan Church.

--MISSIONS

3804 LIND, Marie, ed.
God can do anything; 39 incidents relating to Wesleyan missionaries and their work. Marion, Ind., Wesleyan Publishing House, 1968. 109 p.
Issued also under title: Missionary stories for church programs; 39 incidents relating to missionaries and their work.

II. 1. Christian Holiness Association

3805 LIND, Marie, ed.
Missionary stories for church programs; 39 incidents relating to missionaries and their work. Grand Rapids, Mich., Baker Book House, 1968. 109 p.
Issued also under title: God can do anything; 39 incidents relating to Wesleyan missionaries and their work.

--PASTORAL THEOLOGY

3806 DEAL, William Sanford, 1910-
Counseling Christian parents. Grand Rapids, Mich., Zondervan Publishing House, 1970. 128 p.

--PERIODICALS

3807 BRIDGE. 1- , 1969?- . Marion, Ind.

3808 WESLEYAN ADVOCATE. 127 [i.e. 126, no. 15]-July 15, 1968- . Indianapolis; Marion, Ind.
Formed by merger of Wesleyan Methodist, 1-126, no. 14, 1842-July 3, 1968, and Pilgrim Holiness Advocate, 1-47, no. 13, 1921-June 29, 1968.

3809 WESLEYAN WORLD. 50- , Sept. 1968. Marion, Ind.
Formed by merger of Wesleyan Missionary, 1-49, 1919-July/Aug. 1968, and World Missions Bulletin, 1-30, 1939-1968.

3810 WIND. 33, no. 10- , Oct. 1968- . Marion, Ind.
33-no. 10-36, no. 11 as Win.
Formed by merger of Wesleyan Youth, 1-33, no. 9, 1936-Sept. 1968, and Pilgrim Youth News, 1-20, July 1948-1968.

--RELIGIOUS EDUCATION

3811 McINTYRE, Ralph L.
Talking chemicals; simple object lessons with common chemicals. Kansas City, Mo., Beacon Hill Press, 1972. 52 p.

--WORK WITH YOUTH

3812 WESLEYAN CHURCH. General Department of Youth.
YES Corps looks great to me! Marion, Ind., 1970? Folder.
The Youth Enlisted Serving program.

Part II

Section 2

INTERDENOMINATIONAL HOLINESS CONVENTION (1947-   )

Organized in 1947, this inter-church association serves as an instrument for fellowship among ultra-conservative holiness people. Concerned with the growing worldliness and compromise in standards of conduct since World War II, the convention denies any intention of transforming itself into a denomination. Instead, through conventions and publications it seeks to prod the conscience of the larger movement. Criticism of television, dress, amusements and denominational power loom large in the Convention Herald, its official organ. Under the editorial direction of H.E. Schmul, a Wesleyan Methodist minister who participated in the Allegheny Conference defection of 1966, the paper is published at Salem, Ohio. Monthly editions exceed 10,000 copies. The Convention also operates a bookstore and publishing house at Salem and sponsors a number of regional evangelistic meetings each year. More than twenty groups, including most if not all of the recent splinters from the established holiness denominations, hold membership in the Interdenominational Holiness Convention.

--CLERGY

-- --AUTHORITATIVE SOURCES

3813   KNAPP, Martin Wells, 1853-1901.
Pentecostal preachers. Salem, Ohio, Convention Bookstore; Bicknell, Ind., Fellowship Promoter Press, 19??. 76 p.
Reprint of 189? ed.

--CONDUCT OF LIFE

3814   BOYNTON, R. C.
Fire and fruit: by-products of Pentecost. Milan, Ill., 1965. 145 p.

3815   HARRIS, A.
The case of the parlor movie. Topeka, Kan., Student

II. 2. Interdenominational Convention

of Prophecy & Missionary Evangel, n. d. 24 p.
Foreword by H. Robb French.

3816 SCHMUL, Harold E.
Why are we losing our children?, and other sermons.
Cincinnati, Revivalist Press, c1955. 76 p.
"Messages ... preached and recorded at God's Bible School Camp Meeting or Mid-Year Revival."

3817 WILCOX, Leslie D.
Beacons for youth. Rev. ed. Cincinnati, Revivalist Press, 1967. 95 p.

-- --AUTHORITATIVE SOURCES

3818 HUMPHREY, Jerry Miles, 1872-
Daily guide for the sanctified. Salem, Ohio, Convention Book Store, H. E. Schmul, n. d. 147 p.
Reprint of 1917 ed.

3819 HUMPHREY, Jerry Miles, 1872-
"What ... God hath joined together." Phoenix, Ariz., Rev. Don Hughes, n. d. Cover-title, 22 p.
Autobiographical.

3820 KNAPP, Martin Wells, 1853-1901.
Rescued!, or, The river of death, showing how people perish in it, and how they may be rescued. Rev. ed. Cincinnati, God's Bible School Book Room, n. d. 118 p.
Reprint of 1898 ed.

--DEVOTIONAL LITERATURE

-- --AUTHORITATIVE SOURCES

3821 SHAW, Solomon Benjamin, 1854-   , comp.
Children's edition of Touching incidents and remarkable answers to prayer. 1968 ed. Guthrie, Okla., Faith Publishing House, 1968. 135 p.
Revision of 1895 ed.

--DOCTRINAL AND CONTROVERSIAL WORKS

3822 COWAN, James
Wresting the scriptures; the Revised Standard Version and the New English Bible--NT. Satan's subtle, subversive masterpieces, the most dangerous books of the twentieth century.... n. p., 1962? 35 p.

3823 McCONKEY, James H.
The way of victory; a series of studies upon victory over sin. Pittsburgh, Silver, 1959. 108 p.

3824 YOCUM, Dale Morris
Conformed to Christ. Cincinnati, Revivalist Press, 1962. 215 p.

-- --AUTHORITATIVE SOURCES

3825 BRENGLE, Samuel Logan, 1860-1936.
The guest of the soul; preface by General Edward J. Higgins. 1971 ed. Noblesville, Ind., J. Edwin Newby, Newby Book Room, 1971. 127 p.
Reprint of 1934 ed.

3826 CHADWICK, Samuel, 1860-1932.
Humanity and God. Rochester, Pa., H.E. Schmul, 19??.

3827 CULPEPPER, John B.
Malice. Kokomo, Ind., Rev. J. Edwin Newby, n.d. 29 p.

3828 DANE, Charles Walter, 1875-1944.
Why, when and how of sanctification. 1972 ed. Noblesville, Ind., J. Edwin Newby, Newby Book Room, 1972. 92 p.
Cover-title: Sanctification: why, when, how.
Reprint of 1904 ed.

3829 DOTY, Thomas K., 1833-1913.
Lessons in holiness. Salem, Ohio, Convention Book Store, H.E. Schmul, n.d. 239 p.
Reprint of 1887 ed.

3830 THE DOUBLE cure; or, Echoes from National camp-meetings. Salem, Ohio, Convention Bookstore, 1965. xix, 206 p.
Partial reprint of 1887 ed.

3831 GODBEY, William B., 1833-1920.
Christian perfection. Dallas, Tex., Evangel Press, n.d. 96 p.

3832 GODBEY, William B., 1833-1920.
Sanctification. Dallas, Tex., Holiness Echoes, 1956. 112 p.
Reprint of 1884 ed.

3833 HILLS, Aaron Merritt, 1848-1935.
Holiness and power for the church and the ministry.

II. 2. Interdenominational Convention

Cincinnati, Revivalist Office, 197?. 382 p.
Reprint of 1897 ed.

3834 HOLINESS MISCELLANY: essays [of] Dr. Adam Clarke, and Richard Watson; experiences of Bishop Foster, Rev. Geo. Peck, D.D., Rev. Alfred Cookman, Rev. J.A. Wood, Rev. E.M. Levy, D.D., [and] D. Steele, D.D. Salem, Ohio, Convention Book Store, H.E. Schmul, 1971. 175 p.
Cover-title: Holiness essays and experiences.
John S. Inskip, comp.
Facsimile reprint of 1882 ed.

3835 KNAPP, Martin Wells, 1853-1901.
The double cure. Dallas, Evangel Press, 195?. 96 p.
Reprint of 1895 ed.

3836 McCLURKAN, James O., 1861-1914.
How to keep sanctified. Noblesville, Ind., J. Edwin Newby, Newby Book Room, n.d. 31 p.
Reprint of 1903 ed.

3837 McLAUGHLIN, George Asbury, 1851-1933.
Inbred sin. Dallas, Tex., Evangel Press, n.d. 96 p.
Reprint of 1887 ed.

3838 MAHAN, Asa, 1799-1889.
Christian perfection. New ed., with prefatory letter by the author, and an introd. by George Warner. Salem, Ohio, H.E. Schmul, 1962. 187 p.
Reprint of 1874 ed.

3839 MAHAN, Asa, 1800-1889.
Misunderstood texts of scripture explained and elucidated and the doctrine of the higher life thereby verified. Salem, Ohio, H.E. Schmul, n.d. 181 p.

3840 MARSH, Elmer G.
The old man. 1972 ed. Noblesville, Ind., Newby Books, 1972, c1931. 111 p.
Reprint of 1931 ed.

3841 ROBERTS, Benjamin Titus, 1823-1893.
Holiness teachings, comp. from the editorial writings of the late Rev. Benjamin T. Roberts, A.M., by Benson Howard Roberts, A.M. Salem, Ohio, H.E. Schmul, 1964. 256 p.
Reprint of 1893 ed.

3842 RUTH, Christian Wismer, 1865-1941.
The second crisis in Christian experience. Chicago, Christian Witness Co., c1912; Salem, Ohio, Convention Book Store, 1971. 155 p.

3843 SCHMUL, Harold E., comp.
Christian perfection; a compilation of six holiness classics in one. Salem, Ohio, 1972? Cover-title, 1 v. (various pagings)
Contents: A plain account of Christian perfection, by John Wesley.--Fletcher on perfection, by John Fletcher.--Entire sanctification, by Adam Clarke.--Christian purity, by Bishop R.S. Foster.--The central idea of Christianity, by Bishop Jesse T. Peck.--Faith papers, by S.A. Keen.

3844 SHELHAMER, Elmer Ellsworth, 1869-1947.
Bible holiness, how obtained and how retained. Salem, Ohio, Convention Book Store, H.E. Schmul, 19??. 128 p.
First published under title: Bible standard of regeneration and holiness; reprinted first under title: Popular and radical holiness contrasted.

3845 SHEPARD, William Edward, 1862-
The palm tree blessing; a discourse on the various characteristics of the palm tree, illustrating the many features of the sanctified Christian life. Noblesville, Ind., J. Edwin Newby, Newby Book Room, 1972. 167 p.
Reprint of 1913 ed.

3846 STEELE, Daniel, 1824-1914.
The gospel of the Comforter. Rochester, Pa., H.E. Schmul, 1960. 308 p.

3847 STEELE, Daniel, 1824-1914.
Half-hours with St. Paul, and other Bible readings. Rochester, Pa., H.E. Schmul, n.d. 329 p.

3848 STEELE, Daniel, 1824-1914.
Love enthroned. Salem, Ohio, H.E. Schmul, 1961. 293 p.

3849 WATSON, George Douglas, 1845-1924.
Holiness manual. Dallas, Tex., Chandler Publications, 195?. 144 p.
Reprint of 1882 ed.

3850 WATSON, George Douglas, 1845-1924.
White robes; or, Garments of salvation; and, Spiritual feasts. Cincinnati, God's Revivalist Press, c1883. 162 p.

--ESCHATOLOGY

-- --AUTHORITATIVE SOURCES

3851 HUMPHREY, Jerry Miles, 1872-
The lost soul's first day in eternity. Chicago, Christian Witness Co., c1912; Phoenix, Ariz., Book Nook, n.d. 128 p.

II. 2. Interdenominational Convention

3852 LUDWIGSON, Raymond
Simplified classroom notes on prophecy. Salem, Ohio, Convention Bookstore. Publication, 19??. 142 p.
Reprint of 1951 ed.
Reprinted on recommendation of S. I. Emery.

--EVANGELISTIC WORK

-- --AUTHORITATIVE SOURCES

3853 GLASCOCK, James Luther, 1852-1942.
Revivals of religion; before they occur, how to promote them, while they are in progress, and after they are over; with an introd. by Rev. H. C. Morrison. Cincinnati, God's Bible School Book Room, n. d. 109 p.
Reprint of 1911 ed.

3854 HUMPHREY, Jerry Miles, 1872-
Fire from the pulpit. Chicago, W. B. Rose, 1917; Phoenix, Ariz., Book Nook, n. d. 96 p.

3855 HUMPHREY, Jerry Miles, 1872-
The worker's secret of unction. Chicago, Christian Witness Co., c1920; Phoenix, Ariz., Book Nook, n. d. 89 p.

3856 KNAPP, Martin Wells, 1853-1901.
Revival kindlings. Cincinnati, God's Bible School Book Room, n. d. 336 p.
Reprint of 1890 ed.

--PERIODICALS

3857 CONVENTION HERALD. 1- , 1947- . Salem, Ohio.
1947-1966 as I. H. Convention Herald.

3858 EVANGELIST OF Truth. 1- , 19??- . Knoxville, Tenn.

3859 GOSPEL EMANCIPATOR. 1- , 1959- . Morrisville, Mo.

3860 REVIVAL HERALD. 1- , 19??-1962. Pinellas Park, Fla.
Merged with I. H. Convention Herald.

3861 TORCH. 1- , 1967- . Hobe Sound, Fla., Florida Evangelistic Association.

--SERMONS

3862 COX, Enos Kincheloe
"Where is the Lord God of Elijah?" With introd. by

Byron Hoover DeMent. Salem, Ohio, Convention Book Store, H.E. Schmul, 19??. 127 p.
Reprint of 1929 ed.

3863 HUMPHREY, Jerry Miles, 1872-
X-ray sermons. Salem, Ohio, Convention Book Store, H.E. Schmul, n.d. 247 p.
Reprint of 1924 ed.

3864 KULP, George B., 1845-1939.
The departed Lord; or, Words that burn. Salem, Ohio, Convention Book Store, H.E. Schmul, 19??. 313 p.
Reprint of 1921 ed.

3865 SCHMUL, Harold E.
The church in the wilderness. Knoxville, Evangelist of Truth, 196?. 44 p.
"Messages ... originally printed in ... No Uncertain Sound."

3866 SCHMUL, Harold E., comp.
No uncertain sound; compilation of sermons by holiness preachers and writers. Rochester, Pa., 195?. 120 p.

3867 SCHMUL, Harold E., comp.
Valiant for truth; compilation of sermons by holiness preachers and writers. Rochester, Pa., H.E. Schmul, 195?. 232 p.

BIBLE MISSIONARY CHURCH (1955-   )

[Nov. 1955 to Sept. 1956 as Bible Missionary Union]

The first of at least eight separatist movements within established holiness denominations in the 1950's and 1960's, the Bible Missionary Church originated in protest against worldliness in the Church of the Nazarene. In the ten months following establishment of the first congregation at Caldwell, Idaho, in November 1955, the Bible Missionary Union (soon re-named Bible Missionary Church) spread to twenty states and three foreign countries. In the summer of 1956 the group was augmented by a large number of ministers and laymen who had recently failed in efforts to get the Nazarene General Assembly to condemn television. Led at first by Glenn Griffith and Elbert Dodd, former Nazarene district superintendents of Idaho and Louisiana respectively, the Bible Missionary Church has stressed plain dress and separation from the world. It plays down centralized authority (general and district leaders are called moderators), but has been as aggressively expansionist in its planning as its parent. By 1967 it reported

II. 2. Interdenominational Convention

churches in thirty-four states, Canada, and Mexico and was supporting missionary work in Guyana, Barbados, St. Vincent Island, India, New Guinea, Japan, Okinawa, and among American Indians in New Mexico. Since 1958, it has maintained the Bible Missionary Institute and a bookstore in Rock Island, Illinois. From headquarters in Denver it issues The Missionary Revivalist. Although the Bible Missionary Church does not publish membership statistics, an estimate based on proportional representation in the quadrennial General Conference would indicate a total of more than 3000 full adult members in the United States.

3868   BIBLE MISSIONARY Church. General Conference.
        Journal. 1st- , 1956- . n.p., 1956- .
        Quadrennial, 1959- .

3869   BIBLE MISSIONARY Church.
        Manual, 1956- . n.p., 1956- .
        Quadrennial, 1959- .

--APOLOGETIC WORKS

3870   BIBLE MISSIONARY Church.
        Introducing--The Bible Missionary Church: Arminian in theology, Wesleyan in doctrine, holiness in experience, scriptural in standards, informal in worship. Denver, Department of Publications of the General Board, The Bible Missionary Church, n.d. 12 p.

--CONDUCT OF LIFE

3871   GRIFFITH, Glenn, 1894-
        "Until death do us part." Dundee, Ill., Metropolitan Press, 1958. 32 p.

--DOCTRINAL AND CONTROVERSIAL WORKS

3872   ERDMANN, H. A.
        The carnal mind and the cure for it. Rock Island, Ill., Bible Missionary Church Book Store, 1960. 61 p.
        Reprint of 1934 ed.

3873   ERDMANN, H. A.
        Office work of the Holy Spirit. Jerome, Ida., n.d. 96 p.

3874   JOHNSON, Spencer
        The offence of the cross. Denver, Colo., 19??. Folder.

-- --GLOSSOLALIA

3875 CHESNUT, Lawrence J.
True Bible tongues: their proper place and use in the church. Oklahoma City, Okla., c1948. 96 p.

--MISSIONS

3876 ENCYCLOPEDIA OF modern Christian missions; the agencies. Burton L. Goddard, ed.... Camden, N.J., T. Nelson, 1967. xix, 743 p.
"Bible Missionary Church, Foreign Missions Committee": p. 87.

--PERIODICALS

3877 MISSIONARY REVIVALIST. 1- , June 1956- . Denver, Colo.; Rock Island, Ill.

--SERMONS

3878 JOHNSON, Spencer
Good news; [a message from God]. Rock Island, Ill., Bible Missionary Church Book Store, n.d. Folder.

CHURCH OF THE BIBLE COVENANT (1967-)

When the Bible Missionary Church was formed, a large sympathetic group remained in the Church of the Nazarene intent on stemming the tide of worldliness they claimed was inundating it. Including the General Secretary of Foreign Missions and several district superintendents, the group controlled several districts and undoubtedly exercised a powerful conservative influence in denominational affairs. In 1960, the foreign missions secretary, Remiss Rehfeldt, was removed. For a time he served as an evangelist, then was elected superintendent of the Indianapolis District, a conservative stronghold. Feeling that the parent body was set on an irreversible course toward "lowering of the standards of holiness and ... regression from true spirituality," Rehfeldt withdrew from the Church of the Nazarene. Rallying several younger ministers around him as a General Steering Committee, "articles" were drawn up and a General Convention called to meet at the John T. Hatfield Campground in Cleveland, Indiana during August 1967. At the convention, the Church of the Bible Covenant was formed with Rehfeldt and Marvin Powers, a young minister, as the General Presiding Officers. During the first year,

II. 2. Interdenominational Convention

about one hundred ministers affiliated with the group, and churches were established in a large arc from western Pennsylvania through Indiana and Iowa to Oklahoma and Texas, in much the same area as the Bible Missionary Church. In 1968 the group assumed responsibility for missionary work of Joseph Pitts in the Philippine Islands and more recently has begun work in Mexico. It sponsors the Covenant Foundation College near Knightstown, Indiana, and issues a monthly paper, The Covenanter, from offices in Tulsa, Oklahoma. The official headquarters is Indianapolis.

3879   CHURCH OF the Bible Covenant.
    Articles: first General Convention, August 10-13, 1967, Cleveland, Indiana. n.p., 1967. 23 p.
    Mimeographed.

3880   CHURCH OF the Bible Covenant.
    Articles of the Church of the Bible Covenant, 1968. Bethany, Okla., 1968. 75 p.
    Published by the authority of the Church of the Bible Covenant; headquarters: Indianapolis, Indiana.

3881   CHURCH OF the Bible Covenant.
    Articles of the Church of the Bible Covenant, 1970. Knightstown, Ind., 1970. 86 p.
    Published by the authority of the Church of the Bible Covenant; headquarters: Indianapolis, Indiana.

3882   CHURCH OF the Bible Covenant. General Convention.
    Moments of memory; excerpts from the First General Convention of the Church of the Bible Covenant, held in Cleveland, Indiana, August 10-13, 1967. n.p., Century Records, 1968. 2 sides 33 rpm (31730).

--APOLOGETIC WORKS

3883   CHURCH OF the Bible Covenant. Milesburg, Pa., 1968.
    Folder.

--PERIODICALS

3884   COVENANTER. 1- , 1967- . Tulsa, Okla.

EVANGELICAL WESLEYAN CHURCH (1963-)

The product of the union of the Midwest Holiness Association and the Evangelical Wesleyan Church of North America at

Grand Island, Nebraska, in July 1963, this group is concentrated in Nebraska and Pennsylvania. Both parent bodies had originated in protest against compromise of older doctrinal and disciplinary standards by the Free Methodist Church. As a result, the new group committed itself to rigorous enforcement of its reformulation of these standards. Denominational headquarters is at Grand Island, Nebraska, where The Earnest Christian is also published. The Evangelical Wesleyan Church sponsors Bible training schools at Kearney, Nebraska, and Northville, New York.

3885   EVANGELICAL WESLEYAN Church.
Doctrines & discipline of the Evangelical Wesleyan Church, 1967. Grand Island, Neb., Evangelical Wesleyan Book Concern, 1968. 199 p.

3886   EVANGELICAL WESLEYAN Church.
Directory and general combined minutes; containing the minutes of the annual conferences and the complete journal of the 1971 General Conference. Dannebrog, Neb., Evangelical Wesleyan Book Concern, 1971. 52 p.

--CATECHISMS AND CREEDS

3887   EVANGELICAL WESLEYAN Church.
A Methodist catechism containing the doctrines of the Christian religion; prepared especially for the members of the Evangelical Wesleyan Church, published by order of the General Board of Administration. Grand Island, Neb., Evangelical Wesleyan Book Concern, 1970. 16 p.

--HYMNS

3888   EVANGELICAL WESLEYAN Church.
Hymns of our heritage; published by authority of the General Board of Administration of the Evangelical Wesleyan Church. Grand Island, Neb., Evangelical Wesleyan Book Concern, 1969. Unpaged.
With music.

--PERIODICALS

3889   EARNEST CHRISTIAN. 1- , 1962- . Ansley, Neb.

EVANGELICAL WESLEYAN CHURCH OF NORTH AMERICA (1958-1

A splinter of the Free Methodist Church of North America

the Evangelical Wesleyan Church of North America was formed by a convention held near Centerville, Crawford County, Pennsylvania, on July 19, 1958. Committed to conservation of old-time Free Methodism, the Pennsylvania group united with former Free Methodists of the Nebraska-based Midwest Holiness Association to form the Evangelical Wesleyan Church in July 1963.

3890   EVANGELICAL WESLEYAN Church of North America.
       Doctrines and discipline. Titusville, Pa., 1960. vii, 139 p.

Evangelistic Associations

MIDWEST HOLINESS ASSOCIATION (1962-1963)

A protest against worldliness and "apostacy" in the Free Methodist Church of North America, the Midwest Holiness Association was organized during a convention held in Ansley, Custer County, Nebraska, on June 5, 1962. A year later the Association united with the Evangelical Wesleyan Church of North America, a like-minded group of former Free Methodists in Pennsylvania, to form the Evangelical Wesleyan Church.

--PERIODICALS

3891   EARNEST CHRISTIAN. 1- , 1962- . Ansley, Neb.

VOICE OF THE NAZARENE ASSOCIATION OF CHURCHES (195?-)

The conservative reaction which swept the Church of the Nazarene following World War II and which resulted in the eventual formation of the Bible Missionary Church and the Church of the Bible Covenant, was to a large extent coordinated by a small western Pennsylvania paper called The Voice of the Nazarene. Begun by W. L. King in 1951 the paper attacked the growing worldliness and institutionalization of the denomination. In the ten years following their 1956 General Assembly defeat in relation to television, most of the leaders of the radical conservatives left the Church of the Nazarene. Instead of joining the new church bodies, the Voice of the Nazarene publishers became independent. They then formed a loose association of autonomous congregations called the Voice of the Nazarene Association of Churches, Inc., which by 1967 had seven member and eighteen cooperating congregations. In recent years extreme conservatism in political and social matters has characterized both the paper and the churches.

--PERIODICALS

3892　UNIVERSAL CHALLENGER. 1- , 1962-196?. Finleyville, Pa.
196? merged with Voice of the Nazarene to form Voice of the Nazarene, a Universal Challenger.

3893　VOICE OF the Nazarene, a Universal Challenger. 1- , 1951- . Finleyville, Pa.
1951-196? as Voice of the Nazarene.

INDEPENDENT HOLINESS CHURCHES (1958-)

The Association of Independent Holiness Churches, chartered in 1958, partially continues the work of the Holiness Movement Church of Canada, which formally merged with the Free Methodist Church in 1959. Puritanical in behavioral standards and congregational in church government, the group makes a distinction between entire sanctification and the Baptism of the Holy Ghost. Entire sanctification, it teaches freeing the believer from inbred sin; the Baptism of the Holy Ghost empowers him for Christian service. Churches are located in Ontario and Saskatchewan, and missions conducted in Hong Kong, Formosa, and West Africa. The Association issues a monthly periodical, Gospel Tidings, and sponsors the Calvary Holiness College at Wellesley, Ontario. The total membership appears to be less than a thousand.

3894　INDEPENDENT HOLINESS Churches.
　　　Declaration of rules and doctrine. n.p., 1960. Unpaged.
　　　Mimeographed.

3895　INDEPENDENT HOLINESS Churches.
　　　Declaration of rules and doctrine, by authority of General Conference, 1971. n.p., 1971. 56 p.
　　　Mimeographed.

--PERIODICALS

3896　GOSPEL TIDINGS. 1- , 1960- . Kingston, Ont., Can.; Burnaby, B.C., Can.; Wellesley, Ont., Can.

II. 2. Interdenominational Convention

Methodists

ALLEGHENY WESLEYAN METHODIST CONNECTION (Original Allegheny Conference) (1966-)

Opposed to the proposed merger of the Wesleyan Methodist Church of America and the Pilgrim Holiness Church, most of the Wesleyan Methodist churches in western Pennsylvania and eastern Ohio left the main body in 1966. Alarmed at the growing centralization of denominational administration and feeling that compromise inherent in merger must of necessity increase worldliness and diminish fervor, the Allegheny Connection set out to restore original Wesleyan Methodist patterns of church government and personal behavior. The group, which adopted the present name in 1968 when it reached a property settlement with the parent body, is strongly committed to congregational autonomy. Though the conference is headed by an elected president, the churches cooperate in sponsoring ventures such as publishing and missionary work, not feasible for individual church sponsorship. Between sessions of the annual conference, connectional activity is directed from offices in Titusville, Pennsylvania, by five elected boards. In 1971, Allegheny Wesleyans reported having 98 organized churches and 2908 members. As an adjunct to missionary work among American Indians, the group sponsored a Bible school at Alberton, Montana.

3897   ALLEGHENY WESLEYAN Methodist Connection (Original Allegheny Conference)
        Discipline. 1970 ed. Titusville, Pa., 1970. 168 p.

3898   ALLEGHENY WESLEYAN Methodist Connection (Original Allegheny Conference)
        Minutes. 125th- , 1968- .
        Annual.

--CONDUCT OF LIFE

3899   MORRISON, Joseph Grant, 1871-1939.
        Achieving faith. Titusville, Pa., Allegheny Wesleyan Methodist Connection, 19??. 80 p.
        Partial reprint of 1926 ed.

3900   VAN WORMER, Ivah B.
        Keep thy garments. n.p., 196?. 11 p.
        Mimeographed.

--DEVOTIONAL LITERATURE

3901   McLAUGHLIN, George Asbury, 1851-1933.
        On eagle's wings; or, Spiritual aviation; a devotional

book, containing daily meditations on devotional subjects for one month. Titusville, Pa., Allegheny Wesleyan Methodist Connection, 19??. 64 p.

--DOCTRINAL AND CONTROVERSIAL WORKS

-- --AUTHORITATIVE SOURCES

3902 COOKMAN, Alfred, 1828-1871.
    Familiar talks on the subject of the higher Christian life. Titusville, Pa., Allegheny Wesleyan Methodist Connection, 19??. 71 p.
    Reprint of 1900 ed.

BIBLE METHODIST CONNECTION OF CHURCHES (1966-)

[1966-1970 as Wesleyan Connection of Churches, and 1968-1970 as Bible Methodist Church]

    Besides the departure of most of the Allegheny Conference churches, merger with the Pilgrim Holiness Church was the occasion for secession movements in the Wesleyan Methodist conferences of Ohio, Tennessee and Alabama. Most of the dissidents in Tennessee have remained independent, but by 1968 separatists in the other areas had organized: in Alabama as the Bible Methodist Church; and in southwestern Ohio as the Wesleyan Connection of Churches. Like the Allegheny group, they were deeply committed to congregationalism and to conservative standards of dress and behavior, also to nineteenth-century forms of Wesleyan Methodist organization. As a result, when the two merged in 1970 they called themselves the Bible Methodist Connection of Churches and adopted a constitution calling for cooperation solely to support connectional interests rather than as a means of denominational coercion. In 1970, with thirty churches from the Alabama group and eleven in the Ohio one, the Bible Methodist Connection numbered 794 members. That year it started publishing the Bible Methodist at Brent, Alabama.

3903 BIBLE METHODIST Connection of Churches.
    Bible Methodist discipline, 1970. n.p., 1970. 119 p.

3904 BIBLE METHODIST Connection of Churches. Conferences. Ohio.
    Minutes. 1st- , 1966- .

3905 BIBLE METHODIST Connection of Churches. General Conference.
    Minutes. 1st- , 1970- . n.p., 1970- .
    Quadrennial.

II. 2. Interdenominational Convention

--PERIODICALS

3906 BIBLE METHODIST. 1- , 1970- . Brent, Ala.

PILGRIM HOLINESS CHURCH OF NEW YORK (1963-)

An emergency meeting of the New York District conference of the Pilgrim Holiness Church held at Utica in February 19, 1963, voted unanimously to declare itself an independent denomination. Fearing the trend toward centralized power in the national body, the New York group claimed autonomy on the basis of incorporation as a district following merger with the national group in 1922. The conference reconvened February 25 and 26, 1963, in Schenectady and organized a separate body to be known as the Pilgrim Holiness Church of New York, Inc. In June the annual conference of the new body reported 801 members in 25 congregations in New York, Pennsylvania, and Massachusetts. Eight years later there were 1032 members in 44 churches in the three original states and Ohio, Manitoba and Ontario.

The Pilgrim Holiness Church of New York cooperates with the Interdenominational Holiness Convention, and contributes to foreign missionary work of the Evangelistic Faith Missions and Evangelical Bible Missions. In addition it continues to support some foreign missionary projects of The Wesleyan Church. <u>Pilgrim News</u> is the official denominational organ.

3907 PILGRIM HOLINESS Church of New York.
   Discipline; adopted by the Annual Conference of 1964. Albany, N.Y., Rev. Andrew J. Whitney, 1964. 90 p.

3908 PILGRIM HOLINESS Church of New York.
   Discipline, 1971. Albany, N.Y., Pilgrim Holiness Church of New York, Inc., 1971. ii, 113 p.

3909 PILGRIM HOLINESS Church of New York. Annual Conference.
   Minutes. 42d- , 1963- . Lake Placid, N.Y.

--HISTORY

3910 THE PENTECOSTAL Rescue Mission: Pilgrim Holiness Church of New York; seventy-fifth anniversary diamond jubilee. Binghamton, N.Y., 1972. Unpaged.
   Added t.-p.: Celebrating the 75th anniversary of the Pentecostal Rescue Mission. Motto: "Holiness unto the Lord." A brief history. Christ our way, truth, life:

Pilgrim Holiness Church of New York, Inc.

3911 THOMAS, Paul Westphal, 1894-1972.
"The days of our pilgrimage; a history of the Pilgrim Holiness Church," by Paul Westphal Thomas and Paul William Lee Thomas. Unpublished paper, 1968. 1 v. (variour pagings)
In archives of The Wesleyan Church, Marion, Indiana.
Account of separation of the New York District: ℓ. 356-358.

--PERIODICALS

3912 PILGRIM NEWS. 1- , 1949- . Lake Placid, N.Y.; Northville, N.Y.

PILGRIM HOLINESS CHURCH OF THE MIDWEST (1970-)

In 1967 ten congregations affiliated with the Pilgrim Holiness Church of New York but located in Indiana and Illinois, form the Midwest Conference of the New York group. Three years late the Midwest Conference adopted its own discipline and incorporated as the Pilgrim Holiness Church of the Midwest. Although an independent, governmentally autonomous body, the group enjoys a warm relationship with the New York group. In 1969 it reported 246 members in thirteen churches.

The Midwest group cooperates with the program of the Interdenominational Holiness Convention and supports foreign missionary work of the Evangelistic Faith Missions and the Evangelical Bible Missions.

3913 PILGRIM HOLINESS Church of New York. Conferences. Midwest.
Minutes of the Midwest Conference. 1st-3d, 1967-1969 Massena, N.Y., Lake Placid, N.Y., Pilgrim Press, 1967-1969. 3 v.
Annual.

UNITED HOLINESS CHURCH OF NORTH AMERICA (1966-)

This group is the result of conservative dissent within the Free Methodist Church. Organized on June 15, 1955 during a camp meeting held at Carson City, Michigan. The body purports

II. 2. Interdenominational Convention

to perpetuate the fervor and lack of worldliness which its spokesmen think once characterized the parent body. The United Holiness Church maintains a Bible college at Cedar Springs, Michigan, which has become the center of the movement. The official organ, the United Holiness Sentinel, is published there. Except for stricter discipline, the United Holiness Church strongly resembles the Free Methodist Church. Like other newly formed holiness denominations, the church works in cooperation with the Interdenominational Holiness Convention.

3914   UNITED HOLINESS Church of North America.
        Discipline of the United Holiness Church of North America, 1969. n.p., 1969. 46 p.

--PERIODICALS

3915   UNITED HOLINESS Sentinel. 1- , Feb. 1966- . Cedar Springs, Mich.
        Also as Sentinel.

WESLEYAN HOLINESS ASSOCIATION OF CHURCHES (1959-)

In 1959 Glenn Griffith, a former district superintendent of the Church of the Nazarene and founder of the Bible Missionary Church, formed this group in protest of an alleged compromise by the Bible Missionary Church receiving divorced people as members or ministers. Directed from Phoenix, Arizona, where Griffith makes his home, the Wesleyan Holiness Association is a loose federation of widely dispersed independent congregations held together by commitment to the conservative ideas of its leaders. The Association appears to have neither schools, foreign missionary work, nor an official periodical. Governmental and doctrinal standards are outlined in the Declaration of Principles (1971). Maintaining a friendly stance toward other radically conservative holiness churches, the Association is affiliated with the Interdenominational Holiness Convention.

3916   WESLEYAN HOLINESS Association of Churches.
        Declaration of principles, 1971. Phoenix, Ariz., 1971. vi, 76 p.

--CONDUCT OF LIFE

3917   GRIFFITH, Glenn, 1894-
        "Until death do us part." Dundee, Ill., Metropolitan Press, 1958. 32 p.

--PERIODICALS

3917a ELEVENTH HOUR Messenger. 1- , 1960- . Phoenix, Ariz.

--SERMONS

3918 GRIFFITH, Glenn, 1894-
"I sought for a man." Phoenix, Ariz., n.d. vi, 112 p.
Autobiography and sermons.

3919 GRIFFITH, Glenn, 1894-
Jesus' last words, a sermon by Glenn Griffith, general superintendent of Wesleyan Holiness Association of Churches; "He giveth more grace" sung by L. Wayne States. Produced by Delbert H. Willoughby. Phoenix, Ariz., Wesleyan Holiness Association of Churches, 197?. 2 sides 33 rpm (ARA 31169).

3920 GRIFFITH, Glenn, 1894-
A voice in the midnight hour; comp. for printing by Donald Hughes. Denver, Rev. Glenn Griffith, n.d. 167 p.
Sermons.

Part III

KESWICK MOVEMENT

Unlike the Holiness Movement, the Keswick Movement has been productive neither of significant institutionalism nor new church movements. It was founded and has continued largely as an annual convention. Inclusion of individuals and church bodies within the Keswick Movement, therefore, implies sympathy with the teachings promulgated by the annual meeting. It does not indicate any organic or institutional relationship.

KESWICK CONVENTION (1875-   )

An annual gathering held at Keswick in northwestern England, the Keswick Convention aims at promoting "Practical Holiness" by encouraging prayer, Bible study and personal discipline. Begun in 1875 as a result of the impact of American perfectionists such as William E. Boardman, a Presbyterian, Asa Mahan, a Congregationist, and Robert Pearsal Smith and his wife, Hannah Whitall Smith, Quakers, this interdenominational meeting has been largely supported by evangelicals in the Church of England and the free churches. Suspect in the eyes of Wesleyan holiness people because of its emphasis on the suppression of evil tendencies (the Wesleyan group believes the carnal nature can be eradicated), the Keswick Movement has enjoyed only limited fraternity with the Holiness Movement. Although Wesleyan perfectionists have occasionally spoken at Keswick, they have traditionally supported the Southport Methodist Holiness Convention (recently called the Southport International Revival Convention), which is also held annually.

3921   ACCOUNT OF the Union Meeting for the Promotion of Scriptural Holiness, held at Oxford, Aug. 29 to Sept. 7, 1874. London, Daldy, Isbister & Co., 1874. vii, 17-388 p.

3922   ACCOUNT OF the Union Meeting for the Promotion of Scriptural Holiness, held at Oxford, August 29 to September 7, 1874. Boston and New York, Willard

Tract Repository, 1874. vii, 17-388 p.

3923 KESWICK CONVENTION.
The Keswick week [proceedings of the convention] 1st ed.; 1872-1928, 1950- . London, Marshall, Morgan & Scott. v. Annual.

3924 KESWICK CONVENTION.
Keswick Convention for the Promotion of Practical Holiness, 1897; programme and note book.... Liverpool, Thompson & Co., 1897. 18 p.

3925 KESWICK CONVENTION.
Programme & note book, 1930-1939, 1947- . London. v. Annual.

--APOLOGETIC WORKS

3926 HARFORD, Charles Forbes, 1864- , ed.
The Keswick Convention: its message, its method and its men. London, Marshall Bros., 1907. xi, 249 p.

3927 PIERSON, Arthur Tappan, 1837-1911.
The Keswick Movement in precept and practise; with an introd. by Rev. Evan H. Hopkins. New York and London, Funk & Wagnalls Co., 1903. 124 p.

--CONDUCT OF LIFE

3928 MEYER, Frederick Brotherton, 1847-1929.
The directory of the devout life. London, Morgan & Scott, 1904. 191 p.

3929 MEYER, Frederick Brotherton, 1847-1929.
Saved and kept; counsels to young believers.... London, Morgan & Scott, 1897. 154 p.

3930 MURRAY, Andrew, 1828-1917.
Abide in Christ, thoughts on the blessed life of fellowship with the Son of God. Philadelphia, H. Altemus, 1895. 236 p.
Continued by the author's Like Christ, 1895.

3931 MURRAY, Andrew, 1828-1917.
The inner chamber and the inner life. New York, Chicago, Fleming H. Revell Co., c1905. 170 p.
"The most of these chapters ... appeared in the South African Pioneer."

Part III. Keswick Movement 487

3932 MURRAY, Andrew, 1828-1917.
Like Christ, thoughts on the blessed life of conformity to the Son of God. A sequel to Abide in Christ. Philadelphia, H. Altemus, 1895. 282 p.

3933 TORREY, Reuben Archer, 1856-1928.
How to succeed in the Christian life. New York, Chicago, Fleming H. Revell Co., c1906. 121 p.

--CRITICAL WORKS

3934 HILLS, Aaron Merritt, 1848-1935.
Scriptural holiness and Keswick teaching compared. Manchester, Eng., Star Hall, 1910? 182 p.

3935 JOHNSON, Elias Henry, 1841-1906.
The highest life; a story of shortcomings and a goal, including a friendly analysis of the Keswick Movement. New York, A.C. Armstrong and Son, 1901. ix, 183 p.

--DEVOTIONAL LITERATURE

3936 MURRAY, Andrew, 1828-1917.
Be perfect! A message from the Father in heaven to His children on earth. Meditations for a month. London, J. Nisbet & Co., 1894. 156 p.

3937 MURRAY, Andrew, 1828-1917.
The spiritual life. A series of lectures delivered before the students of the Moody Bible Institute, Chicago, August 1895. Chicago, Tupper & Robertson, 1896. 243 p.

3938 MURRAY, Andrew, 1828-1917.
Thy will be done; the blessedness of a life in the will of God; meditations for a month. New York, Chicago, F.H. Revell Co., 1900. 201 p.

3939 MURRAY, Andrew, 1828-1917.
With Christ in the school of prayer; thoughts on our training for the ministry of intercession. Toronto, S.R. Briggs, Willard Tract Depository, 1886. xii, 274 p.

3940 MURRAY, Andrew, 1828-1917.
With Christ in the school of prayer; thoughts on our training for the ministry of intercession. Philadelphia, H. Altemus, 1895. 307 p.

--DOCTRINAL AND CONTROVERSIAL WORKS

3941 KESWICK CONVENTION.
The Keswick library; ed. by Rev. Evan H. Hopkins. London, Marshall Bros., 1894- .

3942 KESWICK CONVENTION.
The message of Keswick and its meaning.... London, Edinburgh, Marshall, Morgan & Scott, 1939. 124 p.

3943 ASKWITH, Edward Harrison, 1864-
The Christian conception of holiness. London, Macmillan, 1900. xv, 258 p.

3944 GORDON, Adoniram Judson, 1836-1895.
In Christ; or, The believer's union with his Lord. Boston, Gould and Lincoln, 1872. 309 p.

3945 GORDON, Adoniram Judson, 1836-1895.
In Christ; or, The believer's union with his Lord. 6th ed. Boston, H. Gannett, 1883. 209 p.

3946 GORDON, Adoniram Judson, 1836-1895.
The ministry of the Spirit; with an introd. by F.B. Meyer. Philadelphia, American Baptist Publication Society, 1894. 225 p.

3947 GORDON, Adoniram Judson, 1836-1895.
The ministry of the Spirit; with an introd. by Rev. F.B. Meyer.... New York, F.H. Revell Co., c1894. 229 p.

3948 GORDON, Adoniram Judson, 1836-1895.
The two fold life; or, Christ's work for us and Christ's work in us. Boston, H. Gannett, 1883. 259 p.

3949 IRONSIDE, Henry Allan, 1876-1951.
Holiness, the false and the true. New York, Loizeaux Bros., 1953. 142 p.
Reprint of 1912 ed.

3950 IRONSIDE, Henry Allan, 1876-1951.
Praying in the Holy Spirit. Oakland, Calif., Western Book and Tract Co., n.d. 61 p.

3951 MAHAN, Asa, 1800-1889.
The baptism of the Holy Ghost; with a new preface to which is added, The enduement with power, by Rev. C.G. Finney. West Summerland (Okamagan), B.C., Can., Printed from the Home of the Friendless Publishing House of Pure Religious Literature at Mizpah Heights, 1932. 156 p.
Imprint covered by label.

Part III. Keswick Movement 489

3952 MARSH, Frederick Edward, 1858-
Emblems of the Holy Spirit. Grand Rapids, Mich., Kregel Publications, 1957. ix, 257 p.
"First American reprint edition."

3953 MEYER, Frederick Brotherton, 1847-1929.
The call & challenge of the Unseen. London, Morgan & Scott, 1928. 183 p.

3954 MEYER, Frederick Brotherton, 1847-1929.
Calvary to Pentecost. London, Marshall Bros., 1894. 110 p.

3955 MEYER, Frederick Brotherton, 1847-1929.
Calvary to Pentecost. London, Marshall Bros., 1898. 111 p.

3956 MEYER, Frederick Brotherton, 1847-1929.
Love to the uttermost; expositions of John XIII-XVI. London, Morgan & Scott, 1898. 254 p.

3957 MEYER, Frederick Brotherton, 1847-1929.
The present tenses of the blessed life. London, Morgan and Scott, 1889. 149 p.

3958 MEYER, Frederick Brotherton, 1847-1929.
The soul's pure intention. London, Samuel Bagster & Sons, 1906. vi, 207 p.

3959 MEYER, Frederick Brotherton, 1847-1929.
The way into the holiest; expositions of the Epistle to the Hebrews. London, Morgan & Scott, 1893. viii, 234 p.

3960 MOODY, Dwight Lyman, 1837-1899.
Power from on high. London, Morgan and Scott, n.d.

3961 MOODY, Dwight Lyman, 1837-1899.
Secret power. Chicago, Fleming H. Revell Co., 1881.

3962 MORGAN, George Campbell, 1863-1945.
God's perfect will. New York, Chicago, Fleming H. Revell Co., 1901. 164 p.

3963 MORGAN, George Campbell, 1863-1945.
Hosea, the heart and holiness of God. New York, Fleming H. Revell Co., c1934. 159 p.

3964 MORGAN, George Campbell, 1863-1945.
The Spirit of God. New York, Chicago, Fleming H. Revell Co., c1900. 246 p.

3965   MORGAN, George Campbell, 1863-1945.
         The Spirit of God. London, Westminster City Publishing Co., 1938. 237 p.

3966   MOULE, Handley Carr Glyn, bp. of Durham, 1841-1920.
         The cross and the Spirit: studies in the Epistle to the Galatians. London, Seeley & Co., 1898. viii, 96 p.

3967   MOULE, Handley Carr Glyn, bp. of Durham, 1841-1920.
         Holiness by faith; a manual of Keswick teaching, by H.C.G. Moule, H. Brooke, J.E. Cumming [and] F.B. Meyer. London, Religious Tract Society, 1904. 156 p.

3968   MOULE, Handley Carr Glyn, bp. of Durham, 1841-1920.
         Need and fulness. London, Marshall Bros., 1895. 112 p. (The Keswick library)

3969   MOULE, Handley Carr Glyn, bp. of Durham, 1841-1920.
         Thoughts on Christian sanctity. London, Seeley & Co., 1885. 126 p.

3970   MOULE, Handley Carr Glyn, bp. of Durham, 1841-1920.
         Veni Creator: thoughts on the person and work of the Holy Spirit of promise. London, Hodder & Stoughton, 1890. xv, 252 p.

3971   MURRAY, Andrew, 1828-1917.
         Absolute surrender and other addresses. New York, Chicago, Fleming H. Revell Co., c1897. 126 p.

3972   MURRAY, Andrew, 1828-1917.
         The deeper Christian life, an aid to its attainment. Chicago, New York, Fleming H. Revell Co., 1896. 127 p.

3973   MURRAY, Andrew, 1828-1917.
         The full blessing of Pentecost; the one thing needful. New York, Chicago, F.H. Revell Co., c1908. 158 p.

3974   MURRAY, Andrew, 1828-1917.
         Holy in Christ; thoughts on the calling of God's children to be holy as He is holy.... New York, Anson D.F. Randolph & Co., 1887. 302 p.

3975   MURRAY, Andrew, 1828-1917.
         "Jesus himself." New York, Chicago, Fleming H. Revell Co., 1893. 68 p.
         "Revision of two addresses, which originally appeared in the South African Pioneer."

3976   MURRAY, Andrew, 1828-1917.
         "Love made perfect." Chicago, New York, Fleming H. Revell Co., 1894. 73 p.

Part III. Keswick Movement 491

"The substance of addresses delivered at the South African Keswick of 1893." First published in the South African Pioneer.

3977 MURRAY, Andrew, 1828-1917.
The Master's indwelling. Chicago, New York, Fleming H. Revell Co., 1896. 180 p.
"Substance ... of addresses [delivered] at the Northfield Conference of 1895."

3978 MURRAY, Andrew, 1828-1917.
The spirit of Christ: thoughts on the indwelling of the Holy Spirit in the believer and the church. Toronto, A. G. Watson, 1888. 394 p.

3979 MURRAY, Andrew, 1828-1917.
The two covenants and the second blessing. New York, Chicago, Fleming H. Revell Co., 1898. 206 p.

3980 PENTECOST, George Frederick, 1842-1920.
"Out of Egypt!"; Bible readings on the Book of Exodus, by G. F. Pentecost.... New York, London, Funk & Wagnalls, 1884. ix, 214 p.

3981 PIERSON, Arthur Tappan, 1837-1911.
The acts of the Holy Spirit, being an examination of the active mission and ministry of the Spirit of God, the divine Paraclete, as set forth in the Acts of the Apostles. New York, Chicago, Fleming H. Revell Co., 1895. 142 p.

3982 PIERSON, Arthur Tappan, 1837-1911.
Catharine of Siena, an ancient lay preacher; a story of sanctified womanhood and power in prayer. New York and London, Funk & Wagnalls Co., 1898. 68 p.

3983 PIERSON, Arthur Tappan, 1837-1911.
Dr. Pierson and his message; a sketch of the life and work of a great preacher, together with a varied selection from his unpublished manuscripts. Ed. by J. Kennedy Maclean. New York, Association Press, 1911. 280 p.

3984 SMITH, Robert Pearsall, 1827-1898.
Holiness through faith. London, Morgan and Chase, 1870. vi, 118 p.

3985 SMITH, Robert Pearsall, 1827-1898.
Holiness through faith; light on the way of holiness, by R. P. S.... Rev. ed. New York, A. D. F. Randolph & Co., 1870. 156 p.

3986 STEVENSON, Herbert F.
A galaxy of saints; lesser known Bible men and women.

Foreword by Paul S. Rees. Westwood, N.J., Revell, 1958. 158 p.

3987 STEVENSON, Herbert F., ed.
The ministry of Keswick; a selection from the Bible readings delivered at the Keswick Convention. Grand Rapids, Mich., Zondervan Publishing House, 1963- .
Contents.--ser. 1. 1892-1919: First recorded Bible readings, by H. Brooke. Grace and peace in four Pauline epistles, by H.W. Webb-Peploe. The work of Christ for the believer, by A.T. Pierson. Lord, teach us to pray, by G.C. Morgan. The Bible and spiritual life, by W.H.G. Thomas. Perplexities of the divine providence, by J.S. Holden. The practice of Christ's presence, by W.Y. Fullerton. We beheld His glory, by A. Smellie.

3988 STEVENSON, Herbert F.
The road to the cross. Foreword by Rev. Paul S. Rees. London, Marshall, Morgan & Scott, 1963. 128 p.

3989 STEVENSON, Herbert F.
Titles of the triune God; studies in divine self-revelation. Foreword by Paul S. Rees. Westwood, N.J., F.H. Revell Co., 1956. 190 p.

3990 STOCKMAYER, Otto
Abraham der Vater der Gläubigen. Basel, Brunnen-Verlag, 1943. 151 p.

3991 STOCKMAYER, Otto
Sanctified ones. New York, n.d. 184 p.

3992 STOCKMAYER, Otto
Sanctified ones. New York, 1904? 203 p.

3993 TORREY, Reuben Archer, 1856-1928.
The baptism with the Holy Spirit. New York, Chicago, Fleming H. Revell Co., 1895. 67 p.

3994 TORREY, Reuben Archer, 1856-1928.
The fundamental doctrines of the Christian faith. New York, George H. Doran Co., c1918. 328 p.

3995 TORREY, Reuben Archer, 1856-1928, ed.
The higher criticism and the new theology; unscientific, unscriptural, and unwholesome. Montrose, Pa., Montrose Christian Literature Society, c1911. 284 p.

3996 TORREY, Reuben Archer, 1856-1928, ed.
The higher criticism and the new theology; unscientific, unscriptural, and unwholesome. New York, Gospel Publishing House, 192?. 283 p.

Part III. Keswick Movement

3997 TORREY, Reuben Archer, 1856-1928.
The Holy Spirit, who He is and what He does and how to know Him in all the fullness of His gracious and glorious ministry. New York, Chicago, Fleming H. Revell Co., c1927. 201 p.

3998 TORREY, Reuben Archer, 1856-1928.
How to be saved, and how to be lost; the way of salvation and the way of condemnation made as plain as day. New York, Chicago, Fleming H. Revell Co., c1923. 218 p.

3999 TORREY, Reuben Archer, 1856-1928.
"Ought Christians to keep the Sabbath?" Chicago, New York, Fleming H. Revell Co., 1899. 45 p.

4000 TORREY, Reuben Archer, 1856-1928.
The person and work of the Holy Spirit as revealed in the Scriptures and in personal experience. New York, Chicago, Fleming H. Revell Co., c1910. 262 p.

4001 TORREY, Reuben Archer, 1856-1928.
What the Bible teaches; a thorough and comprehensive study of all the Bible has to say concerning the great doctrines of which it treats. Chicago, New York, Fleming H. Revell Co., c1898. 539 p.

4002 WEBB-PEPLOE, Hanmer William, 1837-1923.
Christ and His church; chapters on the Protestant faith. London, James Nisbet & Co., 1900. 181 p.

4003 WEBB-PEPLOE, Hanmer William, 1837-1923.
Consider Him; or, Sketches of the four Gospels. London, Marshall Bros., 1906. 88 p.

4004 WEBB-PEPLOE, Hanmer William, 1837-1923.
The faithfulness of God. London, Marshall Brothers, 1900. 30 p.

4005 WEBB-PEPLOE, Hanmer William, 1837-1923.
"I follow after." London, Marshall Brothers, 1894. 106 p.

4006 WEBB-PEPLOE, Hanmer William, 1837-1923.
Remarkable letters of St. Paul. London, Marshall Bros., 1904. 112 p.
Four addresses.

4007 WEBB-PEPLOE, Hanmer William, 1837-1923.
That beautiful name ... Bible readings given at the Keswick Convention, July, 1910. London and Edinburgh, Marshall Brothers, 1910. vi, 118 p.

4008 WEBB-PEPLOE, Hanmer William, 1837-1923.
Within and without; or, The Christian's foes. London, Marshall Bros., 1900. 91 p.

-- --ESCHATOLOGY

4009 MORGAN, George Campbell, 1863-1945.
Sunrise. "Behold, he cometh!" An introduction to a study of the second advent. New York, Chicago, Fleming H. Revell Co., c1912. 95 p.
"The chapters in this book were preached as sermons."

4010 PIERSON, Arthur Tappan, 1837-1911.
The second coming of Our Lord. Philadelphia, H. Altemus, c1896. 50 p.

4011 TORREY, Reuben Archer, 1856-1928.
The return of the Lord Jesus; the key to the Scripture, and the solution to all our political and social problems; or, The golden age that is soon coming to the earth, Los Angeles, Printed by Grant's Publishing House, c1913. 160 p.

4012 TORREY, Reuben Archer, 1856-1928.
Will Christ come again?; an exposure of the foolishness, fallacies and falsehoods of Shailer Mathews. Los Angeles, Bible Institute of Los Angeles, c1918. Cover-title, 31 p.

4013 WEBB-PEPLOE, Hanmer William, 1837-1923.
He cometh! London, Marshall Bros., 1905. vi, 116 p.

-- --FAITH-HEALING

4014 GORDON, Adoniram Judson, 1836-1895.
The ministry of healing; or, Miracles of cure in all ages. Boston, H. Gannett, 1882. v, 236 p.

-- --SPIRITUALISM

4015 MEYER, Frederick Brotherton, 1847-1929.
The modern craze of spiritualism. London, Morgan & Scott, 1919. 46 p.

--EVANGELISTIC WORK

4016 TORREY, Reuben Archer, 1856-1928.
How to bring men to Christ. Chicago, New York, Fleming H. Revell Co., 1893. 121 p.

4017 TORREY, Reuben Archer, 1856-1928.
How to work for Christ; a compendium of effective methods. Chicago, New York, Fleming H. Revell Co.,

Part III. Keswick Movement   495

      c1901. 518 p.

4018 TORREY, Reuben Archer, 1856-1928.
      Real salvation and whole-hearted service. New York,
      Chicago, Fleming H. Revell Co., 1905. 267 p.

      --HISTORY

4019 KESWICK CONVENTION.
      The Keswick Jubilee souvenir; the story of the Convention's fifty years' ministry and influence. London, Edinburgh, Marshall Bros., 1925. 50 p.

4020 KESWICK CONVENTION.
      The story of Keswick, eighteenth convention, 1892, ed. by ... E. H. Hopkins. London, The Life of Faith, 1892.

4021 BARNABAS, Steven
      So great salvation; the history and message of the Keswick Convention, with a foreword by Fred Mitchell. London, Marshall, Morgan & Scott, 1952. 207 p.

4022 BARNABAS, Steven
      So great salvation; the history and message of the Keswick Convention, with a foreword by Fred Mitchell. Westwood, N.J., Revell, 1953. 207 p.

4023 BATTERSBY, Thomas Dundas Harford, 1823?-1883.
      Memoir of T.D. Harford-Battersby ... together with some account of the Keswick Convention by two of his sons, with a preface by H.C.G. Moule. London, Seeley & Co., 1890. xv, 230 p.

4024 BATTERSBY, Thomas Dundas Harford, 1823?-1883.
      Reminiscences of the Keswick Convention, 1879, with addresses by Pastor Otto Stockmayer [ed. by T.D.H. Battersby]. London, S.W. Partridge & Co., 1879. 80 p.

4025 HOPKINS, Evan Henry
      A standard bearer of faith and holiness; reminiscences [with a memoir of the author]. London, Morgan & Scott, 1919. 47 p.

4026 POLLOCK, John Charles
      The Keswick story; the authorized history of the Keswick Convention. London, Hodder and Stoughton, 1964. 192 p.

4027 SLOAN, Walter B.
      These sixty years; the story of the Keswick Convention. London, Pickering & Inglis, 1935. 114 p.

--HISTORY OF DOCTRINES

4028 CUMMING, J. Elder
"An exposition of recent teaching on holiness," Expository Times, V (1893-1894), 164-168.

--HYMNS

4029 KESWICK CONVENTION.
The Keswick hymn-book; comp. by the trustees of the Keswick Convention. London, Edinburgh, Marshall, Morgan & Scott, 1938. xi, 239 p.

4030 KESWICK CONVENTION.
The Keswick hymn-book, comp. by the trustees of the Keswick Convention. London, Edinburgh, Marshall Morgan & Scott, 1938. xi, 666 p.

4031 FABER, Frederick William, 1814-1863.
Hymns selected from Faber, by R. Pearsall Smith. Boston, New York, Willard Tract Repository, 1874. xv, 170 p.

4032 GORDON, Adoniram Judson, 1836-1895, ed.
The vestry hymn and tune book. Boston, H.A. Young & Co., 1872. 297 p.

--MISSIONS

4033 GORDON, Adoniram Judson, 1836-1895.
The Holy Spirit in missions; six lectures. New York, F.H. Revell Co., 1893. 241 p.

4034 NEILL, Stephen Charles, bp., 1900-
Concise dictionary of the Christian world mission, ed. by Stephen Neill, Gerald H. Anderson [and] John Goodwin. Nashville, Abingdon Press, 1971. xxi, 682 p.
"Keswick Convention," by John Pollock: p. 322.

--PERIODICALS

4035 LIFE OF Faith; a weekly record of spiritual life and work. 1- , 1874- . London.
1874-1878 as Christian's pathway to power.

4036 SOUTH AFRICAN Pioneer. 1- , 1887- . London.

4037 SOUTH AFRICAN Pioneer. American ed. 1- , Dec. 1920- . Brooklyn, N.Y.

Part III. Keswick Movement

Aug. /Sept. 1936-Dec. 1941 merged with British ed.

--SERMONS

4038 GORDON, Adoniram Judson, 1836-1895.
Grace and glory; sermons for the life that now is and that which is to come. Boston, H. Gannett, 1880. iv, 355 p.

4039 GORDON, Adoniram Judson, 1836-1895.
Yet speaking; a collection of addresses, by A. J. Gordon.... New York, F. H. Revell Co., 1897. 155 p.

4040 STEVENSON, Herbert F.
James speaks for today. Foreword by Rev. Paul S. Rees. London, Marshall, Morgan & Scott, 1966. 127 p.

4041 STEVENSON, Herbert F., ed.
Keswick's authentic voice; sixty-five dynamic addresses delivered at the Keswick Convention, 1875-1957. London, Edinburgh, Marshall, Morgan & Scott, 1959. 528 p.

4042 STEVENSON, Herbert F., ed.
Keswick's triumphant voice; forty-eight outstanding addresses delivered at the Keswick Convention, 1882-1962. London, Edinburgh, Marshall, Morgan & Scott, 1962. 408 p.

4043 STEVENSON, Herbert F., ed.
Keswick's triumphant voice; forty-eight outstanding addresses delivered at the Keswick Convention, 1882-1962. Grand Rapids, Mich., Zondervan Publishing House, 1963. 408 p.

4044 STOCKMAYER, Otto
Transformation. London, Bethshan Book-room, 1909. 176 p.
Sermons, chiefly on the Epistles of Peter. "This little book is a translation of notes taken down in German at morning worship at the Schloss (castle) in Hauptweil.... It has not been revised by the author."

4045 WEBB-PEPLOE, Hanmer William, 1837-1923.
All one; sermons preached by H. W. Webb-Peploe. London, Marshall Brothers, 1896. 96 p.

4046 WEBB-PEPLOE, Hanmer William, 1837-1923.
Calls to holiness.... London, Marshall Brothers, 1900. 251 p.
Sermons.

4047 WEBB-PEPLOE, Hanmer William, 1837-1923.
The grace of God. London, Marshall Bros., 1893.
32 p.
Sermon.

4048 WEBB-PEPLOE, Hanmer William, 1837-1923.
The life of privilege: possession, peace, and power.
London, J. Nisbet & Co., 1896. 202 p.
Sermons.

4049 WEBB-PEPLOE, Hanmer William, 1837-1923.
The titles of Jehovah: a course of sermons. London, James Nisbet & Co., 1901. vii, 194 p.

4050 WEBB-PEPLOE, Hanmer William, 1837-1923.
The victorious life. London, Nisbet & Co., 1897.
208 p.
Sermons.

4051 WEBB-PEPLOE, Hanmer William, 1837-1923.
The walk on the water. London, Marshall Bros., 1896. 16 p.
Sermon.

CHRISTIAN AND MISSIONARY ALLIANCE (1887-)

[1887-1897 as Christian Alliance, and International Missionary Alliance]

Preferring to be known as an evangelistic and missionary movement rather than a denomination, the Christian and Missionary Alliance is the outgrowth of the work of A.B. Simpson, a Presbyterian minister who in 1881 left the denomination to work among the poor and neglected people outside the established churches. Two societies representing the domestic and foreign aspects of the work, called the Christian Alliance and the International Missionary Alliance, formed in 1887, were combined under the present name in 1897. Emphasizing Christ's role as savior, sanctifier, healer, and coming King, the Alliance, though not eradicationist, has maintained cordial relationships with the Wesleyan holiness churches. Alliance writers such as Simpson and A.W. Tozer are widely read in the Holiness Movement and quoted in holiness periodicals. With headquarters until recently located in New York City (now at Nyack on the Hudson), the group operates four Bible training colleges in the United States and Canada. With 26 mission fields in South America, Africa, and Asia, it supports 865 American workers. In these areas it has over four thousand national workers, 2894 organized churches, and 195,000 members. By comparison, in 1967 it claimed 1292 congregations and 80,381 members in the United States.

Part III. Keswick Movement   499

4052   CHRISTIAN AND Missionary Alliance.
        Annual report.... n.p.

4053   CHRISTIAN AND Missionary Alliance.
        Manual of the Christian and Missionary Alliance, authorized and approved by the Board of Managers. New York, Christian Alliance Publishing Co., 1917. 120 p.

4054   CHRISTIAN AND Missionary Alliance.
        Manual of the Christian and Missionary Alliance, containing services for marriage, funeral and dedication of children, together with the revised constitution and by-laws. New York, Christian and Missionary Alliance, 1936. 78 p.

4055   CHRISTIAN AND Missionary Alliance.
        Report of the president ... for the year 1920. New York,?, 1920. 32 p.

           --APOLOGETIC WORKS

4056   STOESZ, Samuel J.
        Understanding my church. Harrisburg, Pa., Christian Publications, 1968. 223 p.

           --CHURCH WORK

4057   SMITH, Oswald J.
        The man God uses. New York, Christian Alliance Publishing Co., c1925. 135 p.

           --CONDUCT OF LIFE

4058   SIMPSON, Albert Benjamin, 1843-1919.
        A larger Christian life. Harrisburg, Pa., Christian Publications, n.d.

4059   SMITH, Oswald J.
        From death to life. New York, Christian Alliance Publishing Co., c1925. 128 p.

4060   SMITH, Oswald J.
        The man in the well. Chicago, Bible Institute Colportage Association, c1934. 31 p.

4061   SMITH, Oswald J.
        The Spirit-filled life. New York, Christian Alliance Publishing Co., c1926. 126 p.

4062   TOZER, Aiden Wilson, 1897-1963.
       Of God and men. Harrisburg, Pa., Christian Publications, 1960. 133 p.

4063   TOZER, Aiden Wilson, 1897-1963.
       Paths to power. London, Oliphants, 1964. 60 p.

4064   TOZER, Aiden Wilson, 1897-1963.
       The pursuit of God; introd. by Samuel M. Zwemer. Harrisburg, Pa., Christian Publications, 1948. 128 p.

4065   TOZER, Aiden Wilson, 1897-1963.
       That incredible Christian. Harrisburg, Pa., Christian Publications, c1964. 137 p.
       "Most of the chapters of this book appeared as editorials in The Alliance Witness.... 1960-1963."

--DEVOTIONAL LITERATURE

4066   ESSAYS ON prayer; His reader on conversing with God, by A.W. Tozer and others. Chicago, Inter-Varsity Press, 1968. 89 p.
       A collection of articles that had originally appeared in His magazine.

4067   TOZER, Aiden Wilson, 1897-1963.
       The Christian book of mystical verse; selected and with an introd. and notes by A.W. Tozer. Harrisburg, Pa., Christian Publications, c1963. xiv, 152 p.

--DOCTRINAL AND CONTROVERSIAL WORKS

4068   McCROSSAN, Thomas J.
       The Bible: its Christ and modernism. Introduction by Rev. Kenneth Mackenzie. New York, Christian Alliance Publishing Co., c1925. 212 p.

4069   SIMPSON, Albert Benjamin, 1843-1919.
       The Christ life; with an introd. by Rev. Walter M. Turnbull, D.D. New York, Christian Alliance Publishing Co., 1925. 121 p.
       On cover: New edition with select poems.

4070   SIMPSON, Albert Benjamin, 1843-1919.
       Christ our sanctifier. Harrisburg, Pa., Christian Publications, 1947.

4071   SIMPSON, Albert Benjamin, 1843-1919.
       The cross of Christ. New York, Alliance Press Co., c1910. 157 p.

Part III. Keswick Movement

4072 SIMPSON, Albert Benjamin, 1843-1919.
The four-fold Gospel. New York, Christian Alliance Publishing Co., 1890. 154 p.

4073 SIMPSON, Albert Benjamin, 1843-1919.
The four-fold Gospel; with an introd. by Rev. Fredric H. Senft. New York, Christian Alliance Publishing Co., c1925. 128 p.

4074 SIMPSON, Albert Benjamin, 1843-1919.
The fulness of Jesus; or, Christian life in the New Testament. New York, Christian Alliance Publishing Co., 1890. 475 p.

4075 SIMPSON, Albert Benjamin, 1843-1919.
The Holy Spirit. New York, Christian Alliance Publishing Co., 1924. 2 v.

4076 SIMPSON, Albert Benjamin, 1843-1919.
Life more abundantly. New York, Christian Alliance Publishing Co., c1912. 134 p.

4077 SIMPSON, Albert Benjamin, 1843-1919.
The name of Jesus. New York, Christian Alliance Publishing Co., 1892. 285 p.

4078 SIMPSON, Albert Benjamin, 1843-1919.
Walking in the Spirit. Harrisburg, Pa., Christian Publications, n.d.

4079 SIMPSON, Albert Benjamin, 1843-1919.
When the Comforter came. New York, Alliance Press Co., c1911. [128] p.

4080 SIMPSON, Albert Benjamin, 1843-1919.
Wholly sanctified; with introd. by Rev. Alfred C. Snead. New York, Christian Alliance Publishing Co., c1925. 136 p.

4081 SMITH, Oswald J.
Back to Pentecost. New York, Christian Alliance Publishing Co., c1926. 124 p.

4082 SMITH, Oswald J.
The baptism with the Holy Spirit. New York, Christian Alliance Publishing Co., c1925. 54 p.

4083 TOZER, Aiden Wilson, 1897-1963.
Born after midnight. Harrisburg, Pa., Christian Publications, c1959. 142 p.

4084 TOZER, Aiden Wilson, 1897-1963.
The divine conquest; introd. by William L. Culbertson.

New York, Revell, 1950. 128 p.

4085 TOZER, Aiden Wilson, 1897-1963.
The knowledge of the holy; the attributes of God: their meaning in the Christian life. New York, Harper, 1961. 128 p.

4086 TOZER, Aiden Wilson, 1897-1963.
Man, the dwelling place of God. Harrisburg, Pa., Christian Publications, 1966. 174 p.

4087 TOZER, Aiden Wilson, 1897-1963.
The root of the righteous. Harrisburg, Pa., Christian Publications, 1955. 160 p.

-- --ESCHATOLOGY

4088 CARTER, Russell Kelso, 1849-1926.
Alpha and omega; or, The birth and death of the world, the science of the creation, the coming crisis and the golden age. San Francisco, O.H. Elliott, 1894. 613 p.

4089 CARTER, Russell Kelso, 1849-1926.
Behold! The bridegroom! New Britain, 189?. 20 p.
A tract on the Second Advent.

4090 SIMPSON, Albert Benjamin, 1843-1919.
The coming One. New York, Christian Alliance Publishing Co., c1912. 228 p.

4091 SIMPSON, Albert Benjamin, 1843-1919.
Heaven opened; or, Expositions of the book of Revelation. Nyack, N.Y. and New York, Christian Alliance Publishing Co., 1899. 299 p.

4092 SMITH, Oswald J.
Is the antichrist at hand?--What of Musolini. 7th ed. 22d thousand. New York, Christian Alliance Publishing Co., c1927. 128 p.

4093 SMITH, Oswald J.
Prophecy--what lies ahead? London, Edinburgh, Marshall, Morgan & Scott, 1943. x, 11-190 p.

4094 SMITH, Oswald J.
When Antichrist reigns. New York, Christian Alliance Publishing Co., c1927. 148 p.

-- --FAITH-HEALING

4095 McCROSSAN, Thomas J.
Bodily healing and the atonement. Seattle, T.J. McCrossan, c1930. 112 p.

Part III. Keswick Movement 503

4096 SIMPSON, Albert Benjamin, 1843-1919.
The gospel of healing. Rev. ed. New York, Christian Alliance Publishing Co., 1915. 186 p.

4097 SIMPSON, Albert Benjamin, 1843-1919.
The Lord for the body, with questions and answers on divine healing; foreword by Rev. Walter M. Turnbull, D.D., introd. by Rev. Kenneth Mackenzie. New York, Christian Alliance Publishing Co., c1925. 142 p.
An enlargement of the author's The Discovery of Divine Healing, published in 1903.

4098 SMITH, Oswald J.
The Great Physician. New York, Christian Alliance Publishing Co., c1927. 128 p.

--EDUCATION

4099 TROUTEN, Donald James
"Changes in educational policies in the Christian and Missionary Alliance." Unpublished Ph.D. dissertation, New York University, 1962. 511ℓ.

--EVANGELISTIC WORK

4100 SIMPSON, Albert Benjamin, 1843-1919.
We would see Jesus. New York, Alliance Press Co., c1910. [64] p.

4101 SMITH, Oswald J.
The revival we need. New York, Christian Alliance Publishing Co., c1925. 125 p.

--HISTORY

4102 AFTER FIFTY years; a record of God's working through the Christian and Missionary Alliance; written in collaboration by Robert B. Eckvall, Harry M. Shuman, Alfred C. Snead [and others].... Harrisburg, Pa., Christian Publications, c1939. vi, 278 p.

4103 CLARK, Elmer Talmage, 1886-1966.
The small sects in America. Rev. ed. New York, Abingdon Press, c1965. 256 p.
Account of the Christian and Missionary Alliance: p. 76-77.

4104 MEAD, Frank Spencer, 1898-
Handbook of denominations in the United States. New

5th ed. Nashville, Abingdon Press, c1970. 265 p.
"Christian and Missionary Alliance": p. 62-63.

4105 SCHAFF, Philip, 1819-1893.
New Schaff-Herzog encyclopedia of religious knowledge.... S. M. Jackson, editor-in-chief. New York, Funk, 1908-1912. 12 v.
"Christian and Missionary Alliance, " by A. B. Simpson: v. 3, p. 4.

4106 TWENTIETH CENTURY encyclopedia of religious knowledge; an extension of the New Schaff-Herzog Encyclopedia of Religious Knowledge. Editor-in-chief: Lefferts A. Loetscher. Grand Rapids, Mich., Baker Book House, 1955. 2 v. (xx, 1205 p.)
"Christian and Missionary Alliance, " by William F. Smalley: p. 239-240.

--HYMNS

4107 CHRISTIAN AND Missionary Alliance.
Hymns of the Christian life; a book of worship in song emphasizing evangelism, missions, and the deeper life. Harrisburg, Pa., Christian Publications, c1936. 480 p.
With music.

4108 CHRISTIAN AND Missionary Alliance.
Hymns of the Christian life; a book of worship in song emphasizing evangelism, missions, and the deeper life. 1962 rev. and enl. ed. Harrisburg, Pa., Christian Publications, 1963. 657 p.
"Second edition."

4109 CARTER, Russell Kelso, 1849-1926.
Hymns of the Christian life; new and standard songs for the sanctuary, Sunday schools, prayer meetings, mission work and revival services, ed. by Capt. R. Kelso Carter and Rev. A. B. Simpson.... New York, Christian Alliance Publishing Co., c1891. 320 p.
With music.

4110 SIMPSON, Albert Benjamin, 1843-1919.
Hymns and songs of the fourfold Gospel, and the fullness of Jesus. New York, Christian Alliance Publishing Co., 1891. 130 p.
Without music.

--MISSIONS

4111 CHRISTIAN AND Missionary Alliance.
Missionary atlas; a manual of the foreign work of the

Part III. Keswick Movement 505

Christian and Missionary Alliance, by Alfred C. Snead ... illus. with maps, charts and photographs.... Harrisburg, Pa., Christian Publications, 1936. 127 p.

4112 CHRISTIAN AND Missionary Alliance.
Missionary atlas; a manual of the foreign work of the Christian and Missionary Alliance, prepared by the Foreign Department under the direction of Alfred C. Snead, foreign secretary. Harrisburg, Pa., Christian Publications, 1950. 155 p.

4113 CHRISTIAN AND Missionary Alliance.
Missionary atlas; a manual of the foreign work of the Christian and Missionary Alliance, prepared by the Foreign Department, Louis L. King, foreign secretary, revised as of June 30, 1964. Harrisburg, Pa., Christian Publications, 1964. 207 p.

4114 CHRISTIAN AND Missionary Alliance. Foreign Department.
Building Christ's church in a crumbling world; a missionary survey showing the work of God in the foreign fields of the Christian and Missionary Alliance. New York, Foreign Department, Christian and Missionary Alliance, 1941. 97 p.
"Report of the Foreign Department for 1940."

4115 CHRISTIAN AND Missionary Alliance. Foreign Department.
Hearts aflame in a world on fire; a story of God's working through devoted missionaries and nationals in foreign fields of the Christian and Missionary Alliance. New York, 1942. 79 p.
"Report of the Foreign Department for 1941 as delivered to General Council, May, 1942."--p. 79.

4116 CHRISTIAN AND Missionary Alliance. Foreign Department.
Fields ... "white already to harvest"; voices of the past year and visions for days to come in the foreign missionary work of the Christian and Missionary Alliance. New York, 1943. 47 p.
"Report of the Foreign Department for 1942 as delivered to General Council, May, 1943."

4117 CHRISTIAN AND Missionary Alliance. Foreign Department.
God's garden amid man's desert, recounting the goodness and grace of God in the foreign fields of the Christian and Missionary Alliance.... New York, Foreign Department, Christian and Missionary Alliance, 1944. 47 p.
"Report of the Foreign Department for 1943 as delivered to General Council, June, 1944."
"By Rev. A.C. Snead."--p. 3.

4118 SIMPSON, Albert Benjamin, 1843-1919.
The challenge of missions. New York, Christian Alliance Publishing Co., 1926. 68 p.

4119 SIMPSON, Albert Benjamin, 1843-1919.
Larger outlooks on missionary lands; descriptive sketches of a missionary journey through Egypt, Palestine, India, Burmah, Malaysia, China, Japan and the Sandwich Islands. New York, Christian Alliance Publishing Co., c1893. 595 p.

4120 TAYLOR, John Floyd
"Indigenous churches of the Christian and Missionary Alliance." Unpublished Ph.D. dissertation, New York University, 1966. 483ℓ.

-- --HISTORY

4121 ENCYCLOPEDIA OF modern Christian missions; the agencies. Burton L. Goddard, ed.... Camden, N.J., T. Nelson, 1967. xix, 743 p.
"The Christian and Missionary Alliance," by Louis L. King: p. 133-137.

4122 HUNTER, James Hogg, 1890-
Beside all waters; the story of seventy-five years of world-wide ministry: the Christian and Missionary Alliance; with an introd. by Nathan Bailey. Harrisburg, Pa., Christian Publications, 1964. 245 p.

--PERIODICALS

4123 ALLIANCE WITNESS. 1- , 1887- . New York; Harrisburg, Pa.
v. 24-34 repeated in numbering.
1887 as The Word, the Work, and the World; 1887-1896 as Christian Alliance and Foreign Missionary Weekly; 1897-Sept. 1911 as Christian and Missionary Alliance; Oct. 1911-Dec. 25, 1957 as Alliance Weekly.

--SERMONS

4124 SIMPSON, Albert Benjamin, 1843-1919.
Evangelistic addresses. New York, Christian Alliance Publishing Co., c1926. 96 p.

4125 SIMPSON, Albert Benjamin, 1843-1919.
Missionary messages; with an introd. by Rev. Walter M. Turnbull, D.D. New York, Christian Alliance Publishing Co., c1925. 131 p.

4126 SIMPSON, Albert Benjamin, 1843-1919.
Salvation sermons; with an introd. by Rev. Walter M. Turnbull, D.D. New York, Christian Alliance Publishing Co., c1925. 123 p.

Part III. Keswick Movement 507

--STATISTICS

4127 U.S. BUREAU of the Census.
...Census of religious bodies, 1926; Christian and Missionary Alliance: statistics, denominational history, doctrine, and organization.... Washington, U.S. Government Printing Office, 1928. 10 p.

--AFRICA

4128 WIBERG, Erik, 1912-
100 [i.e. Hundra] dagar i Afrika. Jönköping, Samforlaget, 1967. 67 p.

--CHINA

4129 OLDFIELD, Walter Herbert, 1879-
Pioneering in Kwangsi; the story of Alliance missions in South China. Harrisburg, Pa., Christian Publications, c1936. 208 p.

--CONGO

4130 CHRISTIAN AND Missionary Alliance.
Nkunga mia moyo wa bankwa Klisto. Boma, 1954. 347 p.
Most of the "hymns have been taken from the Hymns of the Christian life, Alliance hymnal, and translated into Kikongo."

--INDONESIA

4131 CHRISTIAN AND Missionary Alliance.
Njanjian kenenangen iman. Suatu buku mjanjian rohani untuk dipergunakan didalum segala rupa kebatian umat Keristen. Bandung, Kantor Kalam Hidup, 1965. 253, xix p.

4132 CHRISTIAN AND Missionary Alliance.
Prayer manual for the Indonesia mission of the Christian and Missionary Alliance, 1955. Bandung, 1955. 76 p.

--JAPAN

4133 ENCYCLOPEDIA OF modern Christian missions; the agencies. Burton L. Goddard, ed.... Camden, N.J., T. Nelson, 1967. xix, 743 p.
"Nippon Araiance Kyodan (Japan Alliance Church)," by Anne F. Dievendorf: p. 486-487.

--LATIN AMERICA

4134 CHRISTIAN AND Missionary Alliance.
Himnos de la vida cristiana; una colección de antiguos y nuevos himnos de alabanza á Dios. New York, Alianza cristiana y misionera, 1939. 320 p.
With music.

4135 CLARK, Raymond Brooke, 1889-
Under the Southern Cross; the story of Alliance missions in South America. Harrisburg, Pa., Christian Publications, c1938. 232 p.

--NEAR EAST

4136 CHRISTIAN AND Missionary Alliance. Missions and mission conferences. Palestine and Arabian Mission.
...Annual report. 19??. Jerusalem, 19??.

--NEW GUINEA

4137 MICHELSON, Einar H.
God can; story of God's faithfulness to a pioneer missionary explorer in New Guinea. n.p., 1969, c1966. 301 p.

--NIGERIA

4138 ROSEBERRY, Robert Sherman, 1883-
The Niger vision. Harrisburg, Pa., Christian Publications, c1934. 254 p.

--TIBET

4139 EKVALL, Robert Brainerd, 1898-
Gateway to Tibet: the Kansu-Tibetan border; introd. [by] Rev. William Christie. Harrisburg, Pa., Christian Publications, c1938. 198 p.

--VIETNAM

4140 HEFLEY, James C.
By life or by death; the dramatic story of the valiant missionary martyrs who have lived and died for Christ in war-torn Vietnam. Grand Rapids, Mich., Zondervan Publishing House, 1969. 208 p.

Part III. Keswick Movement 509

4141 IRWIN, Edwin Franklin, 1888-
With Christ in Indo-China; the story of Alliance missions in French Indo-China and eastern Siam. Harrisburg, Pa., Christian Publications, c1937. 164 p.

Evangelistic Associations

MISSIONARY CHURCH ASSOCIATION (1898-1969)

Formed at Berne, Indiana, in 1898, this evangelistic association, as its name implies, stressed missionary activity. Like the United Missionary Church, with which it merged in 1969, the Missionary Church Association sprang from Mennonite roots and was in part the result of the impact of holiness teaching on Mennonite people. Stressing foreign missions, the group sponsored the Fort Wayne Bible College in Indiana and worked in the Dominican Republic, Haiti, Jamaica, Ecuador and Sierra Leone. Until 1945, it did not develop its own fields but sent out missionaries under other boards, a policy it continued to a limited extent after establishing its own fields. Many of its members served under the Christian and Missionary Alliance, a group with which it enjoyed cordial relations. Concentrated in the eastern Middle West, the group had scattered congregations as far west as the Pacific coast. In 1966 it reported 130 churches and more than 9000 members, and had 84 foreign missionaries, twelve of them working under other mission boards.

4142 MISSIONARY CHURCH Association.
Constitution and General Conference by-laws of the Missionary Church Association as adopted by the General Conference in 1956 and revised by the General Conference in 1962, 1964, 1966; a study guide in doctrines and church government. Fort Wayne, Ind., Bible Truth Publishers, 1966. Cover-title, 36 p.

--HISTORY

4143 CLARK, Elmer Talmage, 1886-1966.
The small sects in America. Rev. ed. New York, Abingdon Press, c1965. 256 p.
"The Missionary Church Association": p. 78.

4144 LUGIBIHL, Walter H., 1883-
The Missionary Church Association; historical account of its origin and development, by Walter H. Lugibihl and Jared F. Gerig. Berne, Ind., Economy Printing Concern, 1950, c1951. 164 p.

4145 MEAD, Frank Spencer, 1898-
Handbook of denominations in the United States. 2d rev. ed. New York, Abingdon Press, c1961. 272 p.
"Missionary Church Association": p. 105.

4146 RAMSEYER, Macy (Garth)
Joseph E. Ramseyer--"yet speaking." Fort Wayne, Ind., Fort Wayne Bible Institute, 1945. 293 p.

4147 SCHAFF, Philip, 1819-1893.
New Schaff-Herzog encyclopedia of religious knowledge.... S. M. Jackson, editor-in-chief. New York, Funk, 1908-1912. 12 v.
"Missionary Church Association," by E. M. Bliss: v. 7, p. 393.

4148 TWENTIETH CENTURY encyclopedia of religious knowledge; an extension of the New Schaff-Herzog Encyclopedia of Religious Knowledge. Editor-in-chief: Lefferts A. Loetscher. Grand Rapids, Mich., Baker Book House, 1955. 2 v. (xx, 1205 p.)
"Missionary Church Association," by Jonas A. Ringenberg.

--MISSIONS

4149 ENCYCLOPEDIA OF modern Christian missions; the agencies. Burton L. Goddard, ed.... Camden, N.J., T. Nelson, 1967. xix, 743 p.
"The Missionary Church Association, Board of Missions," by Tillman Habegger: p. 440.

--PERIODICALS

4150 EMPHASIS. 1-2, Feb. 1967-Feb. 1969. Fort Wayne, Ind.
Supersedes Missionary Worker.
Merged with Gospel Banner and Missionary Banner to form Emphasis on Faith and Living.

4151 MISSIONARY WORKER. 1-63, Sept. 1, 1904-Jan. 1967.
Fort Wayne, Ind.
Superseded by Emphasis.

--RELATIONS

-- --UNITED MISSIONARY CHURCH

4152 CONSTITUTION PROPOSED as basis for union of the Missionary Church Association and the United Missionary Church. n.p., 196?. 31, 3 p.

--STATISTICS

4153 U. S. BUREAU of the Census.
...Census of religious bodies; Missionary Church Association: statistics, denominational history, doctrine, and organization.... Washington, U. S. Government Printing Office, 1928. 9 p.

Part IV

HOLINESS-PENTECOSTAL MOVEMENT

General

4154 ATTER, Gordon Francis, 1905-
"The Third Force"; a Pentecostal answer to the question so often asked by both our own young people and by members of other churches: "Who are the Pentecostals?" Peterborough, Ont., College Press, 1962. 314 p.

4155 BATTLE, Allen Overton
"Status personality in a Negro Holiness sect." Unpublished Ph.D. dissertation, Catholic University of America, 1961. v, 114ℓ.

4156 BATTLE, Allen Overton
Status personality in a Negro Holiness sect. Washington, Catholic University of America Press, 1961. 21 p.
Abstract of thesis (Ph.D.)--Catholic University of America, 1961.

4157 BIANCHI, E.
"Ecumenism and the Spirit-filled communities," Thought, XLI (Fall 1966), 390-412.

4158 BOIS, Jules, 1871-
"The new religions of America: 1. The Holy Rollers, the American Dervishes," Forum LXXIII (February 1925), 145-155.

4159 BOISEN, Anton T.
"Religion and hard times; a study of the Holy Rollers," Social Action, V (Mar. 15, 1939), 8-35.

4160 BROWN, James Stephen
"Social class, intermarriage, and church membership in a Kentucky community," American Journal of Sociology, LVII (November 1951), 232-242.

4161 DAMBORIENA, P.
"The Pentecostal fury," Catholic World, CCII (Jan. 1966), 217-223.

4162 GAUSTAD, Edwin Scott, 1923-
Historical atlas of religion in America. New York, Harper & Row, 1962. 179 p.
"Holiness and Pentecostal bodies": p. 121-126.

4163 HARRELL, David Edwin, 1930-
White sects and black men in the recent South; foreword by Edwin S. Gaustad. Nashville, Vanderbilt University Press, 1971. xvii, 161 p.

4164 HOLLENWEGER, Walter J.
The Pentecostals; the charismatic movement in the churches. Minneapolis, Augsburg Publishing House, 1972. xx, 572 p.
Translation of Enthusiastisches Christentum: die Pfingstbewegung in Geschichte und Gegenwart.

4165 HOLLIDAY, Robert Kelvin, 1933-
Tests of faith. Oak Hill, W. Va., Fayette Tribune, 1966. 104 p.

4166 HOLT, John B.
"Holiness religion: cultural shock and reorganization," American Sociological Review, V (Oct. 1940), 740-747.

4167 McDONNELL, K.
"The ecumenical significance of the Pentecostal Movement," Worship, XL (Dec. 1966), 608-629.

4168 ROBERTSON, Archibald Thomas
That old-time religion. Boston, Houghton, Mifflin, 1950. 282 p.
"Tongues and snakes": p. 156-181.

4169 SCHWARTZ, Gary
Sect ideologies and social status. Chicago, University of Chicago Press, 1970. x, 260 p.

4170 VAN DUSEN, Henry Pitney, 1897-
"Third force in Christendom; gospel-singing, doomsday-preaching sects," Life, XLIV (June 9, 1958), 113-122, 124.

4171 WASHINGTON, Joseph R., 1930-
Black sects and cults. Garden City, N.Y., Doubleday, 1972. xii, 176 p.
"Holiness and Pentecostal blacks: the permanent sects": p. 58-82.

--ANECDOTES, REMINISCENCES, SATIRE, ETC.

4172 GOSS, Howard Archibald, 1883-
The winds of God; the story of the early Pentecostal

Part IV. Holiness-Pentecostal Movement 515

      days (1901-1914) in the life of Howard A. Goss, as told by Ethel E. Goss. New York, Comet Press Books, 1958. 178 p.

4173 HOLMES, Nickels John, 1847-1919.
      Life sketches and sermons, by Reverend N.J. Holmes and wife. Royston, Ga., Press of the Pentecostal Holiness Church, c1920. 310 p.

--CRITICAL WORKS

4174 HILLS, Aaron Merritt, 1848-1935.
      The Tongues Movement. Manchester, Eng., Star Hall, 1910? 39 p.

--DOCTRINAL AND CONTROVERSIAL WORKS

-- --BIBLIOGRAPHY

4175 MARTIN, Ira Jay, 1911-
      Glossolalia, the gift of tongues; a bibliography. Cleveland, Tenn., Pathway Press, 1970. 72 p.

--HISTORY

4176 BLOCH-HOELL, Nils
      The Pentecostal Movement: its origin, development, and distinctive character. Oslo, Universitetsforlaget, 1964. 255 p.
      Translation of the author's Pinsebevegelsen first published in 1956.

4177 CLARK, Elmer Talmage, 1886-1966.
      The small sects in America. Rev. ed. New York, Abingdon Press, c1965. 256 p.
      "Charismatic or Pentecostal sects": p. 85-132.

4178 HARPER, Michael
      At the beginning; the twentieth century Pentecostal revival. London, Hodder and Stoughton, 1965. 128 p.

4179 KENDRICK, Klaude
      "The history of the modern Pentecostal Movement. Unpublished Ph.D. dissertation, University of Texas, 1959.

4180 KENDRICK, Klaude
      The promise fulfilled; a history of the modern Pentecostal Movement. Springfield, Mo., Gospel Publishing House, c1961. 237 p.

Based on thesis (Ph.D.), University of Texas, 1959.

4181 SYNAN, Vinson, 1934-
The Holiness-Pentecostal Movement in the United States. Grand Rapids, Mich., Eerdmans, 1971. 248 p.

4182 TWENTIETH CENTURY encyclopedia of religious knowledge; an extension of the New Schaff-Herzog Encyclopedia of Religious Knowledge. Editor-in-chief: Lefferts A. Loetscher. Grand Rapids, Mich., Baker Book House, 1955. 2 v. (xx, 1205 p.)
"Pentecostal Churches," by Elmer T. Clark: p. 864-865.

--HISTORY OF DOCTRINES

4183 MARTIN, Ira Jay, 1911-
Glossolalia in the Apostolic Church; a survey study of tongue-speech. Berea, Ky., Berea College, 1960. 100 p.

--HYMNS

4184 BUFFUM, Herbert, 1879-1939.
White flag of peace. Song special. Words by Marie Pauline Sass. A beautiful song for Christians suggested by "Star Spangled Banner." Haegler, Neb., Marie Pauline Sass, c1937.

4185 GOSPEL SONGS.... Chicago, T. Harris, c1931. [256] p.

4186 HARRIS, Thoro, 1874-1955.
Gospel quintet songs. Chicago, Thoro Harris, 192?. Unpaged.
With music.

4187 HARRIS, Thoro, 1874-1955, ed.
Songs of His coming. Chicago, T. Harris, 1915? Cover-title, [256] p.

4188 HARRIS, Thoro, 1874-1955, ed.
Songs of His coming. Chicago, T. Harris, 1923? Cover-title, unpaged.
Hymns with music, principally by Thoro Harris.

4189 HARRIS, Thoro, 1874-1955, ed.
Songs of power, edited by Thoro Harris. Special contributors: L.C. Hall and J.O. Olsen.... Chicago, T. Harris, c1914. Cover-title, [160] p.

Part IV. Holiness-Pentecostal Movement 517

4190 HARRIS, Thoro, 1874-1955.
Songs of summerland. Prepared in cooperation with
Rev. Floyd Humble [by] Thoro Harris. Eureka Springs,
Ark., T. Harris, c1943. Cover-title, [192] p.

--PERIODICALS

4191 ALTAMONT WITNESS. 1- , Oct. 1911-May 1918. Greenville, S.C., Altamont Bible and Missionary Institute, etc.

4192 APOSTOLIC EVANGEL. 1- , Feb. 15, 1909-1928. Goldsboro, N.C.; Falcon, N.C.

4193 BRIDEGROOM'S MESSENGER. 1- , 1908-19??. Atlanta, Ga.

4194 CHRISTIAN EVANGEL. 1- , July 1913-Mar. 1915. Plainfield, Ind., Findlay, Ohio, St. Louis.

4194a THE FINISHED Work of Calvary ... Holiness without Carnality ... Truth without Error ... The Baptism in the Holy Ghost (Acts 2:4). I- , 19??-191?. Topeka, Kan. 19??-Nov. 1910 as Tried by Fire; Dec. 1910-Mar. 1913 as Holiness without Carnality ... Truth without Error.

4195 HERALD OF Truth. 1- , Dec. 1927-1928. Greenville, S.C., Holmes Bible and Missionary Institute.

4196 INTERCESSORY MISSIONARY. 1, 1907. Fort Wayne, Ind.

4197 VICTORY. 1, 1910.

4198 VOICE OF Holmes. 1- , 1936- . Greenville, S.C., Holmes Bible and Missionary Institute, etc. 1936-1946 as Holmes Bulletin.

--CANADA

4199 KULBECK, Gloria G.
What God hath wrought; a history of the Pentecostal Assemblies of Canada. Edited by Walter E. McAlister and George R. Upton. Foreword by A.G. Ward. Toronto, Pentecostal Assemblies of Canada, 1958. 364 p.

--GREAT BRITAIN

4200 CALLEY, Malcolm J.
God's people; West Indian Pentecostal sects in England. London, Issued under the auspices of the Institute of Race

Relations [by the] Oxford University Press, 1965. 182 p.

--LATIN AMERICA

4201 KESSLER, J. B. A., 1925-
A study of the older Protestant missions and churches in Peru and Chile. With special reference to the problems of division, nationalism and native ministry. Goes, Oosterbaan & Le Cointre, 1967. xii, 372 p.
Thesis--Utrecht.

4202 WILLEMS, Emilio
Followers of the new faith; culture change and the rise of Protestantism in Brazil and Chile. Nashville, Vanderbilt University Press, 1967. x, 290 p.

Baptists

HOLINESS BAPTISTS (1903-1914)

[Also as Pentecostal Baptists]

Originating in southwestern Arkansas about 1903, this tiny group early considered union with other holiness people. A participant in the talks which led to merger of the Independent Holiness Church and the New Testament Church of Christ in 1904, it insisted upon immersion as the only valid mode of baptism and disqualified itself from the union. The founder, W. Jethro Walthall, who was removed from the Baptist ministry for professing entire sanctification, had for twenty-five years occasionally spoken in unknown tongues. As a consequence, he welcomed tongues-speaking workers associated with the Pentecostal Movement when they reached the area after 1906. By 1916 he had led the Holiness Baptists into the Assemblies of God, a newly formed Pentecostal group, which denied the Wesleyan interpretation of entire sanctification.

4203 HOLINESS BAPTISTS. Arkansas. Convocation.
Minutes of the first annual convocation of the Holiness Baptist churches of southeastern Arkansas, held with the church at Sutton, Arkansas, Nov. 6, 7, 8, 1903. n.p., 1903. 7 p.

--HISTORY

4204 JERNIGAN, Charles Brougher, 1863-1930.
Pioneer days of the Holiness Movement in the South-

Part IV. Holiness-Pentecostal Movement

west. Kansas City, Mo., Pentecostal Nazarene Publishing House, 1919. 157 p.
"The Holiness Movement in Arkansas": p. 33-36.

PENTECOSTAL FREE-WILL BAPTIST CHURCH (190?-)

[1855-190? as Cape Fear Conference of the Free-Will Baptist Church]

Originating in opposition to the Calvinism which by the eighteenth century pervaded most Baptist churches, many Free-Will Baptists early joined the Holiness Movement. By 1883 the Cape Fear Conference in North Carolina had become committed to the doctrine of entire sanctification as taught by the National Holiness evangelists. Acceptance of glossolalia after 1906, however, effectively barred the group from fellowship with non-tongues-speaking Free-Will Baptists as well as other holiness people. As a result they organized the Pentecostal Free-Will Baptist Church and established headquarters at Dunn, North Carolina. Factionalism and poor organization inhibited growth until 1959 when the three Free-Will Baptist Conferences in North Carolina amalgamated to form the present organization. The denomination reported 150 congregations and 13,500 members in 1970.

4205 PENTECOSTAL FREE-WILL Baptist Church.
Discipline of the Pentecostal Free-Will Baptist Church. Dunn, N.D., 190?.

Church of God

CHURCH OF GOD (General Assembly) (1886-)

[1886-18?? as Christian Union; 1902-1907 as Holiness Church. Also as Church of God (Cleveland, Tenn.)]

Like the (Original) Church of God, the Church of God (General Assembly) traces its origins to the Christian Union organized by Richard G. Spurling on August 19, 1886, in Monroe County, Tennessee. Known from 1902 to 1907 as the Holiness Church, the group early accepted tongues speaking as evidence of Holy Spirit baptism. Under A.J. Tomlinson, who served as General Overseer from 1909 to 1923, the group committed itself to the Pentecostalist position and lost contact with the conservative Holiness Movement. Church headquarters and the related Lee College are located at Cleveland, Tenn. At present the group has over 7500 ministers, 4600 churches, and 242,000 members in the United States and Canada and an extensive foreign missionary work.

--ANECDOTES, REMINISCENCES, SATIRE, ETC.

4206 TOMLINSON, Ambrose Jessup, bp., 1865-1943.
Diary of A.J. Tomlinson; editorial notes by his son, Homer A. Tomlinson. Queens Village, N.Y., Church of God, World Headquarters, 1949-1955. 3 v.

--DOCTRINAL AND CONTROVERSIAL WORKS

4207 SLAY, James L.
Rescue the perishing. Cleveland, Tenn., Pathway Press, 1961. 166 p.

-- --FAITH-HEALING

4208 CROSS, James A., 1911- , ed.
Healing in the church. Cleveland, Tenn., Pathway Press, 1962. 141 p.

--HISTORY

4209 CONN, Charles W.
Like a mighty army moves the Church of God, 1886-1955. Cleveland, Tenn., Church of God Publishing House, 1955. 380 p.

4210 GAUSTAD, Edwin Scott, 1923-
Historical atlas of religion in America. New York, Harper & Row, 1962. xii, 179 p.
Account of Church of God (General Assembly): p. 124-125.

4211 SIMMONS, Ernest Lesley, 1893-
History of the Church of God. Cleveland, Tenn., Church of God Publishing House, 1938. 156 p.

--MISSIONS

4212 ENCYCLOPEDIA OF modern Christian missions; the agencies. Burton L. Goddard, ed.... Camden, N.J., T. Nelson, 1967. xix, 743 p.
"Church of God, World Missions Board," by Duran M. Palmertree: p. 171-173.

4213 HUGHES, Ray Harrison
"The influence of Lee College on the development of the world missions program of the Church of God." Unpublished M.S. thesis, University of Tennessee, 1964. vi, 77ℓ.

Part IV. Holiness-Pentecostal Movement 521

--PERIODICALS

4214 CHURCH OF God Evangel. 1- , Mar. 1, 1910- . Cleveland, Tenn.
1910-1911 as Evening Light and Church of God Evangel.

--PUBLISHERS AND PUBLISHING

4215 CONN, Charles W., ed.
The Evangel reader; selections from the Church of God Evangel, 1910-1958. Compiled and ed., with introd. and notes by Charles W. Conn. 256 p.

--RELIGIOUS EDUCATION

4216 CHURCH OF God (General Assembly).
Workers training course. Cleveland, Tenn., Pathway Press, 19??- .
"Prepared under the auspices of the Church of God, National Sunday School and Youth Board."

--SERMONS

4217 CROSS, James A., 1911- , ed.
The glorious gospel. Cleveland, Tenn., Church of God Publishing House, 1956. 135 p.

4218 LEE, Flavius Josephus, 1875-1928.
Life sketch and sermons of F.J. Lee, comp. by Mrs. F.J. Lee. Cleveland, Tenn., Church of God Publishing House, 192?. 373 p.

4219 LEMMONS, Frank W., 1901-
Perennial Pentecost. Cleveland, Tenn., Pathway Press, 1971. 126 p.

4220 LEMMONS, Frank W., 1901-
Profiles of faith. Cleveland, Tenn., Pathway Press, 1971. 103 p.

4221 PAULK, Earl P.
Forward in faith sermons; sermons preached on the national radio broadcast "Forward in Faith." Cleveland, Tenn., Pathway Press, 1960. 275 p.

CHURCH OF GOD IN CHRIST (1897-)

Rejected by Negro Baptists in Arkansas because of their emphasis on holiness, C.H. Mason and C.P. Jones founded the

Church of God in Christ in a cotton gin house at Lexington, Mississippi, in 1897. Both of the original leaders stressed entire sanctification. When Mason received the gift of tongues and declared it to be evidence of the baptism with the Holy Spirit, the group split, the Holiness faction following Jones into a reorganized body called the Church of Christ (Holiness) U.S.A., in 1907. Tongues-speaking and racial prejudice have largely isolated the Church of God in Christ from the Holiness fellowship. Denominational headquarters and the church-sponsored Saints Junior College are in Lexington. At present the group claims 419,466 members in 4150 congregations. The Church of God in Christ sponsors missionary work in Jamaica, Haiti and on the west coast of Africa.

--HISTORY

4222 CLARK, Elmer Talmage, 1886-1966.
The small sects in America. Rev. ed. New York, Abingdon Press, c1965. 256 p.
Account of the Church of God in Christ: p. 119.

4223 MASON, Charles H., 1866-
The history and life work of Elder C.H. Mason, chief apostle and his co-laborers. Memphis, Howe Printing Dept., 1920. 87 p.
Compiled by Prof. Jas. Courts.

4224 MEAD, Frank Spencer, 1898-
Handbook of denominations in the United States. New 5th ed. Nashville, Abingdon Press, c1970. 265 p.
"Church of God in Christ": p. 76.

--MISSIONS

4225 ENCYCLOPEDIA OF modern Christian missions; the agencies. Burton L. Goddard, ed.... Camden, N.J., T. Nelson, c1967. xix, 743 p.
"Church of God in Christ, Board of Home and Foreign Missions": p. 174.

--TENNESSEE

4225a BATTLE, Allen Overton, 1927-
"Status personality in a Negro Holiness sect." Unpublished Ph.D. dissertation, Catholic University of America, 1961. v, 114ℓ.
Account of the Church of God in Christ in Memphis, Tennessee, led by C.H. Mason.

Part IV. Holiness-Pentecostal Movement 523

(ORIGINAL) CHURCH OF GOD (1886-)

[1886-18?? as Christian Union; 1902-1907 as Holiness Church]

Formed in 1886 by followers of the Rev. Richard G. Spurling, this eastern Tennessee group was originally part of the group which became the Church of God (General Assembly). A split occurred in 1917, and with legal incorporation in 1922, this group added "Original" to its name. Like other holiness denominations it emphasizes justification, entire sanctification, faith healing and the second coming of Christ. Unlike most holiness groups, however, after the Azusa Street revival, the Church of God accepted tongues speaking as evidence of the baptism of the Holy Spirit and lost contact with the older Holiness Movement. Headquarters are located at Chattanooga, Tennessee. At present there are about 50 churches and 6000 members.

4226 CLARK, Elmer Talmage, 1886-1966.
The small sects in America. Rev. ed. New York, Abingdon Press, c1965. 256 p.
Account of the (Original) Church of God: p. 102.

4227 MEAD, Frank Spencer, 1898-
Handbook of denominations in the United States. New 5th ed. Nashville, Abingdon Press, c1970. 265 p.
"The (Original) Church of God": p. 73-74.

Evangelistic Associations

APOSTOLIC FAITH MISSION (1907-)

[Also as Apostolic Faith]

A product of the impact of the Pentecostal revival on the Holiness Movement, the Apostolic Faith Mission was organized at Portland, Oregon, by the Rev. Mrs. Florence L. Crawford in 1907. The Mission teaches justification by faith, entire sanctification, and the baptism of the Holy Spirit, as evidenced by speaking in unknown tongues. It emphasizes city mission work and, in keeping with its holiness background, requires its members to eschew worldly attire and amusements and to refrain from marriage with non-believers. Church headquarters and a publishing plant are located in Portland, Oregon. In 1970 the Apostolic Faith claimed 4678 members in 43 churches. Foreign missionary emphasis, begun with publication of a bimonthly paper called the Light of Hope in 1907, has been instrumental in establishment of indigenous churches in Africa (150), the Caribbean (50), Europe (15), and Japan (2). Like other tongues-speaking groups, the Apostolic Faith Mission has little contact with groups in fellowship with the Christian Holiness Association.

--DOCTRINAL AND CONTROVERSIAL WORKS

4228 APOSTOLIC FAITH Mission.
A series of Bible studies; a course of brief outlines and notes on Biblical teachings formulated and compiled with the intention of aiding all who are earnestly desiring the truth. Portland, Ore., The Apostolic Faith, 19??. v.

4229 APOSTOLIC FAITH Mission.
Studies in the scriptures, as given at the Apostolic Faith Camp Ground, 1940. Portland, Ore., 1940? 98 p.

--EVANGELISTIC WORK

4230 CRAWFORD, Raymond Robert, 1891-1965.
A gleam across the wave; a brief account of the purpose and travels of the missionary motor vessel Lower Light. Portland, Ore., Apostolic Faith Publishing House, 195?. 32 p.

--HISTORY

4231 APOSTOLIC FAITH Mission.
A historical account of the Apostolic Faith, a Trinitarian-fundamental evangelistic organization: its origin, functions, doctrinal heritage, and departmental activities of evangelism. Portland, Ore., Apostolic Faith Publishing House, 1965. 315 p.
Written by R.R. Crawford.

4232 MEAD, Frank Spencer, 1898-
Handbook of denominations in the United States. New 5th ed. Nashville, Abingdon Press, c1970. 265 p.
"Apostolic Faith": p. 26-27.

--MISSIONS

4233 ENCYCLOPEDIA OF modern Christian missions; the agencies. Burton L. Goddard, editor.... Camden, N.J., T. Nelson, 1967. xix, 743 p.
"The Apostolic Faith": p. 39.

--PASTORAL THEOLOGY

4234 APOSTOLIC FAITH Mission.
Minister's manual. Portland, Ore., 1950. 400 p.

--SERMONS

4235 CRAWFORD, Florence Louise, 1872-1936.
Sermons and scriptural studies. Portland, Ore., Apostolic Faith, 19??. 2 v.

APOSTOLIC FAITH MOVEMENT (1900-   )

[Also as Apostolic Faith, and Apostolic Faith Mission]

The foundation of the modern Pentecostal Movement, the Apostolic Faith Movement originated in meetings conducted by two holiness evangelists at Topeka, Kansas, in 1900. An outbreak of tongues-speaking among students of the Bethel Bible College in Topeka that year caused the group as a whole to espouse glossolalia and brought to the forefront Charles Fox Parham, a key figure in the early history of Pentecostalism. Placing emphasis on tongues-speaking and faith healing, the Apostolic Faith Movement concentrated on city mission work. Determinedly anti-sectarian, it has steadily lost converts to other better-organized groups and as late as 1965 claimed only 2200 members. Although the Movement has no official foreign missionary program, members support evangelistic workers in India, Central America and Alaska. The Apostolic Faith, the official organ, is issued from Baxter Springs, Kansas.

--DOCTRINAL AND CONTROVERSIAL WORKS

4236 WHITE, Kent, 1860-1940.
The Word of God coming again; return of the apostolic faith and works now due on the earth ... with a sketch of the life of Pastor W. Oliver Hutchinson. Bournemouth, Eng., Apostolic Faith Church, 1919. 296 p.

--HISTORY

4237 CLARK, Elmer Talmage, 1886-1966.
The small sects in America. Rev. ed. New York, Abingdon Press, c1965. 256 p.
Account of the Apostolic Faith Mission: p. 111-112.

--MISSIONS

4238 ENCYCLOPEDIA OF modern Christian missions; the agencies. Burton L. Goddard, ed.... Camden, N.J., T. Nelson, 1967. xix, 743 p.
"The Apostolic Faith Movement" by F.E. Waterbury: p. 39.

FIRE-BAPTIZED HOLINESS CHURCH (1898-1911)

[1898-1902 as Fire-Baptized Holiness Association of America]

This group was the outgrowth of the third blessing teaching which troubled Midwestern holiness adherents during the last decade of the nineteenth century. Starting as Fire-Baptized Holiness associations organized on the state level in Iowa, Kansas, Oklahoma and Texas in 1895, the movement spread rapidly to the Southeast. Led by the popular evangelist Benjamin Hardin Irwin, the movement soon became bi-racial. Extreme emotional displays characterized many of Irwin's meetings. Dietary and dress regulations were introduced, and at Lincoln, Nebraska, in October 1899, the first issue of Live Coals of Fire, the official organ, appeared. Although in 1898 the first national convention which met at Anderson, South Carolina, made Irwin the General Overseer, "open and gross sin" necessitated his removal two years later. Within a decade his successor, J. E. King, once a minister in Methodist Episcopal Church, South, led the group into the Pentecostal Movement, thus severing whatever fellowship its members enjoyed in the older Holiness Movement. In 1911 the Fire Baptized Holiness Church and the Pentecostal Holiness Church merged, taking the name of the latter.

4239 CAMPBELL, Joseph Enoch
The Pentecostal Holiness Church, 1898-1948: its background and history; presenting complete background material which adequately explains the existence of this organization, also the existence of other kindred Pentecostal and holiness groups, as an essential and integral part of the total church set-up. Franklin Springs, Ga., Publishing House of the Pentecostal Holiness Church, 1951. 573 p.
Account of the Fire-Baptized Holiness Church: p. 192-215.

--PERIODICALS

4240 LIVE COALS of Fire. 1, nos. 1-21, Oct. 6, 1899-June 15, 1900; 1, no. 22?- , 1902-1907. Lincoln, Neb., (Chariton, Iowa), Mercer, Mo., Royston, Ga.
1902-1907 as Live Coals; 1907 as Apostolic Evangel.
Fire-Baptized Holiness Association of America, 1899-1902; Fire-Baptized Holiness Church, 1902-1907.

PENTECOSTAL HOLINESS CHURCH (1900-1911)

[1901-1909 as Holiness Church; Also as Holiness Church of North Carolina]

Part IV. Holiness-Pentecostal Movement   527

The Pentecostal Holiness Church organized at Fayetteville, North Carolina, in the spring of 1900 by A.B. Crumpler, former minister in the Methodist Episcopal Church, South. (The North Carolina Convention of the Holiness Church, held in October 1899 in Goldsboro and composed of Crumpler's followers, apparently laid the ground work for formation of the new church.) The Pentecostal Holiness Church adhered to second-crisis sanctification, premillennialism, and faith-healing. It stood in opposition to "worldliness," entertainments and "oyster stews" for support of the church, "needless ornamentation," and "tobacco." In 1901 the group dropped "Pentecostal" from its name. After joining the tongues movement, however, it restored the original name in 1909. Use of the title continued even after the merger with the Fire-Baptized Holiness Church two years later. From 1900 to 1907 the church's quasi-official journal was Crumpler's Holiness Advocate which was published at Fayetteville, North Carolina.

4241   HOLINESS CHURCH. North Carolina Convention.
Constitution and by-laws, and minutes of the first session, held October 26-28, in Goldsboro, 1899. Goldsboro, N.C., Nash Brothers, 1899. 8 p.

--HISTORY

4242   CAMPBELL, Joseph Enoch
The Pentecostal Holiness Church, 1898-1948: its background and history; presenting complete background material which adequately explains the existence of this organization, also the existence of other kindred Pentecostal and holiness groups, as an essential and integral part of the total church set-up. Franklin Springs, Ga., Publishing House of the Pentecostal Holiness Church, 1951. 573 p.
"The Pentecostal Holiness Church, 1900-1910": p. 233-253.

--PERIODICALS

4243   HOLINESS ADVOCATE. 1- , 1900-1907. Fayetteville, N.C.

PENTECOSTAL HOLINESS CHURCH (1911-)

This group represents a fusion of elements from both Holiness and Pentecostal movements. It was formed in 1911 when the South Carolina-based Fire-Baptized Holiness Church, founded in 1898, merged with the North Carolina centered Pentecostal Holiness Church, founded in 1900 (known from 1901 to 1909 as the Holiness Church). Both had been influenced by the third blessing movement which agitated the Holiness Movement in the Midwest and South during the last two decades of the nineteenth century. Before World War I, they linked tongues speaking with a third experience called the baptism with fire and moved into the Pentecostal Movement.

Emphasizing divine healing, the second coming of Christ, and strict standards of personal conduct, the Pentecostal Holiness Church's espousal of glossolalia largely alienated it from the National Holiness Movement. At present there are more than 65,000 members and 1380 churches in the United States and over 27,000 members and 480 congregations in foreign missionary areas. Franklin Springs, Georgia, is the site of the church-related Emmanual College and of the denominational headquarters. Although he has recently become a Methodist, Oral Roberts was raised and for many years served as a minister in the Pentecostal Holiness Church.

4244 PENTECOSTAL HOLINESS Church.
Discipline of the Pentecostal Holiness Church, 1933. Franklin Springs, Ga., Publishing House of the Pentecostal Holiness Church, 1933. 73 p.

4245 PENTECOSTAL HOLINESS Church.
Discipline of the Pentecostal Holiness Church, 1945. Franklin Springs, Ga., Publishing House of the Pentecostal Holiness Church, 1945.

4246 PENTECOSTAL HOLINESS Church.
Discipline of the Pentecostal Holiness Church, 1961. Franklin Springs, Ga., Advocate Press, 1961.

4247 WOOD, William W.
Culture and personality aspects of the Pentecostal Holiness religion. The Hague, Mouton & Co., 1965. 125 p.

--CATECHISMS AND CREEDS

4248 BEACHAM, Paul Franklin, 1888-
Advanced catechism for the home, Sunday school, and Bible classes.... Franklin Springs, Ga., Publishing House, Pentecostal Holiness Church, 19??. 32 p.

--CONDUCT OF LIFE

4249 MONTGOMERY, G. H.
Why people like you; a Christian approach to human

relations. New York, Taplinger Publishing Co., 1963. 277 p.

4250 ROBERTS, Oral, 1918-
God is a good God; believe it and come alive. Indianapolis, Bobbs-Merrill, 1960. 188 p.

4251 ROBERTS, Oral, 1918-
God's formula for success and prosperity, ed. by Oral Roberts and G.H. Montgomery. Tulsa, Okla., 1956. 158 p.

4252 ROBERTS, Oral, 1918-
God's formula for success and prosperity, ed. by the editorial staff, Abundant Life Magazine. Rev. ed. Tulsa, Okla., Abundant Life Publication, 1966. 128 p.
First ed. by O. Roberts and G.H. Montgomery, published in 1956.

--DOCTRINAL AND CONTROVERSIAL WORKS

4253 BROOKS, Noel
Scriptural holiness. Franklin Springs, Ga., Advocate Press, 1967. 70 p.
Four lectures delivered as the King Memorial lectures.

4254 KING, Joseph Hillery, bp., 1869-1946.
From Passover to Pentecost. 3d ed., rev. and enlarged. Franklin Springs, Ga., Publishing House of the Pentecostal Holiness Church, 1955. 208 p.

4255 KING, Joseph Hillery, bp., 1869-1946.
From Passover to Pentecost. 2d ed., rev. and enlarged. Franklin Springs, Ga., Publishing House of the Pentecostal Holiness Church, c1934. 219 p.

4256 MUSE, Dan Thomas, bp., 1882-1950.
The Song of Songs. Franklin Springs, Ga., Pentecostal Holiness Publishing House, 1947. 231 p.

4257 ROBINSON, Albert Ernest
A layman and the Book. Takoma Park, Md., c1936. 192 p.

4258 SPENCE, Othniel Talmadge, 1926-
The quest for Christian purity. Richmond?, 1964. xxxiv, 286 p.

-- --ESCHATOLOGY

4259 ROBERTS, Oral, 1918-
The drama of the end-time. Franklin Springs, Ga.,

Publishing House P.H. Church, c1941. 79 p.

4260   ROBERTS, Oral, 1918-
        How to be personally prepared for the second coming of Christ. n.p., 19??. 64 p.

4261   TAYLOR, George Floyd, 1881-
        The rainbow. Franklin Springs, Ga., Publishing House of the Pentecostal Holiness Church, c1924. 223 p.

4262   TAYLOR, George Floyd, 1881-
        The second coming of Jesus. Falcon, N.C., Press of the Falcon Publishing Co., c1916. viii, 264 p.

-- --FAITH-HEALING

4263   ROBERTS, Oral, 1918-
        Deliverance from fear and from sickness. Tulsa, Okla., 1954. 94 p.

4264   ROBERTS, Oral, 1918-
        Exactly how you may receive your healing--through faith; including a heart-to-heart talk on your salvation. Tulsa, Okla., Oral Roberts Evangelistic Association, 1958. 64 p.

4265   ROBERTS, Oral, 1918-
        If you need healing do these things. 2d rev. ed. Tulsa, Okla., Oral Roberts Evangelistic Association, 1957. 126 p.

4266   ROBERTS, Oral, 1918-
        If you need healing, do these things. 3d rev. ed. Tulsa, Okla., 1965. 92 p.

-- --GLOSSOLALIA

4267   ROBERTS, Oral, 1918-
        The baptism with the Holy Spirit and the value of speaking in tongues today. Tulsa, Okla., 1964. 96 p.

4268   TURNER, William H.
        The difference between regeneration, sanctification, and the Pentecostal baptism. Franklin Springs, Ga., Publishing House of the Pentecostal Holiness Church, 1947.

4269   TURNER, William H.
        Pentecost and tongues. Shanghai, Shanghai Modern Publishing House, 1939.

Part IV. Holiness-Pentecostal Movement 531

--EDUCATION

4270 CORVIN, R. O.
"History of education by the Pentecostal Holiness Church in South Carolina and Georgia." Unpublished M.A. thesis, University of South Carolina, 1942.

--EVANGELISTIC WORK

4271 ROBERTS, Oral, 1918-
A master plan for 10 million souls. Tulsa, Okla., Oral Roberts, 195?. 32 p.

--HISTORY

4272 CAMPBELL, Joseph Enoch
The Pentecostal Holiness Church, 1898-1948: its background and history; presenting complete background material which adequately explains the existence of this organization, also the existence of other kindred Pentecostal and holiness groups, as an essential and integral part of the total church set-up. Franklin Springs, Ga., Publishing House of the Pentecostal Holiness Church, 1951. 573 p.

4273 KING, Joseph Hillery, 1869-1946.
Yet speaketh; memoirs of the late Bishop Joseph H. King, written by himself and supplemented by Mrs. Blanche L. King. Franklin Springs, Ga., Publishing House of the Pentecostal Holiness Church, 1949. 387 p.

4274 SYNAN, Vinson, 1934-
The Holiness-Pentecostal Movement in the United States. Grand Rapids, Mich., Eerdmans, 1971. 248 p.
Includes account of the origins of the Pentecostal Holiness Church.

--HYMNS

4275 PENTECOSTAL HOLINESS Church.
Pentecostal holiness hymnal, for use in all services of the church, comp. and ed. by Rev. I.H. Presley; published by Board of Education and Publication of the Pentecostal Holiness Church.... Franklin Springs, Ga., Publishing House P.H. Church, 1938. [192] p.

4276 PENTECOSTAL HOLINESS Church.
Pentecostal holiness hymnal no. 2, comp. and ed. by Rev. I.H. Presley; published by Board of Publication of the Pentecostal Holiness Church.... Franklin Springs, Ga.,

Publishing House P.H. Church, 1941. [240] p.
With music (shaped notes)

--MISSIONS

4277 ENCYCLOPEDIA OF modern Christian missions; the agenciew. Burton L. Goddard, ed.... Camden, N.J., T. Nelson, 1967. xix, 743 p.
"Pentecostal Holiness Church, Department of Foreign Missions," by W.H. Turner: p. 529-530.

--PERIODICALS

4278 PENTECOSTAL HOLINESS Advocate. 1- , 1918- .
Franklin Springs, Ga.
Scattered numbers as Advocate.

4279 PENTECOSTAL SUNDAY School Magazine for Teachers and Superintendents. 1- , 1922- . Franklin Springs, Ga.

4280 VIRGINIA CONFERENCE Messenger. 1- , 1939- . Franklin Springs, Ga., Virginia Conference of the Pentecostal Holiness Church.

--RELIGIOUS EDUCATION

4281 TARKENTON, Dallas M., 1912-
"The history and development of the Sunday school as an educational unit in the Pentecostal Holiness Church since 1911." Unpublished M.S. in Education thesis, University of Georgia, 1953. iii, 103ℓ.

--SERMONS

4282 ROBERTS, Oral, 1918-
Oral Roberts' best sermons and stories, as presented in his great evangelistic campaigns around the world. Tulsa, Okla., 1956. 124 p.

4283 ROBERTS, Oral, 1918-
The 4th man, and other famous sermons exactly as Oral Roberts preached them from the revival platform. Tulsa, Okla., Healing Waters, Inc., 1951. 139 p.

4284 ROBERTS, Oral, 1918-
The fourth man. Rev. ed. Tulsa, Okla., Summit Book Co., 1960. 124 p.
First ed. published in 1951 under title: The fourth man, and other famous sermons.

Part IV. Holiness-Pentecostal Movement 533

4285 ROBERTS, Oral, 1918-
"Faith against life's storms." Tulsa?, Okla., 1957. 95 p.

-- --OUTLINES

4286 AARON, Thomas Lee, 1897-1951.
Sermon notes and outlines. Franklin Springs, Ga., Advocate Press, 1964. 126 p.

--YEARBOOKS

4287 PENTECOSTAL HOLINESS Church.
Year book.... Franklin Springs, Ga., Publishing House of the Pentecostal Holiness Church.

--AFRICA, SOUTH

4288 FREEMAN, Dallas Dolphus, 1900-
Observe the African. Franklin Springs, Ga., Printed by Publishing House P.H. Church, c1937. 121 p.

--CHINA

4289 TURNER, William H.
Pioneering in China. Introduction by Rev. J.H. King. Franklin Springs, Ga., Printed by the Publishing House of the P.H. Church, c1928. 312 p.

--NORTH CAROLINA

4290 POPE, Liston
Millhands & preachers; a study of Gastonia. New Haven, Yale University Press, 1942. 369 p.
Account of Pentecostal Holiness Church: p. 96-103, 129, 164-165.

--OKLAHOMA

4291 PAUL, George Harold, 1910-
"The religious frontier: Dan T. Muse and the Pentecostal Holiness Church." Unpublished Ph.D. dissertation, University of Oklahoma, 1965. 302ℓ.

TABERNACLE PENTECOSTAL CHURCH (1899-1915)

[1899-1910 as Brewerton Independent Presbyterian Church; 1910-191? as Tabernacle Presbyterian Church]

One of the few Presbyterian bodies to accept the Wesleyan view of sanctification, this holiness group was founded in 1899 as the Brewerton Presbyterian Church. N.J. Holmes, a Presbyterian minister disfellowshipped for his stand on holiness, soon joined. The Altamount Bible and Missionary Institute near Greenville, South Carolina, which Holmes had founded in 1898, soon became the center of the movement. Re-named the Tabernacle Pentecostal Church, the group accepted tongues-speaking after the Azusa Street revival and in 1915 merged with the Pentecostal Holiness Church. While in sympathy with the union, Holmes did not join the Pentecostal Holiness Church because of his belief that such action might offend the non-denominational constituency of his school.

4292   CAMPBELL, Joseph Enoch
The Pentecostal Holiness Church, 1898-1948: its background and history; presenting complete background material which adequately explains the existence of this organization, also the existence of other kindred Pentecostal and holiness groups, as an essential and integral part of the total church set-up. Franklin Springs, Ga., Publishing House of the Pentecostal Holiness Church, 1951. 573 p.
Account of the Tabernacle Presbyterian Church: p. 263-266.

TRIUMPH THE CHURCH AND KINGDOM OF GOD IN CHRIST (1902-)

In 1897 "Father" E.D. Smith, a Southern black man, received a divine revelation to found a church. It was not until 1902, however, that the plan was "speeded to the earth," nor until 1904 that it "opened to the world." Holding to second-crisis sanctification, the group soon accepted tongues. Although in 1920 Smith departed for Addis Ababa, Ethiopia, and never returned, the movement survived. In 1970 the church claimed 433 congregations and 50,080 members. Denominational offices are in Atlanta.

4293   CLARK, Elmer Talmage, 1886-1966.
The small sects in America. Rev. ed. New York, Abingdon Press, c1965. 256 p.
Account of Triumph the Church and Kingdom of God in Christ: p. 128-129.

Part IV. Holiness-Pentecostal Movement 535

4294 MEAD, Frank Spencer, 1898-
       Handbook of denominations in the United States. New
    5th ed. Nashville, Abingdon Press, c1970. 265 p.
       "Triumph the Church and Kingdom of God in Christ":
    p. 202.

4295 TWENTIETH CENTURY encyclopedia of religious knowledge;
          an extension of the New Schaff-Herzog Encyclopedia of
          Religious Knowledge. Editor-in-chief: Lefferts A.
          Loetscher. Grand Rapids, Mich., Baker Book House,
          1955. 2 v. (xx, 1205 p.)
       "Triumph the Church and Kingdom of God in Christ,"
    by D.H. Harris: p. 1125.

UNITED HOLY CHURCH OF AMERICA (1886-)

[1886-1900 as United Holiness Convention, and the Kahara Holiness Association; 1900-19?? as Holy Church of North Carolina; 19??-1916 as Holy Church of North Carolina and Virginia]

The outgrowth of a revival meeting conducted by the Rev. Isaac Cheshier at Method, a suburb of Raleigh, North Carolina, in 1886, the United Holy Church was among those Negro Holiness groups which joined the Pentecostal Movement early in the twentieth century. At first not all revival participants left the older denominations. By 1900 when the group became known as the Holy Church of North Carolina, however, most adherents had left other churches and joined the new body. As the result of expansion "and Virginia" was soon added to the name. The present title was chosen in 1916. The denomination claims 870 churches and 28,980 members. In addition to glossolalia, the group emphasizes justification, instantaneous sanctification, faith healing, and the imminent second coming of Christ. The Holiness Union, the official organ, is published in Montclair, New Jersey.

4296 CLARK, Elmer Talmage, 1886-1966.
       The small sects in America. Rev. ed. New York,
    Abingdon Press, c1965. 256 p.
       Account of the United Holy Church of America: p. 118-119.

4297 FISHER, H. L.
       History of the United Holy Church of America. n.p.,
    n.d.

4298 TWENTIETH CENTURY encyclopedia of religious knowledge;
          an extension of the New Schaff-Herzog Encyclopedia of
          Religious Knowledge. Editor-in-chief: Lefferts A.

Loetscher. Grand Rapids, Mich., Baker Book House, 1955. 2 v. (xx, 1205 p.)
"United Holy Church of America," by H.H. Hairston: p. 1135.

Part V

SCHOOLS

Unlike parts II through IV, which consist of summary histories of associations and churches and related bibliography, Part V combines directory information and related bibliography. In this section schools are listed alphabetically disregarding denominational sponsorship or affiliation. Listing is generally under the most recent name, followed by present and former locations with dates and former names with dates. When appropriate, the sponsoring association or church is recorded at the end of the entry. If bibliography is included it comes immediately after the entry. Official publications are given first, followed by works written by individuals.

4299 ADIRONDACK BIBLE College. Est. 19??. Northville, N.Y., 19??-Present.
Evangelical Wesleyan Church.

4300 ADRIAN COLLEGE. Est. 1859. Adrian, Mich., 1859-Present.
Wesleyan Methodist Connection of America, 1859-1866.

4301 ALBERTA BIBLE Institute. Est. 1933. Edmonton, Alta., 1933-19??; Camrose, Alta., 19??-Present.
Church of God (Anderson, Indiana).

4302 ALDERSGATE COLLEGE. Est. 1940. Moose Jaw, Sask., 1940-Present.
1940-195? as Moose Jaw Bible School; 195?-1959 as Moose Jaw Bible College.
Free Methodist Church of North America.

4303 ALDERSGATE SCHOOL of Religion. Est. 1969. Hobe Sound, Fla., 1969-1971; Salem, Ohio, 1971-Present.
Interchurch Holiness Association.

4304 ALMA PREPATORY School. Est. 1912. Zarephath, N.J., 1912-Present.
Pentecostal Union, 1912-1917; Pillar of Fire Church, 1917-Present.

4305 ALMA WHITE Bible College. Est. 190?. London, Eng.,
      190?-19??.
          Pentecostal Union, 190?-1917; Pillar of Fire Church,
      1917-19??.

4306 ALMA WHITE College. Est. 1921. Zarephath, N.J., 1921-
          Present.
          Pillar of Fire Church.
4307 Lawrence, Evan Jerry, 1918-
          "Alma White College; a history of its relationship to the
      development of the Pillar of Fire." Unpublished Ed.D. dis-
      sertation, Columbia University, 1966.

4308 AMANDA SMITH Industrial School for Girls. Est. 1899.
          Harvey, Ill., 1899-1918.
4309 Helper. 1- , 1899-190?. Harvey, Ill., Amanda Smith In-
      dustrial School for Girls.

4310 ANDERSON COLLEGE. Est. 1917. Anderson, Ind., 1917-
          Present.
          1917-1925 as Anderson Bible Training School; 1925-1929
      as Anderson Bible School and Seminary; 1929-1964 as An-
      derson College and Theological Seminary.
          Church of God (Anderson, Indiana).

4311 ANNESLEY COLLEGE. Est. 1896. Ottawa, Ont., 1896-
          1948.
          1896-1907 as Bible School.
          1948 affiliated (later merged) with Brockville Bible
      School.
          Holiness Movement Church.

4312 ARKANSAS HOLINESS Academy and Bible School. Est.
          1900. Vilonia, Ark., 1900-1931.
          1900-190? as Arkansas Holiness Literary School; 190?-
      1920 as Arkansas Holiness College; 1920-1923 as Arkansas
      Nazarene Seminary and Normal Training High School.
          1931 merged with Bethany-Peniel College.
          Pentecostal Church of the Nazarene, 1914-1919; Church
      of the Nazarene, 1919-1931.

4313 ARLINGTON COLLEGE. Est. 1954. Arlington, Calif.,
          1954-195?; Long Beach, Calif., 195?-1968.
          1968 merged with Azusa Pacific College.
          Church of God (Anderson, Indiana).

4314 ASBURY COLLEGE. Est. 1890. Wilmore, Ky., 1890-
          Present.
          1890-1891 as Kentucky Holiness School.
4315 Anderson, Tony Marshall, 1888- , ed.
          Our holy faith. Kansas City, Mo., Printed for Asbury
      College by Beacon Hill Press, 1966. 347 p.

Part V. Schools

4316 Barker, Earl Pickett
"The contribution of Methodism to education in Kentucky."
Unpublished Ph.D. dissertation, George Peabody College for Teachers, 1937.

4317 Church, John Robert, 1899-
Why do the righteous suffer?; and, The all-sufficiency of Christ; radio talks delivered at Asbury College extension studio of WHAS, Wilmore, Kentucky. Louisville, Herald Press, 1936. 64 p.

4318 Coleman, Robert Emerson, 1928- , ed.
One divine moment. Old Tappan, N.J., Fleming H. Revell Co., 1970. 123 p.
Concerns the Asbury revival, February 1970.

4319 James, Henry C.
Halls aflame; an account of the spontaneous revivals at Asbury College in 1950 and 1958, by Henry C. James and Paul Rader; introd. by Robert E. Coleman. Wilmore, Ky., Asbury Seminary Press, 1959. 60 p.

4320 James, Henry C.
Halls aflame; an account of the spontaneous revivals at Asbury College in 1950 and 1958, by Henry C. James and Paul Rader; introd. by Robert E. Coleman. Wilmore, Ky., Department of Evangelism, Asbury Theological Seminary, 1966. 60 p.
"Third edition."

4321 Johnson, Zachary Taylor, 1897-
We believe; a study of the practical aspects of our Christian faith. Louisville, Pentecostal Publishing Co., n.d. 101 p.
"A study in the fundamental doctrines of the Wesleyan faith as advocated in the charter of Asbury College."

4322 Kenyon, Jay B., 1885-
Ten college generations. New York, American Press, 1956. 144 p.

4323 McKee, Earl Stanley, 1897-
"The early history of Asbury College (1890-1910)."
Unpublished M.A. thesis, University of Kentucky, 1926.

4324 Nee, Gilbert Chibee
Voices from many lands; foreword by Henry Clay Morrison. Louisville, Pentecostal Publishing Co., 1936. 208 p.

4325 Paul, John Haywood, 1877-1967.
What is new theology? Wilmore, Ky., Department of Publications, Asbury College, 1921.

4326 ASBURY THEOLOGICAL Seminary. Est. 1923. Wilmore, Ky., 1923-Present.

4327 Asbury Theological Seminary. Fortieth Anniversary Committee.
The doctrinal distinctives of Asbury Theological Seminary, Harold B. Kuhn, general editor. Wilmore, Ky., 1963. 100 p.

4328 Abel, Paul Frederick
"An historical study of the origin and development of Asbury Theological Seminary." Unpublished M.A. thesis, Columbia University, 1951.

4329 Asbury Seminarian. 1- , Spring 1946- . Wilmore, Ky.

4330 Fraley, Robert Owen
"A complete history of Asbury Theological Seminary." Unpublished Th.M. thesis, Asbury Theological Seminary, 1949.

4331 Shipps, Howard Fenimore
A short history of Asbury Theological Seminary. Wilmore, Ky., Asbury Theological Seminary, 1963. 96 p.

4332 AZUSA PACIFIC College. Est. 1900. Whittier, Calif., 1900-1901; East Los Angeles, Calif., 1901-1902; Los Angeles, Calif., 1902-1907; Huntington Park, Calif., 1907-1946; Azusa, Calif., 1946-Present.
1900-1939 as Training School for Christian Workers; 1907-1946 also as Huntington Park Bible School; 1939-1957 as Pacific Bible College; 1957-1965 as Azusa College.
1965 merged with Los Angeles Pacific College; 1968, with Arlington College.
California Yearly Meeting of Friends, 1900-1933; Church of God (Anderson, Indiana), Evangelical Methodist Church, Free Methodist Church of North America, Missionary Church, Salvation Army, and Wesleyan Church, 196?-Present.

4333 Brackett, Charles H.
"The history of Azusa College and the Friends, 1900-1965." Unpublished M.A. thesis, University of Southern California, 1967. iv, 152ℓ.

4334 Robertson, Malcolm Ray, 1922-
"A comparative analysis of the general education programs in church related colleges and public junior colleges of California." Unpublished Ed.D. dissertation, University of Southern California, 1967.

4335 B. T. ROBERTS Seminary. Est. 1907. Atlanta, Ga., 1907-191?.
Free Methodist Church of North America.

4336 BARTLESVILLE WESLEYAN College. Est. 1959. Bartlesville, Okla., 1959-Present.
1959-1968 as Central Pilgrim College.
Pilgrim Holiness Church, 1959-1968; Wesleyan Church, 1968-Present.

4337 BEECH LAWN Bible College. Est. 1947. Stalybridge, Cheshire, Eng., 1947-1955.
1955 merged with Hurlet Nazarene College to form British Isles Nazarene College.
Calvary Holiness Church.

Part V. Schools 541

4338 BELL CITY College. Est. 1906? Bell City, La., 1906?-190?.

4339 BELLEVIEW PREPATORY School. Est. 1921. Denver, i.e. Westminster, Colo., 1921-Present.
1921-19?? as Belleview College, Academy, and Bible Seminary; 19??-19?? as Belleview Junior College, Academy, and Bible Seminary.
Pillar of Fire Church.

4340 BETHANY BIBLE College. Est. 1945. Woodstock, N.B., 1945-1947; Yarmouth, N.S., 1947-Present.
1945-1947 as Holiness Bible Institute.
Alliance of the Reformed Baptist Church, 1945-1966; Wesleyan Methodist Church of America, 1966-1968; Wesleyan Church, 1968-Present.

4341 BETHANY FELLOWSHIP Bible and Missionary Training Institute. Est. 1948. Minneapolis, Minn., 1948-Present.
1948-196? as Bethany Fellowship Missionary Training Center.
Bethany Fellowship.

4342 BETHANY NAZARENE College. Est. 1899. Bethany, Okla., 1909-Present.
1909-1920 as Oklahoma Holiness College; 1920 merged with Peniel College (est. 1899); 1920-1955 as Bethany-Peniel College.
Pentecostal Church of the Nazarene, 1909-1919; Church of the Nazarene, 1919-Present.

4343 Bethany Nazarene College Today. 1- , 1943- . Bethany Okla.
1943-1955 as Bethany-Peniel College Today.

4344 Cantrell, Roy Herbert, 1904-
"A history of Bethany Nazarene College." Unpublished D.R.E. dissertation, Southwestern Baptist Theological Seminary, 1955.

4345 Danskin, Donald Ralph, 1910-
"Education for business in church-related liberal arts colleges." Unpublished Ed.D. dissertation, University of Oklahoma, 1955.

4346 McConnell, Leona (Bellew)
"A history of the town and college of Bethany, Oklahoma." Unpublished M.A. thesis, University of Oklahoma, 1935.

4347 Vaughn, Ruth (Wood)
Fools have no miracles; the story of the $100,000 "miracle offering" at Bethany Nazarene College. Kansas City, Mo., Printed for Bethany Nazarene College by Nazarene Publishing House, 1971. 69 p.

4348 BETHEL BIBLE College. Est. 1900. Topeka, Kan., 1900-1901.
Also as Bethel Bible School, College of Bethel, Bethel College.
Apostolic Faith Movement.

4349 BETHEL BIBLE School. Est. 1959? Kimberley, Cape, S. Afr., 1959?-Present.
Africa Evangelistic Band.

4350 Bethel News. 1- , 1959- . Kenilworth, Cape, S. Afr., Bethel Bible School, Kimberley.

4351 BETHEL COLLEGE. Est. 1947. Mishawaka, Ind., 1947-Present.
United Missionary Church, 1947-1969; Missionary Church, 1969-Present.

4352 BETHEL HOLINESS School. Est. 1903. Rose Hill, N.C., 1903-1907.

4353 BETHEL INSTITUTE. Est. 1914. Milton, Pa., 1914-1922.
International Apostolic Holiness Church, 1914-1919; International Holiness Church, 1919-1922.

4354 BEULAH BIBLE Institute. Est. 1916. Edmonton, Alta., 1916-192?.
1916-191? as Edmonton Bible Institute.
Alberta and Saskatchewan Holiness Association.

4355 BEULAH HEIGHTS College and Bible School. Est. 1906. Oklahoma City, Okla., 1906-1909.
1906-190? as Apostolic Holiness Bible School.
1909 merged with Oklahoma Holiness College.

4356 BEULAH HOLINESS Academy. Est. 192?. Shackelfords, Va., 192?-193?.
Pilgrim Holiness Church.

4357 BEULAH SEMINARY. Est. 189?. Clarksville, Mich., 189?-189?.

4358 BIBLE COLLEGE. Est. 1926. Motherwell, Scot., Oct. 1926-June 1928.
Church of the Nazarene.

4359 BIBLE MISSIONARY Institute. Est. 1958. Rock Island, Ill., 1958-Present.
Bible Missionary Church.

4360 BIBLE SCHOOL. Est. 192?. Proton, Ont., 192?-192?.
Pilgrim Holiness Church.

Part V. Schools 543

4361 BIBLE SCHOOL and Rescue Home. Est. 190?. Memphis, Tenn., 190?-190?.

4362 BIBLE TRAINING College. Est. 1911. Clapham, London, Eng., 1911-July 1915.
Pentecostal League.

4363 B. T. C. Journal. 1- , 19??- . London, Bible Training College, Clapham.

4364 BIBLE TRAINING Institute. Est. 1905. Pilot Point, Tex., 1905-1912.
1905-1909 also as Missionary and Bible Training School; 1909-1912 as Nazarene Bible Institute.
1912 merged with Central Nazarene University.
Holiness Church of Christ, 1905-1908; Pentecostal Church of the Nazarene, 1908-1912.

4365 BRAINERD INDIAN School. Est. 1946. Hot Springs, S.D., 1946-Present.
Hephzibah Faith Missionary Association, 1946-1948; Wesleyan Methodist Church of America, 1948-1968; Wesleyan Church, 1968-Present.

4366 Broken Tomahawk. 1- , 1967- . Hot Springs, S.D., Brainard Indian School.

4367 Wesleyan Methodism among the Indians: Onondaga Indian Mission, by Hugh Newcomb; Brainerd Training School, by J. R. Swauger. Syracuse, N.Y., Department of Home Missions of the Wesleyan Methodist Church of America, 1950. 37 p.

4368 BRESEE COLLEGE. Est. 1905. Hutchinson, Kan., 1905-1940.
1905-1908 as Apostolic Holiness Bible School; 1908-1910 as Holiness Bible School; 1910-1914 as Kansas Holiness Institute and Bible School; 1914-1918 as Kansas Holiness College and Bible School (legal name until 1922); 1918-1922 as Nazarene Bible School and Academy; 1922-1925 as Bresee Theological College.
Pentecostal Church of the Nazarene, 1909-1919; Church of the Nazarene, 1919-1940.

4369 BRITISH ISLES Nazarene College. Est. 1955. Manchester, Eng., 1955-Present.
Church of the Nazarene.

4370 BROCKVILLE BIBLE College. Est. 1918. Prescott, Ont., 1918-1920; Brockville, Ont., 1920-Present.
1918-192? as Standard Church Seminary; 192?-195? as Brockville Bible School.
Standard Church of America.

4371 CALIFORNIA COLLEGE and Holiness Bible School. Est. 191?. Los Angeles, Calif., 191?-192?.

4372 CALVARY CHRISTIAN College. Est. 1970. Paris, Ohio, 1970-Present.

4373 CALVARY HOLINESS College. Est. 1969. Wellesley, Ont., 1969-Present.
Independent Holiness Churches.

4374 CANADIAN NAZARENE College. Est. 1921. Calgary, Alta., 1921-1927; Red Deer, Alta., 1927-1961; Winnipeg, Man., 1961-Present.
1921 as Alberta Bible School; 1922-1923 as Canadian Bible School; 1925-1927 as Calgary Bible Institute; 1927-1928 as Alberta School of Evangelism; 1928-1940 as Northern Bible College.
Church of the Nazarene.

4375 Parker, John Fred
From East to western sea; a brief history of the Church of the Nazarene in Canada. Kansas City, Mo., Nazarene Publishing House, 1971. 107 p.
A 50th anniversary project of Canadian Nazarene College.

4376 Thomson, Charles Edward
The story of Canadian Nazarene College. Red Deer, Alta., Canadian Nazarene College, n.d.

4377 Thomson, Dorothy J.
Vine of His planting; history of Canadian Nazarene College. Edmonton, Alta., Can., Commercial Printers, 196?. 34 p.
Fortieth anniversary year, 1960-61.

4378 CARIBBEAN PILGRIM College. Est. 19??. Bridgetown, Barbados, 19??-Present.
Pilgrim Holiness Church, 19??-1968; Wesleyan Church, 1968-Present.

4379 CASCADE COLLEGE. Est. 1918. Portland, Ore., 1918-1969.
1918-1930 as North Pacific Evangelistic Institute; 1930-1939 as Portland Bible Institute.

4380 CEDAREDGE BIBLE School. Est. 19??. Cedaredge, Colo., 19??-194?.
Church of God (Holiness).

4381 CENTRAL COLLEGE. Est. 1884. Orleans, Neb., 1884-1914; McPherson, Kan., 1914-Present.
1884-1914 as Orleans Seminary; 1914-1940 as Central Academy and College.
Free Methodist Church of North America.

Part V. Schools 545

4382 CENTRAL NAZARENE Academy. Est. 1910. Hamlin, Tex., 1910-1929.
1910-1917 as Central Nazarene University; 1917-1923 as Central Nazarene College; 1923-1929 also as Central Nazarene Academy and Bible School.
Pentecostal Church of the Nazarene, 1910-1919; Church of the Nazarene, 1919-1929.

4383 CENTRAL WESLEYAN College. Est. 1906. Central, S.C., 1906-Present.
1906-1909 as Wesleyan Methodist Bible Institute; 1909-1959 as Wesleyan Methodist College.
Wesleyan Methodist Connection (or Church) of America, 1906-1947; Wesleyan Methodist Church of America, 1947-1968; Wesleyan Church, 1968-Present.

4384 CHRIST MISSIONARY and Industrial College. Est. 19??. Jackson, Miss., 19??- .
Church of Christ (Holiness) U.S.A.

4385 CHRISTIAN WORKERS' Training School and Bible Institute. Est. 189?.
LeGrand, Iowa, 189?-190?; Marshalltown, Iowa, 190?-190?.

4386 CIRCLEVILLE BIBLE College. Est. 1948. Circleville, Ohio, 1948-Present.
Churches of Christ in Christian Union.

4387 CLIFF COLLEGE. Est. 1884. Calver, Derbys. near Sheffield, Eng., 1884-Present.
Methodist Church.

4388 COLEGIO DIXON. Est. 19??. San Juanito, Chihuahua, Mex., 19??-Present. Mexican Evangelistic Mission.

4389 COLORADO SPRINGS Bible College. Est. 1905. Colorado Springs, Colo., 1905-1959.
1905-1910 as Rocky Mountain Missionary and Evangelistic Institute; 1910-194? as Colorado Springs Bible Training School; 1959 moved to Bartlesville, Okla., and became Central Pilgrim College.
People's Mission Church, 1905-1925; with Pilgrim Holiness Church, 1925-1959.

4390 CORN BIBLE Academy. Est. 19??. Corn, Okla., 19??-Present.

4391 COVENANT FOUNDATION College. Est. 1968. Knightstown, Ind., 1968-Present.
Church of the Bible Covenant.

4392 EASTERN NAZARENE College. Est. 1900. Saratoga Springs, N.Y., 1900-1902; North Scituate, R.I., 1902-1919; Wollaston Park, Quincy, Mass., 1919-Present.
1900-1902 as Pentecostal Collegiate Institute and Bible Training School; 1902-1918 as Pentecostal Collegiate Institute.
Association of Pentecostal Churches of America, 1900-1907; Pentecostal Church of the Nazarene, 1907-1919; Church of the Nazarene, 1919-Present.

4393 Cameron, James Reese, 1929-
Eastern Nazarene College: the first fifty years, 1900-1950. Kansas City, Mo., Printed for Eastern Nazarene College by the Nazarene Publishing House, 1968. 420 p.

4394 Heart, Head, and Hand; P.C.I. monthly devoted to industrial education. 1- , 1912-191?. North Scituate, R.I., Pentecostal Collegiate Institute.

4395 EASTMAN SEMINARY. Est. 189?. Clarksville, Mich., 189?-189?.

4396 EDEN GROVE Academy and Grammar School. Est. 19??. Cincinnati, Ohio, 19??-196?.
19??-194? as Mt. Hermon Academy and Grammar School.
Pillar of Fire Church.

4397 ELHANAN TRAINING and Industrial Institute. Est. 190?. Marion, N.C., 190?-19??.

4398 EMMANUEL BIBLE College. Est. 1916. Birkenhead, Cheshire, Eng., 1916-Present.
1916-19?? as Emmanuel Missionary Training Home.
Emmanuel Holiness Church.

4399 Emmanuel. 1- , 1927- . Birkenhead, Cheshire, Eng., Emmanuel Bible College.

4400 EMMANUEL BIBLE College. Est. 1940. Kitchener, Ont., 1940-Present.
Mennonite Brethren in Christ, 1940-1947; United Missionary Church, 1947-1969; Missionary Church, 1969-Present.

4401 EMMANUEL COLLEGE. Est. 1919. Franklin Springs, Ga., 1919-1931, 1933-Present.
1919-1939 as Franklin Springs Institute.
Pentecostal Holiness Church.

4402 Campbell, Joseph Enoch
The Pentecostal Holiness Church, 1898-1948: its background and history; presenting complete background material which adequately explains the existence of this organization, also the existence of other kindred Pentecostal and Holiness groups, as an essential and integral part of the total church set-up. Franklin Springs, Ga., Publishing

Part V. Schools 547

      House of the Pentecostal Holiness Church, 1951. 573 p.
      "The Emmanuel College, Franklin Springs, Georgia":
      p. 477-501.
4403 Melton, C. Y.
      "A study of the students who enrolled in Emmanuel College from September 1952 through September 1955." Unpublished M.A. thesis, University of North Carolina, 1956.
4404 Synan, Vinson, 1934-
      Emmanuel College: the first fifty years, 1919-1969. Franklin Springs, Ga., Emmanuel College Library, 1968. xvi, 159 p.

4405 EMMANUEL ORPHANAGE and Bible School. Est. 19??. Lindrith, N. Mex., 19??-1946.

4406 ESCUELA HEROES de Mexico. Est. 19??. El Salvador, Zacatecas, Mex., 19??-Present.
      Mexican Evangelistic Mission.

4407 EUROPEAN NAZARENE Bible College. Est. 1966. Busingen, Ger., 1966-Present.
      Church of the Nazarene.

4408 EVANSVILLE SEMINARY. Est. 1880. Evansville, Wis., 1880-1926.
      1910-1920 as Evansville Junior College.
      Free Methodist Church of North America.

4409 FAIRMOUNT BIBLE School. Est. 1906. Fairmount, Ind., 1906-1920.
      1906-19?? as Theological Seminary of the Indiana Conference of the Wesleyan Methodist Connection (or Church) of America, also as Theological Institute and Bible Training School; 1920 merged with Marion College.
      Wesleyan Methodist Connection (or Church) of America.

4410 FAITH BIBLE School. Est. 1921. Mitchell, S.D., 1921-Present.
      Also as Faith Home and School.
      Hephzibah Faith Missionary Association, 1935-1948.
4411 Crouch, Winnie, 1880-1970.
      Room on the rock. 2d ed., rev. and enl. Phoenix, Ariz., 1957. 56 p.
      Autobiography.
      First issued as Some experiences of an inhabitant of the rock in 1943.
4412 Crouch, Winnie, 1880-1970.
      Some experiences of an inhabitant of the rock. Tabor, Iowa, Good Tidings Press, 1943. 47 p.
      Autobiography.
      Issued also under title: Room on the rock.

4413   FAITH HOME and Training School. Est. 1893. Tabor, Iowa, 1893-1951.
Hephzibah Faith Missionary Association, 1893-1949; Church of the Nazarene, 1949-1951.

4414   FAITH MISSION Training Home and Bible College. Est. 19??. Edinburgh, Scot., 19??-Present.
Also as Faith Mission Bible College.
Faith Mission.

4415   FALCON HOLINESS School. Est. 1902. Falcon, N.C., 1902-1952.
Pentecostal Holiness Church, 1943-1952.

4416   FORT SCOTT Christian Heights. Est. 1947. Fort Scott, Kan., 1947-Present.
1947-1971 as Fort Scott Bible School.
Church of God (Holiness).

4417   FORT WAYNE Bible College. Est. 1904. Fort Wayne, Ind., 1904-Present.
1904-1930 as Fort Wayne Bible Training School; 1930-1950 as Fort Wayne Bible Institute.
Missionary Church Association, 1904-1969; Missionary Church, 1969-Present.

4418   Warner, Timothy Marcus, 1924-
"A study of the place of general education in the Bible college curriculum." Unpublished Ed.D. dissertation, Indiana University, 1967.

4419   FRANCIS ASBURY Bible College. Est. 1960. Moline, Ill., 1960-1965; Milan, Ill., 1965-1969.
1960-1965 as Asbury Bible College.

4420   FRANKFORT WESLEYAN Bible College. Est. 1927. Frankfort, Ind., 1927-1932, 1939-1972.
1927-1932 as Frankfort Pilgrim Bible School; 1939-1969 as Frankfort Pilgrim College.
1972 merged with Penn Wesleyan College and Kernersville Wesleyan College to form United Wesleyan College.
Pilgrim Holiness Church, 1927-1932 and 1938-1968; Wesleyan Church, 1968-1972.

4421   FRIENDS BIBLE College. Est. 1917. Haviland, Kan., 1917-Present.
1917-1930 as Kansas Central Bible Training School.

4422   GALILEAN TRAINING School. Est. 19??. Los Angeles, Calif., 19??-19??.
Pillar of Fire Church.

Part V. Schools 549

4423 GEORGE FOX College. Est. 1891. Newberg, Ore., 1891-
Present.
1891-1949 as Pacific College.
Oregon Yearly Meeting of Friends Church, 1891-1971;
Northwest Yearly Meeting of Friends Churches, 1971-
Present.

4424 GERRY SEMINARY. Est. 1884. Gerry, N.Y., 1884-1888.
Free Methodist Church of North America.

4425 GOD'S BIBLE School. Est. 1900. Cincinnati, Ohio, 1900-
Present.
Also as God's Bible School and Missionary Training
Home, and God's Bible School and College.

4426 God's Bible School. Missionary Prayer Band.
Unveiling the missionary world, comp. by God's Bible
School Missionary Prayer Band, Alice M. White, director.
Cincinnati, God's Bible School and Missionary Training
Home, 1936. 191 p.

4427 Day, Lloyd Raymond
"A history of God's Bible School in Cincinnati, 1900-
1949." Unpublished M.Ed. thesis, University of Cincinnati,
1949.

4428 GREAT COMMISSION Schools. Est. 19??. Anderson, Ind.,
19??-19??.

4429 GREENLEAF FRIENDS Academy. Est. 1908. Greenleaf,
Ida., 1908-Present.
1918-1928 as Greenleaf Seminary.
Oregon Yearly Meeting of Friends Church, 1908-1971;
Northwest Yearly Meeting of Friends Churches, 1971-
Present.

4430 GREENSBORO BIBLE and Literary School. Est. 1903.
Greensboro, N.C., 1903-193?.
Pilgrim Holiness Church, 1924-193?.

4431 GREENVILLE COLLEGE. Est. 1892. Greenville, Ill.,
1892-Present.
Free Methodist Church of North America.

4432 GULF COAST Bible College. Est. 1953. Houston, Tex.,
1953-19??.
Church of God (Anderson, Indiana).

4433 HOBE SOUND Bible College. Est. 1960. Hobe Sound,
Fla., 1960-Present.
1960-1966 as Hobe Sound Bible Institute.
Also as Hobe Sound Bible College & Academy.

4434 HOLINESS BIBLE College. Est. 1936. McCord, Sask., 1936-195?; Winnipeg, Man., 195?-1957.
1936-195? as Western Holiness Bible School.
1957 merged with Moose Jaw Bible College.
Holiness Movement Church.

4435 HOLINESS BIBLE Institute. Est. 19??. Philadelphia, Pa., 19??-191?.
Holiness Christian Church.

4436 HOLINESS BIBLE School. Est. 1906. Beulah, Okla., 1906-1910.

4437 HOLINESS BIBLE School. Est. 1927. Gravette, Ark., 1927-Present. Church of God (Holiness).

4438 HOLINESS BIBLE School and Faith Missionary Training Home. Est. 1901. New London, Ind., etc., 1901-1905; Carlinville, Ill., 1905-191?.
Holiness Christian Church.

4439 HOLINESS COLLEGIATE Institute. Est. 1891. New Florence, Mo., 1891-1897.
Church of God (Unity Holiness People).

4440 HOLINESS COLLEGIATE Institute. Est. 1906. Clarence, Mo., 1906-1919.
1906-19?? as Clarence Bible Seminary.
1919 merged with Missouri Holiness College.
Church of God (Independent Holiness People).

4441 HOLINESS GOSPEL School. Est. 19??. Newberrytown, Pa., 19??-Present.

4442 HOLINESS METHODIST School of Theology. Est. 1914. Minneapolis, Minn., 1914-196?.
Northwestern Holiness Association, 1914-1920; Holiness Methodist Church, 1920-196?.

4442a HOLINESS SCHOOL. Projected 1916 (no students). Artesia, N.M.

4443 HOLINESS SCHOOL. Est. 1914. Ava, Mo., 1914-1932.
Ozark Holiness Association.

4444 HOLINESS SCHOOL. Est. 190? Buffalo Gap, Tex., 190?-1909.
1910 merged with Central Nazarene University.
Holiness Church of Christ, 190?-1908; Pentecostal Church of the Nazarene, 1908-1910.

4445 HOLINESS SCHOOL. Est. 189?. Highway, Ky., 189?-190?.

Part V. Schools   551

4446   HOLINESS SCHOOL. Est. 1918. Hutchinson, Kan., 1918-
       19??.
       Pilgrim Church.

4447   HOLINESS SCHOOL. Est. 190?. Old Cove, Ark., 190?-
       1906.
       Southwestern Arkansas Holiness Association.

4448   HOLINESS SCHOOL. Est. 190?. Plainview, Tex., 190?-
       19??.

4449   HOLMES THEOLOGICAL Seminary. Est. 1898. Paris
       Mountain, S.C., 1898-1900; Atlanta, Ga., 1901-1903;
       Columbia, S.C., 1903-1905; Paris Mountain, S.C.,
       1905-1915; Greenville, S.C., 1916-Present.
       1898-1900 and 1903-1915 as Altamont Bible and Missionary Institute; 1901-1903 as Bible and Missionary Institute of Atlanta; 1916-1940 as Holmes Bible and Missionary Institute; 1940-1958 as Holmes Bible College.

4450   Campbell, Joseph Enoch
       The Pentecostal Holiness Church, 1898-1948: its background and history; presenting complete background material which adequately explains the existence of this organization, also the existence of other kindred Pentecostal and Holiness groups, as an essential and integral part of the total church set-up. Franklin Springs, Ga., Publishing House of the Pentecostal Holiness Church, 1951. 573 p.
       "Holmes Bible College, Greenville, S.C.": p. 423-476.

4451   Thomas, Iva
       History of Holmes Theological Seminary. Franklin Springs, Ga., 1959. 47 p.

4452   HOUGHTON COLLEGE. Est. 1883. Houghton, N.Y., 1883-
       Present.
       1883-1923 as Houghton Wesleyan Methodist Seminary; high school 1923-Present as Houghton Academy.
       Wesleyan Methodist Connection of America, 1883-1891; Wesleyan Methodist Connection (or Church) of America, 1891-1947; Wesleyan Methodist Church of America, 1947-1968; Wesleyan Church, 1968-Present.

4453   Houghton College.
       Consider the years: Houghton College. [Dr. Kenneth L. Wilson, compilation editor; sketches by H. Willard and Aimee E. Ortlip]. Houghton, N.Y., 1958. Unpaged.
       Cover-title
       Seventy-fifth anniversary brochure.

4454   Moon, Wesley G., 1911-
       "The relationship of certain factors to persistence in the teaching profession of Houghton College graduates prepared for teaching." Unpublished Ed.D. dissertation, University of Buffalo, 1952. xii, 159ℓ.

4455 HUNTINGTON COLLEGE. Est. 1897. Huntington, Ind., 1897-Present.
1897-1917 as Central College.
Church of the United Brethren in Christ (Old Constitution).

4456 HURLET NAZARENE College. Est. 1945. Glasgow, Scot., 1945-1955.
1955 merged with Beech Lawn Bible College to form British Isles Nazarene College.
Church of the Nazarene.

4457 ILLINOIS INSTITUTE. Est. 1848. Wheaton, Ill., 1848-1860.
Wesleyan Methodist Connection of America.

4458 IMMANUEL BIBLE Training College. Est. 19??. Tokyo, Japan, 19??-Present.
Immanueru Sogo Dendo Dan (Immanuel General Mission of Japan).

4459 INDEPENDENCE BIBLE College. Est. 1949. Independence, Kan., 1949-Present.
1949-19?? as Independence Bible School.
Fire-Baptized Holiness Church (Wesleyan).

4460 INSTITUTO BIBLICO Vida y Verdad. Est. 19??. Parral, Chihuahua, Mex., 19??-Present.
Mexican Evangelistic Mission.

4461 INTERCESSION CITY Christian Schools. Est. 1934. Intercession City, Fla., 1934-Present.
1934-195? as Central Florida Bible Institute.

4462 Jessop, Harry Edward, 1884-
Spiritual security; a meditation on the mutual responsibility of the Lord and the believing soul for eternal salvation. Intercession City, Fla., Central Florida Bible Institute; University Park, Iowa, Chicago Evangelistic Institute, 1953. 24 p.

4463 JABBOK BIBLE School. Est. 1925. Thomas, Okla., 1925-Present.
1925-196? as Jabbok Bible and Missionary Training School.
Brethren in Christ Church.

4464 JOHN FLETCHER Bible College. Est. 196?. Kearney, Neb., 196?-Present.
Evangelical Wesleyan Church.

4465 JOHN WESLEY College. Est. 1909. Owosso, Mich., 1909-Present.

Part V. Schools 553

1909-194? as Bible Holiness Seminary; 194?-1957 as Owosso Bible College; 1957-1972 as Owosso College.
International Apostolic Holiness Union and Churches, 1909-1913; International Apostolic Holiness Church, 1913-1919; International Holiness Church, 1919-1922; Pilgrim Holiness Church, 1922-1968; Wesleyan Church, 1968-1970.

4466 McCallum, Floyd Frederick, 1920-
"An investigation of the need for a liberal arts college for the Pilgrim Holiness Church." Unpublished Ed.D. dissertation, Michigan State University, 1955. 190ℓ.

4467 Nicholson, Roy Stephen, 1903-
The Arminian emphases. Owosso, Mich., Owosso College, 196?. 167 p. (M.L. Goodman lecture series)

4468 JOHN WESLEY College. Est. 1932. Greensboro, N.C., 1932-Present.
1932-1959 as People's Bible School and College.

4469 JORDAN COLLEGE. Est. 1967. Cedar Springs, Mich., 1967-Present.
1967-1972 as Wesleyan Bible Institute.
United Holiness Church of North America.

4470 Jordan College.
"Report to the Cedar Springs Rotary from the administration of Jordan College (Wesleyan Bible Institute)." Unpublished paper, 1972. [3]ℓ.

4471 KANSAS CITY College and Bible School. Est. 1938. Kansas City, Mo., 1938-1941; Overland Park, Kan., 1941-Present.
1938-1941 as Kansas City Bible School.
Church of God (Holiness).

4472 KENTUCKY MOUNTAIN Bible Institute. Est. 1931. Vancleve, Ky., 1931-Present.
Kentucky Mountain Holiness Association.

4473 KERNERSVILLE WESLEYAN Academy. Est. 1946. Kernersville, N.C., 1946-Present.
1946-1957 as high school department of Pilgrim Bible College; 1957-1970 as high school department of Southern Pilgrim College; 1970-1972 as high school department of Kernersville Wesleyan College.
Pilgrim Holiness Church, 1946-1968; Wesleyan Church, 1968-Present.

4474 KERNERSVILLE WESLEYAN College. Est. 1946. Kernersville, N.C., 1946-1972.
1946-1957 as Pilgrim Bible College; 1957-1970 as Southern Pilgrim College.
1972 merged with Penn Wesleyan College and Frankfort Wesleyan Bible College to form United Wesleyan College.

Pilgrim Holiness Church, 1946-1968; Wesleyan Church, 1968-1972.

4475 KING'S COLLEGE. Est. 1925. Checotah, Okla., 1925-1926; Kingfisher, Okla., 1925-1932.
Pentecostal Holiness Church.

4476 KINGSWOOD HOLINESS College. Est. 1906. Kingswood, Ky., 1906-1931.
1906-1914? as Kingswood College.
International Holiness Church, 1919-1922; Pilgrim Holiness Church, 1922-1931.

4477 KIRKLAND BIBLE Institute. Est. 19??. Decatur, Ind., 19??-Present.

4478 KIRKSVILLE BIBLE School. Est. 1954. Kirksville, Mo., 1954-Present.
Church of God (Holiness).

4479 KLETZING COLLEGE. Est. 1906. University Park, Iowa, 1906-1951.
1906-1924 as Central Holiness University; 1924-1946 as John Fletcher College.

4480 Brasher, John Lakin, 1868-1971.
Reckoning with the eternals, and other themes; introd. by President Joseph Owen. University Park, Iowa, John Fletcher College Press, 1927. 144 p.

4481 Dewey, Clifford Sherwood
"A history of John Fletcher College with special reference to its religious traditions." Unpublished M.A. thesis, State University of Iowa, 1940.

4482 LAMAR BIBLE School. Est. 1932. Lamar, Colo., 1932-Present.
Church of God (Holiness).

4483 LAWRENCE SEMINARY. Est. 1889. Lawrence, Tex., 1889-189?.
Free Methodist Church of North America.

4484 LEBANON MISSIONARY Bible College. Est. 1947. Berwick upon Tweed, Northumb., Eng., 1947-Present.

4485 LEE COLLEGE. Est. 1918. Cleveland, Tenn., 1918-1938; Sevierville, Tenn., 1938-1947; Cleveland, Tenn., 1947-Present.
1918-1941 as Bible Training School; 1941-1947 as Bible Training School and College.
Church of God (General Assembly).

4486 Hughes, Ray Harrison
"The influence of Lee College on the development of

Part V. Schools 555

the world missions program of the Church of God." Unpublished M.S. thesis, University of Tennessee, 1964. vi, 77ℓ.

4487 LORNE PARK College. Est. 1924. Port Credit, Ont., 1924-1966.
1924-1927 as Lorne Park Seminary.
Free Methodist Church of North America.

4488 LOS ANGELES Pacific College. Est. 1903. Los Angeles, Calif., 1903-1965.
1903-1911 as Los Angeles Free Methodist Seminary; 1911-1926 as Los Angeles Junior College; 1926-1954 as Los Angeles Pacific College and High School.
1965 merged with Azusa College to form Azusa Pacific College.
Free Methodist Church of North America.

4489 McGEE COLLEGE. Est. 1889. College Mound, Mo., 1889-189?.
Methodist Episcopal Church.

4490 McGEE HOLINESS College. Est. 1896. College Mound, Mo., 1896-1922.
Church of God (Unity Holiness People).

4491 McKINNEY JUNIOR College. Est. 1910. Campbell, Tex., 1910-1920; McKinney, Tex., 1920-1922.
1910-1920 as Campbell Free Methodist Seminary.
Free Methodist Church of North America.

4492 MALONE COLLEGE. Est. 1892. Cleveland, Ohio, 1892-1956; Canton, Ohio, 1956-Present.
1892-1911 as Friends Bible Institute and Training School; 1911-1937 as Cleveland Bible Institute; 1937-1956 as Cleveland Bible College.
Ohio Yearly Meeting of Friends Church, 1892-1971; Evangelical Friends Church, Eastern Division, 1971-Present.

4493 Buss, Edith (Mitchell)
"History of Malone College with Special Emphasis upon its Founders." Unpublished M.A. thesis, Wheaton College, 1957.

4494 Smith, Joseph Henry, 1855-1946.
Educational limitation in the Holiness Movement. Cleveland, Ohio, Cleveland Bible Institute, 1922. Unpaged.

4495 MARION COLLEGE. Est. 1920. Marion, Ind., 1920-Present.
Wesleyan Methodist Connection (or Church) of America, 1920-1947; Wesleyan Methodist Church of America, 1947-1968; Wesleyan Church, 1968-Present.

4496 MARITIME NAZARENE Bible Institute. Est. 1946. St.
John, N.B., 1946-1950.
Church of the Nazarene.

4497 MERIDIAN FEMALE College. Est. 1896. Meridian, Miss.,
1896-19??.
1896-1903 as East Mississippi Female College.

4498 MERIDIAN MALE College. Est. 1902. Meridian, Miss.,
1902-192?.

4499 MESSIAH COLLEGE. Est. 1909. Harrisburg, Pa., 1909-
1911; Grantham, Pa., 1911-Present.
1909-1924 as Messiah Bible School and Missionary
Training Home; 1924-1951 as Messiah Bible College.
1965 merged with Upland College.
Brethren in Christ Church.

4500 METROPOLITAN BIBLE School. Est. 19??. Waukesha,
Wis., 19??-19??.
Metropolitan Church Association.

4501 MICHIGAN UNION College. Est. 1849. Leoni, Mich.,
1849-186?.
Wesleyan Methodist Connection of America, 1849-1859;
Church of the United Brethren in Christ, 1859-196?.

4502 MID-AMERICA NAZARENE College. Est. 1968. Olathe, Kan.,
1968-Present.
Church of the Nazarene.

4503 MILTONVALE WESLEYAN College. Est. 1909. Miltonvale,
Kan., 1909-Present.
Also as Miltonvale College.
Wesleyan Methodist Connection (or Church) of America,
1909-1947; Wesleyan Methodist Church of America, 1947-
1968; Wesleyan Church, 1968-Present.

4504 MISSIONARY BIBLE Institute. Est. 191?. St. Louis, Mo.,
191?-192?.
191?-191? as Beulah Bible School.
Holiness Christian Church, 191?-1919; International
Holiness Church, 1919-192?.

4505 MISSOURI HOLINESS College. Est. 190?. DesArc, Mo.,
190?-1919; Clarence, Mo., 1919-1921.
1919 merged with Holiness Collegiate Institute.
Pentecostal Church of the Nazarene, 1908-1919; Church
of the Nazarene, 1919-1921.

4506 MIZPAH ACADEMY. Est. 1884. Coldwater, Mich., 1884-
1886; Dutton, Mich., 1886-189?.

Part V. Schools 557

        1884-1889 as Holiness School.
        Michigan Holiness Association, 1884-1889; Primitive
Holiness Mission, 1889-189?.

4507 MT. CARMEL High School. Est. 1925. Lawson, Ky.,
      1925-Present.
      Kentucky Mountain Holiness Association.

4508 MOUNT VERNON Nazarene College. Est. 1968. Mount
      Vernon, Ohio, 1968-Present.
      Church of the Nazarene.

4509 MT. ZION Bible School. Est. 1936. Ava, Mo., 1936-
      Present.
      Church of God (Holiness).

4510 Reporter. 1- , 193?- . Ava, Mo., Mt. Zion Bible
      School.

4511 MOUNTAIN STATE Christian School. Est. 1966. Culloden,
      W. Va., 1966-Present.
      Also as Mountain State Bible School.
      Church of God (Holiness).

4512 MOUNTAIN VIEW Bible College. Est. 1926. Didsbury,
      Alta., 1926-Present.
      Mennonite Brethren in Christ, 1926-1947; United Missionary Church, 1947-1969; Missionary Church, 1969-Present.

4513 NAZARENE BIBLE College. Est. 1967. Colorado Springs,
      Colo., 1967-Present.
      Church of the Nazarene.

4514 NAZARENE BIBLE College. Est. 1954. Potchefstroom,
      Transval, S. Afr., 1954-19??; Florida, Transval, S.
      Afr., 19??-Present.
      Church of the Nazarene.

4515 NAZARENE BIBLE College. Est. 1953. Thornleigh, N. S.
      W., Austl., 1953-Present.
      Church of the Nazarene.

4516 NAZARENE BIBLE School. Est. 1920. Parkhead, Glasgow, Scot., 1920-1923.
      Church of the Nazarene.

4517 NAZARENE INDIAN Bible School. Est. 1948. Lindrith,
      N. Mex., 1948-1954; Albuquerque, N. Mex., 1954-
      Present.
      1948-196? as C. Warren Jones Indian Bible Training
School; 196?-1971 as Nazarene Indian School.
      Church of the Nazarene.

4518 NAZARENE THEOLOGICAL Seminary. Est. 1945. Kansas City, Mo., 1945-Present.
Church of the Nazarene.

4519 NAZARENE THEOLOGICAL Seminary.
Master bibliography of holiness works. Kansas City, Mo., Prepared by Nazarene Theological Seminary and published by Beacon Hill Press, 1965. 45 p.

4520 Seminary Tower. 1- , Winter 1945- . Kansas City, Mo., Nazarene Theological Seminary.

4521 NAZARENE TRAINING College. Est. 1948. Institute, W. Va., 1948-1970.
1948-19?? as Nazarene Bible Institute.
1970 merged with Nazarene Bible College.
Church of the Nazarene.

4522 NEOSHO RAPIDS Seminary. Est. 1887. Neosho Rapids, Kan., 1887-1895.
Free Methodist Church of North America.

4523 NIAGARA CHRISTIAN College. Est. 19??. Fort Erie, Ont., 19??-Present.
Brethren in Christ Church.

4524 NORTHWEST INDIAN Bible School. Est. 1969. Alberton, Mont., 1969-Present.
Allegheny Wesleyan Methodist Connection (Original Allegheny Conference).

4525 NORTHWEST NAZARENE College. Est. 1913. Nampa, Ida., 1913-Present.
1913-1916 as Idaho-Oregon Holiness School; 1916-191? as Northwest Holiness School.
Pentecostal Church of the Nazarene, 1913-1919; Church of the Nazarene, 1919-Present.

4526 Northwest Nazarene College.
Twenty-five years of progress. Nampa, Ida., 1938. 83 p.

4527 Marsh, Marian, 1913-
"An appraisal of the undergraduate program of elementary teacher education, Northwest Nazarene College, Nampa, Idaho." Unpublished Ed. D. dissertation, Colorado State College, 1961.

4528 Nazarene Messenger. 1- , 1917-19??. Nampa, Ida.

4529 OAKDALE VOCATIONAL School. Est. 1921. Oakdale, Ky., 1921-Present.
Free Methodist Church of North America, 1921-196?.

4530 OLD PATHS Bible School. Est. 1912. Glendale, Ariz., 1912-194?; Sunny Slope, Phoenix, Ariz., 194?-1965.

Part V. Schools

194?-1965 as Sunny Slope Bible School.
Church of God (Holiness).

4531 OLIVET NAZARENE College. Est. 1907. Olivet, Ill.,
1907-1940; Kankakee, i.e. Bourbonnais, Ill., 1940-
Present.
1907-1917 as Illinois Holiness University; 1917-1921 as
Olivet University; 1921-1940 as Olivet College.
Illinois Holiness Association, 1907-1912; Pentecostal
Church of the Nazarene, 1912-1919; Church of the Nazarene,
1919-Present.

4532 Olivet Nazarene College.
Olivet chapel hymnal, ed. by Carl Bangs. Kankakee,
Ill., 1959. Unpaged.
Mimeographed.

4533 OZARK INDUSTRIAL College. Est. 1928. Monte Ne, Ark.,
1928-1931.
Pentecostal Holiness Church.

4534 PACIFIC BIBLE Institute. Est. 1920. Boise, Ida., 1920-
1922; Seattle, Wash., 1922-1923.
Church of God (Anderson, Indiana).

4535 PACIFIC COAST Bible Institute. Est. 1945. Chilliwack,
B.C., Can., 1945-19??.
Pentecostal Holiness Church.

4536 PAULINE HOLINESS College. Est. 1883. College Mound,
Mo., 1883-1888.
Southwestern Holiness Association.

4537 PENIEL COLLEGE. Est. 1899. Peniel, Tex., 1889-1920.
1899-1911 as Texas Holiness University; 1911-1918 as
Peniel University.
1920 merged with Oklahoma Holiness College to form
Bethany-Peniel College.
Holiness Association of Texas, 1899-1909; Pentecostal
Church of the Nazarene, 1909-1919; Church of the Nazarene,
1919-1920.

4538 PENN VIEW Bible Institute. Est. 1966. Penns Creek, Pa.,
1966-Present.
God's Missionary Church.

4539 PENN WESLEYAN College. Est. 1921. Allentown, Pa.,
1921-1972.
1921-1934 as Beulah Park Bible School; 1934-1954 as
Allentown Bible Institute; 1954-1970 as Eastern Pilgrim College.
1972 merged with Kernersville Wesleyan College and
Frankfort Wesleyan Bible College to form United Wesleyan

College.
International Holiness Church, 1921-1922; Pilgrim Holiness Church, 1922-1968; Wesleyan Church, 1968-1972.

4540 PENTECOSTAL BIBLE College. Est. 1908. Parkhead, Glasgow, Scot., 1908-1916.
1908-1913 as Parkhead Holiness Bible School.
Pentecostal Church of Scotland, 1908-1915; Pentecostal Church of the Nazarene, 1915-1916.

4541 PENTECOSTAL MISSION Bible School. Est. 1908. Binghamton, N.Y., 1908-1911.
Pentecostal Rescue Mission.

4542 PEOPLES BIBLE College. Est. 193?. Colorado Springs, Colo., 193?-Present.
Emmanuel Association.

4543 PILGRIM BIBLE College. Est. 1917. Pasadena, Calif., 1917-193?.
1946 assets taken over by Holiness Evangelistic Institute, then re-named Pilgrim Evangelistic Institute.
Pilgrim Church, 1917-1922; Pilgrim Holiness Church, 1922-193?.

4544 POINT LOMA College. Est. 1902. Los Angeles, Calif., 1902-1910; Pasadena, Calif., 1910-1973; San Diego, Calif., 1973-Present.
1902-1906 as Pacific Bible College; 1906-1910 as Deets Pacific Bible College of the Nazarene University; 1910-1918 as Nazarene University; 1918-1924 as Pasadena University; 1924-1973 as Pasadena College.
Church of the Nazarene, 1902-1907; Pentecostal Church of the Nazarene, 1907-1919; Church of the Nazarene, 1919-Present.

4545 Knott, James Proctor, 1886-1963.
History of Pasadena College. Pasadena, Calif., Pasadena College, 1960. 124 p. illus.

4546 Price, Ross Eugene, 1907-
Faith in these times; sermons by Pasadena College ministers, commemorating fifty years of service by Pasadena College in the city of Pasadena, California, 1910 to 1960. ed. by Ross E. Price [and] Oscar F. Reed. Kansas City. Mo., Beacon Hill Press, 1961. 117 p.

4547 Purkiser, Westlake Taylor, 1910-
"Toward a definition of Christian education," Vital Speeches, XV (July 15, 1949), 602-605.

4548 Stropko, Andrew John, 1945-
"Values of Nazarene college students on a public and a church sponsored compus." Unpublished M.A. thesis, University of Arizona, 1969. 70(.

Part V. Schools 561

4549 ROBERTS COLLEGE. Est. 18??. Purdy, Tenn., 18??-1887.
Wesleyan Methodist Connection of America.

4550 ROBERTS WESLEYAN College. Est. 1866. North Chili, N.Y., 1866-Present.
1866-1884 as Chili Seminary; 1885-1945 as A.M. Chesbrough Seminary; 1945-1949 as Roberts Junior College.
Free Methodist Church of North America.

4551 ROCKY MOUNTAIN Christian School. Est. 1970. Littleton, Colo., 1970-Present.
Church of God (Holiness).

4552 RUSKIN CAVE College. Est. 1904. Ruskin Cave, Tenn., 1904-191?.

4553 SALEM BIBLE College. Est. 1946. Salem, Ohio, 1946-Present.
1946-1961 as Salem Bible Institute.
Also as Salem Bible College and Academy.

4554 Salem Sentinel. 1- , Sept. 1970- . Salem, Ohio, Salem Bible College.

4555 SAMARITAN HOSPITAL School of Nursing. Est. 1920. Nampa, Ida., 1920-1954.
1920-19?? as Nazarene Missionary Sanitarium and Institute.
Church of the Nazarene.

4556 Nazarene Missionary Sanitarium and Institute.
Samaritan Hospital, a unit of the Nazarene Missionary Sanitarium and Institute. Nampa, Ida., 1936. Unpaged.

4557 SCHOOL OF Theology. Est. 1918. Regina, Sask., 1918-1919.
Pentecostal Church of the Nazarene.

4558 SEATTLE PACIFIC College. Est. 1891. Seattle, Wash., 1891-Present.
1891-1916 as Seattle Seminary.
Free Methodist Church of North America.

4559 SEMINARIO NAZARENO de México. Est. 1922. Mexico City, Mex., 1922-1947.
Church of the Nazarene.

4560 SEMINARIO NAZARENO Hispanoamericano. Est. 1942. Los Angeles, Calif., 1942-1947; San Antonio, Tex., 1947-Present.
1942-1947 as Spanish Bible College (extension of Pasadena College); 1947-1963 as Instituto Biblico Nazareno.
Church of the Nazarene.

4561   SHARON BIBLE and High School. Est. 1944. Madera, Calif., 1944-19??.
Pentecostal Holiness Church.

4562   SOUTHEASTERN HOLINESS College. Est. 1912. Donalsonville, Ga., 1912-1918.
Also as Shingler Holiness College.
1918 merged with Trevecca College.
Pentecostal Church of the Nazarene, 1916-1918.

4563   SOUTHWESTERN COLLEGE. Est. 1946. Oklahoma City, Okla., 1946-Present.
1946-19?? as Southwestern Pentecostal Holiness Bible College; 19??-1962 as Southwestern Bible College.
Pentecostal Holiness Church.

4564   SPOKANE PILGRIM Bible School. Est. 1937. Spokane, Wash., 1937-1939; Clarkston, Wash., 1939-1942.
Pilgrim Holiness Church.

4565   SPRING ARBOR College. Est. 1873. Spring Arbor, Mich., 1873-Present.
1873-1947 as Spring Arbor Seminary; 1947-1960 as Spring Arbor Junior College.
Free Methodist Church of North America.

4566   Killion, Mead W.
"A history of Spring Arbor Seminary and Junior College." Unpublished M.A. thesis, University of Michigan, 1941. v, 106ℓ.

4567   Smith, Roderick Jackson
"An analysis of the transition from the junior college program to that of a four-year liberal arts institution at Spring Arbor Junior College." Unpublished Ed.D. dissertation, Michigan State University, 1961. 145ℓ.

4568   Snyder, Howard Albert
One hundred years at Spring Arbor; a history of Spring Arbor College, 1873-1973. Spring Arbor, Mich., Spring Arbor College, 1973. xx, 160 p.

4569   The urban crisis; a symposium on the racial problem in the inner city. General editor: David McKenna. Grand Rapids, Mich., Zondervan Publishing House, 1969. 146 p.
Papers presented at a seminar held at Spring Arbor College in Jan. 1968.

4570   TAYLOR UNIVERSITY. Est. 1846. Fort Wayne, Ind., 1846-1890; Upland, Ind., 1890-Present.
1846-1852 as Fort Wayne Female College; 1852 merged with Collegiate Institute of Fort Wayne; 1852-1890 as Fort Wayne College.

Part V. Schools

4571 TRAINING HOME and Bible College. Est. 19??. Edinburgh, Scot., 19??-Present.
Faith Mission.

4572 TRANSYLVANIA BIBLE School. Est. 1938. Freeport, Pa., 1938-Present.

4573 Shilling, Henry, 1902-
Seven years of faith; or, Explorations in the realm of prayer. Freeport, Pa., Fountain Press, 1972. 224 p.
Reprint of 1945 ed.

4574 Shilling, Henry, 1902-
The second seven years of faith (1945-1952); Transylvania Bible School, a name that has circled the globe in only fourteen years. Freeport, Pa., Fountain Press, 195?. 332 p.

4575 Shilling, Henry, 1902-
Thirty years of faith in pictures: Transylvania Bible School. Freeport, Pa., 1971. 288 p.

4576 Wintermantel, Ed
"The state of Transylvania; faith, hope and Henry Shilling have guided this western Pennsylvania Bible school through 33 frugal years, and the end's not yet in sight," Pittsburgh Press, Nov. 14, 1971, 4-5.

4577 TREVECCA NAZARENE College. Est. 1901. Nashville, Tenn., 1901-Present.
1901-1910 as Pentecostal Bible and Training School, also as Missionary Training Institute; 1910-1935 as Trevecca College.
Pentecostal Mission, 1901-1915; Pentecostal Church of the Nazarene, 1915-1919; Church of the Nazarene, 1919-Present.

4578 Williams, Eugene
"History of Trevecca Nazarene College." Unpublished B.D. thesis, Nazarene Theological Seminary, 1956. 147ℓ.

4579 UNION BIBLE Seminary. Est. 1911. Westfield, Ind., 1911-Present.
Central Yearly Meeting of Friends.

4580 UNITED WESLEYAN College. Est. 1972. Allentown, Pa., 1972-Present.
Wesleyan Church.

4581 UPLAND COLLEGE. Est. 1920. Upland, Calif., 1920-1965.
1920-1949 as Beulah College.
1965 merged with Messiah College.
Brethren in Christ Church.

4582 VENNARD COLLEGE. Est. 1910. Chicago, Ill., 1910-1951; University Park, Iowa, 1951-Present.

1910-1959 as Chicago Evangelistic Institute.
4583 Eckert, Ruth M., 1922-
"Plans and materials for use in the teaching of Bible biographies, a course offered at Vennard College, University Park, Iowa." Unpublished M.S.E. thesis (field report), Drake University, 1963. 125¢.
4584 Jessop, Harry Edward, 1884-
Foundations of doctrine in scripture and experience; a students' handbook on holiness. Chicago, Chicago Evangelistic Institute, 1938. 252 p.
4585 Jessop, Harry Edward, 1884-
The heritage of holiness. Chicago, Chicago Evangelistic Institute, 1950. 94 p.
4586 Jessop, Harry Edward, 1884-
Spiritual security; a meditation on the mutual responsibility of the Lord and the believing soul for eternal salvation. Intercession City, Fla., Central Florida Bible Institute; University Park, Iowa, Chicago Evangelistic Institute, 1953. 24 p.
4587 Jessop, Harry Edward, 1884-
We the Holiness people; the things we believe and teach. Chicago, Chicago Evangelistic Institute, 1948. 110 p.
"Endorsed and recommended by the National Association for the Promotion of Holiness."
4588 Jessop, Harry Edward, 1884-
We the holiness people; endorsed and recommended by the National Association for the Promotion of Holiness. Chicago, Chicago Evangelistic Institute, 1948. 95 p.
4589 Wesley, John, 1703-1791.
On patience. Chicago, Chicago Evangelistic Institute Press, n.d. Unpaged. (Spiritual life classics, no. 1)

4590 VIRGINIA SEMINARY. Est. 188?. Spotsylvania, Va., 188?-189?.
Free Methodist Church of North America.

4591 WARNER MEMORIAL University. Est. 1929. Eastland, Tex., 1929-1932.
Church of God (Anderson, Indiana).

4592 WARNER PACIFIC College. Est. 1937. Spokane, Wash., 1937-1940; Portland, Ore., 1940-Present.
Church of God (Anderson, Indiana).

4593 WASIOJA INSTITUTE. Est. 1873. Wasioja, Minn., 1873-1892.
Wesleyan Methodist Connection of America.

4594 WESLEYAN INSTITUTE. Est. 1844. Dracut, Mass., 1844-1846.
Weslayan Methodist Connection of America.

Part V. Schools 565

4595 WESLEYAN METHODIST Bible College. Est. 1949. Melbourne, Austl., 1949-Present.
Wesleyan Methodist Church of America, 1949-1968; Wesleyan Church, 1968-Present.

4596 WESSINGTON SPRINGS College. Est. 1887. Wessington Springs, S.D., 1887-1968.
1887-1918 as Wessington Springs Seminary; 1964-1968 as Wessington Springs Academy.
Free Methodist Church of North America.

4597 WESTERN CHRISTIAN High School. Est. 1920. Upland, Calif., 1920-1963; Pomona, Calif., 1963-1970; Glendora, Calif., 1970-Present.
1920-1963 as Upland Academy, high school department of Upland College.
Brethren in Christ Church, 1920-1963.

4598 WESTERN EVANGELICAL Seminary. Est. 1947. Portland, Ore., 1947-Present.
4599 Wynkoop, Mildred (Bangs)
An existential interpretation of the doctrine of holiness; a message presented in chapel service, Western Evangelical Seminary, Portland, Oregon, November 3, 1955. Portland, Ore., Western Evangelical Seminary, 195?. 15 p.

4600 WESTERN PILGRIM College. Est. 1932. El Monte, Calif., 1932-1960.
1932-1946 as Holiness Evangelistic Institute; 1946-195? as Pilgrim Evangelistic Institute; 195?-1955 as Pilgrim Bible Institute.
1960 merged with Central Pilgrim College.
Holiness Church, 1932-1946; Pilgrim Holiness Church, 1946-1960.

4601 WESTMINSTER COLLEGE and Bible Institute. Est. 1953. Tehuacana, Tex., 1953-1972; Florence, Miss., 1972-Present.
Congregational Methodist Church.

4602 WHEATON SEMINARY. Est. 1881. Wheaton, Ill., 1881-1890.
Theological program affiliated with Wheaton College.
Wesleyan Methodist Connection of America.

4603 ZAREPHATH BIBLE Seminary. Est. 19??. Zarephath, N.J., 19??-Present.
19??-19?? as Pillar of Fire Bible and Missionary Training School; 19??-19?? as Zarephath Bible Institute.
Pillar of Fire Church.

Part VI

BIOGRAPHY

As with Part V, this part contains directory information and related bibliography. Individuals are listed alphabetically regardless of their denominational affiliation. The name of the person, with birth and death dates, is followed by abbreviations for collective works where biographical information may be found. This in turn is followed by a record of denominational affiliation(s), occupation(s), and dates and places of birth and death. If bibliography is included, works written by the person listed precede those about him. For collective biography or testimonials of a particular association or church, see --BIOGRAPHY as a subdivision under the group.

4604 AARON, Thomas Lee (1897-1951). SEC (1968), 78-103.
PeHC. Pastor, college pres.
b. Aug. 4, 1897, Jackson County, Ga.
d. Jan. 20, 1951, Franklin Springs, Ga.

4605 ABBOTT, Hollis F. GTWATD (1965), 292-305.
WM, W. Pastor?, missionary (WGM)

4606 ABBOTT, John D. (1922-   ). TDOOP (1968), 346-347.
PHC, W. Pastor, district supt., denominational official, general supt.
b. 1922, Wyoming, Del.
4607 "Conference elects 11 officers," Wesleyan Advocate, CXXVII (July 15, 1968), 8.
4608 "Elected officials of The Wesleyan Church," Wesleyan Advocate, CXXX (July 24, 1972), 14.

4609 ACKERS, Hiram.
Attended GHA, 1901 (Chicago).
WM. Pastor, conference pres.

4610 ACORNLEY, Agnes Rebecca
PrimM. Pastor's wife.
4611 Acornley, John Holmes
Sunshine among the mountains; or, The young pastor's wife: being memorials of Mrs. Agnes Rebecca Acornley ... by her husband.... Brooklyn, H. Daisley, 1876. 130 p.

4612 ACORNLEY, John Holmes
PrimM. Pastor.

4613 Acornley, John Holmes
Scraps from my valise; or, A trip to Europe, with incidents by the way. To be sold for the benefit of the P.M. Church at Williamstown. Lykens, Pa., "Register" print, 1876. 23 p.

4614 ADAMS, Benjamin Mathias (1823-1902). MAWACOSM (1925), 320.
N.Y. Times (Dec. 24, 1902), 9:6
HConf., 1877 (New York), Founding member, NHA
ME. Pastor, evangelist.

4615 ADAMS, Charles Jackson (1925-   ). WWACUA (1970-1971), 2.
PHC. Pastor, college admin.
b. Dec. 8, 1925, Indianapolis, Ind.

4616 ADAMS, Homer James (1921-   ). WWACUA (1970-1971), 2-3.
CN. College prof., college admin.
b. July 2, 1921, Andalusia, Ala.

4617 AGNEW, George Harry Augustus (1964-1903) LLITW (1951), 215.
FM. Missionary.

4618 Hogue, Wilson Thomas, 1852-1920.
G. Harry Agnew, a pioneer missionary; introd. by the Rev. Edward Payson Hart. Chicago, Free Methodist Publishing House, 1905. 317 p.

4619 AGNEW, Lillie Smith (-1939). LLITW (1951), 215.
FM. Missionary.

4620 AGNEW, Milton Seccombe. GTWATD (1965), 352-362.
SA. Officer, officer training school prin.

4621 AGNEW, Susie Sherman (-1895). LLITW (1951), 215.
FM. Missionary.

4622 AGNEW, T. H. (-1924). FYAB (1954), 89-91.
Attended GHA, 1901 (Chicago).
ME, CN. District supt., college bus. mgr.
d. Mar. 19, 1924.

4623 AKERS, John W.
ME, CN, PCN. Public school prin., lay preacher.

4624 AKERS, Lewis Robeson (1881-   ). WW in the Clergy (1935-1936), 22. RLOA (1941-1942), 11. ATY (1930), 144-155.
ME, M. Pastor, college pres., college prof.
b. Aug. 25, 1881, Asheville, N.C.

Part VI. Biography

4625 ALDERFER, Owen Hiram (1923-). DAS (1969), IV, 4.
BIC. College prof., seminary prof.
b. June 7, 1923, Upland, Calif.

4626 ALEJANDRO, D. D. NVFML (1936), 27-40.
Cath., ME. National worker, pastor.

4627 ALEXANDER, John Wesley (1918-). CA. AMS (1965-1968), VII, 19.
FM, Bapt. Leader's child, university prof., youth worker.
b. Apr. 7, 1918, Greenville, Ill.
4628 Alexander, John Wesley, 1918-
Thoughts from the sea. Winona Lake, Ind., Young People's Missionary Society, 1947. 159 p.
Autobiographical.
4629 Belleau Wood (Aircraft carrier)
"Flight quarters"; the story of the U.S.S. Belleau Wood. Los Angeles, Cole-Holmquist Press, 1946. 192 p.
"Editor: Lt. John W. Alexander."

4630 ALLAN, David (-1940). SBWTL (1960), 184.
Pres., FM. Lumber camp foreman, pastor, district elder.
b. 18??, Barkway, Ont.

4631 ALLEE, George Franklin (1897-).
CN. Pastor, evangelist.
b. 1897, Minnesota.

4632 ALLEN, Edric Drell (1917-). WWACUA (1970-1971), 6.
CN. Pastor, college prof., college admin.
b. Oct. 12, 1917, South Fork, Pa.

4633 ALLEN, Jacob Randolph (1838-1924).
Member, IowaHA.
Attended GHA, 1901 (Chicago)
ME. Pastor.
b. Apr. 5, 1838
d. Apr. 27, 1924

4634 ALLEN, John (1795-1887). SCM (1881), 973.
ME. Pastor, evangelist.
4635 Allen, Stephen, 1810-1888.
The life of Rev. John Allen, better known as "Camp-meeting John"; to which is added tributes and eulogies, by Dr. Charles Cullis, Rev. R. B. Howard ... and others. Boston, B.B. Russell, 1888. 140 p.
"Biographical sketch of Rev. John Allen, by Rev. William McDonald," p. 87-101.

4636   ALLING, Jacob Hart (1837-1919).
        Attended GHA, 1901 (1901)
        ME. Pastor
        b. June 25, 1837
        d. Dec. 25, 1919

4637   ALLYN, Robert (1917-1894). SCM (1881), 30. WWW in
            Am. (1607-1896), 21. PPE (1868), 71-75.
        ME. Pastor, academy prin., public schools commissioner, university prof., college pres., university pres.
        b. Jan. 25, 1817, Ledyard, Conn.
        d. Jan. 7, 1894, Carbondale, Ill.

4638   AMOLIK, B. D. HNTB (1934), 103.
        FM, CN. National worker, Bible school teacher.
        b. 189?, India

4639   AMSDEN, F. W. (-1940). LLITW (1951), 215.
        FM. Missionary.

4640   ANDERSON, Alfred (1851-1921). WW in Am. Meth. (1916), 4.
        Attended GHA, 1901 (Chicago)
        ME. Pastor, presiding elder, mgr., Swedish Book Concern.
        b. Mar. 3, 1851, Sweden
        d. Feb. 11, 1921

4641   ANDERSON, August Magnus (1878-   ). WW among N.A. Authors (1933-1935), 23.
        FM. Missionary
        b. May 18, 1878, Norway

4642   ANDERSON, Mack. MLA (1935), 21-25.
        CN. Evangelist, district supt.

4643   ANDERSON, Richard Simpson (1882-1945).
        PM, CN. Missionary
        b. Nov. 30, 1882, Laurens, S.C.
        d. May 17, 1945, Coban, Guatemala
4644   Birchard, Russell
            Richard Simpson Anderson, pioneer missionary to Central America, by Russell and Margaret Anderson Birchard. Kansas City, Mo., Beacon Hill Press, 1951. 112 p.

4645   ANDERSON, T. H. B.
        ME? Pastor?
4646   Anderson, T. H. B.
            A remarkable experience. n.p., n.d. 8 p.
            Caption title.

Part VI. Biography

4647 ANDERSON, Tony Marshall (1888-   ). MLA (1935), 27-30.
      ME, CN. Evangelist
      b. Apr. 30, 1888, Westport, Ky.

4648 ANDREE, Paul. CIOCC (1959), 14-15.
      ME, CN. Pastor.

4649 ANGELL, Ernest E. (-1939).
      Cong., APCA, CN. Pastor, district supt., college
          prof., college pres.
      d. May 12, 1939

4650 APPLETON, C. Floyd (1881-1932). LLITW (1951), 215.
          SBWTL (1960), 202-203.
      FM. Missionary, college prof.
      b. 1881, Vivian, Ont.
      d. 1932, Seattle, Wash.

4651 APPLETON, Laura Millican (-1939). LLITW (1951), 215.
      FM. Missionary.

4652 ARKSEY, Lawrence E. (1898-   ). SBWTL (1960), 204-205.
      FM, Pres. Pastor, missionary
      b. 1898, Belhaven, Ont.

4653 ARMS, Goodsil Filley (1854-   ). WW in Am. Meth. (1916),
          6.
      ME. Pastor, missionary
      b. Jan. 22, 1854, Sutton, Que., Can.

4654 ARMSTRONG, Chauncey Irwin (1896-   ). WW in the Clergy
          (1935-1936), 42-43. SCC (1947), 9-16.
      President, NHA, 1942-1946
      WM, W. Pastor, missionary, evangelistic singer
      b. Feb. 23, 1896

4655 ARMSTRONG, William T. DCSWM (1946), 131-134.
      CN. Military chaplain

4656 ARNETT, William Melvin (1915-   ). DAS (1969), IV, 11.
          GIIH (1962), 54-72. GTWATD (1965), 156-170.
          BPOH (1969), 86-111.
      M, UM. Seminary prof., pastor, evangelist
      b. Jan. 23, 1915, Clay Center, Kan.

4657 ARNOLD, John Motte (1824-1884).
      ME. Pastor, editor
4658 Arnold, John Motte, 1824-1884.
          Selections from the autobiography of Rev. J.M. Arnold, and from his editorial writings on the doctrine of sanctification, comp. and arranged by M.A. Broughton.

Ann Arbor, Mich., Index Publishing House, 1885. 113 p.
Autobiography.

4659 ARNOLD, Thomas B.
Attended GHA, 1901 (Chicago)
FM. Publisher

4660 ARNOLD, William Erastus (1862-   ). WW in the Clergy (1935-1936), 44.
ME, S. Pastor, editor, presiding elder
b. Jan. 9, 1862, Bourbon County, Ky.

4661 ARTHUR, William (1819-1901). MWWW in Ch. Hist. (1968).
Pres., WM (Eng.). Missionary, pastor, college prin., writer
b. 1819, Kells, County Antrim, Ire.
d. 1901, France

4662 ASLIN, Bessie Ruth (1905-1967). ETWF (196?).
PHC. Pastor's wife, missionary
b. Dec. 24, 1905, Peabody, Kan.
d. Apr. 24, 1967

4663 ASLIN, Thomas Elbert (1904-   ). ETWF (196?).
PHC. Pastor, missionary
b. Nov. 5, 1904, Idalia, Mo.

4664 ATKINSON, Elbert L. DCSWM (1946), 150-153.
CN. Military chaplain.

4665 ATWOOD, Anthony (1801-1888). SCM (1881), 70.
Offered resolution at meeting, June 13, 1867, suggesting camp meeting as potential means of promoting holiness. Adopted unanimously by meeting at Philadelphia. NHA formed.
ME. Pastor
b. June 27, 1801, Burlington County, N.J.
d. Nov. 19, 1888

4666 Atwood, Anthony, 1801-1888.
A pastor's legacy to those for whose benefit he has spent his life; or, A final appeal to the careless, the inquiring and the believing in relation to life and usefulness. Philadelphia, Perkinpine & Higgins, 1866. 211 p.

4667 AUSTEL, Kathe P. NVFML (1936), 41-56.
ME? Missionary?

4668 AVERY, Arietta M. (1910-   ). ETWF (196?).
PHC. Pastor's wife, missionary
b. Dec. 22, 1910, Montebello, Calif.

Part VI. Biography

4669 AVERY, Gordon Coleman (1913-). ETWF (196?).
PHC. Pastor, evangelist, missionary
b. Sept. 23, 1913, Panola County, Miss.

4670 AWE, Benjamin A. (-1960). TDOOP (1968), 342.
PHC. Pastor, district supt.
d. Sept. 7, 1960
4671 Pilgrim Holiness Advocate, XL (Oct. 8, 1960), 5.

4672 AWESU, Jonathan. SWGHW (1948), 41.
MBIC, UMC. National worker, mission school headmaster.
4673 Darrell, Lila M.
Africa's challenge: story of Jonathan Awesu. n.p., n.d. 44 p.

4674 AYARS, John E.
ME. Pastor, evangelist

4675 AYCOCK, Dell Davis (-1967). MLA (1935), 32-38.
ME, S; CN. Pastor's wife, evangelistic singer
4676 Aycock, Dell (Davis) -1967.
From darkness to dawn, an autobiography. Kansas City, Mo., Nazarene Publishing House, 1941. 79 p.
4677 Aycock, Jarrette E. -1966.
The story of two prodigals, a true story by Evangelist Jarrette E. Aycock.... Kansas City, Mo., Nazarene Publishing House, 1930. 48 p.
Autobiographical.

4678 AYCOCK, Jarrette E. (-1966). MLA (1935), 32-38. NP (1925), 161-173.
ME, S; CN. Pastor, evangelist, district supt.
4679 Aycock, Jarrette E. -1966.
He lifted me, an autobiography; the life story of Jarrette Aycock, D.D. Kansas City, Mo., Beacon Hill Press, 1962. 23 p.
4680 Aycock, Jarrette E. -1966.
The story of two prodigals, a true story by Evangelist Jarrette E. Aycock.... Kansas City, Mo., Nazarene Publishing House, 1930. 48 p. front. (Port.)
4681 Henry, Helga (Bender)
Mission on Main Street. Boston, W.A. Wilde Co., 1955. 200 p.
Contains chapter on Jarrette Aycock.

4682 BACKENSTOE, William Alfred (-1932). LLITW (1951), 215.
FM. Missionary

4683 BAILEY, Bertram Henry. FHOP (1964).
CN. Pastor, evangelist

4684 BAILEY, Bessie A. FHOP (1964).
CN. Pastor's wife

4685 BAKER, Harold Edwin (1896-   ).
FM. Evangelist, missionary
b. 1896, Angola, N.Y.
4686 Baker, Harold Edwin, 1896-
Sackcloth and purple. East Liverpool, Ohio, 1945. 158 p.
Autobiography.

4687 BAKER, Mrs. Harriet
PrimM. Evangelist
4688 Acornley, John Holmes
The colored lady evangelist; being the life, labors and experiences of Mrs. Harriet Baker. Brooklyn, N.Y., 1892. 78 p.

4689 BAKER, Leonidas H. (1850-1933).
Attended GHA, 1901 (Chicago)
ME. Pastor
b. Mar. 23, 1850
d. Apr. 30, 1933

4690 BAKER, Mrs. Sarah. ROG (1854), 223-225.
ME? Lay member

4691 BAKER, Sheridan (1824-1890).
Unable to attend H. Conf., 1877 (Cincinnati)
ME. Pastor
d. Mar. 30, 1890
4692 Baker, Sheridan, 1824-1890.
The hidden manna; being a view of Christian holiness taken from the standpoint of personal and general experience, with scriptural confirmations introduced with the author's experience. Boston, McDonald, Gill & Co., 1887. 278 p.
4693 Baker, Sheridan, 1824-1890.
The hidden manna; being a view of Christian holiness taken from the standpoint of personal and general experience, with scriptural confirmations, introduced with the author's experience. Salem, Ohio, Convention Book Store, H.E. Schmul, 1971. 278 p.
Reprint of 1887 ed.
4694 Baker, Sheridan, 1824-1890.
Living waters; being Bible expositions and addresses given at different camp-meetings and to ministers and Christian workers on various other occasions, introduced with the author's experience in spreading holiness. 3d ed., corrected and enl. New York, Phillips & Hunt; Cincinnati, Cranston & Stowe, 1888. 314 p.

4695 Baker, Sheridan, 1824-1890.
A peculiar people: being expositions, addresses, and posthumous papers; ed. by Rev. G. F. Oliver, introd. by Bishop Isaac W. Joyce. Boston, McDonald, Gill & Co., 1890. 195 p.

4696 BALDWIN, Harmon Allen (1869-1936). WW in the Clergy (1935-1936), 62. WWW in Am. (1897-1942), 50.
FM. Evangelist, missionary, pastor, writer
b. June 3, 1869, Pierpont, Ashtabula County, Ohio
d. Mar. 11, 1936, Pittsburgh, Pa.

4697 BALL, Ephraim (1812-1872). SCM (1881), 79-80. WWW in Am. (1607-1896), 38.
ME. Inventor, local preacher
b. Aug. 12, 1812, Lake Township, Ohio
d. Jan. 1, 1872, Stark County, Ohio

4698 BALLARD, Aaron Edward (1820-1919). WW in Am. Meth. (1916), 11-12. WWW in Am. (1897-1942), 51-52.
N.Y. Times (Nov. 28, 1919), 13:1.
Signed call to form NHA, 1867 (Philadelphia)
Endorsed call, GHA, 1901 (Chicago)
ME. Pastor, presiding elder
b. Dec. 25, 1820, Bloomfield, N.J.
d. Nov. 27, 1919, Ocean Grove, N.J.

4699 BALSMEIER, A. F. NP (1925), 194-201.
CN. Pastor, evangelist, district supt.

4700 BANFIELD, A. W. (1878-   ). SWGHW (1948), 29-37, 53, 78, 79, 130.
MBIC. Missionary, linguist
b. Aug. 3, 1878, Quebec City, Que., Can.

4701 Banfield, A. W., 1878-
Dictionary of the Nupe language. Shonga, Nigeria, Niger Press, 1914-1916. 2 v.

4702 [Banfield, A. W., 1878-   ]
Gamaga Nupe (Nupe proverbs) [comp. and tr. by] A. W. B. Shonga, Nigeria, Niger Press, 1916.

4703 Banfield, A. W., 1878-
A grammar of the Nupe language, together with a vocabulary, by A.W. Banfield and J.L. Macintyre. London, Society for Promoting Christian Knowledge, 1915. 186 p.

4704 Banfield, A. W., 1878-
Life among the Nupe tribe in West Africa. Berlin, Ont., Can., H.S. Hallman, 1905. 79 p.

4705 BANGS, Carl Oliver (1922-   ). DAS (1969), IV, 16.
CN, UM. Pastor, college prof., seminary prof.
b. Apr. 5, 1922, Seattle Wash.

4706   Bangs, Carl Oliver, 1922-
          Arminius: a study in the Dutch Reformation. Nashville, Abingdon Press, 1971. 382 p.
4707   Bangs, Carl Oliver, 1922-
          "Arminius and Reformed theology." Unpublished Ph.D. dissertation, University of Chicago, 1958. 285ℓ.
4708   Bangs, Carl Oliver, 1922-
          Arminius and reformed theology. Chicago, Department of Photoduplication, University of Chicago Library, 1958.
            Microfilm copy (positive) of typescript.
            Collation of the original: 285ℓ.
            Thesis--University of Chicago.
4709   Bangs, Carl Oliver, 1922-
          German-English theological word list. Rev. ed. Kansas City, Mo., 1962. 16 p.
4710   Bangs, Carl Oliver, 1922-
          "James Arminius and the Remonstrants." Unpublished B.D. thesis, Nazarene Theological Seminary, 1949.

4711   BANGS, Nathan (1778-1862). WWW in Am. (1607-1896), 38. SCM (1881), 85-86. Nat. Cy. Am. Biog., 9:429. DAB.
          ME. Pastor, presiding elder, editor, acting univ. pres.
          b. May 2, 1778, Stratford, Conn.
          d. May 3, 1862
4712   Janes, Edmund Storer, bp., 1807-1876.
          Sermon on the death of Nathan Bangs. New York, Carlton and Porter, 1862. 31 p.
4713   Stevens, Abel, 1815-1897.
          The life and times of Nathan Bangs. New York, Carlton & Porter, 1863. 426 p.
4714   Tuttle, Alexander Harrison, 1844-1932.
          Nathan Bangs. New York, Eaton & Mains; Cincinnati, Jennings & Graham, 1909. 127 p.

4715   BANKER, E. Stanley (1918-   ). WWACUA (1970-1971), 24.
          WM, W. College prof., college admin.
          b. Feb. 3, 1918, Shelbyville, Ind.

4716   BANKER, Max Emerson (1920-   ). WWACUA (1970-1971), 24.
          WM, W. Missionary, college admin.
          b. Apr. 10, 1920, Shelbyville, Ind.

4717   BANKS, Stanley
          JEB, EBCM, FM. Missionary, Bible college prin.

4718   BAREFOOT, Adlie E. (1925-   ). ETWF (196?).
          PHC. Missionary
          b. Mar. 12, 1925, Erwin, N.C.

Part VI. Biography 577

4719 BAREFOOT, Laurette Ilene (1929-). ETWF (196?).
PHC. Missionary
b. Sept. 24, 1929, Whitley County, Ind.

4720 BARNES, Grace Elizabeth (1890-1918).
FM. Missionary
b. Apr. 9, 1890, Pennsylvania
d. Oct. 19, 1918, Yeotmal, India
4721 Root, Helen Isabel, 1873-1945.
An alabaster box; the life story of Grace E. Barnes. Introduction by Mrs. Mary L. Coleman. Chicago, Woman's Missionary Society, Free Methodist Church, 1929. 102 p.

4722 BARNES, O. W. (-1965).
PHC. Pastor
d. Oct. 4, 1965.

4723 BARRETT, Clifford Bean (1821-1899).
FM. Evangelist
b. May 6, 1821, Bethlehem, Grafton County, N.H.
d. Dec. 17, 1899, Gerry, N.Y.
4724 Rhodes, M. L.
Clifford B. Barrett, the "Happy Alleghenian"; introd. by Bishop Walter A. Sellew. Salem, Ohio, Convention Book Store, n.d. 192 p.

4725 BARRETT, Earl Edward (1893-). DAS (1969), IV, 18.
RLOA (1941-1942), 58.
WM, CN. Pastor, college prof., college admin.
b. Sept. 22, 1893, South Dayton, N.Y.

4726 BARRETT, William H. SCC (1947), 17-21.
SA. Denominational official, commissioner

4727 BASSETT, Helen Fair (1917-). ETWF (196?).
PHC. Missionary
b. Jan. 26, 1917, Westville, Ill.

4728 BASSETT, Roger Garfield (1921-). ETWF (196?).
PHC. Missionary
b. Apr. 11, 1921, Roseville, Mich.

4729 BATES, Lewis Benton. GFW (1888), 135-137.
ME. Pastor

4730 BAUER, Betty May (1928-). ETWF (196?).
PHC. Pastor's wife, missionary
b. Mar. 25, 1928, Muncy, Pa.

4731 BAUER, Lawrence Paul (1926-). ETWF (196?).
PHC. Pastor, missionary
b. Sept. 30, 1926, Camden, N.J.

4732 BAXTER, Mrs. M. GFW (1888), 277-279.
      Ch. of Eng. Lay member

4733 BEACHAM, Paul Franklin (1888-). RLOA (1941-1942), 67-68.
      PeHC. Pastor, Bible college pres., denominational official, editor
      b. Sept. 18, 1888, Oconee County, S.C.
4734   Thomas, Iva
          History of Holmes Theological Seminary. Franklin Springs, Ga., 1959. 47 p.
          "Dr. Paul F. Beacham, now president and treasurer": p. 24-47.

4735 BEALS, Charles Arthur (1906-). RLOA (1941-1942), 68.
      Fr. Academy teacher, Bible college prof., pastor, Bible college pres.
      b. July 26, 1906, Searsboro, Iowa

4736 BEARE, Thomas J. (-1919). LLITW (1951), 215.
      FM. Missionary

4737 BEARSE, Joseph C. (1869-1931).
      CEHA, APCA, PCN, ME. Pastor, Bible school principal
      b. Oct. 24, 1869, South Chatham, Mass.
      d. July 2, 1931, South Portland, Me.

4738 BEATTY, Charles L. (1934-). WWACUA (1970-1971), 32.
      CN. College admin.
      b. Feb. 12, 1934, Grand Rapids, Mich.

4739 BECKWITH, Berdina (-1950). LLITW (1951), 215.
      FM. Missionary

4740 BEEBE, Theodore Eaton
      ME, CN. Pastor, district supt.

4741 BEEGLE, Gladys Smith (-1947). LLITW (1951), 215.
      FM. Missionary, pastor's wife

4742 BEEMAN, Samuel David (1922-). WWACUA (1970-1971), 33.
      CN. Pastor, college prof., college admin.
      b. Sept. 20, 1922, Tucumcari, N.M.

4743 BEERS, Adelaide Lionne Newton (-1940).
      FM. Missionary
4744   Beers, Adelaide Lionne Newton, -1940.
          The romance of a consecrated life. Chicago, Free Methodist Publishing House, 1922.

Part VI. Biography

4745   BEET, Joseph Agar (1940-1924). MWWW in Ch. Hist. (1968), 35-36.
          WM (Eng.). College prof., university prof.
          b. 1840, Sheffield, Eng.
          d. 1924

4746   BEIRNES, George (-1942).
          PHC, CN. Missionary, pastor, district supt.
          d. Aug. 1942

4747   BEIRNES, William F.
          IHC, PHC. Pastor, evangelist, missionary, district supt., editor
4748   Beirnes, William F.
              On angel wings. Tequesta, Fla., Midnight Cry, 19??. 16 p.
              On the death of the author's son, Billy.

4749   BELDEN, Henry (1813-1884). PPE (1868), 109-118.
          Pres., Cong. Pastor, abolitionist
          b. 1813, Greenfield, Conn.
          d. June 24, 1884, New York, N.Y.

4750   BELEW, Pascal Perry (1894-).
          HCC, CN. Pastor, evangelist
          b. 1894, Dry Ridge, Grant Co., Ky.
4751   Belew, Pascal Perry, 1894-
              My old Kentucky home; or, Experiences from life. Kansas City, Mo., Printed for Rev. P.P. Belew by the Nazarene Publishing House, 1925? 48 p.

4752   BELL, Dewayne Bert (1920-). WWACUA (1970-1971), 35.
          CG (A). College pres., college admin.
          b. May 12, 1920, Sacramento, Calif.

4753   BELL, Thomas
          Meth. (Can.), CN. Pastor, evangelist
4754   Bell, Thomas
              Breaking new trails. Edmonton, Alta., Can., Commercial Printers, Ltd., n.d.

4755   BELTZ, Roy Allen (1905-). TDOOP (1968), 284-285.
          PHC, W. Pastor, district supt., denominational official
          b. 1905, Marshall, Ill.

4756   BENARGEES, Mrs. Sukhoda
          CN. National worker
          b. 18??, Calcutta, India
4757   The story of Mrs. Sokhoda Benargees and Hope School, Calcutta, India. Los Angeles, Nazarene Publishing Co., 1906.

4758   BENN, Miles S. (1867-   ). SBWTL (1960), 184-185.
        FM. Pastor, district elder

4759   BENNARD, George (1873-1958). LMGSS (1952), 69. SFLF
            (1950), 9-11. CHHMH (1970), 486-487. N.Y. Times
            (Oct. 11, 1958), 23:6. LDML (1953), 74.
        SA, ME, M. Gospel song writer, evangelist
        b. Feb. 4, 1873, Youngstown, Ohio
        d. Oct. 10, 1958, Reed City, Mich.

4760   BENNER, Elias Stephen (1867-1957).
        ME, CN. Farmer
        b. 1867, Randolph County, Ind.
        d. 1957, Pasadena, Calif.
4761   Benner, Hugh Clifford, 1899-
            Rendevous with abundance. Kansas City, Mo., Beacon Hill Press, 1958. 126 p.

4762   BENNER, Hugh Clifford (1899-   ). RLOA (1941-1942), 82.
        CN. College prof., pastor, seminary pres., general
            supt.
        b. Apr. 4, 1899, Marion, Ohio

4763   BENNER, Rol Welbourn (1901-   ). RLOA (1941-1942), 82.
            WW in Am. (1946-1947).
        CN, Univ. College prof., pastor, seminary dean
        b. June 12, 1901, Marion, Ohio

4764   BENNET, P. C. PPE (1868), 262-268.
        ME. Pastor

4765   BENNETT, J. D. (-1899). LLITW (1951), 215.
        FM. Missionary

4766   BENNETT, Willis G. NP (1925), 21-31.
        ME, LAH, CN. Pastor, evangelist
4767   Bennett, Willis G.
            History of the great Cumberland revival of 1800 and
            other revivals. n.p., 1945. 114 p.
4768   Bennett, Willis G.
            The supreme command of Jesus. n.p., 192?.
            Includes discussion of the author's attitudes toward
            the Methodist Episcopal Church.
4769   Gibson, William, 1808-1867.
            More thrilling than fiction; a history of the great revival in the north of Ireland in 1858-9, rev. and abbreviated by W.G. Bennett. Nashville, Bennett, 1943.
            133 p.

4770   BENSON, Erwin George (1905-   ). RLOA (1941-1942), 83.
        CN. Pastor, college admin., denominational official
        b. July 28, 1905, Oviatt, Mich.

Part VI. Biography 581

4771 BENSON, Eva (1865-1932).
PM, CN. Lay leader
d. Aug. 3, 1932

4772 BENSON, John T. (1861-1930). MOUS (1941), 86-91.
ME, S; PM; CN. Gospel music publisher
b. Feb. 18, 1861, Nashville, Tenn.
d. June 24, 1930, Nashville, Tenn.

4773 BENT, John
Member, NHA
ME? Publisher

4774 BERG, Clifton Fletcher (1908-). ETWF (196?).
PHC, W. Pastor, missionary
b. July 21, 1908, Hallstead, Pa.

4775 BERG, Emeline Ilda Hamel (1914-). ETWF (196?).
PHC. Pastor's wife, missionary, evangelistic singer
b. Nov. 16, 1914, Haverhill, Mass.

4776 BERRY, John A. (-1936).
CN. Evangelist

4777 BERRY, Robert Lee (1874-).
CG (A). Pastor

4778 BEVIN, Karl Heinz Martin (1914-). ETWF (196?).
AEB, PHC. Missionary
b. Sept. 7, 1914, Ermelo, Transvaal

4779 BEVIN, Ruth Ralston (1912-). ETWF (196?).
PHC. Missionary
b. Aug. 19, 1912, Pratt, Kan.

4780 BEVINGTON, Guy C.
ME, IHC, PHC. Rescue mission worker, evangelist
4781 Bevington, Guy C.
Remarkable incidents and modern miracles through
prayer and faith. Cincinnati, God's Bible School and
Revivalist, 1921. 272 p.
Autobiographical.
4782 Bevington, Guy C.
Remarkable incidents and modern miracles through
prayer and faith. Niles, Mich., Newby Book Room,
n.d. 272 p.
Autobiographical.
Reprint of 1921 ed.

4783 BHEMBE, Lillian. HNTB (1934), 114-115.
CN. National worker, mission school teacher, preacher
b. 191?, Swaziland, Afr.

4784 BHUJABAL, David. HNTB (1934), 82-83, 85-87.
CN. National worker, pastor
b. 189?, India

4785 BHUJABAL, Jacob Johns (-1917). HNTB (1934), 83-85.
CN. National worker
d. 1917, India

4786 BHUJABAL, Samuel (1906-). HNTB (1934), 87-89.
CN. National worker, pastor, district supt.
b. 1906, Vasind?, India

4787 BHUJABAL, Yeshodabai. HNTB (1934), 89.
CN. National worker, Bible woman

4788 BICKMORE, Edward C. TDOOP (1968), 287.
HC, PHC. Lay leader

4789 BINNEY, Amos (1802-1878).
ME. Pastor, theologian

4790 BISHOP, Charles H. S. PPE (1868), 343-345.
WM (Eng.). Missionary

4791 BLACK, Ernest Watson (1890-1948). WW in the Clergy (1935-1936), 109.
WM. Pastor
b. Apr. 24, 1890, Rock Hill, S.C.
d. 1948, Kannapolis?, N.C.

4792 BLACK, Harry (1895-).
FM. Pastor, evangelist.
b. June 11, 1895, Pittsburgh, Pa.
4793 Black, Harry, 1895-
From newsboy to preacher; the story of my life. Introductions by Bishop George W. Griffith, Rev. L. Glenn Lewis [and] Rev. Joseph H. Smith. Los Angeles, 19??. 171 p.

4794 BLACK, Lillie F.
HCC, CN. Pastor, evangelist
b. 18??, Indiana

4795 BLACK, Warren
CN. Layman, accountant
b. 192?, Oklahoma
4796 Black, Warren
"A Nazarene finds a new dimension," Full Gospel Business Men's Voice, XX (June 1972), 3-7, 26-28.

4797 BLAKESLEE, G. H. PPE (1868), 326-327.
ME. Pastor

Part VI. Biography 583

4798 BLANCHARD, Charles Lorraine (1902-).
 WM, W. Home missionary worker, pastor, conference pres.
 b. Sept. 17, 1902

4799 BLANEY, Harvey Judson Smith (1905-). WWACUA (1970-1971), 45.
 RB, CN. Pastor, college prof., college admin.
 b. Dec. 21, 1905, Hainesville, N.B., Can.

4800 BLANN, Eva Isabel (1920-). ETWF (196?).
 PHC. Missionary
 b. Nov. 17, 1920, Henderson, N.Y.

4801 BLANN, Henry John (1920-). ETWF (196?).
 PHC. Missionary
 b. Mar. 21, 1920, Northville, N.Y.

4802 BLUMHARDT, John Christoph (1805-1880).
 Luth. Pastor
4803 Carter, Russell Kelso, 1849-1926.
 Pastor Blumhardt; a record of the wonderful spiritual and physical manifestations of God's power ... through the prayers of His servant, Christoph Blumhardt. Boston, Willard Tract Repository, 1883? 92 p.

4804 BOARDMAN, William Edwin (1910-1886).
 Pres. Evangelist, home missionary worker, military chaplain
4805 Boardman, Mary M.
 Life and labours of the Rev. W.E. Boardman; with a preface by Rev. Mark Guy Pearse. New York, D. Appleton, 1887. x, 260 p.

4806 BOLT, E. A. J. (-1924).
 Ch. of Eng., IHM. Curate, pastor
 d. June 15, 1924
4807 Bolt, E. A. J., -1924.
 From the Church of England to the International Holiness Mission. London, International Holiness Mission, 1920.

4808 BOLTON, L. Donald. DCSWM (1946), 106-113.
 CN. Military chaplain

4809 BONE, Lawrence. DCSWM (1946), 92-105.
 CN. Military chaplain

4810 BONNER, Norman Neal (1917-). WWACUA (1970-1971), 50.
 PHC, W. Missionary, college pres., seminary prof.
 b. Apr. 4, 1917, Tabor, Iowa

4811 BOOTH, Bramwell (1856-1929). WW (1929-1940), 134-135.
N.Y. Times (June 17, 1929), 1:4.
SA. Officer, commander-in-chief
b. Mar. 8, 1856, Halifax, Eng.
d. June 16, 1929

4812 Booth, Bramwell, 1856-1929.
Echoes and memories. London, Hodder and Stoughton, 1925. vii, 223 p.

4813 Booth, Catherine Bramwell, 1883-
Bramwell Booth. London, Rich & Cowan, 1933. ix, 541 p.

4814 BOOTH, Catherine Mumford (1829-1890). DNB, XXII, 233-235. MMAWODP (1920), 26-39. MWWW in Ch. Hist. (1968), 50.
WM (Eng.), SA. Pastor's wife, officer
b. Jan 17, 1829, Ashbourne, Derbyshire, Eng.
d. Oct. 4, 1890, Clacton-on-Sea, Essex, Eng.

4815 Booth, Catherine Bramwell, 1883-
Catherine Booth: the story of her loves. London, Hodder and Stoughton, 1970. 477 p.

4816 Booth Tucker, Frederick St. George de Latour, 1853-1929.
The life of Catherine Booth, the mother of the Salvation Army. London, International Headquarters, 18??. 2 v.

4817 BOOTH, William (1829-1912). DNB, suppl. 3, 50-52. LDEFC (1911), 354-363. WWW (1897-1915), 75. MCV (1901), 172-179. MWWW in Ch. Hist. (1968), 51.
Meth. N.C. (Eng.), SA. Pastor, commander-in-chief
b. Apr. 10, 1829, Nottingham, Eng.
d. Aug. 20, 1912, London, Eng.

4818 Begbie, Harold, 1871-
The life of General William Booth, the founder of the Salvation Army. New York, Macmillan, 1920. 2 v.

4819 Collier, Richard, 1924-
The general next to God; the story of William Booth and the Salvation Army. New York, Dutton, 1965. 320 p.

4820 Ervine, St. John Greer, 1883-
God's soldier: General William Booth. New York, Macmillan, 1935. 2 v.

4821 Ives, Charles Edward, 1874-1954.
[General William Booth enters into heaven].
Charles Ives: music for chorus, conducted by Gregg Smith Singers, Ithaca College Concert Choir, the Texas Boys Choir of Fort Worth, the Columbia Chamber Orchestra. New York, Columbia Masterworks, 196?.
1 band 33 rpm (MS 6921)

Part VI. Biography 585

Text by Vachel Lindsay.
Duration: about 6 min.

4822   Nelson, William Hamilton, 1878-
Blood & fire: General William Booth. New York, The Century Co., c1929. xv, 269 p.

4823   Smith, John Evan, 1886-
Booth the beloved; personal recollections of William Booth, founder of the Salvation Army. London, Oxford University Press, 1949. 132 p.

4824   Steele, Harold C.
I was a stranger; the faith of William Booth, founder of the Salvation Army. With a foreword by B.O. Williams. New York, Exposition Press, 1954. 183 p.

4825   BORDE, G. S. HNTB (1934), 102.
WM (Eng.)?, CN. National worker
b. 19??, Ahmednagar District, India

4826   BOSMA, Myrtle Evelyn (1926-). ETWF (196?).
PHC. Missionary
b. June 14, 1926, Waukesha, Wis.

4827   BOTTOME, Francis (1823-1894).
ME. Pastor, gospel song writer
b. May 26, 1823, Derbyshire, Eng.
d. June 29, 1894, England

4828   Bottome, Francis, 1823-1894.
Songs from the parsonage. New York, A.D.F. Randolph and Co., 1894. 166 p.
Dedication signed: Margaret Bottome; biographical sketch (p. 15-24) signed W.M.B. [i.e. William McDonald Bottome].

4829   BOTTOME, Margaret McDonald (1827-1906). WWW in Am. (1897-1942), 119.
ME. Pastor's wife.
b. Dec. 29, 1827, New York, N.Y.

4830   Bottome, Margaret (McDonald), 1827-1906.
Crumbs from the King's table. New York, For the author [by] W. McDonald & Co., 1887. 366 p.

4831   Bottome, Margaret (McDonald), 1827-1906.
Heart to heart letters; being extracts from the letters of Margaret Bottome to a son. New York, Hodder and Stoughton, 1909. 125 p.
Preface signed: William McDonald Bottome.

4832   Bottome, Margaret (McDonald), 1827-1906.
A sunshine trip: glimpses of the Orient; extracts from letters written by Margaret Bottome. New York, E. Arnold, 1897. viii, 215 p.

4833   BOUNDS, Edward McKendree (1835-1913). N.Y. Times (Aug. 26, 1913), 9:4. MWWW in Ch. Hist. (1968), 53.

ME, S. Pastor, evangelist, editor, writer
b. 1835, Shelby County, Mo.
d. Aug. 24, 1913, Washington, Ga.

4834   BOWEN, Elias (1791-1871). SCM (1881), 127.
ME, FM. Pastor
b. June 16, 1791, Warwick, Mass.
d. Oct. 25, 1871

4835   Bowen, Elias, 1791-1871.
History of the origin of the Free Methodist Church. Rochester, N.Y., B.T. Roberts, 1871. 350 p.
"Sketch of the life of the author, by Rev. B.T. Roberts": p. iii-viii.

4836   BOWEN, George (1816-1888). DAB. WWW in Am. (1607-1896), 66. MWWW in Ch. Hist. (1968), 53-54.
Pres., ME. Missionary
b. Apr. 30, 1816, Middlebury, Vt.
d. Feb. 5, 1888, Bombay, India

4837   Bowen, George, 1816-1888.
George Bowen of Bombay, missionary, scholar, mystic saint; a memoir by Robert E. Speer. Printed privately for distribution to missionaries. New York, Sold by the Missionary Review of the World, 1938. 366 p.

4838   BOWES, Alpin Marshall (1881-1930).
CN. Pastor

4839   BOWMAN, Carl Ray (1926-   ). Am. Architects Dir. (1970), 92.
CN. Lay member, architect, college prof.
b. Oct. 26, 1926, Eureka, Calif.

4840   BOWMAN, Ruth Mildred (1904-   ). ETWF (196?).
PHC. Bible college teacher, missionary, pastor
b. Dec. 24, 1904, Bowmanstown, Pa.

4841   BOWMAN, Thomas (1817-1914). DAB. LMB (1948), 33. Nat. Cy. of Am. Biog. SCM (1881), 128, 129. WWW in Am. (1897-1942), 124. N.Y. Times (Mar. 4, 1914), 11:5.
Endorsed call, GHA, 1901 (Chicago)
ME. College prof., bishop
b. July 15, 1817, Berwick, Pa.
d. Mar. 3, 1914, Orange, N.J.

4842   BOWMAN, Thomas (1836-1923). WWW in Am. (1897-1942), 124.
EA. Pastor, presiding elder, bishop
b. May 18, 1836, Lehigh Gap, Northampton County, Pa.
d. Mar. 19, 1923, Allentown, Pa.

Part VI. Biography

4843 BOYD, Myron F. (1908-). BPOH (1969), 112-121.
President, NHA, 1954-1958, 1968-1972
FM. Pastor, radio preacher, bishop
b. July 19, 1908, Shelbyville, Ill.

4844 Boyd, Myron F., bp., 1908-
To tell the world; thirty radio messages by Myron F. Boyd, speaker and director, The Light and Life Hour. Winona Lake, Ind., Light and Life Hour, 1964. 196 p.
Biographical sketch by C. Dorr Demaray.

4845 BOYNTON, Jeremy (1824-1883). PPE (1868), 145-149.
ME. Pastor

4846 BOYNTON, R. C.
CN, I. Pastor, evangelist, Bible school pres.

4847 BRACKEN, Archie Kay (1884-1966). WW in Am. (1940-1941), 390. RLOA (1941-1942), 127. FHOP (1964).
ME, S; FBHC; ME; CN; FM; CN. College prof., College pres.
b. Sept. 13, 1884, Inman, Tenn.

4848 BRADLEY, Hilda Aldene (1914-). ETWF (196?).
PHC. Pastor's wife, missionary
b. May 14, 1914, Holbrook, Pa.

4849 BRADLEY, William Calvin (1914-). ETWF (196?).
PHC. Pastor, missionary
b. Jan. 27, 1914, Secretary, Md.

4850 BRANDT, Martin E. (1907-). WWACUA (1970-1971), 57.
FM, WM, W. College admin.
b. June 14, 1907, Caldwell, Kan.

4851 BRASHER, John Lakin (1868-1971). RLOA (1941-1942), 133.
WW in the Clergy (1935-1936), 140. ATY (1930), 56-63.
ME, M, UM. Pastor, evangelist, college pres.
b. July 20, 1868, Attalla, Ala.
d. Jan. 25, 1971, Attalla, Ala.

4852 Brasher, John Lakin, 1868-1971.
Glimpses; some personal glimpses of holiness preachers whom I have known, and with whom I have labored in evangelism, who have answered to their names in the roll call of the skies. Cincinnati, Revivalist Press, 1954. 97 p.

4853 Brasher, John Lakin, 1868-1971.
A simple statement of Christian experience. n.p., 1962. 12 p.
Autobiography.

4854   Brasher, John Lakin, 1868-1971.
          A tribute and some other writings. n.p., 1926.
          86 p.
4855   Murphree, Jon Tal, 1936-
          Giant of a century trail; the life and labors of John
          Lakin Brasher, great southern orator. Introd. by Paul
          S. Rees; preface by Bishop W. Kenneth Goodson.
          Apollo, Pa., West Publishing Co., 1969. 127 p.

4856 BRENGLE, Samuel Logan (1860-1936). N.Y. Times (May
      21, 1936), 23:5; (May 24, 1936), II, 8:8; (June 1,
      1936), 13:1.
      Attended GHA, 1901 (Chicago)
      ME, SA. Pastor, evangelist, Salvation Army officer
      b. June 1, 1860, Fredericksburg, Ind.
      d. May 20, 1936, Scarsdale, N.Y.
4857   Hall, Clarence Wilbur, 1902-
          Samuel Logan Brengle, portrait of a prophet. Chicago, Salvation Army Supply and Purchasing Dept.,
          1933. 254 p.

4858 BRESEE, Phineas Franklin (1838-1915). N.Y. Times (Nov.
      14, 1915), II, 19:5. COPN (1958), 11-25. MHTWW
      (n.d.), 42-44. MOUS (1941), 12-15. DC (1965,
      c1887), ix-xix.
      Member, NHA
      Attended, GHA, 1901 (Chicago)
      ME, CN, PCN. Pastor, evangelist, editor, presiding
      elder, general supt.
      b. Dec. 31, 1838, Franklin, Delaware County, N.Y.
      d. Nov. 13, 1915, Los Angeles, Calif.
4859   Bresee, Phineas Franklin, 1838-1915.
          The certainties of faith; ten sermons by the founder
          of the Church of the Nazarene, with an introd. and
          notes on the author's life by Timothy L. Smith, Ph.D.
          Kansas City, Mo., Nazarene Publishing House, 1958.
          95 p.
4860   Bresee, Phineas Franklin, 1838-1915.
          Sayings of our founder, comp. by Ward B. Chandler.
          Houston, Chandler and Roach Publications, 1948. 50 p.
          First published in 1903; reproduced in 1948 and 1951.
4861   Brickley, Donald Paul
          "The life and work of Phineas F. Bresee." Unpublished Ph.D. dissertation, University of Pittsburgh,
          1958.
4862   Brickley, Donald Paul
          Man of the morning; the life and work of Phineas F.
          Bresee. Kansas City, Mo., Nazarene Publishing House,
          1960. 297 p.
4863   Brown, Harrison D., 1846-1940.
          Personal memories of the early ministry of Dr.
          Phineas F. Bresee: character study. Seattle, Wash.,
          1930. 40 p.

Part VI. Biography

4864 Girvin, Ernest Alexander, 1857-
Phineas F. Bresee: a prince in Israel, a biography. Kansas City, Mo., Pentecostal Nazarene Publishing House, 1916. 463 p.

4865 Hills, Aaron Merritt, 1848-1935.
[Biographical sketch of P. F. Bresee]. Nazarene Magazine, I (January 1930).

4866 Hills, Aaron Merritt, 1848-1935.
Phineas F. Bresee, a life sketch. Kansas City, Mo., Nazarene Publishing House, circa 1930. 84 p.

4867 McGraw, James, 1913-
"The preaching of Phineas F. Bresee," Preacher's Magazine, XXIX (Feb. 1954), 4-6.

4868 Martin, Isaiah Guyman, 1862-1957.
Dr. P. F. Bresee and the church he founded. Kansas City, Mo., Printed for I.G. Martin, Mansfield, Ill. by the Nazarene Publishing House, 1937. 53 p.

4869 BREWER, Elizabeth Luella Alexander (1856-   ).
SA, ME. Evangelist, evangelistic singer

4870 Brewer, Elizabeth Luella (Alexander), 1856-
Stepping nearer, or life and lessons of Mrs. D.A. Brewer, Whiteland, Indiana. Louisville, Ky., Pentecostal Publishing Co., 1911. 93 p.

4871 BRICKLEY, Donald Paul (1920-   ). WWACUA (1970-1971), 59. AMS (1965-1968), VII, 179.
CN. College prof., college admin.
b. Jan. 10, 1920, Johnstown, Pa.

4872 BRINDELL, G. W.   DC (1965, c1887), 77-89.
Member, NHA
ME. Pastor

4873 BROCKETT, Henry E.
EHC? Pastor, evangelist, home missionary worker

4874 Brockett, Henry E.
The riches of holiness: a testimony and message. London, Marshall, Morgan & Scott, Ltd., 1936. 144 p.
Autobiographical.

4875 Brockett, Henry E.
Riches of holiness. Kansas City, Mo., Beacon Hill Press, 1951. 128 p.
Reprint of 1936 ed.
Autobiographical.

4876 BRODHEAD, Anna Sanford (-1927). LLITW (1951), 215.
FM. Missionary

4877 BRODHEAD, John Pearson (-1947). LLITW (1951), 215.
FM. Missionary

4878 BROMLEY, William Ewart (1905-1969).
Meth. (Eng.), I, CN. Pastor, missionary
b. Aug. 15, 1905, Worcester, Worcestershire, Eng.
d. Mar. 19, 1969, Kudjip, New Guinea
4879 Berg, A. A. E.
Arrows of the Almighty; a biography of William Ewart Bromley, pioneer missionary to New Guinea. Kansas City, Mo., Beacon Hill Press, 1972. 116 p.

4880 BROOKMILLER, Frederick H. (1854-1903).
Member, IowaHA
Attended GHA, 1901 (Chicago)
ME. Pastor

4881 BROOKS, Cyrus. PPE (1868), 217-226.
ME. Pastor

4882 BROOKS, Delos Ferdinand (1845-1935).
Endorsed call, GHA, 1901 (Chicago)
ME. Pastor, Bible school principal
b. Oct. 26, 1845
d. May 30, 1935
4883 Brooks, Delos Ferdinand, 1845-1935.
From Bethabara to Pentecost; or, Two and a half years walking and talking with Jesus. Chicago, Christian Witness Co., 1905. 220 p.

4884 BROOKS, Harriet Bennett (-1940). LLITW (1951), 215.
FM. Missionary

4885 BROOKS, John P.
ME, CG (IHP), CG (UHP). Pastor, editor
b. 183?, Madison County, Ill.
4886 Oblinger, Carl D.
"John P. Brooks: separatist tendencies in the Holiness Movement." Unpublished student paper, Northern Illinois University, 1968. 51ℓ.

4887 BROUGH, Lyman (1869-1940).
MP, ME, CN. Pastor, district supt.
b. Dec. 28, 1869, Clyde, Ohio
4888 Brough, Lyman, 1869-1940.
"He lifted me"; the experiences of Rev. Lyman Brough, a pioneer holiness preacher of the Northwest. Kansas City, Mo., Nazarene Publishing House, 1921. 131 p.

4889 BROWN, Arthur Lee (1891-). RLOA (1941-1942), 148.
FM. Pastor, district elder, denominational official, editor
b. Jan. 16, 1891, Pittsburgh, Pa.

Part VI. Biography

4890 BROWN, Charles A. FYAB (1954).
CN, PHC. Pastor, district supt.

4891 BROWN, Charles Calvin (1868-1957). TDOOP (1968), 98-101, 325.
HCC, IHC, PHC. Pastor, evangelist, general supt.
b. Sept. 18, 1868, Crawford County, Ind.
d. Feb. 14, 1957

4892 BROWN, Charles Ewing (1883-). RLOA (1941-1942), 148. SFLF (1950), 12-17. SCC (1947), 22-27.
CG (A). Pastor, editor
b. Dec. 30, 1883, Elizabethtown, Ill.

4893 BROWN, D. Wayne (1913-).
PHC, W. Pastor, denominational official
b. 1913, Maywood, Neb.
4894 "Conference elects 11 officers," Wesleyan Advocate, CXXVII (July 15, 1968), 9.
4895 "Elected officials of The Wesleyan Church," Wesleyan Advocate, CXXX (July 24, 1972), 14.

4896 BROWN, George. ROG (1854), 430-434.
ME. Lay member

4897 BROWN, H. N. DC (1965, c1887), 180-191. SCUH (1962), 55, 60-61, 65-66, 68, 71-72, 76, 79, 81, 83, 88, 206-207, 209.
Member, NHA
ME, APCA, PCN. Pastor

4898 BROWN, Harrison D. (1846-1940). MOUS (1941), 79-85.
ME, CN, PCN, CN. Pastor, evangelist, district supt., social worker
b. Nov. 1, 1846, Burlington, Iowa
d. Feb. 13, 1940
4899 Seals, B. V.
"Pen sketch of H.D. Brown, the Northwest's great pioneer," Preacher's Magazine, XXXIII (June 1958), 8-11.

4900 BROWN, Irwin L. GFIIH (1963), 162-177.
SCA. Bible college prin., missionary, college dean, pastor, conference supt., general supt.

4901 BROWN, Lena Marie (1920-). ETWF (196?).
PHC. Rescue mission worker, evangelistic singer, missionary
b. Jan. 29, 1920, Connersville, Ind.

4902 BROWN, Melza H.
CN. Pastor, evangelist, district supt.

4903　　　　Smith, Hannah (Brown),　　-195?.
　　　　　　For heaven's sake. Boston, Little, Brown, 1949.
　　　　　　266 p.
　　　　　　An autobiographical novel of a girlhood spent in a
　　　　　　Nazarene parsonage.

4904　　　BROWN, Robert. GHAI (1960).
　　　　　　CN. Missionary

4905　　　BROWN, Warren Shelburne (1918-　). WW in Am. (1968-
　　　　　　1969), 310. WWACUA (1970-1971), 65.
　　　　　　CN. Pastor, district supt., college pres.
　　　　　　b. Jan. 1918, Olivet, Ill.

4906　　　BROWNING, Raymond (1879-1953).
　　　　　　ME, S; CN. Evangelist, pastor, district supt.
　　　　　　b. Mar. 30, 1879, Asper Hill, Giles County, Tenn.
　　　　　　d. Aug. 1953.
4907　　　　Browning, Raymond, 1879-1953.
　　　　　　After-study meditations. Durham, N.C., Press of
　　　　　　the Seeman Printery, 1906. 31 p.
　　　　　　Poems.
4908　　　　Browning, Raymond, 1879-1953.
　　　　　　The phantom anvil and other melodies. n.p., n.d.
　　　　　　37 p.
　　　　　　Poems.
4909　　　　Browning, Raymond, 1879-1953.
　　　　　　"The preaching of Raymond Browning," Preacher's
　　　　　　Magazine, XXXIII (Nov. 1958), 8-11.

4910　　　BROWNING, William Garritson (1825-1910). PPE (1868),
　　　　　　332-334.
　　　　　　Endorsed call, GHA, 1901 (Chicago)
　　　　　　ME. Pastor
　　　　　　b. Mar. 20, 1825, New York, N.Y.
　　　　　　d. May 2, 1910, Poughkeepsie, N.Y.
4911　　　　Browning, William Garritson, 1825-1910.
　　　　　　Grace magnified; incidents in the life, ministry, ex-
　　　　　　periences, and travels of William Garritson Browning.
　　　　　　New York, Pub. for the author by Palmer & Hughes,
　　　　　　1887. 451 p.
4912　　　　Browning, William Garritson, 1825-1910.
　　　　　　A few more words. Poughkeepsie, N.Y., A.V.
　　　　　　Haight, 1902. 173 p.
4913　　　　Browning, William Garritson, 1825-1910.
　　　　　　Once again. Poughkeepsie, N.Y., A.V. Haight,
　　　　　　1905. 198 p.
4914　　　　Browning, William Garritson, 1825-1910.
　　　　　　Beyond forescore. Poughkeepsie, N.Y., A.V.
　　　　　　Haight, 1907.

Part VI. Biography 593

4915 BRUSHINGHAM, John Patrick (1855-1927). WW in Am.
(1897-1942), 157. N.Y. Times (Apr. 8, 1927), 23:2.
Nat. Cy. of Am. Biog.
Attended GHA, 1885 (Chicago)
Endorsed call and attended GHA, 1901 (Chicago)
ME. Pastor
b. Feb. 16, 1855, Cuba, N.Y.
d. Apr. 7, 1927, Chicago, Ill.

4916 BRYANT, Thomas J. (1828-1893).
ME. Business college pres., lay leader
4917 [Bryant, Thomas J.], 1828-1893.
Complete chart of bookkeeping by double entry ...
by Bryant's Business College. St. Joseph, Mo., 1876.
8 p.
4918 Bryant, Thomas J., 1828-1893.
Rules for detecting counterfeit gold and silver coin
and bank bills. St. Joseph, Mo., Posegate Printing
and Lithographing Co., 1891. 12 p.

4919 BUDENSIEK, Harold Lyle (1931-   ). WWACUA (1970-1971),
69.
WM, W. College admin.
b. June 8, 1931, Charles City, Iowa

4920 BUFFUM, Herbert (1879-1939). LMGSS (1952), 71. SCUH
(1962), 137, 146. N.Y. Times (Oct. 11, 1939),
30:2.
ME, CN, CGIC, AG. Editor, evangelist, pastor, gospel song writer
b. Nov. 13, 1879, Lafayette, Ill.
d. Oct. 9, 1939, Los Angeles, Calif.

4921 BUFFUM, Lillie. SCUH (1962), 137, 146.
ME, CN, CGIC, AG. Editor, evangelist
4922 Buffum, Lillie
Lillies from the valley. Los Angeles, B.W. Robertson Publishing Co., c1941. 43 p.
Poems.

4923 BULKLEY, C. H. A. PPE (1868), 361-368.
Pres. Pastor

4924 BUNCE, D. S. (1838-   ).
ME? Evangelist
4925 Bunce, D. S., 1838-
From gambling table to pulpit.... Chicago, Christian
Witness Co., 1909. 158 p.

4926 BURNETT, Clyde J. LLITW (1951), 183.
FM. Missionary

4927   BURNETT, Lillian M. Pool. LLITW (1951), 183-184.
        HWP (1905), 67-69.
        HChuC, PCN, FM. Missionary, evangelist

4928   BURNHAM, Richard (1857-). SBWTL (1960), 183.
        FM. Farmer, pastor
        b. 1857, Uxbridge, Ont.

4929   BURNS, Nelson (-1904).
        President, Canadian Holiness Association
        Attended GHA, 1885 (Chicago)
        Meth. (Can.)
4930   Pointen, Harold William
        "The Holiness Movement Church in Canada." Unpublished B.D. thesis, Victoria University, 1950. 179ℓ.
        Account of work of Nelson Burns: p. 71-72, 76-78.

4931   BURRITT, Eldon Grant (1868-1927). WWW in Am. (1897-1942), 172.
        FM. College prof., college pres.
        b. Sept. 9, 1868, Hilton, N.Y.
        d. 1927

4932   BURSCH, Daniel Ray (1918-). ETWF (196?). WWACUA (1970-1971), 73.
        PHC, W. Pastor, Bible school admin., missionary, college pres.
        b. June 13, 1918, Chanute, Kan.

4933   BURSCH, Madge Serna Edwards (1922-). ETWF (196?).
        PHC, W. Pastor's wife, missionary
        b. May 7, 1922, Mitchell, S.D.

4934   BUTLER, Charles William (1873-1960). WW in Am. (1950-1951), 394. RLOA (1941-1942), 174. SFLF (1950), 19-23. ATY (1930), 112-125.
        President, NHA, 1928-1942
        ME, M. Pastor, evangelist, Bible school pres., college pres.
        b. May 13, 1873, Caro, Mich.
        d. Apr. 17, 1960

4935   BUTLER, William (1818-1899). GFW (1888), 200-208.
        SCM (1881), 150. WWW in Am. (1607-1896), 89.
        Ch. of Ire., WM (Eng.), ME. Pastor, missionary
        b. Jan. 30, 1818, Dublin, Ire.
4936   Butler, William, 1818-1899.
        From Boston to Bareilly and back. New York,
        Phillips & Hunt; Cincinnati, Cranston & Stowe, 1885.
        512 p.
4937   Butler, William, 1818-1899.
        The land of the Veda; being the personal reminis-

Part VI. Biography 595

cences of India; its people, castes, thugs, and fakirs; its religions, mythology, principal monuments, palaces, and mausoleums; together with the incidents of the great Sepoy rebellion, and its results to Christianity and civilization ... also, statistical tables of Christian missions, and glossary of Indian terms used in this work and in missionary correspondence. 5th ed. New York, Nelson & Phillips; Cincinnati, Hitchcock & Walden, 1873. 557 p.

4938 Butler, William, 1818-1899.
The land of the Veda; being personal reminiscences of India, its people, castes, thugs and fakirs, its religions, mythology, principal monuments, palaces, and mausoleums, together with the incidents of the great Sepoy rebellion. Jubilee ed. New York, Eaton & Mains; Cincinnati, Jennings & Graham, c1906. 564 p.

4939 Butler, William, 1818-1899.
Roman Catholicism and the Reformation in Mexico, with details of the horrors of the Inquisition and the expulsion of the Jesuits; an address by the Rev. William Butler, to which is prefixed a brief sketch of his life. Belfast, University Printing and Publishing House, 1883. 32 p.

4940 BUXTON, Barclay Fowell (1860-1946).
Ch. of Eng., JEB. Missionary
4941 Buxton, Barclay Godfrey
The reward of faith in the life of Barclay Fowell Buxton, 1860-1946. London, Lutterworth Press, 1949. 274 p.

4942 BYERS, Charles Edgar (1883-). RLOA (1941-1942), 176.
SCC (1947), 44.
CG (A). Pastor
b. May 21, 1883, Edgar County, Ill.

4943 BYRUM, Enoch Edwin (1861-1942). RLOA (1941-1942), 177.
SHBD (1955), 51-75.
UB, CG (A). Pastor, Bible school teacher, editor
b. Oct. 13, 1861, Union City, Ind.
d. Jan. 1942, Anderson, Ind.
4944 Byrum, Enoch Edwin, 1861-1942.
Life experiences; containing narratives, incidents, and experiences in the life of the author. Anderson, Ind., Gospel Trumpet Co., 1928. 432 p.
4945 Byrum, Enoch Edwin, 1861-1942.
Travels and experiences in other lands. Moundsville, W. Va., Gospel Trumpet Co., 1905. 600 p.

4946 BYRUM, Isabel Coston (1870-1938).
CG (A). Religious writer

4947   Byrum, Isabel (Coston), 1870-1938.
        The tread of years. Anderson, Ind., Gospel Trumpet Co., 1938. 136 p.
        Autobiography.

4948   CAFFRAY, Daisy Willia Bourquard (1880-   ).
        Epis., ME, M. Evangelist, missionary
        b. Dec. 17, 1880, Baton Rouge, La.
4949   Robinson, Kenneth L.
        From brass to gold; the life and ministry of Dr. D. Willia Caffray. University Park, Iowa, Vennard College, 1971. 344 p.

4950   CAGLE, H. C. SCUH (1962), 155, 158.
        CN. Pastor, evangelist, district supt.

4951   CAGLE, Mary Lee Wasson Harris (1864-1955). HWP (1905), 70-74. SCUH (1962), 154, 158-159, 169, 171-173, 176, 216-217.
        NTCOC, HChuC, PCN, CN. Pastor, evangelist
        b. 1864, Alabama
        d. Sept. 27, 1955, Texas
4952   Cagle, Mary Lee (Wasson) Harris, 1864-
        Life and work of Mary Lee Cagle, an autobiography. Kansas City, Mo., Nazarene Publishing House, 1928. 176 p.
4953   Parker, John Fred
        "The preaching of Mary Lee Cagle," Preacher's Magazine, XXXIII (Aug. 1958), 7-9.

4954   CALDWELL, Sallie Kitchen (1831-1855).
        ME. Lay member
4955   Gaddis, Maxwell Pierson, 1811-1888.
        The sacred hour. Cincinnati, The author, 1856. 364 p.
        Life and letters of Sallie K. Caldwell.

4956   CAMERON, James Reese (1929-   ). DAS (1969), I, 74.
        CN. College prof.
        b. Aug. 27, 1929, Columbus, Ohio

4957   CANTRELL, Roy Herbert (1904-   ). WW in Am. (1960-1961), 463. WW in Am. (1968-1969), 372. WWACUA (1970-1971), 80. LIE (1971), 148.
        CN. College prof., pastor, district supt., college pres.
        b. Nov. 4, 1904, Kansas City, Mo.

4958   CARDIEL, Adolfo (1903-   ). RWBTB (1953), 19-22.
        CN. Baker, pastor
        b. Sept. 12, 1903, Ascensión, Nuevo León, Mex.

Part VI. Biography

4959 CARMAN, Albert (1833-1917). SCM (1881), 167. LMB
(1948), 40-41. WW in Am. Meth. (1916), 37.
WMDCB (1963), 114.
Endorsed call, GHA, 1901 (Chicago)
ME, Meth (Can.). Headmaster, college prof., university chancellor, bishop, general supt.
b. June 27, 1833, Iroquois, Upper Can.
d. Nov. 3, 1917, Toronto, Ont., Can.

4960 CARMICHAEL, Amy Wilson (1867-1951).
Ch. of Eng. (KesC). Missionary
b. 1867, Northern Ireland
4961 Carmichael, Amy Wilson, 1867-1951.
Gold cord; the story of a fellowship. London, Society for Promoting Christian Knowledge, 1932. viii, 375 p.
Account of Dohnavur Fellowship.
4962 Carmichael, Amy Wilson, 1867-1951.
Things as they are; mission work in southern India. With preface by Eugene Stock. London, Morgan and Scott, 1905. xvi, 304 p.
4963 Dahlquist, Siri
Led milda ljus; Amy Carmichaels liv och gärning som tempelbarnens moder i Dohnavur Stockholm, Svenska kyrkans diakonistyrelses bokförlag, 1954. 128 p.
4964 Houghton, Frank, bp., 1894-
Amy Carmichael of Dohnavur; the story of a lover and her beloved. London, S.P.C.K., 1953. xv, 390 p.
4965 Neill, Stephen Charles, bp., 1900-
Concise dictionary of the Christian world mission, ed. by Stephen Neill, Gerald H. Anderson [and] John Goodwin. Nashville, Abingdon Press, 1971. xxi, 682 p.
Account of Amy Beatrice Carmichael, by John Pollock: p. 90.

4966 CARMONY, Byron M. (1916-).
CN. Pastor, gospel song writer.

4967 CARPENTER, Mary E. (-1886). LLITW (1951), 215.
FM. Missionary

4968 CARRADINE, Beverly (1848-1931). PM (1898), 10-14. DC (1965, c1887), 169-179.
Member, NHA
Endorsed call, GHA, 1901 (Chicago)
ME, S. Pastor, evangelist
b. Apr. 4, 1848, Yazoo County, Miss.
4969 Carradine, Beverly, 1848-1931.
Graphic scenes. Cincinnati, God's Revivalist Office, 1911. 327 p.
Autobiographical.

4970 Carradine, Beverly, 1848-1931.
A journey to Palestine. St. Louis, Mo., C.B. Woodward Printing Co., 1891. 455 p.
4971 Carradine, Beverly, 1848-1931.
A journey to Palestine. Syracuse, N.Y., A.W. Hall, 1892. 489 p.

4972 CARROLL, H. H. (-1921).
PCN, CN. Pastor

4973 CARROLL, John H. (1884-1961).
UB, PHC, EA, PHC. Pastor, evangelist, missionary
b. Oct. 17, 1884, Orange County, Ind.
d. Dec. 23, 1961
4974 Carroll, John H., 1884-1961.
Forty-seven years with the gospel plow; or, The life story of John H. Carroll. Shoals, Ind., Old Paths Tract Society, 195?. 152 p.

4975 CARROLL, Nellie Mae (1918-). ETWF (196?).
PHC. Missionary
b. May 1, 1918, Ava, Mo.

4976 CARTER, Charles Webb (1905-). DAS (1969), IV, 56.
WM, W. Pastor, missionary, college prof., editor
b. May 4, 1905, Indianapolis, Ind.

4977 CARTER, Marjorie. GHAI (1960), 56-63.
CN. Pastor's wife, missionary

4978 CARTER, Melissa Booth (1845-).
ME. Lay leader
4979 Carter, Melissa (Booth), 1845-
Beulah land, an autobiography. Boston, Earle, 1888. 258 p.

4980 CARTER, Russell Kelso (1849-1926). GFW (1888), 98-105. RHOOF (1964), 263. CHHMH (1970), 506.
Pres., ME, CMA, Pres. Military academy instructor, sheep rancher, pastor, evangelist, gospel song writer, physician
b. Nov. 18, 1849, Baltimore, Md.
d. Aug. 23, 1926, Catonsville, Baltimore County, Md.
4981 [Carter, Russell Kelso], 1849-1926.
Amor victor; a novel of Ephesus and Rome, 95-105 A.D., by Orr Kenyon [pseud.].... New York, Frederick A. Stokes Co., 1902. 424 p.
4982 Carter, Russell Kelso, 1849-1926.
Caleb Koons, a 'postle of common sense. Boston, C.M. Clark Publishing Co., c1910. xiii, 440 p.
4983 Carter, Russell Kelso, 1849-1926.
The sleeping car "Twilight"; or, Motherhood without

Part VI. Biography

pain. The whole truth about "Twilight sleep" and the new anesthesia; the marvelous French discovery, the most wonderful of all; and a special chapter for every man on the conquest of pain. Boston, Chapple, 1915. 181 p.

4984 Carter, Russell Kelso, 1849-1926.
Trigonometrical formulae from modern surveying. Advance print for the use of the cadets of the Pennsylvania Military Academy. n.p., 1885. 6 p.

4985 [Carter, Russell Kelso], 1849-1926.
What God hath (not) joined, by Orr Kenyon [pseud.]... New York, Dodge Publishing Co., c1905. vi, 377 p. Novel.

4986 Speer, Robert Elliott, 1867-1947.
Report on India and Persia of the deputation sent by the Board of Foreign Missions of the Presbyterian Church in the U.S.A. to visit these fields in 1921-22; presented by Mr. Robert E. Speer and Mr. Russell Carter. New York, Board of Foreign Missions of the Presbyterian Church in the U.S.A., 1922.

4987 CASE, Orpha Mae (1909-   ). ETWF (196?).
PHC. Bible school teacher, missionary
b. Mar. 8, 1909, Dowling, Mich.

4988 CASSLER, La Fayette
ME?, PCN. Evangelist, district supt.

4989 Cassler, La Fayette
Thrilling experiences of frontier life in the early days of western Oklahoma, embracing the pathetic story of Abe, the tramp: startling providences, touching incidents, miracles of grace, visions and revelations. Cincinnati, Pub. for the author by God's Bible School and Revivalist, n.d. 197 p.

4990 CASTILLEJOS, José. RWBTB (1953), 43-45.
CN. Pastor

4991 CASTLE, Nicholas (1837-1922). WWW in Am. (1897-1942), 203.
Endorsed call, GHA, 1901 (Chicago)
UB. Pastor, presiding elder, bishop
b. Oct. 4, 1837, Bristol, Ind.
d. Apr. 18, 1922

4992 Castle, Nicholas, bp., 1837-1922.
Fifty years in the ministry; an address by Bishop Nicholas Castle, delivered before the St. Joseph Conference; the ideal ministry as viewed from the heights of one who has been pastor, presiding elder, and bishop. Dayton, Ohio, U.B. Publishing House, 1908. Cover-title, 16 p.

4993 Castle, Nicholas, bp., 1837-1922.
My experience. Chambersburg, Pa., Holiness Association, Church of the United Brethren in Christ, 1877? Cover-title, 8 p.

4994 CATALAN P., Apolinar (1915-   ). RWBTB (1953), 33-38.
Bapt., CN. Pastor
b. Jan. 8, 1915, San Nicolás, Michoacán, Mex.

4995 CATTELL, Catherine DeVol (1906-   ). WMAMH (1957), 121-155.
Fr. Pastor's wife, missionary
b. Jan. 30, 1906, Luho, Ch.

4996 CATTELL, Everett Lewis (1905-   ). WW in the Midwest (1969-1970), 184. CA. WWACUA (1970-1971), 86. GIIH (1962), 262-280. GTWATD (1965), 396-411. WMAMH (1957), 131-155.
Fr. Pastor, missionary, general supt., college pres.
b. Sept. 16, 1905, Kensington, Ohio

4997 CAUDILL, Rodney C. SCC (1947), 66-68.
CG (A). Pastor, evangelist

4998 CHADWICK, Grace E. (1873-1911). MMAWOPD (1920), 106-108.
WM. Pastor
d. May 5, 1911

4999 CHADWICK, Samuel (1860-1932).
WM (Eng.). Pastor, evangelist, conference pres., college lecturer, college prin.
b. Sept. 16, 1860, Burnley, Lancs., Eng.
d. Oct. 16, 1932, Calver, Derbys., Eng.

5000 Chadwick, Samuel, 1860-1932.
The testament of Samuel Chadwick, 1860-1932; comp. by D.W. Lambert. London, Epworth Press, 1957. 109 p.

5001 Chadwick, Samuel, 1860-1932.
25 Sunday mornings with Samuel Chadwick; selected and arranged by D.W. Lambert. London, Epworth Press, 1951. 108 p.

5002 Chadwick, Samuel, 1860-1932.
Twenty-five Sunday evenings with Samuel Chadwick; selected and arranged by D.W. Lambert. London, Epworth Press, 1954. 109 p.

5003 Dunning, Norman Grove
Samuel Chadwick; with a foreword by David Lloyd George. London, Hodder & Stoughton, 1933. 250 p.

5004 Smart, William James, 1895-
Six mighty men. London, Hodder and Stoughton, 1956. 151 p.
Sketch of Samuel Chadwick: p. 61-91.

Part VI. Biography 601

5005 CHALFANT, Everette Otis (1882-1953). FYAB (1954), 96-98.
UB, CN. Pastor, district supt.
b. Mar. 22, 1882, Muncie, Ind.
d. Apr. 22, 1954, Detroit, Mich.
5006 Chalfant, Everette Otis, 1882-1953.
Forty years on the firing line (E.O. Chalfant tells his life's story). Kansas City, Mo., Beacon Hill Press, 1951. 80 p.
5007 Chalfant, Everette Otis, 1882-1953.
Getting the glory down, comp. by Morris Chalfant. n.p., n.d. 61 p.
5008 McGraw, James, 1913-
"The preaching of E.O. Chalfant," Preacher's Magazine, XXXIII (i.e. XXXIV) (Oct. 1959), 9-12.

5009 CHAMBERLAIN, Marianne. TDOOP (1968), 287.
HC, PHC. Pastor?

5010 CHAMBERLAIN, Ray W. TDOOP (1968), 287.
HC, PHC. Pastor?

5010a CHAMBERS, George Augustus (1879-1957).
Bi. Chr., Meth. (Can.), MBIC, PeAC. Pastor, evangelist, general supt., district supt.
b. Oct. 8, 1879, Opps, County of Victoria, Ont.
d. Dec. 27, 1957, Kitchener, Ont.
5010b Chambers, George Augustus, 1879-1957.
Fifty years in the service of the King; autobiography of George Augustus Chambers. Foreword by Walter E. McAlister. Toronto, Testimony Press, 1960. viii. 48 p.
"Authorized by the National Publications Committee, the Pentecostal Assemblies of Canada."

5011 CHAMBERS, Joseph Leon
CN. Pastor, evangelist, district supt., college prof., college admin.

5012 CHAMBERS, Oswald (1874-1917).
Bapt., PL, Y.M.C.A. Evangelist, missionary
b. July 24, 1874, Aberdeen, Scot.
d. Nov. 15, 1917, Cairo, Eg.
5013 Chambers, Oswald, 1874-1917.
Oswald Chambers, his life and work; with a foreword by Rev. Dinsdale T. Young. London, Edinburgh, Oswald Chambers Publications Association and Marshall, Morgan & Scott, 1959. 357 p.
5014 Chambers, Oswald, 1874-1917.
The philosophy of Swedenborg.... Paisley, Scot., Meikleriggs, 1902. 16 p.
A paper read before the New-Church Doctrinal Union

in the hall of the Church of the New Jerusalem, Queen's Park, Glasgow, on March 10th, 1902.

5015 Lambert, David Willoughby
Oswald Chambers, an unbridled soul. Fort Washington, Pa., Christian Literature Crusade, 1968. 94 p.

5016 CHANDLER, Letitia (-1937). LLITW (1951), 215.
FM. Missionary

5017 CHANG, Chien Hsun. HNTB (1934), 50-51.
CN. National worker, pastor

5018 CHAO, Kui Suan. HNTB (1934), 44-47.
CN. National worker

5019 CHAPMAN, James Blaine (1884-1947). NP (1925), 42-52. WMK (1966), 45. RLOA (1941-1942), 206. WWW in Am. (1943-1950), 111. N.Y. Times (July 31, 1947), 21:4.
WFMA, HATex, IndHC, HChuC, PCN, CN. Pastor, evangelist, college pres., editor, general supt.
b. Aug. 30, 1884, Yale, Ill.
d. July 30, 1947, Vicksburg, Mich.

5020 Chapman, James Blaine, 1884-1947.
Let the winds blow; selected writings comp. by Samuel Young. Kansas City, Mo., Beacon Hill Press, 1957. 102 p.

5021 Chapman, James Blaine, 1884-1947.
30,000 miles of missionary travel. Kansas City, Mo., Nazarene Publishing House, 193?. 167 p.

5022 Chapman, James Blaine, 1884-1947.
The wit and wisdom of J.B. Chapman; unusual stories Dr. Chapman told, comp. by Grace Chapman Ramquist. Grand Rapids, Mich., Zondervan Publishing House, 1948. 72 p.

5023 Corlett, David Shelby, 1894-
Spirit-filled; the life of the Rev. James Blaine Chapman, D.D. Kansas City, Mo., Beacon Hill Press, 194?. 206 p.

5024 McGraw, James, 1913-
"The preaching of James B. Chapman," Preacher's Magazine, XXIX (Aug. 1954), 4-7.

5025 Moore, George Chapman
"An analytical study of invention and style in selected sermons of James Blaine Chapman." Unpublished M.A. thesis, University of Oklahoma, 1948.

5026 CHAPMAN, Louise (Robinson). CIOCC (1959), 5-6. SFLF (1950), 24-29.
CN. Missionary, missionary society pres.

5027 Chapman, Louise (Robinson)
Africa, O Africa; twenty years a missionary on the

dark continent. Kansas City, Mo., Beacon Hill Press, 1945. 221 p.

5028 Scott, Mary
"Mrs. Chapman retires," Herald of Holiness, LIII (Aug. 12, 1964), 10.

5029 CHAPMAN, Maud Frederick (1880-1940).
Bapt., ME, IndHC, HChuC, CN. Pastor's wife.
b. Dec. 3, 1880, Longview, Tex.
d. Feb. 18, 1940, Oklahoma City, Okla.

5030 Chapman, Maud (Frederick), 1880-1940.
"Diary, Mar. 4, 1902-Mar. 24, 1903." In the possession of Grace Chapman Ramquist, Kansas City, Missouri.

5031 Chapman, James Blaine, 1884-1947.
My wife, arranged by James B. Chapman. Kansas City, Mo., Nazarene Publishing House, 1940. 64 p.

5032 CHENEY, L. Keith (1908-   ). LIE (1971), 166.
WM, W. Lay leader, public school teacher, public school prin., college prof.
b. Feb. 6, 1908, Hillsdale, Mich.

5033 CHILSON, Arthur Benton (1872-1939).
Fr. Missionary

5034 Chilson, Edna (Hill)
Ambassador of the King, by Edna H. Chilson (Mrs. Arthur B. Chilson). Wichita, Kan., 1943. 269 p.

5035 CHILTON, Claude L. DCSWM (1960), 78-91.
CN. Military chaplain

5036 CHISM, Fairy Steele (1899-1971).
ME, PCN, CN. Pastor, missionary, evangelist
b. Jan. 1899, Booneville, Ark.

5037 Gish, Carol (Spell)
Touched by the divine; the story of Fairy Chism. Kansas City, Mo., Beacon Hill Press, 1952. 108 p.

5038 CHISHOLM, Thomas O. (1866-1960). LMGSS (1952), 19.
N.Y. Times (Mar. 2, 1960), 37:2.
ME. Gospel song writer
b. July 29, 1866, Kentucky.

5039 CHRISTIE, G. A.
HMoC. Pastor

5040 Christie, G. A.
Out of bondage into liberty; ed. by Rev. G. A. Christie, with introd. by Patrick Morgan. Ottawa, Can., Holiness Movement Publishing House, 1912. xi, 224 p.

5041 CHUNG, Robert. FHOP (1964). NVFML (1936), 175-179.
I, CN. Evangelist
b. 18??, Korea

5042 CHURCH, John Robert (1899-). WW in Meth. (1952), 133.
SCC (1947), 30-35.
ME, S; M

5043 CHYNOWETH, Mary E. (-1908). LLITW (1951), 215.
FM. Missionary
5044   Clarke, M. C., -1936.
Mary E. Chynoweth, a missionary, by Rev. and Mrs. M.C. Clarke. Chicago, Free Methodist Publishing House, 1915.

5045 CLARK, Dougan (1828-1896). GFW (1888), 19-24.
Fr. College prof., evangelist
b. May 17, 1828, Randolph County, N.C.
5046   Jones, Rufus Matthew, 1863-1948.
"Dr. Dougan Clark--at rest," American Friend, III (Oct. 15, 1896), 997.

5047 CLARK, Esther D. (-1938). LLITW (1951), 215.
FM. Missionary

5048 CLARK, John W.
HCC, IHC. Pastor

5049 CLARK, William Henry (1854-1925). BMW (1960), 197-211.
FM. Pastor, district elder, bishop
b. Apr. 8, 1854, Racine, Wis.
d. Nov. 8, 1925, Rome, N.Y.

5050 CLARK, William Warner (1838-). PPE (1868), 227-231.
Meth. (Can.). Pastor
b. Mar. 16, 1838, London, Upper Can.

5051 CLARKE, M. C. (-1936). LLITW (1951), 215.
FM. Missionary

5052 CLARKE, Mary Lane (1872-1970).
WM, W. Missionary, children's worker
d. 1970, Cleveland, Tenn.
5053   Clarke, Mary Lane, 1872-1970.
A Limba-English dictionary; or, Tampeṅ ta ka taluṅ ta ka Hulimb ha in huinkilisi ha. Houghton, N.Y., 1922. 150 p.

5054 CLIMENHAGA, Arthur Merlin (1916-). WW in Am. (1970-1971), 423. WW in Am. (1972-1973), 592.
GFIIH (1963), 14-29. GTWATD (1965), 372-383.
BIC. Missionary, college pres.
b. Feb. 21, 1916, Grantham, Pa.

5055 CLIMENHAGA, Asa W. (1889-). RLOA (1941-1942), 221-222.
BIC. Pastor, college admin.
b. July 1, 1889, Stevensville, Ont., Can.

5056 COATES, Lola Mae (1931-). ETWF (196?).
CN, PHC, BMC. Missionary
b. July 7, 1931, Dallas, Tex.

5057 COATS, Eugenia Phillips (1883-). FHOP (1964).
EC, CN. Missionary
b. 1883, Perry, Mo.

5058 COBB, Eunice Parsons (1793-1877).
ME, FM. Lay member
b. Feb. 13, 1793, Litchfield, Conn.
d. Jan. 3, 1877, Marengo, Ill.

5059 Chapman, Mary (Weems)
Mother Cobb; or, Sixty years' walk with God. Salem, Ohio, H.E. Schmul, Convention Bookstore, 1965. 277 p.
Contains excerpts from Mrs. Cobb's journals.
Reprint of original ed.

5060 COCHRAN, Albert S. (1850-1914).
Member, NHA
Member, IowaHA
ME, PCN. Pastor, evangelist, district supt.
b. Jan. 7, 1850, Pleasant Prairie, Kenosha County, Wisc.
d. Aug. 22, 1914, Kansas City, Mo.

5061 Jones, Charles Edwin, 1932-
"Disinherited or rural?; a historical case study in urban Holiness religion," Missouri Historical Review, LXVI (Apr. 1972), 395-412.
Includes biography of A.S. Cochran.

5062 COLEMAN, George Whitefield (1830-1907). BMW (1960), 75-89. WWW in Am. (1897-1942), 243.
FM. Pastor, district elder, seminary prin., bishop
b. Oct. 10, 1830, Perry Center, N.Y.
d. July 3, 1907. Gainesville, N.Y.

5063 COLEMAN, John Paul
ME, CN, PCN, PC, PHC. Pastor

5064 COLEMAN, John V. (1885-1928). N.Y. Times (Aug. 16, 1928), 21:5.
IHC, PHC. Pastor, evangelist
b. Sept. 24, 1885, Harris City, Ind.
d. Aug. 14, 1928, Springfield, Ohio

5065 COLEMAN, Robert Emerson (1928-).
M, UM. Seminary prof.

5066 COLLETT, Ronald. SBWTL (1960), 205-206.
FM. Pastor, missionary
b. 19??, London, Eng.

5067 COLLINS, Mahlen Day (1838-1904). DC (1965, c1887), 130-138.
Member, NHA
Attended GHA, 1901 (Chicago)
ME. Pastor, evangelist

5068 COLT, W. B. M.
Attended WUHC, 1880 (Jacksonville, Ill.)
Endorsed GHA, 1885 (Chicago)
FM. Pastor, evangelist

5069 COOK, C. O. PPE (1868), 300-302.
ME. Pastor

5070 COOK, Esta Virginia Bangle (1925-). ETWF (196?).
PHC. Pastor's wife, missionary
b. Jan. 14, 1925, Lucerne, Kan.

5071 COOK, Ethel (-1925). LLITW (1951), 215.
FM. Missionary

5072 COOK, Oliver James (1922-). ETWF (196?).
PHC. Pastor, missionary
b. May 21, 1922, Gove, Kan.

5073 COOKE, Sarah Ann Bass (1827-).
Attended WUHC, 1880 (Jacksonville, Ill.)
Attended GHA, 1901 (Chicago)
FM. Evangelist

5074 Cooke, Sarah Ann (Bass), 1827-
The handmaiden of the Lord; or, Wayside sketches. Introd. by L.B. Kent. Chicago, T.B. Arnold, 1896. 382 p.

5075 Cooke, Sarah Ann (Bass), 1827-
Wayside sketches; or, The handmaiden of the Lord. Rev. and enl. ed. Grand Rapids, Mich., Shaw Publishing Co., 18??

5076 COOKMAN, Alfred (1828-1871). SCM (1881), 255. N.Y. Times (Nov. 15, 1871), 1-6. HM (1882). GFW (1888), 237-245. WWW in Am. (1607-1896), 120. Nat. Cy. Am. Biog., XIII, 167-168. PPE (1868), 76-84. EAP (1890, c1879), 109-113.
Member, NHA
ME. Pastor, evangelist, U.S. Senate chaplain

Part VI. Biography 607

        b. Jan. 4, 1828, Columbia, Pa.
        d. Nov. 13, 1871, Newark, N.J.

5077   Cookman, Alfred, 1828-1871.
        Familiar talks on the subject of the higher Christian life. New ed. University Park, Iowa, Christian Witness Association, 1947. 71 p.
        "Experience": p. 68-71.

5078   McDonald, William, 1820-1901.
        Life sketches of Rev. Alfred Cookman. Cincinnati, Freedmen's Aid and Southern Education Society, 1900. 239 p.

5079   Ridgaway, Henry Bascom, 1830-1895.
        The life of the Rev. Alfred Cookman; with some account of his father, the Rev. George Grimston Cookman, with an introd. by the Rev. R.S. Foster. New York, Nelson & Phillips; Cincinnati, Hitchcock & Walden, 1874. 480 p.

5080   COOKMAN, John Emory (1836-1891). Nat. Cy. Am. Biog., X, 154.
        Member, NHA
        ME, Epis. Pastor, evangelist
        b. June 8, 1836, Carlisle, Pa.
        d. Mar. 29, 1891, New York, N.Y.

5081   COON, Mrs. H. Arvilla Damon (1829-).
        ME, FM. Lay leader
        b. Feb. 9, 1829, Geauga County, Ohio

5082   Coon, Mrs. H. Arvilla (Damon), 1829-
        Life and labors of Auntie Coon, as related to Rev. E.E. Shelhamer. Atlanta, Repairer Office, 1905.

5083   Coon, Mrs. H. Arvilla Damon, 1829-
        Life and labors of Auntie Coon, as related to Rev. E.E. Shelhamer. Salem, Ohio, H.E. Schmul, 1964. 301 p.
        Reprint of 1905 ed.

5084   COOPER, Mary May (1898-1970).
        ME, UB, CN. Pastor, missionary
        b. Feb. 1, 1898, Hillsboro, Ind.

5085   Emslie, Betty (Levenson)
        With both hands; the story of Mary Cooper of Gazaland. Kansas City, Mo., Nazarene Publishing House, 1970. 88 p.

5086   COOPER, Sherman E. (-1951). LLITW (1951), 215.
        FM. Missionary

5087   COREY, James Benijah (1832-).
        ME? Coal mine owner, lay leader

5088   Corey, James Benijah, 1832-
        Memoir and personal recollection.... Pittsburgh,

Pa., Pittsburgh Printing Co., 1914. 405 p.
Autobiography.

5089 Corey, James Benijah, 1832-
Restore the ancient land-marks thy fathers (and mothers) have set; J.B. Corey's opinion of the 400 layman's effort to reform the manners of the people. Pittsburgh, 1906? 40 p.
Caption title.

5090 CORLETT, David Shelby (1894-). RLOA (1941-1942), 246. FHOP (1964). WW in the Clergy (1935-1936), 247-248.
CN. Pastor, editor
b. Jan. 28, 1894, Homestead, Pa.

5091 CORLETT, Lewis Thomas (1896-). RLOA (1941-1942), 246. LIE (1948), 225. WW in Am. (1960-1961), 620. GFIIH (1963), 332-349. MHP (1957), 53-61.
CN. Pastor, college prof., college pres., seminary pres.
b. Feb. 8, 1896, Homestead, Pa.

5092 CORNELL, Clarence Ellsworth
ME, CN, PCN, CN. Pastor, evangelist
b. 186?, Pennsylvania
5093 McGraw, James, 1913-
"The preaching of C.E. Cornell," Preacher's Magazine, XXIX (Mar. 1954), 3-5.

5094 CORYELL, Ernest. CIOCC (1959), 17-19.
CN. Pastor, evangelist

5095 COUCHENOUR, H.M. SFLF (1950), 29-34.
President, NHA, 1946-1950
ME, M, UM. Pastor, evangelist, Bible college pres.

5096 COULTER, George. MHP (1957), 23-32.
CN. Pastor, evangelist, district supt., denominational official, general supt.
b. 19??, Ireland

5097 COWEN, Clarence Eugene (1904-).
CG (H). Pastor, Bible college pres., evangelist
b. Sept. 24, 1904, Fordland, Mo.

5098 COWHERD, Effie Grace (-1950). LLITW (1951), 215. SBWTL (1960), 203.
FM. Missionary, supply pastor, evangelist
b. 18??, Brantford, Ont.

5099 COWMAN, Charles Elmer (1868-1924). Nat. Cy. of Am. Biog., XIX, 295.

Part VI. Biography 609

   Founder, OMS
   ME, IAHU, IAHC, IHC, PHC. Telegrapher, missionary (OMS)
   b. Mar. 13, 1868, Toulon, Ill.
   d. Sept. 25, 1924, Los Angeles, Calif.

5100 Cowman, Lettie (Burd), 1870-1960.
   Charles E. Cowman, missionary warrior; with portraits, illustrations and maps. Los Angeles, Oriental Missionary Society, c1939. 433 p.

5101 Erny, Edward
   No guarantee but God; the story of the founders of the Oriental Missionary Society, by Edward and Esther Erny. Greenwood, Ind., Oriental Missionary Society, 1969. 116 p.
   "Charles Cowman": p. 1-24.

5102 Kilbourne, Ernest Albert, 1865-1928.
   The story of a mission in Japan. Tokyo, Cowman and Kilbourne, n.d.

5103 Pearson, Benjamin Harold, 1893-
   But if it dies; illustrated in the life of Charles E. Cowman. Fort Washington, Pa., Christian Literature Crusade, 1970. 109 p.

5104 COWMAN, Lettie Burd (1870-1960).
   ME, IAHU, IAHC, IHC, PHC. Missionary (OMS)
   b. Mar. 3, 1870, Afton, Iowa
   d. Apr. 17, 1960, Los Angeles, Calif.

5105 Erny, Edward
   No guarantee but God; the story of the founders of the Oriental Missionary Society, by Edward and Esther Erny. Greenwood, Ind., Oriental Missionary Society, 1969. 116 p.
   "Lettie B. Cowman": p. 67-103.

5106 Pearson, Benjamin Harold, 1893-
   The vision lives; a profile of Mrs. Charles E. Cowman. Los Angeles, Cowman Publications, 1961. 341 p.

5107 Pearson, Benjamin Harold, 1893-
   The vision lives; a profile of Mrs. Charles E. Cowman. Los Angeles, Cowman Publishing Co., 1961. 205 p.
   Abridged ed.

5108 COX, Anna Lee. FHOP (1964).
   ME, CN. Missionary
   b. 18??, Farmington, Mo.

5109 COX, Edward F.
   CN. Pastor, evangelist, district supt.

5110 COX, Homer L. (-1929). LDML (1953), 67.
   Fr. Pastor, evangelist, gospel song writer, Bible institute teacher, yearly meeting supt.
   d. Nov. 1929

5111 COX, Leo George (1912-). GFIIH (1963), 178-195.
WM, W. College prof., Bible college prin., pastor, college pres.

5112 COX, Rose (-1938). LLITW (1951), 215.
FM. Missionary

5113 COX, Sidney. LDML (1953), 75.
SA. Salvation Army officer, gospel song writer

5114 COX, Winfred R. TDOOP (1968), 114-116.
IAHU, IAHC, IHC, PHC. Editor, Bible school pres., pastor, general supt.

5115 CRAIG, James (1844-1919). SBWTL (1960), 180-181.
ME, FM. Pastor, district chairman
b. 1844, Scotland
d. 1919, California

5116 CRANE, Olive. FHOP (1964).
CN. Pastor, missionary

5117 CRANE, R. H. PPE (1868), 210-211.
Bapt., ME. Pastor

5118 CRARY, B. F. (1821-). GFW (1888), 85-89. PPE (1868), 137-141.
ME. Pastor, evangelist
b. Dec. 12, 1821, Jennings County, Ind.

5119 CRAWFORD, James H. (1879-1958?).
CN. Evangelist, pastor
b. Aug. 30, 1879, Fallsville, Ark.
d. 1958?

5120 McGraw, James, 1913-
"The preaching of J. H. Crawford." Preacher's Magazine, XXXVI (Oct. 1961), 4-6.

5121 CRITTENTON, Charles Nelson (1833-1909). MCV (1901), 70-81. MHTWW (n.d.), 28-30. DAB. N.Y. Times (Nov. 17, 1909), 9:4.
Attended GHA, 1901 (Chicago)
Epis. Merchant, philanthropist, rescue mission founder, rescue home founder, lay evangelist
b. Feb. 20, 1833, Henderson, Jefferson County, N.Y.
d. Nov. 16, 1909, San Francisco, Calif.

5122 Crittenton, Charles Nelson, 1833-1909.
Around the world with Jesus. Chicago, World's Woman's Christian Temperance Union, 1894.

5123 Crittenton, Charles Nelson, 1833-1909.
The brother of girls; the life story of Charles N. Crittenton, as told by himself. Chicago, World's

Events Co., 1910. 247 p.
Autobiography.
5124 Crittenton, Charles Nelson, 1833-1910.
Life sketch and work of Evangelist Charles N. Crittenton. Washington, 1897. 19 p.

5125 CROCKETT, Abbie Lord (-1937). LLITW (1951), 215.
FM. Missionary

5126 CROOKS, Adam (1824-1874). SCM (1881), 269-270.
MP, WM. Pastor, home missionary, editor
b. May 3, 1824, Leesville, Ohio
d. Dec. 15, 1874, Syracuse, N.Y.
5127 Crooks, Elizabeth (Willets)
Life of Rev. A. Crooks, written and comp. by his wife, Mrs. E.W. Crooks. Syracuse, N.Y., Wesleyan Methodist Publishing House, 1875. 312 p.

5128 CROSSLEY, Francis William (1839-1897).
I. Rescue mission supt. (Star Hall, Manchester)
5129 Crossley, Ella Kathleen
He heard from God; the story of Frank Crossley.
London, Salvationist Publishing & Supplies, 1959.
122 p.
5130 Harris, James Rendel, 1852- , ed.
The life of Francis William Crossley, ed. by J.R. Harris. 2d ed. London, J. Nisbet & Co., 1899.
xiii, 249 p.

5131 CROUCH, Charles. DCSWM (1946), 54-60.
CN. Military chaplain

5132 CROUCH, Winnie (1880-1970).
ME, HFMA. Pastor, evangelist, orphanage worker, Bible school founder, Bible school teacher
b. 1880, Custer County, Neb.
d. Nov. 20, 1970, Phoenix, Ariz.
5133 Crouch, Winnie, 1880-1970.
Room on the rock. 2d ed., rev. and enl. Phoenix, Ariz., 1957. 56 p.
Autobiography.
First issued as Some experiences of an inhabitant of the rock in 1943.
5134 Crouch, Winnie, 1880-1970.
Some experiences of an inhabitant of the rock.
Tabor, Iowa, Good Tidings Press, 1943. 47 p.
Autobiography.
Issued also under title: Room on the rock.

5135 CROWDER, Thomas J. PPE (1868), 328-329.
ME. Pastor

5136 CROY, Ima B. Lehman. FHOP (1964).
      CN. Pastor's wife

5137 CROY, J. W. FHOP (1964).
      CN. Pastor, evangelist

5138 CRUZ, Javier de la. HNTB (1934), 136-138.
      R. Cath., CN. National worker, pastor
      b. 18??, Guatemala

5139 CUBIE, David Livingston (1928-). DAS (1969), IV, 76.
      CN, Cong., CN. Pastor, college prof.
      b. Feb. 12, 1928, Perth, Scot.

5140 CULBERTSON, Paul Thomas
      CN. Pastor?, college prof., college dean
5141 Culbertson, Paul Thomas
      "A history of the initiative and referendum in Oregon." Unpublished Ph.D. dissertation, University of Oregon, 1941. 544ℓ.

5142 CULLIS, Charles (1833-1892). GFW (1888), 174-175.
      WWW in Am. (1607-1896), 130. DAB.
      Epis. Physician, faith healer
      b. Mar. 7, 1833, Boston, Mass.
      d. June 18, 1892
5143 Cullis, Charles, 1833-1892.
      History of the Consumptives' Home, no. 11 Willard St. ... being the five annual reports to ... 1869. Boston, 1869.
5144 [Cullis, Charles], 1833-1892.
      Intervale Park, Intervale, N.H. Boston, Willard Tract Repository, 1883. Cover-title, 32 p.
5145 Cullis, Charles, 1833-1892.
      Work of faith; history of the Consumtives' Home. Boston, 1866.
5146 Boardman, William Edwin, 1810-1886.
      Faith work under Dr. Cullis. Boston, Willard Tract Repository, 1874. ix, 296 p.

5147 CULLIS, Lucretia Ann. GFW (1888), 169-173.
      Epis. Lay member

5148 CULVER, Thelma Blanche (1909-). WW in Am. (1968-1969), 525. WWACUA (1970-1971), 114. LIE (1971), 211.
      FM, CN. College prof., college admin.
      b. Mar. 29, 1909, Corsica, S.D.

5148a CUNNINGHAM, James Barber (1887-). RLOA (1941-1942), 266-267.
      FM. Pastor, district supt.
      b. Nov. 11, 1887, Upton County, Ga.

Part VI. Biography

5149 CURNICK, Edward T. (1850-1923).
Endorsed call, GHA, 1901 (Chicago)
ME. Pastor
b. Sept. 23, 1850
d. Sept. 14, 1923
5150 Curnick, Edwart T., 1850-1923.
The Kentucky ranger. Chicago, Christian Witness Co., 1923. 198 p.

5151 CURTIS, J. Samuel (1890-   ). FHOP (1964).
ME, S; CN. Pastor
b. Oct. 30, 1890
Parents: tenant farmers

5152 CUTHBERTSON, James (1882-1957).
JEB. Missionary
5153 Gosden, Eric William
Take fire! James Cuthbertson of Japan; introd. by Paul S. Rees. London, Marshall, Morgan & Scott, 1960. 110 p.
5154 Gosden, Eric William
Take fire! James Cuthbertson of Japan. Fort Washington, Pa., Christian Literature Crusade, 1960. 110 p.

5155 DADMUN, John William (1819-1890). MAWACOSM (1925), 315-317.
ME. Academy teacher, pastor, military chaplain, prison chaplain, gospel song writer
b. Dec. 20, 1819, Hubbardston, Mass.
d. May 6, 1890, Boston, Mass.

5156 DAKE, Vivian Adelbert (1854-1892).
FM (PB). Pastor, evangelist, district chairman, missionary
d. 1892, Africa
5157 Nelson, Thomas Hiram, 1863-
Life and labors of Rev. Vivian A. Dake, organizer and leader of Pentecost Bands, embracing an account of his travels in America, Europe and Africa, with selections from his sketches, poems and songs. Chicago, Pub. for the author by T.B. Arnold, 1894. 508 p.
5158 Parsons, Ida Dake
Kindling watch-fires; being a brief sketch of the life of Rev. Vivian A. Dake, together with a compilation of selections from his writings, sermons, and poems, to which is appended a few of his best songs with the music. Chicago, Pub. for the author by Free Methodist Publishing House, 1915. 209 p.

5159 DAMON, C. M.
FM. Pastor, seminary (academy) founder

5160	Damon, C. M.
Sketches and incidents; or, Reminiscence of interest in the life of the author with an appendix containing treatises on "the ministration of the Spirit," "National religion," and "on holiness," with other matter. Chicago, Free Methodist Publishing House, 1900. 366 p.

5161	DAMON, Herbert Milton (-1924). LLITW (1951), 215.
FM. Missionary

5162	DANE, Charles Walter (1875-1944). WW in the Clergy (1935-1936), 274. N.Y. Times (July 4, 1944), 19:3.
ME, U. Pres. Pastor, Pres. moderator
b. Aug. 23, 1875, Lexington, Mass.
d. July 1, 1944, Montclair, N.J.

5163	DANFORD, Samuel Alexander (1865-)
ME. Pastor, evangelist, presiding elder

5164	DANIELS, Josiah R. (1836?-1908). PPE (1868), 234-239.
ME. Pastor
d. Aug. 22, 1908, Ocean Grove, N.J.

5165	DANSKIN, Donald Ralph (1910-). WWACUA (1970-1971), 119.
CN. Public school teacher, college prof., college admin.
b. Nov. 3, 1910, Ragan, Neb.

5166	DASHIELL, Edward Honeywood (1873-1931). PM (1898), 43-48.
Epis.; ME, S. Pastor, evangelist
b. Feb. 15, 1873, Elizabeth, N.C.

5167	D'AUBIGNE, Merle. EAP (1890, c1879), 101-103.
Bapt. ? Layman

5168	DAVIES, Edward (1830-).
ME. Pastor, evangelist, publisher

5169	DAVIS, Grace Weiser
Endorsed call, GHA, 1901 (Chicago)
ME? Evangelist

5170	DAVIS, Harrison. GHAI (1960), 51-55.
CN. College prof., missionary

5171	DAVIS, Henry Turner (1832-). SCM (1881), 278.
ME. Pastor
b. July 29, 1832, Springfield, Ohio

5172	Davis, Henry Turner, 1832-
Solitary places made glad; being observations and

Part VI. Biography

experiences for thirty-two years in Nebraska, with sketches and incidents touching the discovery, early settlement, and development of the state. Cincinnati, Printed for the author by Cranston & Stowe, 1890. 422 p.

5173 DAVIS, Melba S. (-1937). LLITW (1951), 215.
FM. Missionary

5174 DAVIS, Samuel M. (1835-1892).
Attended GHA, 1885 (Chicago)
ME. Pastor
d. Dec. 7, 1892.

5175 DAW, Francis Ambrose (1894-1951). SBWTL (1960), 189-190.
Ch. of Eng., WM, FM. Pastor, district supt., editor
b. 1894, London, Eng.
d. 1951, Newmarket, Ont.

5176 DAY, William (1833?-). PPE (1868), 85-89.
ME. Pastor

5177 DAYHOFF, Irvin E.
IAHU, IHM, CN. Missionary
5178 Dayhoff, Irvin E.
Missionary vicissitudes, by Mr. and Mrs. Dayhoff. Cincinnati, Published for the authors by God's Bible School and Revivalist, 1938.

5179 DAYTON, Wilber Thomas (1916-). DAS (1969), IV, 82. WW in Am. Ed. (1967-1968), 193. GFIIH (1963), 88-104. GTWATD (1965), 196-209. BPOH (1969), 16-27.
WM, W. College prof., college dean, seminary prof., college pres.
b. Oct. 29, 1916, Hadley, N.Y.

5180 DEAL, William Sanford (1910-). CA. WW in the West (1967-1968), 225.
PHC, W. Pastor, evangelist, district supt., Bible college pres., counselor
b. Apr. 9, 1910, Taylorsville, N.C.

5181 DEAN, William Ward (1924-). DAS (1969), IV, 83.
UMC. College Prof.
b. Sept. 7, 1924, Brown City, Mich.

5182 DECH, George L. FHOP (1964).
CN. Pastor

5183 DeLONG, Russell Victor (1901-   ). WW in Am. (1960-
      1961), 733. RLOA (1941-1942), 289. MLA (1935),
      90-93.
      CN. Pastor, evangelist, college prof., college pres.,
      radio preacher, seminary prof.
      b. Aug. 24, 1901, Dover, N.H.
5184 DeLong, Russell Victor, 1901-
      "The concept of personality in the philosophy of Ralph
      Barton Perry." Unpublished Ph.D. dissertation, Boston
      University, 1940.

5185 DEMARAY, Donald Eugene (1926-   ). WWACUA (1970-1971),
      127. DAS (1969), IV, 85. LIE (1971), 230. GIIH
      (1962), 208-221. GTWATD (1965), 270-281.
      FM. Pastor, college prof., seminary prof., seminary
      admin.
      b. Dec. 6, 1926, Adrian, Mich.

5186 DeMILLE, Wesley C. SBWTL (1960), 206.
      FM. Pastor, missionary

5187 DEMPSTER, Joseph S.
      Attended GHA, 1901 (Chicago)
      R. Cath., ME. Pastor, evangelist, editor
5188 Dempster, Joseph S.
      From Romanism to Pentecost; or, The spiritual auto-
      biography of Rev. Joseph S. Dempster. Cincinnati,
      M.W. Knapp, 1898. 105 p. (Pentecostal holiness
      library, vol. 1, no. 3)

5189 DENMAN, Mary R. GFW (1888), 106-109.
      Epis. Lay member

5190 DENTON, Ronald. GHAI (1960), 66-67.
      CN. Missionary

5191 DePASQUALE, Frances. GHAI (1960), 68-69.
      CN. Missionary

5192 DePAUW, Washington Charles (1822-1887). DAB. SCM
      (1881), 287-289. WWW in Am. (1607-1896), 146.
      Member, NHA
      Attended HConf., 1877 (Cincinnati)
      ME. Lay leader, banker, manufacturer, philanthropist
      b. Jan. 4, 1822, Salem, Ind.
      d. May 5, 1887
5193 O'Brien, Michael F.
      "A nineteenth century Hoosier business man: Wash-
      ington Charles DePauw." Unpublished B.A. thesis,
      DePauw University, 1966.

Part VI. Biography 617

5194 DESH, Frank. LLITW (1951), 215.
FM. Missionary

5195 DESH, Rose Myers. LLITW (1951), 216.
FM. Missionary

5196 DeSHAZER, Jacob (1912-).
FM. Missionary
b. Nov. 15, 1912, Salem, Ore.
5197 DeShazer, Jacob, 1912-
I was a prisoner of Japan. Osaka, Japan?, Bible Meditation League, 1950.
In Japanese.
5198 Watson, Charles Hoyt, 1888-
De Shazer: the Doolittle raider who turned missionary; a true and thrilling story of how the practical demonstration of the law of love is bringing international understanding and the spirit of Christ to Japan. Winona Lake, Ind., Light and Life Press, 1950. 181 p.

5199 DeVOL, Charles Edward (1903-). WMAMH (1957), 90-120.
Fr. Missionary
b. Oct. 2, 1903, Luho, Ch.

5200 DeVOL, George Fox (1871-1917).
Fr. Physician, missionary
b. Mar. 8, 1871, Maryland
d. Dec. 30, 1917, Luho, Ch.
5201 Williams, Walter Rollin, 1884-
Me and my house, by Walter R. and Myrtle M. Williams; pen drawings by Anna Talbott McPherson.
Grand Rapids, Mich., Wm. B. Eerdmans Publishing Co., 1957. 187 p.

5202 DeVOL, Isabella French (1869-1920). WMAMH (1957), 30-89.
Fr. Physician, missionary
b. Nov. 18, 1869, Damascus, Ohio
d. Dec. 22, 1920, Glens Falls, N.Y.

5203 DeVOL, William Ezra (1909-). WMAMH (1957), 156-186.
Fr. Physician, missionary
b. Sept. 7, 1909, Kuling, Ch.

5204 DeWEERD, Mrs. Fred.
IHC, PHC. Missionary
5205 DeWeerd, Mrs. Fred
The last mile of the way. Fairmount, Ind., Mrs. Fred DeWeerd, 1923.

5206 DeWEERD, James Arthur (1916-1972).
WM, W. Pastor, evangelist, college pres., military chaplain
d. Mar. 29, 1972, Fairmount, Ind.

5207 DeWITT, Pearl L. FHOP (1964).
CN. Pastor, evangelistic singer

5208 DHLAMINI, Samuel. HNTB (1934), 110-112.
CN. National worker, pastor
b. 189?, Swaziland
5209 Burne, Marjory
Thy servant heareth; the story of Samuel Dlamini of Swaziland, by Marjory Burne and Helen Temple. Kansas City, Mo., Nazarene Publishing House, 1967. 80 p.

5210 DHLAMINI, Zakeu (-1931). HNTB (1934), 112-114.
CN. National worker, pastor

5211 DIAZ, John Joseph (1873-1964). HNTB (1934), 13-19.
APCA, PCN, CN. Missionary
b. May 23, 1873, Brava, Cape Verde Islands
d. Nov. 24, 1964, Oakland, Calif.

5212 DICKERMAN, Ethel King
CN. Pastor's wife, college prof.
5213 Dickerman, Ethel (King)
Not by bread alone; a factual narrative of one family who found meaning in life on a cotton farm. Kansas City, Mo., Pedestal Press, 1970. 63 p.

5214 DIETER, Harold D. (1906-1948).
PHC. Pastor, Bible institute pres.
d. Sept. 6, 1948, Allentown, Pa.

5215 DIETER, Melvin Easterday (1924-). WW in the East (1968-1969), 277.
PHC, WC. Pastor, Bible college pres., denominational admin.
b. Oct. 12, 1924, Cherryville, Pa.
5216 "Elected officials of The Wesleyan Church," Wesleyan Advocate, CXXX (July 24, 1972), 15.

5217 DILBECK, Lula May (-1918).
HChuC, PCN. Evangelist
d. Oct. 1918
5218 Lula May, our preacher girl. Bethany, Okla., 1918.

5219 DILLINGHAM, Michael Vance (1863-1944?).
PCN, CN. Pastor
b. May 20, 1863, Gladewater, Tex.
d. 1944?, Shreveport, La.

Part VI. Biography

5220 "The preaching of M. V. Dillingham," Preacher's Magazine, XXXVI (June 1961), 8-10.

5221 DIRKSE, Neal C. DCSWM (1946), 140-142.
CN. Military chaplain, pastor

5222 DITMER, Russell P. (1897-). RLOA (1941-1942), 301.
MBIC, UMC. Pastor, district supt., editor
b. July 10, 1897, Laura, Ohio

5223 DIXON, Bertha Pinkham
Fr., Bapt., CMA, ET. Evangelist, missionary
5224 Dixon, Bertha (Pinkham)
A romance of faith. Los Angeles, Bedrock Press, 194?. xvi, 206 p.
Imprint on label.
Autobiography.

5225 DIXON, Elmer P. (-1957).
PCN, PHC. Lay leader
d. Aug. 23, 1957

5226 DODGE, William Asbury (1844-1904).
ME, S. Pastor, evangelist
d. Jan. 16, 1904
5227 Garbutt, Mrs. J. William
Rev. W.A. Dodge as we knew him.... Atlanta, 1906.

5228 DODSON, E. H.
PCN, CN. Lay leader
d. 19??, Dodson?, Tex.

5229 DOLBOW, Andrew J. (1846-1934).
ME, CN. Evangelist
b. May 30, 1846, Perkintown, Salem County, N.J.
d. 1934.
5230 Dolbow, Andrew J., 1846-1934.
The dark and the bright side of life. Elmer, N.J., Elmer Times print, 1895. 37 p.
Autobiography.
5231 Dolbow, Andrew J., 1846-1934.
Story of my life: its dark and bright side; written from dictation by Rev. S.H. Hann. Chicago, Christian Witness Co., 1904? 64 p.
Autobiography.

5232 DONNELLY, John T. DCSWM (1960), 64-77.
CN. Military chaplain

5233 DOOLEY, Gladys Emmeline (1906-). ETWF (196?).
PHC. Pastor, missionary
b. Mar. 21, 1906, Terre Haute, Ind.

5234 DOOLEY, Hannah M. Lippincott (1868-   ). SCUH (1962), 147.
Attended GHA, 1901 (Chicago)
ME, CN, PCN, CN. Pastor's wife, evangelist, rescue mission worker
5235 Dooley, John Alexander, 1860-
Fifty years winning souls, by Rev. and Mrs. J.A. Dooley. 3d ed. Minneapolis, 1938. 33 p.

5236 DOOLEY, John Alexander (1860-   ). SCUH (1962), 147.
Attended GHA, 1901 (Chicago)
ME, I, CN, PCN, CN. Pastor, evangelist, rescue mission supt.
5237 Dooley, John Alexander, 1860-
Fifty years winning souls, by Rev. and Mrs. J.A. Dooley. 3d ed. Minneapolis, 1938. 33 p.

5238 DORSEY, Morton W. GFIIH (1963), 56-71. GTWATD (1965), 384-395. BPOH (1969), 122-129.
President, NHA, 1958-1960
COCICU. Pastor, Bible college pres., evangelist

5239 DOTY, Thomas K. (1833-1913).
Attended HConf., 1877 (Cincinnati)
Signed call, GHA, 1885 (Chicago)
Attended GHA, 1901 (Chicago)
WM. Pastor, evangelist, editor
b. June 6, 1833, Massachusetts
d. Oct. 13, 1913, Cleveland, Ohio
5240 McLeister, Ira Ford, 1879-1963.
History of the Wesleyan Methodist Church of America. Rev. ed. [i.e. 3d ed.] by Roy Stephen Nicholson. Marion, Ind., Wesley Press, 1959. 558 p.
Reference made to Thomas K. Doty: p. 108, 118, 338, 407-409.

5241 DOUGLAS, John Henry (1832-1919)
Fr. Pastor, yearly meeting supt., evangelist
b. 1832, Fairfield, Me.
5242 Douglas, John Henry, 1832-1919.
"My early experience in the ministry," American Friend, XIX (Feb. 15, 1912).
5243 Douglas, John Henry, 1832-1919.
"The boyhood of John Henry Douglas," ed. by Mabel H. Douglas, American Friend, XVIII (Jan. 5, 1911); XVIII (Feb. 6, 1911).
5244 Mott, Edward, 1866-1954.
Sixty years of gospel ministry. Portland, Ore., 1947. 206 p.
"John Henry Douglas--the evangelist," by Bernard E. Mott: p. 168-175.

Part VI. Biography 621

5245 DOWNEY, Lois Jean Baumgardner (1931-). ETWF (196?).
    PHC. Pastor's wife, missionary
    b. Feb. 11, 1931, Hamilton, Ohio

5246 DOWNEY, Paul Roger (1930-). ETWF (196?).
    PHC. Pastor, missionary
    b. June 21, 1930, Columbus, Ohio

5247 DROWN, Walter Forbes (1896-1972). ETWF (196?).
    PHC. Pastor, evangelist, district supt., missionary
        evangelist
    b. Nov. 12, 1896, Kimball, S.D.
    d. Mar. 10, 1972, Colorado Springs, Colo.

5248 DRUM, Woodard Glenn (1903-). SEC (1968), 104-124.
    PeHC. Lay leader; public school teacher, prin., supt.;
        Bible academy teacher, college dean, college pres.
    b. Sept. 11, 1903, Catawba County, N.C.

5249 DRYSDALE, John Douglas (1880-1953).
    EHC. Pastor, evangelist, Bible school prin.
5250   Grubb, Norman Percy, 1895- , ed.
        J.D. Drysdale, prophet of holiness ... autobiography
    by J.D. Drysdale; biography of N. Grubb; postscript by
    Stanley Banks; ed. by N. Grubb. London, Lutterworth
    Press, 1955. 265 p.

5251 DUCKWORTH, Bonita Lois (1934-). ETWF (196?).
    PHC. Evangelist, evangelistic singer, missionary
    b. Apr. 7, 1934, Portageville, Mo.

5252 DUCKWORTH, Jack Raymond (1934-). ETWF (196?).
    PHC. Evangelist, evangelistic singer, Bible school
        teacher, missionary
    b. Mar. 3, 1934, Savannah, Tenn.

5253 DUDA, Rachel Grace Fair (1926-). ETWF (196?).
    PHC. Pastor's wife, missionary
    b. Nov. 14, 1926, New Marshfield, Ohio

5254 DUDA, Robert Clarence (1924-). ETWF (196?).
    PHC. Pastor, missionary
    b. Aug. 14, 1924, Boswell, Pa.

5255 DUDLEY, Dora Griffin
    Cong. Rescue mission worker
5256   Dudley, Mrs. Dora Griffin
        Beulah; or, Some of the fruits of one consecrated
    life. Rev. and enl. ed. Grand Rapids, Mich., 1896.
    269 p.

5257 DUDMAN, Charlotte
        Attended WUHC, 1880 (Jacksonville, Ill.)
        Attended GHA, 1901 (Chicago)
        FM. Lay member

5258 DUNHAM, R. E.
        ME, PCN. Pastor, district supt.

5259 DUNN, Lewis Romaine (1822-1898). SCM (1881), 318.
        PPE (1868), 60-64.
        Attended H. Conf. 1877 (New York)
        Member, NHA
        ME. Pastor, evangelist
        b. 1822, New Brunswick, N.J.
        d. Aug. 6, 1898

5260 DURYEA, John Ackerly (1878-1946). RLOA (1941-1942), 321.
        Member, NHA
        CN (OMS). Rescue mission supt., evangelist, college admin., missionary soc. promoter
        b. Sept. 30, 1878, Huntington (Elwood), N.Y.
        d. 1946, Freeport?, L.I., N.Y.
5261   Duryea, Jennie Sworn
        John A. Duryea; a Spirit-filled evangel. Louisville, Ky., Herald Press, n.d. 249 p.

5262 DUSTMAN, J. M.
        Attended GHA, 1901 (Chicago)
        ME? Pastor?

5263 DYGOSKI, Louise Annie (1911-   ). DAS (1969), II, 147.
        CN. College prof.
        b. July 26, 1911, New York, N.Y.

5264 EAGLE, J. M. (-1936). SBWTL (1960), 183.
        FM. Harness maker, pastor, district elder
        b. 18??, Yarker, Ont.
        d. 1936, Hamilton, Ont.

5265 EARLE, Absalom Backas (-1892). LDEFC (1921), 300-310.
        Bapt. Pastor, evangelist
5266   Earle, Absalom Backas,   -1892.
        Bringing in sheaves. Boston, J.H. Earle, 1868. 384 p.
5267   Earle, Absalom Backas,   -1892.
        Incidents used in his meetings. Boston, J.H. Earle?, 1888. 210 p.
5268   Earle, Absalom Backas,   -1892.
        Work of an evangelist; review of fifty years. Boston, J.H. Earle, 1881. 66 p.
        "Fiftieth anniversary sermon [delivered in Tremont

Part VI. Biography

Temple, Boston, Mass., Nov. 14, 1880]": p. 35-66.

5269 EARLE, Ralph (1907-   ). CA. GIIH (1962), 74-88.
GTWATD (1965), 172-179.
CN. Pastor, college prof., seminary prof.
b. Jan. 27, 1907, Dighton, Mass.

5270 EATON, Joel W. (1836-   ). SCM (1881), 325.
ME. Pastor, military chaplain

5271 EBY, Blanche Remington (1885-1925). SWGHW (1948), 88, 91-92.
MBIC. Missionary
d. June 1923, Syria

5272 Eby, Blanche (Remington), 1885-
At the mercy of Turkish brigands, a true story; introd. by Rev. J.A. Huffman. New Carlisle, Ohio, Bethel Publishing Co., c1922. 285 p.
Account of siege and massacre.

5273 EBY, D. C. SWGHW (1948), 88, 91-93.
MBIC. Missionary
b. 188?, Southampton, Ont., Can.

5274 ECKEL, Howard. SCUH (1962), 276-279, 328.
Cong., APCA, PCN, CN. Pastor, district supt.

5275 ECKEL, William A.
PCN, CN. Pastor, district supt., missionary

5276 ECKERT, Ruth M. (1922-   ). WWACUA (1970-1971), 144.
WM?, W? Bible college prof., Bible college admin.
b. July 27, 1922, Kingston, N.Y.

5277 EDMONDS, L. M. PPE (1868), 248-250.
ME. Pastor

5278 EDWARDS, Frank C.
ME, CN, ME. Pastor, evangelist
b. 18??, Iowa
d. 19??, Pasadena, Calif.

5279 EDWARDS, Grace Morris. MLA (1935), 41-54.
ME, CN. Orphanage worker, pastor, evangelist, evangelistic singer
b. 18??, Benton, Ill.

5280 EDWARDS, Grace Smith (-1944). LLITW (1951), 216.
FM. Missionary

5281 EDWARDS, Maud W. (-1933). LLITW (1951), 216.
FM. Missionary

5282   EISENHOWER, Abraham Lincoln (-1944). WMK (1966), 55.
       BIC (HFMA). Evangelist, orphanage supt.
       b. 18??, Pennsylvania
       d. Dec. 13, 1944, Upland, Calif.
5283   Dodd, Gladys
       "The early career of Abraham L. Eisenhower, pioneer preacher," Kansas Historical Quarterly, XXIX (Autumn 1963), 233-249.
       In 1892 Abraham Lincoln Eisenhower, veterinarian of Hope and Abilene, Kansas, became an itinerant preacher. Turning his home in Abilene over to his brother, Dwight Eisenhower's father, Abraham Eisenhower toured Kansas in his Gospel wagon. In 1899 he and his wife started an orphanage in Oklahoma, a work which was ultimately turned over to the Brethren in Christ Church.
5284   Dodd, Gladys
       "The religious background of the Eisenhower family." Unpublished B.D. thesis, Nazarene Theological Seminary, 1959. vi, iv, 436ℓ.

5285   EISENHOWER, Ira (1870-1943). WMK (1966), 52-55.
       BIC, HFMA, CG (H). Evangelist, pastor, rescue mission supt.
       d. Mar. 1943
5286   Dodd, Gladys
       "The religious background of the Eisenhower family." Unpublished B.D. thesis, Nazarene Theological Seminary, 1959. vi, iv, 436ℓ.

5287   EKVALL, Robert Brainerd (1898-   ). CA.
       CMA. Missionary's child, anthropologist, translator
       b. Feb. 18, 1898, Kansu, Ch.
5288   Ekvall, Robert Brainerd, 1898-
           Cultural relations on the Kansu-Tibetan border. Chicago, University of Chicago Press, c1939. xiii, 87 p.
5289   Ekvall, Robert Brainerd, 1898-
           Faithful echo; foreword by Arthur H. Dean. New York, Twayne Publishers, 1960. 125 p.
           Autobiographical.
5290   Ekvall, Robert Brainerd, 1898-
           Religious observances in Tibet: patterns and function. Chicago, University of Chicago Press, 1964. xiii, 313 p.
5291   Ekvall, Robert Brainerd, 1898-
           Tents against the sky; a novel of Tibet. London, V. Gollancz, 1954. 264 p.
5292   Ekvall, Robert Brainerd, 1898-
           Tents against the sky; a novel of Tibet. New York, Farrar, Strauss & Young, 1955?. 264 p.

Part VI. Biography

5293 Ekvall, Robert Brainerd, 1898-
 Tibetan sky lines. New York, Farrar, Straus and Young, 1952. 240 p.
5294 Ekvall, Robert Brainerd, 1898-
 Tibetan voices; drawings by Jean Hammond. New York and London, Harper & Brothers, 1946. 63 p.
 Poems.

5295 ELIZONDO, Santos (1869-). HNTB (1934), 181-184.
 R. Cath., CN, PCN, CN. National worker, pastor
 b. 1869, Chihuahua, Mex.

5296 ELLIOT, Henry Bond (-1912). PPE (1868), 196-202.
 N.Y. Times (Aug. 26, 1912), 9:6.
 Cong., Pres. Pastor
 d. Aug. 25, 1912, Port Jefferson, L.I., N.Y.

5297 ELLIOTT, Esther Cantrell (1929-). ETWF (196?).
 PHC. Missionary, Bible school teacher
 b. May 10, 1929, Knoxville, Tenn.

5298 ELLIOTT, Harry Joseph
 CN. Pastor, evangelist
5299 Elliott, Harry Joseph
 From sinking sands. Kansas City, Mo., Nazarene Publishing House, 1922. 39 p.
 Autobiography.

5300 ELLIOTT, Paul Frederick (1869-1944).
 ME, IAHU, IAHC, IHC, PHC. Pastor, evangelist, district supt.
 d. June 2, 1944

5301 ELLIOTT, Paul Frederick (1904-). WW in Am. Ed. (1967-1968). BPOH (1969), 78-84. TDOOP (1968), 187-189.
 President, NHA, 1950-1954
 PHC, W. Pastor, Bible college pres., denominational official, evangelist, college pres., general supt.
 b. Mar. 26, 1904, Mason, Mich.
5302 Pilgrim Holiness Church. Department of Sunday Schools and Youth.
 The life of Paul F. Elliott.... Indianapolis, Pilgrim Publishing House, 1964. 16 p.

5303 ELLIS, William T.
 Attended WUHC, 1880 (Jacksonville, Ill.)
 Attended GHA, 1885 (Chicago)
 ME. Pastor, editor

5304 ELLYSON, Edgar Painter (1869-1954). NP (1925), 32-41.
 Fr., CN. General supt., district supt., editor, de-

nominational official
b. Aug. 4, 1869, Damascus, Ohio
d. Aug. 24, 1954, Kansas City, Mo.

5305 Akers, Lyle Everette
"The life and works of E. P. and M. Emily Ellyson."
Unpublished B. D. thesis, Nazarene Theological Seminary, 1953.

5306 ELLYSON, Mary Emily Soul (1869-1943).
Fr., CN, PCN, CN. Pastor
b. Aug. 12, 1869, Dunham, Que., Can.
d. June 26, 1943, Vicksburg, Mich.

5307 Akers, Lyle Everette
"The life and works of E. P. and M. Emily Ellyson."
Unpublished B. D. thesis, Nazarene Theological Seminary, 1953.

5308 EMERY, O. Dale (1927-). TDOOP (1968), 348.
Executive director, CHA, 1970-1972
PHC, W. Pastor, district supt., denominational official
b. 1927, Indianapolis, Ind.

5309 "Conference elects 11 officers," Wesleyan Advocate, CXXVII (July 15, 1968), 10.

5310 "Elected officials of The Wesleyan Church," Wesleyan Advocate, CXXX (July 24, 1972), 15.

5311 ENYART, Paul C. (1908-1971).
Fr. Pastor, missionary, Bible school teacher
b. Jan. 29, 1908, near Celina, Ohio
d. Aug. 3, 1971, Farmersburg, Ind.

5312 Enyart, Mary H.
"Dear Papa" (Biography). n.p., 197?. 42 p.
Cover-title: "Dear Papa"; a biography of Paul C. Enyart.

5313 ERWIN, S. H. FHOP (1964).
CN. Pastor, college prof.

5314 EUBANKS, Annie Laurie (1926-). ETWF (196?).
PHC. Missionary, editor
b. Nov. 3, 1926, Birmingham, Ala.

5315 FAILING, George Edgar (1912-). WW in Am. (1968-1969), 702. WW in Am. (1972-1973), I, 960. GIIH (1962), 10-31. GTWATD (1965), 422-429.
WM, W. Pastor, college prof., editor
b. Nov. 25, 1912, Kingston, Ont., Can.

5316 FAIRBAIRN, Charles Victor (1890-). RLOA (1941-1942), 351. SBWTL (1960), 210-215.
Meth. (Can.), FM. Evangelist, district elder, pastor,

bishop
b. Nov. 22, 1890, Ventnor, Ont., Can.

5317 Fairbairn, Charles Victor, bp., 1890-
I call to remembrance. Winona Lake, Ind., Light and Life Press, 1960. 185 p.
Autobiography.

5318 FANT, David Jones (1897-). RLOA (1941-1942), 352.
Bapt., CMA. Pastor
b. Jan. 27, 1897, Atlanta, Ga.

5319 FARSON, Duke M.
ME, MetCA. Evangelist
5320 Farson, Duke
Raised a communist; life in a religious commune, illus. by the author. Los Angeles, Farson Studio Publications, 1936. 142 p.
Fictionalized account by son of Duke M. Farson, a founder of the Metropolitan Church Association, concerning his boyhood.

5321 FEE, John Gregg (1816-1901). DAB. Nat. Cy. Am. Biog., XXIV, 301. N.Y. Times (Jan. 12, 1901), 1:6.
Endorsed call, GHA, 1901 (Chicago)
Cong. Pastor, college pres.
b. 1816, Bracken County, Ky.
d. Jan. 11, 1901, Berea, Ky.
5322 Fee, John Gregg, 1816-1901.
An anti-slavery manual, being an examination, in the light of the Bible, and of facts, into the moral and social wrongs of American slavery, with a remedy for the evil. Maysville, Ky., Printed at the Herald Office, 1848. 230 p.
5323 Fee, John Gregg, 1816-1901.
An anti-slavery manual, being an examination, in the light of the Bible, and of facts, into the moral and social wrongs of American slavery, with a remedy for the evil. New York, Arno Press, 1969. 230 p.
Reprint of 1848 ed.
5324 Fee, John Gregg, 1816-1901.
Autobiography of John G. Fee of Berea, Kentucky. Chicago, National Christian Association, 1891. 211 p.
5325 Fee, John Gregg, 1816-1901.
The sinfulness of slaveholding shown by appeals to reason and Scripture. New York, Printed by J.A. Gray, 1851. 36 p.

5326 FELKER, Dean George (1918-). ETWF (196?).
PHC. Missionary
b. Oct. 9, 1918, Bethlehem, Pa.

5327 FELKER, Lillie Beatrice Flexon (1916-   ). ETWF (196?).
      PHC. Missionary
      b.   Oct. 22, 1916, McKeesport, Pa.

5328 FERGUSON, Frank (1880-   ). FHOP (1964).
      PM, CN. Missionary
      b.   Nov. 12, 1880, Salem, Va.

5329 FERGUSON, Lula Hutcherson (1867-1944).
      PM, CN. Missionary
      d.   May 8, 1944, Nashville, Tenn.
5330   Hutcherson, Faith Luce
          Rich in faith; life of Mrs. Frank Fergurson [sic].
      Louisville, Ky., Pentecostal Publishing Co., 1945.
      136 p.

5331 FERGUSON, Manie Payne (1850-   ). LMGSS (1952), 67.
      LDML (1953), 77. PFT (n.d.), 3-35.
      PenielM. Rescue mission worker, gospel song writer,
          editor
      b.   1850, Carlow, Ire.

5332 FERGUSON, Theodore Pollock (1853-1920). PFT (n.d.),
      3-35.
      UPres., PenielM. Rescue mission supt., evangelist
      b.   Jan. 10, 1853, Mansfield, Ohio
      d.   July 12, 1920, Los Angeles, Calif.
5333   Ferguson, Manie (Payne), 1850-
          T.P. Ferguson, the love slave of Jesus Christ and
          His people and founder of Peniel Missions. Los Angeles, 192?. 240 p.

5334 FERNANDEZ, Eugenio (1898-   ). NVFML (1936), 57-69.
      ME. Pastor
      b.   Sept. 6, 1898, Binalman, Pangasian, P.I.

5335 FINCH, Oscar J. (1901-   ). WW in Am. (1954-1955), 865.
      WW in the West (1965-1966), 261.
      CN. Pastor, district supt., college pres.
      b.   Feb. 27, 1901, Somerton, Ohio.

5336 FINCH, Paul W.
      PHC, EmA, CG (H). Pastor, evangelist, missionary,
          Bible school pres.

5337 FINCH, Ralph Goodrich (1881-1950). TDOOP (1968), 115-
      118, 165-168. Colorado Springs Morning Free
      Press (July 26, 1950), 2.
      ME, IHC, PHC, EmA. Pastor, missionary, evangelist,
          general supt. for missions, general supt., editor

Part VI. Biography

        b. July 17, 1881, Terrace Park, Hamilton County, Ohio
        d. July 23, 1950, Tolesboro, Ky.

5338   Finch, Ralph Goodrich, 1881-1950.
        Campaigning for God in southern waters, by Ralph G. Finch and Charles L. Slater. Louisville, Ky., Pentecostal Publishing Co., 1923.

5339   Finch, Ralph Goodrich, 1881-1950.
        My early years and five revival sermons. Cincinnati, Pub. for the author by God's Bible School and Revivalist, 1929. 172 p.
        Autobiography.

5340   Ives, R. Wingrove
        A missionary's cry from Barbados; last chapter by Rev. R.G. Finch, General Missionary Superintendent of the Pilgrim Holiness Church. Kingswood, Ky., Missionary Office, 192?. 72 p.

5340a FINCH, Ruth Wood (1885-1971). Church Herald and Holiness Banner, XCII (Sept. 23, 1971), 14.
        ME, IHC, PHC, EmA, CG (H). Pastor's wife, missionary
        b. Jan. 8, 1885, Glen Rose, Claremont County, Ohio
        d. Aug. 19, 1971, Kansas City, Mo.

5341   FINNEY, Spencer S. PPE (1868), 172-174.
        Pres. Pastor

5342   FIRESTONE, Elvira R. Englund
        CG (H), EM. Missionary (CG (H); W-WM)

5343   Firestone, Elvira R. (Englund)
        Wonderful works of God. n.p., 1951? 126 p.
        Autobiographical.

5344   FIRESTONE, Homer Leon (1921-). National Directory of Latin Americanists. 2d ed. Washington, Library of Congress, 1971, 194.
        CG (H), EMC. Missionary (CG (H), W-WM)
        b. Dec. 10, 1921, Fargo, Okla.

5345   Firestone, Homer Leon, 1921-
        "A description and classification of Sirionó, a Tupí-Guaraní language." Unpublished Ph.D. dissertation, University of New Mexico, 1963. 101ℓ.

5346   Firestone, Homer Leon, 1921-
        Description and classification of Sirionó, a Tupí-Guaraní language. The Hague, Mouton, 1965. 69 p. (Janua linguarum. Series practica, 16)

5347   FISCHER, William Gustavus (1835-1912). CHHMH (1970), 543. MAWACOSM (1925), 322-323. LMGSS (1952), 73. SCM (1881), 361-362. MOHMMH (1937), 286-

289. N.Y. Times (Aug. 15, 1912), 9:2.
ME. College prof., choir director, gospel song writer
b. Oct. 14, 1835, Baltimore, Md.
d. Aug. 12, 1912, Philadelphia, Pa.

5348 FISHER, Annie May Johnson. HWP (1905), 62-64.
Luth., NTCOC, HChuC, PCN, CN. Evangelist, pastor's wife
b. 18??, Swedonia, Tex.

5349 FISHER, Charles William (1916-). CA.
CN. Evangelist, radio preacher
b. Dec. 23, 1916, Blackwell, Okla.

5350 FISHER, William Edgar. SCUH (1962), 155, 158-159, 169, 172, 178, 221.
NTCOC, HChuC, PCN, CN. Evangelist, editor, pastor, district supt.

5351 FITCH, Charles. EAP (1890, c1879), 100-101.
Bapt. ? Pastor

5352 FITKIN, Abram Edward (1878-1933). WWW in Am. (1897-1942), 403. N.Y. Times (Mar. 19, 1933), 33:3.
Fr., APCA. Evangelist, stock broker
b. Sept. 18, 1878, Brooklyn, N.Y.
d. Mar. 18, 1933

5353 FITKIN, Susan Norris (1870-1951). N.Y. Times (Oct. 20, 1951), 15.
Fr., APCA, PCN, CN. Evangelist, missionary soc. pres.
b. Mar. 31, 1870, Ely, Que., Can.
d. Oct. 1951, Oakland, Calif.

5354 Fitkin, Susan (Norris), 1870-1951.
Grace much more abounding; a story of the triumphs of redeeming grace during two score years in the Master's service. Kansas City, Mo., Nazarene Publishing House, 19??. 112 p.

5355 Fitkin, Susan (Norris), 1870-1951.
Over in old Mexico. Kansas City, Mo., Printed for the Woman's Foreign Missionary Society by the Nazarene Publishing House, 193?. 39 p.

5356 Fitkin, Susan (Norris), 1870-1951.
A trip to Africa, New York, 192?. 58 p.
An account of trip to Africa to visit Church of the Nazarene missionary work.

5357 Fitkin, Susan (Norris), 1870-1951.
Under tropical skies. Kansas City, Mo., Printed for the Woman's Foreign Missionary Society by the Nazarene Publishing House, 192?. 96 p.
Account of trip to Barbados, the Leeward Islands

Part VI. Biography

and Trinidad to visit Church of the Nazarene missionary work.
5358   Miller, Basil William, 1897-
       Susan N. Fitkin; for God and missions. Kansas City, Mo., Nazarene Publishing House, n.d. 206 p.

5359   FITZGERALD, Osie M. Boylan (1813-). GFW (1888), 138-147.
       Endorsed call, GHA, 1901 (Chicago)
       ME. Lay leader
       b. 1813, Bernardsville, N.J.

5360   FLEMING, Bona. COPN (1958), 115-120. NP (1925), 78-88.
       IAHC, IHC, CN. Evangelist
5361   Fleming, Bona
       Bona Fleming: his testimony and red hot sermon preached at God's Bible School. n.p., 196?. 2 sides 33 rpm (19572)
       Introduction by Marshall Smart
5362   Fleming, John, -1935.
       Truth on fire, by John and Bona Fleming. Cincinnati, Revivalist Press, n.d. 168 p.
       Autobiographical sermons.

5363   FLEMING, E. J. (1871-1954). SCUH (1962), 295, 322, 338, 341, 347.
       PCN, CN. Pastor, denominational official
       b. Mar. 27, 1871, Ohio
       d. Dec. 18, 1954, Spokane, Wash.

5364   FLEMING, John (-1935). COPN (1958), 115-120.
       IAHC, IHC, CN. Pastor, evangelist
5365   Fleming, John, -1935.
       Truth on fire, by John and Bona Fleming. Cincinati, Revivalist Press, n.d. 168 p.
       Autobiographical sermons.

5366   FLEXON, Richard G. TDOOP (1968), 283-284.
       IAHU, IAHC, IHC, PHC, WC. Pastor, evangelist, Bible academy pres., district supt., denominational official, general supt.
       b. 189?, New Jersey

5367   FLINNER, Lyle Payson (1918-). DAS (1969), IV, 113.
       CN. College prof.
       b. Aug. 11, 1918, New Castle, Pa.
5368   Flinner, Lyle Payson, 1918-
       "Relation between authoritarianism and attitudes toward authority figures." Unpublished Ph.D. dissertation, University of Pittsburgh, 1968.

5369   FLORES, Catarino C. (1896-   ). HNTB (1934), 177-179.
        R. Cath., CN. National worker, Bible school teacher,
           pastor
        b. Nov. 1896, Mexico City, Mex.

5370   FLOWERS, Sumpter Lee (1881-1945).
        ME, CN. Pastor, evangelist
5371   Flowers, Sumpter Lee, 1881-1945.
              The circuit rider; or, Suffering for Christ's sake,
           by Evangelist S. L. Flowers. Olivet-Georgetown, Ill.,
           Flowers Publishing Co., 1912. 183 p.
              Fictionalized autobiography.
5372   Flowers, Sumpter Lee, 1881-1945.
              The mystery of Lookout Mountain. Boston, Christopher Publishing House, c1935. 183 p.

5373   FOGG, L. N.
        APCA, PCN, CN. Pastor, district supt.

5374   FOOTE, John Bartlit (1826-1911). SCM (1881), 368.
        Member, NHA
        Endorsed and attended GHA, 1901 (Chicago)
        ME. Pastor, evangelist
        b. July 1, 1826, Martinsburg, N.Y.
        d. Dec. 30, 1911, Syracuse, N.Y.

5375   FOOTE, Mrs. Julia A. J. (1823-   ).
        Attended WUHC, 1880 (Jacksonville, Ill.)
        Endorsed call, GHA, 1901 (Chicago)
        Cong., AME. Evangelist
5376   Foote, Julia A. J., 1823-
              A brand plucked from the fire, an autobiographical
           sketch. Cleveland, Printed for the author by W. F.
           Schneider, 1879. 124 p.
5377   Foote, Julia A. J., 1823-
              A brand plucked from the fire, an autobiographical
           sketch. Cleveland, Lauer & Yost, 1886. 124 p.

5378   FORD, C. B. PPE (1868), 337-338.
        ME. Pastor

5379   FORD, Jack (1908-   ).
        IHM, CHC, CN. Pastor, evangelist, Bible college
           principal
        b. 1908, Hull, Eng.

5380   FOSS, Cyrus David (1834-1910). DAB. GFW (1888), 219-
           222. LMB (1948), 68-69. SCM (1881), 371. WWW
           in Am. (1897-1942), 415. N.Y. Times (Jan. 30,
           1910), II, 11:4.
        Endorsed call, GHA, 1901 (Chicago)
        ME. Pastor, university pres., bishop

Part VI. Biography

b. Jan. 17, 1834, Kingston, N.Y.
d. Jan. 29, 1910, Philadelphia, Pa.

5381 Foss, Cyrus David, bp., 1834-1910.
From the Himalayas to the equator; letters, sketches and addresses, giving some account of a tour in India and Malaysia, New York and Cincinnati, Eaton & Mains, 1899. 262 p.

5382 Foss, Cyrus David, bp., 1834-1910.
In sickness and in "accidents"; experiences.... Cincinnati, Cranston & Curts, 1895. 16 p.

5383 Foss, Cyrus David, bp., 1834-1910.
My experience in sickness. Cincinnati, Cranston & Stowe, 1887. 8 p.

5384 Funeral service held in Philadelphia in the Arch Street Methodist Episcopal Church on Feb. 1, 1910, conducted by the Rev. Geo. Bickley. Philadelphia, 1911. Funeral of Cyrus David Foss.

5385 Public reception given to the Rev. Bishop Cyrus D. Foss ... on his return from India and Malaysia by the ministry and membership of the Methodist Episcopal Church in Philadelphia and vicinity in the Arch Street Methodist Episcopal Church, Philadelphia, Thursday evening, April 21, 1898. Philadelphia, Philadelphia Laymen's Association of the Methodist Episcopal Church, 1898.

5386 FOSTER, Randolph Sinks (1820-1903). DAB. HM (1882). LMB (1948), 69-70. SCM (1881), 371-372. WWW in Am. (1897-1942), 417.
ME. Pastor, university pres., bishop
b. Feb. 22, 1820, Williamsburg, Ohio
d. May 2, 1903, Newton, Mass.

5387 FOWLER, A. M.
ME. Pastor?
5388 McDonald, William, 1820-1901.
Christian perfection. New York?, 1893. 16 p.
Contents.--Christian perfection [as taught by John Wesley] by William McDonald.--An experience of more than fifty years ago, by A.M. Fowler.--The Pentecost, by A.M. Fowler.

5389 FOWLER, Anderson (1843-1906). N.Y. Times (Feb. 11, 1906, 7:6; (Feb. 27, 1906), 9:5 (buried at sea).
ME. Lay leader, promoter of self-supporting missions, businessman, industrialist
b. 1843, Northern Ireland
d. Feb. 9, 1906, at sea near Naples, Italy

5390 FOWLER, Charles J. (circa 1848-1919). DC (1965, c1887), 102-114.
President, NHA, 1893-1919

Endorsed call and attended, GHA, 1901 (Chicago)
ME. Pastor, evangelist

5391 FOX, Henry J. (1821-). SCM (1881), 374.
ME. Pastor, seminary (academy) prin., university prof.
b. 1821, Hull, Eng.

5392 FRAME, George
CN. Pastor, district supt., Bible school prin.
b. 190?, Scotland

5393 FREDERICK, Daisy E. (-1946). LLITW (1951), 216.
FM. Missionary

5394 FRYE, William Arthur (-1967).
IHC, PHC. Pastor
d. June 14, 1967

5395 FUGE, Frederick Thomas (1872-). WW in the Clergy (1935-1936), 401.
IAHU, IAHC, IHC, PHC, CN. Missionary, pastor, editor, evangelist.
b. Dec. 2, 1872, Notre Dame Bay, Nfld., Can.

5396 Fuge, Frederick Thomas, 1872-
Sixteen years among the Zulus. Kansas City, Mo., Published for the author by the Nazarene Publishing House, n.d.

5397 Fuge, Frederick Thomas, 1872-
Soul hunting in Africa. Cincinnati, God's Revivalist Office, n.d.

5398 Fuge, Frederick Thomas, 1872-
With Christ in Kaffir land. Port Elizabeth, S. Africa, Africa's Revivalist Office, n.d.

5399 FUGGETT, C. B.
CN. Evangelist, pastor

5400 FUHRMAN, Eldon Ralph (1918-). DAS (1969), IV, 121. GTWATD (1965), 138-154. BPOH (1969), 150-157.
EUB, ECNA. Seminary prof., pastor, evangelist
b. Apr. 24, 1918, Mound City, Mo.

5401 FULLER, Harold L. (1908-1972).
CN, PHC, CG (H), WHC. Pastor, evangelist
b. Sept. 22, 1908, Green Island, N.Y.
d. June 13, 1972, Dixon, Mo.

5402 Church Herald and Holiness Banner, XCIII (July 20, 1972), 11.

5403 FUNK, John Fretz (1835-1930).
Menn. Pastor

Part VI. Biography

b. 1835, Bucks County, Pa.
d. 1930

5404   Funk, John Fretz, bp., 1835-1930.
The Mennonite Church and her accusers; a vindication of the character of the Mennonite Church of America from her first organization in this country to the present time. Elkhart, Ind., Mennonite Publishing Co., 1878. 206 p.

5405   Dean, William Ward, 1924-
"John F. Funk and the Mennonite awakening." Unpublished Ph.D. dissertation, State University of Iowa, 1965. 299ℓ.

5406   GAAR, J. E. NP (1925), 116-124.
MP, CN. Pastor, conference pres., evangelist

5407   GABRIEL, Charles Hutchinson (1856-1932). LMGSS (1952), 137. RHOOF (1964), 295-296.
ME. Gospel song writer
b. Aug. 18, 1856, Wilton, Iowa
d. Sept. 15, 1932, Los Angeles, Calif.

5408   Gabriel, Charles Hutchinson, 1856-1932.
Personal memoirs of Charles H. Gabriel. Chicago, Printed by K. G. Bottorf, 1918. xi, 51 p.

5409   GADDIS, Maxwell Pierson (1811-1888). PPE (1868), 351-354.
ME. Pastor

5410   Gaddis, Maxwell Pierson, 1811-1888.
Footprints of an itinerant. Cincinnati, Printed at the Methodist Book Concern, for the author, 1856. 546 p.
Autobiography.

5411   Gaddis, Maxwell Pierson, 1811-1888.
Last words and old-time memories; original and compiled from the most authentic records, with an introd. by Bishop Randolph S. Foster. New York, Phillips & Hunt, 1880. 430 p.

5412   GAEKWAD, Wamanrao. HNTB (1934), 100-101.
CN. National worker, pastor
b. 189?, India

5413   GARCIA, Estanislao. HNTB (1934), 134-136.
R. Cath., CN. National worker, evangelist
b. 19??, Guatemala

5414   GARCIA, Lucia Carmen. HNTB (1934), 189-195.
R. Cath., CN. National worker
b. 189?, Argentina

5415   GARDNER, James Russell (1891-). DAS (1969), IV, 125. SFLF (1950), 35-40.

EC, IHC, PHC, CN. Pastor, evangelist, college prof.
b. Aug. 25, 1891, Howard, Pa.

5416 Gardner, James Russell, 1891-
"The role of experience and value in naturalistic and personalistic thought as represented by the philosophies of Clarence Irving Lewis and Edgar Sheffield Brightman." Unpublished Ph.D. dissertation, University of Illinois, 1953.

5417 GARDNER, Nary Crilley.
ME. Lay member

5418 Gardner, Mary Crilley
The useful disciple; or, A narrative of Mrs. M. Gardner [ed.] by Mrs. P. Palmer. Cincinnati, Swormstedt and Power for the Methodist Episcopal Church, 1851. 175 p.

5419 Gardner, Mary Crilley
The useful disciple; or, A narrative of Mrs. M.G. (sketched as taken from the lips of Mrs. G. by Mrs. L.A. Baily); [ed.] by Mrs. P. Palmer.... First English ed. London, 1857.

5420 GARDNER, Robert Wayne (1894-   ). WW in Am. (1964-1965), 715.
CN. Pastor, college prof., college pres., military chaplain, college admin.
b. May 16, 1894, Tidioute, Pa.

5421 GARRETT, "Aunt Puss" (1838-   ). MCV (1901), 146-154.
ME, S; PM. Exhorter, evangelistic singer
b. July 17, 1838, Nashville, Tenn.

5422 GARRETT, Paul Hamilton (1908-   ). WW in the South and Southwest (1967-1968), 342.
CN. Pastor, district supt.
b. Jan 26, 1908, Erick, Okla.

5423 GARRETT, William L.
CN, PCN. Evangelist

5424 GARRISON, Harold Allen (1918-   ). WWACUA (1970-1971), 182.
PHC, W. College prof., college admin.
b. Aug. 16, 1918, Glassboro, N.J.

5425 GARSEE, Jarrell Willis (1930-   ).
CN. Pastor, missionary, college prof., college admin., college chaplain
b. Sept. 26, 1930.

5426 Garsee, Jarrell Willis, 1930-
Samoa diary. Kansas City, Mo., Nazarene Publishing House, 1963. 96 p.

Part VI. Biography

5427 Garsee, Jarrell Willis, 1930-
"Samoan interpersonal values," by Jarrell W. Garsee and Alfred F. Flixman, Journal of Social Psychology, LXXII (June 1967), 45-60.

5428 Garsee, Jarrell Willis, 1930-
"A study of Samoan interpersonal values." Unpublished M.S. thesis, University of Oklahoma, 1965. 74ℓ.

5429 "MVNC professor completes doctoral studies," Herald of Holiness, LXI (Dec. 6, 1972), 21-22.

5430 GASSAWAY, Percy Lee (1885-1937). Biog. Dir. Am. Cong. (1774-1961), 933. WWW in Am. (1897-1942), 443.
N.Y. Times (May 16, 1937), II, 9:1.
ME, S. Pastor, attorney, judge, Congressman, leader's child
b. Aug. 30, 1885, Waco, Tex.
d. May 15, 1937, Coalgate, Okla.

5431 GATES, Charles W. GHAI (1964), 14-16.
ME, CN. Missionary

5432 GAY, David. PPE (1868), 306-308.
ME. Pastor

5433 GAYJIKIAN, Krikor (circa 1887-1972).
PHC, W. Rescue mission supt.
b. circa 1887, Armenia
d. Nov. 13, 1972, Cincinnati, Ohio

5434 Gayjikian, Krikor, circa 1887-1972.
A life full of miracles. Cincinnati, c1964. 173 p.
Autobiography.

5435 Gayjikian, Krikor, circa 1887-1972.
Martyred Armenia and the story of my life. Cincinnati, God's Revivalist Press, c1920. 308 p.

5436 [Obituary of the Rev. Krikor Gayjikian], Wesleyan Advocate, CXXXI (Apr. 2, 1973), 18.

5437 GEIGER, Kenneth E. (1916-   ). GTWATD (1965), 12-23.
BPOH (1969), 130-136.
President, NHA, 1960-1964
MBIC, UMC, MC. Pastor, evangelist, conference supt., general supt.

5438 GEORGE, J. Lowell. DCSWM (1946), 31-35.
CN. Military chaplain

5439 GERBER, Wayne Jay (1927-   ). WWACUA (1970-1971), 184.
UMC, MC. College prof., college admin.
b. Nov. 24, 1927, Tremont, Ill.

5440 GERIG, Jared Franklin (1907-   ). WWACUA (1970-1971), 184. GIIH (1962), 222-238.
MCA, MC. College dean, church pres., college pres., pastor
b. June 29, 1907, Grabill, Ind.

5441 GHORMLEY, Newton Baxter (-1940).
FM. Missionary

5442 GIBBS, Donna D. (1925-   ). ETWF (196?).
PHC. Pastor's wife, missionary
b. July 10, 1925, Findlay, Ohio

5443 GIBBS, Frederick W. (1914-   ). ETWF (196?).
PHC. Pastor, missionary
b. Apr. 28, 1914, Grand Rapids, Mich.

5444 GIBSON, Charles Arthur (1888-   ). RLOA (1941-1942), 418. COPN (1958), 91-96.
Bapt., HCC, CN. Pastor, evangelist, district supt.
b. Feb. 23, 1888, Greensberg, Ind.

5445 GIBSON, James. NVFML (1936), 15-25.
ME. Pastor, evangelist
b. 19??, Ireland

5446 GIBSON, Julia Roberts
APCA, PCN, CN. Physician, missionary
5447 Gibson, Julia Roberts
A cry from India's night. Kansas City, Mo., Publishing House of the Pentecostal Church of the Nazarene, 1914. 216 p.

5448 GILL, Joshua
Member, NHA
ME, EA. Pastor, editor, presiding elder, publisher

5449 GILLETTE, Frieda Almira (1899-   ).
WM, W. College prof.
b. 1899, Fillmore, N.Y.
5450 Gillette, Frieda Almira, 1899-
"The New York State Constitutional Convention of 1938." Unpublished Ph.D. dissertation, Cornell University, 1944. 157ℓ.

5451 GILLETTE, Philip Goode (1833-   ). SCM (1881), 413.
Attended HConf., 1877 (Cincinnati)
ME. Lay leader, educator
b. Mar. 24, 1833, Madison, Ind.

5452 GILLEY, Ruth Evelyn (1904-   ). WWACUA (1970-1971), 187.

Part VI. Biography

        CN. College librarian
        b. Oct. 19, 1904, Russell, Ky.

5453 GILLEY, William Richard (1879-1949).
        ME, CN. Pastor
        b. Nov. 30, 1879
        d. Sept. 1949

5454 GILLIES, James W. (-1915).
        APCA, PCN. Pastor

5455 GILMOUR, Henry Lake (1836-1920). RHOOF (1964), 300.
        ME. Dentist, evangelistic singer, gospel song writer
        b. Jan. 19, 1836, Londonderry, Ire.
        d. May 20, 1920, Delair, N.J.

5456 GILPATRICK, Emma Appling (-1913). LLITW (1951), 216.
        FM. Missionary

5457 GINDER, Henry A. GTWATD (1965), 78-87.
        President, CHA, 1972-
        BIC. Pastor, evangelist, bishop

5458 GIRVIN, Ernest Alexander (1857-). SCUH (1962).
        ME, PenielM, CN, PCN. Court reporter, pastor
5459   Girvin, Ernest Alexander, 1857-
        Domestic duels; or, Evening talks on the woman
        question. San Francisco, E.D. Bronson & Co., 1898.
        277 p.

5460 GISH, Carol Spell
        CN. College prof., writer

5461 GLASCOCK, James Luther (1852-1942).
        Endorsed call, GHA, 1901 (Chicago)
        ME. Pastor, evangelist
        b. 1852, Phillipi, Barber County, W.Va.
        d. Oct. 30, 1942, Cincinnati, Ohio
5462   Glascock, James Luther, 1852-1942.
        Some grapes from Eschol, a sermon on perfect
        love--what it is, and how to obtain it ... also his ex-
        perience, with introductions by Rev. E.I.D. Pepper
        and Rev. John Thompson. Cincinnati, M.W. Knapp,
        1896. 53 p.

5463 GLENN, Jennie
        I (EFM). Missionary society director's wife
5464   Evangelistic Faith Missions.
        Losing to win: Victor Glenn, God's man in times
        like these. Bedford, Ind., 196?. 32 p.

5465 GLENN, Victor
I (EFM). Missionary society director
5466 Glenn, Victor
Crossing continents with Christ; the amazing story of the miracle ministry of faith missions. Bedford, Ind., Evangelistic Faith Missions, 196?. 31 p.
"Sixth printing (revised)."
5467 Glenn, Victor
The price and product of missions. Bedford, Ind., Missionary-Evangelistic Ministries of the Evangelical Faith Missions, 1972. 40 p.
Autobiographical.
5468 Evangelistic Faith Missions.
Losing to win: Victor Glenn, God's man in times like these. Bedford, Ind., 196?. 32 p.

5469 GLIDE, Mrs. Lizzie Helen Snyder (1852-1936?)
ME. Philanthropist
5470 McPheeters, Julian C., 1889-
The life story of Lizzie H. Glide. San Francisco, Calif., Eagle Printing Co., 1936. 110 p.

5471 GODBEY, Emma Durham (1839-1915).
ME, S. Evangelist's wife
5472 Godbey, William B., 1833-1920.
My better half. Cincinnati, God's Revivalist Press, 1918? 32 p.

5473 GODBEY, William B., (1833-1920). PM (1898), 15-25.
ME, S. Pastor, college pres., evangelist, writer
b. June 3, 1833, Pulaski County, Ky.
d. 1920, Zarephath, N.J.
5474 Godbey, William B., 1833-1920.
The apocalyptic angel. Cincinnati, God's Revivalist Press, 1914. 509 p.
5475 Godbey, William B., 1833-1920.
Around the world, garden of Eden, latter day prophecies, and missions. Cincinnati, God's Revivalist Office, 1907. 596 p.
5476 Godbey, William B., 1833-1920.
Autobiography. Cincinnati, God's Revivalist Office, 1909. 509 p.
5477 Godbey, William B., 1833-1920.
Footprints of Jesus in the Holy Land. Cincinnati, M.W. Knapp, 1900. 272 p.
5478 Godbey, William B., 1833-1920.
Happy nonagenarian. Zarephath, N.J., Pillar of Fire, 1919. 184 p.
5479 Godbey, William B., 1833-1920.
Holy land. Cincinnati, M.W. Knapp, 1895. 87 p.

Part VI. Biography

5480 GOFF, Frank D.
HMoC, GWC. Evangelist, pastor
b. 18??, Gananoque, Ont., Can.

5481 GOFF, H. H.
FW Bapt., PeFW Bapt., PeHC. Pastor
5482 Goff, Florence
Tests and triumphs. Falcon, N.C., 1924. 96 p.
Autobiography

5483 GOFF, Reginald F. NVFML (1936), 105-119.
GWC. Pastor
b. 19??, Ontario, Can.

5484 GOFF, Walter Roy (1877-).
Attended GHA, 1901 (Chicago)
ME. Pastor

5485 GOODMAN, Woodrow I. (1915-). WWACUA (1970-1971), 193.
UMC, WM, W. Editor, college admin., college pres.
b. Aug. 21, 1915, Olive Hill, Ky.

5486 GOODSELL, Daniel Ayres (1840-1909). DAB. LMB (1948), 77. WWW in Am. (1897-1942), 468. N.Y. Times (Dec. 6, 1909), 9:3.
Endorsed call, GHA, 1901 (Chicago)
ME. Pastor, editor, bishop
b. Nov. 5, 1840, Newburgh, N.Y.
d. Dec. 5, 1909, New York, N.Y.

5487 GOODWIN, John Wesley (1869-1945). RLOA (1941-1942), 437.
Ad. Chr., CN, PCN, CN. Pastor, district supt., college admin., general supt.
b. Mar. 13, 1869, North Berwick, Me.
d. Jan. 26, 1945, Pasadena, Calif.
5488 Goodwin, John Wesley, 1869-1945.
Tithing, the touchstone of stewardship. Kansas City, Mo., Nazarene Publishing House, n.d. 39 p.
"Personal experiences": p. 35-39.
5489 McGraw, James, 1913-
"The preaching of John W. Goodwin," Preacher's Magazine, XXIX (May 1954), 3-4, 9, 12.
5490 Sanner, Asa Everette, 1890-
John W. Goodwin, a biography. Kansas City, Mo., Nazarene Publishing House, 1945. 160 p.

5491 GOODWIN, Paul John (1896-). RLOA (1941-1942), 437.
CN, Pres. Leader's child, teacher, pastor
b. Sept. 6, 1896, Haverhill, Mass.

5492 GORDON, Adoniram Judson (1836-1895). LDEFC (1911),
        328-336. WWW in Am. (1607-1896), 211. Nat. Cy.
        of Am. Biog., XI, 263.
        Bapt. Pastor, evangelist
        b. Apr. 19, 1836, New Hampton, Belknap County, N.H.
        d. Feb. 2, 1895, Boston, Mass.
5493   Gordon, Adoniram Judson, 1836-1895.
        How Christ came to church; the pastor's dream: a
        spiritual autobiography, by A.J. Gordon ... with the
        life-story, and the dream as interpreting the man, by
        A.T. Pierson.... Philadelphia, American Baptist Publication Society, 1895. 149 p.
        Autobiography.

5494 GORHAM, B. Weed. MAWACOSM (1925), 320. PPE (1868),
        240-244.
        ME. Pastor

5495 GOSS, Howard Archibald (1883-).
        AFM, CGIC. Pastor
5496   Goss, Howard Archibald, 1883-
        The winds of God; the story of the early Pentecostal
        days (1901-1914) in the life of Howard A. Goss, as told
        by Ethel E. Goss. New York, Comet Press Books,
        1958. 178 p.

5497 GOULD, Joseph Glenn (1896-). DAS (1969), IV, 135-136.
        RLOA (1941-1942), 441.
        CN. Pastor, denominational official, college prof.
        b. Mar. 8, 1896, Rogers, Ohio

5498 GOVAN, John George (1861-1927).
        FaM. Evangelist, missionary promoter
5499   Govan, John George, 1861-1927.
        [Religious tracts]. London, 1889-1896. 3 pts.
5500   Govan Stewart, Isabel Rosie, 1900-
        Spirit of revival; biography of J.B. Govan, founder
        of the Faith Mission, by I.R. Govan. Edinburgh, Faith
        Mission; London, Edinburgh, Marshall, Morgan & Scott,
        1938. 208 p.

5501 GOVAN STEWART, Isabel Rosie (1900-).
        FaM. Evangelist, missionary

5502 GOWLAND, Frank B. FHOP (1964).
        ME, CN. Pastor
        b. 18??, Marshalltown, Iowa

5503 GRACEY, Samuel Levis (1835-1911). PPE (1868), 185-189.
        ME. Pastor, consul
        b. Sept. 8, 1835, Philadelphia, Pa.
        d. 1911

Part VI. Biography

5504 GRANBERY, John Cowper (1829-1907). WWW in Am. (1897-1942), 476. N.Y. Times (Apr. 2, 1907), 11:5.
ME, S. Pastor, military chaplain, university prof., bishop
b. Dec. 5, 1829, Norfolk, Va.
d. Apr. 1907

5505 GRANT, Abraham (1848-1911). WWW in Am. (1897-1942), 476.
Endorsed call, GHA, 1901 (Chicago)
AME. Pastor, bishop
b. Aug. 25, 1848, Lake City, Fla.
d. 1911

5506 GRAVES, Albert Phelps (1829-1911). PPE (1868), 150-156.
Bapt. Pastor

5507 GRAVES, Albert Schuyler (1824-1887). SCM (1881), 417.
Attended HConf., 1877 (New York)
ME. Pastor, seminary prin.
b. Jan. 17, 1824, Salisbury, Vt.
d. Sept. 14, 1887

5508 GRAVES, Edith D. (-1941). LLITW (1951), 216.
FM. Missionary

5509 GRAY, Forrest Burton (1913-). ETWF (196?).
PHC. Pastor, missionary
b. July 22, 1913, Byrnedale, Pa.

5510 GRAY, Minnie Mae (1920-). ETWF (196?).
PHC. Pastor's wife, missionary
b. Mar. 8, 1920, Mt. Savage, Md.

5511 GRAY, W. C. LLITW (1951), 216.
FM. Missionary

5512 GRAY, Willetta. LLITW (1951), 216.
FM. Missionary

5513 GRAY, William L. (1821-1902).
Member, NHA
ME. Pastor, evangelist

5514 GREATHOUSE, William M. (1919-). DAS (1969), IV, 138. GTWATD (1965), 210-227.
M, CN. Pastor, college prof., college pres., seminary pres.
b. Apr. 29, 1919, Van Buren, Ark.

5515 GREEN, Cora Lee. GHAI (1960), 26-29.
CN. Missionary

5516 GREEN, John Dryer (-1947). LLITW (1951), 216.
FM. Missionary

5517 GREENE, T. W. EAP (1890, c1879), 96-100. PPE (1868), 183-184.
Bapt. Pastor

5518 GREENLEE, Jacob Harold (1918-). DAS (1969), IV, 139. GFIIH (1963), 72-87.
M? Seminary prof., missionary?
b. May 12, 1918, Charleston, W.Va.

5519 GREER, Naoma Adelaid (1910-). ETWF (196?).
HC, PHC. Missionary
b. July 12, 1910, Chiclayo, Peru

5520 GREGORY, James F. GFIIH (1963), 30-39.
FM. Pastor, district supt., college prof., college pres., editor

5521 GREGORY, W. H. SBWTL (1960), 188-189.
FM. Pastor, district elder
b. 186?, Verona, Ont.

5522 GRENTZENBERG, Herman A. (1835-1934). N.Y. Times (May 9, 1934), 19:5.
Endorsed call and attended, GHA, 1901 (Chicago)
ME. Pastor?, editor
b. Oct. 15, 1835
d. May 8, 1934

5523 GRESHAM, L. Paul (1911-). WWACUA (1970-1971), 200. LIE (1971), 364.
CN. College prof., college dean
b. Jan. 3, 1911, Portales, N.M.

5524 GRIDER, Joseph Kenneth (1921-). WW in Am. Ed. (1967-1968). GTWATD (1965), 68-77.
CN. Pastor, college prof., seminary prof.
b. Oct. 22, 1921, Madison, Ill.

5525 GRIFFITH, George William (1869-1936). BMW (1960), 231-247.
ME, FM. Pastor, seminary (academy) pres., editor, bishop
b. Jan. 6, 1869, Oneida, Ill.
d. Feb. 13, 1936

5526 Griffith, Lillian (Bushnell), 1875-
Living embers, the life and writings of George William Griffith, by Mrs. G.W. Griffith. Winona Lake, Ind., Printed by Light and Life Press for the author, Los Angeles, Calif., 1937. 319 p.
"List of published works": p. 309-319.

Part VI. Biography

5527 GRIFFITH, Glenn (1894-).
ME, CN, BMiU, BMiC, WHAC. Oil company foreman, pastor, evangelist, district supt., general moderator, general supt.
b. Aug. 17, 1894, near Augusta, Kan.
5528 Griffith, Glenn, 1894-
"I sought for a man." Phoenix, Ariz., n.d. vi, 112 p.
Autobiography and sermons.

5529 GRINNELL, A. Lee (-1923). LLITW (1951), 216.
FM. Missionary

5530 GRINNELL, Maud. LLITW (1951), 216.
FM. Missionary

5531 GROVES, Vernon Thomas (1911-). LIE (1971), 371.
CN. College prof.
b. Aug. 15, 1911, Viroqua, Wisc.

5532 GUILL, J. E. (-1962). TDOOP (1968), 343.
PHC. Pastor, district supt.
d. Dec. 11, 1962
5533 Pilgrim Holiness Advocate, XLIII (Jan. 26, 1963), 11.

5534 GUNN, Elihu. EAP (1890, c1879), 103-107. PPE (1868), 46-51.
Bapt. Pastor

5535 GUNN, M. W. FHOP (1964).
Pres., SA, CN. Pastor, evangelist
b. 1891, Nova Scotia

5536 GUY, Augusta Oakes (1892-).
ME, CN. Pastor's wife, temperance worker
b. Mar. 22, 1892, Stonington, Baca County, Colo.
5537 Guy, Augusta (Oakes), 1892-
Pioneering with God. Bethany, Okla., Printed by Yukon Printing Co., Yukon, Okla., c1972. viii, 128 p.
On label: Written by Vada Lee Barkley.
Autobiography.

5538 GUY, Francis Ridley (1889-).
ME, CN. Pastor
b. Apr. 28, 1889, McConnelsville, Ohio
5539 Guy, Augusta (Oakes), 1892-
Pioneering with God. Bethany, Okla., Printed by Yukon Printing Co., Yukon, Okla., c1972. viii, 128 p.
On label: Written by Vada Lee Barkley.
Autobiography of Mrs. Francis Ridley Guy.

5540 HAGGARD, Cornelius Paul (1911-). WWACUA (1970-1971), 208. LIE (1971), 380. GFIIH (1963), 196-210.
ET, PHC, EMC. Pastor, college prof., college pres., asst. general supt.
b. Sept. 11, 1911, Pomona, Calif.

5541 HAHN, Martha Sophia (1892-). ETWF (196?).
PHC. Bible school admin., missionary, pastor
b. Feb. 12, 1892, Sioux City, Iowa

5542 HALE, Edwin E. (1894-). FHOP (1964). DCSWM (1946), 135.
CN. Pastor, district supt., army chaplain, Bible school pres.
b. Dec. 4, 1894, Altus, Okla.

5543 HALEY, John Wesley (1879-1951). LLITW (1951), 216. SBWTL (1960), 201-202.
FM. Missionary
b. 1879, Muskoka, Ont.
5544 Haley, John Wesley, 1879-1951.
Life in Mozambique and South Africa; introd. by Rev. William B. Olmstead. Chicago, Free Methodist Publishing House, 1926. 174 p.

5545 HALEY, Matilda Deyo (-1947). LLITW (1951), 216.
FM. Missionary

5546 HALL, Alvin Willard (1852-).
Endorsed call, GHA, 1901 (Chicago)
WM. Pastor, denominational official
5547 Hall, Alvin Willard, 1852-
Three hundred miles in a hammock; or, Six weeks in Africa. Houghton, N.Y., Houghton Index Print, 1889. 165 p.

5548 HALL, Bert Harold (1921-). DAS (1969), IV, 145. GTWATD (1965), 180-194.
WM, W. College prof., college dean
b. Feb. 6, 1921

5549 HALL, Henry P. (1814-). GFW (1888), 148-151.
Bapt., ME. Pastor
b. Sept. 20, 1814, Portsmouth, N.H.

5550 HALL, J. Walter (1878-1964).
PCN, CN. Pastor, district supt., college admin.
d. 1964, Norman, Okla.
5551 Herald of Holiness, LIII (June 17, 1964), 15.

5552 HALLER, Lola Marie (1929-). LIE (1971), 384.
WM, W. College prof.
b. July 11, 1929, Lake Odessa, Mich.

Part VI. Biography

5553 HALT, Eulice Vern (1896-   ). RLOA (1941-1942), 477.
TDOOP (1968), 161-162, 282.
PHC, W. Pastor, evangelist, denominational official
b. Aug. 9, 1896, Cory, Ind.

5554 HALT, Raymond J. (1905-   )
PHC, W. Denominational official
b. Dec. 12, 1905, Cory, Ind.
5555 "Conference elects 11 officers," Wesleyan Advocate, CXXVII (July 15, 1968), 10.
5556 "Publisher-treasurer appointed by General Board," Wesleyan Advocate, CXXX (Aug. 7, 1972), 15.

5557 HAMBLEN, James Henry (1877-1971). WW in the Clergy (1935-1936), 475.
ME, S; M; EMC. Pastor, general supt.
b. Nov. 13, 1877, Kaufman County, Tex.
d. Nov. 1971, Abilene, Tex.
5558 Hamblen, James Henry, 1877-1971.
A look into life: an autobiography. Abilene, Tex., The author, 1969. 184 p.
5559 Hamblen, Oberia, 1905-
My brother Stuart Hamblen. Los Angeles, Cowman Publications, 1950. vi, 130 p.

5560 HAMES, J. M.
WM. Evangelist

5561 HAMILTON, R. H. (1883-1954). SBWTL (1960), 187-188.
FM (GWC). Pastor, conference supt., editor, evangelist
b. 1883, Kent County, Ont.
d. 1954, Welland, Ont.

5562 HAMLIN, George Edwin
CN. Lay leader

5563 HAMLIN, Howard H.
CN. Physician, missionary

5564 HAMLINE, Leonidas Lent (1797-1865). SCM (1881), 424-426. WWW in Am. (1607-1896), 231. ROG (1854), 9-19. Nat. Cy. of Am. Biog., XIII, 88-89.
ME. Pastor, editor, bishop, philanthropist
b. May 10, 1797, Burlington, Conn.
d. Feb. 22, 1865, Mount Pleasant, Iowa
5565 Hamline, Leonidas Lent, bp., 1797-1865.
Works, ed. by F.G. Hibbard. Cincinnati, Hitchcock and Walden; New York, Carlton and Lanahan, 1869-1871. 2 v.
5566 Hibbard, Freeborn Garrettson, 1811-1895.
Biography of Rev. Leonidas L. Hamline. Cincinnati, Jennings and Pye, 1881.

5567　　Palmer, Walter Clark, 1804-1883.
　　　　Life and letters of Leonidas L. Hamline, D.D., late one of the bishops of the Methodist Episcopal Church, by Walter C. Palmer, M.D., with introductory letters by Bishops Morris, Janes and Thomson. New York, Carlton & Porter, 1866. 544 p.

5568　　HAMLINE, Melinda Truesdell (1801-). ROG (1854), 286-290. SCM (1881), 426.
　　　　ME.　Bishop's wife
　　　　b.　Sept. 29, 1801, Hillsdale, Columbia County, N.Y.

5569　　HAMMER, Anna Maria Nichols (1840-1910). GFW (1888), 110-114. WWOTC (1893), 354. N.Y. Times (May 1, 1910), II, 11:4.
　　　　Epis., REpis. Lay leader, temperance worker
　　　　b.　Sept. 14, 1840, Pottsville, Pa.
　　　　d.　Apr. 29, 1910, Westfield, N.J.

5570　　HAMMOND, George M.
　　　　HChuC, PCN, CN.　Pastor

5571　　HAMMOND, Robert Bruce
　　　　VC, VCA.　Missionary
5572　　Hammond, Robert Bruce
　　　　Bondservants of the Japanese. San Pedro, Calif., Sheffield Press, c1943. 89 p.
5573　　Hammond, Robert Bruce
　　　　Bondservants of the Lord; our experiences during the siege of Hong Kong, internment in Stanley Prison Concentration Camp, the establishment of Voice of China and Asia missionary work. Pasadena, Calif., Vancouver, B.C., Can., Voice of China and Asia (Missionary Society), 1963, c1943. 84 p.
　　　　Ninth ed.
　　　　First ed. published under title: Bondservants of the Japanese.

5574　　HAMRIC, Lee L. NP (1925), 185-193.
　　　　HChuC, PCN, CN.　Evangelist

5575　　HANEY, Milton Lorenzo (1825-1922).
　　　　Member, IowaHA
　　　　Member, NHA
　　　　Attended GHA, 1901 (Chicago)
　　　　ME.　Pastor, evangelist, military chaplain
　　　　b.　1825, Ohio
　　　　d.　1922, Pasadena, Calif.
5576　　Haney, Milton Lorenzo, 1825-1922.
　　　　Pentecostal possibilities; or, Story of my life. Chicago, Christian Witness Co., 1906. 398 p.

Part VI. Biography

5577 HANKINS, Margaret Bell Edwards (1897-   ). ETWF (196?).
PHC, W. Pastor, evangelist, missionary
b. Oct. 29, 1897, Rio Grande, N.J.

5578 HANLEY, Charles S. WMK (1966), 45, 50.
Endorsed call, GHA, 1901 (Chicago)
WFMA. Newspaper editor, evangelistic asso. pres.
b. 18??, Iowa

5579 HANLEY, Richard R. WMK (1966), 25, 29, 45, 50.
Bapt., WFMA, HFMA. Physician, pastor, evangelist, evangelistic asso. pres.
d. 19??, Iowa

5580 HANNA, Philip C. (1857-1929). WWW in Am. (1897-1942), 516.
FM, --. Evangelist, U.S. consul general at Monterey, Mex.
b. June 27, 1857, Waterloo, Iowa
d. Feb. 17, 1929
5581 Dake, Vivian Adelbert, 1854-1892.
From the pit to the pulpit; or, A sot at sixteen, a true account of Phil C. Hanna. Chicago, Baker & Arnold, 1880. 67 p.

5582 HARDING, Ulla Earl (1883-1958). NP (1925), 64-71.
FM, CN. Pastor, evangelist, district supt.
b. May 16, 1883, Shoals, Ind.
d. May 8, 1958
5583 Harding, Ulla Earl, 1883-1958.
Is the young man safe? Georgetown, Ill., [Silent Evangel Society Press, Indianapolis], 1911. 103 p.
Autobiography.
"Dedicated to the Young Men's Holiness League and to all who work and pray to lead young men to our Savior."
5584 Harding, Ulla Earl, 1883-1958.
A new grip on God. 2d ed. University Park, Iowa, College Press, n.d. 68 p.
5585 Harding, Ulla Earl, 1883-1958.
Pen pictures from life's pathway. Kansas City, Mo., Nazarene Publishing House, 1938. 63 p.
5586 Harding, Ulla Earl, 1883-1958.
Pen pictures from life's pathway. 5th ed. Pasadena, Calif., Mission Press, 1938. 63 p.
5587 McGraw, James, 1913-
"The preaching of U.E. Harding," Preacher's Magazine, XXXVI (Feb. 1961), 5-8.

5588 HARDY, Chester Ernest (1882-1972). WW in Am. (1942-1943), 1000. WW in the Clergy (1935-1936), 481.
Bapt., PM, CN. Pastor, evangelist, college prof.,

college pres.
b. Sept. 2, 1882, Alexander City, Ala.

5589 HARGRAVE, Richard. PPE (1868), 119-121.
ME. Pastor

5590 HARLOW, William Thompson (1815-). SCM (1881), 428.
Member, NHA
ME. Pastor, seminary (academy) prin., college prof., evangelist
b. Apr. 18, 1815, Duxbury, Mass.

5591 HARMON, Frank H. (-1957).
IHC, PHC. Pastor
d. Dec. 5, 1957

5592 HARPER, Albert Foster (1907-). WW in Am. Ed. (1967-1968), 349.
CN. College prof., college dean, denominational official
b. July 9, 1907, Boulder, Colo.

5593 HARPER, Charles Howard
PCN, CN. Pastor

5594 HARRELL, John R.
M. Building contractor, politician
5595 Comer, A. Vance
The manifestation of God to John R. Harrell. Louisville, Ky., Herald Press, 1959. 43 p.
Cover-title: The manifestation of God in the healing of John R. Harrell.

5596 HARRIS, John M. LMGSS (1952), 65. LDML (1953), 73.
Attended GHA, 1901 (Chicago)
ME. Gospel song writer, evangelistic singer

5597 HARRIS, John William (1870-)
ME? Pastor, evangelist
5598 Harris, John William, 1870-
Tears and triumphs; the life story of a pastor-evangelist. Louisville, Ky., Pentecostal Publishing Co., 1948. 445 p.

5599 HARRIS, Margaret J. (1865-1919). LMGSS (1952), 65. LDML (1953), 73.
Member, IowaHA
Attended GHA, 1901 (Chicago)
ME. Gospel song writer, evangelistic singer

5600 HARRIS, Mary Griffin Bristow
Ch. of Eng., PL, PLOP. Rescue mission worker

Part VI. Biography 651

5601 HARRIS, Merne Arthur. GIIH (1962), 32-52. GTWATD (1965), 88-117. GPOH (1969), 42-54.
WM, W. Pastor, evangelist, Bible college prof., Bible college dean, Bible college pres.

5602 HARRIS, Reader (1847-1909). WWW (1897-1916), 316.
Ch. of Eng., PL. Attorney (King's counsel), engineer, rescue mission supt.
b. July 5, 1847, Worcester, Eng.
d. Mar. 30, 1909, London, Eng.

5603 Harris, Reader, 1847-1909.
How I became an agnostic and how God saved me; recollections of a lecture by the late Reader Harris, K.C., comp. by his daughters. London, S.W. Partridge & Co., 1910. 58 p.

5604 Harris, Reader, 1847-1909.
In memoriam; being a series of fourteen addresses by the late Reader Harris. London, S.W. Partridge & Co.; Speke Hall Bookroom, 1910. 14 pt.

5605 Harris, Reader, 1847-1909.
Reader Harris, 1847-1909; thanksgiving and remembrance after twenty five years, November 8th, 1934, ed. by M.R. Hooker. London, Westminster City Publishing Co., 1934. 31 p.

5606 Harris, Reader, 1847-1909.
Why I believe; or, The case against atheism. London, P.L. Publishing Co., 1915. 93 p.

5607 Hooker, Mary Reader (Harris), 1881-
Adventures of an agnostic; life and letters of Reader Harris, Q.C., by Mary Reader Hooker. London, Marshall, Morgan & Scott, 1959. 152 p.

5608 Storrs, William Townsend, Vicar of Sandown, I.O.W.
Christian perfection: what it is not, and what it is; notes on a booklet of the Pentecostal League. Sandown, I.O.W., Eng., I.W. Chronicle Printing Works, 1900. 19 p.
Notes on Christian Perfection, by Reader Harris.

5609 HARRIS, Robert Lee (-1894).
FM, ME, S; NTCOC. Pastor, evangelist, missionary
b. 18??, Texas
d. Nov. 26, 1894, Milan, Tenn.

5610 Harris, Robert Lee, -1894.
In America and Africa. Chicago, J.L. Regan Printing Co., 1887.

5611 Harris, Robert Lee, -1894.
My trip to Africa, by Robert Lee Harris (cow-boy preacher), who has made three trips to the Dark Continent. Nashville, Tenn., Cumberland Presbyterian Publishing House, 1890. 24 p.

5612 Harris, Robert Lee, -1894.
Why we left the Methodist Episcopal Church, South. Milan, Tenn., 1894.

5613 HARRISON, Thomas (1854-).
          ME. Evangelist
5614   Davies, Edward, 1830-
              The boy preacher; or, The life and labors of Rev.
          Thomas Harrison, together with sketches of the most
          remarkable revivals in which he has been engaged.
          Reading, Mass., Holiness Book Concern, 1881. 290 p.

5615 HART, Edward Payson (-1919). BMW (1960), 47-73.
          ME, FM. Pastor, district chairman, seminary prin.,
              bishop
          d. Mar. 15, 1919, Alameda, Calif.
5616   Hart, Edward Payson, bp., -1919.
              Reminiscences of early Free Methodism; with an introd. by Burton R. Jones. Chicago, Free Methodist
          Publishing House, 1913. xxi, 259 p.

5617 HARTMAN, Lucy A. (-1950). LLITW (1951), 216.
          FM. Missionary

5618 HARTSOUGH, Lewis (1828-1919). MAWACOSM (1925), 312-
          313. RHOOF (1964), 308-309.
          ME. Pastor, presiding elder, gospel song writer
          b. Aug. 31, 1828, Ithaca, N.Y.
          d. Jan. 1, 1919, Mount Vernon, Iowa

5619 HARVEY, John W. (1854-).
          ME, S? Lay leader, physician
          b. 1854
          d. 19??, Texas
5620   Harvey, John W., 1854-
              The treatment of skin cancers by chemical means.
          Fort Worth, Tex., Kimble Printery, 1914. 12 p.

5621 HATFIELD, John Thomas (1851-1934).
          Attended GHA, 1901 (Chicago)
          ME, CN. Evangelist, pastor?
          b. Aug. 8, 1851
          d. Dec. 14, 1934
5622   Hatfield, John Thomas, 1851-1934.
              Thirty-three years a live wire; life of John T. Hatfield, the "Hoosier evangelist," by himself. Cincinnati,
          God's Revivalist Office, 1913. 317 p.

5623 HAVEN, Gilbert (1821-1880). DAB. WWW in Am. (1607-
              1896), 240.
          ME. Seminary (academy) teacher and prin., pastor,
              military chaplain, editor, bishop
          b. Sept. 19, 1821, Malden, Mass.
          d. Jan. 3, 1880, Malden, Mass.
5624   Prentice, George
              The life of Gilbert Haven, bishop of the Methodist

Part VI. Biography 653

Episcopal Church. New York, Phillips & Hunt; Cincinnati, Walden & Stowe, 1883. 526 p.

5625 HAVERGAL, Frances Ridley (1836-1879). GFW (1888), 188-194. CHHMH (1970), 564. LDEFC (1911), 312-326. MCV (1901), 82-92. MMAWODP (1920), 218-224.
Ch. of Eng. Lay member, gospel song writer
b. Dec. 14, 1836, Astley, Eng.
d. June 3, 1879, Oystermouth, Glamorganshire, Wales

5626 Havergal, Frances Ridley, 1836-1879.
Frances Ridley Havergal, a saint of God; a new memoir by T.H. Darlow, with a selection of extracts from her prose and verse and an introd. by the Bishop of Worcester. London, Nisbet & Co., 1927. 269 p.
"A list of works by Frances Ridley Havergal": p. 267-269.

5627 Davies, Edward, 1830-
Frances Ridley Havergal: a full sketch of her life, with choice selections from her prose and poetical writings, by Rev. E. Davies.... Reading, Mass., Holiness Book Concern; Boston, Willard Tract Repository; etc., etc., 1884. 192 p.

5628 Davies, Edward, 1830-
Frances Ridley Havergal, a full sketch of her life, with choice selections from her prose and poetical writings, by E. Davies. Cincinnati, M.W. Knapp, c1884. 192 p.

5629 Havergal, Maria Vernon Graham, 1821-1887.
Memorials of Frances Ridley Havergal, by her sister, M.V.G.H. London, James Nisbet, 1886. 250 p.

5630 HAVILAND, Emma Hillmon (1863-1940).
FM. Missionary

5631 Haviland, Emma (Hillmon), 1863-1940.
Under the Southern cross; or, A woman's life work for Africa. Cincinnati, God's Bible School and Revivalist, 1928. 461 p.

5632 HAWKINS, Floyd W. (1904-). LMGSS (1952), 45.
CN. Pastor, gospel song writer

5633 HAWKINS, Richard C. TDOOP (1968), 317-318.
ME, PHC. Pastor, district supt., denominational official

5634 HAWKINS, Richard Watson (-1892). MHWMCOA (1959), 116-117, 265-266. MFATALW (1960), 295-296. PPE (1868), 309-312.
ME, FM, WM. Pastor, presiding elder, evangelist
d. Jan. 13, 1892.

5635 HAYDEN, Clara M. (-1926). LLITW (1951), 216.
      FM. Missionary

5636 HAYES, Richard Baxter (1858-1937).
      PeHC. Pastor, evangelist
5637   Hayes, W. M.
            Memoirs of Richard Baxter Hayes, comp. and ed. by
            W.M. Hayes.... Greer, S.C. [Philadelphia, Dunlap
            Printing Co., 1945]. xvi, 204 p.

5638 HAYGOOD, Atticus Greene (1839-1896). SCM (1881), 436-437. WWW in Am. (1607-1896), 242.
      ME, S. Pastor, presiding elder, denominational official, college pres., bishop
      b. Nov. 19, 1839, Watkinsville, Ga.
      d. Jan. 19, 1896, Oxford, Ga.
5639   Mann, Harold William
            Atticus Greene Haygood, Methodist bishop, editor,
            and educator. Athens, University of Georgia Press,
            1965. viii, 254 p.
            Includes comment on the Holiness Movement in
            Georgia.

5640 HAYNES, Benjamin Franklin (1851-1923). MOUS (1941), 72-78.
      ME, S; PCN; CN. Pastor, presiding elder, college pres., editor
      b. 1851, Franklin, Tenn.
      d. Oct. 2, 1923, Nashville, Tenn.
5641   Haynes, Benjamin Franklin, 1851-1923.
            Tempest-tossed on Methodist seas; or, A sketch of
            my life. Louisville, Pentecostal Publishing Co., 1921.
            310 p.
            Autobiography.

5642 HEATH, Frank Stowe. PM (1898), 49-53.
      ME. Evangelist

5643 HECKART, Robert H.
      PHC, W. Pastor, evangelist, Bible college pres., district supt.
      b. 19??, Palo Alto, Pa.
5644   Heckart, Robert H.
            Behold the Lamb of God. Butler, Ind., Higley Press,
            1959. xv, 62 p.
            Biographical sketch: p. vii-viii.

5645 HELLING, Hubert W. GHAI (1960), 71-73.
      CN. Missionary

5646 HENDREN, Evelyn Webb (-1921). LLITW (1951), 216.
      FM. Missionar

Part VI. Biography

5647 HENDRICKS, Andrew Oliver (1879-1965).
Luth., CN, PCN, CN. Pastor, evangelist, college pres., missionary
b. Sept. 27, 1879, Sweden
d. 1965, Pasadena, Calif.
5648 Hendricks, Andrew Oliver, 1879-1965.
"The theory of evolution according to Herbert Spencer and Henri Bergson." Unpublished M.A. thesis, University of Southern California, 1919. 127ℓ.
5649 Hathaway, Evelyn (Hendricks)
Hallelujah chariot. Richmond, Va., John Knox Press, 1969. 213 p.
"A story drawn from the life of my father, Dr. Andrew O. Hendricks."

5650 HENDRICKS, Fawn Galbraith (-1947).
CN. Pastor's wife
5651 Hathaway, Evelyn (Hendricks)
Hallelujah chariot. Richmond, Va., John Knox Press, 1969. 213 p.
"A story drawn from the life of my father, Dr. Andrew O. Hendricks."

5652 HENSON, Jacob Cornelius (1875-).
Bapt., MP, NTCOC, HChuC, PCN, CN. Pastor, district supt., college admin., evangelist
b. Sept. 15, 1875, McLennan County, Tex.
5653 "The preaching of J.C. Henson," Preacher's Magazine, XXXVI (Aug. 1961), 5-8.

5654 HERRELL, Noah Benjamin (1877-1953). COPN (1958), 79-84. LMGSS (1952), 149-151. LDML (1953), 78.
HCC, CN. Pastor, evangelist, district supt., gospel song writer
b. Mar. 8, 1877, Muncie, Ind.
d. May 10, 1953, Pasadena, Calif.
5655 "The preaching of N.B. Herrell," Preacher's Magazine, XXXVI (July 1961), 5-8.

5656 HERSHEY, Eusebius (1823-1891). SWGHW (1948), 13-20, 22.
MBIC. Missionary
b. 1823, Elstonville, Lancaster County, Pa.
d. 1891, Liberia
5657 Hershey, Eusebius, 1823-1891.
The living poem. Philadelphia, Craig, Finley & Co., 1877. Cover-title, 88 p.

5658 HERTENSTEIN, Ralph. FHOP (1964).
CN. Pastor

5659 HERTENSTEIN, Zylphia. FHOP (1964).
CN. Pastor's wife

5660 HESLOP, William Greene (1886-   ). SCC (1947), 69-76.
WW in the Clergy (1935-1936), 520.
PHC, CN. Pastor, college prof.
b. July 11, 1886, England

5661 HESS, Weaver W. (1890-   ). WW in the Clergy (1935-1936), 520. FHOP (1964).
CN. Pastor, evangelist, district supt.
b. Sept. 15, 1890, Newton, Kan.

5662 HIBBARD, Freeborn Garrettson (1811-1895). PPE (1868), 34-45. DAB. WWW in Am. (1607-1896), 250.
ME. Pastor, editor
b. Feb. 22, 1811, New Rochelle, N.Y.
d. Jan. 27, 1895

5663 HICKS, Lawrence B. MHP (1957), 103-111.
CN. Pastor, evangelist, district supt.
b. 19??, Tennessee

5664 HIGGINS, Edward John
SA. Officer
5665 Atkinson, John Edward
Here is a man: E.J. Higgins. London, Salvationist Publishing & Supplies, 1954. 15 p.

5666 HIGGINS, Nota Rose (1914-   ). ETWF (196?).
PHC. Rescue mission worker, missionary
b. June 11, 1914, Columbus, Ohio

5667 HIGGS, Daniel E. (1887-1944). COPN (1958), 73-78.
ME, PCN, CN. Pastor, district supt.
b. Apr. 4, 1887, New Market, Marys County, Md.
d. Jan. 1944

5668 HILL, A. PPE (1868), 313-316.
ME. Pastor

5669 HILLMAN, Joseph (1833-1890). MAWACOSM (1925), 313-315. SCM (1881), 444-445.
ME. Lay leader, camp meeting promoter, song book comp.
b. 1833, Schoharie County, N.Y.

5670 HILLS, Aaron Merritt (1848-1935). MOUS (1941), 50-57. NP (1925), 233-239. PM (1898), 33-42.
Attended GHA, 1901 (Chicago)
Cong., PCN, CN. Pastor, college pres., college prof., writer

Part VI. Biography 657

        b. Feb. 4, 1848, Dowagiac, Mich.
        d. Sept. 11, 1935, Altadena, Calif.
5671   "Dr. A.M. Hills," Herald of Holiness, XL (July 2, 1951).
5672   McGraw, James, 1913-
        "The preaching of A.M. Hills," Preacher's Magazine, XXXIII (Feb. 1958), 6-8.

5673 HIWALE, Jacobrao. HNTB (1934), 96-97.
        Pres., CN. National worker, pastor
        b. 18??, India

5674 HOBART, Maurice Arden (1925-). ETWF (196?).
        RMC, PHC. Pastor, missionary
        b. Aug. 29, 1925, Otisco, N.Y.

5675 HOBART, Ruth Elizabeth Elwine (1932-). ETWF (196?).
        PHC. Pastor's wife, missionary
        b. Nov. 20, 1932, Pocono Lake, Pa.

5676 HODGIN, George Arnold (-1967).
        PCN, PC, PHC. College prof., college admin.,
          evangelist, asst. general supt., Bible college pres.
        d. Jan. 2, 1967.

5677 HOGUE, Wilson Thomas (1852-1920). BMW (1960), 109-141. DAB. LMB (1948), 93-94. WW in Am. Meth. (1916), 99. WWW in Am. (1897-1942), 576.
        Attended GHA, 1901 (Chicago)
        FM. Pastor, district elder, college pres., bishop
        b. Mar. 6, 1852, Lyndon, N.Y.
        d. Feb. 13, 1920

5678 HOKE, Edna Wells (1875-).
        CN. Evangelist
5679   Hoke, Edna (Wells), 1875-
        He faileth not; or, The triumphs of faith. Kansas City, Mo., Nazarene Publishing House, 1927. 160 p.

5680 HOLLAND, William Webster (1884-). RLOA (1941-1942), 539.
        ME. Pastor, Bible school teacher, college prof.
        b. June 28, 1884, Queen Anne County, Md.

5681 HOLLENBACK, R. L. NP (1925), 53-63.
        PCN, CN. Evangelist

5682 HOLLMANN, Paul H. (-1963). TDOOP (1968), 343.
        PHC. Pastor
        d. Dec. 6, 1963
5683   Pilgrim Holiness Advocate, XLIII (Feb. 23, 1963), 5.

5684 HOLMES, Nickels John (1847-1919).
Pres., (HU), Pent. Pastor, Bible school founder
d. Dec. 17, 1919
5685 Holmes, Nickels John, 1847-1919.
Life sketches and sermons, by Reverend N.J. Holmes and wife. Royston, Ga., Press of the Pentecostal Holiness Church, c1920. 310 p.
5685 Thomas, Iva
History of Holmes Theological Seminary. Franklin Springs, Ga., 1959. 47 p.
Account of N.J. Holmes, the founder: p. 2-22.

5687 HONN, Alice Griffith (-1940). LLITW (1951), 216.
FM. Missionary

5688 HOOPLE, William Howard (1868-1922). N.Y. Times (Sept. 30, 1922), 13:5. MOUS (1941), 65-71.
Bapt., APCA, PCN, CN. Merchant, pastor, Y.M.C.A. worker
b. Aug. 6, 1868, Herkimer, N.Y.
d. Sept. 29, 1922

5689 HOOVER, J. W. PPE (1868), 256-261.
ME. Pastor

5690 HOPKINS, Harlow Eugene (1931-). LIE (1971), 442.
CN. College prof.
b. Jan. 25, 1931, Flint, Mich.

5691 HORINE, Ruth. TDOOP (1968), 287.
HC, PHC. Lay member

5692 HORNE, James Wesley (1823-18??). SCM (1881), 455.
PPE (1868), 203-206.
Member, NHA
ME. Missionary, pastor, evangelist
b. Mar. 24, 1823, Jamaica, W.I.

5693 HORNER, Ralph Cecil (1854-1921). MHWMCOA (1959), 395-396.
Meth. (Can.), WM, HMoC, SCA. Evangelist, bishop
b. Dec. 22, 1854, Shawville, Pontiac Co., Que., Can.
d. Sept. 12, 1921, Ivanhoe, Que.?, Can.
5694 Horner, Ralph Cecil, 1854-1921.
Conference and evangelistic relations no. II. Ottawa, Can., Holiness Movement Publishing House, 1905.
5695 Horner, Ralph Cecil, 1854-1921.
From the altar to the upper room. Toronto, 1891.
5696 Horner, Ralph Cecil, 1854-1921.
Ralph C. Horner, evangelist; reminiscences from his own pen. Brockville, Ont., Can., Pub. for Mrs. A.E. Horner by Standard Publishing House, n.d. xxi, 215 p.

Part VI. Biography 659

5697 Pointen, Harold William
"The Holiness Movement Church in Canada." Unpublished B.D. thesis, Victoria University, 1950. 179ℓ.
Contains account of the work of R.C. Horner.

5698 HOTCHKISS, Willis Ray (1873-1948).
Fr. Missionary
5699 Hotchkiss, Willis Ray, 1873-1948.
Then and now in Kenya colony; forty adventurous years in East Africa. New York, Fleming H. Revell Co., c1937. 160 p.

5700 HOUGHTON, Willard J. (1825-1896).
WM. Evangelist, seminary (academy) founder
b. July 19, 1825, Rushford?, N.Y.
d. Apr. 21, 1896, Houghton, N.Y.
5701 Houghton, Willard J., 1825-1896.
Retrospection; ed. by Frieda A. Gillette. Houghton, N.Y., Houghton College, 1964. (Issued as Houghton College Bulletin, XXXIX, 12).

5702 HOUSE, Elsie Elizabeth (1927-). ETWF (196?).
PHC. Pastor, missionary
b. Jan. 26, 1927, Newaygo County, Mich.

5703 HOUSE, Meredith Carl (1923-). ETWF (196?).
PHC. Pastor's wife, missionary
b. Aug. 21, 1923, Genoa, Ohio

5704 HOUSTON, L. S. (-1964). TDOOP (1968), 344.
PHC. Pastor, district supt.
d. June 24, 1964

5705 HOWARD, Ivan Cushing (1900-). DAS (1969), IV, 171.
GFIIH (1963), 230-246.
EMC. Bible college prof., college dean, seminary prof., pastor, evangelist
b. Dec. 14, 1900, Galena, Ohio

5706 HOWLAND, Carl LeRoy (1881-). RLOA (1941-1942), 555.
FM. Pastor, district elder, college prof., editor
b. Mar. 24, 1881, Havelock, Neb.

5707 HOYT, Harold Baldwin (1917-). DAS (1969), IV, 171.
CN. Pastor, Bible school teacher, college prof.
b. Oct. 23, 1917, Wellington, Kan.

5708 HUDSON, Oscar (1874-). FHOP (1964).
Pres., CN. College bus. manager, pastor, district supt.
b. Apr. 24, 1874, Fayetteville, Ark.

5709   Hudson, Oscar, 1874-
         This I remember; true incidents of pioneer days related by Oscar Hudson. Kansas City, Mo., Beacon Hill Press, 1965. 63 p.

5710   HUFF, George E. (-1956).
         IHC, PHC. Pastor
         d. Mar. 9, 1956.

5711   HUFF, William H.
         President, NHA, 1919-1921
         ME. Evangelist

5712   HUFFMAN, Jasper Abraham (1880-). WW in the Clergy (1935-1936), 559. RLOA (1941-1942), 559-560. WW in Am. (1952-1953), 1201. SFLF (1950), 41-44.
         MBIC, UMC. Pastor, college prof., seminary prof.
         b. Feb. 28, 1880, Elkhart County, Ind.

5713   Huffman, Jasper Abraham, 1880-
         A guide to the study of the Old and New Testaments, for use in the high schools of Indiana, prepared by J.A. Huffman ... for Indiana Board of Control for High School Bible Study for Credit in Indiana by the Committee of Five. Dayton, Ohio, 1926. 176 p.
         "Approved by the Indiana State Board of Education, June 1926."

5714   Huffman, Lambert
         Not of this world. Canton?, Ohio, c1951. 159 p.

5715   HUGHES, George (1823-1904). GFW (1888), 270-276. PPE (1868), 127-131. N.Y. Times (Oct. 11, 1904), 9:5.
         Founding member, NHA
         Chairman, GHA, 1885 (Chicago)
         Temporary chairman, GHA, 1901 (Chicago)
         ME. Pastor, evangelist, editor
         b. Feb. 22, 1823, Manchester, Eng.
         d. Oct. 9, 1904, South Orange, N.J.

5716   HUGHES, J. PPE (1868), 341-342.
         ME. Pastor

5717   HUGHES, John Wesley (1852-1932).
         ME, S. Pastor, college founder, college pres.
         b. 1852, Wilmore?, Ky.
         d. 1932, Wilmore, Ky.

5718   Hughes, John Wesley, 1852-1923.
         Autobiography; with biographical contributions by Rev. Andrew Johnson ... and appreciations by others. Louisville, Ky., Pentecostal Publishing Co., 1923. 295 p.

5719   Hughes, T. Walt
         Wilmore, Kentucky. Compton, Calif., M & A Books, 1965. 202 p.

Part VI. Biography

5720 HUMPHREY, Jerry Miles (1872-).
FM. Evangelist
b. June 30, 1872, near Memphis, Tenn.
d. 19??, California

5721 Humphrey, Jerry Miles, 1872-
"What ... God hath joined together." Phoenix, Ariz., Rev. Don Hughes, n.d. Cover-title, 22 p.
Autobiographical.

5722 HUNT, Marion Palmer (1860-). WW in the Clergy (1935-1936), 566.
Bapt. Pastor
b. July 1, 1860, Williamsburg, Mo.

5723 Hunt, Marion Palmer, 1860-
The story of my life. Louisville, Herald Press, 1941. 171 p.

5724 HUNTER, Fannie McDowell. HWP (1905), 48-61.
ME, S; VanM; NTCOC. Evangelist
b. 18??, Missouri

5725 HUNTER, Nora Siens (1873-1951). SHBD (1955), 123-144.
CG (A). Evangelistic worker, pastor's wife, missionary society pres.
b. Aug. 16, 1873, Chanute, Kan.
d. Jan. 1951

5726 Neal, Hazel G.
Madam President: the story of Nora Siens Hunter, founder and first president of the National Woman's Missionary Society of the Church of God, by Hazel G. Neal and Axchie A. Bolitho. Anderson, Ind., Gospel Trumpet Co., 1951. 148 p.

5727 HUNTER, William (1811-1877). MAWACOSM (1925), 318.
SCM (1881), 459.
ME. Pastor, presiding elder, editor, college prof., gospel song writer
b. May 26, 1811, Ireland
d. Oct. 18, 1877

5728 HUNTINGTON, Rev. Dr. PPE (1868), 355-357.
Cong. Pastor

5729 HUNTINGTON, DeWitt Clinton (1830-1912). WWW in Am. (1897-1942), 609-610. N.Y. Times (Feb. 9, 1912), 9:5.
ME. Pastor, presiding elder, college prof., college admin., gospel song writer
b. Apr. 27, 1830, Townsend, Vt.
d. Feb. 1912

5730 HUSSEY, Ashabel H. (1833-   ). GFW (1888), 131-134.
         Fr. Pastor
         b. Nov. 23, 1833, Mount Pleasant, Ohio

5731 HYND, Agnes Kanema Sharpe. GHAI (1960), 78-81.
         CN. Missionary

5732 HYND, David (1895-   ). GHAI (1960), 78-81.
         CN. Missionary
5733   Frame, George
            Blood brother of the Swazis; the life story of David
         Hynd.... Kansas City, Mo., Beacon Hill Press, 1952.
         121 p.

5734 INGLER, Arthur F. (1873-1935). LDML (1953), 77.
         APCA, MetCA, PCN, CN. Pastor, gospel song writer,
            evangelist
         b. May 12, 1873, Montandon, Pa.
         d. Aug. 8, 1935.

5735 INGRAM, Pearl. FHOP (1964).
         CN. Missionary

5736 INGRAM, Robert Clinton (1886-1958).
         CN. Missionary
         d. Mar. 17, 1958
5737   Williamson, Gideon Brooks, 1898-
            Sent forth by the Holy Ghost; the life of R.C. Ingram.
         Kansas City, Mo., Nazarene Publishing House, 1960.
         96 p.

5738 INSKIP, John Swanel (1816-1884). DAB. PPE (1868), 34-
            45. MMAWODP (1920), 236-245. SCM (1881), 478-
            480. WWW in Am. (1607-1896), 272. N.Y. Times
            (Mar. 8, 1884), 2:7.
         President, NHA, 1867-1884
         ME. Pastor, evangelist
         b. Aug. 10, 1816, Huntingdon, Eng.
         d. Mar. 7, 1884, Ocean Grove, N.J.
5739   Bottome, Francis, 1823-1894.
            An eleventh hour laborer; reminiscences of the life
         and character of the late Edward S. Inskip, Esq., de-
         livered on the occasion of his funeral, in the Gothic M.
         E. Church, Brooklyn, E.D. Published by request.
         New York, Hosford & Ketcham, Stationers and Printers,
         1863. 23 p.
5740   McDonald, William, 1820-1901.
            The life of Rev. John S. Inskip, by W. McDonald
         and John E. Searles. Chicago, Christian Witness Co.,
         1885. 374 p.
            At head of title: I am, O Lord, wholly and forever
         Thine.

Part VI. Biography

5741   Pepper, Eleuthera I. D.,   -1908, ed.
               Memorial of Rev. John S. Inskip. Philadelphia, National Publishing Association for the Promotion of Holiness, 1884? 51 p.

5742   IRICK, Allie (-1949)
               ME, S; NTCOC; HChuC; PCN; CN. Evangelist, district supt.
               b. 18??, Lamasco, Fannin County, Tex.
               d. Dec. 28, 1949
5743   Irick, Allie,   -1949.
               A journey 'round the world. Louisville, Pentecostal Herald Print, 1907. 306 p.
5744   McGraw, James, 1913-
               "The preaching of Allie Irick," Preacher's Magazine, XXX (Jan. 1958), 6-8.

5745   IRICK, Emma
               HChuC, PCN, CN. Evangelist, pastor

5746   IRONSIDE, Henry Allan (1876-1951). WW in the Clergy (1935-1936), 577. RLOA (1941-1942), 576. N.Y. Times (Jan. 17, 1951), 28:4.
               SA, Ply. Br. Pastor, evangelist, college prof.
               b. Oct. 14, 1876, Toronto, Ont., Can.
               d. Jan. 16, 1951, Rotu Rua, N.Z.
5747   Ironside, Henry Allan, 1876-1951.
               Holiness, the false and the true. New York, Loizeaux Bros., 1953. 142 p.
               Reprint of 1912 ed.
               Includes spiritual autobiography and unfavorable critique of the Holiness Movement.

5748   IRWIN, A. W. FHOP (1964).
               ME, PCN, ME, CN. Pastor

5749   IRWIN, Hazel I. FHOP (1964).
               ME, PCN, ME, CN. Pastor's wife.

5750   ISAAC, Eben M.
               ME, PCN. Pastor
5751   Isaac, Eben M.
               The extremely spiritual man; or, Holiness in action. Chicago, Christian Witness Co., 1907. 193 p.
               Fictionalized autobiography.

5752   ISAYAMA, N. HNTB (1934), 74-76.
               CN. National worker, pastor
               b. 18??, Japan

5753   IVES, R. Wingrove
               IHC, PHC. Pastor, missionary
               b. 18??, England

5754 Ives, R. Wingrove
A missionary's cry from Barbados; last chapter by Rev. R.G. Finch, General Missionary Superintendent of the Pilgrim Holiness Church. Kingswood, Ky., Missionary Office, 192?. 72 p.

5755 JACKSON, James Harvey (1920-   ). WWACUA (1970-1971), 260.
CN. Pastor, college admin.
b. June 24, 1920, Stroll, S.D.

5756 JACOBS, Simon P. (1847-1921).
President, Southwestern HA
Attended GHA, 1901
ME. Pastor, missionary
d. Mar. 6, 1921

5757 JAFFRAY, Robert Alexander (1873-1945).
CMA. Missionary
5758 Tozer, Aiden Wilson, 1897-1963.
Let my people go!; the life of Robert A. Jaffray. Harrisburg, Pa., Christian Publications, c1947. 127 p.

5759 JAMES, Eldon LeRoy (-1945). LLITW (1951), 216.
FM. Missionary

5670 JAMES, Mary Dagworthy Yard (1810-1883). GFW (1888), 195-199. MAWACOSM (1925), 323-324.
ME. Lay leader, gospel song writer, temperance worker
b. Aug. 7, 1810, Trenton, N.J.
d. Oct. 4, 1883, New York, N.Y.

5761 JAMES, Maynard G. (1902-   ). MHP (1957), 63-73.
IHM, CHC, CN. Evangelist, editor, pastor
b. Apr. 17, 1902, Bargoed, S. Wales

5762 JANES, Edmund Storer (1807-1876). SCM (1881), 493-494.
N.Y. Times (Sept. 19, 1876), 4:6; (Sept. 22, 1876), 8:2; (Nov. 17, 1876), 2:7. LMB (1948).
ME. Pastor, college admin., bishop
b. Apr. 27, 1807, Sheffield, Berkshire County, Mass.
d. Sept. 18, 1876, New York
5763 Ridgaway, Henry Bascom, 1830-1895.
The life of Edmund S. Janes, D.D., LL.D., late senior bishop of the Methodist Episcopal Church. New York, Phillips & Hunt; Cincinnati, Walden & Stowe, 1882. 428 p.

5764 JENKINS, Charles S.
Bapt., PCN, CN. Pastor, missionary
b. 189?, Lynn, Mass.

Part VI. Biography

5765 Young, Samuel, 1901-
God's unfailing faithfulness (the life of Charles S. Jenkins). Kansas City, Mo., Nazarene Publishing House, 1961. 87 p.

5766 JENKINS, Orville W.
CN. Pastor, district supt., denominational official, general supt.

5767 JENKINS, Pearl May Kent
Bapt., PCN, CN. Nurse, pastor's wife, missionary
b. 189?, Lyndon, Vt.

5768 Young, Samuel, 1901-
God's unfailing faithfulness (the life of Charles S. Jenkins). Kansas City, Mo., Nazarene Publishing House, 1961. 87 p.
Includes account of Pearl Jenkins.

5769 JENNINGS, Arthur T. (1858-1914).
Endorsed call, GHA, 1901 (Chicago)
WM. Pastor, editor
b. July 21, 1858, Kinney's Corners, Yates County, N.Y.
d. Mar. 24, 1914, Houghton, N.Y.

5770 JENNINGS, Otho (1911-). AMS (1965-1968), VII, 781. GFIIH (1963), 140-160.
PHC, CN. Pastor, Bible college prof., Bible college pres., college prof.
b. Dec. 9, 1911, Marthaville, La.

5771 JERNIGAN, Charles Brougher (1863-1930). MOUS (1941), 29-35. NP (1925), 72-77.
Attended GHA, 1901 (Chicago)
ME, S; IAHU; IndHC; HChuC; PCN, CN. Pastor, evangelist, district supt., editor
b. Sept. 4, 1863, Casilla, Miss.
d. 1930, Bethany, Okla.

5772 Jernigan, Charles Brougher, 1863-1930.
From the prairie schooner to a city flat. Brooklyn, N.Y., 1926. 140 p.
Autobiography.

5773 Jernigan, Charles Brougher, 1863-1930.
Pioneer days of the Holiness Movement in the Southwest. Kansas City, Mo., Pentecostal Nazarene Publishing House, 1919. 157 p.

5774 McGraw, James, 1913-
"The preaching of Charles B. Jernigan," Preacher's Magazine, XXXIII (Mar. 1958), 8-10.

5775 JERNIGAN, Johnny Hill. HWP (1905), 79-83.
ME, S; IAHU; IndHC; HChuC; PCN; CN. Evangelist, rescue home supt.

5776   JESSOP, Harry Edward (1884-). SFLF (1950), 45-49.
            Bapt. (Scot.), PCN, IHM, CN. Pastor, evangelist,
            Bible college pres.
5777   Jessop, Harry Edward, 1884-
            I met a man with a shining face; an autobiography in
            the things of God. Chicago, Humboldt Park Gospel
            Tabernacle, 1941. 75 p.

5778   JOHNSON, Andrew (1875-). WW in Meth. (1952), 369.
            SFLF (1950), 50-54.
            ME, M. Pastor, evangelist, temperance worker

5779   JOHNSON, Benjamin Edgar (1921-). WW in Am. (1972-
            1973), I, 1600.
            CN. Pastor, denominational official
            b. Oct. 30, 1921, Sterling, Colo.

5780   JOHNSON, Harry Fred (1889-1945). LLITW (1951), 216.
            RLOA (1941-1942), 592.
            FM. Pastor, missionary, denominational official
            b. Apr. 15, 1889, Wessington Springs, S.D.

5781   JOHNSON, Herbert S.
            CN, PCN. Pastor

5782   JOHNSON, Ithiel Town (1849-1931).
            Endorsed call, GHA, 1901 (Chicago)
            ME. Pastor, evangelist
            b. July 26, 1849, Douglas, Mass.
            d. July 4, 1931, Springfield, Mass.
5783   Johnson, Ithiel Town, 1849-1931.
            The story of my life; or, Forty busy years. Bur-
            lington, Vt., Free Press Printing Co., 1912. 231 p.

5784   JOHNSON, John Prescott (1921-). DAS (1969), IV, 182.
            CG (H), CN. Pastor, Bible school teacher, college
            prof.
            b. Apr. 24, 1921, Tumalo, Ore.

5785   JOHNSON, Walter Henry (1917-). DAS (1969), IV, 183.
            GIIH (1962), 282-294.
            FM. Pastor, college prof.
            b. Feb. 24, 1917, Pontiac, Ill.

5786   JOHNSON, Zachary Taylor (1897-). WW in Am. (1960-
            1961), 1499. RLOA (1941-1942), 595.
            ME, S. Pastor, college admin., college pres., evange-
            list
            b. June 18, 1897, Athens, Ga.

5787   JOHNSTON, U. G.
            ME? Pastor?

Part VI. Biography

5788 Johnston, U. G.
Letters from Beulah, by Joshua Satisfied (Rev. U. G. Johnston). Chicago and Boston, Christian Witness Co., 1906. 104 p.

5789 JONES, Anna (-1936). LLITW (1951), 216.
FM. Missionary

5790 JONES, Burton Rensselaer (1845-1933). BMW (1960), 95-107. WW in Am. Meth. (1916), 114. WWW in Am. (1897-1942), 646.
FM. Pastor, district elder, editor, bishop
b. Dec. 3, 1845, Livingston County, N.Y.
d. Apr. 20, 1933, Pasadena, Calif.
5791 Jones, Burton Rensselaer, bp., 1845-1933.
Incidents in the life and labors of Burton R. Jones. Chicago, Free Methodist Publishing House, 1909. 315 p.
Autobiography.

5792 JONES, Byon A. (1896-). SEC (1968), 63-66.
PeHC. Printer's helper, bricklayer, Bible academy teacher, Bible academy supt.
b. 1896, Mount Olive, N.C.

5793 JONES, Carl Warren (1882-1963). RLOA (1941-1942), 597. COPN (1958), 97-102.
ME, PCN, CN. Pastor, college prof., district supt., denominational official
b. Mar 2, 1882, Garfield, Wash.
d. Apr. 22, 1963, Bethany, Okla.

5794 JONES, Carlos Edward (1926-). ETWF (196?).
PHC. Pastor, college admin., denominational official
b. Mar. 2, 1926, Port Clinton, Ohio

5795 JONES, Charles P.
Bapt., CC (H). Pastor, denominational leader, gospel song writer

5796 JONES, David B. (1885-1950).
IHM. Missionary
b. Nov. 1885, Ferndale, Wales
d. Jan. 1950, Durban, Natal, S. Afr.
5797 Jones, Mrs. D. B.
David Jones, ambassador to the Africans, by Mrs. D.B. Jones and her sons, Reginald and Harold. Kansas City, Mo., Beacon Hill Press, 1955. 122 p.

5798 JONES, Dess Dain (1895-). The Transit Scout (Kansas City, Mo.), (Dec. 1960).
CG (H), CN. Lay member, streetcar conductor
b. July 9, 1895, Iola, Kan.

5799   Smith, Harlie W.
        "Something better than divorce!," Church Herald and Holiness Banner, XCI (Mar. 26, 1970), 15-16.

5800   JONES, Edith Frances (-1951). LLITW (1951), 216.
        FM. Missionary

5801   JONES, Eli Stanley (1884-1973). WW in Am. (1966-1967), 1092. Twentieth Cent. Ency. of Rel. Know., I, 612. SFLF (1950), 55-57. NVFML (1936), 201-207.
        ME, M, UM. Missionary
        b. Jan. 3, 1884, Clarksville, Howard Co., Md.
        d. Jan. 25, 1973, India

5802   Jones, Eli Stanley, 1884-1973.
        A song of ascents. New York, Abingdon, 1968.
        Autobiography.

5803   Paul, John Haywood, 1877-1967.
        Main Street in Jericho; viewing social justice at its fountain head, with a friendly examination of "Christ's alternative to Communism," by E. Stanley Jones. Chicago, Christian Witness Co., 1937. 98 p.

5804   Wilson, Francis C.
        "E. Stanley Jones, world ambassador of 'The Way'," Zion's Herald (May 17, 1950), 3, 4, 18.

5805   JONES, Lum. NP (1925), 98-106.
        CN. Pastor, evangelist

5806   Jones, Lum
        The new pastor. Kansas City, Mo., Nazarene Publishing House, 1926. 96 p.
        Fictionalized autobiography.

5807   JONES, Margaret Louise Hatten (1925-). ETWF (196?).
        PHC. Pastor's wife
        b. Apr. 12, 1925, Jackson, Ohio

5808   JONES, Samuel Porter (1847-1906). MCV (1901), 162-170. SCUH (1962), 181. WWW in Am. (1897-1942), 650. N.Y. Times (Oct. 16, 1906), 9:4. DAB.
        ME, S. Pastor, evangelist
        b. Oct. 16, 1847, Chambers County, Ala.
        d. Oct. 1906

5809   Jones, Samuel Porter, 1847-1906.
        Living words.... Toronto, William Briggs, 1886. 595 p.

5810   Jones, Samuel Porter, 1847-1906.
        Sam Jones' own book; a series of sermons collected and ed. under the author's own supervision, with an autobiographical sketch. Cincinnati, Cranston and Stowe, 1887. 539 p.

5811   Jones, Laura (McElwain)
        The life and sayings of Sam P. Jones, by his wife

assisted by Rev. Walt Holcomb, a co-worker of Mr. Jones.... Atlanta, Franklin-Turner Co., 1907. 464 p.

5812 McGraw, James, 1913-
"The preaching of Sam Jones," Preacher's Magazine, XXXII (Nov. 1957), 10-13.

5813 JONES, William. GFW (1888), 152-157. DC (1965, c1887), 26-44.
Unable to attend H. Conf., 1877 (Cincinnati)
Member, NHA
ME. Physician, pastor, evangelist

5814 JOPPIE, Alton S. (1906-).
PHC, W. Pastor, evangelist

5815 JORDAN, Ethel (1882-). ETWF (196?).
PHC. Pastor, rescue mission and orphanage work, missionary
b. Aug. 24, 1882, Vernon County, Wis.

5816 JOY, Bertha Lucile (1918-1966). ETWF (196?).
PHC. Missionary
b. Oct. 10, 1918, Lourenco Marques, Port. E. Afr.
d. Dec. 1, 1966

5817 JOY, Donald Marvin (1928-). GTWATD (1965), 246-254.
FM. Pastor, editor, seminary prof.

5818 JOYCE, Isaac Wilson (1836-1905). DAB. LMB (1948), 104-105. SCM (1881), 503. WWW in Am. (1897-1942), 653.
Endorsed call, GHA, 1901 (Chicago)
ME. Pastor, presiding elder, bishop
b. Oct. 11, 1836, Hamilton County, Ohio
d. July 28, 1905, Minneapolis, Minn.?

5819 JUDD, F. Emerson. PPE (1868), 269-274.
Epis. Priest

5820 JURICH, Alroma B. FHOP (1964).
CN. Pastor's wife

5821 KAHL, Maud H. (1885-1971).
Dis. Chr., PB, MB, CG (H). Missionary, pastor
b. Apr. 27, 1885, Young America, Ind.
d. Jan. 23, 1971, Pittsburgh, Kan.

5822 Kahl, Maude H., 1885-1971.
His guiding hand, an autobiography. Overland Park, Kan., Herald and Banner Press, 1970. 280 p.
Autobiography.

5823 KAHN, Ida (1872-1932). MWWW in Ch. Hist. (1968), 228.
      ME, BM. Physician, missionary
      b. 1872, Kiukiang, Kiangsu Provimce, Ch.
      d. 1932

5824 KANO, Shiro (1911-1944).
      CN. Pastor's asst., sailor
      b. 1911, Kyoto, Jap.
      d. Jan. 19, 1944, Solomon Islands
5825   Spangenberg, Alice
          Oriental pilgrim; story of Shiro Kano. Rev. ed.
        Kansas City, Mo., Beacon Hill Press, 1963. 96 p.

5826 KARNS, Donald Monroe (1930-). ETWF (196?).
      PHC. Pastor, missionary
      b. May 2, 1930, Evansville, Ind.

5827 KARNS, Mrs. Elizabeth Canterbury (1932-). ETWF (196?).
      PHC. Pastor's wife, missionary
      b. July 24, 1932, Evansville, Ind.

5828 KEELER, George H. FHOP (1964).
      ME, CN. Pastor

5829 KEEN, Samuel Ashton (1842-1895). PM (1898), 26-32.
      ME. Pastor, evangelist
      b. May 12, 1842, Harrison, Hamilton Co., Ohio
5830   Keen, Samuel Ashton, 1842-1895.
          Praise papers. Cincinnati, Cranston & Curts, 1894.
        144 p.
5831   Keen, Samuel Ashton, 1842-1895.
          Praise papers, a spiritual autobiography; introd. by
        Daniel Steele. Chicago, Christian Witness Co., c1894.
        83 p.
5832   Keen, Mrs. Mary J. (Palmer)
          Memorial papers; or, The record of a spirit-filled
        life. Cincinnati, M.W. Knapp, 1899. 217 p.

5833 KEEN, Sarah L. SCM (1881), 985.
      ME. Lay leader

5834 KEITH, Clarence Gault (1903-). ETWF (196?).
      PHC, W. Missionary
      b. Oct. 6, 1903, Austin, Ind.

5835 KEITH, David Livingstone (1930-). ETWF (196?).
      PHC, W. Missionary, pastor, editor, denominational
        official
      b. May 23, 1930, Swaziland
5836   "Elected officials of The Wesleyan Church," Wesleyan
        Advocate, CXXX (July 24, 1972), 15.

Part VI. Biography

5837 KEITH, Huberta Letha Carver (1928-   ). ETWF (196?).
PHC, W. Missionary
b. June 29, 1928, Portsmouth, Ohio

5838 KEITH, Verna Roberta (1905-   ). ETWF (196?).
PHC, W. Missionary
b. July 10, 1905, North Vernon, Ind.

5839 KELLEY, Augusta Tullis (-1887). LLITW (1951), 216.
FM. Missionary

5840 KELLEY, John William Walker
FM. Evangelist, pastor, conference supt.

5841 KELLEY, Selden Dee (1897-1949). WWW in Am. (1943-1950), 293.
CN. Pastor, radio preacher, college pres.
b. Aug. 6, 1897, Livingston County, Mich.
d. Apr. 9, 1949, Kankakee, Ill.
5842 "The preaching of Selden Dee Kelley," Preacher's Magazine, XXXVI (Dec. 1961), 6-9.

5843 KELLEY, Walter W. (-1899). LLITW (1951), 216.
FM. Missionary

5844 KENT, Lyman Blackmarr (1830-1911). FYAB (1954), 88-89.
Attended GHA, 1885 (Chicago)
Attended GHA, 1901 (Chicago)
ME, PCN. Pastor, presiding elder, editor, district supt.
b. 1830, Wyoming County, N.Y.
5845 Kent, Lyman Blackmarr, 1830-1911.
A stalwart of the old guard; the life and labors of Lyman Blackmarr Kent. Edited by Bertha Corson and Iva Durham Vennard. Chicago, Christian Witness Co., 1912. 178 p.

5846 KENWORTHY, Amos M. (1831-1917).
Fr. Pastor, evangelist
b. June 19, 1831, Springboro, Ohio
d. Feb. 28, 1917, Denair, Calif.
5847 Williams-Cammack, Lydia M.
Life and works of Amos M. Kenworthy, by Lydia M. Williams-Cammack and Truman C. Kenworthy. 1972 ed. Noblesville, Ind., J. Edwin Newby, Newby Book Room, 1972. xiii, 292 p.
Reprint of 1918 ed.

5848 KENYON, Jay B. (1885-   ).
M. College dean
5849 Kenyon, Jay B., 1885-
Ten college generations. New York, American Press, 1956. 144 p.

5850 KESSEL, G. G. (-1945). LLITW (1951), 216.
FM. Missionary

5851 KESSEL, Hattie Flenniken (-1935). LLITW (1951), 216.
FM. Missionary

5852 KEY, Joseph Staunton (1829-1920). LMB (1948), 108. WW in Am. Meth. (1916), 119. WWW in Am. (1897-1942), 672. N.Y. Times (Apr. 7, 1920), 11:5.
Member, NHA
ME, S. Pastor, evangelist, bishop
b. July 18, 1829, La Grange, Ga.
d. Apr. 6, 1920, Sherman, Tex. ?

5853 KHARAT, Wamanrao. HNTB (1934), 91-93.
CN. National worker, pastor
b. 18??, India

5854 KIEHN, Anna Schmidt. FHOP (1964).
Men., CN. Missionary

5855 KIEHN, Peter. FHOP (1964).
Men., CN. Missionary, pastor

5856 KIERGAN, Arthur M. (1848-1933).
Attended GHA, 1885 (Chicago)
ME, S; CG (IHP). Pastor, evangelist, editor
b. Dec. 22, 1848, Wakenda, Carroll County, Mo.
d. Feb. 14, 1933, Sapulpa, Okla.

5857 Kiergan, Arthur M., 1848-1933.
Historical sketches of the revival of true holiness and local church polity from 1865-1916. Fort Scott, Kan., Board of Publication of the Church Advocate and Good Way, 1972. Cover-title, 87 p.
Double columns.
Published at the decision of the convention of 1971 of the churches of God (commonly known as the Independent Holiness People).
Autobiographical.

5858 KILBOURNE, Edwin L.
IHC, PHC. Missionary (OMS)

5859 KILBOURNE, Ernest Albert (1865-1928).
Co-founder, OMS
Meth. (Can.) Telegrapher, missionary (OMS)
b. Mar. 13, 1865, Niagra Falls, Ont., Can.
d. Apr. 13, 1928

5860 Kilbourne, Ernest Albert, 1865-1928.
The story of a mission in Japan. Tokyo, Cowman and Kilbourne, n.d.

Part VI. Biography

5861   Erny, Edward
No guarantee but God; the story of the founders of the Oriental Missionary Society, by Edward and Esther Erny. Greenwood, Ind., Oriental Missionary Society, 1969. 116 p.
"Ernest Kilbourne": p. 49-64.

5862   KIMBROUGH, Mary D. Kiplinger (1918-1968)
FM, CG (H). Missionary, pastor's wife
b. May 18, 1918, Nebraska
d. Jan. 5, 1968, York, Ala.

5863   Kimbrough, Mary D. (Kiplinger), 1918-1968.
His way with me; life story and poems. Overland Park, Kan., Printed by the Herald and Banner Press, 1967. 235 p.
Autobiography.

5864   KINDSCHI, Paul L. (1917-). BPOH (1969), 10-15.
President, NHA, 1964-1968
WM, W. Pastor, evangelist, conference pres., denominational official
b. Jan. 17, 1917, Houghton, S.D.

5865   "Conference elects 11 officers," Wesleyan Advocate, CXXVII (July 15, 1968), 10.

5866   KING, Dexter S.
ME. Editor

5867   King, Dexter S., comp.
Fireside poetical readings, illustrative of American scenery, rural life, and historical incidents, and also religious feelings, designed as a domestic and religious offering. Boston, D.S. King, 1843, c1842. ii, 313 p.

5868   KING, Elizabeth DeCamp (1884-1964). ETWF (196?).
PHC. Pastor's wife, missionary
b. Sept. 8, 1884, Ladoga, Ind.
d. Apr. 7, 1964

5869   KING, Ida Ethel Adkins (1884-).
MP, Bapt., CN. Lay member
b. Oct. 11, 1884, Fort Mill, S.C.

5870   Dickerman, Ethel (King)
Not by bread alone; a factual narrative of one family who found meaning in life on a cotton farm. Kansas City, Mo., Pedestal Press, 1970. 63 p.

5871   KING, Joseph Hillery (1869-1946). RLOA (1941-1942), 628.
ME, PeHC. Pastor, evangelist, editor, general supt., bishop
b. Aug. 11, 1869, Anderson Co., S.C.
d. Apr. 23, 1946, Anderson, S.C.

5872   King, Joseph Hillery, 1869-1946.
            Yet speaketh; memoirs of the late Bishop Joseph H.
            King, written by himself and supplemented by Mrs.
            Blanche L. King. Franklin Springs, Ga., Publishing
            House of the Pentecostal Holiness Church, 1949. 387 p.

5873   KING, Oscar L. (1872-1925). SBWTL (1960), 186-187.
            FM. Pastor, district elder, editor, missionary
            b. 1872, Michigan
            d. 1925, Alaska

5874   KING, Oscar Logan (1887-1964). ETWF (196?). TDOOP
                (1968), 344.
            PHC. Pastor, evangelist, missionary
            b. May 3, 1887, Crawford County, Ind.
            d. Jan. 8, 1964.
5875   King, Oscar Logan, 1887-1964.
            The price of a cocoanut. Indianapolis, Ind., Pilgrim
            Publishing House, 1936. 40 p.

5876 *   KINGHORN, Kenneth Cain (1930-   ). DAS (1969), IV, 196.
                BPOH (1969), 30-40.
            M, UM. Seminary prof.
            b. June 23, 1930, Albany, Okla.

5877   KINLAW, Dennis Franklin (1922-   ). WWACUA (1970-1971),
                286. GFIIH (1963), 40-53. GTWATD (1965), 118-
                125.
            M, UM. Pastor, seminary prof., college pres., evange-
                list, missionary
            b. June 26, 1922, Lumberton, N.C.

5878   KINNE, Clarence James (1869-1932). MOUS (1941), 43-49.
            ME, CN. Pastor, publishing house mgr.
            b. Dec. 12, 1869, Knoxville, Iowa
            d. Oct. 19, 1932

5879   KIRBY, William (1881-1957).
            Fr., ET. Pastor, Bible school teacher
5880   Coffin, T. Eugene
            "History of California Yearly Meeting of Friends
            Churches, 1895-1955." Unpublished M.A. thesis, Uni-
            versity of Southern California, 1956. vi, 83ℓ.
            "Doctrinal difficulties": 48-57.
5881   Phillips, Isaac N.
            "A History of the Evangelistic Tabernacles." Unpub-
            lished M.A. thesis, Pacific Bible College, 1955. 74ℓ.

5882   KIRKPATRICK, William James (1838-1921). MAWACOSM
                (1925), 333-334. CHHMH (1970), 589-590. WWW in
                Am. (1897-1942), 682. MWWW in Ch. Hist. (1968),
                234-235.

ME. Gospel song writer, publisher, editor
b. Feb. 27, 1838, Duncannon, Pa.
d. Sept. 20, 1921, Philadelphia, Pa.

5883 KIRN, John (1858-1933).
Endorsed call and attended, GHA, 1901 (Chicago)
PrimHM, EA, EC. Pastor, evangelist
b. Mar. 14, 1858, New Haven, Mich.
d. June 15, 1933
5884 Watson, William H.
History of the Michigan Conference of the Evangelical Church, 1838-1940. Harrisburg, Pa., Evangelical Press, 1942.
Includes biographical sketch of John Kirn: p. 278.

5885 KITAGAWA, Hiroshi (1888-   ). HNTB (1934), 62-72.
PCN, CN. Pastor, district supt., Bible school teacher
b. Jan. 11, 1888, Kumamoto, Kyushu, Jap.
5886 Eckel, Catherine P.
Kitagawa of Japan. Kansas City, Mo., Nazarene Publishing House, 1966. 84 p.

5887 KLETZING, Elmer L. (1864?-1947). N.Y. Times (Aug. 24, 1947), 57:1.
EA?, EC? Businessman, lay leader
b. 1864?, Norristown, Pa.
d. Aug. 21, 1947, Chicago, Ill.

5888 KLETZING, Henry Frick (1850-1910).
Member, IowaHA.
Attended GHA, 1901 (Chicago)
EA? Pastor, evangelist
5889 Kletzing, Henry Frick, 1850-1910.
Progress of a race; or, The remarkable advancement of the American Negro from the bondage of slavery, ignorance and poverty, to freedom of citizenship, intelligence, affluence, honor and trust, by H.F. Kletzing ... and W.H. Crogman ... with an introd. by Booker T. Washington. Atlanta, Ga., Naperville, Ill., J.L. Nichols & Co., 1897. 663 p.

5890 KNAPP, Ethel Alice (1896-   ). RLOA (1941-1942), 637.
I, FM. Evangelist
b. Dec. 11, 1896, Greenfield, Mass.

5891 KNAPP, Joseph Fairchild (1832-1891). Nat. Cy. of Am. Biog., XXIV, 114-115.
ME. Lay leader, insurance underwriter
b. July 1, 1832, New York, N.Y.
d. Sept. 14, 1891, at sea returning from France

5892   KNAPP, Martin Wells (1853-1901). PM (1898), 61-75.
            TDOOP (1968), 10-14, 53-54.
            Attended GHA, 1901 (Chicago)
            ME, IAHUPL. Pastor, evangelist, editor, Bible school
                prin.
            b. Mar. 27, 1853, Clarendon, Calhoun County, Mich.
            d. Dec. 7, 1901, Cincinnati, Ohio
5893   Knapp, Martin Wells, 1853-1901.
                Pentecostal aggressiveness; or, Why I conducted the
            meetings of the Chesapeake Holiness Union at Bowens,
            Maryland. Cincinnati, M.W. Knapp, 1899? 188 p.
5894   Knapp, Martin Wells, 1853-1901.
                Pentecostal letters; selected from the correspondence
            of M.W. Knapp. Cincinnati, Office of God's Revivalist,
            1902. 153 p.
5895   Hills, Aaron Merritt, 1848-1935.
                A hero of faith and prayer; or, Life of Rev. Martin
            Wells Knapp. Cincinnati, O., Mrs. M.W. Knapp, 1902.
            424 p. (Pentecostal Holiness Library)

5896   KNAPP, Mrs. Minnie C. Ferle (1868-1923).
            IAHUPL, IAHU, IAHC, IHC, PHC. Deaconess, Bible
                school admin.
            b. Mar. 4, 1868, Michigan
            d. Jan. 24, 1923, Cincinnati, Ohio
5897   Knapp, Minnie C. (Ferle), 1868-1923.
                Diary letters, a missionary trip through the West
            Indies and South America. Cincinnati, God's Revivalist
            Office, 1918.

5898   KNAPP, Phoebe Palmer (1839-1908). MAWACOSM (1925),
            324-325. MOHMMH (1937), 279-280. CHHMH (1970),
            590-591.
            ME. Lay leader, gospel song writer
            b. Mar. 9, 1839, New York, N.Y.
            d. July 10, 1908, Poland Springs, Me.

5899   KNIGHT, John Allan.
            CN. College prof., pastor, college pres.

5900   KNIGHT, John L. CIOCC (1959), 26-28.
            CN. Pastor, district supt., denominational official

5901   KNOTT, James Proctor (1886-1963). WW in Calif. (1942-
            1943), 500. FHOP (1964). RLOA (1941-1942), 640.
            CN, PCN, Bapt., CN. Pastor, college prof.
            b. Nov. 11, 1886, Lebanon, Ky.

5902   KNOTT, Lucy Stanton Pierce (1856-19??). WW in Calif.
            (1942-1943), 500.
            ME, CN, PCN, CN. Rescue mission worker, pastor,
                evangelist
            b. July 18, 1856, Lancaster, Ky.

Part VI. Biography 677

5903 KNUPP, Clarence Jean (1918-). ETWF (196?).
PHC. Missionary
b. May 24, 1918, Warren, Pa.

5904 KNUPP, Mildred Marcella Beck (1919-). ETWF (196?).
PHC. Missionary
b. Dec. 18, 1919, Kragon, Ky.

5905 KOBAYASHI, F. HNTB (1934), 72-74.
CN. National worker, pastor
b. 19??, Japan

5906 KRAGERUD, Ole (-1921). LLITW (1951), 216.
FM. Missionary

5907 KRESGE, Bessie Reid (1897-). SBWTL (1960), 204.
FM. Teacher, pastor, missionary, editor, temperance worker
b. 1897, Kingston, Ont.

5908 KRIGBAUM, Clellie Lee (-1970).
ME, CN. Pastor, evangelist
d. Apr. 13, 1970, Bartlesville, Okla.
5909 Krigbaum, Ella M., 1900-
Our pilgrimage together. Kansas City, Mo., Pedestal Press, 1971. 216 p.
Reminiscences of the wife of C.L. (Ted) Krigbaum, minister in the Church of the Nazarene.

5910 KRIKORIAN, Samuel C. (1893-). HNTB (1934), 29-37.
Cong., PCN, CN. Missionary
b. 1893, Aintab, Turk.
5911 Krikorian, Rebecca K.
Jerusalem; the life sketch of Miss Rebecca Krikorian and her nephew, Rev. Samuel Krikorian, together with their divine call to open a field of work in Jerusalem. Rev. ed. Kansas City, Mo., General Board of Foreign Missions, Church of the Nazarene, 1919. 153 p.

5912 KRING, James Arthur (1873-).
ME, CG (UHP), CN. Pastor, evangelist, editor, Bible college admin.
b. Oct. 5, 1873, Tuscola, Douglas County, Ill.
5913 Kring, James Arthur, 1873-
The conquest of Canaan. Kansas City, Mo., Printed for J.A. Kring by the Nazarene Publishing House, 1930. 263 p.
Includes biographical sketch of the author by H. Orton Wiley.

5914 KUHN, Harold Barnes (1911-). DAS (1969), IV, 204.
GIIH (1962), 240-261.

Fr. Pastor, seminary prof., evangelist, military chaplain
b. Aug. 21, 1911, Belleville, Kan.

5915 KULP, George B. (1845-1939). TDOOP (1968), 66-73.
ME, IAHUPL, IAHU, IAHC, IHC, PHC. Pastor, evangelist, general supt.
b. July 23, 1845, Philadelphia, Pa.
d. July 21, 1939, Battle Creek, Mich.

5916 KUMALO, Alice. HNTB (1934), 119-121.
CN. National worker, pastor
b. 190?, Swaziland, S. Afr.

5917 KUNZ, George J. (1862-1925).
President, NHA, 1921-1924.
ME. Pastor, evangelist
d. Jan. 6, 1925, Kalamazoo, Mich.
5918 Sharpe, George, 1865-1948.
This is my story, by Rev. George Sharpe, D.D., founder of the Church of the Nazarene in the British Isles. Glasgow, Messenger Publishing Co., 1948. 142 p.
Autobiography.
Reference to George J. Kunz: p. 34.

5919 KUNZE, R. J. FHOP (1964).
CN. Pastor

5920 KUO, Heng Chun. HNTB (1934), 53-54.
CN. National worker, pharmacist
b. 19??, China

5921 LaDUE, Wilson Cathey (1902-). WW in Am. Ed. (1967-1968), 468.
FM. College prof., college dean
b. Jan. 5, 1902, Greenville, Ill.

5922 LADY, Jesse F. GIIH (1962), 172-189.
BIC. Pastor, college prof., college pres., missionary

5923 LAMBERT, Rose (1878-). SWGHW (1948), 83-84, 88.
MBIC. Missionary
b. 1878, Vera Cruz, Pa.

5924 LANE, Neva (-1956)
CN. Missionary
5925 Coats, Eugenia (Phillips), 1883-
Beloved of Guatemala (the life of Neva Lane). Kansas City, Mo., Beacon Hill Press, 1957. 77 p.

5926 LANPHER, Carroll P. (1876-). COPN (1958), 33-37.
ME, APCA, PCN, CN. Pastor
b. June 11, 1876, West Berkshire, Vt.

5927 LARSEN, Walter Burdick (-1957). CIOCC (1959), 10-12.
CN. College prof.
d. June 15?, 1957, Kankakee, Ill.

5928 LASHBROOK, Jack Walton (1912-1960). ETWF (196?).
TDOOP (1968), 343.
PHC. Pastor, missionary
b. Nov. 19, 1912, Cincinnati, Ohio
d. Sept. 22, 1960, Kentucky

5929 LASHBROOK, Ruth Elizabeth Raisch (1917-). ETWF (196?).
PHC. Pastor's wife, missionary
b. Jan. 3, 1917, Belfast, Ohio

5930 LAWLOR, Edward
CN. Pastor, evangelist, district supt., denominational official, general supt.
5931 Mann, William Edward
Sect, cult and church in Alberta. Toronto, University of Toronto Press, 1955. xiii, 166 p.
Includes references to Edward Lawlor: p. 14, 116, 127, 129.

5932 LAWRENCE, Evan Jerry (1918-). WWACUA (1970-1971), 304.
POF. Pastor, college admin.
b. Oct. 5, 1918, Morgan County, Ga.

5933 LAWRENCE, Ruliff Vanclief (1825-1872). PPE (1868), 207-209.
Signed call to meeting to form NHA, 1867.
ME. Pastor
d. July 1, 1872.

5934 LEE, Byron D. DCSWM (1946), 143.
CN. Military chaplain

5935 LEE, Flavius Josephus (1875-1928).
Bapt., CG (GA). Carpenter, pattern maker, pastor, state overseer, general overseer
b. July 18, 1875, Polk County, Tenn.
d. Oct. 28, 1928, Cleveland, Tenn.
5936 Lee, Flavius Josephus, 1875-1928.
Life sketch and sermons of F.J. Lee, comp. by Mrs. F.J. Lee. Cleveland, Tenn., Church of God Publishing House, 192?. 373 p.

5937   LEE, Hazel C. GHAI (1960), 9-11.
       CN. Pastor's wife, missionary

5938   LEE, John Wesley
       Attended GHA, 1901 (Chicago)
       ME?, PCN. Pastor

5939   LEE, Luther (1800-1889). SCM (1881), 535. WWW in Am. (1607-1896), 309.
       ME, WM, ME. Pastor, editor, college prof.
       b. Nov. 30, 1800, Schoharie, N.Y.
       d. Dec. 13, 1889, Flint, Mich.
5940   Lee, Luther, 1800-1889.
           Autobiography of the Rev. Luther Lee.... New York,
       Phillips & Hunt; Cincinnati, Walden & Stowe, 1882.
       345 p.

5941   LEE, Thomas E. TDOOP (1968), 287.
       HC, PHC, W. Pastor, district supt.

5942   LEE, William H. (1855-1919). TDOOP (1968), 123-126.
       ME, SA, PeoMC, PCN, PeoMC. Pastor, evangelist,
           rescue mission worker, district supt.
       d. Nov. 1, 1919, Colorado Springs, Colo.
5943   The Mission Advance, I (Feb. 1920), 2.

5944   LEFFINGWELL, Clara (1863-1905). LLITW (1951), 216.
       FM. Missionary
5945   Sellew, Walter Ashbel, bp., 1844-1929.
           Clara Leffingwell, a missionary; introd. by the Rev.
       Wilson T. Hogue.... Chicago, Free Methodist Publishing House, 1907. xv, 320 p.

5946   LEHMAN, Frederick Martin (1868-   ). LMGSS (1952), 125.
       LDML (1953), 75.
       ME, PCN, CN. Pastor, rescue worker, gospel song writer
5947   Lehman, Frederick Martin, 1868-
           The man in black. Kansas City, Mo., Publishing
       House of the Pentecostal Church of the Nazarene, 1913.
       192 p.
           Autobiographical allegory on the carnal mind.

5948   LEIST, J. F. (-1972).
       CN. College prof.
       d. May 2, 1972, Kankakee, Ill.

5949   LEITZEL, Leonard Winfield (1918-   ). ETWF (196?).
       PHC. Pastor, missionary
       b. July 22, 1918, Ashland, Pa.

Part VI. Biography

5950 LEITZEL, Pauline Marie Burden (1920-). ETWF (196?).
PHC. Pastor's wife, missionary
b. Mar. 24, 1920, Syracuse, N.Y.

5951 LE SHANA, David Charles (1932-). WWACUA (1970-1971), 309.
Fr. Pastor, college admin., college pres.
b. Nov. 15, 1932, Lucknow, India

5952 LEVY, Edgar M. (1822-1906). WWW in Am. (1897-1942), 724. HM (1882). GFW (1888), 46-62.
Endorsed call, GHA, 1901 (Chicago)
Bapt. Pastor, evangelist
b. Nov. 23, 1822, St. Mary's, Ga.

5953 LEWIS, Charles Elwood (1928-). ETWF (196?).
PHC. Pastor, denominational official
b. Jan. 23, 1928, Selbyville, Del.

5954 LEWIS, David J. (1846-1918).
Fr. Pastor, evangelist

5955 LEWIS, David J. (1859-1899).
ME, Fr. Pastor, evangelist
b. May 20, 1859, Pittsburgh, Pa.
d. Feb. 16, 1899, East Richland, Ohio

5956 Lewis, David J., 1859-1899.
Word and work of David J. Lewis. Cincinnati, M. W. Knapp, Office of the Revivalist, 1900. 320 p.
Sermons of David J. Lewis: p. 82-320.

5957 LEWIS, Dorothy Carroll Baker (1928-). ETWF (196?).
PHC. Pastor's wife
b. Aug. 7, 1928, Dover, Del.

5958 LEWIS, Voyle H. MHP (1957), 33-41.
CN. Pastor, evangelist, district supt., denominational official, general supt.

5959 LILLENAS, Bertha Mae Wilson (1889-1945). NP (1925), 142-148. LMGSS (1952), 19.
CN. Pastor's wife, evangelist, evangelistic singer, gospel song writer
b. Mar. 3, 1889, Hansen, Ky.
d. Apr. 13, 1945

5960 LILLENAS, Haldor (1885-1959). LMGSS (1952).
Luth., PenielM, PCN, CN. Pastor, gospel song writer, music editor, evangelist
b. Nov. 19, 1885, Stord, Norway
d. Aug. 18, 1959

5961   Lillenas, Haldor, 1885-1959.
        Down Melody Lane, an Autobiography. Kansas City,
        Mo., Beacon Hill Press, 1953. 80 p.
5962   Lillenas, Haldor, 1885-1959.
        Motoring 11,000 miles through Norway; a guide for
        tourists with sixty suggested tours. With 25 photos.
        New York, Exposition Press, 1955. 131 p.
5963   Lillenas, Haldor, 1885-1959.
        Raking leaves, and other poems. Kansas City, Mo.,
        Nazarene Publishing House, 1929. 40 p.
5964   McGraw, James, 1913-
        "The preaching of Haldor Lillenas," Preacher's Magazine, XXXVI (May 1961), 5-8.

5965   LNCICOME, Forman (1880-   ). SFLF (1950), 58-61.
        FM. Evangelist
        b. Feb. 2, 1880, southern Ohio

5966   LINCOLN, Arthur D. (-1888). LLITW (1951), 216.
        FM. Missionary

5967   LINCOLN, Polly Abbie Mudge (-1888). LLITW (1951),
        216.
        FM. Missionary

5968   LIND, Abraham A. LLITW (1951), 216.
        FM. Missionary

5969   LINDSAY, Arthur L. (1934-   ). WWACUA (1970-1971), 313.
        UM? College admin.
        b. Jan. 18, 1934, Kokomo, Ind.

5970   LINDSEY, Leroy E., Jr. GTWATD (1965), 282-290.
        EMC. Pastor, missionary, Bible college prof.

5971   LISHALI, Philip
        IHM. Evangelist
5972   Bedwell, H. Kenneth
        Philip Lishali, a African firebrand. North Rand,
        Trans., S. Afr., International Holiness Mission, 1937.
        20 p.

5973   LONDON, Allie S. SCC (1947), 92-96.
        CN. Bible school teacher, evangelist

5974   LONDON, Holland Bryan (1908-   ). MLA (1935), 56-61.
        CN, Bapt. Pastor, evangelist, district supt.

5975   LONG, Lois Eileen (1937-   ). ETWF (196?).
        PHC. Missionary
        b. Jan. 21, 1937, Petoskey, Mich.

Part VI. Biography

5976 LONG, Richard Eugene (1927-). ETWF (196?).
PHC. Missionary
b. Oct. 11, 1927, Osawatomie, Kan.

5977 LONG, Ruby Irene Berkgren (1927-). ETWF (196?).
PHC. Missionary, Bible school teacher
b. Oct. 16, 1927, Oakley, Kan.

5978 LONGACRE, Andrew (1831-1906). SCM (1881), 990. N.Y. Times (Feb. 19, 1906), 9:4.
Signed call to meeting to form NHA, 1867 (Philadelphia)
ME. Pastor
b. June 12, 1831, Philadelphia, Pa.
d. Feb. 16, 1906

5979 LONGHURST, Sarah (1860-1940).
HMoC. Missionary
5980 Longhurst, Sarah, 1860-1940.
Reminiscences of my life in Egypt. Ottawa, Ont., Can.?, Holiness Movement Publishing House?, 1937.

5981 LOPEZ, Antonio. HNTB (1934), 195-199.
CN. National worker
b. 19??, Spain

5982 LORD, Edwin Jay (18??-1942).
APCA, CN. Pastor, district supt.

5983 LORD, Luella N. (1877-1964).
APCA, CN. Pastor's wife
5984 Herald of Holiness, LIII (July 29, 1964), 16.

5985 LORING, W. T.
Attended GHA, 1901 (Chicago)
ME? Pastor

5986 LOUGHLIN, Delia (-1892).
DH. Convert
5987 Whittemore, Emma (Mott), 1850-1931.
Delia; formerly the Bluebird of Mulberry Bend. New York, The Door of Hope, 1893. 136 p.
5988 Whittemore, Emma (Mott), 1850-1931.
Delia, the blue-bird of Mulberry Bend. New and rev. ed. New York, Revell, 1914. 126 p.

5989 LOVE, Mrs. L. Belle
Attended GHA, 1901 (Chicago)
CN, PCN. Deaconess, carpenter's wife

5990 LOVE, Louise Calkins (-1946). LLITW (1951), 216.
FM. Missionary

5991 LOVELESS, Robert (-1909). SBWTL (1960), 61-65.
PrimM, FM. Pastor

5992 LOVELL, Ora D. GFIIH (1963), 122-138. GTWATD (1965), 46-56.
Fr. Pastor, college prof., college dean

5993 LOVIN, C. Wesley (1918-).
WM, W. Pastor, conference pres., denominational official
b. 1918, Kannapolis, N.C.
5994 "Conference elects 11 officers," Wesleyan Advocate, CXXVII (July 15, 1968), 9.
5995 "Elected officials of The Wesleyan Church," Wesleyan Advocate, CXXX (July 24, 1972), 15.

5996 LOWE, Thomas O.
Attended HConf., 1877 (Cincinnati)
ME? Lay leader

5997 LOWREY, Asbury (1816-1898). SCM (1881), 552.
Member, NHA
ME. Pastor, presiding elder, editor
b. Mar. 20, 1816, Goodwin's Point, N.Y.
d. Aug. 5, 1898, Germantown, Pa.

5998 LOWREY, Sarah Ann (1884-). FHOP (1964).
FM, CN. Pastor, evangelist
b. Oct. 4, 1884, Jasper County, Tex.

5999 LUCK, H. B. (-1960). SBWTL (1960), 188.
FM. Pastor, district elder
d. 1960, West Summerland, B.C.

6000 LUCKEY, James Seymour (1867-1937). MHWMCOA (1959), 342-344. N.Y. Times (Apr. 8, 1937), 23:5.
WM. College pres.
b. Aug. 1, 1867, Short Tract, N.Y.
d. Apr. 7, 1937, Houghton, N.Y.

6001 LUDWIG, Minnie E. Brink (1877-1958). COPN (1958), 85-90.
ME, CN. Pastor's wife, evangelist
b. Feb. 1, 1877, Huegely, Ill.
d. June 20, 1958, Nashville, Ill.

6002 LUDWIG, Sylvester Theodore (1903-1964). RLOA (1941-1942), 709. WWW in Am. (1961-1968), 591.
CN. Pastor, college pres., denominational official
b. Apr. 2, 1903, Moewequa, Ill.
d. Mar. 3, 1964, Kansas City, Mo.

Part VI. Biography

6003 LUDWIG, Theodore (1871-1957). COPN (1958), 85-90.
NP (1925), 107-115.
ME, CN. Pastor, evangelist, district supt.
b. Oct. 23, 1871, Moweaqua, Ill.
d. June 30, 1957, Nashville, Ill.
6004 Ludwig, Sylvester Theodore, 1903-1964.
"The preaching of Theodore Ludwig," Preacher's Magazine, XXXIII (Apr. 1958), 5-8.

6005 LUND, Oscar. CIOCC (1959), 21-23.
CN. Layman

6006 LUNN, Mervel
PCN, CN. Publishing house mangr.

6007 LYON, David D. (1841-1919).
Member, Iowa HA
Attended GHA, 1901 (Chicago)
ME. Pastor

6008 LYTLE, Robert N. (1917-).
WM, W. Missionary, denominational official
b. 1917, Angelica, N.Y.
6009 "Elected officials of The Wesleyan Church," Wesleyan Advocate, CXXX (July 24, 1972), 15.

6010 McALL, Robert Whitaker (1821-1893). MCV (1901), 24-31.
Ch. of Eng.? Pastor, rescue mission supt.
b. 1821, McClesfield, Eng.
d. 1893, Paris, Fr.

6011 McBRIDE, Hamilton Cree (1840-1917).
Attended GHA, 1901 (Chicago)
ME. Pastor

6012 McBRIDE, Joseph Benjamine (1873-).
Member, Texas HA
TexHA, PCN, CN. Pastor, evangelist
6013 McBride, Joseph Benjamine, 1873-
Knowing God; life story and selected sermons. Cincinnati, God's Bible School and Revivalist, 1923. 220 p.

6014 McCALLUM, Floyd Frederick (1920-). LIE (1971).
GFIIH (1963), 314-330.
FM, PHC, W. Evangelist, Bible school teacher, college prof., college admin.
b. Feb. 13, 1920, Lapeer County, Mich.

6015 McCARTY, Joseph Hendrickson (1830-1897). PPE (1868), 122-126. SCM (1881), 572-573.
ME. Physican, pastor
b. Sept. 20, 1830, Berlin, Pa.

6016   McCarty, Joseph Hendrickson, 1830-1897.
           The olive branch; containing the latest information on
           the use of anaesthesia in labor, by David Miller Barr....
           Ocean Grove, N.J., 1892. viii, 196 p.
6017   McCarty, Joseph Hendrickson, 1830-1897.
           Two thousand miles through the heart of Mexico.
           New York, Phillips & Hunt; Cincinnati, Cranston &
           Stowe, 1886. 288 p.

6018   McCLAIN, Carl Sheldon (1899-). WW in Am. (1952-1953),
           1611. CIOCC (1959), 23-25.
       CN. College prof., college admin.

6019   McCLANAHAN, Burl Austin
       CG (H). Pastor, Bible school pres.
6020   McClanahan, Burl Austin
           "School board policy and its implementation relating
           to religious activities in Missouri public schools."
           Unpublished Ed.D. dissertation, University of Missouri,
           1965.

6021   McCLURKAN, James O. (1861-1914).
           Cumb. Pres., PM. Evangelist, pastor, Bible school
               pres., editor
           b. Nov. 13, 1861, Yellow Creek, Houston County,
               Tenn.
           d. Sept. 16, 1914, Nashville, Tenn.
6022   Heath, Merle (McClurkan)
           A man sent of God; the life of J. O. McClurkan.
           Kansas City, Mo., Beacon Hill Press, 1947. 95 p.
6023   McGraw, James, 1913-
           "The preaching of James O. McClurkan," Preacher's
           Magazine, XXIX (Oct. 1954), 4-6.
6024   Strickland, Samuel Walker
           A new look at Rev. J.O. McClurkan. Nashville,
           Tenn., Parthenon Press, 1960. 95 p.
6025   Strickland, Samuel Walker
           "Reverend J.O. McClurkan as I knew him." Nash-
           ville, Tenn., 1957. (Typescript)
           At head of title: Founder's day address.

6026   McCONN, William Finney (1888-). WW in the Clergy
           (1935-1936), 762-763. RLOA (1941-1942), 753.
           WW in Am. (1956-1957), 1697.
       WM. Temperance worker, college pres.
       b. Sept. 4, 1888, Colony, Kan.

6027   McCONNELL, Charles Allen (1860-1955).
       ME, S; CN. Editor, college prof.
       b. June 19, 1860, Valparaiso, Ind.
6028   McConnell, Charles Allen, 1860-1955.
           Boys of the old sea bed; tales of nature and adventure.

Kansas City, Mo., Publishing House of the Pentecostal Church of the Nazarene, 1913. 176 p.
A true story of frontier life in Juneau County, Wisconsin.

6029 McConnell, Charles Allen, 1860-1955.
Caleb of the hill country. Kansas City, Mo., Publishing House of the Pentecostal Church of the Nazarene, 1914. 163 p.

6030 McConnell, Charles Allen, 1860-1955.
The lost frontier. Kansas City, Mo., Beacon Hill Press, 1927. 157 p.

6031 McConnell, Charles Allen, 1860-1955.
The Potter's vessel; my life story as told to my children at their request. Kansas City, Mo., Beacon Hill Press, 1946. 79 p.
Autobiography.

6032 McCONNELL, Lela Grace (1884-).
ME, KMHA. Evangelist, Bible school prin., evangelistic asso. pres.
b. June 1, 1884, Honey Brook, Chester County, Pa.

6033 McConnell, Lela Grace, 1884-
Faith victorious in the Kentucky mountains; the story of twenty-two years of Spirit-filled ministry. Winona Lake, Ind., Printed for the author by Light and Life Press, 1946. 237 p.
Autobiography.

6034 McConnell, Lela Grace, 1884-
God answers prayer in the mountains of Kentucky. Jackson, Kentucky Mountain Holiness Association, 1968. 2 sides 33 rpm (80450)

6035 McConnell, Lela Grace, 1884-
Hitherto and henceforth in the Kentucky mountains; a quarter of a century of adventures in faith--the year of jubilee. n.p., c1949. 221 p.

6036 McConnell, Lela Grace, 1884-
The Pauline ministry in the Kentucky mountains; or, A brief account of the Kentucky Mt. Holiness Association. Berne, Ind., Printed by Economy Printing Concern, 1942. 200 p.
Autobiography.

6037 McConnell, Lela Grace, 1884-
The power of prayer plus faith. n.p., 1952. 229 p.

6038 McConnell, Lela Grace, 1884-
Rewarding faith plus works. n.p., c1962. 174 p.

6039 McCONNELL, Leona Bellew
PCN, CN. Missionary, college prof., college admin.

6040 McCUMBER, W. E.
CN. Pastor

6041 McDONALD, William (1820-1901). DC (1965, c1887), 56-76. SCM (1881), 573-574. WWW in Am. (1897-1942), 809. CHHMH (1970), 606. MOHMMH (1937), 286-287. MAWACOSM (1925), 321-322. LMGSS (1952), 158.
President, NHA, 1884-1893
ME. Pastor, evangelist, editor, gospel song writer
b. Mar. 1, 1820, Belmont, Me.
d. Sept. 11, 1901, Monrovia, Calif.

6042 MacGEARY, John Samuel (1853-1931). BMW (1960), 165-179. N.Y. Times (Jan. 21, 1931), 19:2.
Attended GHA, 1901 (Chicago)
ME, FM. Pastor, bishop
b. Feb. 13, 1853, Pittsburgh, Pa.
d. Jan. 20, 1931, Oakland, Calif.

6043 McGOVERN, Joseph C. (1868-1944).
WM. Pastor, evangelist, conference pres.
b. 1868, Sharon, Pa.
d. Dec. 4, 1944, Mitchell, S.D.
6044 Anson, Robert Sam
McGovern: a biography. New York, Holt, Rinehart and Winston, 1972. xiii, 303 p.
6045 McIntyre, Robert W., 1922-
"Senator McGovern's Wesleyan heritage," Wesleyan Advocate, CXXX (Sept. 18, 1972), 2-3.

6046 McGRADY, Paul (1925-1967).
CN. Pastor, college prof.
b. June 29, 1925, Delta, Pa.
d. Aug. 3, 1967, Tulsa, Okla.
6047 Culbertson, Howard
Paul McGrady: Mr. Evangelism. Kansas City, Mo., Pedestal Press, 1969. 76 p.

6048 McGRAW, James (1913-). CA.
CN. Pastor, college prof., college admin., seminary prof.
b. Oct. 25, 1913, Greenville, Tex.

6049 McGRAW, William David (1870-).
ME,S?; FM; HChuC; PCN; CN. Pastor
b. Aug. 21, 1870, Sabine County, Tex.
6050 McGraw, James, 1913-
"The preaching of W.D. McGraw," Preacher's Magazine, XXXVI (Jan. 1961), 6-9.

6051 McGRAW, William David, Jr.
CN. Pastor, district supt., college admin.

Part VI. Biography 689

6052 McINTYRE, Robert W. (1922-   ).
WM, W. Pastor, denominational official, editor
b. 1922, Bethlehem, Pa.
6053 "Conference elects 11 officers," Wesleyan Advocate, CXXVII (July 15, 1968), 9.
6054 "Elected officials of The Wesleyan Church," Wesleyan Advocate, CXXX (July 24, 1972), 14-15.

6055 McKAY, John (1896-   ). GHAI (1960), 17-19.
Ch. of Scot., CN. Missionary

6056 McKENNA, David Loren (1929-   ). LIE (1971).
FM. College dean, university prof., college pres.
b. May 5, 1929, Detroit, Mich.
6057 McKenna, David Loren, 1929-
"A study of power and interpersonal relationships in the administration of higher education." Unpublished Ph.D. dissertation, University of Michigan, 1958. 227ℓ.

6058 MACKEY, Alexander Benjamin (1897-1973). WW in Am. (1960-1961), 1814. RLOA (1941-1942), 719.
CN. College prof., college pres.
b. Apr. 16, 1897, Highway, Ky.

6059 McLAUGHLIN, George Asbury (1851-1933). ATY (1930), 42-54. DC (1965, c1887), 159-168. WWW in Am. (1897-1942), 818.
Member, NHA
Endorsed and attended, GHA, 1901 (Chicago)
ME. Pastor, evangelist, editor, Bible school pres.
b. 1851, Nashua, N.H.
d. Mar. 10, 1933, Walnut Park, Calif.
6060 McLaughlin, George Asbury, 1851-1933.
Autobiography of George Asbury McLaughlin, editor of the Christian Witness for 45 years, killed in the Los Angeles earthquake on March 10, 1933. Chicago, Christian Witness Co., n.d. 192 p.

6061 McLEAN, Alexander (1826-1910). PPE (1868), 167-171.
N.Y. Times (Dec. 18, 1910), 13:4.
Member, NHA
HConf., 1877 (New York)
Endorsed call and attended, GHA, 1901 (Chicago)
ME. Pastor, evangelist
b. Apr. 15, 1826, New York, N.Y.
d. Dec. 17, 1910, Brooklyn, N.Y.

6062 McLEISTER, Clara Orrell (1882-1958).
ME, WM. Pastor's wife, missionary society pres.
b. Aug. 8, 1882, Newport, Ky.
d. Jan. 2, 1958, Syracuse, N.Y.

6063   McLeister, Ira Ford, 1879-1963.
            The life and work of Rev. Mrs. Clara McLeister.
            Syracuse, N.Y., Rev. I.F. McLeister, 1958. 54 p.

6064   McLEISTER, Ira Ford (1879-1963). RLOA (1941-1942), 770-
            771.
            WM. Pastor, denominational official, editor
            b. Apr. 22, 1879, Taylorsville, Pa.

6065   McMICHAEL, Wanda Winifred Davis (1921-). WWACUA
            (1970-1971), 351.
            CN. College admin.
            b. Oct. 21, 1921, Kirkland, Wash.

6066   McMURRY, Celia Ferries (-1946). LLITW (1951), 216.
            FM. Missionary

6067   McNEEL, Myrtle. FHOP (1964).
            CN. Public school teacher
            b. 18??, Johnson County, Mo.

6068   McPHEETERS, Julian C. (1889-). WW in Am. (1950-
            1951). WW in the Clergy (1935-1936), 788. SFLF
            (1950), 62-67. GTWATD (1965), 228-235.
            ME, M. Pastor, seminary pres., editor
            b. July 6, 1889, Oxley, Mo.
6069   McPheeters, Julian C., 1889-
            Sunshine and victory. Nashville, Cokesbury Press,
            1933. 121 p.
            Autobiography.
6070   McPheeters, Julian C., 1889-
            Sunshine and victory. Louisville, Ky., Pentecostal
            Publishing Co., 1933. 64 p.
            Autobiography.

6071   McREYNOLDS, Margaret Glyn Wiman (1921-). LIE
            (1971), 613.
            CN. Public school teacher, college prof., college
            admin.
            b. Oct. 24, 1921, Kobe, Jap.

6072   MACRORY, H. B. (1883-).
            CN. Pastor
            b. May 24, 1883, Pittsburgh, Pa.
6073   McGraw, James, 1913-
            "The preaching of H.B. Macrory," Preacher's Maga-
            zine, XXXVI (Mar. 1961), 6-8.

6074   MADDUX, Rose Mary (1925-). ETWF (196?).
            PHC. Missionary
            b. Oct. 18, 1925, Westport, Ind.

Part VI. Biography 691

6075 MAGAR, John B. HNTB (1934), 101.
 CN. National worker, pastor
 b. 19??, India

6076 MAHAN, Asa (1799-1889). GFW (1888), 176-187. MWWW
 in Ch. Hist. (1968), 267. PPE (1868), 11-19. ROG
 (1854), 46-54. WWW in Am. (1607-1896), 329. DAB.
 Cong. Pastor, evangelist, college pres., editor
 b. Nov. 9, 1799, Vernon, N.Y.
 d. Apr. 4, 1889, Eastbourne, Eng.
6077 Mahan, Asa, 1799-1889.
 Autobiography, intellectual, moral, and spiritual.
 London, T. Woolmer, 1882. 458 p.
6078 Mahan, Asa, 1799-1889.
 A critical history of the late American war; with an
 introd. letter by Lieut.-Gen. M.W. Smith. New York,
 A.S. Barnes & Co., 1877. 461 p.
6079 Mahan, Asa, 1799-1889.
 Out of darkness into light; or, The hidden life made
 manifest through facts of observation ane experience,
 facts elucidated by the Word of God. London, Published
 for the author at the Wesleyan Conference Office, 1877.
 366 p.
 Autobiographical.
6080 Mahan, Asa, 1799-1889.
 Out of darkness into light; or, The hidden life made
 manifest. Louisville, Pickett Publishing Co., n.d.
 366 p.
 Autobiographical.
6081 Mahan, Asa, 1799-1889.
 The science of logic; or, An analysis of the laws of
 thought. New York, A.S. Barnes & Co., 1857. 387 p.
6082 Mahan, Asa, 1799-1889.
 A system of intellectual philosophy. Rev. and enl.
 from the 2d ed. New York, A.S. Barnes & Co.; Cincinnati, H.W. Derby, 1857. 476 p.

6083 MAINS, Lura Ann (1847-).
 FWBapt., PrimHM. Evangelist, orphanage supt., Bible
 school prin.
6084 Mains, Lura Ann, 1847-
 Mizpah: autobiographical sketches. Grand Rapids,
 Mich., Hensen & Reynders, 1892. 107 p.

6085 MALLALIEU, Willard Francis (1828-1911). LMB (1948),
 118-119. WWW in Am. (1897-1942), 770. N.Y.
 Times (Aug. 2, 1911), 7:6.
 Endorsed call, GHA, 1901 (Chicago)
 ME. Pastor, bishop
 b. 1828, Sutton, Mass.
 d. Aug. 1, 1911, Auburndale, Mass.

6086 MALONE, John Walter (1857-1935). WWW in Am. (1897-1942), 771. WW in the Clergy (1935-1936), 734.
Endorsed call, GHA, 1901 (Chicago)
Fr. Pastor, businessman, Bible school pres.
b. Aug. 11, 1857, Clermont County, Ohio

6087 MALONE, John Walter (1888-1962). WW in the Clergy (1935-1936), 734-735. WWW in Am. (1961-1968), 607-608.
Fr., Pres. Pastor
b. Mar. 4, 1888, Cleveland, Ohio

6088 MANERIKER, Prasadrao (1908-   ). HNTB (1934), 93-94.
CN. National worker, pastor
b. 1908, Rajapur, Ratnagir District, India

6089 MANGUM, Thomas Emmett (1884-   ).
ME, S, PCN, CN. Lay leader, physician
b. Aug. 11, 1884, Voca, Tex.

6090 Swann, L. Alline (McGraw), 1908-
Song in the night; the story of Dr. and Mrs. Thomas E. Mangum. Kansas City, Mo., Beacon Hill Press, 1957. 112 p.

6091 MANN, Edward Stebbins (1908-   ). WW in Am. (1960-1961), 1841. WW in Am. (1968-1969), 1401. WWACUA (1970-1971), 328. WW in New England (1949), 400. LIE (1971), 620.
CN. College prof., college pres., denominational official
b. Sept. 24, 1908, Waterville, Vt.

6092 MARQUEZ, Raúl (1909-   ). RWBTB (1953), 67-71.
CN. Pastor
b. Apr. 17, 1909, Mexico City, Mex.

6093 MARSH, Elmer G.
IHC, PHC. Bible school teacher, evangelist

6094 MARSH, James D.
Attended GHA, 1901 (Chicago)
FM. Pastor

6095 MARSH, Marian (1913-   ). WW in Am. Ed. (1967-1968), 548.
CN. College prof.
b. Oct. 27, 1913, Fairmount, N.D.

6096 MARSHALL, Ann Louise Martin (1930-   ). ETWF (196?).
PHC. Pastor's wife, missionary
b. May 19, 1930, Marion, Ohio

Part VI. Biography

6097 MARSHALL, Wallace Gene (1930-). ETWF (196?).
    PHC. Pastor, missionary
    b. Feb. 17, 1930, Roseland, Kan.

6098 MARSHBURN, William V. (1855-).
    Fr. Physician
6099   Marshburn, William V., 1855-
        Spiritual experiences in business life. Richmond,
    Ind., Nicholson, 1929. 141 p.

6100 MARSTON, Leslie Ray (1894-). RLOA (1941-1942), 732-
        733. SFLF (1950), 68-71. WW in Am. (1964-1965),
        1290. GFIIH (1963), 284-313. MHP (1957), 43-52.
    FM. College dean, college admin., college pres.,
        bishop
    b. Sept. 24, 1894, Maple Ridge, Mich.
6101   Marston, Leslie Ray, bp., 1894-
        ...Directory of research in child development, comp.
    for National Research Council Committee on Child De-
    velopment. Washington, D.C., National Research Coun-
    cil, 1927. iii, 38 p.
6102   Marston, Leslie Ray, bp., 1894-
        ...The emotions of young children. Iowa City, Uni-
    versity of Iowa, 1925. 99 p.
        Thesis (Ph.D.)--University of Iowa, 1925.

6103 MARSTON, Lorena (-1916). LLITW (1951), 216.
    FM. Missionary

6104 MARTIN, Edward Everett (1887-1951). RLOA (1941-1942),
        733.
    R. Cath., CN. Pastor, district supt., college prof.,
        college pres.
    b. Dec. 29, 1887, Sawyer, Wisc.
    d. Dec. 25, 1951
6105   "The preaching of E.E. Martin," Preacher's Magazine,
        XXXVI (Sept. 1961), 4-6.

6106 MARTIN, Ernest W. MHP (1957), 93-102.
    CN. Pastor, evangelist, district supt.
    b. 19??, Wyoming

6107 MARTIN, Isaiah Guyman (1862-1957). LMGSS (1952), 29.
        FYAB (1954), 93. LDML (1953), 71.
    ME, CN. Pastor, evangelist, district supt., gospel
        song writer
    b. Apr. 18, 1862, Kirksville, Mo.
    d. Aug. 23, 1957, Pasadena, Calif.
6108   Martin, Isaiah Guyman, 1862-1957.
        My scrapbook. Mansfield, Ill., 1936.

6109   MARTIN, Paul La Rush (1915-).
            CN. Pastor, evangelist
6110   Martin, Paul La Rush, 1915-
                Life in a Nazarene parsonage. Kansas City, Mo.,
            Nazarene Publishing House, 195?.

6111   MASON, Charles Harrison (1866-1961). WWW in Am.
            (1961-1968), 618. WWW in Ch. Hist. (1968), 274-
            275.
            Bapt., CGIC. Pastor, evangelist, bishop
            b. Sept. 9, 1866, Bartlett, Tenn.
            d. Nov. 28, 1961, Memphis, Tenn.
6112   Mason, Charles H., 1866-1961.
                The history and life work of Elder C.H. Mason,
            chief apostle and his co-laborers. Memphis, Howe
            Printing Dept., 1920. 97 p.
            Compiled by Prof. Jas. Courts.

6113   MASON, Evelee Doris (1923-). ETWF (196?).
            HFMA, PHC. Pastor, missionary
            b. July 15, 1923, Tecumseh, Neb.

6114   MASON, Genevie Fern (1923-). ETWF (196?).
            HFMA, PHC. Pastor, missionary
            b. July 15, 1923, Tecumseh, Neb.

6115   MATA, José (1932-). RWBTB (1953), 39-42.
            R. Cath., I, CN. Pastor
            b. Aug. 27, 1932, Dallas, Tex.

6116   MATHIS, I. C. (1898-). MLA (1935), 63-66.
            CN. Pastor, evangelist, district supt.
            b. July 1, 1898, Buffalo, Mo.

6117   MATLACK, Lucius Columbus (1816-1883). SCM (1881), 568-
            569.
            Member, NHA
            ME, WM, ME. Pastor, evangelist, editor, military
                chaplain
            b. Apr. 28, 1816, Baltimore, Md.
            d. June 24, 1883, Cambridge, Md.
6118   Matlack, Lucius Columbus, 1816-1883.
                Secession: a personal narrative of proscription for
            being an abolitionist. Syracuse, N.Y., 1856. 65 p.
            Autobiography.

6119   MATTHEWS, John
            CN. Pastor, evangelist

6120   MATTHEWSON, Minnie W. (-1935). LLITW (1951), 216.
            FM. Missionary

Part VI. Biography

6121 MATTHEWSON, Wesley F. (-1947). LLITW (1951), 216.
 FM. Missionary

6122 MATUSI, Anna. HNTB (1934), 129-132.
 CN. National worker, pastor's wife
 b. 19??, Swaziland, S. Afr.

6123 MAVIS, Walter Curry (1905-). CA. GTWATD (1965), 306-315.
 FM. Pastor, district supt., seminary prof.
 b. Dec. 20, 1905, West Salem, Ill.

6124 Mavis, Walter Curry, 1905-
 "The emergence and early development of the Christian pastoral ministry." Unpublished Ph.D. dissertation, University of Southern California, 1945.

6125 MAXWELL, Mrs. Mary. ROG (1854), 62-68.
 ME? Lay member

6126 MAY, John W.
 CN. Pastor

6127 MAZIVILA, John. HNTB (1934), 126-129.
 CN. National worker, pastor, evangelist
 b. 19??, Portuguese East Africa

6128 MEEK, J. H. FYAB (1954), 14, 89.
 WM, CN, PCN. Pastor, conference pres.

6129 MEEKS, Darlene Carol Laffoon (1933-). ETWF (196?).
 PHC, W. Pastor's wife, evangelistic singer, missionary
 b. Nov. 12, 1933, Robinson, Ill.

6130 MEEKS, Paul Wesley (1929-). ETWF (196?).
 PHC, W. Pastor, evangelistic singer, missionary
 b. Oct. 9, 1929, Zafarbad, India

6131 MEGGERS, L. D. FHOP (1964).
 CN. Pastor

6132 MEIKLE, Grace Livingston (-1949). LLITW (1951), 216.
 FM. Missionary

6133 MEIKLE, W. L. LLITW (1951), 216.
 FM. Missionary

6134 MENDELL, Fred H. (1883-1918).
 PCN. Pastor, denominational official
 b. Feb. 18, 1883, Homer, Mich.
 d. Nov. 20, 1918, Hutchinson, Kan.

6135   MERCER, Jerry L. GTWATD (1965), 256-268.
        M, UM. Pastor, college prof.

6136   MEREDITH, Archel. DCSWM (1946), 153-157.
        CN. Military chaplain

6137   MEREDITH, Clyde W. (1901-   ). RLOA (1941-1942), 783.
            SFLF (1950), 72-74.
        WM. Pastor, college prof., college pres.
        b. Aug. 5, 1901, Marion, Ind.

6138   MERRILL, A. D. PPE (1868), 105-108.
        ME. Pastor

6139   MERRITT, Timothy (1775-1845). SCM (1881), 992.
        ME. Pastor, editor
        b. Oct. 1775, Barkhamstead, Conn.
        d. May 2, 1845, Lynn, Mass.
6140   Hughes, George, 1828-1904.
            Fragrant memories of the Tuesday Meeting and the Guide to Holiness, and their fifty years' work for Jesus. Introd. to part I. by Rev. Bishop W. F. Mallalieu; and to part II. by Rev. Bishop William Taylor. New York, Palmer & Hughes, c1886. iv, 242 p.
            Includes account of activities of Timothy Merritt.

6141   MESSENGER, Frank Mortimer (1852-   ).
        ME, MetCA, CN. Evangelist, businessman (publisher)

6142   METHVIN, Rayford H. (1921-   ). WWACUA (1970-1971),
            357-358.
        PMC, EMC. College pres., missionary
        b. Jan. 20, 1921, Cullman, Ala.

6143   METZ, Donald S. (1916-   ). DAS (1969), IV, 247. LIE
            (1971), 646. GTWATD (1965), 316-333.
        ME, CN. Pastor, college prof., college dean
        b. Mar. 17, 1916, Frank, Pa.
6144   Metz, Donald S., 1916-
            "The interaction of naturalism and idealism in American educational philosophy, 1860-1960." Unpublished Ph.D. dissertation, University of Oklahoma, 1962.

6145   MEYERS, Hazeldean (1932-   ). ETWF (196?).
        PHC. Missionary
        b. Mar. 4, 1932, West Portsmouth, Ohio

6146   MICHEL, John W. (1885-   ). FHOP (1964).
        Cath., CN. College teacher
        b. 1885, Lazarfeld, Austria

Part VI. Biography 697

6147 MIENERT, Rudolph William (1934-). WWACUA (1970-1971), 360.
PF. College prof., college admin.
b. Apr. 13, 1934, New York, N.Y.

6148 MILBY, Luke G. (1876-).
Ind., CN. Pastor evangelist
b. Mar. 15, 1876, Summersville, Ky.
6149 Milby, Luke G., 1876-
L.G. Milby: life, works and peculiarities. Kansas City, Mo., Printed for L.G. Milby by the Nazarene Publishing House, n.d. 71 p.
Autobiography.

6150 MILLER, Basil William (1897-). SCC (1947), 97-100.
WW in the Clergy (1935-1936), 803.
CN. Pastor, evangelist, missionary promoter (ind.)
b. Feb. 26, 1897, Laconia, Ind.
6151 Miller, Basil William, 1897-
Those were the days: remembering my youth. Pasadena, Calif., World-Wide Missions, 1970. 125 p. [Autobiography, vol. 1]
6152 Miller, Basil William, 1897-
Years to remember: winning my wings. Pasadena, Calif., World-Wide Missions, 1971. 134 p. [Autobiography, vol. 2]
6153 Miller, Basil William, 1897-
Dreams fulfilled: my mission career. Pasadena, Calif., World-Wide Missions, 1971. 109 p. [Autobiography, vol. 3]
6154 Miller, Basil William, 1897-
Arms around the world: Missions world wide. Pasadena, Calif., World-Wide Missions, 1971. 109 p. [Autobiography, vol. 4]

6155 MILLER, Esther Elnetta Kirk (1894-1970).
CN. Pastor's wife
b. May 19, 1894, Columbus, Ohio
d. June 9, 1970, Pasadena, Calif.
6156 Miller, Basil William, 1897-
A beautiful life; the story of Esther K. Miller. Pasadena, Calif., World-Wide Missions, 1970. 139 p.

6157 MILLER, Hale H. (1856-1922).
ME, PCN, ME. Pastor, Bible college pres., district supt.
b. May 25, 1856, Lakeside, Mich.
d. Aug. 1, 1922, Alhambra, Calif.

6158 MILLER, Howard Vasser (1894-1948). N.Y. Times (Dec. 30, 1948), 19:4. CIOCC (1959), 8-10.
Bapt., CN. Pastor, district supt., general supt.,

evangelist, college prof.
d. Dec. 1948, Brooktondale, N.Y.

6159 McGraw, James, 1913-
"The preaching of Howard V. Miller," Preacher's Magazine, XXIX (Dec. 1954), 3-5.

6160 MILLER, J. PPE (1868), 321-322.
ME. Pastor

6161 MILLER, Merline Ivorita Mack (1930-). ETWF (196?).
PHC. Pastor's wife, missionary
b. Dec. 17, 1930, Washougal, Wash.

6162 MILLER, Nettie
CN. Evangelist

6163 Miller, Nettie
My satisfied quest. Kansas City, Mo., Nazarene Publishing House, 1942. 35 p.
Autobiography.

6164 MILLER, Paul D. (1934-). LIE (1971), 656.
CN. Public school teacher, college prof.
b. Sept. 2, 1934, Molalla, Ore.

6165 MILLER, Paul Elmer (1930-). ETWF (196?).
PHC. Pastor, missionary
b. June 28, 1930, Glendale, Ariz.

6166 MILLER, Ruth Elma (1904-). ETWF (196?).
PHC. Missionary
b. May 29, 1904, Brownsville, Pa.

6167 MILLER, S. PPE (1868), 99-104.
ME. Pastor

6168 MILLIKAN, Roy William (-1949). LLITW (1951), 216.
FM. Missionary

6169 MILLIKEN, A. PPE (1868), 330-331.
ME. Pastor

6170 MILLS, Abbie (-1909). LLITW (1951), 216.
FM. Missionary

6171 MILLS, Abbie C. (1829-1917).
Member, Iowa HA
Attended GHA, 1885 (Chicago)
ME. Evangelist

6172 MILLS, F. J. SCUH (1962), 305.
ME, LHA. Pastor, evangelist

Part VI. Biography 699

6173 MILLS, Howard T. (1887-1973). TDOOP (1968), 318-320.
 ME, PHC, W. Public school teacher, public school admin., Bible school pres., denominational official
 b. Sept. 13, 1887, Sanilac County, Mich.
 d. Mar. 16, 1973, Owosso, Mich.
6174 "Dr. Howard T. Mills, 1887-1973," Wesleyan Advocate, CXXXI (May 14, 1973), 6.
6175 Mitchell, Virgil Allen, 1914-
 "A tribute to a Christian educator," Wesleyan Advocate, CXXXI (May 14, 1973), 6-7.

6176 MILLS, Samuel E. (-1913). LLITW (1951), 216.
 FM. Missionary

6177 MINEER, Trula Frances (1928-). ETWF (196?).
 PHC. Missionary
 b. Oct. 26, 1928, Dalesburg, Ky.

6178 MINTZER, Frederick S. (1825-). PPE (1868), 323-324.
 ME. Pastor

6179 MISCHKE, Carl. FHOP (1964).
 CN. Pastor, missionary
 b. 19??, Yakima, Wash.

6180 MISCHKE, Velma. FHOP (1964). GHAI (1960), 44-50.
 CN. Pastor's wife, missionary
 b. 19??, Beatrice, Neb.

6181 MITCHELL, Elizabeth Ann Oldacre (1876-).
 CG (A).
6182 Mitchell, Elizabeth Ann (Oldacre), 1876-
 Anchored to the rock. Anderson, Ind., Printed for the author by Gospel Trumpet Co., 1950. 142 p.

6183 MITCHELL, J. S. PPE (1868), 157-159.
 ME. Pastor

6184 MITCHELL, Virgil Allen (1914-). WW in the Midwest (1965-1966), 669. WW in Am. (1972-1973), 2211.
 WM, W. Pastor, college prof., conference pres., denominational official, general supt.
 b. Apr. 21, 1914, Six Mile, S.C.
6185 "Conference elects 11 officers," Wesleyan Advocate, CXXVII (July 15, 1968), 8-9.
6186 "Elected officials of The Wesleyan Church," Wesleyan Advocate, CXXX (July 24, 1972), 14.

6187 MITCHUM, Donie. HWM (1905), 75-78. SCUH (1962), 48, 153, 155.
 ME, S; NTCOC; HChuC; PCN; CN. Evangelist

6188 MITCHUM, Robert Bailey. SCUH (1962), 156-157, 169-170, 173, 176, 191, 199.
ME, S; NTCOC; HChuC; PCN; CN. Lay leader, general council pres., businessman

6189 MKETI, Daniel. HNTB (1934).
CN. National worker, pastor, evangelist
b. 189?, Portuguese East Africa

6190 MKWANAZI, Josefa. HNTB (1934), 106-110.
CN. National worker, evangelist
b. 188?, Swaziland, S.Afr.

6191 MOE, Mrs. Cevira Ann (1848-1909).
WM. Housewife
b. 1848, Groton, Tomkins County, N.Y.
d. 1909, Houghton, N.Y.
6192 Moe, Mrs. Cevira Ann, 1848-1909.
Religious experience of Mrs. Cevira Ann Moe. n.p., 1904. 70 p.

6193 MONTGOMERY, Area (-1965).
IHC, PHC. Pastor
d. Sept. 26, 1965.

6194 MONTGOMERY, Mrs. Carrie Judd (1858-).
I. Editor, faith healer
6195 Montgomery, Mrs. Carrie (Judd), 1858-
The prayer of faith. Buffalo, N.Y., H.H. Otis, 1880. 163 p.
6196 Montgomery, Mrs. Carrie (Judd), 1858-
Secrets of victory. Oakland, Calif., Office of Triumphs of Faith, 1921. 168 p.
6197 Montgomery, Mrs. Carrie (Judd), 1858-
"Under His wings"; the story of my life. Oakland, Calif., Office of Triumphs of Faith, 1936. 256 p.

6198 MONTGOMERY, James William (1898-). RLOA (1941-1942), 805.
CN. Pastor, district supt., radio preacher
b. Apr. 27, 1898, Dennis, Miss.

6199 MOODY, Dwight Lyman (1837-1899). DAB. GFW (1888), 223-225. WWW in Am. (1897-1942), 857. LDEFC (1911), 338-352. MMAWODP (1920), 324-335. MHTWW (n.d.), 53-54. N.Y. Times (Dec. 23, 1899), 4:4.
Cong. Evangelist
b. Feb. 5, 1837, Northfield, Mass.
d. Dec. 22, 1899, Northfield, Mass.
6200 Torrey, Reuben Archer, 1856-1928.
Lessons from the life and death of D.L. Moody.

Part VI. Biography

New York, Chicago, Fleming H. Revell Co., 1900. 32 p.
6201 Torrey, Reuben Archer, 1856-1928.
Why God used D.L. Moody. New York, Chicago, Fleming H. Revell Co., c1923. 59 p.

6202 MOON, Wesley G. (1911-). LIE (1971), 666.
WM, CN. Academy teacher, college prof.
b. Apr. 20, 1911, Rushford, N.Y.

6203 MOORE, Altha Honea (-1973).
FM, CN. Pastor's wife
6204 Moore, Altha (Honea), -1973.
The Lord's leadings, by Mrs. J.E. Moore. Kansas City, Mo., Beacon Hill Press, 1949. 60 p.
Autobiography.

6205 MOORE, Arthur James (1888-). ATY (1930), 64-72.
WW in Am. (1956-1957), 1811. WW in the Clergy (1935-1936), 822. RLOA (1941-1942), 807.
ME, S; M. Pastor, bishop
b. Dec. 26, 1888, Waycross, Ga.

6206 MOORE, David Hastings (1838-1915). LMB (1948), 134-135.
SCM (1881), 628-629. WWW in Am. (1897-1942), 859. N.Y. Times (Nov. 24, 1915), 15:6; 22:5.
Endorsed call, GHA, 1901 (Chicago)
ME. Pastor, college pres., bishop
b. Sept. 4, 1838, Athens, Ohio

6207 MOORE, J. M. LLITW (1951), 217.
FM. Missionary

6208 MOORE, John E. MLA (1935), 69-72.
ME, CN. Pastor, evangelist, evangelistic singer

6209 MOORE, John Edgar Littleton (-1935). NP (1925), 149-160.
PCN, CN. Evangelist, college prof., college pres.
d. Jan. 26, 1935, Indianapolis, Ind.

6210 MOORE, Josiah Erben (1889-). COPN (1958), 55-60.
CN. Pastor, district supt.

6211 MOORE, Josiah Erben, Jr. DCEWM (1946), 46-54.
CN. Pastor, military chaplain

6212 MOORE, Mark Reynolds (1916-). DCSWM (1946), 126-131. WWACUA (1970-1971), 369. FYAB (1954), 99-100.
CN. College prof., military chaplain, district supt., college pres.
b. Sept. 30, 1916, Vilonia, Ark.

6213   Moore, Mark Reynolds, 1916-
          Prisoner of the Germans. Kansas City, Mo., Nazarene Publishing House, 194?. 64 p.

6214   MOORE, Norman Lowell (1916-). WW in the Midwest (1969-1970), 725.
          CN. Pastor, college admin.

6215   MORALES, Christobal E. (1892-). HNTB (1934), 174-177. RWBTB (1953), 28-32.
          Bapt., CN. Physician, national worker, pastor, evangelist, Bible seminary prof.
          b. May 8, 1892, Villa Guerrero, Mex.

6216   MOREHOUSE, Alonzo Church (1820-1903).
          Attended GHA, 1901 (Chicago)
          ME. Pastor, leader of Tuesday Meeting, New York
          b. Nov. 17, 1820, Blenheim, Schoharie County, N.Y.
          d. July 26, 1903, Sing Sing Camp-meeting ground, N.Y.
6217   Morehouse, Alonzo Church, 1820-1903.
          Autobiography of A.C. Morehouse, an itinerant minister of the New York and New York East conferences of the Methodist Episcopal Church; with an introd. by Bishop Newman. New York, Tibbals Book Co., 1895. 306 p.

6218   MOREHOUSE, Frank Eugene (1854-1908).
          Attended GHA, 1901 (Chicago)
          ME. Pastor
          b. Aug. 24, 1854, Hillsdale County, Mich.
          d. Jan. 16, 1908, Jackson, Mich.
6219   Moore, Charles
          History of Michigan. Chicago, Lewis Publishing Co., 1915.
          Includes biographical sketch of Frank Eugene Morehouse: v. 3, p. 1220.

6220   MORGAN, Clifford L. TDOOP (1968), 287.
          HC, PHC. Pastor

6221   MORGAN, Mattie Mallory
          IAHU?, PCN, CN. Rescue mission worker, orphanage operator, Bible school teacher

6222   MORRIS, Benjamin S. (-1914).
          Attended GHA, 1901 (Chicago)
          ME? Pastor?
          d. 1914, Oakland, Iowa

6223   MORRIS, Elsie Emma (1929-). ETWF (196?).
          PHC. Evangelist, evangelistic singer
          b. Aug. 30, 1929, Delmar, Md.

Part VI. Biography

6224 MORRIS, Lelia Naylor (1862-1929). N.Y. Times (July 24, 1929), 25:3. LDML (1953), 70. LMGSS (1952), 11.
ME. Gospel song writer
b. Apr. 15, 1862, Pennsville, Ohio
d. July 23, 1929, Auburn, N.Y.
6225 Wiess, Mary Ethel
Singing at her work; a biography of Mrs. C.H. Morris. Kansas City, Mo., Nazarene Publishing House, 19??. 48 p.

6226 MORRIS, Samuel (1872-1893).
ME? Student
6227 Baldwin, Lindley J.
The march of faith; the challenge of Samuel Morris to undying life and leadership. Chicago, National Institute of Applied Religion, 1941. 94 p.
6228 Baldwin, Lindley J.
The march of faith; the challenge of Samuel Morris to undying life and leadership. Chicago, Mary E. Baldwin, Publisher, 1942. 92 p.
6229 Baldwin, Lindley J.
The march of faith; the challenge of Samuel Morris to undying life and leadership. Victory Center ed. New York, Distributed by Christian Business Men's Committee, Inc., of New York, 1944. 94 p.
6230 Evans, Alec Richard
Sammy Morris. London, Edinburgh, Oliphants, 1958. 95 p.
6231 Evans, Alec Richard
Sammy Morris. Grand Rapids, Mich., Zondervan, 1958. 95 p.
6232 Masa, Jorge O.
The angel in ebony; or, The life and message of Sammy Morris; published by class of 1928 of Taylor University. Upland, Ind., Taylor University Press, 1928. 131 p.
6233 Merritt, Stephen
En time med Sammy Morris, av Stephen Merrit og T.C. Reade. Oslo, Filadelfiaforlaget, 1949?. 32 p.
6234 Merritt, Stephen
Samuel Morris, a true story. Colorado Springs, Colo., Gospel Stationery & Tract House, n.d. Folder.
6235 Reade, Thaddeus Constantine, 1846-1902.
Samuel Morris. Upland, Ind., Taylor University, 1921. 40 p.
6236 Reade, Thaddeus Constantine, 1846-1902.
Samuel Morris, Prince Kaboo of the Kru Tribe-- seamen of Africa. Berne, Ind., Golden Rule Book Shop, n.d. 30 p.
Cover title: Samuel Morris: the story of a Spirit-filled life.

6237 [Reade, Thaddeus Constantine, 1846-1902.]
Samuel Morris: the story of a Spirit-filled life.
Louisville, Ky., Pentecostal Publishing Co., n.d. 31 p.

6238 [Reade, Thaddeus Constantine, 1846-1902.]
Sketch of the life of Samuel Morris (Prince Kaboo)....
Upland, Ind., Taylor University, 1896. Cover-title,
19 p.

6239 Wengatz, John Christian, 1880-
Sammy Morris: Spirit-filled life. Upland, Ind.,
Taylor University Press, 1954. 67 p.

6240 MORRISON, Henry Clay (1857-1942). ATY (1930), [6]-13.
Nat. Cy. of Am. Biog., 33:276. WW in the Clergy
(1935-1936), 834. WWW in Am. (1943-1950), 385.
N.Y. Times (Mar. 25, 1942), 21:1.
Member, NHA
Attended GHA, 1901 (Chicago)
ME, S. Pastor, evangelist, editor, college pres.,
seminary pres.
b. Mar. 10, 1857, Bedford, Ky.
d. Mar. 24, 1942

6241 Morrison, Henry Clay, 1857-1942.
The confessions of a backslider. Louisville, Pentecostal Publishing Co., n.d. 93 p.
Autobiography.

6242 Morrison, Henry Clay, 1857-1942.
Life sketches and sermons. Louisville, Ky., Pentecostal Publishing Co., 1903. 112 p.

6243 Morrison, Henry Clay, 1857-1942.
Remarkable conversions, interesting incidents and
striking illustrations. Louisville, Ky., Pentecostal Publishing Co., 1925. 125 p.

6244 Morrison, Henry Clay, 1857-1942.
Some chapters from my life story. Louisville, Ky.,
Pentecostal Publishing Co., 1941. 269 p.

6245 Morrison, Henry Clay, 1857-1942.
World tour of evangelism. Louisville, Ky., Pentecostal Publishing Co., 1911. 280 p.

6246 Arnold, William Erastus, 1862-
The H.C. Morrison case: a statement of facts; an
investigation of the law. Louisville, Kentucky Methodist
Publishing Co., 1897. 34 p.

6247 Olson, Bessie Goldie, 1909-1973.
Henry Clay Morrison. Des Moines, Iowa, Boone
Publishing Co., 1946. 47 p.

6248 Ridout, George Whitefield, 1870-
Henry Clay Morrison: prophet, warrior, orator.
Louisville, Ky., Pentecostal Publishing Co., 1944. 31 p.

6249 Wesche, Percival A.
Henry Clay Morrison: crusader saint. Berne, Ind.,
Herald Press, 1963. 208 p.

Part VI. Biography

6250 Wesche, Percival A.
"The life, theology and influence of Henry Clay Morrison." Unpublished Ph.D. dissertation, University of Oklahoma, 1955.

6251 Wimberly, Charles Franklin, 1866-1946.
A biographical sketch of Henry Clay Morrison, D.D., editor of The Pentecostal Herald; the man and his ministry. New York, Revell, 1922. 214 p.

6252 MORRISON, John Arch (1893-1965). RLOA (1941-1942), 816. WW in Am. (1956-1957), 1834. WWW in Am. (1961-1968), 681.
CG (A). Pastor, Bible school prin., college teacher, college pres.
b. Feb. 6, 1893, St. James, Mo.
d. Dec. 23, 1965

6253 Morrison, John Arch, 1893-1965.
As the river flows; the autobiography of John A. Morrison. Anderson, Ind., Anderson College Press, 1962. 214 p.

6254 MORRISON, Joseph Grant (1871-1939). MOUS (1941), 58-64. NP (1925), 174-184. N.Y. Times (Nov. 24, 1939), 23:5. WW in the Clergy (1935-1936), 834.
ME, LHA, CN. Pastor, evangelist, editor, district supt., college pres., denominational official, general supt.
b. Mar. 27, 1871, Oskaloosa, Iowa

6255 Morrison, Joseph Grant, 1871-1939.
Interesting incidents; continuing the sketches published in an earlier booklet entitled, Other Days. Kansas City, Mo., Nazarene Publishing House, 19??. 96 p.

6256 Morrison, Joseph Grant, 1871-1939.
Other days; boyhood reminiscences of frontier hardships. Kansas City, Mo., Nazarene Publishing House, n.d. 64 p.

6257 Corbett, C. T.
Soldier of the cross; the life story of J.G. Morrison, 1871-1939. Kansas City, Mo., Beacon Hill Press, 1956. 128 p.

6258 McGraw, James, 1913-
"The preaching of Joseph Grant Morrison," Preacher's Magazine, XXIX (July 1954), 4-7.

6259 MORROW, Abbie Clemens. PM (1898), 54-60.
Endorsed call, GHA, 1901 (Chicago)
--. Evangelist, editor

6260 Morrow, Abbie (Clemens)
Autograph album selections. New York, N. Tibbals & Sons, 1883 [i.e. 1882]. 190 p.

6261 MORSE, George M. SCUH (1962).
 Endorsed call and attended, GHA, 1901 (Chicago)
 Bapt., PCN. Evangelist, pastor?

6262 MOSTELLER, Earl. GHAI (1960), 32-35.
 CN. Pastor, missionary

6263 MOSTELLER, Gladys. GHAI (1960), 32-35.
 CN. Pastor's wife, missionary

6264 MOTA, Jose S. (1885-). HNTB (1934), 180-181.
 R. Cath., PCN, CN. National worker, pastor
 b. 1885, San Pablo, Oztotepec, Mex.

6265 MOTT, Edward (1866-1954).
 Fr. Pastor, evangelist, Bible school teacher.
 b. Dec. 9, 1866, Moreau, Saratoga County, N.Y.
6266 Mott, Edward, 1866-1954.
 Sixty years of gospel ministry, by Edward Mott, author and publisher, preacher and teacher in Friends churches and schools, also in interdenominational service. Portland, Ore., 1947. 206 p.
 Autobiography.

6267 MOULE, Handley Carr Glyn (1841-1920). MWWW in Ch. Hist. (1968), 295. N.Y. Times (May 9, 1920), 22:4.
 Ch. of Eng. Asst. school master, curate, college prin., university prof., bishop, writer
 b. 1841, Fordington, Dorset, Eng.
 d. 1920

6268 MOULTON, Cyrus Orlando (-1909).
 ME, CM, IAHU. Missionary
 d. 1909, Georgetown, Brit. Guiana
6269 Moulton, Cyrus Orlando,   -1909.
 Exploits in the tropics. Bridgetown, Barbados, B.W.I., Christian Mission Book Room, 1907.

6270 MOULTON, Morris Kimber (1904-). RLOA (1941-1942), 819-820. SCC (1947), 101-105.
 CN. Pastor
 b. July 18, 1904

6271 MOUZON, Edwin DuBose (1869-1937). WW in the Clergy (1935-1936), 840. WWW in Am. (1897-1942), 875.
 N.Y. Times (Feb. 11, 1937), 23:3.
 MÈ, S. Pastor, college prof., bishop
 b. May 19, 1869, Spartanburg, S.C.
 d. Feb. 10, 1937
6272 Mouzon, Edwin DuBose, bp., 1869-1937.
 "Papers, 1910-1937." In Methodist Historical Library, Southern Methodist University.

Contain record of controversy concerning the "Second Blessing" movement in the Methodist Episcopal Church, South.

6273 MUDGE, James (1844-1918). GFW (1888), 63-68. WW in Am. Meth. (1916), 154-155. SCM (1881), 634. WWW in Am. (1897-1942), 876.
ME. Pastor, missionary, editor, writer
b. Apr. 5, 1844, West Springfield, Mass.
d. May 7, 1918, Malden, Mass.

6274 MUELLER, Duane K. (1928-). WWACUA (1970-1971), 375.
PHC, W. College admin.
b. Nov. 28, 1928, Stafford, Kan.

6275 MULDER, Chester O. DCSWM (1960), 60-63.
CN. Military chaplain

6276 MULLEN, Wilbur Handley (1919-). DAS (1969), IV, 261.
RB, W. Missionary, college prof.
b. Feb. 19, 1919, North Head, N.B., Can.

6277 MULLER, D. N. PPE (1868), 327.
ME. Pastor

6278 MUNGER, Charles
Member, NHA
ME. Pastor, evangelist

6279 MUNHALL, Leander Whitcomb (1843-1934). WW in Am. Meth. (1916), 155. WWW in Am. (1897-1942), 879.
ME. Evangelist, editor
b. June 7, 1843, Zanesville, Ohio
d. Jan. 7, 1934, Germantown?, Pa.

6280 MUNRO, Bertha (1887-).
APCA, CN. College prof., college dean
b. Feb. 19, 1887, Saugus, Mass.
6281 Munro, Bertha, 1887-
The years teach: remembrances to bless, an autobiography. Kansas City, Mo., Beacon Hill Press of Kansas City, 1970. 359 p.
Autobiography.

6282 MUNROE, Elizabeth (1793-1873).
--. Lay leader
6283 James, Mary Dagworthy (Yard), 1810-1883.
"Mother Munroe"; the shining path as illustrated in the life and experience of Elizabeth Munroe. Boston, J.H. Earle, 1880. 192 p.

6284 MUNROE, Florence
      ME? Missionary (OMS)
6285 Munroe, Florence
      For me to live. Greenwood, Ind., Oriental Missionary Society, 196?. 87 p.

6286 MURDICK, Perry Harvey (1879-). WW in Am. Meth. (1916), 156.
      Attended GHA, 1901 (Chicago)
      ME. Pastor
      b. July 8, 1879, Peru, Vt.

6287 MURRAY, M. Grace (-1934). LLITW (1951), 217.
      FM. Missionary

6288 MURRISH, Thomas
      ME?, CN. Pastor
      b. 18??, Cornwall, Eng.

6289 MUSE, Dan Thomas (1882-1950).
      Bapt., PeHC. Pastor, evangelist, conference supt., denominational official, bishop
      b. 1882, Boyd, Wise County, Tex.
      d. Feb. 4, 1950
6290 Paul, George Harold, 1910-
      "The religious frontier: Dan T. Muse and the Pentecostal Holiness Church." Unpublished Ph.D. dissertation, University of Oklahoma, 1965. 302ℓ.

6291 MYNETT, Frederick G. LLITW (1951), 217.
      FM. Missionary

6292 NAKADA, Juji (1870-1939)
      JHC. Bishop
      b. 1870, Hirosake, Japan
      d. Sept. 24, 1939, Tokyo?, Japan
6293 Erny, Edward
      No guarantee but God; the story of the founders of the Oriental Missionary Society, by Edward and Esther Erny. Greenwood, Ind., Oriental Missionary Society, 1969. 116 p.
      "Juji Nakada": p. 27-47.

6294 NARDI, Michele (1850-1914).
      CMA. Evangelist
6295 Simpson, Albert Benjamin, 1843-1919, comp.
      Michele Nardi, the Italian evangelist; his life and work. New York, Blanche P. Nardi, c1916. 143 p.

6296 NASH, David. PPE (1868), 251-255.
      ME. Pastor

Part VI. Biography

6297 NAST, Albert Julius (1846-1936). WW in Am. Meth. (1916), 157. WWW in Am. (1897-1942), 888. N.Y. Times (Mar. 28, 1936), 15:4.
       Endorsed call, GHA, 1901 (Chicago)
       ME. Pastor?, editor
       b. Apr. 4, 1846
       d. Mar. 27, 1936

6298 NAST, William (1807-1899). DAB. Nat. Cy. of Am. Biog., 10:223. SCM (1881), 994.
       Member, NHA
       Luth., ME. Seminary prof., college prof., editor
       b. 1807, Stuttgart, Wurtemberg, Ger.
6299   Wittke, Carl Frederick
       William Nast, patriarch of German Methodism. Detroit, Wayne State University Press, 1959. 248 p.

6300 NAYLOR, Jasper Ross (1908-   ). WWACUA (1970-1971), 381.
       CN. College prof., college admin.
       b. May 7, 1908, Buffalo, N.Y.

6301 NEASE, Floyd William (1893-1930). NP (1925), 209-220.
       IAHC, CN. Pastor, college prof., district supt., college pres.
       b. Dec. 21, 1893, Vassar, Mich.
       d. Oct. 26, 1930, Pittsburgh, Pa.
6302   Nease, Floyd William, 1893-1930.
       Symphonies of praise; introd. by the Rev. Roy T. Williams. Kansas City, Mo., Nazarene Publishing House, 1931. 192 p.
       Includes biographical sketch by Orval J. Nease.
6303   Munro, Bertha, 1887-
       "The preaching of Floyd William Nease," Preacher's Magazine, XXXIII (Dec. 1958), 4-7.

6304 NEASE, Orval John (1891-1950). RLOA (1941-1942), 835. SFLF (1950), 75-80. FHOP (1964).
       UB, IAHU, PCN, CN. Pastor, evangelist, college pres., general supt., denominational official
       b. Dec. 25, 1891, Nashville, Mich.
       d. Nov. 7, 1950, Pasadena, Calif.
6305   Nease, Orval John, 1891-1950.
       A vessel unto honor; seven sermons and a life sketch. Kansas City, Mo., Beacon Hill Press, 1952.
6306   McGraw, James, 1913-
       "The preaching of Orval J. Nease," Preacher's Magazine, XXIX (Nov. 1954), 5-8.

6307 NEASE, Stephen W. (1925-   ). WWACUA (1970-1971), 381.
       CN. Pastor, college admin., college pres.
       b. Jan. 15, 1925, Everett, Mass.

6308 NEE, Gilbert Chibee. NVFML (1936), 93-104.
--. National worker, evangelist
b. 190?, S. China

6309 NEELY, Benjamin Franklin (1876-1967). NP (1925), 125-134.
NTCOC, HChuC, PCN, CN. Pastor, evangelist, district supt.

6310 NEES, L. G. (-1954). CIOCC (1959), 19-21.
CN. Pastor
d. Oct. 1954.

6311 NEFF, H. PPE (1868), 340.
ME. Pastor

6312 NEFF, William H. (1902-). TDOOP (1968), 323-324.
IAHC, IHC, PHC, W. Pastor, evangelist, asst. general supt., general supt.
b. Dec. 4, 1902, McKeesport, Pa.

6313 NELSON, Eldon Byron (1926-). ETWF (196?).
PHC. Pastor, missionary
b. Oct. 11, 1926, Good Harbor, Mich.

6314 NELSON, Flora B.
Endorsed and attended, GHA, 1901 (Chicago)
FM, PB. Rescue mission worker

6315 NELSON, John O. (-1912).
Attended GHA, 1901 (Chicago)
ME. Pastor

6316 NELSON, Thomas Hiram (1863-).
Endorsed and attended, GHA, 1901 (Chicago)
FM, PB, I? Rescue mission supt.
6317 Nelson, Thomas Hiram, 1863-
Modern proverbs ... selected and arranged by James Gilchrist Lawson.... Grand Rapids, Mich., Zondervan Publishing House, 1937. 164 p.

6318 NELSON, Wilda Arlene (1926-). ETWF (196?).
PHC. Pastor's wife, missionary
b. Apr. 23, 1926, Buckley, Mich.

6319 NEUFELD, Frank A. FHOP (1964).
CN. Pastor, public school teacher

6320 NEWBY, John Melvin (1928-). ETWF (196?).
PHC. Pastor, college prof., missionary
b. Jan. 31, 1928, Westfield, Ind.

Part VI. Biography

6321   NEWBY, Rebecca Jean Hall (1929-   ). ETWF (196?).
        PHC. Missionary
        b. July 30, 1929

6322   NEWSOM, Reuben J. DCSWM (1946), 114-125.
        CN. Military chaplain

6323   NEWTON, George. PPE (1868), 334.
        Attended GHA, 1885 (Chicago)
        ME, CN, PCN. Pastor, editor, rescue mission supt.

6324   NICHOLSON, Roy Stephen (1903-   ). WW in Am. (1968-
        1969), 1615. RLOA (1941-1942), 844. SFLF (1950),
        81-84. GIIH (1962), 144-171. GTWATD (1965), 24-
        44. MHP (1957), 83-92.
        WM, W. Pastor, editor, denominational official, president.
        b. July 12, 1903, Walhalla, S.C.
6325   Wesleyan Methodist Church of America.
        A boy with a dream; the life of Roy S. Nicholson.
        Marion, Ind., 1964. 33 p.

6326   NIELSON, John Bechtold (1918-   ).
        CN. Pastor, Bible college teacher
6327   Nielson, John Bechtold, 1918-
        "The significance of the phrase, en Christo, in the
        writings of Paul, the apostle." Unpublished M.A. thesis, Brown University, 1957. viii, 154ℓ.

6328   NORBECK, Mildred E.
        (HIM), FM. Missionary
6329   Haiti Inland Mission.
        Ten years in Haiti, 1949-1959: Haiti Inland Mission.
        Intercession City, Fla., 1960. Folder
        Includes information on Mildred E. Norbeck, the
        founder.

6330   NOVAK, Frank (1884-   ).
        CN? Prison chaplain
6331   Allee, George Franklin, 1897-
        Beyond prison walls; the story of Frank Novak, once
        a desperate criminal and convict, now national prison
        chaplain no. 1 by the grace of God. Kansas City, Mo.,
        Beacon Hill Press, 1960. 96 p.

6332   NOYES, A. D. (-1923). LLITW (1951), 217.
        FM. Missionary

6333   NOYES, Sophia (-1933). LLITW (1951), 217.
        FM. Missionary

6334 NUSBAUM, Cyrus Silvester (1861-1937). WW in Am. Meth. (1916), 161. LMGSS (1952), 147. LDML (1953), 68. DC (1965, c1887), 115-129.
Member, NHA
ME. Pastor, evangelist, presiding elder, gospel song writer
b. July 27, 1861, Middlebury, Ind.

6335 NUSSEY, Wesley B. (1912-   ). WWACUA (1970-1971), 391.
WM, W. Pastor, college admin.
b. Nov. 18, 1912, Powerscourt, Que., Can.

6336 OLDHAM, William Dale (1903-   ). CA. SFLF (1950), 85-87.
CG (A). Pastor, evangelist, radio preacher
b. Mar. 30, 1903, Ripley, Okla.

6337 OLMSTEAD, Benjamin Luce (1886-   ). RLOA (1941-1942), 858.
FM. Pastor, college prof., editor
b. Sept. 14, 1886, Cedar Springs, Mich.

6338 OLSEN, Abner C. (-1958). CIOCC (1959), 12-13.
CN. Pastor
d. Oct. 2, 1958

6339 OLSEN, Gordon T. CIOCC (1959), 12-13.
CN. Layman

6340 OLSEN, Henry John (1879-1972).
Luth., IAHU, IAHC, IHC, PHC, W. Pastor, evangelist, editor, Bible college prof.
b. Jan. 19, 1879, West Golden, Oceana County, Mich.
d. May 5, 1972, Kernersville, N.C.
6341 Conklin, Mary (Olsen)
"Henry John Olsen, 1879-1972," Wesleyan Advocate, CXXX (July 10, 1972), 11.

6342 OLSEN, Kenneth I. CIOCC (1959), 12-13.
CN. Layman

6343 OLSEN, Mary Lillian Brown (1883-1942).
IAHU, IAHC, IHC, PHC. Pastor's wife (ordained minister), rescue mission worker
b. Sept. 12, 1883
d. Jan. 17, 1942

6344 OLSON, Heddie T.
CMA? Evangelist
6345 Olson, Heddie T.
My personal experience of Divine healing. 2d ed. Hollis, N.Y., 1939. 31 p.

Part VI. Biography 713

6346 OLSON, O. Joe (1910-). WW in the Midwest (1970-1971), 508.
   CN. Pastor, denominational official, journalist
   b. Aug. 30, 1910, Jamestown, N.Y.

6347 OLT, George Russell (1895-). RLOA (1941-1942), 859.
   CG (A). Pastor, college dean
   b. 1895, Dayton, Ohio

6348 ORJALA, Paul Richard (1925-).
   CN. Missionary, seminary prof.
6349 Orjala, Paul Richard, 1925-
   Ambassador diary, by Paul R. Orjala, in collaboration with John Smee. Kansas City, Mo., Nazarene Publishing House, 1967. 96 p.
6350 Orjala, Paul Richard, 1925-
   "A dialect survey of Haitian Creole." Unpublished Ph.D. dissertation, Hartford Seminary Foundation, 1970. 222ℓ.
6351 Orjala, Paul Richard, 1925-
   Haiti diary; the intimate story of a modern young missionary couple's first two years in a foreign country, comp. from the letters of Paul Orjala and ed. by Kathleen Spell. Kansas City, Mo., Beacon Hill Press, 1953. 125 p.

6352 ORMSTON, Mark D. (1890-). RLOA (1941-1942), 860.
   FM. Pastor, district elder, bishop
   b. Dec. 17, 1890, St. Johns, Mich.

6353 ORSBORN, Albert. SFLF (1950), 88-91.
   SA. Salvation Army officer

6354 OSBORN, Leon Clarence
   CN. Missionary
6355 Osborn, Leon Clarence
   From the mouth of the lion, told by a prisoner of Japan. Cleveland, Ohio, 1943. 64 p.

6356 OSBORN, Lucy Reed Drake (1844-).
   ME. Missionary (ind.), Bible school principal
6357 Osborn, Lucy Reed (Drake), 1844-
   Heavenly pearls set in a life; a record of experiences and labors in America, India and Australia. New York, Revell, 1894. 364 p.
   Autobiography.

6358 OSBORN, T. H.
   Endorsed call, GHA, 1901 (Chicago)
   ME? Evangelist

6359 OSBORN, William Bramwell (1832-1902).
Member, NHA
Endorsed call, GHA, 1901 (Chicago)
ME. Pastor, evangelist, missionary, presiding elder
d. Aug. 1902
6360 "The Rev. W. B. Osborn," Christian Advocate (New York), LXXVII (Sept. 18, 1902), 1488-1489.

6361 OSEPOFF, V. G. NVFML (1936), 159-173.
Russ. Orth., ME, S. Evangelist
b. 190?, Russia

6362 OVERHOLT, Elbert David (1925-). LIE (1971), 724.
CN. Public school teacher, college prof.
b. Nov. 23, 1925, Cincinnati, Ohio

6363 OWEN, E. PPE (1868), 331-332.
ME. Pastor

6364 OWEN, George Frederick (1897-). NP (1925), 89-97.
DAS (1951), 711.
CN. Evangelist, college prof.
b. Mar. 13, 1897, Mart, Tex.
6365 Owen, George Frederick, 1897-
Abraham to Allenby. Grand Rapids, Mich., Eerdmans, 1939. 351 p.
6366 Owen, George Frederick, 1897-
Abraham to the Middle-East crisis. 4th ed., rev. Grand Rapids, Mich., Eerdmans, 1957. 429 p.
An enlarged ed. of the author's work first published in 1939 under title: Abraham to Allenby.
6367 Owen, George Frederick, 1897-
Abraham to the Middle-East crisis. 4th ed., rev. London, Pickering & Inglis, 1957. 429 p.
Printed in U.S.A.
An enlarged ed. of the author's work first published in 1939 under title: Abraham to Allenby.
6368 Owen, George Frederick, 1897-
Archaeology and the Bible. Westwood, N.J., Revell, 1961. 384 p.
6369 Owen, George Frederick, 1897-
I caught a lovely thing today. Los Angeles, Cowman Publications, 1953. 120 p.
Poems.
6370 Owen, George Frederick, 1897-
Jerusalem; introd. by Lowell Thomas. Kansas City, Mo., Beacon Hill Press, 1972. 180 p.
6371 Owen, George Frederick, 1897-
The Shepherd Psalm of Palestine; photos. by G. Eric Matson. Grand Rapids, Mich., Eerdmans, 1958. 84 p.

Part VI. Biography

6372 OWEN, George S. (1882-1962).
IHC, PHC. Pastor, evangelist, editor, Bible school principal

6373 OWEN, John Frederick (1881-   ). ATY (1930), 74-81.
ME. Pastor, evangelist
b. Dec. 20, 1881, Boaz, Ala.

6374 OWEN, Joseph Parkes (1886-   ). WW in the Clergy (1935-1936), 883. ATY (1930), 126-134.
ME, S. Pastor, evangelist, college pres.
b. Mar. 14, 1886, Marshall Co., Ala.

6375 PADDOCK, Benjamin Green (1789-1871). SCM (1881), 689. PPE (1868), 335-337. N.Y. Times (Oct. 9, 1871), 1:2.
ME. Pastor, presiding elder
b. Jan. 24, 1789, Bennington, Vt.
d. Oct. 7, 1871, Metuchen, N.J.

6376 PAGE, Isaac E. (1839-1926).
Endorsed call, GHA, 1901 (Chicago)
WM (Eng.). Pastor

6377 PAINE, Stephen William (1908-   ). WW in Am. (1968-1969), 1671. CA. WWACUA (1970-1971), 401-402. Leaders in Ed. (1971), 727.
WM, W. College prof., college dean, college pres.
b. Oct. 28, 1908, Grand Rapids, Mich.

6378 Paine, Stephen William, 1908-
"Aspects of the appropriate name in Greek." Unpublished Ph.D. dissertation, University of Illinois, 1933.

6379 Paine, Stephen William, 1908-
Beginning Greek: a functional approach. New York, Oxford University Press, 1961. 325 p.

6380 Paine, Stephen William, 1908-
"Separation"--is separating Evangelicals. Boston, Fellowship Press, c1951. 43 p.

6381 PALMER, Miles W.
Endorsed call, GHA, 1901 (Chicago)
ME. Lay leader, physician

6382 PALMER, Phoebe Worrell (1807-1874). GFW (1888), 252-261. LDEFC (1911), 378-379. NAW (1607-1950), III, 12-14. SCM (1881), 691-692. MMAWODP (1920), 350-353.
ME. Lay leader, evangelist, editor
b. Dec. 18, 1807, New York, N.Y.
d. Nov. 2, 1874, New York, N.Y.

6383 Palmer, Phoebe (Worrell), 1807-1874.
  Four years in the Old World; comprising the travels, incidents, and evangelistic labors of Dr. and Mrs. Palmer in England, Ireland, Scotland and Wales. New York, Foster & Palmer, 1867. 700 p.

6384 Palmer, Phoebe (Worrell), 1807-1874.
  Mrs. Phoebe Palmer's testimony to the faithfulness of the covenant-keeping God. New York, W.C. Palmer, Jr., 1875. 7 p.
  "A fac-simile of Mrs. Palmer's handwriting, and the last communication that her busy hand ever wrote for the Christian public."
  On cover: Crowning testimony.

6385 [Palmer, Phoebe (Worrell)], 1807-1874.
  The way of holiness, with notes by the way; being a narrative of experience resulting from a determination to be a Bible Christian. New York, Piercy and Reed, 1843. ix, 256 p.

6386 Palmer, Phoebe (Worrell), 1807-1874.
  The way of holiness, with notes by the way; being a narrative of religious experience resulting from a determination to be a Bible Christian. New York, G. Lane & C.B. Tippett, 1845. 288 p.

6387 Hughes, George, 1828-1904.
  Fragrant memories of the Tuesday Meeting and the Guide to Holiness, and their fifty years' work for Jesus. Introd. to part I. by Rev. Bishop W.F. Mallalieu; and to part II. by Rev. Bishop William Taylor. New York, Palmer & Hughes, c1886. iv, 242 p.
  Includes account of activities of Phoebe Palmer.

6388 Wall, Ernest
  "I commend unto you Phoebe," Religion in Life, XXVI (Summer 1957), 396-408.

6389 Wheatley, Richard, 1831-
  The life and letters of Mrs. Phoebe Palmer. New York, W.C. Palmer, Jr., 1876. 636 p.

6390 PALMER, Sarah A. Worrell Lankford (1806-1896). GFW (1888), 262-269. ROG (1854), 150-161.
  ME. Lay leader
  b. Apr. 23, 1806

6391 Hughes, George, 1828-1904.
  Fragrant memories of the Tuesday Meeting and the Guide to Holiness, and their fifty years' work for Jesus. Introd. to part I. by Rev. Bishop W.F. Mallalieu; and to Part II. by Rev. Bishop William Taylor. New York, Palmer & Hughes, c1886. iv, 242 p.
  Includes account of activities of Sarah A. Worrell Lankford Palmer.

6392 Roche, John Alexander
  The life of Mrs. Sarah A. Lankford Palmer, who for sixty years was the able teacher of entire holiness,

Part VI. Biography

with an introd. by John P. Newman, bishop of the Methodist Episcopal Church. New York, George Hughes & Co., 1898. 286 p.

6393 PALMER, Walter Clark (1804-1883). SCM (1881), 692. N.Y. Times (July 22, 1883), 5:3. Nat. Cy. of Am. Biog., V, 182.
ME. Lay leader, physician, lay preacher, editor
b. Feb. 6, 1804, New Jersey
d. July 20, 1883, Ocean Grove, N.J.

6394 Hughes, George, 1828-1904.
The beloved physician, Walter C. Palmer, M.D.: his sun-lit journey to the celestial city, by his colleague, Rev. George Hughes, with an introd. by Rev. F.G. Hibbard. New York, Published for the author by Palmer & Hughes, 1884. 400 p.

6395 Hughes, George, 1828-1904.
Fragrant memories of the Tuesday Meeting and the Guide to Holiness, and their fifty years' work for Jesus. Introd. to part I. by Rev. Bishop W.F. Mallalieu; and to part II. by Rev. Bishop William Taylor. New York, Palmer & Hughes, c1886. iv, 242 p.
Includes account of activities of Dr. Walter C. Palmer.

6396 PANNABECKER, Ray Plowman (1913-). WWACUA (1970-1971), 402-403.
UMC, MC. Pastor, district supt., college prof., college pres.
b. June 27, 1913, Elkton, Mich.

6397 PAPPAS, Paul John (1898-). HVFML (1936), 121-143. RLOA (1941-1942), 868.
Gr. Orth., ME, OMS. Missionary, evangelist, pastor
b. May 24, 1898, Bazapalliona, Zara, Asia Minor

6398 Pappas, Paul John, 1898-
Experiences of Rev. Paul J. Pappas. Louisville, Pentecostal Publishing Co., n.d. 40 p.
Autobiography.

6399 Pappas, Paul John, 1898-
Experiences of Rev. Paul J. Pappas. Louisville, Pentecostal Publishing Co., 1938? 126 p.
Autobiography.

6400 Pappas, Paul John, 1898-
From Greek Catholicism to Christ, and World War experiences. Louisville, Pentecostal Publishing Co., 1926. 68 p.
Autobiography.

6401 PARKER, John (1825-1911). GFW (1888), 93-97. PPE (1868), 291-294.
HConf., 1877 (New York)

Endorsed call, GHA, 1901 (Chicago)
WM (Eng.), ME. Pastor, evangelist
b. Feb. 1825, England
d. Sept. 18, 1911, Asbury Park, N.J.

6402 PARROTT, Alonzo Leslie (1891-   ). RLOA (1941-1942), 870.
PCN, CN. Pastor, evangelist, college pres.
b. 1891, Monterey, Tenn.

6403 PARROTT, Leslie (1922-   ).
CN. Pastor, college pres.

6404 PARROTT, Lora Lee Montgomery (1923-   ). CA.
CN. Pastor's wife
b. Apr. 7, 1923, Wilmore, Ky.

6405 PATTEE, John W. (1903-   ). GHAI (1960), 82-87.
CN. Pastor, missionary
b. Sept. 23, 1903, North Dakota
6406 Pattee, John W., 1903-
Hazardous days in China. Pasadena, Calif., 1942? 106 p.

6407 PATTEE, Lillian Kerr (1902-   ). GHAI (1960), 82-87.
CN. Pastor's wife, missionary
b. Sept. 5, 1902, North Ireland

6408 PATTERSON, James Howard (1867-   ).
BIC? Layman
6409 Patterson, James Howard, 1867-
Of me I sing; or, Me and education.... Nappanee, Ind., E.V. Publishing House, 1940. 304 p.

6410 PAUL, John Haywood (1877-1967). RLOA (1941-1942), 873. WW in Am. (1950-1951), 2135. SFLF (1950), 92-93. ATY (1930), 136-143.
ME, M. Pastor, college admin., college pres., seminary prof.
b. Sept. 23, 1877, Rapides Parish, La.
d. Dec. 31, 1967
6411 Paul, John Haywood, 1877-1967.
The climax of the Bible; a Question Bureau study of Revelation, with a sermon on The music of the River of Life and a Brief professional biography of the author. Louisville, Herald Press, n.d. 54 p.
"A sketch of John Paul's life," by Joel Brown: p. 50-54.

6412 PAULK, John Chester (1876-   ). RLOA (1941-1942), 873.
ME, S; CG (A). Pastor, evangelist
b. Dec. 24, 1876, Cloverdale, Ala.

Part VI. Biography 719

6413 PAULSON, David (1868-1916).
I. Medical worker in rescue mission
6414 Paulson, David, 1868-1916.
Footprints of faith. Hinsdale, Ill., Life Boat Publishing Co., 1921. v, 118 p.
Autobiography.

6415 PAWAR, Dagadu. HNTB (1934), 101-102.
CN. National worker, pastor
b. 19??, India

6416 PAWAR, Gopal Govind. HNTB (1934), 103.
CN. National worker, pastor
b. 19??, India

6417 PEARCE, William (1862-1947). BMW (1960), 283-303.
WW in Am. Meth. (1916), 167. WW in the Clergy (1935-1936), 899.
WM (Eng.), FM. Pastor, district elder, bishop
b. Oct. 15, 1862, Hayle, Cornwall, Eng.

6418 PEARSE, Mark Guy (1842-1930). SCM (1881), 697-698. WWW (1929-1940).
WM (Eng.). Pastor, rescue mission worker
b. Jan. 3, 1842, Camborne, Cornwall, Eng.
d. Jan. 1, 1930, London Eng.

6419 PEARSON, Benjamin Harold (1893-   ). RLOA (1941-1942), 875.
FM. Missionary, denominational official, editor
b. Apr. 25, 1893, Los Angeles, Calif.

6420 PEAVEY, Leroy Deering (1876-1937). WWW in Am. (1897-1942), 951. N.Y. Times (Mar. 26, 1937), 22:1.
APCA, CN. Lay leader, businessman

6421 PECK, George (1797-1876). DAB. HM (1882). SCM (1881), 698. WWW in Am. (1607-1896), 401.
ME. Pastor, conference seminary principal, presiding elder, editor
b. Aug. 8, 1797, Middlefield, Otsego County, N.Y.
d. May 20, 1876, Scranton, Pa.
6422 Peck, George, 1797-1876.
The life and times of Rev. George Peck, D.D. New York, Nelson & Phillips, 1874. 409 p.

6423 PECK, Jesse Truesdell (1811-1883). DAB. SCM (1881), 698-699. WWW in Am. (1607-1896), 401.
ME. Pastor, conference seminary principal, editor, bishop
b. Apr. 4, 1811, Middlefield, Otsego County, N.Y.
d. May 17, 1883, Syracuse, N.Y.

6424   PECK, Jonas Oramel (1836-   ). GFW (1888), 246-251.
        SCM (1881), 698.
        ME. Pastor
        b. Sept. 4, 1836, Groton, Vt.

6425   PECK, Kathryn Blackburn (1904-   ). CA.
        CN. Lay member, editorial writer
        b. July 9, 1904, Jacksonville, Ill.

6426   PEGLER, George (1799-   ). SCM (1881), 699-700.
        MP, WM. Pastor
        b. Oct. 11, 1799, London, Eng.
6427   Pegler, George, 1799-
        Autobiography of the life and times of the Rev.
        George Pegler.... Beaver, Minn., 1875. 532 p.
6428   Pegler, George, 1799-
        Autobiography of the life and times of the Rev.
        George Pegler. Syracuse, NY., Wesleyan Methodist
        Publishing House, 1879. 532 p.

6429   PEIRCE, Bradford Kinney (1819-1889). GFW (1888), 115-
        118. SCM (1881), 700.
        ME. Pastor, editor, state institutional supt. and chaplain
        b. Feb. 3, 1819, Royalton, Windsor County, Vt.
        d. Apr. 19, 1889, Newton Center, Mass.

6430   PEIRCE, E. W. PPE (1868), 193-195.
        ME. Pastor
        b. 18???, New York

6431   PEISKER, Armor D. GTWATD (1965), 180-194. TDOOP
        (1968), 347-348.
        PeoMC, PHC, W. Bible school teacher, Bible school
            pres., denominational official, editor
        b. 190?, Colorado

6432   PENN, Joseph H. (1850-1934).
        CN. Pastor

6433   PENNER, Opal Good. FHOP (1964).
        CN, FM, CN. Pastor, missionary to Japanese in Calif.

6434   PENNER, William A. FHOP (1964).
        CN, FM, CN. Pastor, missionary

6435   PENNINGTON, Levi Talbott (1875-   ).
        Fr. Pastor, college pres.
        b. Aug. 29, 1875, Amo, Ind.
6436   Pennington, Levi Talbott, 1875-
        Rambling recollections of ninety happy years. Portland, Ore., Metropolitan Press, 1967. xvi, 187 p.
        Autobiography.

6437 PEPPER, Eleuthera I. D. (-1908). DC (1965, c1887), 90-101.
Member, NHA
ME. Pastor, evangelist, editor

6438 PEREZ, Benjamin. HNTB (1934), 142-143.
CN. National worker, pastor
b. 19??, San Jeronimo, Guatemala

6439 PEREZ, Francisco R. (1889-). HNTB (1934), 179-180.
CN. National worker, pastor
b. 1889, Iguala, Guerrero, Mex.

6440 PERKINS, Ethel (1875-). GFW (1888), 216-218.
Pres., ME.
b. June 24, 1875

6441 PETERSON, Fern Annabelle Nelson (1916-). ETWF (196?).
PHC. Pastor's wife, evangelistic singer, missionary
b. Dec. 17, 1916, Omaha, Neb.

6442 PETERSON, Lily M. (-1908). LLITW (1951), 217.
FM. Missionary

6443 PETERSON, Martin Luther (1912-). ETWF (196?).
PHC. Pastor, evangelist, evangelistic singer, missionary
b. July 1, 1912, Greeley, Colo.

6444 PETTEE, I. I. ROG (1854), 30-38.
ME. Pastor

6445 PETTICORD, Emory W. (1880-). WW in the Clergy (1935-1936), 910.
EC. Pastor, evangelist, district supt.
b. July 25, 1880, Greenspring, Ohio

6446 PETTICORD, Paul Parker (1907-). WWACUA (1970-1971), 416.
EUB, ECNA. Seminary pres.
b. June 22, 1907, Lost Springs, Kan.

6447 PETTIT, Charles Warren (1869-1931). N.Y. Times (Dec. 2, 1931), 25:2.
MP, APCA, PCN, ME. Pastor
b. May 10, 1869, Garasevoort, N.Y.
d. Nov. 30, 1931

6448 PEYTON, Claudie (1894-). ETWF (196?).
PHC. Orphanage worker, missionary
b. Dec. 15, 1894, Barboursville, W.Va.

6449   Peyton, Claudie, 1894-
         Twenty years in Africa. Pittsburgh, Pa., Salvation
         Tract Society, n.d.

6450   PHAUP, Bernard Hugo (1912-). WW in Am. (1972-1973),
         II, 2486. WW in the Midwest (1965-1966), 757.
         WM, W. Pastor, evangelist, conference pres., general
             supt.
           b. July 17, 1912, Farmville, Va.
6451   "Conference elects 11 officers," Wesleyan Advocate,
         CXXVII (July 15, 1968), 8.
6452   "Elected officials of The Wesleyan Church," Wesleyan
         Advocate, CXXX (July 24, 1972), 14.

6453   PHILLIPPE, Edward Everett (1904-). ETWF (196?).
         PHC. Missionary
           b. July 15, 1904, Rural Retreat, Va.

6454   PHILLIPPE, Eunice Leona (1903-). ETWF (196?).
         PHC. Missionary
           b. May 31, 1903, Canton, Ohio

6455   PHILLIPPE, Paul Samuel (1929-). ETWF (196?).
         PHC. Pastor, missionary
           b. Dec. 9, 1929, Saba, Netherlands Antilles

6456   PHILLIPPE, Vivian Virginia Hart (1932-). ETWF (196?).
         PHC. Pastor's wife, missionary
           b. Mar. 8, 1932, LaGrange, Ind.

6457   PHILLIPS, Dean Howard (1921-). ETWF (196?).
         PHC. Missionary
           b. Apr. 23, 1921, Millville, N.J.

6458   PHILLIPS, Elizabeth Ann Clark (1922-). ETWF (196?).
         PHC. Missionary
           b. July 16, 1922, Denton, Md.

6459   PHILLIPS, Koy Wright (1915-). WWACUA (1970-1971),
         418.
         CN. College prof., college admin.
           b. Jan. 23, 1915, Bedford County, Tenn.

6460   PHILLIPS, William I.
         Endorsed call, GHA, 1901 (Chicago)
         National Christian Asso. General secretary

6461   PHILO, L. C. (1907-1972). DAS (1969), IV, 290.
         PHC, CN. Bible college dean, Bible college pres.,
             college prof.
           b. June 1, 1907, Lansing, Mich.
           d. Apr. 10, 1972, Kankakee, Ill.

Part VI. Biography

6462 PICKETT, Jarrell Waskom (1890-). RLOA (1941-1942), 888. CA. WW in the Clergy (1935-1936), 917.
ME, M. Missionary, district supt., editor, bishop
b. Feb. 21, 1890, Marshall, Tex.

6463 PICKETT, Leander Lycurgus (1859-1928). N.Y. Times (May 10, 1928), 27:5. LDML (1952), 74.
Attended, GHA, 1901 (Chicago)
ME, S. Pastor, evangelist, editor, gospel song writer
b. 1859, Burnsville, Ky.
d. May 8, 1928

6464 PIERCE, David Rand
ME, APCA, PCN, CN. Pastor, evangelist

6465 PIERCE, G. M. PPE (1868), 285-290.
ME. Pastor

6466 PIERCE, Lovick (1785-1879). SCM (1881), 717-718.
Member, GeorgiaHA
ME; ME, S. Pastor
b. Mar. 24, 1785, Halifax County, N.C.

6467 PIERCE, Phoebe
CN, IHC, PHC. Missionary, deaconess

6468 PIERCE, Robert
CN. Pastor, general secretary
b. 18??, Liverpool, Eng.

6469 PIKE, John M. DC (1965, c1887), 1-25.
Member, NHA
Attended, GHA, 1901 (Chicago)
ME? Evangelist, rescue mission supt., editor
6470 Browning, Raymond, 1879-1953.
God's melting pot: Romans 8:28. Kansas City, Mo., Beacon Hill Press, 1951. 32 p.
Includes account of John M. Pike: p. 23-26.

6471 PINKHAM, William Penn (1841-1919).
Fr. Bible school teacher
6472 Pinkham, William Penn, 1841-1919.
His voice to me. Huntington Park, Calif., Privately printed, n.d.

6473 PITTS, Joseph S. DCSWM (1946), 9-30.
CN, I, CBC. Pastor, military chaplain, missionary
6474 Pitts, Joseph S.
Voices from the Philippines. Wilmore, Ky., 1958. 26 p.

6475 PLEDGER, Clifton Pryor (1875-1909).
Attended GHA, 1901 (Chicago)
ME. Pastor
d. Feb. 11, 1909

6476 PLUMB, Roselle John (1886-   ). COPN (1958), 61-66. WW in Calif. (1942-1943), 727. WW in the Clergy (1935-1936), 921-922.
PeoMC, PCN, CN. Pastor, district supt.
b. Apr. 7, 1886, Eastonville, Colo.

6477 POLOVINA, Samuel (1888-   ).
R. Cath., I? Coal miner
b. Jan. 14, 1888, Austria
6478 Polovina, Samuel, 1888-
From heathenism to Christ; life story of Samuel Polovina, the converted Austrian. Eldorado, Ill.?, 1920. 31 p.
Autobiography.

6479 POOLE, W. H. PPE (1868), 20-33.
ME. Pastor

6480 POPE, Gladys M. GHAI (1960), 12-13.
CN. Missionary

6481 POTTS, John. SCM (1881), 730.
Endorsed call, GHA, 1901 (Chicago)
Meth. (Can.)
Pastor, denominational official

6482 POWERS, Hardy Carroll (1900-1972). CIOCC (1959), 6-8.
CN. Pastor, district superintendent, general superintendent
b. June 7, 1900, Oglesby, Tex.
d. June 10, 1972, Bethany, Okla.
6483 "Hardy C. Powers," Herald of Holiness, LXI (July 19, 1972), 9-11.

6484 PRATT, Melvin F. (1860-1939).
ME, HCC, IHC, PHC. Rescue mission supt., Bible school principal, pastor, evangelist, district supt.
b. Apr. 21, 1860, Cedar Rapids, Mich.
d. May 11, 1939
6485 Pratt, William H.
God amid the shadows; thrilling sketches from the lives of Rev. and Mrs. Melvin Pratt, well-known spiritual leaders and founders of missions and homes for penitent, erring girls. Indianapolis, Ind., n.d. 151 p.

6486 PRATT, William H.
IHC, PHC. Pastor, evangelist

Part VI. Biography

6487 PRESCOTT, Grace. GHAI (1960), 20-22.
CN. Pastor's wife, missionary

6488 PRESCOTT, Lyle (1913-1970). GHAI (1960), 20-22.
CN. Pastor, missionary
b. May 26, 1913
d. Feb. 12, 1970
6489 Prescott, Lyle, 1913-1970.
Our 25 years in the Caribbean. Kansas City, Mo.,
Nazarene Publishing House, 1970. 88 p.
Autobiography.

6490 PRICE, Ross Eugene (1907-). WW in the West (1969-1970), 740. DAS (1969), IV, 295.
CN. Pastor, college prof., district supt.
b. July 15, 1907, Culbertson, Mont.

6491 PRINDLE, Cyrus (1800-1885). SCM (1881), 736.
ME, WM, ME. Pastor
b. 1800, Vermont
d. Dec. 1, 1885

6492 PRITCHARD, M. C.
HMoC. Pastor?
6493 Pritchard, M. C., ed.
Gleaned from life's pathway. ed. Ottawa, Holiness
Movement Publishing House, 1908. 256 p.

6494 PURDY, Jessie Amelia (1870-). ETWF (196?).
BHFMSNE, PHC. Missionary
b. July 1, 1870, Wentworth, N.S., Can.

6495 PURKISER, Westlake Taylor (1910-). WW in Am. (1960-1961), 2347. CA. DAS (1969), IV, 296. GFIIH (1963), 248-266.

6496 RAGER, Mary Ellen (1935-). ETWF (196?).
PHC. Missionary
b. Mar. 15, 1935, Lancaster, Ohio

6497 RAGSDALE, Dorothy Frances (1917-). ETWF (196?).
PHC. Missionary
b. Nov. 20, 1917, Alexandria, Ind.

6498 RAGSDALE, Paul Wesley (1917-). ETWF (196?).
PHC. Missionary
b. Sept. 6, 1917, Petersburg, Ind.

6499 RAIDABAUGH, Peter W.
Endorsed call, GHA, 1901 (Chicago)
Fr. Publisher

6500 RAMOS, Rosula. HNTB (1934), 142.
      CN. National worker, pastor
      b. 19??, Guatemala

6501 RAMSEYER, Joseph Eicher (1868 or 9-1944).
      MCA. Pastor?
6502   Ramseyer, Macy (Garth)
          Joseph E. Ramseyer--"yet speaking." Fort Wayne, Bible Institute, 1945. 293 p.

6503 RANF, M. Louisa (-1890). LLITW (1951), 217.
      FM. Missionary

6504 RANKS, Swanton. PPE (1868), 245-247.
      ME. Pastor

6505 RANSOM, Arthur S.
      PM, PCN. Lay leader, businessman

6506 RAY, Emma J. (1859-).
      FM. Lay leader, temperance worker, hospital worker
6507   Ray, Emma J., 1859-
          Twice sold, twice ransomed; autobiography of Mr. and Mrs. L.P. Ray. Introduction by Rev. C.E. McReynolds. Chicago, Free Methodist Publishing House, c1926. 320 p.

6508 READE, Thaddeus Constantine (1846-1902).
      Endorsed call, GHA, 1901 (Chicago)
      ME. Pastor, college pres.
6509   Reade, Thaddeus Constantine, 1846-1902.
          The elder brother. Hartford City, Ind., T.C. Reade, 1900. 46 p.
6510   Reade, Thaddeus Constantine, 1846-1902.
          The exodus and other poems. Cincinnati, Walden and Stowe, 1883. 100 p.

6511 REDDY, William (1813-). GFW (1888), 209-215.
      Pres., ME. Pastor
      b. Sept. 28, 1813, Ledyard Township, Cayuga County, N.Y.

6512 REDFIELD, John Wesley (1810-1863). MMAWODP (1920), 360-365.
      ME, FM. Pastor, evangelist
      b. Jan. 23, 1810, Clarendon, N.H.
      d. Nov. 2, 1863, Marengo, Ill.
6513   Terrill, Joseph Goodwin, -1895.
          The life of Rev. John Wesley Redfield, M.D. Chicago, The author, 1889. 464 p.
6514   Terrill, Joseph Goodwin, -1895.
          The life of Rev. John Wesley Redfield, M.D. Titus-

Part VI. Biography 727

ville, Pa., Allegheny Wesleyan Methodist Connection, n.d. xx, 464 p.
Reprint of 1889 ed.

6515 REED, David S. (1867-).
FM, PenielM, CN. Pastor, evangelist, district supt.
b. 1867, Wisconsin
6516 Reed, David S., 1867-
The circuit rider. Louisville, Ky., Pentecostal Publishing Co., 195?. 162 p.
Autobiography.

6517 REED, Harold William (1909-). WW in the Midwest (1969-1970), 846. WW in Am. (1968-1969), 1800. WWACUA (1970-1971), 437. LIE (1971), 780.
PHC, CN. Pastor, college prof., college pres.
b. July 14, 1909, Haigler, Neb.

6518 REED, Louis Archibald (1892-1952). WW in Clergy (1935-1936), 951.
CN. Pastor, college prof., seminary prof.
b. May 30, 1892, Brooklyn, N.Y.

6519 REED, Oscar Ferguson
CN. Pastor, college prof.

6520 REEDY, Edward Napoleon (1883-).
CG (A). Pastor
6521 Reedy, Edward Napoleon, 1883-
Valleys and hilltops. n.p., c1956. 172 p.

6522 REES, Byron Johnson (1877-1920). WWW in Am. (1897-1942), 1018.
IAHUPL. Evangelist, college prof.
b. 1877, Westfield, Ind.
d. Feb. 18, 1920, Williamstown, Mass.
6523 Rees, Byron Johnson, 1877-1920, ed.
Modern American prose selections. New York, Harcourt, Brace and Howe, 1920. 181 p.
6524 Rees, Byron Johnson, 1877-1920, ed.
Nineteenth century letters, selected and ed. with an introd. by Byron Johnson Rees. New York, Scribners, 1919. 543 p. (Modern student's library)

6525 REES, Frida Marie Stromberg (-1958).
IAHUPL, PCN, PC, PHC. Deaconess, pastor's wife
d. July 28, 1958

6526 REES, Hulda A. Johnson (1855-1898).
Fr., IAHUPL. Evangelist, pastor's wife
6527 Rees, Byron Johnson, 1877-1920.
Hulda A. Rees, the Pentecostal prophetess (Title

suggested by Rev. E.I.D. Pepper); or, A sketch of her life and triumph, together with seventeen of her sermons. Philadelphia, Christian Standard Co., 1898. 152 p.

6528 REES, Paul Stromberg (1900-). WW in Am. (1968-1969), 1802. CA. SFLF (1950), 94-97. MHP (1957), 113-128.
PC, PHC, Miss. Cov. Evangelist, pastor, missionary promoter (ind.)
b. Sept. 4, 1900, Providence, R.I.

6529 McGraw, James, 1913-
"The preaching of Paul S. Rees." Preacher's Magazine, XXXV (July 1960), 9-12.

6530 REES, Seth Cook (1854-1933). PM (1898), 4-14. TDOOP (1868), 14-22, 152, 156, 159, 162a-165.
Fr., IAHUPL, I, PCN, PC, PHC. Pastor, evangelist, general supt.
b. Aug. 6, 1854, Westfield, Hamilton Co., Ind.
d. May 22, 1933, Pasadena, Calif.

6531 Rees, Seth Cook, 1854-1933.
The wings of the morning; a record of recent travel, by Seth C. Rees and Paul S. Rees. Greensboro, N.C., Winfred R. Cox, 1926. 253 p.

6532 Rees, Paul Stromberg, 1900-
Seth Cook Rees, the warrior-saint. Indianapolis, Pilgrim Book Room, 1934. 194 p.

6533 Rees, Paul Stromberg, 1900-
The life of Seth Cook Rees; a pen portrait series (abbreviated from Paul S. Rees' book--Seth Cook Rees--the warrior saint) for the CYC cadet award. Indianapolis, Ind., Pilgrim Publishing House, 1964. 15 p.

6534 Scopino, Aldorigo Joseph, 1947-
"Seth Cook Rees: perfectionist preacher; the Rhode Island years, 1890-1896." Unpublished student paper, Brown University, 1972. 32ℓ.

6535 REHFELDT, Remiss (1915-).
CN, CBC. Pastor, evangelist, district supt., denominational official, general presiding officer

6536 REID, Alex J. NVFML (1936), 145-158.
ME, S. Missionary

6537 REID, Isaiah (1836-1911).
Member, IowaHA
Member, NHA
Attended GHA, 1885 (Chicago)
Attended GHA, 1901 (Chicago)
Pres., CG (IHP), CN, PCN. Pastor, publisher, editor, evangelist

Part VI. Biography

6538 REID, Pearl. SBWTL (1960), 205.
FM. Nurse, missionary
b. 19??, Kingston, Ont.

6539 REILEY, J. McKendree. PPE (1868), 160-166.
ME. Pastor

6540 REISDORPH, Rufus Deland (1896-   ). RLOA (1941-1942), 920.
WM. Conf. pres., denominational official, editor
b. Sept. 1896, Leola, S.D.

6541 RENNELLS, Charles Stephen (1873-1962).
WM. Pastor
6542 Rennels, Charles Stephen, 1873-1962.
"Papers, 1852-1958." 60 items and 2 v. In University of Michigan, Michigan Historical Collections.
Personal papers and miscellanea collected by Rennells on Wesleyan Methodist churches in Michigan; ms. of his History of the Michigan Conference, Wesleyan Methodist Church of America (1940); a history of the Rennells family; a photograph album; and sermon records.

6543 REYNOLDS, Alfred (1903-1937). TDOOP (1968), 229.
PHC. Missionary
d. Mar. 8, 1937, N. Rhodesia

6544 REYNOLDS, E. E. (1862?-1930).
Member, Vermont HA
Endorsed call, GHA, 1901 (Chicago)
ME, PCN, ME. Pastor, evangelist
d. June 16, 1930, St. Petersburg, Fla.

6545 REYNOLDS, Eleanor Margaret Ann Morrow. ETWF (196?).
PHC. Missionary

6546 REYNOLDS, Hiram Farnham (1854-1938). MOUS (1941), 16-22. N.Y. Times (July 14, 1938), 21:5.
Member, Vermont HA
ME, APCA, CN. Pastor, evangelist, denominational official, general supt.
b. May 12, 1854, Lyons, Ill.
d. July 13, 1938, Wollaston, Mass.
6547 Hinshaw, Amy N.
In labors abundant; a biography of H.F. Reynolds, D.D. Kansas City, Mo., Nazarene Publishing House, 1938. 287 p.
6548 Lunn, Mervel
Hiram F. Reynolds: Mr. World Missionary. Kansas City, Mo., Nazarene Publishing House, 1968. 64 p.

6549   McGraw, James, 1913-
         "The preaching of Hiram F. Reynolds," Preacher's Magazine, XXIX (Apr. 1954), 3-5.

6550   REYNOLDS, Paul David (1928-   ). ETWF (196?).
         PHC. Pastor, evangelist, Bible school teacher, missionary
         b. Aug. 21, 1928, Oshkosh, Neb.

6551   REYNOLDS, William Henry (1880-1963). ETWF (196?).
         PHC. Missionary
         b. Jan. 16, 1880, Kimberly, Cape Province, Union of South Africa
         d. Nov. 27, 1963.

6552   REYNOLDS, Wilma Lucille Waggoner (1927-   ). ETWF (196?).
         PHC. Evangelistic singer, missionary
         b. July 12, 1927, Daviess County, Ind.

6553   RICE, Edward Ordello. WIWBA (1946), 209-211.
         ME? Lay leader, businessman
6554   Rowley, Charles E.
         Apples of gold. Findlay, Ohio, C.E. Rowley, 1925. 257 p.

6555   RICE, James Silas (-1942). LLITW (1951), 217.
         FM. Missionary

6556   RICE, Paul (1951-1968).
         CN. Student
         d. Aug. 16, 1968, Kansas City, Mo.
6557   Rice, George
         Facing the dawn; the Paul Rice story. Kansas City, Mo., Pedestal Press, 1970. 48 p.

6558   RICE, Squire (-1911).
         Endorsed call and attended, GHA, 1901 (Chicago)
         WM, PU. Evangelist, rescue mission supt., editor
         d. 1911, Seattle, Wash.

6559   RICE, W. S.
         CG (UHP), CN, PCN, CN. Pastor, evangelist

6560   RICHMAN, C. J. PPE (1868), 324-325.
         ME. Pastor

6561   RICKER, William A.
         Attended HConf., 1877 (Cincinnati)
         ME. Pastor

6562 RICKMAN, Claude R. (1917-). WWACUA (1970-1971), 444.
WM, W. College dean, college pres.
b. Nov. 10, 1917, Brevard, N.C.

6563 RIDGAWAY, Henry Bascom (1830-1895). SCM (1881), 757.
WWW in Am. (1607-1896), 443.
ME. Pastor
b. Sept. 7, 1830, Talbot County, Md.
d. Mar. 30, 1895, Evanston, Ill.

6564 Funeral service, held Tuesday, April 2nd, A.D. 1895, at the First Methodist Church, Evanston, Ill., over the remains of the late H.B. Ridgaway ... President of the Garrett Biblical Institute.... n.p., 1895? 23ℓ.

6565 RIDOUT, George Whitefield (1870-1954). SFLF (1950), 98-102. N.Y. Times (Mar. 20, 1954), 15:5.
Endorsed call and attended GHA, 1901 (Chicago)
Pastor, evangelist, college prof., military chaplain, missionary, author
b. Apr. 1, 1870, Bonne Bay, St. Johns, N.F.
d. Mar. 19, 1954, Philadelphia, Pa.

6566 Ridout, George Whitefield, 1870-1954.
The cross and the flag; experiences in the great World War. Louisville, Pentecostal Publishing Co., c1919. 175 p.

6567 RIES, Claude Arden (1893-). DAS (1969), IV, 307. GIIH (1962), 190-206.
WM, W. Pastor, college prof., college admin.
b. Sept. 13, 1893, Akron, Ohio

6568 RIGGLE, Herbert McClellan (1872-). RLOA (1941-1942), 927-928. SHBD (1955), 76-99.
Luth., WM-MBIC, CG (A). Pastor, evangelist, missionary
b. Feb. 18, 1872, Cochran's Mills, Pa.

6569 Riggle, Herbert McClellan, 1872-
Pioneer evangelism; or, Experiences and observations at home and abroad. Anderson, Ind., Gospel Trumpet Co., 1924. 351 p.

6570 RIGGS, Albert B.
ME, APCA, CN. Pastor, district supt.

6571 RILEY, John Eckel (1909-). WW in Am. (1968-1969), 1832. WWACUA (1970-1971), 445-446. GIIH (1962), 90-104. MHP (1957), 75-82.
CN. Pastor, college pres.
b. Jan. 23, 1909, Haverhill, Mass.

6572 RILEY, William E.
APCA, CN. Pastor, district supt.

6573 RIPPER, Carl Harold (1905-). WW in Am. (1964-1965), 1685. WW in Am. (1968-1969), 1834. WW in Am. (1972-1973), II, 2656.
PHC, CN. Pastor, college prof., college dean
b. June 14, 1905, Denver, Colo.

6574 RITTER, L. H. (1878-). FHOP (1964).
ME, S; CN. Pastor
b. 1878, LaMar County, Ala.

6575 RIXSE, Eva. FHOP (1964).
ME, CN. Missionary
b. 18??, Oklahoma Territory?

6576 ROBERTS, Arthur Owen (1923-). WWACUA (1970-1971), 448.
Fr. Pastor, college prof., college dean
b. Jan. 7, 1923, Caldwell, Ida.

6577 ROBERTS, Benjamin Titus (1823-1893). BMW (1960), 13-46. DAB. WWW in Am. (1607-1896), 446. MWWW in Ch. Hist. (1968), 351-352.
Attended GHA, 1885 (Chicago)
ME, FM. Pastor, editor, general supt.
b. July 25, 1823, Gowanda, N.Y.
d. Feb. 27, 1893, Cattaraugus, N.Y.
6578 Roberts, Benjamin Titus, 1823-1893.
First lessons on money. Rochester, N.Y., 1886. 160 p.
6579 Roberts, Benson Howard, 1853-1930.
Benjamin Titus Roberts, late general superintendent of the Free Methodist Church, a biography by his son. North Chili, N.Y., The Earnest Christian, 1900. vi, 570 p.
6580 Roberts, Esther M.
The bishop and his lady. Winona Lake, Ind., Light and Life Press, 1962. 104 p.
6581 Zahniser, Clarence Howard, 1902-
Earnest Christian; life and works of Benjamin Titus Roberts. Circleville, Ohio, Advocate Publishing House, 1957. 349 p.
6582 Zahniser, Clarence Howard, 1902-
"The life and works of Benjamin Titus Roberts."
Unpublished Ph.D. dissertation, University of Pittsburgh, 1951.

6583 ROBERTS, Benson Howard (1853-1930). WW in Am. Meth. (1916), 185. WWW in Am. (1897-1942), 1039. N.Y. Times (Mar. 4, 1930), 27:2.

Part VI. Biography

    Endorsed call and attended, GHA, 1901 (Chicago)
    FM, Pres. Editor, private school principal
    b. Oct. 9, 1853, Brockport, N.Y.
    d. Mar. 2, 1930, Catonsville, Md.

6584 ROBERTS, Florence
    CG (A). Rescue mission worker
6585   Roberts, Florence
    Fifteen years with the outcast. Anderson, Ind., Gospel Trumpet Co., 1912. 472 p.

6586 ROBERTS, George C. M. (1806-1870). SCM (1881), 759. PPE (1868), 175-178.
    Member, NHA
    ME. Local preacher, physician, military chaplain
    d. Jan. 15, 1870

6587 ROBERTS, Oral (1918-).
    PeHC, UM. Pastor, evangelist
    b. Jan. 24, 1918, near Ada, Okla.
6588   Roberts, Oral, 1918-
    The call, an autobiography. Garden City, N.Y., Doubleday, 1972. 216 p.
6589   Roberts, Oral, 1918-
    Oral Roberts' Life story as told by himself. Illustrations by Eloise Gray. Tulsa, Okla., Oral Roberts, c1952. 160 p.
6590   Roberts, Oral, 1918-
    My story. Tulsa, Okla., Summit Book Co., 1961. 213 p.
    Autobiography
6591   Roberts, Oral, 1918-
    My twenty years of a miracle ministry. Tulsa?, Okla., 1967. 96 p.

6592 ROBINSON, Charles. NP (1925), 135-141.
    CN. Evangelist

6593 ROBINSON, Reuben (1860-1942). COPN (1958), 44-49. MLA (1935), 13-19. N.Y. Times (Nov. 4, 1942), 24:2. NP (1925), 5-20.
    Endorsed call, GHA, 1901 (Chicago)
    ME, S; SA; ME; CN. Evangelist
    b. Jan. 27, 1860, White County, Tenn.
    d. Nov. 2, 1942, Pasadena, Calif.
6594   Robinson, Reuben, 1860-1942.
    Bud Robinson's Religion, philosophy and fun. Kansas City, Mo., Beacon Hill Press, 1942. 48 p.
6595   Robinson, Reuben, 1860-1942.
    My hospital experience, by Bud Robinson. Louisville Ky., Herald Press, 1919? 35 p.

6596 Robinson, Reuben, 1860-1942.
[My hospital experience].
Uncle Bud Robinson's hospital experience; introduced by Dr. D.I. Vanderpool. Kansas City, Mo., Beacon Hill Records, 196?. 2 sides 33 rpm (L-114)

6597 Robinson, Reuben, 1860-1942.
My travels in the Holy Land, by Bud Robinson. Louisville, Ky., Herald Press, 1934? 36 p.

6598 Robinson, Reuben, 1860-1942.
Sunshine and smiles: life story, flash lights, sayings and sermons, by Bud Robinson. 2d ed. Chicago, Christian Witness Co., 1903. 191 p.
Autobiography.

6599 Chapman, James Blaine, 1884-1947.
Bud Robinson, a brother beloved. Kansas City, Missouri, Beacon Hill Press, 1943. 200 p.

6600 Corbett, C. T.
Bud Robinson: stories, sketch. Garden City, Kan., Lloyd Jackson Co., 1957. 32 p.

6601 Corbett, C. T.
"Bud Robinson stories and life sketch." Noblesville, Ind., J. Edwin Newby, 1970, c1957. 31 p.
First published in 1957 under title: Bud Robinson: stories, sketch.

6602 McGraw, James, 1913-
"The preaching of Bud Robinson," Preacher's Magazine, XXIX (Jan. 1954), 9-12.

6603 Miller, Basil William, 1897-
Bud Robinson, miracle of grace. Kansas City, Mo., Beacon Hill Press, 1947. 207 p.

6604 Wise, George C.
Rev. Bud Robinson. Louisville, Ky., Pentecostal Publishing Co., 1946. 96 p.

6605 ROBY, Eva Carpenter (1880-). FHOP (1964).
PM, CN. Missionary, pastor's wife
b. June 28, 1880, Davidson County, Tenn.

6606 ROBY, John L. (-1958). FHOP (1964).
PM, CN. Pastor
d. Aug. 10, 1958, Miami, Fla.?

6607 ROGERS, Dennis (1858-).
HC, HChuC, CN. Pastor, evangelist, editor
b. Mar. 21, 1858, northern Texas

6608 Rogers, Dennis, 1858-
Holiness pioneering in the Southland. Hemet, Calif., 1944. 36 p.

6609 ROMERO, Ignacio (19??-1952). RWBTB (1953), 55-57.
CN. Pastor
b. 19??, Deming, N.Mex.
d. June 22, 1952, Pasadena, Calif.

Part VI. Biography

6610 ROOT, Helen Isabel (1873-1945). LLITW (1951), 217.
RLOA (1941-1942), 939.
Am. Bd. Com. For. Mis., FM. Missionary, denominational official
b. Apr. 13, 1873, Port Byron, N.Y.
6611 Tapper, Ruth M.
The full years; the life story of Helen I. Root. Winona Lake, Ind., Young People's Missionary Society, 1948. 96 p.

6612 ROSA, Maria de la. HNTB (1934), 140-142.
R. Cath., CN. National worker, pastor's wife

6613 ROSA, Pablo de la. HNTB (1934), 140-142.
R. Cath., CN. National worker, colporteur, pastor

6614 ROSALES, D. Enrique (1910-). RWBTB (1953), 46-51.
R. Cath., CN. Insurance agent, pastor, district supt.
b. Nov. 30, 1910, Esperanza, Coahuila, Mex.

6615 ROSE, Alvin C. MAWACOSM (1925), 321.
ME. Pastor, evangelist, gospel music arranger

6616 ROSE, Delbert Roy (1912-). DAS (1969), IV, 313. GIIH (1962), 106-128. GTWATD (1965), 126-136.
EUB, UM. College prof., pastor, evangelist, seminary admin., seminary prof.
b. Sept. 17, 1912, Corunna, Mich.

6617 ROSE, Olin Ward (1863-1940).
ME, PCN, ME. Pastor
b. July 7, 1863, Caroline, N.Y.
d. June 3, 1940, Redlands, Calif.

6618 ROSE, William Brewster (1849-1926).
Attended GHA, 1901 (Chicago)
FM. Pastor?, publisher

6619 ROTHWELL, Mel-Thomas (1905-). DAS (1969), IV, 315.
PHC, CN. Evangelist, Bible college prof., college prof.
b. June 24, 1905, Port Huron, Mich.

6620 ROWLAND, Charles W. SCM (1881), 768.
Attended HConf., 1877 (Cincinnati)
ME. Lay leader, manufacturer

6621 ROWLEY, Charles E.
ME. Evangelist, editor
6622 Rowley, Charles E.
Apples of gold. Finley, Ohio, C.E. Rowley, 1925. 257 p.
Autobiography.

6623   RUNDELL, Emma Mitchell (1919-   ). ETWF (196?).
        PHC. Bible school admin., missionary
        b. Nov. 2, 1919, Carlisle, Ky.

6624   RUNDELL, Merton Russell (1923-   ). ETWF (196?).
        PHC. Bible school admin., missionary
        b. Nov. 13, 1923, Austin, Tex.

6625   RUTH, Christian Wismer (1865-1941). COPN (1958), 26-32.
            N.Y. Times (May 28, 1941), 25:5.
        Endorsed call and attended GHA, 1901 (Chicago)
        HCC, IAHUPL, CN. Evangelist
        b. Sept. 1, 1865, Bucks County, Pa.
        d. May 27, 1941, Wilmore, Ky.
6626   Ruth, Christian Wismer, 1865-1941.
            Entire sanctification, a second blessing; together with life sketch, Bible readings and sermon outlines. Chicago and Boston, Christian Witness Co., 1903. 192 p.
6627   [Ruth, Laura]
            Short sketches from the life of Rev. and Mrs. C.W. Ruth. Louisville, Ky., Pentecostal Publishing Co., n.d. 31 p.

6628   RUTHERFORD, Eliza J. HWP (1905), 65-67.
        MP. Evangelist

6629   RYDING, I. S. W. (-1956). SBWTL (1960), 203.
        FM. Missionary
        b. 18??, Manchester, Eng.

6630   RYFF, Ethel Davey (1887-1949). LLITW (1951), 217.
            SBWTL (1960), 204.
        FM. Teacher, pastor, missionary
        b. 1887, Verona (Oak Flats), Ont.

6631   RYFF, Jules. LLITW (1951), 199.
        FM. Missionary

6632   RYFF, Lilla Eva (-1920). LLITW (1951), 199.
        FM. Missionary

6633   SABIN, Benjamin (1790-   ). PPE (1868), 142-144.
        ME. Pastor
        b. Mar. 1, 1790, Thompson, Windham County, Conn.

6634   SAGE, Charles H. (1825-1908). SBWTL (1960), 179-180.
        ME, FM. Blacksmith, farmer, pastor, district chairman
        b. 1825, New York

6635   SALVE, S. Y. (1892-   ). HNTB (1934), 79-82.
        CN. National worker, pastor
        b. 1892, India

6636 SAMUDRA, Joseph. HNTB (1934), 104.
     CMA, CN. National worker
     b. 19??, India

6637 SAN JOSE, Vicente. HNTB (1934), 138-140.
     R. Cath., PM, PCN, CN. National worker, pastor
     b. 18??, San Jeronimo, Guatemala

6638 SANNER, Asa Everette (1890-). COPN (1958), 103-108.
        FHOP (1964). RLOA (1941-1942), 952. WW in
        Calif. (1942-1943), 800-801.
     CG (UHP), CN. Evangelist, pastor, college prof.,
        district supt., missionary retirement home supt.
     b. Feb. 13, 1890, Macon, Mo.

6639 SANTIN, Vicente G (1870-1948). HNTB (1934), 171-174.
        RWBTB (1953), 13-18.
     ME, S; PCN; CN. Pastor, district supt.
     b. July 19, 1870, Toluca, near Mexico City, Mex.
     d. Feb. 4, 1948, Mexico City, Mex.

6640 SARIAN, Nerses S. (1886-1964).
     JEB?
6641   Sarian, Nerses S., 1886-1964.
     I shall not die; a tribute to the faithfulness of God;
     introd. by Eric W. Gosden. London, Oliphants, 1967.
     176 p.

6642 SAUNDERS, Dallas Roy (1912-). ETWF (196?).
     PHC. Pastor, missionary
     b. Aug. 21, 1912, Troy, N.C.

6643 SAUNDERS, Vivian Taylor (1914-). ETWF (196?).
     PHC. Pastor's wife, missionary
     b. June 30, 1914, Hagerstown, Ind.

6644 SAWYER, Robert Leonard (1922-). DAS (1969), IV, 322.
     CN. Pastor, college prof.
     b. July 16, 1922, Akron, Ohio

6645 SAXON, John Davis (1893-1956?).
     Cong., CN. Pastor, college field rep., district supt.
     b. Oct. 20, 1893, Houston, Miss.
     d. 1956?, Merigold, Miss.
6646   "The preaching of John D. Saxon," Preacher's Magazine, XXXVI (Nov. 1961), 12-14.

6647 SAYES, James Ottis (1922-). DAS (1969), IV, 322. LIE
     (1971), 835.
     CN. Pastor, college prof.
     b. Nov. 16, 1922, Hudson, La.

6648 SCARLETT, John (1803-1889). PPE (1868), 179-182.
ME. Pastor
6649 Scarlett, John, 1803-1889.
Almond, a true story; in five parts. Orange, N.J., The author, 1883. 106 p.
Introduction signed: N. Vansant.
Author's autobiography in verse.
6650 Scarlett, John, 1803-1889.
The itinerant on foot; or, Life-scenes recalled, with an introd. by Rev. George Hughes.... New York, W.C. Palmer, 1882. 256 p.
6651 Scarlett, John, 1803-1889.
The life and experience of a converted infidel. New York, Carlton & Phillips, 1854. 274 p.
Autobiography.

6652 SCHAFFER, Jacob (-1937). LLITW (1951), 217.
FM. Missionary

6653 SCHIRMER, William C.
Attended GHA, 1901 (Chicago)
ME? Layman, physician

6654 SCHLOSSER, George Donald (-1936). LLITW (1951), 217.
FM. Missionary

6655 SCHMELZENBACH, Harmon Faldine (1882-1929). MHTWW (n.d.), 18-20.
R. Cath., PCN, CN. Missionary
b. 1882, Archers Fork, Ohio
d. May 22, 1929, Pigg's Peak, Swaziland, S.Afr.
6656 Schmelzenbach, Harmon Faldine, III
Schmelzenbach of Africa; the story of Harmon F. Schmelzenbach, missionary pioneer to Swaziland, South Africa. Kansas City, Mo., Nazarene Publishing House, 1971. 103 p.
6657 Schmelzenbach, Lula
The missionary prospector; a life story of Harmon Schmelzenbach, missionary to South Africa. Kansas City, Mo., Beacon Hill Press, 194?. 205 p.

6658 SCHOCKE, Albert J. FHOP (1964).
SA, CN. Pastor

6659 SCHOCKE, Hazel M. FHOP (1964).
SA, CN. Pastor's wife

6660 SCHOENHALS, Lawrence R. (1912-). WWACUA (1970-1971), 471.
FM. College prof., college admin., college pres.
b. Mar. 24, 1912, Brown City, Mich.

Part VI. Biography

6661 SCHUH, Charles Gottlob (1856-).
 Attended GHA, 1901 (Chicago)
 ME? Evangelist
6662 Schuh, Charles Gottlob, 1856- , ed.
 Deutsch-englisches handbuch über Chicago und die weltausstellung.... Chicago, 1893. 34 p.

6663 SCHURMAN, Wenford G. (1871-1932). COPN (1958), 38-43. FYAB (1954), 94-95. NP (1925), 202-208.
 APCA, CN. Pastor, district supt.
 b. Aug. 14, 1871, Arcadia Mines, N.S.
 d. Aug. 16, 1932, Chicago, Ill.
6664 Ludwig, Sylvester Theodore, 1903-1964.
 "The preaching of W.G. Schurman," Preacher's Magazine, XXXIII (Sept. 1958), 7-10.

6665 SCHWAB, Bertha Goss. FHOP (1964).
 MB, CN. Asst. pastor
 b. 18??, Indianapolis, Ind.

6666 SCHWAB, Otho. MLA (1935), 75-77.
 CN. Pastor, evangelist

6667 SCOFIELD, Florence R. Myers. LLITW (1951), 217.
 FM. Missionary

6668 SCOFIELD, George H. LLITW (1951), 217.
 FM. Missionary

6669 SCOTT, David E.
 PM, PCN, ME. Pastor

6670 SCOTT, Janice Delores (1934-). ETWF (196?).
 PHC. Missionary
 b. Aug. 26, 1934, Albemarle, N.C.

6671 SCOTT, Orange (1800-1847). SCM (1881), 791. WWW in Am. (1607-1896), 470. DAB. MAWACOSM (1925), 331-332.
 ME, WM. Pastor, presiding elder, editor
 b. Feb. 13, 1800, Brookfield, Vt.
 d. July 31, 1847, Newark, N.J.
6672 Matlack, Lucius Columbus, 1816-1883.
 The life of Rev. Orange Scott, comp. from his personal narrative, correspondence, and other authentic sources of information. New York, C. Prindle and L. C. Matlack at the Wesleyan Methodist Book Room, 1847-1848. 2 pts. in 1 v. (307 p.)

6673 SCOTT, Peter Cameron (1867-1897).
 DH

6674   Whittemore, Emma (Mott), 1850-1931.
              Promoted!; or, A brief life sketch of P. Cameron
          Scott. New York, Door of Hope Publishing House,
          1897. 125 p.

6675   SEARS, Angeline Brooks (1817-1848). SCM (1881), 792.
              ME. Pastor's wife
              b. Sept. 20, 1817, Cincinnati, Ohio
              d. Dec. 16, 1848, Ohio?
6676   Hamline, Melinda Truesdell
              Memoirs of Mrs. Angeline B. Sears, with extracts
          from her correspondence. Cincinnati, Swormstedt and
          Power, for the Methodist Episcopal Church, 1850.
          294 p.
6677   Hamline, Melinda Truesdell
              Memoirs of Mrs. Angeline B. Sears, with extracts
          from her correspondence. Cincinnati, Swormstedt &
          Poe, 1854. 294 p.

6678   SEBREE, Herbert T. GTWATD (1965), 334-351.
              FM. Pastor, conference supt.

6679   SEE, Isaac M. PPE (1868), 132-136.
              Dutch Ref. Pastor

6680   SELLE, Robert L. (1865-1929).
              Attended GHA, 1901 (Chicago)
              ME. Pastor, presiding elder
              b. Jan. 30, 1865, Stanley Co., N.C.
              d. Sept. 2, 1929, Rogers, Ark.
6681   Selle, Robert L., 1865-1929.
              Apples of gold in pictures of silver. Louisville, Ky.,
          Pentecostal Publishing Co., 1917. 266 p.
              Poems.

6682   SELLECK, Harold A. SCC (1947), 111-115.
              Fr. Pastor
              b. 190?, Emporia, Kan.

6683   SELLEW, Walter Ashbel (1844-1929). BMW (1960), 147-
          163. WWW in Am. (1897-1942), 1103. WW in Am.
          Meth. (1916), 196-197.
              FM. Pastor, presiding elder, bishop
              b. Feb. 27, 1844, Gowanda, N.Y.
              d. Jan. 16, 1929

6684   SENSENSEY, J. H.
              Member, NHA
              ME

6685   SHANNON, Ernest Boyd (1911-1968). AMS (1965-1968),
          VIII, 1445.

Part VI. Biography

        CN. Chemist, college prof., college admin.
        b. July 17, 1911, Morgan County, Tenn.
        d. Mar. 12, 1968, Pasadena, Calif.

6686   SHANTZ, Ward M. GIIH (1962), 130-142.
        UMC, MC. Pastor, Bible college pres., district supt.

6687   SHARP, B. S. PPE (1868), 190-192.
        ME. Pastor

6688   SHARPE, George (1865-1948).
        ME, Cong. (Scot.), PCS, PCN, CN. Pastor, evangelist, district supt., missionary supt.
        b. Apr. 17, 1865, Graigneuk, Lanarkshire, Scot.
        d. Mar. 26, 1948, Glasgow, Scot.
6689   Sharpe, George, 1865-1948.
        This is my story. Glasgow, Messenger Publishing Co., 1948. 142 p.
        Autobiography.
6690   Ford, Jack, 1908-
        In the steps of John Wesley; the Church of the Nazarene in Britain. Kansas City, Mo., Printed by Nazarene Publishing House, 1968. 300 p.
        Thesis (Ph.D.)--University of London, 1967.
        Account of activities of George Sharpe: p. 35-74.
6691   Frame, George
        "The preaching of George Sharpe," Preacher's Magazine, XXXIII (July 1958), 8-11.

6692   SHATTUCK, Burdette O. (-1958).
        IAHC, IHC, PHC. Pastor
        d. Oct. 20, 1958

6693   SHAVER, Charles
        CN. Evangelist, seminary prof.

6694   SHAW, Solomon Benjamin (1854-). SCUH (1962), 28, 33-35, 153.
        President, MichiganHA
        Signed call and attended, GHA, 1885 (Chicago)
        Attended GHA, 1901 (Chicago)
        ME, WM, FM, PrimHM. Pastor, evangelist, editor, publisher

6695   SHEA, George Beverly (1909-).
        WM, I. Evangelistic singer
        b. Feb. 1, 1909, Winchester, Ont., Can.
6696   Shea, George Beverly, 1909-
        Songs that lift the heart; a personal story by George Beverly Shea with Fred Bauer. Old Tappan, N.J., Fleming H. Revell Co., 1972. 125 p.
        Autobiography.

6697   Shea, George Beverly, 1909-
        Then sings my soul, [by] George Beverly Shea with Fred Bauer. Old Tappan, N.J., Fleming H. Revell Co., 1968. 176 p.
        Autobiography.

6698   SHEARER, Daniel Clyde (1878?-1940).
        IHC, PHC. Pastor, Bible school teacher, district supt.
        b. 1878?
        d. Feb. 16, 1940, Marion, Ohio

6699   SHEEKS, Mrs. E. J. SCUH (1962), 153, 155, 157, 174, 176, 214-215. HWP (1905), 84-89.
        ME, S; NTCOC; HChuC; PCN; CN. Pastor, evangelist, rescue mission worker, rescue home worker

6700   SHEEKS, Edwin H. (1839-1935). SCUH (1962), 153, 155, 157, 170, 172, 174, 176, 214-215, 254.
        ME, S; NTCOC; HChuC; PCN; CN. Lay leader, merchant, traveling salesman
        b. Oct. 21, 1839, Lebanon, Ind.
        d. Dec. 30, 1935, Hutchinson, Kan.

6701   SHEETS, Harold Kenneth (1903-   ). WW in the Midwest (1965-1966), 874.
        WM, W. Pastor, denominational official, general supt.
        b. Mar. 29, 1903, Detroit, Kan.

6702   SHEFFER, B. F.
        ME, S; ME; PCN; CN. Pastor, district supt.

6703   SHELDON, Henry Olcott (1799-1882).
        Attended HConf., 1877 (Cincinnati)
        ME. Pastor
        d. Dec. 21, 1882

6704   Sheldon, Henry Olcott, 1799-1882.
        The Sheldon magazine; or, A genealogical list of the Sheldons in America, with biographical and historical notices of other families with which this intermarried.... Loudonville, Ohio, 1855-1857. 113 p.

6705   SHELHAMER, Elmer Ellsworth (1869-1947).
        FM. Pastor, district elder, evangelist, missionary, editor
        b. Dec. 16, 1869, Mateer, Armstrong County, Pa.
        d. Jan. 21, 1947, Joplin, Mo.

6706   Shelhamer, Elmer Ellsworth, 1869-1947.
        Heart searching sermons and sayings. Atlanta, Repairer Publishing Co., 1917. 320 p.

6707   Shelhamer, Elmer Ellsworth, 1869-1947.
        How we escaped, by Rev. E.E. Shelhamer and wife.

Part VI. Biography

Cincinnati, God's Revivalist Office, n.d. 30 p.
6708 Shelhamer, Elmer Ellsworth, 1869-1947.
Plain preaching for practical people. Cincinnati, God's Bible School and Revivalist, 1929. 287 p.
Includes "A bit of my experience."
6709 Shelhamer, Elmer Ellsworth, 1869-1947.
Sixty years of thorns and roses. Cincinnati, God's Bible School and Missionary Training Home, 1930. 224 p.
Autobiography.
6710 Shelhamer, Elmer Ellsworth, 1869-1947.
Sixty years of thorns and roses. Noblesville, Ind., Newby Book Room; Cincinnati, God's Bible School Bookroom, 1969. 224 p.
Reprint of 1930 ed.
Autobiography.
6711 Shelhamer, Elmer Ellsworth, 1869-1947.
A Spartan evangel; life story of E.E. Shelhamer, as told by himself and wife. Winona Lake, Ind., Light and Life Press, 1951. 236 p.
6712 Shelhamer, Elmer Ellsworth, 1869-1947.
The ups and downs of a pioneer preacher; also, Some of my mistakes and what they taught me. Atlanta, Repairer Pub. Co., 1915. 272 p.

6713 SHELHAMER, Julia Arnold
FM. Evangelist
6714 Shelhamer, Elmer Ellsworth, 1869-1947.
How we escaped, by Rev. E.E. Shelhamer and wife. Cincinnati, God's Revivalist Office, n.d. 30 p.
6715 Shelhamer, Julia (Arnold)
Trials and triumphs of a minister's wife. Atlanta, Repairer Publishing Co., 1923. 223 p.

6716 SHELHAMER, Minnie Baldwin (-1902). MMAWODP (1920), 398-411.
FM, PB. Evangelist
d. Mar. 28, 1902, Atlanta, Ga.

6717 SHEMELD, Catherine. LLITW (1951), 217.
FM. Missionary

6718 SHEMELD, Robert R. LLITW (1951), 217.
FM. Missionary

6719 SHEPARD, William Edward (1862-).
Attended GHA, 1901 (Chicago)
ME, CN, PCN, MetCA?, CN? Evangelist
6720 Shepard, William Edward, 1862-
Fads, fakes, freaks, frauds and fools. Anderson, Ind., Published for the author by the Commercial Service Co., 1923. 420 p.

6721 Shepard, William Edward, 1862-
Nuts to crack; or, Mental gymnastics; practical problems for mental training and entertainment. Pasadena, Calif., The Arts Press, c1930. 87 p.

6722 SHERMAN, Charles W.
Attended WUHC, 1880 (Jacksonville, Ill.)
Attended GHA, 1885 (Chicago)
VanM, NTCOC. Rescue mission supt., evangelist, editor

6723 SHILLING, Henry (1902-   ).
ME, M, UM. Pastor, Bible school founder and pres.
b. 1902, New Bethlehem, Pa.

6724 SHINGLER, T. J.
ME, S?; I; HChuC; PCN; CN. Pastor, businessman, Bible school founder

6725 SHIPLEY, David Clark (1907-   ). DAS (1969), IV, 335-336.
M, UM. Univ. prof., seminary prof.
b. Mar. 6, 1907, McKeesport, Pa.

6726 SHIPPS, Howard Fenimore (1903-   ). DAS (1969), IV, 336.
ME?, M?, UM?. Pastor?, seminary prof.
b. May 7, 1903, Delanco, N.J.

6727 SHONGWE, Kelina. HNTB (1934), 115-116.
CN. National worker, nurse
b. 19??, Swaziland, S.Afr.

6728 SHORT, James Wiley (1880-1967). COPN (1958), 67-72.
CN. Pastor, district supt.
b. June 9, 1880, Greensboro, N.C.
d. 1967, Greenfield, Ind.

6729 SHORT, John N. (1841-1922). MOUS (1941), 36-42. PPE (1868), 338-339. DC (1965, c1887), 192-206.
Member, NHA
ME, APCA, PCN, CN. Pastor, evangelist
b. Sept. 24, 1841, Middlefield, Mass.
d. Apr. 12, 1922, Cambridge, Mass.
6730 Gould, Joseph Glenn, 1896-
"The preaching of John N. Short (a personal appraisal)," Preacher's Magazine, XXXIII (Oct. 1958), 6-8.

6731 SHOWERMAN, R. E.
Attended GHA, 1901 (Chicago)
SA? Officer

Part VI. Biography

6732 SHULER, Robert Pierce (1880-). RLOA (1941-1942), 986.
SCC (1947), 116-118. PP in Am. Meth. (1945), 328.
WW in Am. Meth. (1952), 616-617. WW in the
Clergy (1935-1936), 1029-1030.
ME, S; M. Pastor, editor
b. Aug. 4, 1880, Grayson Co., Va.

6733 SIBREL, Joseph H. (-1957).
IHC, PHC. Pastor
d. Dec. 4, 1957

6734 SILSBEE, R. N. PPE (1868), 317-320.
ME. Pastor

6735 SIMMONS, Ichabod (1831-1898).
Member, NHA
Attended HConf., 1877 (New York)
ME. Pastor, evangelist
d. Apr. 14, 1898

6736 SIMPSON, Albert Benjamin (1843-1919). DAB. WWW in
Am. (1897-1942), 1128. N.Y. Times (Oct. 30,
1919), 13:3. MWWW in Ch. Hist. (1968), 374.
Pres., CMA. Pastor, editor, general supt.
b. Dec. 15, 1843, Bayview, P.E.I., Can.
d. Oct. 29, 1919, Nyack, N.Y.
6737 Simpson, Albert Benjamin, 1843-1919.
Larger outlooks on missionary lands; descriptive
sketches of a missionary journey through Egypt, Palestine, India, Burmah, Malaysia, China, Japan and the
Sandwich Islands. New York, Christian Alliance Publishing Co., c1893. 595 p.
6738 Thompson, Albert Edward, 1870-
The life of A.B. Simpson, with special chapters by
Paul Rader, James M. Gray, J. Gregory Mantle, R.H.
Glover, Kenneth Mackenzie, F.H. Senft and W.M. Turnbull. Brooklyn, N.Y., Christian Alliance Publishing
Co., 1920. 300 p.
6739 Tozer, Aiden Wilson, 1897-
Wingspread; Albert B. Simpson, a study in spiritual
altitude. Centenary ed. Harrisburg, Pa., Christian
Publications, 1943. 143 p.

6740 SIMPSON, Matthew (1811-1884). DAB. PFT (n.d.), 63-64.
SCM (1881), 801. WWW in Am. (1607-1896), 484.
N.Y. Times (June 19, 1884), 4:7. MWWW in Ch.
Hist. (1968), 374-375.
Member, NHA
ME. Pastor, college pres., editor, bishop
b. June 21, 1811, Cadiz, Ohio
d. June 18, 1884, Philadelphia, Pa.

6741 Clark, Robert Donald, 1910-
 The life of Matthew Simpson. New York, Macmillan, 1956. 344 p.
6742 Crooks, George Richard, 1822-1897.
 The life of Bishop Matthew Simpson of the Methodist Episcopal Church. New York, Harper, 1890. 512 p.

6743 SIMS, Albert (1851-). SBWTL (1960), 181-182.
 PrimM, FM. Pastor, traveling chairman, writer, editor
 b. Sept. 26, 1851, Stroud, Gloucestershire, Eng.
6744 Sims, Albert, 1851-
 Yet not I; or, A brief sketch of the early life, conversion, call to the ministry, and some of the subsequent labors in the Master's vineyard of A. Sims. Toronto, 19??. 89 p.
 "Published and for sale ... at the office of 'The Lamp of Life'."

6745 SLATER, Charles Livingstone (1884-1950).
 IAHU, IAHC, IHC, PHC. Missionary, pastor, evangelist
 b. 1884, Afton, Iowa
 d. May 24, 1950, Orange Free State, S. Africa
6746 Finch, Ralph Goodrich, 1881-1949.
 Campaigning for God in southern waters, by Ralph G. Finch and Charles L. Slater. Louisville, Pentecostal Publishing Co., 1923.
6747 Slater, Maude E., 1883-1973.
 Missionary evangelist; a biography of Charles L. Slater. n.p., 1951. 163 p.
6748 Slater, Maude E., 1883-1973.
 Safe in the midst of submarines; thrilling experiences during the World War. n.p., n.d.

6749 SLATER, Flora Belle (1906-). ETHF (196?).
 PHC, W. Missionary
 b. Jan. 31, 1906, Monroe, Wash.

6750 SLOAT, L. Russell. SWGHW (1948), 43, 66-67, 78.
 MBIC. Missionary

6751 SMITH, A. B. PPE (1868), 303-305.
 ME. Pastor

6752 SMITH, Amanda Berry (1837-1915). MMAWODP (1920), 384-393. NAW (1607-1950), III, 304-305. WW of the Colored Race (1915), 246. N.Y. Times (Mar. 6, 1915), 11:6.
 HConf., 1877 (New York)
 Endorsed and attended, GHA, 1901 (Chicago)
 AME. Evangelist, missionary

Part VI. Biography 747

b. Jan. 23, 1837, Long Green, Md.
d. Feb. 24, 1915, Sebring, Fla.

6753 Smith, Amanda (Berry), 1837-1915.
Autobiography; the story of the Lord's dealings with Mrs. Amanda Smith, the colored evangelist, containing an account of her life work of faith, and her travels in America, England, Ireland, Scotland, India and Africa, as an independent missionary, with an introd. by Bishop Thoburn, of India. Chicago, Meyer & Bros., 1893. 506 p.

6754 Smith, Amanda (Berry), 1837-1915.
Autobiography; the story of the Lord's dealings with Mrs. Amanda Smith, the colored evangelist, containing an account of her life work of faith, and her travels in America, England, Ireland, Scotland, India and Africa, as an independent missionary, with an introd. by Bishop Thoburn, of India. Noblesville, Ind., J. Edwin Newby, 1962. 506 p.
Reprint of 1893 ed.

6755 Cadbury, M. H.
The life of Amanda Smith, "the African sybil, the Christian saint"; with an introd. by J. Rendel Harris.... Birmingham, Eng., Cornish Bros., Ltd., 1916. 84 p.

6756 Taylor, Marshall William, 1846-1887.
The life, travels, labors, and helpers of Mrs. Amanda Smith, the famous Negro missionary evangelist, by Rev. Marshall W. Taylor ... with an introd. by Rev. J. Krehbiel.... Cincinnati, .Printed by Cranston & Stowe for the author, 1886. 63 p.

6757 SMITH, Arlis Milton (1903-).
CN. Pastor, district supt.
b. 1903, Arkansas

6758 SMITH, Aura
Attended GHA, 1885 (Chicago)
Attended GHA, 1901 (Chicago)
ME? Pastor?

6759 SMITH, Bernie (1920-).
CN, Bapt. Evangelist

6760 Smith, Bernie, 1920-
Journey to Calvary. Grand Rapids, Mich., Baker Book House, 1967. 88 p.

6761 Smith, Bernie, 1920-
Meditations on prayer; introd. by Robert G. Lee. Grand Rapids, Mich., Baker Book House, 1966. 81 p.

6762 SMITH, Carroll (-1949). LLITW (1951), 217.
FM. Missionary

6763 SMITH, Donnell J. (-1936).
PCN, CN. Pastor, college field rep.
d. Feb. 1936

6764 SMITH, Emma French. FHOP (1964).
CN. Pastor

6765 SMITH, Frederick George (1880-1947). SCC (1947), 119-121. SHBD (1955), 100-122. RLOA (1941-1942), 999.
CG (A). Pastor, evangelist, missionary, editor
b. Nov. 12, 1880, Lacota, Mich.
d. 1947

6766 SMITH, George H.
CG (UHP), CG (H), FM. Pastor, editor

6767 SMITH, Hannah Whitall (1832-1911). GFW (1888), 119-130. DAB. NAW (1607-1950), III, 313-316. N.Y. Times (May 8, 1911), 11:5.
Fr. Author
b. Feb. 7, 1832, Philadelphia, Pa.
d. May 1911, Iffley, Eng.

6768 Smith, Hannah (Whitall), 1832-1911.
Philadelphia Quaker; the letters of Hannah Whitall Smith edited by her son, Logan Pearsall Smith, with a biographical preface by Robert Gathorne-Hardy. New York, Harcourt, Brace, 1950. xxii, 234 p.
First published in London in 1949 under title: A religious rebel.

6769 Smith, Hannah (Whitall), 1832-1911.
The record of a happy life: being memorials of Franklin Whitall Smith, a student of Princeton College, by his mother, H. W. S. Philadelphia, Printed for private circulation, 1873. 13-209 p.

6770 Smith, Hannah (Whitall), 1832-1911.
A religious rebel; the letters of "H. W. S." (Mrs. Pearsall Smith), ed. by her son, Logan Pearsall Smith, with a pref. and memoir by Robert Gathorne-Hardy. London, Nisbet, 1949. 232 p.

6771 Smith, Hannah (Whitall), 1832-1911.
The science of motherhood. New York, Revell, 1894. 47 p.

6772 Smith, Hannah (Whitall), 1832-1911.
The unselfishness of God and how I discovered it. New York, Revell, 1903. 312 p.

6773 Parker, Robert Allerton
A family of Friends; the story of the transatlantic Smiths. London, Museum Press, 1960. 232 p.
First published in New York in 1959 under title: The transatlantic Smiths.

Part VI. Biography 749

6774 Parker, Robert Allerton
 The transatlantic Smiths. New York, Random House, 1959. xvii, 237 p.
6775 Smith, Logan Pearsall, 1865-1946.
 "Old diary," Atlantic, LXXXVIII (July 1901), 92-100.

6776 SMITH, J. A.
 ME, CN, PCN, PHC. Pastor, district supt.

6777 SMITH, Jennie (1842-).
 Endorsed call and attended, GHA, 1901 (Chicago)
 ME. Railroad evangelist
6778 Smith, Jennie, 1842-
 From Baca to Beulah; sequel to Valley of Baca. Philadelphia, Garrigues Bros., 1880. 358 p.
6779 Smith, Jennie, 1842-
 Ramblings in Beulah land; a continuation of experiences in the life of Jennie Smith. Philadelphia, Garrigues Brothers, 1886-1888. 2 v.
6780 Smith, Jennie, 1842-
 The valley of Baca; a record of suffering and triumph. Cincinnati, Hitchcock and Walden, 1876. 288 p.

6781 SMITH, Joseph Henry (1855-1946). ATY (1930), 14-22.
 President, NHA, 1924-1928
 Attended GHA, 1901 (Chicago)
 ME, M. Pastor, evangelist
 b. June 4, 1855, Philadelphia, Pa.
 d. Apr. 8, 1946, Redlands, Calif.
6782 Rose, Delbert Roy, 1912-
 A theology of Christian experience. Wilmore, Ky., Seminary Press, 1958. 234 p.
 Thesis (Ph.D.)--State University of Iowa. School of Religion and Graduate College, 1952.
6783 Rose, Delbert Roy, 1912-
 A theology of Christian experience; interpreting the historic Wesleyan message. Minneapolis, Minn., Bethany Fellowship, 1965. 314 p.
 Thesis (Ph.D.)--State University of Iowa. School of Religion and Graduate College, 1952.
6784 Rose, Delbert Roy, 1912-
 "The theology of Joseph H. Smith." Unpublished Ph.D. dissertation, State University of Iowa, 1952.
6785 Teed, Florence (Schleicher), 1901-1954.
 "Papers, 1924-1954." 4 feet. In University of Michigan, Michigan Historical Collections.
 Methodist minister and civic leader of Ann Arbor, Michigan; contain student papers, sermon materials, and sermons, including miscellanea relating to the Detroit Holiness Tabernacle, Chicago Evangelistic Institute and holiness association activities and leaders, particularly Joseph H. Smith.

6786   SMITH, Joseph Thomas (1851-   ). WW in Am. Meth.
        (1916), 206.
        ME, S. Pastor, presiding elder
        b. Nov. 25, 1851, Campbell County, Tenn.

6787   SMITH, Julia Ann (1937-   ). ETHF (196?).
        PHC. Pastor's wife, missionary
        b. Sept. 8, 1937, Howard County, Ind.

6788   SMITH, Lizzie O. (1823-18??)
6789   Davies, Edward, 1830-
            History of a modern martyr; or, The life, sufferings and religious experience of Miss Lizzie O. Smith. n.p., Published by the author, 187?. 96 p.
6790   Davies, Edward, 1830-
            History of a modern martyr; or, The life, sufferings, and religious experience of Miss Lizzie O. Smith. Enl. ed. Reading, Mass., Published by the author, 1874? 104 p.

6791   SMITH, Mrs. Lizzie R. PFT (n.d.), 34-42 (2d group).
        Endorsed call and attended GHA, 1901 (Chicago)
        ME. Evangelist

6792   SMITH, Merlin Grant (1894-   ). WW in Am. (1958-1959).
        FM. College prof., college pres.
        b. Aug. 26, 1894, Delta, Ohio
6793   Killion, Mead W.
            "A history of Spring Arbor Seminary and Junior College." Unpublished M.A. thesis, University of Michigan, 1941. v, 106ℓ.
            Account of the administration of Merlin G. Smith: ℓ. 50-54.

6794   SMITH, Myrta. LLITW (1951), 217.
        FM. Missionary

6795   SMITH, Nathaniel B. (-1911). LLITW (1951), 217.
        FM. Missionary

6796   SMITH, Oswald J.
        CMA. Pastor, evangelist
6797   Smith, Oswald J.
            The story of my life, and the Peoples Church. Foreword by Redd Harper. London, Marshall, Morgan & Scott, 1962. 128 p.
            "Previous editions published in Canada under the title: The Peoples Church and its Founder."

6798   SMITH, Robert Eugene (1937-   ). ETHF (196?).
        PHC. Pastor, missionary
        b. Feb. 25, 1937, Fall River, Kan.

Part VI. Biography 751

6799 SMITH, Robert Pearsall (1827-1898).
 Fr. Evangelist
6800 Parker, Robert Allerton
 A family of Friends; the story of the transatlantic
 Smiths. London, Museum Press, 1960. 232 p.
 First published in New York in 1959 under title:
 The transatlantic Smiths.
6801 Parker, Robert Allerton
 The transatlantic Smiths. New York, Random House,
 1959. xvii, 237 p.

6802 SMITH, Rosa Hunter (-1932). LLITW (1951), 217.
 FM. Missionary

6803 SMITH, Royal Curtis (1915-). WWACUA (1970-1971),
 495.
 CN. Pastor, evangelist, college admin., college pres.
 b. Feb. 3, 1915, Cameron, Tex.

6804 SMITH, Samuel Roger. WIWBA (1946), 41-44.
 BIC. Bible school pres., bishop

6805 SMITH, Timothy Lawrence (1924-). DAS (1969), I, 479.
 WW in Am. Ed. (1967-1968), 796.
 CN. Pastor, college prof., univ. prof.
 b. Apr. 13, 1924, Central, S.C.

6806 SMITH, Wilbur K. (1913-). NVFML (1936), 83-92.
 --. Missionary
 b. 1913, Brazil

6807 SMITH, Willard Garfield (1911-).
 WM, W. Lay leader, college prof., college admin.,
 denominational official
 b. July 23, 1911, Houghton?, N.Y.
6808 "Publisher-treasurer appointed by General Board,"
 Wesleyan Advocate, CXXX (Aug. 7, 1972), 15.

6809 SMITH, William Martin (1872-).
 Fr. Evangelist, Bible seminary supt., editor, writer
6810 Smith, William Martin, 1872-
 The infidel's grave and some strange incidents about
 it. Westfield, Ind., Gospel Minister, 19??. 40 p.
 First published in the Gospel Minister in 1933.
 Reprint with revisions of 1933 ed.
 Impressions of Chester Bedell of North Benton,
 Mahoning County, Ohio.

6811 SNAPP, Hickman Corbin
 ME, IHC, PHC. Pastor?

6812 SNEAD, Alfred Cookman (1884-   ). RLOA (1941-1942), 1004.
CMA. Pastor, Bible school teacher, denominational official
b. Aug. 16, 1884, Ellisburg, Pa.

6813 SNEED, J. A. (-1944).
CG (UHP), CG (H). Pastor, editor
d. 1944, College Mound, Mo.

6814 SNOW, O. L.
Attended GHA, 1901 (Chicago)
ME. Pastor

6815 SNOWBARGER, Samuel
ME, PCN, CN. Lay leader, farmer

6816 SNOWBARGER, Vernon A. (1915-   ). LIE (1971).
CN. College prof., college admin.
b. May 15, 1915, Sylvia, Kan.

6817 SNOWBARGER, Willis Edward (1921-   ). DAS (1969), I, 480. WW in Am. (1956-1957), 2407. WW in the Midwest (1965-1966), 898. LIE (1971), 891.
CN. College prof., college dean, denominational official
b. Aug. 24, 1921, Sylvia, Kan.

6818 SNYDER, Emerson (1868-195?). SBWTL (1960), 183-184.
FM. Pastor, district supt.
b. 1868, Yarker, Ont.
d. 195?, Verona, Ont.

6819 SNYDER, Melvin Harold (1912-   ). WW in the Midwest (1969-1970), 956-957. WW in Am. (1972-1973), II, 2975. TDOOP (1968), 326-327.
PHC, W. Pastor, district supt., general supt.
b. Jan. 1, 1912, Evansville, Ind.

6820 "Conference elects 11 officers," Wesleyan Advocate, CXXVII (July 15, 1968), 8.

6821 "Elected officials of The Wesleyan Church," Wesleyan Advocate, CXXX (July 24, 1972), 14.

6822 SOL, David J. (1902-   ). RWBTB (1953), 23-27.
R. Cath., CN. Pastor, district supt.
b. Oct. 30, 1902, Villa Flores, Chiapas, Mex.

6823 SOL MOLINA, Lauro (1911-   ). RWBTB (1953), 58-61.
CN. Pastor
b. July 10, 1911, Villa Flores, Chiapas, Mex.

Part VI. Biography

6824 SOLTERO, Francisco H. (1892-). ETWF (196?). TDOOP (1968), 140-143.
PC, PHC, W. Missionary
b. Nov. 9, 1892, Parral, Chihuahua, Mexico

6825 SOLTERO, Nettie Winans (-1957). ETWF (196?).
PC, PHC. Missionary
d. June 5, 1957

6826 SPALDING, Ida Heffner (-1930). LLITW (1951), 217.
FM. Missionary

6827 SPANGENBERG, Leonard (1906-). WW in Am. (1968-1969), 2061. WW in New England (1949), 569. SFLF (1950), 103-107.
CN. Lay leader, economist
b. Sept. 13, 1906, Plainfield, N.J.

6828 SPANGENBERG, Robert Leonard (1933-). WW in the East (1968-1969), 990. WW in the East (1972-1973), 706.
CN? Lay leader's child
b. May 16, 1933, Newton, Mass.

6829 SPARKES, Fannie J. (1844-1919). GFW (1888), 31-38.
ME. Missionary teacher, orphanage supt.
b. 1844, Binghamton, N.Y.

6830 SPARKS, Samuel F.
Bapt., CN. Evangelist
b. 191?, Boyd County, Ky.
6831 Sparks, Samuel F.
I met Jesus. Louisville, Pentecostal Publishing Co., n.d. 45 p.
Autobiography.

6832 SPEAKES, Joseph Nicholas (1879-1959). COPN (1958), 50-54.
ME, S; HChuC; PCN; CN. Pastor, district supt.
b. Jan. 12, 1879, Lake City, Ark.
d. Apr. 18, 1959, Nampa, Ida.
6833 McGraw, James, 1913-
"The preaching of Joseph N. Speakes," Preacher's Magazine, XXXVI (Apr. 1961), 8-10.

6834 SPICER, Tobias (1788-1862).
ME. Pastor
6835 Spicer, Tobias, 1788-1862.
Autobiography; containing incidents and observations, also some account of his visit to England. Boston, C.H. Pierce and Co., 1851. 312 p.

6836   Spicer, Tobias, 1788-1862.
        Autobiography; containing incidents and observations, also some account of his visit to England. New York, Lane & Scott, 1852. 312 p.

6837   SPRING, Worthy Allen (1896-). RLOA (1941-1942), 1013.
        UB, EUB? Pastor, Bible college pres., college pres.
        b. July 22, 1896, Millersburg, Ohio

6838   SPRUCE, Elizabeth Woolsey (1873-1969).
        ME, S; CN. Lay member, farmer's wife
        b. Aug. 24, 1873, Weimar, Tex.
        d. Jan. 2, 1969, Bethany, Okla.
6839   Spruce, Elizabeth (Woolsey), 1873-1969.
        "Extracts from my lessons." Bethany, Okla., 1966. (Mimeographed).

6840   SPRUCE, Fletcher Clarke
        CN. Pastor, district supt.

6841   SPRUILL, William F. T. (1830-1903).
        Attended GHA, 1901 (Chicago)
        ME. Pastor

6842   STAFFORD, S. M. SCUH (1962).
        I, HChuC, PCN, CN. Missionary, pastor?

6843   STALKER, Charles Henry (1876-).
        Fr. Evangelist
6844   Stalker, Charles Henry, 1876-
        Twice around the world with the Holy Ghost; or, The impressions and convictions of the mission field. Columbus, Ohio, C. H. Stalker, 1906. 237 p.

6845   STAMBAUGH, Mrs. Emma
        Attended GHA, 1901 (Chicago)
        ME? Lay member?

6846   STANDLEY, Meredith Goslin (1879-).
        IAHU, IAHC, IHC, PHC. Bible school pres., editor
6847   Standley, Meredith Goslin, 1879-
        My life as I have lived it for Christ and others. Cincinnati, Published by the author, 1949.

6848   STANGER, Frank Bateman (1914-). WWACUA (1970-1971), 504. LIE (1971), 903. GFIIH (1963), 212-229.
        ME, M, UM. Pastor, seminary pres.
        b. Aug. 31, 1914, Cedarville, N. J.

6849   STAPLES, Rob Lyndal
        CN. College prof.

Part VI. Biography 755

6850 STARK, Kenneth. GHAI (1960), 64-65.
CN. Missionary

6851 STARR, Roy V. (1885-1949). COPN (1958), 109-114.
RLOA (1941-1942), 1018.
I, CN. Rescue mission supt., editor, pastor, district supt.
b. Oct. 14, 1885, Argyle, Mich.
d. Dec. 18, 1949, Illinois

6852 STAUFFER, Joshua (1891-1971).
Fr., PHC, W. Bible seminary teacher, Bible seminary pres., district supt., Bible college teacher, religious writer
d. May 19, 1971, Kernersville, N.C.

6853 Dieter, Melvin Easterday, 1924-
"A tribute to service," Wesleyan Advocate, CXXIX (July 12, 1971), 15.

6854 STAYT, E. H. (-1933). LLITW (1951), 217.
FM. Missionary

6855 STEARNS, Daniel Miner (1844-1920).
Endorsed call, GHA, 1901 (Chicago)
ME? Editor

6856 STEEL, Henry (1929?-1961).
FM. Pastor, missionary promoter (OMS)
b. 1929?, Clio, Mich.
d. May 1961, Duarte, Calif.

6857 Erny, Edward
Mission accomplished under sentence of death.
Greenwood, Ind., Oriental Missionary Society, 1967.
96 p.

6858 STEELE, A. M. PPE (1868), 295-299.
ME. Pastor

6859 STEELE, Daniel (1824-1914). DAB. HM (1882). Nat. Cy.
of Am. Biog., XII, 490-491. SCM (1881), 830.
WWW in Am. (1897-1942), 1174. N.Y. Times
(Sept. 3, 1914), 7:5. GFW (1888), 39-45.
Unable to attend H. Conf., 1877 (New York)
Attended GHA, 1901 (Chicago)
ME. Pastor, college prof., university pres., university prof.
b. Oct. 5, 1824, Windham, N.Y.
d. Sept. 2, 1914, Milton, Mass.

6860 STEELE, Evangeline Ruth Felsburg (1931-   ). ETWF (196?).
PHC. Pastor's wife, missionary
b. Dec. 28, 1931, Johnson, Kan.

6861 STEELE, Paul Wesley (1929-). ETWF (196?).
PHC. Pastor, missionary
b. Feb. 18, 1929, Covington, Ky.

6862 STEWART, Grace M. (-1916). LLITW (1951), 217.
FM. Missionary

6863 STEWART, John H. PPE (1868), 232-233.
ME. Pastor

6864 STIKELEATHER, Shirley M. (1878-1962). RLOA (1941-1942), 1025.
IAHU, IAHC, IHC, PHC. Pastor, denominational official, Bible college admin., district supt.
b. July 20, 1878, Turnersburg, N.C.
d. June 13, 1962, Kingswood, Ky.

6865 "He trusted God and did well," Pilgrim Holiness Advocate, XLII (Aug. 4, 1962), 3.

6866 STITES, Edgar Page (1836-1921). LMGSS (1952), 75.
N.Y. Times (Jan. 9, 1921), 23:2. RHOOF (1964), 415.
ME. Gospel song writer
b. Mar. 22, 1836, Cape May, N.J.
d. Jan. 7, 1921, Cape May, N.J.

6867 STOCKTON, J. N. PPE (1868), 279-284.
ME. Pastor

6868 STOCKTON, John
CN. Banker, college admin., denominational official
b. 189?, Chico, Tex.

6869 Stockton, John
Investments here and hereafter. Kansas City, Mo., Nazarene Publishing House, 1964. 84 p.
Autobiographical.

6870 STOCKTON, John Hart (1813-1877). RHOOF (1964), 416.
CHHMH (1970), 617.
ME. Gospel song writer
b. Apr. 19, 1813, New Hope, Pa.
d. Mar. 25, 1877, Philadelphia, Pa.

6871 STOKES, Ellwood Haines (1815-1897). SCM (1881), 835.
ME. Pastor, presiding elder, camp-meeting asso. pres.
b. 1815, Medford, Burlington County, N.J.
d. July 16, 1897, Ocean Grove, N.J.

6872 Stokes, Ellwood Haines, 1815-1897.
Footprints in my own life. Asbury Park, N.J., M.W. & C. Pennypacker, 1898. 164 p.

Part VI. Biography

6873 Stokes, Ellwood Haines, 1815-1897.
The story of fifty years. Ocean Grove, N.J., Press of J.B. Rodgers Printing Co., 1893. 50 p.

6874 STOLL, Charles Augustus (1872-1939). WWW in Am. (1897-1942).
FM, PCN?, FM. Pastor?, college dean, college pres.
b. Oct. 28, 1872, Brookfield, Wisc.
d. Apr. 5, 1939, McPherson, Kan.?

6875 STONE, Mary (1873-1954). MWWW in Ch. Hist. (1968), 389-390.
BM. Physician, missionary
b. 1873, Kiukiang, Kiangsi, Ch.
d. 1954, Pasadena, Calif.

6876 STONE, Wilmot C. (1876-1941).
ME, PCN, IHC, PHC. Pastor, college prof., Bible school prin., editor
b. Oct. 15, 1876, Canton, Pa.
d. Apr. 18, 1941
6877 "Rev. W.C. Stone," Pilgrim Holiness Advocate, XXI (May 8, 1941), 2-4.

6878 STOPANI, Carlos (1911-). RWBTB (1953), 62-66.
R. Cath., CN. Pastor, district supt.
b. July 10, 1911, Durango (state), Mex.

6879 STOREY, R. K. TDOOP (1968), 265, 273-274, 282-283.
PHC. Missionary
6880 Storey, R. K.
The Storeys' own story. Indianapolis, Ind., Foreign Missionary Office, Pilgrim Holiness Church, 1945.

6881 STRANG, Clifford Benjamin (1895-). RLOA (1941-1942), 1029-1030.
CN, M. Pastor
b. Mar. 15, 1895, Homestead, Pa.

6882 STREET, Abram K. (1807-1898).
Signed call to form NHA, 1867 (Philadelphia)
ME. Pastor

6883 STRICKLAND, William Jefferson (1932-). DAS (1969), IV, 357.
CN. College prof., military chaplain (res.)
b. Oct. 15, 1932, Nashville, Tenn.
6884 Strickland, William Jefferson, 1932-
"John Goodwin as seen through his controversies of 1640-1660." Unpublished Ph.D. dissertation, Vanderbilt University, 1967. 270ℓ.

6885 STUART, Robert Lee (1883-). RLOA (1941-1942), 1032.
ME. Pastor, college pres.
b. Sept. 12, 1883, Basham, Va.

6886 STUDD, G. B. SCUH (1962).
PenielM. Rescue mission worker

6887 STURK, Louis Willard (1895-1955). N.Y. Times (June 15, 1955), 31:5. TDOOP (1968), 279-280, 321-322.
IHC, PHC. Pastor, district supt., general supt.
b. Feb. 1, 1895, Bad Axe, Mich.
d. June 13, 1955, Defiance, Ohio

6888 "Rev. Louis Willard Sturk, D.D.," Pilgrim Holiness Advocate, XXXV (July 2, 1955), 3-10.

6889 SUDDARTH, Mrs. Fannie E. HWP (1905), 90-93. SCUH (1962), 172.
Pres.; Epis.; ME, S; NTCOC; HChuC; PCN. Evangelist, Bible school prin.
b. 18??, Harrodsburg, Ky.

6890 SUMLIN, H. H.
HChuC, PCN. Pastor, district supt.

6891 SUMMERS, Ancel (1871-).
Meth. (Can.), WM, FM. Pastor
b. Mar. 24, 1871, Wincester, Ont., Can.
6892 Cowan, James
Sanctified wholly: Rev. Ancel and Grace Summers. Estevan, Sask., Can., 1952. 56 p.

6893 SUMMERS, Grace Langman (1886-).
Fr., Meth. (Can.), FM. Pastor's wife.
b. July 7, 1886, Collingwood?, Ont., Can.
6894 Cowan, James
Sanctified wholly: Rev. Ancel and Grace Summers. Estevan, Sask., Can., 1952. 56 p.

6895 SURBROOK, Evangeline Shelhamer (-1930).
FM, PHC. Minister's wife
d. 1930
6896 Shelhamer, Elmer Ellsworth, 1869-1947.
Sixty years of thorns and roses. Cincinnati, God's Bible School and Missionary Training Home, 1930. 224 p.
Account of life of Evangeline Shelhamer Surbrook: p. 206-224.

6897 SURBROOK, Walter Lewis (1891-). RLOA (1941-1942), 1034. SFLF (1950), 108-112. TDOOP (1968), 173-178, 180-181, 206-207, 211, 262-263, 277-278.
Member, NHA

Part VI. Biography 759

       IHC, PHC, W. Bible college teacher, Bible college pres., general supt.
       b. Mar. 4, 1891, Croswell, Mich.

6898 SUTTON, B. D. (-1951). LMGSS (1952), 151.
       CN? Evangelistic singer, gospel song writer
       d. May 25, 1951

6899 SWAIN, F. M. (-1926). FYAB (1954).
       Member, IowaHA
       CN, PCN, CN. Physician, lay preacher, lay leader
       d. 1926

6900 SWANN, L. Alline McGraw (1908-).
       CN. College prof.
       b. 1908, Texas
6901   Swann, L. Alline (McGraw), 1908-
       Distant drums; an anthology of meditations, epigrams, and poems, illus. by Alvin H. Kauffman and Ruth Long. Boston, Christopher Publishing House, 1958. 105 p.
6902   Swann, L. Alline (McGraw), 1908-
       The uttermost part; a layman visits India. Kansas City, Mo., Nazarene Publishing House, 1969. 77 p.

6903 SWARTH, Dowie. FHOP (1964).
       CN. Pastor, evangelist, district supt., missionary to Am. Indians

6904 SWARTH, Thressa (-1952). FHOP (1964).
       CN. Missionary, pastor's wife

6905 SWAUGER, John Robert (1900-1955). MHWMCOA (1959).
       WM. Pastor?, denominational official
       d. Sept. 23, 1955, Pasadena, Calif.

6906 SWEETEN, Howard W.
       CN. Evangelist

6907 SWENEY, John Robson (1837-1899). LMGSS (1952), 75. RHOOF (1964), 418.
       Pres., ME. Music teacher, evangelistic singer, gospel song writer
       b. Dec. 31, 1837, West Chester, Pa.
       d. Apr. 10, 1899, Chester, Pa.

6908 SWIM, Roy Elliott (1899-). LIE (1948), 1046.
       CN. Pastor, college prof., seminary prof., editorial writer
       b. Jan. 4, 1899, Olney, Ill.

6909 SWING, James W. TDOOP (1968), 288.
       President, Southern California and Arizona HA, 1883-

1896
ME, HBd, HC. Pastor, evangelist, editor

6910 SYNAN, Vinson (1934-). SEC (1968), xiv-xv.
PeHC. Evangelist, pastor, college prof., college dean
b. Dec. 1, 1934, Hopewell, Va.

6911 TAKARO, Magdalene P. NVFML (1936), 71-82.
Hung. Ref.

6912 TALBEE, Frank E. (1869-1929).
PCN, ME. Pastor
b. Dec. 15, 1869, Bristol, R.I.
d. Apr. 25, 1929, Putney, Vt.

6913 TAMBLYN, Jeremiah W. (1851-).
FM. Pastor
b. 1851
6914 Tamblyn, Jeremiah W., 1851-
Sweet memories of a trustful life. Morristown, Pa.,
E.A. Smith & Sons, Printers, 1924. 85 p.

6915 TAYLOR, Arthur M. (1896-). SEC (1968), 61-63.
PeHC. Denominational official, Bible academy supt.
b. 1896, Darlington, S.C.

6916 TAYLOR, Bushrod Shedden (1849-1935).
Attended GHA, 1901 (Chicago)
ME. Pastor, evangelist
b. 1849, Poultney, Vt.
d. Oct. 8, 1935, Marcy, N.Y.
6917 Taylor, Bushrod Shedden, 1849-1935.
Bible readings and spiritual essays. Cincinnati, M.
W. Knapp, 1886-1900. 3 v.
Contents.--v. 1. Personal experience. Full salvation. The old stump.--v. 2. Hot shot. Holy fire. Dakota campaign. Pipe and quid.--v. 3. The Gibeonites. The Canaanites. Death, hell, and judgment.

6918 TAYLOR, Cary G. (-1954).
IHC, PHC. Pastor, district supt., Bible college pres.,
editor
d. Jan. 24, 1954

6919 TAYLOR, Donald M. GTWATD (1965), 58-66.
UMC, MC. Pastor?, college prof., Bible college
prof., editor

6920 TAYLOR, George Floyd (1881-1934). SEC (1968), 6-11,
18-86.
ME, S; PeHC. Bible school teacher, Bible school
supt., editor, pastor, denominational official

b. Aug. 10, 1881, Duplin County, N.C.
d. Nov. 16, 1934, Franklin Springs, Ga.

6921 TAYLOR, J. T. (-1945). LLITW (1951), 217.
FM. Missionary

6922 TAYLOR, James Milburn (1873-). WW in Am. Meth. (1916), 218.
ME. Missionary evangelist (founded mission work taken over by IAHC)
b. July 27, 1873, Maryville, Tenn.

6923 TAYLOR, James Morgan. SCUH (1962).
ME?, LHA, Pent. Evangelist

6924 TAYLOR, Jesse Paul (1895-). LMB (1948), 174. WW in the Midwest (1965-1966), 949.
FM. Pastor, district supt., bishop
b. Apr. 1, 1895, Mt. Vernon, Ill.

6925 TAYLOR, Margaret Fallon (-1919). LLITW (1951), 217.
FM. Missionary

6926 TAYLOR, Mendell
CN. College prof., college dean, seminary prof., seminary dean, evangelist
6927 Taylor, Mendell
50,000 miles of people, places, and practices. Kansas City, Mo., Nazarene Publishing House, 1966. 89 p.

6928 TAYLOR, Richard Shelley (1912-). GFIIH (1963), 268-282. GTWATD (1965), 88-117. BPOH (1969), 56-77.
CN. Pastor, Bible college prin., seminary prof.

6929 TAYLOR, Willard Harlan
CN. Pastor, college pres., seminary prof., seminary dean
6930 Taylor, Willard Harlan
"The antithetic method in Pauline theology." Unpublished Ph.D. dissertation, Northwestern University, 1959.

6931 TAYLOR, William (1821-1902). DAB. LMB (1948), 175. MWWW in Ch. Hist. (1968), 398. SCM (1881), 1002. WWW in Am. (1897-1942), 1221. N.Y. Times (May 20, 1902), 9:5.
Member, NHA
ME. Pastor, evangelist, missionary, bishop
b. May 2, 1821, Rockbridge County, Va.
d. May 18, 1902, Palo Alto, Calif.

6932 Taylor, William, bp., 1821-1902.
Address to young America, and a word to the old folks.... Philadelphia, Perkinpine & Higgins, 1860. 83 p.

6933 Taylor, William, bp., 1821-1902.
California life illustrated. New York, Published for the author by Carlton & Porter, 1858. 348 p.

6934 Taylor, William, bp., 1821-1902.
Christian adventures in South Africa. New York, Phillips & Hunt, 1881. 557 p.

6935 Taylor, William, bp., 1821-1902.
Christian adventures in South Africa, by Rev. William Taylor, of the South India Conference.... New York, Hunt and Eaton; Cincinnati, Cranston and Stowe, 1867. 557 p.

6936 Taylor, William, bp., 1821-1902.
The flaming torch in darkest Africa; with an introd. by Henry M. Stanley. New York, Eaton & Mains, 1898. 675 p.

6937 Taylor, William, bp., 1821-1902.
Four years' campaign in India. London, Hodder and Stoughton; New York, Nelson & Phillips, 1876. 416 p.

6938 Taylor, William, bp., 1821-1902.
Our South American cousins. New York, Nelson and Phillips; London, Hodder and Stoughton, 1879. 318 p.

6939 Taylor, William, bp., 1821-1902.
Our South American cousins.... New York, Phillips & Hunt; Cincinnati, Walden & Stowe, 1881. 318 p.

6940 Taylor, William, bp., 1821-1902.
Seven years' street preaching in San Francisco, California; embracing incidents, triumphant death scenes, etc., ed. by W. P. Strickland. New York, Phillips & Hunt [pref. 1856]. 394 p.

6941 Taylor, William, bp., 1821-1902.
Seven years' street preaching in San Francisco, California; embracing incidents, triumphant death scenes, etc., ed. by W. P. Strickland. New York, Published for the author by Carlton & Porter, 1857. 394 p.

6942 Taylor, William, bp., 1821-1902.
Story of my life; an account of what I have thought and said and done in my ministry of more than fifty-three years in Christian lands and among the heathen; ed. by John Clark Ridpath, copiously embellished with original engravings and sketches by Frank Beard. New York, Eaton & Mains, 1896, c1895. 748 p.

6943 Taylor, William, bp., 1821-1902.
Ten years of self-supporting missions in India. New York, Phillips & Hunt, 1882. 484 p.

6944 Taylor, William, bp., 1821-1902.
William Taylor of California, bishop of Africa; an autobiography; rev., with a preface by the Rev. C. G. Moore. London, Hodder and Stoughton, 1897. 411 p.

Part VI. Biography 763

6945 Arms, Goodsil Filley, 1854-
History of the William Taylor self-supporting missions in South America. New York, Methodist Book Concern, 1921. 263 p.
6946 Barchwitz-Krauser, Oscar von
Six years with William Taylor in South America. Boston, Published for the author by McDonald & Gill, 1885. 332 p.
6947 Belew, Pascal Perry, 1894-
My old Kentucky home; or, Experiences from life. Kansas City, Mo., Printed for Rev. P. P. Belew by the Nazarene Publishing House, 1925?. 48 p.
Essay on Bishop William Taylor: p. 42-44.
6948 Davies, Edward, 1830-
The Bishop of Africa; or, The life of William Taylor, with an account of the Congo country, and mission.... Reading, Mass., Holiness Book Concern, 1885. 216 p.
6949 Davies, Edward, 1830-
The Bishop of Africa; or, The life of William Taylor, D.D., with an account of the Congo country, and mission. Reading, Mass., Published for the benefit of the building and transit fund of William Taylor's missions by Holiness Book Concern, 1885. 192 p.
6950 James, George Wharton
Heroes of California. Boston, Little, Brown, 1910. xxii, 515 p.
Biographical sketch of William Taylor: p. 137-153.
6951 McCoy, B. H.
"Bishop William Taylor." Proceedings of Rockbridge County Historical Society, IV, 16-18.
6952 Methodist Episcopal Church. Missions and mission conferences. South Central Africa. Angola District.
"Records, 1885-1897, including minutes of regular and special meetings of the district, presiding elder's reports, and records of births, deaths, baptisms, marriages, ordinations, etc." In Library, Pacific School of Religion. 1 v.
6953 Paul, John Haywood, 1877-1967.
The soul digger; or, Life and times of William Taylor. Upland, Ind., Taylor University Press, 1928. 318 p.
6954 Paul, John Haywood, 1877-1967.
William Taylor, a sketch of his life. Kansas City, Mo., Nazarene Publishing House, n.d. 63 p.

6955 TAYLOR, Wingrove. BPOH (1969), 138-149.
PHC, W. Pastor, evangelist, Bible college pres.

6956 TEDROW, Blanche Ione (1909-). ETWF (196?).
PHC. Pastor, missionary
b. July 9, 1909, Martin County, Ind.

6957 TEED, Florence Schleicher (1901-1954).
ME, M. Evangelist
6958 Teed, Florence (Schleicher), 1901-1954.
"Papers, 1924-1954." 4 feet. In University of Michigan, Michigan Historical Collections.
Methodist minister and civic leader of Ann Arbor, Michigan; contain student papers, sermon materials, and sermons, including miscellanea relating to the Detroit Holiness Tabernacle, Chicago Evangelistic Institute, Asbury College, and holiness association activities and leaders, particularly Joseph H. Smith.

6959 TEMPLETON, Charles Bradley (1915-).
CN, Pres. Pastor, evangelist, youth worker.
6960 Templeton, Charles Bradley, 1915-
Evangelism for tomorrow. New York, Harper, 1957. 175 p.
6961 Templeton, Charles Bradley, 1915-
Life looks up. New York, Harper, c1955. 192 p.

6962 TERRILL, Joseph Goodwin (-1895). MFATALW (1960).
Attended GHA, 1885 (Chicago)
ME, FM. Pastor, evangelist, denominational official

6963 TETRICK, D. C. W.
HChuC, PCN. Evangelist

6964 THAHABEYAH, Milhem (1893-). HNTB (1934).
Gr. Orth., R. Cath., PCN, CN. Pastor, missionary
b. 1893, Bludan, Syria

6965 THAYER, Clarence E. FHOP (1964).
CN. Pastor

6966 THOBURN, Isabella (1840-1901). N.Y. Times (Sept. 4, 1901), 7:7. DAB. MWWW in Ch. Hist. (1968), 404.
ME. Missionary
b. 1840, St. Clairsville, Ohio
d. 1901, Lucknow, India
6967 Thoburn, James Mills, bp., 1836-1922.
Life of Isabella Thoburn. Cincinnati, Jennings and Pye; New York, Eaton and Mains, 1903. 373 p.

6968 THOBURN, James Mills (1836-1922). N.Y. Times (Nov. 29, 1922), 17:5. SCM (1881), 858-859. WWW in Am. (1897-1942), 1227. DAB. LMB (1948), 177-178. MWWW in Ch. Hist. (1968), 404.
ME. Missionary, missionary bishop
b. Mar. 7, 1836, St. Clairsville, Ohio
d. Nov. 28, 1922, Meadville, Pa.
6969 Thoburn, James Mills, 1836-1922.
My missionary apprenticeship. New York, Phillips

Part VI. Biography

        & Hunt, 1887. 386 p.
        Autobiography.

6970   THOMAS, Clifford William (1916-). WWACUA (1970-1971), 526-527. TDOOP (1968), 287.
        PHC, CN, PHC, W. Pastor, college prof., college dean
        b. Nov. 27, 1916, El Centro, Calif.

6971   THOMAS, David (1860-1930).
        Cong., PL, IHM. Draper, rescue mission worker, mission supt.
        b. Sept. 29, 1860, Llanllanddog, Carmarthenshire
        d. June 16, 1930, London
6972   David Thomas, founder of the International Holiness Mission. London, International Holiness Mission, 1933.

6973   THOMAS, Fred (1909-). MLA (1935), 79-83.
        SA, PCN, CN. Evangelist, pastor
        b. Oct. 7, 1909, Bloomington, Ill.

6974   THOMAS, Hazel Marie (1926-). ETWF (196?).
        PHC. Missionary
        b. Jan. 19, 1926, Danville, Va.

6975   THOMAS, Lois Adams (-1937). LLITW (1951), 217.
        FM. Missionary

6976   THOMAS, Minnie Frances Emery (1928-). ETWF (196?).
        PHC, W. Missionary
        b. Aug. 26, 1928, Indianapolis, Ind.

6977   THOMAS, Paul Westphal (1894-1972). TDOOP (1968), 126, 345-346.
        SA, PeoMC, PHC, W. Pastor, rescue mission worker, evangelist, mission supt., Bible school pres., denominational official, editor, general supt.
        b. Sept. 28, 1894, Stockton, Calif.
        d. Mar. 1, 1972, Baywood Park, Calif.
6978   "Dr. Paul Westphal Thomas," Wesleyan Advocate, CXXX (Apr. 17, 1972), 5.

6979   THOMAS, Paul William (1921-). ETWF (196?).
        PHC, W. Missionary
        b. Nov. 29, 1921, Colorado Springs, Colo.

6980   THOMAS, Theodore J. LLITW (1951), 213.
        FM. Missionary

6981   THOMPSON, C. A.
        ME, PCN. Pastor, evangelist, district supt.

6982 THOMPSON, Edward W.
ME, S; PM. Businessman, lay leader

6983 THOMPSON, Herbert W. (1908-   ).
CG (A). Pastor

6984 Thompson, Herbert W., 1908-
An adventure in the will of God; the story of how Herb and Lola Thompson sought earnestly and found the will of God for their lives together in good times and in dark days. Anderson, Ind., Warner Press, 1963. 96 p.

6985 THOMPSON, John (-1899). DC (1965, c1887), 45-55. Member, NHA
ME. Pastor, evangelist

6986 THOMPSON, Raymond Duane (1931-   ). WW in Am. Ed. (1967-1968), 852. GTWATD (1965), 364-371.
WM, W. Pastor, college prof.
b. Jan. 10, 1931, Marion, Ind.

6987 THOMPSON, Walter Lee (1876-   ). MHWMCOA (1959), 178, 196, 201-202, 204, 266, 279, 350, 424. RLOA (1941-1942), 1109.
WM. Pastor, college pres., evangelist, conference pres., connectional official
b. May 4, 1876, Anderson, Ind.

6988 THOMPSON, William Ralph (1910-   ). DAS (1969), IV, 367. GFIIH (1963), 106-121. GTWATD (1965), 236-245.
FM. Pastor, missionary, college prof.
b. May 23, 1910, Illinois

6989 THOMSON, Charles Edward
Meth. (Can.), PCN, CN. Pastor, Bible school teacher, evangelist, district supt., college pres.

6990 TILLETT, J. PPE (1868), 358-360.
ME. Pastor

6991 TILLMAN, Charlie Davis (1861-1943). LDML (1953), 74. LMGSS (1952), 49. N.Y. Times (Sept. 4, 1943), 13:5.
ME, S. Gospel song writer, evangelistic singer
b. Mar. 20, 1861, Tallassee, Ala.
d. Sept. 2, 1943

6992 Tillman, Charlie Davis, 1861-1943.
The assembly book, with Scriptures for each school day. Atlanta, Charlie Tillman Song Book Co., c1936. Cover-title, 128 (i.e. 130) p.
Georgia edition. Also published, with appropriate

Part VI. Biography 767

alternations, as South Carolina assembly book.
6993 Tillman, Charlie Davis, 1861-1943.
Father and mother songs. Atlanta, Charlie Tillman Song Book Co., 1939? 32 p.
In both ordinary and shape-note notation.
6994 Tillman, Charlie Davis, 1861-1943.
South Carolina assembly book, with Scriptures for each school day. Atlanta, Charlie Tillman Song Book Co., c1936. Cover-title, 128 (i.e. 130) p.
Georgia edition published under title: The Assembly book, with Scriptures for each day.

6995 TINSLEY, James N. FHOP (1964).
FM, CN. Pastor, district supt.

6996 TITUS, W. S. PPE (1868), 212-216.
ME. Pastor

6997 TODE, Runjaji K. HNTB (1934), 95-96.
PCN, CN. National worker, pastor
b. 189?, India

6998 TOMLINSON, Ambrose Jessup (1865-1943). MWWW in Ch. Hist. (1968), 408. N.Y. Times (Oct. 3, 1943), 49:2.
Fr., CU(NC), HC (T), CG (GA), CG (T). Colporteur, evangelist, bishop
b. 1865, Westfield, Ind.
d. 1943
6999 Tomlinson, Ambrose Jessup, bp., 1865-1943.
Diary of A.J. Tomlinson; editorial notes by his son, Homer A. Tomlinson. Queens Village, N.Y., Church of God, World Headquarters, 1949-1955. 3 v.

7000 TOWNSEND, Lewis A.
Attended GHA, 1901 (Chicago)
Cong., CN, PCN. Pastor

7001 TOWNSEND, Socrates (1816-). PPE (1868), 275-278.
ME. Pastor

7002 TOZER, Aiden Wilson (1897-1963). N.Y. Times (May 14, 1963), 39:3.
CMA. Pastor, editor
b. 1897, Newburg, Pa.
d. May 13, 1963, Toronto, Ont., Can.
7003 Fant, David Jones, 1897-
A.W. Tozer: a twentieth century prophet. Harrisburg, Pa., Christian Publications, 1964. 180 p.

7004 TRACY, Gertrude Perry
APCA, PCN, CN. Missionary, pastor's wife

7005   Tracy, Gertrude (Perry)
            Beth and I in India; ed. by Amy N. Hinshaw and
            Mary E. Cove. Kansas City, Mo., Nazarene Publishing House, 1932. 94 p.
            Autobiographical.

7006   TRACY, Leighton Stanley (1882-1942). SCUH (1962).
            APCA, PCN, CN. Missionary, pastor
            d. Sept. 28, 1942.
7007   Tracy, Leighton Stanley, 1882-1942.
            "A comparative study of the Toda and Banyankole tribes." Unpublished M.A. thesis, Hartford Seminary Foundation, 1926. 52ℓ.
7008   Tracy, Olive Gertrude, 1908-
            Tracy Sahib of India. Kansas City, Mo., Beacon Hill Press, 1954. 191 p.

7009   TRAINA, Robert Angelo (1921-   ). WWACUA (1970-1971), 536. LIE (1971), 950.
            FM? Seminary prof., seminary admin.
            b. Aug. 27, 1921, Chicago, Ill.

7010   TRAUGH, Hubert Lee (1929-   ). ETWF (196?).
            PHC. Missionary
            b. Aug. 6, 1929, Nelsonville, Ohio

7011   TRAUGH, Joanne Marilyn (1931-   ). ETWF (196?).
            PHC. Missionary
            b. Sept. 9, 1931, Memphis, Tenn.

7012   TRAVELLER, Abram Dow (1839-1923). WW in Am. Meth. (1916), 224.
            Attended GHA, 1901 (Chicago)
            Meth. (Can.), ME. Pastor, presiding elder
            b. Dec. 24, 1839, Ottawa, Ont., Can.
            d. 1923, Chicago?, Ill.

7013   TRONNES, Cora Cook Thomas
            CN. Pastor?
7014   Tronnes, Cora (Cook) Thomas
            "Prepare ye the way." Yacolt, Wash., 1956. (Mimeographed)
            Autobiography.

7015   TROUTMAN, Gladys Virginia (1933-   ). ETWF (196?).
            PHC. Missionary
            b. Dec. 26, 1933, Gold Hill, N.C.

7016   TROXEL, Cecil Warren (1879-1944).
            ME. Missionary (NHMS)
            b. Apr. 1, 1879, El Paso, Ill.
            d. June 9, 1944, University Park, Iowa

Part VI. Biography

7017   Troxel, Ellen (Armour), 1875-
          Cecil Troxel, the man and the work; missionary to China with the National Holiness Missionary Society from its inception in 1910 until his promotion on June 9, 1944, by Mrs. Cecil Troxel and Mrs. John J. Trachsel. Chicago, National Holiness Missionary Society, 1948. 261 p.

7018   TRUE, Ira L. (1898-   ). FHOP (1964).
          CN. Pastor, missionary, college bus. manager, district supt.
          b. July 16, 1898, Omaha, Neb.

7019   TRUE, Valora (1898-   ). FHOP (1964).
          CN. Missionary, Pastor's wife
          b. June 8, 1898, Spokane, Wash.

7020   TRUMBAUER, Horace G. SCUH (1962), 77.
          HCC, PCN. Pastor, presiding elder, district supt.

7021   TRUMBAUER, Jonas (1848-1920).
          HCC, PCN, CN. Pastor, presiding elder

7022   TRUSLOW, Julietta
          ME
7023   Bottome, Francis, 1823-1894.
          Memoir of Julietta Truslow. New York, W.C. Palmer, 1866. 114 p.

7024   TSUCHIYA, Kenichi (1883-   ). NVFML (1936), 181-200.
          JHC. Pastor
          b. Feb. 1, 1883, Japan

7025   TSUTADA, David Tsugio (-1971).
          IGMJ. Pastor, national mission leader, president
          b. 19??, Singapore
          d. July 25, 1971, Tokyo, Japan
7026   Tsutada, David Tsugio,   -1971.
          20 years retrospect of Immanuel General Mission in Japan. Tokyo, Immanuel General Mission in Japan, 1965. 270 p.
          Text mostly in Japanese with English captions.
7027   Lytle, Robert N., 1917-
          "Japan's 'John Wesley' dies, " Wesleyan Advocate, CXXIX (July 12, 1971), 12.

7028   TURKINGTON, William David (1893-   ). RLOA (1941-1942), 1068. WW in the Clergy (1935-1936), 1127.
          ME. Pastor, seminary prof., college prof.
          b. Apr. 25, 1893, Acme, Wash.

7029   TURNBULL, Walter Mason (1881-1930). WWW in Am. (1897-1942), 1258.
        CMA. Missionary, rescue mission worker, academy prin., Bible institute dean
        b. Oct. 10, 1881, Peterboro, Ont., Can.
        d. May 12, 1930, Nyack, N.Y.

7030   TURNER, George Allen (1908-   ). DAS (1969), IV, 372-373. GTWATD (1965), 412-421.
        FM. College prof., pastor, conference supt., seminary prof.
        b. Aug. 28, 1908, Willsboro, N.Y.

7031   TUTTLE, Alexander Harrison (1844-1932). WW in Am. Meth. (1916), 226-227. WWW in Am. (1897-1942), 1260. N.Y. Times (Dec. 5, 1932), 20:1.
        Endorsed call, GHA, 1901 (Chicago)
        ME. Pastor
        b. Feb. 28, 1844, Bordentown, N.J.
        d. Dec. 4, 1932, East Orange, N.J.

7032   TYSINGER, J. Walden (1909-1971).
        WM, W. Pastor, academy pres., college admin.
        b. 1909, Lexington, N.C.
        d. May 24, 1971, Anderson, S.C.
7033   Dieter, Melvin Easterday, 1924-
        "A tribute to service," Wesleyan Advocate, CXXIX (July 12, 1971), 15.
7034   "Dr. J. Walden Tysinger, 1909-1971," Wesleyan Advocate, CXXIX (July 12, 1971), 12.
7035   Rickman, Claude R., 1917-
        "A tribute," Wesleyan Advocate, CXXIX (July 12, 1971), 12.

7036   UHRIG, Henry E. (1889?-1948). N.Y. Times (Jan. 27, 1948), 25:1.
        IHC, PHC. Pastor, district supt.
        b. 1889?
        d. Jan. 26, 1948, Allentown, Pa.

7037   UPCHURCH, James T. (1870-   ).
        HChuC, PCN, CN. Rescue home supt., evangelist?

7038   UPDEGRAFF, David Brainerd (1830-1894). DAB. GFW (1888), 25-30. WWW in Am. (1607-1896), 544.
        Fr. Pastor, evangelist, editor
        b. Aug. 23, 1830, Mount Pleasant, Ohio
        d. May 23, 1894, Mount Pleasant, Ohio
7039   Clark, Dougan
        David B. Updegraff and his work, by Dougan Clark and Joseph H. Smith. Cincinnati, Published for Joseph H. Smith by M. W. Knapp, Revivalist Office, 1895. 310 p.

Part VI. Biography

7040 UPHAM, Phebe Lord. ROG (1854), 435-456.
Cong. Lay member

7041 UPHAM, Thomas Cogswell (1799-1872). DAB. GFW (1888), 226-236. WWW in Am. (1607-1896), 544. N.Y. Times (Apr. 3, 1872), 8:5. ROG (1854), 20-29. PPE (1868), 90-98.
Cong. College prof.
b. Jan. 30, 1799, Deerfield, N.H.
d. Apr. 2, 1872, New York, N.Y.

7042 Upham, Thomas Cogswell, 1799-1872.
African colonization; letter from Professor Thomas C. Upham, D.D. Washington, American Colonization Society, 1870. 4 p.
Caption title.
Notes on Liberia: p. 3-4.

7043 [Upham, Thomas Cogswell], 1799-1872.
Domestic and religious offering; illustrative of American scenery, rural life, and historical incidents, and also of religious feelings. 2d ed. With additions by the author. Boston, Waite, Peirce & Co., 1845. 321 p.
Added t.-p., with vignette: American cottage life.
Compiled by Dexter S. King.

7044 Upham, Thomas Cogswell, 1799-1872.
Letters aesthetic, social, and moral, written from Europe, Egypt, and Palestine. Private ed. Brunswick, Me., J. Griffin, 1855. 58 p.

7045 Packard, Alpheus Spring, 1798-1884.
Address on the life and character of Thomas C. Upham, D.D., late professor of mental and moral philosophy in Bowdoin College; delivered at the interment, Brunswick, Me., April 4, 1872, by Alpheus S. Packard. Brunswick, Me., J. Griffin, 1873. 24 p.

7046 VALLERY, Abden J. (-1937).
PCN, CN. Pastor, rescue home supt.
d. 1937, Memphis?, Tenn.

7047 VAN ANDA, Carmi A. (1833-1899).
Member, NHA
Sent paper to be read, HConf., 1877 (Cincinnati)
ME. Pastor, evangelist
b. 1833, Lewiston, Pa.
d. Sept. 3, 1899, Mackinac Island, Mich.

7048 VAN COTT, Maggie Newton (1830-1914). SCM (1881), 885. NAW (1607-1950), III, 506-507.
ME. Evangelist, rescue mission worker
b. Mar. 25, 1830, New York, N.Y.
d. Aug. 29, 1914, Catskill, N.Y.

7049 Van Cott, Maggie (Newton), 1830-1914.
The harvest of the reaper. New York, N. Tibbals,

1876. 360 p.
A dictated account by an evangelist who served the Methodist Church in New England and the Middle East.

7050 VANDALL, N. B. LMGSS (1952), 37. LDML (1953), 78.
ME. Businessman, evangelistic singer, gospel song writer

7051 VANDERPOOL, Daniel I. (1891-). SFLF (1950), 113-117.
CG (UHP), CN. Pastor, evangelist, district supt., general supt.
b. Sept. 6, 1891, Pollock, Mo.
7052 Vanderpool, Daniel I., 1891-
Living waters. Kansas City, Mo., Nazarene Publishing House, 1964. 123 p.
7053 Purkiser, Westlake Taylor, 1910-
"General Superintendent D.I. Vanderpool retires," Herald of Holiness, LIII (July 1, 1964), 369-370.

7054 VANDERPOOL, Wilford. DCSWM (1946), 144-149.
CN. Military chaplain, pastor

7055 VAN DE VENTER, Judson W. (1855-1939). LMGSS (1952), 77. RHOOF (1964), 427.
ME. Gospel song writer
b. Dec. 5, 1855, Dundee, Mich.
d. July 17, 1939, Tampa, Fla.

7056 VAN NAME, Nettie (-1892).
ME? Evangelistic singer?
7057 Hughes, George, 1828-1904.
The sweet singer, Nettie Van Name, and her seven years' work for Jesus, by George Hughes assisted by Mrs. Lidie H. Kennedy; introd. by Rev. E.I.D. Pepper. Philadelphia, National Holiness Publishing House, 1892? 89 p.

7058 VANSANT, Nicholas (1823-1902).
Endorsed call, GHA, 1901 (Chicago)
ME. Pastor
7059 Vansant, Nicholas, 1823-1902.
Sunset memories; with an introd. by General James F. Rusling. New York, Eaton & Mains; Cincinnati, Curts & Jennings, 1896. 271 p.
Autobiography.

7060 VAN SLYKE, D.C. (1898-1970).
FM, CN. Evangelist
b. Jan. 15, 1898, Elmore, Minn.
7061 Van Slyke, D.C., 1898-1970.
The wail of a drug addict. Grand Rapids, Mich., Wm. B. Eerdmans Publishing Co., 1945. 121 p.
Autobiography.

Part VI. Biography

7062 VARGAS, Ezequiel B. (-1965).
      ME, S; MEM; EMC. Pastor, presiding elder, general supt.
      d. Jan. 1965, Chihuahua, Chih., Mex.

7063 VAUGHN, Bill Edward
      CN. College prof.
7064   Vaughn, Bill Edward
      "Billy Graham: a rhetorical study in adaptation."
      Unpublished Ph.D. dissertation, University of Kansas, 1972. 258ℓ.

7065 VELAZQUEZ, Juan'(-1951). RWBTB (1953), 52-55.
      CN. Pastor
      d. Jan. 5, 1951, La Noria, Guanajuato, Mex.

7066 VENNARD, Iva May Durham (1871-1945). N.Y. Times (Sept. 15, 1945), 15:4. ATY (1930), 102-110.
      ME. Deaconess, evangelist, Bible college pres.
      b. Dec. 27, 1871, Prairie City, Ill.
      d. Sept. 12, 1945, Chicago, Ill.
7067   Bowie, Mary Ella
      Alabaster and spikenard; the life of Iva Durham Vennard, D.D., founder of Chicago Evangelistic Institute. Chicago, Chicago Evangelistic Institute, 1947. 317 p.

7067a VESTAL, Blum (1874-).
      IHC. Evangelist
7067b   Vestal, Blum, 1874-
      From the saloon to the pulpit. Greensboro, N.C., Printed by Apostolic Messenger Co., 1911. 61 p.
      Autobiography.

7068 VINCENT, Burton Jones (1877-1931). BMW (1960), 249-265. LMB (1948), 181. N.Y. Times (July 19, 1931), 22:1.
      Attended GHA, 1901 (Chicago)
      FM. Pastor, seminary (academy) prin., college pres., bishop
      b. Aug. 15, 1877, Ypsilanti, Mich.
      d. July 1931, Evanston, Ill.

7069 WACHTEL, Alexander. GHAI (1960), 30-31.
      CN. Missionary

7070 WADDELL, Lloyd L. (-1954). TDOOP (1968), 204.
      IHC, PHC. Pastor, evangelist, district supt.
      d. Sept. 7, 1954.

7071 WADDLE, G. E.
      HChuC, PCN. Pastor, district supt.

7072 WALDEN, John Morgan (1831-1914). DAB. LMB (1948), 183-184. SCM (1881), 894. WWW in Am. (1897-1942), 1288. N.Y. Times (Jan. 22, 1914), 7:7; (Jan. 23, 1914), 11:5.
Endorsed call, GHA, 1901 (Chicago)
ME. Pastor, editor, Freedmen's Aid Soc. corr. sec., pub. agent, bishop
b. Feb. 11, 1831, Lebanon, Ohio
d. Jan. 21, 1914

7073 WALKER, Edward Franklin (1852-1918). MOUS (1941), 23-28.
Endorsed call and attended, GHA, 1901 (Chicago)
ME, Pres., PCN. Pastor, evangelist, general supt.
b. Jan. 20, 1852, Steubenville, Ohio
d. May 6, 1918, Glendora, Calif.

7074 McGraw, James, 1913-
"The preaching of Edward F. Walker," Preacher's Magazine, XXIX (Sept. 1954), 3-5.

7075 WALKER, George C. FYAB (1954), 89.
ME?, CN, ME? Pastor, evangelist, district supt.

7076 WALKER, Jennie Reeves
ME?, CN, PCN, ME? Pastor's wife, evangelist

7077 WALKER, W. B.
CN. Pastor, evangelist

7078 WALLACE, Adam (1825-1903). SCM (1881), 896. N.Y. Times (Sept. 24, 1903), 9:6.
ME. Pastor, presiding elder, editor, camp meeting asso. member
b. Jan. 1825, Manor Hamilton, Ire.
d. Sept. 23, 1903, Germantown, Pa.

7079 WALLACE, DeLance (186?-193?). SCUH (1962).
ME, CN, PCN, CN. Rescue mission worker, pastor, pub. house mgr., district supt.

7080 WALLACE, Elsie M. SCUH (1962).
ME, CN, PCN, CN. Rescue mission supt., pastor

7081 WALLIN, Henry Bradford (1890-). RLOA (1941-1942), 1086. FHOP (1964). WW in the Clergy (1935-1936), 1148.
CN. Pastor
b. May 22, 1890, Vernon, Tex.

7082 WALLS, Alice E. (1887-1959). SBWTL (1960), 195-196.
FM. Pastor, Bible college teacher, Bible college prin., editor

Part VI. Biography

        b. 1887, Walsingham Centre, Ont.
        d. Feb. 1, 1959, London, Ont.

7083   WALLS, W. C. (-1900). SBWTL (1960), 182.
        PrimM, FM. Pastor, district elder

7084   WALTERS, Alexander (1858-1917). DAB. WW in Am.
        Meth. (1916), 232-233. WWW in Am. (1897-1942),
        1295. N.Y. Times (Feb. 3, 1917), 13:5.
        Endorsed call, GHA, 1901 (Chicago)
        AME Zion
        Pastor, bishop
        b. Aug. 1, 1858, Bardstown, Ky.
        d. Feb. 2, 1917, New York, N.Y.
7085   Walters, Alexander, bp., 1858-1917.
        My life and work. New York, Fleming H. Revell,
        1917. 272 p.
        Autobiography.

7086   WANG, Wen T'san. HNTB (1934), 47-50.
        CN. National worker, evangelist
        b. 18??, Chaocheng, Ch.

7087   WARD, Elizabeth Tucker (-1915). LLITW (1951), 217.
        FM. Missionary

7088   WARD, Ernest F. (-1938). LLITW (1951), 217.
        FM. Missionary

7089   WARD, J. A. (-1940).
        PCN, CN. Pastor
        d. 1940, Brooklyn?, N.Y.

7090   WARD, Phebe E. Cox (-1910). LLITW (1951), 217.
        FM. Missionary

7091   WARNER, Daniel Sidney (1842-1895). SHBD (1955), 17-50.
        MWWW in Ch. Hist. (1968), 427.
        CG (General Eldership), CG (N. Indiana Eldership),
        CG (A). Evangelist, editor, pastor
        b. June 25, 1842, Marshallville, Ohio (then Bristol)
        d. Dec. 12, 1895
7092   Warner, Daniel Sidney, 1842-1895.
        Innocence, a poem giving a description of the author's
        experience from innocence into sin, and from sin to full
        salvation. Grand Junction, Mich., Gospel Trumpet,
        1896. 26 p.
7093   Warner, Daniel Sidney, 1842-1895.
        "Papers, 1866-1885." 1 reel of microfilm. In
        Anderson College and Theological Seminary, School of
        Theology Library.
        Diary, personal notes, budget, record of sermons

preached, sermon outline book, a history of the Gospel Trumpet Co., and papers relating to Warner's business transactions on behalf of the Gospel Trumpet Co.

7094 Warner, Daniel Sidney, 1842-1895.
Poems of grace and truth. Grand Junction, Mich., Gospel Trumpet Publishing House, 1890. 343 p.

7095 Warner, Daniel Sidney, 1842-1895.
Salvation, present, perfect, now or never. Moundsville, W. Va., Gospel Trumpet, n.d. viii, 118 p.
Biographical sketch of author: p. [v]-viii.

7096 Byers, Andrew L., 1869-
Birth of a reformation; or, The life and labors of Daniel S. Warner. Anderson, Ind., Gospel Trumpet Co., 1921. 467 p.

7097 WARNER, David Snethen (1857-1927). BMW (1960), 181-196. LMB (1948), 189.
FM. Pastor, seminary (academy) teacher, seminary (academy) prin., editor, bishop
b. Oct. 29, 1857, Livingston County, N.Y.
d. May 13, 1927, Rochester, Minn.

7098 Warner, David Snethen, bp., 1857-1927.
Glimpses of Palestine and Egypt. Chicago, W. B. Rose, 1914. 229 p.

7099 WARNER, George R. (1900-). GTWATD (1965), 396-411. IHTA, EMC. Missionary, editor, missionary Society pres. (WGM)
b. July 1900

7100 WARREN, Barney Elliott (1867-1951). LMGSS (1952), 35. N.Y. Times (Apr. 23, 1951), 25:3.
CG (A). Gospel song writer, evangelist
b. 1867
d. Apr. 21, 1951, Springfield, Ohio

7101 WARREN, Robert Hopkins (1876-1938). BMW (1960), 267-281.
FM. Pastor, district elder, bishop
b. Mar. 6, 1876, Glenwood, N.Y.
d. 1938, Seattle, Wash.

7102 WARRINGTON, Uriah (1828-1913).
Member, IowaHA
Attended GHA, 1901 (Chicago)
ME. Pastor
d. Nov. 16, 1913, Chicago, Ill.

7103 WASHBURN, B. A.
Signed call, GHA, 1885 (Chicago)
HBd, HC. Pastor, evangelist

Part VI. Biography

7104 WASHBURN, James F. SCUH (1962).
Attended GHA, 1901 (Chicago)
HC. Pastor, evangelist, editor
7105 Washburn, Josephine F.
History and reminiscences of Holiness Church work in southern California and Arizona. South Pasadena, Calif., Record Press, 1912? 463 p.

7106 WASHBURN, Nathan H. (1865-1941). SCUH (1962).
APCA, PCN, CN. Pastor, district supt.

7107 WATERMAN, Anna (1874-   ). LMGSS (1952), 51.
CN? Gospel song writer
b. Oct. 29, 1874, New Market, Ind.

7108 WATERMAN, Charles C. (1870-   ). LMGSS (1952), 51.
WIWBA (1946), 68-77.
CN? Prison and hospital chaplain
b. 1870, Eugene, Ind.
7109 Waterman, Charles C., 1870-
Experience of Charles C. Waterman, conductor, Pasadena, Calif. Colorado Springs, Colo., Gospel Stationary & Tract House, n.d. 8 p.

7110 WATKINS, Aura Clay (1885-1945). WW in the Central States (1929), 1031. Kansas City Star (Nov. 8, 1945).
CG (UHP), CG (H). Pastor, evangelist, Bible school pres.
b. Aug. 24, 1885, College Mound, Mo.
d. Nov. 7, 1945, Kansas City, Mo.
7111 Watkins, Aura Clay, 1885-1945.
Pacific coast evangelistic tour; or, The opening of new fields for holiness. Louisville, Pentecostal Publishing Co., 1914. 118 p.
7112 Jones, Charles Edwin, 1932-
"Disinherited or rural?; a historical case study in urban Holiness religion," Missouri Historical Review, LXVI (Apr. 1972), 395-412.
Includes biography of A. C. Watkins.

7113 WATKINS, Mildred Eugenia (1913-   ). WWACUA (1970-1971), 560.
PF. College admin.
b. Feb. 10, 1913, Weehawken, N.J.

7114 WATSON, Charles Hoyt (1888-   ). RLOA (1941-1942), 1094. WW in Am. (1956-1957), 2706.
FM. Pastor, university prof., college prof., college pres.
b. Dec. 12, 1888, Eudora, Kan.

7115 WATSON, Claude A. (1885-). RLOA (1941-1942), 1094.
WW in Am. (1956-1957), 2706-2707.
FM. Pastor, district supt., attorney
b. June 26, 1885, Wexford County, Mich.

7116 WATSON, George Douglas (1845-1924). WWW in Am.
(1897-1942), 1308. GFW (1888), 78-84. PFT (n.d.),
32-34 (2d group).
HConf., 1877 (Cincinnati)
Endorsed GHA, 1885 (Chicago)
ME, WM, IHC, WM. Pastor, evangelist
b. Mar. 26, 1845, Accomac County, Va.
d. 1924, Los Angeles?, Calif.

7117 WATSON, James. TDOOP (1968), 234-237.
R. Cath., PHC. National worker, evangelist
b. 19??, Barbados

7118 WEATHERFORD, Fred Merle (1888-). RLOA (1941-1942), 1095.
CN. Pastor
b. Jan. 18, 1888, Arlington, Ore.

7119 WEAVERS, George (1840-1914). WMK (1966).
Bapt., WFMA, HFMA. Farmer, pastor, evangelist,
missionary, evangelistic asso. pres.
b. Feb. 18, 1840, Soham, Cambridgeshire, Eng.
d. 1914, Waverly, N.Y.
7120 McCord, James Bennett
My patients were Zulus, by James B. McCord with
John Scott Douglas. New York, Rinehart, 1951.
308 p.
Congregationalist missionary doctor who found natives inculcated with belief in faith healing as taught by George Weavers, Hephzibah Faith Missionary Association missionary, before McCord arrived.

7121 WEBB, Bruce Darrell (1933-). WWACUA (1970-1971),
562.
CN. College admin.
b. Feb. 11, 1933, Okemah, Okla.

7122 WEBER, Joseph Hulse (1855-).
R. Cath., ME. Pastor, evangelist
b. Oct. 12, 1855, Cincinnati, Ohio
7123 Knapp, Martin Wells, 1853-1901.
Revival tornadoes; or, Life and labors of Rev.
Joseph H. Weber, evangelist, the converted Roman
Catholic. Cincinnati, Revivalist Publishing House,
1889. 326 p.

Part VI. Biography

7124 WEEDEN, Winfield Scott (1847-1908). LMGSS (1952), 77. RHOOF (1964), 435.
ME? Gospel song writer, evangelistic singer
b. Mar. 29, 1847, Middleport, Ohio
d. July 31, 1908, Bisby Lake, N.Y.

7125 WEEKS, Sherwood (1907-1968).
ME, CN, I, FM, EWC. Pastor, Bible college pres.
b. June 6, 1907, Erie, Pa.
d. Nov. 1, 1968

7126 Weeks, Sherwood, 1907-1968.
The delusion of the holiness mystics and heresy in the holiness pulpits. Wauseon, Ohio, Gilson Press, 1955. Unpaged.
Cover title: Mysticism, antinomianism and the positive gospel.

7127 The Earnest Christian, VII (Nov. 1968).
Includes obituary of Sherwood Weeks.

7128 WEEKS, Sylvester (1836-1921).
Attended HConf., 1877 (Cincinnati)
ME. Pastor
b. Nov. 28, 1836, Cincinnati, Ohio
d. Dec. 29, 1921, Florida?

7129 WEES, F. M. (1874-). SBWTL (1960), 185-186.
FM. Pastor
b. 1874, Stratford, Ont.

7130 WEIDMAN, J. C. (-1910).
Attended HConf., 1877 (Cincinnati)
ME. Pastor

7131 WELCH, Charles Edgar (1852-1925). WW in Am. Meth. (1916), 238. WWW in Am. (1897-1942), 1318. N.Y. Times (Jan. 7, 1925), 25:3.
ME. Manufacturer, temperance worker, missionary promoter, editor
b. Mar. 2, 1852, Watertown, N.Y.
d. Jan. 6, 1925

7132 WELLMAN, George L. (-1967).
IHC, PHC. Pastor
d. Feb. 10, 1967

7133 WELLS, Charlotte Johns (-1936). LLITW (1951), 217.
FM. Missionary

7134 WELLS, Edward Thompson (1842-1912).
Attended HConf., 1877 (Cincinnati)
ME. Pastor
b. July 29, 1842, Norwalk, Ohio
d. Oct. 23, 1912, Toledo, Ohio

7135 WELLS, Elbert H. (-1948). LLITW (1951), 217.
FM. Missionary

7136 WELLS, Fred K. TDOOP (1968), 287, 290.
HC, PHC. Pastor, church pres.

7137 WELLS, George C. (1819-1873). MAWACOSM (1925), 320-321.
Member, NHA
ME. Pastor, evangelist, gospel song writer
b. 1819, Colchester, Conn.
d. May 31, 1873, Minneapolis, Minn.

7138 WELLS, Kenneth H. LDML (1953), 77.
CN. Evangelist, evangelistic singer, gospel song writer, Bible college teacher

7139 WERT, Clarence E. (-1963). TDOOP (1968), 344.
PHC. Bible college prof., Bible college pres.
d. Dec. 7, 1963.
7140 Pilgrim Holiness Advocate, XLIV (Jan. 25, 1964), 7.

7141 WESTCOTT, John Bunyan (1839-1930). N.Y. Times (Apr. 11, 1930), 27:5.
Endorsed call, GHA, 1901 (Chicago)
ME. Pastor
b. 1839
d. Apr. 10, 1930, Camden, N.J.

7142 WESTERGREEN, Nels O. (1834-1919).
Attended GHA, 1901 (Chicago)
ME. Pastor
b. July 25, 1834, Blekinge, Swed.
d. Oct. 22, 1919, Chicago, Ill.

7143 WHEATON, Elizabeth Ryder (1844-). WMK (1966), 16-17.
Attended GHA, 1901 (Chicago)
HFMA. Evangelist, prison worker
7144 Wheaton, Elizabeth (Ryder), 1844-
Prisons and prayer; or, A labor of love, an account of nearly twenty-two years of gospel work, seeking the lost, in prisons, reformatories, stockades, rescue homes, saloons and dives, and on the streets, railroad trains, etc.... Tabor, Iowa, C.M. Kelley, 1906. 634 p.

7145 WHEELER, Elizabeth
CN. Missionary
7146 Tracy, Gertrude (Perry)
Beth and I in India; ed. by Amy N. Hinshaw and Mary E. Cove. Kansas City, Mo., Nazarene Publishing House, 1932. 94 p.
Autobiographical.

Part VI. Biography

7147 WHEELER, Mary Sparkes (1835-1919). GFW (1888), 158-168. WWW in Am. (1897-1942), 1329.
ME. Evangelist, temperance worker, writer
b. June 21, 1835, Tinturn Abbey, Eng.
d. Jan. 21, 1919, Ocean Grove, N.J.
7148 Wheeler, Mary (Sparkes), 1835-1919, comp.
Poems for the fireside; in three parts: childhood, youth and mature age, original and selected. Cincinnati, Walden and Stowe, 1883. 200 p.

7149 WHIFFEN, Nellie M. (-1946). LLITW (1951), 217.
FM. Missionary

7150 WHITAKER, Charles B. (1855-).
Endorsed and attended, GHA, 1901 (Chicago)
UB. Pastor, presiding elder
7151 Whitaker, Charles B., 1855-
Whitaker's system of rapid writing, for the typewriter, especially adapted to be used with the new model Hall typewriter. Spring Grove?, Mich., 1890. [4] p.

7152 WHITCOMB, A. L.
Attended GHA, 1901 (Chicago)
President, NHA, 1928
ME, FM, PCN, FM. Pastor, college pres., evangelist

7153 WHITCOMB, L. B.
Endorsed call, GHA, 1901 (Chicago)
FM. Pastor

7154 WHITE, Alma Bridwell (1862-1946). MWWW in Ch. Hist. (1968), 435. Nat. Cy. of Am. Biog., XXXV, 151-152. WW on the Pacific Coast (1947), 1008. RLOA (1941-1942), 1106. N.Y. Times (June 27, 1946), 21:4. School & Society, LXIV (July 6, 1946), 11. NAW (1607-1950), III, 581-583. WWW in Am. (1943-1950), 571.
Attended GHA, 1901 (Chicago)
ME, MetCA?, PU, POF. Evangelist, pastor, Bible college pres., bishop
b. June 16, 1862, Lewis County, Ky.
d. June 26, 1946, Zarephath, N.J.
7155 White, Alma (Bridwell), 1862-1946.
Jerusalem; Egypt; Palestine; Syria. Zarephath, N.J., Pillar of Fire, 1936. 2 v. in 1.
Part I first published in 1911 under title: My trip to the Orient.
7156 White, Alma (Bridwell), 1862-1946.
Looking back from Beulah; on the overruling and forming hand of God in the poverty and struggles of

childhood and the hardships of later years; the battles, victories, and joys of the sanctified life, and the discovery of the path that led to it. The apostasy of the modern churches, with scriptural subjects and comments. Evangelistic labors.... Denver, Colo., The Pentecostal Union, 1902. 307 p.
Autobiography.

7157 White, Alma (Bridwell), 1862-1946.
Looking back from Beulah; on the overruling and forming hand of God in the poverty and struggles of childhood and the hardships of later years; the battles, victories, and joys of the sanctified life.... Zarephath, N.J., Pillar of Fire, 1929. 392 p.
Autobiography.

7158 White, Alma (Bridwell), 1862-1946.
Musings of the past; illustrated by Rev. Branford Clarke. Zarephath, N.J., Pillar of Fire, 1927. 112 p.

7159 White, Alma (Bridwell), 1862-1946.
My heart and my husband. Zarephath, N.J., 1923. 94 p.
Contains music.

7160 White, Alma (Bridwell), 1862-1946.
My trip to the Orient. Bound Brook, N.J., The Pentecostal Union (Pillar of Fire), 1911. 215 p.

7161 White, Alma (Bridwell), 1862-1946.
Ein rückblick aus Canaan (Beulah); über die alles leitende und formende hand Gottes in der armut und den kämpfen der kindheit; die beschwerden späterer jahre; die kämpfe, siege und freuden des geheiligten lebens.... Zarephath, N.J., Pillar of Fire, 1919. 365 p.
Translation of Looking back from Beulah.

7162 White, Alma (Bridwell), 1862-1946.
The story of my life and the Pillar of Fire. Zarephath, N.J., Pillar of Fire, 1935-1943. 5 v.
Autobiography.

7163 White, Alma (Bridwell), 1862-1946.
The voice of nature; illustrated by Rev. Branford Clarke. Zarephath, N.J., Pillar of Fire, 1927. 116 p.
Poems.

7164 White, Alma (Bridwell), 1862-1946.
With God in the Yellowstone. Zarephath, N.J., Pillar of Fire, 1920. 138 p.

7165 Paige, Clara R., 1869-   , comp.
Alma White's evangelism; press reports, comp. by C.R. Paige [and] C.K. Ingler. Zarephath, N.J., Pillar of Fire, 1939-1940. 2 v.
"Drawings by Branford Clarke."

7166 "Pillar," American Magazine, CXXIII (May 1937), 101.
7167 White, Arthur Kent, 1889-
Some White family history. Denver, Colo., Pillar of Fire, 1948. 432 p.

Part VI. Biography 783

7168   Wolfram, Gertrude (Metlen), 1888-
        The widow of Zarephath, a church in the making.
        Zarephath, N.J., Pillar of Fire, 1954. 244 p.

7169   WHITE, Arthur Kent (1889-   ). Nat. Cy. of Am. Biog.,
        cur. v. F, 219. RLOA (1941-1942), 1106.
        PU, POF. Evangelist, pastor, Bible college pres.,
            bishop
        b. Mar. 15, 1889, Denver, Colo.

7170   WHITE, Kent (1860-1940). Nat. Cy. of Am. Biog., XXXV,
            152.
        ME, PU, Pent. Pastor, evangelist, editor, Bible
            school teacher
        b. Aug. 16, 1860, Beverly, Randolph County, Va.
            (now W.Va.)
        d. July 31, 1940, Denver, Colo.
7171   White, Kent, 1860-1940.
        The hostel of the Good Shepherd. London, Hodder
        & Stoughton, 1938. 126 p.

7172   WHITE, Levi
        Attended GHA, 1901 (Chicago)
        Cong. Pastor

7173   WHITE, Myrtle Mangum. FHOP (1964).
        ME, HChuC, CN. Pastor, missionary, teacher
        b. 18??, Mason, Iowa

7174   WHITE, Ray Bridwell (1892-1946). Nat. Cy. of Am. Biog.,
            35:152-153; cur. v. F, 219-220. RLOA (1941-1942),
            1109. WW in Am. (1926-1927), 2020.
        PU, POF. Pastor, Bible college pres., bishop
        b. Aug. 24, 1892, Morrison, Colo.
        d. Nov. 5, 1946, Zarephath, N.J.

7175   WHITE, Stephen Solomon (1890-1971). SFLF (1950), 118-
            122. LIE (1941), 1073. Herald of Holiness, LX
            (Apr. 14, 1971), 27. NP (1925), 221-232.
        CN. Pastor, college prof., seminary prof., editor,
            college pres.
        b. Jan. 25, 1890, Walnut Springs, Tex.
        d. Mar. 21, 1971, Kankakee, Ill.
7176   White, Stephen Solomon, 1890-1971.
        ...A comparison of the philosophies of F.C.S.
        Schiller and John Dewey. Chicago, 1940. iv, 80 p.
        Thesis (Ph.D.)--University of Chicago, 1938.
7177   McGraw, James, 1913-
        "The preaching of Stephen S. White," Preacher's
        Magazine, XXXV (Aug. 1960), 5-8.

7178 WHITESIDE, Edward D.
       Endorsed call, GHA, 1901 (Chicago)
       CMA. Pastor?, rescue mission supt.

7179 WHITTEMORE, Emma Mott (1850-1931). MCV (1901), 110-
       118. MMAWODP (1920), 496-507. N.Y. Times
       (Jan. 3, 1931), 17:4.
       Endorsed call, GHA, 1901 (Chicago)
       DH. Rescue mission supt., rescue home supt.
       d. Jan. 2, 1931, New York, N.Y.
7180   Whittemore, Emma (Mott), 1850-1931.
       Mother Whittemore's records of modern miracles;
       foreword by her son and daughter and by Commander
       Evangeline Booth; tribute by Miss Sara Wray of the
       Eighth Avenue Mission. New York City, ed. by Rev.
       F.A. Robinson. Toronto, Missions of Biblical Educa-
       tion, 1931. 310 p.
7181   Whittemore, Emma (Mott), 1850-1931.
       Frankie; or, The little conqueror.... New York,
       Door of Hope Repository, 1894. 67 p.
7182   Meredith, Isaac Hickman, 1872-
       The story of the pink rose, by Mrs. E.M. Whitte-
       more; with music arranged by I.H. Meredith. New
       York, Tullar-Meredith Co., c1899. 31 p.
       With the music.

7183 WHITTLE, J. A. G. LLITW (1951), 217.
       FM. Missionary

7184 WIDMEYER, Charles Brenton (1884-19??). RLOA (1941-
       1942), 1113-1114. WW in the Clergy (1935-1936),
       1181-1182. WW in Calif. (1942-1943), 979-980. WW
       on the Pacific Coast (1950), 1009. LMGSS (1952),
       131. LDML (1953), 79. FHOP (1964).
       CN. Evangelist, college prof., pastor, district supt.,
       gospel song writer
       b. July 19, 1884, Berkeley Springs, W.Va.

7185 WIDNEY, Joseph Pomeroy (1841-1938). DAB (2d suppl.).
       N.Y. Times (July 5, 1938), 17:2.
       ME, CN, ME, I. Physician, pastor, rescue mission
       worker, general supt., university pres.
       b. Dec. 26, 1841, Miami County, Ohio
       d. July 4, 1938, Los Angeles, Calif.
7186   Widney, Joseph Pomeroy, 1841-1938.
       Civilizations and their diseases; and, Rebuilding a
       wrecked world civilization. Los Angeles, Pacific Pub-
       lishing Co., 1937. 2 v. in 1.
7187   Widney, Joseph Pomeroy, 1841-1938.
       The faith that has come to me. Los Angeles, Paci-
       fic Publishing Co., 1932. 272 p.

Part VI. Biography

7188 Widney, Joseph Pomeroy, 1841-1938.
The genesis and evolution of Islam and Judaeo-Christianity. Los Angeles, Pacific Publishing Co., 1932. 238 p.
Companion to The faith that has come to me.

7189 Widney, Joseph Pomeroy, 1841-1938.
Race life and race religions; modern light on their growth, their shaping and their future, a survey. Los Angeles, Pacific Publishing Co., 1936. 133, 253 p.

7190 Widney, Joseph Pomeroy, 1841-1938.
The three Americas; their racial past and the dominant racial factors of their future. Los Angeles, Pacific Publishing Co., Times-Mirror Press, 1935. 306 p.
A continuation of the story of race migrations told in Race-life of the Aryan Peoples.

7191 Widney, Joseph Pomeroy, 1841-1938.
Whither away?; the problem of death and the hereafter. Los Angeles, Pacific Publishing Co., 1934. 152 p.
Prose and poetry.

7192 Bay, Leslie F., Jr.
"History of the University of Southern California." Unpublished M.A. thesis, University of Southern California, 1910. xiii, 301, 8ℓ.
Includes account of the presidency of J.P. Widney.

7193 Potter, Edward Lawrence
"The Widney family." Unpublished M.A. thesis, University of Southern California, 1966. iii, 130ℓ.

7194 W., E. T.
"Joseph Pomeroy Widney, A.M., M.D., D.D., LL.D.," California and Western Medicine, XLIV (Apr.-June 1936), 3-6.

7195 Warner, J. J.
An historical sketch of Los Angeles County, California, from the Spanish occupancy, by the founding of the Mission San Gabriel Archangel, September 8, 1771, to July 4, 1876, prepared by J.J. Warner, Benjamin Hayes [and] J.P. Widney; a reprint of the original ed. published by Louis Lewin & Co., no. 14, Spring St., 1876, to which is added an invaluable introd. written by J.P. Widney, the surviving member of the trio, July 4, 1936. Los Angeles, O.W. Smith, 1936. 159 p.

7196 WILCOX, Mrs. Tabitha McSween
ME? Rescue mission worker

7197 Wilcox, Mrs. Tabitha McSween
Incidents of a city missionary's life. Louisville, Ky., Pentecostal Publishing Co., 1916. 121 p.
Autobiography.

7198 WILEY, Arlene Maudie Likes (1923-   ). ETWF (196?).
I, PHC. Missionary, Bible college teacher
b. Sept. 3, 1923, Corunna, Ind.

7199 WILEY, Charles A. (1925-1963). ETWF (196?).
I, PHC. Missionary
b. Jan. 8, 1925, Muncie, Ind.
d. Apr. 26, 1963

7200 WILEY, Henry Orton (1877-1961). WW on the Pacific Coast (1947), 604. WW on the Pacific Coast (1950), 1013. WW in Calif. (1961), 49. WW in Am. (1948-1949), 2682. LIE (1948), 1150. WW in the Clergy (1935-1936), 1184. RLOA (1941-1942), 1116.
UB, CN, PCN, CN. Pastor, editor, college pres.
b. Nov. 15, 1877, Marquette, Neb.
d. Aug. 22, 1961, Pasadena, Calif.

7201 WILKENS, John Charles (1923-   ). WWACUA (1970-1971), 575
WM. College admin.
b. Jan. 17, 1923, Niota, Ill.

7202 WILKES, Alphaeus Nelson Paget (1871-1934). MWWW in Ch. Hist. (1968), 439.
Ch. of Eng., JEB. Missionary, evangelist
b. 1871, Tichwell, Suffolk, Eng.

7203 Wilkes, Alphaeus Nelson Paget, 1871-1934.
Missionary joys in Japan; or, Leaves from my journal ... with an introd. by the Rev. Barclay F. Buxton. London, Morgan & Scott, 1913. xvi, 321 p.

7204 Govan Stewart, Isabel Rosie, 1900-
Dynamic: Paget Wilkes of Japan; foreword by B.G. Buxton. London, Edinburgh, Marshall, Morgan & Scott, 1957. 96 p.

7205 Japan Evangelistic Band.
Memorial series. London, 1935. 6 pts.
In memory of A. Paget Wilkes.

7206 Pattison, Mary Winifred Dunn
Ablaze for God; the life story of Paget Wilkes.... London, Japan Evangelistic Band, 1936. xii, 317 p.

7207 WILKINS, Chester (1918-   ). WWACUA (1970-1971), 576.
PHC, W. College prof., college admin.
b. Dec. 26, 1918, Evansville, Ind.

7208 WILLARD, Amy Hankins (-1951). LLITW (1951), 217.
FM. Missionary

7209 WILLARD, Frances Elizabeth (1839-1898). DAB. MCV (1901), 16-22. WWW in Am. (1607-1896), 581. GFW (1888), 69-77. NAW (1607-1950), III, 613-619.

MMAWODP (1920), 486-495.
ME. Seminary (academy) teacher, college pres., temperance worker
b. Sept. 28, 1839, Churchville, N.Y.
d. Feb. 18, 1898, New York, N.Y.

7210 Willard, Frances Elizabeth, 1839-1898.
Glimpses of fifty years.... Chicago, Woman's Temperance Publishing Association, 1889. 698 p.

7211 Willard, Frances Elizabeth, 1839-1898.
My happy half-century; the autobiography of an American woman; ed. by Frances E. Cook ... with an introd. by Lady Henry Somerset.... London, Ward, Lock & Bowden, 1894. 392 p.

7212 Earhart, Mary
Frances Willard: from prayers to politics. Chicago, University of Chicago Press, 1944. 417 p.

7213 WILLARD, Francis Burleigh. LLITW (1951), 202-203.
FM. Missionary

7214 WILLETT, John Starbuck (1876-). MHWMCOA (1959), 164-166. WW in Am. Meth. (1916), 242.
WM. Pastor, conference pres., denominational official
b. Oct. 30, 1876, Measham, Eng.

7215 WILLIAMS, Mrs. E. E.
Attended GHA, 1901 (Chicago)
ME? Evangelistic worker

7216 WILLIAMS, Eunice Harvey
ME, S; HChuC; PCN; CN. College prof., pastor's wife

7217 McConnell, Charles Allen, 1860-1955.
Daughter of the hill country. Kansas City, Mo., Beacon Hill Press, 1949. 142 p.
First published under title: Happy Day.
Fictional biography of Eunice Harvey Williams.

7218 McConnell, Charles Allen, 1860-1955.
Happy Day. Kansas City, Mo., Nazarene Publishing House, c1921. 170 p.
Fictional biography of Eunice Harvey Williams.

7219 WILLIAMS, J. E.
CN. Evangelist

7220 Williams, J. E.
Fireside chats of "Your friendly philosopher."
Louisville, Pentecostal Publishing Co., 19??. 32 p.

7221 WILLIAMS, Lewis Milton (1862-). FYAB (1954), 92.
SA, CN. Evangelist, district supt.

7222 WILLIAMS, Reginald Stille (1910-). WW in the West (1970-1971), 674.

CN, Epis. Leader's child, attorney
b. Feb. 19, 1910, Peniel, Tex.

7223 WILLIAMS, Roy Tilman (1883-1946). WWW in Am. (1943-1950), 531.
ME, S; PCN; CN. College prof., evangelist, pastor, general supt.
b. Feb. 14, 1883, Many, La.
d. Mar. 25, 1946, Tuscambia, Mo.

7224 Williams, Roy Tilman, 1883-1946.
Glimpses abroad. Kansas City, Mo., Nazarene Publishing House, 1930. 250 p.
Account of foreign travel supervising missionary activity of the Church of the Nazarene.

7225 Emmel, James Robert, 1923-
"Speeches and speaking of Roy Tilman Williams."
Unpublished M.A. thesis, University of Oklahoma, 1950.

7226 McGraw, James, 1913-
"The preaching of Roy T. Williams," Preacher's Magazine, XXIX (June 1954), 5-8.

7227 Williamson, Gideon Brooks, 1898-
Roy T. Williams, servant of God. Kansas City, Mo., Nazarene Publishing House, 1947. 230 p.

7228 Williamson, Gideon Brooks, 1898-
Roy T. Williams, servant of God. Rev. ed. Kansas City, Mo., Nazarene Publishing House, 1970. 112 p.

7229 WILLIAMS, Roy Tilman, Jr.
CN. Pastor, college admin., college prof.

7230 Williams, Roy Tilman
"A study of the problems of self-development of a selected number of aspiring and practicing school superintendents." Unpublished Ed.D. dissertation, Boston University, 1964. 329ℓ.

7231 WILLIAMS, W. H. EAP (1890, c1879), 107-109. PPE (1868), 65-70.
Asso. Ref., Pres. Pastor

7232 WILLIAMSON, Audrey Johnston
ME, CN. College prof., pastor's wife

7233 WILLIAMSON, Gideon Brooks (1898-   ). RLOA (1941-1942), 1121. WW in the Midwest (1965-1966), 1043. MHP (1957), 13-22.
CG (H), CN. Pastor, college pres., general supt.
b. Nov. 26, 1898, New Florence, Mo.

7234 WILLING, Herman S.
Attended GHA, 1901 (Chicago)
PB. Rescue mission worker

Part VI. Biography

7235 WILLING, Jennie Fowler (1834-1916). SCM (1881), 952-953. NAW (1607-1950), III, 623-625. GFW (1888), 280-285.
Endorsed call, GHA, 1901 (Chicago)
ME. Pastor's wife, missionary promoter, temperance worker
b. Jan. 22, 1834, Burford, Ont., Can.
d. Oct. 6, 1916, New York, N.Y.

7236 WILLING, William C. LLITW (1951), 217.
FM. Missionary, physician

7237 WILLINGHAM, Theodore Weber (1893-). WW in the Midwest (1949), 1320. RLOA (1941-1942), 1121-1122.
CN. Pastor, college admin., college pres., evangelist, district supt., denominational admin.
b. Jan. 20, 1893, Sebree, Ky.

7238 WILSON, Albert H. (1888-1956). TDOOP (1968), 102-104, 325.
PRM, PHC. Pastor, evangelist, district supt.
b. Sept. 1, 1888, Saranac, N.Y.
d. Aug. 15, 1956

7239 WILSON, Clarence True (1872-1939). ATY (1930), 24-40. WW in Am. Meth. (1916), 244. WW in the Clergy (1935-1936), 1191. WWW in Am. (1897-1942), 1359. N.Y. Times (Feb. 17, 1939), 19:1.
ME. Pastor, reformer, denominational official
b. Apr. 24, 1872, Milton, Del.
d. Feb. 16, 1939

7240 WILSON, David Emerson (1893-1963). TDOOP (1968), 343. RLOA (1941-1942), 1123.
PRM, PHC. Pastor, evangelist
b. Sept. 8, 1893, Saranac, N.Y.
d. Jan. 17, 1963

7241 Pilgrim Holiness Advocate, XLIII (Feb. 23, 1963), 5.

7242 WILSON, Ermal Leroy (1917-). ETWF (196?). TDOOP (1968), 316-317.
PHC, W. Evangelist, missionary, denominational official
b. Mar. 3, 1917, Daviess County, Ind.

7243 "Conference elects 11 officers," Wesleyan Advocate, CXXVII (July 15, 1968), 9-10.

7244 WILSON, George Washington (1853-1929). DC (1965, c1887), 149-158.
ME. Pastor, evangelist
d. Jan. 25, 1929

7245   Wilson, George Washington, 1853-1929.
        Truths as I have seen them. Cincinnati, Jennings &
        Pye, 1897.

7246   WILSON, Guy L. ATY (1930), 92-101. SCUH (1962), 305.
        CN, PCN, LHA, ME. Pastor, evangelist

7247   WILSON, Henry. MCW (1901), 130-136.
        Epis., CMA. Asst. minister, field supt.
        b. 18??, Peterborough, Ont., Can.
        d. 19??, Atlanta, Ga.

7248   WILSON, Isaiah (1842-1932).
        Attended GHA, 1901 (Chicago)
        ME. Pastor
        b. July 17, 1842
        d. Feb. 28, 1932

7249   WILSON, John
        Attended GHA, 1901 (Chicago)
        ME? Pastor?

7250   WILSON, Madgel Howard (1915-1967). ETWF (196?).
        PHC. Missionary, evangelist
        b. May 23, 1915, Jackson, Mich.
        d. Jan. 24, 1967

7251   WILSON, Oliver G. (1891-1959).
        WM. Pastor, conference pres., college prof., denomi-
            national official, editor
        b. 1891, Oak Hill, Kan.
        d. June 28, 1959, Houghton, N.Y.
7252   Wilson, Charles
        Climbing the hills; the life of Oliver G. Wilson, ed.
        by the Department of Sunday Schools, Wesleyan Metho-
        dist Church of America. Marion, Ind., Wesley Press,
        1963. 19 p.

7253   WILSON, W. H. SBWTL (1960), 185.
        FM. Teacher, pastor, Bible college admin.
        d. 19??, Seattle, Wash.

7254   WILSON, William Columbus (1866-1915).
        ME, S; CN; PCN. Pastor, evangelist, general supt.
        b. Dec. 22, 1866, Hopkins County, Ky.
        d. Dec. 19, 1915, Pasadena, Calif.
7255   McGraw, James, 1913-
        "The preaching of William C. Wilson," Preacher's
        Magazine, XXXIV (July 1959), 4-6.

7256   WIMBERLY, Charles Franklin (1866-1946). ATY (1930),
        82-91. WW in Am. Meth. (1916), 245. WWW in

Part VI. Biography

Am. (1943-1950), 585. WW in the Clergy (1935-1936), 1194.
ME, S. Pastor, editor, evangelist
b. Nov. 19, 1866, Jefferson County, Ill.
d. July 10, 1946, Columbia, S.C.

7257 Wimberly, Charles Franklin, 1866-1946.
The mills of the gods, a tale of tomorrow; illustrated by Newell Wimberly. Louisville, Pentecostal Publishing Co., c1929. 255 p.

7258 Wimberly, Charles Franklin, 1866-1946.
The vulture's claw; a tale of rural life. New York, R.F. Fenno & Co., c1910. 356 p.

7259 WINANS, Esther Carson (1891-1928).
WM, CN. Missionary
b. Sept. 11, 1891, Big Prairie, Ohio
d. Nov. 6, 1928, Jaen, Chiclayo, Peru

7260 Winans, Esther (Carson), 1891-1928.
Letters; ed. by Carol Gish, with personal recollections of Esther Carson Winans by Dr. H. Orton Wiley. Kansas City, Mo., Beacon Hill Press, 1951. 126 p.

7261 Winans, Esther (Carson), 1891-1928.
Letters of Esther Carson Winans, missionary to the Aguaruna Indians, comp. and ed. by Carol Gish. Rev. ed. Kansas City, Mo., Nazarene Publishing House, 1967. 103 p.

7262 Hinshaw, Amy N.
The trail of the Aguaruna (a life story of Esther Carson Winans). Kansas City, Mo., Nazarene Publishing House, n.d. 188 p.

7263 WINANS, J. W. (1864-1929). LLITW (1951), 217. SBWTL (1960), 203.
FM. Pastor, missionary
b. 1864, North Cayuga township, Haldimande County, Ont.
d. 1929, Hamilton, Ont.

7264 WINANS, Roger S. (1886-). FHOP (1964).
CN. Missionary
b. Dec. 15, 1886, Osawkie, Kan.

7265 Winans, Roger S., 1886-
Gospel over the Andes; notes of Roger S. Winans. Kansas City, Mo., Beacon Hill Press, 1955. 141 p. Autobiography.

7266 WINCHESTER, Charles Wesley (1843-1917). WWW in Am. (1897-1942), 1364.
ME. Pastor, seminary (academy) prin., presiding elder, editor, college pres.
b. July 2, 1843, Westminster, Vt.

7267   Winchester, Charles Wesley, 1843-1917.
            Reminiscences of fifty years in Christian service.
        Louisville, Pentecostal Publishing Co., 1915. 255 p.
            First pub. in the Northern Christian Advocate.

7268   WINCHESTER, Olive May (1880-1947). WW in the Clergy
            (1935-1936), 1195. RLOA (1941-1942), 1127. LIE
            (1941), 1096.
            CN. Pastor?, college prof., college admin.
            b. Nov. 22, 1880, Monson, Me.

7269   WINES, John Maurice (1857-). FYAB (1954), 91-92.
            ME, CN. Pastor, district supt.
7270   Wines, John Maurice, 1857-
            Hoosier happenings. Kansas City, Mo., Nazarene
        Publishing House, 1926. 106 p.
            Autobiography.

7271   WINGET, Benjamin
            Attended GHA, 1901 (Chicago)
            FM. Pastor, denominational official

7272   WINGET, Wilfred Lamont (1930-). DAS (1969), IV, 398.
            CN. Pastor, college prof.
            b. July 25, 1930, Dover, N.J.

7273   WINSLOW, Carolyn Van Valin. LLITW (1951), 203.
            FM. Missionary

7274   WINSLOW, Harold H. (-1944). LLITW (1951), 217.
            FM. Missionary

7275   WISE, Daniel (1813-1898). DAB. SCM (1881), 959.
            ME. Pastor, editor
            b. Jan. 10, 1813, Portsmouth, Eng.
            d. 1898, Englewood, N.J.

7276   WISE, Forest Franklyn (1920-). WWACUA (1920-1921),
            584. LIE (1971), 1026.
            CN. Pastor?, college prof., college admin.
            b. Oct. 21, 1920, Akron, Ohio

7277   WISE, H. H. (1888-1948).
            Pres., F.W. Bapt., CN. Pastor, district supt.
            b. Jan. 29, 1888, Johnson County, Tenn.
            d. Aug. 21, 1948, Nashville, Tenn.
7278   Cox, Edward F.
            "The preaching of H. H. Wise." Preacher's Magazine, XXXIII (May 1958), 5-8.

7279   WISEMAN, Peter (1883-). SFLF (1950), 123-127.
            HMoC. Pastor, evangelist, Bible college teacher,
                college prof.

Part VI. Biography 793

7280 WISLER, R. L.
Attended GHA, 1901 (Chicago)
HCC, PCN?, CN. Pastor

7281 WISSBROECKER, Edwin Kenneth. GHAI (1960), 36-43.
Luth., CN, W. Missionary

7282 WOERTENDYKE, James H. (1869-).
Attended GHA, 1901 (Chicago)
ME. Pastor

7283 WOLFE, J. E. (1872-1955).
PHC. Evangelist, pastor, editor, Bible colporteur
d. Aug. 21, 1955

7284 WOLFE, R. W. TDOOP (1968), 204, 215-217.
PHC. Pastor, district supt., denominational official, evangelist
b. 18??, West Virginia

7285 WOOD, Bernice M. (-1941). LLITW (1951), 217.
FM. Missionary

7286 WOOD, John Allen (1828-19??). HM (1882). PPE (1868), 346-350. DC (1965, c1887), 139-148.
Signed call to meeting to form NHA, 1867 (Philadelphia)
Attended H. Conf., 1877 (New York)
Attended GHA, 1885 (Chicago)
Attended GHA, 1901 (Chicago)
Member, NHA
ME. Pastor, evangelist
7287 Wood, John Allen, 1828-
Autobiography. Chicago, Christian Witness Co., 1904. 113 p.
7288 Wood, John Allen, 1828-
Sunset echoes. Chicago, Christian Witness Co., 1904. 179 p.

7289 WOOD, M. D.
ME, APCA, Advent. Missionary
7290 Wood, M. D.
Fruit from the jungle. Mountain View, Calif., Pacific Press Publishing Association, 1919. 331 p.
Autobiography, p. 6-14.

7291 WOODARD, Luke (1832-). GFW (1888), 90-92.
Fr. Pastor
b. Mar. 12, 1832, New Garden, Wayne County, Ind.
7292 Woodard, Luke, 1832-
Sketches of a life at 75.... Richmond, Ind., Nicholson Printing Co., 1907. 246 p.

7293 WOODBRIDGE, Mary Ann Brayton (1830-1894).
Cong. ? Temperance worker?
7294 Hills, Aaron Merritt, 1848-1935.
Life and labors of Mrs. Mary A. Woodbridge ... with an introd. by Miss Frances E. Willard, and contributions by Lady Henry Somerset, Joseph Cook, John G. Wooley and others. Ravenna, Ohio, F. W. Woodbridge, 1895. 401 p.

7295 WOODRUFF, Arnold Bond (1920-   ). AMS (1968). DCSWM (1946), 36-45.
CN, UM. Military chaplain, college prof.
b. Sept. 15, 1920, Columbus, Ohio

7296 WOODRUM, Lon Riley (1901-   ). MLA (1935), 85-89.
Cath., CN, EUB. Evangelist
b. Dec. 8, 1901, Petersburg, Ill.

7297 WOODS, Harry F.
IHC, PHC. Missionary (OMS)

7298 WOODS, John Franklin (1865-   ).
ME, IHC, PHC. Railroad worker, pastor, evangelist
b. Nov. 19, 1865, Chambersburg, Pa.
7299 Woods, John Franklin, 1865-
God's marvelous grace to me; a short history of the life of the author, with a few Bible readings and sermons, with an introd. by Rev. W. L. Surbrook, General Superintendant of the Pilgrim Holiness Church. Huntington, W. Va. ?, 1936. 175 p.
Autobiography.

7300 WOODS, W. S. (-1950). LLITW (1951), 217.
FM. Missionary

7301 WORCESTER, Leonard Beacher (-1926). WMK (1966).
Pres., WFMA, HFMA. Pastor, editor, missionary, Bible school teacher, evangelist, evangelistic asso. pres.
d. 1926, Tabor, Iowa

7302 WORDSWORTH, E. E. SCUH (1962), 312-313.
PCN, CN. Pastor, district supt.

7303 WORTHEIM, Mrs. R. L.
Attended GHA, 1901 (Chicago)
ME? Lay member?

7304 WRIGHT, Virginia Fern Meeks (1925-   ). ETWF (196?).
PHC. Bible college teacher, missionary
b. Feb. 6, 1925, Babatpur, India

Part VI. Biography

7305 WRIGHT, Wayne Wible (1926-   ). ETWF (196?).
PHC. Bible college teacher, missionary
b. Oct. 22, 1926, Terre Haute, Ind.

7306 WU, Tung Tai. HNTB (1934), 42-44.
CN. National worker, pastor
b. 18??, China

7307 WYMAN, Edward G.
CN. Missionary, evangelist
7308 Wyman, Edward G.
Along the Latin trail; [trophies for the Master in Latin-American evangelism]. Kansas City, Mo., Nazarene Publishing House, 1963. 71 p.
Autobiographical.

7309 WYNKOOP, Mildred Bangs
CN. Missionary, pastor's wife, seminary prof., college prof.
7310 Wynkoop, Mildred (Bangs)
"A historical and semantic analysis of methods of Biblical interpretation as they relate to views of inspiration." Unpublished Th.D. dissertation, Northern Baptist Theological Seminary, 1955.

7311 YARD, Edmund Jones (1792-1876).
ME. Lay leader?
7312 James, Mary Dagworthy (Yard), 1810-1883.
The soul-winner; a sketch of facts and incidents in the life and labors of Edmund J. Yard ... by his sister, Mrs. Mary D. James ... with an introd. by D.P. Kidder, D.D. New York, Phillips & Hunt; Cincinnati, Walden & Stowe, 1883. 231 p.

7313 YOCUM, Dale Morris
CG (H). Bible college dean, Bible college pres., missionary, pastor
7314 Yocum, Dale Morris
"A study of exceptional students who entered the University of Kansas in the fall of 1954." Unpublished Ed.D. dissertation, University of Kansas, 1957.
7315 Yocum, Dale Morris
A study of exceptional students who entered the University of Kansas in the fall of 1954, by Dale M. Yocum and Kenneth E. Anderson. Lawrence, [University of Kansas] School of Education, 1957. 40 p.

7316 YODER, Carrie A.
IAHC, IHC. Evangelist

7317 YOUNG, Donald L. (1931-   ). WWACUA (1970-1971), 594.
CN. College prof., college dean
b. Nov. 23, 1931, Portland, Me.

7318 YOUNG, Egerton Ryerson (1840-1909). WMDCB (1963), 818.
MWWW in Ch. Hist. (1968), 449.
Endorsed call, GHA, 1901 (Chicago)
Meth. (Can.). Public school teacher, missionary, pastor
b. Apr. 7, 1840, Crosby, Upper Can.
d. Oct. 5, 1909, Bradford, Ont., Can.

7319 Young, Egerton Ryerson, 1840-1909.
By canoe and dog-train among the Cree and Salteaux Indians; with an introd. by Mark Guy Pearse. Toronto, W. Briggs, 1890. x, 267 p.

7320 Young, Egerton Ryerson, 1840-1909.
By canoe and dog-train among the Cree and Salteaux Indians; with an introd. by Mark Guy Pearse. New York, Hunt & Eaton; Cincinnati, Cranston & Stowe, 1891. xvi, 267 p.

7321 Young, Egerton Ryerson, 1840-1909.
On the Indian trail; stories of missionary work among the Cree and Saulteaux Indians. New York, Fleming H. Revell, 1897. 214 p.

7322 Young, Egerton Ryerson, 1840-1909.
Oowikapun; or, How the gospel reached the Nelson River Indians. New York, Hunt & Eaton; Cincinnati, Cranston & Curts, 1894. 240 p.

7323 Young, Egerton Ryerson, 1840-1909.
Oowikapun; or, How the gospel reached the Nelson River Indians. London, C.H. Kelly, 1895. 162 p.

7324 Young, Egerton Ryerson, 1840-1909.
Stories from Indian wigwams and northern campfires. New York, Hunt & Eaton; Cincinnati, Cranston & Curts, 1893. 293 p.

7325 YOUNG, G. A. LMGSS (1952), 27.
CN? Carpenter, gospel song writer

7326 YOUNG, George W.
Attended GHA, 1901 (Chicago)
ME? Pastor?

7327 YOUNG, Samuel (1901-).
CN. Pastor, district supt., college pres., general supt.
b. Sept. 8, 1901, Glasgow, Scot.

7328 Herald of Holiness, LXI (June 7, 1972), 5-9.

7329 YOUNG, Willie. HNTB (1934), 121-123.
CN. National worker, teacher, evangelist
b. 19??, Swaziland, S.Afr.

7330 YOUNGREN, Anna Millikan (-1941). LLITW (1951), 217.
FM. Missionary

Part VI. Biography

7331 YOUNGREN, August. LLITW (1951), 214.
FM. Missionary

7332 YOUNGREN, Ethel Helm Clarke (-1947). LLITW (1951), 217.
FM. Missionary

7333 YUNGRED, Kison. HNTB (1934), 103-104.
Hindu, CN. National worker
b. 19??, India

7334 ZAHNISER, Arthur DeFrance (1865-1935). BMW (1960), 213-230. N.Y. Times (Aug. 15, 1935), 19:2. WWW in Am. (1897-1942), 1394.
Pres., FM. Pastor, district elder, evangelist, bishop
b. Aug. 26, 1865, Five Points near Mercer, Pa.
d. Aug. 14, 1935, Laramie, Wyo.

7335 Zahniser, Arthur DeFrance, bp., 1865-1935.
Servant of God; life story and selected articles of Bishop Arthur D. Zahniser, by Lefa E. Snyder and Bernice E. Weidman. Winona Lake, Ind., Light and Life Press, 1940. 185 p.

7336 ZELLEY, Henry J. (1859-1942). LMGSS (1952), 17. N.Y. Times (Mar. 18, 1942), 23:3.
ME. Pastor, gospel song writer
d. Mar. 18, 1942, Roselle Park, N.J.

7337 ZIMMERMAN, Julia. LLITW (1951), 217.
FM. Missionary

7338 ZURBRIGG, William (1873-1958). SBWTL (1960), 186.
FM. Pastor
b. 1873, Perth County, Ont.
d. Nov. 1958, Toronto, Ont.

INDEX

A. M. Chesbrough Seminary see Roberts Wesleyan College
Aaron, T. L. see Aaron, Thomas Lee (1897-1951)
Aaron, Thomas Lee (1897-1951) 4286, 4604
Abbott, Hollis F. 4605
Abbott, J. D. see Abbott, John D. (1922-)
Abbott, John D. (1922-) 4606-4608
Abel, Paul Frederick 4328
Abolition of Slavery see Slavery
Abstinence see Temperance
Abundant Life Magazine 4252
Ackerman, George Everett 222, 2879
Ackers, Hiram 4609
Acornley, Agnes Rebecca 4610-4611
Acornley, J. H. see Acornley, John Holmes
Acornley, John Holmes 3106-3107, 4611-4613, 4688
Acornley, Mrs. John Holmes see Acornley, Agnes Rebecca
Action (periodical) 3382
Adams, B. M. see Adams, Benjamin Mathias (1823-1902)
Adams, Benjamin Mathias (1823-1902) 4614
Adams, Charles Jackson (1925-). 4615
Adams, Homer James (1921-) 4616
Adams, J. 3783

Adams, John Quincy (1825-1881) 103
Adams, Joseph 2589
Adams, Roy P. 2067
Adirondack Bible College 4299, 7127
Adrian, Mich. 4300
Adrian College 4300
Advocate (periodical) see Pentecostal Holiness Advocate (periodical)
Advocate for Primitive Christian Union (periodical) 1963
Advocate of Bible Holiness (periodical see Christian Witness and Advocate of Bible Holiness (periodical)
Advocate of Christian Holiness (periodical) see Christian Witness and Advocate of Bible Holiness (periodical)
Advocate of Holiness (periodical) 756
Advocate of Holiness and the Speedy Coming of the Lord (periodical) 757
Africa 977, 1862, 2177, 2748-2752, 3429, 3574, 4128, 4288, 5027, 5037, 5085, 5157, 5610-5611, 5631, 6227-6239, 6753-6756, 6934-6936, 6942, 6944, 6948-6948, 6952, 7042, 7120
Africa, Central 1863, 6952
Africa, South 1864-1865, 2072, 2476-2479, 3033-3035, 3575-3576, 4036-4037, 4514, 5178, 5205, 5396-5398, 5544, 5797, 5765, 5768, 5972, 6656-6657, 6747, 6934-6935, 6948-6949, 7120

Africa Evangelistic Band
3249-3253, 4349 see also
Faith Mission
Africa Evangelistic Mission
3254-3256
African (periodical) 758, 2372
African Methodist Episcopal
Church 5376-5377, 6753-
6756
African Methodist Episcopal
Zion Church 7085
African News (Vineland, N.J.)
759
African News (Vineland, N.J.,
Chicago, etc.) 760
Africa's Revivalist (periodical)
3545
Africa's Silent Messenger (periodical) 2473
Agnew, G. Harry see Agnew,
George Harry Augustus
(1864-1903)
Agnew, George Harry Augustus
(1864-1903) 4617-4618
Agnew, Mrs. George Harry
Augustus see Agnew, Lillie
Smith (-1939); Agnew,
Susie Sherman (-1895)
Agnew, Lillie Smith (-1939)
4619
Agnew, Milton Seccombe 3626,
4620
Agnew, Susie Sherman (-1895)
4621
Agnew, T. H. (-1924) 4622
Agnosticism 5603, 5607 see
also Atheism
Ahrendt, Edward Henry (1878-)
1146
Ahrendt, Vivian 1146
Aiken, Irene 1320
Akers, J. W. see Akers,
John W.
Akers, John W. 4623
Akers, Lewis Robeson (1881-)
223, 959, 4624
Akers, Lyle Everette 5305,
5307
Alabama 4855
Alaska 4230
Alberta 1868, 2753, 3771,
4301, 4354, 4374, 4512,
5931

Alberta and Saskatchewan Holiness Association 4354
Alberta Bible Institute 4301
Alberta Bible School see
Canadian Nazarene College
Alberta School of Evangelism
see Canadian Nazarene College
Alberton, Mont. 4524
Albright, Raymond Wolf (1901-
) 1988, 3719
Albuquerque, N. Mex. 4517
Alcoholism see Liquor problem
Alderfer, Owen Hiram (1923-)
1011, 4625
Aldersgate College 4302
Aldersgate School of Religion
4303
Alejandro, D. D. 4626
Alexander, John Wesley (1918-)
2632, 4627-4629
All the World (periodical) 3672
Allan, David (-1940) 4630
Allee, G. Franklin see Allee,
George Franklin (1897-)
Allee, George Franklin (1897-)
1417, 1568, 1654, 4631, 6331
Allegheny Wesleyan Methodist
Connection (Original Allegheny Conference) 3897-
3902, 4524
Allen, Charles Bosne (1857-)
224, 873
Allen, Drell see Allen, Edric
Drell (1917-)
Allen, Edric Drell (1917-)
4632
Allen, Jacob Randolph (1838-
1924) 4633
Allen, John (1795-1887) 4634
Allen, Stephen (1810-1888) 4635
Allentown, Pa. 4539, 4580
Allentown Bible Institute see
Penn Wesleyan College
Alliance of the Reformed Baptist Church 1004-1009, 4340
Alliance of the Reformed Baptist Church. Department of
Foreign Missions. 1008
Alliance of the Reformed Baptist Church of Canada see
Alliance of the Reformed

Baptist Church
Alliance Weekly (periodical)
see Alliance Witness (periodical)
Alliance Witness (periodical) 4065, 4123
Alling, J. H. see Alling, Jacob Hart (1837-1919)
Alling, Jacob Hart (1837-1919) 4636
Allis, Mrs. Matilda 225
Allyn, R. see Allyn, Robert (1817-1894)
Allyn, Robert (1817-1894) 4637
Alma Prepatory School 4304
Alma White Bible College 4305
Alma White College 2223, 4306-4307
Altamont Bible and Missionary Institute see Holmes Theological Seminary
Altamont Witness (periodical) 4191
Alwood, J. K. 226
Amanda Smith Industrial School for Girls 4308-4309
American Baptist Publication Society 3946
American Holiness Journal (periodical) 191, 761
American Indians see Indians of North America
American Methodist (periodical) see Lamp of Life (Bay City, Mich., etc.)
American Methodist League 2507
American Outlook (periodical) 762
American Wesleyan (periodical) see Wesleyan Methodist (periodical)
Amillennialism see Millennialism
Amolik, B. D. 4638
Amsden, F. W. (-1940) 4639
Anabaptist and Wesleyan Tradition Seminar, Goshen College Biblical Seminary, Goshen, Ind., 1960 2545

Anderson, Alfred (1851-1921) 4640
Anderson, August Magnus (1878-) 2748, 4641
Anderson, J. Grant 1146
Anderson, Kenneth Eugene (1926-) 7315
Anderson, Mack 4642
Anderson, R. S. see Anderson, Richard Simpson (1882-1945)
Anderson, Richard Simpson (1882-1945) 4643-4644
Anderson, T. H. B. 4645-4646
Anderson, T. M. see Anderson, Tony Marshall (1888-)
Anderson, Tony Marshall (1888-) 227, 1321, 1418, 1783, 1960-1961, 4315, 4647
Anderson, William Ketcham (1888-1947) 2483
Anderson, Ind. 1187, 4310, 4428
Anderson Bible School and Seminary see Anderson College
Anderson Bible Training School see Anderson College
Anderson College 4310, 6253
Anderson College and Theological Seminary see Anderson College
Andree, Paul 4648
Angell, E. E. see Angell, Ernest E. (-1939)
Angell, Edward D. 2546
Angell, Ernest E. (-1939) 2546, 4649
Angelo, Valenti 39
Anglo-Israelism 626, 2106-2107
Ann Arbor, Mich. 6958
Annesley College 4311
Anson, Robert Sam 6044
Antichrist 591, 1575, 3410, 4092, 4094
Antigua 3577
Antislavery see Slavery
La Antorcha Dominical (periodical) 1727
Apostolic Christian Church see

Apostolic Christian Church (Nazarean); Apostolic Christian Church of America
Apostolic Christian Church (Nazarean) 2009-2011
Apostolic Christian Church of America 2012-2020
Apostolic Evangel (Goldsboro, N.C., etc.) 4192
Apostolic Evangel (Royston, Ga.) see Live Coals of Fire (periodical)
Apostolic Evangelist (periodical) 3546
Apostolic Faith see Apostolic Faith Mission (1907-); Apostolic Faith Movement (1900-)
Apostolic Faith Mission 4228-4235 see also Apostolic Faith Movement
Apostolic Faith Movement 4236-4238, 4348
Apostolic Holiness Bible School see Beulah Heights College and Bible School; Bresee College
Apostolic Messenger (periodical) 3547
Apostolic Methodist Church 2596-2597
Apostolic succession 2880, 2882
Apostolic Visitor (periodical) see International Holiness Church Paper (periodical)
Appleton, C. Floyd (1881-1932) 4650-4651
Appleton, Mrs. C. Floyd see Appleton, Laura Millican (-1939)
Appleton, Laura Millican (-1939) 4651
Argentina 5330
Arizona 2823, 4530
Arkansas 2782, 3225, 4203, 4312, 4437, 4447, 4533
Arkansas Holiness Academy and Bible School 4312
Arkansas Holiness College see Arkansas Holiness Academy and Bible School
Arkansas Holiness Literary School see Arkansas Holiness Academy and Bible School
Arkansas Nazarene Seminary and Normal Training High School see Arkansas Holiness Academy and Bible School
Arksey, Lawrence E. (1898-) 4652
Arlington, Calif. 4313
Arlington College 4313
Armenian question 3774-3775, 5272, 5911
Armenians 3471, 5435, 5911, 6641
Arminius, Jacobus (1560-1609) 4706-4708, 4710
Arms, Goodsil Filley (1854-) 4653, 6945
Armstrong, C. I. see Armstrong, Chauncey Irwin (1896-)
Armstrong, Chauncey Irwin (1896-) 4654
Armstrong, Kenneth Shelby 1677-1678, 1849-1850
Armstrong, William T. 4655
Arnett, William Melvin (1915-) 659, 4656
Arnold, E. Irena 3621
Arnold, J. M. see Arnold, John Motte (1824-1884)
Arnold, John Motte (1824-1884) 4657-4658
Arnold, T.B. see Arnold, Thomas B.
Arnold, Thomas B. 2709, 2736, 4659
Arnold, Mrs. William C. see Arnold, E. Irena
Arnold, William Erastus (1862-) 3042, 3058, 4660, 6246
Arrién, J. J. see Arrién, Juan J. Uriarte
Arrién, Juan J. U. see Arrién, Juan J. Uriarte
Arrién, Juan J. Uriarte 2157
Arthur, William (1819-1901) 2512, 4661

Asbury, Francis (1745-1816)
2828-2829, 2967
Asbury, Herbert (1891-   )
4496
Asbury Bible College see
Francis Asbury Bible College
Asbury College 382, 435, 865,
903, 1418, 4314-4325, 5718-
5719, 5849, 6249-6251,
6398-6400, 6958
Asbury Collegian (periodical)
763
Asbury Seminarian (periodical)
4329
Asbury Theological Seminary
4326-4331
Asbury Theological Seminary.
Fortieth Anniversary Committee 4327
Ash, Edward (1797-1873) 2279
Ashton, Albert E. 2266, 3227
Ashton, Bessie Sherman 2266
Askwith, Edward Harrison
(1864-   ) 25, 3943
Aslin, Bessie Ruth (1905-1967)
4662
Aslin, Thomas Elbert (1904-   )
4663
Aslin, Mrs. Thomas Elbert
see Aslin, Bessie Ruth
(1905-1967)
Association of Evangelical
Friends see Evangelical
Friends Alliance
Association of Free Methodist
Colleges 2682
Association of Pentecostal
Churches of America 1002-
1003, 4392-4394, 6547,
7290
Atheism 2334, 5606, 6651,
6810 see also Agnosticism
Atkinson, Elbert L. 4664
Atkinson, John Edward 5665
Atkinson, Joseph Baines 2513
Atlanta, Ga. 4335, 4449-4451,
6709-6711
Atter, Gordon Francis (1905-   )
4154
Atwood, Alvin Ray (1924-   )
1593

Atwood, Anthony (1801-1888)
229, 864, 2856-2858, 2880-
2882, 3048, 4665-4666
Austel, Kathe P. 4667
Australia 1869-1870, 3226,
4515, 4595
Austrian-Americans 6478
Ava, Mo. 4443, 4509-4510
Avery, Arietta M. (1910-   )
4668
Avery, Gordon Coleman (1913-   )
4669
Avery, Mrs. Gordon Coleman
see Avery, Arietta M.
(1910-   )
Awe, Ben A. see Awe, Benjamin A. (-1960)
Awe, Benjamin A. (-1960)
4670-4671
Awesu, Jonathan 4672-4673
Ayars, J. E. see Ayars,
John E.
Ayars, John E. 646, 4674
Aycock, Dell Davis (-1967)
1322, 1784-1785, 4675-4676,
4677
Aycock, Jarrette E. (-1966)
892, 1323, 1609-1611, 1713,
1786-1789, 4677-4681
Aycock, Mrs. Jarrette E. see
Aycock, Dell Davis (-1967)
Azusa, Calif. 4313, 4332
Azusa College see Azusa Pacific College
Azusa Pacific College 2308,
4332-4334

B. T. C. Journal (periodical)
3297
B. T. Roberts Seminary 4335
Babcock, C. H. 230
Babson, Roger Ward (1875-   )
1637
Backenstoe, William Alfred
(-1932) 4682
Bailey, Bertram Henry 4683
Bailey, Mrs. Bertram Henry
see Bailey, Bessie A.
Bailey, Bessie A. 4684
Bailey, Nathan 4122
Baily, Mrs. L. A. 5419
Baird, Mr. 231

Baker, Archibald Gillies (1875-) 3764
Baker, H. E. see Baker, Harold Edwin (1896-)
Baker, Harold Edwin (1896-) 2740, 4685-4686
Baker, Mrs. Harriet 4687-4688
Baker, L. H. see Baker, Leonidas H. (1850-1933)
Baker, Leonidas H. (1850-1933) 4689
Baker, Richard Terrill (1913-) 3386
Baker, Mrs. Sarah 4690
Baker, Sheridan (1824-1890) 232-233, 3022, 4691-4695
Baldwin, Harmon Allen (1869-1936) 234, 1544, 2643-2649, 2678, 4696
Baldwin, Lindley J. 6227-6229
Ball, Charles S. 2307
Ball, Ephraim (1812-1872) 2883, 4697
Ballard, Aaron Edward (1820-1919) 4698
Balsmeier, A. F. 4699
Banfield, A. W. (1878-) 4700-4704
Bangs, Carl Oliver (1922-) 1751, 4532, 4705-4710
Bangs, Mildred see Wynkoop, Mildred Bangs
Bangs, Nathan (1778-1862) 2884, 4711-4714
Banker, E. Stanley (1918-) 4715
Banker, Floyd E. 2267, 3228
Banker, Mrs. Floyd E. see Banker, Hazel Rodgers (-1959)
Banker, Hazel Rodgers (-1959) 2267, 3228
Banker, Max Emerson (1920-) 4716
Banks, Stanley 449, 1973, 3307-3308, 4717, 5250
Banner of Holiness (periodical) see Church Voice and Banner of Holiness (periodical)
Banner of Hope (periodical) 764

Banner of Love (periodical) 765
Baptism 247, 281, 320-321, 333, 2384, 2881, 2933, 3706, 7039
Barbados 3578-3579, 4378, 5338, 5340, 5754
Barchwitz-Krauser, Oscar von 6946
Barclay, Robert (1648-1690) 2271
Barclay, Wade Crawford (1874-) 2820
Barefoot, Adlie E. (1925-) 4718
Barefoot, Mrs. Adlie E. see Barefoot, Laurette Ilene (1929-)
Barefoot, Laurette Ilene (1929-) 4718-4719
Barker, Earl Pickett 4316
Barker, John Henry James 2514, 2676
Barkley, Vada Lee Beard 5537, 5539
Barnabas, Steven 4021-4022
Barnard, Allison F. 1080
Barnes, Grace Elizabeth (1890-1918) 4720-4721
Barnes, Horatio Nelson (1806-1896) 2370
Barnes, O. W. (-1965) 4722
Barnesville, Ohio 2367-2368
Barnett, Paul W. 2272
Barnhart, Kenneth Edwin (1893-) 2484
Barr, David Miller 6016
Barr, Josiah Henry 191
Barrett, Clifford Bean (1821-1899) 4723-4724
Barrett, Earl Edward (1893-) 4725
Barrett, William H. 4726
Barth, Karl (1886-1968) 54, 57
Bartlesville, Okla. 4336
Bartlesville Wesleyan College 4336
Barton, Bruce (1886-1963) 3649
Bassett, Ancel H. (1809-1886) 3101
Bassett, Helen Fair (1917-) 4727

Bassett, Roger Garfield (1921-) 4728
Bassett, Mrs. Roger Garfield see Bassett, Helen Fair (1917-)
Bates, Lewis Benton 4729
Batt, John Herridge 2590
Battersby, Thomas Dundas Harford (1823?-1883) 4023-4024
Battle, Allen Overton 4155-4156, 4225a
Bauer, Betty May (1928-) 4730
Bauer, Fred 6696-6697
Bauer, Lawrence Paul (1926-) 4731
Bauer, Mrs. Lawrence Paul see Bauer, Betty May (1928-)
Baugh, Stanley T. 2782
Baumgartner, S. H. see Baumgartner, Samuel Henry (1860-)
Baumgartner, Samuel Henry (1860-) 1983
Bautz, Friedrich Wilhelm 2012
Baxter, Mrs. M. 4732
Beacham, Paul Franklin (1888-) 4248, 4733-4734
Beals, Charles Arthur (1906-) 2383, 4735
Beals, Prescott L. 1898
Beard, Charles Austin (1874-1948) 1
Beard, Frank 6942
Beare, Thomas J. (-1919) 4736
Bearse, Joseph C. (1869-1931) 4737
Beatty, Charles L. (1934-) 4738
Beauty of Holiness (periodical) 3011
Beckwith, Berdina (-1950) 4739
Bedell, Chester 6810
Bedsole, Adolph 2399
Bedwell, H. Kenneth 2476-2479, 5972
Beebe, Ralph K. (1932-) 2388

Beebe, T. E. see Beebe, Theodore Eaton
Beebe, Theodore Eaton 198, 1285, 1747, 2871, 4740
Beech Lawn Bible College 4337
Beegle, Mrs. Burton L. see Beegle, Gladys Smith (-1947)
Beegle, Gladys Smith (-1947) 4741
Beeman, David see Beeman, Samuel David (1922-)
Beeman, Samuel David (1922-) 4742
Beers, Adelaide Lionne Newton (-1940) 4743-4744
Beers, Forest William 856
Beet, Joseph Agar (1840-1924) 2885, 4745
Begbie, Harold (1871-) 3650, 4818
Beirnes, Billy 4748
Beirnes, George (-1942) 1569, 3583, 4746
Beirnes, William F. 3500-3507, 4747-4748
Belden, Henry (1813-1884) 4749
Belew, P. P. see Belew, Pascal Perry (1894-)
Belew, Pascal Perry (1894-) 1420, 1790, 4750-4751, 6947
Belgian Congo see Congo
Bell, Dewayne Bert (1920-) 4752
Bell, Thomas 4753-4754
Bell, W. M. see Bell, William Melvin (1860-1933)
Bell, William Melvin (1860-1933) 3726
Bell City, La. 4338
Bell City College 4338
Belleau Wood (Aircraft carrier) 4629
Belleview College Academy, and Bible Seminary see Belleview Prepatory School
Belleview Junior College, Academy, and Bible Seminary see Belleview Prepatory School
Belleview Prepatory School 4339
Bellew, Leona see McConnell,

Leona Bellew
Beltz, Roy Allen (1905-   )
   3485, 4755
Bemesderfer, James Orville
   2007
Benargees, Mrs. Sukhoda
   4756-4757
Benn, M. S. see Benn,
   Miles S. (1867-   )
Benn, Miles S. (1867-   ) 4758
Bennard, George (1873-1958)
   4759
Benner, Elias Stephen (1867-
   1957) 4760-4761
Benner, Forest T. 2547
Benner, H. C. see Benner,
   Hugh Clifford (1899-   )
Benner, Hugh Clifford (1899-   )
   1387, 1712, 4761-4762
Benner, Rol Welbourn (1901-   )
   4763
Bennet, P. C. 4764
Bennett, Harriet see Brooks,
   Harriet Bennett (-1940)
Bennett, J. D. (-1899)
   4765
Bennett, Merril 1931
Bennett, Willis G. 1324-1325,
   1421, 4766-4769
Bennis, Eliza (1725-1802)
   2515
Benson, Erwin George (1905-   )
   1759, 4770
Benson, Eva (1865-1932) 4771
Benson, John T. (1861-1930)
   2191, 4772
Benson, Mrs. John T. see
   Benson, Eva (1865-1932)
Benson, Joseph (1749-1821)
   550-551, 2544, 2591
Bent, John 4773
Berea, Ky. 5324
Berg, A. A. E. 4879
Berg, Clifton Fletcher (1908-   )
   4774
Berg, Mrs. Clifton Fletcher
   see Berg, Emeline Ilda
   Hamel (1914-   )
Berg, Emeline Ilda Hamel
   (1914-   ) 4775
Bergson, Henri (1859-1941)
   5648

Berkouwer, Gerrit Cornelis
   (1903-   ) 55
Berry, J. A. see Berry, John
   A. (-1936)
Berry, Jack see Berry, John
   A. (-1936)
Berry, John A. (-1936) 4776
Berry, Joseph Flintoft (1856-
   1931) 3024
Berry, Robert Lee (1874-   )
   1081, 4777
Bert, Norman A. 1019
Berwick upon Tweed, Eng.
   4484
Bethany, Okla. 1936, 4342-
   4347
Bethany Bible College 4340
Bethany Fellowship 3257-3264,
   4341
Bethany Fellowship Bible and
   Missionary Training Institute
   4341
Bethany Fellowship Missionary
   Training Center see Bethany
   Fellowship Bible and Mis-
   sionary Training Institute
Bethany Nazarene College
   1378a, 4342-4347
Bethany Nazarene College Today
   (periodical) 4343
Bethany-Peniel College see
   Bethany Nazarene College
Bethany-Peniel College Today
   (periodical) see Bethany
   Nazarene College Today (per-
   iodical)
Bethel Bible College 4348
Bethel Bible School, Kimberley,
   S. Afr. 3252, 4349-4350
Bethel Bible School, Topeka,
   Kan. see Bethel Bible Col-
   lege
Bethel College, Mishawaka, Ind.
   4351
Bethel College, Topeka, Kan.
   see Bethel Bible College
Bethel Herald (periodical) 3548
Bethel Holiness School 4352
Bethel Institute 4353
Bethel Mission of China 3265-
   3269
Bethel Mission of China. News-

letter 3269
Bethel News (periodical) 3252
Beulah, Okla. 4436
Beulah, Okla. Holiness Bible School see Holiness Bible School, Beulah, Okla.
Beulah Bible Institute 4354
Beulah Bible School see Missionary Bible Institute
Beulah Christian (Oklahoma City, Okla.) 766
Beulah Christian (Providence, R.I.) 1003, 2027
Beulah College see Upland College
Beulah Heights College and Bible School 4355
Beulah Holiness Academy 4356
Beulah Holiness Bible School see Holiness Bible School, Beulah, Okla.
Beulah Items (periodical) 2026
Beulah Land (periodical) 767
Beulah Park Bible School see Penn Wesleyan College
Beulah Seminary 4357
Bevin, Karl Heinz Martin (1914-) 4778
Bevin, Mrs. Karl Heinz Martin see Bevin, Ruth Ralston (1912-)
Bevin, Ruth Ralston (1912-) 4779
Bevington, G. C. see Bevington, Guy C.
Bevington, Guy C. 4780-4782
Beyer, Herman E. 1113
Bhembe, Lillian 4783
Bhujabal, Mrs. Bandu see Bhujabal, Yeshodabai
Bhujabal, Bulwantrao see Bhujabal, Jacob Johns (-1917)
Bhujabal, David 1784
Bhujabal, Jacob Johns (-1917) 4785
Bhujabal, Samuel (1906-) 4786
Bhujabal, Yeshodabai 4787
Bianchi, E. 4157
Bible and Missionary Institute of Atlanta see Holmes Theological Seminary
Bible Christian (periodical) 2028
Bible colleges see Education
Bible Evangelist (periodical) 768
Bible Holiness Mission see Bible Holiness Movement
Bible Holiness Movement 2021-2023
Bible Holiness Seminary see John Wesley College, Owosso, Mich.
Bible Home and Foreign Missionary Society 3270-3271
Bible Institute of Los Angeles 4012
Bible Methodist (periodical) 3906
Bible Methodist Church see Bible Methodist Connection of Churches
Bible Methodist Connection of Churches 2120, 3903-3906
Bible Methodist Connection of Churches. Conferences. Ohio 3904
Bible Methodist Connection of Churches. General Conference 3905
Bible Methodist Missions 2609
Bible Missionary Church 3868-3878, 4359
Bible Missionary Church. Foreign Missions Committee 3876
Bible Missionary Church. General Conference 3868
Bible Missionary Institute 4359
Bible Missionary Union see Bible Missionary Church
Bible School and Missionary Training Institute see Holmes Theological Seminary
Bible School and Rescue Home 4361
Bible School Journal (periodical) 1728
Bible School Teacher's Journal (periodical) see Bible School Journal (periodical)
Bible schools see Education
Bible Standard (periodical) 3212

Bible Training College 3324, 4362-4363
Bible Training Institute 4364
Bible Training School see Lee College
Bible Training School and College see Lee College
Bickley, George Harvey, bp., (1868-1924) 5384
Bickmore, Edward C. 4788
Binghamton, N.Y. 4541
Binney, Amos (1802-1878) 4789
Binney, Amos (1802-1878). Binney's Theological compend., improved. 1207, 2886
Biola see Bible Institute of Los Angeles
Birch, Zola Dee Kinnison (1892-1950) 3232
Birchard, Margaret (Anderson) 4644
Birchard, Russell 4644
Birkenhead, Eng. 4398
Birkenhead, Eng. Emmanuel Bible College see Emmanuel Bible College, Birkenhead, Eng.
Birmingham, Eng. 2593
Bishop, Charles H. S. 4790
Bishop Taylor's Magazine see African News (Vineland, N.J.)
Black, E. W. see Black, Ernest Watson (1890-1948)
Black, Ernest Watson (1890-1948) 3162, 3223, 4791
Black, Harry (1895-) 4792, 4793
Black, Lillie F. 4794
Black, Warren 1585, 4795-4796
Blacks see Negroes
Blackwelder, Boyce W. 1082, 1113
Blakeslee, G. H. 4797
Blanchard, C. L. see Blanchard, Charles Lorraine (1902-)
Blanchard, Charles Lorraine (1902-) 120, 4798

Blanchard, Pierre 34
Blaney, Harvey Judson Smith (1905-) 1313, 1439, 4799
Blann, Eva Isabel (1920-) 4800
Blann, Henry John (1920-) 4801
Blann, Mrs. Henry John see Blann, Eva Isabel (1920-)
Blews, Richard R. 2627
Bliss, E. M. see Bliss, Edwin Munsell (1848-1919)
Bliss, Edwin Munsell (1848-1919) 2029, 2033, 2057, 2065, 2142, 2768, 4147
Bloch-Hoell, Nils 4176
Bloede, Louis William 2006
Blumhardt, John Christoph (1805-1880) 4802-4803
Boardman, Mary M. 4805
Boardman, William Edwin (1810-1886) 235-237, 426, 4804-4805, 5146
Bob Shuler's Magazine (periodical) see Methodist Challenge (periodical)
Bois, Jules (1871-) 4158
Boise, Ida. 4534
Boisen, Anton T. 4159
Boland, J. M. see Boland, Jeremiah McCartha (1835-1907)
Boland, Jeremiah McCartha (1835-1907) 3063, 3065
Boland, Jeremiah McCartha. The problem of Methodism 374, 3064, 3084
Bolitho, Axchie A. 1171, 5726
Bolivia 2772, 5312, 5343, 5345-5346
Bolt, E. A. J. (-1924) 4806-4807
Bolton, L. Donald 4808
Bone, Lawrence 4809
Bonner, Norman Neal (1917-) 3575, 3795, 4810
Booth, Ballington (1859-1940) 3662
Booth, Bramwell (1856-1929) 3627, 3640, 3651, 3686, 4811-4813
Booth, Catherine Bramwell

(1883-) 4813, 4815
Booth, Catherine Mumford
 (1829-1890) 141-142, 238,
 893-895, 2128, 3606-3608,
 3616-3618, 3622, 3628-3634,
 3675-3678, 4814-4816
Booth, Evangeline Cory (1865-
 1950) 117, 3621, 3663,
 7180
Booth, Herbert H. 3664
Booth, Mrs. Herbert H. 3666
Booth, W. Bramwell see
 Booth, Bramwell (1856-1929)
Booth, William (1829-1912)
 3614, 3619-3620, 3635-3638,
 3650, 3653, 3665-3666,
 3667-3668, 3681-3682, 3687,
 4817-4824
Booth, Mrs. William see
 Booth, Catherine Mumford
 (1829-1890)
Booth, William Bramwell see
 Booth, Bramwell (1856-1929)
Booth Tucker, Frederick St.
 George de Latour (1853-
 1929) 3611, 4816
Borde, G. S. 4825
Borders, M. Edward 572-573
Bosma, Myrtle Evelyn (1926-)
 4826
Boston, Mass. 21, 5143-5144,
 5146, 5266
Bottome, Francis (1823-1894)
 4827-4829, 5739, 7023
Bottome, Mrs. Francis see
 Bottome, Margaret McDonald
 (1827-1906)
Bottome, Margaret McDonald
 (1827-1906) 239, 4828-4832
Bottome, William McDonald
 4828, 4831
Bounds, E. M. see Bounds,
 Edward McKendree (1835-1913)
Bounds, Edward McKendree
 (1835-1913) 205, 4833
Bourbonnais, Ill. 4531
Bourne, Hugh (1768-1829)
 3107
Bowen, Elias (1791-1871) 2689,
 4834-4835
Bowen, George (1816-1888)
 240-241, 4836-4837

Bowens, Md. 98, 5893
Bower, Reuben Edward (1874-)
 1269, 1683, 1892
Bowes, Alpin Marshall (1881-
 1930) 873, 4838
Bowes, Alpin P. 1607
Bowie, Mary Ella 7067
Bowman, Carl Ray (1926-)
 4839
Bowman, Hezekiah J. 1985
Bowman, Ray see Bowman,
 Carl Ray (1926-)
Bowman, Ruth Mildred (1904-)
 4840
Bowman, Thomas (1817-1914)
 4841
Bowman, Thomas (1836-1923)
 1986, 4842
Boyce, William B. (1804-)
 3034
Boyd, Myron F. (1908-) 568,
 2741, 4843-4844
Boyer, Harold W. 1083
Boynton, J. see Boynton,
 Jeremy (1824-1883)
Boynton, Jeremy (1824-1883)
 242, 4845
Boynton, R. C. 3814, 4846
Bracken, A. K. see Bracken,
 Archie Kay (1884-1966)
Bracken, Archie Kay (1884-
 1966) 4847
Brackenbury, T. 2533
Brackett, Charles H. 1977,
 2308, 4333
Bradley, Hilda Aldene (1914-)
 4848
Bradley, William Calvin (1914-)
 4849
Bradley, Mrs. William Calvin
 see Bradley, Hilda Aldene
 (1914-)
Brady, J. W. 243
Brainerd Indian School 3211,
 4365-4367
Bramwell, William (1759-1818)
 1556
Bramwell-Booth, Catherine see
 Booth, Catherine Bramwell,
 (1883-)
Brandon, Vt. 1001
Brandt, Martin E. (1907-)

4850
Brash, John 2533
Brasher, J. L. see Brasher, John Lakin (1868-1971)
Brasher, John Lakin (1868-1971) 244-245, 896, 4480, 4851-4855
Brazil 3772-4202
Breckbill, W. W. 2609
Brengle, S. L. see Brengle, Samuel Logan (1860-1936)
Brengle, Samuel Logan (1860-1936) 3340, 3623, 3639-3644, 3647, 3683, 3825, 4856-4857
Bresee, P. F. see Bresee, Phineas Franklin (1838-1915)
Bresee, Phineas Franklin (1838-1915) 1253, 1422, 1639, 1791-1794, 4858-4868
Bresee College 4368
Bresee Theological College see Bresee College
Brethren in Christ Church 1012-1039, 4463, 4499, 4523, 4581, 4597, 5283-5284, 5286, 6409
Brethren in Christ Church. Board for Missions 1029
Brethren in Christ Church. Peace and Social Concerns Commission 1032a
Brethren in Christ Church in India 1035
Brethren in Christ Church in Rhodesia 1036-1039
Brewer, Mrs. D. A. see Brewer, Elizabeth Luella Alexander (1856-)
Brewer, E. D. C. 2485
Brewer, Elizabeth Luella Alexander (1856-) 4869-4870
Brewerton Independent Presbyterian Church see Tabernacle Pentecostal Church
Brewster, William H. 3207
Breyfogel, Sylvanus Charles (1851-1934) 1982
Brice, J. I. 2521

Brickley, Donald Paul 4861-4862, 4871
Bridegroom's Messenger (periodical) 4193
Bridge (periodical) 3807
Bridgetown, Barbados 4378
Bridwell, Lillian O. 2038
Brightman, Edgar Sheffield (1884-1953) 5416
Brindell, G. W. 4872
Bristol, Frank Milton (1851-1932) 2952
Bristow, P. S. 2044
British Columbia 4535
British Guiana 3580-3581
British Isles Nazarene College 4369
Broadcasting (Radio) see Radio
Broadcasting (Television) see Television
Brockett, Henry E. 1545-1546, 4873-4875
Brockville, Ont. 4370
Brockville Bible College 4370
Brockville Bible School see Brockville Bible College
Brodhead, Anna Sanford see Brodhead, Chloe Anna Sanford (-1927)
Brodhead, Chloe Anna Sanford (-1927) 2751, 4876
Brodhead, John Pearson (-1947) 4877
Brodhead, Mrs. John Pearson see Brodhead, Anna Sanford (-1927)
Broken Tomahawk (periodical) 4366
Bromley, Henry W. 2076
Bromley, Will see Bromley, William Ewart (1905-1969)
Brooke, H. 3967, 3987
Brooklyn, N. Y. 5739
Brookmiller, F. H. see Brookmiller, Frederick H. (1854-1903)
Brookmiller, Frederick H. (1854-1903) 4880
Brooks, Cyrus 4881
Brooks, Delos Ferdinand (1845-1935) 246, 857, 4882-4883

Brooks, Harriet Bennett (-1940) 4884
Brooks, J. P. see Brooks, John P.
Brooks, John P. 1202-1203, 4885-4886
Brooks, John P. A Survey of the Field, and Strictures Thereon 250
Brooks, John Rives (1836-) 3066-3067
Brooks, Noel 4253
Brough, Lyman (1869-1940) 4887-4888
Broughton, M. A. 4658
Brown, Antoinette L. 3152
Brown, Arthur Lee (1891-) 4889
Brown, C. A. see Brown, Charles A.
Brown, C. C. see Brown, Charles Calvin (1868-1957)
Brown, Charles A. 4890
Brown, Charles Calvin (1868-1957) 4891
Brown, Charles Ewing (1883-) 1061, 1084-1089, 1147, 1152, 4892
Brown, D. J. 2478
Brown, D. Wayne (1913-) 4893-4895
Brown, George 4896
Brown, H. D. see Brown, Harrison D. (1846-1940)
Brown, H. N. 4897
Brown, Harrison D. (1846-1940) 4863, 4898-4899
Brown, Irwin L. 3693, 4900
Brown, James Stephen 4160
Brown, Joel 6411
Brown, Lena Marie (1920-) 4901
Brown, Melza H. 4902-4903
Brown, Robert 4904
Brown, W. Shelburne see Brown, Warren Shelburne (1918-)
Brown, Warren Shelburne (1918-) 1326, 4905
Browning, Raymond (1879-1953) 1795, 4906-4909, 6470

Browning, W. G. see Browning, William Garritson (1825-1910)
Browning, William Garritson (1825-1910) 4910-4914
Brushingham, John Patrick (1855-1927) 2945-2946, 4915
Bryant, John R. 721
Bryant's Business College, St. Joseph, Mo. 4917
Buck, E. Parker 3183
Bucke, Emory Stevens 2810
Buckley, James Monroe (1836-1920) 2948
Buckwalter, Leoda A. 1035, 1037
Bud, Uncle see Robinson, Reuben (1860-1942)
Buddy, Uncle see Robinson, Reuben (1860-1942)
Budensiek, Harold Lyle (1931-) 4919
Buffalo Gap, Tex. 4444
Buffum, Herbert (1879-1939) 4184, 4920
Buffum, Mrs. Herbert see Buffum, Lillie
Buffum, Lillie 4921-4922
Bugle of Holiness (periodical) 2455
Bulkley, C. H. A. 4923
Bunce, D. S. (1838-) 4924-4925
Bunyan, John (1628-1688). The Pilgrim's Progress 1405
Burkholder, Lewis J. (1875-) 3777
Burkholder, M. I. 3729
Burne, Marjory 5209
Burnett, Clyde J. 4926
Burnett, Mrs. Clyde J. see Burnett, Lillian M. Pool
Burnett, Lillian M. Pool 4927
Burnett family 3387
Burnham, Richard (1857-) 4928
Burning Bush (periodical) 2149
Burns, Nelson (-1904) 251, 4929, 5697
Burns, W. G. 2446
Burritt, Carrie Turrell 2719
Burritt, Eldon Grant (1868-

1927) 4931
Bursch, Daniel Ray (1918-) 4932
Bursch, Mrs. Daniel Ray see Bursch, Madge Serna Edwards (1922-)
Bursch, Madge Serna Edwards (1922-) 4933
Bury, John Bagnell (1861-1927) 1
Busingen, Ger. 4407
Buss, Edith Mitchell 4493
Bustin, Charles M. 3272
Bustin, G. T. 3272
Butler, C. W. see Butler, Charles William (1873-1960)
Butler, Charles William (1873-1960) 252-253, 960, 4934
Butler, William (1818-1899) 2887, 3006, 3044, 4935-4939
Butts, B. F. 724
Buxton, Barclay Fowell (1860-1946) 4940-4941, 7204
Buxton, Barclay Godfrey 3295-3296, 3309-3313, 3341, 3343, 4941
Byers, A. L. see Byers, Andrew L. (1869-)
Byers, Andrew L. (1869-) 1062-1063, 1077, 1141, 1153, 1164-1165, 1169-1170, 1180, 1182-1186, 7096
Byers, Charles B. 1016
Byers, Charles Edgar (1883-) 4942
Byers, Charlie B. see Byers, Charles B.
Byrum, Bessie L. 1164
Byrum, E. E. see Byrum, Enoch Edwin (1861-1942)
Byrum, Enoch Edwin (1861-1942) 1064, 1078, 1090-1096, 1142-1145, 1150, 4943-4945
Byrum, Isabel Coston (1870-1938) 1065, 1071, 1192, 4946-4947
Byrum, N. H. 1068, 1181
Byrum, Russell Raymond (1888-) 1070, 1097-1099

C. Warren Jones Indian Bible Training School see Nazarene Indian Bible School
Cadbury, Henry Joel (1883-) 2273
Cadbury, M. H. 6755
Caffray, D. Willia see Caffray, Daisy Willia Bourquard (1880-)
Caffray, Daisy Willia Bourquard (1880-) 4948-4949
Cagle, H. C. 4950
Cagle, Mrs. H. C. see Cagle, Mary Lee Wasson Harris (1864-1955)
Cagle, Mary Lee Wasson Harris (1864-1955) 4951-4953
Calcutta, India 1254
Caldwell, Sallie Kitchen (1831-1855) 4954-4955
Caldwell, Wayne 3123
Calgary, Alta. 4374
Calgary Bible Institute see Canadian Nazarene College
California 1246-1247, 1251-1252, 1254-1255, 1258, 1871, 2824, 4313, 4332, 4371, 4422, 4488, 4543-4548, 4560-4561, 4597, 4600, 4681, 5224, 5333, 5356-5357, 5649, 5880-5881, 6151-6154, 6156, 6595-6596, 6933, 6940-6941, 6944, 6950
California College and Holiness Bible School 4371, 6060
California Yearly Meeting of Friends see Friends, Society of. California Yearly Meeting
Calkins, Louise see Love, Louise Calkins (-1946)
The Call from Haitian Hills (periodical) 3288
Call to Prayer (periodical) 3427
Calley, Malcolm J. 4200
Calvary Christian College 4372
Calvary Holiness Church 1042-1047, 1889-1890, 4337
Calvary Holiness Church. Missionary Society 1046
Calvary Holiness College 4373
Calver, Eng. 4387
Calvin, Jean (1509-1564) 56, 58

Calvin, John see Calvin, Jean (1509-1564)
Cameron, James Reese (1929-) 1594, 4393, 4956
Cameron, Richard Morgan (1898-) 2774
Cammack, Phyllis 2390
Camp meetings 119-130, 2628-2629, 2782, 2836-2852, 4635
Campbell, Duncan 2044, 2046, 2050-2051
Campbell, Joe E. see Campbell, Joseph Enoch
Campbell, Joseph Enoch 4239, 4242, 4272, 4292, 4402, 4450
Campbell, L. M. 1423
Campbell, Tex. 4491
Campbell Free Methodist Seminary see McKinney Junior College
Camrose, Alta. 4301
Canada 1194, 1263, 1868, 1872-1874, 2754-2755, 3771, 4199, 6892, 6894, 7319-7324
Canadian Bible School see Canadian Nazarene College
Canadian Free Methodist Herald (periodical) 2723
Canadian Nazarene College 4374-4377
Cann, A. D. 1008
Cannon, William Ragsdale (1916-) 2548
Canton, N.Y. 128
Canton, Ohio 4492-4494
Cantrell, Roy Herbert (1904-) 4344, 4957
Cape Island, N. J. 3048
Cape Verde Islands 1875-1878
Capehart, John C. 535
Capital punishment 2369
Cardiel, Adolfo (1903-) 4958
Carey, Alfred Belmont 3679
Caribbean Pilgrim College 4378
Caribbean Region 978, 1879, 3582-3584, 5338, 5340, 5897, 6269, 6746
Carlinville, Ill. 4438
Carman, Albert (1833-1917) 2516, 2527, 4959
Carmichael, Amy Beatrice see Carmichael, Amy Wilson (1867-1951)
Carmichael, Amy Wilson (1867-1951) 3364, 4960-4965
Carmony, Byron M. (1916-) 4966
Carpenter, Eva see Roby, Eva Carpenter (1880-)
Carpenter, Mary E. (-1886) 4967
Carradine, B. see Carradine, Beverly (1848-1931)
Carradine, Beverly (1848-1931) 73-83, 110, 143-145, 209, 254-266, 667-668, 701, 897-898, 963, 3059, 3068, 3094-3095, 3096, 3115, 3153, 3161, 3180-3181, 4968-4971
Carroll, H. H. (-1921) 4972
Carroll, H. K. see Carroll, Henry King (1848-1931)
Carroll, Henry King (1848-1931) 1648
Carroll, J. H. see Carroll, John H. (1884-1961)
Carroll, John H. (1884-1961) 2037, 4973-4974
Carroll, Nellie Mae (1918-) 4975
Carruth, Wallace E. 1265
Carson, Esther see Winans, Esther Carson (1891-1928)
Carswell, Pamela 36
Carter, Charles Webb (1905-) 522, 3224, 3233-3234, 4976
Carter, Mrs. Clarence see Carter, Marjorie
Carter, Marjorie 4977
Carter, Melissa Booth (1845-) 4978-4979
Carter, R. Kelso see Carter, Russell Kelso (1849-1926)
Carter, Russell Kelso (1849-1926) 608-611, 625, 669, 685, 4088-4089, 4109, 4803, 4980-4986
Carvosso, William (1750-1835) 2129, 2868
Cary, W. W. see Cary, William Walter (1887-)
Cary, William Walter (1887-)

121, 3425
Cascade College 4379
Case, Orpha Mae (1909-) 4987
Cassels, Louis 2517
Cassler, L. F. see Cassler, La Fayette
Cassler, La Fayette 4988-4989
Castillejos, José 4990
Castle, Nicholas (1837-1922) 3703-3705, 4991-4993
Catalán P., Apolinar (1915-) 4994
Caterina de Siena (1347-1380) 3982
Catharine of Siena see Caterina de Siena (1347-1380)
Catholicism 853-855, 1178, 1744, 2157-2159, 2246, 2345-2346, 2460, 2734, 3384, 4939, 5188, 5330, 7123
Cattell, Catherine DeVol (1906-) 2375, 4995
Cattell, Everett Lewis (1905-) 2280, 4996
Cattell, Mrs. Everett Lewis see Cattell, Catherine DeVol (1906-)
Caudill, Rodney C. 4997
Cavit, Marshal 2281, 3424
Cedar Springs, Mich. 4469-4470
Cedar Springs, Mich. Rotary Club see Rotary Club, Cedar Springs, Mich.
Cedaredge, Colo. 4380
Cedaredge Bible School 4380
Cell, George Croft (1875-1937) 2549
Central, S.C. 4383
Central Academy and College see Central College
Central America 3585
Central College, Huntington, Ind. see Huntington College
Central College, McPherson, Kan. 4381
Central Evangelical Holiness Association 2024-2028
Central Florida Bible Institute see Intercession City Christian Schools
Central Holiness University see Kletzing College
Central Nazarene Academy 4382
Central Nazarene Academy and Bible School see Central Nazarene Academy
Central Nazarene College see Central Nazarene Academy
Central Nazarene University see Central Nazarene Academy
Central Pilgrim College see Bartlesville Wesleyan College
Central Wesleyan College 4383
Central Yearly Meeting of Friends see Friends, Society of. Central Yearly Meeting
Cessna, W. Conrad 2462
Chadwick, Grace E. (1873-1911) 4998
Chadwick, Samuel (1860-1932) 267-269, 1547-1548, 2509-2510, 2518-2521, 2878, 3826, 4999-5004
Chalfant, E. O. see Chalfant, Everette Otis (1882-1953)
Chalfant, Everette Otis (1882-1953) 5005-5008
Chalfant, Morris 1424, 1586, 1640, 1796, 5007
Chamberlain, Marianne 5009
Chamberlain, Ray W. 5010
Chambers, G. A. see Chambers, George Augustus (1879-1957)
Chambers, George Augustus (1879-1957) 5010a, 5010b
Chambers, Joseph Leon 1314, 5011
Chambers, Leon see Chambers, Joseph Leon
Chambers, Oswald (1874-1917) 270-271, 3297, 3301-3306, 3314-3328, 3347, 5012-5015
Chandler, Letitia (-1937) 5016
Chandler, Ward B. 965, 1327,

1639, 4860
Chang, Chien Hsun 5017
Chang Chien Hsun see Chang, Chien Hsun
Chao, Kui Suan 5018
Chao Kui Suan see Chao, Kui Suan
Chaplains, Military see U.S. Army--Chaplains
Chapman, J. B. see Chapman, James Blaine (1884-1947)
Chapman, James Blaine (1884-1947) 1272, 1301, 1328-1330, 1394-1396, 1425-1430, 1489, 1612, 1641, 1655, 1684, 1714, 1797-1803, 1847, 2436, 5019, 5025, 5031, 6599
Chapman, Mrs. James Blaine see Chapman, Louise Robinson; Chapman, Maud Frederick (1880-1940)
Chapman, John A. M. (1829-1905) 899
Chapman, Louise Robinson 1947, 5026-5028
Chapman, Mary Weems 5059
Chapman, Maud Frederick (1880-1940) 5029-5031
Chappell, L. W. 3468
Charitable institutions see Charities
Charities 654-655, 3147-3148, 3610-3614, 3701
Chase, William R. 574
Chavchavadze, Maria 35
Checotah, Okla 4475
Cheney, L. Keith (1908-) 5032
Chesapeake Holiness Union 98, 5893
Chesham, Sallie 3652
Chesnut, Lawrence J. 1148
Chicago 192-193, 4582-4589, 6622, 7067
Chicago. Humboldt Park Gospel Tabernacle 5777
Chicago. World's Columbian Exposition, 1893. 6662
Chicago Evangelistic Institute see Vennard College

Children's work see Work with youth
Child's Treasure (periodical) 2456
Chile 4201-4202
Chiles, Robert Eugene (1923-) 2550-2552
Chili Seminary see Roberts Wesleyan College
Chilliwack, B. C. 4535
Chilson, Arthur Benton (1872-1939) 5033-5034
Chilson, Edna Hill 5034
Chilton, Claude L. 1715, 5035
China 1881-1884, 2373-2374, 3385, 3422, 3431-3432, 4129, 5201, 5945, 6355, 6406, 7017
China Peniel Missionary Society see Voice of China and Asia
Chisholm, Thomas O. (1866-1960) 5038
Chism, Fairy Steele (1899-1971) 1331, 1864, 1948, 5036-5037
Christ Action (periodical) 3289
Christ Missionary and Industrial College 4384
Christian Advance and Volunteers' Gazette (periodical) see Volunteer Gazette (periodical)
Christian Advocate (Pittsburgh) 2883
Christian Advocate (St. Louis) 3096
Christian Alliance see Christian and Missionary Alliance
Christian Alliance and Foreign Missionary Weekly (periodical) see Alliance Witness (periodical)
Christian and Missionary Alliance 4052-4141, 5758, 6295, 6737-6739, 6797, 7003
Christian and Missionary Alliance. Foreign Department 4112-4117
Christian and Missionary Alliance. Missions and Mission Conferences. Palestine and Arabian Mission 4136
Christian and Missionary Alliance (periodical) see

Alliance Witness (periodical)
Christian and Missionary Alliance in Africa 4128
Christian and Missionary Alliance in China 4129
Christian and Missionary Alliance in Indonesia 4131-4132, 5758
Christian and Missionary Alliance in Japan 4133
Christian and Missionary Alliance in Latin America 4134-4135
Christian and Missionary Alliance in New Guinea 4137
Christian and Missionary Alliance in Nigeria 4138
Christian and Missionary Alliance in the Congo 4130
Christian and Missionary Alliance in the Near East 4136
Christian and Missionary Alliance in Tibet 4139, 5289
Christian and Missionary Alliance in Vietnam 4140-4141
Christian Congregation 2029-2030
Christian education see Religious education
Christian ethics see Conduct of life
Christian Evangel (periodical) 4194
Christian Faith Band Church see Church of God (Apostolic)
Christian family see Family Life, Marriage
Christian Harvester (periodical) 769
Christian Holiness Association 69-72, 96-97, 119, 122-123, 426, 566, 568-571, 646, 650, 652-653, 657-658, 837, 3691, 3830, 4587-4588, 5740-5741, 6782-6785, 7287-7288
Christian Holiness Association. Commission on Social Action 1032a
Christian home see Family life, Marriage
Christian life see Conduct of life
Christian Life (periodical) see International Purity Journal (periodical)
Christian Messenger (periodical) 770, 2413
Christian Minister (periodical) 2724
Christian Nation Church 1048-1049
Christian Science 856-859, 1745
Christian sociology see Social criticism
Christian Standard (Brockville, Ont.) 3695
Christian Standard (London) 772
Christian Standard (Philadelphia, etc.) 147, 771
Christian Union see Church of God (General Assembly); (Original) Church of God
Christian union see Church union
Christian Witness (periodical) see Christian Witness and Advocate of Bible Holiness (periodical)
Christian Witness and Advocate of Bible Holiness (periodical) 356, 773, 2873, 6060
Christian Worker (periodical) 2300
Christian Workers' Training School and Bible Institute 4385
Christian's Companion (periodical) 3549
Christian's pathway to power (periodical) see Life of Faith (periodical)
Christie, G. A. 5039-5040
Der Christliche Apologete (periodical) 3012
Christ's Sanctified Holy Church 1050-1051
Chung, Robert 5041
Church, John Robert (1899-) 146, 272-282, 575, 619, 900-903, 4317, 5042
Church Advocate and Good Way (periodical) 1218, 1234, 5857

Church Advocate and Holiness Banner (periodical) see Church Herald and Holiness Banner (periodical)
Church entertainments 3151
Church finance 1636-1638, 3649, 6869
Church government 1122-1123, 1201-1204, 2880, 2882
Church Herald (periodical) 1223
Church Herald and Holiness Banner (periodical) 1219, 1224, 1226, 5402
Church music 1031, 1712, 3671 see also Hymns--History and criticism
Church of Christ (Holiness) U.S.A. 1052-1059, 4384
Church of Christ (Holiness) U.S.A. Foreign Mission Board 1058
Church of Christ (Holiness) U.S.A. Liturgy and ritual 1052
Church of Christ Advocate (periodical) see Advocate for Primitive Christian Union (periodical)
Church of Daniel's Band 2031-2035
Church of England 4807
Church of God see Church of the Gospel; Churches of God in North America (General Eldership)
Church of God (Anderson, Ind.) 1060-1194, 4301, 4310, 4313, 4332, 4432, 4534, 4591-4592, 4944-4945, 4947, 5726, 6182, 6253, 6521, 6569, 6585, 6984, 7093, 7036
Church of God (Anderson, Ind.) Executive Council 1193
Church of God (Anderson, Ind.) Missionary Board 1171
Church of God (Anderson, Ind.) National Woman's Missionary Society 5726
Church of God (Anderson, Ind.) in Canada 1194

Church of God (Apostolic) 1195-1196
Church of God (Cleveland, Tenn.) see Church of God (General Assembly)
Church of God (General Assembly) 4206-4221, 4485-4486, 5936, 6999
Church of God (General Assembly). National Sunday School and Youth Board 4216
Church of God (General Assembly). World Mission Board 4212
Church of God (Holiness) 1197-1230, 4380, 4416, 4437, 4439-4440, 4471, 4478, 4490, 4509-4511, 4530, 4551, 5343, 5822, 5857, 5863, 5913, 7111
Church of God (Holiness). Department of Missions 1221
Church of God (Holiness). Unification Commission 1201
Church of God (Holiness) in Bolivia 1228, 5343
Church of God (Holiness) in Jamaica 1227
Church of God (Holiness) in Missouri 1229-1230
Church of God (Independent Holiness people) see Church of God (Holiness); Churches of God (Independent Holiness People)
Church of God (Northern Indiana Eldership) 1231
Church of God (Unity Holiness people) see Church of God (Holiness)
Church of God Evangel (periodical) 4214-4215
Church of God in Christ 4222-4225, 6112
Church of God in Christ. Board of Home and Foreign Missions 4225
Church of God in Christ in Tennessee 4225a
Church of God in North America (General Eldership) see Churches of God in North America (General Eldership)

Church of God Missions (periodical) 1173
Church of Jesus Christ of Latter-Day Saints see Mormonism
Church of the Bible Covenant 3879-3884, 4391
Church of the Bible Covenant. General Convention 3882
Church of the Gospel 1245
Church of the Nazarene (1895-1907) 1246-1254, 1280-1284, 4544, 4555, 4859-4868
Church of the Nazarene (1895-1907). Assembly 1246
Church of the Nazarene 1255-1953, 4312, 4342-4347, 4364, 4368-4369, 4374, 4382, 4392-4394, 4407, 4413, 4444, 4456, 4496, 4502, 4505, 4508, 4513-4521, 4525, 4531, 4537, 4540, 4544-4548, 4557, 4559-4560, 4562, 4577-4578, 4675-4681, 4751, 4754, 4761, 4796, 4859-4868, 4889, 4899, 4903, 4909, 4952, 5006, 5020-5025, 5085, 5093, 5120, 5209, 5220, 5230-5231, 5235, 5237, 5261, 5299, 5305, 5307, 5354-5358, 5490, 5537, 5539, 5551, 5585-5587, 5649, 5651, 5653, 5655, 5671-5672, 5679, 5709, 5737, 5744, 5772-5774, 5777, 5806, 5842, 5909, 5913, 5947, 5961, 5964, 5984, 6004, 6013, 6031, 6047, 6050, 6073, 6105, 6108, 6110, 6159, 6163, 6204, 6257-6258, 6281, 6302-6303, 6305-6306, 6349, 6406, 6483, 6547-6549, 6557, 6595-6604, 6627, 6646, 6664, 6689-6691, 6730, 6831, 6833, 6839, 6869, 6927, 7053-7054, 7061, 7074, 7177, 7224-7228, 7255, 7270, 7278, 7328
Church of the Nazarene. Board of General Superintendents 1257, 1630
Church of the Nazarene. Commission of the Mid-Century Crusade for Souls 1607
Church of the Nazarene. Commission on Christian Service Training 1305
Church of the Nazarene. Department of Church Schools 1764, 1766, 1769, 1778
Church of the Nazarene. Department of Education 1312
Church of the Nazarene. Department of Evangelism 1316, 1608
Church of the Nazarene. Department of Foreign Missions see Church of the Nazarene. Department of World Missions
Church of the Nazarene. Department of Home Missions and Evangelism. 1303
Church of the Nazarene. Department of World Missions 1682, 1688, 1697, 5737
Church of the Nazarene. Districts. Canada Central 1263
Church of the Nazarene. Districts. Chicago Central 1264, 5006
Church of the Nazarene. Districts. Louisiana 1265
Church of the Nazarene. Districts. Michigan 1266
Church of the Nazarene. Districts. New England 1267
Church of the Nazarene. Districts. Northwest 1268
Church of the Nazarene. Districts. Southern California 1871
Church of the Nazarene. Districts. Washington-Philadelphia 1269-1270
Church of the Nazarene. Districts. Wisconsin 1271
Church of the Nazarene. General Assembly 1258, 1769
Church of the Nazarene. Gene-

ral Board 1892
Church of the Nazarene. General Board of Foreign Missions 1530, 1683, 1707, 5911
Church of the Nazarene. General Secretary 1416
Church of the Nazarene. General Stewardship Committee 1290, 1369
Church of the Nazarene. Missions and mission districts. India 1897
Church of the Nazarene. Missions and mission districts. Peru 1937
Church of the Nazarene. Nazarene Young People's Society 1858
Church of the Nazarene. Woman's Foreign Missionary Society 1663, 1690, 1710, 5355
Church of the Nazarene. Woman's Missionary Society see Church of the Nazarene. Woman's Foreign Missionary Society
Church of the Nazarene in Africa 1862-1867, 5027, 5037, 5085, 5209, 5733, 5765, 5768, 5797
Church of the Nazarene in Alberta 1868, 5931
Church of the Nazarene in Argentina 5330
Church of the Nazarene in Australia 1869-1870
Church of the Nazarene in California 1871, 5649, 6516
Church of the Nazarene in Canada 1872-1874
Church of the Nazarene in China 1881-1884, 6355, 6406
Church of the Nazarene in Cuba 6489
Church of the Nazarene in Europe 1888
Church of the Nazarene in Great Britain 1889-1891
Church of the Nazarene in Guatemala 1892-1893, 4644, 5737, 5925
Church of the Nazarene in Haiti 1894-1896, 6351
Church of the Nazarene in Idaho 1268
Church of the Nazarene in Illinois 1264, 5006
Church of the Nazarene in India 1254, 1897-1901, 4757, 5447, 6902, 7005, 7008, 7146
Church of the Nazarene in Indiana 7270
Church of the Nazarene in Italy 1902-1904
Church of the Nazarene in Japan 1905-1907, 5825, 5886
Church of the Nazarene in Kansas 1908
Church of the Nazarene in Korea 1909
Church of the Nazarene in Latin America 1910-1917, 7308
Church of the Nazarene in Louisiana 1265
Church of the Nazarene in Maine 1918
Church of the Nazarene in Maryland 1269-1270
Church of the Nazarene in Mexico 1919-1920, 5355
Church of the Nazarene in Michigan 1266
Church of the Nazarene in Missouri 1921, 6557
Church of the Nazarene in New England 1267
Church of the Nazarene in New Guinea 1925, 4879
Church of the Nazarene in Nicaragua 1926
Church of the Nazarene in North Carolina 5213, 5870
Church of the Nazarene in Oceania 1927-1930
Church of the Nazarene in Okinawa 1931-1932
Church of the Nazarene in Oklahoma 1933-1936, 5772-5773
Church of the Nazarene in Ontario 1263

Church of the Nazarene in
  Oregon 1268
Church of the Nazarene in
  Palestine 5911
Church of the Nazarene in
  Pennsylvania 1269-1270
Church of the Nazarene in
  Peru. 1937-1938 7260-
  7262, 7265
Church of the Nazarene in
  Puerto Rico 6489
Church of the Nazarene in
  Quebec 1263
Church of the Nazarene in
  Rhode Island 1943
Church of the Nazarene in
  Samoa 5426
Church of the Nazarene in
  Swaziland 1947-1949,
  5733, 6656-6657
Church of the Nazarene in
  Tennessee 1950-1951
Church of the Nazarene in
  Texas 1952, 4952, 5709
Church of the Nazarene in the
  Cape Verde Islands 1875-
  1878
Church of the Nazarene in the
  Caribbean region 1879-
  1880, 6489
Church of the Nazarene in the
  Far East 1885-1887
Church of the Nazarene in the
  Near East 1922-1924
Church of the Nazarene in the
  Pacific Northwest 1268,
  7061
Church of the Nazarene in the
  Philippine Islands 1939-
  1942, 6474
Church of the Nazarene in the
  Republic of South Africa
  1865
Church of the Nazarene in the
  Southern states 1944
Church of the Nazarene in the
  Southwestern states 1945-
  1946, 5773-5774, 6204
Church of the Nazarene in
  Trinidad 1953
Church of the Nazarene in
  Washington 1268, 7014
Church of the Nazarene in Wis-
  consin 1271
Church of the Pillar of Fire
  see Pillar of Fire Church
Church of the United Brethren
  in Christ 3698-3726, 4501,
  4992-4993
Church of the United Brethren
  in Christ. Board of Administration 3700
Church of the United Brethren
  in Christ. Conferences 3699
Church of the United Brethren
  in Christ. Foreign Missionary Society 3726
Church of the United Brethren
  in Christ. General Con-
  ference 3699
Church of the United Brethren
  in Christ. Historical Society
  see United Brethren Historical Society
Church of the United Brethren
  in Christ. Holiness Association 4993
Church of the United Brethren
  in Christ in China 3726
Church of the United Brethren
  in Christ (Old Constitution)
  3727-3733, 4455
Church of the United Brethren
  in Christ (Old Constitution).
  Department of Christian Education 3729
Church of the United Brethren
  in Christ (Old Constitution).
  Parent Board of Missions
  3730
Church of the United Brethren
  in Christ (Old Constitution).
  Woman's Missionary Association 3730
Church of the United Brethren
  in Christ (Old Constitution)
  in Sierra Leone 3733
Church School Builder (periodical) 1729
Church union 64, 317, 1086,
  4157, 4167
Church Voice and Banner of
  Holiness (periodical) 199,
  250, 774

Church Witness (periodical) 1225
Churches of Christ see Independent Holiness Church of Christ
Churches of Christ in Christian Union 1954-1965, 4386
Churches of Christ in Christain Union. Annual Council. Ohio 1956
Churches of Christ in Christian Union of Ohio see Churches of Christ in Christian Union
Churches of God (Independent Holiness People) 1232-1237, 5857
Churches of God, Holiness 1238-1240
Churches of God in North America (General Eldership) 1241-1244
Churches of God in North America (General Eldership). Board of Missions. 1244
Chynoweth, Mary E. (-1908) 5043-5044
Cincinnati, Ohio 196, 952, 989-992, 4396, 4425-4427, 5895, 6299, 6847
Circleville, Ohio 4386
Circleville Bible College 4386
Clapham, Eng. see London, Eng.
Clarence, Mo. 4440, 4505
Clarence Bible Seminary see Holiness Collegiate Institute
Clark, Dougan (1828-1896) 283-287, 2282, 5045-5046, 7039
Clark, Elmer Talmage (1886-1966) 647
Clark, Esther D. (-1938) 5047
Clark, John W. 2407, 5048
Clark, L. A. 2422
Clark, Raymond Brooke (1889-) 4135
Clark, Robert Donald (1910-) 6741
Clark, Samuel Delbert (1910-) 2447
Clark, William A. 660
Clark, William Henry (1854-1925) 5049
Clark, William Warner (1838-) 5050
Clarke, Adam (1762?-1832) 105, 552-553, 2523, 3182, 3834, 3843
Clarke, Branford 2209, 2218, 2224, 2249-2251, 7158, 7163, 7165
Clarke, Ethel Helm see Youngren, Ethel Helm Clarke (-1947)
Clarke, George H. (-1929) 3235
Clarke, Mrs. George H. see Clarke, Mary Lane (1872-1970)
Clarke, M. C. (-1936) 5044, 5051
Clarke, Mary Lane (1872-1970) 3235, 5052-5053
Clarkson, Nester K. 876
Clarkston, Wash. 4564
Clarksville, Mich. 4357, 4395
Clear, Valorous Bernard (1915-) 1060
Clergy 2631, 3058, 3152, 3444, 3615-3616, 3784-3785, 3813 see also Women as ministers
Clergy--Wives see Women in church work
Cleveland, Ohio 4492-4494
Cleveland, Tenn. 4485, 6999
Cleveland Bible College see Malone College
Cleveland Bible Institute see Malone College
Clevenger, Jerry 83a
Cliff College 4387
Climenhaga, Arthur Merlin (1916-) 5054
Climenhaga, Asa W. (1889-) 1021, 5055
Climenhaga, John A. 1035, 1037
Clothier, M. James 3249
Clothing and dress 3391, 3393
Coates, Lola Mae (1931-) 5056
Coats, Mrs. see Coates, Eugenia Phillips (1883-)

Coats, Eugenia Phillips
    (1883-   ) 5057, 5925
Cobb, Mother see Cobb,
    Eunice Parsons (1793-1877)
Cobb, Eunice Parsons (1793-
    1877) 5058-5059
Cobb, Mrs. Whiteman see
    Cobb, Eunice Parsons
    (1793-1877)
Cobbins, Otho Beale 1054
Cochran, A. S. see Cochran,
    Albert S. (1850-1914)
Cochran, Albert S. (1850-
    1914) 5060-5061
Cochrane, Rollin E. 2701
Coffin, Merrill M. 2376
Coffin, T. Eugene 1978,
    2309, 5880
Coldwater, Mich. 4506
Colegio Dixon 4388
Coleman, George Whitefield
    (1830-1907) 5062
Coleman, J. P. see Coleman,
    John Paul
Coleman, John Paul 3458,
    5063
Coleman, John V. (1885-1928)
    5064
Coleman, Mrs. Mary L. 4721
Coleman, Robert Emerson
    (1928-   ) 2789-2790, 3005,
    4318-4319, 4320, 5065
College Mound, Mo. 4489-
    4490, 4536
College of Bethel see Bethel
    Bible College
Colleges see Education
Collett, Ronald 5066
Collett, Sidney. All about the
    Bible 1206
Collier, Richard (1924-   )
    3653, 4819
Collier, William (1803-   )
    3101
Collins, J. H. 288, 3069-3070
Collins, M. D. see Collins,
    Mahlen Day (1838-1904)
Collins, Mahlen Day (1838-
    1904) 289, 5067
Colorado 2199-2202, 4339,
    4380, 4389, 4482, 4513,
    4542, 4551, 5943, 6978,
7156-7157, 7161-7162
Colorado Springs, Colo. 4389,
    4513, 4542, 5943, 6978
Colorado Springs Bible College
    4389
Colorado Springs Bible Training
    School see Colorado Springs
    Bible College
Colorado Springs Bible Training
    School and Christian Academy
    3595
Colored Church, South see
    Christ's Sanctified Holy
    Church
Colored people see Negroes
Colt, W. B. M. 5068
Columbia, S. C. 4449-4451
Columbia, S. C. Oliver Gospel
    Mission 842, 6470
Comer, A. Vance 5595
Commandments, Ten see Ten
    Commandments
Communion see Lord's Supper
Communism 1751, 3422-3423
Composers see Song writers
Concern (periodical) 2301
Concord, N. H. Theological
    Seminary of the Methodist
    Episcopal Church see Theo-
    logical Seminary of the Metho-
    dist Episcopal Church, Con-
    cord, N. H.
Conduct of life 2093-2095,
    2632-2640, 2856-2868, 3059-
    3060, 3274, 3284-3285, 3295-
    3300, 3363, 3391-3394, 3473-
    3478, 3617-3620, 3742, 3786,
    3814-3817, 4058-4065, 4249-
    4252
Congo 3251, 4130
Congregational Methodist Church
    2598-2601, 4601
Congregational Methodist Church.
    General Mission Board 2600
Congregational Methodist Mes-
    senger (periodical) 2601
Conklin, Mrs. Floyd see Conk-
    lin, Mary Olsen
Conklin, Mary Olsen 6341
Conn, Charles W. 4209, 4215
Conneautville, Pa. 995
Conquest (periodical) 1730

Consecrated Life and Guide to
   Holiness (periodical) 775,
   789, 986, 6140, 6387-6389,
   6394-6395
Contributor (periodical) 776
Convention for Deepening of
   Spiritual Life, Karnizawa,
   Japan 434
Convention Herald (periodical)
   3857
Conway, L. W. 1236
Cook, Arnold Willis 2631, 3784
Cook, C. O. 5069
Cook, Esta Virginia Bangle
   (1925-) 5070
Cook, Ethel (-1925) 5071
Cook, Frances E. 7211
Cook, Franklin 1685, 1852
Cook, Joseph (1838-1901) 7294
Cook, Oliver James (1922-)
   5072
Cook, Mrs. Oliver James see
   Cook, Esta Virginia Bangle
   (1925-)
Cook, Thomas (1867-) 2522
Cooke, Mrs. John see Cooke,
   Sarah Ann Bass (1827-)
Cooke, Sarah Ann Bass (1827-)
   5073-5075
Cookman, Alfred (1828-1871)
   105, 290-291, 3834, 3902,
   5076-5079
Cookman, George Grimston
   (1800-1841) 5079
Cookman, J. E. see Cookman,
   John Emory (1836-1891)
Cookman, John Emory (1836-
   1891) 5080
Coon, Mrs. H. Arvilla Damon
   (1829-) 5081-5083
Coone, J. M. 3583
Cooper, Mary May (1898-1970)
   5084-5085
Cooper, Sherman E. (-1951)
   5086
Copelin, Roy E. 1939
Copes, V. Earle 2813
Copplestone, J. Tremayne
   2819
Corbett, C. T. 1294-1295,
   1570, 6257, 6600-6601
Cordell, Bessie Bell 3432

Corey, James Benijah (1832-)
   5087-5089
Corlett, D. Shelby see Cor-
   lett, David Shelby (1894-)
Corlett, David Shelby (1894-)
   1332-1333, 1431-1436, 1591,
   1752, 5023, 5090
Corlett, L. T. see Corlett,
   Lewis Thomas (1896-)
Corlett, Lewis Thomas (1896-)
   1437-1438, 5091
Corn, Okla. 4390
Corn Bible Academy 4390
Cornell, C. E. see Cornell,
   Clarence Ellsworth
Cornell, Clarence Ellsworth
   147, 209, 628, 904, 1397,
   1613, 5092-5093
Corson, Bertha 5845
Corvin, R. O. 4270
Coryell, Ernest 5094
Couchenour, H. M. 292, 5095
Coulter, George 5096
Courts, James 4223, 6112
Coutts, Frederick Lee 3645
Cove, Mary Elizabeth 1664,
   7005, 7146
Covenant Foundation College
   4391
Covenanter (periodical) 3884
Cowan, James 3822, 6892-6894
Coward, Samuel L. C. 293,
   661
Cowen, C. E. see Cowen,
   Clarence Eugene (1904-)
Cowen, Clarence Eugene (1904-)
   1215-1216, 5097
Cowherd, Effie Grace (-1950)
   5098
Cowman, Charles Elmer (1868-
   1924) 3377, 3379, 3383,
   5099-5103, 5105, 5860-5861,
   6293
Cowman, Mrs. Charles Elmer
   see Cowman, Lettie Burd
   (1870-1960)
Cowman, Lettie Burd (1870-
   1960) 3365-3372, 3377, 3379-
   3380, 5100-5101, 5104, 5105-
   5107, 5861, 6293
Cowman and Kilbourne Work
   see Oriental Missionary So-

ciety
Cowper, William (1731-1800) 2511
Cox, Anna Lee 5108
Cox, E. K. see Cox, Enos Kincheloe
Cox, Edward F. 5109, 7278
Cox, Emmett D. 3733
Cox, Enos Kincheloe 3862
Cox, Homer L. (-1929) 5110
Cox, Leo George (1912-) 1549, 2553-2554, 3163-3165, 5111
Cox, Rose (-1938) 5112
Cox, Sidney 5113
Cox, W. R. see Cox, Winfred R.
Cox, Winfred R. 5114
Crabtree, Robert E. 1726
Craig, James (1844-1919) 5115
Cramer, Raymond L. (1908-) 3363, 3373-3374
Crane, Jonathan Townley (1819-1880) 229, 2888
Crane, Olive 5116
Crane, R. H. 5117
Crary, B. F. (1821-) 5118
Crawford, Florence Louise (1872-1936) 4235
Crawford, J. H. see Crawford, James H. (1879-1958?)
Crawford, James H. (1879-1958?) 5119-5120
Crawford, R. R. see Crawford, Raymond Robert (1891-1965)
Crawford, Raymond Robert (1891-1965) 4231
Crittenton, Charles Nelson (1833-1909) 5121-5124
Crockett, Abbie Lord (-1937) 5125
Crockett, Mrs. Horace Leeds see Crockett, Abbie Lord (-1937)
Crogman, William Henry (1841-) 5889
Croisades de la Grande Commission (Great Commission Crusades) see Haiti Inland Mission
Crooks, A. see Crooks, Adam (1824-1874)
Crooks, Adam (1824-1874) 5126-5127
Crooks, Elizabeth Willets 5127
Crooks, George Richard (1822-1897) 2499, 2872, 6742
Crose, Lester A. 1171
Cross, James A. (1911-) 4208, 4217
Crossley, Ella Kathleen 5129
Crossley, Francis William (1839-1897) 5128-5130
Crossley, Frank see Crossley, Francis William (1839-1897)
Crouch, Charles 5131
Crouch, Winnie (1880-1970) 4411-4412, 5132-5134
Crow, Linda 1894
Crow, Walter 1894
Crowder, Thomas J. 5135
Crown of Glory (periodical) 777, 2414
Croy, Ima B. Lehman 5136
Croy, J. W. 5137
Croy, Mrs. J. W. see Croy, Ima B. Lehman
Crump, Simpson 2533
Cruz, Javier de la 5138
Cuba 6489
Cubie, David Livingston (1928-) 2555, 5139
Culbertson, Howard 6047
Culbertson, Paul Thomas 1398, 1533, 5140-5141
Culbertson, William L. (1905-) 4084
Cullis, Charles (1833-1892) 302, 612-614, 670-673, 905, 4635, 5142-5146
Cullis, Mrs. Charles see Cullis, Lucretia Ann
Cullis, Lucretia Ann 5147
Culloden, W. Va. 4511
Culpepper, John B. 294, 592, 3827
Culpepper, O. Burke 718-720, 723
Culver, Thelma Blanche (1909-) 5148
Cumming, J. E. see Cumming,

J. Elder
Cumming, J. Elder 3967, 4028
Cummings, M. Homer 2191
Cundiff, B. A. 131, 295
Cunningham, James Barber (1887-) 5148a
Curnick, E. T. see Curnick, Edward T. (1850-1923)
Curnick, Edward T. (1850-1923) 132, 5149-5150
Curtis, Geoffrey 35
Curtis, J. Samuel (1890-) 5151
Cuthbertson, James (1882-1957) 3355, 5152-5154

Dadmun, John William (1819-1890) 5155
Dahlquist, Siri 4963
Dake, V. A. see Dake, Vivian Adelbert (1854-1892)
Dake, Vivian Adelbert (1854-1892) 2163-2164, 5156-5158, 5581
Dale, Edith M. 1220
Damboriena, P. 4161
Damon, C. M. 5159-5160
Damon, H. M. see Damon, Herbert Milton (-1924)
Damon, Herbert Milton (-1924) 5161
Dancing 148, 178
Dane, Charles Walter (1875-1944) 296, 3828, 5162
Danford, Samuel Alexander (1865-) 206, 988, 1100, 2827, 5163
Daniels, J. R. see Daniels, Josiah R. (1836?-1908)
Daniels, Josiah R. (1836?-1908) 5164
Danskin, D. R. see Danskin, Donald Ralph (1910-)
Danskin, Donald Ralph (1910-) 1595, 4345, 5165
Darlow, Thomas Herbert (1858-) 5626
Darrell, Lila M. 4373
Darwinism see Evolution
Dashiell, Edward Honeywood (1873-1931) 110, 209, 297, 576, 5166

D'Aubigné, Merle 5167
Davenport, Frederick Morgan (1866-) 2486
Davey, Ethel see Ryff, Ethel Davey (-1949)
Davidson, Hannah Frances (1860-) 1036
Davies, Edward (1830-) 298-302, 358, 561, 906, 977, 984, 1001, 5168, 5614, 5627-5628, 6789-6790, 6948-6949
Davies, Rupert Eric (1909-) 2487
Davis, Frank M. 2998
Davis, Grace Weiser 674-676, 968, 5169
Davis, Harrison 5170
Davis, Henry Turner (1832-) 303-304, 615, 2859, 3047, 5171-5172
Davis, Leo C. 1304
Davis, Lyman Edwyn (1854-1930) 3102
Davis, Melba S. (-1937) 5173
Davis, Mrs. R. N. see Davis, Melba A. (-1937)
Davis, Mrs. Roland Newton see Davis, Melba S. (-1937)
Davis, Samuel M. (1835-1892) 5174
Daw, F. A. see Daw, Francis Ambrose (1894-1951)
Daw, Francis Ambrose (1894-1951) 5175
Dawson, Edith J. 3493
Day, Lloyd Raymond 4427
Day, William (1833?-) 5176
Dayhoff, I. E. see Dayhoff, Irvin E.
Dayhoff, Irvin E. 1571, 5177-5178
Dayton, Donald W. 100
Dayton, Mrs. Donald W. see Dayton, Lucille S.
Dayton, Lucille S. 1032a
Dayton, Wilber Thomas (1916-) 5179
Deal, William Sanford (1910-) 1384, 3473-3476, 3481, 3486, 3536, 3786, 3789, 3806, 5180
Dean, Arthur Hobson (1898-) 5289

Dean, W. W. see Dean, William Ward (1924-)
Dean, William Ward (1924-) 3743, 5181, 5405
Death penalty see Capital punishment
Decatur, Ind. 4477
Dech, George L. 5182
Deets Pacific Bible College of the Nazarene University see Point Loma College
Delanco, N. J. 126
De la Rosa, Maria see Rosa, Maria de la
De la Rosa, Pablo see Rosa, Pablo de la
DeLong, Russell Victor (1901-) 1334-1335, 1550, 1614, 1686, 1709, 1804-1811, 5183-5184
Demaray, C. Dorr 2741, 4844
Demaray, Donald Eugene (1926-) 5185
DeMent, Byron Hoover (1863-1933) 3862
DeMille, Wesley C. 5186
Demonology 327
Dempster, Joseph S. 305, 5187-5188
Denman, Mary R. 5189
Denton, Ronald 5190
Denver, Colo. 4339, 7156-7157, 7161-7162
DePasquale, Mrs. Don see DePasquale, Frances
DePasquale, Frances 5191
DePauw, Washington Charles (1822-1887) 2944, 5192-5193
DePauw University 2944
DesArc, Mo. 4505
Desh, Frank 5194
Desh, Mrs. Frank see Desh, Rose Myers
Desh, Rose Myers 5195
DeShazer, Jacob (1912-) 5196-5198
Des Plaines, Ill. 2837
Detroit, Mich. Holiness Tabernacle 6958
DeVol, Catherine Isabella see Cattell, Catherine DeVol (1906-)
DeVol, Charles Edward (1903-) 5199
DeVol, George Fox (1871-1917) 2363, 5200-5201
DeVol, Mrs. George Fox see DeVol, Isabella French (1869-1920)
DeVol, Isabella French (1869-1920) 5202
DeVol, William Ezra (1909-) 5203
DeVol family 2363, 5201
DeWeerd, Mrs. Fred 5204-5205
DeWeerd, James Arthur (1916-1972) 3166, 5206
Dewey, Clifford Sherwood 4481
Dewey, John (1859-1952) 7176
DeWitt, Mrs. C. E. see DeWitt, Pearl L.
DeWitt, Pearl L. 5207
Dhlamini, Samuel 5208-5209
Dhlamini, Zakeu (-1931) 5210
Diaz, John Joseph (1873-1964) 5211
Dickerman, Mrs. Charles Burton see Dickerman, Ethel King
Dickerman, Ethel King 1938, 5212-5213, 5870
Dickinson College 2943
Didsbury, Alta. 4512
Dieter, Harold D. (1906-1948) 5214
Dieter, M. E. see Dieter, Melvin Easterday (1924-)
Dieter, Melvin Easterday (1924-) 648, 662, 5215-5216, 6853, 7033
Dievendorf, Anne F.
Dilbeck, Lula May (-1918) 5217-5218
Dillingham, M. V. see Dillingham, Michael Vance (1863-1944?)
Dillingham, Michael Vance (1863-1944?) 5219-5220
Dimond, Sydney George (1882-) 2488
Dinius, Will L. 1204

Dirkse, Neal C. 1336, 5221
Ditmer, R. P. see Ditmer, Russell P. (1897-)
Ditmer, Russell P. (1897-) 3765, 5222
Divine Life (periodical) 778
Divorce see Marriage
Dixon, Bertha Pinkham 5223-5224
Dixon, E. P. see Dixon, Elmer P. (-1957)
Dixon, Elmer P. (-1957) 5225
Dixon, Mrs. W. T. see Dixon, Bertha Pinkham
Dlamini, Samuel see Dhlamini, Samuel
Doctors see Physicians
Dodd, Gladys 1022-1023, 2062, 5283-5284, 5286
Dodds, Gil 3156
Dodge, Asbury see Dodge, William Asbury (1844-1904)
Dodge, W. A. see Dodge, William Asbury (1844-1904)
Dodge, William Asbury (1844-1904) 5226-5227
Dodson, E. H. 5228
Dodsworth, Jeremiah 149, 3060
Dohnavur Fellowship 4961
Dolbow, Andrew J. (1846-1934) 5229-5231
Dolbow, Maggie Miller 5231
Dominican Republic 2756
Donalsonville, Ga. 2430, 4562
Donnelly, John T. 5232
Dooley, Bertha R. 4526
Dooley, Gladys Emmeline (1906-) 5233
Dooley, Hannah M. Lippincott (1868-) 5234-5235, 5237
Dooley, J. A. see Dooley, John Alexander (1860-)
Dooley, John Alexander (1860-) 1582, 5235-5237
Dooley, Mrs. John Alexander see Dooley, Hannah M. Lippincott (1868-)
Dorsey, Morton W. 5238
Doty, T. K. see Doty, Thomas K. (1833-1913)

Doty, Thomas K. (1833-1913) 306-307, 3167, 3829, 5239-5240
Douglas, John Henry (1832-1919) 5241-5244
Douglas, John Scott 2072, 7120
Douglas, Mabel H. 5243
Douglas, Major 2283
Douglas, Wilson 180
Douglas, Mass. 984
Douglass, Paul Franklin (1904-) 2953
Downey, Lois Jean Baumgardner (1931-) 5245
Downey, Paul Roger (1930-) 5246
Downey, Mrs. Paul Roger see Downey, Lois Jean Baumgardner (1931-)
Dracut, Mass. 4594
Drake, Lucy Reed see Osborn, Lucy Reed Drake (1844-)
Dress see Clothing and dress
Drinking see Liquor problem
Drown, Walter Forbes (1896-1972) 5247
Drug habit see Narcotic habit
Drum, W. G. see Drum, Woodard Glenn (1903-)
Drum, Woodard Glenn (1903-) 5248
Drunkenness see Liquor problem
Drury, A. W. see Drury, Augustus Waldo (1851-1935)
Drury, Augustus Waldo (1851-1935) 3698, 3699, 3706-3709, 3715-3718
Dry Legion (periodical) 2240
Drysdale, John Douglas (1880-1953) 1966-1972, 5249-5250
DuBois, Lauriston J. 1296, 1337-1340, 1615, 1687
Duckworth, Bonita Lois (1934-) 5251
Duckworth, Jack Raymond (1934-) 5252
Duckworth, Mrs. Jack Raymond see Duckworth, Bonita Lois (1934-)
Duda, Rachel Grace Fair (1926-) 5253

Duda, Robert Clarence (1924-   ) 5254
Duda, Mrs. Robert Clarence see Duda, Rachel Grace Fair (1926-   )
Dudley, Dora Griffin 5255-5256
Dudman, Charlotte 5257
Dudman, Mrs. George S. see Dudman, Charlotte
Dunham, R. E. 5258
Dunkle, William Frederick 2818
Dunn, Lewis Romaine (1822-1898) 2889-2891, 3023, 5259
Dunning, H. Ray 1341, 1652
Dunning, Norman Grove 5003
Duren, William Larkin (1905-   ) 3086
Duryea, Jennie Sworn 5261
Duryea, John Ackerly (1878-1946) 5260-5261
Dustman, J. M. 327, 5262
Dutton, Mich. 4506
Dygoski, Louise Annie (1911-   ) 2587, 5263

Eagle, J. M. (-1936) 5264
Earhart, Mary 7212
Earle, A. B. see Earle, Absalom Backas (-1892)
Earle, Absalom Backas (-1892) 104, 309-310, 629, 677-679, 907-909, 5265-5268
Earle, Ralph (1907-   ) 522, 1304, 1439-1446, 1885, 1899, 1927, 5269
Earnest Christian (periodical) 3889, 3891, 7127
Earnest Christian and Golden Rule (periodical) 2725
East (Far East) 1885-1887, 3386
East and West Indies Bible Mission see Evangelical Bible Mission
East Los Angeles, Calif. 4332
East Mississippi Female College see Meridian Female College
Eastern Nazarene College 1415, 1475a, 1594, 4392-4394, 5825, 6281, 6302
Eastern Pilgrim College see Penn Wesleyan College
Eastland, Tex. 4591
Eastman, C. S. 3024
Eastman Seminary 4395
Eaton, J. W. see Eaton, Joel W. (1836-   )
Eaton, Joel W. (1836-   ) 127, 5270
Eberstein, John G. 2047, 2050
Eby, Blanche Remington (1885-1925) 5271-5272
Eby, D. C. 5273
Eby, Mrs. D. C. see Eby, Blanche Remington (1885-1925)
Eckel, Catherine P. 5886
Eckel, Howard 910, 1871, 3459, 5274
Eckel, W. A. see Eckel, William A.
Eckel, William A. 1905, 5275
Eckel, William Dohn 1906
Eckert, Ruth M. (1922-   ) 4583, 5276
Eden Grove Academy and Grammar School 4396
Edinburgh, Scot. 4414, 4571
Edmonds, L. M. 5277
Edmonton, Alta. 4301, 4354
Edmonton Bible Institute see Beulah Bible Institute
Education 626-627, 865, 1593-1606, 2223, 2308, 2682-2684, 2943-2944, 3185-3187, 3513, 3795-3798, 4099, 4270, 4300-4603
Education, Christian see Religious education
Education, Higher see Education
Education, Religious see Religious education
Edwards, F. C. see Edwards, Frank C.
Edwards, Frank C. 5278
Edwards, Mrs. G. G. see Edwards, Grace Smith

(-1944)
Edwards, Grace Morris 5279-5280
Edwards, Grace Smith (-1944) 5280
Edwards, Jonathan (1703-1758) 2130-2131, 2939
Edwards, Maud W. (-1933) 5281
Edwards, Mildred Speakes (1904-) 1853
Effusion, Baptismal see Baptism
Egypt 2177, 5980
Ehlers, W. C. 94
Eicken, Erich von 2556
Eisenhower, A. L. see Eisenhower, Abraham Lincoln (-1944)
Eisenhower, Abe see Eisenhower, Abraham Lincoln (-1944)
Eisenhower, Abraham Lincoln (-1944) 1022, 5282-5284
Eisenhower, Dwight David (1890-1969) 2062
Eisenhower, Ira (1870-1943) 5285-5286
Eisenhower family 2062
Ekvall, Robert Brainerd (1898-) 4102, 4139, 5287-5294
Election (Theology) see Predestination
Electric Messages (periodical) see OMS Outreach (periodical)
Eleventh Hour Messenger 3917a
Elhanan Training and Industrial Institute 4397
Eliade, Mircea 14
Elijah, the prophet 311
Elizondo, Santos (1869-) 5295
Elliot, H. B. see Elliot, Henry Bond (-1912)
Elliot, Henry Bond (-1912) 5296
Elliott, Charles (1792-1869) 2954
Elliott, Esther Cantrell (1929-) 5297
Elliott, Harry Joseph 5298-5299
Elliott, Paul Frederick (1869-1944) 3560, 5300
Elliott, Paul Frederick (1904-) 5301-5302
Elliott, Paul Frederick, Jr. see Elliott, Paul Frederick (1904-)
Elliott, Paul Frederick, Sr. see Elliott, Paul Frederick (1869-1944)
Ellis, J. William 1616
Ellis, W. T. see Ellis, William T.
Ellis, William T. 5303
Ellyson, E. P. see Ellyson, Edgar Painter (1869-1954)
Ellyson, Edgar Painter (1869-1954) 150-151, 207, 311-313, 1447-1451, 1716, 1760-1769, 5304-5305, 5307
Ellyson, Mrs. Edgar Painter see Ellyson, Mary Emily Soul (1869-1943)
Ellyson, M. Emily see Ellyson, Mary Emily Soul (1869-1943)
Ellyson, Mary Emily Soul (1869-1943) 5305-5307
El Monte, Calif. 4600
El Salvador, Mex. 4406
Emancipation of slaves see Slavery
Emery, O. D. see Emery, O. Dale (1927-)
Emery, O. Dale (1927-) 5308-5310
Emery, S. I. 3852
Emmanuel (periodical) 1974, 4399
Emmanuel Association 2036-2041, 4542, 4974
Emmanuel Association. General Council 2039
Emmanuel Bible College, Birkenhead, Eng. 663, 1974, 4398-4399, 5250
Emmanuel Bible College, Kitchener, Ont. 4400
Emmanuel Bible College and

Missions see Emmanuel Holiness Church
Emmanuel College 4401-4404
Emmanuel Herald (periodical) 2040
Emmanuel Holiness Church 1966-1975, 4398, 5250
Emmanuel Missionary Church see Emmanuel Association
Emmanuel Missionary Training Home see Emmanuel Bible College
Emmanuel News Bulletin (periodical) 1975
Emmanuel Orphanage and Bible School 4405
Emmel, J. Robert see Emmel, James Robert (1923-)
Emmel, James Robert (1923-) 7225
Emotion display in worship see Shouting
Emphasis (periodical) 4150
Emphasis on Faith and Living (periodical) 3247
Emslie, Betty Levenson 5085
End of the world see Eschatology
Endsley, Andrew J. (1824-) 2883
England 194-195, 364, 367, 371, 2593, 4337, 4362-4363, 4369, 4387, 4398, 4484, 6972 see also Great Britain
Engle, Albert H. 1026
Engle, Anna R. 1035, 1037
Englund, Elvira see Firestone, Elvira R. Englund
Engstrom, Theodore Wilhelm (1916-) 960
Entertainments see Church entertainments
Entwisle, J. Howard 1982, 2997-2998
Enyart, Mary H. 2343, 5312
Enyart, Paul C. (1908-1971) 2343, 5311-5312
Era of Holiness (periodical) 779
Erdman, Charles Rosenbury (1866-) 3750, 3752

Erdmann, H. A. 1452, 3872-3873
Erny, Edward 3379, 3451, 5101, 5105, 5861, 6293, 6857
Erny, Esther 3379, 3451, 5101, 5105, 5861, 6293
Ervine, St. John Greer (1883-) 4820
Erwin, S. H. 5313
Eschatology 572-607, 1134-1140, 1568-1581, 2113-2115, 2185, 2218-2219, 2335-2341, 2678-2681, 2940, 3406-3410, 3500-3512, 3792-3794, 3851-3852, 4088-4094, 4259-4262
Escuela Heroes de Mexico 4406
Eshelman, Wiler J. 1024
Esselstyn, William C. 1866
Eternal punishment see Hell
Eternal security see Predestination
Ethics, Christian see Conduct of life
Ethics, Political see Political criticism
Ethics, Social see Social criticism
Eubanks, Annie Laurie (1926-) 3470, 3542, 3574, 3582, 3598, 5314
Europe 1888, 4407
European Nazarene Bible College 4407
European War, 1914-1918. 587, 2113-2114, 6400, 6566, 6748
Evangel Church 1976-1980, 2042-2043, 2312, 5880-5881
Evangelical Advocate (periodical) 1999
Evangelical Association of North America see Evangelical Church
Evangelical Baptist Society see Apostolic Christian Church of America
Evangelical Bible Mission 3272
Evangelical Church 1981-1997, 5884
Evangelical Church in Indiana 1983
Evangelical Church in Kansas 1984

Evangelical Church of North America 1998-1999
Evangelical Congregational Church 2000-2003
Evangelical Congregational Church. Board of Missions 2002
Evangelical Friend (Cleveland, Ohio) 2302
Evangelical Friend (Damascus, Ohio) see Evangelical Friend and Oriental News
Evangelical Friend (Newberg, Ore.) 2303
Evangelical Friend and Oriental News 2364
Evangelical Friends Alliance 2270, 2299, 2303
Evangelical Friends Association see Evangelical Friends Alliance
Evangelical Friends Church, Eastern Division see Friends, Society of. Ohio Yearly Meeting
Evangelical Mennonites see United Missionary Church
Evangelical Messenger (periodical) 1986, 1993
Evangelical Methodist Church 2602-2611, 3104, 4332, 5558 see also Mexican Evangelistic Mission
Evangelical Methodist Church. Board of World Missions 2608
Evangelical Methodist Church. Conferences 2603
Evangelical Methodist Church. Conferences. Mexican 2154
Evangelical Tidings (periodical) 780
Evangelical United Brethren Church 2004-2008
Evangelical United Brethren Church. Board of Missions 2008
Evangelical United Brethren Church. Board of Missions. Division of Women's Service 2008
Evangelical United Mennonites see United Missionary Church
Evangelical Visitor (periodical) 2030, 1032
Evangelical Wesleyan Church 3885-3889, 4299, 4464, 7127
Evangelical Wesleyan Church. General Board of Administration 3887
Evangelical Wesleyan Church of North America 3890
Evangelicalism 2658, 6380
Evangelische Magazin für die Sonntags-schule und den Familienkreis 1994
Evangelist (Huntington Park, Calif.) 1980
Evangelist (Waco, Tex.) 3448
Evangelist of Truth (periodical) 3858, 3865
Evangelistic Faith Missions 3273-3280a, 5464, 5466-5468
Evangelistic Tabernacle 2042-2043
Evangelistic Tabernacles see Evangel Church
Evangelistic work 628-645, 648, 654-655, 662, 1043, 1150-1151, 1214, 1607-1635, 2044-2045, 2139, 2186, 2685-2688, 2789-2790, 2945-2951, 3188, 3262, 3514-3515, 3647, 3799, 3853-3856, 4100-4101, 4230, 4271, 6960, 7111, 7123, 7144
Evangelists see Clergy
Evangeliums Posaune (periodical) 1174
Evans, Alec Richard 6230-6231
Evans, Christmas (1766-1838) 2132
Evans, James Harrington 3
Evanston, Ill. 6564
Evansville, Wis. 4408
Evansville Junior College see Evansville Seminary
Evansville Seminary 4408
Evening Light and Church of God Evangel (periodical) see Church of God Evangel (periodical)
Everett, Walter Goodnow (1860-

1936) 4
Eves, Norma A. 2452
Evil spirits see Demonology
Evolution 1450, 5648
Expositor of the Christ Life (periodical) 781
Eyre, John 2525
Eyre, Marion 2454

Faber, Frederick William (1814-1863) 37, 4031
Failing, George Edgar (1912-) 3154, 5315
Fairbairn, C. V. see Fairbairn, Charles Victor (1890-)
Fairbairn, Charles Victor (1890-) 2685, 5316-5317
Fairmount, Ind. 4409
Fairmount Bible School 4409
Faith Bible School 4410, 5133-5134
Faith cure see Faith-healing
Faith-healing 608-618, 1141-1146, 1582-1584, 4014, 4095-4098, 4208, 4263-4266, 5266, 5595, 6069-6070, 6345
Faith Home and School see Faith Bible School
Faith Home and Training School 4413
Faith Mission 2044-2051, 4414, 4571, 5500
Faith Mission Bible College see Faith Mission Training Home and Bible College
Faith Mission in Canada see Faith Mission
Faith Mission Training Home and Bible College 4414
Faith Missions see Evangelistic Faith Missions
Falcon, N. C. 4415
Falcon Holiness School 4415
Family see Marriage
Family life 3816
Family relations see Family life; Marriage
Fanaticism 447
Fant, David Jones (1897-) 5318, 7003

Far East see East (Far East)
Farish, Hunter Dickinson (1897-) 3087
Farrar, Frederic William (1831-1903) 3686
Farson, Duke 2123
Farson, Duke M. 2145-2146, 5319-5320
Fee, John Gregg (1816-1901) 5321-5325
Felker, Beatrice see Felker, Lillie Beatrice Flexon (1916-)
Felker, Dean George (1918-) 5326
Felker, Mrs. Dean George see Felker, Lillie Beatrice Flexon (1916-)
Felker, Lillie Beatrice Flexon (1916-) 5327
Feminism see Woman
Fenelon, Francois de Salignac de La Mothe (1651-1715) 556, 563
Fergerson, E. A. 314, 911-912
Ferguson, Charles Wright (1901-) 2792
Ferguson, Frank (1880-) 5328, 5330
Ferguson, Mrs. Frank see Ferguson, Lula Hutcherson (1867-1944)
Ferguson, Lula Hutcherson (1867-1944) 5329-5330
Ferguson, Mannie Payne (1850-) 2174-2175, 5331, 5333
Ferguson, T. P. see Ferguson, Theodore Pollock (1853-1920)
Ferguson, Theodore Pollock (1853-1920) 5332-5333
Ferguson, Mrs. Theodore Pollock see Ferguson, Mannie Payne (1850-)
Ferle, Minnie C. see Knapp, Minne C. Ferle (1868-1923)
Ferm, Lois Roughan 3796
Ferm, Vergilius Ture Anselm (1896-) 1061
Fernandez, Eugenio (1898-) 5334

Feucht, Werner Christian Martin (1929-1959) 45
Finance, Church see Church finance
Finch, Oscar J. (1901-) 1453, 5335
Finch, Paul W. 2041, 5336
Finch, R. G. see Finch, Ralph Goodrich (1881-1950)
Finch, Ralph Goodrich (1881-1950) 3290, 3579, 3583, 5337-5340, 5754, 6746
Finch, Mrs. Ralph Goodrich see Finch, Ruth Wood (1885-1971)
Finch, Ruth Wood (1885-1971) 5340a
The Finished Work of Calvary ... Holiness with Carnality ... Truth without Error ... The Baptism in the Holy Ghost (Acts 2:4) (periodical) 4194a
Fink, Newton W. 2707
Fink, Mrs. Newton W. 2707
Finnemore, J. 2533
Finney, Charles Grandison (1792-1875) 5, 190, 558, 664, 2139, 3391, 3951
Finney, Spencer S. 5341
Fire and Hammer (periodical) 782
Fire-Baptized Holiness Association of America see Fire-Baptized Holiness Church
Fire-Baptized Holiness Church 4239-4240, 5872
Fire Baptized Holiness Church (Wesleyan) 2052-2054, 4459
Fire-brand (periodical) see Missionary World (periodical)
Firestone, Elvira R. Englund 1228, 5342-5343
Firestone, Homer Leon (1921-) 5344-5346
Firestone, Mrs. Homer Leon see Firestone, Elvira R. Englund
Fischer, W. G. see Fischer, William Gustavus (1835-1912)

Fischer, William Gustavus (1835-1912) 5347
Fisher, Annie May Johnson 5348
Fisher, Bill see Fisher, Charles William (1916-)
Fisher, C. William see Fisher, Charles William (1916-)
Fisher, Charles William (1916-) 1286, 1342, 1388, 1617-1619, 1689, 1744-1746, 1749-1750, 1812, 5349
Fisher, H. L. 4297
Fisher, W. E. see Fisher, William Edgar
Fisher, William see Fisher, Charles William (1916-)
Fisher, William Edgar 1454, 5350
Fisher, Mrs. William Edgar see Fisher, Annie May Johnson
Fitch, Charles 5351
Fitch, Ross L. 691
Fitkin, A. E. see Fitkin, Abram Edward (1878-1933)
Fitkin, Mrs. A. E. see Fitkin, Susan Norris (1870-1951)
Fitkin, Abram Edward (1878-1933) 152, 5352
Fitkin, Mrs. Abram Edward see Fitkin, Susan Norris (1870-1951)
Fitkin, Mrs. S. N. see Fitkin, Susan Norris (1870-1951)
Fitkin, Susan Norris (1870-1951) 1690, 1711, 1886, 5353-5358
Fitzgerald, Mrs. John D. see Fitzgerald, Osie M. Boylan (1813-)
Fitzgerald, John Newbury (1837-1907) 2849
Fitzgerald, Osee M. Boylan see Fitzgerald, Osie M. Boylan (1813-)
Fitzgerald, Osie M. Boylan (1813-) 5359
Flame (periodical) 783, 1047
Flaming Sword (periodical 2053
Flashlight (periodical) 3421
Fleming, Bona 913-914, 5360-5362, 5365
Fleming, E. J. (1871-1954)

1860-1861, 5363
Fleming, John (-1935) 914, 5362, 5364-5365
Fletcher, John William (1729-1785) 550-551, 554, 1551, 2524, 2476, 2592, 2892-2894, 3843
Flew, Robert Newton (1886-) 6, 2583
Flexon, Mrs. Emma Laura 3537
Flexon, R. G. see Flexon, Richard G.
Flexon, Richard G. 3487-3489, 3508, 3590, 3790-3791, 5366
Flinner, Lyle Payson (1918-) 5367-5368
Florence, Miss. 4601
Flores, Catarino C. (1896-) 5369
Florida 3861, 4303, 4433, 4461-4462
Florida, S. Afr. 4514
Florida Evangelistic Association 3861
Flowers, S. L. see Flowers, Sumpter Lee (1881-1945)
Flowers, S. Lee see Flowers, Sumpter Lee (1881-1945)
Flowers, Sumpter Lee (1881-1945) 694, 874, 1343, 2830, 5370-5372
Floyd, Fred (1900-) 1389
Fogg, L. N. 5373
Follin, N. Hammond 617
Foot-washing (rite) 1087, 1091
Foote, J. B. see Foote, John Bartlit (1826-1911)
Foote, John Bartlit (1826-1911) 5374
Foote, Mrs. Julia A. J. (1823-) 5375-5377
Ford, C. B. 5378
Ford, Jack (1908-) 663, 1044-1045, 1889-1890, 2077-1078, 2080, 2118, 2471-2472, 3358, 3453, 5379, 6690
Ford, Paul D. 3589
Foreign missions see Missions

Foreign Missions Bulletin see World Missions Bulletin
Foreordination see Predestination
Formosa 2757
Forrest, Aubrey Leland 1155
Fort Erie, Ont. 4523
Fort Scott, Kan. 1233, 1234, 4416
Fort Scott Christian Heights 4416
Fort Wayne, Ind. 4417, 4570
Fort Wayne, Ind. Bible Institute see Fort Wayne Bible College
Fort Wayne Bible College 4146, 4417-4418, 6502
Fort Wayne Bible Institute see Fort Wayne Bible College
Fort Wayne Bible Training School see Fort Wayne Bible College
Fort Wayne Female College see Taylor University
Forward in Faith (radio broadcast) 4221
Fosdick, Harry Emerson (1878-1969) 448
Foss, Cyrus David (1834-1910) 3018, 3025-3028, 5380-5385
Foss, Martin (1889-) 7
Foster, John Onesiumus (1833-1920) 2837
Foster, R. S. see Foster, Randolph Sinks (1820-1903)
Foster, Randolph Sinks (1820-1903) 105, 1552, 2895-2896, 3834, 3843, 5386, 5411
Fountain (periodical) 784
Fowler, A. M. 405, 5387-5388
Fowler, Anderson (1843-1906) 5389
Fowler, C. J. see Fowler, Charles J. (circa 1848-1919)
Fowler, Charles J. (circa 1848-1919) 133, 208, 315-317, 667-668, 689, 701, 712, 715, 915, 5390
Fowler, Wilton R. 2599
Fox, George (1624-1691) 2273, 2277, 2283, 2298
Fox, Henry J. (1821-) 112,

5391
Fraley, Robert Owen 4330
Frame, George 5392, 5733, 6691
Francis Asbury Bible College 4419
Francis of Assisi (1182-1226) 40
Francis of Sales (1567-1622) 40
Francois de Sales, Saint see Francis of Sales (1567-1622)
Frankfort, Ind. 4420
Frankfort Pilgrim Bible School see Frankfort Wesleyan Bible College
Frankfort Pilgrim College see Frankfort Wesleyan Bible College
Frankfort Wesleyan Bible College 4420
Franklin Springs, Ga. 4401, 5872
Franklin Springs Institute see Emmanuel College
Fraternities see Secret societies
Frazee, E. W. 916
Frederick, Daisy E. (-1946) 5393
Free Baptist Church 1010
Free Methodist (periodical) see Light and Life (periodical)
Free Methodist Church of North America 2163-2164, 2612-2765, 3205, 3220, 4302, 4332, 4335, 4381, 4408, 4424, 4431, 4483, 4487-4488, 4491, 4522, 4529, 4550, 4558, 4565-4569, 4590, 4596, 4617-4618, 4628, 4685-4686, 4723-4724, 4744, 4793, 4835, 4844, 5044, 5059, 5074-5075, 5082-5083, 5157-5158, 5160, 5197-5198, 5317, 5526, 5544, 5616, 5631, 5721, 5791, 5945, 6507, 6513-6514, 6516, 6579-6582, 6611, 6706-6712, 6714-6715, 6744, 6793, 6857, 6892, 6894, 6914, 7126, 7335

Free Methodist Church of North America. Commission on Christian Education 2682
Free Methodist Church of North America. Conferences. East Ontario 2618-2619
Free Methodist Church of North America. Conferences. Kentucky-Tennessee 2620
Free Methodist Church of North America. Conferences. Oklahoma 2621
Free Methodist Church of North America. General Conference 2614
Free Methodist Church of North America. General Missionary Board 2716, 2720
Free Methodist Church of North America. General Missionary Secretary 2713-2714
Free Methodist Church of North America. Hymnal Commission 2699
Free Methodist Church of North America. Woman's Missionary Society 2728, 2756-2757, 2760, 2765, 4721
Free Methodist Church of North America. Young People's Missionary Society 2632, 2718, 4628, 6611
Free Methodist Haiti Inland Mission see Haiti Inland Mission
Free Methodist World Fellowship 2615-2616, 2720, 2729 see also Free Methodist Church of North America
Free Methodists in Africa 2748-2752, 5544, 5631
Free Methodists in Alberta 2753
Free Methodists in California 6516
Free Methodists in Canada 2754-2755, 6892, 6894
Free Methodists in China 5945
Free Methodists in Dominican Republic 2756
Free Methodists in Formosa 2757

Free Methodists in Haiti 3281-3289
Free Methodists in Illinois 2758, 6513-6514
Free Methodists in India 2759, 4721, 5044, 6611
Free Methodists in Japan 2760-2762
Free Methodists in Kentucky 2620
Free Methodists in Michigan 6857
Free Methodists in New York 6579-6582
Free Methodists in Oklahoma 2621
Free Methodists in Ontario 2618-2619, 6744
Free Methodists in Panama 2763
Free Methodists in Paraguay 2764
Free Methodists in Tennessee 2620
Free Methodists in the Philippine Islands 2765
Free-Will Baptist Church. Conferences. Cape Fear see Pentecostal Free-Will Baptist Church
Freeman, D. D. see Freeman, Dallas Dolphus (1900-)
Freeman, Dallas Dolphus (1900-) 4288
Freeman, Harry C. 153
Freemasons see Secret societies
Freeport, N.Y. 803
Freeport, Pa. 4572-4576
French, Alfred J. 2593
French, H. Robb 3815
French, Mary Isabella see DeVol, Isabella French (1869-1920)
Frey, Howard J. 3468
Friederichs, Hulda 3609
Friendly Endeavor (periodical) see Northwest Friend (periodical)
Friends, Society of 2270-2306, 5034, 5046, 5242-5244, 5847, 5956, 6099, 6266, 6436, 6472, 6768-6770, 6773-6775, 6800-6801, 6844, 7039, 7292
Friends, Society of. California Yearly Meeting 2307-2314, 4332, 5880-5881
Friends, Society of. Central Yearly Meeting 2315-2350, 4579, 5312, 6853
Friends, Society of. Central Yearly Meeting. Missionary Committee 2342
Friends, Society of. Kansas Yearly Meeting 2351-2357
Friends, Society of. Kansas Yearly Meeting. Board of Missions 2357
Friends, Society of. Ohio Yearly Meeting of the Friends Church 2358-2376
Friends, Society of. Ohio Yearly Meeting of the Friends Church. Friends Foreign Missionary Society 2362
Friends, Society of. Oregon Yearly Meeting of Friends Church 2377-2393, 4423, 4429, 6436
Friends, Society of. Oregon Yearly Meeting of Friends Church. Board of Christian Education 2379
Friends, Society of. Oregon Yearly Meeting of Friends Church. Board of Missions 2391
Friends, Society of. Oregon Yearly Meeting of Friends Church. Board of Peace and Service 2385
Friends, Society of. Oregon Yearly Meeting of Friends Church. Board of Publication 2382-2383
Friends, Society of. Pacific Yearly Meeting 2310-2311
Friends, Society of. Rocky Mountain Yearly Meeting 2394-2396
Friends Bible College 4421
Friends Bible Institute and Training School see Malone

College
Friends Evangel (periodical) 2344
Friends' Expositor (periodical) 2304
Friends Herald (periodical) 2365
Friends in Africa 2372, 5034, 5699
Friends in China 2373-2374, 5201
Friends in India 2375-2376
Friends in Ohio 2358-2376, 7039
Friends' Minister (periodical) 3413
Friends Oriental News (periodical) 2366
Fruit of the Vine (periodical) 2392
Frye, W. A. see Frye, William Arthur (-1967)
Frye, William Arthur (-1967) 5394
Fuge, Fred T. see Fuge, Frederick Thomas (1872-)
Fuge, Frederick Thomas (1872-) 1656, 3576, 5395-5398
Fuggett, C. B. 5399
Fuhrman, Eldon Ralph (1918-) 2557, 5400
Full Gospel and Rescue Journal 785
Full Salvation Quarterly 786
Fuller, H. L. see Fuller, Harold L. (1908-1972)
Fuller, Harold L. (1908-1972) 5401-5402
Fundamentalism see Evangelicalism; Modernism
Funk, J. F. see Funk, John Fretz (1835-1930)
Funk, John Fretz (1835-1930) 5403-5405

G., W. see G. W.
G. W. 2079
Gaar, J. E. 5406
Gabriel, Charles Hutchinson (1856-1932) 5407-5408
Gaddis, B. H. 2701

Gaddis, M. P. see Gaddis, Maxwell Pierson (1811-1888)
Gaddis, Maxwell Pierson (1811-1888) 4955, 5409-5411
Gaddis, Merrill Elmer (1891-) 649
Gaekwad, Wamanrao 5412
Gaines, Ina 3236
Galilean Training School 4422
Gall, Shirley J. 3763
Galloway, C. Dean 1926
Gambling 3095-3096
Garber, Paul Neff (1899-) 2775
Garbutt, Mrs. J. William 5227
Garcia, Estanislao 5413
Garcia, Lucia Carmen 5414
Gardner, J. Russell see Gardner, James Russell (1891-)
Gardner, James Russell (1891-) 5415-5416
Gardner, Mary Crilley 5417-5419
Gardner, R. Wayne see Gardner, Robert Wayne (1894-)
Gardner, Robert Wayne (1894-) 5420
Gardner, Russell see Gardner, James Russell (1891-)
Garrett, "Aunt Puss" (1838-) 5421
Garrett, Paul Hamilton (1908-) 5422
Garrett, W. L. see Garrett, William L.
Garrett, William L. 5423
Garrett Biblical Institute 3025
Garrett County, Md. 983
Garrison, Harold Allen (1918-) 5424
Garsee, Jarrell Willis (1930-) 1344, 1679, 5425-5429
Gassaway, Percy Lee (1885-1937) 5430
Gaston County, N. C. 3231, 4290
Gates, Charles W. 5431
Gaustad, Edwin Scott (1923-) 60, 1156, 1242, 1643, 4162-4163, 4210
Gay, David 5432

Gay, Leslie F., Jr. 7192
Gayjikian, Hosanna Gabooshian (1892-1941) 3471
Gayjikian, Krikor (circa 1887-1972) 3471, 5433-5436
Gayjikian, Osanna Gaboshian see Gayjikian, Hosanna Gabooshian (1892-1941)
Gaza, Afr. see Gazaland
Gazaland 5085
Gealy, Fred Daniel 2810
Geiger, K. E. see Geiger, Kenneth E. (1916-)
Geiger, Kenneth E. (1916-) 569-571, 5437
General Holiness Assembly. Chicago, 1885 192
General Holiness Assembly. Chicago, 1901 193
General Holiness League 2055
George, J. Lowell 5438
George Fox College 4423, 6436
Georgia 2430, 3097-3098, 3147-3148, 4270, 4335, 4401, 4449-4451, 4562, 5227, 5872, 6709-6711
Gerber, Wayne Jay (1927-) 5439
Gerig, Jared Franklin (1907-) 4144, 5440
German Guide to Holiness (periodical) see Guide to Holiness (Wegweiser zur Heiligung (periodical)
German Methodists see Methodists, German
Germans in the United States 3012
Germany 3685, 4407
Gerry, N.Y. 4424
Gerry Seminary 4424
Ghormley, Newton Baxter (-1940) 2633, 2752, 5441
Gibbs, Donna D. (1925-) 5442
Gibbs, Frederick W. (1914-) 5443
Gibbs, Mrs. Frederick W. see Gibbs, Donna D. (1925-)
Gibson, C. A. see Gibson, Charles Arthur (1888-)
Gibson, Charles Arthur (1888-) 1717, 5444
Gibson, James 5445
Gibson, Julia Roberts (-196?) 5446-5447
Gibson, William (1808-1867) 4769
Gift Box Missionary (periodical) see World Missions Bulletin
Gill, Joshua 318-319, 680-685, 708-709, 714, 5448
Gillette, Frieda Almira (1899-) 5449-5450, 5701
Gillette, Philip Goode (1833-) 5451
Gilley, Ruth Evelyn (1904-) 5452
Gilley, W. R. see Gilley, William Richard (1879-1949)
Gilley, William Richard (1879-1949) 5453
Gillies, J. W. see Gillies, James W. (-1915)
Gillies, James W. (-1915) 5454
Gilliland, Ponder W. 1620
Gillmore, Calvin 2970
Gilmour, H. L. see Gilmour, Henry Lake (1836-1920)
Gilmour, Henry Lake (1836-1920) 667, 682-683, 685, 700-703, 715, 2990-2991, 2994-2997, 3001-3002, 5455
Gilpatrick, Emma Appling (-1913) 5456
Gilpatrick, Mrs. T. H. see Gilpatrick, Emma Appling (-1913)
Gilpin, Joshua, vicar of Wrockwardine 550-551
Ginder, Henry A. 119, 5457
Girandola, Anthony 3132
Girvin, Ernest Alexander (1857-) 1248, 4864, 5458-5459
Gish, Carol Spell 1297, 1345, 1691, 1875, 1879, 1902, 1922, 5037, 5460, 6351, 7260-7261
Gish, Mrs. Delbert see Gish, Carol Spell

Glascock, J. L. see Glascock, James Luther (1852-1942)

Glascock, James Luther (1852-1942) 154, 630, 917, 3853, 5461-5462

Glasgow, Scot. 4456, 4516, 4540, 6689-6690

Glasgow, Scot. Metropolitan Mission 2136

Glendale, Ariz. 4530

Glendora, Calif. 4597

Glenn, Jennie 5463-5464

Glenn, Victor 3273-3276, 3278-3279, 3280a, 5465-5468

Glenn, Mrs. Victor see Glenn, Jennie

Glide, Mrs. Lizzie Helen Snyder (1852-1936?) 5469-5470

Glixman, Alfred F. 5427

Glossbrenner, J. J. see Glossbrenner, Jacob John (1812-1887)

Glossbrenner, Jacob John (1812-1887) 3717

Glossolalia 619-623, 1147-1149, 1213, 1583, 1585-1590, 2220-2222, 3244, 3875, 4175, 4267-4269, 4796, 6516

Glover, Robert Hall (1871-1947) 6738

Godbey, Emma Durham (1839-1915) 5471-5472

Godbey, W. B. see Godbey, William B. (1833-1920)

Godbey, William B. (1833-1920) 110, 137-139, 200, 209, 320-338, 616, 631, 747, 858, 860, 918-919, 963, 2180, 2185, 2247, 3071, 3831-3832, 5472-5479

Godbey, Mrs. William B. see Godbey, Emma Durham (1839-1915)

God's Bible School 913, 3816, 4425-4427, 5361, 6847

God's Bible School. Missionary Prayer Band 4426

God's Bible School and College see God's Bible School

God's Bible School and Missionary Training Home see God's Bible School

God's Messenger (periodical) 3550

God's Messenger and Bible Advocate (periodical) 3551

God's Missionary Church 2397-2401, 4538

God's Missionary Standard (periodical) 2401

God's Revivalist and Bible Advocate (periodical) 787

Göhler, Alfred 56

Goff, Florence 5482

Goff, Frank D. 2403, 5480

Goff, H. H. 5481-5482

Goff, Reginald F. 5483

Goff, W. Roy see Goff, Walter Roy (1877-)

Goff, Walter Roy (1877-) 577-578, 5484

Golden Gate Pentecost (periodical) see Kingdom (periodical)

Golliher, Clyde 1938

Gomer, Thelma 2187

Good Citizen (periodical) 2218, 2241, 2251

Good Tidings (periodical) 788

Good Tidings Sent of God (periodical) 2068

Good Way (periodical) see Church Herald and Holiness Banner (periodical)

Good Way Association 1226

Goodell, Charles LeRoy (1854-1937) 201, 2955

Goodman, Woodrow I. (1915-) 5485

Goodnow, Edith P. 1692-1693

Goodsell, Daniel Ayres (1840-1909) 5486

Goodson, Walter Kenneth, bp. (1912-) 4855

Goodwin, J. W. see Goodwin, John Wesley (1869-1945)

Goodwin, John (1593-1665) 6884

Goodwin, John Wesley (1869-1945) 1346-1347, 1399, 1455-1456, 1813, 5487-5490

Goodwin, Paul John (1896-) 5491

Gordon, A. J. see Gordon, Adoniram Judson (1836-1895)
Gordon, Adoniram Judson (1836-1895) 136, 3944-3948, 4014, 4032-4033, 4038-4039, 5492-5493
Gorham, B. W. see Gorham, B. Weed
Gorham, B. Weed 124, 686, 2897, 2971, 5494
Gosden, Eric William 3342, 3353-3356, 5153-5154, 6641
Goshen College 2545
Gospel Banner (periodical) 3766
Gospel Emancipator (periodical) 3859
Gospel Flame (periodical) 2726
Gospel Minister (periodical) 949, 2320, 2329, 2331, 2333, 2338, 2340-2344, 2347, 3391-3392, 3407, 3409-3411, 3414, 6810
Gospel songs see Hymns
Gospel Tabernacle Association 2056
Gospel Tidings (periodical) 3896
Gospel Trumpet (periodical) see Vital Christianity (periodical)
Gospel Trumpet Company 1162, 1166, 1180-1181, 7093
Gospel Trumpet Company. Editorial Staff 1157-1158
Gospel Trumpet for the Blind (periodical) 1175
Gospel Worker (periodical) 2406
Gospel Workers Church 2402-2406
Goss, Bertha see Schwab, Bertha Goss
Goss, Ethel Elizabeth 4172, 5496
Goss, Howard Archibald (1883-) 4172, 5495-5496
Gossip see Slander
Gould, J. Glenn see Gould, Joseph Glenn (1896-)
Gould, Joseph Glenn (1896-) 1457-1459, 1596, 1672, 1694, 1718, 5497, 6730
Gouthey, A. P. 155, 339
Govan, I. R. see Govan Stewart, Isabel Rosie (1900-)
Govan, Isabel Rosie see Govan Stewart, Isabel Rosie (1900-)
Govan, John George (1861-1927) 2045, 2048-2049, 5498-5500
Govan Stewart, Isabel Rosie (1900-) 2048, 2049, 3343, 5500-5501, 7204
Government, Church see Church government
Gowland, Frank B. 5502
Grace, John 3670
Gracey, S. L. see Gracey, Samuel Levis (1835-1911)
Gracey, Samuel Levis (1835-1911) 5503
Graham, Mrs. Billy see Graham, Ruth McCue Bell (1920-)
Graham, Ruth McCue Bell (1920-) 1318
Graham, William Franklin (1918-) 7064
Granbery, J. C. see Granbery, John Cowper (1829-1907)
Granbery, John Cowper (1829-1907) 3072, 5504
Grant, Abraham (1848-1911) 5505
Grantham, Pa. 4499
Graves, A. P. see Graves, Albert Phelps (1829-1911)
Graves, Albert Phelps (1829-1911) 156-159, 687-688, 5506
Graves, Albert Schuyler (1824-1887) 5507
Graves, Edith D. (-1941) 5508
Gravette, Ark. 4437
Gravette, Ark. Holiness Bible School see Holiness Bible School, Gravette, Ark.
Gravette Holiness Bible School see Holiness Bible School, Gravette, Ark.

Gray, Eloise 6589
Gray, Forrest Burton (1913-   )
    5509
Gray, Mrs. Forrest Burton
    see Gray, Minnie Mae
    (1920-   )
Gray, James M. 6738
Gray, Joseph 1814
Gray, Minnie Mae (1920-   )
    5510
Gray, W. C. 5511
Gray, Mrs. W. C. see
    Gray, Willetta
Gray, W. L. see Gray,
    William L. (1821-1902)
Gray, Willetta 5512
Gray, William L. (1821-1902)
    5513
Great Britain 1889-1891,
    3686-3688, 4200
Great Commission Crusades
    see Haiti Inland Mission
Great Commission Schools
    4428
Greathouse, William M.
    (1919-   ) 1460-1461, 5514
Greaves, J. C. 2533
Greek-Americans 6398-6400
Greek Catholicism 6400
Green, Cora Lee 5515
Green, David E. 14
Green, Mrs. Edward see
    Green, Cora Lee
Green, John Dryer (-1947)
    5516
Greencastle, Ind. DePauw
    University see DePauw
    University
Greencastle. Indiana Asbury
    University see DePauw
    University
Greene, T. W. 5517
Greenleaf, Ida 4429
Greenleaf Friends Academy
    4429
Greenleaf Seminary see
    Greenleaf Friends Academy
Greenlee, J. Harold see
    Greenlee, Jacob Harold
    (1918-   )
Greenlee, Jacob Harold
    (1918-   ) 5518

Greensboro, N. C. 4430, 4468
Greensboro Bible and Literary
    School 4430
Greenville, Ill. 4431
Greenville, S. C. 4449-4451
Greenville College 2636, 4431
Greer, George Dixon 61
Greer, Naoma Adelaid (1910-   )
    5519
Gregory, Benjamin 2533
Gregory, James F. 5520
Gregory, John 340
Gregory, W. H. 5521
Grentzenberg, H. see Grent-
    zenberg, Herman A. (1835-
    1934)
Grentzenberg, Herman A. (1835-
    1934) 5522
Gresham, L. Paul (1911-   )
    5523
Gresham, Lunia Paul see
    Gresham, L. Paul (1911-   )
Grider, J. Kenneth see Grider,
    Joseph Kenneth (1921-   )
Grider, Joseph Kenneth (1921-   )
    1462, 5524
Griffin, Dora see Dudley,
    Dora Griffin
Griffith, G. W. see Griffith,
    George William (1869-1936)
Griffith, George William (1869-
    1936) 4793, 5525-5526
Griffith, Lilliam Bushnell
    (1875-   ) 5526
Griffith, Glenn (1894-   ) 2124,
    3871, 3917-3920, 5527-5528
Grimes, John Franklin 2838
Grinnell, A. Lee (-1923)
    5529
Grinnell, Mrs. A. Lee see
    Grinnell, Maud
Grinnell, Maud 5530
Groves, Vernon Thomas
    (1911-   ) 5531
Grubb, Norman Percy (1895-   )
    1472, 3260, 5250
Gruner, Max 3685
Guatemala 1892-1893, 4644,
    5737, 5925
Guide to Christian Perfection
    (periodical) see Conse-
    crated Life and Guide to Holi-

ness (periodical)
Guide to Holiness (periodical)
see Consecrated Life and
Guide to Holiness (periodical)
Guide to Holiness (Wegweiser
zur Heiligung) (periodical)
790
Guide to Holiness and Class-
leader's Magazine (periodi-
cal) 2588
Guide to Perfect Love (periodi-
cal) 791
Guiding Star (periodical) 1995
Guill, J. E. (-1962) 5532-
5533
Guille, George E. 596
Gulf Coast Bible College 4432
Gunn, Elihu 5534
Gunn, M. W. 5535
Gurney, Joseph John (1788-
1847) 2274
Guy, Augusta Oakes (1892-)
5536-5537, 5539
Guy, F. R. see Guy,
Francis Ridley (1889-)
Guy, Francis Ridley (1889-)
5538
Guy, Mrs. Francis Ridley
see Guy, Augusta Oakes
(1892-)
Guyon, Jeanne Marie Bouvier
de La Motte (1648-1717)
555-557, 563, 2511, 3702
Gyllenkrok, Axel (1910-) 46

H. W. S. see Smith, Hannah
Whitall (1832-1911)
Haas, Frank L. see Haas,
L. Frank (1856-)
Haas, L. Frank (1856-)
2412
Habegger, Tillman 4149
Hadleigh, Eng. 3612
Haggard, C. P. see Haggard,
Cornelius Paul (1911-)
Haggard, Cornelius Paul
(1911-) 5540
Haggard, Henry Rider (1856-
1925) 3612, 3688
Hahn, Martha Sophia (1892-)
5541
Haines, Lee 522
Haines, Marie 2389

Hairston, H. H. 4298
Haiti 1894-1896, 6329, 6350-
6351
Haiti Inland Mission 3281-3289,
6329
Hale, E. E. see Hale, Edwin
E. (1894-)
Hale, Edwin E. (1894-) 5542
Haley, Mrs. Albert E. see
Haley, Matilda Deyo (-1947)
Haley, J. W. see Haley, John
Wesley (1879-1951)
Haley, John Wesley (1879-1951)
5543-5544
Haley, Matilda Deyo (-1947)
5545
Hall, A. W. see Hall, Alvin
Willard (1852-)
Hall, Alvin Willard (1852-)
3168, 5546-5547
Hall, B. Maurice 1863
Hall, Bert Harold (1921-)
5548
Hall, Clarence Wilbur (1902-)
4857
Hall, Henry P. (1814-) 5549
Hall, J. Walter (1878-1964)
5550-5551
Hall, Kenneth F. (1926-)
1102
Hall, L. C. 4189
Hall family 1133
Haller, Lola Marie (1929-)
5552
Halt, E. V. see Halt, Eulice
Vern (1896-)
Halt, Eulice Vern (1896-)
3525-3529, 5553
Halt, R. J. see Halt, Ray-
mond J. (1905-)
Halt, Raymond J. (1905-)
5554-5556
Hamblen, J. H. see Hamblen,
James Henry (1877-1971)
Hamblen, James Henry (1877-
1971) 5557-5559
Hamblen, Oberia (1905-)
5559
Hamblen, Stuart (1908-) 5559
Hames, J. M. 160, 341-354,
920-922, 5560
Hamilton, R. H. (1883-1954)
5561

Hamilton, Mass. 128
Hamilton County (Ind.) Holiness Association 949
Hamlin, George Edwin 5562
Hamlin, Howard H. 1287, 1348, 5563
Hamlin, Tex. 4382
Hamline, L. L. see Hamline, Leonidas Lent (1797-1865)
Hamline, Leonidas Lent (1797-1865) 3019, 5564-5568
Hamline, Mrs. Leonidas Lent see Hamline, Melinda Truesdell (1801-)
Hamline, Melinda Truesdell (1801-) 5568, 6676-6677
Hammer, Anna Maria Nichols (1840-1910) 5569
Hammer, Mrs. William A. see Hammer, Anna Maria Nichols (1840-1910)
Hammond, G. M. see Hammond, George M.
Hammond, George M. 5570
Hammond, Helen Reiton 3420, 5572-5573
Hammond, Robert Bruce 3420, 3423, 5571-5573
Hammond, Mrs. Robert Bruce see Hammond, Helen Reiton
Hammond, Jean 5294
Hamric, L. L. see Hamric, Lee L.
Hamric, Lee L. 5574
Handy, Robert Theodore (1918-) 2489
Haney, M. L. see Haney, Milton Lorenzo (1825-1922)
Haney, Milton Lorenzo (1825-1922) 355-356, 2873, 5575-5576
Hankins, Margaret Bell Edwards (1897-) 5577
Hankins, Mrs. Raymond see Hankins, Margaret Bell Edwards (1897-)
Hanley, C. S. see Hanley, Charles S.
Hanley, Charles S. 5578

Hanley, R. R. see Hanley, Richard R.
Hanley, Richard R. 5579
Hann, Samuel H. (1854-1918) 5231
Hanna, Alfreda Huhnke Wuester see Wuester, Alfreda Huhnke
Hanna, Philip C. (1857-1929) 5580-5581
Hanson, Carl 1439
Happy Pilgrim (periodical) 792
Happy Trio 3659
Harding, U. E. see Harding, Ulla Earl (1883-1958)
Harding, Ulla Earl (1883-1958) 1349, 1489, 5582-5587
Hardy, Chester Ernest (1882-1972) 357, 5588
Harford, Charles Forbes (1864-) 3926
Harford-Battersby, T. D. see Battersby, Thomas Dundas Harford (1823?-1883)
Hargrave, Richard 5589
Harkness, Georgia Elma (1891-) 2776
Harlow, W. T. see Harlow, William Thompson (1815-)
Harlow, William Thompson (1815-) 5590
Harmon, Frank H. (-1957) 5591
Harmon, Nolan Bailey (1892-) 2400, 2791
Harness, Mary M. 3147
Harney, William J. 210
Harper, A. F. see Harper, Albert Foster (1907-)
Harper, Albert Foster (1907-) 1350, 1400, 1621, 1770-1772, 5592
Harper, C. H. see Harper, Charles Howard
Harper, Charles Howard 5593
Harper, J. A. see Harper, James Albert
Harper, James Albert 2097
Harper, Michael 4178
Harrell, David Edwin (1930-) 4163
Harrell, John R. 5594-5595
Harris, A. 3815

Harris, D. H. 4295
Harris, J. M. see Harris, John M.
Harris, James Rendel (1852-) 5130, 6755
Harris, John (1802-1856) 301, 358
Harris, John M. 689-690, 711-713, 716, 1251, 5596
Harris, Mrs. John M. see Harris, Margaret J. (1865-1919)
Harris, John William (1870-) 632, 5597-5598
Harris, M. J. see Harris, Margaret J. (1865-1919)
Harris, Margaret J. (1865-1919) 689, 711-712, 716, 5599
Harris, Mary Griffin Bristow 2098-2099, 2113-2115, 2117, 5600
Harris, Mary Lee see Cagle, Mary Lee Wasson Harris (1864-1955)
Harris, Merne Arthur 571, 5601
Harris, R. L. see Harris, Robert Lee (-1894)
Harris, Mrs. R. L. see Cagle, Mary Lee Wasson Harris (1864-1955)
Harris, Reader (1847-1909) 2093-2095, 2096, 2100-2111, 2112, 2116-2117, 5602-5608
Harris, Mrs. Reader see Harris, Mary Griffin Bristow
Harris, Richard Reader see Harris, Reader (1847-1909)
Harris, Robert Lee (-1894) 5609-5612
Harris, Mrs. Robert Lee see Cagle, Mary Lee Wasson Harris (1864-1955)
Harris, Thoro (1874-1955) 691-694, 2705-2706, 4185-4190
Harrisburg, Pa. 4499
Harrison, Thomas 2987
Harrison, Thomas (1854-) 5613-5614

Hart, E. P. see Hart, Edward Payson (-1919)
Hart, Edward Payson (-1919) 2622, 2690-2691, 4618, 5615-5616
Hartley, John 2533
Hartman, J. 3578
Hartman, Lucy A. (-1950) 5617
Hartsough, Lewis (1828-1919) 695, 706, 5618
Harvey, Edwin Lawrence (1865-) 2145-2146, 2150
Harvey, Eunice see Williams, Eunice Harvey
Harvey, J. W. see Harvey, John W. (1854-19??)
Harvey, John W. (1854-19??) 359, 5619-5620
Harvey, Ill. 4308-4309
Hastings, Cecily 36
Hatfield, John Thomas (1851-1934) 5621-5622
Hathaway, Evelyn Hendricks 5649, 5651
Haven, Gilbert (1821-1880) 125, 5623-5624
Havergal, Frances Ridley (1836-1879) 5625-5628
Havergal, Maria Vernon Graham (1821-1887) 5629
Haviland, Emma Hillmon (1863-1940) 5630-5631
Haviland, Kan. 4421
Hawkins, Floyd W. (1904-) 5632
Hawkins, R. C. see Hawkins, Richard C.
Hawkins, R. W. see Hawkins, Richard Watson (-1892)
Hawkins, Richard C. 3479, 5633
Hawkins, Richard Watson (-1892) 2650, 5634
Hayden, Clara M. (-1926) 5635
Hayes, Benjamin 7195
Hayes, Richard Baxter (1858-1937) 5636-5637
Hayes, W. M. 5637
Haygood, Atticus Greene (1839-1896) 84, 3097, 5638-5639
Haynes, B. F. see Haynes,

Benjamin Franklin (1851-1923)
Haynes, Benjamin Franklin (1851-1923) 95, 933, 1463-1464, 1779, 3061-3062, 5640-5641
Hayse, George R. 1867
Healing see Faith-healing
Heap, Gwladys 1893
Heart and Life (periodical) 793
Heart, Head, and Hand (periodical) 4394
Heath, F. S. see Heath, Frank Stowe
Heath, Frank Stowe 110, 161, 5642
Heath, Merle McClurkan 2188, 6022
Heaven 572-573, 576, 579-580, 603, 604, 1276-1277, 2634, 2897, 3060, 3312, 3566, 3636, 3936, 4091
Heavenly Recruit Church 2057
Heavenly Recruit Association see Holiness Christian Church
Heckart, Robert H. 3561, 5643-5644
Heffner, Ida see Spalding, Ida Heffner (-1930)
Hefley, James C. 4140
Hegre, T. A. see Hegre, Theodore A.
Hegre, Theodore A. 360, 3257-3259
Heironimus, H. T. 361
Heisey, Ruth E. 1034
Hell 575, 598, 2347
Helling, Hubert W. 5645
Helm, Benjamin 362
Helm, Kathryn 85
Helper (periodical) 4309
Hendren, Evelyn Webb (-1921) 5646
Hendren, Mrs. Leslie E. see Hendren, Evelyn Webb (-1921)
Hendricks, A. O. see Hendricks, Andrew Oliver (1879-1965)
Hendricks, Andrew Oliver (1879-1965) 5647-5649, 5651
Hendricks, Mrs. Andrew Oliver see Hendricks, Fawn Galbraith (-1947)
Hendricks, Fawn Galbraith (-1947) 5649-5651
Henley, John H. 3210
Henricks, Andrew Oliver see Hendricks, Andrew Oliver (1879-1965)
Henricks, Mrs. Andrew Oliver see Hendricks, Fawn Galbraith (-1947)
Henricks, Fawn Galbraith see Hendricks, Fawn Galbraith (-1947)
Henry, George W. (1801-) 2133-2134, 2446, 2972
Henry, Helga Bender 4681
Henschen, Walter G. 2558
Henson, H. Hensley see Henson, Herbert Hensley (1863-1947)
Henson, Herbert Hensley (1863-1947) 851
Henson, J. C. see Henson, Jacob Cornelius (1875-)
Henson, Jacob Cornelius (1875-) 1351, 5652
Hepburn, Samuel 3648
Hephzibah Faith Home Association see Hephzibah Faith Missionary Association
Hephzibah Faith Missionary Association 2058-2072, 4365, 4410
Hephzibah Faith Missionary Association in Africa 2072, 7120
Hephzibah Orphanage, Macon, Ga. 3147-3148
Herald, a Journal of Full Salvation and the Way of Faith (periodical) 589, 794, 6249-6251
Herald of Gospel Freedom (periodical) 795
Herald of Holiness (periodical) 1461, 1731, 1736, 1743, 5984
Herald of Light (periodical) 2165
Herald of Light and Zion's

Watchman (periodical) see Herald of Light (periodical)
Herald of Truth (periodical) 4195
Heraldo de Santidad (Kansas City, Mo.) 1732-1733
Heraldo de Santidad (Los Angeles) 1733
Hermiz, Thomas 1959
Herrell, N. B. see Herrell, Noah Benjamin (1877-1953)
Herrell, Noah Benjamin (1877-1953) 1352, 5654-5655
Hershey, Eusebius (1823-1891) 5656-5657
Hertenstein, Ralph 5658
Hertenstein, Mrs. Ralph see Hertenstein, Zylphia
Hertenstein, Zylphia 5659
Heslop, William Greene (1886-) 1353, 1572, 1657-1658, 1815, 1848, 5660
Hess, Weaver W. (1890-) 5661
Hibbard, F. G. see Hibbard, Freeborn Garrettson (1811-1895)
Hibbard, Freeborn Garrettson (1811-1895) 5565-5566, 5662, 6394
Hicks, L. B. see Hicks, Lawrence B.
Hicks, Lawrence B. 363, 1816, 5663
Higgins, Edward John 3825, 5664-5665
Higgins, Nota Rose (1914-) 5666
Higgs, A. R. 3585
Higgs, Mrs. A. R. 3585
Higgs, D. E. see Higgs, Daniel E. (1887-1944)
Higgs, Daniel E. (1887-1944) 5667
Higher criticism 3995-3996
Higher education see Education
Highway (periodical) 796
Highway, Ky. 4445
Highway and Banner (periodical) see Highway (periodical)
Highway of Holiness (periodical) 3721
Highways and Hedges (Bethany, Okla.) 1734
Highways and Hedges (Pilot Point, Tex.) see Holiness Evangel (Pilot Point, Tex.)
Higley, L. H. 162, 890
Hiles, Lewis C. 3580
Hiles, Vera Ann (-1967) 3580
Hill, A. 5668
Hill, Nettie M. 2452-2453
Hill, Paul S. 1817
Hillman, Joseph (1833-1890) 695, 5669
Hills, A. M. see Hills, Aaron Merritt (1848-1935)
Hills, Aaron Merritt (1848-1935) 106, 110, 140, 209, 364-373, 558, 626, 863, 867, 923, 969, 1465-1468, 1719, 2181-2182, 3444, 3833, 3934, 4174, 4865-4866, 5670-5672, 5895
Hilson, James Benjamin (1908-) 3130
Hiltner, Seward (1909-) 1722
Hinshaw, Amy N. 1298, 1695, 1756, 6547, 7005, 7146, 7262
Hirsch, Helen Kathryn Hubbard 2821
Hirst, W. N. see Hirst, William N.
Hirst, William N. 209
His (periodical) 4066
Historical Records Survey. Michigan 3689
Historical Records Survey. New Jersey 3690
Hiwale, Jacobrao 5673
Hobart, Maurice Arden (1925-) 5674
Hobart, Mrs. Maurice Arden see Hobart, Ruth Elizabeth Elwine (1932-)
Hobart, Ruth Elizabeth Elwine (1932-) 5675
Hobbs, James 2526
Hobe Sound, Fla. 4303, 4433

Hobe Sound Bible College 4433

Hobe Sound Bible College & Academy see Hobe Sound Bible College

Hobe Sound Bible Institute see Hobe Sound Bible College

Hodgin, G. Arnold see Hodgin, George Arnold (-1967)

Hodgin, George Arnold (- 1967) 5676

Hoekema, Anthony A. (1913-) 57

Hoell, Nils Bloch- see Bloch-Hoell, Nils

Hoffman, Elisha A. (1839-1929) 674-675, 723

Hoffman, Ira Orwig (-1943) 674-675

Hogue, W. T. see Hogue, Wilson Thomas (1852-1920)

Hogue, Wilson Thomas (1852-1920) 1222, 2651-2653, 2679, 2686, 2691, 2710, 2712, 2715, 2722, 4618, 5677

Hoke, Edna Wells (1875-) 5678-5679

Holcomb, Walt 5811

Holiness Advocate (Fayetteville, N. C.) 4243

Holiness Advocate (London) 2416

Holiness Association of Oklahoma 993

Holiness Association of Texas 2073-2075

Holiness Bands see Holiness Church (1880-1946)

Holiness Baptists 4203-4204

Holiness Baptists. Arkansas. Convocation 4203

Holiness Bible College 4434

Holiness Bible Institute, Philadelphia, Pa. 4435

Holiness Bible Institute, Woodstock, N. B. see Bethany Bible College

Holiness Bible School, Beulah, Okla. 4436

Holiness Bible School, Gravette, Ark. 1206-1209, 4437

Holiness Bible School, Hutchinson, Kan. see Bresee College

Holiness Bible School and Faith Missionary Training Home 4438

Holiness Christian Association see Holiness Christian Church

Holiness Christian Church 2407-2415, 4435, 4438, 4504, 6485, 6626

Holiness Christian Church of the United States of America see Holiness Christian Church

Holiness Christian Messenger (periodical) see Christian Messenger (periodical)

Holiness Church (1880-189?) 2416-2417

Holiness Church (1880-1946) 2418-2429, 4600, 6608, 7105

Holiness Church (1880-1946) in Peru 2429

Holiness Church (1880-1946) in Texas 2423-2424, 6608

Holiness Church (1899). North Carolina Convention 4241

Holiness Church (1901-1909) see Pentecostal Holiness Church (1900-1911)

Holiness Church (1901-1907) see Church of God (General Assembly) (Original) Church of God

Holiness Church, Donalsonville, Georgia 2430-2431

Holiness Church of Christ 2432-2442, 2465, 4444

Holiness Church of Christ (1888-1914) see Independent Holiness Church of Christ

Holiness Church of North Carolina see Holiness Church (1899); Pentecostal Holiness Church (1900-1911)

Holiness Collegiate Institute, Clarence, Mo. 4440

Holiness Collegiate Institute, New Florence, Mo. 4439

Holiness Conservator (periodical) 797

Holiness Era (periodical) 2457
Holiness Evangel (Birmingham, Eng.) 799
Holiness Evangel (Pilot Point, Tex.) 2439
Holiness Evangel (Portland, Ore.) 798
Holiness Evangelist (periodical) 800
Holiness Evangelistic Association see Evangel Church
Holiness Evangelistic Institute see Western Pilgrim College
Holiness Gospel School 4441
Holiness Herald (Bethany, Okla.) 1736
Holiness Herald (Glasgow, Scot.) 1735
Holiness Herald (Seven Kings, Eng.) 801
Holiness Layman (periodical) see Holiness Messenger (periodical)
Holiness Messenger (periodical) 2092
Holiness Methodist Advocate (periodical) 2771
Holiness Methodist Church (1900-) 2766-2768
Holiness Methodist Church (1911-1969) 2769-2772, 4442
Holiness Methodist Church (1911-1969). Bolivian Holiness Mission 2772
Holiness Methodist Church (1911-1969) in Bolivia 2772
Holiness Methodist Church [North Carolina] see Holiness Methodist Church (1900-); Holiness Methodists
Holiness Methodist Church [North Dakota] see Holiness Methodist Church (1911-1969)
Holiness Methodist School of Theology 4442
Holiness Methodists 2773
Holiness Mission see International Holiness Mission

Holiness Mission Journal (periodical) 2474
Holiness Missionary Colporteur (periodical) 802
Holiness Missionary Fellowship 799
Holiness Movement Church 2443-2460, 4311, 4434, 5040, 5696-5697, 5980, 6493
Holiness Movement Church. Young People's Missionary Society 2452
Holiness Movement Church in Canada see Holiness Movement Church
Holiness-Pentecostal Movement see Pentecostal Movement
Holiness School see Mizpah Academy
Holiness Sentinel (periodical) 803
Holiness Union 2076
Holiness with Carnality ... Truth without Error see The Finished Work of Calvary ... Holiness without Carnality ... Truth without Error ... The Baptism in the Holy Ghost (Acts 2:4) (periodical)
Holiness Worker (periodical) see Gospel Worker (periodical)
Holiness Workers Association see Gospel Workers Church
Holland, William Webster (1884-) 748, 5680
Hollenback, R. L. 5681
Hollenweger, W. J. see Hollenweger, Walter J.
Hollenweger, Walter J. 4164
Holliday, Robert Kelvin (1933-) 4165
Hollmann, Paul H. (-1963) 5682-5683
Hollow Rock Glad Tidings (periodical) 804
Holmes, Lucy Elizabeth Simpson (-1922) 4173, 5685
Holmes, N. J. see Holmes, Nickels John (1847-1919)
Holmes, Nickels John (1847-

1919) 4173, 5684-5686
Holmes, Mrs. Nickels John see Holmes, Lucy Elizabeth Simpson (-1922)
Holmes Bible and Missionary Institute see Holmes Theological Seminary
Holmes Bible College see Holmes Theological Seminary
Holmes Bulletin (periodical) see Voice of Holmes (periodical)
Holmes Theological Seminary 4449-4451
Holt, John B. 4166
Holy Church of North Carolina see United Holy Church of America
Holy Church of North Carolina and Virginia see United Holy Church of America
Home see Marriage
Home Herald, the New Voice of the Ram's Horn (periodical) 805
Home life see Family life
Homer, Charlotte G., pseud. see Gabriel, Charles Hutchinson (1856-1932)
Homiletical illustrations 3524, 3802
Honeywell, E. I. 3392
Honn, Alice Griffith (-1940) 5687
Honn, Mrs. Noah S. see Honn, Alice Griffith (-1940)
Hood, John J. 2985
Hooker, H. H. 1469-1470
Hooker, Mary Reader Harris (1881-) 5605, 5607
Hoople, William Howard (1868-1922) 5688
Hoover, J. W. 5689
Hopkins, Mrs. E. B. 696
Hopkins, Evan Henry 507, 3927, 3941, 4020, 4025
Hopkins, Harlow Eugene (1931-) 5690
Horine, Ruth 5691
Horn, Purl 1773
Horne, J. W. see Horne, James Wesley (1823-18??)

Horne, James Wesley (1823-18??) 5692
Horner, Mrs. A. E. 3694, 5696
Horner, Ralph Cecil (1854-1921) 374, 2448, 2527, 3169, 3694, 5693-5697
Hostetter, Henry N. 1029
Hot Springs, S. D. 4365-4367
Hotchkiss, William Ray (1873-1948) 2372, 5698-5699
Hott, James William (1844-1902) 3717
Hough, S. S. see Hough, Samuel Strickler (1864-1944)
Hough, Samuel Strickler (1864-1944) 3700, 3726
Houghton, Frank (1894-) 4964
Houghton, W. J. see Houghton, Willard J. (1825-1896)
Houghton, Walter Edwards (1904-) 8
Houghton, Willard J. (1825-1896) 5700-5701
Houghton, N. Y. 4452-4454, 5701, 6192
Houghton Academy see Houghton College
Houghton College 4452-4454, 5701, 6697
Houghton Wesleyan Methodist Seminary see Houghton College
House, Elsie Elizabeth (1927-) 5702
House, Meredith Carl (1923-) 5703
House, Mrs. Meredith Carl see House, Elsie Elizabeth (1927-)
Houston, L. S. (-1964) 5704
Houston, Tex. 4432
Howard, Ivan Cushing (1900-) 5705
Howard, Rowland Bailey (1834-1892) 4635
Howland, Carl Leroy (1881-) 2692, 2715, 5706
Hoyt, Harold Baldwin (1917-) 5707
Hu, Betty M. 3265, 3268
Hubbard, S. 2976

Hudson, Hilary T. 3056
Hudson, Oscar (1874-)
    5708-5709
Hudson, Ralph E. (1843-1901)
    697, 1818
Hübner, Hans 47
Huff, George E. (-1956)
    5710
Huff, Will see Huff, William H.
Huff, William H. 924-925,
    5711
Huffman, J. 2616
Huffman, J. A. see Huffman, Jasper Abraham
    (1880-)
Huffman, J. L. 3800
Huffman, Jasper Abraham
    (1880-) 375, 970-971,
    3742, 3746-3756, 3759, 3769-
    3770, 5272, 5712-5714
Huffman, Lambert 5714
Hughes, Don see Hughes, Donald
Hughes, Donald 3920
Hughes, Edwin Holt (1866-1950) 202, 2794
Hughes, George (1828-1904)
    125, 976, 985-986, 2874,
    5715, 6140, 6387, 6391,
    6394-6395, 6650, 7057
Hughes, H. Raymond see Hughes, Howard Raymond
Hughes, Howard Raymond 126
Hughes, J. 5716
Hughes, John Wesley (1852-1932) 5717-5719
Hughes, Ray Harrison 4213, 4486
Hughes, T. Walt 5719
Hughes, Walt see Hughes, T. Walt
Hull, Asa 2973
Hull, William (1738-1814)
    2511
Hulme, William Edward (1920-)
    48
Humble, Floyd 4190
Humphrey, J. M. see Humphrey, Jerry Miles (1872-)
Humphrey, Jerry Miles
    (1872-) 163-164, 211-215,
579-580, 633, 926-929, 2634,
2641, 3818-3819, 3851, 3854-
3855, 3863, 5720-5721
Humphries, Hugh Will 9
Hunt, M. P. see Hunt, Marion Palmer (1860-)
Hunt, Marion Palmer (1860-)
    861, 875, 930-931, 5722-
    5723
Hunter, Clarence E. 1170
Hunter, Mrs. Clarence E. see Hunter, Nora Siens (1873-1951)
Hunter, Fannie McDowell 106,
    140, 3444, 5724
Hunter, James Hogg (1890-)
    4122
Hunter, Nora Siens (1873-1951)
    5725-5726
Hunter, Mrs. W. W. see Hunter, Fanie McDowell
Hunter, William (1811-1877)
    5727
Huntington, Rev. Dr. 5728
Huntington, D. W. C. see Huntington, DeWitt Clinton (1830-1912)
Huntington, DeWitt Clinton
    (1830-1912) 2898-2899,
    3029-3030, 5729
Huntington, Ind. 4455
Huntington, W. Va. 7299
Huntington College 4455
Huntington Park, Calif. 4332
Huntington Park Bible School
    see Azusa Pacific College
Hurlet Nazarene College 4456
Hussey, Ashabel H. (1833-)
    5730
Hutcherson, Faith Luce 5330
Hutchinson, Paul (1890-)
    2543
Hutchinson, W. Oliver 4236
Hutchinson, Kan. 4368, 4446
Huxley, Thomas Henry (1825-1895) 3602
Hyde, E. L. 703, 940
Hymn writers see Song writers
Hymns 667-742, 1027, 1056-
    1057, 1163-1170, 1219, 1660-
    1675, 2016-2019, 2144-2146,

2156, 2175, 2191, 2233-2238, 2411-2412, 2582, 2698-2709, 2807-2809, 2967-3002, 3202-3208, 3525-3534, 3658-3669, 3720, 3803, 3888, 4029-4032, 4107-4110, 4184-4190, 4275-4276

Hymns--History and criticism 743, 1676-2583-2586, 2710-2712, 2810-2813, 3003-3004, 3090-3091, 5961 see also Church music

Hymns, Congo 4130

Hymns, Hungarian 2019

Hymns, Indonesia 4131

Hymns, Spanish 4134

Hynd, Agnes Kanema Sharpe 5731

Hynd, David (1895-   ) 1862, 5732-5733

Hynd, Mrs. David see Hynd, Agnes Kanema Sharpe

Hynd, Nema see Hynd, Agnes Kanema Sharpe

I. H. Convention see Interdenominational Holiness Convention

I. H. Convention Herald (periodical) see Convention Herald (periodical)

I. S. L. see Leonard, Isabella S.

Idaho 1268, 4429, 4525, 4534, 4555-4556, 6090

Idaho-Oregon Holiness School see Northwest Nazarene College

Iglesia Nacional Boliviana de los Amigos see Friends, Society of. Oregon Yearly Meeting

Illinois 192-193, 199, 1264, 2758, 2837, 2842, 4308-4309, 4359, 4419, 4431, 4438, 4457, 4531, 4582-4589, 5320, 5576, 5595, 5679, 5845, 6414, 6513-6514, 6564

Illinois Holiness University see Olivet Nazarene College

Illinois Institute 4457

Illustrated Africa (periodical) see Illustrated Christian World (periodical)

Illustrated Christian World (periodical) 806

Imitatio Christi. English 38-39, 2505, 2869

Immanuel Bible Training College 4458

Immanuel General Mission of Japan see Immanueru Sogo Dendo Dan (Immanuel General Mission of Japan)

Immanuel Mission 3290-3291

Immanuel Missionary Church see Emmanuel Association

Immanuel Wesleyan Federation see Immanueru Uesureyan Remmei (Immanuel Wesleyan Federation)

Immanueru Sogo Dendo Dan (Immanuel General Mission of Japan) 2461-2464, 4458

Immanueru Uesureyan Remmei (Immanuel Wesleyan Federation) 2462-2463

Immersion, Baptismal see Baptism

Imprisonment see Prisons

Independence, Kan. 4459

Independence Bible College 4459

Independence Bible School see Independence Bible College

Independent Holiness Church 2465-2467, 4373, 5030

Independent Holiness Church of Christ 2468-2469, 3443

Independent Holiness Churches 3894-3896

Independent Holiness Movement 2077-2079

India 1035, 1254, 1897-1901, 2266-2269, 2375-2376, 2759, 3036-3038, 3227-3229, 3586-3588, 3773, 4721, 4757, 4961-4965, 5044, 5381, 5447, 5863, 6753-6756, 6937, 6942-6943, 6967, 6969, 7005, 7007-7008, 7146, 7290

India North-West Mission 3292
Indian Witness (periodical) 3013
Indiana 1187, 3039, 4310, 4351, 4391, 4409, 4417, 4420, 4428, 4438, 4477, 4495, 4570, 4579, 5193, 5583, 5622, 5714, 5822, 5832, 7270
Indiana. Board of Control for High School Bible Study for Credit 5713
Indiana Asbury University see DePauw University
Indianapolis, Ind. 924, 5583, 5832
Indianapolis, Ind. Young Men's Holiness League see Young Men's Holiness League, Indianapolis
Indians of North America 1683, 1705, 3211, 4365-4367, 7319-7324
Indians of South America 1937, 5345-5346, 7260-7262
Indonesia 4131-4132, 5758
Infant baptism see Baptism
Ingler, Arthur F. (1873-1935) 5734
Ingler, Clifford Knowlton (1876-) 2224, 7165
Ingram, Pearl 5735
Ingram, Robert Clinton (1886-1958) 5736-5737
Ingram, Mrs. Robert Clinton see Ingram, Pearl
Inland Christian Advocate (periodical) 3014
Inskip, Edward S. (1788-1863) 5739
Inskip, J. S. see Inskip, John Swanel (1816-1884)
Inskip, John Swanel (1816-1884) 105, 698, 2500, 2956, 3834, 5738-5741
Institute, W. Va. 4521
Institute of Race Relations, London 4200
Institutions, Charitable and Philanthropic see Charities

Instituto Biblico Nazareno see Seminario Nazareno Hispanoamericano
Instituto Biblico Vida y Verdad 4460
Intemperance see Liquor problem
Inter-American Missionary Society see Oriental Missionary Society
Intercession City, Fla. 4461-4462
Intercession City Christian Schools 380, 4461-4462, 4586
Intercessory Missionary (periodical) 4196
Interchurch Holiness Association 4303
Interdenominational Evangelistic Association see Evangel Church
Interdenominational Holiness Berean (periodical) see Lamp of Life (Toronto)
Interdenominational Holiness Convention 3813-3867
Interior Advance (periodical) 807
International Apostolic Holiness Church see Pilgrim Holiness Church
International Apostolic Holiness Union and Churches see Pilgrim Holiness Church
International Apostolic Holiness Union and Prayer League see Pilgrim Holiness Church
International Holiness Advocate (periodical) see Pilgrim Holiness Advocate (periodical)
International Holiness Church see Pilgrim Holiness Church
International Holiness Church Paper (periodical) 3552
International Holiness Mission 1889-1890, 2470-2479, 4807, 5797, 4972, 6972
International Holiness Mission in Africa 2476-2479
International Missionary Alliance see Christian and

Missionary Alliance
International Purity Journal
  (periodical) 808
International Sunday-school
  lessons 890, 1779, 2736
Intervale, N. H. 5144
Inter-Varsity Fellowship of
  Evangelical Unions 16
Iowa 979, 4385, 4413, 4479-
  4481, 4582-4589
Iowa Holiness Association
  979
Ireland 2080 see also Great
  Britain
Ireland, North see Ulster
Irick, Allie (-1949) 5742-
  5744
Irick, Mrs. Allie see Irick,
  Emma
Irick, Emma 5745
Irish Evangelistic Band 2080
Ironside, H. A. see Iron-
  side, Henry Allan (1876-
  1951)
Ironside, Harry see Ironside,
  Henry Allan (1876-1951)
Ironside, Henry Allan (1876-
  1951) 203, 3949-3950,
  5746-5747
Irwin, A. W. 5748
Irwin, Mrs. A. W. see Ir-
  win, Hazel I.
Irwin, Edwin Franklin (1888-)
  4141
Irwin, Hazel I. 5749
Isaac, E. M. see Isaac,
  Eben M.
Isaac, Eben M. 87, 5750-5751
Isayama, N. 5752
Italian-Americans 6295
Italy 1902-1904
Itineracy (church polity) 2874
Ives, Charles Edward (1874-
  1954) 3007, 4821
Ives, R. Wingrove 3090, 3579,
  5340, 5753-5754

Jabbok Bible and Missionary
  Training School see Jab-
  bok Bible School
Jabbok Bible School 4463
Jackson, Mrs. Elizabeth 2525

Jackson, James Harvey (1920-)
  5755
Jackson, Sheldon Glenn 2356
Jackson, Miss. 4384
Jacksonville, Ill. 199
Jacobs, S. P. see Jacobs,
  Simon P. (1847-1921)
Jacobs, Simon P. (1847-1921)
  165, 376, 5756
Jaffray, Robert Alexander
  (1873-1945) 5757-5758
Jails see Prisons
Jamaica 1227, 3589
Jamaica Church Herald (periodi-
  cal) 1227
James, Eldon LeRoy (-1945)
  5759
James, George Wharton 6950
James, Mrs. Henry B. see
  James, Mary Dagworthy
  Yard (1810-1883)
James, Henry C. 4319-4320
James, John T. 3055
James, Mary Dagworthy Yard
  (1810-1883) 5760, 6283,
  7312
James, Maynard G. (1902-)
  1042-1043, 1471-1472, 1573,
  3260, 5761
James, William (1842-1910)
  10-11
Janes, E. S. see Janes, Ed-
  mund Storer (1807-1876)
Janes, Edmund Storer (1807-
  1876) 109, 2854, 2895-2896,
  2925, 3008, 4712, 5567,
  5762-5763
Janes, Edwin Lines (1807-1875)
  2925
Japan 434, 436, 1905-1907,
  2760-2762, 3353-3357, 3387-
  3388, 4133, 4458, 5100-5103,
  5105-5107, 5153-5154, 5197-
  5198, 5572, 5825, 5860-
  5861, 5886, 6293, 6355,
  7026-7027, 7203-7206
Japan Alliance Church see
  Nippon Araiance Kyodan
  (Japan Alliance Church)
Japan Church of the Nazarene
  see Nihon Nazaren Kyodan
  (Church of the Nazarene)

Japan Evangelistic Band 3293-3357, 4941, 5153-5154, 7203-7206
Japan Evangelistic Band. Magazine see Japan Evangelistic Band (periodical)
Japan Evangelistic Band. News-letter for Prayer 3349
Japan Evangelistic Band. Quarterly Magazine see Japan Evangelistic Band (periodical)
Japan Evangelistic Band. Witness series 3350
Japan Evangelistic Band (periodical) 3348
Japan Holiness Church see Nihon Horinesu Kyodan (Japan Holiness Church)
Japan Rescue Mission 3358
Jehovah's Witnesses 860-862, 1746, 2249
Jenkins, Charles S. 1864, 5764-5765, 5768
Jenkins, Mrs. Charles S. see Jenkins, Pearl May Kent
Jenkins, Orville W. 1622, 5766
Jenkins, Pearl May Kent 5765, 5767-5768
Jenks, Orrin R. 691
Jennings, A. T. see Jennings, Arthur T. (1858-1914)
Jennings, Arthur T. (1858-1914) 2699, 3190, 3205, 5769
Jennings, Otho (1911-) 5770
Jernigan, C. B. see Jernigan, Charles Brougher (1863-1930)
Jernigan, Charles Brougher (1863-1930) 1000, 1302, 1473, 1574, 1933, 1945, 2073, 2170, 2423, 2431-2432, 2437, 2465, 2466, 3443, 3445, 4204, 5771-5774
Jernigan, Mrs. Charles Brougher see Jernigan, Johnny Hill
Jernigan, Johnny Hill 5775
Jerusalem 5911, 6370
Jervey, Edward Drewry (1929-) 2824
Jessop, Harry Edward (1884-) 96-97, 377-380, 1474-1475, 1575, 4462, 4584-4588, 5776-5777
Jester, Helen Irene 1948
Jesus-Marie, Bruno de 36, 44
Jewelry 180
Jews--Restoration see Zionism
Joest, Wilfried (1914-) 49
John Fletcher Bible College 4464
John Fletcher College see Kletzing College
John of the Cross (1542-1591) 40
John Three Sixteen (periodical) 2054, 2069
John Wesley College, Greensboro, N. C. 4468
John Wesley College, Owosso, Mich. 3179, 4465-4467
Johnson, Andrew (1875-) 327, 581, 5718, 5778
Johnson, B. Edgar see Johnson, Benjamin Edgar (1921-)
Johnson, Benjamin Edgar (1921-) 5779
Johnson, Charles Albert (1916-) 2839-2840
Johnson, Elias Henry (1841-1906) 3935
Johnson, Eva R. 1077
Johnson, Guy Benton (1928-) 62-63
Johnson, Harold 2461
Johnson, Harry Fred (1889-1945) 5780
Johnson, Herbert S. 5781
Johnson, I. T. see Johnson, Ithiel Town (1849-1931)
Johnson, Ithiel Town (1849-1931) 699, 5782-5783
Johnson, J. Prescott see

Johnson, John Prescott (1921-   )
Johnson, Jerry 1888
Johnson, John Prescott (1921-   ) 5784
Johnson, Pearl Vennard 2756
Johnson, Spencer 3874, 3878
Johnson, Walter Henry (1917-   ) 5785
Johnson, Z. T. see Johnson, Zachary Taylor (1897-   )
Johnson, Zachary Taylor (1897-   ) 381-383, 634, 4321, 5786
Johnston, Pearl Rose (1856-   ) 1232
Johnston, U. G. 5787-5788
Joint Commission of the Free Methodist and Wesleyan Methodist Churches 3220
Jones, Anna (-1936) 5789
Jones, B. R. see Jones, Burton Rensselaer (1845-1933)
Jones, Burton Rensselaer (1845-1933) 2622, 2647, 2690, 5616, 5790-5791
Jones, Byon A. (1896-   ) 5792
Jones, C. P. see Jones, Charles P.
Jones, C. Warren see Jones, Carl Warren (1882-1963)
Jones, Carlos Edward (1926-   ) 5794
Jones, Mrs. Carlos Edward see Jones, Margaret Louise Hatten (1925-   )
Jones, Carl Warren (1882-1963) 1696-1697, 5793
Jones, Charles Edwin (1932-   ) 101, 650, 994, 1217, 1230, 1737, 1921, 1934, 2777, 3520, 5061, 7112
Jones, Charles P. 1056-1057, 5795
Jones, Mrs. D. B. 5797
Jones, D. D. see Jones, Dess Dain (1895-   )
Jones, David B. (1885-1950) 5796-5797

Jones, Dess Dain (1895-   ) 5798-5799
Jones, E. Stanley see Jones, Eli Stanley (1884-1973)
Jones, Edith Frances (-1951) 5800
Jones, Eli Stanley (1884-1973) 878, 5801-5804
Jones, Elizabeth Brown (1907-   ) 1854
Jones, Harold 5797
Jones, Kenneth E. 1149
Jones, Laura McElwain 5811
Jones, Lum 1273, 1720, 5805-5806
Jones, Margaret Louise Hatten (1925-   ) 5807
Jones, Owen Roger (1922-   ) 12
Jones, Reginald 5797
Jones, Rufus Matthew (1863-1948) 2273, 5046
Jones, Sam P. see Jones, Samuel Porter (1847-1906)
Jones, Samuel Porter (1847-1906) 932-933, 5808-5812
Jones, Thomas W. 3111
Jones, W. 384
Jones, Will O. 694
Jones, William 5813
Joppie, A. S. see Joppie, Alton S. (1906-   )
Joppie, Alton S. (1906-   ) 3490, 5814
Jorchow, Merrill E. 2841
Jordan, Ethel (1882-   ) 5814
Jordan, Oreus E. 1757
Jordan College 4469-4470
Jorden, E. E. 2559
Joy, Bertha Lucile (1918-1966) 5816
Joy, Donald Marvin (1928-   ) 2654-2655, 2737-2738, 2746, 2783, 5817
Joyce, Isaac Wilson (1836-1905) 4695, 5818
Joyful News (periodical) 2521
Juan de la Cruz, Saint see John of the Cross (1542-1591)
Judas Iscariot 915
Judd, F. Emerson 5819
Junior Call (periodical) 3428

Jurich, Alroma B. 5820
Jurich, Mrs. Peter G. see Jurich, Alroma B.

Kahara Holiness Association see United Holy Church of America
Kahl, Maude H. (1885-1971) 5821-5822
Kahn, Ida (1872-1932) 5823
K'ang C'heng see Kahn, Ida (1872-1932)
Kankakee, Ill. 1264, 4531
Kano, Shiro (1911-1944) 5824-5825
Kansas 980, 1233-1234, 1908, 3041, 4348, 4368, 4381, 4416, 4421, 4446, 4459, 4471, 4502-4503, 4522, 5283-5284, 5286, 5822
Kansas Central Bible Training School see Friends Bible College
Kansas City, Mo. 1249-1250, 1253, 1255, 1256, 1258, 1272, 4315, 4471, 4518-4520, 5799
Kansas City, Mo. Church of God (Holiness) 1230, 5799
Kansas City, Mo. First Church of the Nazarene 1921, 6557
Kansas City Bible School see Kansas City College and Bible School
Kansas City College and Bible School 4471, 5863
Kansas Holiness Association see Kansas State Holiness Association
Kansas Holiness College and Bible School see Bresee College
Kansas Holiness Institute and Bible School see Bresee College
Kansas State Holiness Association 980
Kansas Wesleyan University 3041
Kansas Yearly Meeting of Friends see Friends, Society of. Kansas Yearly Meeting
Karnizawa, Japan. Convention for Deepening of Spiritual Life see Convention for Deepening of Spiritual Life, Karnizawa, Japan
Karns, Donald Monroe (1930-) 5826
Karns, Mrs. Donald Monroe see Karns, Elizabeth Canterbury (1932-)
Karns, Elizabeth Canterbury (1932-) 5827
Kauffman, Alvin H. 6901
Kaufman, Edmund George (1891-) 3764
Kearney, Neb. 4464
Keeler, George H. 5828
Keen, Mrs. John F. see Keen, Sarah L.
Keen, Mrs. Mary J. Palmer 5832
Keen, Samuel Ashton (1842-1895) 110, 385-389, 2900, 3843, 5829-5832
Keen, Sarah L. 5833
Keith, C. G. see Keith, Clarence Gault (1903-)
Keith, Clarence Gault (1903-) 5834
Keith, Mrs. Clarence Gault see Keith, Verna Roberta (1905-)
Keith, David Livingstone (1930-) 5835-5836
Keith, Mrs. David Livingstone see Keith, Huberta Letha Carver (1928-)
Keith, Huberta Letha Carver (1928-) 5837
Keith, Roberta see Keith, Verna Roberta (1905-)
Keith, Verna Roberta (1905-) 5838
Keithly, J. W. 390
Kelley, Augusta Tullis (-1887) 5839
Kelley, Edward R. 391, 934

Kelley, J. W. W. see
    Kelley, John William Walker
Kelley, John William Walker
    5840
Kelley, Selden Dee (1897-1949)
    5841-5842
Kelley, Walter W. (-1899)
    5843
Kelley, Mrs. Walter W. see
    Kelley, Augusta Tullis
    (-1887)
Kelly, Charles M. 2271
Kelly, M. Thomas 1774
Kempis, Thomas à see
    Thomas à Kempis (1380-
    1471)
Kendall, Edith Lorna 13
Kendrick, Klaude 4179-4180
Kennedy, Benjamin H. (1804-
    1889) 742
Kennedy, Gerald Hamilton
    (1907-) 2501
Kennedy, Mrs. Lidie H. 7057
Kent, L. B. see Kent, Ly-
    man Blackmarr (1830-1911)
Kent, Lyman Blackmarr (1830-
    1911) 5074, 5844-5845
Kentucky 2081-2086, 2620,
    3042, 3230, 4314, 4326,
    4445, 4472, 4476, 4507,
    4529, 4751, 5324, 5718-
    5719, 5723, 5849, 6033-
    6038, 6241-6251, 6831
Kentucky Holiness School see
    Asbury College
Kentucky Methodist (periodical)
    see Herald, a Journal of
    Full Salvation and the Way
    of Faith (periodical)
Kentucky Mountain Bible Insti-
    tute 4472
Kentucky Mountain Holiness
    Association 2081-2086,
    4472-4507, 6033-6038
Kenworthy, Amos M. (1831-
    1917) 5846-5847
Kenworthy, Truman C. 5847
Kenya 5699
Kenyon, Jay B. (1885-)
    4322, 5848-5849
Kenyon, Orr, pseud. see
    Carter, Russell Kelso

(1849-1926)
Kephart, I. L. see Kephart,
    Isaiah Lafayette (1832-1908)
Kephart, Isaiah Lafayette (1832-
    1908) 3701
Kepler, Thomas Samuel
    (1897-) 33, 38, 2536
Kernersville, N. C. 4473-4474
Kernersville Wesleyan Academy
    4473
Kernersville Wesleyan College
    4474 see also Kernersville
    Wesleyan Academy
Kersey, George E. 719
Kessel, G. G. (-1945) 5850
Kessel, Mrs. G. G. see
    Kessel, Hattie Flenniken
    (-1935)
Kessel, Hattie Flenniken (-
    1935) 5851
Kessler, J. B. A. (1925-)
    4201
Keswick Convention 3923-3925,
    3941-3942, 4019-4020, 4029-
    4030
Keswick Movement 863, 3921-
    4051
Ketcheson, W. G. 2445
Key, Joseph Staunton (1829-
    1920) 933, 5852
Kharat, Wamanrao 5853
Kidder, Daniel Parish (1815-
    1891) 7312
Kiehn, Anna Schmidt 5854
Kiehn, Peter 5855
Kiehn, Mrs. Peter see Kiehn,
    Anna Schmidt
Kiergan, A. M. see Kiergan,
    Arthur M. (1848-1933)
Kiergan, Arthur M. (1848-1933)
    1218, 1233, 5856-5857
Kierkegaard, Søren Aabye
    (1813-1855) 9
Kilbourne, E. A. see Kil-
    bourne, Ernest Albert (1865-
    1928)
Kilbourne, E. L. see Kil-
    bourne, Edwin L.
Kilbourne, Edwin L. 5858
Kilbourne, Ernest Albert (1865-
    1928) 3379, 3388, 5101-
    5102, 5105, 5859, 5861, 6293

Killion, Mead W. 4566, 6793
Kimber, John Shober 392-393, 3375-3376
Kimberley, S. Afr. 4349-4350
Kimbrough, Mary D. Kiplinger (1918-1968) 5862-5863
Kimbrough, Mrs. Ray L. see Kimbrough, Mary D. Kiplinger (1918-1968)
Kindschi, Paul L. (1917-) 3170, 5864-5865
King, Blanche Leon 4273, 5872
King, D. S. see King, Dexter S.
King, Dexter S. 5866-5867, 7043
King, Elizabeth DeCamp (1884-1964) 5868
King, Ethel see Dickerman, Ethel King
King, Ida Ethel Adkins (1884-) 5213, 5869-5870
King, J. H. see King, Joseph Hillery (1869-1946)
King, Joseph Hillery (1869-1946) 4254-4255, 4273, 4289, 5871, 5872
King, Louis L. 4113, 4121
King, O. L. see King, Oscar L. (1872-1925); King, Oscar Logan (1887-1964)
King, Mrs. O. L. see King, Elizabeth DeCamp (1884-1964)
King, Oscar L. (1872-1925) 5873
King, Oscar Logan (1887-1964) 3577, 5874-5875
King, Paul S. 1038
King, Mrs. T. T. see King, Ida Ethel Adkins (1884-)
King, Mrs. Tollie Tate see King, Ida Ethel Adkins (1884-)
Kingdom (periodical) 809
Kingdom Tidings (periodical) 810
Kingfisher, Okla. 4475
Kinghorn, Kenneth Cain (1930-) 5876

King's College 4475
King's Highway (periodical) 811, 1009
Kingswood, Ky. 4476
Kingswood College see Kingswood Holiness College
Kingswood Holiness College 4476, 5718
Kinlaw, Dennis Franklin (1922-) 5877
Kinne, C. J. see Kinne, Clarence James (1869-1932)
Kinne, Clarence James (1869-1932) 1401-1402, 1665, 1698, 1794, 1881, 5878
Kiplinger, Mary D. see Kimbrough, Mary D. Kiplinger (1918-1968)
Kirby, William (1881-1957) 2312, 5879-5880, 5881
Kirkland Bible Institute 4477
Kirkpatrick, W. J. see Kirkpatrick, William James (1838-1921)
Kirkpatrick, William James (1838-1921) 667-668, 682-684, 700-703, 708-709, 713, 715, 732-734, 1251, 1665, 2705, 2981, 2988-2991, 2993-2996, 2999-3002, 5882
Kirksville, Mo. 4478
Kirksville Bible School 4478
Kirn, John (1858-1933) 5883-5884
Kitagawa, Hiroshi (1888-) 5885-5886
Kitchener, Ont. 4400
Kitchener, Ont. Emmanuel Bible College see Emmanuel Bible College, Kitchener, Ont.
Klein, Mattias 2762
Kletzing, Elmer L. (1864?-1947) 166-167, 483, 555, 5887
Kletzing, Henry Frick (1850-1910) 166-167, 5888-5889
Kletzing College 896, 4479-4481
Kline, George E. 2661-2662
Knapp, Ethel Alice (1896-) 5890

Knapp, J. F. see Knapp, Joseph Fairchild (1832-1891)
Knapp, John Franklin 717, 2560
Knapp, Joseph Fairchild (1832-1891) 5891
Knapp, Mrs. Joseph Fairchild see Knapp, Phoebe Palmer (1839-1908)
Knapp, M. W. see Knapp, Martin Wells (1853-1901)
Knapp, Martin Wells (1853-1901) 98, 110, 168, 209, 394-399, 635, 704, 721-722, 749, 989-991, 3813, 3820, 3835, 3856, 5892-5896, 7123
Knapp, Mrs. Martin Wells see Knapp, Minnie C. Ferle (1868-1923)
Knapp, Minnie C. Ferle (1868-1923) 992, 5896-5897
Knapp, Phoebe Palmer (1839-1908) 705, 2974, 5898
Knight, John Allan 1475a, 2561, 5899
Knight, John L. 1608, 1628, 5900
Knight, John William (1729-1785) 2561
Knightstown, Ind. 4391
Knott, J. Proctor see Knott, James Proctor (1886-1963)
Knott, James Proctor (1886-1963) 1775, 4545, 5901
Knott, Lucy Stanton Pierce (1856-19??) 5902
Knott, Mrs. William S. see Knott, Lucy Stanton Pierce (1856-19??)
Knox, Ronald Arbuthnott (1888-1957) 2490
Knudson, Albert (1873-1953) 2551-2552
Knupp, Clarence Jean (1918-) 5903
Knupp, Mrs. Clarence Jean see Knupp, Mildred Marcella Beck (1919-)
Knupp, Mildred Marcella Beck (1919-) 5904
Kobayashi, F. 5905

Kodesh Church of Immanuel 2480-2482
Köberle, Adolf (1898-) 50-51
Koerber, Charles J. 2562
Koglin, Anna E. 1164
Korea 1909
Kragerud, Ole (-1921) 5906
Krauser, Oscar von Barchwitz- see Barchwitz-Krauser, Oscar von
Kreider, Mary C. 1029
Kresge, Bessie Reid (1897-) 5907
Kresge, Mrs. Luther see Kresge, Bessie Reid (1897-)
Krigbaum, C. L. see Krigbaum, Clellie Lee (-1970)
Krigbaum, Clellie Lee (-1970) 5908, 5909
Krigbaum, Ella M. (1900-) 5909
Krigbaum, Ted see Krigbaum, Clellie Lee (-1970)
Krikorian, Rebecca K. 5911
Krikorian, Samuel C. (1893-) 5910-5911
Kring, J. A. see Kring, James Arthur (1873-)
Kring, James Arthur (1873-) 1205, 1476, 1819, 5912-5913
Ku Klux Klan (1915-) 2249-2250
Kuhn, Harold Barnes (1911-) 4327, 5914
Kulbeck, Gloria G. 4199
Kulp, George B. (1845-1939) 2875, 3024, 3477, 3524, 3562-3564, 3864, 5915
Kumalo, Alice 5916
Kunz, George J. (1862-1925) 5917-5918
Kunze, R. J. 5919
Kuo, Heng Chun 5920
Kuo Heng Chun see Kuo, Heng Chun
Kurtz, Henry C. 2772

L., I. S. see Leonard, Isabella S.
Labertew, Dorothy 1237
Labor and laboring classes

3021
Labor unions see Labor and laboring classes
Laborers see Labor and laboring classes
Labouchere, Henry 3686
LaDue, Wilson Cathey (1902-) 5921
Lady, Jesse F. 5922
Lageer, Ellis A. 3741
Lake Bluff, Ill. 2842
Lake Bluff Camp Meeting Association, Lake Bluff, Ill. 2842
Lamar, Colo. 4482
Lamar Bible School 4482
Lamb, R. Ernest 2313
Lambert, David Willoughby 2510, 5000-5002, 5015
Lambert, Rose (1878-) 3774, 5923
Lamp of Life (Bay City, Mich., etc.) 3015
Lamp of Life (Toronto) 812, 6744
Lamson, Byron Samuel (1901-) 2617, 2716, 2720-2721
Lan, Alice Y. 3268
Lancaster, Ohio 2838
Landisville, Pa. 129
Lane, Neva (-1956) 5924-5925
Lang, August (1867-) 58
Lankford, Sarah A. see Palmer, Sarah A. Worrell Lankford (1806-1896)
Lanpher, C. P. see Lanpher, Carroll P. (1876-)
Lanpher, Carroll P. (1876-) 5926
Larsen, Walter Burdick (-1957) 5927
Lashbrook, J. W. see Lashbrook, Jack Walton (1912-1960)
Lashbrook, Jack Walton (1912-1960) 5928
Lashbrook, Mrs. Jack Walton see Lashbrook, Ruth Elizabeth Raisch (1917-)
Lashbrook, Ruth Elizabeth Raisch (1917-) 5929

Latham, Joy 1666, 2703, 3803
Latin America 981-982, 1910-1917, 3433, 4134-4135, 4201-4202, 5330, 5897, 6938-6939, 6945-6946, 7308
Latter-Day Saints see Mormonism
Lavelle, Louis (1883-1951) 40
Law, William (1686-1761) 26-28, 2870
Law and Gospel (periodical) 813
Lawlor, Edward 1623, 5930-5931
Lawrence, Evan Jerry (1918-) 2223, 4307, 5932
Lawrence, R. V. see Lawrence, Ruliff Vanclief (1825-1872)
Lawrence, Ruliff Vanclief (1825-1872) 5933
Lawrence, Tex. 4483
Lawrence Seminary 4483
Lawson, James Gilchrist (1874-) 6317
Lawson, Ky. 4507
Laymen's Holiness Association 2087-2092
Lazenby, Marion Elias (1885-) 118
League for Social Service, New York 3611
League of Prayer 2093-2119, 4362-4363, 5013, 5015, 5603-5608
Leaton, James 530
Lebanon Missionary Bible College 3359, 4484
Lee, Byron D. 5934
Lee, Earl G. 1354
Lee, Mrs. Earl G. see Lee, Hazel C.
Lee, Eva Townsend 4218, 5936
Lee, F. J. see Lee, Flavius Josephus (1875-1928)
Lee, Mrs. F. J. see Lee, Eva Townsend
Lee, Flavius Josephus (1875-1928) 4218, 5935-5936
Lee, Mrs. Flavius Josephus see Lee, Eva Townsend

Lee, Hazel C. 5937
Lee, Jesse (1758-1816) 2957
Lee, John Wesley 5938
Lee, Luther (1800-1889) 2876, 3142, 3152, 3171-3176, 3188, 3218-3219, 5939-5940
Lee, Robert Greene (1886-) 6761
Lee, Thomas E. 5941
Lee, William H. (1855-1919) 5942-5943
Lee College 4213, 4485-4486
Leeuw, Gerardus van der (1890-1950) 14
Leffingwell, Clara (1863-1905) 5944-5945
Leftwich, W. M. 3073
LeGrand, Iowa 4385
Lehman, F. M. see Lehman, Frederick Martin (1868-)
Lehman, Frederick Martin (1868-) 198, 876, 1274, 1477, 1748, 2871, 5946-5947
Leist, J. F. (-1972) 1820, 5007, 5948
Leitzel, Leonard Winfield (1918-) 5949
Leitzel, Mrs. Leonard Winfield see Leitzel, Pauline Marie Burden (1920-)
Leitzel, Pauline Marie Burden (1920-) 5950
Lemieux, Ernest 1345
Lemmons, Frank W. (1901-) 4219-4220
Leonard, I. S. see Leonard, Isabella S.
Leonard, Isabella S. 88, 194-195, 510
Leoni, Mich. 4501
Lerch, David (1903-) 2563
Le Shana, David Charles (1932-) 2310-2311, 5951
Levy, Edgar M. (1822-1906) 105, 400, 984, 3834, 5952
Lewis, Charles Elwood (1928-) 3541, 5953
Lewis, Mrs. Charles Elwood see Lewis, Dorothy Carroll Baker (1928-)
Lewis, Clarence Irving (1883-) 5416
Lewis, David J. (1846-1918) 5954
Lewis, David J. (1859-1899) 2371, 5955-5956
Lewis, Dorothy Carroll Baker (1928-) 5957
Lewis, Esther Lambert 1317
Lewis, L. Glenn 4793
Lewis, V. H. see Lewis, Voyle H.
Lewis, Voyle H. 1306, 1624, 1821, 5958
Lewis, W. F. 3121
Libby Prison 2952
Liberalism see Modernism
Liddick, Ruth Sension 3229
Life-boat (periodical) 814
Life of Faith (periodical) 4020, 4035
Light and Life (periodical) 2727
Light and Life Hour (radio broadcast) 2741
Lighthouse Messenger (periodical) 815
Lighthouse Mission, St. Louis, Mo. see St. Louis, Mo. Lighthouse Mission
Lightwood, James Thomas (1856-) 2584
Lillenas, Bertha Mae Wilson (1889-1945) 5959
Lillenas, Haldor (1885-1959) 743, 1660, 1667-1673, 1674, 5960-5964
Lillenas, Mrs. Haldor see Lillenas, Bertha Mae Wilson (1889-1945)
Lincicome, F. see Lincicome, Forman (1880-)
Lincicome, Forman (1880-) 2635, 2656-2657, 2742, 3166, 5965
Lincoln, Arthur D. (-1888) 5966
Lincoln, Mrs. Arthur D. see Lincoln, Polly Abbie Mudge (-1888)
Lincoln, Polly Abbie Mudge (-1888) 5967
Lind, Abraham A. 5968
Lind, Marie 3804, 3805

Lindrith, N. Mex. 4405, 4517
Lindsay, Arthur L. (1934-) 5969
Lindsay, Vachel (1879-1931) 4821
Lindsey, Leroy E., Jr. 5970
Lindström, Harald Gustaf Ake (1905-) 2564, 2565
Liquor problem 884, 2240, 2248, 2367, 3153, 5581, 7210-7212
Lishali, Philip 2479, 5971-5972
Little Methodist (periodical) see Holiness Messenger (periodical)
Little Rock, Ark. 2782
Littleton, Colo. 4551
Live Coals (periodical) see Live Coals of Fire (periodical)
Live Coals of Fire (periodical) 4240
Living Epistle (periodical) 1996
Living Water (periodical) 2192, 3092
Living Waters from David's Fountain (periodical) 816
Living Words (periodical) 817
Lockport, N. Y. 3124
Löschhorn, Albert 15
Logan, J. T. 2685, 2739
London, Allie S. 1855-1856, 5973
London, Holland Bryan (1908-) 1355-1356, 1674, 5974
London, Eng. 2590, 4305, 4362-4363, 6972
London. Institute of Race Relations see Institute of Race Relations, London
London Pillar of Fire (periodical) see Pillar of Fire (London) (periodical)
Long, Lois Eileen (1937-) 5975
Long, Richard Eugene (1927-) 5976
Long, Mrs. Richard Eugene see Long, Ruby Irene Berkgren (1927-)

Long, Ruby Irene Berkgren (1927-) 5977
Long, Ruth 6901
Long Beach, Calif. 4313
Longacre, Andrew (1831-1906) 5978
Longhurst, Sarah (1860-1940) 5979-5980
Lopez, Antonio 5981
Lord, E. J. see Lord, Edwin Jay (18??-1942)
Lord, Mrs. E. J. see Lord, Luella N. (1877-1964)
Lord, Edwin Jay (18??-1942) 5982
Lord, Mrs. Edwin Jay see Lord, Luella N. (1877-1964)
Lord, J. C. 664
Lord, Luella N. (1877-1964) 5983-5984
Lord's Supper 2384, 7039
Loring, W. T. 5985
Lorne Park College 4487
Lorne Park Seminary see Lorne Park College
Los Angeles, Calif. 1246-1247, 1251-1252, 1254-1255, 1258, 4332, 4371, 4422, 4488, 4544-4548, 4560, 4681, 5333, 5649, 5651
Los Angeles. Bible Institute see Bible Institute of Los Angeles
Los Angeles. Union Rescue Mission 4681
Los Angeles Free Methodist Seminary see Los Angeles Pacific College
Los Angeles Junior College see Los Angeles Pacific College
Los Angeles Pacific College 4488
Los Angeles Pacific College and High School see Los Angeles Pacific College
Lot, Myrrha Borodine (1882-1957) 41
Lotteries see Gambling
Loughlin, Delia (-1892) 5986-5988
Louisiana 1265

Louisiana State Lottery Co. 3094-3095
Louisville, Ill. 5595
Louisville, Ky. 5723
Love, Belle see Love, L. Belle
Love, Mrs. Harry see Love, Louise Calkins (-1946)
Love, Mrs. L. B. see Love, L. Belle
Love, L. Belle 5989
Love, Louise Calkins (-1946) 5990
Love, Mrs. Mark A. see Love, L. Belle
Lovelace, Austin Cole (1919-) 2810
Lovelace, Ora V. 1864
Loveless, Robert (-1909) 5991
Lovell, Ora D. 5992
Lovin, C. Wesley (1918-) 5993-5995
Lowe, Thomas O. 5996
Lower Light (motor boat) 4230
Lower Light Church 2120
Lower Light Mission see Lower Light Church
Lowery, D. D. 3702
Lown, A. J. 1357
Lowrey, Asbury (1816-1898) 1553, 2901-2902, 5997
Lowrey, Mrs. M. M. Lowrey see Lowrey, Sarah Ann (1884-)
Lowrey, Sadie see Lowrey, Sarah Ann (1884-)
Lowrey, Sarah Ann (1884-) 5998
Luccock, Halford Edward (1885-) 2543
Luck, H. B. (-1960) 5999
Luckey, J. S. see Luckey, James Seymour (1867-1937)
Luckey, James Seymour (1867-1937) 6000
Ludwig, Minnie E. Brink (1877-1958) 1358, 1625, 6001
Ludwig, S. T. see Ludwig, Sylvester Theodore (1903-1964)
Ludwig, Sylvester Theodore (1903-1964) 1597, 1650, 6002, 6004, 6664
Ludwig, Theodore (1871-1957) 1359, 6003-6004
Ludwigson, R. see Ludwigson, Raymond
Ludwigson, Raymond 3852
Lugibihl, Walter H. (1883-) 4144
Lumber River Annual Conference of the Holiness Methodist Church see Holiness Methodist Church (1900-)
Lumber River Mission see Holiness Methodist Church (1900-)
Lumber River Mission Conference of the Holiness Methodist Church see Holiness Methodist Church (1900-)
Lummus, Aaron 2903
Lund, Oscar 6005
Lunn, M. see Lunn, Mervel
Lunn, Mervel 1360, 6006, 6548
Lunn, P. H. 1672
Lunsford, Esther 1910
Lunsford, Robert Lloyd 651, 1910
Luther, Martin (1483-1546) 46-47, 49, 2556
Lyall, Leslie T. 3385
Lyles, Albert M. 2491
Lynch, W. M. (1925-) 1952
Lyon, David D. (1841-1919) 6007
Lytle, Robert N. (1917-) 3209, 6008-6009, 7027

McAlister, Walter E. 4199, 5010b
McAll, R. W. see McAll, Robert Whitaker (1821-1893)
McAll, Robert Whitaker (1821-1893) 6010
McBride, H. C. see McBride, Hamilton Cree (1840-1917)
McBride, Hamilton Cree (1840-1917) 6011
McBride, J. B. see McBride,

Joseph Benjamine (1873-19??)
McBride, Joseph Benjamine (1873-19??) 401-402, 6012-6013
McCabe, Charles Cardwell (1836-1906) 2952, 2999-3000
McCallum, Floyd Frederick (1920-) 3513, 4466, 6014
McCarty, J. H. see McCarty, Joseph Hendrickson (1830-1897)
McCarty, J. Hendrickson see McCarty, Joseph Hendrickson (1830-1897)
McCarty, Joseph Hendrickson (1830-1897) 2860, 6015-6017
McClain, C. S. see McClain, Carl Sheldon (1899-)
McClain, Carl Sheldon (1899-) 1361, 6018
McClanahan, Burl Austin 6019-6020
McClurkan, J. O. see McClurkan, James O. (1861-1914)
McClurkan, James O. (1861-1914) 107, 2178-2179, 2183-2184, 2186, 3836, 6021-6025
McConkey, James Henry (1858-1937) 169, 403-404, 582-583, 3823
McConn, W. F. see McConn, William Finney (1888-)
McConn, William Finney (1888-) 6026
McConnell, C. A. see McConnell, Charles Allen (1860-1955)
McConnell, Charles Allen (1860-1955) 1478, 6027-6031, 7217-7218
McConnell, Mrs. Charles Allen see McConnell, Leona Bellew
McConnell, Lela Grace (1884-) 2081-2086, 6032-6038
McConnell, Leona Bellew 1935, 4346, 6039

McCord, James Bennett 2072, 7120
McCord, Sask. 4434
McCoy, B. H. 6951
McCrossan, Charles Wesley (1870-) 216
McCrossan, T. J. see McCrossan, Thomas J.
McCrossan, Thomas J. 4068, 4095
McCullough, Melvin 1362
McCumber, W. E. 1479-1480, 1822, 6040
McCutchan, Robert Guy (1877-) 2811
McDonald, W. see McDonald, William (1820-1901)
McDonald, William (1820-1901) 405-408, 437, 706-710, 730-731, 2904, 2940, 2942, 2975-2976, 3049, 4635, 5078, 5388, 5470, 6041
McDonnell, K. 4167
McDougle, Leonidas I. 2905
McDowell, J. V. 374
MacGeary, John Samuel (1853-1931) 2648, 2693, 6042
McGee College 4489
McGee Holiness College 4490
McGovern, George Stanley (1922-) 6044-6045
McGovern, J. C. see McGovern, Joseph C. (1868-1944)
McGovern, Joseph C. (1868-1944) 6043-6045
McGrady, Paul (1925-1967) 6046-6047
McGraw, James (1913-) 961, 1315, 1554, 4867, 5007-5008, 5024, 5093, 5120, 5489, 5587, 5672, 5744, 5774, 5812, 5964, 6023, 6048, 6050, 6073, 6159, 6258, 6306, 6529, 6549, 6602, 6833, 7074, 7177, 7226, 7255
McGraw, James Paul see McGraw, James (1913-)
McGraw, W. D. see McGraw, William David (1870-)
McGraw, W. D., Jr. see

McGraw, William David, Jr.
McGraw, William David (1870-) 6049-6050
McGraw, William David, Jr. 1481, 6051
McIntosh, Lawrence Dennis 2566
Macintyre, John Lester 4703
McIntyre, Ralph L. 1776, 3811
McIntyre, Robert (1851-1914) 750, 3009
McIntyre, Robert W. (1922-) 3155, 6045, 6052-6054
McKaig, Robert Newton (1842-) 409
McKay, John (1896-) 6055
McKee, Earl Stanley (1897-) 4323
McKenna, David Loren (1929-) 2682, 4569, 6056-6057
MacKenzie, Kenneth M. 2778, 4068, 4097, 6738
Mackey, A. B. see Mackey, Alexander Benjamin (1897-1973)
Mackey, Alexander Benjamin (1897-) 6058
McKinley, O. Glenn (-1970) 1592, 3184
McKinney, Tex. 4491
McKinney Junior College 4491
McLaughlin, G. A. see McLaughlin, George Asbury (1851-1933)
McLaughlin, George Asbury (1851-1933) 253, 410-412, 681, 683-684, 689, 711-716, 3837, 3901, 6059-6060
McLaughlin, Mrs. George Asbury see Walker, Jennie Reeves
McLean, A. see McLean, Alexander (1826-1910)
McLean, Alexander (1826-1910) 127, 6061
Maclean, J. Kennedy 3983
McLeister, Clara Orrell (1882-1958) 6062-6063
McLeister, I. F. see McLeister, Ira Ford (1879-1963)
McLeister, Ira Ford (1879-1963) 2063, 2269, 2463, 3118, 3126, 3191-3192, 5240, 6063-6064
McLeister, Mrs. Ira Ford see McLeister, Clara Orrell (1882-1958)
McMichael, Wanda Winifred Davis (1921-) 6065
Macmillan, Margaret Burnham 3045
McMillen, Sim I. (1898-) 3156-3157, 3792-3793
McMurry, Celia Ferries (-1946) 6066
McMurry, Mrs. Valentine George see McMurry, Celia Ferries (-1946)
McNeel, Myrtle 6067
McNeill, Robert E. 690, 704, 717, 729
Macon, Ga. 3147-3148
Macon County, Mo. 1229
McPheeters, J. C. see McPheeters, Julian C. (1889-)
McPheeters, Julian C. (1889-) 413, 5470, 6068-6070
McPherson, Aimee Semple (1890-1944) 618, 622
McPherson, Anna Talbott 2363, 5201
McPherson, Kan. 4381
McReynolds, C. E. 6507
McReynolds, Mrs. Emory see McReynolds, Margaret Glyn Wiman (1921-)
McReynolds, Margaret Glyn Wiman (1921-) 6071
Macrory, H. B. (1883-19??) 6072-6073
McWherter, Leroy 333
Macy, Herman H. 2384
Maddux, Rose Mary (1925-) 6074
Madera, Calif. 4561
Magar, John B. 6075
Mahan, Asa (1799-1889) 170, 205, 414-418, 664, 870-871, 3838-3839, 3951, 6076-6082
Maine 1918, 7045

Mains, Lura Ann (1847-) 6083-6084
Maiyü, Shih see Stone, Mary (1873-1954)
Major, Rev. Mr. 2880
Malaysia 3043, 5381
Mallalieu, W. F. see Mallalieu, Willard Francis (1828-1911)
Mallalieu, Willard Francis (1828-1911) 565, 985-986, 2806, 2904, 2906, 2947, 6085, 6140, 6387, 6391, 6395
Mallory, Mattie see Morgan, Mattie Mallory
Malone, Mrs. E. J. see Rutherford, Eliza J.
Malone, J. Walter see Malone, John Walter (1857-1935)
Malone, J. Walter, Jr. see Malone, John Walter (1888-1962)
Malone, John Walter (1857-1935) 6086
Malone, John Walter (1888-1962) 6087
Malone College 2372, 4492-4494
Manchester, Eng. 4369
Manchester, Eng. Star Hall 194-195, 364, 367, 371, 844-863, 867, 3934, 4174, 5129-5130
Maneriker, Prasadrao (1908-) 6088
Mangum, Emile Sellman 6090
Mangum, Myrtle see White, Myrtle Mangum (18??-)
Mangum, Thomas Emmett (1884-) 6089-6090
Manheim, Pa. 127-128
Manifold, Orrin Avery 2567
Manitoba 4374, 4434
Mann, E. S. see Mann, Edward Stebbins (1908-)
Mann, Edward Stebbins (1908-) 6091
Mann, Harold William 3097, 5639
Mann, William Edward 1868, 2449, 2753, 3771, 5931

Mantle, J. Gregory 6738
Marie, Bruno de Jesus- see Jesus-Marie, Bruno de
Marion, Ind. 4495
Marion, N. C. 4397
Marion, Ohio 4761
Marion College 4495
Maritime Nazarene Bible Institute 4496
Markey, Joseph B. 3118
Marks, Edie see Marks, William Edie
Marks, William Edie 718, 724
Márquez, Raúl (1909-) 6092
Marriage 1075-1076, 1370, 2124, 2319, 2861, 2866, 3394, 3819, 3871, 3917, 4985, 5459, 5721, 7159
Marsh, E. G. see Marsh, Elmer G.
Marsh, Edward Garrard (1783-1862) 29
Marsh, Elmer G. 3491, 3840, 6093
Marsh, Frederick Edward (1858-) 3952
Marsh, Ida Marian see Marsh, Marian (1913-)
Marsh, J. D. see Marsh, James D.
Marsh, James D. 6094
Marsh, Marian (1913-) 4527, 6095
Marshall, Ann Louise Martin (1930-) 6096
Marshall, Wallace Gene (1930-) 6097
Marshall, Mrs. Wallace Gene see Marshall, Ann Louise Martin (1930-)
Marshall, Walter (1628-1680) 30
Marshalltown, Iowa 4385
Marshburn, William V. (1855-) 6098-6099
Marston, Leslie Ray (1894-) 2636-2638, 2694, 2712, 2747, 6100-6102
Marston, Lorena (-1916) 6103
Martin, E. E. see Martin, Edward Everett (1887-1951)
Martin, E. W. see Martin, Ernest W.

Martin, Ed see Martin, Edward Everett (1887-1951)
Martin, Edward Everett (1887-1951) 6104-6105
Martin, Ernest W. 6106
Martin, Hugh 2540
Martin, I. G. see Martin, Isaiah Guyman (1862-1957)
Martin, Ira Jay (1911-) 4175, 4183
Martin, Ira Jay, III see Martin, Ira Jay (1911-)
Martin, Isaiah Guyman (1862-1957) 4868, 6107-6108
Martin, Joel 3193
Martin, Paul La Rush (1915-) 1275, 1403-1404, 1482-1483, 6109-6110
Martin, Sydney 1483a
Marvin, Edward Payson (1834-) 507
Mary, Virgin 2158
Maryland 98, 128, 983, 5893
Masa, Jorge O. 6232
Mason, C. H. see Mason, Charles Harrison (1866-1961)
Mason, Charles Harrison (1866-1961) 4223, 4225a, 6111-6112
Mason, Evelee Doris (1923-) 6113
Mason, Genevie Fern (1923-) 6114
Masonry see Secret societies
Massachusetts 21, 128, 984, 4392-4394, 4594, 6281
Mata, José (1932-) 6115
Mathews, G. M. see Mathews, George Martin (1848-1921)
Mathews, George Martin (1848-1921) 3726
Mathews, Shailer (1863-1941) Will Christ Come Again? 4012
Mathis, I. C. (1898-) 1484, 6116
Matlack, L. C. see Matlack, Lucius Columbus (1816-1883)
Matlack, Lucius Columbus (1816-1883) 2959-2962, 3050, 3177, 3194-3198, 3218, 6117-6118, 6672

Matson, G. Eric 6371
Mattes, John C. 50-51
Matthews, John 1390, 1485-1486, 1587, 6119
Matthewson, Minnie W. (-1935) 6120
Matthewson, Wesley F. (-1947) 6121
Matthewson, Mrs. Wesley F. see Matthewson, Minnie W. (-1935)
Mattison, Hiram (1811-1868) 2925
Mattison, Hiram (1811-1868) Calm review of Dr. Perry's late article in the Christian Advocate and Journal 2907, 2926
Mattoon, L. C. 3121
Matusi, Anna 6122
Matusi, Mrs. Zakaria see Matusi, Anna
Maupin, William 333
Mavis, Marion 2620
Mavis, W. Curry see Mavis, Walter Curry (1905-)
Mavis, Walter Curry (1905-) 2630, 2658-2660, 6123-6124
Maxwell, Mrs. Mary 6125
May, James William (1912-) 2963
May, John W. 1487, 6126
May, Samuel Joseph (1797-1871) 3218
Mazivila, John 6127
Mead, Amos P. (1829-1886) 2843
Meadley, Thomas Donald 2528
Medical doctors see Physicians
Medical Missions see Missions, Medical
Medici, Lorenzo de' (1449-1492) 84
Medina, N. Y. 3032
Meek, J. H. 3178, 6128
Meek, Leona Bellew McConnell see McConnell, Leona Bellew
Meeks, Darlene Carol Laffoon (1933-) 6129
Meeks, E. A. 3586
Meeks, Mrs. John Wesley see Meeks, Darlene Carol Laf-

foon (1933-)
Meeks, Paul Wesley (1929-) 6130
Meggers, L. D. 6131
Meikle, Grace Livingston (-1949) 6132
Meikle, W. L. 6133
Meikle, Mrs. W. L. see Meikle, Grace Livingston (-1949)
Mekeel, Arthur Jacob 2296
Melbourne, Austl. 4595
Melton, C. Y. 4403
Memphis, Tenn. 4225a, 4361
Men for Missions International 3362, 3382
Mendell, Fred H. (1883-1918) 6134
Mennonite Brethren in Christ see United Missionary Church
Mennonites 5404
Mercer, Jerry L. 6135
Meredith, Archel 6136
Meredith, Clyde W. (1901-) 3201, 6137
Meredith, Isaac Hickman (1872-) 7182
Meridian, Miss. 4497-4498
Meridian Female College 4497
Meridian Male College 4498
Merrill, A. D. 6138
Merritt, Stephen 6233-6234, 6236-6237
Merritt, Timothy (1775-1845) 2908, 6139-6140
Message of the Cross (periodical) 3264
Messenger, Frank Mortimer (1852-) 1576-1578, 2151, 6141
Messiah Bible College see Messiah College
Messiah Bible School and Missionary Training Home see Messiah College
Messiah College 4499
Methodism 864-865, 1747, 1748, 2491
Methodist (periodical) see Herald, a Journal of Full Salvation and the Way of Faith (periodical); Holiness Messenger (periodical)
Methodist and the Way of Life (periodical) see Herald, a Journal of Full Salvation and the Way of Faith (periodical)
Methodist Challenge (periodical) 3093
Methodist Church (United States) 2774-2825, 4387, 5595, 5802
Methodist Church (United States). Board of Social and Economic Relations 2774, 2779-2780
Methodist Church (United States). Conferences. Little Rock 2782
Methodist Church (United States). Conferences. North Dakota. Historical Society 2781
Methodist Church (United States). Conferences. North Georgia. Historical Society 3098
Methodist Church (United States). Conferences. Southern California-Arizona. Historical Society 2823-2824
Methodist Church (United States). General Conference. Commission on Ritual and Orders of Worship see Methodist Church (United States). General Conference. Commission on Worship
Methodist Church (United States). General Conference. Commission on Worship 2814-2817
Methodist Church (United States). General Conference. Commission on Worship. The Book of Worship for Church and Home 2818
Methodist Episcopal Church 2812, 2826-3053, 3699, 4489, 4634-4635, 4691-4695, 4711-4714, 4768, 4828, 4855, 4863-4864, 5078-5079, 5235, 5237, 5339, 5371, 5410-5411, 5418-5419, 5470, 5537, 5539, 5565-5567, 5576, 5624, 5739-5741, 5751, 5763, 5783,

5802, 5832, 5845, 5893-
5895, 5940, 5947, 5956,
6060, 6069-6070, 6140,
6217, 6219, 6225, 6255-
6257, 6360, 6387-6389,
6391-6392, 6394-6395, 6398,
6411, 6422, 6513-6514,
6564, 6566, 6622, 6649-
6651, 6676-6677, 6741-6742,
6778-6780, 6782-6784, 6835-
6836, 6872-6873, 6917,
6932-6954, 6967, 6969,
7049, 7059, 7123, 7192,
7210-7212, 7245, 7267,
7287-7288, 7312

Methodist Episcopal Church. Conferences. Central German 3012

Methodist Episcopal Church. Conferences. East Genesee. Laymen's Association 2899

Methodist Episcopal Church. Conferences. Michigan 3024

Methodist Episcopal Church. Conferences. New York 6217

Methodist Episcopal Church. Conferences. New York East 6217

Methodist Episcopal Church. Conferences. North Dakota 2827

Methodist Episcopal Church. Conferences. Ohio 3011

Methodist Episcopal Church. Conferences. Oklahoma 750, 3009

Methodist Episcopal Church. Conferences. Pittsburgh 3011

Methodist Episcopal Church. General Conference 2876, 3219

Methodist Episcopal Church. Missions and mission conferences. South Central Africa. Angola District 3033, 6952

Methodist Episcopal Church. Tract Society 2937

Methodist Episcopal Church, South 2812, 3054-3100, 5476, 5558, 5612, 5641, 5718, 5809-5811, 6241-6251, 6272

Methodist Home Journal (periodical) see Christian Standard (periodical)

Methodist Monthly (periodical) 3016

Methodist Protestant Church (1830-) 2812, 3101-3103

Methodists, German 2953, 3012, 6299

Methodists in Africa 3033-3035, 6934-6936, 6944, 6948-6949, 6952

Methodists in Arizona 2823

Methodists in California 2824, 6933, 6940-6941, 6944, 6950, 7192

Methodists in Canada 5694

Methodists in Georgia 3097-3098, 5227, 5639

Methodists in Illinois 6513-6514

Methodists in India 3036-3038, 4936-4938, 5381, 5802, 6937, 6942-6943, 6967, 6969

Methodists in Indiana 3039-3040

Methodists in Kansas 3041

Methodists in Kentucky 3042, 5718

Methodists in Latin America 6938-6939, 6945-6946

Methodists in Malaysia 3043, 5381

Methodists in Maryland 5893

Methodists in Mexico 3044, 6017

Methodists in Michigan 3045-3046, 6219, 6958

Methodists in Nebraska 3047, 5172

Methodists in New England 7049

Methodists in New Jersey 3048

Methodists in North Dakota 2781, 2827, 6255-6257

Methodists in Rhode Island 3049

Methodists in Tennessee 5641

Methodists in Texas 3052-3053, 3099-3100, 5558, 7217-7218

Methodists in the Middle West 7049

Methodists in the Southern
  States 3050-3051, 5624,
  6272
Methodists in Virginia 2825,
  6951
Methvin, Rayford H. (1921-)
  6142
Metropolitan Bible School 4500
Metropolitan Church Association
  2121-2152, 4500, 5320
Metropolitan Church Association. General Assembly
  2148
Metropolitan Holiness Church
  see Metropolitan Church
  Association
Metz, Donald S. (1916-)
  1488, 1588, 1777, 6143-6144
Mexican-Americans 3210
Mexican Annual Conference,
  Evangelical Methodist Church
  see Mexican Evangelistic
  Mission
Mexican Evangelistic Mission
  2153-2160, 2609, 4388, 4406,
  4460 see also Evangelical
  Methodist Church
Mexicans in the United States
  see Mexican-Americans
Mexico 1919-1920, 2153-2160,
  3044, 3590-3596, 4388,
  4406, 4460, 4559, 4939,
  5355, 6017
Mexico City, Mex. 4559
Mexico District, Evangelical
  Methodist Church see Mexican Evangelistic Mission
Meyer, F. B. see Meyer,
  Frederick Brotherton (1847-
  1929)
Meyer, Frederick Brotherton
  (1847-1929) 327, 3928-3929,
  3946-3947, 3953-3959, 4015
Meyer, Jacob 2011
Meyer, James (1883-) 42
Meyering, Chester 1598, 1680
Meyers, Hazeldean (1932-)
  6145
Michel, John W. (1885-)
  6146
Michelson, Einar H. 4137
Michigan 1266, 2042-2043,
  3048, 3689, 4300, 4357,
  4395, 4465-4467, 4469-4470,
  4501, 4506, 4565-4569, 5884,
  5940, 6174-6175, 6219, 6857,
  6958
Michigan Christian Advocate
  (periodical) 3015
Michigan Holiness Association
  818, 4506
Michigan Holiness Record (periodical) 818, 2264
Michigan Union College 4501
Mid-America Nazarene College
  4502
Middle East see Near East
Midnight Cry (periodical) 819,
  3500-3507, 4748
Midwest Conference, Pilgrim
  Holiness Church of New York
  see Pilgrim Holiness Church
  of the Midwest
Midwest Holiness Association
  3891
Mienert, Rudolph William
  (1934-) 6147
Milan, Ill. 4419
Milby, L. G. see Milby, Luke
  G. (1876-)
Milby, Luke G. (1876-) 6148-
  6149
Miley, John (1813-1895) 2551-
  2552, 2909
Military chaplains see U.S.
  Army--Chaplains
Millenarians see Millennialism
Millennial Dawnism see Jehovah's Witnesses
Millennialism 581, 585, 594,
  605-606, 2679, 3411
Miller, Basil William (1897-)
  171, 1299, 1307, 1363, 1489,
  1778, 1876, 3435-3437, 5358,
  6150-6154, 6156, 6603
Miller, Mrs. Basil William
  see Miller, Esther Elnetta
  Kirk (1894-1970)
Miller, Esther Elnetta Kirk
  (1894-1970) 6155-6156
Miller, H. H. see Miller,
  Hale H. (1856-1922)
Miller, H. V. see Miller,
  Howard Vasser (1894-1948)

Miller, Hale H. (1856-1922) 6157
Miller, Howard Vasser (1894-1948) 1490-1493, 6158-6159
Miller, J. 6160
Miller, L. J. 419
Miller, L. L. (-1957) 3480, 3538
Miller, Merline Ivorita Mack (1930-) 6161
Miller, Nettie 6162-6163
Miller, Paul D. (1934-) 6164
Miller, Paul Elmer (1930-) 6165
Miller, Mrs. Paul Elmer see Miller, Merline Ivorita Mack (1930-)
Miller, Ruth Elma (1904-) 6166
Miller, S. 6167
Millikan, Roy William (-1949) 6168
Milliken, A. 6169
Mills, Abbie (-1909) 6170
Mills, Abbie C. (1829-1917) 935, 6171
Mills, Albert 2404
Mills, F. J. 936, 6172
Mills, H. T. see Mills, Howard T. (1887-1973)
Mills, Howard T. (1887-1973) 6173-6175
Mills, Paul M. 2385
Mills, Samuel E. (-1913) 6176
Mills, Mrs. Samuel E. see Mills, Abbie (-1909)
Milton, Pa. 4353
Miltonvale, Kan. 4503
Miltonvale College see Miltonvale Wesleyan College
Miltonvale Wesleyan College 4503
Mineer, Trula Frances (1928-) 6177
Ministers' Conference of Greenville College, Greenville, Ill., 12th, 1939 2661
Ministers' Conference of Greenville College, Greenville, Ill., 13th-14th, 1940-1941 2662
Mink, Nelson G. 1869, 1928
Minneapolis, Minn. 4341, 4442, 5235, 5237
Minnesota 2841, 4341, 4442, 6427-6428
Mintzer, F. S. see Mintzer, Frederick S. (1825-)
Mintzer, Frederick S. (1825-) 6178
Mischke, Carl 6179
Mischke, Mrs. Carl see Mischke, Velma
Mischke, Velma 6180
Mishawaka, Ind. 4351
Mission Advance (periodical) 2201, 5943
Mission Foi Evangile see Faith Mission
Missionary Ambassador (periodical) 3696
Missionary and Bible Training School see Bible Training Institute
Missionary Bands of the World 2161-2167, 5157-5158, 5823
Missionary Banner (periodical) 3767
Missionary Bible Institute 4504
Missionary Bureau of the National Association for the Promotion of Holiness see World Gospel Mission
Missionary Challenge (periodical) 2458
Missionary Challenger (periodical) 1235
Missionary Church 3238-3248, 4332, 4351, 4400, 4417, 4512
Missionary Church. General Board 3243
Missionary Church. General Conference 3241
Missionary Church. Merging General Conference 3240
Missionary Church Association 3768-3769, 4142-4153, 6502
Missionary Church Association. Board of Missions 4149
Missionary Evangel (periodical) 2440

Missionary Herald (periodical) 3280, 3392
Missionary Holiness Herald (periodical) see Missionary Herald (periodical)
Missionary Holiness Herald and Vanguard (periodical) see Missionary Herald (periodical)
Missionary Revivalist (periodical) 3877
Missionary Standard (periodical) see OMS Outreach (periodical)
Missionary Tidings (periodical) 1964, 2728
Missionary Training Institute see Trevecca Nazarene College
Missionary Voice of Evangelical Friends (periodical) 2305
Missionary Worker (periodical) 4151
Missionary World (periodical) 3440
Missions 744-746, 1046, 1058, 1171-1172, 1220-1221, 1682-1706, 2020, 2039, 2067, 2147-2148, 2239, 2299, 2313, 2342-2343, 2357, 2362-2363, 2390-2391, 2452-2454, 2600, 2608-2609, 2713-2718, 3006, 3111-3112, 3209-3211, 3246, 3263, 3412, 3536-3540, 3670, 3730, 3736, 3762, 3804-3805, 3876, 4033-4034, 4111-4120, 4149, 4212-4213, 4225, 4233, 4238, 4277, 5475
Missions, Foreign see Missions
Missions, Home see Church Extension
Missions, Medical 1698
Missions, Rescue see Rescue Missions
Mississippi 74, 83, 4384, 4497-4498, 4601
Missouri 144, 1229, 1236, 1249-1250, 1253, 1255, 1258, 1260, 1272, 1921, 4315, 4439, 4440, 4443, 4471, 4478, 4489-4490, 4504, 4505, 4509-4510, 4518-4520, 4536, 5857, 6020
Missouri Holiness College 4505
Mitchel, Louis F. 2146
Mitchell, Elizabeth Ann Oldacre (1876-) 1066, 6181-6182
Mitchell, Fred 4022
Mitchell, J. S. 6183
Mitchell, S. D. 4410
Mitchell, T. Crichton 1494
Mitchell, V. A. see Mitchell, Virgil Allen (1914-)
Mitchell, Virgil Allen (1914-) 6175, 6184-6186
Mitchum, Donie 6187
Mitchum, R. B. see Mitchum, Robert Bailey
Mitchum, Robert Bailey 6188
Mitchum, Mrs. Robert Bailey see Mitchum, Donie
Mizpah Academy 4506
Mketi, Daniel 6189
Mketi, Kufeni see Mketi, Daniel
Mkwanazi, Josefa 6190
Modernism 448, 1489, 2915, 4068
Modernist-fundamentalist controversy see Modernism
Moe, Mrs. Cevira Ann (1848-1909) 6191-6192
Moldenhawer, J. V. 27
Molina, Lauro Sol see Sol Molina, Lauro (1911-)
Moline, Ill. 4419
Money 6578
Monk, Robert Clarence (1930-) 2568-2569, 2571
Monroe, N. C. 5213, 5870
Montafio, Walter Manuel 2734
Montana 4524
Montano, Walter Manuel 3384
Monte Ne, Ark. 4533
Montgomery, Area (-1965) 6193
Montgomery, Mrs. Carrie Judd (1858-) 6194-6197
Montgomery, G. H. 4249, 4251-4252

Montgomery, J. W. see Montgomery, James William (1898-)

Montgomery, James William (1898-) 1627, 1823-1824, 6198

Moody, D. L. see Moody, Dwight Lyman (1837-1899)

Moody, Dwight Lyman (1837-1899) 3960-3961, 6199-6201

Moody Bible Institute 3937

Moon, Wesley G. (1911-) 4454, 6202

Moore, Altha Honea (-1973) 6203-6204

Moore, Arthur James (1888-) 6205

Moore, Charles 6219

Moore, David Hastings (1838-1915) 6206

Moore, Ernest William 1599

Moore, George Chapman 5025

Moore, J. E., Jr. see Moore, Josiah Erben, Jr.

Moore, J. E., Sr. see Moore, Josiah Erben (1899-)

Moore, Mrs. J. E., Sr. see Moore, Altha Honea (-1973)

Moore, J. E. L. see Moore, John Edgar Littleton (-1935)

Moore, J. M. 6207

Moore, John 2533

Moore, John E. 6208

Moore, John Edgar Littleton (-1935) 6209

Moore, Josiah Erben (1889-) 6210

Moore, Josiah Erben, Jr. 6211

Moore, Josiah Erben, Sr. see Moore, Josiah Erben (1889-)

Moore, Mrs. Josiah Erben, Sr. see Moore, Altha Honea (-1973)

Moore, Mark Reynolds (1916-) 1264, 1308, 6212-6213

Moore, Norman Lowell (1916-) 6214

Moose Jaw, Sask. 4302

Moose Jaw Bible College see Aldersgate College

Moose Jaw Bible School see Aldersgate College

Morales, C. E. see Morales, Christobal E. (1892-)

Morales, Christobal E. (1892-) 6215

Morehouse, A. C. see Morehouse, Alonzo Church (1820-1903)

Morehouse, Alonzo Church (1820-1903) 6216-6217

Morehouse, Frank Eugene (1854-1908) 420, 6218-6219

Morgan, Clifford L. 6220

Morgan, G. Campbell see Morgan, George Campbell (1863-1945)

Morgan, George Campbell (1863-1945) 3962-3965, 4009

Morgan, H. P. 2460

Morgan, Mattie Mallory 6221

Morgan, Patrick 5040

Mormonism 866, 1179, 1749

Morris, B. S. see Morris, Benjamin S. (-1914)

Morris, Benjamin S. (-1914) 6222

Morris, Mrs. C. H. see Morris, Lelia Naylor (1862-1929)

Morris, Elsie Emma (1929-) 6223

Morris, Lelia Naylor (1862-1929) 6224-6225

Morris, Samuel (1872-1893) 6226-6239

Morris, Thomas A. (1794-1874) 5567

Morrison, H. C. see Morrison, Henry Clay (1857-1942)

Morrison, Henry Clay (1857-1942) 108, 187, 421, 584-587, 630, 755, 853, 877, 937-938, 2507, 3058, 3074, 3858, 4324, 6241-6251

Morrison, J. G. see Morrison, Joseph Grant (1871-1939)

Morrison, John Arch (1893-1965) 1188, 6252-6253

Morrison, Joseph Grant (1871-1939) 1495-1497, 1636, 1825, 3899, 6254-6258
Morristown, N. J. 2925
Morrow, Abbie Clemens 110, 209, 216-217, 557, 559, 6259-6260
Morrow, Ralph Ernest 3051
Morse, Deacon see Morse, George M.
Morse, George M. 6261
Mosely, Harriett 88
Mosteller, Earl 6262
Mosteller, Mrs. Earl see Mosteller, Gladys
Mosteller, Gladys 6263
Mota, Jose S. (1885-) 6264
Motherwell, Scot. 4358
Motion pictures see Moving pictures
Mott, Bernard E. 5244
Mott, Edward (1866-1954) 2275, 2285, 5244, 6265-6266
Mott, John Raleigh (1865-1955) 3036
Moule, H. C. G. see Moule, Handley Carr Glyn (1841-1920)
Moule, Handley Carr Glyn (1841-1920) 3966-3970, 4023, 6267
Moulton, C. O. see Moulton, Cyrus Orlando (-1909)
Moulton, Cyrus Orlando (-1909) 6268-6269
Moulton, M. Kimber see Moulton, Morris Kimber (1904-)
Moulton, Morris Kimber (1904-) 6270
Mt. Carmel High School 4507
Mt. Hermon Academy and Grammar School see Eden Grove Academy and Grammar School
Mount Vernon, Ohio 4508
Mount Vernon Nazarene College 4508
Mt. Zion Bible School 4509
Mountain Lake Park, Md. 983
Mountain State Bible School see Mountain State Christian School
Mountain State Christian School 4511
Mountain View Bible College 4512
Mourer, C. C. see Mourer, Charles Calvin (1882-)
Mourer, Charles Calvin (1882-) 3492, 3530-3534
Mouzon, Edwin DuBose (1869-1937) 6271-6272
Movies see Moving pictures
Moving pictures 173, 188, 1356, 3158
Mozambique 5544
Mudge, James (1844-1918) 2910-2914, 3072, 6273
Mudge, James (1844-1918) Growth in holiness toward perfection 2891, 2901, 2929
Muelder, Walter George (1907-) 1258, 2779
Mueller, Duane K. (1928-) 6274
Mueller, E. S. 3471
Müller, George (1805-1898) 559
Mulder, Chester O. 6275
Mullen, Handley C. 1007
Mullen, Wilbur Handley (1919-) 6276
Muller, D. N. 6277
Mumme, James H. 2155, 2609
Munger, Charles 868, 6278
Munhall, L. W. see Munhall, Leander Whitcomb (1843-1934)
Munhall, Leander Whitcomb (1843-1934) 2877, 2915, 6279
Munro, Bertha (1887-) 1364, 1405-1407, 6280-6281, 6303
Munroe, Mother see Munroe, Elizabeth (1793-1873)
Munroe, Elizabeth (1793-1873) 6282-6283
Munroe, Florence 6284-6285
Murdick, P. H. see Murdick, Perry Harvey (1879-)
Murdick, Perry Harvey (1879-) 6286

Murphree, Jon Tal (1936-   )
4855
Murray, Andrew (1828-1917)
3930-3932, 3936-3939, 3971-3979
Murray, M. Grace (-1934)
6287
Murray, O. E.   420
Murrish, Thomas   6288
Muse, Dan Thomas (1882-1950)
4256, 4291, 6289-6290
Music see Church music
Music, Church see Church music
Musselman, Mrs. David see Lambert, Rose (1878-   )
Mussman, Robert Byron   2572
Mussolini, Benito (1883-1945)
4092
Myers, Florence R. see Scofield, Florence R. Myers
Mynett, Frederick G.   6291

Nakada, Juji (1870-1939)   3379, 3451, 5101, 5105, 5861, 6292-6293
Nampa, Ida.   4525, 4555-4556
Narcotic habit   7061
Nardi, Michele (1850-1914)
6294-6295
Nash, David   6296
Nashville, Tenn.   1243, 4577-4578, 5330, 5641
Nashville, Tenn. First Church of the Nazarene   1950
Nast, A. J. see Nast, Albert Julius (1846-1936)
Nast, Albert Julius (1846-1936)
6297
Nast, William (1807-1899)
2853, 6298-6299
National Association for the Promotion of Holiness see Christian Holiness Association
National Association for the Promotion of Holiness. Foreign Missionary Department see World Gospel Mission
National Association for the Promotion of Holiness. Missionary Bureau see World Gospel Mission
National Association for the Promotion of Holiness. Missionary Department see World Gospel Mission
National Association for the Promotion of Holiness. Missionary Society see World Gospel Mission
National Camp Meeting Association for the Promotion of Holiness see Christian Holiness Association
National Christian Council of India, Burma and Ceylon
3036
National Holiness Association see Christian Holiness Association
National Holiness Missionary Society see World Gospel Mission
National Publishing Association for the Promotion of Holiness
141, 196, 286, 408, 746, 864, 893
Naylor, Jasper Ross (1908-   )
6300
Nazarene (periodical) see Nazarene Messenger (periodical)
Nazarene Bible College, Colorado Springs, Colo.   4513
Nazarene Bible College, Florida, S. Afr.   4514
Nazarene Bible College, Thornleigh, Austl.   4515
Nazarene Bible Institute, Institute, W. Va. see Nazarene Training College
Nazarene Bible Institute, Pilot Point, Tex. see Bible Training Institute
Nazarene Bible School   4516
Nazarene Bible School and Academy see Bresee College
Nazarene Indian Bible School
4517
Nazarene Indian School see Nazarene Indian Bible School

Nazarene Messenger (Los Angeles) 1252
Nazarene Messenger (Nampa, Ida.) 4528
Nazarene Missionary Sanitarium and Institute see Samaritan Hospital School of Nursing
Nazarene Pastor (periodical) 1290, 1738
Nazarene Preacher (periodical) see Preacher's Magazine (periodical)
Nazarene Publishing House 1756, 1758
Nazarene Theological Seminary 567, 1475a, 1567, 1726, 4518-4520
Nazarene Training College 4521
Nazarene University see Point Loma College
Neal, Harry Edward (1906-) 3655
Neal, Hazel G. 1172, 5726
Near East 1922-1924, 3774-3775, 4136, 5435, 7155
Nease, Floyd William (1893-1930) 1827, 6301-6303
Nease, O. J. see Nease, Orval John (1891-1950)
Nease, Orval John (1891-1950) 1827-1828, 6302-6306
Nease, Stephen W. (1925-) 6307
Nebraska 3047, 4381, 4464
Nee, G. C. see Nee, Gilbert Chibee
Nee, Gilbert Chibee 108, 4324, 6308
Neely, B. F. see Neely, Benjamin Franklin (1876-1967)
Neely, Benjamin Franklin (1876-1967) 1498, 1589, 6309
Nees, L. G. (-1954) 6310
Neff, H. 6311
Neff, William H. (1902-) 6312
Negroes 68, 660, 4155-4156, 4163, 4171, 5376-5377, 5721, 5889, 6118, 6227-6239, 6507, 6753-6756, 7042, 7085
Neill, Stephen Charles (1900-) 31, 4034, 4965
Nelson, Eldon Byron (1926-) 6313
Nelson, Mrs. Eldon Byron see Nelson, Wilda Arlene (1926-)
Nelson, Flora B. 6314
Nelson, J. O. see Nelson, John O. (-1912)
Nelson, J. Robert 2492
Nelson, John O. (-1912) 6315
Nelson, Marven O. 2683, 3185
Nelson, Thomas Hiram (1863-) 422-424, 588, 2163, 5157, 6316-6317
Nelson, Mrs. Thomas Hiram see Nelson, Flora B.
Nelson, Walter O. 2621
Nelson, Wilda Arlene (1926-) 6318
Nelson, William Hamilton (1878-) 4822
Neosho Rapids, Kan. 4522
Neosho Rapids Seminary 4522
Neufeld, Frank A. 6319
New Brunswick 4340, 4496
New England 1267, 7049
New England Christian Herald (periodical) see Zion's Herald (periodical)
New Florence, Mo. 4439
New Guinea 1925, 4137, 4879
New Hampshire 5144
New Jersey 126-128, 2925, 3048, 3690, 4304, 4306, 4603
New London, Ind. 4438
New Mexico 4405, 4517
New Testament Church of Christ 3441-3449, 4952
New York (city) 91, 117, 985-986, 1242, 2925, 2949, 3008, 6140, 6387-6389, 6391-6392, 6394-6395, 7023, 7180-7181
New York (city). Door of Hope 91, 117, 5987-5988, 6674, 7180
New York (state) 91, 117, 127, 196, 985-987, 1242, 2193-2198, 2925, 2949, 3008,

3032, 3120-3121, 3124,
3129, 3467, 3907-3912,
4299, 4392-4394, 4424,
4541, 4550, 5261, 5740-
5741, 6192, 6217, 6579-
6582, 7127
New York Tuesday Meeting
see Tuesday Meeting, New
York
Newberg, Ore. 4423
Newberry, Gene W. 1089,
1103, 1188
Newberrytown, Pa. 4441
Newby, J. Edwin (1898-)
2323-2324, 2335-2336
Newby, John Melvin (1928-)
6320
Newby, Mrs. John Melvin
see Newby, Rebecca Jean
Hall (1929-)
Newby, Rebecca Jean Hall
(1929-) 6321
Newcomb, George T. 2879
Newcomb, Hugh 3211, 4367
Newman, John Henry (1801-
1890) 2559
Newman, John Philip (1826-
1899) 6217
News and Views (periodical)
2729
News from home (periodical)
2198
Newsom, Reuben J. 6322
Newton, G. see Newton,
George
Newton, George 6323
Nfofane see Dhlamini, Samuel
Niagara Christian College
4523
Nicaragua 1926
Nicholson, Roy Stephen
(1903-) 2063, 2269, 2463,
3146, 3179, 3192, 3237,
4467, 5240, 6324-6325
Nielson, John Bechtold (1918-)
6326-6327
Nigeria 3776, 4138, 4673,
4701-4704
Nihon Horinesu Kyodan (Japan
Holiness Church) 3450-
3451, 6293
Nihon Nazaren Kyodan (Church
of the Nazarene) 1932
Ninde, William Xavier (1832-
1901) 605
Nippon Araiance Kyodan (Japan
Alliance Church) 4132
Nofsinger, George F. 3225
Norbeck, Mildred E. 3282-
3283, 3287, 6328-6329
North, C. C. 2834-2835
North American Indians see
Indians of North America
North Carolina 3231, 4241-
4243, 4290, 4296-4299, 4352,
4397, 4415, 4430, 4468,
4473-4474, 5213, 5482, 5870,
7034
North Chili, N. Y. 4550
North Dakota 988, 2781, 2827,
5751, 6255-6257, 6917
North Dakota Methodist (periodi-
cal) see Holiness Messen-
ger (periodical)
North Pacific Evangelistic Insti-
tute see Cascade College
North Scituate, R. I. 4392-
4394
Northern Bible College see
Canadian Nazarene College
Northern Independent (periodical)
820
Northern Ireland see Ulster
Northrup, A. O. 3121
Northville, N. Y. 4299, 7127
Northwest, Pacific see Pacific
Northwest
Northwest Friend (periodical)
2393
Northwest Holiness School see
Northwest Nazarene College
Northwest Indian Bible School
4524
Northwest Nazarene College
1356, 4525-4528
Northwest Texas Holiness Asso-
ciation 2168-2171
Northwest Yearly Meeting of
Friends Churches see
Friends, Society of. Oregon
Yearly Meeting
Northwestern Holiness Associa-
tion see Holiness Methodist
Church (1911-1969)

Nova Scotia 4340
Novak, Frank (1884-) 6330-6331
Noyes, A. D. (-1923) 6332
Noyes, Mrs. A. D. see Noyes, Sophia (-1933)
Noyes, Sophia (-1933) 6333
Nuelsen, John Louis (1867-1946) 2953
Nusbaum, C. S. see Nusbaum, Cyrus Silvester (1861-1937)
Nusbaum, Cyrus Silvester (1861-1937) 6334
Nussey, Wesley B. (1912-) 6335
Nutter, Charles Sumner (1842-) 3003-3004, 3090-3091
Nygren, Ellis Herbert 2573

OMS International see Oriental Missionary Society
OMS Outreach (periodical) 3383
Oakdale, Ky. 4529
Oakdale Vocational School 4529
Oakington, Md. 128
Oblinger, Carl D. 4886
O'Brien, Michael F. 5193
Ocean Grove, N. J. 2844-2851, 6360
Ocean Grove Camp Meeting Association of the Methodist Episcopal Church 2844-2851, 6360, 6872-6873
Ocean Grove Times (periodical) 2851
Oceania 1927-1930
Ockenga, Harold John (1905-) 3792
Ohio 196, 952, 989-992, 2838, 4372, 4386, 4396, 4425-4427, 4492-4494, 4553-4554, 5895, 6225, 6622, 6847, 7039
Ohio Infantry. 122d regt. (1862-1865) 2952
Ohio Yearly Meeting of Friends Church see Friends, Society of. Ohio Yearly Meeting

O'Kane, Tullius Clinton (1830-1912) 2999-3000
Oke, Norman R. 1628
Okinawa 1931
Oklahoma 750, 993-994, 1933-1936, 2621, 4291, 4336, 4342-4347, 4355, 4390, 4436, 4463, 4475, 4563, 4989, 5218, 5772, 6290, 6588-6591
Oklahoma. Holiness Association see Holiness Association of Oklahoma
Oklahoma City, Okla. 4355, 4563
Oklahoma Holiness College see Bethany Nazarene College
Olathe, Kan. 4502
Old Cove, Ark. 4447
Old Methodist (periodical) see Herald, a Journal of Full Salvation and the Way of Faith (periodical)
Old Paths (periodical) 821
Old Paths Bible School 4530
Oldenburger, Teunis 113
Oldfield, Walter Herbert (1879-) 4129
Oldham, Dale see Oldham, William Dale (1903-)
Oldham, W. Dale see Oldham, William Dale (1903-)
Oldham, William Dale (1903-) 1072-1074, 1189-1190, 6336
Oliver, George Fletcher (1853-) 4695
Oliver Gospel Mission, Columbia, S. C. see Columbia, S. C. Oliver Gospel Mission
Olivet, Ill. 4531
Olivet College see Olivet Nazarene College
Olivet Nazarene College 4531
Olivet University see Olivet Nazarene College
Olmstead, B. L. see Olmstead, Benjamin Luce (1886-)
Olmstead, Benjamin Luce (1886-) 6337
Olmstead, William Backus (1862-1941) 2704-2707,

2739, 5544
Olsen, Abner C. (-1958) 6338
Olsen, Gordon T. 6339
Olsen, H. J. see Olsen, Henry John (1879-1972)
Olsen, Henry John (1879-1972) 3493, 6340-6341
Olsen, Mrs. Henry John see Olsen, Mary Lillian Brown (1883-1942)
Olsen, J. O. 4189
Olsen, Kenneth I. 6342
Olsen, Mary Lillian Brown (1883-1942) 6343
Olson, Bessie Goldie (1909-1973) 6247
Olson, Heddie T. 6344-6345
Olson, O. Joe (1910-) 6346
Olson, Olof Joe Julius see Olson, O. Joe (1910-)
Olt, George Russell (1895-) 6347
Ontario 1263, 2618-2619, 3777, 4311, 4360, 4370, 4373, 4400, 4487, 4523, 5696
Oral Roberts Evangelistic Association 4264-4265
Oregon 1268, 4379, 4423, 4592, 4598-4599, 6436
Oregon Yearly Meeting of Friends Church see Friends, Society of. Oregon Yearly Meeting of Friends Church
Oriental and Inter-American Missionary Standard (periodical) see OMS Outreach (periodical)
Oriental Missionary Society 3360-3388, 5100-5103, 5105-5107, 5261, 5860-5861, 6285, 6293, 6398, 6857
Oriental Missionary Standard (periodical) see OMS Outreach (periodical)
(Original) Church of God 4226-4227
Orjala, Paul Richard (1925-) 1895-1896, 6348-6351
Orleans, Neb. 4381
Orleans Seminary see Central College
Ormston, Mark D. (1890-) 6352
Orr, Charles Ebert (1861-) 1079, 1104-1106, 1179
Orsborn, Albert 3656, 6353
Ortlip, Aimee E. 4453
Ortlip, H. Willard 4453
Osborn, Leon Clarence 1882, 6354-6355
Osborn, Lucy Reed Drake (1844-) 425, 6356-6357
Osborn, T. H. 6358
Osborn, W. B. see Osborn, William Bramwell (1832-1902)
Osborn, William Bramwell (1832-1902) 6359-6360
Osborn, Mrs. William Bramwell see Osborn, Lucy Reed Drake (1844-)
Osepoff, V. G. 6361
O'Sullivan, Dorothea 40
Other Sheep (periodical) 1739
Ottawa, Ont. 4311
Otterbein, Philip William (1726-1813) 3718
Outler, Albert Cook (1908-) 2538
Overholt, Elbert David (1925-) 6362
Overland Park, Kan. 4471
Owen, E. 6363
Owen, G. Frederick see Owen, George Frederick (1897-)
Owen, George Frederick (1897-) 6364-6371
Owen, George S. (1882-1962) 6372
Owen, John Frederick (1881-) 6373
Owen, Joseph Parkes (1886-) 896, 4480, 6374
Owosso, Mich. 4465-4467
Owosso Bible College see John Wesley College, Owosso, Mich.
Owosso College see John Wesley College, Owosso, Mich.
Oxford. Union Meeting for the Promotion of Scriptural Holiness, 1874 see Union Meeting for the Promotion of

Scriptural Holiness. Oxford, 1874
Oxford Movement 2559
Ozark Industrial College 4533

Pacific Bible College, Huntington Park, Calif. see Azusa Pacific College
Pacific Bible College, Los Angeles, Calif. see Point Loma College
Pacific Bible Institute 4534
Pacific Coast Bible Institute 4535
Pacific Coast Holiness Association 822
Pacific College see George Fox College
Pacific Friend (periodical) 2314
Pacific Herald of Holiness (periodical) 822
Pacific Northwest 1268, 7061, 7111
Pacifism see Peace
Packard, Alpheus Spring (1798-1884) 7045
Paddock, Father see Paddock, Benjamin Green (1789-1871)
Paddock, B. G. see Paddock, Benjamin Green (1789-1871)
Paddock, Benjamin Green (1789-1871) 6375
Page, I. E. see Page, Isaac E. (1839-1926)
Page, Isaac E. (1839-1926) 426, 2533, 6376
Paige, Clara R. (1869-) 2224, 7165
Paine, Stephen William (1908-) 3158, 6377-6380
Palestine 5477, 5479, 5911, 6365-6368, 6370, 7098, 7155
Palmer, M. W. see Palmer, Miles W.
Palmer, Miles W. 6381
Palmer, Phoebe Worrell (1807-1874) 109, 135, 242, 427-430, 2907, 5418-5419, 6382-6389
Palmer, Sarah A. Worrell Lankford (1806-1896) 6390-6392
Palmer, W. C. see Palmer, Walter Clark (1804-1883)
Palmer, Walter Clark (1804-1883) 431, 5567, 6383, 6393-6395
Palmer, Mrs. Walter Clark see Palmer, Phoebe Worrell (1807-1874); Palmer, Sarah A. Worrell Lankford (1806-1896)
Palmertree, Duran M. 4212
Panama 2763
Pannabecker, Ray Plowman (1913-) 6396
Papadavidiadou, John Paul see Pappas, Paul John (1898-)
Pappas, Paul John (1898-) 432, 636, 6397-6400
Paraguay 2764
Paris, Ohio 4372
Paris Mountain, S. C. 4449-4451
Parker, Fitzgerald Sale (1863-1936) 2811
Parker, J. Fred see Parker, John Fred
Parker, John (1825-1911) 6401
Parker, John Fred 1872-1874, 2405, 4375, 4953
Parker, Robert Allerton 6773-6774, 6800
Parkhead, Scot. see Glasgow, Scot.
Parkhead Holiness Bible School see Pentecostal Bible School
Parr, F. O. 1391
Parral, Mex. 4460
Parrott, A. L. see Parrott, Alonzo Leslie (1891-)
Parrott, Alonzo Leslie (1891-) 6402
Parrott, Leslie (1922-) 1288, 1309-1311, 1365-1366, 1499, 1600, 1721, 6403
Parrott, Lora Lee Montgomery (1923-) 1310, 1318, 1408, 6404
Parsons, Ida Dake 2164, 5158
Pasadena, Calif 1871, 4543-4548, 7109

Pasadena, Calif. Bresee Avenue Church of the Nazarene 1300
Pasadena, Calif. University Pentecostal Church of the Nazarene 1871, 3459
Pasadena College see Point Loma College
Pasadena University see Point Loma College
Pascoe, W. G. 2533
Pastoral psychology see Pastoral theology
Pastoral rotation see Itineracy (Church polity)
Pastoral theology 747-755, 1713-1724, 2587, 2722, 3008-3010, 3347, 3806, 4234
Pastors see Clergy
Pastor's Bulletin (periodical) see South African Nazarene (periodical)
Pattee, John W. (1903-) 6405-6406
Pattee, Mrs. John W. see Pattee, Lillian Kerr
Pattee, Lillian Kerr 6407
Patterson, James Howard (1867-) 6408-6409
Pattison, Mary Winifred Dunn 3344, 7206
Paul, Cecil Rowland 1722
Paul, George Harold (1910-) 4291, 6290
Paul, John Haywood (1877-1967) 89-90, 134, 172, 433-436, 553, 589-590, 637-638, 878-881, 939, 4325, 5803, 6410-6411, 6953-6954
Paul, Thomas E. 2002
Pauline Advocate (periodical) 823
Pauline Holiness College 4536
Pauline Mission Chronicle (periodical) 824
Paulk, Earl P. 4221
Paulk, John Chester (1876-) 6412
Paulson, David (1868-1916) 6413-6414

Pawar, Dagadu 6415
Pawar, Gopal Govind 6416
Payson, Edward (1783-1827) 2135
Payton, Jacob Simpson (1884-) 2829
Peace 1032a, 2368, 2385
Peace of mind 4250
Pearce, Ernest Harold (1865-1930) 5626
Pearce, William (1862-1947) 2636, 2701, 6417
Pearse, Mark Guy (1842-1930) 437, 2916-2918, 4805, 6418, 7319-7320
Pearson, B. H. see Pearson, Benjamin Harold (1893-)
Pearson, Ben see Pearson, Benjamin Harold (1893-)
Pearson, Benjamin Harold (1893-) 2734, 2763, 3362, 3380, 5103, 5106-5107, 6419
Peavey, Leroy Deering (1876-1937) 6420
Peck, George (1797-1876) 105, 2831, 2919-2920, 3834, 6421-6422
Peck, Mrs. Harlan C. see Peck, Kathryn Blackburn (1904-)
Peck, J. O. see Peck, Jonas Oramel (1836-)
Peck, J. Oramel see Peck, Jonas Oramel (1836-)
Peck, J. T. see Peck, Jesse Truesdell (1811-1883)
Peck, Jesse Truesdell (1811-1883) 438-439, 882, 1555, 2136, 2861, 2921-2924, 2943, 3020, 3843, 6423
Peck, Jonas Oramel (1836-) 2948, 6424
Peck, Kathryn Blackburn (1904-) 1857, 6425
Pedobaptism see Baptism
Pegler, George (1799-) 6426-6428
Peirce, B. K. see Peirce, Bradford Kinney (1819-1889)
Peirce, Bradford Kinney (1819-1889) 6429
Peirce, E. W. 6430

Peisker, Armor D.   3584, 3591, 6431
Pelikan, Jaroslav (1923-   )   52-53
Peniel, Tex.   4537
Peniel College   207, 311, 4537
Peniel Herald (periodical)   2176
Peniel Holiness Association   995
Peniel Missionary Society   see Peniel Missions
Peniel Missions   2172-2177, 5333, 5961, 6516
Peniel Missions in Egypt   2177
Peniel University   see Peniel College
Peninsula Methodist (periodical)   2905
Penitentiaries   see Prisons
Penn, Joseph H. (1850-1934)   6432
Penn View Bible Institute   4538
Penn Wesleyan College   4539
Penner, Opal Good   6433
Penner, William A.   6434
Penner, Mrs. William A.   see Penner, Opal Good
Pennington, Levi Talbott (1875-   )   6435-6436
Penns Creek, Pa.   4538
Pennsylvania   127-129, 995, 1269, 2397-2398, 3117-3118, 4353, 4435, 4441, 4499, 4538-4539, 4572-4576, 4580, 4613
Pennsylvania Military Academy   4984
Pentecost, George Frederick (1842-1920)   3980
Pentecost (periodical)   see Standard Bearer of Bible Holiness (periodical)
Pentecost Bands   see Missionary Bands of the World
Pentecost Bands of the World   see Missionary Bands of the World
Pentecost Century (periodical)   825
Pentecost Herald (periodical)   2166
Pentecost-Pilgrim Church   see Pilgrim Church
Pentecost Trumpet (periodical)   see Western Record (periodical)
Pentecostal Advocate (periodical)   311, 2075
Pentecostal Alliance   see Pentecostal Mission
Pentecostal Assemblies of Canada   4199
Pentecostal Assemblies of Canada. National Publications Committee   5010b
Pentecostal Baptists   see Holiness Baptists
Pentecostal Bible and Training School   see Trevecca Nazarene College
Pentecostal Bible College   4540
Pentecostal Brethren in Christ   1040-1041
Pentecostal Christian (periodical)   826
Pentecostal Church of Scotland   3452-3456, 4540, 6689-6690
Pentecostal Church of the Nazarene   see Church of the Nazarene (1908-   )
Pentecostal churches   see Pentecostal Movement
Pentecostal Collegiate Institute   see Eastern Nazarene College
Pentecostal Collegiate Institute and Bible Training School   see Eastern Nazarene College
Pentecostal Era and National Advocate of Perfect Love (periodical)   827
Pentecostal Evangelist (periodical)   828
Pentecostal Free-Will Baptist Church   4205, 5482
Pentecostal Herald (periodical)   see Herald, a Journal of Full Salvation and the Way of Faith (periodical)
Pentecostal Herald and the Way of Faith (periodical)   see Herald, a Journal of Full

Salvation and the Way of Faith (periodical)
Pentecostal Holiness Advocate (periodical) 4278
Pentecostal Holiness Church (1900-1911) 4241-4243
Pentecostal Holiness Church 4244-4291, 4401, 4415, 4475, 4533, 4561, 4563-4564, 5482, 5637, 5872, 6290, 6588-6591
Pentecostal Holiness Church. Conferences. Virginia 4280
Pentecostal Holiness Church. Department of Foreign Missions 4277
Pentecostal Holiness Church in Africa 4288
Pentecostal Holiness Church in China 4289
Pentecostal Holiness Church in North Carolina 4290
Pentecostal Holiness Church in Oklahoma 4297, 6588-6591
Pentecostal League see League of Prayer
Pentecostal League of Prayer see League of Prayer
Pentecostal Mission 2178-2192, 4577-4578, 5330, 6022-6025
Pentecostal Mission Bible School 4541
Pentecostal Mission Prayer Union see League of Prayer
Pentecostal Movement 867, 4154-4202, 4199
Pentecostal Movement in Canada 4199, 5496
Pentecostal Movement in Great Britain 4200
Pentecostal Movement in Latin America 4201-4202
Pentecostal Rescue Evangelist (periodical) 2202
Pentecostal Rescue Mission 2193-2198, 3910, 4541
Pentecostal Rescue Mission. Yearly Meeting 2195
Pentecostal Sunday School Magazine for Teachers (periodical) 4279

Pentecostal Union see Pillar of Fire Church
Pentecostalism see Pentecostal Movement
Penuel (periodical) 829
Peoples Bible College 4542
People's Bible School and College see John Wesley College, Greensboro, N. C.
People's Christian Movement see People's Methodist Church
Peoples Church, Toronto see Toronto. Peoples Church
People's Methodist Church 3104-3105
People's Mission Church 2199-2202, 4389, 5943, 6978
Peploe, Hanmer William Webb- see Webb-Peploe, Hanmer William (1837-1923)
Pepper, E. I. D. see Pepper, Eleuthera I. D. (-1908)
Pepper, Eleuthera I. D. (-1908) 220, 305, 917, 940, 942, 5462, 5741, 6437, 6527, 7057
Perez, Benjamin 6438
Perez, Francisco R. (1889-) 6439
Perkins, Ethel (1875-) 6440
Perkins, Floyd J. 1259
Perry, Gertrude see Tracy, Gertrude Perry
Perry, James H. (1811-1863) 2907
Perry, James H. (1811-1863) Reply to Professor Mattison's Calm review 2926
Perry, Ralph Barton (1876-1957) 5184
Perry, Ralph Edward 1601
Pershall, Roscoe 1629
Peru 1937-1938, 2429, 3597, 4201, 7260-7262, 7265
Peters, John Leland 2800-2801
Peters, Madison Clinton (1859-1918) 941
Peterson, Fern Annabelle Nelson (1916-) 6441
Peterson, Lily M. (-1908) 6442
Peterson, Martin Luther

(1912-) 6443
Peterson, Mrs. Martin Luther see Peterson, Fern Annabelle Nelson (1916-)
Pettee, I. I. 6444
Pettengill, William T. 2146
Petticord, E. W. see Petticord, Emory W. (1880-)
Petticord, Emory W. (1880-) 1670, 1987, 6445
Petticord, Paul Parker (1907-) 6446
Pettit, Charles Warren (1869-1931) 6447
Peyton, Claudie (1894-) 6448-6449
Phaup, Bernard Hugo (1912-) 6450-6452
Phelan, Macum (1874-) 3052-3053, 3099-3100
Phelps, Alexander Alonzo (1836-1904) 440
Philadelphia, Pa. 646, 1269, 4435, 5384-5385
Philanthropy see Charities
Philippine Islands 1939-1942, 2765, 3598, 6474, 6880
Phillippe, E. E. see Phillippe, Edward Everett (1904-)
Phillippe, Edward Everett (1904-) 6453
Phillippe, Mrs. Edward Everett see Phillippe, Eunice Leona (1903-)
Phillippe, Eunice Leona (1903-) 6454
Phillippe, Paul Samuel (1929-) 6455
Phillippe, Mrs. Paul Samuel see Phillippe, Vivian Virginia Hart (1932-)
Phillippe, Sally see Phillippe, Vivian Virginia Hart (1932-)
Phillippe, Vivian Virginia Hart (1932-) 6456
Phillips, Dean Howard (1921-) 6457
Phillips, Dean Howard, Jr. see Phillips, Dean Howard (1921-)
Phillips, Mrs. Dean Howard, Jr. see Phillips, Elizabeth Ann Clark (1922-)
Phillips, Elizabeth Ann Clark (1922-) 6458
Phillips, Eugenia see Coats, Eugenia Phillips (1883-)
Phillips, Isaac N. 1979, 2043, 2312, 5881
Phillips, Koy Wright (1915-) 6459
Phillips, Philip (1834-1895) 2708-2709
Phillips, W. I. see Phillips, William I.
Phillips, William I. 6460
Philo, L. C. (1907-1972) 1602, 6461
Phoenix, Ariz. 4530
Pickett, J. Waskom see Pickett, Jarrell Waskom (1890-)
Pickett, Jarrell Waskom (1890-) 3036, 6462
Pickett, L. L. see Pickett, Leander Lycurgus (1859-1928)
Pickett, Leander Lycurgus (1859-1928) 99, 111, 264, 327, 338, 441-443, 484, 581, 591-594, 620, 718-726, 854-855, 883-887, 972, 2174, 3068, 3075-3077, 3181, 6463
Pickett, Waskom see Pickett, Jarrell Waskom (1890-)
Pierce, Alfred Mann (1874-) 3098
Pierce, D. Rand see Pierce, David Rand
Pierce, David Rand 6464
Pierce, G. M. 6465
Pierce, L. see Pierce, Lovick (1785-1879)
Pierce, Lovick (1785-1879) 3078, 6466
Pierce, Phoebe 6467
Pierce, Robert 6468
Pierson, Arthur Tappan (1837-1911) 3927, 3981-3983, 4010, 5493
Pietism 648, 662, 2007
Pike, John M. 209, 6469-6470
Pike, Mignon 2390
Pike, Ted 2390
Pilgrim (periodical) 830, 3461

Pilgrim Bible College. Kernersville, N. C. see Kernersville Wesleyan Academy; Kernersville Wesleyan College
Pilgrim Bible College, Pasadena, Calif. 4543
Pilgrim Bible Institute see Western Pilgrim College
Pilgrim Church 3457-3461, 4446, 4543
Pilgrim Evangelistic Institute see Western Pilgrim College
Pilgrim Holiness Advocate (periodical) 3519, 3553, 4671, 5533, 7140, 7241
Pilgrim Holiness Church 1010, 3221-3222, 3462-3601, 4336, 4353, 4356, 4360, 4389, 4420, 4430, 4465-4467, 4473-4474, 4476, 4504, 4539, 4543, 4600, 4781-4782, 4974, 5205, 5302, 5338, 5434, 5533, 5644, 5683, 5875, 6174-6175, 6341, 6485, 6531-6533, 6746-6747, 6847, 6853, 6865, 6877, 6880, 6888, 6896, 6983, 7140, 7241, 7299
Pilgrim Holiness Church. Department of Foreign Missions see Pilgrim Holiness Church. Department of World Missions
Pilgrim Holiness Church. Department of Sunday Schools and Youth 5302
Pilgrim Holiness Church. Department of World Missions 3470, 3538-3542, 3544, 3581, 3584, 3590-3593, 3596, 3599-3600, 6746
Pilgrim Holiness Church. Districts. Michigan 3466
Pilgrim Holiness Church. Districts. Pennsylvania-New Jersey 3468
Pilgrim Holiness Church. Districts. New York 3467
Pilgrim Holiness Church. Foreign Missionary Office see Pilgrim Holiness Church. Department of World Missions
Pilgrim Holiness Church. Foreign Missions Department see Pilgrim Holiness Church. Department of World Missions
Pilgrim Holiness Church. Forward Movement Committee 3479
Pilgrim Holiness Church. General Board 3462, 3472
Pilgrim Holiness Church. General Conference see Pilgrim Holiness Church. International Conference
Pilgrim Holiness Church. International Conference 1010, 3255, 3465
Pilgrim Holiness Church. Missionary office 3577, 3580, 3585-3586, 3589
Pilgrim Holiness Church. Pilgrim Information Agency 3469
Pilgrim Holiness Church in Africa 3574-3576, 5205, 6449, 6747
Pilgrim Holiness Church in Antigua 3577
Pilgrim Holiness Church in Barbados 3578-3579, 5338, 5340, 5754
Pilgrim Holiness Church in British Guiana 3580-3581
Pilgrim Holiness Church in Central America 3585
Pilgrim Holiness Church in Colorado 6978
Pilgrim Holiness Church in India 3586-3588
Pilgrim Holiness Church in Jamaica 3589
Pilgrim Holiness Church in Mexico 3590-3596
Pilgrim Holiness Church in Michigan 3466, 6174-6175, 6888
Pilgrim Holiness Church in New Jersey 3468
Pilgrim Holiness Church in New York 3467

Pilgrim Holiness Church in Pennsylvania 3468
Pilgrim Holiness Church in Peru 3597
Pilgrim Holiness Church in Rhodesia 3599-3600
Pilgrim Holiness Church in the Caribbean region 3582-3584, 5338, 5340, 5875, 5897, 6269, 6746
Pilgrim Holiness Church in the Philippine Islands 3598, 6880
Pilgrim Holiness Church in Trinidad 3601
Pilgrim Holiness Church in West Virginia 7299
Pilgrim Holiness Church of New York 3907-3912
Pilgrim Holiness Church of New York. Annual Conference 3909
Pilgrim Holiness Church of New York. Conferences. Midwest 3913
Pilgrim Holiness Church of the Midwest 3913
Pilgrim/Pelgrim (periodical) 3253
Pilgrim News (periodical) 3912
Pilgrim Youth News (periodical) 3554
Pillar of Fire see Pillar of Fire Church
Pillar of Fire (Denver, Colo., Zarephath, N.J.) 2243
Pillar of Fire (London) 2242
Pillar of Fire Bible and Missionary Training School see Zarephath Bible Seminary
Pillar of Fire Church 2203-2261, 4304-4305, 4306-4307, 4339, 4396, 4422, 4603, 7155-7168
Pillar of Fire; devoted to the interests of the sanctified life (periodical) see Pillar of Fire (periodical)
Pillar of Fire Junior (periodical) 2244

Pilot Point, Tex. 1255, 4364
Pinkham, Bertha see Dixon, Bertha Pinkham
Pinkham, William Penn (1841-1919) 2286-2287, 6471-6472
Pitts, Harold E. 2600
Pitts, Joseph S. 1392, 1940-1941, 6473-6474
Plainview, Tex. 4448
Platt, Frederic 2
Platz, M. C. 1984
Pledger, C. P. see Pledger, Clifton Pryor (1875-1909)
Pledger, Clifton Pryor (1875-1909) 6475
Plumb, R. J. see Plumb, Roselle John (1886-)
Plumb, Roselle John (1886-) 6476
Plymouth Brethren 868
Point Loma College 1483a, 4544-4548
Pointen, Harold William 2450, 4930, 5697
Political and social criticism 654-655, 873-889, 1751-1755, 2151, 2248-2252, 2367-2369, 2441, 3018-3021, 3094-3095, 3219, 3557, 5803, 5889
Political criticism see Political and social criticism
Political ethics see Political criticism
Pollock, J. C. see Pollock, John Charles
Pollock, John Charles 4026, 4034, 4965
Polovina, Samuel (1888-) 6477-6478
Pomeroy, B. 128
Pomona, Calif. 4597
Pool, Lillian see Burnett, Lillian M. Pool
Poole, W. H. 6479
Poor relief see Charities
Pope, Gladys M. 6480
Pope, Liston 3231, 4290
Pope, William Burt (1822-1903) 2529-2530
Port Credit, Ont. 4487
Porter, James (1808-1888) 2852

Portland, Ore. 4379, 4592, 4598-4599
Portland Bible Institute see Cascade College
Portsmouth, R. I. 996
Portuguese East Africa see Mozambique
Postmillennialism see Millennialism
Potchefstroom, S. Afr. 4514
Potter, Edward Lawrence 7193
Potts, James Manning (1895-) 2829
Potts, John 6481
Pouring, Baptismal see Baptism
Powers, Hardy Carroll (1900-1972) 1260, 1630, 1925, 6482-6483
Pratt, Julia Mary Ann Judson 6485
Pratt, Melvin F. (1860-1939) 6484-6485
Pratt, William H. 3509-3510, 6485-6486
Preacher (periodical) 831
Preachers see Clergy
Preacher's Magazine (periodical) 1740
Predestination 624, 1591-1592, 2941, 3183-3184, 3411
Premillennialism see Millennialism
Prentice, George 5624
Presbyterian Church in the U.S.A. Board of Foreign Missions 4986
Prescott, Grace 6487
Prescott, Lyle (1913-1970) 1911, 6488-6489
Prescott, Mrs. Lyle see Prescott, Grace
Prescott, Ont. 4370
Presley, I. H. 4275-4276
Price, Ross Eugene (1907-) 1289, 1500, 1539, 1829, 1843, 4546, 6490
Primitive Holiness Church see Primitive Holiness Mission
Primitive Holiness Mission 2262-2264, 4506, 5884, 6084
Primitive Holiness Record (periodical) 818, 2264
Primitive Methodist Church, U.S.A. 3106-3112, 4610-4613, 4687-4688
Primitive Methodist International Mission Board 3111
Primitive Methodist Journal (periodical) 3112
Prindle, Cyrus (1800-1885) 3142, 3203, 3208, 6491
Prior, Kenneth Francis William 16
Prisons 1150, 2952, 3610, 6331, 7144
Pritchard, M. C. 6492-6493
Prohibition 2240
Protestantism 869, 2159, 4002
Proton, Ont. 4360
Providence, R. I. 3049, 6527
Providence, R. I. People's Evangelical Church 996
Providence, R. I. St. Paul's Methodist Episcopal Church 996
Psychology, Pastoral see Pastoral theology
Publishers and publishing 1756-1758, 4215
Puerto Rico 6489
Purdy, Jessie Amelia (1870-) 6494
Purdy, Tenn. 4549
Pure in Heart (periodical) 2417
Pure Religion (periodical) 832
Puritans 2568-2569, 2570-2571
Purity Journal and the Christian Life (periodical) see International Purity Journal (periodical)
Purkiser, W. T. see Purkiser, Westlake Taylor (1910-)
Purkiser, Westlake Taylor (1910-) 1367-1368, 1501-1508, 1583, 1590, 1603, 1631, 4547, 6495, 7053
Putnam, Stan see Putnam, Stanley
Putnam, Stanley 2277, 2288

Pye, Ernest (1881-   ) 3775

Quarterly Review of the United Brethren in Christ see United Brethren Review
Quebec 5694, 5696
Quillian, Joseph D. (1917-   ) 2818
Quincy, Mass. 4392-4394

R. P. S. see Smith, Robert Pearsall (1827-1898)
Rader, Paul 4319-4320, 6738
Radio 1347, 2254, 2741, 4221, 4844
Rager, Mary Ellen (1935-   ) 6496
Ragsdale, Dorothy Frances (1917-   ) 6497
Ragsdale, Paul Wesley (1917-   ) 6498
Ragsdale, Mrs. Paul Wesley see Ragsdale, Dorothy Frances (1917-   )
Raidabaugh, Peter W. 6499
Rairdon, Jack T. 1651
Ralph, Allen W. 2951
Ralston, Ruth see Bevin, Ruth Ralston (1912-   )
Ralston, Thomas Neely (1806-1891) 3079-3083
Ramos, Rosula 6500
Ramquist, A. E. 1672
Ramquist, Grace Chapman (1907-   ) 1883, 1900, 1903, 1909, 1912, 1929, 1942, 5022
Ram's Horn (periodical) see Herald of Light (periodical); Home Herald, the New Voice of the Ram's Horn (periodical)
Ramseyer, J. E. see Ramseyer, Joseph Eicher (1868 or 9-1944)
Ramseyer, Joseph Eicher (1868 or 9-1944) 4146, 6501-6502
Ramseyer, Mrs. Joseph Eicher see Ramseyer, Macy Garth
Ramseyer, Macy Garth 4146, 6502

Ranf, M. Louisa (-1890) 6503
Ranks, Swanton 6504
Ransom, Arthur S. 6505
Rash, R. W. (1904-   ) 3729
Rassman, A. E. 3586-3587
Rattenbury, John Ernest (1870-   ) 2585
Ravenhill, Leonard 218, 444
Rawlings, Elden Everette 64, 1260, 1758
Ray, Emma J. (1859-   ) 6506-6507
Ray, Mrs. L. P. see Ray, Emma J. (1859-   )
Ray, Lloyd P. (1860-   ) 6507
Ray, W. P. 680
Reachout (periodical) 2730
Read, Osceola J. 2030
Reade, Thaddeus Constantine (1846-1902) 6233, 6235-6238, 6508-6510
Red Deer, Alta. 4374
Red Rock, Minn. 2841
Reddy, William (1813-   ) 6511
Redfield, John Wesley (1810-1863) 6512-6514
Redford, M. E. see Redford, Maury English
Redford, Maury English 1249, 1645-1647, 1944, 1951, 2024, 2189, 3446, 3454
Reed, D. S. see Reed, David S. (1867-   )
Reed, David S. (1867-   ) 6515-6516
Reed, Harold William (1909-   ) 1262, 1291, 1830, 6517
Reed, L. A. see Reed, Louis Archibald (1892-1952)
Reed, Louis Archibald (1892-1952) 1369, 1884, 6518
Reed, Marshall Russell (1891-   ) 2784
Reed, Oscar Ferguson 1780, 1829, 4546, 6519
Reedy, Edward Napoleon (1883-   ) 6520-6521
Rees, Byron Johnson (1877-1920) 209, 942, 997, 3494, 3565, 6522-6524, 6527
Rees, Frida Marie Stromberg

(-1958) 6525
Rees, Hulda A. Johnson (1855-1898) 942, 6526, 6527
Rees, O. W. 3601
Rees, Paul Stromberg (1900-) 173, 274-275, 888, 943, 2790, 3355, 3986, 3988-3989, 4040, 4855, 5153, 6528-6529, 6531-6533
Rees, Seth Cook (1854-1933) 110, 209, 751, 889, 963, 3495, 3557, 3566-3568, 6530-6534
Rees, Mrs. Seth Cook see Rees, Frida Marie Stromberg (-1958); Rees, Hulda A. Johnson (1855-1898)
Reformed Baptist Alliance of Canada see Alliance of the Reformed Baptist Church
Reformed Baptist Church see Alliance of the Reformed Baptist Church
Reformed Methodist Church 3113-3114
Refugees, Armenian see Armenian question; Armenians
Regina, Sask. 4537
Rehfeldt, Remiss (1915-) 1393, 1699, 6535
Reid, Alex J. 6536
Reid, Bessie see Kresge, Bessie Reid (1897-)
Reid, Isaiah (1836-1911) 445, 6537
Reid, Pearl 6538
Reiley, J. McKendree 6539
Reinhard, James Arnold (1932-) 2694a
Reisdorph, Rufus Deland (1896-) 6540
Religious education 890-891, 1182-1186, 1759-1782, 2611, 2736-2739, 2821, 3811, 4216
Religious Society of Friends see Friends, Society of
Rennells, Charles Stephen (1873-1962) 3126-3127, 6541-6542
Repairer (periodical) 2731
Report (periodical) 3248

Reporter (periodical) 4510
Rescue homes 2441, 3557, 5122-5124, 6414, 6485, 6532
Rescue missions 3471, 5122-5124, 5129-5130, 5235, 5237, 5256, 5943, 6470, 6485, 6709-6711, 7180-7181, 7197
Rest Cottage Association 2441
Revival Herald (periodical) 180, 3860
Revivalist (periodical) see God's Revivalist and Bible Advocate (periodical)
Revivals see Evangelistic work
Reynolds, Alfred (1903-1937) 6543
Reynolds, E. E. (1862?-1930) 6544
Reynolds, Eleanor Margaret Ann Morrow 6545
Reynolds, H. F. see Reynolds, Hiram Farnham (1854-1938)
Reynolds, Hiram Farnham (1854-1938) 1700, 6546-6549
Reynolds, Paul David (1928-) 6550
Reynolds, Mrs. Paul David see Reynolds, Wilma Lucille Waggoner (1927-)
Reynolds, William Henry (1880-1963) 6551
Reynolds, Mrs. William Henry see Reynolds, Eleanor Margaret Ann Morrow
Reynolds, Wilma Lucille Waggoner (1927-) 6552
Reza, H. T. see Reza, Honorato T.
Reza, Honorato T. 1701, 1913, 1919
Rhode Island 996-999, 1943, 3049, 4392-4394, 6281, 6527, 6534
Rhodes, M. L. 4724
Rhodesia 1036-1039, 3599-3600
Rice, E. O. see Rice, Edward Ordello
Rice, Edward Ordello 6553-6554
Rice, George 6557
Rice, Hillery C. 1107
Rice, James Silas (-1942)

Rice, Paul (1951-1968) 6555-6557
Rice, S. see Rice, Squire (-1911)
Rice, Squire (-1911) 6558
Rice, W. S. 6559
Richman, C. J. 6560
Ricker, William A. 6561
Rickman, Claude R. (1917-) 6562, 7035
Ridgaway, Henry Bascom (1830-1895) 5079, 5763, 6563-6564
Ridout, G. W. see Ridout, George Whitefield (1870-1954)
Ridout, George Whitefield (1870-1954) 446-448, 621, 639, 859, 862, 865, 866, 872, 944, 6248, 6565-6566
Ridpath, John Clark (1841-1900) 6942
Ries, Claude Arden (1893-) 6567
Riggle, Herbert McClellan (1872-) 1108-1112, 1134-1138, 1178, 6568-6569
Riggs, A. B. see Riggs, Albert B.
Riggs, Albert B. 6570
Riggs, E. D. 2664
Riley, John Eckel (1909-) 1076, 1370, 6571
Riley, William E. 6572
Ringenberg, Jonas A. 4148
Ripper, Carl Harold (1905-) 6573
Ritter, L. H. (1878-) 6574
River Brethren see Brethren in Christ Church
Rixse, Eva 6575
Roark, Warren C. (1902-) 1113-1114, 1146
Roberts, Arthur Owen (1923-) 2276-2277, 2278, 2297-2298, 6576
Roberts, B. T. see Roberts, Benjamin Titus (1823-1893)
Roberts, Benjamin Titus (1823-1893) 2625, 2631a, 2663-2665, 2687-2688, 2689, 2695, 3841, 4835, 6577-6582
Roberts, Benson Howard (1853-1930) 2663, 3841, 6579, 6583
Roberts, Ellen Stowe (-1908) 6580
Roberts, Esther M. 6580
Roberts, Evan 2945
Roberts, Florence 6584-6585
Roberts, G. C. M. see Roberts, George C. M. (1806-1870)
Roberts, George C. M. (1806-1870) 6586
Roberts, Oral (1918-) 4250-4252, 4259-4260, 4263-4266-4267, 4271, 4282-4285, 6587-6591
Roberts, Robert Richford (1778-1843) 2954
Roberts College 4549
Roberts Junior College see Roberts Wesleyan College
Roberts Wesleyan College 4550
Robertson, Archibald Thomas 4168
Robertson, Archie see Robertson, Archibald Thomas
Robertson, Malcolm Ray (1922-) 4334
Robinson, A. E. see Robinson, Albert Ernest
Robinson, Albert Ernest 4257
Robinson, Bud see Robinson, Reuben (1860-1942)
Robinson, Charles 6592
Robinson, Frank Alfred (1874-) 117, 7180
Robinson, Frank E. 2986
Robinson, Kenneth Eugene (-1967) 1604
Robinson, Kenneth L. 4949
Robinson, Louise see Chapman, Louise Robinson
Robinson, Reuben (1860-1942) 450-454, 945, 963, 1831-1834, 3748, 6593, 6604
Robson, R. S. 680
Roby, Eva Carpenter (1880-) 6605
Roby, J. L. see Roby, John

L. (-1958)
Roby, Mrs. J. L. see Roby, Eva Carpenter (1880-)
Roby, John L. (-1958) 6606
Roche, John Alexander 6392
Rochester, N. Y. 3129
Rock Island, Ill. 4359
Rocky Mountain Christian School 4551
Rocky Mountain Missionary and Evangelistic Institute see Colorado Springs Bible College
Rocky Mountain Pillar of Fire (periodical) see Pillar of Fire (periodical)
Rocky Mountain Yearly Meeting of Friends see Friends, Society of. Rocky Mountain Yearly Meeting
Rodriguez, Alphonsus 43
Rogers, Dennis (1858-) 1946, 2424, 6607-6608
Rogers, Hester Ann (1756-1794) 560-561
Roman Catholicism see Catholicism
Romero, Ignacio (19??-1952) 6609
Root, Helen Isabel (1873-1945) 2717, 4721, 6610-6611
Rosa, Maria de la 6612
Rosa, Pablo de la 6613
Rosa, Sra. Pablo de la see Rosa, Maria de la
Rosales D., Enrique (1910-) 6614
Rose, Alvin C. 6615
Rose, Delbert Roy (1912-) 652-653, 6616, 6782-6784
Rose, O. W. see Rose, Olin Ward (1863-1940)
Rose, Olin Ward (1863-1940) 6617
Rose, William Brewster (1849-1926) 2665, 6618
Rose Hill, N. C. 4352
Roseberry, Robert Sherman (1883-) 4138
Ross, Milo C. 2382
Rosser, Leonidas (1815-1892) 3084
Rotary Club, Cedar Springs, Mich. 4470
Rothwell, Helen Francis (1908-) 3472
Rothwell, Mel-Thomas (1905-) 3472, 6619
Round Lake, N. Y. 127-128, 987
Routley, Erik (1917-) 2586
Rowland, Charles W. 6620
Rowley, Charles E. 727, 6554, 6621-6622
Royal Priest (periodical) 833
Rundell, Emma Mitchell (1919-) 6623
Rundell, Merton Russell (1923-) 2429, 3597, 6624
Rundell, Merton Russell, Jr. see Rundell, Merton Russell (1923-)
Rundell, Mrs. Merton Russell, Jr. see Rundell, Emma Mitchell (1919-)
Runyan, William Marion (1870-1957) 743, 1676
Ruskin Cave, Tenn. 4552
Ruskin Cave College 4552
Rusling, James Fowler (1834-1918) 7059
Russell, Bernard Curry 2504
Russell, Charles Taze (1852-1916) 860, 2247
Russellism see Jehovah's Witnesses
Ruth, C. W. see Ruth, Christian Wismer (1865-1941)
Ruth, Christian Wismer (1865-1941) 209, 455-460, 1133, 1371, 1509, 3842, 6625, 6627
Ruth, Laura 6627
Rutherford, E. S. 3468
Rutherford, Eliza J. 6628
Rutherford, Thomas 2892-2894
Ryckman, Harold H. 2720
Ryding, I. S. W. (-1956) 6629
Ryff, Ethel Davey (1887-1949) 6630
Ryff, Jules 6631
Ryff, Mrs. Jules see Ryff, Ethel Davey (-1949); Ryff, Lilla Eva (-1920)

Ryff, Lilla Eva (-1920) 6632

S., H. W. see Smith, Hannah Whitall (1832-1911)
S., R. P. see Smith, Robert Pearsall (1827-1898)
Sabbath 1126-1127, 1333, 3999
Sabin, Benjamin (1790-) 6633
Sage, C. H. see Sage, Charles H. (1825-1908)
Sage, Charles H. (1825-1908) 6634
St. Charles, Ill. 2758
St. John, N. B. 4496
St. Joseph, Mo. Bryant's Business College see Bryant's Business College, St. Joseph, Mo.
St. Louis, Mo. 144, 1236, 4504
St. Louis, Mo. Church of God at Baden 1236
St. Louis, Mo. Lighthouse Mission 815
Salem, Ohio 4303, 4553-4554
Salem Bible College 4553-4554
Salem Bible College and Academy see Salem Bible College
Salem Bible Institute see Salem Bible College
Salem Sentinel (periodical) 4554
Salina. Kansas Wesleyan University see Kansas Wesleyan University
Saltzman, Herbert Royce 1031
Salvation Army 3602-3690, 4332, 4857, 5665
Salvation Army in Germany 3685
Salvation Army in Great Britain 3686-3688, 4811-4824
Salvation Army in Michigan 3689
Salvation Army in New Jersey 3690
Salvation News (periodical) see Salvation Telephone (periodical)

Salvation Telephone (periodical) 2732
Salve, S. Y. (1892-) 6635
Samaritan Hospital School of Nursing 4555-4556, 6090
Samoa 5426-5428
Samudra, Joseph 6636
San Antonio, Tex. 4560
San Diego, Calif. 4544-4548
San Francisco, Calif. 5470, 6595-6596, 6940-6941
San Jose, Vicente 6637
San Juanito, Mex. 4388
Sanctified Church of Christ 3691
Sandall, Robert 3656
Sangster, William Edwin (1900-1960) 2508, 2531-2532, 2574, 2594, 2785-2786
Sanner, A. E. see Sanner, Asa Everette (1890-)
Sanner, Asa Everette (1890-) 5490, 6638
Santin, V. G. see Santin, Vicente G. (1870-1948)
Santin, Vicente G. (1870-1948) 6639
Saratoga Springs, N. Y. 4392-4394
Sarian, Nerses S. (1886-1964) 6640-6641
Saskatchewan 4434, 4557
Sass, Marie Pauline 4184
Satisfied, Joshua, pseud. see Johnston, U. G.
Saunders, Dallas Roy (1912-) 6642
Saunders, Mrs. Dallas Roy see Saunders, Vivian Taylor (1914-)
Saunders, Vivian Taylor (1914-) 6643
Savonarola, Girolamo (1452-1498) 84
Sawyer, Joe C. 3128
Sawyer, Robert Leonard (1922-) 6644
Saxon, John Davis (1893-1956?) 6645-6646
Saxon, Ruth O. 1953
Sayes, J. Ottis see Sayes, James Ottis (1922-)

Sayes, James Ottis (1922-) 1781, 6647
Sayes, Ottis see Sayes, James Ottis (1922-)
Scarlet, John see Scarlett, John (1803-1889)
Scarlett, John (1803-1889) 6648, 6651
Schaffer, Jacob (-1937) 6652
Schiller, F. C. S. see Schiller, Ferdinand Canning Scott (1864-1937)
Schiller, Ferdinand Canning Scott (1864-1937) 7176
Schilling, Sylvester Paul (1904-) 2780
Schirmer, William C. 6653
Schlosser, George Donald (-1936) 6654
Schmelzenbach, Harmon Faldine (1882-1929) 6655-6657
Schmelzenbach, Harmon Faldine, III 6656
Schmelzenbach, Lula 6657
Schmul, H. E. see Schmul, Harold E.
Schmul, Harold E. 3816, 3843, 3865-3867
Schocke, Albert J. 6658
Schocke, Mrs. Albert J. see Schocke, Hazel M.
Schocke, Hazel M. 6659
Schoenhals, Lawrence Russell (1912-) 2684, 6660
School of Theology 4557
Schools see Education
Schoombie, G. A. 3599
Schrag, Martin Homer 1015
Schuh, Charles Gottlob (1856-) 2862-2863, 6661-6662
Schurman, W. G. see Schurman, Wenford G. (1871-1932)
Schurman, Wenford G. (1871-1932) 6663-6664
Schwab, Bertha Goss 6665
Schwab, Mrs. Harry see Schwab, Bertha Goss
Schwab, Otho 6666
Schwab, Ralph Kendall 1992

Schwartz, Gary 4169
Scofield, Florence R. Myers 6667
Scofield, George H. 6668
Scofield, Mrs. George H. see Scofield, Florence R. Myers
Scopino, Aldorigo Joseph (1947-) 1943, 6534
Scotland 4358, 4414, 4456, 4540, 4571, 6689-6690 see also Great Britain
Scott, David E. 6669
Scott, Jane A. (-1866) 2927
Scott, Janice Delores (1934-) 6670
Scott, Leland H. 2802-2803
Scott, Mary 5028
Scott, Orange (1800-1847) 2978-2980, 3143, 3197, 6671-6672
Scott, P. Cameron see Scott, Peter Cameron (1867-1897)
Scott, Percy 2575
Scott, Peter Cameron (1867-1897) 6673-6674
Seals, B. V. 1409, 4899
Seamands, John T. 1372
Search, Pamela 3613
Searles, John E. (1819-1893) 5740
Sears, Angeline Brooks (1817-1848) 6675-6677
Sears, Mrs. Clinton William see Sears, Angeline Brooks
Sears, Lawrence Wayne (1917-) 1584, 1908
Seattle, Wash. 4558
Seattle Pacific College 4558
Seattle Seminary see Seattle Pacific College
Sebree, Herbert T. 6678
Second Advent 574, 586, 599, 601-602, 1568, 1579, 2113, 2679-2680, 3503, 4009-4012, 4089-4090, 4259-4262
Second Coming of Christ see Second Advent
Secret societies 144, 3059, 3161
See, Isaac M. 6679
Selle, Robert L. (1865-1929) 174, 461-464, 640, 6680-6681

Selleck, Harold A. 6682
Sellew, Walter Ashbel (1844-1929) 2666, 2759, 4724, 5945, 6683
Semark, H. G. 3250
Seminario Nazarene de Mexico 4559
Seminario Nazareno Hispanoamericano 4560
Seminary Tower (periodical) 1726, 4520
El Sendero de la Verdad (periodical) 1741
Senft, F. H. see Senft, Frederic H.
Senft, Frederic H. 4073, 6738
Sensensey, J. H. 6684
Sent of God (periodical) 2070, 2469
Sentinel (periodical) see United Holiness Sentinel (periodical)
Sermon illustrations see Homiletical illustrations
Sermon Quarterly (periodical) 834
Serrano, Antonio (1899-) 3367
Seventh-Day Adventism 1750, 2160, 3556
Sevierville, Tenn. 4485-4486
Sexual ethics see Conduct of Life
Schackelfords, Va. 4356
Shanghai. Bethel Mission 3266
Shannon, E. Boyd see Shannon, Ernest Boyd (1911-1968)
Shannon, Ernest Boyd (1911-1968) 1605, 6685
Shantz, Ward M. 6686
Sharian, Bedros M. 3775
Sharon Bible and High School 4561
Sharp, B. S. 6687
Sharpe, George (1865-1948) 1510, 1890-1891, 3452, 3455, 5918, 6688-6691
Shattuck, B. O. see Shattuck, Burdette O. (-1958)
Shattuck, Burdette O. (-1958) 6692
Shaver, Charles 1373, 6693
Shaver, Chic see Shaver, Charles
Shaw, S. B. see Shaw, Solomon Benjamin (1854-)
Shaw, Solomon Benjamin (1854-) 113-114, 192-193, 465, 641-642, 2262, 3821, 6694
Shea, Beverly see Shea, George Beverly (1909-)
Shea, George Beverly (1909-) 6695-6697
Shearer, D. C. see Shearer, Daniel Clyde (1878?-1940)
Shearer, Daniel Clyde (1878?-1940) 6698
Sheeks, E. H. see Sheeks, Edwin H. (1839-1935)
Sheeks, Mrs. E. J. 2435, 2442, 6699
Sheeks, Edwin H. (1839-1935) 6700
Sheeks, Mrs. Edwin H. see Sheeks, Mrs. E. J.
Sheets, H. K. see Sheets, Harold Kenneth (1903-)
Sheets, Harold Kenneth (1903-) 6701
Sheffer, B. F. 6702
Sheldon, H. O. see Sheldon, Henry Olcott (1799-1882)
Sheldon, Henry Olcott (1799-1882) 3021, 6703-6704
Sheldon, Joseph G. 65
Sheldon family 6704
Shelhamer, E. E. see Shelhamer, Elmer Ellsworth (1869-1947)
Shelhamer, Elmer Ellsworth (1869-1947) 175, 190, 466, 752-753, 946-948, 973, 1385, 1725, 2667, 3844, 5082-5083, 6705-6712, 6714, 6896
Shelhamer, Mrs. Elmer Ellsworth see Shelhamer, Julia Arnold; Shelhamer, Minnie Baldwin (-1902)
Shelhamer, Evangeline see Surbrook, Evangeline Shel-

hamer (-1930)
Shelhamer, Julia Arnold 176-177, 974, 6707, 6711, 6713-6715
Shelhamer, Minnie Baldwin (-1902) 6716
Shemeld, Catherine 6717
Shemeld, R. R. see Shemeld, Robert R.
Shemeld, Robert R. 6718
Shemeld, Mrs. Robert R. see Shelmeld, Catherine
Shepard, William Edward (1862-) 467-470, 1374, 1511, 3845, 6719-6721
Shepard, William Orville (1862-1931) 2855
Sherman, C. W. see Sherman, Charles W.
Sherman, Charles W. 6722
Sherwood, Mrs. 3133
Shih Maiyü see Stone, Mary (1873-1954)
Shilling, Henry (1902-) 4573-4576, 6723
Shingler, James Simon (1859-) 932
Shingler, T. J. 6724
Shingler Holiness College see Southeastern Holiness College
Shining Light (periodical) 1062-1063, 1182, 1186
Shining Way (periodical) 835
Shipley, David Clark (1907-) 2576, 2804, 6725
Shipps, Howard Fenimore (1903-) 4331, 6726
Shongwe, Kelina 6727
Short, J. N. see Short, John N. (1841-1922)
Short, J. W. see Short, James Wiley (1880-1967)
Short, James Wiley (1880-1967) 6728
Short, John N. (1841-1922) 617, 1512, 6729-6730
Shouting 2133-2134
Showerman, R. E. 6731
Shuler, Robert Pierce (1880-) 618, 622, 2605, 6732

Shumake, C. E. 1513
Shuman, Harry M. 4102
Shupe, H. F. see Shupe, Henry Fox (1860-1926)
Shupe, Henry Fox (1860-1926) 3700
Siberal, J. H. see Sibrel, Joseph H. (-1957)
Sibrel, Joseph H. (-1957) 6733
Siens, Nora see Hunter, Nora Siens (1873-1951)
Sierra Leone 3232-3235, 3733, 5053, 5547
Sigston, James 1556
Sigsworth, John Wilkins 2451, 2755
Silsbee, R. N. 6734
Silver, Jesse Forest 2679
Silver Lake, Vt. 1001
Simla Hill States Mission see India North-West Mission
Simmons, E. L. see Simmons, Ernest Lesley (1893-)
Simmons, Ernest Lesley (1893-) 4211
Simmons, I. see Simmons, Ichabod (1831-1898)
Simmons, Ichabod (1831-1898) 6735
Simpson, A. B. see Simpson, Albert Benjamin (1843-1919)
Simpson, Albert Benjamin (1843-1919) 4058, 4069-4080, 4090-4091, 4096-4097, 4100, 4105, 4109-4110, 4118-4119, 4124-4126, 6295, 6736-6739
Simpson, Matthew (1811-1884) 199, 2137, 2625, 2695-2696, 2964, 3023, 3089, 3103, 3110, 3200, 6740-6742
Sims, A. see Sims, Albert (1851-)
Sims, Albert (1851-) 2623-2624, 2668-2669, 2680-2681, 6743-6744
Sims, Edgar P. 2386
Slander 155, 1343
Slater, Charles Livingstone (1884-1950) 3569, 5338, 6745-6748
Slater, Mrs. Charles Living-

stone see Slater, Maude
  E. (1883-1973)
Slater, Flora Belle (1906-)
  6749
Slater, Maude E. (1883-1973)
  6747-6748
Slater, Richard (1854-1939)
  3671
Slavery 2876, 2959, 2961-
  2962, 3019, 3175-3176,
  3194-3196, 3198, 3219,
  5322-5323, 5325, 6118,
  7042
Slay, James L. 4207
Sloan, Walter B. 4027
Sloat, L. R. see Sloat, L.
  Russell
Sloat, L. Russell 3776, 6750
Smalley, William F. 4106
Smart, Marshall 913, 5361
Smart, William James
  (1895-) 5004
Smee, John 6349
Smelser, F. L. see Smelser, Fred L.
Smelser, Fred L. 1206-1209
Smelser, S. L. [i.e. F. L.]
  see Smelser, Fred L.
Smith, A. B. 6751
Smith, A. Milton see Smith,
  Arlis Milton (1903-)
Smith, Alfred Emanuel (1873-
  1944) 883
Smith, Allister 3298, 3646
Smith, Amanda Berry (1837-
  1915) 6752-6756
Smith, Annie S. 3614
Smith, Arlis Milton (1903-)
  1514, 1835, 6757
Smith, Aura 6758
Smith, Bernie (1920-) 115-
  116, 1836-1837, 6759-6761
Smith, Carroll (-1949)
  6762
Smith, Mrs. Carroll see
  Smith, Rosa Hunter
  (-1932)
Smith, Charles Merrill 2497-
  2498
Smith, Curtis see Smith,
  Royal Curtis (1915-)
Smith, Donnell J. (-1936)
  6763
Smith, Edward (1797-1856)
  2876, 3219
Smith, Emma French 6764
Smith, F. G. see Smith,
  Frederick George (1880-
  1947)
Smith, Florence Ethel 178
Smith, Frank Whitall (1854-
  1872) 6769
Smith, Frederick George (1880-
  1947) 1115-1119, 1139-1140,
  1160, 6765
Smith, G. H. see Smith,
  George H.
Smith, George H. 1213, 6766
Smith, Hannah (-195?) 1276-
  1277, 4903
Smith, Hannah Whitall (1832-
  1911) 851-852, 2288-2292,
  2294, 6767-6775, 6800-6801
Smith, Harlie W. 5799
Smith, Hugh E. 2986
Smith, J. A. 6776
Smith, J. T. see Smith,
  Joseph Thomas (1851-)
Smith, Jennie (1842-) 6777-
  6780
Smith, John (1794-186?) 3477
Smith, John Evan (1886-)
  4823
Smith, John W. V. (1914-)
  1069, 1120, 1161, 1231
Smith, Joseph Henry (1855-
  1946) 102, 219, 471-474,
  627, 652-653, 656, 4494,
  4793, 6781-6785, 6958,
  7039
Smith, Joseph Thomas (1851-)
  3085, 6786
Smith, Julia Ann (1937-)
  6787
Smith, Keith Eugene (1926-)
  1918
Smith, Lizzie O. (1823-18??)
  6788-6789, 6790
Smith, Mrs. Lizzie R. 6791
Smith, Logan Pearsall (1865-
  1946) 6768, 6770, 6775
Smith, M. A. 3076
Smith, M. W. 6078
Smith, Merlin Grant (1894-)

6792-6793
Smith, Myrta 6794
Smith, Nathaniel B. (-1911) 6795
Smith, Oswald J. 4057, 4059-4061, 4081-4082, 4092-4094, 4098, 4101, 6796-6797
Smith, Robert Eugene (1937-) 6798
Smith, Mrs. Robert Eugene see Smith, Julia Ann (1937-)
Smith, Robert Pearsall (1827-1898) 3984-3985, 4031, 6773-6774, 6799-6801
Smith, Roderick Jackson 4567
Smith, Rosa Hunter (-1932) 6802
Smith, Royal Curtis (1915-) 6803
Smith, Samuel Roger 6804
Smith, Simeon O. 2325, 3393, 3396
Smith, Timothy Lawrence (1924-) 654-655, 1002, 1250, 1649, 2025, 2055, 2074, 2190, 2263, 2438, 2467, 3447, 3456, 4859, 6805
Smith, W. C. see Smith, William C. (1818-1891)
Smith, Wilbur K. (1913-) 6806
Smith, Willard Garfield (1911-) 3186, 6807-6808
Smith, William C. (1809-1886) 3039
Smith, William C. (1818-1891) 2832, 2834-2835, 3010
Smith, William Martin (1872-) 477, 595-596, 949, 2326-2330, 2337-2341, 2345, 2347, 3390, 3397-3402, 3406-3410, 3415, 3511-3512, 6809-6810
Smoking see Tobacco
Snake cults (Holiness churches) 4165
Snapp, H. C. see Snapp, Hickman Corbin
Snapp, Hickman Corbin 6811
Snead, Alfred Cookman (1884-) 4080, 4102, 4111-4112, 4117, 6812
Sneed, J. A. (-1944) 1210, 6813
Snow, O. L. 6814
Snowbarger, Samuel 6815
Snowbarger, Vernon A. (1915-) 6816
Snowbarger, W. E. see Snowbarger, Willis Edward (1921-)
Snowbarger, Willis Edward (1921-) 6817
Snyder, Emerson (1868-195?) 6818
Snyder, Howard Albert 66, 4568
Snyder, Lefa Elisabeth Zahniser (1898-) 7335
Snyder, Melvin Harold (1912-) 6819-6821
Social conditions see Social criticism
Social criticism see Political and social criticism
Social ethics see Social criticism
Social problems see Social criticism
Social service see Charities
Social welfare work see Charities
Socials see Church entertainments
Society of Friends see Friends, Society of
Society of Soul Winners 836
Sociology, Christian see Social criticism
Sol, David J. (1902-) 6822
Sol M., Lauro see Sol Molina, Lauro (1911-)
Sol Molina, Lauro (1911-) 6823
Soltero, F. H. see Soltero, Francisco H. (1892-)
Soltero, Francisco H. (1892-) 3592-3593, 6824
Soltero, Mrs. Francisco H. see Soltero, Nettie Winans (-1957)
Soltero, Nettie Winans (-1957)

3592-3594, 6825
Somerset, Isabella Caroline (1851-1921) 7294
Songs see Hymns
Soria, Emiliano 2158
Sororities see Secret societies
Soul-winner (Cleveland, Ohio) 2306
Soul Winner (Wilmore, Ky.) 836
South Africa Annual (periodical) 2475
South African Nazarene (periodical) 1742
South African Pioneer (periodical) 3931, 3975-3976, 4036
South African Pioneer. American ed. (periodical) 4037
South America see Latin America
South American Indians see Indians of South America
South Carolina 3236, 4270, 4383, 4449-4451, 5685-5686, 6470, 6992, 6994
South China Peniel Holiness Missionary Society see Voice of China and Asia
South Dakota 4365-4367, 4410, 4596, 6044-6045, 6917
South Providence Holiness Association 998
South Side Mission, Ypsilanti, Mich. see Evangelistic Tabernacle
Southeast Kansas Fire Baptized Holiness Association see Fire Baptized Holiness Church (Wesleyan)
Southeastern Holiness College 4562
Southern California and Arizona Holiness Association see Holiness Church (1880-1946)
Southern Pilgrim College see Kernersville Wesleyan Academy; Kernersville Wesleyan College
Southern States 1944, 3051, 3237
Southport Methodist Holiness Convention 2493
Southwest, Old 1000, 1945-1946
Southwestern Arkansas Holiness Association 4447
Southwestern Bible College see Southwestern College
Southwestern College 4563
Southwestern Pentecostal Holiness Bible College see Southwestern College
Spalding, Ida Heffner (-1930) 6826
Spangenberg, Alice 1702, 1877, 1923
Spangenberg, Leonard (1906-) 1637, 6827
Spangenberg, Robert Leonard (1933-) 6828
Spanish Bible College see Seminario Nazareno Hispanoamericano
Spanish in the U.S. see Mexican-Americans
Spann, Anna Louise 284-285
Spann, John Richard (1891-) 2787
Sparkes, Fannie J. (1844-1919) 6829
Sparks, Sammy see Sparks, Samuel F.
Sparks, Samuel F. 1838, 6830-6831
Speakes, J. N. see Speakes, Joseph Nicholas (1879-1959)
Speakes, Joseph Nicholas (1879-1959) 6832-6833
Speer, Robert Elliott (1867-1947) 4837, 4986
Spell, Kathleen, pseud. see Gish, Carol Spell
Spence, Othniel Talmadge (1926-) 4258
Spencer, Herbert (1820-1903) 5648
Spicer, T. see Spicer, Tobias (1788-1862)
Spicer, Tobias (1788-1862) 2928, 2965, 6834-6836
Spirits, Evil see Demonology
Spiritual Life (periodical) 2119
Spiritualism 625, 870-872,

2942, 4015
Spokane, Wash. 4564, 4592
Spokane Pilgrim Bible School 4564
Spotsylvania, Va. 4590
Spreng, Samuel P. 1991
Spring, Worthy Allen (1896-) 6837
Spring Arbor, Mich. 4565-4569
Spring Arbor College 4565-4569, 6793
Spring Arbor Junior College see Spring Arbor College
Spring Arbor Seminary see Spring Arbor College
Sprinkling, Baptismal see Baptism
Spruce, Elizabeth Woolsey (1873-1969) 6838-6839
Spruce, Fletcher Clarke 1292, 1375, 1839, 6840
Spruce, Mrs. Robert Elmer see Spruce, Elizabeth Woolsey (1873-1969)
Spruill, W. F. T. see Spruill, William F. T. (1830-1903)
Spruill, William F. T. (1830-1903) 6841
Stafford, S. M. 6842
Stafford, Samuel M. see Stafford, S. M.
Stalder, Kurt 59
Staley, H. J. 2533
Stalker, Charles Henry (1876-) 950, 6843-6844
Stalybridge, Eng. 4337
Stambaugh, Mrs. Emma 6845
Standard Bearer of Bible Holiness (periodical) 2427
Standard Church of America 3692-3697, 4370
Standard Church Seminary see Brockville Bible College
Standard of Holiness (periodical) 837
Standards of conduct see Conduct of life
Standley, M. G. see Standley, Meredith Goslin (1879-)

Standley, Meredith Goslin (1879-) 154, 690, 717, 729, 951, 975, 3524, 6846-6847
Stanger, Frank Bateman (1914-) 6848
Stanley, Sir Henry Morton (1841-1904) 3035, 6936
Staples, Rob Lyndal 2577, 6849
Star Hall, Manchester, Eng. see Manchester, Eng. Star Hall
Star Hall Convention. Manchester, 1890 194
Star Hall Convention. Manchester, 1891 195
Stark, Kenneth 6850
Starkey, Lycurgus Monroe 2788
Starr, R. V. see Starr, Roy V. (1885-1949)
Starr, Roy V. (1885-1949) 6851
States, L. Wayne 3919
Stauffer, Joshua (1891-1971) 475-477, 952, 967, 2319-2320, 2331-2333, 2348-2350, 3394, 3403-3405, 3416, 3478, 3482, 3496-3499, 3514, 3535, 3570-3571, 3573, 6852-6853
Stayt, E. H. (-1933) 6854
Stearns, D. M. see Stearns, Daniel Miner (1844-1920)
Stearns, Daniel Miner (1844-1920) 478, 597, 6855
Steel, Henry (1929?-1961) 6856-6857
Steele, A. M. 6858
Steele, Daniel (1824-1914) 105, 240, 317, 868, 893-895, 1386, 1557-1558, 2886, 3834, 3846-3848, 5831, 6859
Steele, Daniel (1824-1914). Binney's Theological compend. 141-142, 479-483, 1207, 2929-2931, 3261
Steele, Evangeline Ruth Felsburg (1931-) 6860
Steele, Harold C. 4824
Steele, Paul Wesley (1929-) 6861

Steele, Mrs. Paul Wesley
see Steele, Evangeline Ruth
Felsburg (1931-)
Stenbock, Evelyn 1632
Sterner, R. Eugene 1067
Stevens, Abel (1815-1897)
2831, 2966, 4713
Stevens, G. S. 730-731
Stevenson, Herbert F. 3986-3989, 4040-4043
Stewart, Grace M. (-1916) 6862
Stewart, Isabel Rosie Govan
see Govan Stewart, Isabel
Rosie (1900-)
Stewart, John H. 6863
Stikeleather, S. M. see
Stikeleather, Shirley M.
(1878-1962)
Stikeleather, Shirley M. (1878-1962) 6864-6865
Stites, Edgar Page (1836-1921) 6866
Stock, Eugene 4962
Stockmayer, Otto 3990-3992, 4024, 4044
Stockton, J. N. 6867
Stockton, John 1376, 6868-6869
Stockton, John Hart (1813-1877) 6870
Stoesz, Samuel J. 4056
Stokes, Ellwood Haines (1815-1897) 2844-2848, 6871-6873
Stoll, Charles Augustus (1872-1939) 6874
Stone, Mary (1873-1954) 6875
Stone, W. C. see Stone,
Wilmot C. (1876-1941)
Stone, Wilmot C. (1876-1941) 6876-6877
Stopani, Carlos (1911-) 6878
Storey, R. K. 6879-6880
Storms, Everek Richard 3744, 3761, 3765
Storrs, William Townsend 2112, 5608
Strachan, Alexander (1793-1865) 2534-2535
Strachey, Rachel Conn Costelloe (1887-) 851
Strachey, Ray see Strachey,
Strachey, Rachel Conn Costelloe (1887-)
Strang, C. B. see Strang,
Clifford Benjamin (1895-)
Strang, Clifford Benjamin
(1895-) 1278-1279, 6881
Street, A. K. see Street,
Abram K. (1807-1898)
Street, Abram K. (1807-1898) 6882
Strickland, Romey E. 3600
Strickland, Samuel Walker
(1892-1973) 6024-6025
Strickland, William Jefferson
(1932-) 6883-6884
Strong, Marie 1151
Stropko, Andrew John (1945-) 1606, 1681, 4548
Stuart, Charles Macaulay (1853-1932) 577-578
Stuart, George Rutledge (1857-1926) 932
Stuart, Robert Lee (1883-) 269, 6885
Stubbs, Enoch 2927
Studd, G. B. 6886
Student of Prophecy & Missionary Evangel (periodical) 3815
Sturk, L. W. see Sturk,
Louis Willard (1895-1955)
Sturk, Louis Willard (1895-1955) 6887-6888
Success 4251-4252
Suddarth, Mrs. Fannie E. 3442, 6889
Sullivan, Kenneth E. 1416
Sumlin, H. H. 6890
Summers, Ancel (1871-) 6891-6892, 6894
Summers, Mrs. Ancel see
Summers, Grace Langman
(1886-)
Summers, George D. 2956
Summers, Grace Langman
(1886-) 6892-6894
Summers, Thomas Osmond
(1812-1882) 550-551, 2512, 3081
Sunday see Sabbath
Sunday School lessons see In-

ternational Sunday-School lessons

Sunny Slope, Ariz. see Phoenix, Ariz.

Sunny Slope Bible School see Old Paths Bible School

Sunrise; newsletter for boys and girls (periodical) 3351

Sunrise; the junior quarterly magazine of the Japan Evangelistic Band (periodical) 3352

Surbrook, Evangeline Shelhamer (-1930) 6895-6896

Surbrook, W. L. see Surbrook, Walter Lewis (1891-)

Surbrook, Walter Lewis (1891-) 6897, 7299

Surbrook, Mrs. Walter Lewis see Surbrook, Evangeline Shelhamer (-1930)

Sutton, B. D. (-1951) 6898

Sutton, Ark. 4203

Swain, F. M. (-1926) 6899

Swann, Alline see Swann, L. Alline McGraw (1908-)

Swann, L. Alline McGraw (1908-) 6090, 6900-6902

Swarth, D. see Swarth, Dowie

Swarth, Dowie 6903

Swarth, Mrs. Dowie see Swarth, Thressa (-1952)

Swarth, Thressa (-1952) 6904

Swauger, J. R. see Swauger, John Robert (1900-1955)

Swauger, John Robert (1900-1955) 3148, 3150, 3211, 3226, 4367, 6905

Swaziland 1947-1949, 5205, 5209, 5396, 5733, 6656-6657, 7120

Swaziland Church of the Nazarene 1949, 5209, 6656-6657

Swedenborg, Emanuel (1688-1772) 5014

Sweet, William Henry (1843-1919) 3041

Sweet, William Warren (1881-1959) 2796-2797, 2799, 2825, 2944, 3040

Sweeten, Howard W. 484, 1515-1517, 6906

Sweney, John Robson (1837-1899) 669, 684, 708-709, 732-734, 2981-3002, 6907

Swim, Roy Elliott (1899-) 1708, 6908

Swing, J. W. see Swing, James W.

Swing, James W. 6909

Synan, Harold Vinson see Synan, Vinson (1934-)

Synan, Vinson (1934-) 4181, 4274, 4404, 6910

Tabernacle Pentecostal Church 4292

Tabernacle Presbyterian Church see Tabernacle Pentecostal Church

Tabor, Iowa 4413

Takaro, Magdalene P. 6911

Talbee, F. E. see Talbee, Frank E. (1869-1929)

Talbee, Frank E. (1869-1929) 6912

Tambe, Narendra Govind (1926-) 1936

Tamblyn, Jeremiah W. (1851-) 6913-6914

Tapper, Ruth M. 6611

Tappert, Theodore G. 2143, 2482

Tarkenton, Dallas M. (1912-) 4281

Taylor, A. M. see Taylor, Arthur M. (1896-)

Taylor, Arthur M. (1896-) 6915

Taylor, B. S. see Taylor, Bushrod Shedden (1849-1936)

Taylor, Bushrod Shedden (1849-1935) 179, 485-487, 598, 643, 735, 6916-6917

Taylor, C. G. see Taylor, Cary G. (-1954)

Taylor, Cary G. (-1954) 6918

Taylor, Charles Winthrop 3187

Taylor, Donald M. 3757, 6919

Taylor, G. F. see Taylor,

George Floyd (1881-1934)
Taylor, George Floyd (1881-1934) 4261-4262, 6920
Taylor, Isaac (1759-1829) 3135-3136
Taylor, J. M. see Taylor, James Milburn (1873-); Taylor, James Morgan
Taylor, J. Paul see Taylor, Jesse Paul (1895-)
Taylor, J. T. (-1945) 6921
Taylor, Mrs. J. T. see Taylor, Margaret Fallon (-1919)
Taylor, James Milburn (1873-) 744-745, 978, 981-982, 6922
Taylor, James Morgan 488-490, 599, 6923
Taylor, Jeffreys (1792-1853) 3137-3138
Taylor, Jeremy (1613-1667) 32-33
Taylor, Jesse Paul (1895-) 2502, 2626, 2670, 2697, 2711, 6924
Taylor, John Floyd 4120
Taylor, Margaret Fallon (-1919) 6925
Taylor, Marshall William (1846-1887) 6756
Taylor, Mendell 1334, 1410-1411, 1633, 1709, 1753, 1858, 6926-6927
Taylor, Milton H. 1270
Taylor, Richard Shelley (1912-) 1377-1378, 1518-1521, 1870, 1930, 6928
Taylor, Ross 806
Taylor, Willard Harlan 6929-6930
Taylor, William (1821-1902) 746, 754, 759-760, 806, 986, 2932-2934, 2941, 3033-3035, 6140, 6387, 6391, 6395, 6931-6954
Taylor, William Stephens (1905-) 17
Taylor, Wingrove 6955
Taylor University 4570, 6227-6239
Teasley, D. Otis 1170

Tedrow, Blanche Ione (1909-) 6956
Teed, Florence Schleicher (1901-1954) 656, 6785, 6957-6958
Teed, Mrs. Wallace see Teed, Florence Schleicher (1901-1954)
Teel, George M. 2419
Teen Time (periodical) see Reachout (periodical)
Tehuacana, Tex. 4601
Television 3815
Temperance 2240, 2865, 7210-7212, 7294
Temple, Helen Frances 1688, 1703, 1880, 1887, 1907, 1914-1917, 5209
Templeton, Charles Bradley (1915-) 6959-6962
Templeton, Chuck see Templeton, Charles Bradley (1915-)
Ten Commandments 2108, 3155
Tennessee 1243, 1950-1951, 2187-2190, 2620, 4361, 4485-4486, 4549, 4552, 4577-4578, 5330, 5641, 6022, 6024-6025, 6999
Tennessee Methodist (periodical) see Living Water (periodical)
Tenney, Mary Alice (1889-) 2503, 2639-2640, 2671
Teresa, Saint see Teresa of Avila (1515-1582)
Teresa of Avila (1515-1582) 40
Terrill, J. G. see Terrill, Joseph Goodwin (-1895)
Terrill, Joseph Goodwin (-1895) 2628, 2708-2709, 2758, 6513-6514
Teersteegen, Gerhard (1697-1769) 15
Tetley, J. D. 2533
Tetrick, D. C. W. 6963
Texas 1952, 2073-2075, 2168-2171, 2423-2424, 3052-3053, 3099-3100, 4364, 4382, 4432, 4444, 4448, 4483, 4491, 4537, 4560, 4591, 4601, 5709, 6608, 6839, 7217-7218
Texas Holiness Advocate (peri-

odical) see Pentecostal Advocate (periodical)
Texas Holiness Banner (periodical) 2171
Texas Holiness University see Peniel College
Thahabeyah, Milhem (1893-) 6964
Thayer, Clarence E. 6965
Theological Institute and Bible Training School see Fairmount Bible School
Theological Seminary of the Indiana Conference of the Wesleyan Methodist Connection (or Church) of America see Fairmount Bible School
Theological Seminary of the Methodist Episcopal Church, Concord, N. H. Missionary Society 3006
Theology, Pastoral see Pastoral theology
Theresa, Saint see Teresa of Avila (1515-1582)
Thoburn, Isabella (1840-1901) 6966-6967
Thoburn, James Mills (1836-1922) 2935, 3037-3038, 3043, 6753-6754, 6967-6969
Thomas, Clifford William (1916-) 3785, 3797, 6970
Thomas, Cora Cook see Tronnes, Cora Cook Thomas
Thomas, David (1860-1930) 2470, 6971-6972
Thomas, David C. 110
Thomas, Fred (1909-) 6973
Thomas, Hazel Marie (1926-) 6974
Thomas, Iva 4451, 4734, 5686
Thomas, James Melton (1917-) 1840
Thomas, John 963
Thomas, Lois Adams (-1937) 6975
Thomas, Lowell (1892-) 6370
Thomas, Minnie Frances Emery (1928-) 6976
Thomas, P. W. see Thomas, Paul Westphal (1894-1972)

Thomas, Paul Westphal (1894-1972) 1041, 2038, 2056, 2197, 2200, 2425, 3256, 3271, 3291, 3434, 3460, 3523, 3539, 3588, 3595-3596, 3911, 6977-6978
Thomas, Paul William (1921-) 3523, 3543-3544, 6979
Thomas, Paul William Lee see Thomas, Paul William (1921-)
Thomas, Mrs. Paul William Lee see Thomas, Minnie Frances Emery (1928-)
Thomas, Theodore J. 6980
Thomas, Mrs. Theodore J. see Thomas, Lois Adams (-1937)
Thomas, Walter Lee (1938-) 3798
Thomas, Wilhelm 2578
Thomas à Kempis (1380-1471) 38-39, 2505, 2869
Thomas, Okla. 4463
Thompson, Albert Edward (1870-) 6738
Thompson, C. A. 6981
Thompson, Claude Holmes 2805
Thompson, Edward W. 6982
Thompson, Herb see Thompson, Herbert W. (1908-)
Thompson, Herbert W. (1908-) 6983-6984
Thompson, J. see Thompson, John (-1899)
Thompson, John (-1899) 220, 917, 983, 5462, 6985
Thompson, Lola 6984
Thompson, R. Duane see Thompson, Raymond Duane (1931-)
Thompson, Raymond Duane (1931-) 6986
Thompson, W. L. see Thompson, Walter Lee (1876-)
Thompson, W. Ralph see Thompson, William Ralph (1910-)
Thompson, Walter Lee (1876-) 6987
Thompson, William Ralph (1910-) 522, 2764, 6988

Thomson, Charles Edward 4376, 6989
Thomson, Dorothy J. 4377
Thomson, Edward (1810-1870) 5567
Thornleigh, Austl. 4515
Tibet 4139, 5288-5294
Tidwell, W. M. 1579
Tigert, John James (1856-1906) 3067
Tillett, J. 6990
Tillett, Wilbur Fisk (1854-1936) 3004, 3090-3091
Tillman, Charlie Davis (1861-1943) 736-741, 6991-6994
Times of Refreshing (periodical) 838
Tinney, J. S. see Tinney, James S.
Tinney, James S. 72
Tinsley, James N. 6995
Titanic (Steamship) 2252
Tithes 136, 280, 465, 938, 3162, 3569, 3755, 5488
Tithing see Tithes
Titus, W. S. 6996
Tobacco 152, 162, 179, 186, 1373, 3010, 3156
Tode, Runjaji K. 6997
Tokyo, Japan 4458
Tolle, Raymond A. 3128
Tomlinson, A. J. see Tomlinson, Ambrose Jessup (1865-1943)
Tomlinson, Ambrose Jessup (1865-1943) 4206, 6998-6999
Tomlinson, Homer Aubrey (1892-1968) 4206, 6999
Tongue of Fire (periodical) see Way of Life (periodical)
Tongues, Gift of see Glossololia
Tongues of Fire (periodical) see Spiritual Life (periodical)
Tongues, Speaking in see Glossolalia
Toole, I. N. 2346, 3411
Topeka, Kan. 4348
Torch (periodical) 3861
Toronto, Ohio 804

Toronto, Ont. Peoples Church 6797
Torrey, R. A. see Torrey, Reuben Archer (1856-1928)
Torrey, Reuben Archer (1856-1928) 3933, 3993-4001, 4011-4012, 4016-4018, 6200-6201
Towne, J. L. 3729
Townsend, Lewis A. 7000
Townsend, Socrates (1816-   ) 7001
Tozer, A. W. see Tozer, Aiden Wilson (1897-1963)
Tozer, Aiden Wilson (1897-1963) 3262, 4062-4065, 4066-4067, 4083-4087, 5758, 6739, 7002-7003
Trachsel, Mrs. John J. see Trachsel, Laura Cammack (1907-   )
Trachsel, Laura Cammack (1907-   ) 2177, 3430, 3431, 3433, 7017
Tracts for the People, no. 4 2882
Tracy, Gertrude Perry 7004-7005, 7146
Tracy, L. S. see Tracy, Leighton Stanley (1882-1942)
Tracy, Leighton Stanley (1882-1942) 7006-7008
Tracy, Mrs. Leighton Stanley see Tracy, Gertrude Perry
Tracy, Olive Gertrude (1908-   ) 1878, 1904, 1924, 7008
Trade Unions see Labor and laboring classes
Trafton, Norman E. 1006
Traina, Robert Angelo (1921-   ) 665, 7009
Training Home and Bible College 4571
Training School for Christian Workers see Azusa Pacific College
Transylvania Bible School 784, 816, 4572-4576
Traugh, Hubert Lee (1929-   ) 7010
Traugh, Mrs. Hubert Lee see Traugh, Joanne Marilyn

(1931-)
Traugh, Joanne Marilyn (1931-) 7011
Traveller, A. D. see Traveller, Abram Dow (1839-1923)
Traveller, Abram Dow (1839-1923) 7012
Treffry, Richard (1771-1842) 491, 562, 2523, 2544
Tremain, Lloyd Carlos 2629
Trevecca College see Trevecca Nazarene College
Trevecca Nazarene College 4577-4578
Tried by Fire (periodical) see The Finished Work of Calvary ... Holiness without Carnality ... Truth without Error ... The Baptism in the Holy Ghost (Acts 2:4) (periodical)
Trinidad 1953, 3601
Trinity Gospel Tabernacle Association see Gospel Tabernacle Association
Triumph the Church and Kingdom of God in Christ 4293-4295
Triumphs of Faith (periodical) 839
Troke, James Allan 890
Tronnes, Cora Cook Thomas 7013-7014
Trouten, Donald James 4099
Troutman, Gladys Virginia (1933-) 7015
Troxel, Cecil Warren (1879-1944) 3431, 7016-7017
Troxel, Mrs. Cecil Warren see Troxel, Ellen Armour (1875-)
Troxel, Ellen Armour (1875-) 3431, 7017
True, Ira L. (1898-) 7018
True, Ira L., Sr. see True, Ira L. (1898-)
True, Mrs. Ira L., Sr. see True, Valora (1898-)
True, Valora (1898-) 7019
True Holiness (periodical) 840
True Wesleyan (periodical) see Wesleyan Methodist (periodical)
Trueblood, David Elton (1900-) 2311
Truesdell, Mrs. Melinda see Hamline, Melinda Truesdell (1801-)
Trumbauer, Horace G. 7020
Trumbauer, Jonas (1848-1920) 7021
Trumpet (periodical) 3449
Truslow, Julietta 7022-7023
Truth on Fire (periodical) 2023
Tsuchiya, Kenichi (1883-) 7024
Tsutada, David Tsugio (-1971) 2464, 7025-7027
Tsutada, John M. 2462
Tucker, Frederick St. George de Latour Booth see Booth Tucker, Frederick St. George de Latour (1853-1929)
Tuesday Meeting, New York 985-986, 6140, 6384-6389, 6391-6392, 6394-6395
Tulsa, Okla. Oral Roberts Evangelistic Association see Oral Roberts Evangelistic Association
Turkington, W. D. see Turkington, William David (1893-)
Turkington, William David (1893-) 7028
Turnbull, W. M. see Turnbull, Walter Mason (1881-1930)
Turnbull, Walter Mason (1881-1930) 4069, 4097, 4125-4126, 6738, 7029
Turner, George Allen (1908-) 1559, 2579, 2672-2673, 7030
Turner, W. H. see Turner, William H.
Turner, William H. 4268-4269, 4277, 4289
Tushingham, Charles A. 700, 702
Tuttle, A. H. see Tuttle, Alexander Harrison (1844-1932)
Tuttle, Alexander Harrison (1844-1932) 2798, 2936, 3031, 4714, 7031
Tysinger, J. Walden (1909-1971)

905

7032-7035
Tyson, William Ainsworth
(1891-   )   2950

Uhrig, H. E. see Uhrig, Henry E. (1889?-1948)
Uhrig, Henry E. (1889?-1948) 7036
Ulster   2080   see also Great Britain
Union Bible Seminary   949, 2319, 2322, 2325-2328, 2330, 2332, 2337-2340, 2345-2346, 2348-2350, 3389-3416, 4579
Union Biblical Seminary   3707
Union Meeting for the Promotion of Scriptural Holiness. Oxford, 1874   3921-3922
Unitarianism   3218
United Brethren (periodical)   3731
United Brethren Historical Society   3699
United Brethren in Christ see Church of the United Brethren in Christ
United Brethren in Christ (Old Constitution) see Church of the United Brethren in Christ (Old Constitution)
United Brethren Mutual Aid Society of Pennsylvania   3701
United Brethren Publishing House   3723
United Brethren Review   3722
United Christian Church   3734-3737
United Christian Church. Mission Board   3736
United Holiness Church of North America   3914-3915, 4469-4470
United Holiness Convention see United Holy Church of America
United Holiness Sentinel (periodical)   3915
United Holy Church of America   4296-4298
United Mennonites see United Missionary Church

United Methodist Church (United States). Commission on Worship   2818
United Missionary Church   3738-3777, 4152, 4351, 4400, 4512, 5714
United Missionary Church. Board of Evangelism   3744
United Missionary Church. General Board   3745
United Missionary Church. General Conference   3740
United Missionary Church. Missionary Board see United Missionary Society
United Missionary Church. United Missionary Society see United Missionary Society
United Missionary Church in Alberta   3771
United Missionary Church in Brazil   3772
United Missionary Church in India   3773
United Missionary Church in Nigeria   3776, 4672-4673, 4700-4704
United Missionary Church in Ontario   3777
United Missionary Church in the Near East   3774-3775, 5272
United Missionary Society   3762-3763, 3772-3773
U.S. Army--Chaplains   1296, 1687, 1715, 6136, 6213
U.S. Bureau of the Census   1033, 1059, 1191, 1240, 1851, 1997, 2003, 2035, 2071, 2152, 2167, 2259, 2428, 2822, 3572, 3680, 3724, 3732, 3737, 3780, 4141, 4153
United States Christian Commission   2952
U.S. Works Project Administration   1271, 3466
United Wesleyan College   4580
United Zion's Children   1033
Universal Challenger (periodical)   3892
University Park, Iowa   4479-

4481, 4582-4589
Unknown tongues see Glossolalia
Upchurch, J. T. see Upchurch, James T. (1870-)
Upchurch, James T. (1870-) 1754, 7037
Updegraff, David Brainerd (1830-1894) 953, 7038-7039
Upham, Phebe Lord 556, 7040
Upham, T. C. see Upham, Thomas Cogswell (1799-1872)
Upham, Thomas Cogswell (1799-1872) 492-496, 563, 1560, 7041-7045
Upham, Mrs. Thomas Cogswell see Upham, Phebe Lord
Upland, Calif. 4581, 4597
Upland, Ind. 4570
Upland Academy see Western Christian High School
Upland College 4581
Upton, George R. 4199
Uriarte Arrién, Juan J. see Arrién, Juan J. Uriarte

Vallery, A. J. see Vallery, Abden J. (-1937)
Vallery, Abden J. (-1937) 7046
Van Anda, C. A. see Van Anda, Carmi A. (1833-1899)
Van Anda, Carmi A. (1833-1899) 7047
Vancleve, Ky. 4472
Van Cott, Maggie Newton (1830-) 7048-7049
Van Cott, Mrs. Margaret see Van Cott, Maggie Newton (1830-1914)
Vandall, N. B. 7050
Vanderpool, D. I. see Vanderpool, Daniel I. (1891-)
Vanderpool, Daniel I. (1891-) 1704, 1841, 6596, 7051-7053
Vanderpool, Wilford 7054
Van de Venter, J. W. see Van de Venter, Judson W. (1855-1939)
Van de Venter, Judson W. (1855-1939) 7055
Van Dusen, H. P. see Van Dusen, Henry Pitney (1897-)
Van Dusen, Henry Pitney (1897-) 4170
Vanguard (periodical) 2265
Vanguard Mission 2265-2269
Vanguard Mission in India 2266-2269
Van Name, Nettie (-1892) 7056-7057
Vansant, N. see Vansant, Nicholas (1823-1902)
Vansant, Nicholas (1823-1902) 497, 6649, 7058-7059
Van Slyke, D. C. (1898-1970) 7060-7061
Van Wormer, Ivah B. 3159, 3900
Vargas, E. B. see Vargas, Ezequiel B. (-1965)
Vargas, Ezequiel B. (-1965) 2158-2159, 2160, 7062
Vaughn, Bill Edward 7063-7064
Vaughn, Ruth Wood 4347
Vaughters, William C. 1920
Vegetarianism 2216
Velázquez, Juan (-1951) 7065
Vennard, Iva May Durham (1871-1945) 954, 5845, 7066-7067
Vennard, Mrs. Thomas see Vennard, Iva May Durham (1871-1945)
Vennard College 96-97, 378-380, 4462, 4582-4589, 4949, 6958, 7067
Vermont 1001
Verner, Clara 1705
Vess, Arthur L. 180
Vestal, B. H. see Vestal, Blum (1874-)
Vestal, Blum (1874-) 7067a, 7067b
Victory (periodical) 4197
Vietnam 3423, 4140-4141
Vilonia, Ark. 4312
Vincent, B. J. see Vincent, Burton Jones (1877-1931)
Vincent, Burton Jones (1877-1931) 7068

Vincent, John Heyl (1832-1920) 2864, 2974
Vineland, N. J. 127-128
Virginia 2825, 4356, 4590
Virginia Conference Messenger (periodical) 4280
Virginia Seminary 4590
Vital Christianity (periodical) 1101, 1176, 1181
Voice from Canaan (periodical) 2415
Voice of China see Voice of China and Asia
Voice of China and Asia 3417-3423, 5573
Voice of China and Asia Missionary Society see Voice of China and Asia
Voice of Evangelical Methodism (periodical) 2610
Voice of Holmes (periodical) 4198
Voice of the Family Altar (periodical) 841
Voice of the Nazarene (periodical) 3893
Voice of the Nazarene Association of Churches 3892-3893
Volk, Harold 1628
Volunteer Gazette (periodical) 3779
Volunteers' Gazette (periodical) see Volunteer Gazette (periodical)
Volunteers of America 3778-3780

W., E. T. 7194
W., G. see G. W.
Wachtel, Alexander 7069
Waddell, L. L. see Waddell, Lloyd L. (-1954)
Waddell, Lloyd L. (-1954) 7070
Waddle, G. E. 7071
Wade, Bill 3156
Wakefield, Wesley H. 2022
Wakeley, Joseph Burton (1809-1875) 2843
Walden, John Morgan (1831-1914) 7072
Waldron, John 3623

Wales see Great Britain
Walker, E. F. see Walker, Edward Franklin (1852-1918)
Walker, Edward Franklin (1852-1918) 498, 1522, 1779, 7073-7074
Walker, George C. 7075
Walker, Mrs. George C. see Walker, Jennie Reeves
Walker, Jennie Reeves 7076
Walker, W. B. 955-957, 1523, 7077
Wall, Ernest 6388
Wallace, A. see Wallace, Adam (1825-1903)
Wallace, Adam (1825-1903) 129, 7078
Wallace, DeLance (-193?) 1665, 7079
Wallace, Mrs. DeLance see Wallace, Elsie M.
Wallace, Elsie M. 7080
Wallace, John H. 2937
Wallin, H. B. see Wallin, Henry Bradford (1890-)
Wallin, Henry Bradford (1890-) 7081
Walls, Alice E. (1887-1959) 7082
Walls, W. C. (-1900) 7083
Walters, Alexander (1858-1917) 7084-7085
Walton, John Maxey 3540, 3556, 3581
Wang, Wen T'san 7086
Wang Wen T'san see Wang, Wen T'san
War 1032a, 6566
War Cry (New York) 3603, 3673
War Cry (Toronto) 3674
Warburton, T. R. 67
Ward, A. G. 4199
Ward, Cliff (1909-) 3794
Ward, E. F. see Ward, Ernest F. (-1938)
Ward, Elizabeth Tucker (-1915) 7087
Ward, Ernest F. (-1938) 2759, 7088
Ward, Mrs. Ernest F. see Ward, Elizabeth Tucker

(-1915); Ward, Phebe E. Cox (-1910)
Ward, J. A. (-1940) 7089
Ward, Phebe E. Cox (-1910) 2759, 7090
Ward, William Thurman (1871-) 2855
Warfield, Benjamin Breckinridge (1851-1921) 18
Warner, D. S. see Warner, Daniel Sidney (1842-1895); Warner, David Snethen (1857-1927)
Warner, Daniel Sidney (1842-1895) 1153, 1162, 1167-1168, 7091-7096
Warner, Daniel Sidney (1842-1895). Love without Partiality 249, 1075, 1121-1131
Warner, David Snethen (1857-1927) 2674-2675, 7097-7098
Warner, George 415, 3838
Warner, George R. (1900-) 3426, 7099
Warner, J. J. 7195
Warner, Sam Bass, Jr. 20
Warner, Timothy Marcus (1924-) 4418
Warner, Wellman Joel (1897-) 2494
Warner Memorial University 4591
Warner Pacific College 4592
Warren, B. Elliott see Warren, Barney Elliott (1867-1951)
Warren, Barney Elliott (1867-1951) 1165, 1167-1170, 7100
Warren, R. H. see Warren, Robert Hopkins (1876-1938)
Warren, Robert Hopkins (1876-1938) 7101
Warren, William Fairfield (1833-1929) 2913
Warrington, U. see Warrington, Uriah (1828-1913)
Warrington, Uriah (1828-1913) 7102
Washburn, B. A. 2420, 7103
Washburn, Charles Campbell (1868-) 2812
Washburn, Florence M. 1267
Washburn, James F. 7104
Washburn, Josephine F. 2426, 7105
Washburn, Nathan H. (1865-1941) 7106
Washington, Booker Taliaferro (1856-1915) 5889
Washington, Joseph R. (1930-) 68, 4171
Washington, Joseph R., Jr. see Washington, Joseph R. (1930-)
Washington [state] 1268, 4558, 4564, 4592, 7014
Wasioja, Minn. 4593
Wasioja Institute 4593
Waterbury, F. E. 4238
Waterman, Anna (1874-) 7107
Waterman, Charles C. (1870-) 7108-7109
Waterman, Mrs. Charles C. see Waterman, Anna (1874-)
Watkins, A. C. see Watkins, Aura Clay (1885-1945)
Watkins, Aura Clay (1885-1945) 1211, 1214, 7110-7111, 7112
Watkins, Mildred Eugenia (1913-) 7113
Watmough, A. 2523
Watson, C. A. see Watson, Claude A. (1885-)
Watson, C. Hoyt see Watson, Charles Hoyt (1888-)
Watson, Charles Hoyt (1888-) 2744, 5198, 7114
Watson, Claude A. (1885-) 2701, 2745, 7115
Watson, G. D. see Watson, George Douglas (1845-1924)
Watson, George Douglas (1845-1924) 181-185, 499-521, 600-602, 963, 3849-3850, 7116
Watson, James 7117
Watson, Philip S. 2539
Watson, Richard (1781-1833) 105, 2523, 2551-2552, 2938, 3834
Watson, William H. 5884
Watts, Alice 3432
Waukesha, Wis. 4500

The Way; a Holiness Journal
  see Holiness Herald (Glasgow, Scot.)
Way of Faith (periodical) 842
Way of Holiness (Chattanooga, Tenn.) 843
Way of Holiness (Glasgow, Scot.) see Holiness Herald (Glasgow, Scot.)
Way of Holiness (Manchester, Eng.) 844
Way of Holiness (Syracuse, N.Y.) 3213
Way of Life (periodical) 138, 845
Weatherford, Fred Merle (1888-) 1524-1525, 7118
Weaver, George see Weavers, George (1840-1914)
Weaver, J. see Weaver, Jonathan (1824-1901)
Weaver, Jonathan (1824-1901) 3718
Weavers, George (1840-1914) 7119-7120
Webb, Bruce Darrell (1933-) 7121
Webb-Peploe, H. W. see Webb-Peploe, Hanmer William (1837-1923)
Webb-Peploe, Hanmer William (1837-1923) 4002-4008, 4013, 4045-4051
Weber, J. H. see Weber, Joseph Hulse (1855-)
Weber, Joseph Hulse (1855-) 7122-7123
Weeden, W. S. see Weeden, Winfield Scott (1847-1908)
Weeden, Winfield Scott (1847-1908) 7124
Weeks, Sherwood (1907-1968) 2642, 7125-7127
Weeks, Sylvester (1836-1921) 7128
Wees, F. M. (1874-) 7129
Weidman, Bernice Evelyn Zahniser (1899-) 7335
Weidman, J. C. (-1910) 7130
Weise, Arthur James (1838-1910 or 11) 987

Welch, C. E. see Welch, Charles Edgar (1852-1925)
Welch, Charles Edgar (1852-1925) 758, 7131
Welch, T. B. see Welch, Thomas Bramwell
Welch, Thomas Bramwell 759
Welfare work see Charities
Wellesley, Ont. 4373
Wellman, George L. (-1967) 7132
Wellman, Wendell 1379
Wells, Charlotte Johns (-1936) 7133
Wells, E. H. see Wells, Elbert H. (-1948)
Wells, E. T. see Wells, Edward Thompson (1842-1912)
Wells, Edward Thompson (1842-1912) 7134
Wells, Elbert H. (-1948) 7135
Wells, Mrs. Elbert H. see Wells, Charlotte Johns (-1936)
Wells, Fred K. 7136
Wells, G. C. see Wells, George C. (1819-1873)
Wells, George C. (1819-1873) 7137
Wells, Kenneth H. 7138
Wengatz, John Christian (1880-) 6239
Wert, C. E. see Wert, Clarence E. (-1963)
Wert, Clarence E. (-1963) 7139-7140
Wesche, Percival A. 130, 6249-6250
Wesley, Charles (1707-1788) 2539, 2585, 2586, 2712
Wesley, John (1703-1791) 191, 302, 374, 405, 550-551, 564-565, 1494, 1542, 1561, 1718, 2138, 2494, 2504-2505, 2515, 2523, 2524-2525, 2532, 2536-2541, 2546, 2548-2549, 2553-2557, 2562-2575, 2577-2581, 2583, 2586-2587, 2595, 2785, 2869-2870, 2908, 2939, 3085, 3285, 3485, 3843, 4589, 5388

Wesley family 2586
Wesleyan Advocate (periodical) 3808
Wesleyan Bible Institute see Jordan College
Wesleyan Church 3781-3812, 4332, 4336, 4340, 4365, 4378, 4420, 4452-4454, 4465-4467, 4473-4474, 4495, 4503, 4539, 4580, 4595, 4606-4608, 4894-4895, 5216, 5309-5310, 5555-5556, 5836, 5865, 5994-5995, 6009, 6053-6054, 6185-6186, 6451-6452, 6808, 6820-6821, 6978, 7243
Wesleyan Church. Department of Extension and Evangelism see Wesleyan Church. General Department of Extension and Evangelism
Wesleyan Church. Department of Youth see Wesleyan Church. General Department of Youth
Wesleyan Church. General Conference 3782, 4383
Wesleyan Church. General Department of Extension and Evangelism 3787-3788
Wesleyan Church. General Department of Youth 3812
Wesleyan Connection of Churches see Bible Methodist Connection of Churches
Wesleyan Herald (periodical) 3214
Wesleyan Holiness Association of Churches 3916-3920, 5528
Wesleyan Institute 4594
Wesleyan Methodist (periodical) 3215
Wesleyan Methodist Bible College 4595
Wesleyan Methodist Bible Institute see Central Wesleyan College
Wesleyan Methodist Church of America 2702, 2735, 3115-3237, 3558-3559, 4300, 4340, 4365, 4367, 4383, 4452-4454, 4457, 4495, 4501, 4503, 4549, 4593-4595, 4602, 5547, 5701, 5940, 6044-6045, 6063, 6192, 6325, 6427-6428, 6542, 6672, 6696-6697, 7033-7035, 7252
Wesleyan Methodist Church of America. Administrative Department 3140
Wesleyan Methodist Church of America. Conferences. Allegheny 3117-3118
Wesleyan Methodist Church of America. Conferences. Canada 3119
Wesleyan Methodist Church of America. Conferences. Champlain 3120-3121
Wesleyan Methodist Church of America. Conferences. Iowa 3122
Wesleyan Methodist Church of America. Conferences. Kansas 3123
Wesleyan Methodist Church of America. Conferences. Lockport 3124, 5701
Wesleyan Methodist Church of America. Conferences. Michigan 3125-3127, 6542
Wesleyan Methodist Church of America. Conferences. Oklahoma 3128
Wesleyan Methodist Church of America. Conferences. Rochester 3129
Wesleyan Methodist Church of America. Conferences. South Carolina 3130
Wesleyan Methodist Church of America. Conferences. Wisconsin 3131
Wesleyan Methodist Church of America. Department of Church Extension 3141, 3149
Wesleyan Methodist Church of America. Department of Home Missions 3147-3148, 3150, 3210-3211, 3226, 3230, 3236, 4367, 4409
Wesleyan Methodist Church of America. Department of

Sunday Schools 3144, 7252
Wesleyan Methodist Church of America. Department of World Missions 3209, 3229, 4367
Wesleyan Methodist Church of America. Editorial Department 3145
Wesleyan Methodist Church of America. General Conference 3116
Wesleyan Methodist College see Central Wesleyan College
Wesleyan Methodist Connection of America see Wesleyan Methodist Church of America
Wesleyan Methodist Connection (or Church) of America see Wesleyan Methodist Church of America
Wesleyan Methodists in Arkansas 3225
Wesleyan Methodists in Australia 3226
Wesleyan Methodists in India 3227-3229
Wesleyan Methodists in Iowa 3122
Wesleyan Methodists in Kansas 3123
Wesleyan Methodists in Kentucky 3230
Wesleyan Methodists in Michigan 3125, 6542
Wesleyan Methodists in New York 3120, 3124, 3129, 5701
Wesleyan Methodists in North Carolina 2773, 3231, 7034
Wesleyan Methodists in Oklahoma 3128
Wesleyan Methodists in Ontario 3119, 6697
Wesleyan Methodists in Pennsylavnia 3117-3118
Wesleyan Methodists in Sierra Leone 3232-3235, 5053, 5547
Wesleyan Methodists in South Carolina 3130, 3236
Wesleyan Methodists in South Dakota 6044-6045
Wesleyan Methodists in the Southern states 3237
Wesleyan Methodists in Wisconsin 3131
Wesleyan Missionary (periodical) 3216
Wesleyan Theological Journal (periodical) 846
Wesleyan World (periodical) 3809
Wesleyan Young People's Journal (periodical) see Wesleyan Youth (periodical)
Wesleyan Youth (periodical) 3217
Wessington Springs, S. D. 4596
Wessington Springs Academy see Wessington Springs College
Wessington Springs College 4596
Wessington Springs Seminary see Wessington Springs College
West Indies Bible Mission see Evangelical Bible Mission
West Virginia 4511, 4521, 7299
Westcott, J. B. see Westcott, John Bunyan (1839-1930)
Westcott, John Bunyan (1839-1930) 7141
Westergreen, Nels O. (1834-1919) 7142
Western Christian High School 4597
Western Evangelical Seminary 544, 4598-4599
Western Holiness Association 197
Western Holiness Bible School see Holiness Bible College
Western Pilgrim College 4600
Western Record (periodical) 847
Western Union Holiness Convention. Jacksonville, Ill., 1880 197, 199
Westfield, Ind. 4579
Westminster, Colo. 4339

Westminster College and Bible Institute 4601
Wheatley, Richard (1831-) 6389
Wheaton, Mother see Wheaton, Elizabeth Ryder (1844-)
Wheaton, Elizabeth Ryder (1844-) 7143-7144
Wheaton, Ill. 4457, 4602
Wheaton Seminary 4602
Whedon, D. A. 2580
Whedon, Daniel Denison (1808-1885) 2959-2960, 3194-3195
Wheeler, Elizabeth 7005, 7145-7146
Wheeler, Mrs. Henry see Wheeler, Mary Sparkes (1835-1919)
Wheeler, Mrs. James see Wheeler, Elizabeth
Wheeler, Mary Sparkes (1835-1919) 523, 603, 7147-7148
Whiffen, Nellie M. (-1946) 7149
Whispers of Peace (periodical) 848
Whitaker, C. B. see Whitaker, Charles B. (1855-)
Whitaker, Charles B. (1855-) 524, 7150-7151
Whitall, John Mickle (1800-1877) 2294
Whitcomb, A. L. 2743, 7152
Whitcomb, L. B. 7153
White, Alice Minnie (1894-) 4426
White, Alma Bridwell (1862-1946) 2207, 2209, 2211-2216, 2218-2219-2222, 2224, 2227-2229, 2230-2231, 2233-2238, 2246, 2249-2256, 2260, 7154-7168
White, Arthur Kent (1889-) 2210, 2217, 2230, 2233-2235, 2238, 2257, 7167, 7169
White, Edgar 1229
White, Ernest (1887-) 21
White, H. J. 2478
White, Kent (1860-1940) 4236, 7170-7171
White, Mrs. Kent see White, Alma Bridwell (1862-1946)
White, Levi 525, 7172
White, Mollie Alma Bridwell see White, Alma Bridwell (1862-1946)
White, Myrtle Mangum (18??-) 7173
White, Ray Bridwell (1892-1946) 2203, 2217, 2258, 7174
White, Mrs. Robert H. see White, Myrtle Mangum (18??-)
White, S. S. see White, Stephen Solomon (1890-1971)
White, Stephen Solomon (1890-1971) 1526-1529, 7175-7177
White slavery see Prostitution
Whiteside, E. D. see Whiteside, Edward D.
Whiteside, Edward D. 7178
Whitford, Richard 39
Whitney, Arthur P. (1912-) 2495, 3042
Whittemore, Mrs. E. M. see Whittemore, Emma Mott (1850-1931)
Whittemore, Emma Mott (1850-1931) 91, 117, 5987-5988, 6674, 7179-7182
Whittier, Calif. 4332
Whittle, J. A. G. 7183
Wiberg, Erik (1912-) 4128
Widmeyer, Charles Brenton (1884-19??) 692, 7184
Widney, J. P. see Widney, Joseph Pomeroy (1841-1938)
Widney, Joseph Pomeroy (1841-1938) 1247, 7185-7195
Widney, Robert Maclay (1838-1929) 7193
Wiese, Harry A. 1884
Wiess, Mary Ethel 6225
Wiggins, Arch R. 3671
Wight, J. B. 186
Wilcox, Leslie D. 657-658, 3160, 3817
Wilcox, Mrs. Tabitha McSween 7196-7197
Wilde, Earle F. 1530
Wiley, Arlene Maudie Likes

(1923-   ) 7198
Wiley, Charles A. (1925-1963) 7199
Wiley, Charles A., Jr. see Wiley, Charles A. (1925-1963)
Wiley, Mrs. Charles A., Jr. see Wiley, Arlene Maudie Likes (1923-   )
Wiley, H. Orton see Wiley, Henry Orton (1877-1961)
Wiley, Henry Orton (1877-1961) 1531-1533, 1762-1763, 1842-1844, 5913, 7200
Wilkens, John Charles (1923-   ) 7201
Wilkes, A. Paget see Wilkes, Alphaeus Nelson Paget (1871-1934)
Wilkes, Alphaeus Nelson Paget (1871-1934) 1562-1564, 3293-3294, 3299-3300, 3329-3339, 3343-3346, 3357, 7202-7206
Wilkins, Chester (1918-   ) 644-645, 1634, 3222, 3515, 3559, 3799, 7207
Willard, Amy Hankins (-1951) 7208
Willard, Frances Elizabeth (1839-1898) 7209-7212, 7294
Willard, Francis Burleigh 7213
Willard, Mrs. Francis Burleigh see Willard, Amy Hankins (-1951)
Willard, Willis Wardner, Jr. 22
Willcuts, Jack L. 2381, 2390-2391
Willems, Emilio 4202
Willett, J. S. see Willett, John Starbuck (1876-   )
Willett, John Starbuck (1876-   ) 3237, 7214
Williams, B. O. 4824
Williams, Carl Carnelius (1903-   ) 1132
Williams, Colin W. 2581
Williams, Mrs. E. E. 983, 7215

Williams, Eugene 4578
Williams, Eunice Harvey 7216-7218
Williams, J. A. 2582
Williams, J. E. 1380, 1534, 1580, 7219-7220
Williams, L. Milton see Williams, Lewis Milton (1862-   )
Williams, Leewin Bell (1868-   ) 604, 1638, 1659
Williams, Lewis Milton (1862-   ) 526-529, 7221
Williams, Lucille 2342
Williams, Myrtle May Hosack 2363, 5201
Williams, R. T. see Williams, Roy Tilman (1883-1946)
Williams, R. T., Jr. see Williams, Roy Tilman, Jr.
Williams, Ray L. 3802
Williams, Reginald Stille (1910-   ) 7222
Williams, Roy Tilman (1883-1946) 1381-1383, 1535-1537, 1706, 1723, 1827, 6304, 7223-7228
Williams, Mrs. Roy Tilman see Williams, Eunice Harvey
Williams, Roy Tilman, Jr. 1628, 7229-7230
Williams, W. H. 7231
Williams, Walter Rollin (1884-   ) 2295, 2362-2363, 2373-2374, 5201
Williams, Mrs. Walter Rollin see Williams, Myrtle May Hosack
Williams-Cammack, Lydia M. 5847
Williamson, Audrey Johnston 1319, 1412, 1859, 1901, 7232
Williamson, G. B. see Williamson, Gideon Brooks (1898-   )
Williamson, Gideon Brooks (1898-   ) 1538, 1635, 1724, 1755, 1901, 5737, 7227-7228, 7233
Williamson, Mrs. Gideon Brooks see Williamson, Audrey Johnston

Williamstown, Pa. 4613
Willing, H. S. see Willing, Herman S.
Willing, Herman S. 7234
Willing, Jennie Fowler (1834-1916) 7235
Willing, William C. 7236
Willing, Mrs. William C. see Willing, Jennie Fowler (1834-1916)
Willingham, T. W. see Willingham, Theodore Weber (1893-   )
Willingham, Theodore Weber (1893-   ) 1413, 1581, 7237
Willoughby, Delbert H. 3919
Wilmore, Ky. 4314, 4326, 5719
Wilson, A. H. see Wilson, Albert H. (1888-1956)
Wilson, Albert H. (1888-1956) 7238
Wilson, Byron R. 23
Wilson, Charles 7252
Wilson, Clarence True (1872-1939) 7239
Wilson, David Emerson (1893-1963) 7240-7241
Wilson, Ermal Leroy (1917-   ) 7242-7243
Wilson, Mrs. Ermal Leroy see Wilson, Madgel Howard (1915-1967)
Wilson, Francis C. 5804
Wilson, G. W. see Wilson, George Washington (1853-1929)
Wilson, George Washington (1853-1929) 530, 605, 742, 2806, 7244-7245
Wilson, Guy L. 7246
Wilson, Henry 7247
Wilson, Isaiah (1842-1932) 7248
Wilson, John 7249
Wilson, Kenneth L. 4453
Wilson, Lum see Wilson, William Columbus (1866-1915)
Wilson, Luther Barton (1856-1928) 2945
Wilson, Madgel Howard (1915-1967) 7250
Wilson, Oliver G. (1891-1959) 3130, 7251-7252
Wilson, W. C. see Wilson, William Columbus (1866-1915)
Wilson, W. H. 7253
Wilson, William Columbus (1866-1915) 7254-7255
Wiman, Margaret Glyn see McReynolds, Margaret Glyn Wiman (1921-   )
Wimberly, C. F. see Wimberly, Charles Franklin (1866-1946)
Wimberly, Charles Franklin (1866-1946) 118, 187-188, 531-535, 593, 606, 607, 624, 755, 958, 3057, 6251, 7256, 7258
Wimberly, Newell 7257
Winans, Esther Carson (1891-1928) 7259-7262
Winans, J. W. (1864-1929) 7263
Winans, Roger S. (1886-   ) 1937, 7264-7265
Winans, Mrs. Roger S. see Winans, Esther Carson (1891-1928)
Winchester, C. W. see Winchester, Charles Wesley (1843-1917)
Winchester, Charles Wesley (1843-1917) 92, 869, 2865, 3032, 7266-7267
Winchester, Olive May (1880-1947) 1539-1540, 7268
Wind (periodical) 3810
Wines, J. M. see Wines, John Maurice (1857-   )
Wines, John Maurice (1857-   ) 7269-7270
Winget, B. see Winget, Benjamin
Winget, Benjamin 7271
Winget, Wilfred Lamont (1930-   ) 1653, 7272
Winnipeg, Man. 4374, 4434
Winslow, Carolyn Van Valin 2718, 7273
Winslow, Harold H. (-1944)

7274
Winslow, Mrs. Harold H. see Winslow, Carolyn Van Valin
Winslow, Octavius 3
Wintermantel, Ed. 4576
Wisbey, Herbert Andrew (1919-) 3657
Wisconsin 1271, 4408, 4500
Wise, Daniel (1813-1898) 2833, 2866-2868, 2951, 7275
Wise, F. Franklyn see Wise, Forest Franklyn (1920-)
Wise, Forest Franklyn (1920-) 1782, 7276
Wise, George C. 6604
Wise, H. H. (1888-1948) 7277-7278
Wise, Marjorie 1865, 1949
Wiseman, Peter (1883-) 221, 536-539, 7279
Wisler, R. L. 7280
Wissbroecker, Edwin Kenneth 7281
Wittke, Carl Frederick 6299
Woertendyke, J. H. see Woertendyke, James H. (1869-)
Woertendyke, James H. (1869-) 7282
Wolfe, J. E. (1872-1955) 7283
Wolfe, R. W. 7284
Wolfram, Donald J. 2239
Wolfram, Gertrude Metlen (1888-) 2231, 7168
Wollaston, Mass. 4392-4394
Wolter, Gerald A. 3122
Wolverton, Wallace Irving (1905-) 24
Woman 4983, 5459, 6016
Woman--Dress see Clothing and dress
Woman preachers see Women as ministers
Woman's Chains (periodical) 2245
Women as ministers 106, 138-140, 942, 2209, 2245, 3152, 3444, 3616, 3982, 4687-4688, 4869-4870, 4952-4953, 5037, 4074-4075, 5218, 5235, 5354, 5358, 5376-5377, 5679, 5822, 6063, 6084, 6163, 6171, 6187, 6195-6197, 6345, 6527, 6958, 7014, 7049
Women in church work 135, 1317-1319, 2008, 4611, 5027-5028, 5031, 5059, 5082-5083, 5085, 5105-5107, 5133-5134, 5224, 5256, 5330, 5418-5419, 5447, 5470, 5472, 5482, 5537, 5631, 5651, 5726, 5768, 5863, 5909, 5911, 5925, 5945, 5980, 5984, 5987-5988, 6182, 6192, 6195-6197, 6204, 6225, 6281, 6283, 6285, 6329, 6357, 6383-6389, 6391-6392, 6449, 6507, 6611, 6676-6677, 6714-6715, 6753-6756, 6773-6774, 6778-6780, 6839, 6894, 6896, 6902, 6967, 6984, 7005, 7023, 7057, 7067, 7144, 7146, 7180, 7197, 7210-7212, 7260-7262, 7294
Wood, Bernice M. (-1941) 7285
Wood, John Allen (1828-) 105, 540-543, 564-565, 1565-1566, 2677, 3834, 7286-7288
Wood, M. D. 7289-7290
Wood, William W. 4247
Wood-Woods, Lois 2636-2638
Woodard, Luke (1832-) 2293, 7291-7292
Woodbridge, Mary Ann Brayton (1830-1894) 7293-7294
Woodruff, A. Bond see Woodruff, Arnold Bond (1920-)
Woodruff, Arnold Bond (1920-) 7295
Woodruff, Bond see Woodruff, Arnold Bond (1920-)
Woodrum, Lon Riley (1901-) 1845, 7296
Woods, Harry F. 3378, 3381, 7297
Woods, J. F. see Woods, John Franklin (1865-)
Woods, John Franklin (1865-) 7298-7299
Woods, Leonard (1774-1854)

Woods, W. S. (-1950) 7300
Woodstock, N. B. 4340
Woodward, W. D. 999
Wooley, John G. 7294
Worcester, L. B. see Worcester, Leonard Beacher (-1926)
Worcester, Leonard Beacher (-1926) 7301
Worcester, Paul W. 2066, 2468, 3439
Word, Emma B. 1886
The Word, the Work, and the World (periodical) see Alliance Witness (periodical)
Words of Faith (periodical) 849
Wordsworth, E. E. 7302
Work with youth 868-875, 1852-1859, 2261, 2746-2747, 3573, 3681-3683, 3812, 6557, 6932
Working classes see Labor and laboring classes
World Fellowship of Free Methodist Churches see Free Methodist World Fellowship
World Gospel Mission 3424-3433, 7017
World Missionary Association see World's Faith Missionary Association
World Missions Bulletin 3555
World War, 1939-1945 4628, 5197-5198, 5572, 6213, 6355, 6406, 6880
World War I see European War, 1914-1918
World War II see World War, 1939-1945
World-Wide Missionary Society 3434
World-Wide Missions 3435-3438, 6153-6154, 6156
World-Wide Missions (periodical) 3438
Worldliness 1015, 2181
World's Columbia Exposition, 1893 see Chicago, World's Columbia Exposition, 1893
World's Faith Missionary Association 3439-3440
Wortheim, Mrs. R. L. 7303
Wray, Newton (1854-) 136
Wray, Sara 117, 7180
Wright, Stanley W. 3129
Wright, Virginia Fern Meeks (1925-) 7304
Wright, Wayne Wible (1926-) 7305
Wright, Mrs. Wayne Wible see Wright, Virginia Fern Meeks (1925-)
Wrigley, Edgar J. 791
Wu, Tung Tai 7306
Wu Tung Tai see Wu, Tung Tai
Wuester, Alfreda Huhnke 1743
Wyman, Edward G. 7307-7308
Wynkoop, Mildred Bangs 544, 1541-1542, 4599, 7309-7310

Yard, Edmund Jones (1792-1876) 7311-7312
Yard, Mary see James, Mary Dagworthy Yard (1810-1883)
Yarmouth, N. S. 4340
Yellowstone National Park 7164
Yocum, Dale Morris 1201, 1212, 3824, 7313-7315
Yoder, A. B. 3753
Yoder, Carrie A. 7316
Yorker Brethren 1033
Young, Carlton Raymond (1926-) 2810, 2813
Young, Dinsdale T. 5013
Young, Donald L. (1931-) 7317
Young, Egerton Ryerson (1840-1909) 7318-7324
Young, G. A. 7325
Young, George W. 7326
Young, Samuel (1901-) 1293, 1414, 1543, 5020, 5765, 5768, 7327-7328
Young, Willie 7329
Young Men's Holiness League, Indianapolis 5583
Young People's Guide (periodical) 2459
Young People's Leader (periodi-

cal) 3697
Youngren, Anna Millikan (-1941) 7330
Youngren, August 7331
Youngren, Mrs. August see Youngren, Anna Millikan (-1941); Youngren, Ethel Helm Clarke (-1947)
Youngren, Ethel Helm Clarke (-1947) 7332
Youth (periodical) 1177
Youth in Action (periodical) 2733
Youth work see Work with youth
Ypsilanti, Mich. South Side Mission see Evangelistic Tabernacle
Yungred, Kison 7333

Zachary, E. E. 1268
Zahniser, A. D. see Zahniser, Arthur DeFrance (1865-1935)
Zahniser, Arthur DeFrance (1865-1935) 7334-7335
Zahniser, Clarence Howard (1902-) 6581-6582
Zambia see Rhodesia
Zanesville and Putnam Colonization Society, Zanesville, Ohio 3019
Zanesville, Ohio. Zanesville and Putnam Colonization Society see Zanesville and Putnam Colonization Society, Zanesville, Ohio
Zarephath, N. J. 4304, 4306, 4603
Zarephath Bible Institute see Zarephath Bible Seminary
Zarephath Bible Seminary 4603
Zelley, Henry J. (1859-1942) 7336
Zepp, Arthur Carroll (1878-) 189, 545-549, 623
Zimmerman, Julia 7337
Zionism 2219
Zion's Herald (periodical) 3017
Zion's Herald and Wesleyan Journal (periodical) see Zion's Herald (periodical)
Zion's Outlook (periodical) see Living Water (periodical)
Zion's Watchman (periodical) 850
Zook, J. R. 1017-1018
Zurbrigg, William (1873-1958) 7338
Zwemer, Samuel Marinus (1867-) 4064